D0526216

Collins

— POCKET —

Italian
Dictionary

HarperCollins Publishers
Westerhill Road
Bishopbriggs
Glasgow
G64 2QT

Seventh Edition 2013

10 9 8 7 6 5 4 3

© HarperCollins Publishers 2013, 2010, 2008, 2002, 1996

ISBN 978-0-00-748550-5

Collins® is a registered trademark of HarperCollins Publishers Limited

www.collins.co.uk

A catalogue record for this book is available from the British Library

Typeset by Aptara in India and Davidson Publishing Solutions, Glasgow

Printed and bound in Italy by Lego SpA, Lavis (Trento)

Acknowledgements
We would like to thank those authors and publishers who kindly gave permission for copyright material to be used in the Collins Corpus. We would also like to thank Times Newspapers Ltd for providing valuable data.

INDICE

CONTENTS

Introduzione italiana	v
Introduzione inglese	vii
Abbreviazioni	ix
Trascrizione fonetica	xiii
La pronuncia dell'italiano	xv
Verbi	xvi
I numeri	xxiii
L'ora	xxvi
La data	xxvii
ITALIANO–INGLESE	1–282
Italian in focus	1–32
INGLESE–ITALIANO	283–580
Verbi italiani	1–32

Italian introduction	v
English introduction	vii
Abbreviations	ix
Phonetic transcription	xiii
Italian pronunciation	xv
Verb tables	xvi
Numbers	xxiii
Time	xxvi
Dates	xxvii
ITALIAN–ENGLISH	1–282
Italian in focus	1–32
ENGLISH–ITALIAN	283–580
Italian verb tables	1–32

PROJECT MANAGEMENT
Carol McCann

CONTRIBUTORS
Teresa Álvarez García
Gaëlle Amiot-Cadey
Gabriella Bacchelli
Daphne Day
Val McNulty
Complexli

COMPUTING
Thomas Callan

FOR THE PUBLISHER
Lucy Cooper
Kerry Ferguson
Elaine Higgleton
Ruth O'Donovan

SERIES EDITOR
Rob Scriven

INTRODUZIONE

Vi ringraziamo di aver scelto il Dizionario inglese Collins Gem e ci auguriamo che esso si riveli uno strumento utile e piacevole da usare nello studio, in vacanza e sul lavoro.

In questa introduzione troverete alcuni suggerimenti per aiutarvi a trarre il massimo beneficio dal vostro nuovo dizionario, ricco non solo per il suo ampio lemmario ma anche per il gran numero di informazioni contenute in ciascuna voce.

All'inizio del dizionario troverete l'elenco delle abbreviazioni usate nel testo e una guida alla pronuncia.Troverete inoltre un utile elenco delle forme dei verbi irregolari inglesi e italiani, seguito da una sezione finale con i numeri, l'ora e la data.

Come usare il dizionario Collins Gem

Per imparare ad usare in modo efficace il dizionario è importante comprendere la funzione delle differenziazioni tipografiche, dei simboli e delle abbreviazioni usati nel testo. Vi forniamo pertanto qui di seguito alcuni chiarimenti in merito a tali convenzioni.

I lemmi
Sono le parole in **neretto** elencate in ordine alfabetico. Il primo e l'ultimo lemma di ciascuna pagina appaiono al margine superiore.

Dove opportuno, informazioni sull'ambito d'uso o il livello di formalità di certe parole vengono fornite tra parentesi in corsivo e spesso in forma abbreviata dopo l'indicazione della categoria grammaticale (es. (*Comm*), (*inf*)).

In certi casi più parole con radice comune sono raggruppate sotto lo stesso lemma. Tali parole appaiono in neretto ma in un carattere leggermente ridotto (es. **acceptance**).

Esempi d'uso del lemma sono a loro volta in neretto ma in un carattere diverso dal lemma (es. **to be cold**).

La trascrizione fonetica
La trascrizione fonetica che illustra la corretta pronuncia del lemma è tra parentesi quadre e segue immediatamente il lemma (es. **knee** [niː]). L'elenco dei simboli fonetici è alle pagine xiii–xiv.

Le traduzioni

Le traduzioni sono in carattere tondo e,quando il lemma ha più di un significato,le traduzioni sono separate da un punto e virgola. Spesso diverse traduzioni di un lemma sono introdotte da una o più parole in corsivo tra parentesi tonde: la loro funzione è di chiarire a quale significato del lemma si riferisce la traduzione. Possono essere sinonimi, indicazioni di ambito d'uso o di registro del lemma (es. **party** *(Pol)*, *(team)*, *(celebration)*; **laid back** *(inf)* ecc.).

Le 'parole chiave'

Un trattamento particolare è stato riservato a quelle parole che, per frequenza d'uso o complessità, necessitano una strutturazione più chiara ed esauriente (es. **da, di, avere** in italiano, **at, to, be, this** in inglese). Frecce e numeri vi guidano attraverso le varie distinzioni grammaticali e di significato; ulteriori informazioni sono fornite in corsivo tra parentesi.

Informazioni grammaticali

Le parti del discorso (noun, adjective ecc.) sono espresse da abbreviazioni convenzionali in corsivo *(n, adj* ecc.) e seguono la trascrizione fonetica del lemma.

Eventuali ulteriori informazioni grammaticali, come ad esempio le forme di un verbo irregolare o il plurale irregolare di un sostantivo, precedono tra parentesi la parte del discorso (es. **give** *(pt* **gave**, *pp* **given**) *vt*; **man** [...] *(pl* **men**) *n*).

INTRODUCTION

We are delighted that you have decided to buy the Collins Gem Italian Dictionary and hope you will enjoy and benefit from using it at school, at home, on holiday or at work.

This introduction gives you a few tips on how to get the most out of your dictionary – not simply from its comprehensive wordlist but also from the information provided in each entry. This will help you to read and understand modern Italian, as well as communicate and express yourself in the language.

The dictionary begins by listing the abbreviations used in the text and illustrating the sounds shown by the phonetic symbols. You will also find Italian and English verb tables, followed by a section on numbers and time expressions.

Using your Collins Gem dictionary

A wealth of information is presented in the dictionary, using various typefaces, sizes of type, symbols, abbreviations and brackets. The various conventions and symbols used are explained in the following sections.

Headwords

The words you look up in a dictionary – "headwords" – are listed alphabetically. They are printed in **bold type** for rapid identification. The two headwords appearing at the top of each page indicate the first and last word dealt with on the page in question.

Information about the usage or form of certain headwords is given in brackets after the part of speech. This usually appears in abbreviated form and in italics (e.g.(*fam*),(*Comm*)).

Where appropriate, words related to headwords are grouped in the same entry (e.g. **illustrare, illustrazione**) in a slightly smaller bold type than the headword.

Common expressions in which the headword appears are shown in a different bold roman type (e.g. **aver freddo**).

Phonetic spellings

Where the phonetic spelling of headwords (indicating their pronunciation) is given, it will appear in square brackets immediately after the headword (e.g. **calza** ['kaltsa]). A list of these symbols is given on pages xiii–xiv.

Translations

Headword translations are given in ordinary type and, where more than one meaning or usage exists, these are separated by a semicolon. You will often find other words in italics in brackets before the translations. These offer suggested contexts in which the headword might appear (e.g. **duro** (*pietra*) or (*lavoro*)) or provide synonyms (e.g. **duro** (*ostinato*)).

"Key" words

Special status is given to certain Italian and English words which are considered as "key" words in each language. They may, for example, occur very frequently or have several types of usage (e.g. **da**, **di**, **avere** in Italian, **at**, **to**, **be**, **this** in English). A combination of arrows and numbers helps you to distinguish different parts of speech and different meanings. Further helpful information is provided in brackets and italics.

Grammatical information

Parts of speech are given in abbreviated form in italics after the phonetic spellings of headwords (e.g. *vt*, *av*, *cong*).

Genders of Italian nouns are indicated as follows: *sm* for a masculine and *sf* for a feminine noun. Feminine and irregular plural forms of nouns are also shown (e.g. **uovo**, (*pl(f)*) **uova**); **dottore**, **essa**).

Feminine adjective endings are given, as are plural forms (e.g. **opaco**, **a**, **chi**, **che**).

ABBREVIAZIONI		ABBREVIATIONS
abbreviazione	*abbr*	abbreviation
aggettivo	*adj*	adjective
amministrazione	*Admin*	administration
avverbio	*adv*	adverb
aeronautica, viaggi aerei	*Aer*	flying, air travel
aggettivo	*ag*	adjective
agricoltura	*Agr*	agriculture
amministrazione	*Amm*	administration
anatomia	*Anat*	anatomy
architettura	*Archit*	architecture
articolo determinativo	*art def*	definite article
articolo indeterminativo	*art indef*	indefinite article
attributivo	*attrib*	attributive
ausiliare	*aus, aux*	auxiliary
Australia	*Aust*	Australia
automobile	*Aut*	motor car and motoring
avverbio	*av*	adverb
aeronautica, viaggi aerei	*Aviat*	flying, air travel
biologia	*Biol*	biology
botanica	*Bot*	botany
inglese britannico	*BRIT*	British English
consonante	*C*	consonant
chimica	*Chim, Chem*	chemistry
familiare (!da evitare)	*col(!)*	colloquial usage (! particularly offensive)
commercio, finanza	*Comm*	commerce, finance
comparativo	*compar*	comparative
informatica	*Comput*	computing
congiunzione	*cong, conj*	conjunction
edilizia	*Constr*	building
sostantivo usato come aggettivo, ma mai con funzione predicativa	*cpd*	compound element: noun used as adjective and which cannot follow the noun it qualifies

ABBREVIAZIONI

		ABBREVIATIONS
cucina	*Cuc, Culin*	cookery
davanti a	*dav*	before
articolo determinativo	*def art*	definite article
determinativo ; articolo, aggettivo dimostrativo o indefinito ecc	*det*	determiner: article, demonstrative etc
diminutivo	*dimin*	diminutive
diritto	*Dir*	law
economia	*Econ*	economics
edilizia	*Edil*	building
elettricità, elettronica	*Elettr, Elec*	electricity, electronics
esclamazione	*escl, excl*	exclamation
femminile	*f*	feminine
familiare (! da evitare)	*fam(!)*	colloquial usage (! particularly offensive)
ferrovia	*Ferr*	railways
senso figurato	*fig*	figurative use
fisiologia	*Fisiol*	physiology
fotografia	*Fot*	photography
verbo inglese la cui particella è inseparabile dal verbo	*fus*	(phrasal verb) where the particle cannot be separated from the main verb
nella maggior parte dei sensi; generalmente	*gen*	in most or all senses; generally
geografia, geologia	*Geo*	geography, geology
geometria	*Geom*	geometry
storia, storico	*Hist*	history, historical
impersonale	*impers*	impersonal
articolo indeterminativo	*indef art*	indefinite article
infinito	*infin*	infinitive
informatica	*Inform*	computing
insegnamento, sistema scolastico e universitario	*Ins*	schooling, schools and universities

ABBREVIAZIONI		ABBREVIATIONS
invariabile	*inv*	invariable
irregolare	*irreg*	irregular
grammatica, linguistica	*Ling*	grammar, linguistics
maschile	*m*	masculine
matematica	*Mat(h)*	mathematics
termine medico, medicina	*Med*	medical term, medicine
il tempo, meteorologia	*Meteor*	the weather, meteorology
maschile o femminile	*m/f*	masculine or feminine
esercito, linguaggio militare	*Mil*	military matters
musica	*Mus*	music
sostantivo	*n*	noun
nautica	*Naut*	sailing, navigation
numerale (aggettivo, sostantivo)	*num*	numeral adjective or noun
Nuova Zelanda	*NZ*	New Zealand
	o.s.	oneself
peggiorativo	*peg, pej*	derogatory, pejorative
fotografia	*Phot*	photography
fisiologia	*Physiol*	physiology
plurale	*pl*	plural
politica	*Pol*	politics
participio passato	*pp*	past participle
preposizione	*prep*	preposition
pronome	*pron*	pronoun
psicologia, psichiatria	*Psic, Psych*	psychology, psychiatry
tempo passato	*pt*	past tense
qualcosa	*qc*	something
qualcuno	*qn*	someone
religione, liturgia	*Rel*	religions, church service
sostantivo	*s*	noun
	sb	somebody

ABBREVIAZIONI		ABBREVIATIONS
insegnamento, sistema scolastico e universitario	*Scol*	schooling, schools and universities
singolare	*sg*	singular
soggetto (grammaticale)	*sog*	(grammatical) subject
	sth	something
congiuntivo	*sub*	subjunctive
soggetto (grammaticale)	*subj*	(grammatical) subject
superlativo	*superl*	superlative
termine tecnico, tecnologia	*Tecn, Tech*	technical term, technology
telecomunicazioni	*Tel*	telecommunications
tipografia	*Tip*	typography, printing
televisione	*TV*	television
tipografia	*Typ*	typography, printing
università	*Univ*	university
inglese americano	*US*	American English
vocale	*V*	vowel
verbo	*vb*	verb
verbo o gruppo verbale con funzione intransitiva	*vi*	verb or phrasal verb used intransitively
verbo pronominale o riflessivo	*vpr*	pronominal or reflexive verb
verbo o gruppo verbale con funzione transitiva	*vt*	verb or phrasal verb used transitively
zoologia	*Zool*	zoology
marchio registrato	®	registered trademark
introduce un'equivalenza culturale	≈	introduces a cultural equivalent

TRASCRIZIONE FONETICA

Consonanti — Consonants

NB **p, b, t, d, k, g** sono seguite da un'aspirazione in inglese.

NB **p, b, t, d, k, g** are not aspirated in Italian.

padre	p	**p**u**pp**y
bam**b**ino	b	**b**a**b**y
tu**tt**o	t	**t**en**t**
da**d**o	d	**d**a**dd**y
cane **ch**e	k	**c**ork **k**iss **ch**ord
gola **gh**iro	g	**g**a**g** **g**uess
sano	s	**s**o ri**c**e ki**ss**
svago e**s**ame	z	cou**s**in buzz
scena	ʃ	**sh**eep **s**ugar
	ʒ	plea**s**ure bei**g**e
pe**c**e lan**ci**are	tʃ	**ch**ur**ch**
giro **gi**oco	dʒ	**j**udge **g**eneral
a**f**a **f**aro	f	**f**arm ra**ff**le
vero bra**v**o	v	**v**ery re**v**
	θ	**th**in ma**th**s
	ð	**th**at o**th**er
le**tt**o a**l**a	l	**l**itt**l**e ba**ll**
g**l**i	ʎ	mi**lli**on
rete a**r**co	r	**r**at **r**a**r**e
ramo mad**r**e	m	**m**u**mm**y co**m**b
no fuma**n**te	n	**n**o ra**n**
gnomo	ɲ	ca**ny**on
	ŋ	si**ng**ing ba**n**k
	h	**h**at re**h**eat
bu**i**o p**i**acere	j	**y**et
uomo g**u**aio	w	**w**all be**w**ail
lo**ch**	x	

Varie — Miscellaneous

per l'inglese: la "r" finale viene pronunciata se seguita da una vocale	r	
precede la sillaba accentata	ˈ	precedes the stressed syllable

PHONETIC TRANSCRIPTION

Vocali		Vowels

NB La messa in equivalenza di certi suoni indica solo una rassomiglianza approssimativa.

NB The pairing of some vowel sounds only indicates approximate equivalence.

vino idea	i iː	heel bead
	ɪ	hit pity
stella edera	e	
epoca eccetto	ɛ	set tent
mamma amore	a æ	bat apple
	ɑː	after car calm
fiancé	ɑ̃	
	ʌ	fun cousin
müsli	y	
	ə	over above
	əː	urn fern work
rosa occhio	ɔ	wash pot
	ɔː	born cork
ponte ognuno	o	
föhn	ø	
utile zucca	u	full soot
	uː	boon lewd

Dittonghi		Diphthongs
	ɪə	beer tier
	ɛə	tear fair there
	eɪ	date plaice day
	aɪ	life buy cry
	au	owl foul now
	əu	low no
	ɔɪ	boil boy oily
	uə	poor tour

ITALIAN PRONUNCIATION

Vowels

Where the vowel **e** or the vowel **o** appears in a stressed syllable it can be either open [ɛ],[ɔ] or closed [e],[o]. As the open or closed pronunciation of these vowels is subject to regional variation, the distinction is of little importance to the user of this dictionary. Phonetic transcription for headwords containing these vowels will therefore only appear where other pronunciation difficulties are present.

Consonants

c before "e" or "i" is pronounced like the "*tch*" in match.
ch is pronounced like the "*k*" in "kit".
g before "e" or "i" is pronounced like the "*j*" in "jet".
gh is pronounced like the "*g*" in "get".
gl before "e" or "i" is normally pronounced like the "*lli*" in "million", and in a few cases only like the "*gl*" in "glove".
gn is pronounced like the "*ny*" in "canyon"
sc before "e" or "i" is pronounced "*sh*".
z is pronounced like the "*ts*" in "stetson", or like the "*d's*" in "bird's-eye".

Headwords containing the above consonants and consonantal groups have been given full phonetic transcription in this dictionary.

NB All double written consonants in Italian are fully sounded: e.g. the *tt* in "tutto" is pronounced as in "hat trick".

ITALIAN VERB FORMS

a Gerund **b** Past participle **c** Present **d** Imperfect **e** Past historic **f** Future
g Conditional **h** Present subjunctive **i** Imperfect subjunctive **j** Imperative

1 **abbattere e** abbattei, abbattesti
   (*doesn't have alternative forms* -etti,
   -ette, -ettero)
2 **accendere b** acceso **e** accesi,
   accendesti
3 **accludere b** accluso **e** acclusi,
   accludesti
4 **accorgersi b** accorto **e** mi accorsi,
   ti accorgesti
5 **aggiungere b** aggiunto
   e aggiunsi, aggiungesti
6 **andare c** vado, vai, va, andiamo,
   andate, vanno **f** andrò *etc.* **h** vada
   j va'!, vada!, andate!, vadano!
7 **apparire b** apparso **c** appaio,
   appari *or* apparisci, appare *or*
   apparisce, appaiono *or*
   appariscono **e** apparvi *or* apparsi,
   apparisti, apparve *or* apparì *or*
   apparse, apparvero *or* apparirono
   or apparsero **h** appaia *or* apparisca
8 **appendere b** appeso **e** appesi,
   appendesti
9 **aprire b** aperto **c** apro **e** aprii,
   apristi **h** apra
10 **ardere b** arso **e** arsi, ardesti
11 **assistere e** assistei *or* assistesti *or*
   assistetti, assistesti
12 **assumere b** assunto **e** assunsi,
   assumesti
13 AVERE **c** ho, hai, ha, abbiamo,
   avete, hanno **e** ebbi, avesti, ebbe,
   avemmo, aveste, ebbero **f** avrò
   etc. **h** abbia *etc.* **j** abbi!, abbia!,
   abbiate!, abbiano!
14 **baciare** *when the ending begins
   with* -e, *the* i *is dropped* —> bacerò
   (*not* bacierò)
15 **bagnare c** bagniamo, bagniate
   h bagniamo, bagniate (*not*
   bagnamo, bagnate)

16 **bere a** bevendo **b** bevuto **c** bevo
   etc. **d** bevevo *etc.* **e** bevvi *or*
   bevetti, bevesti **f** berrò *etc.* **h** beva
   etc. **i** bevessi *etc.*
17 **bollire c** bollo *or* bollisco, bolli *or*
   bollisci *etc.*
18 **cadere e** caddi, cadesti **f** cadrò *etc.*
19 **cambiare** *drops the* i *of the root if
   the ending starts with* i (cambi,
   cambino *not* cambii, cambiino
   (*cf.* inviare)
20 **caricare** *when* c *in the root is
   followed by* -i *or* -e *an* h *should be
   inserted* (ie carichi, carichiamo,
   caricherò)
21 **chiedere b** chiesto **e** chiesi,
   chiedesti
22 **chiudere b** chiuso **e** chiusi,
   chiudesti
23 **cogliere b** colto **c** colgo, colgono
   e colsi, cogliesti **h** colga
24 **compiere b** compiuto **e** compii,
   compisti
25 **confondere b** confuso **e** confusi,
   confondesti
26 **conoscere b** conosciuto
   e conobbi, conoscesti
27 **consigliare** *when the ending begins
   with* -i, *the* i *of the root is dropped*
   -> consigli (*not* consiglii)
28 **correre b** corso **e** corsi, corresti
29 CREDERE **a** credendo **b** creduto
   c credo, credi, crede, crediamo,
   credete, credono **d** credevo,
   credevi, credeva, credevamo,
   credevate, credevano **e** credei *or*
   credetti, credesti, credé *or*
   credette, credemmo, credeste,
   crederono *or* credettero **f** crederò,
   crederai, crederà, crederemo,
   crederete, crederanno **g** crederei,

credaresti, crederebbe,
credaremmo, credereste,
crederebbero **h** creda, creda,
creda, crediamo, crediate,
credano **i** credessi, credessi,
credesse, credessimo, credeste,
credessero **j** credi!, creda!,
credete!, credano!

30 crescere b cresciuto **e** crebbi,
crescesti

31 cucire when c or g in the root is
followed by -o or -a an i should be
inserted (ie cucio, cucia)

32 cuocere b cotto **c** cuocio,
cociamo, cuociono **e** cossi, cocesti

33 dare b do, dai, dà, diamo, date,
danno **e** diedi or detti, desti **f** darò
etc. **h** dia etc. **i** dessi etc. **j** da'!, dai!,
date!, diano!

34 decidere b deciso **e** decisi,
decidesti

35 deludere b deluso **e** delusi,
deludesti

36 difendere b difeso **e** difesi,
difendesti

37 dipingere b dipinto **e** dipinsi,
dipingesti

38 dire a dicendo **b** detto **c** dico, dici,
dice, diciamo, dite, dicono
d dicevo etc. **e** dissi, dicesti **f** dirò
etc. **h** dica, diciamo, diciate,
dicano **i** dicessi etc. **j** di'!, dica!,
dite!, dicano!

39 dirigere b diretto **e** diressi,
dirigesti

40 discutere b discusso **e** discussi,
discutesti

41 disfare like fare but **c** disfo, disfi
etc. **f** disferò, disferai etc. **i** disfi,
disfi etc. (regular forms)

42 distinguere b distinto **e** distinsi,
distinguesti

43 dividere b diviso **e** divisi,
dividesti

44 dolere c dolgo, duoli, duole,
dolgono **e** dolsi, dolesti **f** dorrò etc.
h dolga

45 DORMIRE a dormendo **b** dormito
c dormo, dormi, dorme,
dormiamo, dormite, dormono
d dormivo, dormivi, dormiva,
dormivamo, dormivate,
dormivano **e** dormii, dormisti,
dormì, dormimmo, dormiste,
dormirono **f** dormirò, dormirai,
dormirà, dormiremo, dormirete,
dormiranno **g** dormirei,
dormiresti, dormirebbe,
dormiremmo, dormireste,
dormirebbero **h** dorma, dorma,
dorma, dormiamo, dormiate,
dormano **i** dormissi, dormissi,
dormisse, dormissimo, dormiste,
dormissero **j** dormi!, dorma!,
dormite!, dormano!

46 dovere c devo or debbo, devi, deve,
dobbiamo, dovete, devono or
debbono **f** dovrò etc. **h** debba,
dobbiamo, dobbiate, devano or
debbano

47 esigere b esatto (not common)
e esigei or esigetti, esigesti

48 espellere b espulso **e** espulsi,
espellesti

49 esplodere b esploso **e** esplosi,
esplodesti

50 esprimere b espresso **e** espressi,
esprimesti

51 ESSERE b stato **c** sono, sei, è,
siamo, siete, sono **d** ero, eri, era,
eravamo, eravate, erano **e** fui,
fosti, fu, fummo, foste, furono
f sarò etc. **h** sia etc. **i** fossi, fossi,
fosse, fossimo, foste, fossero **j** sii!,
sia!, siate!, siano!

52 evadere b evaso **e** evasi, evadesti

53 fare a facendo **b** fatto **c** faccio, fai,
fa, facciamo, fate, fanno **d** facevo
etc. **e** feci, facesti **f** farò etc. **h** faccia
etc. **i** facessi etc. **j** fa'!, faccia!, fate!,
facciano!

54 fingere b finto **e** finsi, fingesti

55 FINIRE a finendo **b** finito **c** finisco,
finisci, finisce, finiamo, finite,

finiscono **d** finivo, finivi, finiva,
finivamo, finivate, finivano **e** finii,
finisti, finì, finimmo, finiste,
finirono **f** finirò, finirai, finirà,
finiremo, finirete, finiranno
g finirei, finiresti, finirebbe,
finiremmo, finireste, finirebbero
h finisca, finisca, finisca, finiamo,
finiate, finiscano **i** finissi, finissi,
finisse, finissimo, finiste, finissero
j finisci!, finisca!, finite!, finiscano!
56 **friggere b** fritto **e** frissi, friggesti
57 **giacere b** giaciuto **e** giacqui,
giacesti
58 **godere f** godrò, godrai *etc.*
g godrei, godresti *etc.*
59 **immergere b** immerso **e** immersi,
immergesti
60 **inviare c** (tu) invii **f** (essi) inviino
61 **leggere b** letto **e** lessi, leggesti
62 **mangiare** *when the ending begins
with* -e, *the* i *is dropped* —> mangerò
(not mangierò)
63 **mettere b** messo **e** misi, mettesti
64 **mordere b** morso **e** morsi,
mordesti
65 **morire b** morto **c** muoio, muori,
muore, moriamo, morite,
muoiono **f** morirò *or* morrò *etc.*
h muoia
66 **muovere b** mosso **e** mossi,
muovesti
67 **nascere b** nato **e** nacqui,
nascesti
68 **nascondere b** nascosto
e nascosi, nascondesti
69 **nuocere b** nuociuto **c** nuoccio,
nuoci, nuoce, nociamo *or*
nuociamo, nuocete, nuocciono
d nuocevo *etc.* **e** nocqui, nuocesti
f nuocerò *etc.* **g** nuoccia
70 **offrire b** offerto **c** offro **e** offersi *or*
offrii, offristi **h** offra
71 **parere b** parso **c** paio, paiamo,
paiono **e** parvi *or* parsi, paresti
f parrò *etc.* **h** paia, paiamo, paiate,
paiano

72 **PARLARE a** parlando **b** parlato
c parlo, parli, parla, parliamo,
parlate, parlano **d** parlavo,
parlavi, parlava, parlavamo,
parlavate, parlavano **e** parlai,
parlasti, parlò, parlammo,
parlaste, parlarono **f** parlerò,
parlerai, parlerà, parleremo,
parlerete, parleranno **g** parlerei,
parleresti, parlerebbe,
parleremmo, parlereste,
parlerebbero **h** parli, parli, parli,
parliamo, parliate, parlino
i parlassi, parlassi, parlasse,
parlassimo, parlaste, parlassero
j parla!, parli!, parlate!, parlino!
73 **perdere b** perso *or* perduto
e persi, perdesti
74 **piacere b** piaciuto **c** piaccio,
piacciamo, piacciono **e** piacqui,
piacesti **h** piaccia *etc.*
75 **piangere b** pianto **e** piansi,
piangesti
76 **piovere b** piovuto **e** piovve
77 **porre a** ponendo **b** posto **c** pongo,
poni, pone, poniamo, ponete,
pongono **d** ponevo *etc.* **e** posi,
ponesti **f** porrò *etc.* **h** ponga,
poniamo, poniate, pongano
i ponessi *etc.*
78 **potere c** posso, puoi, può,
possiamo, potete, possono
f potrò *etc.* **h** possa, possiamo,
possiate, possano
79 **prefiggersi b** prefisso **e** mi
prefissi, ti prefiggesti
80 **pregare** *when* g *in the root is
followed by* -i *or* -e *an* h *should be
inserted (ie* preghi, preghiamo,
pregherò)
81 **prendere b** preso **e** presi,
prendesti
82 **prevedere** *like* vedere *but*
f prevederò, prevederai *etc.*
g prevederei *etc.*
83 **proteggere b** protetto **e** protessi,
proteggesti

84 **pungere b** punto **e** punsi, pungesti

85 **radere b** raso **e** rasi, radesti

86 **redimere b** redento **e** redensi, redimesti

87 **reggere b** retto **e** ressi, reggesti

88 **rendere b** reso **e** resi, rendesti

89 **ridere b** riso **e** risi, ridesti

90 **ridurre a** riducendo **b** ridotto **c** riduco *etc.* **d** riducevo *etc.* **e** ridussi, riducesti **f** ridurrò *etc.* **h** riduca *etc.* **i** riducessi *etc.*

91 **riempire a** riempiendo **c** riempio, riempi, riempie, riempiono

92 **riflettere b** riflettuto *or* riflesso

93 **rimanere b** rimasto **c** rimango, rimangono **e** rimasi, rimanesti **f** rimarrò *etc.* **h** rimanga

94 **risolvere b** risolto **e** risolsi, risolvesti

95 **rispondere b** risposto **e** risposi, rispondesti

96 **rivolgere b** rivolto **e** rivolsi, rivolgesti

97 **rompere b** rotto **e** ruppi, rompesti

98 **salire c** salgo, sali, salgono **h** salga

99 **sapere c** so, sai, sa, sappiamo, sapete, sanno **e** seppi, sapesti **f** saprò *etc.* **h** sappia *etc.* **j** sappi!, sappia!, sappiate!, sappiano!

100 **scegliere b** scelto **c** scelgo, scegli, sceglie, scegliamo, scegliete, scelgono **e** scelsi, scegliesti **h** scelga, scegliamo, scegliate, scelgano **j** scegli!, scelga!, scegliamo!, scegliete!, scelgano!

101 **scendere b** sceso **e** scesi, scendesti

102 **scindere b** scisso **e** scissi, scindesti

103 **sciogliere b** sciolto **c** sciolgo, sciogli, scioglie, sciogliamo, sciogliete, sciolgono **e** sciolsi, sciogliesti **h** sciolga, sciogliamo, sciogliate, sciolgano **j** sciogli!, sciolga!, sciogliamo!, sciogliete!, sciolgano!

104 **sconfiggere b** sconfitto **e** sconfissi, sconfiggesti

105 **scrivere b** scritto **e** scrissi, scrivesti

106 **scuotere b** scosso **e** scossi, scuotesti

107 **sedere c** siedo, siedi, siede, siedono **h** sieda

108 **solere b** solito **e** soglio, suoli, suole, sogliamo, solete, sogliono **h** soglia (*regular imperfect, gerund, past participle; no other verb forms*)

109 **sorgere b** sorto **e** sorse, sorsero

110 **spandere b** spanto **e** spansi, spandesti

111 **spargere b** sorto **e** sorse, sorsero

112 **sparire e** sparii, sparisti

113 **spegnere b** spento **c** spengo, spengono **e** spensi, spegnesti **h** spenga

114 **spingere b** spinto **e** spinsi, spingesti

115 **sporgere b** sporto **e** sporsi, sporgesti

116 **stare b** stato **c** sto, stai, sta, stiamo, state, stanno **e** stetti, stesti **f** starò *etc.* **h** stia *etc.* **i** stessi *etc.* **j** sta'!, stia!, state!, stiano!

117 **stringere b** stretto **e** strinsi, stringesti

118 **succedere b** successo **e** successi, succedesti

119 **tacere b** taciuto **c** taccio, tacciono **e** tacqui, tacesti **h** taccia

120 **tendere b** teso **e** tesi, tendesti

121 **tenere c** tengo, tieni, tiene, tengono **e** tenni, tenesti **f** terrò *etc.* **h** tenga

122 **togliere b** tolto **c** tolgo, togli, toglie, togliamo, togliete, tolgono **e** tolsi, togliesti **h** tolga **j** togli!, tolga!, togliamo!, togliete!, tolgano!

123 **trarre a** traendo **b** tratto **c** traggo, trai, trae, traiamo,

traete, traggono **d** traevo *etc.*
e trassi, traesti **f** trarrò *etc.*
h tragga **i** traessi *etc.*
124 udire c odo, odi, ode, odono **h** oda
125 uscire c esco, esci, esce, escono
h esca
126 valere b valso **c** valgo, valgono
e valsi, valesti **f** varrò *etc.* **h** valga
127 vedere b visto *or* veduto **e** vidi,
vedesti **f** vedrò *etc.*

128 venire b venuto **c** vengo, vieni,
viene, vengono **e** venni, venisti
f verrò *etc.* **h** venga
129 vincere b vinto **e** vinsi,
vincesti
130 vivere b vissuto **e** vissi, vivesti
131 volere c voglio, vuoi, vuole,
vogliamo, volete, vogliono **e** volli,
volesti **f** vorrò *etc.* **h** voglia *etc.* **j** *not
common*

ENGLISH VERB FORMS

present	pt	pp	present	pt	pp
arise	arose	arisen	feed	fed	fed
awake	awoke	awoken	feel	felt	felt
be (am, is, are; being)	was, were	been	fight	fought	fought
			find	found	found
bear	bore	born(e)	flee	fled	fled
beat	beat	beaten	fling	flung	flung
become	became	become	fly	flew	flown
begin	began	begun	forbid	forbade	forbidden
bend	bent	bent	forecast	forecast	forecast
bet	bet, betted	bet, betted	forget	forgot	forgotten
			forgive	forgave	forgiven
bid (at auction, cards)	bid	bid	forsake	forsook	forsaken
			freeze	froze	frozen
bid (say)	bade	bidden	get	got	got, (US) gotten
bind	bound	bound			
bite	bit	bitten	give	gave	given
bleed	bled	bled	go (goes)	went	gone
blow	blew	blown	grind	ground	ground
break	broke	broken	grow	grew	grown
breed	bred	bred	hang	hung	hung
bring	brought	brought	hang (execute)	hanged	hanged
build	built	built	have (has; having)	had	had
burn	burnt, burned	burnt, burned	hear	heard	heard
			hide	hid	hidden
burst	burst	burst	hit	hit	hit
buy	bought	bought	hold	held	held
can	could	(been able)	hurt	hurt	hurt
cast	cast	cast	keep	kept	kept
catch	caught	caught	kneel	knelt, kneeled	knelt, kneeled
choose	chose	chosen			
cling	clung	clung	know	knew	known
come	came	come	lay	laid	laid
cost	cost	cost	lead	led	led
cost (work out price of)	costed	costed	lean	leant, leaned	leant, leaned
creep	crept	crept	leap	leapt, leaped	leapt, leaped
cut	cut	cut			
deal	dealt	dealt	learn	learnt, learned	learnt, learned
dig	dug	dug			
do (does)	did	done	leave	left	left
draw	drew	drawn	lend	lent	lent
dream	dreamed, dreamt	dreamed, dreamt	let	let	let
			lie (lying)	lay	lain
drink	drank	drunk	light	lit, lighted	lit, lighted
drive	drove	driven			
dwell	dwelt	dwelt	lose	lost	lost
eat	ate	eaten	make	made	made
fall	fell	fallen			

present	pt	pp	present	pt	pp
may	might	—	spell	spelt, spelled	spelt, spelled
mean	meant	meant			
meet	met	met	spend	spent	spent
mistake	mistook	mistaken	spill	spilt, spilled	spilt, spilled
mow	mowed	mown, mowed			
			spin	spun	spun
must	(had to)	(had to)	spit	spat	spat
pay	paid	paid	split	split	split
put	put	put	spoil	spoiled, spoilt	spoiled, spoilt
quit	quit, quitted	quit, quitted			
			spread	spread	spread
read	read	read	spring	sprang	sprung
rid	rid	rid	stand	stood	stood
ride	rode	ridden	steal	stole	stolen
ring	rang	rung	stick	stuck	stuck
rise	rose	risen	sting	stung	stung
run	ran	run	stink	stank	stunk
saw	sawed	sawed, sawn	stride	strode	stridden
			strike	struck	struck, stricken
say	said	said			
see	saw	seen	strive	strove	striven
seek	sought	sought	swear	swore	sworn
sell	sold	sold	sweep	swept	swept
send	sent	sent	swell	swelled	swollen, swelled
sew	sewed	sewn			
shake	shook	shaken	swim	swam	swum
shear	sheared	shorn, sheared	swing	swung	swung
			take	took	taken
shed	shed	shed	teach	taught	taught
shine	shone	shone	tear	tore	torn
shoot	shot	shot	tell	told	told
show	showed	shown	think	thought	thought
shrink	shrank	shrunk	throw	threw	thrown
shut	shut	shut	thrust	thrust	thrust
sing	sang	sung	tread	trod	trodden
sink	sank	sunk	wake	woke, waked	woken, waked
sit	sat	sat			
slay	slew	slain	wear	wore	worn
sleep	slept	slept	weave	wove, weaved	woven, weaved
slide	slid	slid			
sling	slung	slung	wed	wedded, wed	wedded, wed
slit	slit	slit			
smell	smelt, smelled	smelt, smelled	weep	wept	wept
			win	won	won
sow	sowed	sown, sowed	wind	wound	wound
			wring	wrung	wrung
speak	spoke	spoken	write	wrote	written
speed	sped, speeded	sped, speeded			

I NUMERI		NUMBERS
uno(a)	1	one
due	2	two
tre	3	three
quattro	4	four
cinque	5	five
sei	6	six
sette	7	seven
otto	8	eight
nove	9	nine
dieci	10	ten
undici	11	eleven
dodici	12	twelve
tredici	13	thirteen
quattordici	14	fourteen
quindici	15	fifteen
sedici	16	sixteen
diciassette	17	seventeen
diciotto	18	eighteen
diciannove	19	nineteen
venti	20	twenty
ventuno	21	twenty-one
ventidue	22	twenty-two
ventitré	23	twenty-three
ventotto	28	twenty-eight
trenta	30	thirty
quaranta	40	forty
cinquanta	50	fifty
sessanta	60	sixty
settanta	70	seventy
ottanta	80	eighty
novanta	90	ninety
cento	100	a hundred
cento uno	101	a hundred and one
duecento	200	two hundred
mille	1 000	a thousand
milleduecentodue	1 202	one thousand two hundred and two
cinquemila	5000	five thousand
un milione	1 000 000	a million

I NUMERI

primo(a)
secondo(a)
terzo(a)
quarto(a)
quinto(a)
sesto(a)
settimo(a)
ottavo(a)
nono(a)
decimo(a)
undicesimo(a)
dodicesimo(a)
tredicesimo(a)
quattordicesimo(a)
quindicesimo(a)
sedicesimo(a)
diciassettesimo(a)
diciottesimo(a)
diciannovesimo(a)
ventesimo(a)
ventunesimo(a)
ventiduesimo(a)
ventitreesimo(a)
ventottesimo(a)
trentesimo(a)
centesimo(a)
centunesimo(a)
millesimo(a)
milionesimo(a)

NUMBERS

first, 1st
second, 2nd
third, 3rd
fourth, 4th
fifth, 5th
sixth, 6th
seventh
eighth
ninth
tenth
eleventh
twelfth
thirteenth
fourteenth
fifteenth
sixteenth
seventeenth
eighteenth
nineteenth
twentieth
twenty-first
twenty-second
twenty-third
twenty-eighth
thirtieth
hundredth
hundred-and-first
thousandth
millionth

Frazioni

mezzo
terzo
due terzi
quarto
quinto
zero virgola cinque, 0,5
tre virgola quattro, 3,4
dieci per cento
cento per cento

Esempi

abita al numero dieci
si trova nel capitolo sette,
 a pagina sette
abita al terzo piano
arrivò quarto
scala uno a venticinquemila

Fractions

half
third
two thirds
quarter
fifth
(nought) point five, 0.5
three point four, 3.4
ten per cent
a hundred per cent

Examples

he lives at number 10
it's in chapter 7, on page 7

he lives on the 3rd floor
he came in 4th
scale 1:25,000

L'ORA

che ora è?, che ore sono?

è ..., sono ...

mezzanotte
l'una (di notte)

le tre del mattino

l'una e cinque
l'una e dieci
l'una e un quarto, l'una e quindici

l'una e venticinque

l'una e mezzo *or* mezza, l'una e
trenta
le due meno venticinque, l'una
e trentacinque
le due meno venti, l'una e
quaranta
le due meno un quarto, l'una e
tre quarti
le due meno dieci, l'una e cinquanta
le dodici, mezzogiorno

l'una, le tredici

le sette (di sera), le diciannove

a che ora?

a mezzanotte
all'una, alle tredici
fra venti minuti
venti minuti fa

THE TIME

what time is it?

it's ...

midnight
one o'clock (in the
  morning), one (a.m.)
three o'clock (in the
  morning), three (a.m.)
five past one
ten past one
a quarter past one,
  one fifteen
twenty-five past one,
  one twenty-five
half past one, one thirty

twenty-five to two,
  one thirty-five
twenty to two, one forty

a quarter to two, one
  forty-five
ten to two, one fifty
twelve o'clock, midday,
  noon
one o'clock (in the
  afternoon), one (p.m.)
seven o'clock (in the
  evening), seven (p.m.)

at what time?

at midnight
at one o'clock
in twenty minutes
twenty minutes ago

LA DATA

oggi	today
ogni giorno, tutti i giorni	every day
ieri	yesterday
stamattina	this morning
domani notte; domani sera	tomorrow night
l'altroieri notte; l'altroieri sera	the night before last
l'altroieri	the day before yesterday
ieri notte; ieri sera	last night
due giorni/sei anni fa	two days/six years ago
domani pomeriggio	tomorrow afternoon
dopodomani	the day after tomorrow
tutti i giovedì, di or il giovedì	every Thursday, on Thursdays
ci va di or il venerdì	he goes on Fridays
"chiuso il mercoledì"	"closed on Wednesdays"
dal lunedì al venerdì	from Monday to Friday
per giovedì, entro giovedì	by Thursday
un sabato di marzo	one Saturday in March
tra una settimana	in a week's time
martedì a otto	a week next or on Tuesday
questa/la prossima/la scorsa settimana	this/next/last week
tra due settimane, tra quindici giorni	in two weeks or a fortnight
lunedì a quindici	two weeks on Monday
il primo/l'ultimo venerdì del mese	the first/last Friday of the month
il mese prossimo	next month
l'anno scorso	last year
il primo giugno	the 1st of June, June first
il due ottobre	the 2nd of October or October 2nd
sono nato nel 1987	I was born in 1987
il suo compleano è il 5 giugno	his birthday is on June 5th (BRIT) or 5th June (US)
il 18 agosto	on 18th August (BRIT) or August 18 (US)
nel 2011	in 2011
nella primavera del '94	in the Spring of '94
dal 19 al 3	from the 19th to the 3rd
quanti ne abbiamo oggi?	what's the date? or what date is it today?

oggi è il 15	today's date is the 15th *or* today is the 15th
1988 - millenovecentottantotto	1988 - nineteen eighty-eight
2011 - duemilaundici	2011 - two thousand and eleven
10 anni esatti	10 years to the day
alla fine del mese	at the end of the month
la settimana del 30/7	week ending 30/7
giornalmente *or* al giorno	daily
settimanalmente *or* alla settimana	weekly
mensilmente, al mese	monthly
annualmente *or* all'anno	annually
due volte alla settimana/al mese/ all'anno	twice a week/month/year
bimestralmente	bi-monthly
nel 4 a.C.	in 4 B.C. *or* B.C. 4
nel 79 d.C.	in 79 A.D *or* A.D. 79
nel tredicesimo secolo	in the 13th century
negli anni '80	in *or* during the 80s
nel 1990 e rotti	in 1990 something

La data nelle lettere
9 ottobre 2011

Headings of letters
9th October 2011 *or*
9 October 2011

A *abbr* (= *autostrada*) ≈ M (BRIT)

PAROLA CHIAVE

a (*a* + *il* = **al**, *a* + *lo* = **allo**, *a* + *l'* = **all'**, *a* + *la* = **alla**, *a* + *i* = **ai**, *a* + *gli* = **agli**, *a* + *le* = **alle**) *prep* **1** (*stato in luogo*) at; (: *in*) in; **essere a casa/a scuola/a Roma** to be at home/at school/in Rome; **essere alla stazione** to be at the station; **è a 10 km da qui** it's 10 km from here, it's 10 km away
2 (*moto a luogo*) to; **andare a casa/a scuola/alla stazione** to go home/to school/to the station
3 (*tempo*) at; (*epoca, stagione*) in; **alle cinque** at five (o'clock); **a mezzanotte/Natale** at midnight/Christmas; **al mattino** in the morning; **a maggio/primavera** in May/spring; **a cinquant'anni** at fifty (years of age); **a domani!** see you tomorrow!
4 (*complemento di termine*) to; **dare qc a qn** to give sb sth
5 (*mezzo, modo*) with, by; **a piedi/cavallo** on foot/horseback; **fatto a mano** made by hand, handmade; **una barca a motore** a motorboat; **a uno a uno** one by one; **all'italiana** the Italian way, in the Italian fashion
6 (*rapporto*) a, per; (: *con prezzi*) a; **prendo 2000 euro al mese** I get 2000 euro a *o* per month; **pagato a ore** paid by the hour; **vendere qc a 2 euro il chilo** to sell sth at 2 euros a *o* per kilo

abbagli'ante [abbaʎ'ʎante] *ag* dazzling; **abbaglianti** *smpl* (Aut): **accendere gli abbaglianti** to put one's headlights on full (BRIT) *o* high (US) beam

abbagli'are [abbaʎ'ʎare] /27/ *vt* to dazzle; (*illudere*) to delude

abbai'are /19/ *vi* to bark

abbando'nare /72/ *vt* to leave, abandon, desert; (*trascurare*) to neglect; (*rinunciare a*) to abandon, give up; **abbandonarsi** *vpr* to let o.s. go; **abbandonarsi a** (*ricordi, vizio*) to give o.s. up to

abbas'sare /72/ *vt* to lower; (*radio*) to turn down; **abbassarsi** *vpr* (*chinarsi*) to stoop; (*livello, sole*) to go down; (*fig: umiliarsi*) to demean o.s.; **~ i fari** (Aut) to dip (BRIT) *o* dim (US) one's lights

ab'basso *escl*: **~ il re!** down with the king!

abbas'tanza [abbas'tantsa] *av* (*a sufficienza*) enough; (*alquanto*) quite, rather, fairly; **non è ~ furbo** he's not shrewd enough; **un vino ~ dolce** quite a sweet wine; **averne ~ di qn/qc** to have had enough of sb/sth

ab'battere /1/ *vt* (*muro, casa, ostacolo*) to knock down; (*albero*) to fell; (: *vento*) to bring down; (*bestie da macello*) to slaughter; (*cane, cavallo*) to destroy, put down; (*selvaggina, aereo*) to shoot down; (*fig: malattia,* *disgrazia*) to lay low; **abbattersi** *vpr* (*avvilirsi*) to lose heart; **abbat'tuto, -a** *ag* (*fig*) depressed

abba'zia [abbat'tsia] *sf* abbey

'abbia *vb vedi* **avere**

abbi'ente *ag* well-to-do, well-off; **abbienti** *smpl:* **gli abbienti** the well-to-do

abbiglia'mento [abbiʎʎa'mento] *sm* dress *no pl*; (*indumenti*) clothes *pl*; (*industria*) clothing industry

abbi'nare /72/ *vt:* **~ (con** *o* **a)** to combine (with)

abboc'care /20/ *vi* (*pesce*) to bite; (*tubi*) to join; **~ (all'amo)** (*fig*) to swallow the bait

abbona'mento *sm* subscription; (*alle ferrovie ecc*) season ticket; **fare l'~ (a)** to take out a subscription (to)

abbo'nare /72/ *vt* to deduct; **abbonarsi** *vpr:* **abbonarsi a un giornale** to take out a subscription to a newspaper; **abbonarsi al teatro/ alle ferrovie** to take out a season ticket for the theatre/the train

abbon'dante *ag* abundant, plentiful; (*giacca*) roomy

abbon'danza [abbon'dantsa] *sf* abundance; plenty

abbor'dabile *ag* (*persona*) approachable; (*prezzo*) reasonable

abbotto'nare /72/ *vt* to button up, do up

abbracci'are [abbrat'tʃare] /14/ *vt* to embrace; (*persona*) to hug, embrace; (*professione*) to take up; (*contenere*) to include; **abbracciarsi** *vpr* to hug *o* embrace (one another); **ab'braccio** *sm* hug, embrace

abbrevi'are /19/ *vt* to shorten; (*parola*) to abbreviate

abbreviazi'one [abbrevjat'tsjone] *sf* abbreviation

abbron'zante [abbron'dzante] *ag* tanning, sun *cpd*

abbron'zare [abbron'dzare] /72/ *vt* to tan; **abbronzarsi** *vpr* to tan, get a tan

abbron'zato, -a [abbron'dzato] *ag* (sun)tanned

abbrusto'lire /55/ *vt* (*pane*) to toast; (*caffè*) to roast; **abbrustolirsi** *vpr* to toast; (*fig, al sole*) to soak up the sun

abbuf'farsi /72/ *vpr* (*fam*): **~ (di qc)** to stuff o.s. (with sth)

abdi'care /20/ *vi* to abdicate; **~ a** to give up, renounce

a'bete *sm* fir (tree); **~ rosso** spruce

'abile *ag* (*idoneo*): **~ (a qc/a fare qc)** fit (for sth/to do sth); (*capace*) able; (*astuto*) clever; (*accorto*) skilful; **~ al servizio militare** fit for military service; **abilità** *sf inv* ability; cleverness; skill

a'bisso *sm* abyss, gulf

abi'tante *smf* inhabitant

abi'tare /72/ *vt* to live in, dwell in ▷ *vi:* **~ in campagna/a Roma** to live in the country/in Rome; **dove abita?** where do you live?; **abitazi'one** *sf* residence; house

'abito *sm* dress *no pl*; (*da uomo*) suit; (*da donna*) dress; (*abitudine, disposizione, Rel*) habit; **abiti** *smpl* (*vestiti*) clothes; **in ~ da sera** in evening dress

abitu'ale *ag* usual, habitual; (*cliente*) regular

abitual'mente *av* usually, normally

abitu'are /72/ *vt:* **~ qn a** to get sb used *o* accustomed to; **abituarsi a** to get used to, accustom o.s. to

abitudi'nario, -a *ag* of fixed habits ▷ *sm/f* creature of habit

abi'tudine *sf* habit; **aver l'~ di fare qc** to be in the habit of doing sth; **d'~** usually; **per ~** from *o* out of habit

abo'lire /55/ *vt* to abolish; (*Dir*) to repeal

abor'tire /55/ *vi* (*Med*) to miscarry, have a miscarriage; (: *deliberatamente*) to have an abortion; (*fig*) to miscarry, fail; **a'borto** *sm* miscarriage; abortion

ABS [abi'ɛsse] *sigla m* (= *Anti-Blockier System*) ABS = **anti-lock braking system**

'**abside** *sf* apse

abu'sare /72/ *vi*: **~ di** to abuse, misuse; (*approfittare, violare*) to take advantage of; **~ dell'alcool/dei cibi** to drink/eat to excess

abu'sivo, -a *ag* unauthorized, unlawful; (**occupante**) **~** (*di una casa*) squatter

> Attenzione! In inglese esiste la parola *abusive*, che però vuol dire *ingiurioso*.

a.C. *abbr* (= *avanti Cristo*) BC

a'cacia, -cie [a'katʃa] *sf* (*Bot*) acacia

ac'cadde *vb vedi* **accadere**

acca'demia *sf* (*società*) learned society; (*scuola: d'arte, militare*) academy

acca'dere /18/ *vb impers* to happen, occur

accal'dato *ag* hot

accalo'rarsi /61/ *vpr* (*fig*) to get excited

accampa'mento *sm* camp

accam'pare /72/ *vt* to encamp; **accamparsi** *vpr* to camp

acca'nirsi /55/ *vpr* (*infierire*) to rage; (*ostinarsi*) to persist; **acca'nito, -a** *ag* (*odio, gelosia*) fierce, bitter; (*lavoratore*) assiduous; (*giocatore, fumatore*) inveterate

ac'canto *av* near, nearby; **~ a** *prep* near, beside, close to

accanto'nare /72/ *vt* (*problema*) to shelve; (*somma*) to set aside

accappa'toio *sm* bathrobe

accarez'zare [akkaret'tsare] /72/ *vt* to caress, stroke, fondle; (*fig*) to toy with

acca'sarsi /27/ *vpr* to set up house; to get married

accasci'arsi [akkaʃ'ʃarsi] /14/ *vpr* to collapse; (*fig*) to lose heart

accat'tone, -a *sm/f* beggar

accaval'lare /72/ *vt* (*gambe*) to cross

acce'care [attʃe'kare] /20/ *vt* to blind ▷ *vi* to go blind

ac'cedere [at'tʃedere] /29/ *vi*: **~ a** to enter; (*richiesta*) to grant, accede to

accele'rare [attʃele'rare] /72/ *vt* to speed up ▷ *vi* (*Aut*) to accelerate; **~ il passo** to quicken one's pace; **accelera'tore** *sm* (*Aut*) accelerator

ac'cendere [at'tʃɛndere] /2/ *vt* (*fuoco, sigaretta*) to light; (*luce, televisione*) to put o switch o turn on; (*Aut: motore*) to switch on; (*Comm: conto*) to open; (*fig: suscitare*) to inflame, stir up; **accen'dino, accendi'sigaro** *sm* (cigarette) lighter

accen'nare [attʃen'nare] /72/ *vt* (*Mus*) to pick out the notes of; to hum ▷ *vi*: **~ a** (*fig*) (*alludere a*) to hint at; (*far atto di*) to make as if; **~ un saluto** (*con la mano*) to make as if to wave; (*col capo*) to half nod; **accenna a piovere** it looks as if it's going to rain

ac'cenno [at'tʃenno] *sm* (*cenno*) sign; nod; (*allusione*) hint

accensi'one [attʃen'sjone] *sf* (*vedi accendere*) lighting; switching on; opening; (*Aut*) ignition

ac'cento [at'tʃento] *sm* accent; (*Fonetica, fig*) stress; (*inflessione*) tone (of voice)

accentu'are [attʃentu'are] /72/ *vt* to stress, emphasize; **accentuarsi** *vpr* to become more noticeable

accerchi'are [attʃer'kjare] /19/ *vt* to surround, encircle

accerta'mento [attʃerta'mento] *sm* check; assessment

accer'tare [attʃer'tare] /72/ *vt* to ascertain; (*verificare*) to check; (*reddito*) to assess; **accertarsi** *vpr*: **accertarsi (di qc/che)** to make sure (of sth/that)

ac'ceso, -a [at'tʃeso] *pp di* **accendere** ▷ *ag* lit; on; open; (*colore*) bright

acces'sibile [attʃes'sibile] *ag* (*luogo*) accessible; (*persona*) approachable; (*prezzo*) reasonable

ac'cesso [at'tʃesso] *sm* (*anche Inform*) access; (*Med*) attack, fit; (*impulso violento*) fit, outburst

acces'sorio, -a [attʃes'sɔrjo] *ag* secondary; **accessori** *smpl* accessories

ac'cetta [at'tʃetta] *sf* hatchet

accet'tabile [attʃet'tabile] *ag* acceptable

accet'tare [attʃet'tare] /72/ *vt* to accept; **~ di fare qc** to agree to do sth; **accettazi'one** *sf* acceptance; *(locale di servizio pubblico)* reception; **accettazione bagagli** *(Aer)* check-in (desk)

acchiap'pare [akkjap'pare] /72/ *vt* to catch

acciaie'ria [attʃaje'ria] *sf* steelworks *sg*

acci'aio [at'tʃajo] *sm* steel

acciden'tato, -a [attʃiden'tato] *ag* *(terreno ecc)* uneven

accigli'ato, -a [attʃiʎ'ʎato] *ag* frowning

ac'cingersi [at'tʃindʒersi] /54/ *vpr*: **~ a fare** to be about to do

acciuf'fare [attʃuf'fare] /72/ *vt* to seize, catch

acci'uga, -ghe [at'tʃuga] *sf* anchovy

ac'cludere /3/ *vt* to enclose

accocco'larsi /72/ *vpr* to crouch

accogli'ente [akkoʎ'ʎɛnte] *ag* welcoming, friendly

ac'cogliere /23/ *vt (ricevere)* to receive; *(dare il benvenuto)* to welcome; *(approvare)* to agree to, accept; *(contenere)* to hold, accommodate

ac'colgo *ecc vb vedi* **accogliere**

ac'colsi *ecc vb vedi* **accogliere**

accoltel'lare /72/ *vt* to knife, stab

accomoda'mento *sm* agreement, settlement

accomo'dante *ag* accommodating

accomo'dare /72/ *vt* to repair; **accomodarsi** *vpr (sedersi)* to sit down; *(fig: risolversi: situazione)* to work out; **si accomodi!** *(venga avanti)* come in!; *(si sieda)* take a seat!

accompagna'mento [akkompaɲɲa'mento] *sm (Mus)* accompaniment

accompa'gnare [akkompaɲ'ɲare] /15/ *vt* to accompany, come *o* go with; *(Mus)* to accompany; *(unire)* to couple; **~ la porta** to close the door gently

accompagna'tore, -'trice *sm/f* companion; **~ turistico** courier

acconcia'tura [akkontʃa'tura] *sf* hairstyle

accondiscen'dente [akkondiʃʃen'dɛnte] *ag* affable

acconsen'tire /17/ *vi*: **~ (a)** to agree *o* consent (to)

acconten'tare /72/ *vt* to satisfy; **accontentarsi** *vpr*: **accontentarsi di** to be satisfied with, content o.s. with

ac'conto *sm* part payment; **pagare una somma in ~** to pay a sum of money as a deposit

acco'rato, -a *ag* heartfelt

accorci'are [akkor'tʃare] /14/ *vt* to shorten; **accorciarsi** *vpr* to become shorter

accor'dare /72/ *vt* to reconcile; *(colori)* to match; *(Mus)* to tune; *(Ling)*: **~ qc con qc** to make sth agree with sth; *(Dir)* to grant; **accordarsi** *vpr* to agree, come to an agreement; *(colori)* to match

ac'cordo *sm* agreement; *(armonia)* harmony; *(Mus)* chord; **essere d'~** to agree; **andare d'~** to get on well together; **d'~!** all right!, agreed!; **~ commerciale** trade agreement

ac'corgersi [ak'kɔrdʒersi] /4/ *vpr*: **~ di** to notice; *(fig)* to realize

ac'correre /28/ *vi* to run up

ac'corto, -a *pp di* **accorgersi** ▷ *ag* shrewd; **stare ~** to be on one's guard

accos'tare /72/ *vt (avvicinarsi a)* to approach; *(socchiudere: imposte)* to half-close; *(: porta)* to leave ajar ▷ *vi*: *(Naut)* to come alongside; **accostarsi** *vpr*: **accostarsi a** to draw near, approach; *(idee politiche)* to come to agree with; **~ qc a** *(avvicinare)* to bring sth near to, put sth near to

accredi'tare /72/ vt (notizia) to confirm the truth of; (Comm) to credit; (diplomatico) to accredit

ac'credito sm (Comm: atto) crediting; (: effetto) credit

accucci'arsi [akkut'tʃarsi] /14/ vpr (cane) to lie down

accu'dire /55/ vi: ~ **a** to attend to

accumu'lare /72/ vt to accumulate; **accumularsi** vpr to accumulate; (Finanza) to accrue

accu'rato, -a ag (diligente) careful; (preciso) accurate

ac'cusa sf accusation; (Dir) charge; **la pubblica ~** the prosecution

accu'sare /72/ vt: ~ **qn di qc** to accuse sb of sth; (Dir) to charge sb with sth; ~ **ricevuta di** (Comm) to acknowledge receipt of

accusa'tore, -'trice sm/f accuser ▷ sm (Dir) prosecutor

a'cerbo, -a [a'tʃerbo] ag bitter; (frutta) sour, unripe; (persona) immature

'acero ['atʃero] sm maple

a'cerrimo, -a [a'tʃerrimo] ag very fierce

a'ceto [a'tʃeto] sm vinegar

ace'tone [atʃe'tone] sm nail varnish remover

'A.C.I. ['atʃi] sigla m (= Automobile Club d'Italia) ≈ AA (BRIT)

'acido, -a ['atʃido] ag (sapore) acid, sour; (Chim) acid ▷ sm (Chim) acid

'acino ['atʃino] sm berry; ~ **d'uva** grape

'acne sf acne

'acqua sf water; (pioggia) rain; **acque** sfpl (di mare, fiume ecc) waters; **fare ~** (Naut) to leak, take in water; ~ **in bocca!** mum's the word!; ~ **corrente** running water; ~ **dolce** fresh water; ~ **minerale** mineral water; ~ **potabile** drinking water; ~ **salata** o **salmastra** salt water; ~ **tonica** tonic water

a'cquaio sm sink

acqua'ragia [akkwa'radʒa] sf turpentine

a'cquario sm aquarium; **A~** Aquarius

acquas'cooter [akkwas'cuter] sm inv Jet Ski®

a'cquatico, -a, -ci, -che ag aquatic; (sport, sci) water cpd

acqua'vite sf brandy

acquaz'zone [akkwat'tsone] sm cloudburst, heavy shower

acque'dotto sm aqueduct; waterworks pl, water system

acque'rello sm watercolour

acqui'rente smf purchaser, buyer

acquis'tare /72/ vt to purchase, buy; (fig) to gain; **a'cquisto** sm purchase; **fare acquisti** to go shopping

acquo'lina sf: **far venire l'~ in bocca a qn** to make sb's mouth water

a'crobata, -i, -e sm/f acrobat

a'culeo sm (Zool) sting; (Bot) prickle

a'cume sm acumen, perspicacity

a'custico, -a, -ci, -che ag acoustic ▷ sf (scienza) acoustics sg; (di una sala) acoustics pl: **apparecchio ~** hearing aid; **cornetto ~** ear trumpet

a'cuto, -a ag (appuntito) sharp, pointed; (suono, voce) shrill, piercing; (Mat, Ling, Med) acute; (Mus) high-pitched; (fig: dolore, desiderio) intense; (: perspicace) acute, keen

a'dagio [a'dadʒo] av slowly ▷ sm (Mus) adagio; (proverbio) adage, saying

adatta'mento sm adaptation

adat'tare /72/ vt to adapt; (sistemare) to fit; **adattarsi** vpr: **adattarsi (a)** (ambiente, tempi) to adapt (to); (essere adatto) to be suitable (for)

a'datto, -a ag: ~ **(a)** suitable (for), right (for)

addebi'tare /72/ vt: ~ **qc a qn** to debit sb with sth

ad'debito sm (Comm) debit

adden'tare /72/ vt to bite into

adden'trarsi /72/ vpr: ~ **in** to penetrate, go into

addestra'mento sm training

addes'trare /72/ vt to train

ad'detto, -a *ag*: **~ a** (*persona*) assigned to; (*oggetto*) intended for ▷ *sm* employee; (*funzionario*) attaché; **~ commerciale/stampa** commercial/press attaché; **gli addetti ai lavori** authorized personnel; (*fig*) those in the know

ad'dio *sm, escl* goodbye, farewell

addirit'tura *av* (*veramente*) really, absolutely; (*perfino*) even; (*direttamente*) directly, right away

addi'tare /72/ *vt* to point out; (*fig*) to expose

addi'tivo *sm* additive

addizi'one *sf* addition

addob'bare /72/ *vt* to decorate; **ad'dobbo** *sm* decoration

addolo'rare /72/ *vt* to pain, grieve; **addolorarsi** *vpr*: **addolorarsi (per)** to be distressed (by)

addolo'rato, -a *ag* distressed, upset; **l'Addolorata** (*Rel*) Our Lady of Sorrows

ad'dome *sm* abdomen

addomesti'care /20/ *vt* to tame

addomi'nale *ag* abdominal; **(muscoli) addominali** stomach muscles

addormen'tare /72/ *vt* to put to sleep; **addormentarsi** *vpr* to fall asleep, go to sleep

ad'dosso *av* on; **~ a** (*sopra*) on; (*molto vicino*) right next to; **mettersi ~ il cappotto** to put one's coat on; **stare ~ a qn** (*fig*) to breathe down sb's neck; **dare ~ a qn** (*fig*) to attack sb

adegu'are /72/ *vt*: **~ qc a** to adjust sth to; **adeguarsi** *vpr* to adapt

adegu'ato, -a *ag* adequate; (*conveniente*) suitable; (*equo*) fair

a'dempiere /24/ *vt* to fulfil, carry out

ade'rente *ag* adhesive; (*vestito*) close-fitting ▷ *smf* follower

ade'rire /55/ *vi* (*stare attaccato*) to adhere, stick; **~ a** to adhere to, stick to; (*fig: società, partito*) to join; (*opinione*) to support; (*richiesta*) to agree to

adesi'one *sf* adhesion; (*fig*) agreement, acceptance; **ade'sivo, -a** *ag, sm* adhesive

a'desso *av* (*ora*) now; (*or ora, poco fa*) just now; (*tra poco*) any moment now

adia'cente [adja'tʃɛnte] *ag* adjacent

adi'bire /55/ *vt* (*usare*): **~ qc a** to turn sth into

adole'scente [adoleʃʃɛnte] *ag, smf* adolescent

adope'rare /72/ *vt* to use

ado'rare /72/ *vt* to adore; (*Rel*) to adore, worship

adot'tare /72/ *vt* to adopt; (*decisione, provvedimenti*) to pass; **adot'tivo, -a** *ag* (*genitori*) adoptive; (*figlio, patria*) adopted; **adozi'one** *sf* adoption; **adozione a distanza** child sponsorship

adri'atico, -a, -ci, -che *ag* Adriatic ▷ *sm*: **l'A~, il mare A~** the Adriatic, the Adriatic Sea

ADSL *sigla m* ADSL = **asymmetric digital subscriber line**

adu'lare /72/ *vt* to flatter

a'dultero, -a *ag* adulterous ▷ *sm/f* adulterer (adulteress)

a'dulto, -a *ag* adult; (*fig*) mature ▷ *sm* adult, grown-up

a'ereo, -a *ag* air *cpd*; (*radice*) aerial ▷ *sm* aerial; (*aeroplano*) plane; **~ da caccia** fighter (plane); **~ di linea** airliner; **~ a reazione** jet (plane); **ae'robica** *sf* aerobics *sg*; **aero'nautica** *sf* (*scienza*) aeronautics *sg*: **aeronautica militare** air force

aero'porto *sm* airport

aero'sol *sm inv* aerosol

'afa *sf* sultriness

affabile *ag* affable

affaccen'dato, -a [affattʃen'dato] *ag* (*persona*) busy

affacci'arsi [affat'tʃarsi] /14/ *vpr*: **~ (a)** to appear (at)

affa'mato, -a *ag* starving; (*fig*): **~ (di)** eager (for)

affan'noso, -a *ag* (*respiro*) difficult; (*fig*) troubled, anxious

affare *sm* (*faccenda*) matter, affair; (*Comm*) piece of business, (business) deal; (*occasione*) bargain; (*Dir*) case; (*fam: cosa*) thing; **affari** *smpl* (*Comm*) business *sg*: **ministro degli Affari Esteri** Foreign Secretary (*BRIT*), Secretary of State (*US*)

affascinante [affaʃʃi'nante] *ag* fascinating

affascinare [affaʃʃi'nare] /72/ *vt* to bewitch; (*fig*) to charm, fascinate

affaticare /20/ *vt* to tire; **affaticarsi** *vpr* (*durar fatica*) to tire o.s. out; **affaticato, -a** *ag* tired

affatto *av* completely; **non ... ~** not ... at all; **niente ~** not at all

affermare /72/ *vt* (*dichiarare*) to maintain, affirm; **affermarsi** *vpr* to assert o.s., make one's name known); **affermato, -a** *ag* established, well-known; **affermazione** *sf* affirmation, assertion; (*successo*) achievement

afferrare /72/ *vt* to seize, grasp; (*fig: idea*) to grasp; **afferrarsi** *vpr*: **afferrarsi a** to cling to

affettare /72/ *vt* (*tagliare a fette*) to slice; (*ostentare*) to affect

affettatrice [affetta'tritʃe] *sf* meat slicer

affettivo, -a *ag* emotional, affective

affetto *sm* affection; **affettuoso, -a** *ag* affectionate

affezionarsi [affettsjo'narsi] /72/ *vpr*: **~ a** to grow fond of

affezionato, -a [affettsjo'nato] *ag*: **~ a qn/qc** fond of sb/sth; (*attaccato*) attached to sb/sth

affiatato, -a *ag*: **essere affiatati** to work well together *o* get on

affibbiare /19/ *vt* (*fig: dare*) to give

affidabile *ag* reliable

affidamento *sm* (*Dir: di bambino*) custody; (*fiducia*): **fare ~ su qn** to rely on sb; **non dà nessun ~** he's not to be trusted

affidare /72/ *vt*: **~ qc** *o* **qn a qn** to entrust sth *o* sb to sb; **affidarsi** *vpr*: **affidarsi a** to place one's trust in

affilare /72/ *vt* to sharpen

affilato, -a *ag* (*gen*) sharp; (*volto, naso*) thin

affinché [affin'ke] *cong* in order that, so that

affittare /72/ *vt* (*dare in affitto*) to let, rent (out); (*prendere in affitto*) to rent; **affitto** *sm* rent; (*contratto*) lease

affliggere [af'fliddʒere] /104/ *vt* to torment; **affliggersi** *vpr* to grieve

afflissi *ecc vb vedi* **affliggere**

afflosciarsi [affloʃ'ʃarsi] /14/ *vpr* to go limp

affluente *sm* tributary

affogare /80/ *vt, vi* to drown

affollare /72/ *vt*, **affollarsi** *vpr* to crowd; **affollato, -a** *ag* crowded

affondare /72/ *vt* to sink

affrancare /20/ *vt* to free, liberate; (*Amm*) to redeem; (*lettera*) to stamp; (*: meccanicamente*) to frank (*BRIT*), meter (*US*)

affresco, -schi *sm* fresco

affrettare /72/ *vt* to quicken; **affrettarsi** *vpr* to hurry; **affrettarsi a fare qc** to hurry *o* hasten to do sth

affrettato, -a *ag* (*veloce: passo, ritmo*) quick, fast; (*frettoloso: decisione*) hurried, hasty; (*: lavoro*) rushed

affrontare /72/ *vt* (*pericolo ecc*) to face; (*nemico*) to confront; **affrontarsi** *vpr* (*reciproco*) to confront each other

affumicato, -a *ag* (*prosciutto, aringa ecc*) smoked

affusolato, -a *ag* tapering

Afghanistan *sm*: **l'~** Afghanistan

afoso, -a *ag* sultry, close

'Africa *sf*: **l'~** Africa; **africano, -a** *ag*, *sm/f* African

agenda [a'dʒɛnda] *sf* diary

> Attenzione! In inglese esiste la parola *agenda*, che però vuol dire *ordine del giorno*.

agente [a'dʒɛnte] *sm* agent; **~ di cambio** stockbroker; **~ di polizia** police officer; **~ segreto** secret agent; **agenzia** *sf* agency;

(*succursale*) branch; **agenzia di collocamento** employment agency; **agenzia immobiliare** estate agent's (office) (BRIT), real estate office (US); **agenzia di stampa** press agency; **agenzia viaggi** travel agency

agevo'lare [adʒevoˈlare] /72/ vt to facilitate, make easy

agevolazi'one [adʒevolatˈtsjone] sf (*facilitazione economica*) facility; **~ di pagamento** payment on easy terms; **agevolazioni creditizie** credit facilities; **agevolazioni fiscali** tax concessions

a'gevole [aˈdʒevole] ag easy; (*strada*) smooth

agganci'are [agganˈtʃare] /14/ vt to hook up; (*Ferr*) to couple

ag'geggio [adˈdʒeddʒo] sm gadget, contraption

agget'tivo [addʒetˈtivo] sm adjective

agghiacci'ante [aggjatˈtʃante] ag chilling

aggior'nare [addʒorˈnare] /72/ vt (*opera, manuale*) to bring up-to-date; (*seduta ecc*) to postpone; **aggiornarsi** vpr to bring (o keep) o.s. up-to-date; **aggior'nato, -a** ag up-to-date

aggi'rare [addʒiˈrare] /72/ vt to go round; (*fig: ingannare*) to trick; **aggirarsi** vpr to wander about; **il prezzo s'aggira sul milione** the price is around the million mark

aggi'ungere [adˈdʒundʒere] /5/ vt to add; (*Inform*): **grazie per avermi aggiunto (come amico)** thanks for the add

aggi'unsi ecc [adˈdʒunsi] vb vedi **aggiungere**

aggius'tare [addʒusˈtare] /72/ vt (*accomodare*) to mend, repair; (*riassettare*) to adjust; (*fig: lite*) to settle

aggrap'parsi /72/ vpr: **~ a** to cling to

aggra'vare /72/ vt (*aumentare*) to increase; (*appesantire: anche fig*) to weigh down, make heavy; (*pena*) to make worse; **aggravarsi** vpr to worsen, become worse

aggre'dire /55/ vt to attack, assault

aggressi'one sf aggression; (*atto*) attack, assault

aggres'sivo, -a ag aggressive

aggres'sore sm aggressor, attacker

aggrot'tare /72/ vt: **~ le sopracciglia** to frown

aggrovigli'are /27/ vt to tangle; **aggrovigliarsi** vpr (*fig*) to become complicated

aggu'ato sm trap; (*imboscata*) ambush; **tendere un ~ a qn** to set a trap for sb

agguer'rito, -a ag fierce

agi'ato, -a [aˈdʒato] ag (*vita*) easy; (*persona*) well-off, well-to-do

'agile [ˈadʒile] ag agile, nimble

'agio [ˈadʒo] sm ease, comfort; **agi** smpl comforts; **mettersi a proprio ~** to make o.s. at home o comfortable; **dare ~ a qn di fare qc** to give sb the chance of doing sth

a'gire [aˈdʒire] /55/ vi to act; (*esercitare un'azione*) to take effect; (*Tecn*) to work, function; **~ contro qn** (*Dir*) to take action against sb

agi'tare [adʒiˈtare] /72/ vt (*bottiglia*) to shake; (*mano, fazzoletto*) to wave; (*fig: turbare*) to disturb; (: *incitare*) to stir (up); (: *dibattere*) to discuss; **agitarsi** vpr (*mare*) to be rough; (*malato, dormitore*) to toss and turn; (*bambino*) to fidget; (*emozionarsi*) to get upset; (*Pol*) to agitate; **agi'tato, -a** ag rough; restless; fidgety; upset, perturbed

'aglio [ˈaʎʎo] sm garlic

a'gnello [aɲˈɲɛllo] sm lamb

'ago (*pl* **aghi**) sm needle

ago'nistico, -a, -ci, -che ag athletic; (*fig*) competitive

agopun'tura sf acupuncture

a'gosto sm August

a'grario, -a ag agrarian, agricultural; (*riforma*) land cpd

a'gricolo, -a ag agricultural, farm cpd; **agricol'tore** sm farmer; **agricol'tura** sf agriculture, farming

agri'foglio [agri'fɔʎʎo] sm holly
agritu'rismo sm farm holidays pl
agro'dolce ag bittersweet; (salsa) sweet and sour
a'grume sm (spesso al pl: pianta) citrus; (: frutto) citrus fruit
a'guzzo, -a [a'guttso] ag sharp
'ahi escl (dolore) ouch!
'Aia sf: **L'~** The Hague
AIDS ['aids] abbr m, abbr f AIDS
airbag sm inv air bag
ai'rone sm heron
aiu'ola sf flower bed
aiu'tante smf assistant ▷ sm (Mil) adjutant; (Naut) master-at-arms; **~ di campo** aide-de-camp
aiu'tare /72/ vt to help; **~ qn (a fare)** to help sb (to do); **aiutarsi** vpr to help each other; **~ qn in qc/a fare qc** to help sb with sth/to do sth; **può aiutarmi?** can you help me?
ai'uto sm help, assistance, aid; (aiutante) assistant; **venire in ~ di qn** to come to sb's aid; **~ chirurgo** assistant surgeon
'ala (pl **ali**) sf wing; **fare ~** to fall back, make way; **~ destra/sinistra** (Sport) right/left wing
ala'bastro sm alabaster
a'lano sm Great Dane
'alba sf dawn
alba'nese ag, smf, sm Albanian
Alba'nia sf: **l'~** Albania
albe'rato, -a ag (viale, piazza) lined with trees, tree-lined
al'bergo, -ghi sm hotel; **~ della gioventù** youth hostel
'albero sm tree; (Naut) mast; (Tecn) shaft; **~ genealogico** family tree; **~ a gomiti** crankshaft; **~ maestro** mainmast; **~ di Natale** Christmas tree; **~ di trasmissione** transmission shaft
albi'cocca, -che sf apricot
'album sm album; **~ da disegno** sketch book
al'bume sm albumen
'alce ['altʃe] sm elk

'alcol sm inv = **alcool**
al'colico, -a, -ci, -che ag alcoholic ▷ sm alcoholic drink
alcoliz'zato, -a [alkolid'dzato] sm/f alcoholic
'alcool sm inv alcohol
al'cuno, -a det (dav sm: **alcun** + C, V, **alcuno** + s impura, gn, pn, ps, x, z; dav sf: **alcuna** + C, **alcun'** + V: nessuno): **non ... ~** no, not any; **alcuni, e** det pl, pron pl some, a few; **non c'è alcuna fretta** there's no hurry, there isn't any hurry; **senza alcun riguardo** without any consideration
alfa'betico, -a, -ci, -che ag alphabetical
alfa'beto sm alphabet
'alga, -ghe sf seaweed no pl, alga
'algebra ['aldʒebra] sf algebra
Alge'ria [aldʒe'ria] sf: **l'~** Algeria; **alge'rino, -a** ag, sm/f Algerian
ali'ante sm (Aer) glider
'alibi sm inv alibi
a'lice [a'litʃe] sf anchovy
ali'eno, -a ag (avverso): **~ (da)** opposed (to), averse (to) ▷ sm/f alien
alimen'tare /72/ vt to feed; (Tecn) to feed, supply; (fig) to sustain ▷ ag food cpd; **alimentari** smpl foodstuffs; (anche: **negozio di alimentari**) grocer's shop; **alimentazi'one** sf feeding; supplying; sustaining; (cibi) diet
a'liquota sf share; **~ d'imposta** tax rate
alis'cafo sm hydrofoil
'alito sm breath
all. abbr (= allegato) encl.
allaccia'mento [allattʃa'mento] sm (Tecn) connection
allacci'are [allat'tʃare] /14/ vt (scarpe) to tie, lace (up); (cintura) to do up, fasten; (luce, gas) to connect; (amicizia) to form
allaccia'tura [allattʃa'tura] sf fastening
alla'gare /80/ vt, **alla'garsi** vpr to flood

allar'gare /80/ vt to widen; (*vestito*) to let out; (*aprire*) to open; (*fig: dilatare*) to extend; **allargarsi** vpr (*gen*) to widen; (*scarpe, pantaloni*) to stretch; (*fig: problema, fenomeno*) to spread

allar'mare /72/ vt to alarm

al'larme sm alarm; **~ aereo** air-raid warning

allat'tare /72/ vt to (breast-)feed

alle'anza [alle'antsa] sf alliance

alle'arsi /72/ vpr to form an alliance; **alle'ato, -a** ag allied ⊳ sm/f ally

alle'gare /80/ vt (*accludere*) to enclose; (*Dir: citare*) to cite, adduce; (*denti*) to set on edge; **alle'gato, -a** ag enclosed ⊳ sm enclosure; (*di e-mail*) attachment; **in allegato** enclosed

allegge'rire [alledd͡ʒe'rire] /55/ vt to lighten, make lighter; (*fig: lavoro, tasse*) to reduce

alle'gria sf gaiety, cheerfulness

al'legro, -a ag cheerful, merry; (*un po' brillo*) merry, tipsy; (*vivace: colore*) bright ⊳ sm (*Mus*) allegro

allena'mento sm training

alle'nare /72/ vt, **alle'narsi** vpr to train; **allena'tore** sm (*Sport*) trainer, coach

allen'tare /72/ vt to slacken; (*disciplina*) to relax; **allentarsi** vpr to become slack; (*ingranaggio*) to work loose

aller'gia, -'gie [aller'd͡ʒia] sf allergy; **al'lergico, -a, -ci, -che** [al'lɛrd͡ʒiko] ag allergic

alles'tire /55/ vt (*cena*) to prepare; (*esercito, nave*) to equip, fit out; (*spettacolo*) to stage

allet'tante ag attractive, alluring

alle'vare /72/ vt (*animale*) to breed, rear; (*bambino*) to bring up

allevi'are /19/ vt to alleviate

alli'bito, -a ag pale; disconcerted; astounded

alli'evo sm pupil; (*apprendista*) apprentice; **~ ufficiale** cadet

alliga'tore sm alligator

alline'are /72/ vt (*persone, cose*) to line up; (*Tip*) to align; (*fig: economia, salari*) to adjust, align; **allinearsi** vpr to line up; (*fig: a idee*): **allinearsi a** to come into line with

al'lodola sf (sky)lark

alloggi'are [allod͡ʒ'd͡ʒare] /62/ vt to accommodate ⊳ vi to live; **al'loggio** sm lodging, accommodation (*BRIT*), accommodations (*US*)

allonta'nare /72/ vt to send away, send off; (*impiegato*) to dismiss; (*pericolo*) to avert, remove; (*estraniare*) to alienate; **allontanarsi** vpr: **allontanarsi (da)** to go away (from); (*estraniarsi*) to become estranged (from)

al'lora av (*in quel momento*) then ⊳ cong (*in questo caso*) well then; (*dunque*) well then, so; **la gente d'~** people then o in those days; **da ~ in poi** from then on

al'loro sm laurel

'alluce ['allut͡ʃe] sm big toe

alluci'nante [allut͡ʃi'nante] ag awful; (*fam*) amazing

allucinazi'one [allut͡ʃinat'tsjone] sf hallucination

al'ludere /35/ vi: **~ a** to allude to, hint at

allu'minio sm aluminium (*BRIT*), aluminum (*US*)

allun'gare /80/ vt to lengthen; (*distendere*) to prolong, extend; (*diluire*) to water down; **allungarsi** vpr to lengthen; (*ragazzo*) to stretch, grow taller; (*sdraiarsi*) to lie down, stretch out

al'lusi ecc vb vedi **alludere**

allusi'one sf hint, allusion

alluvi'one sf flood

al'meno av at least ⊳ cong: **(se) ~** if only; **(se) ~ piovesse!** if only it would rain!

a'logeno, -a [a'lɔd͡ʒeno] ag: **lampada alogena** halogen lamp

a'lone sm halo

'Alpi sfpl: **le ~** the Alps

alpi'nismo *sm* mountaineering, climbing; **alpi'nista, -i, -e** *sm/f* mountaineer, climber

al'pino, -a *ag* Alpine; mountain *cpd*; **alpini** *smpl* (*Mil*) Italian Alpine troops

alt *escl* halt!, stop!

alta'lena *sf* (*a funi*) swing; (*in bilico*) seesaw

al'tare *sm* altar

alter'nare /72/ *vt*, **alter'narsi** *vpr* to alternate; **alterna'tivo, -a** *ag* alternative

al'terno, -a *ag* alternate; **a giorni alterni** on alternate days, every other day

al'tero, -a *ag* proud

al'tezza [al'tettsa] *sf* height; (*di tessuto*) width, breadth; (*di acqua, pozzo*) depth; (*di suono*) pitch; (*Geo*) latitude; (*titolo*) highness; (*fig: nobiltà*) greatness; **essere all'~ di** to be on a level with; (*fig*) to be up to *o* equal to

al'ticcio, -a, -ci, -ce [al'tittʃo] *ag* tipsy

alti'tudine *sf* altitude

'alto, -a *ag* high; (*persona*) tall; (*tessuto*) wide, broad; (*sonno, acque*) deep; (*suono*) high(-pitched); (*Geo*) upper; (*: settentrionale*) northern ▷ *sm* top (part) ▷ *av* high; (*parlare*) aloud, loudly; **il palazzo è ~ 20 metri** the building is 20 metres high; **ad alta voce** aloud; **a notte alta** in the dead of night; **in ~** up, upwards; at the top; **dall'~ in *o* al basso** up and down; **degli alti e bassi** (*fig*) ups and downs; **alta fedeltà** high fidelity, hi-fi; **alta finanza/società** high finance/society; **alta moda** haute couture; **alta definizione** (*TV*) high definition; **alta velocità** (*Ferr*) high speed rail system

altopar'lante *sm* loudspeaker

altopi'ano (*pl* **altipiani**) *sm* upland plain, plateau

altret'tanto, -a *ag, pron* as much; (*pl*) as many ▷ *av* equally; **tanti**

auguri! — grazie, ~ all the best! — thank you, the same to you

altri'menti *av* otherwise

PAROLA CHIAVE

'altro, -a *det* **1** (*diverso*) other, different; **questa è un'altra cosa** that's another *o* a different thing **2** (*supplementare*) other; **prendi un altro cioccolatino** have another chocolate; **hai avuto altre notizie?** have you had any more *o* any other news?

3 (*nel tempo*): **l'altro giorno** the other day; **l'altr'anno** last year; **l'altro ieri** the day before yesterday; **domani l'altro** the day after tomorrow; **quest'altro mese** next month

4: d'altra parte on the other hand ▷ *pron* **1** (*persona, cosa diversa o supplementare*): **un altro, un'altra** another (one); **lo farà un altro** someone else will do it; **altri, e** others; **gli altri** (*la gente*) others, other people; **l'uno e l'altro** both (of them); **aiutarsi l'un l'altro** to help one another; **da un giorno all'altro** from day to day; (*nel giro di 24 ore*) from one day to the next; (*da un momento all'altro*) any day now

2 (*sostantivato: solo maschile*) something else; (*: in espressioni interrogative*) anything else; **non ho altro da dire** I have nothing else *o* I don't have anything else to say; **più che altro** above all; **se non altro** at least; **tra l'altro** among other things; **ci mancherebbe altro!** that's all we need!; **non faccio altro che lavorare** I do nothing but work; **contento? — altro che!** are you pleased? — I certainly am!; *vedi anche* **senza; noialtri; voialtri; tutto**

al'trove *av* elsewhere, somewhere else

altru'ista, -i, -e *ag* altruistic

a'lunno, -a *sm/f* pupil

alve'are *sm* hive

al'zare [al'tsare] /72/ *vt* to raise, lift; (*issare*) to hoist; (*costruire*) to build, erect; **alzarsi** *vpr* to rise; (*dal letto*) to get up; (*crescere*) to grow tall (*o taller*); **~ le spalle** to shrug one's shoulders; **alzarsi in piedi** to stand up, get to one's feet

a'maca, -che *sf* hammock

amalga'mare /72/ *vt*, **amalga'marsi** *vpr* to amalgamate

a'mante *ag*: **~ di** (*musica ecc*) fond of ▷ *smf* lover (mistress)

a'mare /72/ *vt* to love; (*amico, musica, sport*) to like; **amarsi** *vpr* to love each other

amareggi'ato, -a [amared'dʒato] *ag* upset, saddened

ama'rena *sf* sour black cherry

ama'rezza [ama'rettsa] *sf* bitterness

a'maro, -a *ag* bitter ▷ *sm* bitterness; (*liquore*) bitters *pl*

amaz'zonico, -a, -ci, -che [amad'dzɔniko] *ag* Amazonian; Amazon *cpd*

ambasci'ata [ambaʃʃata] *sf* embassy; (*messaggio*) message; **ambascia'tore, -'trice** *sm/f* ambassador (ambassadress)

ambe'due *ag inv*: **~ i ragazzi** both boys ▷ *pron inv* both

ambienta'lista, -i, -e *ag* environmental ▷ *sm/f* environmentalist

ambien'tare /72/ *vt* to acclimatize; (*romanzo, film*) to set; **ambientarsi** *vpr* to get used to one's surroundings

ambi'ente *sm* environment; (*fig: insieme di persone*) milieu; (*stanza*) room

am'biguo, -a *ag* ambiguous

ambizi'one [ambit'tsjone] *sf* ambition; **ambizi'oso, -a** *ag* ambitious

'ambo *ag inv* both ▷ *sm* (*al gioco*) double

'ambra *sf* amber; **~ grigia** ambergris

ambu'lante *ag* itinerant ▷ *sm* peddler

ambu'lanza [ambu'lantsa] *sf* ambulance; **chiamate un ~** call an ambulance

ambula'torio *sm* (*studio medico*) surgery

A'merica *sf*: **l'~** America; **l'~ latina** Latin America; **ameri'cano, -a** *ag*, *sm/f* American

ami'anto *sm* asbestos

ami'chevole [ami'kevole] *ag* friendly

ami'cizia [ami'tʃittsja] *sf* friendship; **amicizie** *sfpl* (*amici*) friends

a'mico, -a, -ci, -che *sm/f* friend; (*amante*) boyfriend (girlfriend); **~ del cuore** *o* **intimo** bosom friend; **aggiungere come ~** (*Internet*) to friend

'amido *sm* starch

ammac'care /20/ *vt* (*pentola*) to dent; (*persona*) to bruise; **ammacca'tura** *sf* dent; bruise

ammaes'trare /72/ *vt* (*animale*) to train

ammai'nare /72/ *vt* to lower, haul down

amma'larsi /72/ *vpr* to fall ill; **amma'lato, -a** *ag* ill, sick ▷ *sm/f* sick person; (*paziente*) patient

ammanet'tare /72/ *vt* to handcuff

ammas'sare /72/ *vt* (*ammucchiare*) to amass; (*raccogliere*) to gather together; **ammassarsi** *vpr* to pile up; to gather

ammat'tire /55/ *vi* to go mad

ammaz'zare [ammat'tsare] /72/ *vt* to kill; **ammazzarsi** *vpr* (*uccidersi*) to kill o.s.; (*rimanere ucciso*) to be killed; **ammazzarsi di lavoro** to work o.s. to death

am'mettere /63/ *vt* to admit; (*riconoscere: fatto*) to acknowledge, admit; (*permettere*) to allow, accept; (*supporre*) to suppose

amminis'trare /72/ *vt* to run, manage; (*Rel, Dir*) to

administer; **amministra'tore** *sm* administrator; (*di condominio*) flats manager; **amministratore delegato** managing director; **amministrazi'one** *sf* management; administration

ammi'raglio [ammi'raʎʎo] *sm* admiral

ammi'rare /72/ *vt* to admire; **ammirazi'one** *sf* admiration

am'misi *ecc vb vedi* **ammettere**

ammobili'ato, -a *ag* furnished

am'mollo *sm*: **lasciare in ~** to leave to soak

ammo'niaca *sf* ammonia

ammo'nire /55/ *vt* (*avvertire*) to warn; (*rimproverare*) to admonish; (*Dir*) reprimand

ammonizi'one [ammonit'tsjone] *sf* (*monito: anche Sport*) warning; (*rimprovero*) reprimand; (*Dir*) caution

ammon'tare /72/ *vi*: **~ a** to amount to ▷ *sm* (*totale*) amount

ammorbi'dente *sm* fabric softener

ammorbi'dire /55/ *vt* to soften

ammortizza'tore [ammortiddza'tore] *sm* (*Aut, Tecn*) shock absorber

ammucchi'are [ammuk'kjare] /19/ *vt* to pile up, accumulate

ammuf'fire /55/ *vi* to go mouldy (*BRIT*) o moldy (*US*)

ammuto'lire /55/ *vi* to be struck dumb

amne'sia *sf* amnesia

amnis'tia *sf* amnesty

'amo *sm* (*Pesca*) hook; (*fig*) bait

a'more *sm* love; **amori** *smpl* love affairs; **il tuo bambino è un ~** your baby's a darling; **fare l'~** o **all'~** to make love; **per ~ o per forza** by hook or by crook; **amor proprio** self-esteem, pride

amo'roso, -a *ag* (*affettuoso*) loving, affectionate; (*d'amore: sguardo*) amorous; (: *poesia, relazione*) love *cpd*

'ampio, -a *ag* wide, broad; (*spazioso*) spacious; (*abbondante: vestito*)

loose; (: *gonna*) full; (: *spiegazione*) ample, full

am'plesso *sm* intercourse

ampli'are /19/ *vt* (*ingrandire*) to enlarge; (*allargare*) to widen; **ampliarsi** *vpr* to grow, increase

amplifica'tore *sm* (*Tecn, Mus*) amplifier

ampu'tare /72/ *vt* (*Med*) to amputate

A.N. *sigla f* (*Pol*) = **Alleanza Nazionale**

anabbagli'ante [anabbaʎ'ʎante] *ag* (*Aut*) dipped; **anabbaglianti** *smpl* dipped *or* dimmed headlights

anaboliz'zante *sm* anabolic steroid

anal'colico, -a, -ci, -che *ag* non-alcoholic ▷ *sm* soft drink

analfa'beta, -i, -e *ag, smf* illiterate

anal'gesico, -a, -ci, -che [anal'dʒɛziko] *ag, sm* analgesic

a'nalisi *sf inv* analysis; (*Med: esame*) test; **~ del sangue** blood test

anali'zzare [analid'dzare] /72/ *vt* to analyse; (*Med*) to test

a'nalogo, -a, -ghi, -ghe *ag* analogous

'ananas *sm inv* pineapple

anar'chia [anar'kia] *sf* anarchy; **a'narchico, -a, -ci, -che** *ag* anarchic(al) ▷ *sm/f* anarchist

anarco-insurreziona'lista *ag* anarcho-revolutionary

'A.N.A.S. *sigla f* (= *Azienda Nazionale Autonoma delle Strade*) national roads department

anato'mia *sf* anatomy

'anatra *sf* duck

'anca, -che *sf* (*Anat*) hip

'anche ['anke] *cong* (*inoltre, pure*) also, too; (*perfino*) even; **vengo anch'io!** I'm coming too!; **~ se** even if

an'cora *av* still; (*di nuovo*) again; (*di più*) some more; (*persino*): **~ più forte** even stronger; **non ~** not yet; **~ una volta** once more, once again; **~ un po'** a little more; (*di tempo*) a little longer

an'dare /6/ *sm*: **a lungo ~** in the long run ▷ *vi* to go; **~ a** (*essere adatto*) to suit; **il suo comportamento non mi va** (*piace*) I don't like the way he behaves; **ti va di ~ al cinema?** do you feel like going to the cinema?; **~ a cavallo** to ride; **~ in macchina/aereo** to go by car/plane; **~ a fare qc** to go and do sth; **~ a pescare/sciare** to go fishing/skiing; **andarsene** to go away; **questa camicia va lavata** this shirt needs a wash *o* should be washed; **~ a male** to go bad; **come va?** (*lavoro, progetto*) how are things?; **come va? — bene, grazie!** how are you? — fine, thanks!; **va fatto entro oggi** it's got to be done today; **ne va della nostra vita** our lives are at stake; **an'data** sf going; (*viaggio*) outward journey; **biglietto di sola andata** single (*BRIT*) *o* one-way ticket; **biglietto di andata e ritorno** return (*BRIT*) *o* round-trip (*US*) ticket

andrò ecc vb vedi **andare**

a'neddoto sm anecdote

a'nello sm ring; (*di catena*) link; **anelli** smpl (*Ginnastica*) rings

a'nemico, -a, -ci, -che ag anaemic

aneste'sia sf anaesthesia

anfeta'mina sf amphetamine

'angelo ['andʒelo] sm angel; **~ custode** guardian angel

anghe'ria [ange'ria] sf vexation

angli'cano, -a ag Anglican

anglo'sassone ag Anglo-Saxon

'angolo sm corner; (*Mat*) angle; **~ cottura** (*di appartamento ecc*) cooking area

an'goscia, -sce [an'goʃʃa] sf deep anxiety, anguish no pl

angu'illa sf eel

an'guria sf watermelon

'anice ['anitʃe] sm (*Cuc*) aniseed; (*Bot*) anise

'anima sf soul; (*abitante*) inhabitant; **~ gemella** soul mate; **non c'era ~ viva** there wasn't a living soul

ani'male sm, ag animal; **~ domestico** pet

anna'cquare /72/ vt to water down, dilute

annaffi'are /19/ vt to water; **annaffia'toio** sm watering can

an'nata sf year; (*importo annuo*) annual amount; **vino d'~** vintage wine

anne'gare /80/ vt, vi to drown

anne'rire /55/ vt to blacken ▷ vi to become black

annien'tare /72/ vt to annihilate, destroy

anniver'sario sm anniversary; **~ di matrimonio** wedding anniversary

'anno sm year; **quanti anni hai? — ho 40 anni** how old are you? — I'm 40 (years old)

anno'dare /72/ vt to knot, tie; (*fig: rapporto*) to form

annoi'are /19/ vt to bore; **annoiarsi** vpr to be bored

> Attenzione! In inglese esiste il verbo *to annoy*, che però vuol dire *dare fastidio a*.

anno'tare /72/ vt (*registrare*) to note, note down; (*commentare*) to annotate

annu'ale ag annual

annu'ire /55/ vi to nod; (*acconsentire*) to agree

annul'lare /72/ vt to annihilate, destroy; (*contratto, francobollo*) to cancel; (*matrimonio*) to annul; (*sentenza*) to quash; (*risultati*) to declare void

annunci'are [annun'tʃare] /14/ vt to announce; (*dar segni rivelatori*) to herald

an'nuncio [an'nuntʃo] sm announcement; (*fig*) sign; **~ pubblicitario** advertisement; **annunci economici** classified advertisements, small ads; **annunci mortuari** (*colonna*) obituary column

'annuo, -a ag annual, yearly

annu'sare /72/ vt to sniff, smell; **~ tabacco** to take snuff

a'nomalo, -a ag anomalous

a'nonimo, -a ag anonymous ▷ sm (*autore*) anonymous writer (*o* painter

anores'sia *sf* anorexia

ano'ressico, -a, -ci, -che *ag* anorexic

anor'male *ag* abnormal ▷ *smf* subnormal person

'ANSA *sigla f* (= *Agenzia Nazionale Stampa Associata*) national press agency

'ansia *sf* anxiety

ansi'mare /72/ *vi* to pant

ansi'oso, -a *ag* anxious

'anta *sf* (*di finestra*) shutter; (*di armadio*) door

An'tartide *sf*: **l'~** Antarctica

an'tenna *sf* (*Radio*, *TV*) aerial; (*Zool*) antenna, feeler; (*Naut*) yard; **~ parabolica** satellite dish

ante'prima *sf* preview; **~ di stampa** (*Inform*) print preview

anteri'ore *ag* (*ruota*, *zampa*) front *cpd*; (*fatti*) previous, preceding

antiade'rente *ag* non-stick

antibi'otico, -a, -ci, -che *ag*, *sm* antibiotic

anti'camera *sf* anteroom; **fare ~** to be kept waiting

antici'pare [antitʃi'pare] /72/ *vt* (*consegna*, *visita*) to bring forward, anticipate; (*somma di denaro*) to pay in advance; (*notizia*) to disclose ▷ *vi* to be ahead of time; **an'ticipo** *sm* anticipation; (*di denaro*) advance; **in anticipo** early, in advance

an'tico, -a, -chi, -che *ag* (*quadro*, *mobili*) antique; (*dell'antichità*) ancient; **all'antica** old-fashioned

anticoncezio'nale [antikontʃettsjo'nale] *sm* contraceptive

anticonfor'mista, -i, -e *ag*, *smf* nonconformist

anti'corpo *sm* antibody

antidolo'rifico, -ci *sm* painkiller

anti'doping *sm inv*, *ag inv* drug testing; **test ~** drugs (*BRIT*) o drug (*US*) test

an'tifona *sf* (*Mus*, *Rel*) antiphon; **capire l'~** (*fig*) to take the hint

anti'forfora *ag inv* anti-dandruff

anti'furto *sm* anti-theft device

anti'gelo [anti'dʒɛlo] *ag inv* antifreeze *cpd* ▷ *sm* (*per motore*) antifreeze; (*per cristalli*) de-icer

antiglobalizza'zione [antiglobaliddza'tsjone] *ag* anti-globalization

An'tille *sfpl*: **le ~** the West Indies

antin'cendio [antin'tʃendjo] *ag inv* fire *cpd*

anti'nebbia *sm inv* (*anche*: **faro ~**) (*Aut*) fog lamp

antin'fiammatorio, -a *ag*, *sm* anti-inflammatory

antio'rario *ag*: **in senso ~** anticlockwise

anti'pasto *sm* hors d'œuvre

antipa'tia *sf* antipathy, dislike; **anti'patico, -a, -ci, -che** *ag* unpleasant, disagreeable

antipro'iettile *ag inv* bulletproof

antiquari'ato *sm* antique trade; **un pezzo d'~** an antique; **anti'quario** *sm* antique dealer; **anti'quato, -a** *ag* antiquated, old-fashioned

anti'rughe [anti'ruge] *ag inv* (*crema*, *prodotto*) anti-wrinkle

antitraspi'rante *ag* antiperspirant

anti'vipera *ag inv*: **siero ~** remedy for snake bites

antivi'rale *ag* antiviral

anti'virus [anti'virus] *sm inv* antivirus software *no pl*

antolo'gia, -'gie [antolo'dʒia] *sf* anthology

anu'lare *ag* ring *cpd* ▷ *sm* ring finger

'anzi ['antsi] *av* (*invece*) on the contrary; (*o meglio*) or rather, or better still

anzi'ano, -a [an'tsjano] *ag* old; (*Amm*) senior ▷ *sm/f* old person; senior member

anziché [antsi'ke] *cong* rather than

a'patico, -a, -ci, -che *ag* apathetic

'ape *sf* bee

aperi'tivo *sm* apéritif

aperta'mente *av* openly

ecc); **società anonima** (*Comm*) joint stock company

a'**perto, -a** pp di **aprire** ▷ ag open ▷ sm: **all'~** in the open (air)

aper'**tura** sf opening; (ampiezza) width; (Fot) aperture; **~ alare** wing span; **~ mentale** open-mindedness

ap'**nea** sf: **immergersi in ~** to dive without breathing apparatus

a'**postrofo** sm apostrophe

ap'**paio** ecc vb vedi **apparire**

ap'**palto** sm (Comm) contract; **dare/ prendere in ~ un lavoro** to let out/ undertake a job on contract

appan'**nare** /72/ vt (vetro) to mist; **appannarsi** vpr to mist over; to grow dim

apparecchi'**are** [apparek'kjare] /19/ vt to prepare; (tavola) to set ▷ vi to set the table

appa'**recchio** [appa'rekkjo] sm piece of apparatus, device; (aeroplano) aircraft inv; **~ acustico** hearing aid; **~ televisivo/telefonico** television set/telephone

appa'**rente** ag apparent

appa'**rire** /7/ vi to appear; (sembrare) to seem, appear

apparta'**mento** sm flat (BRIT), apartment (US)

appar'**tarsi** /72/ vpr to withdraw

apparte'**nere** /121/ vi: **~ a** to belong to

ap'**parvi** ecc vb vedi **apparire**

appassio'**nare** /72/ vt to thrill; (commuovere) to move; **appassionarsi** vpr: **appassionarsi a qc** to take a great interest in sth; **appassio'nato, -a** ag passionate; (entusiasta): **appassionato (di)** keen (on)

appas'**sire** /55/ vi to wither; **appas'sito, -a** ag dead

ap'**pello** sm roll-call; (implorazione, Dir) appeal; **fare ~ a** to appeal to

ap'**pena** av (a stento) hardly, scarcely; (solamente, da poco) just ▷ cong as soon as; **(non) ~ furono arrivati ...** as soon as they had arrived ...; **~ ... che** o **quando** no sooner ... than

ap'**pendere** /8/ vt to hang (up)

appen'**dice** [appen'ditʃe] sf appendix; **romanzo d'~** popular serial; **appendi'cite** sf appendicitis

Appen'**nini** smpl: **gli ~** the Apennines

appesan'**tire** /55/ vt to make heavy; **appesantirsi** vpr to grow stout

appe'**tito** sm appetite

appic'**care** /20/ vt: **~ il fuoco a** to set fire to, set on fire

appicci'**care** [appittʃi'kare] /20/ vt to stick; **appicciccarsi** vpr to stick; (fig: persona) to cling

appiso'**larsi** /72/ vpr to doze off

applau'**dire** /45/ vt, vi to applaud; ap'**plauso** sm applause no pl

appli'**care** /20/ vt to apply; (regolamento) to enforce; **applicarsi** vpr to apply o.s.; **applicazi'one** sf application; **applicazione per il cellulare** mobile app

appoggi'**are** [appod'dʒare] /62/ vt (fig: sostenere) to support; **~ qc a qc** (mettere contro) to lean o rest sth against sth; **appoggiarsi** vpr: **appoggiarsi a** to lean against; (fig) to rely upon; ap'**poggio** sm support

apposita'**mente** av (apposta) on purpose; (specialmente) specially

ap'**posito, -a** ag appropriate

ap'**posta** av on purpose, deliberately

appos'**tarsi** /72/ vpr to lie in wait

ap'**prendere** /81/ vt (imparare) to learn; appren'**dista, -i, -e** sm/f apprentice

apprensi'**one** sf apprehension

apprez'**zare** [appret'tsare] /72/ vt to appreciate

appro'**dare** /72/ vi (Naut) to land; (fig): **non ~ a nulla** to come to nothing

approfit'**tare** /72/ vi: **~ di** (situazione) to make the most of; (persona) to take advantage of

approfon'**dire** /55/ vt to deepen; (fig) to study in depth

appropri'**ato, -a** ag appropriate

approssima'**tivo, -a** ag approximate, rough; (impreciso) inexact, imprecise

appro'vare /72/ vt (condotta, azione) to approve of; (candidato) to pass; (progetto di legge) to approve

appunta'mento sm appointment; (amoroso) date; **darsi ~** to arrange to meet (one another); **ho un ~ con...** I have an appointment with ...; **vorrei prendere un ~** I'd like to make an appointment

ap'punto sm note; (rimprovero) reproach ▷ av (proprio) exactly, just; **per l'~!, ~!** exactly!

apribot'tiglie [apribot'tiʎʎe] sm inv bottleopener

a'prile sm April

a'prire /9/ vt to open; (via, cadavere) to open up; (gas, luce, acqua) to turn on ▷ vi to open; **aprirsi** vpr to open; **aprirsi a qn** to confide in sb, open one's heart to sb

apris'catole sm inv tin (BRIT) o can opener

APT sigla f (= Azienda di Promozione) ≈ tourist board

aquagym [akwa'dʒim] sf aquarobics

'aquila sf (Zool) eagle; (fig) genius

aqui'lone sm (giocattolo) kite; (vento) North wind

A/R abbr (= andata e ritorno) (biglietto) return (ticket) (BRIT), round-trip ticket (US)

A'rabia Sau'dita sf: **l'~** Saudi Arabia

'arabo, -a ag, sm/f Arab ▷ sm (Ling) Arabic

a'rachide [a'rakide] sf peanut

ara'gosta sf crayfish; spiny lobster

a'rancia, -ce [a'rantʃa] sf orange; **aranci'ata** sf orangeade; **aranci'one** ag inv: **(color) arancione** bright orange

a'rare /72/ vt to plough (BRIT), plow (US)

a'ratro sm plough (BRIT), plow (US)

a'razzo [a'rattso] sm tapestry

arbi'trare /72/ vt (Sport) to referee; to umpire; (Dir) to arbitrate

arbi'trario, -a ag arbitrary

'arbitro sm arbiter, judge; (Dir) arbitrator; (Sport) referee; (: Tennis, Cricket) umpire

ar'busto sm shrub

archeolo'gia [arkeolo'dʒia] sf arch(a)eology; **arche'ologo, -a, -gi, -ghe** sm/f arch(a)eologist

architet'tare [arkitet'tare] /72/ vt (fig: ideare) to devise; (: macchinare) to plan, concoct

archi'tetto [arki'tetto] sm architect; **architet'tura** [arkitet'tura] sf architecture

ar'chivio [ar'kivjo] sm archives pl; (Inform) file

'arco sm (arma, Mus) bow; (Archit) arch; (Mat) arc

arcoba'leno sm rainbow

arcu'ato, -a ag curved, bent

'ardere /10/ vt, vi to burn

ar'desia sf slate

'area sf area; (Edil) land, ground; **~ di rigore** (Sport) penalty area; **~ di servizio** (Aut) service area

a'rena sf arena; (per corride) bullring; (sabbia) sand

are'narsi /72/ vpr to run aground

argente'ria [ardʒente'ria] sf silverware, silver

Argen'tina [ardʒen'tina] sf: **l'~** Argentina; **argen'tino, -a** ag, sm/f Argentinian

ar'gento [ar'dʒento] sm silver; **~ vivo** quicksilver

ar'gilla [ar'dʒilla] sf clay

'argine ['ardʒine] sm embankment, bank; (diga) dyke, dike

argo'mento sm argument; (motivo) motive; (materia, tema) subject

'aria sf air; (espressione, aspetto) air, look; (Mus: melodia) tune; (: di opera) aria; **all'~ aperta** in the open (air); **mandare all'~ qc** to ruin o upset sth

'arido, -a ag arid

arieggi'are [arjed'dʒare] /62/ vt (cambiare aria) to air; (imitare) to imitate

ari'ete *sm* ram; (*Mil*) battering ram;
  A~ Aries
a'ringa, -ghe *sf* herring *inv*
arit'metica *sf* arithmetic
'arma, -i *sf* weapon, arm; (*parte
  dell'esercito*) arm; **alle armi!** to
  arms!; **chiamare alle armi** to call
  up (BRIT), draft (US); **sotto le armi**
  in the army (*o* forces); **~ atomica/
  nucleare** atomic/nuclear weapon;
  ~ da fuoco firearm; **armi di
  distruzione de massa** weapons of
  mass destruction
arma'dietto *sm* (*di medicinali*)
  medicine cabinet; (*in palestra ecc*)
  locker; (*in cucina*) (kitchen) cupboard
ar'madio *sm* cupboard; (*per abiti*)
  wardrobe; **~ a muro** built-in
  cupboard
ar'mato, -a *ag*: **~ (di)** (*anche fig*)
  armed (with) ▷ *sf* (*Mil*) army; (*Naut*)
  fleet; **rapina a mano armata** armed
  robbery
arma'tura *sf* (*struttura di sostegno*)
  framework; (*impalcatura*) scaffolding;
  (*Storia*) armour *no pl*, suit of armour
armis'tizio [armis'tittsjo] *sm*
  armistice
armo'nia *sf* harmony
ar'nese *sm* tool, implement; (*oggetto
  indeterminato*) thing, contraption;
  male in ~ (*malvestito*) badly dressed;
  (*di salute malferma*) in poor health; (*di
  condizioni economiche*) down-at-heel
'arnia *sf* hive
a'roma, -i *sm* aroma; fragrance;
  aromi *smpl* (*Cuc*) herbs and spices;
  aromatera'pia *sf* aromatherapy
'arpa *sf* (*Mus*) harp
arrabbi'are /19/ *vi* (*cane*) to be
  affected with rabies; **arrabbiarsi** *vpr*
  (*essere preso dall'ira*) to get angry, fly
  into a rage; **arrabbi'ato, -a** *ag* rabid,
  with rabies; (*persona*) furious, angry
arrampi'carsi /20/ *vpr* to climb (up)
arran'giare [arran'dʒare] /62/ *vt* to
  arrange; **arrangiarsi** *vpr* to manage,
  do the best one can

arreda'mento *sm* (*studio*) interior
  design; (*mobili ecc*) furnishings *pl*
arre'dare /72/ *vt* to furnish
ar'rendersi /88/ *vpr* to surrender
arres'tare /72/ *vt* (*fermare*) to stop,
  halt; (*catturare*) to arrest; **arrestarsi**
  vpr (*fermarsi*) to stop; **ar'resto** *sm*
  (*cessazione*) stopping; (*fermata*)
  stop; (*cattura, Med*) arrest; **subire
  un arresto** to come to a stop *o*
  standstill; **mettere agli arresti**
  to place under arrest; **arresti
  domiciliari** house arrest *sg*
arre'trare /72/ *vt, vi* to withdraw;
  arre'trato, -a *ag* (*lavoro*) behind
  schedule; (*paese, bambino*) backward;
  (*numero di giornale*) back *cpd*;
  arretrati *smpl* arrears
arric'chire [arrik'kire] /55/ *vt* to
  enrich; **arricchirsi** *vpr* to become rich
arri'vare /72/ *vi* to arrive; (*accadere*) to
  happen, occur; **~ a** (*livello, grado ecc*)
  to reach; **lui arriva a Roma alle 7** he
  gets to *o* arrives at Rome at 7; **non ci
  arrivo** I can't reach it; (*fig: non capisco*)
  I can't understand it
arrive'derci [arrive'dertʃi] *escl*
  goodbye!
arri'vista, -i, -e *sm/f* go-getter
ar'rivo *sm* arrival; (*Sport*) finish,
  finishing line
arro'gante *ag* arrogant
arros'sire /55/ *vi* (*per vergogna,
  timidezza*) to blush; (*per gioia*) to flush
arros'tire /55/ *vt* to roast; (*pane*) to
  toast; (*ai ferri*) to grill
ar'rosto *sm, ag inv* roast
arroto'lare /72/ *vt* to roll up
arroton'dare /72/ *vt* (*forma, oggetto*)
  to round; (*stipendio*) to add to;
  (*somma*) to round off
arruggi'nito, -a [arruddʒin'nito]
  ag rusty
'arsi *vb vedi* **ardere**
'arte *sf* art; (*abilità*) skill
ar'teria *sf* artery; **~ stradale** main
  road
'artico, -a, -ci, -che *ag* Arctic

articolazi'one [artikolat'tsjone] *sf* (*Anat*, *Tecn*) joint

ar'ticolo *sm* article; **~ di fondo** (*Stampa*) leader, leading article

artifici'ale [artifi'tʃale] *ag* artificial

artigia'nato [artidʒa'nato] *sm* craftsmanship; craftsmen *pl*

artigi'ano, -a [arti'dʒano] *sm/f* craftsman/woman

ar'tista, -i, -e *sm/f* artist; **un lavoro da ~** (*fig*) a professional piece of work; **ar'tistico, -a, -ci, -che** *ag* artistic

ar'trite *sf* (*Med*) arthritis

a'scella [aʃʃɛlla] *sf* (*Anat*) armpit

ascen'dente [aʃʃen'dɛnte] *sm* ancestor; (*fig*) ascendancy; (*Astr*) ascendant

ascen'sore [aʃʃen'sore] *sm* lift

a'scesso [aʃʃɛsso] *sm* (*Med*) abscess

asciugaca'pelli [aʃʃugaka'pelli] *sm* hair dryer

asciuga'mano [aʃʃuga'mano] *sm* towel

asciu'gare [aʃʃu'gare] /80/ *vt* to dry; **asciugarsi** *vpr* to dry o.s.; (*diventare asciutto*) to dry

asci'utto, -a [aʃʃutto] *ag* dry; (*fig: magro*) lean; (: *burbero*) curt; **restare a bocca asciutta** (*fig*) to be disappointed

ascol'tare /72/ *vt* to listen to

as'falto *sm* asphalt

'Asia *sf*: **l'~** Asia; **asi'atico, -a, -ci, -che** *ag, sm/f* Asiatic, Asian

a'silo *sm* refuge, sanctuary; **~ (d'infanzia)** nursery(-school); **~ nido** crèche; **~ politico** political asylum

'asino *sm* donkey, ass

ASL *sigla f* (= *Azienda Sanitaria Locale*) local health centre

'asma *sf* asthma

as'parago, -gi *sm* asparagus *no pl*

aspet'tare /72/ *vt* to wait for; (*anche Comm*) to await; (*aspettarsi*) to expect ▷ *vi* to wait

as'petto *sm* (*apparenza*) aspect, appearance, look; (*punto di vista*) point of view; **di bell'~** good-looking

aspira'polvere *sm inv* vacuum cleaner

aspi'rare /72/ *vt* (*respirare*) to breathe in, inhale; (*apparecchi*) to suck (up) ▷ *vi*: **~ a** to aspire to

aspi'rina *sf* aspirin

'aspro, -a *ag* (*sapore*) sour, tart; (*odore*) acrid, pungent; (*voce, clima, fig*) harsh; (*superficie*) rough; (*paesaggio*) rugged

assaggi'are [assad'dʒare] /62/ *vt* to taste; **assag'gini** [assad'dʒini] *smpl* (*Cuc*) selection of first courses

as'sai *av* (*molto*) a lot, much; (: *con ag*) very; (*a sufficienza*) enough ▷ *ag inv* (*quantità*) a lot of, much; (*numero*) a lot of, many; **~ contento** very pleased

as'salgo *ecc vb vedi* **assalire**

assa'lire /98/ *vt* to attack, assail

assal'tare /72/ *vt* (*Mil*) to storm; (*banca*) to raid; (*treno, diligenza*) to hold up

as'salto *sm* attack, assault

assassi'nare /72/ *vt* to murder; (*Pol*) to assassinate; (*fig*) to ruin; **assas'sino, -a** *ag* murderous ▷ *sm/f* murderer; assassin

'asse *sm* (*Tecn*) axle; (*Mat*) axis ▷ *sf* board; **~ da stiro** ironing board

assedi'are /19/ *vt* to besiege

asse'gnare [assen'nare] /15/ *vt* to assign, allot; (*premio*) to award

as'segno [as'senno] *sm* allowance; (*anche:* **~ bancario**) cheque (BRIT), check (US); **contro ~** cash on delivery; **~ circolare** bank draft; **~ di malattia** *o* **di invalidità** sick pay/disability benefit; **~ sbarrato** crossed cheque; **~ di viaggio** travel(l)er's cheque; **~ a vuoto** dud cheque; **assegni familiari** ≈ child benefit *sg*

assem'blea *sf* assembly

assen'tarsi /72/ *vpr* to go out; **as'sente** *ag* absent; (*fig*) faraway, vacant; **as'senza** *sf* absence

asse'tato, -a *ag* thirsty, parched

assicu'rare /72/ *vt* (*accertare*) to ensure; (*infondere certezza*) to assure;

(*fermare, legare*) to make fast, secure; (*fare un contratto di assicurazione*) to insure; **assicurarsi** *vpr*: **assicurarsi (di)** (*accertarsi*) to make sure (of); **assicurarsi (contro)** (*il furto ecc*) to insure o.s. (against); **assicurazi'one** *sf* assurance; insurance

assi'eme *av* (*insieme*) together ▷ *prep*: **~ a** (together) with

assil'lare /72/ *vt* to pester, torment

assis'tente *smf* assistant; **~ sociale** social worker; **~ di volo** (*Aer*) steward (stewardess); **assis'tenza** *sf* assistance; **assistenza ospedaliera** free hospital treatment; **assistenza sanitaria** health service; **assistenza sociale** welfare services *pl*; **as'sistere** /11/ *vt* (*aiutare*) to assist, help; (*curare*) to treat ▷ *vi*: **assistere (a qc)** (*essere presente*) to be present (at sth), attend (sth)

'asso *sm* ace; **piantare qn in ~** to leave sb in the lurch

associ'are [assot'ʃare] /14/ *vt* to associate; **associarsi** *vpr* to enter into partnership; **associarsi a** to become a member of, join; (*dolori, gioie*) to share in; **~ qn alle carceri** to take sb to prison

associazi'one [assotʃat'tsjone] *sf* association; (*Comm*) association, society; **~ a o per delinquere** (*Dir*) criminal association

as'solsi *ecc vb vedi* **assolvere**

assoluta'mente *av* absolutely

asso'luto, -a *ag* absolute

assoluzi'one [assolut'tsjone] *sf* (*Dir*) acquittal; (*Rel*) absolution

as'solvere /94/ *vt* (*Dir*) to acquit; (*Rel*) to absolve; (*adempiere*) to carry out, perform

assomigli'are [assomiʎ'ʎare] /27/ *vi*: **~ a** to resemble, look like; **assomigliarsi** *vpr* to look alike; (*nel carattere*) to be alike

asson'nato, -a *ag* sleepy

asso'pirsi /55/ *vpr* to doze off

assor'bente *ag* absorbent ▷ *sm*: **~ igienico/esterno** sanitary towel; **~ interno** tampon

assor'bire /17/ *vt* to absorb

assor'dare /72/ *vt* to deafen

assorti'mento *sm* assortment; **assor'tito, -a** *ag* assorted; (*colori*) matched, matching

assuefazi'one [assuefat'tsjone] *sf* (*Med*) addiction

as'sumere /12/ *vt* (*impiegato*) to take on, engage; (*responsabilità*) to assume, take upon o.s.; (*contegno, espressione*) to assume, put on; (*droga*) to consume

as'sunsi *ecc vb vedi* **assumere**

assurdità *sf inv* absurdity; **dire delle ~** to talk nonsense; **as'surdo, -a** *ag* absurd

'asta *sf* pole; (*modo di vendita*) auction

as'temio, -a *ag* teetotal ▷ *sm/f* teetotaller

> Attenzione! In inglese esiste la parola *abstemious*, che però vuol dire *moderato*.

aste'nersi /121/ *vpr*: **~ (da)** to abstain (from), refrain (from); (*Pol*) to abstain (from)

aste'risco, -schi *sm* asterisk

'astice ['astitʃe] *sm* lobster

astig'matico, -a, -ci, -che *ag* astigmatic

asti'nenza [asti'nɛntsa] *sf* abstinence; **essere in crisi di ~** to suffer from withdrawal symptoms

as'tratto, -a *ag* abstract

'astro... *prefisso* astro; **astrolo'gia** [astrolo'dʒia] *sf* astrology; **astro'nauta, -i, -e** *sm/f* astronaut; **astro'nave** *sf* space ship; **astrono'mia** *sf* astronomy; **astro'nomico, -a, -ci, -che** *ag* astronomic(al)

as'tuccio [as'tuttʃo] *sm* case, box, holder

as'tuto, -a *ag* astute, cunning, shrewd

A'tene *sf* Athens

'ateo, -a ag, sm/f atheist

at'lante sm atlas

at'lantico, -a, -ci, -che ag Atlantic ▷ sm: **l'A~, l'Oceano A~** the Atlantic, the Atlantic Ocean

at'leta, -i, -e sm/f athlete; **at'letica** sf athletics sg: **atletica leggera** track and field events pl: **atletica pesante** weightlifting and wrestling

atmos'fera sf atmosphere

a'tomico, -a, -ci, -che ag atomic; (nucleare) atomic, atom cpd, nuclear

'atomo sm atom

'atrio sm entrance hall, lobby

a'troce [a'trotʃe] ag (che provoca orrore) dreadful; (terribile) atrocious

attac'cante smf (Sport) forward

attacca'panni sm hook, peg; (mobile) hall stand

attac'care /20/ vt (unire) to attach; (cucire) to sew on; (far aderire) to stick (on); (appendere) to hang (up); (assalire: anche fig) to attack; (iniziare) to begin, start; (fig: contagiare) to pass on ▷ vi to stick, adhere; **attaccarsi** vpr to stick, adhere; (trasmettersi per contagio) to be contagious; (afferrarsi): **attaccarsi (a)** to cling (to); (fig: affezionarsi): **attaccarsi (a)** to become attached (to); **~ discorso** to start a conversation; **at'tacco, -chi** sm (azione offensiva: anche fig) attack; (Med) attack, fit; (Sci) binding; (Elettr) socket

atteggia'mento [atteddʒa'mento] sm attitude

at'tendere /120/ vt to wait for, await ▷ vi: **~ a** to attend to

atten'dibile ag (scusa, storia) credible; (fonte, testimone, notizia) reliable

atten'tato sm attack; **~ alla vita di qn** attempt on sb's life

attenta'tore, -'trice sm/f bomber; **~ suicida** suicide bomber

at'tento, -a ag attentive; (accurato) careful, thorough ▷ escl be careful!; **stare ~ a qc** to pay attention to

sth; **attenzi'one** [atten'tsjone] sf attention ▷ escl watch out!, be careful!; **attenzioni** sfpl (premure) attentions; **fare attenzione a** to watch out for; **coprire qn di attenzioni** to lavish attention on sb

atter'raggio [atter'raddʒo] sm landing

atter'rare /72/ vt to bring down ▷ vi to land

at'tesa sf waiting; (tempo trascorso aspettando) wait; **essere in ~ di qc** to be waiting for sth

at'tesi ecc vb vedi **attendere**

at'teso, -a pp di **attendere**

'attico, -ci sm attic

attil'lato, -a ag (vestito) close-fitting

'attimo sm moment; **in un ~** in a moment

atti'rare /72/ vt to attract

atti'tudine sf (disposizione) aptitude; (atteggiamento) attitude

attività sf inv activity; (Comm) assets pl

at'tivo, -a ag active; (Comm) profit-making, credit cpd ▷ sm (Comm) assets pl: **in ~** in credit

'atto sm act; (azione, gesto) action, act, deed; (Dir: documento) deed, document; **atti** smpl (di congressi ecc) proceedings; **mettere in ~** to put into action; **fare ~ di fare qc** to make as if to do sth; **~ di nascita/morte** birth/death certificate

at'tore, -'trice sm/f actor (actress)

at'torno av round, around, about ▷ prep: **~ a** round, around, about

attrac'care /20/ vt, vi (Naut) to dock, berth

at'tracco, -chi sm (Naut) docking; (: luogo) berth

at'trae ecc vb vedi **attrarre**

attra'ente ag attractive

at'traggo ecc vb vedi **attrarre**

at'trarre /123/ vt to attract

at'trassi ecc vb vedi **attrarre**

attraver'sare /72/ vt to cross; (città, bosco, fig: periodo) to go through; (fiume) to run through

attra'verso prep through; (da una parte all'altra) across

attrazi'one [attrat'tsjone] sf attraction

attrezza'tura sf equipment no pl; rigging

at'trezzo sm tool, instrument; (Sport) piece of equipment

at'trice [at'tritʃe] sf vedi **attore**

attu'ale ag (presente) present; (di attualità) topical

> Attenzione! In inglese esiste la parola actual, che però vuol dire effettivo.

attualità sf inv topicality; (avvenimento) current event; **attual'mente** av at the moment, at present

> Attenzione! In inglese esiste la parola actually, che però vuol dire effettivamente oppure veramente.

attu'are /72/ vt to carry out; **attuarsi** vpr to be realized

attu'tire /55/ vt to deaden, reduce

'audio sm (TV, Radio, Cine) sound

audiovi'sivo, -a ag audiovisual

audizi'one [audit'tsjone] sf hearing; (Mus) audition

augu'rare /72/ vt to wish; **augurarsi qc** to hope for sth

au'gurio sm (good) wish; **auguri** smpl best wishes; **fare gli auguri a qn** to give sb one's best wishes; **tanti auguri!** best wishes!; (per compleanno) happy birthday!

'aula sf (scolastica) classroom; (universitaria) lecture theatre; (di edificio pubblico) hall

aumen'tare /72/ vt, vi to increase; ~ **di peso** (persona) to put on weight; **la produzione è aumentata del 50%** production has increased by 50%; **au'mento** sm increase

au'rora sf dawn

ausili'are ag, sm, smf auxiliary

Aus'tralia sf: **l'~** Australia; **australi'ano, -a** ag, sm/f Australian

'Austria sf: **l'~** Austria; **aus'triaco, -a, -ci, -che** ag, sm/f Austrian

au'tentico, -a, -ci, -che ag authentic, genuine

au'tista, -i sm driver

'auto sf inv car

autoabbron'zante ag self-tanning

autoade'sivo, -a ag self-adhesive ▷ sm sticker

autobio'grafico, -a, -ci, -che ag autobiographic(al)

'autobus sm inv bus

auto'carro sm lorry (BRIT), truck

autocertificazi'one [autotʃertifikat'tsjone] sf self-declaration

autodistrut'tivo, -a ag self-destructive

auto'gol sm inv own goal

au'tografo, -a ag, sm autograph

auto'grill® sm inv motorway café

auto'matico, -a, -ci, -che ag automatic ▷ sm (bottone) snap fastener; (fucile) automatic

auto'mobile sf (motor) car; **automobi'lista, -i, -e** sm/f motorist

autono'leggio [autono'leddʒo] sm car hire

autono'mia sf autonomy; (di volo) range; **au'tonomo, -a** ag autonomous; independent

autop'sia sf post-mortem (examination), autopsy

auto'radio sf inv (apparecchio) radio; (autoveicolo) radio car

au'tore, -'trice sm/f author

autoreg'gente [autored'dʒente] ag: **calze autoreggenti** hold ups

auto'revole ag authoritative; (persona) influential

autoricari'cabile ag: **scheda ~** top-up card

autori'messa sf garage

autorità sf inv authority

autoriz'zare [autorid'dzare] /72/ vt (permettere) to authorize; (giustificare) to allow, sanction

autos'contro *sm* dodgem car (BRIT), bumper car (US)
autoscu'ola *sf* driving school
autos'tima *sf* self-esteem
autos'top *sm* hitchhiking; **autostop'pista, -i, -e** *sm/f* hitchhiker
autos'trada *sf* motorway (BRIT), highway (US); **~ informatica** information superhighway

○ **AUTOSTRADE**
○
○ You have to pay to use Italian
○ motorways. They are indicated
○ by an "A" followed by a number on
○ a green sign. The speed limit on
○ Italian motorways is 130 kph.

auto'velox® *sm inv* (police) speed camera
autovet'tura *sf* (motor) car
au'tunno *sm* autumn
avam'braccio [avam'brattʃo] (*pl f* **avambraccia**) *sm* forearm
avangu'ardia *sf* vanguard
a'vanti *av* (*stato in luogo*) in front; (*moto: andare, venire*) forward; (*tempo: prima*) before ▷ *prep* (*luogo*): **~ a** before, in front of; (*tempo*): **~ Cristo** before Christ ▷ *escl* (*entrate*) come (*o go*) in!; (*Mil*) forward!; (*coraggio*) come on! ▷ *sm inv* (*Sport*) forward; **~ e indietro** backwards and forwards; **andare ~** to go forward; (*continuare*) to go on; (*precedere*) to go (on) ahead; (*orologio*) to be fast; **essere ~ negli studi** to be well advanced with one's studies
avan'zare [avan'tsare] /72/ *vt* (*spostare in avanti*) to move forward, advance; (*domanda*) to put forward; (*promuovere*) to promote; (*essere creditore*): **~ qc da qn** to be owed sth by sb ▷ *vi* (*andare avanti*) to move forward, advance; (*progredire*) to make progress; (*essere d'avanzo*) to be left, remain

ava'ria *sf* (*guasto*) damage; (: *meccanico*) breakdown
a'varo, -a *ag* avaricious, miserly ▷ *sm* miser

 PAROLA CHIAVE

a'vere /13/ *sm* (*Comm*) credit; **gli averi** (*ricchezze*) wealth *sg*
▶ *vt* 1 (*possedere*) to have; **ha due bambini/una bella casa** she has (got) two children/a lovely house; **ha i capelli lunghi** he has (got) long hair; **non ho da mangiare/bere** I've (got) nothing to eat/drink, I don't have anything to eat/drink
2 (*indossare*) to wear, have on; **aveva una maglietta rossa** he was wearing *o* he had on a red T-shirt; **ha gli occhiali** he wears *o* has glasses
3 (*ricevere*) to get; **hai avuto l'assegno?** did you get *o* have you had the cheque?
4 (*età, dimensione*) to be; **ha 9 anni** he is 9 (years old); **la stanza ha 3 metri di lunghezza** the room is 3 metres in length; *vedi* **fame**; **paura**; **sonno** *ecc*
5 (*tempo*): **quanti ne abbiamo oggi?** what's the date today?; **ne hai per molto?** will you be long?
6 (*fraseologia*): **avercela con qn** to be angry with sb; **cos'hai?** what's wrong *o* what's the matter (with you)?; **non ha niente a che vedere** *o* **fare con me** it's got nothing to do with me
▶ *vb aus* 1 to have; **aver bevuto/mangiato** to have drunk/eaten
2 (+ *da* + *infinito*): **avere da fare qc** to have to do sth; **non hai che da chiederlo** you only have to ask him

aviazi'one [avjat'tsjone] *sf* aviation; (*Mil*) air force
'avido, -a *ag* eager; (*peg*) greedy
avo'cado *sm* avocado
a'vorio *sm* ivory
Avv. *abbr* = **avvocato**

avvantaggi'are [avvantad'dʒare] /62/ vt to favour; **avvantaggiarsi** vpr: **avvantaggiarsi negli affari/ sui concorrenti** to get ahead in business/of one's competitors

avvele'nare /72/ vt to poison

av'vengo ecc vb vedi **avvenire**

avveni'mento sm event

avve'nire /128/ vi, vb impers to happen, occur ▷ sm future

av'venni ecc vb vedi **avvenire**

avven'tato, -a ag rash, reckless

avven'tura sf adventure; (amorosa) affair

avventu'rarsi /72/ vpr to venture

avventu'roso, -a ag adventurous

avve'rarsi /72/ vpr to come true

av'verbio sm adverb

avverrò ecc vb vedi **avvenire**

avver'sario, -a ag opposing ▷ sm opponent, adversary

avver'tenza [avver'tɛntsa] sf (ammonimento) warning; (cautela) care; (premessa) foreword; **avvertenze** sfpl (istruzioni per l'uso) instructions

avverti'mento sm warning

avver'tire /45/ vt (avvisare) to warn; (rendere consapevole) to inform, notify; (percepire) to feel

avvi'are /60/ vt (mettere sul cammino) to direct; (impresa, trattative) to begin, start; (motore) to start; **avviarsi** vpr to set off, set out

avvici'nare [avvitʃi'nare] /72/ vt to bring near; (trattare con: persona) to approach; **avvicinarsi** vpr: **avvicinarsi (a qn/qc)** to approach (sb/sth), draw near (to sb/sth)

avvi'lito, -a ag discouraged

avvin'cente [avvin'tʃɛnte] ag enthralling

avvi'sare /72/ vt (far sapere) to inform; (mettere in guardia) to warn; **av'viso** sm warning; (annuncio) announcement; (affisso) notice; (inserzione pubblicitaria) advertisement; **a mio avviso** in my opinion; **avviso di chiamata** (servizio) call waiting; (segnale) call waiting signal; **avviso di garanzia** (Dir) notification (of impending investigation and of the right to name a defence laywer)

> Attenzione! In inglese esiste la parola advice, che però vuol dire consiglio.

avvis'tare /72/ vt to sight

avvi'tare /72/ vt to screw down (o in)

avvo'cato, -'essa sm/f (Dir) barrister (BRIT), lawyer; (fig) defender, advocate

av'volgere [av'vɔldʒere] /96/ vt to roll up; (avviluppare) to wrap up; **avvolgersi** vpr (avvilupparsi) to wrap o.s. up; **avvol'gibile** sm roller blind (BRIT), blind

av'volsi ecc vb vedi **avvolgere**

avvol'toio sm vulture

aza'lea [addza'lɛa] sf azalea

azi'enda [ad'dzjɛnda] sf business, firm, concern; **~ agricola** farm

azi'one [at'tsjone] sf action; (Comm) share

a'zoto [ad'dzɔto] sm nitrogen

azzar'dare [addzar'dare] /72/ vt (soldi, vita) to risk, hazard; (domanda, ipotesi) to hazard, venture; **azzardarsi** vpr: **azzardarsi a fare** to dare (to) do

az'zardo [ad'dzardo] sm risk

azzec'care [attsek'kare] /20/ vt (risposta, pronostico) to get right

azzuf'farsi [attsuf'farsi] /72/ vpr to come to blows

az'zurro, -a [ad'dzurro] ag blue ▷ sm (colore) blue; **gli azzurri** (Sport) the Italian national team

'babbo sm (fam) dad, daddy; **B~ Natale** Father Christmas
baby'sitter ['beɪbɪsɪtə'] sm inv, f inv baby-sitter
'bacca, -che sf berry
baccalà sm dried salted cod; (fig: peg) dummy
bac'chetta [bak'ketta] sf (verga) stick, rod; (di direttore d'orchestra) baton; (di tamburo) drumstick; **~ magica** magic wand
ba'checa, -che [ba'kɛka] sf (mobile) showcase, display case; (Università, in ufficio) notice board (BRIT), bulletin board (US)
baci'are [ba'tʃare] /14/ vt to kiss; **baciarsi** vpr to kiss (one another)
baci'nella [batʃi'nɛlla] sf basin
ba'cino [ba'tʃino] sm basin; (Mineralogia) field, bed; (Anat) pelvis; (Naut) dock; **~ d'utenza** catchment area
'bacio ['batʃo] sm kiss

'baco, -chi sm worm; **~ da seta** silkworm
ba'dante smf care worker
ba'dare /72/ vi (fare attenzione) to take care, be careful; **~ a** (occuparsi di) to look after, take care of; (dar ascolto) to pay attention to; **bada ai fatti tuoi!** mind your own business!
'baffi smpl moustache sg; (di animale) whiskers; **leccarsi i ~** to lick one's lips; **ridere sotto i ~** to laugh up one's sleeve
bagagli'aio [bagaʎ'ʎajo] sm luggage van (BRIT) o car (US); (Aut) boot (BRIT), trunk (US)
ba'gaglio [ba'gaʎʎo] sm luggage no pl, baggage no pl; **fare/disfare i bagagli** to pack/unpack; **~ a mano** hand luggage
bagli'ore [baʎ'ʎore] sm flash, dazzling light; **un ~ di speranza** a (sudden) ray of hope
ba'gnante [baɲ'ɲante] smf bather
ba'gnare [baɲ'ɲare] /15/ vt to wet; (inzuppare) to soak; (innaffiare) to water; (fiume) to flow through; (: mare) to wash, bathe; **bagnarsi** vpr to get wet; (al mare) to go swimming o bathing; (in vasca) to have a bath
ba'gnato, -a [baɲ'ɲato] ag wet
ba'gnino [baɲ'ɲino] sm lifeguard
'bagno ['baɲɲo] sm bath; (locale) bathroom; (toilette) toilet; **bagni** smpl (stabilimento) baths; **fare il ~** to have a bath; (nel mare) to go swimming o bathing; **fare il ~ a qn** to give sb a bath; **mettere a ~** to soak
bagnoma'ria [baɲɲoma'ria] sm: **cuocere a ~** to cook in a double saucepan (BRIT) o double boiler (US)
bagnoschi'uma [baɲɲoskj'uma] sm inv bubble bath
'baia sf bay
balbet'tare /72/ vi to stutter, stammer; (bimbo) to babble ▷ vt to stammer out
bal'canico, -a, -ci, -che ag Balkan
bal'cone sm balcony

bal'doria *sf*: **fare ~** to have a riotous time
ba'lena *sf* whale
ba'leno *sm* flash of lightning; **in un ~** in a flash
bal'lare /72/ *vt, vi* to dance
balle'rina *sf* dancer; ballet dancer; (*scarpa*) ballet shoe
balle'rino *sm* dancer; ballet dancer
bal'letto *sm* ballet
'**ballo** *sm* dance; (*azione*) dancing *no pl*; **essere in ~** (*fig: persona*) to be involved; (: *cosa*) to be at stake
balne'are *ag* seaside *cpd*; (*stagione*) bathing
'**balsamo** *sm* (*aroma*) balsam; (*lenimento, fig*) balm; (*per capelli*) conditioner
bal'zare [bal'tsare] /72/ *vi* to bounce; (*lanciarsi*) to jump, leap; '**balzo** *sm* bounce; jump, leap; (*del terreno*) crag
bam'bina *sf vedi* **bambino**
bam'bino, -a *sm/f* child
'**bambola** *sf* doll
bambù *sm* bamboo
ba'nale *ag* banal, commonplace
ba'nana *sf* banana
'**banca, -che** *sf* bank; **~ (di) dati** data bank
banca'rella *sf* stall
banca'rotta *sf* bankruptcy; **fare ~** to go bankrupt
ban'chetto [ban'ketto] *sm* banquet
banchi'ere [ban'kjɛre] *sm* banker
ban'china [ban'kina] *sf* (*di porto*) quay; (*per pedoni, ciclisti*) path; (*di stazione*) platform; **~ cedevole** (*Aut*) soft verge (*BRIT*) *o* shoulder (*US*)
'**banco, -chi** *sm* bench; (*di negozio*) counter; (*di mercato*) stall; (*di officina*) (work)bench; (*Geo, banca*) bank; **~ di corallo** coral reef; **~ degli imputati** dock; **~ di prova** (*fig*) testing ground; **~ dei testimoni** witness box (*BRIT*) *o* stand (*US*); **~ dei pegni** pawnshop; **~ di nebbia** bank of fog

'**Bancomat®** *sm inv* automated banking; (*tessera*) cash card; (*sportello automatico*) cashpoint
banco'nota *sf* banknote
'**banda** *sf* band; (*di stoffa*) band, stripe; (*lato, parte*) side; **~ larga** broadband
bandi'era *sf* flag, banner
ban'dito *sm* outlaw, bandit
'**bando** *sm* proclamation; (*esilio*) exile, banishment; **~ alle ciance!** that's enough talk!; **~ di concorso** announcement of a competition
bar *sm inv* bar
'**bara** *sf* coffin
ba'racca, -che *sf* shed, hut; (*peg*) hovel; **mandare avanti la ~** to keep things going
ba'rare /72/ *vi* to cheat
'**baratro** *sm* abyss
'**baratto** *sm* barter
ba'rattolo *sm* (*di latta*) tin; (*di vetro*) jar; (*di coccio*) pot
'**barba** *sf* beard; **farsi la ~** to shave; **farla in ~ a qn** (*fig*) to do sth to sb's face; **servire qn di ~ e capelli** (*fig*) to teach sb a lesson; **che ~!** what a bore!
barbabi'etola *sf* beetroot (*BRIT*), beet (*US*); **~ da zucchero** sugar beet
barbi'ere *sm* barber
bar'bone *sm* (*cane*) poodle; (*vagabondo*) tramp
'**barca, -che** *sf* boat; **~ a motore** motorboat; **~ a remi** rowing boat; **~ a vela** sailing boat (*BRIT*), sailboat (*US*)
barcol'lare /72/ *vi* to stagger
ba'rella *sf* (*lettiga*) stretcher
ba'rile *sm* barrel, cask
ba'rista, -i, -e *sm/f* barman (barmaid); (*proprietario*) bar owner
ba'rocco, -a, -chi, -che *ag, sm* baroque
ba'rometro *sm* barometer
ba'rone *sm* baron; **baro'nessa** *sf* baroness
'**barra** *sf* bar; (*Naut*) helm; (*linea grafica*) line, stroke
bar'rare /72/ *vt* to bar

barri'care /20/ *vt* to barricade;
 barricarsi *vpr* to barricade o.s.
barri'era *sf* barrier; (*Geo*) reef
ba'ruffa *sf* scuffle
barzel'letta [bardzel'letta] *sf* joke,
 funny story
ba'sare /72/ *vt* to base, found;
 basarsi *vpr*: **basarsi su** (*fatti, prove*)
 to be based *o* founded on; (*persona*) to
 base one's arguments on
basco, -a, -schi, -sche *ag* Basque
 ▷ *sm* (*copricapo*) beret
base *sf* base; (*fig: fondamento*) basis;
 (*Pol*) rank and file; **di ~** basic; **in ~ a**
 on the basis of, according to; **a ~ di**
 caffè coffee-based
baseball ['beisbɔːl] *sm* baseball
ba'silica, -che *sf* basilica
ba'silico *sm* basil
basket ['basket] *sm* basketball
bas'sista, -i, -e *sm/f* bass player
basso, -a *ag* low; (*di statura*) short;
 (*meridionale*) southern ▷ *sm* bottom,
 lower part; (*Mus*) bass; **la bassa**
 Italia southern Italy
bassorili'evo *sm* bas-relief
bas'sotto, -a *ag* squat ▷ *sm* (*cane*)
 dachshund
basta *escl* (that's) enough!, that
 will do!
bas'tardo, -a *ag* (*animale, pianta*)
 hybrid, crossbreed; (*persona*)
 illegitimate, bastard (*peg*) ▷ *sm/f*
 illegitimate child, bastard (*peg*)
bas'tare /72/ *vi, vb impers* to be
 enough, be sufficient; **~ a qn** to be
 enough for sb; **basta chiedere** *o* **che**
 chieda a un vigile you have only to
 o need only ask a policeman; **basta**
 così, grazie that's enough, thanks
basto'nare /72/ *vt* to beat, thrash
baston'cino [baston'tʃino] *sm* (*Sci*)
 ski pole; **bastoncini di pesce** fish
 fingers
bas'tone *sm* stick; **~ da passeggio**
 walking stick
bat'taglia [bat'taʎʎa] *sf* battle;
 fight

bat'tello *sm* boat
bat'tente *sm* (*imposta: di porta*) wing,
 flap; (: *di finestra*) shutter; (*batacchio:*
 di porta) knocker; (: *di orologio*)
 hammer; **chiudere i battenti** (*fig*) to
 shut up shop
'battere /1/ *vt* to beat; (*grano*) to
 thresh; (*percorrere*) to scour ▷ *vi*
 (*bussare*) to knock; (*pioggia, sole*) to
 beat down; (*cuore*) to beat; (*Tennis*)
 to serve; (*urtare*): **~ contro** to hit *o*
 strike against; **battersi** *vpr* to fight;
 ~ le mani to clap; **~ i piedi** to stamp
 one's feet; **~ a macchina** to type; **~**
 bandiera italiana to fly the Italian
 flag; **~ in testa** (*Aut*) to knock; **in**
 un batter d'occhio in the twinkling
 of an eye
batte'ria *sf* battery; (*Mus*) drums *pl*
bat'terio *sm* bacterium
batte'rista, -i, -e *sm/f* drummer
bat'tesimo *sm* (*rito*) baptism;
 christening
battez'zare [batted'dzare] /72/ *vt* to
 baptize; to christen
batti'panni *sm inv* carpet-beater
battis'trada *sm inv* (*di pneumatico*)
 tread; (*di gara*) pacemaker
'battito *sm* beat, throb; **~ cardiaco**
 heartbeat
bat'tuta *sf* blow; (*di macchina da*
 scrivere) stroke; (*Mus*) bar; beat; (*Teat*)
 cue; (*frase spiritosa*) witty remark; (*di*
 caccia) beating; (*Polizia*) combing,
 scouring; (*Tennis*) service
ba'tuffolo *sm* wad
ba'ule *sm* trunk; (*Aut*) boot (BRIT),
 trunk (US)
'bava *sf* (*di animale*) slaver, slobber; (*di*
 lumaca) slime; (*di vento*) breath
bava'glino [bavaʎ'ʎino] *sm* bib
ba'vaglio [ba'vaʎʎo] *sm* gag
'bavero *sm* collar
ba'zar [bad'dzar] *sm inv* bazaar
BCE *sigla f* (= *Banca centrale europea*)
 ECB
be'ato, -a *ag* blessed; (*fig*) happy;
 ~ te! lucky you!

bec'care /20/ vt to peck; (fig: raffreddore) to catch; **beccarsi** vpr (fig) to squabble; **beccarsi qc** to catch sth

beccherò ecc [bekke'rɔ] vb vedi **beccare**

'becco, -chi sm beak, bill; (di caffettiera ecc) spout; lip

Be'fana sf old woman who, according to legend, brings children their presents at the Epiphany; (Epifania) Epiphany; **befana** hag, witch

beffardo, -a ag scornful, mocking

'begli ['bɛʎʎi], **'bei** ag vedi **bello**

beige [bɛʒ] ag inv beige

bel ag vedi **bello**

be'lare /72/ vi to bleat

'belga, -gi, -ghe ag, smf Belgian

'Belgio ['bɛldʒo] sm: **il ~** Belgium

'bella sf (Sport) decider; vedi **bello**

bel'lezza [bel'lettsa] sf beauty

PAROLA CHIAVE

'bello, -a (ag: dav sm **bel** + C, **bell'** + V, **bello** + s impura, gn, pn, ps, x, z, pl **bei** + C, **begli** + s impura ecc o V) ag **1** (oggetto, donna, paesaggio) beautiful, lovely; (uomo) handsome; (tempo) beautiful, fine, lovely; **le belle arti** fine arts

2 (quantità): **una bella cifra** a considerable sum of money; **un bel niente** absolutely nothing

3 (rafforzativo): **è una truffa bella e buona!** it's a real fraud!; **è bell'e finito** it's already finished

▶ sm **1** (bellezza) beauty; (: tempo) fine weather

2: adesso viene il bello now comes the best bit; **sul più bello** at the crucial point; **cosa fai di bello?** are you doing anything interesting?

▶ av: **fa bello** the weather is fine, it's fine

'belva sf wild animal

belve'dere sm inv panoramic viewpoint

benché [ben'ke] cong although

'benda sf bandage; (per gli occhi) blindfold; **ben'dare** /72/ vt to bandage; to blindfold

'bene av well; (completamente, affatto): **è ben difficile** it's very difficult ▷ ag inv: **gente ~** well-to-do people ▷ sm good; **beni** smpl (averi) property sg, estate sg: **io sto ~/poco ~** I'm well/ not very well; **va ~** all right; **volere un ~ dell'anima a qn** to love sb very much; **un uomo per ~** a respectable man; **fare ~** to do the right thing; **fare ~ a** (salute) to be good for; **fare del ~ a qn** to do sb a good turn; **beni di consumo** consumer goods

bene'detto, -a pp di **benedire** ▷ ag blessed, holy

bene'dire /38/ vt to bless; to consecrate

benedu'cato, -a ag well-mannered

benefi'cenza [benefi'tʃentsa] sf charity

bene'ficio [bene'fitʃo] sm benefit; **con ~ d'inventario** (fig) with reservations

be'nessere sm well-being

benes'tante ag well-to-do

be'nigno, -a [be'niɲɲo] ag kind, kindly; (critica ecc) favourable; (Med) benign

benve'nuto, -a ag, sm welcome; **dare il ~ a qn** to welcome sb

ben'zina [ben'dzina] *sf* petrol
(BRIT), gas (US); **fare ~** to get petrol
o gas; **rimanere senza ~** to run out
of petrol *o* gas; **~ verde** unleaded
petrol; **benzi'naio** *sm* petrol (BRIT) *o*
gas (US) pump attendant

'bere /16/ *vt* to drink; **darla a ~ a qn**
(*fig*) to fool sb

ber'lina *sf* (*Aut*) saloon (car) (BRIT),
sedan (US)

Ber'lino *sf* Berlin

ber'muda *smpl* (*calzoncini*) Bermuda
shorts

ber'noccolo *sm* bump; (*inclinazione*)
flair

ber'retto *sm* cap

berrò *ecc vb vedi* **bere**

ber'saglio [ber'saʎʎo] *sm* target

bescia'mella [beʃʃa'mɛlla] *sf*
béchamel sauce

bes'temmia *sf* curse; (*Rel*)
blasphemy; **bestemmi'are** /19/ *vi* to
curse, swear; to blaspheme ▷ *vt* to
curse, swear at; to blaspheme

'bestia *sf* animal; **andare in ~** (*fig*) to
fly into a rage; **besti'ale** *ag* beastly;
animal *cpd*; (*fam*): **fa un freddo
bestiale** it's bitterly cold; **besti'ame**
sm livestock; (*bovino*) cattle *pl*

be'tulla *sf* birch

be'vanda *sf* drink, beverage

'bevo *ecc vb vedi* **bere**

be'vuto, -a *pp di* **bere**

'bevvi *ecc vb vedi* **bere**

bianche'ria [bjanke'ria] *sf* linen;
~ intima underwear; **~ da donna**
ladies' underwear, lingerie; **~
femminile** lingerie

bi'anco, -a, -chi, -che *ag* white; (*non
scritto*) blank ▷ *sm* white; (*intonaco*)
whitewash ▷ *sm/f* white, white man
(woman); **in ~** (*foglio, assegno*) blank;
in ~ e nero (*TV, Fot*) black and white;
mangiare in ~ to follow a bland diet;
pesce in ~ boiled fish; **andare in ~**
(*non riuscire*) to fail; **notte bianca**
o **in ~** sleepless night; **~ dell'uovo**
egg-white

biasi'mare /72/ *vt* to disapprove
of, censure

'Bibbia *sf* (*anche fig*) Bible

bibe'ron *sm inv* feeding bottle

'bibita *sf* (*soft*) drink

biblio'teca, -che *sf* library; (*mobile*)
bookcase

bicarbo'nato *sm*: **~ (di sodio)**
bicarbonate (of soda)

bicchi'ere [bik'kjɛre] *sm* glass

bici'cletta [bitʃi'kletta] *sf* bicycle;
andare in ~ to cycle

bidè *sm inv* bidet

bi'dello, -a *sm/f* (*Ins*) janitor

bi'done *sm* drum, can; (*anche*: **~
dell'immondizia**) (dust)bin; (*fam*:
truffa) swindle; **fare un ~ a qn** (*fam*)
to let sb down; to cheat sb

bien'nale *ag* biennial

> ○ **BIENNALE DI VENEZIA**
>
> ○
> ○ Dating back to 1895, the *Biennale*
> ○ *di Venezia* is an international
> ○ festival of the contemporary arts.
> ○ It takes place every two years in
> ○ the "Giardini Pubblici". The various
> ○ countries taking part each put on
> ○ exhibitions in their own pavilions.
> ○ There is a section dedicated to
> ○ the work of young artists, as well
> ○ as a special exhibition organized
> ○ around a specific theme for that
> ○ year.

bifami'liare *ag* (*villa, casetta*) semidetached

bifor'carsi /20/ *vpr* to fork

bigiotte'ria [bidʒotte'ria] *sf*
costume jewellery (BRIT) *o* jewelry
(US); (*negozio*) jeweller's (shop)
(BRIT) *o* jewelry store (US: *selling only
costume jewellery*)

bigliet'taio, -a *sm/f* (*nei treni*) ticket
inspector; (*in autobus ecc*) conductor

bigliette'ria [biʎʎette'ria] *sf* (*di
stazione*) ticket office; booking office;
(*di teatro*) box office

bigli'etto [biʎ'ʎetto] *sm* (*per viaggi, spettacoli ecc*) ticket; (*cartoncino*) card; **~ di banca** (bank)note; (*anche*: **~ d'auguri/da visita**) greetings/visiting card; **~ di andata e ritorno** return (BRIT) *o* round-trip (US) ticket; **~ di sola andata** single (ticket); **~ elettronico** e-ticket

bignè [biɲ'ɲɛ] *sm inv* cream puff

bigo'dino *sm* roller, curler

bi'gotto, -a *ag* over-pious ▷ *sm/f* church fiend

bi'kini *sm inv* bikini

bi'lancia, -ce [bi'lantʃa] *sf* (*pesa*) scales *pl*; (: *di precisione*) balance; **B~** Libra; **~ commerciale/dei pagamenti** balance of trade/payments

bi'lancio [bi'lantʃo] *sm* (Comm) balance (sheet); (*statale*) budget; **fare il ~ di** (*fig*) to assess; **~ consuntivo** (final) balance; **~ preventivo** budget

biliar'dino *sm* pinball

bili'ardo *sm* billiards *sg*; (*tavolo*) billiard table

bi'lingue *ag* bilingual

bilo'cale *sm* two-room flat (BRIT) *o* apartment (US)

'bimbo, -a *sm/f* little boy (girl)

bi'nario, -a *ag* (*sistema*) binary ▷ *sm* (railway) track *o* line; (*piattaforma*) platform; **~ morto** dead-end track

bi'nocolo *sm* binoculars *pl*

bio... *prefisso* bio; **biocarbu'rante** *sm* biofuel; **biodegra'dabile** *ag* biodegradable; **biodi'namico, -a, -ci, -che** *ag* biodynamic; **biogra'fia** *sf* biography; **biolo'gia** *sf* biology

bio'logico, -a, -ci, -che *ag* (*scienze, fenomeni ecc*) biological; (*agricoltura, prodotti*) organic; **guerra biologica** biological warfare

bi'ondo, -a *ag* blond, fair

biotecnolo'gia [bioteknolo'dʒia] *sf* biotechnology

biri'chino, -a [biri'kino] *ag* mischievous ▷ *sm/f* scamp, little rascal

bi'rillo *sm* skittle (BRIT), pin (US)

'biro® *sf inv* biro®

'birra *sf* beer; **~ chiara/scura** lager/stout; **a tutta ~** (*fig*) at top speed; **birre'ria** *sf* ≈ bierkeller

bis *escl, sm inv* encore

bis'betico, -a, -ci, -che *ag* ill-tempered, crabby

bisbigli'are [bizbiʎ'ʎare] /27/ *vt, vi* to whisper

'bisca, -sche *sf* gambling house

'biscia, -sce ['biʃʃa] *sf* snake; **~ d'acqua** water snake

biscot'tato, -a *ag* crisp; **fette biscottate** rusks

bis'cotto *sm* biscuit

bisessu'ale, -i *smf* bisexual

bises'tile *ag*: **anno ~** leap year

bis'nonno, -a *sm/f* great grandfather/grandmother

biso'gnare [bizoɲ'ɲare] /15/ *vb impers*: **bisogna che tu parta/lo faccia** you'll have to go/do it; **bisogna parlargli** we'll (*o* I'll) have to talk to him

bi'sogno [bi'zoɲɲo] *sm* need; **ha ~ di qualcosa?** do you need anything?

bis'tecca, -che *sf* steak, beefsteak

bisticci'are [bistit'tʃare] /14/ *vi* to quarrel, bicker; **bisticciarsi** *vpr* to quarrel, bicker

'bisturi *sm inv* scalpel

'bivio *sm* fork; (*fig*) dilemma

biz'zarro, -a [bid'dzarro] *ag* bizarre, strange

blate'rare /72/ *vi* to chatter

blin'dato, -a *ag* armoured

bloc'care /20/ *vt* to block; (*isolare*) to isolate, cut off; (*porto*) to blockade; (*prezzi, beni*) to freeze; (*meccanismo*) to jam; **bloccarsi** *vpr* (*motore*) to stall; (*freni, porta*) to jam, stick; (*ascensore*) to get stuck, stop

blocche'rò *ecc* [blokke'rɔ] *vb vedi* **bloccare**

bloc'chetto [blok'ketto] *sm* notebook; (*di biglietti*) book

'blocco, -chi *sm* block; (Mil) blockade; (*dei fitti*) restriction; (*quadernetto*)

pad; (fig: unione) coalition; (il bloccare)
blocking; isolating, cutting-off;
blockading; freezing; jamming; **in
~** (nell'insieme) as a whole; (Comm)
in bulk; **~ cardiaco** cardiac arrest;
~ stradale road block

blog [blog] sm inv blog

blog'gare /80/ vi to blog

blu ag inv, sm inv dark blue

blusa sf (camiciotto) smock;
(camicetta) blouse

boa sm inv (Zool) boa constrictor;
(sciarpa) feather boa ▷ sf buoy

bo'ato sm rumble, roar

bob [bɔb] sm inv bobsleigh

bocca, -che sf mouth; **in ~ al lupo!**
good luck!

boc'caccia, -ce [bok'kattʃa] sf
(malalingua) gossip; **fare le boccacce**
to pull faces

boc'cale sm jug; **~ da birra** tankard

boc'cetta [bot'tʃetta] sf small bottle

boccia, -ce ['bottʃa] sf bottle; (da
vino) decanter, carafe; (palla di legno,
metallo) bowl; **gioco delle bocce**
bowls sg

bocci'are [bot'tʃare] /14/ vt (proposta,
progetto) to reject; (Ins) to fail; (Bocce)
to hit

bocci'olo [bot'tʃolo] sm bud

boc'cone sm mouthful, morsel

boicot'tare /72/ vt to boycott

bolla sf bubble; (Med) blister; **~ di
consegna** (Comm) delivery note; **~
papale** papal bull

bol'lente ag boiling; boiling hot

bol'letta sf bill; (ricevuta) receipt;
essere in ~ to be hard up

bollet'tino sm bulletin; (Comm) note;
~ meteorologico weather forecast;
~ di spedizione consignment note

bolli'cina [bolli'tʃina] sf bubble

bol'lire /17/ vt, vi to boil

bolli'tore sm boiler; (Cuc: per acqua)
kettle

bollo sm stamp; **~ per patente**
driving licence tax; **~ postale**
postmark

bomba sf bomb; **~ atomica** atom
bomb; **~ a mano** hand grenade; **~ ad
orologeria** time bomb

bombarda'mento sm
bombardment; bombing

bombar'dare /72/ vt to bombard; (da
aereo) to bomb

bombola sf cylinder

bombo'letta sf spray can

bomboni'era sf box of sweets
(as souvenir at weddings, first
communions etc)

bo'nifico, -ci sm (riduzione, abbuono)
discount; (versamento a terzi) credit
transfer

bontà sf goodness; (cortesia)
kindness; **aver la ~ di fare qc** to be
good o kind enough to do sth

borbot'tare /72/ vi to mumble

borchia ['borkja] sf stud

bor'deaux [bor'dɔ] ag inv, sm inv
maroon

bordo sm (Naut) ship's side; (orlo)
edge; (striscia di guarnizione) border,
trim; **a ~ di** (nave, aereo) aboard, on
board; (macchina) in

bor'ghese [bor'geze] ag (spesso peg)
middle-class; bourgeois; **abito ~**
civilian dress

borgo, -ghi sm (paesino) village;
(quartiere) district; (sobborgo)
suburb

boro'talco sm talcum powder

bor'raccia, -ce [bor'rattʃa] sf
canteen, water-bottle

borsa sf bag; (anche: **~ da signora**)
handbag; (Econ): **la B~ (valori)** the
Stock Exchange; **~ dell'acqua calda**
hot-water bottle; **~ nera** black
market; **~ della spesa** shopping bag;
~ di studio grant; **borsel'lino** sm
purse; **bor'setta** sf handbag

bosco, -schi sm wood

bos'niaco, -a, -ci, -che ag, sm/f
Bosnian

Bosnia-Erze'govina ['bɔsnja
erdze'govina] sf: **la ~** Bosnia-
Herzegovina

Bot, bot *sigla m inv* (= *buono ordinario del Tesoro*) short-term Treasury bond
bo'tanico, -a, -ci, -che *ag* botanical ▷ *sm* botanist ▷ *sf* botany
'**botola** *sf* trap door
'**botta** *sf* blow; (*rumore*) bang
'**botte** *sf* barrel, cask
bot'tega, -ghe *sf* shop; (*officina*) workshop
bot'tiglia [bot'tiʎʎa] *sf* bottle; **bottiglie'ria** *sf* wine shop
bot'tino *sm* (*di guerra*) booty; (*di rapina, furto*) loot
'**botto** *sm* bang; crash; **di ~** suddenly
bot'tone *sm* button; **attaccare (un) ~ a qn** to buttonhole sb
bo'vino, -a *ag* bovine; **bovini** *smpl* cattle
box [bɔks] *sm inv* (*per cavalli*) horsebox; (*per macchina*) lock-up; (*per macchina da corsa*) pit; (*per bambini*) playpen
boxe [bɔks] *sf* boxing
'**boxer** ['bɔkser] *sm inv* (*cane*) boxer ▷ *smpl* (*mutande*): **un paio di ~** a pair of boxer shorts
BR *sigla fpl* = **Brigate Rosse**
brac'cetto [brat'tʃetto] *sm*: **a ~** arm in arm
braccia'letto [brattʃa'letto] *sm* bracelet, bangle
bracci'ata [brat'tʃata] *sf* (*nel nuoto*) stroke
'**braccio** ['brattʃo] *sm* (*pl f* **braccia**) (*Anat*) arm; (*pl m* **bracci**) (*di gru, fiume*) arm; (*di edificio*) wing; **~ di mare** sound; **bracci'olo** *sm* (*appoggio*) arm
'**bracco, -chi** *sm* hound
'**brace** ['bratʃe] *sf* embers *pl*
braci'ola [bra'tʃola] *sf* (*Cuc*) chop
'**branca, -che** *sf* branch
'**branchia** ['brankja] *sf* (*Zool*) gill
'**branco, -chi** *sm* (*di cani, lupi*) pack; (*di uccelli, pecore*) flock; (*peg: di persone*) gang, pack
bran'dina *sf* camp bed (*BRIT*), cot (*US*)
'**brano** *sm* piece; (*di libro*) passage

Bra'sile *sm*: **il ~** Brazil; **brasili'ano, -a** *ag, sm/f* Brazilian
'**bravo, -a** *ag* (*abile*) clever, capable, skilful; (*buono*) good, honest; (: *bambino*) good; (*coraggioso*) brave; **~!** well done!; (*al teatro*) bravo!
bra'vura *sf* cleverness, skill
Bre'tagna [bre'taɲɲa] *sf*: **la ~** Brittany
bre'tella *sf* (*Aut*) link; **bretelle** *sfpl* (*di calzoni*) braces
bret(t)one *ag, smf* Breton
'**breve** *ag* brief, short; **in ~** in short
brevet'tare /72/ *vt* to patent
bre'vetto *sm* patent; **~ di pilotaggio** pilot's licence (*BRIT*) o license (*US*)
'**bricco, -chi** *sm* jug; **~ del caffè** coffeepot
'**briciola** ['britʃola] *sf* crumb
'**briciolo** ['britʃolo] *sm* (*fig*) bit
'**briga, -ghe** *sf* (*fastidio*) trouble, bother; **pigliarsi la ~ di fare qc** to take the trouble to do sth
bri'gata *sf* (*Mil*) brigade; (*gruppo*) group, party; **le Brigate Rosse** (*Pol*) the Red Brigades
'**briglia** ['briʎʎa] *sf* rein; **a ~ sciolta** at full gallop; (*fig*) at full speed
bril'lante *ag* bright; (*anche fig*) brilliant; (*che luccica*) shining ▷ *sm* diamond
bril'lare /72/ *vi* to shine; (*mina*) to blow up ▷ *vt* (*mina*) to set off
'**brillo, -a** *ag* merry, tipsy
'**brina** *sf* hoarfrost
brin'dare /72/ *vi*: **~ a qn/qc** to drink to o toast sb/sth
'**brindisi** *sm inv* toast
bri'oche [bri'ɔʃ] *sf inv* brioche (bun)
bri'tannico, -a, -ci, -che *ag* British
'**brivido** *sm* shiver; (*di ribrezzo*) shudder; (*fig*) thrill
brizzo'lato, -a [brittso'lato] *ag* (*persona*) going grey; (*barba, capelli*) greying
'**brocca, -che** *sf* jug
'**broccoli** *smpl* broccoli *sg*

'brodo sm broth; (per cucinare) stock; **~ ristretto** consommé

bron'chite [bron'kite] sf (Med) bronchitis

bronto'lare /72/ vi to grumble; (tuono, stomaco) to rumble

'bronzo ['brondzo] sm bronze

'browser ['brauzer] sm inv (Inform) browser

brucia'pelo [brutʃa'pelo]: **a ~** av point-blank

bruci'are [bru'tʃare] /14/ vt to burn; (scottare) to scald ▷ vi to burn; **bruciarsi** vpr to burn o.s.; (fallire) to ruin one's chances; **~ le tappe** o **i tempi** (fig) to shoot ahead; **bruciarsi la carriera** to put an end to one's career

'bruco, -chi sm grub; (di farfalla) caterpillar

'brufolo sm pimple, spot

'brullo, -a ag bare, bleak

'bruno, -a ag brown, dark; (persona) dark(-haired)

'brusco, -a, -schi, -sche ag (sapore) sharp; (modi, persona) brusque, abrupt; (movimento) abrupt, sudden

bru'sio sm buzz, buzzing

bru'tale ag brutal

'brutto, -a ag ugly; (cattivo) bad; (malattia, strada, affare) nasty, bad; **~ tempo** bad weather

Bru'xelles [bry'sɛl] sf Brussels

BSE [biɛssɛ'e] sigla f BSE

'buca, -che sf hole; (avvallamento) hollow; **~ delle lettere** letterbox

buca'neve sm inv snowdrop

bu'care /20/ vt (forare) to make a hole (o holes) in; (pungere) to pierce; (biglietto) to punch; **bucarsi** vpr (con eroina) to mainline; **~ una gomma** to have a puncture

bu'cato sm (operazione) washing; (panni) wash, washing

'buccia, -ce ['buttʃa] sf skin, peel

bucherò ecc [buke'rɔ] vb vedi **bucare**

'buco, -chi sm hole

bud'dismo sm Buddhism

bu'dino sm pudding

'bue sm ox; (anche: **carne di ~**) beef

bu'fera sf storm

'buffo, -a ag funny; (Teat) comic

bu'gia, -'gie [bu'dʒia] sf lie; **dire una ~** to tell a lie; **bugi'ardo, -a** ag lying, deceitful ▷ sm/f liar

'buio, -a ag dark ▷ sm dark, darkness

'bulbo sm (Bot) bulb; **~ oculare** eyeball

Bulga'ria sf: **la ~** Bulgaria; **'bulgaro, -a** ag, sm/f, sm Bulgarian

buli'mia sf bulimia; **bu'limico, -a, -ci, -che** ag bulimic

bullismo [bul'lizmo] sm bullying

bul'lone sm bolt

buona'notte escl good night! ▷ sf: **dare la ~ a** to say good night to

buona'sera escl good evening!

buongi'orno [bwon'dʒorno] escl good morning (o afternoon)!

buongus'taio, -a sm/f gourmet

 PAROLA CHIAVE

bu'ono, -a (ag: dav sm **buon** + C o V, **buono** + s impura, gn, pn, ps, z; dav sf **buon'** + V) ag **1** (gen) good; **un buon pranzo/ristorante** a good lunch/restaurant; **(stai) buono!** behave!

2 (benevolo): **buono (con)** good (to), kind (to)

3 (giusto, valido) right; **al momento buono** at the right moment

4 (adatto): **buono a/da** fit for/to; **essere buono a nulla** to be no good o use at anything

5 (auguri): **buon anno!** happy New Year!; **buon appetito!** enjoy your meal!; **buon compleanno!** happy birthday!; **buon divertimento!** have a nice time!; **buona fortuna!** good luck!; **buon riposo!** sleep well!; **buon viaggio!** bon voyage!, have a good trip!

6: a buon mercato cheap; **di buon'ora** early; **buon senso** common sense; **alla buona** ag simple

▶ *av* in a simple way, without any fuss
▶ *sm* **1** (*bontà*) goodness, good
2 (*Comm*) voucher, coupon; **buono di cassa** cash voucher; **buono di consegna** delivery note; **buono del Tesoro** Treasury bill

buon'senso *sm* = **buon senso**
burat'tino *sm* puppet
'burbero, -a *ag* surly, gruff
buro'cratico, -a, -ci, -che *ag* bureaucratic
burocra'zia [burokrat'tsia] *sf* bureaucracy
bur'rasca, -sche *sf* storm
'burro *sm* butter
bur'rone *sm* ravine
bus'sare /72/ *vi* to knock
'bussola *sf* compass
'busta *sf* (*da lettera*) envelope; (*astuccio*) case; **in ~ aperta/chiusa** in an unsealed/sealed envelope; **~ paga** pay packet
busta'rella *sf* bribe, backhander
bus'tina *sf* (*piccola busta*) envelope; (*di cibi, farmaci*) sachet; (*Mil*) forage cap; **~ di tè** tea bag
'busto *sm* bust; (*indumento*) corset, girdle; **a mezzo ~** (*fotografia, ritratto*) half-length
but'tare /72/ *vt* to throw; (*anche:* **~ via**) to throw away; **buttarsi** *vpr* (*saltare*) to jump; **~ giù** (*scritto*) to scribble down; (*cibo*) to gulp down; (*edificio*) to pull down, demolish; (*pasta, verdura*) to put into boiling water; **buttarsi dalla finestra** to jump out of the window
byte ['bait] *sm inv* byte

C

ca'bina *sf* (*di nave*) cabin; (*da spiaggia*) beach hut; (*di autocarro, treno*) cab; (*di aereo*) cockpit; (*di ascensore*) cage; **~ di pilotaggio** cockpit; **~ telefonica** callbox, (*tele*)phone box *o* booth
cabi'nato *sm* cabin cruiser
ca'cao *sm* cocoa
'caccia ['kattʃa] *sf* hunting; (*con fucile*) shooting; (*inseguimento*) chase; (*cacciagione*) game ▷ *sm inv* (*aereo*) fighter; (*nave*) destroyer; **~ grossa** big-game hunting; **~ all'uomo** manhunt
cacci'are [kat'tʃare] /14/ *vt* to hunt; (*mandar via*) to chase away; (*ficcare*) to shove, stick ▷ *vi* to hunt; **cacciarsi** *vpr*: **~ fuori qc** to whip *o* pull sth out; **~ un urlo** to let out a yell; **dove s'è cacciata la mia borsa?** where has my bag got to?; **cacciarsi nei guai** to get into trouble; **caccia'tore** *sm* hunter; **cacciatore di frodo** poacher

caccia'vite [kattʃa'vite] *sm inv* screwdriver

'cactus *sm inv* cactus

ca'davere *sm* (dead) body, corpse

'caddi *ecc vb vedi* **cadere**

ca'denza [ka'dɛntsa] *sf* cadence; *(andamento ritmico)* rhythm; *(Mus)* cadenza

ca'dere /18/ *vi* to fall; *(denti, capelli)* to fall out; *(tetto)* to fall in; **questa gonna cade bene** this skirt hangs well; **lasciar ~** *(anche fig)* to drop; **~ dal sonno** to be falling asleep on one's feet; **~ dalle nuvole** *(fig)* to be taken aback

cadrò *ecc vb vedi* **cadere**

ca'duta *sf* fall; **la ~ dei capelli** hair loss

caffè *sm inv* coffee; *(locale)* café; **~ corretto** coffee with liqueur; **~ in grani** coffee beans; **~ macchiato** coffee with a dash of milk; **~ macinato** ground coffee

caffel'latte *sm inv* white coffee

caffetti'era *sf* coffeepot

'cagna ['kaɲɲa] *sf (Zool, peg)* bitch

CAI *sigla m* = **Club Alpino Italiano**

cala'brone *sm* hornet

cala'maro *sm* squid

cala'mita *sf* magnet

calamità *sf inv* calamity, disaster

ca'lare /72/ *vt (far discendere)* to lower; *(Maglia)* to decrease ▷ *vi (discendere)* to go (o come) down; *(tramontare)* to set, go down; **~ di peso** to lose weight

cal'cagno [kal'kaɲɲo] *sm* heel

cal'care /20/ *sm (incrostazione)* (lime)scale

'calce ['kaltʃe] *sm*: **in ~** at the foot of the page ▷ *sf* lime; **~ viva** quicklime

cal'cetto [kal'tʃetto] *sm (calcio-balilla)* table football; *(calcio a cinque)* five-a-side (football)

calci'are [kal'tʃare] /14/ *vt, vi* to kick; **calcia'tore** *sm* footballer

'calcio ['kaltʃo] *sm (pedata)* kick; *(sport)* football, soccer; *(di pistola, fucile)* butt; *(Chim)* calcium; **~ d'angolo** *(Sport)* corner (kick); **~ di punizione** *(Sport)* free kick; **~ di rigore** penalty

calco'lare /72/ *vt* to calculate, work out, reckon; *(ponderare)* to weigh (up); **calcola'tore, -'trice** *ag* calculating ▷ *sm* calculator; *(fig)* calculating person ▷ *sf*: **calcolatore elettronico** computer; **calcola'trice** *sf* calculator

'calcolo *sm (anche Mat)* calculation; *(infinitesimale ecc)* calculus; *(Med)* stone; **fare i propri calcoli** *(fig)* to weigh the pros and cons; **per ~** out of self-interest

cal'daia *sf* boiler

'caldo, -a *ag* warm; *(molto caldo)* hot; *(fig: appassionato)* keen; hearty ▷ *sm* heat; **ho ~** I'm warm; I'm hot; **fa ~** it's warm; it's hot

caleidos'copio *sm* kaleidoscope

calen'dario *sm* calendar

'calibro *sm (di arma)* calibre, bore; *(Tecn)* callipers *pl*; *(fig)* calibre; **di grosso ~** *(fig)* prominent

'calice ['kalitʃe] *sm* goblet; *(Rel)* chalice

Cali'fornia *sf* California; **californi'ano, -a** *ag* Californian

calligra'fia *sf (scrittura)* handwriting; *(arte)* calligraphy

'callo *sm* callus; *(ai piedi)* corn

'calma *sf* calm

cal'mante *sm* tranquillizer

cal'mare /72/ *vt* to calm; *(lenire)* to soothe; **calmarsi** *vpr* to grow calm, calm down; *(vento)* to abate; *(dolori)* to ease

'calmo, -a *ag* calm, quiet

'calo *sm (Comm: di prezzi)* fall; *(: di volume)* shrinkage; *(: di peso)* loss

ca'lore *sm* warmth; *(intenso)* heat; **essere in ~** *(Zool)* to be on heat

calo'ria *sf* calorie

calo'rifero *sm* radiator

calo'roso, -a *ag* warm

calpes'tare /72/ *vt* to tread on, trample on; **"è vietato ~ l'erba"** "keep off the grass"

ca'lunnia *sf* slander; *(scritta)* libel

cal'vizie [kal'vittsje] *sf* baldness

'calvo, -a *ag* bald

'calza ['kaltsa] *sf (da donna)* stocking; *(da uomo)* sock; **fare la ~** to knit; **calze di nailon** nylons, (nylon) stockings

calza'maglia [kaltsa'maʎʎa] *sf* tights *pl*; *(per danza, ginnastica)* leotard

calzet'tone [kaltset'tone] *sm* heavy knee-length sock

cal'zino [kal'tsino] *sm* sock

calzo'laio [kaltso'lajo] *sm* shoemaker; *(che ripara scarpe)* cobbler

calzon'cini [kaltson'tʃini] *smpl* shorts; **~ da bagno** (swimming) trunks

cal'zone [kal'tsone] *sm* trouser leg; *(Cuc)* savoury turnover made with pizza dough; **calzoni** *smpl (pantaloni)* trousers (BRIT), pants (US)

camale'onte *sm* chameleon

cambia'mento *sm* change; **cambiamenti climatici** climate change *sg*

cambi'are /19/ *vt* to change; *(modificare)* to alter, change; *(barattare)*: **~ (qc con qn/qc)** to exchange (sth with sb/for sth) ▷ *vi* to change, alter; **cambiarsi** *vpr (variare abito)* to change; **~ casa** to move (house); **~ idea** to change one's mind; **~ treno** to change trains

cambiava'lute *sm inv* exchange office

'cambio *sm* change; *(modifica)* alteration, change; *(scambio, Comm)* exchange; *(corso dei cambi)* rate (of exchange); *(Tecn, Aut)* gears *pl*: **in ~ di** in exchange for; **dare il ~ a qn** to take over from sb

'camera *sf* room; *(anche:* **~ da letto***)* bedroom; *(Pol)* chamber, house; **~**
ardente mortuary chapel; **~ d'aria** inner tube; *(di pallone)* bladder; **C~ di Commercio** Chamber of Commerce; **C~ dei Deputati** Chamber of Deputies, ≈ House of Commons (BRIT), ≈ House of Representatives (US); **~ a gas** gas chamber; **~ a un letto/a due letti/matrimoniale** single/twin-bedded/double room; **~ oscura** *(Fot)* dark room

> Attenzione! In inglese esiste la parola *camera*, che però significa *macchina fotografica*.

came'rata, -i, -e *sm/f* companion, mate ▷ *sf* dormitory

cameri'era *sf (domestica)* maid; *(che serve a tavola)* waitress; *(che fa le camere)* chambermaid

cameri'ere *sm* (man)servant; *(di ristorante)* waiter

came'rino *sm (Teat)* dressing room

'camice ['kamitʃe] *sm (Rel)* alb; *(per medici ecc)* white coat

cami'cetta [kami'tʃetta] *sf* blouse

ca'micia, -cie [ka'mitʃa] *sf (da uomo)* shirt; *(da donna)* blouse; **~ di forza** straitjacket; **~ da notte** *(da donna)* nightdress; *(da uomo)* nightshirt

cami'netto *sm* hearth, fireplace

ca'mino *sm* chimney; *(focolare)* fireplace, hearth

'camion *sm inv* lorry (BRIT), truck (US)

camio'nista, -i *sm* lorry driver (BRIT), truck driver (US)

cam'mello *sm (Zool)* camel; *(tessuto)* camel hair

cammi'nare /72/ *vi* to walk; *(funzionare)* to work, go

cam'mino *sm* walk; *(sentiero)* path; *(itinerario, direzione, tragitto)* way; **mettersi in ~** to set o start off

camo'milla *sf* camomile; *(infuso)* camomile tea

ca'moscio [ka'moʃʃo] *sm* chamois; **di ~** *(scarpe, borsa)* suede *cpd*

cam'pagna [kam'paɲɲa] *sf* country, countryside; *(Pol, Comm, Mil)* campaign; **in ~** in the country; **andare in ~** to go to the country; **fare una ~** to campaign; **~ pubblicitaria** advertising campaign

cam'pana *sf* bell; (*anche:* **~ di vetro**) bell jar; **~ (per la raccolta del vetro)** bottle bank; **campa'nello** *sm* (*all'uscio, da tavola*) bell

campa'nile *sm* bell tower, belfry

cam'peggio *sm* camping; (*terreno*) camp site; **fare (del) ~** to go camping

camper ['kamper] *sm inv* motor caravan (*BRIT*), motor home (*US*)

campio'nario, -a *ag:* **fiera campionaria** trade fair ▷ *sm* collection of samples

campio'nato *sm* championship

campio'ne, -'essa *sm/f* (*Sport*) champion ▷ *sm* (*Comm*) sample

'campo *sm* field; (*Mil*) field; (*: accampamento*) camp; (*spazio delimitato: sportivo ecc*) ground; field; (*di quadro*) background; **i campi** (*campagna*) the countryside; **~ da aviazione** airfield; **~ di battaglia** (*Mil, fig*) battlefield; **~ di concentramento** concentration camp; **~ di golf** golf course; **~ profughi** refugee camp; **~ sportivo** sports ground; **~ da tennis** tennis court; **~ visivo** field of vision

'Canada *sm:* **il ~** Canada; **cana'dese** *ag, smf* Canadian ▷ *sf* (*anche:* **tenda canadese**) ridge tent

ca'naglia [ka'naʎʎa] *sf* rabble, mob; (*persona*) scoundrel, rogue

ca'nale *sm* (*anche fig*) channel; (*artificiale*) canal

'canapa *sf* hemp; **~ indiana** (*droga*) cannabis

cana'rino *sm* canary

cancel'lare [kantʃel'lare] /72/ *vt* (*con la gomma*) to rub out, erase; (*con la penna*) to strike out; (*annullare*) to annul, cancel; (*disdire*) to cancel

cancelle'ria [kantʃelle'ria] *sf* chancery; (*quanto necessario per scrivere*) stationery

can'cello [kan'tʃello] *sm* gate

'cancro *sm* (*Med*) cancer; **C~** Cancer

candeg'gina [kanded'dʒina] *sf* bleach

can'dela *sf* candle; **~ (di accensione)** (*Aut*) spark(ing) plug

cande'labro *sm* candelabra

candeli'ere *sm* candlestick

candi'dare /72/ *vt* to present as candidate; **candidarsi** *vpr* to present o.s. as candidate

candi'dato, -a *sm/f* candidate; (*aspirante a una carica*) applicant

'candido, -a *ag* white as snow; (*puro*) pure; (*sincero*) sincere, candid

can'dito, -a *ag* candied

cane *sm* dog; (*di pistola, fucile*) cock; **fa un freddo ~** it's bitterly cold; **non c'era un ~** there wasn't a soul; **~ da caccia** hunting dog; **~ da guardia** guard dog; **~ lupo** alsatian; **~ pastore** sheepdog

ca'nestro *sm* basket

can'guro *sm* kangaroo

ca'nile *sm* kennel; (*di allevamento*) kennels *pl*: **~ municipale** dog pound

'canna *sf* (*pianta*) reed; (*: indica, da zucchero*) cane; (*bastone*) stick, cane; (*di fucile*) barrel; (*di organo*) pipe; (*fam: Droga*) joint; **~ fumaria** chimney flue; **~ da pesca** (*fishing*) rod; **~ da zucchero** sugar cane

cannel'loni *smpl* pasta tubes stuffed with sauce and baked

cannocchi'ale [kannok'kjale] *sm* telescope

can'none *sm* (*Mil*) gun; (*: Storia*) cannon; (*tubo*) pipe, tube; (*piega*) box pleat; (*fig*) ace

can'nuccia, -ce [kan'nuttʃa] *sf* (drinking) straw

ca'noa *sf* canoe

'canone *sm* canon, criterion; (*mensile, annuo*) rent; fee

canot'taggio [kanot'taddʒo] *sm* rowing

canotti'era *sf* vest

ca'notto *sm* small boat, dinghy; canoe

can'tante *smf* singer

can'tare /72/ *vt, vi* to sing; **cantau'tore, -'trice** *sm/f* singer-composer

canti'ere *sm* (*Edil*) (building) site; (*anche:* **~ navale**) shipyard

can'tina *sf* cellar; (*bottega*) wine shop; **~ sociale** cooperative winegrowers' association

> Attenzione! In inglese esiste la parola *canteen*, che però significa *mensa*.

'canto *sm* song; (*arte*) singing; (*Rel*) chant; chanting; (*Poesia*) poem, lyric; (*parte di una poesia*) canto; (*parte, lato*): **da un ~** on the one hand; **d'altro ~** on the other hand

canzo'nare [kantso'nare] /72/ *vt* to tease

can'zone [kan'tsone] *sf* song; (*Poesia*) canzone

'caos *sm inv* chaos; **ca'otico, -a, -ci, -che** *ag* chaotic

CAP *sigla m* = **codice di avviamento postale**

ca'pace [ka'patʃe] *ag* able, capable; (*ampio, vasto*) large, capacious; **sei ~ di farlo?** can you o are you able to do it?; **capacità** *sf inv* ability; (*Dir, di recipiente*) capacity

ca'panna *sf* hut

capan'none *sm* (*Agr*) barn; (*fabbricato industriale*) (factory) shed

ca'parbio, -a *ag* stubborn

ca'parra *sf* deposit, down payment

ca'pello *sm* hair; **capelli** *smpl* (*capigliatura*) hair *sg*

ca'pezzolo [ka'pettsolo] *sm* nipple

ca'pire /55/ *vt* to understand

capi'tale *ag* (*mortale*) capital; (*fondamentale*) main *cpd*, chief *cpd* ▷ *sf* (*città*) capital ▷ *sm* (*Econ*) capital

capi'tano *sm* captain

capi'tare /72/ *vi* (*giungere casualmente*) to happen to go, find o.s.; (*accadere*) to happen; (*presentarsi:* *cosa*) to turn up, present itself ▷ *vb impers* to happen; **mi è capitato un guaio** I've had a spot of trouble

capi'tello *sm* (*Archit*) capital

ca'pitolo *sm* chapter

capi'tombolo *sm* headlong fall, tumble

'capo *sm* head; (*persona*) head, leader; (: *in ufficio*) head, boss; (: *in tribù*) chief; (*di tavolo, scale*) head, top; (*di filo*) end; (*Geo*) cape; **andare a ~** to start a new paragraph; **da ~** over again; **~ di bestiame** head *inv* of cattle; **~ di vestiario** item of clothing; **Capo'danno** *sm* New Year; **capo'giro** *sm* dizziness *no pl*; **capola'voro, -i** *sm* masterpiece; **capo'linea** (*pl* **capilinea**) *sm* terminus; **capostazi'one** (*pl* **capistazione**) *sm* station master; **capo'tavola** (*mpl* **capitavola**, *fpl* **capotavola**) *smf* (*persona*) head of the table; **sedere a capotavola** to sit at the head of the table; **capo'volgere** /96/ *vt* to overturn; (*fig*) to reverse; **capovolgersi** *vpr* to overturn; (*barca*) to capsize; (*fig*) to be reversed

'cappa *sf* (*mantello*) cape, cloak; (*del camino*) hood

cap'pella *sf* (*Rel*) chapel

cap'pello *sm* hat

'cappero *sm* caper

cap'pone *sm* capon

cap'potto *sm* (over)coat

cappuc'cino [kapput'tʃino] *sm* (*frate*) Capuchin monk; (*bevanda*) cappuccino

cap'puccio [kap'puttʃo] *sm* (*copricapo*) hood; (*della biro*) cap

'capra *sf* (she-)goat

ca'priccio [ka'prittʃo] *sm* caprice, whim; (*bizza*) tantrum; **fare i capricci** to be very naughty; **capricci'oso, -a** *ag* capricious, whimsical; naughty

Capri'corno *sm* Capricorn

capri'ola *sf* somersault

capri'olo *sm* roe deer

'**capro** *sm*: **~ espiatorio** scapegoat

ca'prone *sm* billy-goat

'**capsula** *sf* capsule; (*di arma, per bottiglie*) cap

cap'tare /72/ *vt* (*Radio, TV*) to pick up; (*cattivarsi*) to gain, win

carabini'ere *sm* member of Italian military police force

ca'raffa *sf* carafe

Ca'raibi *smpl*: **il mar dei ~** the Caribbean (Sea)

cara'mella *sf* sweet

ca'rattere *sm* character; (*caratteristica*) characteristic, trait; **avere un buon ~** to be good-natured; **~ jolly** wild card; **caratte'ristico, -a, -ci, -che** *ag* characteristic ▷ *sf* characteristic, trait

car'bone *sm* coal

carbu'rante *sm* (motor) fuel

carbura'tore *sm* carburettor

carce'rato, -a [kartʃe'rato] *sm/f* prisoner

'**carcere** ['kartʃere] *sm* prison; (*pena*) imprisonment

carci'ofo [kar'tʃɔfo] *sm* artichoke

cardel'lino *sm* goldfinch

car'diaco, -a, -ci, -che *ag* cardiac, heart *cpd*

cardi'nale *ag, sm* cardinal

'**cardine** *sm* hinge

'**cardo** *sm* thistle

ca'rente *ag*: **~ di** lacking in

cares'tia *sf* famine; (*penuria*) scarcity, dearth

ca'rezza [ka'rettsa] *sf* caress

'**carica** *sf vedi* **carico**

caricabatte'ria *sm inv* (*Elettr*) battery charger

cari'care /20/ *vt* (*merce*) to load; (*orologio*) to wind up; (*batteria, Mil*) to charge; (*Inform*) to load

'**carico, -a, -chi, -che** *ag* (*fucile*) loaded; (*orologio*) wound up; (*batteria*) charged; (*colore*) deep; (*caffè, tè*) strong; **~ di** (*che porta un peso*) loaded *o* laden with ▷ *sm* (*il caricare*) loading; (*ciò che si carica*) load; (*fig: peso*) burden, weight; **persona a ~** dependent; **essere a ~ di qn** (*spese ecc*) to be charged to sb

'**carie** *sf* (*dentaria*) decay

ca'rino, -a *ag* (*grazioso*) lovely, pretty, nice; (*simpatico*) nice

carità *sf* charity; **per ~!** (*escl di rifiuto*) good heavens, no!

carnagi'one [karna'dʒone] *sf* complexion

'**carne** *sf* flesh; (*bovina, ovina ecc*) meat; **~ di manzo/maiale/pecora** beef/pork/mutton; **~ in scatola** tinned *o* canned meat; **~ tritata** *o* **macinata** mince (*BRIT*), hamburger meat (*US*), minced (*BRIT*) *o* ground (*US*) meat

carne'vale *sm* carnival; **C~**; *see note* **"Carnevale"**

'**caro, -a** *ag* (*amato*) dear; (*costoso*) dear, expensive; **è troppo ~** it's too expensive

ca'**rogna** [ka'roɲɲa] *sf* carrion; (*fig: fam*) swine

ca'**rota** *sf* carrot

caro'**vana** *sf* caravan

car'**poni** *av* on all fours

car'**rabile** *ag* suitable for vehicles; **"passo ~"** "keep clear"

carreggi'**ata** [karred'dʒata] *sf* carriageway (BRIT), roadway

car'**rello** *sm* trolley; (*Aer*) undercarriage; (*Cine*) dolly; (*di macchina da scrivere*) carriage

carri'**era** *sf* career; **fare ~** to get on; **a gran ~** at full speed

carri'**ola** *sf* wheelbarrow

'**carro** *sm* cart, wagon; **~ armato** tank; **~ attrezzi** (*Aut*) breakdown van

car'**rozza** [kar'rɔttsa] *sf* carriage, coach

carrozze'**ria** [karrottse'ria] *sf* body, coachwork (BRIT); (*officina*) coachbuilder's workshop (BRIT), body shop

carroz'**zina** [karrot'tsina] *sf* pram (BRIT), baby carriage (US)

'**carta** *sf* paper; (*al ristorante*) menu; (*Geo*) map; plan; (*documento*) card; (*costituzione*) charter; **carte** *sfpl* (*documenti*) papers, documents; **alla ~** (*al ristorante*) à la carte; **~ assegni** bank card; **~ assorbente** blotting paper; **~ bollata** o **da bollo** official stamped paper; **~ (da gioco)** playing card; **~ di credito** credit card; **~ fedeltà** loyalty card; **~ (geografica)** map; **~ d'identità** identity card; **~ igienica** toilet paper; **~ d'imbarco** (*Aer, Naut*) boarding card; **~ da lettere** writing paper; **~ libera** (*Amm*) unstamped paper; **~ stradale** road map; **~ da pacchi** wrapping paper; **~ da parati** wallpaper; **~ verde** (*Aut*) green card; **~ vetrata** sandpaper; **~ da visita** visiting card

car'**taccia, -ce** [kar'tattʃa] *sf* waste paper

carta'**pesta** *sf* papier-mâché

car'**tella** *sf* (*scheda*) card; (*custodia: di cartone, Inform*) folder; (: *di uomo d'affari ecc*) briefcase; (: *di scolaro*) schoolbag, satchel; **~ clinica** (*Med*) case sheet

carte'**llino** *sm* (*etichetta*) label; (*su porta*) notice; (*scheda*) card; **timbrare il ~** (*all'entrata*) to clock in; (*all'uscita*) to clock out; **~ di presenza** clock card, timecard

car'**tello** *sm* sign; (*pubblicitario*) poster; (*stradale*) sign, signpost; (*in dimostrazioni*) placard; (*Econ*) cartel; **~ stradale** sign; **cartel'lone** (*della tombola*) scoring frame; (*Teat*) playbill; **tenere il cartellone** (*spettacolo*) to have a long run; **cartellone pubblicitario** advertising poster

car'**tina** *sf* (*Aut, Geo*) map

car'**toccio** [kar'tɔttʃo] *sm* paper bag

cartolarizzazi'**one** [kartolariddza'tsjone] *sf* securitization

cartole'**ria** *sf* stationer's (shop)

carto'**lina** *sf* postcard; **~ postale** ready-stamped postcard

car'**tone** *sm* cardboard; (*Arte*) cartoon; **cartoni animati** (*Cine*) cartoons

car'**tuccia, -ce** [kar'tuttʃa] *sf* cartridge

'**casa** *sf* house; (*specialmente la propria casa*) home; (*Comm*) firm, house; **essere a ~** to be at home; **vado a ~ mia/tua** I'm going home/to your house; **vino della ~** house wine; **~ di cura** nursing home; **~ editrice** publishing house; **C~ delle Libertà** *centre-right coalition*; **~ di riposo** (old people's) home, care home; **~ dello studente** student hostel; **case popolari** ≈ council houses (o flats) (BRIT), ≈ public housing units (US)

ca'**sacca, -che** *sf* military coat; (*di fantino*) blouse

casa'lingo, -a, -ghi, -ghe ag household, domestic; (fatto a casa) home-made; (semplice) homely; (amante della casa) home-loving ▷ sf housewife

cas'care /20/ vi to fall; **cas'cata** sf fall; (d'acqua) cascade, waterfall

cascherò ecc [kaske'rɔ] vb vedi **cascare**

'casco (pl **caschi**) sm helmet; (del parrucchiere) hair-dryer; (di banane) bunch; **~ blu** (Mil) blue helmet (UN soldier)

casei'ficio [kazei'fitʃo] sm creamery

ca'sella sf pigeonhole; **~ email** mailbox; **~ postale** post office box

ca'sello sm (di autostrada) tollgate

ca'serma sf barracks

ca'sino sm (fam: confusione) row, racket; (casa di prostituzione) brothel

casinò sm inv casino

'caso sm chance; (fatto, vicenda) event, incident; (possibilità) possibility; (Med, Ling) case; **a ~** at random; **per ~** by chance, by accident; **in ogni ~, in tutti i casi** in any case, at any rate; **al ~** should the opportunity arise; **nel ~ che** in case; **~ mai** if by chance; **~ limite** borderline case

caso'lare sm cottage

'caspita escl (di sorpresa) good heavens!; (di impazienza) for goodness' sake!

'cassa sf case, crate, box; (bara) coffin; (mobile) chest; (involucro: di orologio ecc) case; (macchina) cash register, till; (luogo di pagamento) cash desk, checkout (counter); (fondo) fund; (istituto bancario) bank; **~ automatica prelievi** automatic telling machine, cash dispenser; **~ continua** night safe; **mettere in ~ integrazione** ≈ to lay off; **~ mutua** o **malattia** health insurance scheme; **~ di risparmio** savings bank; **~ toracica** (Anat) chest

cassa'forte (pl **casseforti**) sf safe

cassa'panca (pl **cassapanche** o **cassepanche**) sf settle

casseru'ola, casse'rola sf saucepan

cas'setta sf box; (per registratore) cassette; (Cine, Teat) box-office takings pl: **film di ~** box-office draw; **~ delle lettere** letterbox; **~ di sicurezza** strongbox

cas'setto sm drawer

cassi'ere, -a sm/f cashier; (di banca) teller

casso'netto sm wheelie-bin

cas'tagna [kas'taɲɲa] sf chestnut

cas'tagno [kas'taɲɲo] sm chestnut (tree)

cas'tano, -a ag chestnut (brown)

cas'tello sm castle; (Tecn) scaffolding

casti'gare /80/ vt to punish; **cas'tigo, -ghi** sm punishment; **mettere/essere in castigo** to punish/be punished

cas'toro sm beaver

casu'ale ag chance cpd; (Inform) random cpd

catalizza'tore [kataliddza'tore] sm (anche fig) catalyst; (Aut) catalytic converter

ca'talogo, -ghi sm catalogue

catarifran'gente [katarifran'dʒɛnte] sm (Aut) reflector

ca'tarro sm catarrh

ca'tastrofe sf catastrophe, disaster; **catastro'fista, -i, -e** ag, smf doommonger

catego'ria sf category

ca'tena sf chain; **~ di montaggio** assembly line; **catene da neve** (Aut) snow chains; **cate'nina** sf (gioiello) (thin) chain

cate'ratta sf cataract; (chiusa) sluice gate

ca'tino sm basin

ca'trame sm tar

'cattedra sf teacher's desk; (di università) chair

catte'drale sf cathedral

catti'veria sf wickedness, malice; (di bambino) naughtiness; (azione) spiteful act; (parole) malicious o spiteful remark

cat'tivo, -a ag bad; (malvagio) bad, wicked; (turbolento: bambino) bad, naughty; (: mare) rough; (odore, sapore) nasty, bad

cat'tolico, -a, -ci, -che ag, sm/f (Roman) Catholic

cattu'rare /72/ vt to capture

'causa sf cause; (Dir) lawsuit, case, action; **a ~ di, per ~ di** because of; **fare** o **muovere ~ a qn** to take legal action against sb

cau'sare /72/ vt to cause

cau'tela sf caution, prudence

'cauto, -a ag cautious, prudent

cauzi'one [kaut'tsjone] sf security; (Dir) bail

'cava sf quarry

caval'care /20/ vt (cavallo) to ride; (muro) to sit astride; (ponte) to span; **caval'cata** sf ride; (gruppo di persone) riding party

cavalca'via sm inv flyover

cavalci'oni [kaval't∫oni]: **a ~ di** prep astride

cavali'ere sm rider; (feudale, titolo) knight; (soldato) cavalryman; (al ballo) partner

caval'letta sf grasshopper

caval'letto sm (Fot) tripod; (da pittore) easel

ca'vallo sm horse; (Scacchi) knight; (Aut: anche: **~ vapore**) horsepower; (dei pantaloni) crotch; **a ~** on horseback; **a ~ di** astride, straddling; **~ di battaglia** (fig) hobbyhorse; **~ da corsa** racehorse; **~ a dondolo** rocking horse

ca'vare /72/ vt (togliere) to draw out, extract, take out; (: giacca, scarpe) to take off; (: fame, sete, voglia) to satisfy; **cavarsela** to get away with it; to manage, get on all right

cava'tappi sm inv corkscrew

ca'verna sf cave

'cavia sf guinea pig

cavi'ale sm caviar

ca'viglia [ka'viʎʎa] sf ankle

'cavo, -a ag hollow ▷ sm (Anat) cavity; (grossa corda) rope, cable; (Elettr, Tel) cable

cavo'letto sm: **~ di Bruxelles** Brussels sprout

cavolfi'ore sm cauliflower

'cavolo sm cabbage; **non m'importa un ~** (fam) I don't give a hoot

'cazzo ['kattso] sm (fam!: pene) prick (!); **non gliene importa un ~** (fig: fam!) he doesn't give a damn about it; **fatti i cazzi tuoi** (fig: fam!) mind your own damn business

C.C.D. sigla m (= Centro Cristiano Democratico) party originating from Democrazia Cristiana

C.D. sm inv (= compact disc) CD; (lettore) CD player

CD-Rom [t∫idi'rɔm] sigla m inv CD-Rom

C.d.U. sigla m (= Cristiano Democratici Uniti) United Christian Democrats (Italian centre-right political party)

ce [t∫e] pron, av vedi **ci**

Ce'cenia [t∫e't∫enja] sf Chechnya; **ce'ceno, -a** ag, sm/f Chechen

'ceco, -a, -chi, -che ['t∫ɛko] ag, sm/f, sm Czech; **la Repubblica Ceca** the Czech Republic

'cedere ['t∫edere] /29/ vt (concedere: posto) to give up; (Dir) to transfer, make over ▷ vi (cadere) to give way, subside; **~ (a)** to surrender (to), yield (to), give in (to)

'cedola ['t∫ɛdola] sf (Comm) coupon; voucher

'ceffo ['t∫ɛffo] sm (peg) ugly mug

cef'fone [t∫ef'fone] sm slap, smack

cele'brare [t∫ele'brare] /72/ vt to celebrate

'celebre ['t∫ɛlebre] ag famous, celebrated

ce'leste [t∫e'lɛste] ag celestial; heavenly; (colore) sky-blue

'**celibe** ['tʃɛlibe] *ag* single, unmarried

'**cella** ['tʃɛlla] *sf cell*; **~ frigorifera** cold store

'**cellula** ['tʃɛllula] *sf* (*Biol, Elettr, Pol*) cell; **cellu'lare** *sm* cellphone

cellu'lite [tʃellu'lite] *sf* cellulite

cemen'tare [tʃemen'tare] /72/ *vt* (*anche fig*) to cement

ce'mento [tʃe'mento] *sm* cement; **~ armato** reinforced concrete

'**cena** ['tʃena] *sf* dinner; (*leggera*) supper

ce'nare [tʃe'nare] /72/ *vi* to dine, have dinner

'cenere ['tʃenere] *sf* ash

'**cenno** ['tʃenno] *sm* (*segno*) sign, signal; (*gesto*) gesture; (*col capo*) nod; (*con la mano*) wave; (*allusione*) hint, mention; (*breve esposizione*) short account; **far ~ di sì/no** to nod (one's head)/shake one's head

censi'mento [tʃensi'mento] *sm* census

cen'sura [tʃen'sura] *sf* censorship; censor's office; (*fig*) censure

cente'nario, -a [tʃente'narjo] *ag* (*che ha cento anni*) hundred-year-old; (*che ricorre ogni cento anni*) centennial, centenary *cpd* ▷ *sm/f* centenarian ▷ *sm* centenary

cen'tesimo, -a [tʃen'tɛzimo] *ag, sm* hundredth; (*di euro, dollaro*) cent

cen'tigrado, -a [tʃen'tigrado] *ag* centigrade; **20 gradi centigradi** 20 degrees centigrade

cen'timetro [tʃen'timetro] *sm* centimetre

centi'naio [tʃenti'najo] (*pl f* **centinaia**) *sm*: **un ~ (di)** a hundred; about a hundred

'**cento** ['tʃɛnto] *num* a hundred, one hundred

cento'mila [tʃento'mila] *num* a o one hundred thousand; **te l'ho detto ~ volte** (*fig*) I've told you a thousand times

cen'trale [tʃen'trale] *ag* central ▷ *sf*: **~ elettrica** electric power station; **~ eolica** wind farm; **~ telefonica** (telephone) exchange; **centrali'nista** *smf* operator; **centra'lino** *sm* (telephone) exchange; (*di albergo ecc*) switchboard; **centraliz'zato, -a** [tʃentralid'dzato] *ag* central

cen'trare [tʃen'trare] /72/ *vt* to hit the centre (BRIT) o center (US) of; (*Tecn*) to centre

cen'trifuga [tʃen'trifuga] *sf* spin-dryer

'**centro** ['tʃɛntro] *sm* centre; **~ civico** civic centre; **~ commerciale** shopping centre; (*città*) commercial centre; **~ di permanenza temporanea** reception centre

centro'destra [tʃentro'dɛstra] *sm* (*Pol*) centre right

centrosi'nistra [tʃentrosi'nistra] *sm* (*Pol*) centre left

'**ceppo** ['tʃeppo] *sm* (*di albero*) stump; (*pezzo di legno*) log

'**cera** ['tʃera] *sf* wax; (*aspetto*) appearance

ce'ramica (*pl* **ceramiche**) [tʃe'ramika] *sf* ceramic; (*Arte*) ceramics *sg*

cerbi'atto [tʃer'bjatto] *sm* (*Zool*) fawn

cercaper'sone [tʃerkaper'sone] *sm inv* bleeper

cer'care [tʃer'kare] /20/ *vt* to look for, search for ▷ *vi*: **~ di fare qc** to try to do sth

cercherò *ecc* [tʃerke'rɔ] *vb vedi* **cercare**

'**cerchia** ['tʃerkja] *sf* circle

cer'chietto [tʃer'kjetto] *sm* (*per capelli*) hairband

'**cerchio** ['tʃerkjo] *sm* circle; (*giocattolo, di botte*) hoop

cere'ale [tʃere'ale] *sm* cereal

ceri'monia [tʃeri'mɔnja] *sf* ceremony

ce'rino [tʃe'rino] *sm* wax match

'**cernia** ['tʃernja] *sf* (*Zool*) stone bass

cerni'era [tʃer'njɛra] *sf* hinge;
~ **lampo** zip (fastener) (*BRIT*),
zipper (*US*)
'cero ['tʃero] *sm* (church) candle
ce'rotto [tʃe'rɔtto] *sm* sticking
plaster
certa'mente [tʃerta'mente] *av*
certainly
certifi'cato [tʃertifi'kato] *sm*
certificate; ~ **medico/di nascita/
di morte** medical/birth/death
certificate

PAROLA CHIAVE

'certo, -a ['tʃɛrto] *ag* (*sicuro*): **certo
(di/che)** certain *o* sure (of/that)
▶ *det* **1** (*tale*) certain; **un certo
signor Smith** a (certain) Mr Smith
2 (*qualche: con valore intensivo*)
some; **dopo un certo tempo** after
some time; **un fatto di una certa
importanza** a matter of some
importance; **di una certa età** past
one's prime, not so young
▶ *pron*: **certi, e** (*pl*) some
▶ *av* (*certamente*) certainly; (*senz'altro*)
of course; **di certo** certainly; **no (di)
certo!, certo che no!** certainly not!;
sì certo yes indeed, certainly

cer'vello [tʃer'vɛllo] (*pl* **cervelli**)
sm (*Anat*) (*pl* **cervella**) brain;
~ **elettronico** computer
'cervo, -a ['tʃɛrvo] *sm/f* stag (hind)
▷ *sm* deer; ~ **volante** stag beetle
ces'puglio [tʃes'puʎʎo] *sm* bush
ces'sare [tʃes'sare] /72/ *vi*, *vt* to stop,
cease; ~ **di fare qc** to stop doing sth
ces'tino [tʃes'tino] *sm* basket; (*per
la carta straccia*) wastepaper basket;
(*Inform*) recycle bin; ~ **da viaggio**
(*Ferr*) packed lunch (*o* dinner)
'cesto ['tʃesto] *sm* basket
'ceto ['tʃɛto] *sm* (*social*) class
cetrio'lino [tʃetrio'lino] *sm* gherkin
cetri'olo [tʃetri'ɔlo] *sm* cucumber
Cfr. *abbr* (= *confronta*) cf

C.G.I.L. *sigla f* (= *Confederazione
Generale Italiana del Lavoro*) trades
union organization
chat'line [tʃæt'laen] *sf inv* chat room
chat'tare [tʃat'tare] /72/ *vi* (*online*) to
chat; **chat'tata** [tʃat'tata] *sf* chat

PAROLA CHIAVE

che [ke] *pron* **1** (*relativo: persona:
soggetto*) who; (: *oggetto*) whom,
that; (: *cosa, animale*) which, that;
il ragazzo che è venuto the boy
who came; **l'uomo che io vedo** the
man (whom) I see; **il libro che è sul
tavolo** the book which *o* that is on
the table; **il libro che vedi** the book
(which *o* that) you see; **la sera che ti
ho visto** the evening I saw you
2 (*interrogativo, esclamativo*) what;
che (cosa) fai? what are you doing?;
a che (cosa) pensi? what are you
thinking about?; **non sa che (cosa)
fare** he doesn't know what to do; **ma
che dici!** what are you saying!
3 (*indefinito*): **quell'uomo ha un
che di losco** there's something
suspicious about that man; **un
certo non so che** an indefinable
something
▶ *det* **1** (*interrogativo: tra tanti*) what;
(: *tra pochi*) which; **che tipo di film
preferisci?** what sort of film do
you prefer?; **che vestito ti vuoi
mettere?** what (*o* which) dress do
you want to put on?
2 (*esclamativo: seguito da aggettivo*)
how; (: *seguito da sostantivo*) what;
che buono! how delicious!; **che bel
vestito!** what a lovely dress!
▶ *cong* **1** (*con proposizioni subordinate*)
that; **credo che verrà** I think he'll
come; **voglio che tu studi** I want
you to study; **so che tu c'eri** I know
(that) you were there; **non che
sia sbagliato, ma ...** not that it's
wrong, but ...
2 (*finale*) so that; **vieni qua, che**

ti veda come here, so (that) I can see you

3 (*temporale*): **arrivai che eri già partito** you had already left when I arrived; **sono anni che non lo vedo** I haven't seen him for years

4 (*in frasi imperative, concessive*): **che venga pure!** let him come by all means!; **che tu sia benedetto!** may God bless you!

5 (*comparativo: con più, meno*) than; *vedi anche* **più; meno; così** *ecc*

chemiotera'pia [kemjotera'pia] *sf* chemotherapy

chero'sene [kero'zɛne] *sm* kerosene

⊙ **PAROLA CHIAVE**

chi [ki] *pron* **1** (*interrogativo: soggetto*) who; (: *oggetto*) who, whom; **chi è?** who is it?; **di chi è questo libro?** whose book is this?, whose is this book?; **con chi parli?** who are you talking to?; **a chi pensi?** who are you thinking about?; **chi di voi?** which of you?; **non so a chi rivolgermi** I don't know who to ask

2 (*relativo*) whoever, anyone who; **dillo a chi vuoi** tell whoever you like

3 (*indefinito*): **chi ... chi ...** some ... others ...; **chi dice una cosa, chi dice un'altra** some say one thing, others say another

chiacchie'rare [kjakkje'rare] /72/ *vi* to chat; (*discorrere futilmente*) to chatter; (*far pettegolezzi*) to gossip; **chi'acchiere** *sfpl*: **fare due** o **quattro chiacchiere** to have a chat

chia'mare [kja'mare] /72/ *vt* to call; (*rivolgersi a qn*) to call (in), send for; **chiamarsi** *vpr* (*aver nome*) to be called; **come ti chiami?** what's your name?; **mi chiamo Paolo** my name is Paolo, I'm called Paolo; **~ alle armi** to call up; **~ in giudizio** to summon; **chia'mata** *sf* (*Tel*) call; (*Mil*) call-up

chia'rezza [kja'rettsa] *sf* clearness; clarity

chia'rire [kja'rire] /55/ *vt* to make clear; (*fig: spiegare*) to clear up, explain

chi'aro, -a ['kjaro] *ag* clear; (*luminoso*) clear, bright; (*colore*) pale, light

chi'asso ['kjasso] *sm* uproar, row

chi'ave ['kjave] *sf* key ▷ *ag inv* key *cpd*; **~ d'accensione** (*Aut*) ignition key; **~ inglese** monkey wrench; **~ di volta** keystone; **~ USB** (*Inform*) USB key

chi'cco, -chi ['kikko] *sm* grain; (*di caffè*) bean; **~ d'uva** grape

chi'edere ['kjɛdere] /21/ *vt* (*per sapere*) to ask; (*per avere*) to ask for ▷ *vi*: **~ di qn** to ask after sb; (*al telefono*) to ask for o want sb; **chiedersi** *vpr*: **chiedersi (se)** to wonder (whether); **~ qc a qn** to ask sb sth; to ask sb for sth

chi'esa ['kjɛza] *sf* church

chi'esi *ecc* ['kjɛzi] *vb vedi* **chiedere**

chi'glia ['kiʎʎa] *sf* keel

chi'lo ['kilo] *sm* kilo; **chilo'grammo** *sm* kilogram(me); **chi'lometro** *sm* kilometre

chi'mico, -a, -ci, -che ['kimiko] *ag* chemical ▷ *sm/f* chemist

chi'nare [ki'nare] /72/ *vt* to lower, bend; **chinarsi** *vpr* to stoop, bend

chi'occiola ['kjɔttʃola] *sf* snail; (*di indirizzo e-mail*) at (symbol); **scala a ~** spiral staircase

chi'odo ['kjɔdo] *sm* nail; (*fig*) obsession; **~ di garofano** (*Cuc*) clove

chi'osco, -schi ['kjɔsko] *sm* kiosk, stall

chi'ostro ['kjɔstro] *sm* cloister

chiro'mante [kiro'mante] *smf* palmist

chirur'gia [kirur'dʒia] *sf* surgery; **~ estetica** cosmetic surgery; **chi'rurgo, -ghi** o **-gi** *sm* surgeon

chissà [kis'sa] *av* who knows, I wonder

chi'tarra [ki'tarra] *sf* guitar

chitar'rista, -i, -e [kitar'rista] *sm/f* guitarist, guitar player

chi'udere ['kjudere] /22/ *vt* to close, shut; (*luce, acqua*) to put off, turn off; (*definitivamente: fabbrica*) to close down, shut down; (*strada*) to close; (*recingere*) to enclose; (*porre termine a*) to end ▷ *vi* to close, shut; to close down, shut down, to end; **chiudersi** *vpr* to shut, close; (*ritirarsi: anche fig*) to shut o.s. away; (*ferita*) to close up

chi'unque [ki'unkwe] *pron* (*relativo*) whoever, (*indefinito*) anyone, anybody; **~ sia** whoever it is

'**chiusi** ecc ['kjusi] *vb vedi* **chiudere**

chi'uso, -a ['kjuso] *pp di* **chiudere** ▷ *sf* (*di corso d'acqua*) sluice, lock; (*recinto*) enclosure; (*di discorso ecc*) conclusion, ending; **chiu'sura** *sf* closing; shutting; closing o shutting down; enclosing; putting o turning off; ending; (*dispositivo*) catch; fastening; fastener; **chiusura lampo**® zip (fastener) (BRIT), zipper (US)

PAROLA CHIAVE

ci [tʃi] (*dav lo, la, li, le, ne diventa* **ce**) *pron* **1** (*personale: complemento oggetto*) us; (: *a noi, complemento di termine*) (to) us; (: *riflessivo*) ourselves; (: *reciproco*) each other, one another; (: *impersonale*): **ci si veste** we get dressed; **ci ha visti** he's seen us; **non ci ha dato niente** he gave us nothing; **ci vestiamo** we get dressed; **ci amiamo** we love one another o each other

2 (*dimostrativo, di ciò, su ciò, in ciò ecc*) about (o on o of) it; **non so cosa farci** I don't know what to do about it; **che c'entro io?** what have I got to do with it?

▷ *av* (*qui*) here; (*lì*) there; (*moto attraverso luogo*): **ci passa sopra un ponte** a bridge passes over it;

non ci passa più nessuno nobody comes this way any more; **esserci** *vedi* **essere**

C.I. *abbr* = **carta d'identità**

cia'batta [tʃa'batta] *sf* slipper; (*pane*) ciabatta

ciam'bella [tʃam'bɛlla] *sf* (*Cuc*) ring-shaped cake; (*salvagente*) rubber ring

ci'ao ['tʃao] *escl* (*all'arrivo*) hello!; (*alla partenza*) cheerio! (BRIT), bye!

cias'cuno, -a [tʃas'kuno] (*dav sm:* **ciascun** + *C, V,* **ciascuno** + *s impura, gn, pn, ps, x, z; dav sf:* **ciascuna** + *C,* **ciascun'** + *V*) *det* every, each; (*ogni*) every ▷ *pron* each (one); (*tutti*) everyone, everybody

ci'barie [tʃi'barje] *sfpl* foodstuffs

cibernauta, -i, -e [tʃiber'nauta] *sm/f* Internet surfer

ciberspazio [tʃiber'spattsjo] *sm* cyberspace

'**cibo** ['tʃibo] *sm* food

ci'cala [tʃi'kala] *sf* cicada

cica'trice [tʃika'tritʃe] *sf* scar

'**cicca, -che** ['tʃikka] *sf* cigarette end

'**ciccia** ['tʃittʃa] *sf* (*fam*) fat

cicci'one, -a [tʃit'tʃone] *sm/f* (*fam*) fatty

cicla'mino [tʃikla'mino] *sm* cyclamen

ci'clismo [tʃi'klizmo] *sm* cycling; **ci'clista, -i, -e** *sm/f* cyclist

'**ciclo** ['tʃiklo] *sm* cycle; (*di malattia*) course

ciclomo'tore [tʃiklomo'tore] *sm* moped

ci'clone [tʃi'klone] *sm* cyclone

ci'cogna [tʃi'koɲɲa] *sf* stork

ci'eco, -a, -chi, -che ['tʃɛko] *ag* blind ▷ *sm/f* blind man/woman

ci'elo ['tʃɛlo] *sm* sky; (*Rel*) heaven

'**cifra** ['tʃifra] *sf* (*numero*) figure, numeral; (*somma di denaro*) sum, figure; (*monogramma*) monogram, initials *pl*; (*codice*) code, cipher

'ciglio [ˈtʃiʎʎo] sm (margine) edge, verge; (pl(f) **ciglia**: delle palpebre) (eye) lash; (eye)lid; (sopracciglio) eyebrow

'cigno [ˈtʃiɲɲo] sm swan

cigo'lare [tʃigoˈlare] /72/ vi to squeak, creak

'Cile [ˈtʃile] sm: **il ~** Chile; **ci'leno, -a** [tʃiˈlɛno] ag, sm/f Chilean

cili'egia, -gie o **-ge** [tʃiˈljɛdʒa] sf cherry

cilie'gina [tʃiljeˈdʒina] sf glacé cherry

cilin'drata [tʃilinˈdrata] sf (Aut) (cubic) capacity; **una macchina di grossa ~** a big-engined car

ci'lindro [tʃiˈlindro] sm cylinder; (cappello) top hat

'cima [ˈtʃima] sf (sommità) top; (di monte) top, summit; (estremità) end; **in ~ a** at the top of; **da ~ a fondo** from top to bottom; (fig) from beginning to end

'cimice [ˈtʃimitʃe] sf (Zool) bug; (puntina) drawing pin (BRIT), thumbtack (US)

cimini'era [tʃimiˈnjɛra] sf chimney; (di nave) funnel

cimi'tero [tʃimiˈtɛro] sm cemetery

'Cina [ˈtʃina] sf: **la ~** China

cin'cin, cin cin [tʃinˈtʃin] escl cheers!

'cinema [ˈtʃinema] sm inv cinema

ci'nese [tʃiˈnese] ag, smf, sm Chinese inv

'cinghia [ˈtʃingja] sf strap; (cintura, Tecn) belt

cinghi'ale [tʃinˈgjale] sm wild boar

cinguet'tare [tʃingwetˈtare] /72/ vi to twitter

'cinico, -a, -ci, -che [ˈtʃiniko] ag cynical ▷ sm/f cynic

cin'quanta [tʃinˈkwanta] num fifty; **cinquan'tesimo, -a** num fiftieth

cinquan'tina [tʃinkwanˈtina] sf (serie): **una ~ (di)** about fifty; (età): **essere sulla ~** to be about fifty

'cinque [ˈtʃinkwe] num five; **avere ~ anni** to be five (years old); **il ~ dicembre 2008** the fifth of

December 2008; **alle ~** (ora) at five (o'clock)

cinque'cento [tʃinkweˈtʃɛnto] num five hundred ▷ sm: **il C~** the sixteenth century

cin'tura [tʃinˈtura] sf belt; **~ di salvataggio** lifebelt (BRIT), life preserver (US); **~ di sicurezza** (Aut, Aer) safety o seat belt

cintu'rino [tʃintuˈrino] sm strap; **~ dell'orologio** watch strap

ciò [tʃɔ] pron this; that; **~ che** what; **~ nonostante** o **nondimeno** nevertheless, in spite of that

ci'occa, -che [ˈtʃɔkka] sf (di capelli) lock

ciocco'lata [tʃokkoˈlata] sf chocolate; (bevanda) (hot) chocolate; **cioccola'tino** sm chocolate

cio'è [tʃoˈɛ] av that is (to say)

ci'otola [ˈtʃɔtola] sf bowl

ci'ottolo [ˈtʃɔttolo] sm pebble; (di strada) cobble(stone)

ci'polla [tʃiˈpolla] sf onion; (di tulipano ecc) bulb

cipol'lina [tʃipolˈlina] sf: **cipolline sottaceto** pickled onions

ci'presso [tʃiˈpresso] sm cypress (tree)

ci'pria [ˈtʃiprja] sf (face) powder

'Cipro [ˈtʃipro] sm Cyprus

'circa [ˈtʃirka] av about, roughly ▷ prep about, concerning; **a mezzogiorno ~** about midday

'circo, -chi [ˈtʃirko] sm circus

circo'lare [tʃirkoˈlare] /72/ vi to circulate; (Aut) to drive (along), move (along) ▷ ag circular ▷ sf (Amm) circular; (di autobus) circle (line); **circolazi'one** sf circulation; (Aut): **la circolazione** (the) traffic

'circolo [ˈtʃirkolo] sm circle

circon'dare [tʃirkonˈdare] /72/ vt to surround; **circondarsi** vpr: **circondarsi di** to surround o.s. with

circonvallazi'one [tʃirkonvallatˈtsjone] sf ring road

(BRIT), beltway (US); (*per evitare una città*) by-pass

circos'petto, -a [tʃirkos'pɛtto] *ag* circumspect, cautious

circos'tante [tʃirkos'tante] *ag* surrounding, neighbouring

circos'tanza [tʃirkos'tantsa] *sf* circumstance; (*occasione*) occasion

cir'cuito [tʃir'kuito] *sm* circuit

C.I.S.L. *sigla f* (= *Confederazione Italiana Sindacati Lavoratori*) *trades union organization*

cis'terna [tʃis'tɛrna] *sf* tank, cistern

'cisti ['tʃisti] *sf inv* cyst

cis'tite [tʃis'tite] *sf* cystitis

ci'tare [tʃi'tare] /72/ *vt* (*Dir*) to summon; (*autore*) to quote; (*a esempio, modello*) to cite

ci'tofono [tʃi'tɔfono] *sm* entry phone; (*in uffici*) intercom

città [tʃit'ta] *sf inv* town; (*importante*) city; **~ universitaria** university campus

cittadi'nanza [tʃittadi'nantsa] *sf* citizens *pl*; (*Dir*) citizenship

citta'dino, -a [tʃitta'dino] *ag* town *cpd*; city *cpd* ▷ *sm/f* (*di uno Stato*) citizen; (*abitante di città*) town dweller, city dweller

ci'uccio ['tʃuttʃo] *sm* (*fam*) comforter, dummy (BRIT), pacifier (US)

ci'uffo ['tʃuffo] *sm* tuft

ci'vetta [tʃi'vetta] *sf* (*Zool*) owl; (*fig: donna*) coquette, flirt ▷ *ag inv*: **auto/ nave ~** decoy car/ship

'civico, -a, -ci, -che ['tʃiviko] *ag* civic; (*museo*) municipal, town *cpd*; city *cpd*

ci'vile [tʃi'vile] *ag* civil; (*non militare*) civilian; (*nazione*) civilized ▷ *sm* civilian

civiltà [tʃivil'ta] *sf* civilization; (*cortesia*) civility

'clacson *sm inv* (*Aut*) horn

clandes'tino, -a *ag* clandestine; (*Pol*) underground, clandestine; (*immigrato*) illegal ▷ *sm/f* stowaway;

(*anche*: **immigrato ~**) illegal immigrant

'classe *sf* class; **di ~** (*fig*) with class; of excellent quality; **~ operaia** working class; **~ turistica** (*Aer*) economy class

'classico, -a, -ci, -che *ag* classical; (*tradizionale: moda*) classic(al) ▷ *sm* classic; classical author

clas'sifica, -che *sf* classification; (*Sport*) placings *pl*

classifi'care /20/ *vt* to classify; (*candidato, compito*) to grade; **classificarsi** *vpr* to be placed

'clausola *sf* (*Dir*) clause

clavi'cembalo [klavi'tʃembalo] *sm* harpsichord

cla'vicola *sf* (*Anat*) collarbone

clic'care /20/ *vi* (*Inform*): **~ su** to click on

cli'ente *smf* customer, client

'clima, -i *sm* climate; **climatizza'tore** *sm* air conditioner

'clinico, -a, -ci, -che *ag* clinical ▷ *sf* (*scienza*) clinical medicine; (*casa di cura*) clinic, nursing home; (*settore d'ospedale*) clinic

clo'nare /72/ *vt* to clone; **clona'zione** [klonat'tsjone] *sf* cloning

'cloro *sm* chlorine

club *sm inv* club

cm *abbr* (= *centimetro*) cm

c.m. *abbr* (= *corrente mese*) inst.

coalizi'one [koalit'tsjone] *sf* coalition

'COBAS *sigla mpl* (= *Comitati di base*) *independent trades unions*

'coca *sf* (*bibita*) Coke; (*droga*) cocaine

coca'ina *sf* cocaine

cocci'nella [kottʃi'nɛlla] *sf* ladybird (BRIT), ladybug (US)

cocci'uto, -a [kot'tʃuto] *ag* stubborn, pigheaded

'cocco, -chi *sm* (*pianta*) coconut palm; (*frutto*): **noce di ~** coconut ▷ *sm/f* (*fam*) darling

cocco'drillo *sm* crocodile

cocco'lare /72/ *vt* to cuddle, fondle

cocerò *ecc* [kotʃe'rɔ] *vb vedi* **cuocere**

co'comero *sm* watermelon

'**coda** *sf* tail; (*fila di persone, auto*) queue (BRIT), line (US); (*di abiti*) train; **con la ~ dell'occhio** out of the corner of one's eye; **mettersi in ~** to queue (up) (BRIT), line up (US); to join the queue *o* line; **~ di cavallo** (*acconciatura*) ponytail

co'dardo, -a *ag* cowardly ▷ *sm/f* coward

'**codice** ['kɔditʃe] *sm* code; **~ di avviamento postale** postcode (BRIT), zip code (US); **~ a barre** bar code; **~ civile** civil code; **~ fiscale** tax code; **~ penale** penal code; **~ segreto** (*di tessera magnetica*) PIN (number); **~ della strada** highway code

coe'rente *ag* coherent

coe'taneo, -a *ag, sm/f* contemporary

'**cofano** *sm* (*Aut*) bonnet (BRIT), hood (US); (*forziere*) chest

'**cogliere** ['kɔʎʎere] /23/ *vt* (*fiore, frutto*) to pick, gather; (*sorprendere*) to catch, surprise; (*bersaglio*) to hit; (*fig: momento opportuno ecc*) to grasp, seize, take; (: *capire*) to grasp; **~ sul fatto *o* in flagrante/alla sprovvista** to catch red-handed/ unprepared

co'gnato, -a [koɲ'ɲato] *sm/f* brother-in-law/sister-in-law

co'gnome [koɲ'ɲome] *sm* surname

coinci'denza [kointʃi'dɛntsa] *sf* coincidence; (*Ferr, Aer, di autobus*) connection

coin'cidere [koin'tʃidere] /34/ *vi* to coincide

coin'volgere [koin'vɔldʒere] /96/ *vt*: **~ in** to involve in

cola'pasta *sm inv* colander

co'lare /72/ *vt* (*liquido*) to strain; (*pasta*) to drain; (*oro fuso*) to pour ▷ *vi, vi* (*sudore*) to drip; (*botte*) to leak; (*cera*) to melt; **~ a picco** *vt* (*nave*) to sink

colazi'one [kolat'tsjone] *sf* breakfast; lunch; **fare ~** to have breakfast (*o* lunch)

co'lera *sm* (*Med*) cholera

'**colgo** *ecc vb vedi* **cogliere**

co'lica *sf* (*Med*) colic

co'lino *sm* strainer

'**colla** *prep + det vedi* **con** ▷ *sf* glue; (*di farina*) paste

collabo'rare /72/ *vi* to collaborate; **~ a** to collaborate on; (*giornale*) to contribute to; **collabora'tore, -'trice** *sm/f* collaborator; (*di giornale, rivista*) contributor; **collaboratore esterno** freelance; **collaboratrice familiare** home help

col'lana *sf* necklace; (*collezione*) collection, series

col'lant [kɔ'lã] *sm inv* tights *pl*

col'lare *sm* collar

col'lasso *sm* (*Med*) collapse

collau'dare /72/ *vt* to test, try out

col'lega, -ghi, -ghe *sm/f* colleague

collega'mento *sm* connection; (*Mil*) liaison

colle'gare /80/ *vt* to connect, join, link; **collegarsi** *vpr* (*Radio, TV*) to link up; **collegarsi con** (*Tel*) to get through to

col'legio [kol'lɛdʒo] *sm* college; (*convitto*) boarding school; **~ elettorale** (*Pol*) constituency

'**collera** *sf* anger

col'lerico, -a, -ci, -che *ag* quick-tempered, irascible

col'letta *sf* collection

col'letto *sm* collar

collezio'nare [kollettsjo'nare] /72/ *vt* to collect

collezi'one [kollet'tsjone] *sf* collection

col'lina *sf* hill

col'lirio *sm* eyewash

'**collo** *prep + det vedi* **con** ▷ *sm* neck; (*di abito*) neck, collar; (*pacco*) parcel; **~ del piede** instep

colloca'mento *sm* (*impiego*) employment; (*disposizione*) placing, arrangement

collo'care /20/ *vt* (*libri, mobili*) to place; (*Comm: merce*) to find a market for

collocazi'one [kollokat'tsjone] *sf* placing; (*di libro*) classification

col'loquio *sm* conversation, talk; (*ufficiale, per un lavoro*) interview; (*Ins*) preliminary oral exam

'colsi *ecc vb vedi* **cogliere**

col'mare /72/ *vt*: **~ di** (*anche fig*) to fill with; (*dare in abbondanza*) to load *o* overwhelm with

co'lombo, -a *sm/f* dove; pigeon

co'lonia *sf* colony; (*per bambini*) holiday camp; **(acqua di) ~** (eau de) cologne

co'lonna *sf* column; **~ sonora** (*Cine*) sound track; **~ vertebrale** spine, spinal column

colon'nello *sm* colonel

colo'rante *sm* colouring

colo'rare /72/ *vt* to colour; (*disegno*) to colour in

co'lore *sm* colour; **a colori** in colour, colour *cpd*; **farne di tutti i colori** to get up to all sorts of mischief

colo'rito, -a *ag* coloured; (*viso*) rosy, pink; (*linguaggio*) colourful ▷ *sm* (*tinta*) colour; (*carnagione*) complexion

'colpa *sf* fault; (*biasimo*) blame; (*colpevolezza*) guilt; (*azione colpevole*) offence; (*peccato*) sin; **di chi è la ~?** whose fault is it?; **è ~ sua** it's his fault; **per ~ di** through, owing to; **col'pevole** *ag* guilty

col'pire /55/ *vt* to hit, strike; (*fig*) to strike; **rimanere colpito da qc** to be amazed *o* struck by sth

'colpo *sm* (*urto*) knock; (*fig: affettivo*) blow, shock; (: *aggressivo*) blow; (*di pistola*) shot; (*Med*) stroke; (*furto*) raid; **di ~** suddenly; **fare ~** to make a strong impression; **il motore perde colpi** the engine is misfiring; **~ d'aria** chill; **~ in banca** bank job *o* raid; **~**

basso (*Pugilato, fig*) punch below the belt; **~ di fulmine** love at first sight; **~ di grazia** coup de grâce; **~ di scena** (*Teat*) coup de théâtre; (*fig*) dramatic turn of events; **~ di sole** sunstroke; **colpi di sole** (*nei capelli*) highlights; **~ di Stato** coup d'état; **~ di telefono** phone call; **~ di testa** (*sudden*) impulse *o* whim; **~ di vento** gust (of wind)

'colsi *ecc vb vedi* **cogliere**

coltel'lata *sf* stab

col'tello *sm* knife; **~ a serramanico** clasp knife

colti'vare /72/ *vt* to cultivate; (*verdura*) to grow, cultivate

'colto, -a *pp di* **cogliere** ▷ *ag* (*istruito*) cultured, educated

'coma *sm inv* coma

comanda'mento *sm* (*Rel*) commandment

coman'dante *sm* (*Mil*) commander, commandant; (*di reggimento*) commanding officer; (*Naut, Aer*) captain

coman'dare /72/ *vi* to be in command ▷ *vt* to command; (*imporre*) to order, command; **~ a qn di fare** to order sb to do

combaci'are [komba'tʃare] /14/ *vi* to meet; (*fig: coincidere*) to coincide

com'battere /1/ *vt*, *vi* to fight

combi'nare /72/ *vt* to combine; (*organizzare*) to arrange; (*fam: fare*) to make, cause; **combinazi'one** *sf* combination; (*caso fortuito*) coincidence; **per combinazione** by chance

combus'tibile *ag* combustible ▷ *sm* fuel

PAROLA CHIAVE

'come *av* **1** (*alla maniera di*) like; **ti comporti come lui** you behave like him *o* like he does; **bianco come la neve** (as) white as snow; **come se** as if, as though

2 (*in qualità di*) as a; **lavora come autista** he works as a driver
3 (*interrogativo*) how; **come ti chiami?** what's your name?; **come sta?** how are you?; **com'è il tuo amico?** what is your friend like?; **come?** (*prego?*) pardon?, sorry?; **come mai?** how come?; **come mai non ci hai avvertiti?** how come you didn't warn us?
4 (*esclamativo*): **come sei bravo!** how clever you are!; **come mi dispiace!** I'm terribly sorry!
▸ *cong* **1** (*in che modo*) how; **mi ha spiegato come l'ha conosciuto** he told me how he met him
2 (*correlativo*) as; (*con comparativi di maggioranza*) than; **non è bravo come pensavo** he isn't as clever as I thought; **è meglio di come pensassi** it's better than I thought
3 (*appena che, quando*) as soon as; **come arrivò, iniziò a lavorare** as soon as he arrived, he set to work; *vedi anche* **così; tanto**

'**comico, -a, -ci, -che** *ag* (*Teat*) comic; (*buffo*) comical ▸ *sm* (*attore*) comedian, comic actor
cominci'are [komin'tʃare] /14/ *vt, vi* to begin, start; **~ a fare/col fare** to begin to do/by doing
comi'tato *sm* committee
comi'tiva *sf* party, group
co'mizio [ko'mittsjo] *sm* (*Pol*) meeting, assembly
com'media *sf* comedy; (*opera teatrale*) play; (: *che fa ridere*) comedy; (*fig*) playacting *no pl*
commemo'rare /72/ *vt* to commemorate
commen'tare /72/ *vt* to comment on; (*testo*) to annotate; (*Radio, TV*) to give a commentary on
commerci'ale [kommer'tʃale] *ag* commercial, trading; (*peg*) commercial
commercia'lista, -i, -e [kommertʃa'lista] *sm/f* (*laureato*)

graduate in economics and commerce; (*consulente*) business consultant
commerci'ante [kommer'tʃante] *smf* trader, dealer; (*negoziante*) shopkeeper
commerci'are [kommer'tʃare] /14/ *vi*: **~ in** to deal o trade in ▸ *vt* to deal o trade in
com'mercio [kom'mertʃo] *sm* trade, commerce; **essere in ~** (*prodotto*) to be on the market o on sale; **essere nel ~** (*persona*) to be in business; **~ all'ingrosso/al dettaglio** wholesale/retail trade
com'messo, -a *pp di* **commettere** ▸ *sm/f* shop assistant (BRIT), sales clerk (US) ▸ *sm* (*impiegato*) clerk; **~ viaggiatore** commercial traveller
commes'tibile *ag* edible
com'mettere /63/ *vt* to commit
com'misi *ecc vb vedi* **commettere**
commissari'ato *sm* (*Amm*) commissionership; (: *sede*) commissioner's office; (: *di polizia*) police station
commis'sario *sm* commissioner; (*di pubblica sicurezza*) ≈ (police) superintendent (BRIT), ≈ (police) captain (US); (*Sport*) steward; (*membro di commissione*) member of a committee o board
commissi'one *sf* (*incarico*) errand; (*comitato, percentuale*) commission; (*Comm: ordinazione*) order; **commissioni** *sfpl* (*acquisti*) shopping *sg*: **~ d'esame** examining board; **commissioni bancarie** bank charges
com'mosso, -a *pp di* **commuovere**
commo'vente *ag* moving
commozi'one [kommot'tsjone] *sf* emotion, deep feeling; **~ cerebrale** (*Med*) concussion
commu'overe /66/ *vt* to move, affect; **commuoversi** *vpr* to be moved
como'dino *sm* bedside table

comodità *sf inv* comfort; convenience

'comodo, -a *ag* comfortable; (*facile*) easy; (*conveniente*) convenient; (*utile*) useful, handy ▷ *sm* comfort; convenience; **con ~** at one's convenience *o* leisure; **fare il proprio ~** to do as one pleases; **far ~** to be useful *o* handy

compa'gnia [kompaɲ'ɲia] *sf* company; (*gruppo*) gathering

com'pagno, -a [kom'paɲɲo] *sm/f* (*di classe, gioco*) companion; (*Pol*) comrade

com'paio *ecc vb vedi* **comparire**

compa'rare /72/ *vt* to compare

compara'tivo, -a *ag, sm* comparative

compa'rire /7/ *vi* to appear

com'parvi *ecc vb vedi* **comparire**

compassi'one *sf* compassion, pity; **avere ~ di qn** to feel sorry for sb, pity sb

com'passo *sm* (pair of) compasses *pl*; callipers *pl*

compa'tibile *ag* (*scusabile*) excusable; (*conciliabile, Inform*) compatible

compa'tire /55/ *vt* (*aver compassione di*) to sympathize with, feel sorry for; (*scusare*) to make allowances for

com'patto, -a *ag* compact; (*roccia*) solid; (*folla*) dense; (*fig: gruppo, partito*) united

compen'sare /72/ *vt* (*equilibrare*) to compensate for, make up for; **~ qn di** (*rimunerare*) to pay *o* remunerate sb for; (*risarcire*) to pay compensation to sb for; (*fig: fatiche, dolori*) to reward sb for; **com'penso** *sm* compensation; payment, remuneration; reward; **in compenso** (*d'altra parte*) on the other hand

compe'rare /72/ *vt* = **comprare**

'compere *sfpl*: **fare ~** to do the shopping

compe'tente *ag* competent; (*mancia*) apt, suitable

com'petere /45/ *vi* to compete, vie; (*Dir: spettare*): **~ a** to lie within the competence of; **competizi'one** *sf* competition

compi'angere [kom'pjandʒere] /75/ *vt* to sympathize with, feel sorry for

'compiere /24/ *vt* (*concludere*) to finish, complete; (*adempiere*) to carry out, fulfil; **compiersi** *vpr* (*avverarsi*) to be fulfilled, come true; **~ gli anni** to have one's birthday

compi'lare /72/ *vt* to compile; (*modulo*) to complete, fill in (BRIT), fill out (US)

'compito *sm* (*incarico*) task, duty; (*dovere*) duty; (*Ins*) exercise; (: *a casa*) piece of homework; **fare i compiti** to do one's homework

comple'anno *sm* birthday

complessità *sf* complexity

comples'sivo, -a *ag* (*globale*) comprehensive, overall; (*totale: cifra*) total

com'plesso, -a *ag* complex ▷ *sm* (*Psic, Edil*) complex; (*Mus: corale*) ensemble; (: *orchestrina*) band; (: *di musica pop*) group; **in** *o* **nel ~** on the whole; **~ alberghiero** hotel complex; **~ edilizio** building complex; **~ vitaminico** vitamin complex

completa'mente *av* completely

comple'tare /72/ *vt* to complete

com'pleto, -a *ag* complete; (*teatro, autobus*) full ▷ *sm* suit; **al ~** full; **~ da sci** ski suit

compli'care /20/ *vt* to complicate; **complicarsi** *vpr* to become complicated

'complice ['kɔmplitʃe] *smf* accomplice

complicità [komplitʃi'ta] *sf inv* complicity; **un sorriso/uno sguardo di ~** a knowing smile/look

complimen'tarsi /72/ *vpr*: **~ con** to congratulate

compli'mento *sm* compliment; **complimenti** *smpl* (*cortesia eccessiva*) ceremony *sg*; (*ossequi*) regards, compliments; **complimenti!** congratulations!; **senza complimenti!** don't stand on ceremony!; make yourself at home!; help yourself!

complot'tare /72/ *vi* to plot, conspire

com'plotto *sm* plot, conspiracy

com'pone *ecc vb vedi* **comporre**

compo'nente *smf* member ▷ *sm* component

com'pongo *ecc vb vedi* **comporre**

componi'mento *sm* (*Dir*) settlement; (*Ins*) composition; (*poetico, teatrale*) work

com'porre /77/ *vt* (*musica, testo*) to compose; (*mettere in ordine*) to arrange; (*Dir: lite*) to settle; (*Tip*) to set; (*Tel*) to dial; **comporsi** *vpr*: **comporsi di** to consist of, be composed of

comporta'mento *sm* behaviour

compor'tare /72/ *vt* (*implicare*) to involve; **comportarsi** *vpr* to behave

com'posi *ecc vb vedi* **comporre**

composi'tore, -'trice *sm/f* composer; (*Tip*) compositor, typesetter

com'posto, -a *pp di* **comporre** ▷ *ag* (*persona*) composed, self-possessed; (*: decoroso*) dignified; (*formato da più elementi*) compound *cpd* ▷ *sm* compound

com'prare /72/ *vt* to buy

com'prendere /81/ *vt* (*contenere*) to comprise, consist of; (*capire*) to understand

compren'sibile *ag* understandable

comprensi'one *sf* understanding

compren'sivo, -a *ag* (*prezzo*): **~ di** inclusive of; (*indulgente*) understanding

Attenzione! In inglese esiste la parola *comprehensive*, che però in genere significa *completo*.

com'preso, -a *pp di* **comprendere** ▷ *ag* (*incluso*) included

com'pressa *sf vedi* **compresso**

com'presso, -a *pp di* **comprimere** ▷ *sf* (*Med: garza*) compress; (*: pastiglia*) tablet

com'primere /50/ *vt* (*premere*) to press; (*Fisica*) to compress; (*fig*) to repress

compro'messo, -a *pp di* **compromettere** ▷ *sm* compromise

compro'mettere /63/ *vt* to compromise; **compromettersi** *vpr* to compromise o.s.

com'puter *sm inv* computer

comu'nale *ag* municipal, town *cpd*; **consiglio/palazzo ~** town council/hall

Co'mune *sm* (*Amm*) town council; (*sede*) town hall

co'mune *ag* common; (*consueto*) common, everyday; (*di livello medio*) average; (*ordinario*) ordinary ▷ *sf* (*di persone*) commune; **fuori del ~** out of the ordinary; **avere in ~** to have in common, share; **mettere in ~** to share

comuni'care /20/ *vt* (*notizia*) to pass on, convey; (*malattia*) to pass on; (*ansia ecc*) to communicate; (*trasmettere: calore ecc*) to transmit, communicate; (*Rel*) to administer communion to ▷ *vi* to communicate

comuni'cato *sm* communiqué; **~ stampa** press release

comunicazi'one [komunikat'tsjone] *sf* communication; (*annuncio*) announcement; (*Tel*): **~ (telefonica)** (telephone) call; **dare la ~ a qn** to put sb through; **ottenere la ~** to get through

comuni'one *sf* communion; **~ dei beni** (*Dir*) joint ownership of property

comu'nismo *sm* communism

comuni'tà *sf inv* community; **C~ Economica Europea** European Economic Community

co'munque *cong* however, no matter how ▷ *av* (*in ogni modo*) in any case; (*tuttavia*) however, nevertheless

con prep (nei seguenti casi **con** può
fondersi con l'articolo definito, con +
il = **col**, con + la = **colla**, con + gli =
cogli, con + l = **coi**, con + le = **colle**)
with; **partire col treno** to leave by
train; **~ mio grande stupore** to my
great astonishment; **~ tutto ciò**
for all that

con'cedere [kon'tʃɛdere] /29/ vt
(accordare) to grant; (ammettere) to
admit, concede; **concedersi qc** to
treat o.s. to sth, allow o.s. sth

concen'trare [kontʃen'trare]
/72/ vt, **concen'trarsi** vpr to
concentrate

concentrazi'one sf concentration

conce'pire [kontʃe'pire] /55/ vt
(bambino) to conceive; (progetto,
idea) to conceive (of); (metodo, piano)
to devise

con'certo [kon'tʃɛrto] sm (Mus)
concert; (: componimento) concerto

con'cessi ecc [kon'tʃɛssi] vb vedi
concedere

con'cetto [kon'tʃɛtto] sm (pensiero,
idea) concept; (opinione) opinion

concezi'one [kontʃet'tsjone] sf
conception

con'chiglia [kon'kiʎʎa] sf shell

conci'are [kon'tʃare] /14/ vt
(pelli) to tan; (tabacco) to cure;
(fig: ridurre in cattivo stato) to beat
up; **conciarsi** vpr (sporcarsi) to get
in a mess; (vestirsi male) to dress
badly

concili'are [kontʃi'ljare] /19/ vt to
reconcile; (contravvenzione) to pay
on the spot; (sonno) to be conducive
to, induce; **conciliarsi qc** to gain o
win sth (for o.s.); **conciliarsi qn** to
win sb over; **conciliarsi con** to be
reconciled with

con'cime [kon'tʃime] sm manure;
(chimico) fertilizer

con'ciso, -a [kon'tʃizo] ag concise,
succinct

concitta'dino, -a [kontʃitta'dino]
sm/f fellow citizen

con'cludere /3/ vt to conclude;
(portare a compimento) to conclude,
finish, bring to an end; (operare
positivamente) to achieve ▷ vi (essere
convincente) to be conclusive;
concludersi vpr to come to an
end, close

concor'dare /72/ vt (prezzo) to
agree on; (Ling) to make agree ▷ vi
to agree

con'corde ag (d'accordo) in
agreement; (simultaneo)
simultaneous

concor'rente ag competing; (Mat)
concurrent ▷ smf competitor;
(Ins) candidate; **concor'renza** sf
competition

concorrenzi'ale [konkorren'tsjale]
ag competitive

con'correre /28/ vi: ~ **(in)** (Mat)
to converge o meet (in); ~ **(a)**
(competere) to compete (for);
(Ins: a una cattedra) to apply (for);
(partecipare: a un'impresa) to take part
(in), contribute (to); **con'corso, -a**
pp di **concorrere** ▷ sm competition;
(esame) competitive examination;
concorso di colpa (Dir) contributory
negligence

con'creto, -a ag concrete

con'danna sf condemnation;
sentence; conviction

condan'nare /72/ vt (disapprovare) to
condemn; (Dir): ~ **a** to sentence to;
~ **per** to convict of

conden'sare /72/ vt to condense

condi'mento sm seasoning;
dressing

con'dire /55/ vt to season; (insalata)
to dress

condi'videre /43/ vt to share

condizio'nale [kondittsjo'nale] ag
conditional ▷ sm (Ling) conditional
▷ sf (Dir) suspended sentence

condizio'nare [kondittsjo'nare]
/72/ vt to condition; **ad aria
condizionata** air-conditioned;
condiziona'tore sm air conditioner

ondizi'one [kondit'tsjone] *sf* condition

ondogli'anze [kondoʎ'ʎantse] *sfpl* condolences

ondo'minio *sm* joint ownership; (*edificio*) jointly-owned building

on'dotta *sf vedi* **condotto**

on'dotto, -a *pp di* **condurre** ▷ *sf* (*modo di comportarsi*) conduct, behaviour; (*di un affare ecc*) handling; (*di acqua*) piping; (*incarico sanitario*) country medical practice controlled by a local authority

ondu'cente [kondu'tʃɛnte] *sm* driver

on'duco *ecc vb vedi* **condurre**

on'durre /90/ *vt* to conduct; (*azienda*) to manage; (*accompagnare: bambino*) to take; (*automobile*) to drive; (*trasportare: acqua, gas*) to convey, conduct; (*fig*) to lead ▷ *vi* to lead

on'dussi *ecc vb vedi* **condurre**

onfe'renza [konfe'rɛntsa] *sf* (*discorso*) lecture; (*riunione*) conference; **~ stampa** press conference

on'ferma *sf* confirmation

onfer'mare /72/ *vt* to confirm

onfes'sare /72/ *vt,* **confes'sarsi** *vpr* to confess; **andare a confessarsi** (*Rel*) to go to confession

on'fetto *sm* sugared almond; (*Med*) pill

Attenzione! In inglese esiste la parola *confetti*, che però significa *coriandoli*.

onfet'tura *sf* (*gen*) jam; (*di arance*) marmalade

onfezio'nare [konfettsjo'nare] /72/ *vt* (*vestito*) to make (up); (*merci, pacchi*) to package

onfezi'one [konfet'tsjone] *sf* (*di abiti: da uomo*) tailoring; (*: da donna*) dressmaking; (*imballaggio*) packaging; **~ regalo** gift pack; **confezioni per signora** ladies' wear *no pl*; **confezioni da uomo** menswear *no pl*

confic'care /20/ *vt*: **~ qc in** to hammer *o* drive sth into; **conficcarsi** *vpr* to stick

confi'dare /72/ *vi*: **~ in** to confide in, rely on ▷ *vt* to confide; **confidarsi con qn** to confide in sb

configu'rare /72/ *vt* (*Inform*) to set

configurazi'one [konfigurat'tsjone] *sf* configuration; (*Inform*) setting

confi'nare /72/ *vi*: **~ con** to border on ▷ *vt* (*Pol*) to intern; (*fig*) to confine

CONFIN'DUSTRIA *sigla f* (= *Confederazione Generale dell'Industria Italiana*) employers' association ≈ CBI (BRIT)

con'fine *sm* boundary; (*di paese*) border, frontier

confis'care /20/ *vt* to confiscate

con'flitto *sm* conflict; **~ d'interessi** conflict of interests

conflu'enza [konflu'ɛntsa] *sf* (*di fiumi*) confluence; (*di strade*) junction

con'fondere /25/ *vt* to mix up, confuse; (*imbarazzare*) to embarrass; **confondersi** *vpr* (*mescolarsi*) to mingle; (*turbarsi*) to be confused; (*sbagliare*) to get mixed up

confor'tare /72/ *vt* to comfort, console

confron'tare /72/ *vt* to compare

con'fronto *sm* comparison; **in** *o* **a ~ di** in comparison with, compared to; **nei miei** (*o tuoi ecc*) **confronti** towards me (*o you ecc*)

con'fusi *ecc vb vedi* **confondere**

confusi'one *sf* confusion; (*imbarazzo*) embarrassment; **far ~** (*chiasso*) to make a racket

con'fuso, -a *pp di* **confondere** ▷ *ag* (*vedi confondere*) confused; embarrassed

conge'dare [kondʒe'dare] /72/ *vt* to dismiss; (*Mil*) to demobilize; **congedarsi** *vpr* to take one's leave

con'gegno *sm* device, mechanism

conge'lare [kondʒe'lare] /72/ *vt* to freeze; **congela'tore** *sm* freezer

congesti'one [kondʒes'tjone] *sf* congestion

conget'tura [kondʒet'tura] *sf* conjecture

con'giungere [kon'dʒundʒere] /5/ *vt*, **con'giungersi** *vpr* to join (together)

congiunti'vite [kondʒunti'vite] *sf* conjunctivitis

congiun'tivo [kondʒun'tivo] *sm* (*Ling*) subjunctive

congi'unto, -a [kon'dʒunto] *pp di* **congiungere** ▷ *ag* (*unito*) joined ▷ *sm/f* relative

congiunzi'one [kondʒun'tsjone] *sf* (*Ling*) conjunction

congi'ura [kon'dʒura] *sf* conspiracy

congratu'larsi /72/ *vpr*: **~ con qn per qc** to congratulate sb on sth

congratulazi'oni [kongratulat'tsjoni] *sfpl* congratulations

con'gresso *sm* congress

C.O.N.I. *sigla m* (= *Comitato Olimpico Nazionale Italiano*) Italian Olympic Games Committee

coni'are /19/ *vt* to mint, coin; (*fig*) to coin

co'niglio [ko'niʎʎo] *sm* rabbit

coniu'gare /80/ *vt* (*Ling*) to conjugate; **coniugarsi** *vpr* to get married

'coniuge ['kɔnjudʒe] *smf* spouse

connazio'nale [konnattsjo'nale] *smf* fellow-countryman/woman

connessi'one *sf* connection

con'nettere /63/ *vt* to connect, join ▷ *vi* (*fig*) to think straight

'cono *sm* cone; **~ gelato** ice-cream cone

co'nobbi *ecc vb vedi* **conoscere**

cono'scente [konoʃʃente] *smf* acquaintance

cono'scenza [konoʃʃentsa] *sf* (*il sapere*) knowledge *no pl*; (*persona*) acquaintance; (*facoltà sensoriale*) consciousness *no pl*; **perdere ~** to lose consciousness

co'noscere [ko'noʃʃere] /26/ *vt* to know; **ci siamo conosciuti a Firenze** we (first) met in Florence; **conoscersi** *vpr* to know o.s.; (*reciproco*) to know each other; (*incontrarsi*) to meet; **~ qn di vista** to know sb by sight; **farsi ~** (*fig*) to make a name for o.s.; **conosci'uto, -a** *pp di* **conoscere** ▷ *ag* well-known

con'quista *sf* conquest

conquis'tare /72/ *vt* to conquer; (*fig*) to gain, win

consa'pevole *ag*: **~ di** aware of

'conscio, -a, -sci, -sce ['kɔnʃo] *ag*: **~ di** aware o conscious of

consecu'tivo, -a *ag* consecutive; (*successivo: giorno*) following, next

con'segna [kon'seɲɲa] *sf* delivery; (*merce consegnata*) consignment; (*custodia*) care, custody; (*Mil: ordine*) orders *pl*; (: *punizione*) confinement to barracks; **dare qc in ~ a qn** to entrust sth to sb; **pagamento alla ~** cash on delivery

conse'gnare [konseɲ'ɲare] /15/ *vt* to deliver; (*affidare*) to entrust, hand over; (*Mil*) to confine to barracks

consegu'enza [konse'gwɛntsa] *sf* consequence; **per o di ~** consequently

con'senso *sm* approval, consent; **~ informato** consent

consen'tire /45/ *vi*: **~ a** to consent o agree to ▷ *vt* to allow, permit

con'serva *sf* (*Cuc*) preserve; **~ di frutta** jam; **~ di pomodoro** tomato purée

conser'vante *sm* (*per alimenti*) preservative

conser'vare /72/ *vt* (*Cuc*) to preserve; (*custodire*) to keep; (: *dalla distruzione ecc*) to preserve, conserve

conserva'tore, -'trice *sm/f* (*Pol*) conservative

conserva'torio *sm* (*di musica*) conservatory

conservazi'one [konservat'tsjone] *sf* preservation; conservation

conside'rare /72/ vt to consider; (reputare) to consider, regard; **considerarsi** vpr to consider o.s.

consigli'are [konsiʎˈʎare] /27/ vt (persona) to advise; (metodo, azione) to recommend, advise, suggest; **con'siglio** sm (suggerimento) advice no pl, piece of advice; (assemblea) council; **consiglio d'amministrazione** board; **Consiglio d'Europa** Council of Europe; **il Consiglio dei Ministri** (Pol) ≈ the Cabinet

consis'tente ag thick; solid; (fig) sound, valid

con'sistere /11/ vi: **~ in** to consist of

conso'lare /72/ ag consular ▷ vt (confortare) to console, comfort; (rallegrare) to cheer up; **consolarsi** vpr to be comforted; to cheer up

conso'lato sm consulate

consolazi'one [konsolatˈtsjone] sf consolation, comfort

'console sm consul

conso'nante sf consonant

'consono, -a ag: **~ a** consistent with, consonant with

con'sorte smf consort

consta'tare /72/ vt to establish, verify

consu'eto, -a ag habitual, usual

consu'lente smf consultant

consul'tare /72/ vt to consult; **consultarsi** vpr: **consultarsi con qn** to seek the advice of sb

consul'torio sm: **~ familiare** family planning clinic

consu'mare /72/ vt (logorare: abiti, scarpe) to wear out; (usare) to consume, use up; (mangiare, bere) to consume; (Dir) to consummate; **consumarsi** vpr to wear out; to be used up; (anche fig) to be consumed; (combustibile) to burn out

con'tabile ag accounts cpd, accounting ▷ smf accountant

contachi'lometri [kontakiˈlɔmetri] sm inv ≈ mileometer

conta'dino, -a sm/f countryman/ woman; farm worker; (peg) peasant

contagi'are [kontaˈdʒare] /62/ vt to infect

contagi'oso, -a ag infectious; contagious

conta'gocce [kontaˈgottʃe] sm inv (Med) dropper

contami'nare /72/ vt to contaminate

con'tante sm cash; **pagare in contanti** to pay cash; **non ho contanti** I haven't got any cash

con'tare /72/ vt to count; (considerare) to consider ▷ vi to count, be of importance; **~ su qn** to count o rely on sb; **~ di fare qc** to intend to do sth; **conta'tore** sm meter

contat'tare /72/ vt to contact

con'tatto sm contact

'conte sm count

conteggi'are [kontedˈdʒare] /62/ vt to charge, put on the bill

con'tegno [konˈteɲɲo] sm (comportamento) behaviour; (atteggiamento) attitude; **darsi un ~** to act nonchalant; (ricomporsi) to pull o.s. together

contemporanea'mente av simultaneously; at the same time

contempo'raneo, -a ag, sm/f contemporary

conten'dente smf opponent, adversary

conte'nere /121/ vt to contain; **conteni'tore** sm container

conten'tezza [kontenˈtettsa] sf contentment

con'tento, -a ag pleased, glad; **~ di** pleased with

conte'nuto sm contents pl; (argomento) content

con'tessa sf countess

contes'tare /72/ vt (Dir) to notify; (fig) to dispute

con'testo sm context

continen'tale ag, smf continental

conti'nente *ag* continent ▷ *sm* (Geo) continent; (: *terra ferma*) mainland

contin'gente [kontin'dʒente] *ag* contingent ▷ *sm* (Comm) quota; (Mil) contingent

continua'mente *av* (*senza interruzione*) continuously, nonstop; (*ripetutamente*) continually

continu'are /72/ *vt* to continue (with), go on with ▷ *vi* to continue, go on; **~ a fare qc** to go on o continue doing sth

continuità *sf* continuity

con'tinuo, -a *ag* (*numerazione*) continuous; (*pioggia*) continual, constant; (Elettr: *corrente*) direct; **di ~** continually

'conto *sm* (*calcolo*) calculation; (Comm, Econ) account; (*di ristorante, albergo*) bill; (*fig: stima*) consideration, esteem; **fare i conti con qn** to settle one's account with sb; **fare ~ su qn** to count o rely on sb; **rendere ~ a qn di qc** to be accountable to sb for sth; **tener ~ di qn/qc** to take sb/sth into account; **per ~ di** on behalf of; **per ~ mio** as far as I'm concerned; **a conti fatti**, **in fin dei conti** all things considered; **~ corrente** current account; **~ alla rovescia** countdown

con'torno *sm* (*linea*) outline, contour; (*ornamento*) border; (Cuc) vegetables *pl*

contrabbandi'ere, -a *sm/f* smuggler

contrab'bando *sm* smuggling, contraband; **merce di ~** contraband, smuggled goods *pl*

contrab'basso *sm* (Mus) (double) bass

contraccambi'are /19/ *vt* (*favore ecc*) to return

contraccet'tivo, -a [kontratt'ʃet'tivo] *ag, sm* contraceptive

contrac'colpo *sm* rebound; (*di arma da fuoco*) recoil; (*fig*) repercussion

contrad'dire /38/ *vt* to contradict; **contraddirsi** *vpr* to contradict o.s.; (*uso reciproco: persone*) to contradict each other o one another; (: *testimonianze ecc*) to be contradictory

contraf'fare /41/ *vt* (*persona*) to mimic; (*alterare: voce*) to disguise; (: *firma*) to forge, counterfeit

contraria'mente *av*: **~ a** contrary to

contrari'are /19/ *vt* (*contrastare*) to thwart, oppose; (*irritare*) to annoy, bother

con'trario, -a *ag* opposite; (*sfavorevole*) unfavourable ▷ *sm* opposite; **essere ~ a qc** (*persona*) to be against sth; **al ~** on the contrary; **in caso ~** otherwise; **avere qualcosa in ~** to have some objection

contrasse'gnare [kontrasseɲ'ɲare] /15/ *vt* to mark

contras'tare /72/ *vt* (*avversare*) to oppose; (*impedire*) to bar; (*negare: diritto*) to contest, dispute ▷ *vi*: **~ (con)** (*essere in disaccordo*) to contrast (with); (*lottare*) to struggle (with)

contrat'tacco *sm* counterattack

contrat'tare /72/ *vt, vi* to negotiate

contrat'tempo *sm* hitch

con'tratto, -a *pp di* **contrarre** ▷ *sm* contract

contravvenzi'one *sf* contravention; (*ammenda*) fine

contrazi'one [kontrat'tsjone] *sf* contraction; (*di prezzi ecc*) reduction

contribu'ente *smf* taxpayer; ratepayer (BRIT), property tax payer (US)

contribu'ire /55/ *vi* to contribute

'contro *prep* against; **~ di me/lui** against me/him; **pastiglie ~ la tosse** throat lozenges; **~ pagamento** (Comm) on payment; **controfi'gura** *sf* (Cine) double

control'lare /72/ *vt* (*accertare*) to check; (*sorvegliare*) to watch, control; (*tenere nel proprio potere, fig: dominare*) to control; **controllarsi** vpr to control o.s.; **con'trollo** sm check; watch; control; **controllo delle nascite** birth control; **control'lore** sm (Ferr, Aut) (ticket) inspector

contro'luce [kontro'lutʃe] sf inv (Fot) backlit shot ▷ av: **(in) ~** against the light; (fotografare) into the light

contro'mano av: **guidare ~** to drive on the wrong side of the road; (in un senso unico) to drive the wrong way up a one-way street

controprodu'cente [kontrprodu'tʃɛnte] ag counterproductive

contro'senso sm (contraddizione) contradiction in terms; (assurdità) nonsense

controspio'naggio [kontrospio'naddʒo] sm counterespionage

contro'versia sf controversy; (Dir) dispute

contro'verso, -a ag controversial

contro'voglia [kontro'vɔʎʎa] av unwillingly

contusi'one sf (Med) bruise

convale'scente [konvaleʃ'ʃɛnte] ag, smf convalescent

convali'dare /72/ vt (Amm) to validate; (fig: sospetto, dubbio) to confirm

con'vegno [kon'veɲɲo] sm (incontro) meeting; (congresso) convention, congress; (luogo) meeting place

conve'nevoli smpl civilities

conveni'ente ag suitable; (vantaggioso) profitable; (: prezzo) cheap

> Attenzione! In inglese esiste la parola convenient, che però significa comodo.

conve'nire /128/ vi (riunirsi) to gather, assemble; (concordare) to agree; (tornare utile) to be worthwhile ▷ vb impers: **conviene fare questo** it

is advisable to do this; **conviene andarsene** we should go; **ne convengo** I agree

con'vento sm (di frati) monastery; (di suore) convent

convenzio'nale [konventsjo'nale] ag conventional

convenzi'one [konven'tsjone] sf (Dir) agreement; (nella società) convention

conver'sare /72/ vi to have a conversation, converse

conversazi'one [konversat'tsjone] sf conversation; **fare ~** to chat, have a chat

conversi'one sf conversion; **~ ad U** (Aut) U-turn

conver'tire /45/ vt (trasformare) to change; (Inform, Pol, Rel) to convert; **convertirsi** vpr: **convertirsi (a)** to be converted (to)

con'vesso, -a ag convex

convin'cente [konvin'tʃɛnte] ag convincing

con'vincere [kon'vintʃere] /129/ vt to convince; **convincersi** vpr: **convincersi (di qc)** to convince o.s. (of sth); **~ qn di qc** to convince sb of sth; **~ qn a fare qc** to persuade sb to do sth

convi'vente smf common-law husband/wife

con'vivere /130/ vi to live together

convo'care /20/ vt to call, convene; (Dir) to summon

convulsi'one sf convulsion

coope'rare /72/ vi: **~ (a)** to cooperate (in); **coopera'tiva** sf cooperative

coordi'nare /72/ vt to coordinate

co'perchio [ko'pɛrkjo] sm cover; (di pentola) lid

co'perta sf cover; (di lana) blanket; (da viaggio) rug; (Naut) deck

coper'tina sf (Stampa) cover, jacket

co'perto, -a pp di **coprire** ▷ ag covered; (cielo) overcast ▷ sm place setting; (posto a tavola) place; (al *ristorante*) cover charge; **~ di** covered in o with

coper'tone *sm* (Aut) rubber tyre

coper'tura *sf* (anche Econ, Mil) cover; (di edificio) roofing

'copia *sf* copy; **brutta/bella ~** rough/final copy

copi'are /19/ *vt* to copy

copincol'lare /72/ *vt* to copy and paste

copin'collo *sm* copy and paste

copi'one *sm* (Cine, Teat) script

'coppa *sf* (bicchiere) goblet; (per frutta, gelato) dish; (trofeo) cup, trophy; **~ dell'olio** oil sump (BRIT) o pan (US)

'coppia *sf* (di persone) couple; (di animali, Sport) pair

coprifu'oco, -chi *sm* curfew

copri'letto *sm* bedspread

copripiu'mino *sm inv* duvet cover

co'prire /9/ *vt* to cover; (occupare: carica, posto) to hold; **coprirsi** *vpr* (cielo) to cloud over; (vestirsi) to wrap up, cover up; (Econ) to cover o.s.; **coprirsi di** (macchie, muffa) to become covered in

coque [kɔk] *sf*: **uovo alla ~** boiled egg

co'raggio [ko'raddʒo] *sm* courage, bravery; **~!** (forza!) come on!; (animo!) cheer up!

co'rallo *sm* coral

Co'rano *sm* (Rel) Koran

co'razza [ko'rattsa] *sf* armour; (di animali) carapace, shell; (Mil) armour(-plating)

'corda *sf* cord; (fune) rope; (spago, Mus) string; **dare ~ a qn** to let sb have his (o her) way; **tenere sulla ~ qn** to keep sb on tenterhooks; **tagliare la ~** to slip away, sneak off; **corde vocali** vocal cords

cordi'ale *ag* cordial, warm ▷ *sm* (bevanda) cordial

'cordless ['kɔːdlɪs] *sm inv* cordless phone

cor'done *sm* cord, string; (linea: di polizia) cordon; **~ ombelicale** umbilical cord

Co'rea *sf*: **la ~** Korea

coreogra'fia *sf* choreography

cori'andolo *sm* (Bot) coriander; **coriandoli** *smpl* confetti *no pl*

cor'nacchia [kor'nakkja] *sf* crow

corna'musa *sf* bagpipes *pl*

cor'netta *sf* (Mus) cornet; (Tel) receiver

cor'netto *sm* (Cuc) croissant; (gelato) cone

cor'nice [kor'nitʃe] *sf* frame; (fig) background, setting

cornici'one [korni'tʃone] *sm* (di edificio) ledge; (Archit) cornice

'corno *sm* (Zool) (pl f **corna**) horn; (Mus) (pl m **corni**) horn; **fare le corna a qn** to be unfaithful to sb

Corno'vaglia [korno'vaʎʎa] *sf*: **la ~** Cornwall

cor'nuto, -a *ag* (con corna) horned; (fam!: marito) cuckolded ▷ *sm* (fam!) cuckold; (: insulto) bastard (!)

'coro *sm* chorus; (Rel) choir

co'rona *sf* crown; (di fiori) wreath

'corpo *sm* body; (militare, diplomatico) corps *inv*; **prendere ~** to take shape; **a ~ a ~** hand-to-hand; **~ di ballo** corps de ballet; **~ insegnante** teaching staff

corpora'tura *sf* build, physique

cor'reggere [kor'rɛddʒere] /87/ *vt* to correct; (compiti) to correct, mark

cor'rente *ag* (fiume) flowing; (acqua del rubinetto) running; (moneta, prezzo) current; (comune) everyday ▷ *sm*: **essere al ~ (di)** to be well-informed (about) ▷ *sf* (movimento di liquido) current, stream; (spiffero) draught; (Elettr, Meteor) current; (fig) trend, tendency; **la vostra lettera del 5 ~ mese** (in lettere commerciali) in your letter of the 5th inst.; **~ alternata (c.a.)** alternating current (AC); **~ continua (c.c.)** direct current (DC); **corrente'mente** *av* commonly; **parlare una lingua correntemente** to speak a language fluently

'correre /28/ *vi* to run; (*precipitarsi*) to rush; (*partecipare a una gara*) to run, run; (*fig: diffondersi*) to go round ▷ *vt* (*Sport: gara*) to compete in; (*rischio*) to run; (*pericolo*) to face; **~ dietro a qn** to run after sb; **corre voce che ...** it is rumoured that ...

cor'ressi *ecc vb vedi* **correggere**

correzi'one [korret'tsjone] *sf* correction; marking; **~ di bozze** proofreading

corri'doio *sm* corridor; (*in aereo, al cinema*) aisle

corri'dore *sm* (*Sport*) runner; (: *su veicolo*) racer

corri'era *sf* coach (BRIT), bus

corri'ere *sm* (*diplomatico, di guerra, postale*) courier; (*spedizioniere*) carrier

corri'mano *sm* handrail

corrispon'dente *ag* corresponding ▷ *smf* correspondent

corrispon'denza [korrispon'dɛntsa] *sf* correspondence

corris'pondere /95/ *vi* (*equivalere*): **~ (a)** to correspond (to) ▷ *vt* (*stipendio*) to pay; (*fig: amore*) to return

cor'rodere /49/ *vt* to corrode

cor'rompere /97/ *vt* to corrupt; (*comprare*) to bribe

cor'roso, -a *pp di* **corrodere**

cor'rotto, -a *pp di* **corrompere** ▷ *ag* corrupt

corru'gare /80/ *vt* to wrinkle; **~ la fronte** to knit one's brows

cor'ruppi *ecc vb vedi* **corrompere**

corruzi'one [korrut'tsjone] *sf* corruption; bribery

'corsa *sf* running *no pl*; (*gara*) race; (*di autobus, taxi*) journey, trip; **fare una ~** to run, dash; (*Sport*) to run a race; **~ campestre** cross-country race

'corsi *ecc vb vedi* **correre**

cor'sia *sf* (*Aut, Sport*) lane; (*di ospedale*) ward

'Corsica *sf*: **la ~** Corsica

cor'sivo *sm* cursive (writing); (*Tip*) italics *pl*

'corso, -a *pp di* **correre** ▷ *sm* course; (*strada cittadina*) main street; (*di unità monetaria*) circulation; (*di titoli, valori*) rate, price; **in ~** in progress, under way; (*annata*) current; **~ d'acqua** river; stream; (*artificiale*) waterway; **~ d'aggiornamento** refresher course; **~ serale** evening class

'corte *sf* (court)yard; (*Dir, regale*) court; **fare la ~ a qn** to court sb; **~ marziale** court-martial

cor'teccia, -ce [kor'tettʃa] *sf* bark

corteggi'are [korted'dʒare] /62/ *vt* to court

cor'teo *sm* procession

cor'tese *ag* courteous; **corte'sia** *sf* courtesy; **per cortesia, dov'è ...?** excuse me, please, where is ...?

cor'tile *sm* (court)yard

cor'tina *sf* curtain; (*anche fig*) screen

'corto, -a *ag* short; **essere a ~ di qc** to be short of sth; **~ circuito** short-circuit

'corvo *sm* raven

'cosa *sf* thing; (*faccenda*) affair, matter, business *no pl*; **(che) ~?** what?; **(che) cos'è?** what is it?; **a ~ pensi?** what are you thinking about?

'coscia, -sce ['kɔʃʃa] *sf* thigh; **~ di pollo** (*Cuc*) chicken leg

cosci'ente [koʃʃɛnte] *ag* conscious; **~ di** conscious o aware of

PAROLA CHIAVE

così *av* **1** (*in questo modo*) like this, (in) this way; (*in tal modo*) so; **le cose stanno così** this is the way things stand; **non ho detto così!** I didn't say that!; **come stai? — (e) così** how are you? — so-so; **e così via** and so on; **per così dire** so to speak; **così sia** amen

2 (*tanto*) so; **così lontano** so far away; **un ragazzo così intelligente** such an intelligent boy

▷ *ag inv* (*tale*): **non ho mai visto un film così** I've never seen such a film

▶ *cong* **1** (*perciò*) so, therefore
2: **così ... come** as ... as; **non è così bravo come te** he's not as good as you; **così ... che** so ... that

cosid'detto, -a *ag* so-called
cos'metico, -a, -ci, -che *ag*, *sm* cosmetic
cos'pargere [kos'pardʒere] /111/ *vt*: ~ **di** to sprinkle with
cos'picuo, -a *ag* considerable, large
cospi'rare /72/ *vi* to conspire
'cossi *ecc vb vedi* **cuocere**
'costa *sf* (*tra terra e mare*) coast(line); (*litorale*) shore; (*Anat*) rib; **la C~ Azzurra** the French Riviera
cos'tante *ag* constant; (*persona*) steadfast ▷ *sf* constant
cos'tare /72/ *vi*, *vt* to cost; ~ **caro** to be expensive, cost a lot
cos'tata *sf* (*Cuc*) large chop
costeggi'are [kosted'dʒare] /62/ *vt* to be close to; to run alongside
cos'tiero, -a *ag* coastal, coast *cpd*
costitu'ire /55/ *vt* (*comitato, gruppo*) to set up, form; (*elementi, parti: comporre*) to make up, constitute; (: *rappresentare*) to constitute; (*Dir*) to appoint; **costituirsi** *vpr*: **costituirsi (alla polizia)** to give o.s. up (to the police)
costituzi'one [kostitut'tsjone] *sf* setting up; building up; constitution
'costo *sm* cost; **a ogni** *o* **qualunque ~, a tutti i costi** at all costs
'costola *sf* (*Anat*) rib
cos'toso, -a *ag* expensive, costly
cos'tringere [kos'trindʒere] /117/ *vt*: ~ **qn a fare qc** to force sb to do sth
costru'ire /55/ *vt* to construct, build; **costruzi'one** *sf* construction, building
cos'tume *sm* (*uso*) custom; (*foggia di vestire, indumento*) costume; ~ **da bagno** bathing *o* swimming costume (BRIT), swimsuit; (*da uomo*) bathing *o* swimming trunks *pl*
co'tenna *sf* bacon rind

coto'letta *sf* (*di maiale, montone*) chop; (*di vitello, agnello*) cutlet
co'tone *sm* cotton; ~ **idrofilo** cotton wool (BRIT), absorbent cotton (US)
'cotta *sf* (*fam: innamoramento*) crush
'cottimo *sm*: **lavorare a ~** to do piecework
'cotto, -a *pp di* **cuocere** ▷ *ag* cooked; (*fam: innamorato*) head-over-heels in love; **ben ~** (*carne*) well done
cot'tura *sf* cooking; (*in forno*) baking; (*in umido*) stewing
co'vare /72/ *vt* to hatch; (*fig: malattia*) to be sickening for; (: *odio, rancore*) to nurse ▷ *vi* (*fuoco, fig*) to smoulder
'covo *sm* den
co'vone *sm* sheaf
'cozza ['kɔttsa] *sf* mussel
coz'zare [kot'tsare] /72/ *vi*: ~ **contro** to bang into, collide with
CPT *sigla m inv* = **Centro di Permanenza Temporanea**
crac'care /20/ *vt* (*Inform*) to crack
'crampo *sm* cramp; **ho un ~ alla gamba** I've got cramp in my leg
'cranio *sm* skull
cra'tere *sm* crater
cra'vatta *sf* tie
cre'are /72/ *vt* to create
'crebbi *ecc vb vedi* **crescere**
cre'dente *smf* (*Rel*) believer
cre'denza [kre'dɛntsa] *sf* belief; (*armadio*) sideboard
'credere /29/ *vt* to believe ▷ *vi*: ~ **in**, ~ **a** to believe in; ~ **qn onesto** to believe sb (to be) honest; ~ **che** to believe *o* think that; **credersi furbo** to think one is clever
'credito *sm* (*anche Comm*) credit; (*reputazione*) esteem, repute; **comprare a ~** to buy on credit
'crema *sf* cream; (*con uova, zucchero ecc*) custard; ~ **pasticciera** confectioner's custard; ~ **solare** sun cream
cre'mare /72/ *vt* to cremate
'crepa *sf* crack

cre'paccio [kre'pattʃo] *sm* large crack, fissure; (*di ghiacciaio*) crevasse

crepacu'ore *sm* broken heart

cre'pare /72/ *vi* (*fam: morire*) to snuff it (BRIT), kick the bucket; ~ **dalle risa** to split one's sides laughing

crêpe [krɛp] *sf inv* pancake

cre'puscolo *sm* twilight, dusk

'crescere ['kreʃʃere] /30/ *vi* to grow ▷ *vt* (*figli*) to raise

'cresima *sf* (*Rel*) confirmation

'crespo, -a *ag* (*capelli*) frizzy; (*tessuto*) puckered ▷ *sm* crêpe

'cresta *sf* crest; (*di polli, uccelli*) crest, comb

'creta *sf* chalk; (*argilla*) clay

creti'nata *sf* (*fam*): **dire/fare una ~** to say/do a stupid thing

cre'tino, -a *ag* stupid ▷ *sm/f* idiot, fool

CRI *sigla f* = **Croce Rossa Italiana**

cric *sm inv* (*Tecn*) jack

cri'ceto [kri'tʃeto] *sm* hamster

crimi'nale *ag, smf* criminal

criminalità *sf* crime; ~ **organizzata** organized crime

'crimine *sm* (*Dir*) crime

crip'tare /72/ *vt* (*TV: programma*) to encrypt

crisan'temo *sm* chrysanthemum

'crisi *sf inv* crisis; (*Med*) attack, fit; ~ **di nervi** attack o fit of nerves

cris'tallo *sm* crystal; **cristalli liquidi** liquid crystals

cristia'nesimo *sm* Christianity

cristi'ano, -a *ag, sm/f* Christian

'cristo *sm*: **C~** Christ

cri'terio *sm* criterion; (*buon senso*) (common) sense

'critica, -che *sf vedi* **critico**

criti'care /20/ *vt* to criticize

'critico, -a, -ci, -che *ag* critical ▷ *sm* critic ▷ *sf* criticism; **la critica** (*attività*) criticism; (*persone*) the critics *pl*

cro'ato, -a *ag, sm/f* Croatian, Croat

Cro'azia [kro'attsja] *sf* Croatia

croc'cante *ag* crisp, crunchy

'croce ['krotʃe] *sf* cross; **in ~** (*di traverso*) crosswise; (*fig*) on tenterhooks; **la C~ Rossa** the Red Cross

croci'ato, -a [kro'tʃato] *ag* cross-shaped ▷ *sf* crusade

croci'era [kro'tʃera] *sf* (*viaggio*) cruise; (*Archit*) transept

crol'lare /72/ *vi* to collapse; **'crollo** *sm* collapse; (*di prezzi*) slump, sudden fall; **crollo in Borsa** slump in prices on the Stock Exchange

cro'mato, -a *ag* chromium-plated

'cromo *sm* chrome, chromium

'cronaca, -che *sf* (*Stampa*) news *sg*; (: *rubrica*) column; (*TV, Radio*) commentary; **fatto** *o* **episodio di** ~ news item; ~ **nera** crime news *sg*; crime column

'cronico, -a, -ci, -che *ag* chronic

cro'nista, -i *sm* (*Stampa*) reporter

cro'nometro *sm* chronometer; (*a scatto*) stopwatch

'crosta *sf* crust

cros'tacei [kros'tatʃei] *smpl* shellfish

cros'tata *sf* (*Cuc*) tart

cros'tino *sm* (*Cuc*) croûton; (: *da antipasto*) canapé

cruci'ale [kru'tʃale] *ag* crucial

cruci'verba *sm inv* crossword (puzzle)

cru'dele *ag* cruel

'crudo, -a *ag* (*non cotto*) raw; (*aspro*) harsh, severe

cru'miro *sm* (*peg*) blackleg (BRIT), scab

'crusca *sf* bran

crus'cotto *sm* (*Aut*) dashboard

CSI *sigla f* (= *Comunità di Stati Indipendenti*) CIS

CSM [tʃiɛsse'ɛmme] *sigla m* (= *consiglio superiore della magistratura*) Magistrates' Board of Supervisors

'Cuba *sf* Cuba; **cu'bano, -a** *ag, sm/f* Cuban

cu'betto *sm*: ~ **di ghiaccio** ice cube

'cubico, -a, -ci, -che *ag* cubic

cu'bista, -i, -e *ag* (*Arte*) Cubist ▷ *sf* podium dancer *dancer who performs on stage in a club*

'cubo, -a *ag* cubic ▷ *sm* cube; **elevare al ~** (*Mat*) to cube

cuc'cagna [kuk'kaɲɲa] *sf*: **paese della ~** land of plenty; **albero della ~** greasy pole (*fig*)

cuc'cetta [kut'tʃetta] *sf* (*Ferr*) couchette; (*Naut*) berth

cucchiai'ata [kukkja'jata] *sf* spoonful

cucchia'ino [kukkja'ino] *sm* teaspoon; coffee spoon

cucchi'aio [kuk'kjajo] *sm* spoon

'cuccia, -ce ['kuttʃa] *sf* dog's bed; **a ~!** down!

'cucciolo ['kuttʃolo] *sm* cub; (*di cane*) puppy

cu'cina [ku'tʃina] *sf* (*locale*) kitchen; (*arte culinaria*) cooking, cookery; (*le vivande*) food, cooking; (*apparecchio*) cooker; **~ componibile** fitted kitchen; **cuci'nare** /72/ *vt* to cook

cu'cire [ku'tʃire] /31/ *vt* to sew, stitch; **cuci'trice** *sf* stapler

cucù cuckoo

'cuffia *sf* bonnet, cap; (*da infermiera*) cap; (*da bagno*) (bathing) cap; (*per ascoltare*) headphones *pl*, headset

cu'gino, -a [ku'dʒino] *sm/f* cousin

PAROLA CHIAVE

'cui *pron* **1** (*nei complementi indiretti: persona*) whom; (: *oggetto, animale*) which; **la persona/le persone a cui accennavi** the person/people you were referring to o to whom you were referring; **i libri di cui parlavo** the books I was talking about o about which I was talking; **il quartiere in cui abito** the district where I live; **la ragione per cui** the reason why **2** (*inserito tra articolo e sostantivo*) whose; **la donna i cui figli sono scomparsi** the woman whose children have disappeared; **il**

signore, dal cui figlio ho avuto il libro the man from whose son I got the book

culi'naria *sf* cookery

'culla *sf* cradle

cul'lare /72/ *vt* to rock

'culmine *sm* top, summit

'culo *sm* (*fam !*) arse (*BRIT !*), ass (*US !*); (*fig: fortuna*): **aver ~** to have the luck of the devil

'culto *sm* (*religione*) religion; (*adorazione*) worship, adoration; (*venerazione: anche fig*) cult

cul'tura *sf* culture; (*conoscenza*) education, learning; **cultu'rale** *ag* cultural

cultu'rismo *sm* body-building

cumula'tivo, -a *ag* cumulative; (*prezzo*) inclusive; (*biglietto*) group *cpd*

'cumulo *sm* (*mucchio*) pile, heap; (*Meteor*) cumulus

cu'netta *sf* (*scolo*) gutter; (*avvallamento*) dip

cu'ocere ['kwɔtʃere] /32/ *vt* (*alimenti*) to cook; (*mattoni ecc*) to fire ▷ *vi* to cook; **~ al forno** (*pane*) to bake; (*arrosto*) to roast; **cu'oco, -a, -chi, -che** *sm/f* cook; (*di ristorante*) chef

cu'oio *sm* leather; **~ capelluto** scalp

cu'ore *sm* heart; **cuori** *smpl* (*Carte*) hearts; **avere buon ~** to be kind-hearted; **stare a ~ a qn** to be important to sb

'cupo, -a *ag* dark; (*suono*) dull; (*fig*) gloomy, dismal

'cupola *sf* dome; (*più piccola*) cupola

'cura *sf* care; (*Med: trattamento*) (course of) treatment; **aver ~ di** (*occuparsi di*) to take care of; **a ~ di** (*libro*) edited by; **~ dimagrante** diet

cu'rare /72/ *vt* (*malato, malattia*) to treat; (: *guarire*) to cure; (*aver cura di*) to take care of; (*testo*) to edit; **curarsi** *vpr* to take care of o.s.; (*Med*) to follow a course of treatment; **curarsi di** to pay attention to

curio'sare /72/ *vi* to look round, wander round; (*tra libri*) to browse; **~ nei negozi** to look *o* wander round the shops

curiosità *sf inv* curiosity; (*cosa rara*) curio, curiosity

curi'oso, -a *ag* curious; **essere ~ di** to be curious about

cur'sore *sm* (*Inform*) cursor

'curva *sf* curve; (*stradale*) bend, curve

cur'vare /72/ *vt* to bend ▷ *vi* (*veicolo*) to take a bend; (*strada*) to bend, curve; **curvarsi** *vpr* to bend; (*legno*) to warp

'curvo, -a *ag* curved; (*piegato*) bent

cusci'netto [kuʃʃi'netto] *sm* pad; (*Tecn*) bearing ▷ *ag inv*: **stato ~** buffer state; **~ a sfere** ball bearing

cu'scino [kuʃʃino] *sm* cushion; (*guanciale*) pillow

cus'tode *smf* keeper, custodian

cus'todia *sf* care; (*Dir*) custody; (*astuccio*) case, holder

custo'dire /55/ *vt* (*conservare*) to keep; (*assistere*) to look after, take care of; (*fare la guardia*) to guard

C.V. *abbr* (= *cavallo vapore*) h.p.

cyberca'ffè [tʃiberka'fe] *sm inv* cybercafé

cyber'nauta, -i, -e *sm/f* Internet surfer

cyber'spazio *sm* cyberspace

PAROLA CHIAVE

da (*da + il* = **dal**, *da + lo* = **dallo**, *da + l'* = **dall'**, *da + la* = **dalla**, *da + i* = **dai**, *da + gli* = **dagli**, *da + le* = **dalle**) *prep*
1 (*agente*) by; **dipinto da un grande artista** painted by a great artist
2 (*causa*) with; **tremare dalla paura** to tremble with fear
3 (*stato in luogo*) at; **abito da lui** I'm living at his house *o* with him; **sono dal giornalaio** I'm at the newsagent's; **era da Francesco** she was at Francesco's (house)
4 (*moto a luogo*) to; (*moto per luogo*) through; **vado da Pietro/dal giornalaio** I'm going to Pietro's (house)/to the newsagent's; **sono passati dalla finestra** they came in through the window
5 (*provenienza, allontanamento*) from; **arrivare/partire da Milano** to

arrive/depart from Milan; **scendere dal treno/dalla macchina** to get off the train/out of the car; **si trova a 5 km da qui** it's 5 km from here 6 (*tempo: durata*) for; (: *a partire da: nel passato*) since; (: *nel futuro*) from; **vivo qui da un anno** I've been living here for a year; **è dalle 3 che ti aspetto** I've been waiting for you since 3 (o'clock); **da oggi in poi** from today onwards; **da bambino** as a child, when I (*o* he *ecc*) was a child 7 (*modo, maniera*) like; **comportarsi da uomo** to behave like a man; **l'ho fatto da me** I did it (by) myself 8 (*descrittivo*): **una macchina da corsa** a racing car; **una ragazza dai capelli biondi** a girl with blonde hair; **un vestito da 100 euro** a 100 euro dress

dà *vb vedi* **dare**

dac'capo *av* (*di nuovo*) (once) again; (*dal principio*) all over again, from the beginning

'**dado** *sm* (*da gioco*) dice *o* die; (*Cuc*) stock cube (BRIT), bouillon cube (US); (*Tecn*) (*screw*) nut; **dadi** *smpl* (*game of*) dice; **giocare a dadi** to play dice

'**daino** *sm* (fallow) deer *inv*; (*pelle*) buckskin

dal'tonico, -a, -ci, -che *ag* colour-blind

'**dama** *sf* lady; (*nei balli*) partner; (*gioco*) draughts *sg* (BRIT), checkers *sg* (US)

damigi'ana [dami'dʒana] *sf* demijohn

da'nese *ag* Danish ▷ *smf* Dane ▷ *sm* (*Ling*) Danish; **Dani'marca** *sf*: **la Danimarca** Denmark

dannazi'one [dannat'tsjone] *sf* damnation

danneggi'are [danned'dʒare] /62/ *vt* to damage; (*rovinare*) to spoil; (*nuocere*) to harm

'**danno** *sm* damage; (*a persona*) harm, injury; **danni** *smpl* (*Dir*) damages;

dan'noso, -a *ag*: **dannoso (a** *o* **per)** harmful (to), bad (for)

Da'nubio *sm*: **il ~** the Danube

'**danza** ['dantsa] *sf*: **la ~** dancing; **una ~** a dance; **dan'zare** /72/ *vt, vi* to dance

dapper'tutto *av* everywhere

dap'prima *av* at first

'**dare** /33/ *sm* (*Comm*) debit ▷ *vt* to give; (*produrre: frutti, suono*) to produce ▷ *vi* (*guardare*): **~ su** to look (out) onto; **darsi** *vpr*: **darsi a** to dedicate o.s. to; **~ da mangiare a qn** to give sb something to eat; **~ per certo qc** to consider sth certain; **~ per morto qn** to give sb up for dead; **darsi al bere** to take to drink; **darsi al commercio** to go into business; **darsi per vinto** to give in

'**data** *sf* date; **~ di nascita** date of birth; **~ di scadenza** expiry date; **~ limite d'utilizzo** *o* **di consumo** (*Comm*) best-before date

'**dato, -a** *ag* (*stabilito*) given ▷ *sm* datum; **dati** *smpl* data *pl*: **~ che** given that; **è un ~ di fatto** it's a fact; **dati sensibili** sense data

da'tore, -'trice *sm/f*: **~ di lavoro** employer

'**dattero** *sm* date (*Bot*)

dattilogra'fia *sf* typing

datti'lografo, -a *sm/f* typist

da'vanti *av* in front; (*dirimpetto*) opposite ▷ *ag inv* front ▷ *sm* front; **~ a** in front of; (*dirimpetto a*) facing, opposite; (*in presenza di*) before, in front of

davan'zale [davan'tsale] *sm* windowsill

dav'vero *av* really, indeed

d.C. *abbr* (= *dopo Cristo*) A.D.

'**dea** *sf* goddess

'**debbo** *ecc vb vedi* **dovere**

'**debito, -a** *ag* due, proper ▷ *sm* debt; (*Comm: dare*) debit; **a tempo ~** at the right time

'**debole** *ag* weak, feeble; (*suono*) faint; (*luce*) dim ▷ *sm* weakness; **debo'lezza** *sf* weakness

debut'tare /72/ *vi* to make one's début

deca'denza [deka'dɛntsa] *sf* decline; (*Dir*) loss, forfeiture

decaffei'nato, -a *ag* decaffeinated

decapi'tare /72/ *vt* to decapitate, behead

decappot'tabile *ag, sf* convertible

de'cennio [de'tʃɛnnjo] *sm* decade

de'cente [de'tʃɛnte] *ag* decent, respectable, proper; (*accettabile*) satisfactory, decent

de'cesso [de'tʃɛsso] *sm* death

de'cidere [de'tʃidere] /34/ *vt*: **~ qc** to decide on sth; (*questione, lite*) to settle sth; **decidersi** *vpr*: **decidersi (a fare)** to decide (to do), make up one's mind (to do); **~ di fare/che** to decide to do/that; **~ di qc** (*cosa*) to determine sth

deci'frare [detʃi'frare] /72/ *vt* to decode; (*fig*) to decipher, make out

deci'male [detʃi'male] *ag* decimal

'decimo, -a [dɛtʃimo] *num* tenth

de'cina [de'tʃina] *sf* ten; (*circa dieci*): **una ~ (di)** about ten

de'cisi *ecc* [de'tʃizi] *vb vedi* **decidere**

decisi'one [detʃi'zjone] *sf* decision; **prendere una ~** to make a decision

deci'sivo, -a [detʃi'zivo] *ag* (*gen*) decisive; (*fattore*) deciding

de'ciso, -a [de'tʃizo] *pp di* **decidere**

decli'nare /72/ *vi* (*pendio*) to slope down; (*fig: diminuire*) to decline ▷ *vt* to decline

declinazi'one *sf* (*Ling*) declension

de'clino *sm* decline

decodifica'tore *sm* (*Tel*) decoder

decol'lare /72/ *vi* (*Aer*) to take off; **de'collo** *sm* take-off

deco'rare /72/ *vt* to decorate; **decorazi'one** *sf* decoration

de'creto *sm* decree; **~ legge** *decree with the force of law*

'dedica, -che *sf* dedication

dedi'care /20/ *vt* to dedicate; **dedicarsi** *vpr*: **dedicarsi a** to devote o.s. to

dediche'rò *ecc* [dedike'rɔ] *vb vedi* **dedicare**

'dedito, -a *ag*: **~ a** (*studio ecc*) dedicated o devoted to; (*vizio*) addicted to

de'duco *ecc vb vedi* **dedurre**

de'durre /90/ *vt* (*concludere*) to deduce; (*defalcare*) to deduct

de'dussi *ecc vb vedi* **dedurre**

defici'ente [defi'tʃɛnte] *ag* (*insufficiente*) insufficient; **~ di** (*mancante*) deficient in ▷ *smf* mental defective; (*peg: cretino*) idiot

'deficit ['dɛfitʃit] *sm inv* (*Econ*) deficit

defi'nire /55/ *vt* to define; (*risolvere*) to settle; **defini'tivo, -a** *ag* definitive, final ▷ *sf*: **in definitiva** (*dopotutto*) when all is said and done; (*dunque*) hence; **definizi'one** *sf* definition; (*di disputa, vertenza*) settlement

defor'mare /72/ *vt* (*alterare*) to put out of shape; (*corpo*) to deform; (*pensiero, fatto*) to distort; **deformarsi** *vpr* to lose its shape

de'forme *ag* deformed; disfigured

de'funto, -a *ag* late *cpd* ▷ *sm/f* deceased

degene'rare [dedʒene'rare] /72/ *vi* to degenerate

de'gente [de'dʒɛnte] *smf* (*ricoverato in ospedale*) in-patient

deglu'tire /55/ *vt* to swallow

de'gnare [deɲ'ɲare] /15/ *vt*: **~ qn della propria presenza** to honour sb with one's presence; **degnarsi** *vpr*: **degnarsi di fare qc** to deign o condescend to do sth

'degno, -a *ag* dignified; **~ di** worthy of; **~ di lode** praiseworthy

de'grado *sm*: **~ urbano** urban decline

'delega, -ghe *sf* (*procura*) proxy

dele'terio, -a *ag* damaging; (*per salute ecc*) harmful

del'fino *sm* (*Zool*) dolphin; (*Storia*) dauphin; (*fig*) probable successor

deli'cato, -a *ag* delicate; (*salute*) delicate, frail; (*fig: gentile*) thoughtful, considerate; (: *che dimostra tatto*) tactful

delin'quente *smf* criminal, delinquent; **~ abituale** regular offender, habitual offender; **delin'quenza** *sf* criminality, delinquency; **delinquenza minorile** juvenile delinquency

deli'rare /72/ *vi* to be delirious, rave; (*fig*) to rave

de'lirio *sm* delirium; (*ragionamento insensato*) raving; (*fig*): **andare/ mandare in ~** to go/send into a frenzy

de'litto *sm* crime

delizi'oso, -a [delit'tsjoso] *ag* delightful; (*cibi*) delicious

delta'plano *sm* hang-glider; **volo col ~** hang-gliding

delu'dente *ag* disappointing

de'ludere /35/ *vt* to disappoint; **delusi'one** *sf* disappointment; **de'luso, -a** *pp di* **deludere**

'demmo *vb vedi* **dare**

demo'cratico, -a, -ci, -che *ag* democratic

democra'zia [demokrat'tsia] *sf* democracy

demo'lire /55/ *vt* to demolish

de'monio *sm* demon, devil; **il D~** the Devil

de'naro *sm* money

densità *sf inv* density

'denso, -a *ag* thick, dense

den'tale *ag* dental

'dente *sm* tooth; (*di forchetta*) prong; **al ~** (*Cuc: pasta*) al dente; **denti del giudizio** wisdom teeth; **denti da latte** milk teeth; **denti'era** *sf* (set of) false teeth *pl*

denti'fricio [denti'fritʃo] *sm* toothpaste

den'tista, -i, -e *sm/f* dentist

'dentro *av* inside; (*in casa*) indoors; (*fig: nell'intimo*) inwardly ▷ *prep*: **~ (a)** in; **piegato in ~** folded over; **qui/ là ~** in here/there; **~ di sé** (*pensare, brontolare*) to oneself

de'nuncia, -ce *o* **-cie** [de'nuntʃa] *sf* denunciation; declaration; **~ del reddito** (income) tax return

denunci'are [denun'tʃare] /14/ *vt* to denounce; (*dichiarare*) to declare; **~ qn/qc (alla polizia)** to report sb/sth to the police

denu'trito, -a *ag* undernourished

denutrizi'one [denutrit'tsjone] *sf* malnutrition

deodo'rante *sm* deodorant

depe'rire /55/ *vi* to waste away

depi'larsi /72/ *vpr*: **~ (le gambe)** (*con rasoio*) to shave (one's legs); (*con ceretta*) to wax (one's legs)

depila'torio, -a *ag* hair-removing *cpd*, depilatory

dépli'ant [depli'ã] *sm inv* leaflet; (*opuscolo*) brochure

deplo'revole *ag* deplorable

de'pone, de'pongo *ecc vb vedi* **deporre**

de'porre /77/ *vt* (*depositare*) to put down; (*rimuovere: da una carica*) to remove; (: *re*) to depose; (*Dir*) to testify

depor'tare /72/ *vt* to deport

de'posi *ecc vb vedi* **deporre**

deposi'tare /72/ *vt* (*gen, Geo, Econ*) to deposit; (*lasciare*) to leave; (*merci*) to store; **depositarsi** *vpr* (*sabbia, polvere*) to settle

de'posito *sm* deposit; (*luogo*) warehouse; depot; (: *Mil*) depot; **~ bagagli** left-luggage office

deposizi'one [depozit'tsjone] *sf* deposition; (*da una carica*) removal

depra'vato, -a *ag* depraved ▷ *sm/f* degenerate

depre'dare /72/ *vt* to rob, plunder

depressi'one *sf* depression

de'presso, -a *pp di* **deprimere** ▷ *ag* depressed

deprez'zare [depret'tsare] /72/ *vt* (*Econ*) to depreciate

depri'mente *ag* depressing

de'primere /50/ *vt* to depress

depu'rare /72/ *vt* to purify

depu'tato, -a *sm/f (Pol)* deputy, ≈ Member of Parliament (*BRIT*), ≈ Congressman/woman (*US*)

deragli'are [deraʎ'ʎare] /27/ *vi* to be derailed; **far ~** to derail

de'ridere /89/ *vt* to mock, deride

de'risi *ecc vb vedi* **deridere**

de'riva *sf (Naut, Aer)* drift; **andare alla ~** (*anche fig*) to drift

deri'vare /72/ *vi*: **~ da** to derive from ▷ *vt* to derive; (*corso d'acqua*) to divert

derma'tologo, -a, -gi, -ghe *sm/f* dermatologist

deru'bare /72/ *vt* to rob

des'crivere /105/ *vt* to describe; **descrizi'one** *sf* description

de'serto, -a *ag* deserted ▷ *sm (Geo)* desert; **isola deserta** desert island

deside'rare /72/ *vt* to want, wish for; (*sessualmente*) to desire; **~ fare/ che qn faccia** to want o wish to do/sb to do; **desidera fare una passeggiata?** would you like to go for a walk?

desi'derio *sm* wish; (*più intenso, carnale*) desire

deside'roso, -a *ag*: **~ di** longing o eager for

desi'nenza [dezi'nɛntsa] *sf (Ling)* ending, inflexion

de'sistere /11/ *vi*: **~ da** to give up, desist from

deso'lato, -a *ag (paesaggio)* desolate; (*persona: spiacente*) sorry

'dessi *ecc vb vedi* **dare**

'deste *ecc vb vedi* **dare**

desti'nare /72/ *vt* to destine; (*assegnare*) to appoint, assign; (*indirizzare*) to address; **~ qc a qn** to intend to give sth to sb, intend sb to have sth; **destina'tario, -a** *sm/f (di lettera)* addressee

destinazi'one [destinat'tsjone] *sf* destination; (*uso*) purpose

des'tino *sm* destiny, fate

destitu'ire /55/ *vt* to dismiss, remove

'destra *sf vedi* **destro**

destreggi'arsi [destred'dʒarsi] /62/ *vpr* to manoeuvre (*BRIT*), maneuver (*US*)

des'trezza [des'trettsa] *sf* skill, dexterity

'destro, -a *ag* right, right-hand ▷ *sf (mano)* right hand; (*parte*) right (side); (*Pol*): **la destra** the right; **a destra** (*essere*) on the right; (*andare*) to the right

dete'nuto, -a *sm/f* prisoner

deter'gente [deter'dʒɛnte] *ag (crema, latte)* cleansing ▷ *sm* cleanser

> Attenzione! In inglese esiste la parola *detergent*, che però significa *detersivo*.

determi'nare /72/ *vt* to determine

determina'tivo, -a *ag* determining; **articolo ~** (*Ling*) definite article

determi'nato, -a *ag (gen)* certain; (*particolare*) specific; (*risoluto*) determined, resolute

deter'sivo *sm* detergent

detes'tare /72/ *vt* to detest, hate

de'trae, de'traggo *ecc vb vedi* **detrarre**

de'trarre /123/ *vt*: **~ (da)** to deduct (from), take away (from)

de'trassi *ecc vb vedi* **detrarre**

'detta *sf*: **a ~ di** according to

det'taglio [det'taʎʎo] *sm* detail; (*Comm*): **il ~** retail; **al ~** (*Comm*) retail; separately

det'tare /72/ *vt* to dictate; **~ legge** (*fig*) to lay down the law; **det'tato** *sm* dictation

'detto, -a *pp di* **dire** ▷ *ag* (*soprannominato*) called, known as; (*già nominato*) above-mentioned ▷ *sm* saying; **~ fatto** no sooner said than done

devas'tare /72/ *vt* to devastate; (*fig*) to ravage

devi'are /19/ *vi*: **~ (da)** to turn off (from) ▷ *vt* to divert; **deviazi'one** *sf* (*anche Aut*) diversion

'devo *ecc vb vedi* **dovere**

de'volvere /94/ vt (Dir) to transfer, devolve

de'voto, -a ag (Rel) devout, pious; (affezionato) devoted

devozi'one [devot'tsjone] sf devoutness; (anche Rel) devotion

dezip'pare [dedzip'pare] /72/ vt (Inform) to unzip

PAROLA CHIAVE

di (di + il = **del**, di + lo = **dello**, di + l' = **dell'**, di + la = **della**, di + i = **dei**, di + gli = **degli**, di + le = **delle**) prep **1** (possesso, specificazione) of; (composto da, scritto da) by; **la macchina di Paolo/di mio fratello** Paolo's/my brother's car; **un amico di mio fratello** a friend of my brother's, one of my brother's friends; **un quadro di Botticelli** a painting by Botticelli

2 (caratterizzazione, misura) of; **una casa di mattoni** a brick house, a house made of bricks; **un orologio d'oro** a gold watch; **un bimbo di 3 anni** a child of 3, a 3-year-old child

3 (causa, mezzo, modo) with; **tremare di paura** to tremble with fear; **morire di cancro** to die of cancer; **spalmare di burro** to spread with butter

4 (argomento) about, of; **discutere di sport** to talk about sport

5 (luogo, provenienza) from; out of; **essere di Roma** to be from Rome; **uscire di casa** to come out of o leave the house

6 (tempo) in; **d'estate/d'inverno** in (the) summer/winter; **di notte** by night, at night; **di mattina/sera** in the morning/evening; **di lunedì** on Mondays

▶ det (una certa quantità di) some; (: negativo) any; (interrogativo) any; some; **del pane** (some) bread; **delle caramelle** (some) sweets; **degli amici miei** some friends of mine; **vuoi del vino?** do you want some o any wine?

dia'bete sm diabetes sg

dia'betico, -a, -ci, -che ag, sm/f diabetic

dia'framma, -i sm (divisione) screen; (Anat, Fot: contraccettivo) diaphragm

di'agnosi [di'aɲɲozi] sf diagnosis sg

diago'nale ag, sf diagonal

dia'gramma, -i sm diagram

dia'letto sm dialect

di'alisi sf dialysis sg

di'alogo, -ghi sm dialogue

dia'mante sm diamond

di'ametro sm diameter

diaposi'tiva sf transparency, slide

di'ario sm diary

diar'rea sf diarrhoea

di'avolo sm devil

di'battito sm debate, discussion

'dice ['ditʃe] vb vedi **dire**

di'cembre [di'tʃɛmbre] sm December

dice'ria [ditʃe'ria] sf rumour, piece of gossip

dichia'rare [dikja'rare] /72/ vt to declare; **dichiararsi** vpr to declare o.s.; (innamorato) to declare one's love; **dichiararsi vinto** to admit defeat; **dichiarazi'one** sf declaration; **dichiarazione dei redditi** statement of income; (modulo) tax return

dician'nove [ditʃan'nɔve] num nineteen

dicias'sette [ditʃas'sɛtte] num seventeen

dici'otto [di'tʃɔtto] num eighteen

dici'tura [ditʃi'tura] sf words pl, wording

'dico ecc vb vedi **dire**

didasca'lia sf (di illustrazione) caption; (Cine) subtitle; (Teat) stage directions pl

di'dattico, -a, -ci, -che ag didactic; (metodo, programma) teaching; (libro) educational

di'eci ['djɛtʃi] num ten

di'edi ecc vb vedi **dare**

'diesel ['di:zəl] sm inv diesel engine

dies'sino, -a *sm/f* member of the DS political party

di'eta *sf* diet; **essere a ~** to be on a diet

di'etro *av* behind; (*in fondo*) at the back ▷ *prep* behind; (*tempo: dopo*) after ▷ *sm* back, rear ▷ *ag inv* back *cpd*; **le zampe di ~** the hind legs; **~ richiesta** on demand; (*scritta*) on application

di'fendere /36/ *vt* to defend; **difendersi** *vpr* (*cavarsela*) to get by; **difendersi da/contro** to defend o.s. from/against; **difendersi dal freddo** to protect o.s. from the cold; **difen'sore, -a** *sm/f* defender; **avvocato difensore** counsel for the defence (BRIT) o defense (US); **di'fesa** *sf vedi* **difeso**

di'fesi *ecc vb vedi* **difendere**

di'fetto *sm* (*mancanza*): **~ di** lack of; shortage of; (*di fabbricazione*) fault, flaw, defect; (*morale*) fault, failing, defect; (*fisico*) defect; **far ~** to be lacking; **in ~** at fault; in the wrong; **difet'toso, -a** *ag* defective, faulty

diffe'rente *ag* different

diffe'renza [diffe'rɛntsa] *sf* difference; **a ~ di** unlike

diffe'rire /55/ *vt* to postpone, defer ▷ *vi* to be different

diffe'rita *sf*: **in ~** (*trasmettere*) prerecorded

dif'ficile [dif'fitʃile] *ag* difficult; (*persona*) hard to please, difficult (to please); (*poco probabile*): **è ~ che sia libero** it is unlikely that he'll be free ▷ *sm* difficult part; difficulty; **difficoltà** *sf inv* difficulty

diffi'dente *ag* suspicious, distrustful

diffi'denza *sf* suspicion, distrust

dif'fondere /25/ *vt* (*luce, calore*) to diffuse; (*notizie*) to spread, circulate; **diffondersi** *vpr* to spread

dif'fusi *ecc vb vedi* **diffondere**

dif'fuso, -a *pp di* **diffondere** ▷ *ag* (*fenomeno, notizia, malattia ecc*) widespread

'diga, -ghe *sf* dam; (*portuale*) breakwater

dige'rente [didʒe'rɛnte] *ag* (*apparato*) digestive

dige'rire [didʒe'rire] /55/ *vt* to digest; **digesti'one** *sf* digestion; **diges'tivo, -a** *ag* digestive ▷ *sm* (after-dinner) liqueur

digi'tale [didʒi'tale] *ag* digital; (*delle dita*) finger *cpd*, digital ▷ *sf* (*Bot*) foxglove

digi'tare [didʒi'tare] /72/ *vt* (*dati*) to key (in)

digiu'nare [didʒu'nare] /72/ *vi* to starve o.s.; (*Rel*) to fast; **digi'uno, -a** *ag*: **essere digiuno** not to have eaten ▷ *sm* fast; **a digiuno** on an empty stomach

dignità [diɲɲi'ta] *sf inv* dignity

'DIGOS *sigla f* (= *Divisione Investigazioni Generali e Operazioni Speciali*) police department dealing with political security

digri'gnare [digriɲ'ɲare] /15/ *vt*: **~ i denti** to grind one's teeth

dilapi'dare /72/ *vt* to squander, waste

dila'tare /72/ *vt* to dilate; (*gas*) to cause to expand; (*passaggio, cavità*) to open (up); **dilatarsi** *vpr* to dilate; (*Fisica*) to expand

dilazio'nare [dilattsjo'nare] /72/ *vt* to delay, defer

di'lemma, -i *sm* dilemma

dilet'tante *smf* dilettante; (*anche Sport*) amateur

dili'gente [dili'dʒɛnte] *ag* (*scrupoloso*) diligent; (*accurato*) careful, accurate

dilu'ire /55/ *vt* to dilute

dilun'garsi /80/ *vpr* (*fig*): **~ su** to talk at length on o about

diluvi'are /19/ *vb impers* to pour (down)

di'luvio *sm* downpour; (*inondazione, fig*) flood

dima'grante *ag* slimming *cpd*

dima'grire /55/ *vi* to get thinner, lose weight

dime'nare /72/ vt to wave, shake; **dimenarsi** vpr to toss and turn; (fig) to struggle; **~ la coda** (cane) to wag its tail

dimensi'one sf dimension; (grandezza) size

dimenti'canza [dimenti'kantsa] sf forgetfulness; (errore) oversight, slip; **per ~** inadvertently

dimenti'care /20/ vt to forget; **dimenticarsi** vpr: **dimenticarsi di qc** to forget sth

dimesti'chezza [dimesti'kettsa] sf familiarity

di'mettere /63/ vt: **~ qn da** to dismiss sb from; (dall'ospedale) to discharge sb from; **dimettersi** vpr: **dimettersi (da)** to resign (from)

dimez'zare [dimed'dzare] /72/ vt to halve

diminu'ire /55/ vt to reduce, diminish; (prezzi) to bring down, reduce ▷ vi to decrease, diminish; (rumore) to die down, die away; (prezzi) to fall, go down

diminu'tivo, -a ag, sm diminutive

diminuzi'one [diminut'tsjone] sf decreasing, diminishing

di'misi ecc vb vedi **dimettere**

dimissi'oni sfpl resignation sg: **dare** o **presentare le ~** to resign, hand in one's resignation

dimos'trare /72/ vt to demonstrate, show; (provare) to prove, demonstrate; **dimostrarsi** vpr: **dimostrarsi molto abile** to show o.s. o prove to be very clever; **dimostra 30 anni** he looks about 30 (years old); **dimostrazi'one** sf demonstration; proof

di'namico, -a, -ci, -che ag dynamic ▷ sf dynamics sg

dina'mite sf dynamite

'dinamo sf inv dynamo

dino'sauro sm dinosaur

din'torno av round; **dintorni** smpl outskirts; **nei dintorni di** in the vicinity o neighbourhood of

'dio (pl **dei**) sm god; **D~** God; **gli dei** the gods; **D~ m~!** my God!

diparti'mento sm department

dipen'dente ag dependent ▷ smf employee; **~ statale** state employee

di'pendere /8/ vi: **~ da** to depend on; (finanziariamente) to be dependent on; (derivare) to come from, be due to

di'pesi ecc vb vedi **dipendere**

di'pingere [di'pindʒere] /37/ vt to paint

di'pinsi ecc vb vedi **dipingere**

di'pinto, -a pp di **dipingere** ▷ sm painting

di'ploma, -i sm diploma

diplo'matico, -a, -ci, -che ag diplomatic ▷ sm diplomat

diploma'zia [diplomat'tsia] sf diplomacy

di'porto sm: **imbarcazione da ~** pleasure craft

dira'dare /72/ vt to thin (out); (visite) to reduce, make less frequent; **diradarsi** vpr to disperse; (nebbia) to clear (up)

'dire /38/ vt to say; (segreto, fatto) to tell; **~ qc a qn** to tell sb sth; **~ a qn di fare qc** to tell sb to do sth; **~ di sì/no** to say yes/no; **si dice che ...** they say that ...; **si direbbe che ...** it looks (o sounds) as though ...; **dica, signora?** (in un negozio) yes, Madam, can I help you?

di'ressi ecc vb vedi **dirigere**

di'retta sf: **in ~** (trasmettere) live; **un incontro di calcio in ~** a live football match

di'retto, -a pp di **dirigere** ▷ ag direct ▷ sm (Ferr) through train

diret'tore, -'trice sm/f (di azienda) director, manager (manageress); (di scuola elementare) head (teacher) (BRIT), principal (US); **~ d'orchestra** conductor; **~ vendite** sales director o manager; **direzi'one** sf board of directors; management; (senso: anche fig) direction; **in direzione di** in the direction of, towards

diri'gente [diri'dʒɛnte] *smf* executive; (*Pol*) leader ▷ *ag*: **classe ~** ruling class; **di'rigere** /39/ *vt* to direct; (*impresa*) to run, manage; (*Mus*) to conduct; **dirigersi** *vpr*: **dirigersi verso** *o* **a** to make *o* head for

dirim'petto *av* opposite; **~ a** opposite, facing

di'ritto, -a *ag* straight; (*onesto*) straight, upright ▷ *av* straight, directly ▷ *sm* right side; (*Tennis*) forehand; (*Maglia*) plain stitch; (*prerogativa*) right; (*leggi, scienza*): **il ~** law; **diritti** *smpl* (*tasse*) duty *sg*: **stare ~** to stand up straight; **aver ~ a qc** to be entitled to sth; **andare ~** to go straight on; **diritti (d'autore)** royalties

dirotta'mento *sm*: **~ (aereo)** hijack

dirot'tare /72/ *vt* (*nave, aereo*) to change the course of; (*aereo: sotto minaccia*) to hijack; (*traffico*) to divert ▷ *vi* (*nave, aereo*) to change course; **dirotta'tore, -'trice** *sm/f* hijacker

di'rotto, -a *ag* (*pioggia*) torrential; (*pianto*) unrestrained; **piovere a ~** to pour; **piangere a ~** to cry one's heart out

di'rupo *sm* crag, precipice

di'sabile *smf* disabled person ▷ *ag* disabled; **i disabili** the disabled

disabi'tato, -a *ag* uninhabited

disabitu'arsi /72/ *vpr*: **~ a** to get out of the habit of

disac'cordo *sm* disagreement

disadat'tato, -a *ag* (*Psic*) maladjusted

disa'dorno, -a *ag* plain, unadorned

disagi'ato, -a [diza'dʒato] *ag* poor, needy; (*vita*) hard

di'sagio [di'zadʒo] *sm* discomfort; (*disturbo*) inconvenience; (*fig: imbarazzo*) embarrassment; **essere a ~** to be ill at ease

disappro'vare /72/ *vt* to disapprove of; **disapprovazi'one** *sf* disapproval

disap'punto *sm* disappointment

disar'mare /72/ *vt, vi* to disarm; **di'sarmo** *sm* (*Mil*) disarmament

di'sastro *sm* disaster

disas'troso, -a *ag* disastrous

disat'tento, -a *ag* inattentive; **disattenzi'one** *sf* carelessness, lack of attention

disavven'tura *sf* misadventure, mishap

dis'capito *sm*: **a ~ di** to the detriment of

dis'carica, -che *sf* (*di rifiuti*) rubbish tip *o* dump

di'scendere [diʃʃendere] /101/ *vt* to go (*o come*) down ▷ *vi* to go (*o come*) down; (*strada*) to go down; (*smontare*) to get off; **~ da** (*famiglia*) to be descended from; **~ dalla macchina/ dal treno** to get out of the car/out of *o* off the train; **~ da cavallo** to dismount, get off one's horse

di'scesa [diʃʃesa] *sf* descent; (*pendio*) slope; **in ~** (*strada*) downhill *cpd*, sloping; **~ libera** (*Sci*) downhill (race)

disci'plina [diʃʃi'plina] *sf* discipline

'disco, -schi *sm* disc; (*Sport*) discus; (*fonografico*) record; (*Inform*) disk; **~ orario** (*Aut*) parking disc; **~ rigido** (*Inform*) hard disk; **~ volante** flying saucer

disco'grafico, -a, -ci, -che *ag* record *cpd*, recording *cpd* ▷ *sm* record producer; **casa discografica** record(ing) company

dis'correre /28/ *vi*: **~ (di)** to talk (about)

dis'corso, -a *pp di* **discorrere** ▷ *sm* speech; (*conversazione*) conversation, talk

disco'teca, -che *sf* (*raccolta*) record library; (*luogo di ballo*) disco(theque)

dis'count [dis'kaunt] *sm inv* (*supermercato*) cut-price supermarket

discre'panza [diskre'pantsa] *sf* discrepancy

dis'creto, -a *ag* discreet; (*abbastanza buono*) reasonable, fair

discriminazi'one
[diskriminat'tsjone] *sf*
discrimination

dis'cussi *ecc vb vedi* **discutere**

discussi'one *sf* discussion; (*litigio*)
argument; **fuori ~** out of the
question

dis'cutere /40/ *vt* to discuss, debate;
(*contestare*) to question ▷ *vi* (*litigare*)
to argue; (*conversare*): **~ (di)** to discuss

dis'detto, -a *pp di* **disdire** ▷ *sf*
(*di prenotazione ecc*) cancellation;
(*sfortuna*) bad luck

dis'dire /38/ *vt* (*prenotazione*) to
cancel; **~ un contratto d'affitto**
(*Dir*) to give notice (to quit)

dise'gnare [disen'nare] /15/ *vt* to
draw; (*progettare*) to design; (*fig*) to
outline; **disegna'tore, -'trice** *sm/f*
designer

di'segno [di'zenno] *sm* drawing;
(*su stoffa ecc*) design; (*fig: schema*)
outline; **~ di legge** (*Dir*) bill

diser'bante *sm* weedkiller

diser'tare /72/ *vt, vi* to desert

dis'fare /41/ *vt* to undo; (*valigie*) to
unpack; (*meccanismo*) to take to
pieces; (*neve*) to melt; **disfarsi** *vpr*
to come undone; (*neve*) to melt; **~ il
letto** to strip the bed; **disfarsi di qn**
(*liberarsi*) to get rid of sb; **dis'fatto, -a**
pp di **disfare**

dis'gelo [diz'dʒɛlo] *sm* thaw

dis'grazia [diz'grattsja] *sf* (*sventura*)
misfortune; (*incidente*) accident,
mishap

disgu'ido *sm* hitch; **~ postale** error in
postal delivery

disgus'tare /72/ *vt* to disgust

dis'gusto *sm* disgust; **disgus'toso, -a**
ag disgusting

disidra'tare /72/ *vt* to dehydrate

disimpa'rare /72/ *vt* to forget

disinfet'tante *ag, sm* disinfectant

disinfet'tare /72/ *vt* to disinfect

disini'bito, -a *ag* uninhibited

disinstal'lare /72/ *vt* (*software*) to
uninstall

disinte'grare /72/ *vt, vi* to
disintegrate; **disintegrarsi** *vpr* to
disintegrate

disinteres'sarsi /72/ *vpr*: **~ di** to
take no interest in; **disinte'resse**
sm indifference; (*generosità*)
unselfishness

disintossi'care /20/ *vt* (*alcolizzato,
drogato*) to treat for alcoholism (*o*
drug addiction); **disintossicarsi** *vpr*
to clear out one's system; (*alcolizzato,
drogato*) to be treated for alcoholism
(*o* drug addiction)

disin'volto, -a *ag* casual, free
and easy

dismi'sura *sf* excess; **a ~** to excess,
excessively

disoccu'pato, -a *ag* unemployed
▷ *sm/f* unemployed person;
disoccupazi'one *sf* unemployment

diso'nesto, -a *ag* dishonest

disordi'nato, -a *ag* untidy; (*privo di
misura*) irregular, wild; **di'sordine**
sm (*confusione*) disorder, confusion;
(*sregolatezza*) debauchery; **disordini**
smpl (*Pol: ecc*) disorder *sg*; (*tumulti*)
riots

disorien'tare /72/ *vt* to
disorientate

disorien'tato, -a *ag* disorientated

'dispari *ag inv* odd, uneven

dis'parte: **in ~** *av* (*da lato*) aside,
apart; **tenersi** *o* **starsene in ~** to
keep to o.s., hold aloof

dispendi'oso, -a *ag* expensive

dis'pensa *sf* pantry, larder; (*mobile*)
sideboard; (*Dir*) exemption; (*Rel*)
dispensation; (*fascicolo*) number,
issue

dispe'rato, -a *ag* (*persona*) in despair;
(*caso, tentativo*) desperate

disperazi'one *sf* despair

dis'perdere /73/ *vt* (*disseminare*) to
disperse; (*Mil*) to scatter, rout; (*fig:
consumare*) to waste, squander;
disperdersi *vpr* to disperse;
to scatter; **dis'perso, -a** *pp di*
disperdere ▷ *sm/f* missing person

dis'petto *sm* spite *no pl*, spitefulness *no pl*; **fare un ~ a qn** to play a (nasty) trick on sb; **a ~ di** in spite of; **dispet'toso, -a** *ag* spiteful

dispia'cere [dispja'tʃere] /74/ *sm* (*rammarico*) regret, sorrow; (*dolore*) grief ▷ *vi*: **~ a** to displease ▷ *vb impers*: **mi dispiace (che)** I am sorry (that); **le dispiace se…?** do you mind if …?; **dispiaceri** *smpl* (*preoccupazioni*) troubles, worries

dis'pone, dis'pongo *ecc vb vedi* **disporre**

dispo'nibile *ag* available

dis'porre /77/ *vt* (*sistemare*) to arrange; (*preparare*) to prepare; (*Dir*) to order; (*persuadere*): **~ qn a** to incline *o* dispose sb towards ▷ *vi* (*decidere*) to decide; (*usufruire*): **~ di** to use, have at one's disposal; (*essere dotato*): **~ di** to have the use of …

dis'posi *ecc vb vedi* **disporre**

disposi'tivo *sm* (*meccanismo*) device

disposizi'one [dispozit'tsjone] *sf* arrangement, layout; (*stato d'animo*) mood; (*tendenza*) bent, inclination; (*comando*) order; (*Dir*) provision, regulation; **a ~ di qn** at sb's disposal

dis'posto, -a *pp di* **disporre**

disprez'zare [dispret'tsare] /72/ *vt* to despise

dis'prezzo [dis'prettso] *sm* contempt

'disputa *sf* dispute, quarrel

dispu'tare /72/ *vt* (*contendere*) to dispute, contest; (*gara*) to take part in ▷ *vi* to quarrel; **~ di** to discuss; **disputarsi qc** to fight for sth

'disse *vb vedi* **dire**

dissente'ria *sf* dysentery

dis'sento, -a *pp di* **disporre**...

'dissi *vb vedi* **dire**

dissimu'lare /72/ *vt* (*fingere*) to dissemble; (*nascondere*) to conceal

dissi'pare /72/ *vt* to dissipate; (*scialacquare*) to squander, waste

dissu'adere /88/ *vt*: **~ qn da** to dissuade sb from

dissua'sore *sm*: **~ di velocità** (*Aut*) speed bump

distac'care /20/ *vt* to detach, separate; (*Sport*) to leave behind; **distaccarsi** *vpr* to be detached; (*fig*) to stand out; **distaccarsi da** (*fig*) (*allontanarsi*) to grow away from

dis'tacco, -chi *sm* (*separazione*) separation; (*fig: indifferenza*) detachment; (*Sport*): **vincere con un ~ di …** to win by a distance of …

dis'tante *av* far away ▷ *ag*: **essere ~ (da)** to be a long way (from)

dis'tanza [dis'tantsa] *sf* distance

distanzi'are [distan'tsjare] /19/ *vt* to space out, place at intervals; (*Sport*) to outdistance; (*fig: superare*) to outstrip, surpass

dis'tare /72/ *vi*: **distiamo pochi chilometri da Roma** we are only a few kilometres (away) from Rome; **quanto dista il centro da qui?** how far is the town centre?

dis'tendere /120/ *vt* (*coperta*) to spread out; (*gambe*) to stretch (out); (*mettere a giacere*) to lay; (*rilassare: muscoli, nervi*) to relax; **distendersi** *vpr* (*rilassarsi*) to relax; (*sdraiarsi*) to lie down

dis'teso, -a *pp di* **distendere** ▷ *sf* expanse, stretch

distil'lare /72/ *vt* to distil

distille'ria *sf* distillery

dis'tinguere /42/ *vt* to distinguish; **distinguersi** *vpr* (*essere riconoscibile*) to be distinguished; (*emergere*) to stand out, be conspicuous; distinguish o.s.

dis'tinta *sf* (*nota*) note; (*elenco*) list; **~ di versamento** pay-in slip

distin'tivo, -a *ag* distinctive; distinguishing ▷ *sm* badge

dis'tinto, -a *pp di* **distinguere** ▷ *ag* (*dignitoso ed elegante*) distinguished; **distinti saluti** (*in lettera*) yours faithfully

distinzi'one [distin'tsjone] *sf*
distinction

dis'togliere [dis'tɔʎʎere] /122/
vt: **~ da** to take away from; (*fig*) to
dissuade from

distorsi'one *sf* (*Med*) sprain; (*Fisica*,
Ottica) distortion

dis'trarre /123/ *vt* to distract;
(*divertire*) to entertain, amuse;
distrarsi *vpr* (*non fare attenzione*)
to be distracted, let one's mind
wander; (*svagarsi*) to amuse *o* enjoy
o.s.; **dis'tratto, -a** *pp di* **distrarre**
▷ *ag* absent-minded; (*disattento*)
inattentive; **distrazi'one** *sf* absent-
mindedness; inattention; (*svago*)
distraction, entertainment

dis'tretto *sm* district

distribu'ire /55/ *vt* to distribute;
(*Carte*) to deal (out); (*posta*) to
deliver; (*lavoro*) to allocate, assign;
(*ripartire*) to share out; **distribu'tore**
sm (*di benzina*) petrol (BRIT) *o* gas
(US) pump; (*Aut, Elettr*) distributor;
(*automatico*) vending machine

distri'care /20/ *vt* to disentangle,
unravel; **districarsi** *vpr* (*tirarsi
fuori*): **districarsi da** to get out of,
disentangle o.s. from

dis'truggere [dis'truddʒere]
/83/ *vt* to destroy; **distruzi'one** *sf*
destruction

distur'bare /72/ *vt* to disturb,
trouble; (*sonno, lezioni*) to disturb,
interrupt; **disturbarsi** *vpr* to put o.s.
out; **dis'turbo** *sm* trouble, bother,
inconvenience; (*indisposizione*)
(slight) disorder, ailment

disubbidi'ente *ag* disobedient;
disubbi'dire /55/ *vi*: **disubbidire (a
qn)** to disobey (sb)

disu'mano, -a *ag* inhuman

di'tale *sm* thimble

'dito (*pl f* **dita**) *sm* finger; (*misura*)
finger, finger's breadth; **~ (del
piede)** toe

'ditta *sf* firm, business

ditta'tore *sm* dictator

ditta'tura *sf* dictatorship

dit'tongo, -ghi *sm* diphthong

di'urno, -a *ag* day *cpd*, daytime *cpd*

'diva *sf vedi* **divo**

di'vano *sm* sofa; (*senza schienale*)
divan; **~ letto** bed settee, sofa bed

divari'care /20/ *vt* to open wide

di'vario *sm* difference

dive'nire /128/ *vi* = **diventare**

diven'tare /72/ *vi* to become;
~ famoso/professore to become
famous/a teacher

diversifi'care /20/ *vt* to diversify,
vary; to differentiate; **diversificarsi**
vpr: **diversificarsi (per)** to differ (in)

diversità *sf inv* difference, diversity;
(*varietà*) variety

diver'sivo *sm* diversion, distraction

di'verso, -a *ag* (*differente*): **~ (da)**
different (from); **diversi, e** *det pl*,
pron pl several, various; (*Comm*)
sundry; several people, many
(people)

diver'tente *ag* amusing

diverti'mento *sm* amusement,
pleasure; (*passatempo*) pastime,
recreation

diver'tire /45/ *vt* to amuse,
entertain; **divertirsi** *vpr* to amuse
o enjoy o.s.

di'videre /43/ *vt* (*anche Mat*) to divide;
(*distribuire, ripartire*) to divide (up),
split (up); **dividersi** *vpr* (*persone*) to
separate; (*ramificarsi*) to fork

divi'eto *sm* prohibition; **"~ di sosta"**
(*Aut*) "no waiting"

divinco'larsi /72/ *vpr* to wriggle,
writhe

di'vino, -a *ag* divine

di'visa *sf* (*Mil: ecc*) uniform; (*Comm*)
foreign currency

di'visi *ecc vb vedi* **dividere**

divisi'one *sf* division

'divo, -a *sm/f* star

divo'rare /72/ *vt* to devour

divorzi'are [divor'tsjare] /19/ *vi*:
~ (da qn) to divorce (sb)

di'vorzio [di'vɔrtsjo] *sm* divorce

divul'gare /80/ vt to divulge, disclose; (*rendere comprensibile*) to popularize

dizio'nario sm dictionary

DJ [di'dʒei] sigla m, sigla f (= Disc Jockey) DJ

do sm (Mus) C; (: solfeggiando la scala) do(h)

dobbi'amo vb vedi **dovere**

D.O.C. [dɔk] sigla (= denominazione di origine controllata) label guaranteeing the quality of wine

'doccia, -ce ['dottʃa] sf (bagno) shower; **fare la ~** to have a shower

docciaschi'uma [dottʃas'kjuma] sm inv shower gel

do'cente [do'tʃɛnte] ag teaching ▷ smf teacher; (di università) lecturer

'docile ['dɔtʃile] ag docile

documen'tare /72/ vt to document; **documentarsi** vpr: **documentarsi (su)** to gather information o material (about)

documen'tario, -a sm documentary

docu'mento sm document; **documenti** smpl (d'identità ecc) papers

dodi'cesimo, -a [dodi'tʃɛzimo] num twelfth

'dodici ['doditʃi] num twelve

do'gana sf (ufficio) customs pl; (tassa) (customs) duty; **passare la ~** to go through customs; **dogani'ere** sm customs officer

'doglie ['dɔʎʎe] sfpl (Med) labour sg (BRIT), labour pains

'dolce ['doltʃe] ag sweet; (carattere, persona) gentle, mild; (fig: mite: clima) mild; (non ripido: pendio) gentle ▷ sm (sapore dolce) sweetness, sweet taste; (Cuc: portata) sweet, dessert; (: torta) cake; **dolcifi'cante** sm sweetener

do'lere /44/ vi to be sore

'dollaro sm dollar

Dolo'miti sfpl: **le ~** the Dolomites

do'lore sm (fisico) pain; (morale) sorrow, grief; **dolo'roso, -a** ag painful; sorrowful, sad

'dolsi ecc vb vedi **dolere**

do'manda sf (interrogazione) question; (richiesta) demand; (: cortese) request; (Dir: richiesta scritta) application; (Econ): **la ~** demand; **fare una ~ a qn** to ask sb a question; **fare ~ (per un lavoro)** to apply (for a job)

doman'dare /72/ vt (per avere) to ask for; (per sapere) to ask; (esigere) to demand; **domandarsi** vpr to wonder; to ask o.s.; **~ qc a qn** to ask sb for sth; to ask sb sth

do'mani av tomorrow ▷ sm: **il ~** (il futuro) the future; (il giorno successivo) the next day; **~ l'altro** the day after tomorrow

do'mare /72/ vt to tame

doma'tore, -'trice sm/f (gen) tamer; **~ di cavalli** horsebreaker; **~ di leoni** lion tamer

domat'tina av tomorrow morning

do'menica, -che sf Sunday; **di** o **la ~** on Sundays

do'mestico, -a, -ci, -che ag domestic ▷ sm/f servant, domestic

domi'cilio [domi'tʃiljo] sm (Dir) domicile, place of residence

domi'nare /72/ vt to dominate; (fig: sentimenti) to control, master ▷ vi to be in the dominant position

do'nare /72/ vt to give, present; (per beneficenza ecc) to donate ▷ vi (fig): **~ a** to suit, become; **~ sangue** to give blood; **dona'tore, -'trice** sm/f donor; **donatore di sangue/di organi** blood/organ donor

dondo'lare /72/ vt (cullare) to rock; **dondolarsi** vpr to swing, sway; **'dondolo** sm: **sedia/cavallo a dondolo** rocking chair/horse

'donna sf woman; **~ di casa** housewife; home-loving woman; **~ di servizio** maid

donnai'olo sm ladykiller

'donnola sf weasel

'dono sm gift

'doping sm doping

'**dopo** av (tempo) afterwards; (: più tardi) later; (luogo) after, next ▷ prep after ▷ cong (temporale): **~ aver studiato** after having studied ▷ ag inv: **il giorno ~** the following day; **~ mangiato va a dormire** after having eaten o after a meal he goes for a sleep; **un anno ~** a year later; **~ di me/lui** after me/him; **~, a ~!** see you later!

dopo'barba sm inv after-shave

dopodo'mani av the day after tomorrow

doposci [dopoʃʃi] sm inv après-ski outfit

dopo'sole sm inv: **(lozione/crema) ~** aftersun (lotion/cream)

dopo'tutto av (tutto considerato) after all

doppi'aggio [dop'pjaddʒo] sm (Cine) dubbing

doppi'are /19/ vt (Naut) to round; (Sport) to lap; (Cine) to dub

'**doppio, -a** ag double; (fig: falso) double-dealing, deceitful ▷ sm (quantità): **il ~ (di)** twice as much (o many), double the amount (o number) of; (Sport) doubles pl ▷ av double

doppi'one sm duplicate (copy)

doppio'petto sm double-breasted jacket

dormicchi'are [dormik'kjare] /19/ vi to doze

dormigli'one, -a [dormiʎ'ʎone] sm/f sleepyhead

dor'mire /45/ vi to sleep; **andare a ~** to go to bed; **dor'mita** sf: **farsi una dormita** to have a good sleep

dormi'torio sm dormitory

dormi'veglia [dormi'veʎʎa] sm drowsiness

'**dorso** sm back; (di montagna) ridge, crest; (di libro) spine; **a ~ di cavallo** on horseback

do'sare /72/ vt to measure out; (Med) to dose

'**dose** sf quantity, amount; (Med) dose

do'tato, -a ag: **~ di** (attrezzature) equipped with; (bellezza, intelligenza) endowed with; **un uomo ~** a gifted man

'**dote** sf (di sposa) dowry; (assegnata a un ente) endowment; (fig) gift, talent

Dott. abbr (= dottore) Dr

dotto'rato sm degree; **~ di ricerca** doctorate, doctor's degree

dot'tore, -'essa sm/f doctor

○ DOTTORE
○
○ In Italy, anyone who has a degree in
○ any subject can use the title dottore.
○ Thus a person who is addressed as
○ dottore is not necessarily a doctor
○ of medicine.

dot'trina sf doctrine

Dott.ssa abbr (= dottoressa) Dr

'**dove** av (gen) where; (in cui) where, in which; (dovunque) wherever ▷ cong (mentre, laddove) whereas; **~ sei?/ vai?** where are you?/are you going?; **dimmi dov'è** tell me where it is; **di dov'è?** where are you from?; **per ~ si passa?** which way should we go?; **la città ~ abito** the town where o in which I live; **siediti ~ vuoi** sit wherever you like

do'vere /46/ sm (obbligo) duty ▷ vt (essere debitore): **~ qc (a qn)** to owe (sb) sth ▷ vi (seguito dall'infinito, obbligo) to have to; **devo partire domani** (intenzione) I'm (due) to leave tomorrow; **dev'essere tardi** (probabilità) it must be late; **lui deve farlo** he has to do it, he must do it; **quanto le devo?** how much do I owe you?; **è dovuto partire** he had to leave; **ha dovuto pagare** he had to pay; **rivolgersi a chi di ~** to apply to the appropriate authority o person; **come si deve** (bene) properly; **una persona come si deve** a respectable person

dove'roso, -a ag (right and) proper

dovrò ecc vb vedi **dovere**

do'vunque av (in qualunque luogo) wherever; (dappertutto) everywhere; **~ io vada** wherever I go

do'vuto, -a ag (causato): **~ a** due to

doz'zina [dod'dzina] sf dozen; **una ~ di uova** a dozen eggs

dozzi'nale [doddzi'nale] ag cheap, second-rate

'**drago, -ghi** sm dragon

'**dramma, -i** sm drama; **dram'matico, -a, -ci, -che** ag dramatic

'**drastico, -a, -ci, -che** ag drastic

'**dritto, -a** ag, av = **diritto**

'**droga, -ghe** sf (sostanza aromatica) spice; (stupefacente) drug; **droghe pesanti/leggere** hard/soft drugs

dro'gare /80/ vt to drug; **drogarsi** vpr to take drugs

dro'gato, -a sm/f drug addict

droghe'ria [droge'ria] sf grocer's (shop) (BRIT), grocery (store) (US)

drome'dario sm dromedary

DS [di'esse] smpl (= Democratici di Sinistra) Democrats of the Left (Italian left-wing party)

'**dubbio, -a** ag (incerto) doubtful, dubious; (ambiguo) dubious ▷ sm (incertezza) doubt; **avere il ~ che** to be afraid that, suspect that; **mettere in ~ qc** to question sth

dubi'tare /72/ vi: **~ di** to doubt; (risultato) to be doubtful of

Du'blino sf Dublin

'**duca, -chi** sm duke

du'chessa [du'kessa] sf duchess

'**due** num two

due'cento [due'tʃɛnto] num two hundred ▷ sm: **il D~** the thirteenth century

due'pezzi [due'pɛttsi] sm (costume da bagno) two-piece swimsuit; (abito femminile) two-piece suit

'**dunque** cong (perciò) so, therefore; (riprendendo il discorso) well (then) ▷ sm inv: **venire al ~** to come to the point

du'omo sm cathedral

> Attenzione! In inglese esiste la parola dome, che però significa cupola.

dupli'cato sm duplicate

'**duplice** ['duplitʃe] ag double, twofold; **in ~ copia** in duplicate

du'rante prep during

du'rare /72/ vi to last; **~ fatica a** to have difficulty in

du'rezza [du'rettsa] sf hardness; stubbornness; harshness; toughness

'**duro, -a** ag (pietra, lavoro, materasso, problema) hard; (persona: ostinato) stubborn, obstinate; (: severo) harsh, hard; (voce) harsh; (carne) tough ▷ sm (durezza) hard part; (difficoltà) hard part; (persona) tough one ▷ av: **tener ~** to stand firm, hold out; **~ d'orecchi** hard of hearing

DVD [divu'di] sm inv DVD; (lettore) DVD player

e

E *abbr* (= *est*) E

e (*dav V spesso* **ed**) *cong* and; **e lui?** what about him?; **e compralo!** well buy it then!

è *vb vedi* **essere**

eb'bene *cong* well (then)

'ebbi *ecc vb vedi* **avere**

e'braico, -a, -ci, -che *ag* Hebrew, Hebraic ▷ *sm* (*Ling*) Hebrew

e'breo, -a *ag* Jewish ▷ *sm/f* Jewish person, Jew (Jewess)

EC *abbr* (= *Eurocity*) fast train connecting Western European cities

ecc. *abbr* (= *eccetera*) etc

eccel'lente [ett∫el'lɛnte] *ag* excellent

ec'centrico, -a, -ci, -che [et't∫ɛntriko] *ag* eccentric

ecces'sivo, -a [ett∫es'sivo] *ag* excessive

ec'cesso [et't∫ɛsso] *sm* excess; **all'~** (*gentile, generoso*) to excess, excessively; **~ di velocità** (*Aut*) speeding

ec'cetera [et't∫ɛtera] *av* et cetera, and so on

ec'cetto [et't∫ɛtto] *prep* except, with the exception of; **~ che** except, other than; **~ che (non)** unless

eccezio'nale [ett∫ettsjo'nale] *ag* exceptional

eccezi'one [ett∫et'tsjone] *sf* exception; (*Dir*) objection; **a ~ di** with the exception of, except for; **d'~** exceptional

ecci'tare [ett∫i'tare] /72/ *vt* (*curiosità, interesse*) to excite, arouse; (*folla*) to incite; **eccitarsi** *vpr* to get excited; (*sessualmente*) to become aroused

'ecco *av* (*per dimostrare*): **~ il treno!** here's *o* here comes the train!; (*dav pronome*): **eccomi!** here I am!; **eccone uno!** here's one (of them)!; (*dav pp*): **~ fatto!** there, that's it done!

ec'come *av* rather; **ti piace? — ~!** do you like it? — I'll say! *o* and how! *o* rather! (BRIT)

e'clisse *sf* eclipse

'eco (*pl m* **echi**) *sm o f* echo

ecogra'fia *sf* (*Med*) ultrasound

ecolo'gia [ekolo'dʒia] *sf* ecology

eco'logico, -a, -ci, -che [eko'lɔdʒiko] *ag* ecological

eco'mafia *sf* mafia involved in crimes related to the environment, in particular the illegal disposal of waste

econo'mia *sf* economy; (*scienza*) economics *sg*; (*risparmio, azione*) saving; **fare ~** to economize, make economies; **eco'nomico, -a, -ci, -che** *ag* economic; (*poco costoso*) economical

'ecstasy ['ɛkstasi] *sf inv* ecstasy

'edera *sf* ivy

e'dicola *sf* newspaper kiosk *o* stand (US)

edi'ficio [edi'fit∫o] *sm* building

e'dile *ag* building *cpd*

Edim'burgo *sf* Edinburgh

edi'tore, -'trice *ag* publishing *cpd* ▷ *sm/f* publisher

Attenzione! In inglese esiste la parola *editor*, che però significa *redattore*.

edizi'one [edit'tsjone] *sf* edition; (*tiratura*) printing; **~ straordinaria** special edition

edu'care /20/ *vt* to educate; (*gusto, mente*) to train; **~ qn a fare** to train sb to do; **edu'cato, -a** *ag* polite, well-mannered; **educazi'one** *sf* education; (*familiare*) upbringing; (*comportamento*) (good) manners *pl*: **educazione fisica** (*Ins*) physical training *o* education

educherò *ecc* [eduke'rɔ] *vb vedi* **educare**

effemi'nato, -a *ag* effeminate

efferve'scente [efferveʃʃɛnte] *ag* effervescent

effet'tivo, -a *ag* (*reale*) real, actual; (*impiegato, professore*) permanent; (*Mil*) regular ▷ *sm* (*Mil*) strength; (*di patrimonio ecc*) sum total

ef'fetto *sm* effect; (*Comm: cambiale*) bill; (*fig: impressione*) impression; **in effetti** in fact, actually; **effetti personali** personal effects, personal belongings; **~ serra** greenhouse effect

effi'cace [effi'katʃe] *ag* effective

effici'ente [effi'tʃɛnte] *ag* efficient

E'geo [e'dʒɛo] *sm*: **l'~, il mare ~** the Aegean (Sea)

E'gitto [e'dʒitto] *sm*: **l'~** Egypt; **egizi'ano, -a** [edʒit'tsjano] *ag, sm/f* Egyptian

'egli ['eʎʎi] *pron* he; **~ stesso** he himself

ego'ismo *sm* selfishness, egoism; **ego'ista, -i, -e** *ag* selfish, egoistic ▷ *sm/f* egoist

Egr. *abbr* = **egregio**

e'gregio, -a, -gi, -gie [e'grɛdʒo] *ag* (*nelle lettere*): **E~ Signore** Dear Sir

E.I. *abbr* = **Esercito Italiano**

elabo'rare /72/ *vt* (*progetto*) to work out, elaborate; (*dati*) to process

elasticiz'zato, -a [elastitʃid'dzato] *ag* stretch *cpd*

e'lastico, -a, -ci, -che *ag* elastic; (*fig: andatura*) springy; (: *decisione, vedute*) flexible ▷ *sm* (*gommino*) rubber band; (*per il cucito*) elastic *no pl*

ele'fante *sm* elephant

ele'gante *ag* elegant

e'leggere [e'lɛddʒere] /61/ *vt* to elect

elemen'tare *ag* elementary; **le (scuole) elementari** *sfpl* primary (BRIT) *o* grade (US) school

ele'mento *sm* element; (*parte componente*) element, component, part; **elementi** *smpl* (*della scienza ecc*) elements, rudiments

ele'mosina *sf* charity, alms *pl*: **chiedere l'~** to beg

elen'care /20/ *vt* to list

elencherò *ecc* [elenke'rɔ] *vb vedi* **elencare**

e'lenco, -chi *sm* list; **~ telefonico** telephone directory

e'lessi *ecc vb vedi* **eleggere**

elet'torale *ag* electoral, election *cpd*

elet'tore, -'trice *sm/f* voter, elector

elet'trauto *sm inv* workshop for car electrical repairs; (*tecnico*) car electrician

elettri'cista, -i [elettri'tʃista] *sm* electrician

elettricità [elettritʃi'ta] *sf* electricity

e'lettrico, -a, -ci, -che *ag* electric(al)

elettriz'zante [elettrid'dzante] *ag* (*fig*) electrifying, thrilling

elettriz'zare [elettrid'dzare] /72/ *vt* to electrify; **elettrizzarsi** *vpr* to become charged with electricity

e'lettro... *prefisso*: **elettrodo'mestico, -a, -ci, -che** *ag*: **apparecchi elettrodomestici** domestic (electrical) appliances; **elet'tronico, -a, -ci, -che** *ag* electronic

elezi'one [elet'tsjone] *sf* election; **elezioni** *sfpl* (*Pol*) election(s)

'elica, -che *sf* propeller

eli'cottero *sm* helicopter
elimi'nare /72/ *vt* to eliminate
elisoc'corso *sm* helicopter ambulance
el'metto *sm* helmet
elogi'are [elo'dʒare] /62/ *vt* to praise
elo'quente *ag* eloquent
e'ludere /35/ *vt* to evade
e'lusi *ecc vb vedi* **eludere**
e-'mail [e'mεil] *sf inv* (*messaggio, sistema*) e-mail ▷ *ag inv* email; **indirizzo ~** email address
emargi'nato, -a [emardʒi'nato] *sm/f* outcast; **emarginazione** [emardʒinat'tsjone] *sf* marginalization
embri'one *sm* embryo
emenda'mento *sm* amendment
emer'genza [emer'dʒεntsa] *sf* emergency; **in caso di ~** in an emergency
e'mergere [e'mεrdʒere] /59/ *vi* to emerge; (*sommergibile*) to surface; (*fig: distinguersi*) to stand out
e'mersi *ecc vb vedi* **emergere**
e'mettere /63/ *vt* (*suono, luce*) to give out, emit; (*onde radio*) to send out; (*assegno, francobollo, ordine*) to issue
emi'crania *sf* migraine
emi'grare /72/ *vi* to emigrate
emis'fero *sm* hemisphere; **~ boreale/australe** northern/southern hemisphere
e'misi *ecc vb vedi* **emettere**
emit'tente *ag* (*banca*) issuing; (*Radio*) broadcasting, transmitting ▷ *sf* (*Radio*) transmitter
emorra'gia, -'gie [emorra'dʒia] *sf* haemorrhage
emor'roidi *sfpl* haemorrhoids *pl* (BRIT), hemorrhoids *pl* (US)
emo'tivo, -a *ag* emotional
emozio'nante [emottsjo'nante] *ag* exciting, thrilling
emozio'nare [emottsjo'nare] /72/ *vt* (*appassionare*) to excite; (*commuovere*) to move; (*agitare*) to make nervous; **emozionarsi** *vpr* to be

excited; to be moved; to be nervous; **emozionato, -a** [emottsjo'nato] *ag* (*commosso*) moved; (*agitato*) nervous; (*elettrizzato*) excited
emozi'one [emot'tsjone] *sf* emotion; (*agitazione*) excitement
enciclope'dia [entʃiklope'dia] *sf* encyclop(a)edia
endove'noso, -a *ag* (*Med*) intravenous
'E.N.E.L. *sigla m* (= Ente Nazionale per l'Energia Elettrica) national electricity company
ener'getico, -a, -ci, -che [ener'dʒεtiko] *ag* (*risorse, crisi*) energy *cpd*; (*sostanza, alimento*) energy-giving
ener'gia, -'gie [ener'dʒia] *sf* (*Fisica*) energy; (*fig*) energy, strength, vigour; **~ eolica** wind power; **~ solare** solar energy, solar power; **e'nergico, -a, -ci, -che** [e'nεrdʒiko] *ag* energetic, vigorous
'enfasi *sf* emphasis; (*peg*) bombast, pomposity
en'nesimo, -a *ag* (*Mat, fig*) nth; **per l'ennesima volta** for the umpteenth time
e'norme *ag* enormous, huge
'ente *sm* (*istituzione*) body, board, corporation; (*Filosofia*) being; **~ pubblico** public body; **~ di ricerca** research organization
en'trambi, -e *pron pl* both (of them) ▷ *ag pl*: **~ i ragazzi** both boys, both of the boys
en'trare /72/ *vi* to enter, go (*o come*) in; **~ in** (*luogo*) to enter, go (*o come*) into; (*trovar posto, poter stare*) to fit into; (*essere ammesso a: club ecc*) to join, become a member of; **~ in automobile** to get into the car; **far ~ qn** (*visitatore ecc*) to show sb in; **questo non c'entra** (*fig*) that's got nothing to do with it; **en'trata** *sf* entrance, entry; **dov'è l'entrata?** where's the entrance?; **entrate** *sfpl* (*Comm*) receipts, takings; (*Econ*) income *sg*

'**entro** prep (temporale) within
entusias'mare /72/ vt to excite, fill
with enthusiasm; **entusiasmarsi**
vpr: **entusiasmarsi (per qc/qn)** to
become enthusiastic (about sth/
sb); **entusi'asmo** sm enthusiasm;
entusi'asta, -i, -e ag enthusiastic
▷ sm/f enthusiast
e'olico, -a, -chi, -che ag wind;
energia eolica wind power
epa'tite sf hepatitis
epide'mia sf epidemic
Epifa'nia sf Epiphany
epiles'sia sf epilepsy
epi'lettico, -a, -ci, -che ag, sm/f
epileptic
epi'sodio sm episode
'**epoca, -che** sf (periodo storico) age,
era; (tempo) time; (Geo) age
ep'pure cong and yet, nevertheless
EPT sigla m (= Ente Provinciale per il
Turismo) district tourist bureau
equa'tore sm equator
equazi'one [ekwat'tsjone] sf (Mat)
equation
e'questre ag equestrian
equi'librio sm balance, equilibrium;
perdere l'~ to lose one's balance
e'quino, -a ag horse cpd, equine
equipaggia'mento
[ekwipaddʒa'mento] sm (operazione:
di nave) equipping, fitting out; (: di
spedizione, esercito) equipping, kitting
out; (attrezzatura) equipment
equipaggi'are [ekwipad'dʒare]
/62/ vt (di persone) to man; (di mezzi)
to equip; **equipaggiarsi** vpr to equip
o.s.; **equi'paggio** sm crew
equitazi'one [ekwitat'tsjone] sf
(horse-) riding
equiva'lente ag, sm equivalent
e'quivoco, -a, -ci, -che ag
equivocal, ambiguous; (sospetto)
dubious ▷ sm misunderstanding;
a scanso di equivoci to avoid any
misunderstanding; **giocare sull'~**
to equivocate
'**equo, -a** ag fair, just

'**era** ecc vb vedi **essere**
'**erba** sf grass; **in ~** (fig) budding;
erbe aromatiche herbs; **~ medica**
lucerne; **er'baccia, -ce** sf weed
erboriste'ria sf (scienza) study of
medicinal herbs; (negozio) herbalist's
(shop)
e'rede smf heir(-ess); **eredità** sf (Dir)
inheritance; (Biol) heredity; **lasciare
qc in eredità a qn** to leave o bequeath
sth to sb; **eredi'tare** /72/ vt to inherit;
eredi'tario, -a ag hereditary
ere'mita, -i sm hermit
er'gastolo sm (Dir: pena) life
imprisonment
'**erica** sf heather
er'metico, -a, -ci, -che ag hermetic
'**ernia** sf (Med) hernia
'**ero** vb vedi **essere**
e'roe sm hero
ero'gare /80/ vt (somme) to
distribute; (gas, servizi) to supply
e'roico, -a, -ci, -che ag heroic
ero'ina sf heroine; (droga) heroin
erosi'one sf erosion
e'rotico, -a, -ci, -che ag erotic
er'rato, -a ag wrong
er'rore sm error, mistake; (morale)
error; **per ~** by mistake; **ci
dev'essere un ~** there must be some
mistake; **~ giudiziario** miscarriage
of justice
eruzi'one [erut'tsjone] sf eruption
esacer'bare [ezat∫er'bare] /72/ vt to
exacerbate
esage'rare [ezadʒe'rare] /72/ vt
to exaggerate ▷ vi to exaggerate;
(eccedere) to go too far
esal'tare /72/ vt to exalt;
(entusiasmare) to excite, stir
e'same sm examination; (Ins) exam,
examination; **fare un ~ di coscienza**
to search one's conscience; **~ di
guida** driving test; **~ del sangue**
blood test
esami'nare /72/ vt to examine
esaspe'rare /72/ vt to exasperate;
(situazione) to exacerbate

esatta'mente *av* exactly; accurately, precisely

esat'tezza [ezat'tettsa] *sf* exactitude, accuracy, precision

e'satto, -a *pp di* **esigere** ▷ *ag (calcolo, ora)* correct, right, exact; *(preciso)* accurate, precise; *(puntuale)* punctual

esau'dire /55/ *vt* to grant, fulfil

esauri'ente *ag* exhaustive

esauri'mento *sm* exhaustion; **~ nervoso** nervous breakdown

esau'rire /55/ *vt (stancare)* to exhaust, wear out; *(provviste, miniera)* to exhaust; **esaurirsi** *vpr* to exhaust o.s., wear o.s. out; *(provviste)* to run out; **esau'rito, -a** *ag* exhausted; *(merci)* sold out; **registrare il tutto esaurito** *(Teat)* to have a full house; **e'sausto, -a** *ag* exhausted

'esca *(pl* **esche)** *sf* bait

'esce ['ɛʃʃe] *vb vedi* **uscire**

eschi'mese [eski'mese] *ag, smf* Eskimo

'esci ['ɛʃʃi] *vb vedi* **uscire**

escla'mare /72/ *vi* to exclaim, cry out

esclama'tivo, -a *ag*: **punto ~** exclamation mark

esclamazi'one [esklamat'tsjone] *sf* exclamation

es'cludere /3/ *vt* to exclude

es'clusi *ecc vb vedi* **escludere**

esclusi'one *sf* exclusion; **a ~ di, fatta ~ per** except (for), apart from; **senza ~ (alcuna)** without exception; **procedere per ~** to follow a process of elimination; **senza ~ di colpi** *(fig)* with no holds barred; **~ sociale** social exclusion

esclu'siva *sf vedi* **esclusivo**

esclusiva'mente *av* exclusively, solely

esclu'sivo, -a *ag* exclusive ▷ *sf (Dir, Comm)* exclusive *o* sole rights *pl*

es'cluso, -a *pp di* **escludere**

'esco *vb vedi* **uscire**

escogi'tare [eskodʒi'tare] /72/ *vt* to devise, think up

'escono *vb vedi* **uscire**

escursi'one *sf (gita)* excursion, trip; (: *a piedi)* hike, walk; *(Meteor)*: **~ termica** temperature range

esecuzi'one [ezekut'tsjone] *sf* execution, carrying out; *(Mus)* performance; **~ capitale** execution

esegu'ire /45/ *vt* to carry out, execute; *(Mus)* to perform, execute

e'sempio *sm* example; **per ~** for example, for instance; **fare un ~** to give an example; **esem'plare** *ag* exemplary ▷ *sm* example; *(copia)* copy

eserci'tare [ezertʃi'tare] /72/ *vt (professione)* to practise (*BRIT*), practice (*US*); *(allenare: corpo, mente)* to exercise, train; *(diritto)* to exercise; *(influenza, pressione)* to exert; **esercitarsi** *vpr* to practise; **esercitarsi nella guida** to practise one's driving

e'sercito [e'zertʃito] *sm* army

eser'cizio [ezer'tʃittsjo] *sm* practice; exercising; *(fisico: di matematica)* exercise; *(Econ)*: **~ finanziario** financial year; **in ~** *(medico ecc)* practising (*BRIT*), practicing (*US*)

esi'bire /55/ *vt* to exhibit, display; *(documenti)* to produce, present; **esibirsi** *vpr (attore)* to perform; *(fig)* to show off; **esibizi'one** *sf* exhibition; *(di documento)* presentation; *(spettacolo)* show, performance

esi'gente [ezi'dʒɛnte] *ag* demanding

e'sigere [e'zidʒere] /47/ *vt (pretendere)* to demand; *(richiedere)* to demand, require; *(imposte)* to collect

'esile *ag (persona)* slender, slim; *(stelo)* thin; *(voce)* faint

esili'are /19/ *vt* to exile; **e'silio** *sm* exile

esis'tenza [ezis'tɛntsa] *sf* existence

e'sistere /11/ *vi* to exist

esi'tare /72/ *vi* to hesitate

'esito *sm* result, outcome

'esodo *sm* exodus

esone'rare /72/ *vt*: **~ qn da** to exempt sb from

e'sordio *sm* debut

esor'tare /72/ vt: **~ qn a fare** to urge sb to do

e'sotico, -a, -ci, -che ag exotic

es'pandere /110/ vt to expand; (confini) to extend; (influenza) to extend, spread; **espandersi** vpr to expand; **espansi'one** sf expansion; **espansione di memoria** (Inform) memory upgrade; **espan'sivo, -a** ag expansive, communicative

espatri'are /19/ vi to leave one's country

espedi'ente sm expedient

es'pellere /48/ vt to expel

esperi'enza [espe'rjɛntsa] sf experience

esperi'mento sm experiment

es'perto, -a ag, sm/f expert

espi'rare /72/ vt, vi to breathe out

es'plicito, -a [es'plitʃito] ag explicit

es'plodere /49/ vi (anche fig) to explode ▷ vt to fire

esplo'rare /72/ vt to explore

esplosi'one sf explosion

es'pone ecc vb vedi **esporre**

es'pongo, es'poni ecc vb vedi **esporre**

es'porre /77/ vt (merci) to display; (quadro) to exhibit, show; (fatti, idee) to explain, set out; (porre in pericolo, Fot) to expose; **esporsi** vpr: **esporsi a** (sole, pericolo) to expose o.s. to; (critiche) to lay o.s. open to

espor'tare /72/ vt to export

es'pose ecc vb vedi **esporre**

esposizi'one [espozit'tsjone] sf displaying; exhibiting; setting out; (anche Fot) exposure; (mostra) exhibition; (narrazione) explanation, exposition

es'posto, -a pp di **esporre** ▷ ag: **~ a nord** facing north ▷ sm (Amm) statement, account; (: petizione) petition

espressi'one sf expression

espres'sivo, -a ag expressive

es'presso, -a pp di **esprimere** ▷ ag express ▷ sm (lettera) express letter;

(anche: **treno ~**) express train; (anche: **caffè ~**) espresso

es'primere /50/ vt to express; **esprimersi** vpr to express o.s.

es'pulsi ecc vb vedi **espellere**

espulsi'one sf expulsion

es'senza [es'sɛntsa] sf essence; **essenzi'ale** ag essential ▷ sm: **l'essenziale** the main o most important thing

PAROLA CHIAVE

'essere /51/ sm being; **essere umano** human being

▶ vb copulativo **1** (con attributo, sostantivo) to be; **sei giovane/ simpatico** you are o you're young/ nice; **è medico** he is o he's a doctor

2 (+ di: appartenere) to be; **di chi è la penna?** whose pen is it?; **è di Carla** it is o it's Carla's, it belongs to Carla

3 (+ di: provenire) to be; **è di Venezia** he is o he's from Venice

4 (data, ora): **è il 15 agosto** it is o it's the 15th of August; **è lunedì** it is o it's Monday; **che ora è?, che ore sono?** what time is it?; **è l'una** it is o it's one o'clock; **sono le due** it is o it's two o'clock

5 (costare): **quant'è?** how much is it?; **sono 20 euro** it's 20 euros

▶ vb aus **1** (attivo): **essere arrivato/ venuto** to have arrived/come; **è già partita** she has already left

2 (passivo) to be; **essere fatto da** to be made by; **è stata uccisa** she has been killed

3 (riflessivo): **si sono lavati** they washed, they got washed

4 (+ da + infinito): **è da farsi subito** it must be done o is to be done immediately

▶ vi **1** (esistere, trovarsi) to be; **sono a casa** I'm at home; **essere in piedi/ seduto** to be standing/sitting

2: **esserci**: **c'è** there is; **ci sono** there are; **che c'è?** what's the matter?,

what is it?; **ci sono!** (*ho capito*) I get it!
▶ *vb impers*: **è tardi/Pasqua** it's late/
Easter; **è possibile che venga** he
may come; **è così** that's the way it is

'essi *pron mpl vedi* **esso**

'esso, -a *pron* it; (*riferito a persona:
soggetto*) he (she); (*: complemento*)
him (her)

est *sm* east

es'tate *sf* summer

esteri'ore *ag* outward, external

es'terno, -a *ag* (*porta, muro*) outer,
outside; (*scala*) outside; (*alunno,
impressione*) external ▷ *sm* outside,
exterior ▷ *sm/f* (*allievo*) day pupil;
esterni *smpl* (*Cine*) location shots;
"per uso ~" "for external use only";
all'~ outside

'estero, -a *ag* foreign ▷ *sm*: **all'~**
abroad

es'teso, -a *pp di* **estendere** ▷ *ag*
extensive, large; **scrivere per ~** to
write in full

es'tetico, -a, -ci, -che *ag* aesthetic
▷ *sf* (*disciplina*) aesthetics *sg*; (*bellezza*)
attractiveness; **este'tista, -i, -e** *sm/f*
beautician

es'tinguere /42/ *vt* to extinguish, put
out; (*debito*) to pay off; **estinguersi**
vpr to go out; (*specie*) to become
extinct

es'tinsi *ecc vb vedi* **estinguere**

estin'tore *sm* (fire) extinguisher

estinzi'one *sf* putting out; (*di specie*)
extinction

estir'pare /72/ *vt* (*pianta*) to uproot,
pull up; (*fig: vizio*) to eradicate

es'tivo, -a *ag* summer *cpd*

es'torcere [es'tortʃere] /106/ *vt*: **~ qc
(a qn)** to extort sth (from sb)

estradizi'one [estradit'tsjone] *sf*
extradition

es'trae, es'traggo *ecc vb vedi*
estrarre

es'traneo, -a *ag* foreign ▷ *sm/f*
stranger; **rimanere ~ a qc** to take
no part in sth

es'trarre /123/ *vt* to extract; (*minerali*)
to mine; (*sorteggiare*) to draw

es'trassi *ecc vb vedi* **estrarre**

estrema'mente *av* extremely

estre'mista, -i, -e *sm/f* extremist

estremità *sf inv* extremity, end ▷ *sfpl*
(*Anat*) extremities

es'tremo, -a *ag* extreme; (*ultimo: ora,
tentativo*) final, last ▷ *sm* extreme; (*di
pazienza, forza*) limit, end; **estremi**
smpl (*Amm: dati essenziali*) details,
particulars; **l'E~ Oriente** the Far
East

estro'verso, -a *ag, sm* extrovert

età *sf inv* age; **all'~ di 8 anni** at the
age of 8, at 8 years of age; **ha la mia
~** he (o she) is the same age as me o as
I am; **raggiungere la maggiore ~** to
come of age; **essere in ~ minore** to
be under age

'etere *sm* ether

eternità *sf* eternity

e'terno, -a *ag* eternal

etero'geneo, -a [etero'dʒɛneo] *ag*
heterogeneous

eterosessu'ale *ag, smf*
heterosexual

'etica *sf vedi* **etico**

eti'chetta [eti'ketta] *sf* label;
(*cerimoniale*): **l'~** etiquette

'etico, -a, -ci, -che *ag* ethical ▷ *sf*
ethics *sg*

eti'lometro *sm* Breathalyzer®

etimolo'gia, -'gie [etimolo'dʒia] *sf*
etymology

Eti'opia *sf*: **l'~** Ethiopia

'etnico, -a, -ci, -che *ag* ethnic

e'trusco, -a, -schi, -sche *ag, smf*
Etruscan

'ettaro *sm* hectare (10,000 m²)

'etto *abbr m* (= ettogrammo) 100 grams

'euro *sm inv* (*divisa*) euro

Eu'ropa *sf*: **l'~** Europe

europarlamen'tare *smf* Member of
the European Parliament, MEP

euro'peo, -a *ag, sm/f* European

eutana'sia *sf* euthanasia

evacu'are /72/ *vt* to evacuate

e'vadere /52/ *vi* (*fuggire*): **~ da** to escape from ▷ *vt* (*sbrigare*) to deal with, dispatch; (*tasse*) to evade

evapo'rare /72/ *vi* to evaporate

e'vasi *ecc vb vedi* **evadere**

evasi'one *sf* (*vedi evadere*) escape; dispatch; **~ fiscale** tax evasion

eva'sivo, -a *ag* evasive

e'vaso, -a *pp di* **evadere** ▷ *sm* escapee

e'vento *sm* event

eventu'ale *ag* possible
> Attenzione! In inglese esiste la parola *eventual*, che però significa *finale*.

eventual'mente *av* if necessary
> Attenzione! In inglese esiste la parola *eventually*, che però significa *alla fine*.

evi'dente *ag* evident, obvious

evidente'mente *av* evidently; (*palesemente*) obviously, evidently

evi'tare /72/ *vt* to avoid; **~ di fare** to avoid doing; **~ qc a qn** to spare sb sth

evoluzi'one [evolut'tsjone] *sf* evolution

e'volversi /94/ *vpr* to evolve

ev'viva *escl* hurrah!; **~ il re!** long live the king!, hurrah for the king!

ex *prefisso* ex-, former

'extra *ag inv* first-rate; top-quality ▷ *sm inv* extra; **extracomuni'tario, -a** *ag* non-EU ▷ *sm/f* non-EU citizen (*often referred to non-European immigrant*)

extrater'restre *ag, smf* extraterrestrial

f

fa *vb vedi* **fare** ▷ *sm inv* (*Mus*) F; (: *solfeggiando la scala*) fa ▷ *av*: **10 anni fa** 10 years ago

'fabbrica *sf* factory; **fabbri'care** /20/ *vt* to build; (*produrre*) to manufacture, make; (*fig*) to fabricate, invent
> Attenzione! In inglese esiste la parola *fabric*, che però significa *stoffa*.

fac'cenda [fat'tʃɛnda] *sf* matter, affair; (*cosa da fare*) task, chore

fac'chino [fak'kino] *sm* porter

'faccia, -ce ['fattʃa] *sf* face; (*di moneta, medaglia*) side; **~ a ~** face to face

facci'ata [fat'tʃata] *sf* façade; (*di pagina*) side

fac'cina [fat'tʃina] *sf* (*Inform*) emoticon

'faccio *ecc* ['fattʃo] *vb vedi* **fare**

fa'cessi *ecc* [fa'tʃessi] *vb vedi* **fare**

fa'cevo *ecc* [fa'tʃevo] *vb vedi* **fare**

facile ['fatʃile] *ag* easy; (*disposto*): **~ a** inclined to, prone to; (*probabile*): **è ~ che piova** it's likely to rain

facoltà *sf inv* faculty; (*autorità*) power

facolta'tivo, -a *ag* optional; (*fermata d'autobus*) request *cpd*

faggio ['faddʒo] *sm* beech

fagi'ano [fa'dʒano] *sm* pheasant

fagio'lino [fadʒo'lino] *sm* French (BRIT) *o* string bean

fagi'olo [fa'dʒolo] *sm* bean

fai *vb vedi* **fare**

fai-da-'te *sm inv* DIY, do-it-yourself

falce ['faltʃe] *sf* scythe; **falci'are** /14/ *vt* to cut; (*fig*) to mow down

falcia'trice [faltʃa'tritʃe] *sf* (*per fieno*) reaping machine; (*per erba*) mowing machine

falco, -chi *sm* hawk

falda *sf* layer, stratum; (*di cappello*) brim; (*di cappotto*) tails *pl*; (*di monte*) lower slope; (*di tetto*) pitch

fale'gname [faleɲ'ɲame] *sm* joiner

falli'mento *sm* failure; bankruptcy

fal'lire /55/ *vi* (*Dir*) to go bankrupt; (*non riuscire*): **~ (in)** to fail (in) ▷ *vt* (*colpo, bersaglio*) to miss

fallo *sm* error, mistake; (*imperfezione*) defect, flaw; (*Sport*) foul; fault; **senza ~** without fail

falò *sm inv* bonfire

falsifi'care /20/ *vt* to forge; (*monete*) to forge, counterfeit

falso, -a *ag* false; (*errato*) wrong; (*falsificato*) forged; fake; (: *oro, gioielli*) imitation *cpd* ▷ *sm* forgery; **giurare il ~** to commit perjury

fama *sf* fame; (*reputazione*) reputation, name

fame *sf* hunger; **aver ~** to be hungry

fa'miglia [fa'miʎʎa] *sf* family

famili'are *ag* (*della famiglia*) family *cpd*; (*ben noto*) familiar; (*rapporti, atmosfera*) friendly; (*Ling*) colloquial ▷ *smf* relative, relation

fa'moso, -a *ag* famous, well-known

fa'nale *sm* (*Aut*) light, lamp (BRIT); (*luce stradale, Naut*) light; (*di faro*) beacon

fa'natico, -a, -ci, -che *ag* fanatical; (*del teatro, calcio ecc*): **~ di** *o* **per** mad *o* crazy about ▷ *sm/f* fanatic; (*tifoso*) fan

fango, -ghi *sm* mud

fanno *vb vedi* **fare**

fannul'lone, -a *sm/f* idler, loafer

fantasci'enza [fantaʃ'ʃentsa] *sf* science fiction

fanta'sia *sf* fantasy, imagination; (*capriccio*) whim, caprice ▷ *ag inv*: **vestito ~** patterned dress

fan'tasma, -i *sm* ghost, phantom

fan'tastico, -a, -ci, -che *ag* fantastic; (*potenza, ingegno*) imaginative

fan'tino *sm* jockey

fara'butto *sm* crook

fard *sm inv* blusher

PAROLA CHIAVE

fare /53/ *sm* **1** (*modo di fare*): **con fare distratto** absent-mindedly; **ha un fare simpatico** he has a pleasant manner

2: **sul far del giorno/della notte** at daybreak/nightfall

▶ *vt* **1** (*fabbricare, creare*) to make; (: *casa*) to build; (: *assegno*) to make out; **fare un pasto/una promessa/ un film** to make a meal/promise/a film; **fare rumore** to make a noise

2 (*effettuare: lavoro, attività, studi*) to do; (: *sport*) to play; **cosa fa?** (*adesso*) what are you doing?; (*di professione*) what do you do?; **fare psicologia/ italiano** (*Ins*) to do psychology/ Italian; **fare un viaggio** to go on a trip *o* journey; **fare una passeggiata** to go for a walk; **fare la spesa** to do the shopping

3 (*funzione*) to be; (*Teat*) to play, be; **fare il medico** to be a doctor; **fare il malato** (*fingere*) to act the invalid

4 (*suscitare: sentimenti*): **fare paura a qn** to frighten sb; **(non) fa niente** (*non importa*) it doesn't matter

5 (*ammontare*): **3 più 3 fa 6** 3 and 3 are *o* make 6; **fanno 6 euro** that's 6 euros; **Roma fa oltre 2.000.000 di abitanti** Rome has over 2,000,000 inhabitants; **che ora fai?** what time do you make it?

6 (+ *infinito*): **far fare qc a qn** (*obbligare*) to make sb do sth; (*permettere*) to let sb do sth; **fammi vedere** let me see; **far partire il motore** to start (up) the engine; **far riparare la macchina/costruire una casa** to get *o* have the car repaired/a house built

7: farsi: farsi una gonna to make o.s. a skirt; **farsi un nome** to make a name for o.s.; **farsi la permanente** to get a perm; **farsi tagliare i capelli** to get one's hair cut; **farsi operare** to have an operation

8 (*fraseologia*): **farcela** to succeed, manage; **non ce la faccio più** I can't go on; **ce la faremo** we'll make it; **me l'hanno fatta!** (*imbrogliare*) I've been done!; **lo facevo più giovane** I thought he was younger; **fare sì/no con la testa** to nod/shake one's head

▶ *vi* **1** (*agire*) to act, do; **fate come volete** do as you like; **fare presto** to be quick; **fare da** to act as; **non c'è niente da fare** it's no use; **saperci fare con qn/qc** to know how to deal with sb/sth; **faccia pure!** go ahead!

2 (*dire*) to say; **"davvero?" fece** "really?" he said

3: fare per (*essere adatto*) to be suitable for; **fare per fare qc** to be about to do sth; **fece per andarsene** he made as if to leave

4: farsi: si fa così you do it like this, this is the way it's done; **non si fa così!** (*rimprovero*) that's no way to behave!; **la festa non si fa** the party is off

5: fare a gara con qn to compete with sb; **fare a pugni** to come to blows; **fare in tempo a fare** to be in time to do

▶ *vb impers*: **fa bel tempo** the weather is fine; **fa caldo/freddo** it's hot/cold; **fa notte** it's getting dark

▶ *vpr* **1** (*diventare*) to become; **farsi prete** to become a priest; **farsi grande/vecchio** to grow tall/old

2 (*spostarsi*): **farsi avanti/indietro** to move forward/back

3 (*fam: drogarsi*) to be a junkie

far'falla *sf* butterfly

fa'rina *sf* flour

farma'cia, -'cie [farma'tʃia] *sf* pharmacy; (*negozio*) chemist's (shop) (BRIT), pharmacy; **farma'cista, -i, -e** [farma'tʃista] *sm/f* chemist (BRIT), pharmacist

'farmaco, -ci *o* **-chi** *sm* drug, medicine

'faro *sm* (*Naut*) lighthouse; (*Aer*) beacon; (*Aut*) headlight

'fascia, -sce ['faʃʃa] *sf* band, strip; (*Med*) bandage; (*di sindaco, ufficiale*) sash; (*parte di territorio*) strip, belt; (*di contribuenti ecc*) group, band; **essere in fasce** (*anche fig*) to be in one's infancy; **~ oraria** time band

fasci'are [faʃʃare] /14/ *vt* to bind; (*Med*) to bandage

fa'scicolo [faʃʃikolo] *sm* (*di documenti*) file, dossier; (*di rivista*) issue, number; (*opuscolo*) booklet, pamphlet

fascino ['faʃʃino] *sm* charm, fascination

fa'scismo [faʃʃizmo] *sm* fascism

'fase *sf* phase; (*Tecn*) stroke; **essere fuori ~** (*motore*) to be rough

fas'tidio *sm* bother, trouble; **dare ~ a qn** to bother *o* annoy sb; **sento ~ allo stomaco** my stomach's upset; **avere fastidi con la polizia** to have trouble *o* bother with the police; **fastidi'oso, -a** *ag* annoying, tiresome; (*schifiltoso*) fastidious

> Attenzione! In inglese esiste la parola *fastidious*, che però significa *pignolo*.

'**fata** *sf* fairy

fa'tale *ag* fatal; (*inevitabile*) inevitable; (*fig*) irresistible

fa'tica, -che *sf* hard work, toil; (*sforzo*) effort; (*di metalli*) fatigue; **a ~** with difficulty; **fare ~ a fare qc** to find it difficult to do sth; **fati'coso, -a** *ag* tiring, exhausting; (*lavoro*) laborious

'**fatto, -a** *pp di* **fare** ▷ *ag*: **un uomo ~** a grown man ▷ *sm* fact; (*azione*) deed; (*avvenimento*) event, occurrence; (*di romanzo, film*) action, story; **~ a mano/in casa** hand-/home-made; **cogliere qn sul ~** to catch sb red-handed; **il ~ sta** *o* **è che** the fact remains *o* is that; **in ~ di** as for, as far as … is concerned; **coppia/unione di ~** long-standing relationship

fat'tore *sm* (*Agr*) farm manager; (*Mat: elemento costitutivo*) factor; **~ di protezione** (*di lozione solare*) factor

fatto'ria *sf* farm; (*casa*) farmhouse

Attenzione! In inglese esiste la parola *factory*, che però significa *fabbrica*.

fatto'rino *sm* errand boy; (*di ufficio*) office boy; (*d'albergo*) porter

fat'tura *sf* (*Comm*) invoice; (*di abito*) tailoring; (*malia*) spell

fattu'rato *sm* (*Comm*) turnover

'**fauna** *sf* fauna

'**fava** *sf* broad bean

'**favola** *sf* (*fiaba*) fairy tale; (*d'intento morale*) fable; (*fandonia*) yarn; **favo'loso, -a** *ag* fabulous; (*incredibile*) incredible

fa'vore *sm* favour; **per ~** please; **fare un ~ a qn** to do sb a favour; **favo'rire** /55/ *vt* to favour; (*il commercio, l'industria, le arti*) to promote, encourage; **vuole favorire?** won't you help yourself?; **favorisca in salotto** please come into the sitting room

fax *sm inv* fax; **mandare qc via ~** to fax sth

fazzo'letto [fattso'letto] *sm* handkerchief; (*per la testa*) (head) scarf; **~ di carta** tissue

feb'braio *sm* February

'**febbre** *sf* fever; **aver la ~** to have a high temperature; **~ da fieno** hay fever

'**feci** *ecc* ['fɛtʃi] *vb vedi* **fare**

fecondazi'one [fekondat'tsjone] *sf* fertilization; **~ artificiale** artificial insemination; **fe'condo, -a** *ag* fertile

'**fede** *sf* (*credenza*) belief, faith; (*Rel*) faith; (*fiducia*) faith, trust; (*fedeltà*) loyalty; (*anello*) wedding ring; (*attestato*) certificate; **aver ~ in qn** to have faith in sb; **in buona/cattiva ~** in good/bad faith; **"in ~"** (*Dir*) "in witness whereof"; **fe'dele** *ag*: **fedele (a)** faithful (to) ▷ *smf* follower; **i fedeli** (*Rel*) the faithful

'**federa** *sf* pillowslip, pillowcase

fede'rale *ag* federal

'**fegato** *sm* liver; (*fig*) guts *pl*, nerve

'**felce** ['fɛltʃe] *sf* fern

fe'lice [fe'litʃe] *ag* happy; (*fortunato*) lucky; **felicità** *sf* happiness

felici'tarsi [felitʃi'tarsi] /72/ *vpr* (*congratularsi*): **~ con qn per qc** to congratulate sb on sth

fe'lino, -a *ag, sm* feline

'**felpa** *sf* sweatshirt

'**femmina** *sf* (*Zool, Tecn*) female; (*figlia*) girl, daughter; (*spesso peg*) woman; **femmi'nile** *ag* feminine; (*sesso*) female; (*lavoro, giornale*) woman's, women's; (*moda*) women's ▷ *sm* (*Ling*) feminine

fe'more *sm* thighbone, femur

fe'nomeno *sm* phenomenon

feri'ale *ag*: **giorno ~** weekday

'**ferie** *sfpl* holidays (*BRIT*), vacation *sg* (*US*); **andare in ~** to go on holiday *o* vacation

fe'rire /55/ *vt* to injure; (*deliberatamente: Mil: ecc*) to wound; (*colpire*) to hurt; **ferirsi** *vpr* to hurt o.s., injure o.s.; **fe'rito, -a** *sm/f* wounded *o* injured man/woman ▷ *sf* injury; wound

fer'maglio [fer'maʎʎo] *sm* clasp; (*per documenti*) clip

fer'mare /72/ vt to stop, halt; (Polizia) to detain, hold ▷ vi to stop; **fermarsi** vpr to stop, halt; **fermarsi a fare qc** to stop to do sth

fer'mata sf stop; **~ dell'autobus** bus stop

fer'menti smpl: **~ lattici** probiotic bacteria

fer'mezza [fer'mettsa] sf (fig) firmness, steadfastness

fermo, -a ag still, motionless; (veicolo) stationary; (orologio) not working; (saldo: anche fig) firm; (voce, mano) steady ▷ escl stop!; keep still! ▷ sm (chiusura) catch, lock; (Dir): **~ di polizia** police detention

fe'roce [fe'rotʃe] ag (animale) fierce, ferocious; (persona) cruel, fierce; (fame, dolore) raging; **le bestie feroci** wild animals

ferra'gosto sm (festa) feast of the Assumption; (periodo) August holidays pl (BRIT) o vacation (US)

○ **FERRAGOSTO**

○ Ferragosto, 15 August, is a national
○ holiday. Marking the feast of
○ the Assumption, its origins are
○ religious but in recent years it
○ has simply become the most
○ important public holiday of the
○ summer season. Most people
○ take some extra time off work and
○ head out of town to the holiday
○ resorts. Consequently, most of
○ industry and commerce grinds to
○ a standstill.

ferra'menta sfpl: **negozio di ~** ironmonger's (BRIT), hardware shop o store (US)

ferro sm iron; **una bistecca ai ferri** a grilled steak; **~ battuto** wrought iron; **~ di cavallo** horseshoe; **~ da stiro** iron; **ferri da calza** knitting needles

ferro'via sf railway (BRIT), railroad (US); **ferrovi'ario, -a** ag railway cpd (BRIT), railroad cpd (US); **ferrovi'ere** sm railwayman (BRIT), railroad man (US)

'fertile ag fertile

'fesso, -a pp di **fendere** ▷ ag (fam: sciocco) crazy, cracked

fes'sura sf crack, split; (per gettone, moneta) slot

'festa sf (religiosa) feast; (pubblica) holiday; (compleanno) birthday; (onomastico) name day; (ricevimento) celebration, party; **far ~** to have a holiday; (far baldoria) to live it up; **far ~ a qn** to give sb a warm welcome

festeggi'are [fested'dʒare] /62/ vt to celebrate; (persona) to have a celebration for

fes'tivo, -a ag (atmosfera) festive; **giorno ~** holiday

'feto sm foetus (BRIT), fetus (US)

'fetta sf slice

fettuc'cine [fettut'tʃine] sfpl (Cuc) ribbon-shaped pasta

FF.SS. abbr = **Ferrovie dello Stato**

FI sigla = **Firenze** ▷ abbr (= Forza Italia) Italian centre-right political party

fi'aba sf fairy tale

fi'acca sf weariness; (svogliatezza) listlessness

fi'acco, -a, -chi, -che ag (stanco) tired, weary; (svogliato) listless; (debole) weak; (mercato) slack

fi'accola sf torch

fi'ala sf phial

fi'amma sf flame

fiam'mante ag (colore) flaming; **nuovo ~** brand new

fiam'mifero sm match

fiam'mingo, -a, -ghi, -ghe ag Flemish ▷ sm/f Fleming ▷ sm (Ling) Flemish; **i Fiamminghi** the Flemish

fi'anco, -chi sm side; (Mil) flank; **di ~** sideways, from the side; **a ~ a ~** side by side

fi'asco, -schi sm flask; (fig) fiasco; **fare ~** to fail

fia'tare /72/ vi (fig: parlare): **senza ~** without saying a word

fi'ato *sm* breath; (*resistenza*) stamina; **avere il ~ grosso** to be out of breath; **prendere ~** to catch one's breath

'fibbia *sf* buckle

'fibra *sf* fibre; (*fig*) constitution

fic'care /20/ *vt* to push, thrust, drive; **ficcarsi** *vpr* (*andare a finire*) to get to

ficcherò *ecc* [fikke'rɔ] *vb vedi* **ficcare**

'fico, -chi *sm* (*pianta*) fig tree; (*frutto*) fig; **~ d'India** prickly pear; **~ secco** dried fig

fiction ['fikʃon] *sf inv* TV drama
Attenzione! In inglese esiste la parola *fiction*, che però significa *narrativa* oppure *finzione*.

fidanza'mento [fidantsa'mento] *sm* engagement

fidan'zarsi [fidan'tsarsi] /72/ *vpr* to get engaged; **fidan'zato, -a** *sm/f* fiancé (fiancée)

fi'darsi /72/ *vpr*: **~ di** to trust; **fi'dato, -a** *ag* reliable, trustworthy

fi'ducia [fi'dutʃa] *sf* confidence, trust; **incarico di ~** position of trust, responsible position; **persona di ~** reliable person

fie'nile *sm* barn; hayloft

fi'eno *sm* hay

fi'era *sf* fair

fi'ero, -a *ag* proud; (*audace*) bold

'fifa *sf* (*fam*): **aver ~** to have the jitters

fig. *abbr* (= *figura*) fig

'figlia ['fiʎʎa] *sf* daughter

figli'astro, -a [fiʎ'ʎastro] *sm/f* stepson/daughter

'figlio ['fiʎʎo] *sm* son; (*senza distinzione di sesso*) child; **~ di papà** spoilt, wealthy young man; **~ unico** only child

fi'gura *sf* figure; (*forma, aspetto esterno*) form, shape; (*illustrazione*) picture, illustration; **far ~** to look smart; **fare una brutta ~** to make a bad impression

figu'rare *vi* to appear ▷ *vt*: **figurarsi qc** to imagine sth; **figurarsi** *vr*: **figurati!** imagine that!; **ti do noia?**

— **ma figurati!** am I disturbing you? — not at all!

figu'rina *sf* figurine; (*cartoncino*) picture card

'fila *sf* row, line; (*coda*) queue; (*serie*) series, string; **di ~** in succession; **fare la ~** to queue; **in ~ indiana** in single file

fi'lare /72/ *vt* to spin ▷ *vi* (*baco, ragno*) to spin; (*formaggio fuso*) to go stringy; (*discorso*) to hang together; (*fam: amoreggiare*) to go steady; (*muoversi a forte velocità*) to go at full speed; **~ diritto** (*fig*) to toe the line; **~ via** to dash off

filas'trocca, -che *sf* nursery rhyme

filate'lia *sf* philately, stamp collecting

fi'letto *sm* (*di vite*) thread; (*di carne*) fillet

fili'ale *ag* filial ▷ *sf* (*di impresa*) branch

film *sm inv* film

'filo *sm* (*anche fig*) thread; (*filato*) yarn; (*metallico*) wire; (*di lama, rasoio*) edge; **con un ~ di voce** in a whisper; **per ~ e per segno** in detail; **~ d'erba** blade of grass; **~ interdentale** dental floss; **~ di perle** string of pearls; **~ spinato** barbed wire

fi'lone *sm* (*di minerali*) seam, vein; (*pane*) ≈ Vienna loaf; (*fig*) trend

filoso'fia *sf* philosophy; **fi'losofo, -a** *sm/f* philosopher

fil'trare /72/ *vt, vi* to filter

'filtro *sm* filter; **~ dell'olio** (*Aut*) oil filter

fi'nale *ag* final ▷ *sm* (*di libro, film*) end, ending; (*Mus*) finale ▷ *sf* (*Sport*) final; **final'mente** *av* finally, at last

fi'nanza [fi'nantsa] *sf* finance; **finanze** *sfpl* (*di individuo, Stato*) finances

finché [fin'ke] *cong* (*per tutto il tempo che*) as long as; (*fino al momento in cui*) until; **aspetta ~ io (non) sia ritornato** wait until I get back

'fine *ag* (*lamina, carta*) thin; (*capelli, polvere*) fine; (*vista, udito*) keen, sharp; (*persona: raffinata*) refined, distinguished; (*osservazione*) subtle ▷ sf end ▷ sm aim, purpose; (*esito*) result, outcome; **in** o **alla ~** in the end, finally; **secondo ~** ulterior motive

fi'nestra sf window; fines'trino sm window

'fingere ['findʒere] /54/ vt to feign; (*supporre*) to imagine, suppose; fingersi vpr: fingersi ubriaco/ pazzo to pretend to be drunk/crazy; **~ di fare** to pretend to do

fi'nire /55/ vt to finish ▷ vi to finish, end; **~ di fare** (*compiere*) to finish doing; (*smettere*) to stop doing; **~ in galera** to end up o finish up in prison

finlan'dese ag Finnish ▷ smf Finn ▷ sm (Ling) Finnish; Fin'landia sf: **la Finlandia** Finland

'fino, -a ag (*capelli, seta*) fine; (*oro*) pure; (*fig: acuto*) shrewd ▷ av (*spesso troncato in fin*: pure, anche) even ▷ prep (*spesso troncato in fin*): **fin quando?** till when?; **fin qui** as far as here; **~ a** (*tempo*) until, till; (*luogo*) as far as, (up) to; **fin da domani** from tomorrow onwards; **fin da ieri** since yesterday; **fin dalla nascita** from o since birth

fi'nocchio [fi'nɔkkjo] sm fennel; (*fam, peg: omosessuale*) queer

fi'nora av up till now

'finsi ecc vb vedi fingere

'finto, -a pp di fingere ▷ ag false; (*fiori*) artificial ▷ sf pretence

finzi'one [fin'tsjone] sf pretence , sham

fi'occo, -chi sm (*di nastro*) bow; (*di stoffa, lana*) flock; (*di neve*) flake; (*Naut*) jib; **coi fiocchi** (*fig*) first-rate; **fiocchi di avena** oatflakes; **fiocchi di granoturco** cornflakes

fi'ocina ['fjɔtʃina] sf harpoon

fi'oco, -a, -chi, -che ag faint, dim

fi'onda sf catapult

fio'raio, -a sm/f florist

fi'ore sm flower; **fiori** smpl (*Carte*) clubs; **a fior d'acqua** on the surface of the water; **aver i nervi a fior di**

pelle to be on edge; **fior di latte** cream; **fiori di campo** wild flowers

fioren'tino, -a ag Florentine

fio'retto sm (*Scherma*) foil

fio'rire /55/ vi (*rosa*) to flower; (*albero*) to blossom; (*fig*) to flourish

Fi'renze [fi'rentse] sf Florence

'firma sf signature

> Attenzione! In inglese esiste la parola firm, che però significa ditta.

fir'mare /72/ vt to sign; **un abito firmato** a designer suit

fisar'monica, -che sf accordion

fis'cale ag fiscal, tax cpd; **medico ~** doctor employed by Social Security to verify cases of sick leave

fischi'are [fis'kjare] /19/ vi to whistle ▷ vt to whistle; (*attore*) to boo, hiss; fischi'etto sm (*strumento*) whistle; 'fischio sm whistle

'fisco sm tax authorities pl, ≈ Inland Revenue (BRIT), ≈ Internal Revenue Service (US)

'fisica sf vedi fisico

'fisico, -a, -ci, -che ag physical ▷ sm/f physicist ▷ sm physique

fisiotera'pia sf physiotherapy; fisiotera'pista smf physiotherapist

fis'sare /72/ vt to fix, fasten; (*guardare intensamente*) to stare at; (*data, condizioni*) to fix, establish, set; (*prenotare*) to book; fissarsi vpr: **fissarsi su** (*sguardo, attenzione*) to focus on; (*fig: idea*) to become obsessed with

'fisso, -a ag fixed; (*stipendio, impiego*) regular ▷ av: **guardare ~ qn/qc** to stare at sb/sth; **telefono ~** landline

'fitta sf vedi fitto

fit'tizio, -a ag fictitious, imaginary

'fitto, -a ag thick, dense; (*pioggia*) heavy ▷ sm depths pl, middle; (*affitto, pigione*) rent ▷ sf sharp pain; **una fitta al cuore** (*fig*) a pang of grief; **nel ~ del bosco** in the heart o depths of the wood

fi'ume sm river

fiu'tare /72/ vt to smell, sniff; (animale) to scent; (fig: inganno) to get wind of, smell; **~ tabacco** to take snuff; **~ cocaina** to snort cocaine

fla'grante ag: **cogliere qn in ~** to catch sb red-handed

fla'nella sf flannel

flash [flaʃ] sm inv (Fot) flash; (giornalistico) newsflash

'flauto sm flute

fles'sibile ag pliable; (fig: che si adatta) flexible

flessibili'tà sf (anche fig) flexibility

flessi'one sf (gen) bending; (Ginnastica: a terra) sit-up; (: in piedi) forward bend; (: sulle gambe) knee-bend; (diminuzione) slight drop, slight fall; (Ling) inflection; **fare una ~** to bend; **una ~ economica** a downward trend in the economy

'flettere /92/ vt to bend

'flipper sm inv pinball machine

F.lli abbr (= fratelli) Bros

'flora sf flora

'florido, -a ag flourishing; (fig) glowing with health

'floscio, -a, -sci, -sce ['flɔʃʃo] ag (cappello) floppy, soft; (muscoli) flabby

'flotta sf fleet

'fluido, -a ag, sm fluid

flu'oro sm fluorine

'flusso sm flow; (Fisica, Med) flux; **~ e riflusso** ebb and flow

fluvi'ale ag river cpd, fluvial

FMI sigla m (= Fondo Monetario Internazionale) IMF

'foca, -che sf (Zool) seal

fo'caccia, -ce [fo'kattʃa] sf kind of pizza; (dolce) bun

'foce ['fotʃe] sf (Geo) mouth

foco'laio sm (Med) centre (BRIT) o center (US) of infection; (fig) hotbed

foco'lare sm hearth, fireside; (Tecn) furnace

'fodera sf (di vestito) lining; (di libro, poltrona) cover

'fodero sm (di spada) scabbard; (di pugnale) sheath; (di pistola) holster

'foga sf enthusiasm, ardour

'foglia ['fɔʎʎa] sf leaf; **~ d'argento/d'oro** silver/gold leaf

'foglio ['fɔʎʎo] sm (di carta) sheet (of paper); (di metallo) sheet; **~ di calcolo** (Inform) spreadsheet; **~ rosa** (Aut) provisional licence; **~ di via** (Dir) expulsion order; **~ volante** pamphlet

'fogna ['foɲɲa] sf drain, sewer

föhn [føːn] sm inv hair-dryer

folksono'mia sf (Inform) folksonomy

'folla sf crowd, throng

'folle ag mad, insane; (Tecn) idle; **in ~** (Aut) in neutral

fol'lia sf folly, foolishness; foolish act; (pazzia) madness, lunacy

'folto, -a ag thick

fon sm inv = **föhn**

fondamen'tale ag fundamental, basic

fonda'mento sm foundation; **fondamenta** sfpl (Edil) foundations

fon'dare /72/ vt to found; (fig: dar base): **~ qc su** to base sth on

fon'dente ag: **cioccolato ~** plain o dark chocolate

'fondere /25/ vt (neve) to melt; (metallo) to fuse, melt; (fig: colori) to merge, blend; (: imprese, gruppi) to merge ▷ vi to melt; **fondersi** vpr to melt; (fig: partiti, correnti) to unite, merge

'fondo, -a ag deep ▷ sm (di recipiente, pozzo) bottom; (di stanza) back; (quantità di liquido che resta, deposito) dregs pl; (sfondo) background; (unità immobiliare) property, estate; (somma di denaro) fund; (Sport) long-distance race; **fondi** smpl (denaro) funds; **a notte fonda** at dead of night; **in ~ a** at the bottom of; at the back of; (strada) at the end of; **in ~** (fig) after all, all things considered; **andare fino in ~ a** (fig) to examine thoroughly; **andare a ~** (nave) to sink; **conoscere a ~** to know inside out; **dar ~ a** (provvisti, soldi) to use up; **a ~ perduto** (Comm) without security; **~ comune di investimento** investment trust; **fondi di caffè** coffee grounds; **fondi di magazzino** old o unsold stock sg

fondo'tinta sm inv (cosmetico) foundation

fo'netica sf phonetics sg

fon'tana sf fountain

fonte sf spring, source; (fig) source ▷ sm: **~ battesimale** (Rel) font; **~ energetica** source of energy

fo'raggio [fo'raddʒo] sm fodder, forage

fo'rare /72/ vt to pierce, make a hole in; (pallone) to burst; (biglietto) to punch; **~ una gomma** to burst a tyre (BRIT) o tire (US)

forbici ['fɔrbitʃi] sfpl scissors

forca, -che sf (Agr) fork, pitchfork; (patibolo) gallows sg

for'chetta [for'ketta] sf fork

for'cina [for'tʃina] sf hairpin

fo'resta sf forest

foresti'ero, -a ag foreign ▷ sm/f foreigner

forfora sf dandruff

forma sf form; (aspetto esteriore) form, shape; (Dir: procedura) procedure; (per calzature) last; (stampo da cucina) mould; **mantenersi in ~** to keep fit

formag'gino [formad'dʒino] sm processed cheese

for'maggio [for'maddʒo] sm cheese

for'male ag formal

for'mare /72/ vt to form, shape, make; (numero di telefono) to dial; (fig: carattere) to form, mould; **formarsi** vpr to form, take shape; **for'mato** sm format, size; **formazi'one** sf formation; (fig: educazione) training; **formazione continua** continuing education; **formazione permanente** lifelong learning; **formazione professionale** vocational training

for'mica¹, -che sf ant

formica²® ['fɔrmika] sf (materiale) Formica®

formi'dabile ag powerful, formidable; (straordinario) remarkable

formula sf formula; **~ di cortesia** (nelle lettere) letter ending

formu'lare /72/ vt to formulate; to express

for'naio sm baker

for'nello sm (elettrico, a gas) ring; (di pipa) bowl

for'nire /55/ vt: **~ qn di qc, ~ qc a qn** to provide o supply sb with sth, supply sth to sb

forno sm (di cucina) oven; (panetteria) bakery; (Tecn: per calce ecc) kiln; (: per metalli) furnace; **~ a microonde** microwave oven

foro sm (buco) hole; (Storia) forum; (tribunale) (law) court

forse av perhaps, maybe; (circa) about; **essere in ~** to be in doubt

forte ag strong; (suono) loud; (spesa) considerable, great; (passione, dolore) great, deep ▷ av strongly; (velocemente) fast; (a voce alta) loud(ly); (violentemente) hard ▷ sm (edificio) fort; (specialità) forte, strong point; **essere ~ in qc** to be good at sth

for'tezza [for'tettsa] sf (morale) strength; (luogo fortificato) fortress

for'tuito, -a ag fortuitous, chance cpd

for'tuna sf (destino) fortune, luck; (buona sorte) success, fortune; (eredità, averi) fortune; **per ~** luckily, fortunately; **di ~** makeshift, improvised; **atterraggio di ~** emergency landing; **fortu'nato, -a** ag lucky, fortunate; (coronato da successo) successful

forza ['fɔrtsa] sf strength; (potere) power; (Fisica) force ▷ escl come on!; **forze** sfpl (fisiche) strength sg; (Mil) forces; **per ~** against one's will; (naturalmente) of course; **a viva ~** by force; **a ~ di** by dint of; **per causa di ~ maggiore** due to circumstances beyond one's control; **la ~ pubblica** the police *pl*: **forze dell'ordine** the forces of law and order; **~ di pace** peacekeeping force; **le forze armate** the armed forces; **F~ Italia** *moderate right-wing party*

for'zare [for'tsare] /72/ *vt* to force; **~ qn a fare** to force sb to do

for'zista, -i, -e [for'tsista] *ag* of Forza Italia ▷ *sm/f* member (*o* supporter) of Forza Italia

fos'chia [fos'kia] *sf* mist, haze

'fosco, -a, -schi, -sche *ag* dark, gloomy

'fosforo *sm* phosphorous

'fossa *sf* pit; (*di cimitero*) grave; **~ biologica** septic tank

fos'sato *sm* ditch; (*di fortezza*) moat

fos'setta *sf* dimple

'fossi *ecc vb vedi* **essere**

'fossile *ag*, *sm* fossil (*cpd*)

'fosso *sm* ditch; (*Mil*) trench

'foste *ecc vb vedi* **essere**

'foto *sf inv* photo ▷ *prefisso*: **~ ricordo** souvenir photo; **~ tessera** passport(-type) photo; **foto'camera** *sf*: **fotocamera digitale** digital camera; **foto'copia** *sf* photocopy; **fotocopi'are** /19/ *vt* to photocopy; **fotocopia'trice** [fotokopja'tritʃe] *sf* photocopier; **fotofo'nino** *sm* camera phone; **fotogra'fare** /72/ *vt* to photograph; **fotogra'fia** *sf* (*procedimento*) photography; (*immagine*) photograph; **fare una fotografia** to take a photograph; **una fotografia a colori/in bianco e nero** a colour/black and white photograph; **foto'grafico, -a, -ci, -che** *ag* photographic; **macchina fotografica** camera; **fo'tografo, -a** *sm/f* photographer; **fotoro'manzo** *sm* romantic picture story; **fotovol'taico, -a, -ci, -che** *ag* photovoltaic; **pannelli fotovoltaici** solar panels

fou'lard [fu'lar] *sm inv* scarf

fra *prep* = **tra**

'fradicio, -a, -ci, -ce ['fraditʃo] *ag* (*molto bagnato*) soaking (wet); **ubriaco ~** blind drunk

'fragile ['fradʒile] *ag* fragile; (*fig: salute*) delicate

'fragola *sf* strawberry

fra'grante *ag* fragrant

frain'tendere /120/ *vt* to misunderstand

fram'mento *sm* fragment

'frana *sf* landslide; (*fig: persona*): **essere una ~** to be useless

fran'cese [fran'tʃeze] *ag* French ▷ *smf* Frenchman/woman ▷ *sm* (*Ling*) French; **i Francesi** the French

'Francia ['frantʃa] *sf*: **la ~** France

'franco, -a, -chi, -che *ag* (*Comm*) free; (*sincero*) frank, open, sincere ▷ *sm* (*moneta*) franc; **farla franca** (*fig*) to get off scot-free; **~ di dogana** duty-free; **prezzo ~ fabbrica** ex-works price

franco'bollo *sm* (postage) stamp

'frangia, -ge ['frandʒa] *sf* fringe

frappé *sm* milk shake

'frase *sf* (*Ling*) sentence; (*locuzione, espressione, Mus*) phrase; **~ fatta** set phrase

'frassino *sm* ash (tree)

frastagli'ato, -a [frastaʎ'ʎato] *ag* (*costa*) indented, jagged

frastor'nare /72/ *vt* to daze; (*confondere*) to bewilder

frastu'ono *sm* hubbub, din

'frate *sm* friar, monk

fratel'lastro *sm* stepbrother; (*con genitore in comune*) half brother

fra'tello *sm* brother; **fratelli** *smpl* brothers; (*nel senso di fratelli e sorelle*) brothers and sisters

fra'terno, -a *ag* fraternal, brotherly

frat'tempo *sm*: **nel ~** in the meantime, meanwhile

frat'tura *sf* fracture; (*fig*) split, break

frazi'one [frat'tsjone] *sf* fraction; (*anche: ~ di comune*) hamlet

'freccia, -ce ['frettʃa] *sf* arrow; **~ di direzione** (*Aut*) indicator

fred'dezza [fred'dettsa] *sf* coldness
freddo, -a *ag, sm* cold; **fa ~** it's cold; **aver ~** to be cold; **a ~** *(fig)* deliberately; **freddo'loso, -a** *ag* sensitive to the cold
fre'gare /80/ *vt* to rub; *(fam: truffare)* to take in, cheat; (: *rubare)* to swipe, pinch; **fregarsene** *(fam!)*: **chi se ne frega?** who gives a damn (about it)?
fregherò *ecc* [frege'rɔ] *vb vedi* **fregare**
fre'nare /72/ *vt (veicolo)* to slow down; *(cavallo)* to rein in; *(lacrime)* to restrain, hold back ▷ *vi* to brake; **frenarsi** *vpr (fig)* to restrain o.s., control o.s.
freno *sm* brake; *(morso)* bit; **tenere a ~** to restrain; **~ a disco** disc brake; **~ a mano** handbrake
frequen'tare /72/ *vt (scuola, corso)* to attend; *(locale, bar)* to go to, frequent; *(persone)* to see (often); **frequen'tato, -a** *ag (locale)* busy; **fre'quente** *ag* frequent; **di frequente** frequently
fres'chezza [fres'kettsa] *sf* freshness; **fresco, -a, -schi, -sche** *ag* fresh; *(temperatura)* cool; *(notizia)* recent, fresh ▷ *sm*: **godere il fresco** to enjoy the cool air; **stare fresco** *(fig)* to be in for it; **mettere al fresco** to put in a cool place
fretta *sf* hurry, haste; **in ~** in a hurry; **in ~ e furia** in a mad rush; **aver ~** to be in a hurry
friggere ['friddʒere] /56/ *vt* to fry ▷ *vi (olio ecc)* to sizzle
frigido, -a ['fridʒido] *ag (Med)* frigid
frigo, -ghi *sm* fridge
frigo'bar *sm inv* minibar
frigo'rifero, -a *ag* refrigerating ▷ *sm* refrigerator
fringu'ello *sm* chaffinch
frissi *ecc vb vedi* **friggere**
frit'tata *sf* omelet(te); **fare una ~** *(fig)* to make a mess of things
frit'tella *sf (Cuc)* fritter
fritto, -a *pp di* **friggere** ▷ *ag* fried ▷ *sm* fried food; **~ misto** mixed fry

frit'tura *sf*: **~ di pesce** mixed fried fish
frivolo, -a *ag* frivolous
frizi'one [frit'tsjone] *sf* friction; *(di pelle)* rub, rub-down; *(Aut)* clutch
friz'zante [frid'dzante] *ag (anche fig)* sparkling
fro'dare /72/ *vt* to defraud, cheat
frode *sf* fraud; **~ fiscale** tax evasion
fronda *sf (leafy)* branch; *(di partito politico)* internal opposition; **fronde** *sfpl (di albero)* foliage *sg*
fron'tale *ag* frontal; *(scontro)* head-on
fronte *sf (Anat)* forehead; *(di edificio)* front, façade ▷ *sm (Mil, Pol, Meteor)* front; **a ~, di ~** facing, opposite; **di ~ a** *(posizione)* opposite, facing, in front of; *(a paragone di)* compared with
fronti'era *sf* border, frontier
frottola *sf* fib
fru'gare /80/ *vi* to rummage ▷ *vt* to search
frugherò *ecc* [fruge'rɔ] *vb vedi* **frugare**
frul'lare /72/ *vt (Cuc)* to whisk ▷ *vi (uccelli)* to flutter; **frul'lato** *sm* milk shake; fruit drink; **frulla'tore** *sm* electric mixer
fru'mento *sm* wheat
fru'scio [fruʃʃio] *sm* rustle; rustling; *(di acque)* murmur
frusta *sf* whip; *(Cuc)* whisk
frus'tare /72/ *vt* to whip
frus'trato, -a *ag* frustrated
frutta *sf* fruit; *(portata)* dessert; **~ candita/secca** candied/dried fruit
frut'tare /72/ *vi* to bear dividends, give a return
frut'teto *sm* orchard
frutti'vendolo, -a *sm/f* greengrocer (BRIT), produce dealer (US)
frutto *sm* fruit; *(fig: risultato)* result(s); *(Econ: interesse)* interest; (: *reddito)* income; **frutti di mare** seafood *sg*: **frutti di bosco** berries
FS *abbr* (= *Ferrovie dello Stato*) Italian railways

fu *vb vedi* **essere** ▷ *ag inv:* **il fu Paolo Bianchi** the late Paolo Bianchi

fuci'lare [futʃiˈlare] /72/ *vt* to shoot

fu'cile [fuˈtʃile] *sm* rifle, gun; (*da caccia*) shotgun, gun

fucsia *sf* fuchsia

'fuga, -ghe *sf* escape, flight; (*di gas, liquidi*) leak; (*Mus*) fugue; **~ di cervelli** brain drain

fug'gire [fudˈdʒire] /31/ *vi* to flee, run away; (*fig: passar veloce*) to fly ▷ *vt* to avoid

'fui *vb vedi* **essere**

fu'liggine [fuˈliddʒine] *sf* soot

'fulmine *sm* bolt of lightning; **fulmini** *smpl* lightning *sg*

fu'mare /72/ *vi* to smoke; (*emettere vapore*) to steam ▷ *vt* to smoke; **fuma'tore, -'trice** *sm/f* smoker

fu'metto *sm* comic strip; **giornale a fumetti** comic

'fummo *vb vedi* **essere**

'fumo *sm* smoke; (*vapore*) steam; (*il fumare tabacco*) smoking; **fumi** *smpl* (*industriali ecc*) fumes; **vendere ~** to deceive, cheat; **i fumi dell'alcool** the after-effects of drink; **~ passivo** passive smoking; **fu'moso, -a** *ag* smoky; (*fig*) muddled

'fune *sf* rope, cord; (*più grossa*) cable

'funebre *ag* (*rito*) funeral; (*aspetto*) gloomy, funereal

fune'rale *sm* funeral

'fungere [ˈfundʒere] /5/ *vi:* **~ da** to act as

'fungo, -ghi *sm* fungus; (*commestibile*) mushroom; **~ velenoso** toadstool

funico'lare *sf* funicular railway

funi'via *sf* cable railway

'funsi ecc *vb vedi* **fungere**

funzio'nare [funtsjoˈnare] /72/ *vi* to work, function; (*fungere*): **~ da** to act as

funzio'nario [funtsjoˈnarjo] *sm* official; **~ statale** civil servant

funzi'one [funˈtsjone] *sf* function; (*carica*) post, position; (*Rel*) service; **in ~** (*meccanismo*) in operation; **in ~ di**

(*come*) as; **fare la ~ di qn** (*farne le veci*) to take sb's place

fu'oco, -chi *sm* fire; (*fornello*) ring; (*Fot, Fisica*) focus; **dare ~ a qc** to set fire to sth; **far ~** (*sparare*) to fire; **al ~!** fire!; **~ d'artificio** firework

fuorché [fworˈke] *cong, prep* except

fu'ori *av* outside; (*all'aperto*) outdoors, outside; (*fuori di casa, Sport*) out; (*esclamativo*) get out! ▷ *prep:* **~ (di)** out of, outside ▷ *sm* outside; **lasciar ~ qc/qn** to leave sth/sb out; **far ~ qn** (*fam*) to kill sb, do sb in; **essere ~ di sé** to be beside oneself; **~ luogo** (*inopportuno*) out of place, uncalled for; **~ mano** out of the way, remote; **~ pericolo** out of danger; **~ uso** old-fashioned; obsolete; **fuorigi'oco** *sm* offside; **fuoris'trada** *sm* (*Aut*) cross-country vehicle

'furbo, -a *ag* clever, smart; (*peg*) cunning

fu'rente *ag:* **~ (contro)** furious (with)

fur'fante *sm* rascal, scoundrel

fur'gone *sm* van

'furia *sf* (*ira*) fury, rage; (*fig: impeto*) fury, violence; (: *fretta*) rush; **a ~ di** by dint of; **andare su tutte le furie** to fly into a rage; **furi'bondo, -a** *ag* furious

furi'oso, -a *ag* furious

'furono *vb vedi* **essere**

fur'tivo, -a *ag* furtive

'furto *sm* theft; **~ con scasso** burglary

'fusa *sfpl:* **fare le ~** to purr

fu'seaux *smpl* leggings

'fusi ecc *vb vedi* **fondere**

fu'sibile *sm* (*Elettr*) fuse

fusi'one *sf* (*di metalli*) fusion, melting; (*colata*) casting; (*Comm*) merger; (*fig*) merging

'fuso, -a *pp di* **fondere** ▷ *sm* (*Filatura*) spindle; **~ orario** time zone

fus'tino *sm* (*di detersivo*) tub

'fusto *sm* stem; (*Anat, di albero*) trunk; (*recipiente*) drum, can

fu'turo, -a *ag, sm* future

g

G8 [dʒi'otto] *sm* (= *Gruppo degli Otto*) G8

G20 [dʒi'venti] *sm* (= *Gruppo dei Venti*) G20

gabbia *sf* cage; (*da imballaggio*) crate; **~ dell'ascensore** lift (BRIT) o elevator (US) shaft; **~ toracica** (*Anat*) rib cage

gabbiano *sm* (sea)gull

gabinetto *sm* (*Med: ecc*) consulting room; (*Pol*) ministry; (*di decenza*) toilet, lavatory; (*Ins: di fisica ecc*) laboratory

gaffe [gaf] *sf inv* blunder, boob

galante *ag* gallant, courteous; (*avventura, poesia*) amorous

galassia *sf* galaxy

galera *sf* (*Naut*) galley; (*prigione*) prison

galla *sf*: **a ~** afloat; **venire a ~** to surface, come to the surface; (*fig: verità*) to come out

galleggiare [galled'dʒare] /62/ *vi* to float

galleria *sf* (*traforo*) tunnel; (*Archit, d'arte*) gallery; (*Teat*) circle; (*strada coperta con negozi*) arcade

Galles *sm*: **il ~** Wales; **gallese** *ag* Welsh ▷ *smf* Welshman/woman ▷ *sm* (*Ling*) Welsh; **i Gallesi** the Welsh

gallina *sf* hen

gallo *sm* cock

galoppare /72/ *vi* to gallop

galoppo *sm* gallop; **al** *o* **di ~** at a gallop

gamba *sf* leg; (*asta: di lettera*) stem; **in ~** (*in buona salute*) well; (*bravo, sveglio*) bright, smart; **prendere qc sotto ~** (*fig*) to treat sth too lightly

gamberetto *sm* shrimp

gambero *sm* (*di acqua dolce*) crayfish; (*di mare*) prawn

gambo *sm* stem; (*di frutta*) stalk

gamma *sf* (*Mus*) scale; (*di colori, fig*) range

gancio ['gantʃo] *sm* hook

gara *sf* competition; (*Sport*) competition; contest; match; (*: corsa*) race; **fare a ~** to compete, vie

garage [ga'raʒ] *sm inv* garage

garantire /55/ *vt* to guarantee; (*debito*) to stand surety for; (*dare per certo*) to assure

garanzia [garan'tsia] *sf* guarantee; (*pegno*) security

garbato, -a *ag* courteous, polite

gareggiare [gared'dʒare] /62/ *vi* to compete

gargarismo *sm* gargle; **fare i gargarismi** to gargle

garofano *sm* carnation; **chiodo di ~** clove

garza ['gardza] *sf* (*per bende*) gauze

garzone [gar'dzone] *sm* (*di negozio*) boy

gas *sm inv* gas; **a tutto ~** at full speed; **dare ~** (*Aut*) to accelerate

gasolio *sm* diesel (oil)

gas(s)ato, -a *ag* fizzy

gastrite *sf* gastritis

gastronomia *sf* gastronomy

gatta *sf* cat, she-cat

gat'tino *sm* kitten

'gatto *sm* cat, tomcat; **~ delle nevi** (*Aut, Sci*) snowcat; **~ selvatico** wildcat

'gazza ['gaddza] *sf* magpie

gel [dʒɛl] *sm inv* gel

ge'lare [dʒe'lare] /72/ *vt, vi, vb impers* to freeze

gelate'ria [dʒelate'ria] *sf* ice-cream shop

gela'tina [dʒela'tina] *sf* gelatine; **~ esplosiva** gelignite; **~ di frutta** fruit jelly

ge'lato, -a [dʒe'lato] *ag* frozen ▷ *sm* ice cream

'gelido, -a ['dʒɛlido] *ag* icy, ice-cold

'gelo ['dʒɛlo] *sm* (*temperatura*) intense cold; (*brina*) frost; (*fig*) chill

gelo'sia [dʒelo'sia] *sf* jealousy

ge'loso, -a [dʒe'loso] *ag* jealous

'gelso ['dʒɛlso] *sm* mulberry (tree)

gelso'mino [dʒelso'mino] *sm* jasmine

ge'mello, -a [dʒe'mello] *ag, sm/f* twin; **gemelli** *smpl* (*di camicia*) cufflinks; **Gemelli** Gemini *sg*

'gemere ['dʒɛmere] /29/ *vi* to moan, groan; (*cigolare*) to creak

'gemma ['dʒɛmma] *sf* (*Bot*) bud; (*pietra preziosa*) gem

gene'rale [dʒene'rale] *ag, sm* general; **in ~** (*per sommi capi*) in general terms; (*di solito*) usually, in general

gene'rare [dʒene'rare] /72/ *vt* (*dar vita*) to give birth to; (*produrre*) to produce; (*causare*) to arouse; (*Tecn*) to produce, generate; **generazi'one** *sf* generation

'genere ['dʒɛnere] *sm* kind, type, sort; (*Biol*) genus; (*merce*) article, product; (*Ling*) gender; (*Arte, Letteratura*) genre; **in ~** generally, as a rule; **il ~ umano** mankind; **generi alimentari** foodstuffs

ge'nerico, -a, -ci, -che [dʒe'nɛriko] *ag* generic; (*vago*) vague, imprecise

'genero ['dʒɛnero] *sm* son-in-law

gene'roso, -a [dʒene'roso] *ag* generous

ge'netico, -a, -ci, -che [dʒe'nɛtiko] *ag* genetic ▷ *sf* genetics *sg*

gen'giva [dʒen'dʒiva] *sf* (*Anat*) gum

geni'ale [dʒe'njale] *ag* (*persona*) of genius; (*idea*) ingenious, brilliant

'genio ['dʒɛnjo] *sm* genius; **andare a ~ a qn** to be to sb's liking, appeal to sb

geni'tore [dʒeni'tore] *sm* parent, father *o* mother; **genitori** *smpl* parents

gen'naio [dʒen'najo] *sm* January

'Genova ['dʒɛnova] *sf* Genoa

'gente ['dʒɛnte] *sf* people *pl*

gen'tile [dʒen'tile] *ag* (*persona, atto*) kind; (: *garbato*) courteous, polite; (*nelle lettere*): **G~ Signore** Dear Sir; **G~ Signor Fernando Villa** (*sulla busta*) Mr Fernando Villa

genu'ino, -a [dʒenu'ino] *ag* (*prodotto*) natural; (*persona, sentimento*) genuine, sincere

geogra'fia [dʒeogra'fia] *sf* geography

geolo'gia [dʒeolo'dʒia] *sf* geology

ge'ometra, -i, -e [dʒe'ɔmetra] *smf* (*professionista*) surveyor

geome'tria [dʒeome'tria] *sf* geometry

ge'ranio [dʒe'ranjo] *sm* geranium

gerar'chia [dʒerar'kia] *sf* hierarchy

'gergo, -ghi ['dʒɛrgo] *sm* jargon; slang

geria'tria [dʒerja'tria] *sf* geriatrics *sg*

Ger'mania [dʒer'manja] *sf*: **la ~** Germany; **la ~ occidentale/ orientale** West/East Germany

'germe ['dʒɛrme] *sm* germ; (*fig*) seed

germogli'are [dʒermoʎ'ʎare] /27/ *vi* to sprout; (*germinare*) to germinate

gero'glifico, -ci [dʒero'glifiko] *sm* hieroglyphic

ge'rundio [dʒe'rundjo] *sm* gerund

'gesso ['dʒɛsso] *sm* chalk; (*Scultura, Med, Edil*) plaster; (*statua*) plaster figure; (*minerale*) gypsum

gesti'one [dʒes'tjone] *sf* management

ges'tire [dʒes'tire] /55/ *vt* to run, manage

'gesto ['dʒɛsto] *sm* gesture

Gesù [dʒe'zu] *sm* Jesus

gesu'ita, -i [dʒezu'ita] *sm* Jesuit

get'tare [dʒet'tare] /72/ *vt* to throw; (*anche*: ~ **via**) to throw away o out; (*Scultura*) to cast; (*Edil*) to lay; (*acqua*) to spout; (*grido*) to utter; **gettarsi** *vpr*: **gettarsi in** (*fiume*) to flow into; ~ **uno sguardo su** to take a quick look at

'getto ['dʒɛtto] *sm* (*di gas, liquido, Aer*) jet; **a ~ continuo** uninterruptedly; **di ~** (*fig*) straight off, in one go

get'tone [dʒet'tone] *sm* token; (*per giochi*) counter; (: *roulette ecc*) chip; ~ **telefonico** telephone token

ghiacci'aio [gjat'tʃajo] *sm* glacier

ghiacci'ato, -a *ag* frozen; (*bevanda*) ice-cold

ghi'accio ['gjattʃo] *sm* ice

ghiacci'olo [gjat'tʃɔlo] *sm* icicle; (*tipo di gelato*) ice lolly (BRIT), popsicle (US)

ghi'aia ['gjaja] *sf* gravel

ghi'anda ['gjanda] *sf* (*Bot*) acorn

ghi'andola ['gjandola] *sf* gland

ghi'otto, -a ['gjotto] *ag* greedy; (*cibo*) delicious, appetizing

ghir'landa [gir'landa] *sf* garland, wreath

'ghiro ['giro] *sm* dormouse

'ghisa ['giza] *sf* cast iron

già [dʒa] *av* already; (*ex, in precedenza*) formerly ▷ *escl* of course!, yes indeed!

gi'acca, -che ['dʒakka] *sf* jacket; ~ **a vento** windcheater (BRIT), windbreaker (US)

giacché [dʒak'ke] *cong* since, as

giac'cone [dʒak'kone] *sm* heavy jacket

gia'cere [dʒa'tʃere] /57/ *vi* to ie

gi'ada ['dʒada] *sf* jade

giagu'aro [dʒa'gwaro] *sm* jaguar

gi'allo ['dʒallo] *ag* yellow; (*carnagione*) sallow ▷ *sm* yellow; (*anche*: **romanzo** ~) detective novel; (*anche*: **film** ~) detective film; ~ **dell'uovo** yolk

Gia'maica [dʒa'maika] *sf*: **la ~** Jamaica

Giap'pone [dʒap'pone] *sm*: **il ~** Japan; **giappo'nese** *ag, smf, sm* Japanese *inv*

giardi'naggio [dʒardi'naddʒo] *sm* gardening

giardini'ere, -a [dʒardi'njere] *sm/f* gardener

giar'dino [dʒar'dino] *sm* garden; ~ **d'infanzia** nursery school; ~ **pubblico** public gardens *pl*, (public) park; ~ **zoologico** zoo

giavel'lotto [dʒavel'lɔtto] *sm* javelin

giga *sm inv* (*Inform*) gig

giga'byte [dʒiga'bait] *sm inv* gigabyte

gi'gante, -'essa [dʒi'gante] *sm/f* giant ▷ *ag* giant, gigantic; (*Comm*) giant-size

'giglio ['dʒiʎʎo] *sm* lily

gilè [dʒi'lɛ] *sm inv* waistcoat

gin [dʒin] *sm inv* gin

gine'cologo, -a, -gi, -ghe [dʒine'kɔlogo] *sm/f* gynaecologist

gi'nepro [dʒi'nepro] *sm* juniper

gi'nestra [dʒi'nɛstra] *sf* (*Bot*) broom

Gi'nevra [dʒi'nevra] *sf* Geneva

gin'nastica [dʒin'nastika] *sf* gymnastics *sg*; (*esercizio fisico*) keep-fit exercises *pl*; (*Ins*) physical education

gi'nocchio [dʒi'nɔkkjo] (*pl f* **ginocchia**) *sm* knee; **stare in ~** to kneel, be on one's knees; **mettersi in ~** to kneel (down)

gio'care [dʒo'kare] /20/ *vt* to play; (*scommettere*) to stake, wager, bet; (*ingannare*) to take in ▷ *vi* to play; (*a roulette ecc*) to gamble; (*fig*) to play a part, be important; ~ **a** (*gioco, sport*) to play; (*cavalli*) to bet on; **giocarsi la carriera** to put one's career at risk; **gioca'tore, -'trice** *sm/f* player; gambler

gio'cattolo [dʒo'kattolo] *sm* toy

giocherò ecc [dʒoke'rɔ] vb vedi **giocare**

gi'oco, -chi [dʒɔko] sm game; (divertimento, Tecn) play; (al casinò) gambling; (Carte) hand; (insieme di pezzi ecc necessari per un gioco) set; **per ~** for fun; **fare il doppio ~ con qn** to double-cross sb; **~ d'azzardo** game of chance; **~ degli scacchi** chess set; **i Giochi Olimpici** the Olympic Games

giocoli'ere [dʒoko'ljɛre] sm juggler

gi'oia [dʒɔja] sf joy, delight; (pietra preziosa) jewel, precious stone

gioielle'ria [dʒojelle'ria] sf jeweller's (BRIT) o jeweler's (US) craft; (negozio) jewel(l)er's (shop)

gioielli'ere, -a [dʒojel'ljɛre] sm/f jeweller

gioi'ello [dʒo'jɛllo] sm jewel, piece of jewellery (BRIT) o jewelry (US); **gioielli** smpl (anelli, collane ecc) jewellery sg: **i miei gioielli** my jewels o jewellery; **i gioielli della Corona** the crown jewels

Gior'dania [dʒor'danja] sf: **la ~** Jordan

giorna'laio, -a [dʒorna'lajo] sm/f newsagent (BRIT), newsdealer (US)

gior'nale [dʒor'nale] sm (news) paper; (diario) journal, diary; (Comm) journal; **~ di bordo** (Naut) ship's log; **~ radio** radio news sg

giornali'ero, -a [dʒorna'ljɛro] ag daily; (che varia: umore) changeable ▷ sm day labourer (BRIT) o laborer (US)

giorna'lismo [dʒorna'lizmo] sm journalism

giorna'lista, -i, -e [dʒorna'lista] smf journalist

gior'nata [dʒor'nata] sf day; **~ lavorativa** working day

gi'orno [dʒorno] sm day; (opposto alla notte) day, daytime; (luce del giorno) daylight; **al ~** per day; **di ~** by day; **al ~ d'oggi** nowadays

gi'ostra [dʒɔstra] sf (per bimbi) merry-go-round; (torneo storico) joust

gi'ovane [dʒovane] ag young; (aspetto) youthful ▷ sm youth, young man ▷ sf girl, young woman; **i giovani** young people

gio'vare [dʒo'vare] /72/ vi: **~ a** (essere utile) to be useful to; (far bene) to be good for ▷ vb impers (essere bene, utile) to be useful; **giovarsi** vpr: **giovarsi di qc** to make use of sth

giovedì [dʒove'di] sm inv Thursday; **di** o **il ~** on Thursdays

gioventù [dʒoven'tu] sf (periodo) youth; (i giovani) young people pl, youth

gip [dʒip] sigla m inv (= giudice per le indagini preliminari) judge for preliminary enquiries

gira'dischi [dʒira'diski] sm inv record player

gi'raffa [dʒi'raffa] sf giraffe

gi'rare [dʒi'rare] /72/ vt (far ruotare) to turn; (percorrere, visitare) to go round; (Cine) to shoot; (: come regista) to make; (Comm) to endorse ▷ vi to turn; (più veloce) to spin; (andare in giro) to wander, go around; **girarsi** vpr to turn; **~ attorno a** to go round; to revolve round; **far ~ la testa a qn** to make sb dizzy; (fig) to turn sb's head

girar'rosto [dʒirar'rɔsto] sm (Cuc) spit

gira'sole [dʒira'sole] sm sunflower

gi'revole [dʒi'revole] ag revolving, turning

gi'rino [dʒi'rino] sm tadpole

gi'ro [dʒiro] sm (circuito, cerchio) circle; (di chiave, manovella) turn; (viaggio) tour, excursion; (passeggiata) stroll, walk; (in macchina) drive; (in bicicletta) ride; (Sport: della pista) lap; (di denaro) circulation; (Carte) hand; (Tecn) revolution; **fare un ~** to go for a walk (o a drive o a ride); **andare in ~** to go about, walk around; **prendere in ~ qn** (fig) to take sb for a ride; **a stretto ~ di posta** by return of post; **nel ~ di un mese** in a month's time; **essere nel ~** (fig) to belong to a circle (of friends); **~ d'affari** (*Comm*) turnover; **~ di parole** circumlocution; **~ di prova** (*Aut*) test drive; **~ turistico** sightseeing tour; **giro'collo** *sm*: **a girocollo** crewneck *cpd*

giron'zolare [dʒirondzo'lare] /72/ *vi* to stroll about

'gita ['dʒita] *sf* excursion, trip; **fare una ~** to go for a trip, go on an outing

gi'tano, -a [dʒi'tano] *sm/f* gipsy

giù [dʒu] *av* down; (*dabbasso*) downstairs; **in ~** downwards, down; **~ di lì** (*pressappoco*) thereabouts; **bambini dai 6 anni in ~** children aged 6 and under; **~ per: cadere ~ per le scale** to fall down the stairs; **essere ~** (*fig: di salute*) to be run down; (: *di spirito*) to be depressed

giub'botto [dʒub'bɔtto] *sm* jerkin; **~ antiproiettile** bulletproof vest; **~ salvagente** life jacket

giudi'care [dʒudi'kare] /20/ *vt* to judge; (*accusato*) to try; (*lite*) to arbitrate in; **~ qn/qc bello** to consider sb/sth (to be) beautiful

gi'udice ['dʒuditʃe] *sm* judge; **~ conciliatore** justice of the peace; **~ istruttore** examining (*BRIT*) *o* committing (*US*) magistrate; **~ popolare** member of a jury

giu'dizio [dʒu'dittsjo] *sm* judgment; (*opinione*) opinion; (*Dir*) judgment, sentence; (: *processo*) trial; (: *verdetto*) verdict; **aver ~** to be wise *o* prudent; **citare in ~** to summons

gi'ugno ['dʒuɲɲo] *sm* June

gi'ungere ['dʒundʒere] /5/ *vi* to arrive ▷ *vt* (*mani ecc*) to join; **~ a** to arrive at, reach

gi'ungla ['dʒungla] *sf* jungle

gi'unsi *ecc* ['dʒunsi] *vb vedi* **giungere**

giura'mento [dʒura'mento] *sm* oath; **~ falso** perjury

giu'rare [dʒu'rare] /72/ *vt* to swear ▷ *vi* to swear, take an oath

giu'ria [dʒu'ria] *sf* jury

giu'ridico, -a, -ci, -che [dʒu'ridiko] *ag* legal

giustifi'care [dʒustifi'kare] /20/ *vt* to justify; **giustificazi'one** *sf* justification; (*Ins*) (note of) excuse

gius'tizia [dʒus'tittsja] *sf* justice; **giustizi'are** /19/ *vt* to execute, put to death

gi'usto, -a ['dʒusto] *ag* (*equo*) fair, just; (*vero*) true, correct; (*adatto*) right, suitable; (*preciso*) exact, correct ▷ *av* (*esattamente*) exactly, precisely; (*per l'appunto, appena*) just; **arrivare ~** to arrive just in time; **ho ~ bisogno di te** you're just the person I need

glaci'ale [gla'tʃale] *ag* glacial

gli [ʎi] *det mpl* (*davV, s impura, gn, pn, ps, x, z*) the ▷ *pron* (*a lui*) to him; (*a esso*) to it; (*in coppia con lo, la, li, le, ne, a lui, a lei, a loro ecc*): **~ele do** I'm giving them to him (*o her o them*); *vedi anche* **il**

glo'bale *ag* overall

'globo *sm* globe

'globulo *sm* (*Anat*): **~ rosso/bianco** red/white corpuscle

glocalizzazi'one [glokaliddza'tsjone] *sf* glocalization

'gloria *sf* glory

'gnocchi ['ɲɔkki] *smpl* (*Cuc*) small dumplings made of semolina pasta or potato

'gobba *sf* (*Anat*) hump; (*protuberanza*) bump

'gobbo, -a *ag* hunchbacked; (*ricurvo*) round-shouldered ▷ *sm/f* hunchback

'goccia, -ce ['gottʃa] *sf* drop; **goccio'lare** /72/ *vi, vt* to drip

go'dere /58/ *vi*: **~ (di)** (*compiacersi*) to be delighted (at), rejoice (at); **~ di** (*trarre vantaggio*) to benefit from ▷ *vt* to enjoy; **godersi la vita** to enjoy life; **godersela** to have a good time, enjoy o.s.

godrò *ecc vb vedi* **godere**

'goffo, -a *ag* clumsy, awkward

gol [gɔl] *sm inv* (*Sport*); = **goal**

'gola sf (Anat) throat; (golosità) gluttony, greed; (di camino) flue; (di monte) gorge; **fare ~** (anche fig) to tempt

golf sm inv (Sport) golf; (maglia) cardigan

'golfo sm gulf

go'loso, -a ag greedy

gomi'tata sf: **dare una ~ a qn** to elbow sb; **farsi avanti a (forza o furia di) gomitate** to elbow one's way through; **fare a gomitate per qc** to fight to get sth

'gomito sm elbow; (di strada ecc) sharp bend

go'mitolo sm ball

'gomma sf rubber; (per cancellare) rubber, eraser; (di veicolo) tyre (BRIT), tire (US); **~ da masticare** chewing gum; **~ a terra** flat tyre; **gom'mone** sm rubber dinghy

gonfi'are /19/ vt (pallone) to blow up, inflate; (dilatare, ingrossare) to swell; (fig: notizia) to exaggerate; **gonfiarsi** vpr to swell; (fiume) to rise; **'gonfio, -a** ag swollen; (stomaco) bloated; (vela) full; **gonfi'ore** sm swelling

'gonna sf skirt; **~ pantalone** culottes pl

goo'glare [gu'glare] /72/ vt (Inform) to google

'gorgo, -ghi sm whirlpool

gorgogli'are [gorgoʎ'ʎare] /27/ vi to gurgle

go'rilla sm inv gorilla; (guardia del corpo) bodyguard

'gotico, -a, -ci, -che ag, sm Gothic

'gotta sf gout

gover'nare /72/ vt (stato) to govern, rule; (pilotare, guidare) to steer; (bestiame) to tend, look after

go'verno sm government

GPL [dʒipi'elle] sigla m (= Gas di Petrolio Liquefatto) LPG

GPS [dʒipi'esse] sigla m GPS

graci'dare [gratʃi'dare] /72/ vi to croak

'gracile ['gratʃile] ag frail, delicate

gradazi'one [gradat'tsjone] sf (sfumatura) gradation; **~ alcolica** alcoholic content, strength

gra'devole ag pleasant, agreeable

gradi'nata sf flight of steps; (in teatro, stadio) tiers pl

gra'dino sm step; (Alpinismo) foothold

gra'dire /55/ vt (accettare con piacere) to accept; (desiderare) to wish, like; **gradisce una tazza di tè?** would you like a cup of tea?

'grado sm (Mat, Fisica: ecc) degree; (stadio) degree, level; (Mil, sociale) rank; **essere in ~ di fare** to be in a position to do

gradu'ale ag gradual

graf'fetta sf paper clip

graffi'are /19/ vt to scratch; **graffiarsi** vpr to get scratched; (con unghie) to scratch o.s.

'graffio sm scratch

gra'fia sf spelling; (scrittura) handwriting

'grafico, -a, -ci, -che ag graphic ▷ sm graph; (persona) graphic designer

gram'matica, -che sf grammar

'grammo sm gram(me)

'grana sf (granello, di minerali, corpi spezzati) grain; (fam: seccatura) trouble; (: soldi) cash ▷ sm inv cheese similar to Parmesan

gra'naio sm granary, barn

gra'nata sf (proiettile) grenade

Gran Bre'tagna [granbre'taɲɲa] sf: **la ~** Great Britain

'granchio ['grankjo] sm crab; (fig) blunder; **prendere un ~** (fig) to blunder

'grande (qualche volta **gran** + C, **grand'** + V) ag (grosso, largo, vasto) big, large; (alto) tall; (lungo) long; (in sensi astratti) great ▷ smf (persona adulta) adult, grown-up; (chi ha ingegno e potenza) great man/ woman; **fare le cose in ~** to do things in style; **una gran bella donna** a very beautiful woman; **non**

è una gran cosa o **un gran che** it's nothing special; **non ne so gran che** I don't know very much about it

gran'dezza [gran'dettsa] sf (dimensione) size; magnitude; (fig) greatness; **in ~ naturale** lifesize

grandi'nare /72/ vb impers to hail

'grandine sf hail

gra'nello sm (di cereali, uva) seed; (di frutta) pip; (di sabbia, sale ecc) grain

gra'nito sm granite

'grano sm (in quasi tutti i sensi) grain; (frumento) wheat; (di rosario, collana) bead; **~ di pepe** peppercorn

gran'turco sm maize

'grappa sf rough, strong brandy

'grappolo sm bunch, cluster

gras'setto sm (Tip) bold (type)

'grasso, -a ag fat; (cibo) fatty; (pelle) greasy; (terreno) rich; (fig: guadagno, annata) plentiful ▷ sm (di persona, animale) fat; (sostanza che unge) grease

'grata sf grating

gra'ticola sf grill

'gratis av free, for nothing

grati'tudine sf gratitude

'grato, -a ag grateful; (gradito) pleasant, agreeable

gratta'capo sm worry, headache

grattaci'elo [gratta'tʃɛlo] sm skyscraper

gratta e 'sosta sm inv scratch card used to pay for parking

gratta e 'vinci [grattae'vintʃi] sm (lotteria) lottery; (biglietto) scratchcard

grat'tare /72/ vt (pelle) to scratch; (raschiare) to scrape; (pane, formaggio, carote) to grate; (fam: rubare) to pinch ▷ vi (stridere) to grate; (Aut) to grind; **grattarsi** vpr to scratch o.s.; **grattarsi la pancia** (fig) to twiddle one's thumbs

grat'tugia [grat'tudʒa], **-gie** sf grater; **grattugi'are** /62/ vt to grate; **pane grattugiato** breadcrumbs pl

gra'tuito, -a ag free; (fig) gratuitous

'grave ag (danno, pericolo, peccato ecc) grave, serious; (responsabilità) heavy, grave; (contegno) grave, solemn; (voce, suono) deep, low-pitched; (Ling): **accento ~** grave accent; **un malato ~** a person who is seriously ill

grave'mente av (ammalato, ferito) seriously

gravi'danza [gravi'dantsa] sf pregnancy

gravità sf seriousness; (anche Fisica) gravity

gra'voso, -a ag heavy, onerous

'grazia ['grattsja] sf grace; (favore) favour; (Dir) pardon

'grazie ['grattsje] escl thank you!; **~ mille!** o **tante!** o **infinite!** thank you very much!; **~ a** thanks to

grazi'oso, -a [grat'tsjoso] ag charming, delightful; (gentile) gracious

'Grecia ['grɛtʃa] sf: **la ~** Greece; **'greco, -a, -ci, -che** ag, sm/f, sm Greek

'gregge ['greddʒe] (pl f **greggi**) sm flock

'greggio, -a, -gi, -ge ['greddʒo] ag raw, unrefined; (diamante) rough, uncut; (tessuto) unbleached

grembi'ule sm apron; (sopravveste) overall

'grembo sm lap; (ventre della madre) womb

'grezzo, -a ['greddzo] ag = **greggio**

gri'dare /72/ vi (per chiamare) to shout, cry (out); (strillare) to scream, yell ▷ vt to shout (out), yell (out); **~ aiuto** to cry o shout for help

'grido (pl f **grida**) sm shout, cry; scream, yell; (di animale) (pl m **gridi**) cry; **di ~** famous

'grigio ['gridʒo], **-a, -gi, -gie** ag, sm grey

'griglia ['griʎʎa] sf (per arrostire) grill; (Elettr) grid; (inferriata) grating; **alla ~** (Cuc) grilled

gril'letto sm trigger

'grillo sm (Zool) cricket; (fig) whim

'grinta sf grim expression; (Sport) fighting spirit

gris'sino sm bread-stick

Groen'landia sf: **la ~** Greenland

gron'daia sf gutter

gron'dare /72/ vi to pour; (essere bagnato): **~ di** to be dripping with ▷ vt to drip with

'groppa sf (di animale) back, rump; (fam: dell'uomo) back, shoulders pl

gros'sezza [gros'settsa] sf size; thickness

gros'sista, -i, -e smf (Comm) wholesaler

'grosso, -a ag big, large; (di spessore) thick; (grossolano: anche fig) coarse; (grave, insopportabile) serious, great; (tempo, mare) rough ▷ sm: **il ~ di** the bulk of; **un pezzo ~** (fig) a VIP, a bigwig; **farla grossa** to do something very stupid; **dirle grosse** to tell tall stories (BRIT) o tales (US); **sbagliarsi di ~** to be completely wrong

'grotta sf cave; grotto

grot'tesco, -a, -schi, -sche ag grotesque

gro'viglio [gro'viʎʎo] sm tangle; (fig) muddle

gru sf inv crane

'gruccia, -ce ['gruttʃa] sf (per camminare) crutch; (per abiti) coat-hanger

'grumo sm (di sangue) clot; (di farina ecc) lump

'gruppo sm group; **~ sanguigno** blood group

GSM sigla m (= Global System for Mobile Communication) GSM

guada'gnare [gwadaɲ'ɲare] /15/ vt (ottenere) to gain; (soldi, stipendio) to earn; (vincere) to win; (raggiungere) to reach

gua'dagno [gwa'daɲɲo] sm earnings pl; (Comm) profit; (vantaggio, utile) advantage, gain; **~ lordo/netto** gross/net earnings pl

gu'ado sm ford; **passare a ~** to ford

gu'ai escl: **~ a te** (o lui ecc) **!** woe betide you (o him ecc)!

gu'aio sm trouble, mishap; (inconveniente) trouble, snag

gua'ire /55/ vi to whine, yelp

gu'ancia, -ce ['gwantʃa] sf cheek

guanci'ale [gwan'tʃale] sm pillow

gu'anto sm glove

guarda'linee sm inv (Sport) linesman

guar'dare /72/ vt (con lo sguardo: osservare) to look at; (: film, televisione) to watch; (custodire) to look after, take care of ▷ vi to look; (badare): **~ a** to pay attention to; (luoghi: esser orientato): **~ a** to face; **guardarsi** vpr to look at o.s.; **guardarsi da** (astenersi) to refrain from; (stare in guardia) to beware of; **guardarsi dal fare** to take care not to do; **guarda di non sbagliare** try not to make a mistake; **~ a vista qn** to keep a close watch on sb

guarda'roba sm inv wardrobe; (locale) cloakroom

gu'ardia sf (individuo, corpo) guard; (sorveglianza) watch; **fare la ~ a qc/qn** to guard sth/sb; **stare in ~** (fig) to be on one's guard; **il medico di ~** the doctor on call; **~ carceraria** (prison) warder (BRIT) o guard (US); **~ del corpo** bodyguard; **~ di finanza** (corpo) customs pl; (persona) customs officer; **~ medica** emergency doctor service

○ **GUARDIA DI FINANZA**
○
○ The Guardia di Finanza is a
○ military body which deals with
○ infringements of the laws
○ governing income tax and
○ monopolies. It reports to the
○ Ministers of Finance, Justice or
○ Agriculture, depending on the
○ function it is performing.

guardi'ano, -a *sm/f (di carcere)* warder; *(di villa ecc)* caretaker; *(di museo)* custodian; *(di zoo)* keeper; **~ notturno** night watchman

guarigi'one [gwari'dʒone] *sf* recovery

gua'rire /55/ *vt (persona, malattia)* to cure; *(ferita)* to heal ▷ *vi* to recover, be cured; to heal (up)

guar'nire /55/ *vt (ornare: abiti)* to trim; *(Cuc)* to garnish

guasta'feste *smf inv* spoilsport

guas'tare /72/ *vt* to spoil; **guastarsi** *vpr (cibo)* to go bad; *(meccanismo)* to break down; *(tempo)* to change for the worse

gu'asto, -a *ag (non funzionante)* broken; *(: telefono ecc)* out of order; *(andato a male)* bad, rotten; *(: dente)* decayed, bad; *(fig: corrotto)* depraved ▷ *sm* breakdown; *(avaria)* failure; **~ al motore** engine failure

gu'erra *sf* war; *(tecnica: atomica, chimica ecc)* warfare; **fare la ~ (a)** to wage war (against); **~ mondiale** world war; **~ preventiva** preventive war

'gufo *sm* owl

gu'ida *sf (persona)* guide; *(libro)* guide(book); *(comando, direzione)* guidance, direction; *(Aut)* driving; *(tappeto: di tenda, cassetto)* runner; **~ a destra/sinistra** *(Aut)* right-/left-hand drive; **~ telefonica** telephone directory; **~ turistica** tourist guide

gui'dare /72/ *vt* to guide; *(squadra, rivolta)* to lead; *(auto)* to drive; *(aereo, nave)* to pilot; **sa ~?** can you drive?; **guida'tore, -'trice** *sm/f (conducente)* driver

guin'zaglio [gwin'tsaʎʎo] *sm* leash, lead

'guscio ['guʃʃo] *sm* shell

gus'tare /72/ *vt (cibi)* to taste; *(: assaporare con piacere)* to enjoy, savour; *(fig)* to enjoy, appreciate ▷ *vi:* **~ a** to please; **non mi gusta affatto** I don't like it at all

'gusto *sm* taste; *(sapore)* taste, flavour *(BRIT)*, flavor *(US)*; *(godimento)* enjoyment; **al ~ di fragola** strawberry-flavoured; **mangiare di ~** to eat heartily; **prenderci ~: ci ha preso ~** he's acquired a taste for it, he's got to like it; **gus'toso, -a** *ag* tasty; *(fig)* agreeable

'herpes ['ɛrpes] *sm (Med)* herpes *sg*:
  ~ zoster shingles *sg*
'hi-fi ['haifai] *sm inv, ag inv* hi-fi
ho [ɔ] *vb vedi* **avere**
'hobby ['hɔbi] *sm inv* hobby
'hockey ['hɔki] *sm* hockey; **~ su
  ghiaccio** ice hockey
'home page ['houm'pɛidʒ] *sf inv*
  home page
'Hong Kong ['ɔ̃k'ɔ̃g] *sf* Hong Kong
'hostess ['houstis] *sf inv* air hostess
  (*BRIT*) *o* stewardess
'hot dog ['hɔtdɔg] *sm inv* hot dog
ho'tel *sm inv* hotel
'humour ['jumor] *sm inv* (sense of)
  humour
'humus *sm* humus
'husky ['aski] *sm inv* (*cane*) husky

H, h ['akka] *sf o m inv* (*lettera*) H, h
  ▷ *abbr* (= *ora*) hr; (= *etto, altezza*) h; **H
  come hotel** ≈ H for Harry (*BRIT*), H
  for How (*US*)
ha, hai [a, ai] *vb vedi* **avere**
ha'cker ['haker] *sm inv* hacker
hall [hɔːl] *sf inv* hall, foyer
ham'burger [am'burger] *sm inv*
  (*carne*) hamburger; (*panino*) burger
'handicap ['handikap] *sm inv*
  handicap; **handicap'pato, -a** *ag*
  handicapped ▷ *sm/f* handicapped
  person, disabled person
'hanno ['anno] *vb vedi* **avere**
hard dis'count [ardis'kaunt] *sm inv*
  discount supermarket
hard 'disk [ar'disk] *sm inv* hard disk
'hardware ['ardwer] *sm inv*
  hardware
ha'scisc, hascisch [aʃʃiʃ] *sm*
  hashish
Ha'waii [a'vai] *sfpl*: **le ~** Hawaii *sg*
help [ɛlp] *sm inv* (*Inform*) help

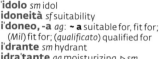

i *det mpl* the

'ibrido, -a *ag, sm* hybrid

IC *abbr* (= Intercity) Intercity

'ICI ['itʃi] *sigla f* (= Imposta Comunale sugli Immobili) ≈ Council Tax

i'cona *sf* (Rel, Inform, fig) icon

i'dea *sf* idea; (opinione) opinion, view; (ideale) ideal; **dare l'~ di** to seem, look like; **neanche** o **neppure per ~!** certainly not!; **~ fissa** obsession

ide'ale *ag, sm* ideal

ide'are /72/ *vt* (immaginare) to think up, conceive; (progettare) to plan

i'dentico, -a, -ci, -che *ag* identical

identifi'care /20/ *vt* to identify; **identificarsi** *vpr*: **identificarsi (con)** to identify o.s. (with)

identità *sf inv* identity

ideolo'gia, -'gie [ideolo'dʒia] *sf* ideology

idio'matico, -a, -ci, -che *ag* idiomatic; **frase idiomatica** idiom

idi'ota, -i, -e *ag* idiotic ▷ *smf* idiot

'idolo *sm* idol

idonei'tà *sf* suitability

i'doneo, -a *ag*: **~ a** suitable for, fit for; (Mil) fit for; (qualificato) qualified for

i'drante *sm* hydrant

idra'tante *ag* moisturizing ▷ *sm* moisturizer

i'draulico, -a, -ci, -che *ag* hydraulic ▷ *sm* plumber

idroe'lettrico, -a, -ci, -che *ag* hydroelectric

i'drofilo, -a *ag*: **cotone ~** cotton wool (BRIT), absorbent cotton (US)

i'drogeno [i'drɔdʒeno] *sm* hydrogen

idrovo'lante *sm* seaplane

i'ena *sf* hyena

i'eri *av, sm* yesterday; **il giornale di ~** yesterday's paper; **~ l'altro** the day before yesterday; **~ sera** yesterday evening

igi'ene [i'dʒɛne] *sf* hygiene; **~ pubblica** public health; **igi'enico, -a, -ci, -che** *ag* hygienic; (salubre) healthy

i'gnaro, -a [iɲ'naro] *ag*: **~ di** unaware of, ignorant of

i'gnobile [iɲ'nɔbile] *ag* despicable, vile

igno'rante [iɲɲo'rante] *ag* ignorant

igno'rare [iɲɲo'rare] /72/ *vt* (non sapere, conoscere) to be ignorant o unaware of, not to know; (fingere di non vedere, sentire) to ignore

i'gnoto, -a [iɲ'nɔto] *ag* unknown

PAROLA CHIAVE

il (pl(m) **i**; diventa **lo** (pl **gli**) davanti a s impura, gn, pn, ps, x, z; f **la** (pl **le**)) *det m*
1 the; **il libro/lo studente/l'acqua** the book/the student/the water; **gli scolari** the pupils
2 (astrazione): **il coraggio/l'amore/la giovinezza** courage/love/youth
3 (tempo): **il mattino/la sera** in the morning/evening; **il venerdì** (abitualmente) on Fridays; (quel giorno) on (the) Friday; **la settimana prossima** next week

4 (*distributivo*) a, an; **2 euro il chilo/paio** 2 euros a *o* per kilo/pair
5 (*partitivo*) some, any; **hai messo lo zucchero?** have you added sugar?; **hai comprato il latte?** did you buy (some *o* any) milk?
6 (*possesso*): **aprire gli occhi** to open one's eyes; **rompersi la gamba** to break one's leg; **avere i capelli neri/il naso rosso** to have dark hair/a red nose
7 (*con nomi propri*): **il Petrarca** Petrarch; **il Presidente Bush** President Bush; **dov'è la Francesca?** where's Francesca?
8 (*con nomi geografici*): **il Tevere** the Tiber; **l'Italia** Italy; **il Regno Unito** the United Kingdom; **l'Everest** Everest

ille'gale *ag* illegal
illeg'gibile [illed'dʒibile] *ag* illegible
ille'gittimo, -a [illeˈdʒittimo] *ag* illegitimate
il'leso, -a *ag* unhurt, unharmed
illimi'tato, -a *ag* boundless; unlimited
ill.mo *abbr* = **illustrissimo**
il'ludere /35/ *vt* to deceive, delude; **illudersi** *vpr* to deceive o.s., delude o.s.
illumi'nare /72/ *vt* to light up, illuminate; (*fig*) to enlighten; **illuminarsi** *vpr* to light up; **~ a giorno** to floodlight; **illuminazi'one** *sf* lighting; illumination; floodlighting; (*fig*) flash of inspiration
il'lusi *ecc vb vedi* **illudere**
illusi'one *sf* illusion; **farsi delle illusioni** to delude o.s.; **~ ottica** optical illusion
il'luso, -a *pp di* **illudere**
illus'trare /72/ *vt* to illustrate; **illustrazi'one** *sf* illustration
il'lustre *ag* eminent, renowned; **illus'trissimo, -a** *ag* (*negli indirizzi*) very revered

imbal'laggio [imbalˈladdʒo] *sm* packing *no pl*
imbal'lare /72/ *vt* to pack; (*Aut*) to race
imbalsa'mare /72/ *vt* to embalm
imbambo'lato, -a *ag* (*sguardo, espressione*) vacant, blank
imbaraz'zante [imbarat'tsante] *ag* embarrassing, awkward
imbaraz'zare [imbarat'tsare] /72/ *vt* (*mettere a disagio*) to embarrass; (*ostacolare: movimenti*) to hamper
imbaraz'zato, -a [imbarat'tsato] *ag* embarrassed; **avere lo stomaco ~** to have an upset stomach
imba'razzo [imbaˈrattso] *sm* (*disagio*) embarrassment; (*perplessità*) puzzlement, bewilderment; **~ di stomaco** indigestion
imbar'care /20/ *vt* (*passeggeri*) to embark; (*merci*) to load; **imbarcarsi** *vpr*: **imbarcarsi su** to board; **imbarcarsi per l'America** to sail for America; **imbarcarsi in** (*fig: affare*) to embark on
imbarcazi'one [imbarkat'tsjone] *sf* (small) boat, (small) craft *inv*; **~ di salvataggio** lifeboat
im'barco, -chi *sm* embarkation; loading; boarding; (*banchina*) landing stage
imbas'tire /55/ *vt* (*cucire*) to tack; (*fig: abbozzare*) to sketch, outline
im'battersi /72/ *vpr*: **~ in** (*incontrare*) to bump *o* run into
imbat'tibile *ag* unbeatable, invincible
imbavagli'are [imbavaʎˈʎare] /27/ *vt* to gag
imbe'cille [imbe'tʃille] *ag* idiotic ▷ *smf* idiot; (*Med*) imbecile
imbian'care /20/ *vt* to whiten; (*muro*) to whitewash ▷ *vi* to become *o* turn white
imbian'chino [imbjanˈkino] *sm* (*house*) painter, painter and decorator
imboc'care /20/ *vt* (*bambino*) to feed; (*entrare: strada*) to enter, turn into

imbocca'tura *sf* mouth; (*di strada, porto*) entrance; (*Mus, del morso*) mouthpiece

imbos'cata *sf* ambush

imbottigli'are [imbottiʎʎare] /27/ *vt* to bottle; (*Naut*) to blockade; (*Mil*) to hem in; **imbottigliarsi** *vpr* to be stuck in a traffic jam

imbot'tire /55/ *vt* to stuff; (*giacca*) to pad; **imbottirsi** *vpr* (*rimpinzarsi*): **imbottirsi di** to stuff o.s. with; **imbot'tito, -a** *ag* stuffed; (*giacca*) padded; **panino imbottito** filled roll

imbra'nato, -a *ag* clumsy, awkward ▷ *sm/f* clumsy person

imbrogli'are [imbroʎʎare] /27/ *vt* to mix up; (*fig: raggirare*) to deceive, cheat; (: *confondere*) to confuse, mix up; **imbrogli'one, -a** *sm/f* cheat, swindler

imbronci'ato, -a *ag* sulky

imbu'care /20/ *vt* to post

imbur'rare /72/ *vt* to butter

im'buto *sm* funnel

imi'tare /72/ *vt* to imitate; (*riprodurre*) to copy; (*assomigliare*) to look like

immagazzi'nare [immagaddzi'nare] /72/ *vt* to store

immagi'nare [immadʒi'nare] /72/ *vt* to imagine; (*supporre*) to suppose; (*inventare*) to invent; **s'immagini!** don't mention it!, not at all!; **immaginazi'one** *sf* imagination; (*cosa immaginata*) fancy

im'magine [im'madʒine] *sf* image; (*rappresentazione grafica, mentale*) picture

imman'cabile *ag* certain; unfailing

im'mane *ag* (*smisurato*) huge; (*spaventoso, inumano*) terrible

immangi'abile [imman'dʒabile] *ag* inedible

immatrico'lare /72/ *vt* to register; **immatricolarsi** *vpr* (*Ins*) to matriculate, enrol

imma'turo, -a *ag* (*frutto*) unripe; (*persona*) immature; (*prematuro*) premature

immedesi'marsi /72/ *vpr*: **~ in** to identify with

immediata'mente *av* immediately, at once

immedi'ato, -a *ag* immediate

im'menso, -a *ag* immense

im'mergere [im'mɛrdʒere] /59/ *vt* to immerse, plunge; **immergersi** *vpr* to plunge; (*sommergibile*) to dive, submerge; (*dedicarsi a*): **immergersi in** to immerse o.s. in

immeri'tato, -a *ag* undeserved

immersi'one *sf* immersion; (*di sommergibile*) submersion, dive; (*di palombaro*) dive

im'mettere /63/ *vt*: **~ (in)** to introduce (into); **~ dati in un computer** to enter data on a computer

immi'grato, -a *sm/f* immigrant

immi'nente *ag* imminent

immischi'are [immis'kjare] /19/ *vt*: **~ qn in** to involve sb in; **immischiarsi** *vpr*: **immischiarsi in** to interfere *o* meddle in

im'mobile *ag* motionless, still; **immobili'are** *ag* (*Dir*) property *cpd*

immon'dizia [immon'dittsja] *sf* dirt, filth; (*spesso al pl: spazzatura, rifiuti*) rubbish *no pl*, refuse *no pl*

immo'rale *ag* immoral

immor'tale *ag* immortal

im'mune *ag* (*esente*) exempt; (*Med, Dir*) immune

immu'tabile *ag* immutable; unchanging

impacchet'tare [impakket'tare] /72/ *vt* to pack up

impacci'ato, -a *ag* awkward, clumsy; (*imbarazzato*) embarrassed

im'pacco, -chi *sm* (*Med*) compress

impadro'nirsi /55/ *vpr*: **~ di** to seize, take possession of; (*fig: apprendere a fondo*) to master

impa'gabile *ag* priceless

impa'lato, -a *ag* (*fig*) stiff as a board

impalca'tura *sf* scaffolding

impalli'dire /55/ *vi* to turn pale; (*fig*) to fade

impa'nato, -a *ag* (*Cuc*) coated in breadcrumbs

impanta'narsi /72/ *vpr* to sink (in the mud); (*fig*) to get bogged down

impappi'narsi /72/ *vpr* to stammer, falter

impa'rare /72/ *vt* to learn

impar'tire /55/ *vt* to bestow, give

imparzi'ale [impar'tsjale] *ag* impartial, unbiased

impas'sibile *ag* impassive

impas'tare /72/ *vt* (*pasta*) to knead

impastic'carsi /20/ *vpr* to pop pills

im'pasto *sm* (*l'impastare: di pane*) kneading; (: *di cemento*) mixing; (*pasta*) dough; (*anche fig*) mixture

im'patto *sm* impact

impau'rire /55/ *vt* to scare, frighten ▷ *vi* (*anche*: **impaurirsi**) to become scared *o* frightened

impazi'ente [impat'tsjente] *ag* impatient

impaz'zata [impat'tsata] *sf*: **all'~** (*precipitosamente*) at breakneck speed

impaz'zire [impat'tsire] /55/ *vi* to go mad; **~ per qn/qc** to be crazy about sb/sth

impec'cabile *ag* impeccable

impedi'mento *sm* obstacle, hindrance

impe'dire /55/ *vt* (*vietare*): **~ a qn di fare** to prevent sb from doing; (*ostruire*) to obstruct; (*impacciare*) to hamper, hinder

impe'gnare [impeɲ'ɲare] /15/ *vt* (*obbligare*) to oblige; **impegnarsi** *vpr* (*vincolarsi*): **impegnarsi a fare** to undertake to do; (*mettersi risolutamente*): **impegnarsi in qc** to devote o.s. to sth; **impegnarsi con qn** (*accordarsi*) to come to an agreement with sb

impegna'tivo, -a *ag* binding; (*lavoro*) demanding, exacting

impe'gnato, -a *ag* (*occupato*) busy; (*fig: romanzo, autore*) committed, engagé

im'pegno [im'peɲɲo] *sm* (*obbligo*) obligation; (*promessa*) promise, pledge; (*zelo*) diligence, zeal; (*compito: d'autore*) commitment

impel'lente *ag* pressing, urgent

impen'narsi /72/ *vpr* (*cavallo*) to rear up; (*Aer*) to go into a climb; (*fig*) to bridle

impensie'rire /55/ *vt* to worry; **impensierirsi** *vpr* to worry

impera'tivo, -a *ag, sm* imperative

impera'tore, -'trice *sm/f* emperor (empress)

imperdo'nabile *ag* unforgivable, unpardonable

imper'fetto, -a *ag* imperfect ▷ *sm* (*Ling*) imperfect (tense)

imperi'ale *ag* imperial

imperi'oso, -a *ag* (*persona*) imperious; (*motivo, esigenza*) urgent, pressing

imperme'abile *ag* waterproof ▷ *sm* raincoat

im'pero *sm* empire; (*forza, autorità*) rule, control

imperso'nale *ag* impersonal

imperso'nare /72/ *vt* to personify; (*Teat*) to play, act (the part of)

imper'territo, -a *ag* unperturbed, undaunted; impassive

imperti'nente *ag* impertinent

'impeto *sm* (*moto, forza*) force, impetus; (*assalto*) onslaught; (*fig: impulso*) impulse; (: *slancio*) transport; **con ~** energetically; vehemently

impet'tito, -a *ag* stiff, erect

impetu'oso, -a *ag* (*vento*) strong, raging; (*persona*) impetuous

impi'anto *sm* (*installazione*) installation; (*apparecchiature*) plant; (*sistema*) system; **~ elettrico** wiring; **~ di riscaldamento** heating system; **~ sportivo** sports complex; **impianti di risalita** (*Sci*) ski lifts

impic'care /20/ *vt* to hang; **impiccarsi** *vpr* to hang o.s.

impicci'are [impit'tʃare] /14/ *vt* to hinder; **impicciarsi** *vpr* (*immischiarsi*):

impicciarsi (in) to meddle (in), interfere (in); **impicciati degli affari tuoi!** mind your own business!

impicci'one, -a [impit't∫one] *sm/f* busybody

impie'gare /80/ *vt* (*usare*) to use, employ; (*spendere: denaro, tempo*) to spend; (*investire*) to invest;

impie'gato, -a *sm/f* employee

impi'ego, -ghi *sm* (*uso*) use; (*occupazione*) employment; (*posto di lavoro*) (regular) job, post; (*Econ*) investment

impieto'sire /55/ *vt* to move to pity; **impietosirsi** *vpr* to be moved to pity

impigli'are [impiʎ'ʎare] /27/ *vt* to catch; **impigliarsi** *vpr* to get caught up *o* entangled

impi'grire /55/ *vt* to make lazy ▷ *vi* (*anche*: **impigrirsi**) to grow lazy

impli'care /20/ *vt* to imply, (*coinvolgere*) to involve; **implicarsi** *vpr*: **implicarsi (in)** to become involved (in)

im'plicito, -a [im'plit∫ito] *ag* implicit

implo'rare /72/ *vt* to implore; (*pietà ecc*) to beg for

impolve'rare /72/ *vt* to cover with dust; **impolverarsi** *vpr* to get dusty

im'pone *ecc vb vedi* **imporre**

impo'nente *ag* imposing, impressive

im'pongo *ecc vb vedi* **imporre**

impo'nibile *ag* taxable ▷ *sm* taxable income

impopo'lare *ag* unpopular

im'porre /77/ *vt* to impose; (*costringere*) to force, make; (*far valere*) to impose, enforce; **imporsi** *vpr* (*persona*) to assert o.s.; (*cosa: rendersi necessario*) to become necessary; (*aver successo: moda, attore*) to become popular; **~ a qn di fare** to force sb to do, make sb do

impor'tante *ag* important; **impor'tanza** *sf* importance; **dare importanza a qc** to attach importance to sth; **darsi importanza** to give o.s. airs

impor'tare /72/ *vt* (*introdurre dall'estero*) to import ▷ *vi* to matter, be important ▷ *vb impers* (*essere necessario*) to be necessary; (*interessare*) to matter; **non importa!** it doesn't matter!; **non me ne importa!** I don't care!

im'porto *sm* (*total*) amount

importu'nare /72/ *vt* to bother

im'posi *ecc vb vedi* **imporre**

imposizi'one [impozit'tsjone] *sf* imposition; (*ordine*) order, command; (*onere, imposta*) tax

imposses'sarsi /72/ *vpr*: **~ di** to seize, take possession of

impos'sibile *ag* impossible; **fare l'~** to do one's utmost, do all one can

im'posta *sf* (*di finestra*) shutter; (*tassa*) tax; **~ sul reddito** income tax; **~ sul valore aggiunto** value added tax (BRIT), sales tax (US)

impos'tare /72/ *vt* (*imbucare*) to post; (*resoconto, rapporto*) to plan; (*problema*) to set out; (*avviare*) to begin, start off; **~ la voce** (*Mus*) to pitch one's voice

impostazi'one [impostat'tsjone] *sf* (*di lettera*) posting (BRIT), mailing (US); (*di problema, questione*) formulation, statement; (*di lavoro*) organization, planning; (*di attività*) setting up; (*Mus: di voce*) pitch; **impostazioni** *sfpl* (*di computer*) settings

impo'tente *ag* weak, powerless; (*anche Med*) impotent

imprati'cabile *ag* (*strada*) impassable; (*campo da gioco*) unplayable

impre'care /20/ *vi* to curse, swear; **~ contro** to hurl abuse at

imprecazi'one [imprekat'tsjone] *sf* abuse, curse

impre'gnare [impreɲ'ɲare] /15/ *vt*: **~ (di)** (*imbevere*) to soak *o* impregnate (with); (*riempire*) to fill (with)

imprendi'tore *sm* (*industriale*) entrepreneur; (*appaltatore*) contractor; **piccolo ~** small businessman

im'presa *sf* (*iniziativa*) enterprise; (*azione*) exploit; (*azienda*) firm, concern

impressio'nante *ag* impressive; upsetting

impressio'nare /72/ *vt* to impress; (*turbare*) to upset; (*Fot*) to expose; **impressionarsi** *vpr* to be easily upset

impressi'one *sf* impression; (*fig: sensazione*) sensation, feeling; (*stampa*) printing; **fare ~** (*colpire*) to impress; (*turbare*) to frighten, upset; **fare buona/cattiva ~ a** to make a good/bad impression on

impreve'dibile *ag* unforeseeable; (*persona*) unpredictable

impre'visto, -a *ag* unexpected, unforeseen ▷ *sm* unforeseen event; **salvo imprevisti** unless anything unexpected happens

imprigio'nare [impridʒo'nare] /72/ *vt* to imprison

impro'babile *ag* improbable, unlikely

im'pronta *sf* imprint, impression, sign; (*di piede, mano*) print; (*fig*) mark, stamp; **~ di carbonio** carbon footprint; **~ digitale** fingerprint

improvvisa'mente *av* suddenly; unexpectedly

improvvi'sare /72/ *vt* to improvise

improv'viso, -a *ag* (*imprevisto*) unexpected; (*subitaneo*) sudden; **all'~** unexpectedly; suddenly

impru'dente *ag* unwise, rash

impu'gnare [impuɲ'ɲare] /15/ *vt* to grasp, grip; (*Dir*) to contest

impul'sivo, -a *ag* impulsive

im'pulso *sm* impulse

impun'tarsi /72/ *vpr* to stop dead, refuse to budge; (*fig*) to be obstinate

impu'tato, -a *sm/f* (*Dir*) accused, defendant

PAROLA CHIAVE

in (*in + il =* **nel**, *in + lo =* **nello**, *in + l' =* **nell'**, *in + la =* **nella**, *in + i =* **nei**, *in + gli** = **negli**, *in + le =* **nelle**) *prep* **1** (*stato in luogo*) in; **vivere in Italia/città** to live in Italy/town; **essere in casa/ ufficio** to be at home/the office; **se fossi in te** if I were you

2 (*moto a luogo*) to; (: *dentro*) into; **andare in Germania/città** to go to Germany/town; **andare in ufficio** to go to the office; **entrare in macchina/casa** to get into the car/ go into the house

3 (*tempo*) in; **nel 1989** in 1989; **in giugno/estate** in June/summer

4 (*modo, maniera*) in; **in silenzio** in silence; **in abito da sera** in evening dress; **in guerra** at war; **in vacanza** on holiday; **Maria Bianchi in Rossi** Maria Rossi née Bianchi

5 (*mezzo*) by; **viaggiare in autobus/ treno** to travel by bus/train

6 (*materia*) made of; **in marmo** made of marble, marble *cpd*; **una collana in oro** a gold necklace

7 (*misura*) in; **siamo in quattro** there are four of us; **in tutto** in all

8 (*fine*): **dare in dono** to give as a gift; **spende tutto in alcool** he spends all his money on drink; **in onore di** in honour of

inabi'tabile *ag* uninhabitable

inacces'sibile [inattʃes'sibile] *ag* (*luogo*) inaccessible; (*persona*) unapproachable

inaccet'tabile [inattʃet'tabile] *ag* unacceptable

ina'datto, -a *ag*: **~ (a)** unsuitable *o* unfit (for)

inadegu'ato, -a *ag* inadequate

inaffi'dabile *ag* unreliable

inami'dato, -a *ag* starched

inar'care /20/ *vt* (*schiena*) to arch; (*sopracciglia*) to raise

inaspet'tato, -a *ag* unexpected

inas'prire /55/ *vt* (*disciplina*) to tighten up, make harsher; (*carattere*) to embitter; **inasprirsi** *vpr* to become harsher; to become bitter; to become worse

inattac'cabile *ag (anche fig)* unassailable; *(alibi)* cast-iron

inatten'dibile *ag* unreliable

inat'teso, -a *ag* unexpected

inattu'abile *ag* impracticable

inau'dito, -a *ag* unheard of

inaugu'rare /72/ *vt* to inaugurate, open; *(monumento)* to unveil

inaugurazi'one [inaugurat'tsjone] *sf* inauguration; unveiling

incal'lito, -a *ag* calloused; *(fig)* hardened, inveterate; *(: insensibile)* hard

incande'scente [inkande∫∫εnte] *ag* incandescent, white-hot

incan'tare /72/ *vt* to enchant, bewitch; **incantarsi** *vpr (rimanere intontito)* to be spellbound; to be in a daze; *(meccanismo: bloccarsi)* to jam; **incan'tevole** *ag* charming, enchanting

in'canto *sm* spell, charm, enchantment; *(asta)* auction; **come per ~** as if by magic; **mettere all'~** to put up for auction

inca'pace [inka'pat∫e] *ag* incapable

incarce'rare [inkart∫e'rare] /72/ *vt* to imprison

incari'care /20/ *vt*: **~ qn di fare** to give sb the responsibility of doing; **incaricarsi** *vpr*: **incaricarsi di** to take care *o* charge of

in'carico, -chi *sm* task, job

incarta'mento *sm* dossier, file

incar'tare /72/ *vt* to wrap (in paper)

incas'sare /72/ *vt (merce)* to pack (in cases); *(gemma: incastonare)* to set; *(Econ: riscuotere)* to collect; *(Pugilato: colpi)* to take, stand up to; **in'casso** *sm* cashing, encashment; *(introito)* takings *pl*

incas'trare /72/ *vt* to fit in, insert; *(fig: intrappolare)* to catch; **incastrarsi** *vpr (combaciare)* to fit together; *(restare bloccato)* to become stuck

incate'nare /72/ *vt* to chain up

in'cauto, -a *ag* imprudent, rash

inca'vato, -a *ag* hollow; *(occhi)* sunken

incendi'are [int∫en'djare] /19/ *vt* to set fire to; **incendiarsi** *vpr* to catch fire, burst into flames

in'cendio [in't∫εndjo] *sm* fire

inceneri'tore [int∫eneri'tore] *sm* incinerator

in'censo [in't∫εnso] *sm* incense

incensu'rato, -a [int∫ensu'rato] *ag (Dir)*: **essere ~** to have a clean record

incenti'vare [int∫enti'vare] /72/ *vt (produzione, vendite)* to boost; *(persona)* to motivate

incen'tivo [int∫en'tivo] *sm* incentive

incep'pare [int∫ep'pare] /72/ *vt* to obstruct; **incepparsi** *vpr* to jam

incer'tezza [int∫er'tettsa] *sf* uncertainty

in'certo, -a [in't∫εrto] *ag* uncertain; *(irresoluto)* undecided, hesitating ▷ *sm* uncertainty

in'cetta [in't∫etta] *sf* buying up; **fare ~ di qc** to buy up sth

inchi'esta [in'kjesta] *sf* investigation, inquiry

inchi'nare [inki'nare] /72/ *vt* to bow; **inchinarsi** *vpr* to bend down; *(per riverenza)* to bow; *(: donna)* to curtsy

inchio'dare [inkjo'dare] /72/ *vt* to nail (down); **~ la macchina** *(Aut)* to jam on the brakes

inchi'ostro [in'kjostro] *sm* ink; **~ simpatico** invisible ink

inciam'pare [int∫am'pare] /72/ *vi* to trip, stumble

inci'dente [int∫i'dεnte] *sm* accident; **~ automobilistico** *o* **d'auto** car accident; **~ diplomatico** diplomatic incident

in'cidere [in't∫idere] /34/ *vi*: **~ su** to bear upon, affect ▷ *vt (tagliare incavando)* to cut into; *(Arte)* to engrave; to etch; *(canzone)* to record

in'cinta [in't∫inta] *ag f* pregnant

incipri'are [intʃi'prjare] /19/ *vt* to powder; **incipriarsi** *vpr* to powder one's face

in'circa [in'tʃirka] *av*: **all'~** more or less, very nearly

in'cisi *ecc* [in'tʃizi] *vb vedi* **incidere**

incisi'one [intʃi'zjone] *sf* cut; (*disegno*) engraving; etching; (*registrazione*) recording; (*Med*) incision

in'ciso, -a [in'tʃizo] *pp di* **incidere**
▷ *sm*: **per ~** incidentally, by the way

inci'tare [intʃi'tare] /72/ *vt* to incite

inci'vile [intʃi'vile] *ag* uncivilized; (*villano*) impolite

incl. *abbr* (= *incluso*) encl.

incli'nare [intʃi'nare] /72/ *vt* to tilt; **inclinarsi** *vpr* (*barca*) to list; (*aereo*) to bank

in'cludere /3/ *vt* to include; (*accludere*) to enclose; **in'cluso, -a** *pp di* **includere** ▷ *ag* included; enclosed

incoe'rente *ag* incoherent; (*contraddittorio*) inconsistent

in'cognito, -a [in'kɔɲɲito] *ag* unknown ▷ *sm*: **in ~** incognito ▷ *sf* (*Mat, fig*) unknown quantity

incol'lare /72/ *vt* to glue, gum; (*unire con colla*) to stick together

inco'lore *ag* colourless

incol'pare /72/ *vt*: **~ qn di** to charge sb with

in'colto, -a *ag* (*terreno*) uncultivated; (*trascurato: capelli*) neglected; (*persona*) uneducated

in'columne *ag* safe and sound, unhurt

incom'benza [inkom'bɛntsa] *sf* duty, task

in'combere /29/ *vi* (*sovrastare minacciando*): **~ su** to threaten, hang over

incominci'are [inkomin'tʃare] /14/ *vi, vt* to begin, start

incompe'tente *ag* incompetent

incompi'uto, -a *ag* unfinished, incomplete

incom'pleto, -a *ag* incomplete

incompren'sibile *ag* incomprehensible

inconce'pibile [inkontʃe'pibile] *ag* inconceivable

inconcili'abile [inkontʃi'ljabile] *ag* irreconcilable

inconclu'dente *ag* inconclusive; (*persona*) ineffectual

incondizio'nato, -a [inkondittsjo'nato] *ag* unconditional

inconfon'dibile *ag* unmistakable

inconsa'pevole *ag*: **~ di** unaware of, ignorant of

in'conscio, -a, -sci, -sce [in'kɔnʃo] *ag* unconscious ▷ *sm* (*Psic*): **l'~** the unconscious

inconsis'tente *ag* insubstantial; (*dubbio*) unfounded

inconsu'eto, -a *ag* unusual

incon'trare /72/ *vt* to meet; (*difficoltà*) to meet with; **incontrarsi** *vpr* to meet

in'contro *av*: **~ a** (*verso*) towards ▷ *sm* meeting; (*Sport*) match; meeting; **~ di calcio** football match

inconveni'ente *sm* drawback, snag

incoraggia'mento [inkoraddʒa'mento] *sm* encouragement

incoraggi'are [inkorad'dʒare] /62/ *vt* to encourage

incornici'are [inkorni'tʃare] /14/ *vt* to frame

incoro'nare /72/ *vt* to crown

in'correre /28/ *vi*: **~ in** to meet with, run into

incosci'ente [inkoʃʃente] *ag* (*inconscio*) unconscious; (*irresponsabile*) reckless, thoughtless

incre'dibile *ag* incredible, unbelievable

in'credulo, -a *ag* incredulous, disbelieving

incremen'tare /72/ *vt* to increase; (*dar sviluppo a*) to promote

incre'mento *sm* (*sviluppo*) development; (*aumento numerico*) increase, growth

incresci'oso, -a [inkreʃʃoso] *ag* (*incidente ecc*) regrettable

incrimi'nare /72/ *vt* (*Dir*) to charge

incri'nare /72/ *vt* to crack; (*fig: rapporti, amicizia*) to cause to deteriorate; **incrinarsi** *vpr* to crack; to deteriorate

incroci'are [inkro'tʃare] /14/ *vt* to cross; (*incontrare*) to meet ▷ *vi* (*Naut, Aer*) to cruise; **incrociarsi** *vpr* (*strade*) to cross, intersect; (*persone, veicoli*) to pass each other; **~ le braccia/ le gambe** to fold one's arms/cross one's legs

in'crocio [in'krotʃo] *sm* (*anche Ferr*) crossing; (*di strade*) crossroads

incuba'trice [inkuba'tritʃe] *sf* incubator

'incubo *sm* nightmare

incu'rabile *ag* incurable

incu'rante *ag*: **~ (di)** heedless (of), careless (of)

incuriosire /55/ *vt* to make curious; **incuriosirsi** *vpr* to become curious

incursi'one *sf* raid

incur'vare /72/ *vt* to bend, curve; **incurvarsi** *vpr* to bend, curve

incusto'dito, -a *ag* unguarded, unattended

in'cutere /40/ *vt*: **~ timore/rispetto a qn** to strike fear into sb/command sb's respect

'indaco *sm* indigo

indaffa'rato, -a *ag* busy

inda'gare /80/ *vt* to investigate

in'dagine [in'dadʒine] *sf* investigation, inquiry; (*ricerca*) research, study; **~ di mercato** market survey

indebi'tare /72/ *vt*: **~ qn** to get sb into debt; **indebitarsi** *vpr* to run *o* get into debt

indebo'lire /55/ *vt, vi* (*anche*: **indebolirsi**) to weaken

inde'cente [inde'tʃɛnte] *ag* indecent

inde'ciso, -a [inde'tʃizo] *ag* indecisive; (*irresoluto*) undecided

indefi'nito, -a *ag* (*anche Ling*) indefinite; (*impreciso, non determinato*) undefined

in'degno, -a [in'deɲɲo] *ag* (*atto*) shameful; (*persona*) unworthy

indemoni'ato, -a *ag* possessed (by the devil)

in'denne *ag* unhurt, uninjured

indenniz'zare [indennid'dzare] /72/ *vt* to compensate

indetermina'tivo, -a *ag* (*Ling*) indefinite

'India *sf*: **l'~** India; **indi'ano, -a** *ag* Indian ▷ *sm/f* (*d'India*) Indian; (*d'America*) Native American, (*American*) Indian

indi'care /20/ *vt* (*mostrare*) to show, indicate; (*: col dito*) to point to, point out; (*consigliare*) to suggest, recommend; **indica'tivo, -a** *ag* indicative ▷ *sm* (*Ling*) indicative (mood); **indicazi'one** *sf* indication; (*informazione*) piece of information

'indice ['inditʃe] *sm* (*Anat: dito*) index finger, forefinger; (*fig*) sign; (*nei libri*) index; **~ di gradimento** (*Radio, TV*) popularity rating

indicherò *ecc* [indike'rɔ] *vb vedi* **indicare**

indi'cibile [indi'tʃibile] *ag* inexpressible

indietreggi'are [indjetred'dʒare] /62/ *vi* to draw back, retreat

indi'etro *av* back; (*guardare*) behind, back; (*andare, cadere: anche*: **all'~**) backwards; **rimanere ~** to be left behind; **essere ~** (*col lavoro*) to be behind; (*orologio*) to be slow; **rimandare qc ~** to send sth back

indi'feso, -a *ag* (*città, confine*) undefended; (*persona*) defenceless

indiffe'rente *ag* indifferent

in'digeno, -a [in'didʒeno] *ag* indigenous, native ▷ *sm/f* native

indigesti'one [indidʒes'tjone] *sf* indigestion

indi'gesto, -a [indi'dʒɛsto] *ag* indigestible

indi'gnare [indiɲ'ɲare] /15/ *vt* to fill with indignation; **indignarsi** *vpr* to be (o get) indignant

indimenti'cabile *ag* unforgettable

indipen'dente *ag* independent

in'dire /38/ *vt* (*concorso*) to announce; (*elezioni*) to call

indi'retto, -a *ag* indirect

indiriz'zare [indirit'tsare] /72/ *vt* (*dirigere*) to direct; (*mandare*) to send; (*lettera*) to address

indi'rizzo [indi'rittso] *sm* address; (*direzione*) direction; (*avvio*) trend, course

indis'creto, -a *ag* indiscreet

indis'cusso, -a *ag* unquestioned

indispen'sabile *ag* indispensable, essential

indispet'tire /55/ *vt* to irritate, annoy ▷ *vi* (*anche:* **indispettirsi**) to get irritated o annoyed

individu'ale *ag* individual

individu'are /72/ *vt* (*dar forma distinta a*) to characterize; (*determinare*) to locate; (*riconoscere*) to single out

indi'viduo *sm* individual

indizi'ato, -a *ag* suspected ▷ *sm/f* suspect

in'dizio [in'dittsjo] *sm* (*segno*) sign, indication; (*Polizia*) clue; (*Dir*) piece of evidence

'indole *sf* nature, character

indolen'zito, -a [indolen'tsito] *ag* stiff, aching; (*intorpidito*) numb

indo'lore *ag* painless

indo'mani *sm*: **l'~** the next day, the following day

Indo'nesia *sf*: **l'~** Indonesia

indos'sare /72/ *vt* (*mettere indosso*) to put on; (*avere indosso*) to have on; **indossa'tore, -'trice** *sm/f* model

indottri'nare /72/ *vt* to indoctrinate

indovi'nare /72/ *vt* (*scoprire*) to guess; (*immaginare*) to imagine, guess; (*il futuro*) to foretell; **indovi'nello** *sm* riddle

indubbia'mente *av* undoubtedly

in'dubbio, -a *ag* certain, undoubted

in'duco *ecc vb vedi* **indurre**

indugi'are [indu'dʒare] /62/ *vi* to take one's time, delay

in'dugio [in'dudʒo] *sm* (*ritardo*) delay; **senza ~** without delay

indul'gente [indul'dʒente] *ag* indulgent; (*giudice*) lenient

indu'mento *sm* article of clothing, garment

indu'rire /55/ *vt* to harden ▷ *vi* (*anche:* **indurirsi**) to harden, become hard

in'durre /90/ *vt*: **~ qn a fare qc** to induce o persuade sb to do sth; **~ qn in errore** to mislead sb

in'dussi *ecc vb vedi* **indurre**

in'dustria *sf* industry; **industri'ale** *ag* industrial ▷ *sm* industrialist

inecce'pibile [inettʃe'pibile] *ag* unexceptionable

i'nedito, -a *ag* unpublished

ine'rente *ag*: **~ a** concerning, regarding

i'nerme *ag* unarmed, defenceless

inerpi'carsi /72/ *vpr*: **~ (su)** to clamber (up)

i'nerte *ag* inert; (*inattivo*) indolent, sluggish

ine'satto, -a *ag* (*impreciso*) inexact; (*erroneo*) incorrect; (*Amm: non riscosso*) uncollected

inesis'tente *ag* non-existent

inesperi'enza [inespe'rjɛntsa] *sf* inexperience

ines'perto, -a *ag* inexperienced

inevi'tabile *ag* inevitable

i'nezia [i'nɛttsja] *sf* trifle, thing of no importance

infagot'tare /72/ *vt* to bundle up, wrap up; **infagottarsi** *vpr* to wrap up

infal'libile *ag* infallible

infa'mante *ag* defamatory

in'fame *ag* infamous; (*fig: cosa, compito*) awful, dreadful

infan'gare /80/ *vt* to cover with mud; (*fig: nome, reputazione*) to sully; **infangarsi** *vpr* to get covered in mud; to be sullied

infan'tile *ag* child *cpd*; childlike; (*adulto, azione*) childish; **letteratura ~** children's books *pl*

in'fanzia [in'fantsja] *sf* childhood; (*bambini*) children *pl*: **prima ~** babyhood, infancy

infari'nare /72/ *vt* to cover with (*o* sprinkle with *o* dip in) flour; **infarina'tura** *sf* (*fig*) smattering

in'farto *sm* (*Med*): **~ (cardiaco)** coronary

infasti'dire /55/ *vt* to annoy, irritate; **infastidirsi** *vpr* to get annoyed *o* irritated

infati'cabile *ag* tireless, untiring

in'fatti *cong* as a matter of fact, actually
⚠ Attenzione! In inglese esiste l'espressione *in fact*, che però vuol dire *in effetti*.

infatu'arsi /72/ *vpr*: **~ di** *o* **per** to become infatuated with, fall for

infe'dele *ag* unfaithful

infe'lice [infe'litʃe] *ag* unhappy; (*sfortunato*) unlucky, unfortunate; (*inopportuno*) inopportune, ill-timed; (*mal riuscito: lavoro*) bad, poor

inferi'ore *ag* lower; (*per intelligenza, qualità*) inferior ▷ *smf* inferior; **~ a** (*numero, quantità*) less *o* smaller than; (*meno buono*) inferior to; **~ alla media** below average; **inferiorità** *sf* inferiority

inferme'ria *sf* infirmary; (*di scuola, nave*) sick bay

infermi'ere, -a *smf* nurse

infermità *sf inv* illness; infirmity; **~ mentale** mental illness; (*Dir*) insanity

in'fermo, -a *ag* (*ammalato*) ill; (*debole*) infirm

infer'nale *ag* infernal; (*proposito, complotto*) diabolical

in'ferno *sm* hell

inferri'ata *sf* grating

infes'tare /72/ *vt* to infest

infet'tare /72/ *vt* to infect; **infettarsi** *vpr* to become infected; **infezi'one** *sf* infection

infiam'mabile *ag* inflammable

infiam'mare /72/ *vt* to set alight; (*fig, Med*) to inflame; **infiammarsi** *vpr* to catch fire; (*Med*) to become inflamed; **infiammazi'one** *sf* (*Med*) inflammation

infie'rire /55/ *vi*: **~ su** (*fisicamente*) to attack furiously; (*verbalmente*) to rage at

infi'lare /72/ *vt* (*ago*) to thread; (*mettere: chiave*) to insert; (: *vestito*) to slip *o* put on; (*strada*) to turn into, take; **infilarsi** *vpr*: **infilarsi in** to slip into; (*indossare*) to slip on; **~ un anello al dito** to slip a ring on one's finger; **~ l'uscio** to slip in; to slip out

infil'trarsi /72/ *vpr* to penetrate, seep through; (*Mil*) to infiltrate

infil'zare [infil'tsare] /72/ *vt* (*infilare*) to string together; (*trafiggere*) to pierce

'infimo, -a *ag* lowest

in'fine *av* finally; (*insomma*) in short

infinità *sf* infinity; (*in quantità*): **un'~ di** an infinite number of

infi'nito, -a *ag* infinite; (*Ling*) infinitive ▷ *sm* infinity; (*Ling*) infinitive; **all'~** (*senza fine*) endlessly

infinocchi'are [infinok'kjare] /19/ *vt* (*fam*) to hoodwink

infischi'arsi [infis'kjarsi] /19/ *vpr*: **~ di** not to care about

in'fisso *sm* fixture; (*di porta, finestra*) frame

inflazi'one [inflat'tsjone] *sf* inflation

in'fliggere [in'fliddʒere] /104/ *vt* to inflict

in'flissi *ecc vb vedi* **infliggere**

influ'ente *ag* influential; **influ'enza** *sf* influence; (*Med*) influenza, flu; **influenza aviaria** bird flu; **influenza suina** swine flu

influen'zare [influen'tsare] /72/ *vt* to influence, have an influence on

influ'ire /55/ *vi*: **~ su** to influence

in'flusso *sm* influence

infon'dato, -a *ag* unfounded, groundless

in'fondere /25/ *vt*: **~ qc in qn** to instill sth in sb

infor'mare /72/ *vt* to inform, tell; **informarsi** *vpr*: **informarsi (di o su)** to inquire (about)

infor'matico, -a, -ci, -che *ag* computer *cpd* ▷ *sf* computer science

informa'tivo, -a *ag* informative

infor'mato, -a *ag* informed; **tenersi ~** to keep o.s. (well-) informed

informa'tore *sm* informer

informazi'one [informat'tsjone] *sf* piece of information; **informazioni** *sfpl* information *sg*: **chiedere un'~** to ask for (some) information

in'forme *ag* shapeless

informico'larsi /72/ *vpr*: **mi si è informicolata una gamba** I've got pins and needles in my leg

infortu'nato, -a *ag* injured, hurt ▷ *sm/f* injured person

infor'tunio *sm* accident; **~ sul lavoro** industrial accident, accident at work

infra'dito *sm inv* (*calzatura*) flip flop (BRIT), thong (US)

infrazi'one [infrat'tsjone] *sf*: **~ a** breaking of, violation of

infredda'tura *sf* slight cold

infreddo'lito, -a *ag* cold, chilled

infu'ori *av* out; **all'~** outwards; **all'~ di** (*eccetto*) except, with the exception of

infuri'are /19/ *vi* to rage; **infuriarsi** *vpr* to fly into a rage

infusi'one *sf* infusion

in'fuso, -a *pp di* **infondere** ▷ *sm* infusion

Ing. *abbr* = **ingegnere**

ingaggi'are [ingad'dʒare] /62/ *vt* (*assumere con compenso*) to take on, hire; (*Sport*) to sign on; (*Mil*) to engage

ingan'nare /72/ *vt* to deceive; (*fisco*) to cheat; (*eludere*) to dodge, elude; (*fig: tempo*) to while away ▷ *vi* (*apparenza*) to be deceptive;

ingannarsi *vpr* to be mistaken, be wrong

in'ganno *sm* deceit, deception; (*azione*) trick; (*menzogna, frode*) cheat, swindle; (*illusione*) illusion

inge'gnarsi [indʒeɲ'narsi] /15/ *vpr* to do one's best, try hard; **~ per vivere** to live by one's wits

inge'gnere [indʒe'ɲɛre] *sm* engineer; **~ civile/navale** civil/ naval engineer; **ingegne'ria** *sf* engineering; **ingegnere genetica** genetic engineering

in'gegno [in'dʒeɲɲo] *sm* (*intelligenza*) intelligence, brains *pl*; (*capacità creativa*) ingenuity; (*disposizione*) talent; **inge'gnoso, -a** *ag* ingenious, clever

ingelo'sire /55/ *vt* to make jealous ▷ *vi* (*anche*: **ingelosirsi**) to become jealous

in'gente [in'dʒente] *ag* huge, enormous

ingenuità [indʒenui'ta] *sf* ingenuousness

in'genuo, -a [in'dʒɛnuo] *ag* naïve

Attenzione! In inglese esiste la parola *ingenious*, che però significa *ingegnoso*.

inge'rire [indʒe'rire] /55/ *vt* to ingest

inges'sare [indʒes'sare] /72/ *vt* (*Med*) to put in plaster; **ingessa'tura** *sf* plaster

Inghil'terra [ingil'tɛrra] *sf*: **l'~** England

inghiot'tire [ingjot'tire] /17/ *vt* to swallow

ingial'lire [indʒal'lire] /55/ *vi* to go yellow

inginocchi'arsi [indʒinok'kjarsi] /19/ *vpr* to kneel (down)

ingiù [in'dʒu] *av* down, downwards

ingi'uria [in'dʒurja] *sf* insult; (*fig: danno*) damage

ingius'tizia [indʒus'tittsja] *sf* injustice

ingi'usto, -a [in'dʒusto] *ag* unjust, unfair

in'glese *ag* English ▷ *smf* Englishman/woman ▷ *sm* (*Ling*) English; **gli Inglesi** the English; **andarsene** *o* **filare all'~** to take French leave

ingoi'are /19/ *vt* to gulp (down); (*fig*) to swallow (up)

ingol'fare /72/ *vt*, **ingol'farsi** *vpr* to flood

ingom'brante *ag* cumbersome

ingom'brare /72/ *vt* (*strada*) to block; (*stanza*) to clutter up

in'gordo, -a *ag*: **~ di** greedy for; (*fig*) greedy *o* avid for

in'gorgo, -ghi *sm* blockage, obstruction; (*anche*: **~ stradale**) traffic jam

ingoz'zare [ingot'tsare] /72/ *vt* (*persona*) to stuff; **ingozzarsi** *vpr*: **ingozzarsi (di)** to stuff o.s. (with)

ingra'naggio [ingra'naddʒo] *sm* (*Tecn*) gear; (*di orologio*) mechanism; **gli ingranaggi della burocrazia** the bureaucratic machinery

ingra'nare /72/ *vi* to mesh, engage ▷ *vt* to engage; **~ la marcia** to get into gear

ingrandi'mento *sm* enlargement; extension

ingran'dire /55/ *vt* (*anche Fot*) to enlarge; (*estendere*) to extend; (*Ottica, fig*) to magnify ▷ *vi* (*anche*: **ingrandirsi**) to become larger *o* bigger; (*aumentare*) to grow, increase; (*espandersi*) to expand

ingras'sare /72/ *vt* to make fat; (*animali*) to fatten; (*lubrificare*) to oil, lubricate ▷ *vi* (*anche*: **ingrassarsi**) to get fat, put on weight

in'grato, -a *ag* ungrateful; (*lavoro*) thankless, unrewarding

ingredi'ente *sm* ingredient

in'gresso *sm* (*porta*) entrance; (*atrio*) hall; (*l'entrare*) entrance, entry; (*facoltà di entrare*) admission; **"~ libero"** "admission free"

ingros'sare /72/ *vt* to increase; (*folla, livello*) to swell ▷ *vi* (*anche*: **ingrossarsi**) to increase; to swell

in'grosso *av*: **all'~** (*Comm*) wholesale; (*all'incirca*) roughly, about

ingua'ribile *ag* incurable

'inguine *sm* (*Anat*) groin

ini'bire /55/ *vt* to forbid, prohibit; (*Psic*) to inhibit; **inibirsi** *vpr* to restrain o.s.

ini'bito, -a *ag* inhibited ▷ *sm/f* inhibited person

iniet'tare /72/ *vt* to inject; **iniezi'one** *sf* injection

ininterrotta'mente *av* non-stop, continuously

ininter'rotto, -a *ag* unbroken; (*rumore*) uninterrupted

inizi'ale [init'tsjale] *ag*, *sf* initial

inizi'are [init'tsjare] /19/ *vt* to begin, start; **~ qn a** to initiate sb into; (*pittura ecc*) to introduce sb to; **~ a fare qc** to start doing sth

inizia'tiva [inittsja'tiva] *sf* initiative; **~ privata** private enterprise

i'nizio [i'nittsjo] *sm* beginning; **all'~** at the beginning, at the start; **dare ~ a qc** to start sth, get sth going

innaffi'are *ecc* = **annaffiare** *ecc*

innamo'rare /72/ *vt* to enchant; **innamorarsi** *vpr*: **innamorarsi (di qn)** to fall in love (with sb)

innamo'rato, -a *ag*: **innamorato (di)** (*che nutre amore*) in love (with); **innamorato di** (*appassionato*) very fond of ▷ *sm/f* lover; (*anche scherzoso*) sweetheart

innanzi'tutto [innantsi'tutto] *av* first of all

in'nato, -a *ag* innate

innatu'rale *ag* unnatural

inne'gabile *ag* undeniable

innervo'sire /55/ *vt*: **~ qn** to get on sb's nerves; **innervosirsi** *vpr* to get irritated *o* upset

innes'care /20/ *vt* to prime

'inno *sm* hymn; **~ nazionale** national anthem

inno'cente [inno'tʃɛnte] *ag* innocent

in'nocuo, -a *ag* innocuous, harmless

innova'tivo, -a *ag* innovative

innume'revole *ag* innumerable

inol'trare /72/ *vt* (*Amm*) to pass on, forward

i'noltre *av* besides, moreover

inon'dare /72/ *vt* to flood

inoppor'tuno, -a *ag* untimely, ill-timed; (*poco adatto*) inappropriate; (*momento*) inopportune

inorri'dire /55/ *vt* to horrify ▷ *vi* to be horrified

inosser'vato, -a *ag* (*non notato*) unobserved; (*non rispettato*) not observed, not kept

inossi'dabile *ag* stainless

INPS *sigla m* (= Istituto Nazionale Previdenza Sociale) social security service

inqua'drare /72/ *vt* (*foto, immagine*) to frame; (*fig*) to situate, set

inqui'eto, -a *ag* restless; (*preoccupato*) worried, anxious

inqui'lino, -a *sm/f* tenant

inquina'mento *sm* pollution

inqui'nare /72/ *vt* to pollute

insabbi'are /19/ *vt* (*fig: pratica*) to shelve; **insabbiarsi** *vpr* (*arenarsi: barca*) to run aground; (*fig: pratica*) to be shelved

insac'cati *smpl* (*Cuc*) sausages

insa'lata *sf* salad; **~ mista** mixed salad; **~ russa** (*Cuc*) Russian salad (*comprised of cold diced cooked vegetables in mayonnaise*); **insalati'era** *sf* salad bowl

insa'nabile *ag* (*piaga*) which cannot be healed; (*situazione*) irremediable; (*odio*) implacable

insa'puta *sf*: **all'~ di qn** without sb knowing

insedi'are /19/ *vt* (*Amm*) to install; **insediarsi** *vpr* to take up office; (*colonia, profughi ecc*) to settle

in'segna [in'seɲɲa] *sf* sign; (*emblema*) sign, emblem; (*bandiera*) flag, banner

insegna'mento [inseɲɲa'mento] *sm* teaching

inse'gnante [inseɲ'ɲante] *ag* teaching ▷ *smf* teacher; **~ di sostegno** teaching assistant

inse'gnare [inseɲ'ɲare] /15/ *vt, vi* to teach; **~ a qn qc** to teach sb sth; **~ a qn a fare qc** to teach sb (how) to do sth

insegui'mento *sm* pursuit, chase

insegu'ire /45/ *vt* to pursue, chase

insena'tura *sf* inlet, creek

insen'sato, -a *ag* senseless, stupid

insen'sibile *ag* (*anche fig*) insensitive

inse'rire /55/ *vt* to insert; (*Elettr*) to connect; (*allegare*) to enclose; (*annuncio*) to put in, place; **inserirsi** *vpr* (*fig*): **inserirsi in** to become part of

inservi'ente *smf* attendant

inserzi'one [inser'tsjone] *sf* insertion; (*avviso*) advertisement; **fare un'~ sul giornale** to put an advertisement in the newspaper

insetti'cida, -i [insetti'tʃida] *sm* insecticide

in'setto *sm* insect

insi'curo, -a *ag* insecure

insi'eme *av* together ▷ *prep*: **~ a** *o* **con** together with ▷ *sm* whole; (*Mat, servizio, assortimento*) set; (*Moda*) ensemble, outfit; **tutti ~** all together; **tutto ~** all together; (*in una volta*) at one go; **nell'~** on the whole; **d'~** (*veduta ecc*) overall

in'signe [in'siɲɲe] *ag* (*persona*) famous, distinguished; (*città, monumento*) notable

insignifi'cante [insiɲɲifi'kante] *ag* insignificant

insinu'are /72/ *vt* (*fig*) to insinuate, imply; **~ qc in** (*introdurre*) to slip *o* slide sth into; **insinuarsi** *vpr*: **insinuarsi in** to seep into; (*fig*) to creep into; to worm one's way into

in'sipido, -a *ag* insipid

insis'tente *ag* insistent; (*pioggia, dolore*) persistent

in'sistere /11/ *vi*: **~ su qc** to insist on sth; **~ in qc/a fare** (*perseverare*) to persist in sth/in doing

insoddis'fatto, -a *ag* dissatisfied

insoffe'rente *ag* intolerant

insolazi'one [insolat'tsjone] *sf* (*Med*) sunstroke

inso'lente *ag* insolent

in'solito, -a *ag* unusual, out of the ordinary

inso'luto, -a *ag* (*non risolto*) unsolved

in'somma *av* (*in breve, in conclusione*) in short; (*dunque*) well ▷ *escl* for heaven's sake!

in'sonne *ag* sleepless; **in'sonnia** *sf* insomnia, sleeplessness

inson'nolito, -a *ag* sleepy, drowsy

insoppor'tabile *ag* unbearable

in'sorgere [in'sordʒere] /109/ *vi* (*ribellarsi*) to rise up, rebel; (*apparire*) to come up, arise

in'sorsi *ecc vb vedi* **insorgere**

insospet'tire /55/ *vt* to make suspicious ▷ *vi* (*anche:* **insospettirsi**) to become suspicious

inspi'rare /72/ *vt* to breathe in, inhale

in'stabile *ag* (*carico, indole*) unstable; (*tempo*) unsettled; (*equilibrio*) unsteady

instal'lare /72/ *vt* to install

instan'cabile *ag* untiring, indefatigable

instau'rare /72/ *vt* to establish, introduce

insuc'cesso [insut'tʃɛsso] *sm* failure, flop

insuffici'ente [insuffi'tʃɛnte] *ag* insufficient; (*compito, allievo*) inadequate; **insuffici'enza** *sf* insufficiency; inadequacy; (*Ins*) fail; **insufficienza di prove** (*Dir*) lack of evidence; **insufficienza renale** renal insufficiency

insu'lina *sf* insulin

in'sulso, -a *ag* (*sciocco*) inane, silly; (*persona*) dull, insipid

insul'tare /72/ *vt* to insult, affront

in'sulto *sm* insult, affront

intac'care /20/ *vt* (*fare tacche*) to cut into; (*corrodere*) to corrode; (*fig:*

cominciare ad usare: risparmi) to break into; (: *ledere*) to damage

intagli'are [intaʎ'ʎare] /27/ *vt* to carve

in'tanto *av* (*nel frattempo*) meanwhile, in the meantime; (*per cominciare*) just to begin with; **~ che** while

inta'sare /72/ *vt* to choke (up), block (up); (*Aut*) to obstruct, block; **intasarsi** *vpr* to become choked o blocked

intas'care /20/ *vt* to pocket

in'tatto, -a *ag* intact; (*puro*) unsullied

intavo'lare /72/ *vt* to start, enter into

inte'grale *ag* complete; (*pane, farina*) wholemeal (BRIT), wholewheat (US); **calcolo ~** (*Mat*) integral calculus

inte'grante *ag*: **parte ~** integral part

inte'grare /72/ *vt* to complete; (*Mat*) to integrate; **integrarsi** *vpr* (*persona*) to become integrated

integra'tore *sm*: **integratori alimentari** nutritional supplements

integrità *sf* integrity

'integro, -a *ag* (*intatto, intero*) complete, whole; (*retto*) upright

intelaia'tura *sf* frame; (*fig*) structure, framework

intel'letto *sm* intellect; **intellettu'ale** *ag, smf* intellectual

intelli'gente [intelli'dʒɛnte] *ag* intelligent

intem'perie *sfpl* bad weather *sg*

in'tendere /120/ *vt* (*comprendere*) to understand; (*udire*) to hear; (*significare*) to mean; (*avere intenzione*): **~ fare qc** to intend o mean to do sth; **intendersi** *vpr* (*conoscere*): **intendersi di** to know a lot about, be a connoisseur of; (*accordarsi*) to get on (well); **intendersela con qn** (*avere una relazione amorosa*) to have an affair with sb; **intendi'tore, -'trice** *sm/f* connoisseur, expert

inten'sivo, -a *ag* intensive

in'tenso, -a *ag* intense

in'tento, -a *ag* (*teso, assorto*): **~ (a)** intent (on), absorbed (in) ▷ *sm* aim, purpose

intenzio'nale [intentsjo'nale] *ag* intentional

intenzi'one [inten'tsjone] *sf* intention; (*Dir*) intent; **avere ~ di fare qc** to intend to do sth, have the intention of doing sth

interat'tivo, -a *ag* interactive

intercet'tare [intertʃet'tare] /72/ *vt* to intercept

intercity [inter'siti] *sm inv* (*Ferr*) ≈ intercity (train)

inter'detto, -a *pp di* **interdire** ▷ *ag* forbidden, prohibited; (*sconcertato*) dumbfounded ▷ *sm* (*Rel*) interdict

interes'sante *ag* interesting; **essere in stato ~** to be expecting (a baby)

interes'sare /72/ *vt* to interest; (*concernere*) to concern, be of interest to; (*far intervenire*): **~ qn a** to draw sb's attention to ▷ *vi*: **~ a** to interest, matter to; **interessarsi** *vpr* (*mostrare interesse*): **interessarsi a** to take an interest in, be interested in; (*occuparsi*): **interessarsi di** to take care of

inte'resse *sm* (*anche Comm*) interest

inter'faccia, -ce [inter'fattʃa] *sf* (*Inform*) interface

interfe'renza [interfe'rɛntsa] *sf* interference

interfe'rire /55/ *vi* to interfere

interiezi'one [interjet'tsjone] *sf* exclamation, interjection

interi'nale *ag*: **lavoro ~** temporary work (*through an agency*)

interi'ora *sfpl* entrails

interi'ore *ag* inner *cpd*; **parte ~** inside

inter'medio, -a *ag* intermediate

inter'nare /72/ *vt* (*arrestare*) to intern; (*Med*) to commit (to a mental institution)

inter'nauta *smf* Internet user

internazio'nale [internattsjo'nale] *ag* international

'Internet ['internet] *sf* Internet; **in ~** on the Internet

in'terno, -a *ag* (*di dentro*) internal, interior, inner; (*: mare*) inland; (*nazionale*) domestic; (*allievo*) boarding ▷ *sm* inside, interior; (*di paese*) interior; (*fodera*) lining; (*di appartamento*) flat (BRIT) o apartment (US) (number); (*Tel*) extension ▷ *sm/f* (*Ins*) boarder; **interni** *smpl* (*Cine*) interior shots; **all'~** inside; **Ministero degli Interni** Ministry of the Interior, ≈ Home Office (BRIT), ≈ Department of the Interior (US)

in'tero, -a *ag* (*integro, intatto*) whole, entire; (*completo, totale*) complete; (*numero*) whole; (*non ridotto: biglietto*) full; (*latte*) full-cream

interpel'lare /72/ *vt* to consult

interpre'tare /72/ *vt* to interpret; **in'terprete** *smf* interpreter; (*Teat*) actor (actress), performer; (*Mus*) performer; **farsi interprete di** to act as a spokesman for

interregio'nale [interredʒo'nale] *sm train that travels between two or more regions of Italy*

interro'gare /80/ *vt* to question; (*Ins*) to test; **interrogazi'one** *sf* questioning *no pl*; (*Ins*) oral test

inter'rompere /97/ *vt* to interrupt; (*studi, trattative*) to break off, interrupt; **interrompersi** *vpr* to break off, stop

interrut'tore *sm* switch

interruzi'one [interrut'tsjone] *sf* interruption; break

interur'bano, -a *ag* inter-city ▷ *sf* long-distance call

inter'vallo *sm* interval; (*spazio*) space, gap

interve'nire /128/ *vi* (*partecipare*): **~ a** to take part in; (*intromettersi*) (*anche Pol*) to intervene; (*Med: operare*) to operate; **inter'vento** *sm* participation; (*intromissione*) intervention; (*Med*) operation;

fare un intervento nel corso di
(dibattito, programma) to take part in
inter'vista sf interview;
intervis'tare /72/ vt to interview
intes'tare /72/ vt (lettera) to address;
(proprietà): **~ a** to register in the name
of; **~ un assegno a qn** to make out a
cheque to sb
intes'tato, -a ag (proprietà, casa, conto)
in the name of; (assegno) made out to;
carta intestata headed paper
intes'tino sm (Anat) intestine
intimidazi'one [intimidat'tsjone]
sf intimidation
intimi'dire /55/ vt to intimidate ▷ vi
(anche: **intimidirsi**) to grow shy
inti'mità sf intimacy; privacy;
(familiarità) familiarity
'intimo, -a ag intimate; (affetti, vita)
private; (fig: profondo) inmost ▷ sm
(persona) intimate o close friend;
(dell'animo) bottom, depths pl: **parti
intime** (Anat) private parts
in'tingolo sm sauce; (pietanza) stew
intito'lare /72/ vt to give a title to;
(dedicare) to dedicate; **intitolarsi** vpr
(libro, film) to be called
intolle'rabile ag intolerable
intolle'rante ag intolerant
in'tonaco, -ci o **-chi** sm plaster
into'nare /72/ vt (canto) to start
to sing; (armonizzare) to match;
intonarsi vpr (colori) to go together;
intonarsi a (carnagione) to suit;
(abito) to go with, match
inton'tito, -a ag stunned, dazed; **~
dal sonno** stupid with sleep
in'toppo sm stumbling block,
obstacle
in'torno av around; **~ a** (attorno a)
around; (riguardo, circa) about
intossi'care /20/ vt to poison;
intossicazi'one sf poisoning
intralci'are [intral'tʃare] /14/ vt to
hamper, hold up
intransi'tivo, -a ag, sm intransitive
intrapren'dente ag enterprising,
go-ahead

intra'prendere /81/ vt to undertake
intrat'tabile ag intractable
intratte'nere /121/ vt to entertain;
(chiacchierando) to engage in
conversation; **intrattenersi** vpr
to linger; **intrattenersi su qc** to
dwell on sth
intrave'dere /127/ vt to catch a
glimpse of; (fig) to foresee
intrecci'are [intret'tʃare] /14/ vt
(capelli) to plait, braid; (intessere:
anche fig) to weave, interweave,
intertwine
intri'gante ag scheming ▷ smf
schemer, intriguer
in'trinseco, -a, -ci, -che ag intrinsic
in'triso, -a ag: **~ (di)** soaked (in)
intro'durre /90/ vt to introduce;
(chiave ecc): **~ qc in** to insert sth
into; (persona: far entrare) to show
in; **introdursi** vpr (moda, tecniche)
to be introduced; **introdursi in**
(persona: penetrare) to enter; (entrare
furtivamente) to steal o slip into;
introduzi'one sf introduction
in'troito sm income, revenue
intro'mettersi /63/ vpr to interfere,
meddle; (interporsi) to intervene
in'truglio [in'truʎʎo] sm concoction
intrusi'one sf intrusion; interference
in'truso, -a sm/f intruder
intu'ire /55/ vt to perceive by
intuition; (rendersi conto) to realize;
in'tuito sm intuition; (perspicacia)
perspicacity
inu'mano, -a ag inhuman
inumi'dire /55/ vt to dampen,
moisten; **inumidirsi** vpr to become
damp o wet
i'nutile ag useless; (superfluo)
pointless, unnecessary
inutil'mente av (senza risultato)
in vain; (senza utilità, scopo)
unnecessarily
inva'dente ag (fig) interfering, nosey
in'vadere /52/ vt to invade; (affollare)
to swarm into, overrun; (acque)
to flood

inva'ghirsi [invaˈɡirsi] /55/ vpr: **~ di** to take a fancy to

invalidità sf infirmity; disability; (Dir) invalidity

in'valido, -a ag (infermo) infirm, invalid; (al lavoro) disabled; (Dir: nullo) invalid ▷ sm/f invalid; disabled person

in'vano av in vain

invasi'one sf invasion

inva'sore, invadi'trice [invadiˈtritʃe] ag invading ▷ sm/f invader

invecchi'are [invekˈkjare] /19/ vi (persona) to grow old; (vino, popolazione) to age; (moda) to become dated ▷ vt to age; (far apparire più vecchio) to make look older

in'vece [inˈvetʃe] av instead; (al contrario) on the contrary; **~ di** instead of

inve'ire /55/ vi: **~ contro** to rail against

inven'tare /72/ vt to invent; (pericoli, pettegolezzi) to make up, invent

inven'tario sm inventory; (Comm) stocktaking no pl

inven'tore, -'trice sm/f inventor

invenzi'one [invenˈtsjone] sf invention; (bugia) lie, story

inver'nale ag winter cpd; (simile all'inverno) wintry

in'verno sm winter

invero'simile ag unlikely

inversi'one sf inversion; reversal; **"divieto d'~"** (Aut) "no U-turns"

in'verso, -a ag opposite; (Mat) inverse ▷ sm contrary, opposite; **in senso ~** in the opposite direction; **in ordine ~** in reverse order

inver'tire /45/ vt to invert, reverse; **~ la marcia** (Aut) to do a U-turn

investi'gare /80/ vt, vi to investigate; **investiga'tore, -'trice** sm/f investigator, detective; **investigatore privato** private investigator

investi'mento sm (Econ) investment

inves'tire /45/ vt (denaro) to invest; (veicolo: pedone) to knock down; (: altro veicolo) to crash into; (apostrofare) to assail; (incaricare): **~ qn di** to invest sb with

invi'are /60/ vt to send; **invi'ato, -a** sm/f envoy; (Stampa) correspondent; **inviato speciale** (Pol) special envoy; (di giornale) special correspondent

in'vidia sf envy; **invidi'are** /19/ vt: **invidiare qn (per qc)** to envy sb (for sth); **invidiare qc a qn** to envy sb sth; **invidi'oso, -a** ag envious

in'vio, -'vii sm sending; (insieme di merci) consignment; (tasto) Return (key), Enter (key)

invipe'rito, -a ag furious

invi'sibile ag invisible

invi'tare /72/ vt to invite; **~ qn a fare** to invite sb to do; **invi'tato, -a** sm/f guest; **in'vito** sm invitation

invo'care /20/ vt (chiedere: aiuto, pace) to cry out for; (appellarsi: la legge, Dio) to appeal to, invoke

invogli'are [invoʎˈʎare] /27/ vt: **~ qn a fare** to tempt sb to do, induce sb to do

involon'tario, -a ag (errore) unintentional; (gesto) involuntary

invol'tino sm (Cuc) roulade

in'volto sm (pacco) parcel; (fagotto) bundle

invo'lucro sm cover, wrapping

inzup'pare [intsupˈpare] /72/ vt to soak; **inzupparsi** vpr to get soaked

'io pron I ▷ sm inv: **,io** the ego, the self; **io stesso(a)** I myself

i'odio sm iodine

l'onio sm: **lo ~, il mar ~** the Ionian (Sea)

ipermer'cato sm hypermarket

ipertensi'one sf high blood pressure, hypertension

iper'testo sm hypertext; **ipertestu'ale** ag (Inform): **collegamento o link ipertestuale** hyperlink

ip'nosi sf hypnosis; **ipnotiz'zare** /72/ vt to hypnotize

ipocri'sia sf hypocrisy

i'pocrita, -i, -e ag hypocritical ▷ smf hypocrite

ipo'teca, -che sf mortgage

i'potesi sf inv hypothesis

'ippico, -a, -ci, -che ag horse cpd ▷ sf horseracing

ippocas'tano sm horse chestnut

ip'podromo sm racecourse

ippo'potamo sm hippopotamus

'ipsilon sf o m inv (lettera) Y, y; (: dell'alfabeto greco) epsilon

IR abbr (= Interregionale) long distance train which stops frequently

ira'cheno, -a [ira'kɛno] ag, sm/f Iraqi

I'ran sm: **I'~** Iran

irani'ano, -a ag, smf Iranian

I'raq sm: **I'~** Iraq

'iride sf (arcobaleno) rainbow; (Anat, Bot) iris

'iris sm inv iris

Ir'landa sf: **I'~** Ireland; **I'~ del Nord** Northern Ireland, Ulster; **la Repubblica d'~** Eire, the Republic of Ireland; **irlan'dese** ag Irish ▷ smf Irishman/woman; **gli Irlandesi** the Irish

iro'nia sf irony; **i'ronico, -a, -ci, -che** ag ironic(al)

irragio'nevole [irradʒo'nevole] ag irrational; (persona, pretese, prezzo) unreasonable

irrazio'nale [irrattsjo'nale] ag irrational

irre'ale ag unreal

irrego'lare ag irregular; (terreno) uneven

irremo'vibile ag (fig) unshakeable, unyielding

irrequi'eto, -a ag restless

irresis'tibile ag irresistible

irrespon'sabile ag irresponsible

irri'gare /80/ vt (annaffiare) to irrigate; (fiume ecc) to flow through

irrigi'dire [irridʒi'dire] /55/ vt to stiffen; **irrigidirsi** vpr to stiffen

irri'sorio, -a ag derisory

irri'tare /72/ vt (mettere di malumore) to irritate, annoy; (Med) to irritate; **irritarsi** vpr (stizzirsi) to become irritated o annoyed; (Med) to become irritated

ir'rompere /97/ vi: **~ in** to burst into

irru'ente ag (fig) impetuous, violent

ir'ruppi ecc vb vedi **irrompere**

irruzi'one [irrut'tsjone] sf: **fare ~ in** to burst into; (polizia) to raid

is'crissi ecc vb vedi **iscrivere**

is'critto, -a pp di **iscrivere** ▷ smf member; **per o in ~** in writing

is'crivere /105/ vt to register, enter; (persona) : **~ (a)** to register (in), enrol (in); **iscriversi** vpr: **iscriversi (a)** (club, partito) to join; (università) to register o enrol (at); (esame, concorso) to register o enter (for); **iscrizi'one** sf (epigrafe ecc) inscription; (a scuola, società ecc) enrolment, registration; (registrazione) registration

Is'lam sm: **I'~** Islam

Is'landa sf: **I'~** Iceland

islan'dese ag Icelandic ▷ smf Icelander ▷ sm (Ling) Icelandic

'isola sf island; **~ pedonale** (Aut) pedestrian precinct

isola'mento sm isolation; (Tecn) insulation

iso'lante ag insulating ▷ sm insulator

iso'lare /72/ vt to isolate; (Tecn) to insulate; (: acusticamente) to soundproof; **isolarsi** vpr to isolate o.s.; **iso'lato, -a** ag isolated; insulated ▷ sm (edificio) block

ispet'tore, -'trice sm/f inspector

ispezio'nare [ispettsjo'nare] /72/ vt to inspect

'ispido, -a ag bristly, shaggy

ispi'rare /72/ vt to inspire

Isra'ele sm: **I'~** Israel; **israeli'ano, -a** ag, sm/f Israeli

is'sare /72/ vt to hoist

istan'taneo, -a ag instantaneous ▷ sf (Fot) snapshot

is'tante sm instant, moment; **all'~, sull'~** instantly, immediately

is'terico, -a, -ci, -che *ag* hysterical

isti'gare /80/ *vt* to incite

is'tinto *sm* instinct

istitu'ire /55/ *vt* (*fondare*) to institute, found; (*porre: confronto*) to establish; (*intraprendere: inchiesta*) to set up

isti'tuto *sm* institute; (*di università*) department; (*ente, Dir*) institution; **~ di bellezza** beauty salon; **~ di credito** bank, banking institution; **~ di ricerca** research institute

istituzi'one [istitut'tsjone] *sf* institution

'istmo *sm* (*Geo*) isthmus

'istrice ['istritʃe] *sm* porcupine

istru'ito, -a *ag* educated

istrut'tore, -'trice *sm/f* instructor ▷ *ag*: **giudice ~** examining (*BRIT*) *o* committing (*US*) magistrate

istruzi'one [istrut'tsjone] *sf* (*gen*) training; (*Ins, cultura*) education; (*direttiva*) instruction; **istruzioni** *sfpl* (*norme*) instructions; **istruzioni per l'uso** instructions (for use); **~ obbligatoria** (*Ins*) compulsory education

l'talia *sf*: **l'~** Italy

itali'ano, -a *ag* Italian ▷ *sm/f* Italian ▷ *sm* (*Ling*) Italian; **gli Italiani** the Italians

itine'rario *sm* itinerary

'ittico, -a, -ci, -che *ag* fish *cpd*; fishing *cpd*

Iugos'lavia *sf* = **Jugoslavia**

'I.V.A. *sigla f* (= *imposta sul valore aggiunto*) VAT

jazz [dʒaz] *sm* jazz

jeans [dʒinz] *smpl* jeans

jeep® [dʒip] *sm inv* jeep

'jogging ['dʒɔgin] *sm* jogging; **fare ~** to go jogging

'jolly ['dʒɔli] *sm inv* joker

joys'tick [dʒois'tik] *sm inv* joystick

ju'do [dʒu'dɔ] *sm* judo

Jugos'lavia [jugoz'lavja] *sf* (*Storia*): **la ~** Yugoslavia; **la ex-~** former Yugoslavia; **jugos'lavo, -a** *ag, sm/f* (*Storia*) Yugoslav(ian)

K l

K, k ['kappa] *sf o m inv* (*lettera*) K, k
  ▷ *abbr* (= *kilo-, chilo-*) k; (*Inform*) K; **K
  come Kursaal** ≈ K for King
kami'kaze [kami'kaddze] *sm inv*
  kamikaze
kara'oke [kara'oke] *sm inv* karaoke
karatè *sm* karate
ka'yak [ka'jak] *sm inv* kayak
'Kenia ['kenja] *sm*: **il ~** Kenya
kg *abbr* (= *chilogrammo*) kg
'killer *sm inv* gunman, hired gun
kitsch [kitʃ] *sm* kitsch
'kiwi ['kiwi] *sm inv* kiwi (fruit)
km *abbr* (= *chilometro*) km
K.'O. [kappa'o] *sm inv* knockout
ko'ala [ko'ala] *sm inv* koala (bear)
koso'varo, -a *ag, sm/f* Kosovan
'Kosovo *sm* Kosovo
'krapfen (*Cuc*) *sm inv* doughnut
Ku'wait [ku'vait] *sm*: **il ~** Kuwait

l *abbr* (= *litro*) l
l' *det vedi* **la; lo; il**
la *det f* (*davV* **l'**) the ▷ *pron* (*davV* **l'**:
  oggetto: persona) her; (: *cosa*) it;
  (: *forma di cortesia*) you; *vedi anche* **il**
là *av* there; **di là** (*da quel luogo*) from
  there; (*in quel luogo*) in there; (*dall'altra
  parte*) over there; **di là di** beyond;
  per di là that way; **più in là** further
  on; (*tempo*) later on; **fatti in là** move
  up; **là dentro/sopra/sotto** in/up o
  on/under there; *vedi anche* **quello**
'labbro *sm* (*pl f* **labbra**) (*Anat*) lip
labi'rinto *sm* labyrinth, maze
labora'torio *sm* (*di ricerca*) laboratory;
  (*di arti, mestieri*) workshop; **~
  linguistico** language laboratory
labori'oso, -a *ag* (*faticoso*) laborious;
  (*attivo*) hard-working
'lacca, -che *sf* lacquer
'laccio ['lattʃo] *sm* noose; (*legaccio,
  tirante*) lasso; (*di scarpa*) lace;
  ~ emostatico tourniquet

lace'rare [latʃe'rare] /72/ vt to tear to shreds, lacerate; **lacerarsi** vpr to tear

'lacrima sf tear; **in lacrime** in tears; **lacri'mogeno, -a** ag: **gas lacrimogeno** tear gas

la'cuna sf (fig) gap

'ladro sm thief

laggiù [lad'dʒu] av down there; (di là) over there

la'gnarsi [laɲ'ɲarsi] /15/ vpr: **~ (di)** to complain (about)

'lago, -ghi sm lake

la'guna sf lagoon

'laico, -a, -ci, -che ag (apostolato) lay; (vita) secular; (scuola) non-denominational ▷ sm/f layman/woman

'lama sf blade ▷ sm inv (Zool) llama; (Rel) lama

lamen'tare /72/ vt to lament; **lamentarsi** vpr (emettere lamenti) to moan, groan; (rammaricarsi): **lamentarsi (di)** to complain (about)

lamen'tela sf complaining no pl

la'metta sf razor blade

'lamina sf (lastra sottile) thin sheet (o layer o plate); **~ d'oro** gold leaf; gold foil

'lampada sf lamp; **~ a petrolio/a gas** oil/gas lamp; **~ da tavolo** table lamp

lampa'dario sm chandelier

lampa'dina sf light bulb; **~ tascabile** pocket torch (BRIT), flashlight (US)

lam'pante ag (fig: evidente) crystal clear, evident

lampeggi'are [lamped'dʒare] /62/ vi (luce, fari) to flash ▷ vb impers: **lampeggia** there's lightning; **lampeggia'tore** sm (Aut) indicator

lampi'one sm street light o lamp (BRIT)

'lampo sm (Meteor) flash of lightning; (di luce, fig) flash

lam'pone sm raspberry

'lana sf wool; **~ d'acciaio** steel wool; **pura ~ vergine** pure new wool; **~ di vetro** glass wool

lan'cetta [lan'tʃetta] sf (indice) pointer, needle; (di orologio) hand

'lancia, -ce ['lantʃa] sf (arma) lance; (: picca) spear; (di pompa antincendio) nozzle; (imbarcazione) launch; **~ di salvataggio** lifeboat

lanciafi'amme [lantʃa'fjamme] sm inv flamethrower

lanci'are [lan'tʃare] /14/ vt to throw, hurl, fling; (Sport) to throw; (far partire: automobile) to get up to full speed; (bombe) to drop; (razzo, prodotto, moda) to launch; **lanciarsi** vpr: **lanciarsi contro/su** to throw o hurl o fling o.s. against/on; **lanciarsi in** (fig) to embark on

lanci'nante [lantʃi'nante] ag (dolore) shooting, throbbing; (grido) piercing

'lancio ['lantʃo] sm throwing no pl; throw; dropping no pl; drop; launching no pl; launch; **~ del disco** (Sport) throwing the discus; **~ del peso** (Sport) putting the shot

'languido, -a ag (fiacco) languid, weak; (tenero, malinconico) languishing

lan'terna sf lantern; (faro) lighthouse

'lapide sf (di sepolcro) tombstone; (commemorativa) plaque

'lapsus sm inv slip

'lardo sm bacon fat, lard

lar'ghezza [lar'gettsa] sf width; breadth; looseness; generosity; **~ di vedute** broad-mindedness

'largo, -a, -ghi, -ghe ag wide; broad; (maniche) wide; (abito: troppo ampio) loose; (fig) generous ▷ sm width; breadth; (mare aperto): **il ~** the open sea ▷ sf: **stare o tenersi alla larga (da qn/qc)** to keep one's distance (from sb/sth), keep away (from sb/sth); **~ due metri** two metres wide; **~ di spalle** broad-shouldered; **di larghe vedute** broad-minded; **su larga scala** on a large scale; **di manica larga** generous, open-handed; **al ~ di Genova** off (the coast of) Genoa;

farsi ~ tra la folla to push one's way through the crowd

'larice ['laritʃe] *sm* (*Bot*) larch

larin'gite [larin'dʒite] *sf* laryngitis

'larva *sf* larva; (*fig*) shadow

la'sagne [la'zaɲɲe] *sfpl* lasagna *sg*

lasci'are [laʃʃare] /14/ *vt* to leave; (*abbandonare*) to leave, abandon, give up; (*cessare di tenere*) to let go of ▷ *vb aus*: **~ qn fare qc** to let sb do sth; **lasciarsi** *vpr* (*persone*) to part; (*coppia*) to split up; **~ andare o correre o perdere** to let things go their own way; **~ stare qc/qn** to leave sth/sb alone; **lasciarsi andare/truffare** to let o.s. go/be cheated

'laser ['lazer] *ag, sm inv*: **(raggio) ~** laser (beam)

lassa'tivo, -a *ag, sm* laxative

'lasso *sm*: **~ di tempo** interval, lapse of time

las'sù *av* up there

'lastra *sf* (*di pietra*) slab; (*di metallo, Fot*) plate; (*di ghiaccio, vetro*) sheet; (*radiografica*) X-ray (plate)

lastri'cato *sm* paving

late'rale *ag* lateral, side *cpd*; (*uscita, ingresso ecc*) side *cpd* ▷ *sm* (*Calcio*) half-back

la'tino, -a *ag, sm* Latin

lati'tante *smf* fugitive (from justice)

lati'tudine *sf* latitude

'lato, -a *ag* (*fig*) wide, broad; **in senso ~** broadly speaking ▷ *sm* side; (*fig*) aspect, point of view

'latta *sf* tin (plate); (*recipiente*) tin, can

lat'tante *ag* unweaned

'latte *sm* milk; **~ detergente** cleansing milk o lotion; **~ intero** full-cream milk; **~ a lunga conservazione** UHT milk, long-life milk; **~ magro o scremato** skimmed milk; **~ secco o in polvere** dried o powdered milk; **~ solare** suntan lotion; **latti'cini** *smpl* dairy o milk products

lat'tina *sf* (*di birra ecc*) can

lat'tuga, -ghe *sf* lettuce

'laurea *sf* degree; **~ in ingegneria** engineering degree; **~ in lettere** ≈ arts degree

LAUREA

The *laurea* is awarded to students who successfully complete their degree courses. Traditionally, this takes between four and six years; a major element of the final examinations is the presentation and discussion of a dissertation. A shorter, more vocational course of study, taking from two to three years, is also available; at the end of this time students receive a diploma called the *laurea breve*.

laure'are /72/ *vt* to confer a degree on; **laurearsi** *vpr* to graduate

laure'ato, -a *ag, sm/f* graduate

'lauro *sm* laurel

'lauto, -a *ag* (*pranzo, mancia*) lavish

'lava *sf* lava

la'vabo *sm* washbasin

la'vaggio [la'vaddʒo] *sm* washing *no pl*; **~ del cervello** brainwashing *no pl*; **~ a secco** dry-cleaning

la'vagna [la'vaɲɲa] *sf* (*Geo*) slate; (*di scuola*) blackboard; **~ interattiva** interactive whiteboard

la'vanda *sf* (*anche Med*) wash; (*Bot*) lavender; **lavande'ria** *sf* laundry; **lavanderia automatica** launderette; **lavanderia a secco** dry-cleaner's; **lavan'dino** *sm* sink

lavapi'atti *smf inv* dishwasher

la'vare /72/ *vt* to wash; **lavarsi** *vpr* to wash, have a wash; **~ a secco** to dry-clean; **lavarsi le mani/i denti** to wash one's hands/clean one's teeth

lava'secco *sf o m inv* dry-cleaner's

lavasto'viglie [lavasto'viʎʎe] *sf o m inv* (*macchina*) dishwasher

lava'trice [lava'tritʃe] *sf* washing machine

la'vello *sm* (kitchen) sink

lavo'rare /72/ *vi* to work; (*fig: bar, studio ecc*) to do good business ▷ *vt* to work; **~ a** to work on; **~ a maglia** to knit; **lavorarsi qn** (*fig: convincere*) to work on sb; **lavora'tivo, -a** *ag* working; **lavora'tore, -'trice** *sm/f* worker ▷ *ag* working

la'voro *sm* work; (*occupazione*) job, work *no pl*; (*opera*) work, job; (*Econ*) labour; **che ~ fa?** what do you do?; **lavori forzati** hard labour *sg*: **~ interinale** *o* **in affitto** temporary work

le *det fpl* the ▷ *pron* (*oggetto*) them; (: *a lei, a essa*) (to) her; (: *forma di cortesia*) (to) you; *vedi anche* **il**

le'ale *ag* loyal; (*sincero*) sincere; (*onesto*) fair

'lecca 'lecca *sm inv* lollipop

leccapi'edi *smf inv* (*peg*) toady, bootlicker

lec'care /20/ *vt* to lick; (*gatto: latte ecc*) to lick o lap up; (*fig*) to flatter; **leccarsi i baffi** to lick one's lips

leccherò *ecc* [lekke'rɔ] *vb vedi* **leccare**

'leccio ['lettʃo] *sm* holm oak, ilex

leccor'nia *sf* titbit, delicacy

'lecito, -a ['lεtʃito] *ag* permitted, allowed

'lega, -ghe *sf* league; (*di metalli*) alloy

le'gaccio [le'gattʃo] *sm* string, lace

le'gale *ag* legal ▷ *sm* lawyer; **legaliz'zare** /72/ *vt* to legalize; (*documento*) to authenticate

le'game *sm* (*corda, fig: affettivo*) tie, bond; (*nesso logico*) link, connection

le'gare /80/ *vt* (*prigioniero, capelli, cane*) to tie (up); (*libro*) to bind; (*Chim*) to alloy; (*fig: collegare*) to bind, join ▷ *vi* (*far lega*) to unite; (*fig*) to get on well

le'genda [le'dʒɛnda] *sf* (*di carta geografica ecc*); = **leggenda**

'legge ['leddʒe] *sf* law

leg'genda [led'dʒɛnda] *sf* (*narrazione*) legend; (*di carta geografica ecc*) key, legend

'leggere ['lɛddʒere] /61/ *vt, vi* to read

legge'rezza [leddʒe'rettsa] *sf* lightness; thoughtlessness; fickleness

leg'gero, -a [led'dʒεro] *ag* light; (*agile, snello*) nimble, agile, light; (*tè, caffè*) weak; (*fig: non grave, piccolo*) slight; (: *spensierato*) thoughtless; (: *incostante*) fickle; free and easy; **alla leggera** thoughtlessly

leg'gio, -'gii [led'dʒio] *sm* lectern; (*Mus*) music stand

legherò *ecc* [lege'rɔ] *vb vedi* **legare**

legisla'tivo, -a [ledʒizla'tivo] *ag* legislative

legisla'tura [ledʒizla'tura] *sf* legislature

le'gittimo, -a [le'dʒittimo] *ag* legitimate; (*fig: giustificato, lecito*) justified, legitimate; **legittima difesa** (*Dir*) self-defence (BRIT), self-defense (US)

'legna ['leɲɲa] *sf* firewood

'legno ['leɲɲo] *sm* wood; (*pezzo di legno*) piece of wood; **di ~** wooden; **~ compensato** plywood

le'gume *sm* (*Bot*) pulse; **legumi** *smpl* pulses

'lei *pron* (*soggetto*) she; (*oggetto: per dare rilievo, con preposizione*) her; (*forma di cortesia: anche:* **L~**) you ▷ *sm*: **dare del ~ a qn** to address sb as "lei"; **~ stessa** she herself; you yourself

---

  ● **LEI**
  ●
  ● *lei* is the third person singular
  ● pronoun. It is used in Italian to
  ● address an adult whom you do not
  ● know or with whom you are on
  ● formal terms.

---

lenta'mente *av* slowly

'lente *sf* (*Ottica*) lens *sg*: **~ d'ingrandimento** magnifying glass; **lenti** *sfpl* (*occhiali*) lenses; **lenti a contatto, lenti corneali** contact lenses; **lenti (a contatto) morbide/ rigide** soft/hard contact lenses

len'tezza [len'tettsa] *sf* slowness
len'ticchia [len'tikkja] *sf* (*Bot*) lentil
len'tiggine [len'tiddʒine] *sf* freckle
'lento, -a *ag* slow; (*molle: fune*) slack; (*non stretto: vite, abito*) loose ▷ *sm* (*ballo*) slow dance
'lenza ['lɛntsa] *sf* fishing line
lenzu'olo [len'tswɔlo] *sm* sheet
le'one *sm* lion; **L~** Leo
lepo'rino, -a *ag*: **labbro ~** harelip
'lepre *sf* hare
'lercio, -a, -ci, -ce ['lɛrtʃo] *ag* filthy
lesi'one *sf* (*Med*) lesion; (*Dir*) injury, damage; (*Edil*) crack
les'sare /72/ *vt* (*Cuc*) to boil
'lessi *ecc vb vedi* **leggere**
'lessico, -ci *sm* vocabulary; (*dizionario*) lexicon
'lesso, -a *ag* boiled ▷ *sm* boiled meat
le'tale *ag* lethal; fatal
leta'maio *sm* dunghill
le'tame *sm* manure, dung
le'targo, -ghi *sm* lethargy; (*Zool*) hibernation
'lettera *sf* letter; **lettere** *sfpl* (*letteratura*) literature *sg*; (*studi umanistici*) arts (subjects); **alla ~** literally; **in lettere** in words, in full
letteral'mente *av* literally
lette'rario, -a *ag* literary
lette'rato, -a *ag* well-read, scholarly
lettera'tura *sf* literature
let'tiga, -ghe *sf* (*barella*) stretcher
let'tino *sm* cot (*BRIT*), crib (*US*); (*per il sole*) sun lounger; **~ solare** sunbed
'letto, -a *pp di* **leggere** ▷ *sm* bed; **andare a ~** to go to bed; **~ a castello** bunk beds *pl*: **~ a una piazza/a due piazze** *o* **matrimoniale** single/double bed
let'tore, -'trice *sm/f* reader; (*Ins*) (foreign language) assistant (*BRIT*), (foreign) teaching assistant (*US*) ▷ *sm* (*Tecn*): **~ ottico (di caratteri)** optical character reader; **~ CD/DVD** CD/DVD player; **~ MP3/MP4** MP3/MP4 player

let'tura *sf* reading

> Attenzione! In inglese esiste la parola *lecture*, che però significa *lezione* oppure *conferenza*.

leuce'mia [leutʃe'mia] *sf* leukaemia
'leva *sf* lever; (*Mil*) conscription; **far ~ su qn** to work on sb; **~ del cambio** (*Aut*) gear lever
le'vante *sm* east; (*vento*) East wind; **il L~** the Levant
le'vare /72/ *vt* (*occhi, braccio*) to raise; (*sollevare, togliere: tassa, divieto*) to lift; (*: indumenti*) to take off, remove; (*rimuovere*) to take away; (*: dal di sopra*) to take off; (*: dal di dentro*) to take out
leva'toio, -a *ag*: **ponte ~** drawbridge
lezi'one [let'tsjone] *sf* lesson; (*all'università, sgridata*) lecture; **fare ~** to teach; to lecture; **dare una ~ a qn** to teach sb a lesson; **lezioni private** private lessons
li *pron pl* (*oggetto*) them
lì *av* there; **di** *o* **da lì** from there; **per di lì** that way; **di lì a pochi giorni** a few days later; **lì per lì** there and then; at first; **essere lì (lì) per fare** to be on the point of doing, be about to do; **lì dentro** in there; **lì sotto** under there; **lì sopra** on there; up there; *vedi anche* **quello**
liba'nese *ag, sm/f* Lebanese *inv*
Li'bano *sm*: **il ~** the Lebanon
'libbra *sf* (*peso*) pound
li'beccio [li'bettʃo] *sm* south-west wind
li'bellula *sf* dragonfly
libe'rale *ag, sm/f* liberal
liberaliz'zare [liberalid'dzare] /72/ *vt* to liberalize
libe'rare /72/ *vt* (*rendere libero: prigioniero*) to release; (*: popolo*) to free, liberate; (*sgombrare: passaggio*) to clear; (*: stanza*) to vacate; (*produrre: energia*) to release; **liberarsi** *vpr*: **liberarsi di qc/qn** to get rid of sth/sb; **liberazi'one** *sf* (*di prigioniero*)

release, freeing; (*di popolo*) liberation; rescuing

- LIBERAZIONE
-
- The *Liberazione* is a national
- holiday which falls on 25 April. It
- commemorates the liberation of
- Italy in 1945 from German forces
- and Mussolini's government
- and marks the end of the war on
- Italian soil.

'**libero, -a** *ag* free; (*strada*) clear; (*non occupato: posto ecc*) vacant; free; not taken; empty; not engaged; **~ di fare qc** free to do sth; **~ da** free from; **~ arbitrio** free will; **~ professionista** self-employed professional person; **~ scambio** free trade; **libertà** *sf inv* freedom; (*tempo disponibile*) free time ▷ *sfpl* (*licenza*) liberties; **essere in libertà provvisoria/vigilata** to be released without bail/be on probation

'**Libia** *sf*: **la ~** Libya; '**libico, -a, -ci, -che** *ag*, *sm/f* Libyan

li'**bidine** *sf* lust

li'**braio** *sm* bookseller

li'**brarsi** /72/ *vpr* to hover

libre'**ria** *sf* (*bottega*) bookshop; (*mobile*) bookcase

> Attenzione! In inglese esiste la parola *library*, che però significa *biblioteca*.

li'**bretto** *sm* booklet; (*taccuino*) notebook; (*Mus*) libretto; **~ degli assegni** chequebook; **~ di circolazione** (*Aut*) logbook; **~ di risparmio** (savings) bankbook, passbook; **~ universitario** student's report book

'**libro** *sm* book; **~ di cassa** cash book; **~ mastro** ledger; **~ paga** payroll; **~ di testo** textbook

li'**cenza** [li'tʃɛntsa] *sf* (*permesso*) permission, leave; (*di pesca, caccia, circolazione*) permit, licence; (*Mil*)

leave; (*Ins*) school-leaving certificate; (*libertà*) liberty; licence; (*sfrenatezza*) licentiousness; **andare in ~** (*Mil*) to go on leave

licenzia'**mento** [litʃentsja'mento] *sm* dismissal

licenzi'**are** [litʃen'tsjare] /19/ *vt* (*impiegato*) to dismiss; (*Comm: per eccesso di personale*) to make redundant; (*Ins*) to award a certificate to; **licenziarsi** *vpr* (*impiegato*) to resign, hand in one's notice; (*Ins*) to obtain one's school-leaving certificate

li'**ceo** [li'tʃɛo] *sm* (*Ins*) secondary (*BRIT*) o high (*US*) school (*for 14- to 19-year-olds*)

'**lido** *sm* beach, shore

'**Liechtenstein** ['liktənstain] *sm*: **il ~** Liechtenstein

li'**eto, -a** *ag* happy, glad; **"molto ~"** (*nelle presentazioni*) "pleased to meet you"

li'**eve** *ag* light; (*di poco conto*) slight; (*sommesso: voce*) faint, soft

lievi'**tare** /72/ *vi* (*anche fig*) to rise ▷ *vt* to leaven

li'**evito** *sm* yeast; **~ di birra** brewer's yeast

'**ligio, -a, -gi, -gie** ['lidʒo] *ag* faithful, loyal

'**lilla, lillà** *sm inv* lilac

'**lima** *sf* file; **~ da unghie** nail file

limacci'**oso, -a** [limat'tʃoso] *ag* slimy; muddy

li'**mare** /72/ *vt* to file (down); (*fig*) to polish

limi'**tare** /72/ *vt* to limit, restrict; (*circoscrivere*) to bound, surround; **limitarsi** *vpr*: **limitarsi nel mangiare** to limit one's eating; **limitarsi a qc/a fare qc** to limit o.s. to sth/to doing sth

'**limite** *sm* limit; (*confine*) border, boundary; **~ di velocità** speed limit

limo'**nata** *sf* lemonade (*BRIT*), (lemon) soda (*US*); (*spremuta*) lemon squash (*BRIT*), lemonade (*US*) li'mone *sm (pianta)* lemon tree; *(frutto)* lemon

'limpido, -a *ag (acqua)* limpid, clear; *(cielo)* clear

'lince ['lintʃe] *sf* lynx

linci'are [lin'tʃare] /14/ *vt* to lynch

'linea *sf* line; *(di mezzi pubblici di trasporto: itinerario)* route; *(: servizio)* service; **a grandi linee** in outline; **mantenere la ~** to look after one's figure; : **aereo di ~** airliner; **nave di ~** liner; **volo di ~** scheduled flight; **~ aerea** airline; **~ di partenza/d'arrivo** *(Sport)* starting/finishing line; **~ di tiro** line of fire

linea'menti *smpl* features; *(fig)* outlines

line'are *ag* linear; *(fig)* coherent, logical

line'etta *sf (trattino)* dash; *(d'unione)* hyphen

lin'gotto *sm* ingot, bar

'lingua *sf (Anat, Cuc)* tongue; *(idioma)* language; **mostrare la ~** to stick out one's tongue; **di ~ italiana** Italian-speaking; **~ madre** mother tongue; **una ~ di terra** a spit of land

lingu'aggio [lin'gwaddʒo] *sm* language

lingu'etta *sf (di strumento)* reed; *(di scarpa, Tecn)* tongue; *(di busta)* flap

'lino *sm (pianta)* flax; *(tessuto)* linen

li'noleum *sm inv* linoleum, lino

liposuzi'one [liposut'tsjone] *sf* liposuction

liqui'dare /72/ *vt (società, beni, persona: uccidere)* to liquidate; *(persona: sbarazzarsene)* to get rid of; *(conto, problema)* to settle; *(Comm: merce)* to sell off, clear; **liquidazi'one** *sf* liquidation; *(di conto)* settlement; *(di merce)* clearance sale

liquidità *sf* liquidity

'liquido, -a *ag, sm* liquid; **~ per freni** brake fluid

liqui'rizia [likwi'rittsja] *sf* liquorice

li'quore *sm* liqueur

'lira *sf (unità monetaria)* lira; *(Mus)* lyre; **~ sterlina** pound sterling

'lirico, -a, -ci, -che *ag* lyric(al); *(Mus)* lyric; **cantante/teatro ~** opera singer/house

Lis'bona *sf* Lisbon

'lisca, -sche *sf (di pesce)* fishbone

lisci'are [liʃ'ʃare] /14/ *vt* to smooth; *(fig)* to flatter

'liscio, -a, -sci, -sce ['liʃʃo] *ag* smooth; *(capelli)* straight; *(mobile)* plain; *(bevanda alcolica)* neat; *(fig)* straightforward, simple ▷ *av:* **andare ~** to go smoothly; **passarla liscia** to get away with it

'liso, -a *ag* worn out, threadbare

'lista *sf (elenco)* list; **~ elettorale** electoral roll; **~ delle spese** shopping list; **~ dei vini** wine list; **~ delle vivande** menu

lis'tino *sm* list; **~ dei cambi** (foreign) exchange rate; **~ dei prezzi** price list

'lite *sf* quarrel, argument; *(Dir)* lawsuit

liti'gare /80/ *vi* to quarrel; *(Dir)* to litigate

li'tigio [li'tidʒo] *sm* quarrel

lito'rale *ag* coastal, coast *cpd* ▷ *sm* coast

'litro *sm* litre

livel'lare /72/ *vt* to level, make level

li'vello *sm* level; *(fig)* level, standard; **ad alto ~** *(fig)* high-level; **~ del mare** sea level

'livido, -a *ag* livid; *(per percosse)* bruised, black and blue; *(cielo)* leaden ▷ *sm* bruise

Li'vorno *sf* Livorno, Leghorn

'lizza ['littsa] *sf* lists *pl:* **scendere in ~** to enter the lists

lo *det m (dav s impura, gn, pn, ps, x, z; dav V l')* the ▷ *pron (dav V l', oggetto: persona)* him; *(: cosa)* it; **lo sapevo** I knew it; **lo so** I know; **sii buono, anche se lui non lo è** be good, even if he isn't; *vedi anche* **il**

lo'cale *ag* local ▷ *sm* room; *(luogo pubblico)* premises *pl:* **~ notturno** nightclub; **località** *sf inv* locality

lo'canda *sf* inn

locomo'tiva *sf* locomotive

locuzi'one [lokut'tsjone] *sf* phrase, expression
lo'dare /72/ *vt* to praise
'lode *sf* praise; (*Ins*): **laurearsi con 110 e ~** ≈ to graduate with first-class honours (*BRIT*), ≈ to graduate summa cum laude (*US*)
'loden *sm inv* (*stoffa*) loden; (*cappotto*) loden overcoat
lo'devole *ag* praiseworthy
loga'ritmo *sm* logarithm
log'garsi /72/ *vpr* (*Inform*) to log in
'loggia, -ge ['lɔddʒa] *sf* (*Archit*) loggia; (*circolo massonico*) lodge; **loggi'one** *sm* (*di teatro*): **il loggione** the Gods *sg*
'logico, -a, -ci, -che ['lɔdʒiko] *ag* logical
logo'rare /72/ *vt* to wear out; (*sciupare*) to waste; **logorarsi** *vpr* to wear out; (*fig*) to wear o.s. out
'logoro, -a (*stoffa*) worn out, threadbare; (*persona*) worn out
Lombar'dia *sf*: **la ~** Lombardy
lom'bata *sf* (*taglio di carne*) loin
lom'brico, -chi *sm* earthworm
londi'nese *ag* London *cpd* ▷ *smf* Londoner
'Londra *sf* London
lon'gevo, -a [lon'dʒevo] *ag* long-lived
longi'tudine [londʒi'tudine] *sf* longitude
lonta'nanza [lonta'nantsa] *sf* distance; absence
lon'tano, -a *ag* (*distante*) distant, faraway; (*assente*) absent; (*vago: sospetto*) slight, remote; (*tempo: remoto*) far-off, distant; (*parente*) distant, remote ▷ *av* far; **è lontana la casa?** is it far to the house?, is the house far from here?; **è ~ un chilometro** it's a kilometre away *o* a kilometre from here; **più ~** farther; **da** *o* **di ~** from a distance; **~ da** a long way from; **è molto ~ da qui?** is it far from here?; **alla lontana** slightly, vaguely

lo'quace [lo'kwatʃe] *ag* talkative, loquacious; (*fig: gesto ecc*) eloquent
'lordo, -a *ag* dirty, filthy; (*peso, stipendio*) gross
'loro *pron pl* (*oggetto, con preposizione*) them; (*complemento di termine*) to them; (*soggetto*) they; (*forma di cortesia: anche*: **L~**) you; to you; **il (la) ~, i (le) ~** *det* their; (*forma di cortesia: anche*: **L~**) your ▷ *pron* theirs; (*forma di cortesia: anche*: **L~**) yours; **~ stessi(e)** they themselves; you yourselves
'losco, -a, -schi, -sche *ag* (*fig*) shady, suspicious
'lotta *sf* struggle, fight; (*Sport*) wrestling; **~ libera** all-in wrestling; **lot'tare** /72/ *vi* to fight, struggle; to wrestle
lotte'ria *sf* lottery; (*di gara ippica*) sweepstake
'lotto *sm* (*gioco*) (state) lottery; (*parte*) lot; (*Edil*) site

- **LOTTO**
-
- The *Lotto* is an official lottery run
- by the Italian Finance Ministry.
- It consists of a weekly draw of
- numbers and is very popular.

lozi'one [lot'tsjone] *sf* lotion
lubrifi'cante *sm* lubricant
lubrifi'care /20/ *vt* to lubricate
luc'chetto [luk'ketto] *sm* padlock
lucci'care [luttʃi'kare] /20/ *vi* to sparkle; (*oro*) to glitter; (*stella*) to twinkle
'luccio ['luttʃo] *sm* (*Zool*) pike
'lucciola ['luttʃola] *sf* (*Zool*) firefly; glow-worm
'luce ['lutʃe] *sf* light; (*finestra*) window; **alla ~ di** by the light of; **fare ~ su qc** (*fig*) to shed *o* throw light on sth; **~ del sole/della luna** sun/moonlight
lucer'nario [lutʃer'narjo] *sm* skylight
lu'certola [lu'tʃertola] *sf* lizard
luci'dare [lutʃi'dare] /72/ *vt* to polish

lucida'trice [lutʃida'tritʃe] *sf* floor polisher

'lucido, -a ['lutʃido] *ag* shining, bright; (*lucidato*) polished; (*fig*) lucid ▷ *sm* shine, lustre; (*per scarpe ecc*) polish; (*disegno*) tracing

'lucro *sm* profit, gain

'luglio ['luʎʎo] *sm* July

'lugubre *ag* gloomy

'lui *pron* (*soggetto*) he; (*oggetto: per dare rilievo, con preposizione*) him; **~ stesso** he himself

lu'maca, -che *sf* slug; (*chiocciola*) snail

lumi'noso, -a *ag* (*che emette luce*) luminous; (*cielo, colore, stanza*) bright; (*sorgente*) of light, light *cpd*; (*fig: sorriso*) bright, radiant

'luna *sf* moon; **~ nuova/piena** new/full moon; **~ di miele** honeymoon

'luna park *sm inv* amusement park, funfair

lu'nare *ag* lunar, moon *cpd*

lu'nario *sm* almanac; **sbarcare il ~** to make ends meet

lu'natico, -a, -ci, -che *ag* whimsical, temperamental

lunedì *sm inv* Monday; **di** *o* **il ~** on Mondays

lun'ghezza [lun'gettsa] *sf* length; **~ d'onda** (*Fisica*) wavelength

'lungo, -a, -ghi, -ghe *ag* long; (*lento: persona*) slow; (*diluito: caffè, brodo*) weak, watery, thin ▷ *sm* length ▷ *prep* along; **~ 3 metri** 3 metres long; **a ~** for a long time; **a ~ andare** in the long run; **di gran lunga** (*molto*) by far; **andare in ~** *o* **per le lunghe** to drag on; **saperla lunga** to know what's what; **in ~ e in largo** far and wide, all over; **~ il corso dei secoli** throughout the centuries

lungo'mare *sm* promenade

lu'notto *sm* (*Aut*) rear *o* back window; **~ termico** heated rear window

lu'ogo, -ghi *sm* place; (*posto: di incidente ecc*) scene, site; (*punto, passo di libro*) passage; **in ~ di** instead of; **in**

primo ~ in the first place; **aver ~** to take place; **dar ~ a** to give rise to; **~ comune** commonplace; **~ di nascita** birthplace; (*Amm*) place of birth; **~ di provenienza** place of origin

'lupo, -a *sm/f* wolf/she-wolf

'luppolo *sm* (*Bot*) hop

'lurido, -a *ag* filthy

lusin'gare /80/ *vt* to flatter

Lussem'burgo *sm* (*stato*): **il ~** Luxembourg ▷ *sf* (*città*) Luxembourg

'lusso *sm* luxury; **di ~** luxury *cpd*; **lussu'oso, -a** *ag* luxurious

lus'suria *sf* lust

lus'trino *sm* sequin

'lutto *sm* mourning; **essere in/portare il ~** to be in/wear mourning

m. *abbr* = **mese**; **metro**; **miglia**; **monte**

ma *cong* but; **ma insomma!** for goodness sake!; **ma no!** of course not!

'**macabro, -a** *ag* gruesome, macabre

macché [mak'ke] *escl* not at all!, certainly not!

macche'roni [makke'roni] *smpl* macaroni *sg*

'**macchia** ['makkja] *sf* stain, spot; (*chiazza di diverso colore*) spot, splash, patch; (*tipo di boscaglia*) scrub; **darsi/vivere alla ~** (*fig*) to go into/live in hiding; **macchi'are** /19/ *vt* (*sporcare*) to stain, mark; **macchiarsi** *vpr* (*persona*) to get o.s. dirty; (*stoffa*) to stain; to get stained *o* marked

macchi'ato, -a [mak'kjato] *ag* (*pelle, pelo*) spotted; **~ di** stained with; **caffè ~** coffee with a dash of milk

'**macchina** ['makkina] *sf* machine; (*motore, locomotiva*) engine;

(*automobile*) car; (*fig: meccanismo*) machinery; **andare in ~** (*Aut*) to go by car; (*Stampa*) to go to press; **~ da cucire** sewing machine; **~ fotografica** camera; **~ da presa** cine *o* movie camera; **~ da scrivere** typewriter; **~ a vapore** steam engine

macchi'nario [makki'narjo] *sm* machinery

macchi'nista, -i [makki'nista] *sm* (*di treno*) engine-driver; (*di nave*) engineer

Mace'donia [matʃe'dɔnja] *sf* Macedonia

mace'donia [matʃe'dɔnja] *sf* fruit salad

macel'laio [matʃel'lajo] *sm* butcher

macelle'ria *sf* butcher's (shop)

ma'cerie [ma'tʃɛrje] *sfpl* rubble *sg*, debris *sg*

ma'cigno [ma'tʃiɲɲo] *sm* (*masso*) rock, boulder

maci'nare [matʃi'nare] /72/ *vt* to grind; (*carne*) to mince (BRIT), grind (US)

macrobi'otico, -a *ag* macrobiotic ▷ *sf* macrobiotics *sg*

Ma'donna *sf* (*Rel*) Our Lady

mador'nale *ag* enormous, huge

'**madre** *sf* mother; (*matrice di bolletta*) counterfoil ▷ *ag inv* mother *cpd*; **ragazza ~** unmarried mother; **scena ~** (*Teat*) principal scene; (*fig*) terrible scene

madre'lingua *sf* mother tongue, native language

madre'perla *sf* mother-of-pearl

ma'drina *sf* godmother

maestà *sf inv* majesty

ma'estra *sf vedi* **maestro**

maes'trale *sm* north-west wind, mistral

ma'estro, -a *sm/f* (*Ins: anche:* **~ di scuola** *o* **elementare**) primary (BRIT) *o* grade school (US) teacher; (*esperto*) expert ▷ *sm* (*artigiano, fig: guida*) master; (*Mus*) maestro ▷ *ag* (*principale*) main; (*di grande abilità*)

masterly, skilful; **maestra d'asilo**
nursery teacher; **~ di cerimonie**
master of ceremonies

'**mafia** sf Mafia

'**maga, -ghe** sf sorceress

ma'**gari** escl (esprime desiderio): **~**
fosse vero! if only it were true!; **ti**
piacerebbe andare in Scozia? — ~!
would you like to go to Scotland? — I
certainly would! ▷ av (anche) even;
(forse) perhaps

magaz'**zino** [magad'dzino] sm
warehouse; **grande ~** department
store

> Attenzione! In inglese esiste
la parola magazine, che però
significa rivista.

'**maggio** ['maddʒo] sm May

maggio'**rana** [maddʒo'rana] sf (Bot)
(sweet) marjoram

maggio'**ranza** [maddʒo'rantsa]
sf majority

maggior'**domo** [maddʒor'dɔmo]
sm butler

maggi'**ore** [mad'dʒore] ag
(comparativo: più grande) bigger,
larger; taller; greater; (: più vecchio:
sorella, fratello) older, elder; (: di grado
superiore) senior; (: più importante:
Mil, Mus) major; (superlativo)
biggest, largest; tallest; greatest;
oldest, eldest ▷ smf (di grado)
superior; (di età) elder; (Mil) major;
(: Aer) squadron leader; **la maggior**
parte the majority; **andare per**
la ~ (cantante, attore ecc) to be very
popular; **maggio'renne** ag of age
▷ smf person who has come of age

ma'**gia** [ma'dʒia] sf magic;
'**magico, -a, -ci, -che** ag magic; (fig)
fascinating, charming, magical

magis'**trato** [madʒis'trato] sm
magistrate

'**maglia** ['maʎʎa] sf stitch; (lavoro ai
ferri) knitting no pl; (tessuto, Sport)
jersey; (maglione) jersey, sweater; (di
catena) link; (di rete) mesh; **~ diritta/**
rovescia plain/purl; **magli'etta**

sf (canottiera) vest; (tipo camicia)
T-shirt

magli'**one** [maʎ'ʎone] sm jumper,
sweater

ma'**gnetico, -a, -ci, -che** ag
magnetic

ma'**gnifico, -a, -ci, -che**
[maɲ'ɲifiko] ag magnificent,
splendid; (ospite) generous

ma'**gnolia** [maɲ'ɲɔlja] sf magnolia

'**mago, -ghi** sm (stregone) magician,
wizard; (illusionista) magician

ma'**grezza** [ma'gretsa] sf thinness

'**magro, -a** ag (very) thin, skinny;
(carne) lean; (formaggio) low-fat;
(fig: scarso, misero) meagre , poor;
(: meschino: scusa) poor, lame;
mangiare di ~ not to eat meat

'**mai** av (nessuna volta) never; (talvolta)
ever; **non ... ~** never; **~ più** never
again; **come ~?** why (o how) on
earth?; **chi/dove/quando ~?**
whoever/wherever/whenever?

mai'**ale** sm (Zool) pig; (carne) pork

mail ['meil] sf inv = **e-mail**

maio'**nese** sf mayonnaise

'**mais** sm maize

mai'**uscolo, -a** ag (lettera) capital;
(fig) enormous, huge

mala'**fede** sf bad faith

malan'**dato, -a** ag (persona: di
salute) in poor health; (: di condizioni
finanziarie) badly off; (trascurato)
shabby

ma'**lanno** sm (disgrazia) misfortune;
(malattia) ailment

mala'**pena** sf: **a ~** hardly, scarcely

ma'**laria** sf (Med) malaria

ma'**lato, -a** ag ill, sick; (gamba) bad;
(pianta) diseased ▷ sm/f sick person;
(in ospedale) patient; **malat'tia** sf
(infettiva ecc) illness, disease; (cattiva
salute) illness, sickness; (di pianta)
disease

mala'**vita** sf underworld

mala'**voglia** [mala'vɔʎʎa]: **di ~** av
unwillingly, reluctantly

Mala'ysia sf Malaysia

m

mal'concio, -a, -ci, -ce
[mal'kontʃo] *ag* in a sorry state
malcon'tento *sm* discontent
malcos'tume *sm* immorality
mal'destro, -a *ag* (*inabile*) inexpert,
inexperienced; (*goffo*) awkward
'**male** *av* badly ▷ *sm* (*ciò che è ingiusto,
disonesto*) evil; (*danno, svantaggio*)
harm; (*sventura*) misfortune; (*dolore
fisico, morale*) pain, ache; **sentirsi ~**
to feel ill; **aver mal di cuore/fegato**
to have a heart/liver complaint;
**aver mal di denti/d'orecchi/di
testa** to have toothache/earache/a
headache; **aver mal di gola** to have
a sore throat; **aver ~ ai piedi** to have
sore feet; **far ~** (*dolere*) to hurt; **far ~
alla salute** to be bad for one's health;
far del ~ a qn to hurt o harm sb;
restare o **rimanere ~** to be sorry; to
be disappointed o be hurt; **trattar
~ qn** to ill-treat sb; **andare a ~** to go
off o bad; **come va? — non c'è ~** how
are you? — not bad; **di ~ in peggio**
from bad to worse; **mal d'auto**
carsickness; **mal di mare** seasickness
male'detto, -a *pp di* **maledire** ▷ *ag*
cursed, damned; (*fig fam*) damned,
blasted
male'dire /38/ *vt* to curse;
maledizi'one *sf* curse; **maledizione!**
damn it!
maledu'cato, -a *ag* rude, ill-
mannered
maleducazi'one
[maledukat'tsjone] *sf* rudeness
ma'lefico, -a, -ci, -che *ag* (*influsso,
azione*) evil
ma'lessere *sm* indisposition, slight
illness; (*fig*) uneasiness
malfa'mato, -a *ag* notorious
malfat'tore, -'trice *sm/f*
wrongdoer
mal'fermo, -a *ag* unsteady, shaky;
(*salute*) poor, delicate
mal'grado *prep* in spite of, despite
▷ *cong* although; **mio** o **tuo** *ecc* **~**
against my (o your *ecc*) will

ma'ligno, -a [ma'liɲɲo] *ag*
(*malvagio*) malicious, malignant;
(*Med*) malignant
malinco'nia *sf* melancholy, gloom;
malin'conico, -a, -ci, -che *ag*
melancholy
malincu'ore: a ~ *av* reluctantly,
unwillingly
malin'teso, -a *ag* misunderstood;
(*riguardo, senso del dovere*) mistaken,
wrong ▷ *sm* misunderstanding;
c'è stato un ~ there's been a
misunderstanding
ma'lizia [ma'littsja] *sf* (*malignità*)
malice; (*furbizia*) cunning;
(*espediente*) trick; **malizi'oso, -a** *ag*
malicious; cunning; (*vivace, birichino*)
mischievous
malme'nare /72/ *vt* to beat up
ma'locchio [ma'lɔkkjo] *sm* evil eye
ma'lora *sf*: **andare in ~** to go to
the dogs
ma'lore *sm* (sudden) illness
mal'sano, -a *ag* unhealthy
'malta *sf* (*Edil*) mortar
mal'tempo *sm* bad weather
'malto *sm* malt
maltrat'tare /72/ *vt* to ill-treat
malu'more *sm* bad mood; (*irritabilità*)
bad temper; (*discordia*) ill feeling; **di ~**
in a bad mood
'malva *sf* (*Bot*) mallow ▷ *ag, sm inv*
mauve
mal'vagio, -a, -gi, -gie [mal'vadʒo]
ag wicked, evil
malvi'vente *sm* criminal
malvolenti'eri *av* unwillingly,
reluctantly
'mamma *sf* mum(my); **~ mia!** my
goodness!
mam'mella *sf* (*Anat*) breast; (*di vacca,
capra ecc*) udder
mam'mifero *sm* mammal
ma'nata *sf* (*colpo*) slap; (*quantità*)
handful
man'canza [man'kantsa] *sf*
lack; (*carenza*) shortage, scarcity;
(*fallo*) fault; (*imperfezione*) failing,

shortcoming; **per ~ di tempo** through lack of time; **in ~ di meglio** for lack of anything better

man'care /20/ *vi (essere insufficiente)* to be lacking; *(venir meno)* to fail; *(sbagliare)* to be wrong, make a mistake; *(non esserci)* to be missing, not to be there; *(essere lontano)*: **~ (da)** to be away (from) ▷ *vt* to miss; **~ di** to lack; **~ a** *(promessa)* to fail to keep; **tu mi manchi** I miss you; **mancò poco che morisse** he very nearly died; **mancano ancora 10 sterline** we're still £10 short; **manca un quarto alle 6** it's a quarter to 6

mancherò *ecc* [manke'rɔ] *vb vedi* **mancare**

'**mancia, -ce** ['mantʃa] *sf* tip; **~ competente** reward

manci'ata [man'tʃata] *sf* handful

man'cino, -a [man'tʃino] *ag (braccio)* left; *(persona)* left-handed; *(fig)* underhand

manda'rancio [manda'rantʃo] *sm* clementine

man'dare /72/ *vt* to send; *(far funzionare: macchina)* to drive; *(emettere)* to send out; *(: grido)* to give, utter, let out; **~ avanti** *(fig: famiglia)* to provide for; *(: fabbrica)* to run, look after; **~ giù** to send down; *(anche fig)* to swallow; **~ via** to send away; *(licenziare)* to fire

manda'rino *sm* mandarin (orange); *(cinese)* mandarin

man'data *sf (quantità)* lot, batch; *(di chiave)* turn; **chiudere a doppia ~** to double-lock

man'dato *sm (incarico)* commission; *(Dir: provvedimento)* warrant; *(di deputato ecc)* mandate; *(ordine di pagamento)* postal *o* money order; **~ d'arresto** warrant for arrest

man'dibola *sf* mandible, jaw

'**mandorla** *sf* almond; '**mandorlo** *sm* almond tree

'**mandria** *sf* herd

maneggi'are [maned'dʒare] /62/ *vt (creta, cera)* to mould , work, fashion; *(arnesi, utensili)* to handle; *(: adoperare)* to use; *(fig: persone, denaro)* to handle, deal with; **ma'neggio** *sm* moulding; handling; use; *(intrigo)* plot, scheme; *(per cavalli)* riding school

ma'nesco, -a, -schi, -sche *ag* free with one's fists

ma'nette *sfpl* handcuffs

manga'nello *sm* club

mangi'are [man'dʒare] /62/ *vt* to eat; *(intaccare)* to eat into *o* away; *(Carte, Scacchi: ecc)* to take ▷ *vi* to eat ▷ *sm* eating; *(cibo)* food; *(cucina)* cooking; **mangiarsi le parole** to mumble; **mangiarsi le unghie** to bite one's nails

man'gime [man'dʒime] *sm* fodder

'**mango, -ghi** *sm* mango

ma'nia *sf (Psic)* mania; *(fig)* obsession, craze; **ma'niaco, -a, -ci, -che** *ag* suffering from a mania; **maniaco (di)** obsessed (by), crazy (about)

'**manica, -che** *sf* sleeve; *(fig: gruppo)* gang, bunch; *(Geo)*: **la M~, il Canale della M~** the (English) Channel; **essere di ~ larga/stretta** to be easy-going/strict; **~ a vento** *(Aer)* wind sock

mani'chino [mani'kino] *sm (di sarto, vetrina)* dummy

'**manico, -ci** *sm* handle; *(Mus)* neck

mani'comio *sm* mental hospital; *(fig)* madhouse

mani'cure *sf o m inv* manicure ▷ *sf inv* manicurist

mani'era *sf* way, manner; *(stile)* style, manner; **maniere** *sfpl (comportamento)* manners; **in ~ che** so that; **in ~ da** so as to; **in tutte le maniere** at all costs

manifes'tare /72/ *vt* to show, display; *(esprimere)* to express; *(rivelare)* to reveal, disclose ▷ *vi* to demonstrate; **manifestazi'one** *sf* show, display, expression; *(sintomo)* sign, symptom; (*dimostrazione pubblica*) demonstration; (*cerimonia*) event

mani'festo, -a *ag* obvious, evident ▷ *sm* poster, bill; (*scritto ideologico*) manifesto

ma'niglia [ma'niʎʎa] *sf* handle; (*sostegno: negli autobus ecc*) strap

manipo'lare /72/ *vt* to manipulate; (*alterare: vino*) to adulterate

man'naro, -a *ag*: **lupo ~** werewolf

'mano, -i *sf* hand; (*strato: di vernice ecc*) coat; **a ~** by hand; **di prima ~** (*notizia*) first-hand; **di seconda ~** second-hand; **man ~** little by little, gradually; **man ~ che** as; **darsi** *o* **stringersi la ~** to shake hands; **mettere le mani avanti** (*fig*) to safeguard o.s.; **restare a mani vuote** to be left empty-handed; **venire alle mani** to come to blows; **mani in alto!** hands up!

mano'dopera *sf* labour

ma'nometro *sm* gauge, manometer

mano'mettere /63/ *vt* (*alterare*) to tamper with; (*aprire indebitamente*) to break open illegally

ma'nopola *sf* (*dell'armatura*) gauntlet; (*guanto*) mitt; (*di impugnatura*) hand-grip; (*pomello*) knob

manos'critto, -a *ag* handwritten ▷ *sm* manuscript

mano'vale *sm* labourer

mano'vella *sf* handle; (*Tecn*) crank

ma'novra *sf* manoeuvre (BRIT), maneuver (US); (*Ferr*) shunting

man'sarda *sf* attic

mansi'one *sf* task, duty, job

mansu'eto, -a *ag* gentle, docile

man'tello *sm* cloak; (*fig: di neve ecc*) blanket, mantle; (*Zool*) coat

mante'nere /121/ *vt* to maintain; (*adempiere: promesse*) to keep, abide by; (*provvedere a*) to support, maintain; **mantenersi** *vpr*: **mantenersi calmo/giovane** to stay calm/young

'Mantova *sf* Mantua

manu'ale *ag* manual ▷ *sm* (*testo*) manual, handbook

ma'nubrio *sm* handle; (*di bicicletta ecc*) handlebars *pl*; (*Sport*) dumbbell

manutenzi'one [manuten'tsjone] *sf* maintenance, upkeep; (*d'impianti*) maintenance, servicing

'manzo ['mandzo] *sm* (*Zool*) steer; (*carne*) beef

'mappa *sf* (*Geo*) map; **mappa'mondo** *sm* map of the world; (*globo girevole*) globe

mara'tona *sf* marathon

'marca, -che *sf* (*Comm: di prodotti*) brand; (*contrassegno, scontrino*) ticket, check; **prodotti di (gran) ~** high-class products; **~ da bollo** official stamp

mar'care /20/ *vt* (*munire di contrassegno*) to mark; (*a fuoco*) to brand; (*Sport: gol*) to score; (: *avversario*) to mark; (*accentuare*) to stress; **~ visita** (*Mil*) to report sick

marcherò *ecc* [marke'rɔ] *vb vedi* **marcare**

mar'chese, -a [mar'keze] *sm/f* marquis *o* marquess/marchioness

marchi'are [mar'kjare] /19/ *vt* to brand

'marcia, -ce ['martʃa] *sf* (*anche Mus, Mil*) march; (*funzionamento*) running; (*il camminare*) walking; (*Aut*) gear; **mettere in ~** to start; **mettersi in ~** to get moving; **far ~ indietro** (*Aut*) to reverse; (*fig*) to back-pedal

marciapi'ede [martʃa'pjɛde] *sm* (*di strada*) pavement (BRIT), sidewalk (US); (*Ferr*) platform

marci'are [mar'tʃare] /14/ *vi* to march; (*andare, treno, macchina*) to go; (*funzionare*) to run, work

'marcio, -a, -ci, -ce ['martʃo] *ag* (*frutta, legno*) rotten, bad; (*Med*) festering; (*fig*) corrupt, rotten

mar'cire [mar'tʃire] /55/ *vi* (*andare a male*) to go bad, rot; (*suppurare*) to fester; (*fig*) to rot, waste away

'**marco, -chi** sm (unità monetaria) mark

'**mare** sm sea; **in ~** at sea; **andare al ~** (in vacanza ecc) to go to the seaside; **il ~ del Nord** the North Sea

ma'**rea** sf tide; **alta/bassa ~** high/low tide

mareggi'**ata** [mared'dʒata] sf heavy sea

mare'**moto** sm seaquake

maresci'**allo** [mareʃʃallo] sm (Mil) marshal; (sottufficiale) warrant officer

marga'**rina** sf margarine

marghe'**rita** [marge'rita] sf (ox-eye) daisy, marguerite

'**margine** ['mardʒine] sm margin; (di bosco, via) edge, border

mariju'**ana** [mæri'wa:nə] sf marijuana

ma'**rina** sf navy; (costa) coast; (quadro) seascape; **~ mercantile** merchant navy (BRIT) o marine (US); **~ militare** ≈ Royal Navy (BRIT), ≈ Navy (US)

mari'**naio** sm sailor

mari'**nare** /72/ vt (Cuc) to marinate; **~ la scuola** to play truant

ma'**rina, -a** ag sea cpd, marine

mario'**netta** sf puppet

ma'**rito** sm husband

ma'**rittimo, -a** ag maritime, sea cpd

marmel'**lata** sf jam; (di agrumi) marmalade

mar'**mitta** sf (recipiente) pot; (Aut) silencer; **~ catalitica** catalytic converter

'**marmo** sm marble

mar'**motta** sf (Zool) marmot

maroc'**chino, -a** [marok'kino] ag, sm/f Moroccan

Ma'**rocco** sm: **il ~** Morocco

mar'**rone** ag inv brown ▷ sm (Bot) chestnut

> Attenzione! In inglese esiste la parola maroon, che però indica un altro colore, il rosso bordeaux.

mar'**supio** sm (Zool) pouch, marsupium

marte'**dì** sm inv Tuesday; **di** o **il ~** on Tuesdays; **~ grasso** Shrove Tuesday

martel'**lare** /72/ vt to hammer ▷ vi (pulsare) to throb; (: cuore) to thump

mar'**tello** sm hammer; (di uscio) knocker; **~ pneumatico** pneumatic drill

'**martire** smf martyr

mar'**xista, -i, -e** ag, smf Marxist

marza'**pane** [martsa'pane] sm marzipan

'**marzo** ['martso] sm March

mascal'**zone** [maskal'tsone] sm rascal, scoundrel

'**mascara** sm inv mascara

ma'**scella** [maʃʃella] sf (Anat) jaw

'**maschera** ['maskera] sf mask; (travestimento) disguise; (per un ballo ecc) fancy dress; (Teat, Cine) usher/usherette; (personaggio del teatro) stock character; **masche'rare** /72/ vt to mask; (travestire) to disguise; to dress up; (fig: celare) to hide, conceal; (Mil) to camouflage; **mascherarsi** vpr: **mascherarsi da** to disguise o.s. as; to dress up as; (fig) to masquerade as

mas'**chile** [mas'kile] ag masculine; (sesso, popolazione) male; (abiti) men's; (per ragazzi, scuola) boys'

mas'**chilista, -i, -e** ag, smf (uomo) (male) chauvinist, sexist; (donna) sexist

'**maschio, -a** ['maskjo] ag (Biol) male; (virile) manly ▷ sm (anche Zool, Tecn) male; (uomo) man; (ragazzo) boy; (figlio) son

masco'**lino, -a** ag masculine

'**massa** sf mass; (di gente) mass, multitude; (Elettr) earth; **una ~ di** (di errori ecc) heaps of, masses of; **in ~** (Comm) in bulk; (tutti insieme) en masse; **adunata in ~** mass meeting; **manifestazione/cultura di ~** mass demonstration/culture

mas'**sacro** sm massacre, slaughter; (fig) mess, disaster

massaggi'**are** [massad'dʒare] /62/ vt to massage

mas'saggio [mas'saddʒo] *sm* massage; **~ cardiaco** cardiac massage

mas'saia *sf* housewife

masse'rizie [masse'rittsje] *sfpl* (household) furnishings

mas'siccio, -a, -ci, -ce [mas'sittʃo] *ag* (*oro, legno*) solid; (*palazzo*) massive; (*corporatura*) stout ▷ *sm* (*Geo*) massif

'**massima** *sf vedi* **massimo**

massi'male *sm* maximum; (*Comm*) ceiling, limit

'**massimo, -a** *ag, sm* maximum ▷ *sf* (*sentenza, regola*) maxim; (*Meteor*) maximum temperature; **in linea di massima** generally speaking; **al ~** at (the) most

'**masso** *sm* rock, boulder

masteriz'zare [masterid'dzare] /72/ *vt* (*CD, DVD*) to burn

masteriz'zatore [masteriddza'tore] *sm* CD burner *o* writer

masti'care /20/ *vt* to chew

'**mastice** ['mastitʃe] *sm* mastic; (*per vetri*) putty

mas'tino *sm* mastiff

ma'tassa *sf* skein

mate'matico, -a, -ci, -che *ag* mathematical ▷ *sm/f* mathematician ▷ *sf* mathematics *sg*

materas'sino *sm* mat; **~ gonfiabile** air bed

mate'rasso *sm* mattress; **~ a molle** spring *o* interior-sprung mattress

ma'teria *sf* (*Fisica*) matter; (*Tecn, Comm*) material, matter *no pl*; (*disciplina*) subject; (*argomento*) subject matter, material; **in ~ di** (*per quanto concerne*) on the subject of; **materie prime** raw materials

materi'ale *ag* material; (*fig: grossolano*) rough, rude ▷ *sm* material; (*insieme di strumenti ecc*) equipment *no pl*, materials *pl*

materni'tà *sf* motherhood, maternity; (*reparto*) maternity ward

ma'terno, -a *ag* (*amore, cura ecc*) maternal, motherly; (*nonno*) maternal; (*lingua, terra*) mother *cpd*

ma'tita *sf* pencil; **matite colorate** coloured pencils; **~ per gli occhi** eyeliner (pencil)

ma'tricola *sf* (*registro*) register; (*numero*) registration number; (*nell'università*) freshman, fresher

ma'trigna [ma'triɲa] *sf* stepmother

matrimoni'ale *ag* matrimonial, marriage *cpd*

matri'monio *sm* marriage, matrimony; (*durata*) marriage, married life; (*cerimonia*) wedding

mat'tina *sf* morning

'**matto, -a** *ag* mad, crazy; (*fig: falso*) false, imitation ▷ *sm/f* madman/ woman; **avere una voglia matta di qc** to be dying for sth

mat'tone *sm* brick; (*fig*): **questo libro/film è un ~** this book/film is heavy going

matto'nella *sf* tile

matu'rare /72/ *vi* (*anche:* **maturarsi**) (*frutta, grano*) to ripen; (*ascesso*) to come to a head; (*fig: persona, idea, Econ*) to mature ▷ *vt* to ripen, to (make) mature

maturi'tà *sf* maturity; (*di frutta*) ripeness, maturity; (*Ins*) school-leaving examination, ≈ GCE A-levels (*BRIT*)

ma'turo, -a *ag* mature; (*frutto*) ripe, mature

max. *abbr* (= *massimo*) max

maxis'chermo [maksis'kermo] *sm* giant screen

'**mazza** ['mattsa] *sf* (*bastone*) club; (*martello*) sledge-hammer; (*Sport: da golf*) club; (: *da baseball, cricket*) bat

maz'zata [mat'tsata] *sf* (*anche fig*) heavy blow

'**mazzo** ['mattso] *sm* (*di fiori, chiavi ecc*) bunch; (*di carte da gioco*) pack

me *pron* me; **me stesso, me stessa** myself; **sei bravo quanto me** you are as clever as I (am) *o* as me

mec'canico, -a, -ci, -che *ag*
mechanical ▷ *sm* mechanic
mecca'nismo *sm* mechanism
me'daglia [me'daʎʎa] *sf* medal
me'desimo, -a *ag* same; (*in persona*):
io ~ I myself
'media *sf vedi* **medio**
medi'ante *prep* by means of
media'tore, -'trice *sm/f* mediator;
(*Comm*) middle man, agent
medi'care /20/ *vt* to treat; (*ferita*)
to dress
medi'cina [medi'tʃina] *sf* medicine;
~ legale forensic medicine
'medico, -a, -ci, -che *ag* medical
▷ *sm* doctor; **~ generico** general
practitioner, GP
medie'vale *ag* medieval
'medio, -a *ag* average; (*punto, ceto*)
middle; (*altezza, statura*) medium
▷ *sm* (*dito*) middle finger ▷ *sf* average;
(*Mat*) mean; (*Ins: voto*) end-of-term
average; **medie** *sfpl vedi* **scuola
media**; **licenza media** *leaving
certificate awarded at the end of 3 years
of secondary education*; **in media** on
average
medi'ocre *ag* mediocre; poor
medi'tare /72/ *vt* to ponder over,
meditate on; (*progettare*) to plan,
think out ▷ *vi* to meditate
mediter'raneo, -a *ag*
Mediterranean; **il (mare) M~** the
Mediterranean (Sea)
me'dusa *sf* (*Zool*) jellyfish
mega *sm inv* (*Inform*) meg
mega'byte *sm inv* (*Inform*) megabyte
me'gafono *sm* megaphone
'meglio ['meʎʎo] *av, ag inv* better;
(*con senso superlativo*) best ▷ *sm* (*la
cosa migliore*) best; **il ~** the best (thing);
faresti ~ ad andartene you had
better leave; **alla ~** as best one can;
andar di bene in ~ to get better and
better; **fare del proprio ~** to do one's
best; **per il ~** for the best; **aver la ~
su qn** to get the better of sb
'mela *sf* apple; **~ cotogna** quince

mela'grana *sf* pomegranate
melan'zana [melan'dzana] *sf*
aubergine (BRIT), eggplant (US)
melato'nina *sf* melatonin
'melma *sf* mud, mire
'melo *sm* apple tree
melo'dia *sf* melody
me'lone *sm* (*musk*) melon
'membro *sm* (*pl m* **membri**) member;
(*pl f* **membra**) (*arto*) limb
memo'randum *sm inv*
memorandum
me'moria *sf* memory; **memorie**
sfpl (*opera autobiografica*) memoirs;
a ~ (*imparare, sapere*) by heart; **a ~
d'uomo** within living memory
mendi'cante *smf* beggar

PAROLA CHIAVE

'meno *av* **1** (*in minore misura*) less;
dovresti mangiare meno you
should eat less, you shouldn't eat
so much
2 (*comparativo*): **meno … di** not as …
as, less … than; **sono meno alto di
te** I'm not as tall as you (are), I'm less
tall than you (are); **meno … che** not
as … as, less … than; **meno che mai**
less than ever; **è meno intelligente
che ricco** he's more rich than
intelligent; **meno fumo più mangio**
the less I smoke the more I eat
3 (*superlativo*) least; **il meno dotato
degli studenti** the least gifted of
the students; **è quello che compro
meno spesso** it's the one I buy
least often
4 (*Mat*) minus; **8 meno 5** 8 minus 5,
8 take away 5; **sono le 8 meno un
quarto** it's a quarter to 8; **meno 5
gradi** 5 degrees below zero, minus
5 degrees; **mille euro in meno** a
thousand euros less
5 (*fraseologia*): **quanto meno
poteva telefonare** he could at least
have phoned; **non so se accettare
o meno** I don't know whether to

accept or not; **fare a meno di qc/qn** to do without sth/sb; **non potevo fare a meno di ridere** I couldn't help laughing; **meno male!** thank goodness!; **meno male che sei arrivato** it's a good job that you've come

▶ ag inv (tempo, denaro) less; (errori, persone) fewer; **ha fatto meno errori di tutti** he made fewer mistakes than anyone, he made the fewest mistakes of all

▶ sm inv **ɪ: il meno** (il minimo) the least; **parlare del più e del meno** to talk about this and that

2 (Mat) minus

▶ prep (eccetto) except (for), apart from; **a meno che, a meno di** unless; **a meno che non piova** unless it rains; **non posso, a meno di prendere ferie** I can't, unless I take some leave

meno'pausa sf menopause
'mensa sf (locale) canteen; (: Mil) mess; (: nelle università) refectory
men'sile ag monthly ▷ sm (periodico) monthly (magazine); (stipendio) monthly salary
'mensola sf bracket; (ripiano) shelf; (Archit) corbel
'menta sf mint; (anche: **~ piperita**) peppermint; (bibita) peppermint cordial; (caramella) mint, peppermint
men'tale ag mental; **mentalità** sf inv mentality
'mente sf mind; **imparare/sapere qc a ~** to learn/know sth by heart; **avere in ~ qc** to have sth in mind; **passare di ~ a qn** to slip sb's mind
men'tire /17/ vi to lie
'mento sm chin
'mentre cong (temporale) while; (avversativo) whereas
menù sm inv (set) menu; **~ turistico** set o tourists' menu
menzio'nare [mentsjo'nare] /72/ vt to mention

men'zogna [men'tsoɲɲa] sf lie
mera'viglia [mera'viʎʎa] sf amazement, wonder; (persona, cosa) marvel, wonder; **a ~** perfectly, wonderfully; **meravigli'are** /27/ vt to amaze, astonish; **meravigliarsi** vpr: **meravigliarsi (di)** to marvel (at); (stupirsi) to be amazed (at), be astonished (at); **meravigli'oso, -a** ag wonderful, marvellous (BRIT), marvelous (US)
mer'cante sm merchant; **~ d'arte** art dealer
merca'tino sm (rionale) local street market; (Econ) unofficial stock market
mer'cato sm market; **~ dei cambi** exchange market; **~ nero** black market
'merce ['mertʃe] sf goods pl, merchandise
mercé [mer'tʃe] sf mercy
merce'ria [mertʃe'ria] sf (articoli) haberdashery (BRIT), notions pl (US); (bottega) haberdasher's shop (BRIT), notions store (US)
mercoledì sm inv Wednesday; **di o il ~** on Wednesdays; **~ delle Ceneri** Ash Wednesday
mer'curio sm mercury
'merda sf (fam!) shit (!)
me'renda sf afternoon snack
meren'dina sf snack
meridi'ano, -a ag (di mezzogiorno) midday cpd, noonday ▷ sm meridian ▷ sf (orologio) sundial
meridio'nale ag southern ▷ smf southerner
meridi'one sm south
me'ringa, -ghe sf (Cuc) meringue
meri'tare /72/ vt to deserve, merit ▷ vb impers: **merita andare** it's worth going
meri'tevole ag worthy
'merito sm merit; (valore) worth; **dare ~ a qn di** to give sb credit for; **finire a pari ~** to finish joint first (o second ecc); (to tie); **in ~ a** as regards, with regard to

mer'letto sm lace

'merlo sm (Zool) blackbird; (Archit) battlement

mer'luzzo [mer'luttso] sm (Zool) cod

mes'chino, -a [mes'kino] ag wretched; (scarso) scanty, poor; (persona: gretta) mean; (: limitata) narrow-minded, petty

mesco'lare /72/ vt to mix; (vini, colori) to blend; (mettere in disordine) to mix up, muddle up; (carte) to shuffle

'mese sm month

'messa sf (Rel) mass; **~ in moto** starting; **~ in piega** set; **~ a punto** (Tecn) adjustment; (Aut) tuning; (fig) clarification; **~ in scena** = **messinscena**

messag'gero [messad'dʒero] sm messenger

messaggi'arsi [messad'dʒarsi] /72/ vpr to text; **messaggiamoci** we'll text each other

messag'gino [messad'dʒino] sm (di telefonino) text (message)

mes'saggio [mes'saddʒo] sm message

messag'gistica [messad'dʒistica] sf: **~ immediata** (Inform) instant messaging; **programma di ~ immediata** instant messenger

mes'sale sm (Rel) missal

messi'cano, -a ag, sm/f Mexican

'Messico sm: **il ~** Mexico

messin'scena [messin'ʃɛna] sf (Teat) production

'messo, -a pp di **mettere** ▷ sm messenger

mesti'ere sm (professione) job; (: manuale) trade; (: artigianale) craft; (fig: abilità nel lavoro) skill, technique; **essere del ~** to know the tricks of the trade

'mestolo sm (Cuc) ladle

mestruazi'one [mestruat'tsjone] sf menstruation

'meta sf destination; (fig) aim, goal

metà sf inv half; (punto di mezzo) middle; **dividere qc a** o **per ~** to divide sth in half, halve sth; **fare a ~ (di qc con qn)** to go halves (with sb in sth); **a ~ prezzo** at half price; **a ~ strada** halfway

meta'done sm methadone

me'tafora sf metaphor

me'tallico, -a, -ci, -che ag (di metallo) metal cpd; (splendore, rumore ecc) metallic

me'tallo sm metal

metalmec'canico, -a, -ci, -che ag engineering cpd ▷ sm engineering worker

me'tano sm methane

meteoro'logico, -a, -ci, -che [meteoro'lɔdʒiko] ag meteorological, weather cpd

me'ticcio, -a, -ci, -ce [me'tittʃo] sm/f half-caste, half-breed

me'todico, -a, -ci, -che ag methodical

'metodo sm method

'metro sm metre; (nastro) tape measure; (asta) (metre) rule

metropoli'tano, -a ag metropolitan ▷ sf underground (BRIT), subway (US)

metroses'suale ag metrosexual

'mettere /63/ vt to put; (abito) to put on; (: portare) to wear; (installare: telefono) to put in; (fig: provocare): **~ fame/allegria a qn** to make sb hungry/happy; (supporre): **mettiamo che ...** let's suppose o say that ...; **mettersi** vpr (persona) to put o.s.; (oggetto) to go; (disporsi: faccenda) to turn out; **mettersi a** (cominciare) to begin to, start to; **mettersi a sedere** to sit down; **mettersi al lavoro** to set to work; **mettersi a letto** to get into bed; (per malattia) to take to one's bed; **mettersi il cappello** to put on one's hat; **mettersi con qn** (in società) to team up with sb; (in coppia) to start going out with sb; **metterci: metterci molta cura/molto tempo** to take a lot of care/a lot of time; **mettercela tutta** to do one's best;

m

~ a tacere qn/qc to keep sb/sth quiet; **~ su casa** to set up house; **~ su un negozio** to start a shop; **~ via** to put away

mezza'notte [meddza'nɔtte] *sf* midnight

'**mezzo, -a** ['mɛddzo] *ag* half; **un ~ litro/panino** half a litre/roll ▷ *av* half-; **~ morto** half-dead ▷ *sm* (*metà*) half; (*parte centrale: di strada ecc*) middle; (*per raggiungere un fine*) means *sg*; (*veicolo*) vehicle; (*nell'indicare l'ora*): **le nove e ~** half past nine; **mezzogiorno e ~** half past twelve; **mezzi** *smpl* (*possibilità economiche*) means; **di mezza età** middle-aged; **un soprabito di mezza stagione** a spring (*o* autumn) coat; **di ~** middle, in the middle; **andarci di ~** (*patir danno*) to suffer; **levarsi** *o* **togliersi di ~** to get out of the way; **in ~ a** in the middle of; **per** *o* **a ~ di** by means of; **mezzi di comunicazione di massa** mass media *pl*: **mezzi pubblici** public transport *sg*: **mezzi di trasporto** means of transport

mezzogi'orno [meddzo'dʒorno] *sm* midday, noon; **a ~** at 12 (o'clock) *o* midday *o* noon; **il ~ d'Italia** southern Italy

mi *pron* (*dav lo, la, li, le, ne diventa* **me**: *oggetto*) me; (*complemento di termine*) (to) me; (*riflessivo*) myself ▷ *sm* (*Mus*) E; (: *solfeggiando la scala*) mi

miago'lare /72/ *vi* to miaow, mew

'**mica** *av* (*fam*): **non ... ~** not ... at all; **non sono ~ stanco** I'm not a bit tired; **non sarà ~ partito?** he wouldn't have left, would he?; **~ male** not bad

'**miccia, -ce** ['mittʃa] *sf* fuse

micidi'ale [mitʃi'djale] *ag* fatal; (*dannosissimo*) deadly

micro'fibra *sf* microfibre

mi'crofono *sm* microphone

micros'copio *sm* microscope

mi'dollo (*pl f* **midolla**) *sm* (*Anat*) marrow; **~ osseo** bone marrow

mi'ele *sm* honey

'**miglia** ['miʎʎa] *sfpl di* **miglio¹**

migli'aio [miʎ'ʎajo] (*pl f* **migliaia**) *sm* thousand; **un ~ (di)** about a thousand; **a migliaia** by the thousand, in thousands

'**miglio¹** ['miʎʎo] (*pl f* **miglia**) *sm* (*unità di misura*) mile; **~ marino** *o* **nautico** nautical mile

'**miglio²** ['miʎʎo] *sm* (*Bot*) millet

migliora'mento [miʎʎora'mento] *sm* improvement

miglio'rare [miʎʎo'rare] /72/ *vt, vi* to improve

migli'ore [miʎ'ʎore] *ag* (*comparativo*) better; (*superlativo*) best ▷ *sm*: **il ~** the best (thing) ▷ *smf*: **il (la) ~** the best (person); **il miglior vino di questa regione** the best wine in this area

'**mignolo** ['miɲɲolo] *sm* (*Anat*) little finger, pinkie; (: *dito del piede*) little toe

Mi'lano *sf* Milan

miliar'dario, -a *sm/f* millionaire

mili'ardo *sm* thousand million , billion (*US*)

mili'one *sm* million

mili'tante *ag, smf* militant

mili'tare /72/ *vi* (*Mil*) to be a soldier, serve; (*fig: in un partito*) to be a militant ▷ *ag* military ▷ *sm* serviceman; **fare il ~** to do one's military service

'**mille** (*pl* **mila**) *num* a *o* one thousand; **diecimila** ten thousand; **~ euro** one thousand euros

mil'lennio *sm* millennium

millepi'edi *sm inv* centipede

mil'lesimo, -a *ag, sm* thousandth

milli'grammo *sm* milligram(me)

mil'limetro *sm* millimetre

'**milza** ['miltsa] *sf* (*Anat*) spleen

mimetiz'zare [mimetid'dzare] /72/ *vt* to camouflage; **mimetizzarsi** *vpr* to camouflage o.s.

'**mimo** *sm* (*attore, componimento*) mime

mi'mosa sf mimosa

min. abbr (= minuto, minimo) min

'mina sf (esplosiva) mine; (di matita) lead

mi'naccia, -ce [mi'nattʃa] sf threat; **minacci'are** /14/ vt to threaten; **minacciare qn di morte** to threaten to kill sb; **minacciare di fare qc** to threaten to do sth

mi'nare /72/ vt (Mil) to mine; (fig) to undermine

mina'tore sm miner

mine'rale ag, sm mineral

mine'rario, -a ag (delle miniere) mining; (dei minerali) ore cpd

mi'nestra sf soup; **~ in brodo** noodle soup; **~ di verdura** vegetable soup

minia'tura sf miniature

mini'bar sm inv minibar

mini'era sf mine

mini'gonna sf miniskirt

'minimo, -a ag minimum, least, slightest; (piccolissimo) very small, slight; (il più basso) lowest, minimum ▷ sm minimum; **al ~** at least; **girare al ~** (Aut) to idle

minis'tero sm (Pol, Rel) ministry; (governo) government; **M~ delle Finanze** Ministry of Finance, ≈ Treasury

mi'nistro sm (Pol, Rel) minister

mino'ranza [mino'rantsa] sf minority

mi'nore ag (comparativo) less; (più piccolo) smaller; (numero) lower; (inferiore) lower, inferior; (meno importante) minor; (più giovane) younger; (superlativo) least; smallest; lowest, least important, youngest ▷ smf = **minorenne**

mino'renne ag under age ▷ smf minor, person under age

minu'scolo, -a ag (scrittura, carattere) small; (piccolissimo) tiny ▷ sf small letter

mi'nuto, -a ag tiny, minute; (pioggia) fine; (corporatura) delicate, fine

▷ sm (unità di misura) minute; **al ~** (Comm) retail

'mio (f **'mia**, pl **mi'ei** o **'mie**) det: **il ~, la mia** ecc my ▷ pron: **il ~, la mia** ecc mine; **i miei** my family; **un ~ amico** a friend of mine

'miope ag short-sighted

'mira sf (anche fig) aim; **prendere la ~** to take aim; **prendere di ~ qn** (fig) to pick on sb

mi'racolo sm miracle

mi'raggio [mi'raddʒo] sm mirage

mi'rare /72/ vi: **~ a** to aim at; **mi'rato, -a** ag targetted

mi'rino sm (Tecn) sight; (Fot) viewer, viewfinder

mir'tillo sm bilberry (BRIT), blueberry (US), whortleberry

mi'scela [miʃ'ʃela] sf mixture; (di caffè) blend

'mischia ['miskja] sf scuffle; (Rugby) scrum, scrummage

mis'cuglio [mis'kuʎʎo] sm mixture, hotchpotch, jumble

'mise vb vedi **mettere**

mise'rabile ag (infelice) miserable, wretched; (povero) poverty-stricken; (di scarso valore) miserable

mi'seria sf extreme poverty; (infelicità) misery

miseri'cordia sf mercy, pity

'misero, -a ag miserable, wretched; (povero) poverty-stricken; (insufficiente) miserable

'misi vb vedi **mettere**

mi'sogino [mi'zɔdʒino] sm misogynist

'missile sm missile

missio'nario, -a ag, smf missionary

missi'one sf mission

misteri'oso, -a ag mysterious

mis'tero sm mystery

'misto, -a ag mixed; (scuola) mixed, coeducational ▷ sm mixture

mis'tura sf mixture

mi'sura sf measure; (misurazione, dimensione) measurement; (taglia) size; (provvedimento) measure, step;

(*moderazione*) moderation; (*Mus*) time; (: *divisione*) bar; (*fig*: *limite*) bounds *pl*, limit; **nella ~ in cui** inasmuch as, insofar as; **su ~** made to measure

misu'rare /72/ *vt* (*ambiente, stoffa*) to measure; (*terreno*) to survey; (*abito*) to try on; (*pesare*) to weigh; (*fig*: *parole ecc*) to weigh up; (: *spese, cibo*) to limit ▷ *vi* to measure; **misurarsi** *vpr*: **misurarsi con qn** to have a confrontation with sb; (*competere*) to compete with sb

'mite *ag* mild

'mitico, -a, -ci, -che *ag* mythical

'mito *sm* myth; **mitolo'gia, -'gie** *sf* mythology

'mitra *sf* (*Rel*) mitre ▷ *sm inv* (*arma*) sub-machine gun

mit'tente *smf* sender

mm *abbr* (= *millimetro*) mm

'mobile *ag* mobile; (*parte di macchina*) moving; (*Dir*: *bene*) movable, personal ▷ *sm* (*arredamento*) piece of furniture; **mobili** *smpl* (*mobilia*) furniture *sg*

mocas'sino *sm* moccasin

'moda *sf* fashion; **alla ~, di ~** fashionable, in fashion

modalità *sf inv* formality

mo'della *sf* model

mo'dello *sm* model; (*stampo*) mould ▷ *ag inv* model *cpd*

'modem *sm inv* modem

modera'tore, -'trice *sm/f* moderator

mo'derno, -a *ag* modern

mo'desto, -a *ag* modest

'modico, -a, -ci, -che *ag* reasonable, moderate

mo'difica, -che *sf* modification

modifi'care /20/ *vt* to modify, alter

'modo *sm* way, manner; (*mezzo*) means, way; (*occasione*) opportunity; (*Ling*) mood; (*Mus*) mode; **modi** *smpl* (*maniere*) manners; **a suo ~, a ~ suo** in his own way; **ad** o **in ogni ~** anyway; **di** o **in ~ che** so that; **in ~ da** so as to; **in tutti i modi** at all costs;

(*comunque sia*) anyway; (*in ogni caso*) in any case; **in qualche ~** somehow or other; **~ di dire** turn of phrase; **per ~ di dire** so to speak

'modulo *sm* (*modello*) form; (*Archit*: *lunare, di comando*) module

mo'gano *sm* mahogany

'mogio, -a, -gi, -gie ['mɔdʒo] *ag* down in the dumps, dejected

'moglie ['moʎʎe] *sf* wife

mo'ine *sfpl* cajolery *sg*; (*leziosità*) affectation *sg*

mo'lare /72/ *sm* (*dente*) molar

'mole *sf* mass; (*dimensioni*) size; (*edificio grandioso*) massive structure

moles'tare /72/ *vt* to bother, annoy; mo'lestia *sf* annoyance, bother; **recar molestia a qn** to bother sb; **molestie sessuali** sexual harassment *sg*

'molla *sf* spring; **molle** *sfpl* (*per camino*) tongs

mol'lare /72/ *vt* to release, let go; (*Naut*) to ease; (*fig*: *ceffone*) to give ▷ *vi* (*cedere*) to give in

'molle *ag* soft; (*muscoli*) flabby

mol'letta *sf* (*per capelli*) hairgrip; (*per panni stesi*) clothes peg (BRIT) o pin (US)

mol'lica, -che *sf* crumb, soft part

mol'lusco, -schi *sm* mollusc

'molo *sm* breakwater; jetty

moltipli'care /20/ *vt* to multiply; **moltiplicarsi** *vpr* to multiply; (*richieste*) to increase in number; **moltiplicazi'one** *sf* multiplication

○ **PAROLA CHIAVE**

'molto, -a *det* (*quantità*) a lot of, much; (*numero*) a lot of, many; **molto pane/carbone** a lot of bread/coal; **molta gente** a lot of people, many people; **molti libri** a lot of books, many books; **non ho molto tempo** I haven't got much time; **per molto (tempo)** for a long time
▷ *av* **1** a lot, (very) much; **viaggia**

molto he travels a lot; **non viaggia molto** he doesn't travel much o a lot 2 (intensivo: con aggettivi, avverbi) very; (: con participio passato) (very) much; **molto buono** very good; **molto migliore, molto meglio** much o a lot better
▶ pron much, a lot

momentanea'mente av at the moment, at present

momen'taneo, -a ag momentary, fleeting

mo'mento sm moment; **da un ~ all'altro** at any moment; (all'improvviso) suddenly; **al ~ di fare** just as I was (o you were o he was ecc) doing; **a momenti** (da un mo'mento all'altro) any time o moment now; (quasi) nearly; **per il ~** for the time being; **dal ~ che** ever since; (dato che) since

monaca, -che sf nun

Monaco sf Monaco; **~ (di Baviera)** Munich

monaco, -ci sm monk

monar'chia sf monarchy

monas'tero sm (di monaci) monastery; (di monache) convent

mon'dano, -a ag (anche fig) worldly; (dell'alta società) society cpd; fashionable

mondi'ale ag (campionato, popolazione) world cpd; (influenza) world-wide

mondo sm world; (grande quantità): **un ~ di** lots of, a host of; **il gran o bel ~** high society

mo'nello, -a sm/f street urchin; (ragazzo vivace) scamp, imp

mo'neta sf coin; (Econ: valuta) currency; (denaro spicciolo) (small) change; **~ estera** foreign currency; **~ legale** legal tender

mongol'fiera sf hot-air balloon

monitor sm inv (Tecn, TV) monitor

monolo'cale sm ≈ studio flat

mono'polio sm monopoly

mo'notono, -a ag monotonous

monovo'lume sf inv (anche: **automobile ~**) people carrier, MPV

mon'sone sm monsoon

monta'carichi [monta'kariki] sm inv hoist, goods lift

mon'taggio [mon'taddʒo] sm (Tecn) assembly; (Cine) editing

mon'tagna [mon'taɲɲa] sf mountain; (zona montuosa): **la ~** the mountains pl: **andare in ~** to go to the mountains; **montagne russe** roller coaster sg, big dipper sg (BRIT)

monta'naro, -a ag mountain cpd ▷ sm/f mountain dweller

mon'tano, -a ag mountain cpd; alpine

mon'tare /72/ vt to go (o come) up; (cavallo) to ride; (apparecchiatura) to set up, assemble; (Cuc) to whip; (Zool) to cover; (incastonare) to mount, set; (Cine) to edit; (Fot) to mount ▷ vi to go (o come) up; (aumentare di livello, volume) to rise; (a cavallo): **~ bene/male** to ride well/badly

monta'tura sf assembling no pl; (di occhiali) frames pl; (di gioiello) mounting, setting; (fig): **~ pubblicitaria** publicity stunt

monte sm mountain; **a ~** upstream; **mandare a ~ qc** to upset sth, cause sth to fail; **il M~ Bianco** Mont Blanc; **~ di pietà** pawnshop; **~ premi** prize

mon'tone sm (Zool) ram; **carne di ~** mutton

montu'oso, -a ag mountainous

monu'mento sm monument

mo'quette [mɔ'kɛt] sf fitted carpet

mora sf (del rovo) blackberry; (del gelso) mulberry; (Dir) delay; (: somma) arrears pl

mo'rale ag moral ▷ sf (scienza) ethics sg, moral philosophy; (complesso di norme) moral standards pl, morality; (condotta) morals pl; (insegnamento morale) moral ▷ sm morale; **essere giù di ~** to be feeling down

'morbido, -a *ag* soft; (*pelle*) soft, smooth

> Attenzione! In inglese esiste la parola *morbid*, che però significa *morboso*.

mor'billo *sm* (*Med*) measles *sg*

'morbo *sm* disease

mor'boso, -a *ag* (*fig*) morbid

'mordere /64/ *vt* to bite; (*addentare*) to bite into

mor'fina *sf* morphine

mori'bondo, -a *ag* dying, moribund

mo'rire /65/ *vi* to die; (*abitudine, civiltà*) to die out; **~ di fame** to die of hunger; (*fig*) to be starving; **~ di noia/paura** to be bored/scared to death; **fa un caldo da ~** it's terribly hot

mormo'rare /72/ *vi* to murmur; (*brontolare*) to grumble

'moro, -a *ag* dark(-haired), dark-complexioned

'morsa *sf* (*Tecn*) vice; (*fig: stretta*) grip

morsi'care /20/ *vt* to nibble (at), gnaw (at); (*insetto*) to bite

'morso, -a *pp di* **mordere** ▷ *sm* bite; (*di insetto*) sting; (*parte della briglia*) bit; **i morsi della fame** pangs of hunger

morta'della *sf* (*Cuc*) mortadella (*type of salted pork meat*)

mor'taio *sm* mortar

mor'tale *ag, sm* mortal

'morte *sf* death

'morto, -a *pp di* **morire** ▷ *ag* dead ▷ *sm/f* dead man/woman; **i morti** the dead; **fare il ~** (*nell'acqua*) to float on one's back; **il Mar M~** the Dead Sea

mo'saico, -ci *sm* mosaic

'Mosca *sf* Moscow

'mosca, -sche *sf* fly; **~ cieca** blind-man's buff

mosce'rino [moʃʃe'rino] *sm* midge, gnat

mos'chea [mos'kɛa] *sf* mosque

'moscio, -a, -sci, -sce ['moʃʃo] *ag* (*fig*) lifeless

mos'cone *sm* (*Zool*) bluebottle; (*barca*) pedalo; (*: a remi*) *kind of pedalo with oars*

'mossa *sf* movement; (*nel gioco*) move

'mossi *ecc vb vedi* **muovere**

'mosso, -a *pp di* **muovere** ▷ *ag* (*mare*) rough; (*capelli*) wavy; (*Fot*) blurred

mos'tarda *sf* mustard; **~ di Cremona** pickled fruit with mustard

'mostra *sf* exhibition, show; (*ostentazione*) show; **in ~** on show; **far ~ di** (*fingere*) to pretend; **far ~ di sé** to show off

mos'trare /72/ *vt* to show

'mostro *sm* monster; **mostru'oso, -a** *ag* monstrous

mo'tel *sm inv* motel

moti'vare /72/ *vt* (*causare*) to cause; (*giustificare*) to justify, account for

mo'tivo *sm* (*causa*) reason, cause; (*movente*) motive; (*letterario*) (*central*) theme; (*disegno*) motif, design, pattern; (*Mus*) motif; **per quale ~?** why?, for what reason?

'moto *sm* (*anche Fisica*) motion; (*movimento, gesto*) movement; (*esercizio fisico*) exercise; (*sommossa*) rising, revolt; (*commozione*) feeling, impulse ▷ *sf inv* (*motocicletta*) motorbike; **mettere in ~** to set in motion; (*Aut*) to start up

motoci'cletta *sf* motorcycle

motoci'clista, -i, -e *smf* motorcyclist

mo'tore, -'trice *ag* motor; (*Tecn*) driving ▷ *sm* engine, motor; **a ~** motor *cpd*, power-driven; **~ a combustione interna/a reazione** internal combustion/jet engine; **~ di ricerca** (*Inform*) search engine; **moto'rino** *sm* moped; **motorino di avviamento** (*Aut*) starter

motos'cafo *sm* motorboat

'motto *sm* (*battuta scherzosa*) witty remark; (*frase emblematica*) motto, maxim

'mouse ['maus] *sm inv* (*Inform*) mouse

mo'vente sm motive

movi'mento sm movement; (fig) activity, hustle and bustle; (Mus) tempo, movement

mozi'one [mot'tsjone] sf (Pol) motion

mozza'rella [mottsa'rɛlla] sf mozzarella

mozzi'cone [mottsi'kone] sm stub, butt, end; (anche: ~ **di sigaretta**) cigarette end

mucca, -che sf cow; ~ **pazza**; mad cow disease

mucchio ['mukkjo] sm pile, heap; (fig): **un ~ di** lots of, heaps of

muco, -chi sm mucus

muffa sf mould, mildew

mug'gire [mud'dʒire] /55/ vi (vacca) to low, moo; (toro) to bellow; (fig) to roar

mu'ghetto [mu'getto] sm lily of the valley

mu'lino sm mill; ~ **a vento** windmill

mulo sm mule

multa sf fine

multi'etnico, -a, -ci, -che ag multiethnic

multiraz'ziale [multirat'tsjale] ag multiracial

multi'sala ag inv multiscreen

multivitami'nico, -a, -ci, -che ag: **complesso ~** multivitamin

mummia sf mummy

mungere ['mundʒere] /5/ vt (anche fig) to milk

munici'pale [munitʃi'pale] ag municipal; town cpd

muni'cipio [muni'tʃipjo] sm town council, corporation; (edificio) town hall

munizi'oni [munit'tsjoni] sfpl (Mil) ammunition sg

munsi ecc vb vedi **mungere**

mu'oio ecc vb vedi **morire**

mu'overe /66/ vt to move; (ruota, macchina) to drive; (sollevare: questione, obiezione) to raise, bring up; (: accusa) to make, bring forward;

muoversi vpr to move; **muoviti!** hurry up!, get a move on!

mura sfpl vedi **muro**

mu'rale ag wall cpd; mural

mura'tore sm mason; (con mattoni) bricklayer

muro sm wall

muschio ['muskjo] sm (Zool) musk; (Bot) moss

musco'lare ag muscular, muscle cpd

muscolo sm (Anat) muscle

mu'seo sm museum

museru'ola sf muzzle

musica sf music; ~ **da ballo/camera** dance/chamber music; **musi'cale** ag musical; **musi'cista, -i, -e** smf musician

müsli ['mysli] sm muesli

muso sm muzzle; (di auto, aereo) nose; **tenere il ~** to sulk

mus(s)ul'mano, -a ag, sm/f Muslim, Moslem

muta sf (di animali) moulting; (di serpenti) sloughing; (per immersioni subacquee) diving suit; (gruppo di cani) pack

mu'tande sfpl (da uomo) (under)pants

muto, -a ag (Med) dumb; (emozione, dolore: Cine) silent; (Ling) silent, mute; (carta geografica) blank; ~ **per lo stupore** ecc speechless with amazement etc

mutuo, -a ag (reciproco) mutual ▷ sm (Econ) (long-term) loan

m

N *abbr* (= nord) N

n *abbr* (= numero) no.

'nafta *sf* naphtha; (*per motori diesel*) diesel oil

nafta'lina *sf* (Chim) naphthalene; (*tarmicida*) mothballs *pl*

'naia *sf* (Mil) slang term for national service

na'ïf [na'if] *ag inv* naïve

'nanna *sf* (*linguaggio infantile*): **andare a ~** to go to beddy-byes

'nano, -a *ag, sm/f* dwarf

napole'tano, -a *ag, sm/f* Neapolitan

'Napoli *sf* Naples

nar'ciso [nar'tʃizo] *sm* narcissus

nar'cotico, -ci *sm* narcotic

na'rice [na'ritʃe] *sf* nostril

nar'rare /72/ *vt* to tell the story of, recount

narra'tivo, -a *ag* narrative ▷ *sf* (*branca*) fiction

na'sale *ag* nasal

'nascere ['naʃʃere] /67/ *vi* (*bambino*) to be born; (*pianta*) to come o spring up; (*fiume*) to rise, have its source; (*sole*) to rise; (*dente*) to come through; (*fig: derivare, conseguire*): **~ da** to arise from, be born out of; **è nata nel 1952** she was born in 1952; **'nascita** *sf* birth

nas'condere /68/ *vt* to hide, conceal; **nascondersi** *vpr* to hide; **nascon'diglio** *sm* hiding place; **nascon'dino** *sm* (*gioco*) hide-and-seek; **nas'cosi** *ecc vb vedi* **nascondere**; **nas'costo, -a** *pp di* **nascondere** ▷ *ag* hidden; **di nascosto** secretly

na'sello *sm* (Zool) hake

'naso *sm* nose

'nastro *sm* ribbon; (*magnetico, isolante: Sport*) tape; **~ adesivo** adhesive tape; **~ trasportatore** conveyor belt

nas'turzio [nas'turtsjo] *sm* nasturtium

na'tale *ag* of one's birth ▷ *sm* (Rel): **N~** Christmas; (*giorno della nascita*) birthday; **nata'lizio, -a** *ag* (*del Natale*) Christmas *cpd*

'natica, -che *sf* (Anat) buttock

'nato, -a *pp di* **nascere** ▷ *ag*: **un attore ~** a born actor; **nata Pieri** née Pieri

na'tura *sf* nature; **pagare in ~** to pay in kind; **~ morta** still life

natu'rale *ag* natural

natural'mente *av* naturally; (*certamente, sì*) of course

natu'rista, -i, -e *ag, sm/f* naturist, nudist

naufra'gare /80/ *vi* (*nave*) to be wrecked; (*persona*) to be shipwrecked; (*fig*) to fall through; **'naufrago, -ghi** *sm* castaway, shipwreck victim

'nausea *sf* nausea; **nause'ante** *ag* (*odore*) nauseating; (*sapore*) disgusting; (*fig*) sickening

'nautico, -a, -ci, -che *ag* nautical

na'vale *ag* naval

na'vata *sf* (*anche:* **~ centrale**) nave; (*anche:* **~ laterale**) aisle

'nave *sf* ship, vessel; **~ cisterna** tanker; **~ da guerra** warship; **~ passeggeri** passenger ship

na'vetta *sf* shuttle; (*servizio di collegamento*) shuttle (service)

navi'cella [navi'tʃɛlla] *sf* (*di aerostato*) gondola; **~ spaziale** spaceship

navi'gare /80/ *vi* to sail; **~ in Internet** to surf the Net; **naviga'tore** *sm*: **navigatore satellitare** satnav; **navigazi'one** *sf* navigation

nazio'nale [nattsjo'nale] *ag* national ▷ *sf* (*Sport*) national team; **nazionalità** *sf inv* nationality

nazi'one [nat'tsjone] *sf* nation

naziskin ['nɑːtsiskin] *sm inv* Nazi skinhead

NB *abbr* (= nota bene) NB

○ **PAROLA CHIAVE**

ne *pron* 1 (*di lui, lei, loro*) of him/her/them; about him/her/them; **ne riconosco la voce** I recognize his (*o* her) voice

2 (*di questa, quella cosa*) of it; about it; **ne voglio ancora** I want some more (of it *o* them); **non parliamone più!** let's not talk about it any more!

3 (*con valore partitivo*): **hai dei libri? — sì, ne ho** have you any books? — yes, I have (some); **hai del pane? — no, non ne ho** have you any bread? — no, I haven't any; **quanti anni hai? — ne ho 17** how old are you? — I'm 17

▷ *av* (*moto da luogo, da lì*) from there; **ne vengo ora** I've just come from there

né *cong*: **né ... né** neither ... nor; **né l'uno né l'altro lo vuole** neither of them wants it; **non parla né l'italiano né il tedesco** he speaks neither Italian nor German, he doesn't speak either Italian or German; **non piove né nevica** it isn't raining or snowing

ne'anche [ne'anke] *av, cong* not even; **non ... ~** not even; **~ se volesse potrebbe venire** he couldn't come even if he wanted to; **non l'ho visto — neanch'io** I didn't see him — neither did I o I didn't either; **~ per idea** o **sogno!** not on your life!

'nebbia *sf* fog; (*foschia*) mist

necessaria'mente *av* necessarily

neces'sario, -a [netʃes'sarjo] *ag* necessary

necessità [netʃessi'ta] *sf inv* necessity; (*povertà*) need, poverty

necro'logio [nekro'lɔdʒo] *sm* obituary notice

ne'gare /80/ *vt* to deny; (*rifiutare*) to deny, refuse; **~ di aver fatto/che** to deny having done/that; **nega'tivo, -a** *ag, sf, sm* negative

negherò *ecc* [nege'rɔ] *vb vedi* **negare**

negli'gente [negli'dʒɛnte] *ag* negligent, careless

negozi'ante [negot'tsjante] *smf* trader, dealer; (*bottegaio*) shopkeeper (BRIT), storekeeper (US)

negozi'are [negot'tsjare] /19/ *vt* to negotiate ▷ *vi*: **~ in** to trade o deal in; **negozi'ato** *sm* negotiation

ne'gozio [ne'gɔttsjo] *sm* (*locale*) shop (BRIT), store (US)

'negro, -a *ag, sm/f* Negro

ne'mico, -a, -ci, -che *ag* hostile; (*Mil*) enemy *cpd* ▷ *sm/f* enemy; **essere ~ di** to be strongly averse o opposed to

nem'meno *av, cong* = **neanche**

'neo *sm* mole; (*fig*) (slight) flaw

'neon *sm* (*Chim*) neon

neo'nato, -a *ag* newborn ▷ *sm/f* newborn baby

neozelan'dese [neoddzelan'dese] *ag* New Zealand *cpd* ▷ *smf* New Zealander

Ne'pal *sm*: **il ~** Nepal

nep'pure *av, cong* = **neanche**

'nero, -a *ag* black; (*scuro*) dark ▷ *sm* black; **il Mar N~** the Black Sea

'nervo *sm* (*Anat*) nerve; (*Bot*) vein; **avere i nervi** to be on edge; **dare sui nervi a qn** to get on sb's nerves; **ner'voso, -a** *ag* nervous; (*irritabile*) irritable ▷ *sm* (*fam*) **far venire il nervoso a qn** to get on sb's nerves

'nespola *sf* (*Bot*) medlar; (*fig*) blow, punch

'nesso *sm* connection, link

PAROLA CHIAVE

nes'suno, -a (*det: dav sm* **nessun** + C, V, **nessuno** + *s impura, gn, pn, ps, x, z*; *dav sf* **nessuna** + C, **nessun'** +V) *det* **1** (*non uno*) no; (: *espressione negativa*) + any; **non c'è nessun libro** there isn't any book, there is no book; **nessun altro** no one else, nobody else; **nessun'altra cosa** nothing else; **in nessun luogo** nowhere
2 (*qualche*) any; **hai nessuna obiezione?** do you have any objections?
▷ *pron* **1** (*non uno*) no one, nobody; (*espressione negativa*) + any(one); **nessuno è venuto, non è venuto nessuno** nobody came
2 (*cosa: espressione negativa*) none; (: *espressione negativa*) + any
3 (*qualcuno*) anyone, anybody; **ha telefonato nessuno?** did anyone phone?

net'tare *vt* to clean

net'tezza [net'tettsa] *sf* cleanness, cleanliness; **~ urbana** cleansing department

'netto, -a *ag* (*pulito*) clean; (*chiaro*) clear, clear-cut; (*deciso*) definite; (*Econ*) net

nettur'bino *sm* dustman (BRIT), garbage collector (US)

neu'trale *ag* neutral

'neutro, -a *ag* neutral; (*Ling*) neuter ▷ *sm* (*Ling*) neuter

'neve *sf* snow; **nevi'care** /20/ *vb impers* to snow; **nevi'cata** *sf* snowfall

ne'vischio [ne'viskjo] *sm* sleet

ne'voso, -a *ag* snowy; snow-covered

nevral'gia [nevral'dʒia] *sf* neuralgia

nevras'tenico, -a, -ci, -che *ag* (*Med*) neurasthenic; (*fig*) hot-tempered

ne'vrosi *sf inv* neurosis

ne'vrotico, -a, -ci, -che *ag, sm/f* (*anche fig*) neurotic

'nicchia ['nikkja] *sf* niche; (*naturale*) cavity, hollow; **~ di mercato** (*Comm*) niche market

nicchi'are [nik'kjare] /19/ *vi* to shilly-shally, hesitate

'nichel ['nikel] *sm* nickel

nico'tina *sf* nicotine

'nido *sm* nest; **a ~ d'ape** (*tessuto ecc*) honeycomb *cpd*

PAROLA CHIAVE

ni'ente *pron* **1** (*nessuna cosa*) nothing; **niente può fermarlo** nothing can stop him; **niente di niente** absolutely nothing; **grazie! — di niente!** thank you! — not at all!; **nient'altro** nothing else; **nient'altro che** nothing but, just, only; **niente affatto** not at all, not in the least; **come se niente fosse** as if nothing had happened; **cose da niente** trivial matters; **per niente** (*gratis, invano*) for nothing
2 (*qualcosa*) **hai bisogno di niente?** do you need anything?
3: **non ... niente** nothing; (*espressione negativa*) + anything; **non ho visto niente** I saw nothing, I didn't see anything; **non ho niente da dire** I have nothing *o* haven't anything to say
▷ *sm* nothing; **un bel niente** absolutely nothing; **basta un niente per farla piangere** the slightest thing is enough to make her cry
▷ *av* (*in nessuna misura*): **non ... niente** not ... at all; **non è (per) niente buono** it isn't good at all

Ni'geria [ni'dʒɛrja] *sf*: **la ~** Nigeria
'ninfa *sf* nymph
nin'fea *sf* water lily
ninna'nanna *sf* lullaby
'ninnolo *sm* (*gingillo*) knick-knack
ni'pote *smf* (*di zii*) nephew (niece);
(*di nonni*) grandson(-daughter),
grandchild
'nitido, -a *ag* clear; (*specchio*) bright
ni'trire /55/ *vi* to neigh
ni'trito *sm* (*di cavallo*) neighing *no pl*;
neigh; (*Chim*) nitrite
nitroglice'rina [nitroglitʃe'rina] *sf*
nitroglycerine
no *av* (*risposta*) no; **vieni o no?** are
you coming or not?; **perché no?** why
not?; **lo conosciamo? — tu no ma
io sì** do we know him? — you don't
but I do; **verrai, no?** you'll come,
won't you?
'nobile *ag* noble ▷ *smf* noble,
nobleman/woman
'nocca, -che *sf* (*Anat*) knuckle
'noccio *ecc* ['nɔttʃo] *vb vedi* **nuocere**
nocci'ola [not'tʃɔla] *sf* hazelnut ▷ *ag
inv* (*anche*: **color ~**) hazel, light brown
noccio'lina [nottʃo'lina] *sf* (*anche*: **~
americana**) peanut
'nocciolo ['nɔttʃolo] *sm* (*di frutto*)
stone; (*fig*) heart, core
'noce ['notʃe] *sm* (*albero*) walnut
tree ▷ *sf* (*frutto*) walnut; **~ di cocco**
coconut; **~ moscata** nutmeg
no'cevo *ecc* [no'tʃevo] *vb vedi*
nuocere
no'civo, -a [no'tʃivo] *ag* harmful,
noxious
nocqui *ecc vb vedi* **nuocere**
'nodo *sm* (*di cravatta, legname, Naut*)
knot; (*Aut, Ferr*) junction; (*Med, Astr,
Bot*) node; (*fig: legame*) bond, tie;
(: *punto centrale*) heart, crux; **avere
un ~ alla gola** to have a lump in
one's throat
no-'global [no-'global] *smf inv*
anti-globalization protester ▷ *ag
inv* (*movimento, manifestante*) anti-
globalization

'noi *pron* (*soggetto*) we; (*oggetto: per
dare rilievo, con preposizione*) us; **~
stessi(e)** we ourselves; (*oggetto*)
ourselves
'noia *sf* boredom; (*disturbo, impaccio*)
bother *no pl*, trouble *no pl*; **avere
qn/qc a ~** not to like sb/sth; **mi è
venuto a ~** I'm tired of it; **dare ~ a** to
annoy; **avere delle noie con qn** to
have trouble with sb
noi'oso, -a *ag* boring; (*fastidioso*)
annoying, troublesome

> Attenzione! In inglese esiste la
> parola *noisy*, che però significa
> *rumoroso*.

noleggi'are [noled'dʒare] /62/ *vt*
(*prendere a noleggio*) to hire (BRIT),
rent; (*dare a noleggio*) to hire out
(BRIT), rent out; (*aereo, nave*) to
charter; **no'leggio** *sm* hire (BRIT),
rental; charter
'nomade *ag* nomadic ▷ *smf* nomad
'nome *sm* name; (*Ling*) noun; **in
o a ~ di** in the name of; **di o per ~**
(*chiamato*) called, named; **conoscere
qn di ~** to know sb by name; **~
d'arte** stage name; **~ di battesimo**
Christian name; **~ di famiglia**
surname; **~ utente** login
no'mignolo [no'miɲɲolo] *sm*
nickname
'nomina *sf* appointment
nomi'nale *ag* nominal; (*Ling*)
noun *cpd*
nomi'nare /72/ *vt* to name; (*eleggere*)
to appoint; (*citare*) to mention
nomina'tivo, -a *ag* (*intestato*)
registered; (*Ling*) nominative ▷ *sm*
(*Amm*) name; (*Ling*) nominative
non *av* not ▷ *prefisso* non-; **grazie —
non c'è di che** thank you — don't
mention it; *vedi anche* **affatto,
appena** *ecc*
nonché [non'ke] *cong* (*tanto più,
tanto meno*) let alone; (*e inoltre*) as
well as
noncu'rante *ag*: **~ (di)** careless (of),
indifferent (to)

'nonno, -a *sm/f* grandfather/
mother; (*in senso più familiare*)
grandma/grandpa; **nonni** *smpl*
grandparents

non'nulla *sm inv*: **un ~** nothing,
a trifle

'nono, -a *num* ninth

nonos'tante *prep* in spite of,
notwithstanding ▷ *cong* although,
even though

nontiscordardimé *sm inv* (*Bot*)
forget-me-not

nord *sm* north ▷ *ag inv* north;
northern; **il Mare del N~** the
North Sea; **nor'dest** *sm* north-east;
nor'dovest *sm* north-west

'norma *sf* (*principio*) norm; (*regola*)
regulation, rule; (*consuetudine*)
custom, rule; **a ~ di legge** according
to law, as laid down by law; **norme
di sicurezza** safety regulations;
norme per l'uso instructions
for use

nor'male *ag* normal; standard *cpd*

normal'mente *av* normally

norve'gese [norve'dʒese] *ag, sm/f,
sm* Norwegian

Nor'vegia *sf*: **la ~** Norway

nostal'gia [nostal'dʒia] *sf* (*di casa,
paese*) homesickness; (*del passato*)
nostalgia

nos'trano, -a *ag* local; national;
(*pianta, frutta*) home-produced

'nostro, -a *det*: **il (la) ~(a)** *ecc* our
▷ *pron*: **il (la) ~(a)** *ecc* ours ▷ *sm*: **il ~**
our money; our belongings; **i nostri**
our family; our own people; **è dei
nostri** he's one of us

'nota *sf* (*segno*) mark; (*comunicazione
scritta*: *Mus*) note; (*fattura*) bill;
(*elenco*) list; **degno di ~** noteworthy,
worthy of note

no'taio *sm* notary

no'tare /72/ *vt* (*segnare*: *errori*) to
mark; (*registrare*) to note (down),
write down; (*rilevare, osservare*)
to note, notice; **farsi ~** to get o.s.
noticed

no'tevole *ag* (*talento*) notable,
remarkable; (*peso*) considerable

no'tifica, -che *sf* notification

no'tizia [no'tittsja] *sf* (*piece of*)
news *sg*; (*informazione*) piece of
information; **notizi'ario** *sm* (*Radio,
TV, Stampa*) news *sg*

'noto, -a *ag* (well-)known

notorietà *sf* fame; notoriety

no'torio, -a *ag* well-known; (*peg*)
notorious

not'tambulo, -a *sm/f* night-bird (*fig*)

not'tata *sf* night

'notte *sf* night; **di ~** at night; (*durante
la notte*) in the night, during the
night; **~ bianca** sleepless night

not'turno, -a *ag* nocturnal; (*servizio,
guardiano*) night *cpd*

no'vanta *num* ninety; **novan'tesimo,
-a** *num* ninetieth

'nove *num* nine

nove'cento [nove'tʃɛnto] *num* nine
hundred ▷ *sm*: **il N~** the twentieth
century

no'vella *sf* (*Letteratura*) short story

no'vello, -a *ag* (*piante, patate*) new;
(*insalata, verdura*) early; (*sposo*)
newly-married

no'vembre *sm* November

novità *sf inv* novelty; (*innovazione*)
innovation; (*cosa originale, insolita*)
something new; (*notizia*) (piece of)
news *sg*; **le ~ della moda** the latest
fashions

nozi'one [not'tsjone] *sf* notion, idea

'nozze ['nɔttse] *sfpl* wedding *sg*,
marriage *sg*; **~ d'argento/d'oro**
silver/golden wedding *sg*

'nubile *ag* (*donna*) unmarried, single

'nuca, -che *sf* nape of the neck

nucle'are *ag* nuclear

'nucleo *sm* nucleus; (*gruppo*) team,
unit, group; (*Mil, Polizia*) squad; **il ~
familiare** the family unit

nu'dista, -i, -e *smf* nudist

'nudo, -a *ag* (*persona*) bare, naked,
nude; (*membra*) bare, naked;
(*montagna*) bare ▷ *sm* (*Arte*) nude

'nulla *pron, av* = **niente** ▷ *sm*: **il ~**
nothing
nullità *sf inv* nullity; (*persona*)
nonentity
'nullo, -a *ag* useless, worthless; (*Dir*)
null (and void); (*Sport*): **incontro
~** draw
nume'rale *ag, sm* numeral
nume'rare /72/ *vt* to number
nu'merico, -a, -ci, -che *ag*
numerical
'numero *sm* number; (*romano,
arabo*) numeral; (*di spettacolo*) act,
turn; **~ civico** house number; **~ di
scarpe** shoe size; **~ di telefono**
telephone number; **nume'roso, -a**
ag numerous, many; (*folla, famiglia*)
large
nu'occio *ecc* ['nwɔttʃo] *vb vedi*
nuocere
nu'ocere ['nwɔtʃere] /69/ *vi*: **~ a** to
harm, damage
nu'ora *sf* daughter-in-law
nuo'tare /72/ *vi* to swim; (*galleggiare:
oggetti*) to float; **nuota'tore, -'trice**
sm/f swimmer; **nu'oto** *sm* swimming
nu'ova *sf vedi* **nuovo**
nuova'mente *av* again
Nu'ova Ze'landa [-dze'landa] *sf*: **la
~** New Zealand
nu'ovo, -a *ag* new ▷ *sf* (*notizia*)
(piece of) news *sg*: **di ~** again; **~
fiammante** *o* **di zecca** brand-new
nutri'ente *ag* nutritious, nourishing
nutri'mento *sm* food, nourishment
nu'trire /45/ *vt* to feed; (*fig:
sentimenti*) to harbour, harbor
(*us*), nurse; **nutrirsi** *vpr*: **nutrirsi di**
to feed on, to eat
'nuvolo, -a *ag* cloudy ▷ *sf* cloud;
nuvo'loso, -a *ag* cloudy
nuzi'ale [nut'tsjale] *ag* nuptial;
wedding *cpd*
'nylon ['nailən] *sm* nylon

o *cong* (*dav V spesso* **od**) or; **o ... o**
either ... or; **o l'uno o l'altro** either
(of them)
O. *abbr* (= *ovest*) W
'oasi *sf inv* oasis
obbedi'ente *ecc vedi* **ubbidiente** *ecc*
obbli'gare /80/ *vt* (*Dir*) to bind;
(*costringere*): **~ qn a fare** to force *o*
oblige sb to do; **obbliga'torio, -a** *ag*
compulsory, obligatory; **'obbligo,
-ghi** *sm* obligation; (*dovere*) duty;
avere l'obbligo di fare to be obliged
to do; **essere d'obbligo** (*discorso,
applauso*) to be called for
o'beso, -a *ag* obese
obiet'tare /72/ *vt*: **~ che** to object
that; **~ su qc** to object to sth, raise
objections concerning sth
obiet'tivo, -a *ag* objective ▷ *sm*
(*Ottica, Fot*) lens *sg*, objective; (*Mil,
fig*) objective
obiet'tore *sm* objector; **~ di
coscienza** conscientious objector

obiezi'one [objet'tsjone] *sf*
objection

obi'torio *sm* morgue

o'bliquo, -a *ag* oblique; *(inclinato)*
slanting; *(fig)* devious, underhand

oblite'rare /72/ *vt (francobollo)* to
cancel; *(biglietto)* to stamp

oblò *sm inv* porthole

'oboe *sm (Mus)* oboe

'oca *(pl* **oche)** *sf* goose

occasi'one *sf (caso favorevole)*
opportunity; *(causa, motivo,
circostanza)* occasion; *(Comm)*
bargain; **d'~** *(a buon prezzo)* bargain
cpd; *(usato)* secondhand

occhi'aia [ok'kjaja] *sf* eye socket;
avere le occhiaie to have shadows
under one's eyes

occhi'ali [ok'kjali] *smpl* glasses,
spectacles; **~ da sole/da vista**
sunglasses/(prescription) glasses

occhi'ata [ok'kjata] *sf* look, glance;
dare un'~ a to have a look at

occhi'ello [ok'kjɛllo] *sm* buttonhole;
(asola) eyelet

'occhio ['ɔkkjo] *sm* eye; **~!** careful!,
watch out!; **a ~ nudo** with the naked
eye; **a quattr'occhi** privately, tête-à-
tête; **dare all'~** *o* **nell'~** to catch
sb's eye; **fare l'~ a qc** to get used to
sth; **tenere d'~ qn** to keep an eye on
sb; **vedere di buon/mal ~ qc** to look
favourably/unfavourably on sth

occhio'lino [okkjo'lino] *sm*: **fare l'~
a qn** to wink at sb

occiden'tale [ottʃiden'tale] *ag*
western ▷ *smf* Westerner

occi'dente [ottʃi'dɛnte] *sm* west;
(Pol): **l'O~** the West; **a ~** in the west

occor'rente *ag* necessary ▷ *sm* all
that is necessary

occor'renza [okkor'rɛntsa] *sf*
necessity, need; **all'~** in case of need

oc'correre /28/ *vi* to be needed, be
required ▷ *vb impers*: **occorre farlo** it
must be done; **occorre che tu parta**
you must leave, you'll have to leave;
mi occorrono i soldi I need the money

Attenzione! In inglese esiste il
verbo *to occur*, che però significa
succedere.

oc'culto, -a *ag* hidden, concealed;
(scienze, forze) occult

occu'pare /72/ *vt* to occupy;
(manodopera) to employ; *(ingombrare)*
to occupy, take up; **occuparsi**
vpr to occupy o.s., keep o.s. busy;
(impiegarsi) to get a job; **occuparsi
di** *(interessarsi)* to take an interest
in; *(prendersi cura di)* to look after,
take care of; **occu'pato, -a** *ag (Mil,
Pol)* occupied; *(persona: affaccendato)*
busy; *(posto, sedia)* taken; *(toilette,
Tel)* engaged; **la linea è occupata**
the line's engaged; **occupazi'one**
sf occupation; *(impiego, lavoro)* job;
(Econ) employment

o'ceano *sm* ocean

'ocra *sf* ochre

'OCSE *sigla f* (= *Organizzazione per la
Cooperazione e lo Sviluppo Economico)*
OECD

ocu'lare *ag* ocular, eye *cpd*;
testimone ~ eye witness

ocu'lato, -a *ag (attento)* cautious,
prudent; *(accorto)* shrewd

ocu'lista, -i, -e *smf* eye specialist,
oculist

odi'are /19/ *vt* to hate, detest

odi'erno, -a *ag* today's, of today;
(attuale) present

'odio *sm* hatred; **avere in ~ qc/qn** to
hate *o* detest sth/sb; **odi'oso, -a** *ag*
hateful, odious

'odo *ecc vb vedi* **udire**

odo'rare /72/ *vt (annusare)* to smell;
(profumare) to perfume, scent ▷ *vi*:
~ (di) to smell (of)

o'dore *sm* smell; **gli odori** *(Cuc)*
(aromatic) herbs

offendere /36/ *vt* to offend; *(violare)*
to break, violate; *(insultare)* to insult;
(ferire) to hurt; **offendersi** *vpr (con
senso reciproco)* to insult one another;
(risentirsi): **offendersi (di)** to take
offence (at), be offended (by)

offe'rente *sm (in aste)*: **al migliore ~** to the highest bidder

of'ferto, -a *pp di* **offrire** ▷ *sf* offer; *(donazione: anche Rel)* offering; *(in gara d'appalto)* tender; *(in aste)* bid; *(Econ)* supply; **fare un'offerta** to make an offer; *(per appalto)* to tender; *(ad un'asta)* to bid; **"offerte d'impiego"** "situations vacant"; **offerta speciale** special offer

of'feso, -a *pp di* **offendere** ▷ *ag* offended; *(fisicamente)* hurt, injured ▷ *sm/f* offended party ▷ *sf* insult, affront; *(Mil)* attack; *(Dir)* offence

offi'cina [offi'tʃina] *sf* workshop

of'frire /70/ *vt* to offer; **offrirsi** *vpr (proporsi)* to offer (o.s.), volunteer; *(occasione)* to present itself; *(esporsi)*: **offrirsi a** to expose o.s. to; **ti offro da bere** I'll buy you a drink

offus'care /20/ *vt* to obscure, darken; *(fig: intelletto)* to dim, cloud; *(: fama)* to obscure, overshadow; **offuscarsi** *vpr* to grow dark; to cloud, grow dim; to be obscured

ogget'tivo, -a [oddʒet'tivo] *ag* objective

og'getto [od'dʒetto] *sm* object; *(materia, argomento)* subject (matter); **oggetti smarriti** lost property *sg*

'oggi ['ɔddʒi] *av, sm* today; **~ a otto** a week today; **oggigi'orno** *av* nowadays

OGM [ɔdʒi'ɛmme] *sigla mpl* (= *organismi geneticamente modificati*) GMO

'ogni ['oɲɲi] *det* every, each; *(tutti)* all; *(con valore distributivo)* every; **~ uomo è mortale** all men are mortal; **viene ~ due giorni** he comes every two days; **~ cosa** everything; **ad ~ costo** at all costs, at any price; **in ~ luogo** everywhere; **~ tanto** every so often; **~ volta che** every time that

Ognis'santi [oɲɲis'santi] *sm* All Saints' Day

o'gnuno [oɲ'ɲuno] *pron* everyone, everybody

O'landa *sf*: **l'~** Holland; **olan'dese** *ag* Dutch ▷ *sm (Ling)* Dutch ▷ *smf* Dutchman/woman; **gli Olandesi** the Dutch

ole'andro *sm* oleander

oleo'dotto *sm* oil pipeline

ole'oso, -a *ag* oily; *(che contiene olio)* oil-yielding

ol'fatto *sm* sense of smell

oli'are /19/ *vt* to oil

oli'era *sf* oil cruet

Olim'piadi *sfpl* Olympic Games; **o'limpico, -a, -ci, -che** *ag* Olympic

'olio *sm* oil; **sott'~** *(Cuc)* in oil; **~ di fegato di merluzzo** cod liver oil; **~ d'oliva** olive oil; **~ di semi** vegetable oil; **oli essenziali** essential oils

o'liva *sf* olive; **o'livo** *sm* olive tree

'olmo *sm* elm

OLP *sigla f* (= *Organizzazione per la Liberazione della Palestina*) PLO

ol'traggio [ol'traddʒo] *sm* outrage; offence , insult; *(Dir)*: **~ a pubblico ufficiale** insulting a public official; *(Dir)*: **~ al pudore** indecent behaviour (BRIT) o behavior (US)

ol'tranza [ol'trantsa] *sf*: **a ~** to the last, to the bitter end

'oltre *av (più in là)* further; *(di più: aspettare)* longer, more ▷ *prep (di là da)* beyond, over, on the other side of; *(più di)* more than, over; *(in aggiunta a)* besides; *(eccetto)*: **~ a** except, apart from; **oltrepas'sare** /72/ *vt* to go beyond, exceed

o'maggio [o'maddʒo] *sm (dono)* gift; *(segno di rispetto)* homage, tribute; **omaggi** *smpl (complimenti)* respects; **in ~** *(copia, biglietto)* complimentary; **rendere ~ a** to pay homage o tribute to

ombe'lico, -chi *sm* navel

'ombra *sf (zona non assolata, fantasma)* shade; *(sagoma scura)* shadow; **sedere all'~** to sit in the shade; **restare nell'~** *(fig)* to remain in obscurity

om'brello sm umbrella; **ombrel'lone** sm beach umbrella

om'bretto sm eyeshadow

O.M.C. sigla f (= Organizzazione Mondiale del Commercio) WTO

ome'lette [ɔmə'lɛt] sf inv omelet(te)

ome'lia sf (Rel) homily, sermon

omeopa'tia sf hom(o)eopathy

omertà sf conspiracy of silence

o'mettere /63/ vt to omit, leave out; **~ di fare** to omit o fail to do

omi'cida, -i, -e [omi'tʃida] ag homicidal, murderous ▷ smf murderer/murderess

omi'cidio [omi'tʃidjo] sm murder; **~ colposo** culpable homicide

o'misi ecc vb vedi **omettere**

omissi'one sf omission; **~ di soccorso** (Dir) failure to stop and give assistance

omogeneiz'zato [omodʒeneid'dzato] sm baby food

omo'geneo, -a [omo'dʒɛneo] ag homogeneous

o'monimo, -a sm/f namesake ▷ sm (Ling) homonym

omosessu'ale ag, smf homosexual

O.M.S. sigla f = **Organizzazione Mondiale della Sanità**

On. abbr (Pol) = **onorevole**

'onda sf wave; **mettere** o **mandare in ~** (Radio, TV) to broadcast; **andare in ~** (Radio, TV) to go on the air; **onde corte/medie/lunghe** short/medium/long wave sg

'onere sm burden; **oneri fiscali** taxes

onestà sf honesty

o'nesto, -a ag (probo, retto) honest; (giusto) fair; (casto) chaste, virtuous

ONG sigla f inv (= Organizzazione Non Governativa) NGO

onnipo'tente ag omnipotent

ono'mastico, -ci sm name day

ono'rare /72/ vt to honour (BRIT), honor (US); (far onore a) to do credit to

ono'rario, -a ag honorary ▷ sm fee

o'nore sm honour (BRIT), honor (US); **in ~ di** in honour of; **fare gli onori di casa** to play host (o hostess); **fare ~ a** to honour; (pranzo) to do justice to; (famiglia) to be a credit to; **farsi ~** to distinguish o.s.; **ono'revole** ag honourable (BRIT), honorable (US) ▷ smf (Pol) ≈ Member of Parliament (BRIT), ≈ Congressman/woman (US)

on'tano sm (Bot) alder

'O.N.U. sigla f (= Organizzazione delle Nazioni Unite) UN, UNO

o'paco, -a, -chi, -che ag (vetro) opaque; (metallo) dull, matt

o'pale sm o f opal

'opera sf work; (azione rilevante) action, deed, work; (Mus) work; opus; (: melodramma) opera; (: teatro) opera house; (ente) institution, organization; **~ d'arte** work of art; **~ lirica** (grand) opera; **opere pubbliche (OO.PP.)** public works

ope'raio, -a ag working-class; workers' ▷ sm/f worker; **classe operaia** working class

ope'rare /72/ vt to carry out, make; (Med) to operate on ▷ vi to operate, work; (rimedio) to act, work; (Med) to operate; **operarsi** vpr (Med) to have an operation; **operarsi d'appendicite** to have one's appendix out; **operazi'one** sf operation

ope'retta sf (Mus) operetta, light opera

opini'one sf opinion; **l'~ pubblica** public opinion

'oppio sm opium

op'pongo ecc vb vedi **opporre**

op'porre /77/ vt to oppose; **opporsi** vpr: **opporsi (a qc)** to oppose (sth); to object (to sth); **~ resistenza/un rifiuto** to offer resistance/to refuse

opportu'nista, -i, -e smf opportunist

opportunità sf inv opportunity; (convenienza) opportuneness, timeliness

oppor'tuno, -a ag timely, opportune

op'posi ecc vb vedi **opporre**

opposizi'one [oppozit'tsjone] sf
opposition; (*Dir*) objection

op'posto, -a pp di **opporre** ▷ ag
opposite; (*opinioni*) conflicting ▷ sm
opposite, contrary; **all'~** on the
contrary

oppressi'one sf oppression

oppri'mente ag (*caldo, noia*)
oppressive; (*persona*) tiresome;
(*deprimente*) depressing

op'primere /50/ vt (*premere, gravare*)
to weigh down; (*estenuare: caldo*) to
suffocate, oppress; (*tiranneggiare:
popolo*) to oppress

op'pure cong or (else)

op'tare /72/ vi: **~ per** to opt for

o'puscolo sm booklet, pamphlet

opzi'one [op'tsjone] sf option

'ora sf (60 *minuti*) hour; (*momento*)
time; **che ~ è?, che ore sono?** what
time is it?; **non veder l'~ di fare** to
long to do, look forward to doing;
di buon'~ early; **alla buon'~!** at
last!; **~ legale** o **estiva** summer time
(BRIT), daylight saving time (US);
~ di cena dinner time; **~ locale** local
time; **~ di pranzo** lunchtime; **~ di
punta** (*Aut*) rush hour

o'racolo sm oracle

o'rale ag, sm oral

o'rario, -a ag hourly; (*fuso, segnale*)
time cpd; (*velocità*) per hour ▷ sm
timetable, schedule; (*di ufficio, visite
ecc*) hours pl; time(s); **in ~** on time

o'rata sf (*Zool*) sea bream

ora'tore, -'trice sm/f speaker;
orator

'orbita sf (*Astr, Fisica*) orbit; (*Anat*)
(eye-)socket

or'chestra [or'kɛstra] sf orchestra

orchi'dea [orki'dɛa] sf orchid

or'digno [or'diɲɲo] sm: **~ esplosivo**
explosive device

ordi'nale ag, sm ordinal

ordi'nare /72/ vt (*mettere in ordine*) to
arrange, organize; (*Comm*) to order;
(*prescrivere: medicina*) to prescribe;

(*comandare*): **~ a qn di fare qc** to
order o command sb to do sth; (*Rel*)
to ordain

ordi'nario, -a ag (*comune*) ordinary;
everyday; standard; (*grossolano*)
coarse, common ▷ sm ordinary; (*Ins:
di università*) full professor

ordi'nato, -a ag tidy, orderly

ordinazi'one [ordinat'tsjone] sf
(*Comm*) order; (*Rel*) ordination;
eseguire qc su ~ to make sth to
order

'ordine sm order; (*carattere*): **d'~
pratico** of a practical nature;
all'~ (*Comm*) (*assegno*) to order; **di
prim'~** first-class; **fino a nuovo
~** until further notice; **essere in ~**
(*documenti*) to be in order; (*persona,
stanza*) to be tidy; **mettere in ~** to
put in order, tidy (up); **~ del giorno**
(*di seduta*) agenda; (*Mil*) order of
the day; **~ di pagamento** (*Comm*)
order for payment; **l'~ pubblico**
law and order; **ordini (sacri)** (*Rel*)
holy orders

orec'chino [orek'kino] sm earring

o'recchio [o'rekkjo] (*pl f* **orecchie**)
sm (*Anat*) ear

orecchi'oni [orek'kjoni] smpl (*Med*)
mumps sg

o'refice [o'refitʃe] sm goldsmith;
jeweller; **orefice'ria** sf (*arte*)
goldsmith's art; (*negozio*) jeweller's
(shop)

'orfano, -a ag orphan(ed) ▷ sm/f
orphan; **~ di padre/madre**
fatherless/motherless

orga'netto sm barrel organ; (*fam:
armonica a bocca*) mouth organ;
(: *fisarmonica*) accordion

or'ganico, -a, -ci, -che ag organic
▷ sm personnel, staff

organi'gramma, -i sm organization
chart

orga'nismo sm (*Biol*) organism;
(*Anat, Amm*) body, organism

organiz'zare [organid'dzare] /72/
vt to organize; **organizzarsi** vpr to

get organized; **organizzazi'one** *sf* organization

'organo *sm* organ; (*di congegno*) part; (*portavoce*) spokesman/woman, mouthpiece

'orgia, -ge ['ɔrdʒa] *sf* orgy

or'goglio [or'ɡoʎʎo] *sm* pride; **orgogli'oso, -a** *ag* proud

orien'tale *ag* (*paese, regione*) eastern; (*tappeti, lingua, civiltà*) oriental; east

orienta'mento *sm* positioning; orientation; direction; **senso di ~** sense of direction; **perdere l'~** to lose one's bearings; **~ professionale** careers guidance

orien'tare /72/ *vt* (*situare*) to position; **orientarsi** *vpr* to find one's bearings; (*fig: tendere*) to tend, lean; (*indirizzarsi*): **orientarsi verso** to take up, go in for

ori'ente *sm* east; **l'O~** the East, the Orient; **a ~** in the east

o'rigano *sm* oregano

origi'nale [oridʒi'nale] *ag* original; (*bizzarro*) eccentric ▷ *sm* original

origi'nario, -a [oridʒi'narjo] *ag* original; **essere ~ di** to be a native of; (*provenire da*) to originate from; (*animale, pianta*) to be native to

o'rigine [o'ridʒine] *sf* origin; **all'~** originally; **d'~ inglese** of English origin; **dare ~ a** to give rise to

origli'are [oriʎ'ʎare] /27/ *vi*: **~ (a)** to eavesdrop (on)

o'rina *sf* urine

ori'nare /72/ *vi* to urinate ▷ *vt* to pass

orizzon'tale [oriddzon'tale] *ag* horizontal

oriz'zonte [orid'dzonte] *sm* horizon

'orlo *sm* edge, border; (*di recipiente*) rim, brim; (*di vestito ecc*) hem

'orma *sf* (*di persona*) footprint; (*di animale*) track; (*impronta, traccia*) mark, trace

or'mai *av* by now, by this time; (*adesso*) now; (*quasi*) almost, nearly

ormeggi'are [ormed'dʒare] /62/ *vt* (*Naut*) to moor

or'mone *sm* hormone

ornamen'tale *ag* ornamental, decorative

or'nare /72/ *vt* to adorn, decorate; **ornarsi** *vpr*: **ornarsi (di)** to deck o.s. (out) (with)

ornitolo'gia [ornitolo'dʒia] *sf* ornithology

'oro *sm* gold; **d'~, in ~** gold *cpd*; **d'~** (*colore, occasione*) golden; (*persona*) marvellous

oro'logio [oro'lɔdʒo] *sm* clock; (*da tasca, da polso*) watch; **~ da polso** wristwatch; **~ al quarzo** quartz watch

o'roscopo *sm* horoscope

or'rendo, -a *ag* (*spaventoso*) horrible, awful; (*bruttissimo*) hideous

or'ribile *ag* horrible

or'rore *sm* horror; **avere in ~ qn/qc** to loathe *o* detest sb/sth; **mi fanno ~** I loathe *o* detest them

orsacchi'otto [orsak'kjɔtto] *sm* teddy bear

'orso *sm* bear; **~ bruno/bianco** brown/polar bear

or'taggio [or'taddʒo] *sm* vegetable

or'tensia *sf* hydrangea

or'tica, -che *sf* (*stinging*) nettle

orti'caria *sf* nettle rash

'orto *sm* vegetable garden, kitchen garden; (*Agr*) market garden (*BRIT*), truck farm (*US*); **~ botanico** botanical garden(s)

orto'dosso, -a *ag* orthodox

ortogra'fia *sf* spelling

orto'pedico, -a, -ci, -che *ag* orthopaedic ▷ *sm* orthopaedic specialist

orzai'olo [ordza'jɔlo] *sm* (*Med*) stye

'orzo ['ɔrdzo] *sm* barley

o'sare /72/ *vt, vi* to dare; **~ fare** to dare (to) do

oscenità [oʃʃeni'ta] *sf inv* obscenity

o'sceno, -a [oʃʃɛno] *ag* obscene; (*ripugnante*) ghastly

oscil'lare [oʃʃil'lare] /72/ *vi* (*pendolo*) to swing; (*dondolare: al vento ecc*) to rock; (*variare*) to fluctuate; (*Tecn*) to oscillate; (*fig*): **~ fra** to waver o hesitate between

oscu'rare /72/ *vt* to darken, obscure; (*fig*) to obscure; **oscurarsi** *vpr* (*cielo*) to darken, cloud over; (*persona*): **si oscurò in volto** his face clouded over

oscurità *sf* (*vedi ag*) darkness; obscurity

os'curo, -a *ag* dark; (*fig*) obscure; (*vita, natali*) humble, lowly ▷ *sm*: **all'~** in the dark; **tenere qn all'~ di qc** to keep sb in the dark about sth

ospe'dale *sm* hospital

ospi'tale *ag* hospitable

ospi'tare /72/ *vt* to give hospitality to; (*albergo*) to accommodate

'ospite *smf* (*persona che ospita*) host/hostess; (*persona ospitata*) guest

os'pizio [os'pittsjo] *sm* (*per vecchi ecc*) home

osser'vare /72/ *vt* to observe, watch; (*esaminare*) to examine; (*notare, rilevare*) to notice, observe; (*Dir: la legge*) to observe, respect; (*mantenere: silenzio*) to keep, observe; **far ~ qc a qn** to point sth out to sb; **osservazi'one** *sf* observation; (*di legge ecc*) observance; (*considerazione critica*) observation, remark; (*rimprovero*) reproof; **in osservazione** under observation

ossessio'nare /72/ *vt* to obsess, haunt; (*tormentare*) to torment, harass

ossessi'one *sf* obsession

os'sia *cong* that is, to be precise

'ossido *sm* oxide; **~ di carbonio** carbon monoxide

ossige'nare [ossidʒe'nare] /72/ *vt* to oxygenate; (*decolorare*) to bleach; **acqua ossigenata** hydrogen peroxide

os'sigeno *sm* oxygen

'osso (*pl f* **ossa**) *sm* (*Anat*) bone; **d'~** (*bottone ecc*) of bone, bone *cpd*; **~ di seppia** cuttlebone

ostaco'lare /72/ *vt* to block, obstruct

os'tacolo *sm* obstacle; (*Equitazione*) hurdie, jump

os'taggio [os'taddʒo] *sm* hostage

os'tello *sm* hostel; **~ della gioventù** youth hostel

osten'tare /72/ *vt* to make a show of, flaunt

oste'ria *sf* inn

os'tetrico, -a, -ci, -che *ag* obstetric ▷ *sm* obstetrician

'ostia *sf* (*Rel*) host; (*per medicinali*) wafer

'ostico, -a, -ci, -che *ag* (*fig*) harsh; difficult, tough; unpleasant

os'tile *ag* hostile

osti'narsi /72/ *vpr* to insist, dig one's heels in; **~ a fare** to persist (obstinately) in doing; **osti'nato, -a** *ag* (*caparbio*) obstinate; (*tenace*) persistent, determined

'ostrica, -che *sf* oyster

> Attenzione! In inglese esiste la parola *ostrich*, che però significa *struzzo*.

ostru'ire /55/ *vt* to obstruct, block

o'tite *sf* ear infection

ot'tanta *num* eighty

ot'tavo, -a *num* eighth

otte'nere /121/ *vt* to obtain, get; (*risultato*) to achieve, obtain

'ottico, -a, -ci, -che *ag* (*della vista: nervo*) optic; (*dell'ottica*) optical ▷ *sm* optician ▷ *sf* (*scienza*) optics *sg*; (*Fot: lenti, prismi ecc*) optics *pl*

ottima'mente *av* excellently, very well

otti'mismo *sm* optimism; **otti'mista, -i, -e** *smf* optimist

'ottimo, -a *ag* excellent, very good

'otto *num* eight

ot'tobre *sm* October

otto'cento [otto'tʃɛnto] *num* eight hundred ▷ *sm*: **l'O~** the nineteenth century

ot'tone *sm* brass; **gli ottoni** (*Mus*) the brass

ottu'rare /72/ *vt* to close (up); (*dente*) to fill; **otturarsi** *vpr* to become o get

blocked up; **otturazi'one** *sf* closing
(up); (*dentaria*) filling
ot'tuso, -a *ag* (*Mat*, *fig*) obtuse;
(*suono*) dull
o'vaia *sf* (*Anat*) ovary
o'vale *ag*, *sm* oval
o'vatta *sf* cotton wool; (*per imbottire*)
padding, wadding
'ovest *sm* west
o'vile *sm* pen, enclosure
ovulazi'one [ovulat'tsjone] *sf*
ovulation
'ovulo *sm* (*Fisiol*) ovum
o'vunque *av* = **dovunque**
ovvi'are /19/ *vi*: **~ a** to obviate
'ovvio, -a *ag* obvious
ozi'are [ot'tsjare] /19/ *vi* to laze
around, idle
'ozio ['ɔttsjo] *sm* idleness; (*tempo
libero*) leisure; **ore d'~** leisure time;
stare in ~ to be idle
o'zono [od'dzɔno] *sm* ozone

P *abbr* (= *parcheggio*) P; (*Aut*)
(= *principiante*) L
p. *abbr* (= *pagina*) p
pac'chetto [pak'ketto] *sm* packet;
~ azionario (*Finanza*) shareholding
'pacco, -chi *sm* parcel; (*involto*)
bundle; **~ postale** parcel
'pace ['patʃe] *sf* peace; **darsi ~** to
resign o.s.; **fare (la) ~ con qn** to
make it up with sb
pa'cifico, -a, -ci, -che [pa'tʃifiko]
ag (*persona*) peaceable; (*vita*)
peaceful; (*fig*: *indiscusso*)
indisputable; (: *ovvio*) obvious, clear
▷ *sm*: **il P~, l'Oceano P~** the Pacific
(Ocean)
paci'fista, -i, -e [patʃi'fista] *smf*
pacifist
pa'della *sf* frying pan; (*per infermi*)
bedpan
padigli'one [padiʎ'ʎone] *sm*
pavilion
'Padova *sf* Padua

'padre sm father
pa'drino sm godfather
padro'nanza [padro'nantsa] sf command, mastery
pa'drone, -a sm/f master/mistress; (proprietario) owner; (datore di lavoro) employer; **essere ~ di sé** to be in control of o.s.; **~/padrona di casa** master/mistress of the house; (per gli inquilini) landlord/lady
pae'saggio [pae'zaddʒo] sm landscape
pa'ese sm (nazione) country, nation; (terra) country, land; (villaggio) village; **~ di provenienza** country of origin; **i Paesi Bassi** the Netherlands
'paga, -ghe sf pay, wages pl
paga'mento sm payment
pa'gare /80/ vt to pay; (acquisto, fig, colpa) to pay for; (contraccambiare) to repay, pay back ▷ vi to pay; **quanto l'ha pagato?** how much did you pay for it?; **~ con carta di credito** to pay by credit card; **~ in contanti** to pay cash
pa'gella [pa'dʒella] sf (Ins) report card
paghe'rò [page'rɔ] sm inv acknowledgement of a debt, IOU
'pagina ['padʒina] sf page; **Pagine bianche** phone book, telephone directory; **Pagine Gialle®** Yellow Pages®
'paglia ['paʎʎa] sf straw
pagli'accio [paʎ'ʎattʃo] sm clown
pagli'etta [paʎ'ʎetta] sf (cappello per uomo) (straw) boater; (per tegami ecc) steel wool
pa'gnotta [paɲ'ɲɔtta] sf round loaf
'Pakistan sm: **il ~** Pakistan
'pala sf shovel; (di remo, ventilatore, elica) blade; (di ruota) paddle
pa'lato sm palate
pa'lazzo [pa'lattso] sm (reggia) palace; (edificio) building; **~ di giustizia** courthouse; **~ dello sport** sports stadium

'palco, -chi sm (Teat) box; (tavolato) platform, stand; (ripiano) layer
palco'scenico, -ci [palkoʃ'ʃɛniko] sm (Teat) stage
pa'lese ag clear, evident
Pales'tina sf: **la ~** Palestine
palesti'nese ag, smf Palestinian
pa'lestra sf gymnasium; (esercizio atletico) exercise, training; (fig) training ground, school
pa'letta sf spade; (per il focolare) shovel; (del capostazione) signalling disc
pa'letto sm stake, peg; (spranga) bolt
'palio sm (gara): **il P~** horse race run at Siena; **mettere qc in ~** to offer sth as a prize

---

  ● **PALIO**

  ●
  ● The *Palio* is a horse race which
  ● takes place in a number of Italian
  ● towns, the most famous being
  ● the 'Palio di Siena'. The Tuscan
  ● race dates back to the thirteenth
  ● century; nowadays it is usually
  ● held twice a year, on 2 July and 16
  ● August, in the Piazza del Campo. 10
  ● of the 17 city districts or 'contrade'
  ● take part; the winner is the first
  ● horse to complete the course,
  ● whether or not it still has its
  ● rider. The race is preceded by a
  ● procession of 'contrada' members
  ● in historical dress.

'palla sf ball; (pallottola) bullet; **~ di neve** snowball; **~ ovale** rugby ball; **pallaca'nestro** sf basketball; **pallamano** [palla'mano] sf handball; **pallanu'oto** sf water polo; **palla'volo** sf volleyball
palleggi'are [palled'dʒare] /62/ vi (Calcio) to practise (BRIT) o practice (US) with the ball; (Tennis) to knock up
pallia'tivo sm palliative; (fig) stopgap measure
'pallido, -a ag pale

p

pal'lina *sf* (*bilia*) marble
pallon'cino [pallon'tʃino] *sm* balloon; (*lampioncino*) Chinese lantern
pal'lone *sm* (*palla*) ball; (*Calcio*) football; (*aerostato*) balloon; **gioco del ~** football
pal'lottola *sf* pellet; (*proiettile*) bullet
'palma *sf* (*Anat*); = **palmo**; (*Bot, simbolo*) palm; **~ da datteri** date palm
'palmo *sm* (*Anat*) palm; **restare con un ~ di naso** to be badly disappointed
'palo *sm* (*legno appuntito*) stake; (*sostegno*) pole; **fare da** *o* **il ~** (*fig*) to act as look-out
palom'baro *sm* diver
pal'pare /72/ *vt* to feel, finger
'palpebra *sf* eyelid
pa'lude *sf* marsh, swamp
pancar'rè *sm* sliced bread
pan'cetta [pan'tʃetta] *sf* (*Cuc*) bacon
pan'china [pan'kina] *sf* garden seat; (*di giardino pubblico*) (park) bench
'pancia, -ce ['pantʃa] *sf* belly, stomach; **mettere** *o* **fare ~** to be getting a paunch; **avere mal di ~** to have stomach ache *o* a sore stomach
panci'otto [pan'tʃotto] *sm* waistcoat
'pancreas *sm inv* pancreas
'panda *sm inv* panda
pande'mia *sf* pandemic
'pane *sm* bread; (*pagnotta*) loaf (of bread); (*forma*): **un ~ di burro/cera** *ecc* a pat of butter/bar of wax *etc*; **guadagnarsi il ~** to earn one's living; **~ a cassetta** sliced bread; **~ integrale** wholemeal bread; **~ di Spagna** sponge cake; **~ tostato** toast
panette'ria *sf* (*forno*) bakery; (*negozio*) baker's (shop), bakery
panetti'ere, -a *sm/f* baker
panet'tone *sm a kind of spiced brioche with sultanas (eaten at Christmas)*
pangrat'tato *sm* breadcrumbs *pl*

'panico, -a, -ci, -che *ag, sm* panic
pani'ere *sm* basket
pani'ficio [pani'fitʃo] *sm* (*forno*) bakery; (*negozio*) baker's (shop), bakery
pa'nino *sm* roll; **~ caldo** toasted sandwich; **~ imbottito** filled roll; sandwich
panino'teca, -che *sf* sandwich bar
'panna *sf* (*Cuc*) cream; (*Aut*); = **panne**; **~ da cucina** cooking cream; **~ montata** whipped cream
'panne [pan] *sf inv* (*Aut*): **essere in ~** to have broken down
pan'nello *sm* panel; **~ solare** solar panel
'panno *sm* cloth; **panni** *smpl* (*abiti*) clothes; **mettiti nei miei panni** (*fig*) put yourself in my shoes
pan'nocchia [pan'nɔkkja] *sf* (*di mais ecc*) ear
panno'lino *sm* (*per bambini*) nappy (BRIT), diaper (US)
panno'lone *sm* incontinence pad
pano'rama, -i *sm* panorama
panta'loni *smpl* trousers (BRIT), pants (US), pair *sg* of trousers *o* pants
pan'tano *sm* bog
pan'tera *sf* panther
pan'tofola *sf* slipper
'papa, -i *sm* pope
pa'pà *sm inv* dad(dy)
pa'pavero *sm* poppy
'pappa *sf* baby cereal; **~ reale** royal jelly
pappa'gallo *sm* parrot; (*fig: uomo*) Romeo, wolf
pa'rabola *sf* (*Mat*) parabola; (*Rel*) parable
para'bolico, -a, -ci, -che *ag* (*Mat*) parabolic; *vedi anche* **antenna**
para'brezza [para'breddza] *sm inv* (*Aut*) windscreen (BRIT), windshield (US)
paraca'dute *sm inv* parachute
para'diso *sm* paradise
parados'sale *ag* paradoxical

para'fulmine *sm* lightning conductor

pa'raggi [pa'raddʒi] *smpl*: **nei ~** in the vicinity, in the neighbourhood (BRIT) o neighborhood (US)

parago'nare /72/ *vt*: **~ con/a** to compare with/to

para'gone *sm* comparison; (*esempio analogo*) analogy, parallel; **reggere al ~** to stand comparison

pa'ragrafo *sm* paragraph

pa'ralisi *sf inv* paralysis

paral'lelo, -a *ag* parallel ▷ *sm* (Geo) parallel; (*comparazione*): **fare un ~ tra** to draw a parallel between

para'lume *sm* lampshade

pa'rametro *sm* parameter

para'noia *sf* paranoia; **para'noico, -a, -ci, -che** *ag*, *sm/f* paranoid

para'occhi [para'ɔkki] *smpl* blinkers

paraolim'piadi *sfpl* paralympics

para'petto *sm* parapet

pa'rare /72/ *vt* (*addobbare*) to adorn, deck; (*proteggere*) to shield, protect; (*scansare: colpo*) to parry; (Calcio) to save ▷ *vi*: **dove vuole andare a ~?** what are you driving at?

pa'rata *sf* (Sport) save; (Mil) review, parade

para'urti *sm inv* (Aut) bumper

para'vento *sm* folding screen; **fare da ~ a qn** (*fig*) to shield sb

par'cella [par'tʃɛlla] *sf* account, fee (*of lawyer etc*)

parcheggi'are [parked'dʒare] /62/ *vt* to park; **parcheggia'tore, -'trice** [parkeddʒa'tore] *sm/f* parking attendant

par'cheggio *sm* parking *no pl*; (*luogo*) car park; (*singolo posto*) parking space

par'chimetro [par'kimetro] *sm* parking meter

'parco, -chi *sm* park; (*spazio per deposito*) depot; (*complesso di veicoli*) fleet

par'cometro *sm* (Pay and Display) ticket machine

pa'recchio, -a [pa'rekkjo] *det* quite a lot of; (*tempo*) quite a lot of, a long

pareggi'are [pared'dʒare] /62/ *vt* to make equal; (*terreno*) to level, make level; (*bilancio, conti*) to balance ▷ *vi* (Sport) to draw; **pa'reggio** *sm* (Econ) balance; (Sport) draw

pa'rente *smf* relative, relation
> ▌ Attenzione! In inglese esiste la parola *parent*, che però significa *genitore*.

paren'tela *sf* (*vincolo di sangue, fig*) relationship

pa'rentesi *sf* (*segno grafico*) bracket, parenthesis; (*frase incisa*) parenthesis; (*digressione*) parenthesis, digression

pa'rere /71/ *sm* (*opinione*) opinion; (*consiglio*) advice, opinion; **a mio ~** in my opinion ▷ *vi* to seem, appear ▷ *vb impers*: **pare che** it seems o appears that, they say that; **mi pare che** it seems to me that; **mi pare di sì/no** I think so/don't think so; **fai come ti pare** do as you like; **che ti pare del mio libro?** what do you think of my book?

pa'rete *sf* wall

'pari *ag inv* (*uguale*) equal, same; (*in giochi*) equal, drawn, tied; (Mat) even ▷ *sm inv* (Pol: *di Gran Bretagna*) peer ▷ *smf inv* peer, equal; **copiato ~ ~** copied word for word; **alla ~** on the same level; **ragazza alla ~** au pair (girl); **mettersi alla ~ con** to place o.s. on the same level as; **mettersi in ~ con** to catch up with; **andare di ~ passo con qn** to keep pace with sb

Pa'rigi [pa'ridʒi] *sf* Paris

pari'gino, -a [pari'dʒino] *ag*, *sm/f* Parisian

parità *sf* parity, equality; (Sport) draw, tie

parlamen'tare /72/ *ag* parliamentary ▷ *smf* ≈ Member of Parliament (BRIT), ≈ Congressman/woman (US) ▷ *vi* to negotiate, parley

parla'mento *sm* parliament

⊚ The Italian constitution, which
⊚ came into force on 1 January 1948,
⊚ states that the *Parlamento* has
⊚ legislative power. It is made up
⊚ of two chambers, the 'Camera
⊚ dei deputati' and the 'Senato'.
⊚ Parliamentary elections are held
⊚ every 5 years.

parlan'tina *sf* (*fam*) talkativeness;
avere ~ to have the gift of the gab
par'lare /72/ *vi* to speak, talk;
(*confidare cose segrete*) to talk ▷ *vt* to
speak; **~ (a qn) di** to speak *o* talk (to
sb) about
parmigi'ano, -a [parmi'dʒano] *sm*
(*grana*) Parmesan (cheese)
pa'rola *sf* word; (*facoltà*) speech;
parole *sfpl* (*chiacchiere*) talk *sg*:
chiedere la ~ to ask permission to
speak; **prendere la ~** to take the
floor; **~ d'onore** word of honour; **~
d'ordine** (*Mil*) password; **parole
incrociate** crossword (puzzle)
sg; **paro'laccia, -ce** *sf* bad word,
swearword
parrò *ecc vb vedi* **parere**
par'rocchia [par'rɔkkja] *sf* parish;
(*chiesa*) parish church
par'rucca, -che *sf* wig
parrucchi'ere, -a [parruk'kjɛre]
sm/f hairdresser ▷ *sm* barber
'**parte** *sf* part; (*lato*) side; (*quota
spettante a ciascuno*) share; (*direzione*)
direction; (*Pol*) party; faction;
(*Dir*) party; **a ~** *ag* separate ▷ *av*
separately; **scherzi a ~** joking aside;
a ~ ciò apart from that; **da ~** (*in
disparte*) to one side, aside; **mettere/
prendere da ~** to put/take aside;
d'altra ~ on the other hand; **da ~ di**
(*per conto di*) on behalf of; **da ~ mia**
as far as I'm concerned, as for me;
da ~ a ~ right through; **da nessuna
~** nowhere; **da questa ~** (*in questa
direzione*) this way; **da ogni ~** on all

sides, everywhere; (*moto da luogo*)
from all sides; **prendere ~ a qc** to
take part in sth; **mettere qn a ~ di
qc** to inform sb of sth
parteci'pare [partetʃi'pare] /72/
vi: **~ a** to take part in, participate
in; (*utili ecc*) to share in; (*spese ecc*) to
contribute to; (*dolore, successo di qn*)
to share (in)
parteggi'are [parted'dʒare] /62/
vi: **~ per** to side with, be on the side of
par'tenza [par'tɛntsa] *sf* departure;
(*Sport*) start; **essere in ~** to be about
to leave, be leaving
parti'cipio [parti'tʃipjo] *sm*
participle
partico'lare *ag* (*specifico*) particular;
(*proprio*) personal, private; (*speciale*)
special, particular; (*caratteristico*)
distinctive, characteristic; (*fuori
dal comune*) peculiar ▷ *sm* detail,
particular; **in ~** in particular,
particularly
par'tire /45/ *vi* to go, leave;
(*allontanarsi*) to go (*o* drive *ecc*) away *o*
off; (*petardo, colpo*) to go off; (*fig: avere
inizio, Sport*) to start; **sono partita
da Roma alle 7** I left Rome at 7; **il
volo parte da Ciampino** the flight
leaves from Ciampino; **a ~ da** from
par'tita *sf* (*Comm*) lot, consignment;
(*Econ: registrazione*) entry, item;
(*Carte, Sport: gioco*) game; **~ di
caccia** hunting party; **numero di ~
IVA** VAT registration number
par'tito *sm* (*Pol*) party; (*decisione*)
decision, resolution; (*persona da
maritare*) match
'**parto** *sm* (*Med*) labour (BRIT), labor
(US), delivery, (child)birth
'**parvi** *ecc vb vedi* **parere**
parzi'ale [par'tsjale] *ag* (*limitato*)
partial; (*non obiettivo*) biased, partial
pasco'lare *vt, vi* to graze
'**pascolo** *sm* pasture
'**Pasqua** *sf* Easter
Pasqu'etta *sf* Easter Monday

pas'sabile ag fairly good, passable
pas'saggio [pas'saddʒo] sm passing
no pl, passage; (traversata) crossing
no pl, passage; (luogo, prezzo della
traversata, brano di libro ecc) passage;
(su veicolo altrui) lift (BRIT), ride; (Sport)
pass; **di ~** (persona) passing through; **~
pedonale/a livello** pedestrian/level
(BRIT) o grade (US) crossing
passamon'tagna
[passamon'taɲɲa] sm inv balaclava
pas'sante smf passer-by ▷ sm loop
passa'porto sm passport
pas'sare /72/ vi (andare) to go;
(veicolo, pedone) to pass (by), go by;
(fare una breve sosta: postino ecc) to
come, call; (: amico: per fare una visita)
to call o drop in; (sole, aria, luce) to get
through; (trascorrere: giorni, tempo) to
pass, go by; (: proposta di legge) to
be passed; (: dolore) to pass, go away;
(Carte) to pass ▷ vt (attraversare) to
cross; (trasmettere: messaggio): **~
qc a qn** to pass sth on to sb; (dare):
~ qc a qn to pass sth to sb, give sb
sth; (trascorrere: tempo) to spend;
(superare: esame) to pass; (triturare:
verdura) to strain; (approvare) to pass,
approve; (oltrepassare, sorpassare:
anche fig) to go beyond, pass; (fig:
subire) to go through; **~ da ... a** to
pass from ... to; **~ di padre in figlio**
to be handed down o to pass from
father to son; **~ per** (anche fig) to go
through; **~ per stupido/un genio**
to be taken for a fool/a genius; **~
sopra** (anche fig) to pass over; **~
attraverso** (anche fig) to go through;
~ alla storia to pass into history;
~ a un esame to go up (to the next
class) after an exam; **~ inosservato**
to go unnoticed; **~ di moda** to go
out of fashion; **le passo il Signor X**
(al telefono) here is Mr X; I'm putting
you through to Mr X; **lasciar ~ qn/
qc** to let sb/sth through; : **come
te la passi?** how are you getting
on o along?

passa'tempo sm pastime, hobby
pas'sato, -a ag past; (sfiorito) faded
▷ sm past; (Ling) past (tense); **~
prossimo** (Ling) present perfect; **~
remoto** (Ling) past historic; **~ di
verdura** (Cuc) vegetable purée
passeg'gero, -a [passed'dʒero] ag
passing ▷ sm/f passenger
passeggi'are [passed'dʒare] /62/
vi to go for a walk; (in veicolo) to go
for a drive; **passeggi'ata** sf walk;
drive; (luogo) promenade; **fare una
passeggiata** to go for a walk o
drive); **passeg'gino** [passed'dʒino]
sm pushchair (BRIT), stroller (US)
passe'rella sf footbridge; (di nave,
aereo) gangway; (pedana) catwalk
'passero sm sparrow
passi'one sf passion
pas'sivo, -a ag passive ▷ sm (Ling)
passive; (Econ) debit; (complesso dei
debiti) liabilities pl
'passo sm step; (andatura) pace;
(rumore) (foot)step; (orma) footprint;
(passaggio, fig: brano) passage;
(valico) pass; **a ~ d'uomo** at walking
pace; **~ (a) ~** step by step; **fare due
o quattro passi** to go for a walk o a
stroll; **di questo ~** at this rate; **"~
carraio"** "vehicle entrance — keep
clear"
'pasta sf (Cuc) dough; (: impasto per
dolce) pastry; (anche: **~ alimentare**)
pasta; (massa molle di materia)
paste; (fig: indole) nature; **paste**
sf pl (pasticcini) pastries; **~ in brodo**
noodle soup; **~ sfoglia** puff pastry
o paste (US)
pastasci'utta [pastaʃʃutta] sf pasta
pas'tella sf batter
pas'tello sm pastel
pas'ticca, -che sf = **pastiglia**
pasticce'ria [pastittʃe'ria] sf
(pasticcini) pastries pl, cakes
pl; (negozio) cake shop; (arte)
confectionery
pasticci'ere, -a [pastit'tʃere] sm/f
pastrycook; confectioner

pastic'cino [pastit'tʃino] *sm* petit four

pas'ticcio [pas'tittʃo] *sm* (*Cuc*) pie; (*lavoro disordinato, imbroglio*) mess; **trovarsi nei pasticci** to get into trouble

pas'tiglia [pas'tiʎʎa] *sf* pastille, lozenge

pas'tina *sf* small pasta shapes used in soup

'pasto *sm* meal

pas'tore *sm* shepherd; (*Rel*) pastor, minister; (*anche*: **cane ~**) sheepdog; **~ tedesco** (*Zool*) Alsatian (dog) (*BRIT*) German shepherd (dog)

pa'tata *sf* potato; **patate fritte** chips (*BRIT*), French fries; **pata'tine** *sfpl* (potato) crisps (*BRIT*) o chips (*US*); **patatine fritte** chips

pâté [pa'te] *sm inv* pâté

pa'tente *sf* licence; (*anche*: **~ di guida**) driving licence (*BRIT*), driver's license (*US*); **~ a punti** driving licence with penalty points

> Attenzione! In inglese esiste la parola *patent*, che però significa *brevetto*.

paterni'tà *sf* paternity, fatherhood

pa'tetico, -a, -ci, -che *ag* pathetic; (*commovente*) moving, touching

pa'tibolo *sm* gallows *sg*, scaffold

'patina *sf* (*su rame ecc*) patina; (*sulla lingua*) fur, coating

pa'tire /55/ *vt, vi* to suffer

pa'tito, -a *sm/f* enthusiast, fan, lover

patolo'gia [patolo'dʒia] *sf* pathology

'patria *sf* homeland

pa'trigno [pa'triɲɲo] *sm* stepfather

patri'monio *sm* estate, property; (*fig*) heritage

pa'trono *sm* (*Rel*) patron saint; (*socio di patronato*) patron; (*Dir*) counsel

patteggi'are [patted'dʒare] /62/ *vt, vi* to negotiate; (*Dir*) to plea-bargain

patti'naggio [patti'naddʒo] *sm* skating; **~ a rotelle/sul ghiaccio** roller-/ice-skating

patti'nare /72/ *vi* to skate; **~ sul ghiaccio** to ice-skate; **pattina'tore, -'trice** *sm/f* skater

'pattino *sm* skate; (*di slitta*) runner; (*Aer*) skid; (*Tecn*) sliding block; **pattini (da ghiaccio)** (ice) skates; **pattini in linea** rollerblades®; **pattini a rotelle** roller skates

'patto *sm* (*accordo*) pact, agreement; (*condizione*) term, condition; **a ~ che** on condition that

pat'tuglia [pat'tuʎʎa] *sf* (*Mil*) patrol

pattu'ire /55/ *vt* to reach an agreement on

pattumi'era *sf* (dust)bin (*BRIT*), ashcan (*US*)

pa'ura *sf* fear; **aver ~ di/di fare/che** to be frightened o afraid of/of doing/ that; **far ~ a** to frighten; **per ~ di/ che** for fear of/that; **pau'roso, -a** *ag* (*che fa paura*) frightening; (*che ha paura*) fearful, timorous

'pausa *sf* (*sosta*) break; (*nel parlare, Mus*) pause

pavi'mento *sm* floor

> Attenzione! In inglese esiste la parola *pavement*, che però significa *marciapiede*.

pa'vone *sm* peacock

pazien'tare [pattsjen'tare] /72/ *vi* to be patient

pazi'ente [pat'tsjɛnte] *ag, smf* patient; **pazi'enza** *sf* patience

paz'zesco, -a, -schi, -sche [pat'tsesko] *ag* mad, crazy

paz'zia [pat'tsia] *sf* (*Med*) madness, insanity; (*di azione, decisione*) madness, folly

'pazzo, -a ['pattso] *ag* (*Med*) mad, insane; (*strano*) wild, mad ▷ *sm/f* madman/woman; **~ di** (*gioia, amore ecc*) mad o crazy with; **~ per qc/qn** mad o crazy about sth/sb

PC *sigla m inv* (= *personal computer*) PC; **PC portatile** laptop

pec'care /20/ *vi* to sin; (*fig*) to err

pec'cato *sm* sin; **è un ~ che** it's a pity that; **che ~!** what a shame o pity!

pecche'rò ecc [pekke'rɔ] vb vedi
peccare

'**pece** ['petʃe] sf pitch

Pe'chino [pe'kino] sf Beijing

'**pecora** sf sheep; **peco'rino** sm
sheep's milk cheese

pe'daggio [pe'daddʒo] sm toll

pedago'gia [pedago'dʒia] sf
pedagogy, educational methods pl

peda'lare /72/ vi to pedal; (andare in
bicicletta) to cycle

pe'dale sm pedal

pe'dana sf footboard; (Sport: nel
salto) springboard; (: nella scherma)
piste

pe'dante ag pedantic ▷ smf pedant

pe'data sf (impronta) footprint; (colpo)
kick; **prendere a pedate qn/qc** to
kick sb/sth

pedi'atra, -i, -e smf paediatrician

pedi'cure sm inv, f inv chiropodist

pe'dina sf (della dama) draughtsman
(BRIT), draftsman (US); (fig) pawn

pedi'nare /72/ vt to shadow, tail

pe'dofilo, -a ag, sm/f paedophile

pedo'nale ag pedestrian

pe'done, -a sm/f pedestrian ▷ sm
(Scacchi) pawn

'**peggio** ['peddʒo] av, ag inv worse
▷ sm o f: **il** o **la ~** the worst; **alla ~**
at worst, if the worst comes to the
worst; **peggio'rare** /72/ vt to make
worse, worsen ▷ vi to grow worse,
worsen; **peggi'ore** ag (comparativo)
worse; (superlativo) worst ▷ smf: **il
(la) peggiore** the worst (person)

'**pegno** ['peɲɲo] sm (Dir) security,
pledge; (nei giochi di società) forfeit;
(fig) pledge, token; **dare in ~ qc** to
pawn sth

pe'lare /72/ vt (spennare) to pluck;
(spellare) to skin; (sbucciare) to peel;
(fig) to make pay through the nose

pe'lato, -a ag peeled; **(pomodori)
pelati** peeled tomatoes

'**pelle** sf skin; (di animale) skin, hide;
(cuoio) leather; **avere la ~ d'oca** to
have goose pimples o goose flesh

pellegri'naggio [pellegri'naddʒo]
sm pilgrimage

pelle'rossa (pl **pellerosse**) smf (peg)
Red Indian (pej)

pelli'cano sm pelican

pel'liccia, -ce [pel'littʃa] sf (mantello
di animale) coat, fur; (indumento) fur
coat; **~ ecologica** fake fur

pel'licola sf (membrana sottile) film,
layer; (Fot, Cine) film

'**pelo** sm hair; (pelame) coat, hair;
(pelliccia) fur; (di tappeto) pile; (di
liquido) surface; **per un ~: per
un ~ non ho perduto il treno;** I
very nearly missed the train; **c'è
mancato un ~ che affogasse** he
narrowly escaped drowning; **pe'loso,
-a** ag hairy

'**peltro** sm pewter

pe'luche [pə'lyʃ] sm plush;
giocattoli di ~ soft toys

pe'luria sf down

'**pena** sf (Dir) sentence; (punizione)
punishment; (sofferenza) sadness
no pl, sorrow; (fatica) trouble no pl,
effort; (difficoltà) difficulty; **far ~** to
be pitiful; **mi fai ~** I feel sorry for you;
prendersi o **darsi la ~ di fare** to go
to the trouble of doing; **~ di morte**
death sentence; **~ pecuniaria** fine;
pe'nale ag penal

pen'dente ag hanging; leaning ▷ sm
(ciondolo) pendant; (orecchino) drop
earring

pendere /8/ vi (essere appeso): **~ da** to
hang from; (essere inclinato) to lean;
(fig: incombere): **~ su** to hang over

pen'dio, -ii sm slope, slant; (luogo in
pendenza) slope

'**pendola** sf pendulum clock

pendo'lare smf commuter

pendo'lino sm high-speed train

pene'trante ag piercing,
penetrating

pene'trare /72/ vi to come o get
in ▷ vt to penetrate; **~ in** to enter;
(proiettile) to penetrate; (acqua, aria)
to go o come into

penicil'lina [penitʃil'lina] *sf* penicillin

pe'nisola *sf* peninsula

penitenzi'ario [peniten'tsjarjo] *sm* prison

'penna *sf* (*di uccello*) feather; (*per scrivere*) pen; **penne** *sfpl* (*Cuc*) quills (*type of pasta*); **~ a feltro/ stilografica/a sfera** felt-tip/ fountain/ballpoint pen

penna'rello *sm* felt(-tip) pen

pen'nello *sm* brush; (*per dipingere*) (paint)brush; **a ~** (*perfettamente*) to perfection, perfectly; **~ per la barba** shaving brush

pennetta *sf*: **~ USB** memory stick

pe'nombra *sf* half-light, dim light

pen'sare /72/ *vi* to think ▷ *vt* to think; (*inventare, escogitare*) to think out; **~ a** to think of; (*amico, vacanze*) to think of o about; (*problema*) to think about; **~ di fare qc** to think of doing sth; **ci penso io** I'll see to o take care of it

pensi'ero *sm* thought; (*modo di pensare, dottrina*) thinking *no pl*; (*preoccupazione*) worry, care, trouble; **stare in ~ per qn** to be worried about sb; **pensie'roso, -a** *ag* thoughtful

'pensile *ag* hanging ▷ *sm* (*in cucina*) wall cupboard

pensio'nato, -a *sm/f* pensioner

pensi'one *sf* (*al prestatore di lavoro*) pension; (*vitto e alloggio*) board and lodging; (*albergo*) boarding house; **andare in ~** to retire; **mezza ~** half board; **~ completa** full board

pen'tirsi /45/ *vpr*: **~ di** to repent of; (*rammaricarsi*) to regret, be sorry for

'pentola *sf* pot; **~ a pressione** pressure cooker

pe'nultimo, -a *ag* last but one (BRIT), next to last, penultimate

penzo'lare [pendzo'lare] /72/ *vi* to dangle, hang loosely

'pepe *sm* pepper; **~ macinato/in grani/nero** ground/whole/black pepper

peperon'cino [peperon'tʃino] *sm* chilli pepper

pepe'rone *sm*: **~ (rosso)** red pepper, capsicum; (*piccante*) chili

pe'pita *sf* nugget

PAROLA CHIAVE

per *prep* **1** (*moto attraverso luogo*) through; **i ladri sono passati per la finestra** the thieves got in (o out) through the window; **l'ho cercato per tutta la casa** I've searched the whole house o all over the house for it

2 (*moto a luogo*) for, to; **partire per la Germania/il mare** to leave for Germany/the sea; **il treno per Roma** the Rome train, the train for o to Rome

3 (*stato in luogo*): **seduto/sdraiato per terra** sitting/lying on the ground

4 (*tempo*) for; **per anni/lungo tempo** for years/a long time; **per tutta l'estate** throughout the summer, all summer long; **lo rividi per Natale** I saw him again at Christmas; **lo faccio per lunedì** I'll do it for Monday

5 (*mezzo, maniera*) by; **per lettera/ ferrovia/via aerea** by letter/ rail/airmail; **prendere qn per un braccio** to take sb by the arm

6 (*causa, scopo*) for; **assente per malattia** absent because of o through o owing to illness; **ottimo per il mal di gola** excellent for sore throats

7 (*limitazione*) for; **è troppo difficile per lui** it's too difficult for him; **per quel che mi riguarda** as far as I'm concerned; **per poco che sia** however little it may be; **per questa volta ti perdono** I'll forgive you this time

8 (*prezzo, misura*) for; (: *distributivo*) a, per; **venduto per 3 milioni** sold for 3 million; **15 euro per persona** 15 euros a o per person; **uno per volta**

one at a time; **uno per uno** one by one; **5 per cento** 5 per cent; **3 per 4 fa 12** 3 times 4 equals 12; **dividere/moltiplicare 12 per 4** to divide/multiply 12 by 4

9 (*in qualità di*) as; (*al posto di*) for; **avere qn per professore** to have sb as a teacher; **ti ho preso per Mario** I mistook you for Mario, I thought you were Mario; **dare per morto qn** to give sb up for dead

10 (*seguito da vb: finale*): **per fare qc** (so as) to do sth, in order to do sth; (*: causale*): **per aver fatto qc** for having done sth; (*: consecutivo*): **è abbastanza grande per andarci da solo** he's big enough to go on his own

'pera *sf* pear

per'bene *ag inv* respectable, decent ▷ *av* (*con cura*) properly, well

percentu'ale [pertʃentu'ale] *sf* percentage

perce'pire [pertʃe'pire] /55/ *vt* (*sentire*) to perceive; (*ricevere*) to receive

PAROLA CHIAVE

perché [per'ke] *av* why; **perché no?** why not?; **perché non vuoi andarci?** why don't you want to go?; **spiegami perché l'hai fatto** tell me why you did it

▷ *cong* **1** (*causale*) because; **non posso uscire perché ho da fare** I can't go out because *o* as I've a lot to do

2 (*finale*) in order that, so that; **te lo do perché tu lo legga** I'm giving it to you so (that) you can read it

3 (*consecutivo*): **è troppo forte perché si possa batterlo** he's too strong to be beaten

▷ *sm inv* reason; **il perché di** the reason for

perciò [per'tʃɔ] *cong* so, for this *o* that reason

per'correre /28/ *vt* (*luogo*) to go all over; (*: paese*) to travel up and down, go all over; (*distanza*) to cover

per'corso, -a *pp di* **percorrere** ▷ *sm* (*tragitto*) journey; (*tratto*) route

percu'otere /106/ *vt* to hit, strike

percussi'one *sf* percussion; **strumenti a ~** (*Mus*) percussion instruments

'perdere /73/ *vt* to lose; (*lasciarsi sfuggire*) to miss; (*sprecare: tempo, denaro*) to waste ▷ *vi* to lose; (*serbatoio ecc*) to leak; **perdersi** *vpr* (*smarrirsi*) to get lost; (*svanire*) to disappear, vanish; **saper ~** to be a good loser; **lascia ~!** forget it!, never mind!

perdigi'orno [perdi'dʒorno] *sm inv, f inv* idler, waster

'perdita *sf* loss; (*spreco*) waste; (*fuoriuscita*) leak; **siamo in ~** (*Comm*) we are running at a loss; **a ~ d'occhio** as far as the eye can see

perdo'nare /72/ *vt* to pardon, forgive; (*scusare*) to excuse, pardon

per'dono *sm* forgiveness; (*Dir*) pardon

perduta'mente *av* desperately, passionately

pe'renne *ag* eternal, perpetual, perennial; (*Bot*) perennial

perfetta'mente *av* perfectly; **sai ~ che ...** you know perfectly well that ...

per'fetto, -a *ag* perfect ▷ *sm* (*Ling*) perfect (tense)

perfeziona'mento [perfettsjona'mento] *sm*: **~ (di)** improvement (in), perfection (of); **corso di ~** proficiency course

perfezio'nare [perfettsjo'nare] /72/ *vt* to improve, perfect; **perfezionarsi** *vpr* to improve

perfezi'one [perfet'tsjone] *sf* perfection

per'fino *av* even

perfo'rare /72/ *vt* to perforate, to punch a hole (*o* holes) in; (*banda, schede*) to punch; (*trivellare*) to drill

perga'mena *sf* parchment

P

perico'lante *ag* precarious

pe'ricolo *sm* danger; **mettere in ~** to endanger, put in danger; **perico'loso, -a** *ag* dangerous

perife'ria *sf (di città)* outskirts *pl*

pe'rifrasi *sf inv* circumlocution

pe'rimetro *sm* perimeter

peri'odico, -a, -ci, -che *ag* periodic(al); *(Mat)* recurring ▷ *sm* periodical

pe'riodo *sm* period

peripe'zie [peripet'tsie] *sfpl* ups and downs, vicissitudes

pe'rito, -a *ag* expert, skilled ▷ *sm/f* expert; *(agronomo, navale)* surveyor; **un ~ chimico** a qualified chemist

peri'zoma, -i [peri'dzɔma] *sm* G-string

'perla *sf* pearl; **per'lina** *sf* bead

perlus'trare /72/ *vt* to patrol

perma'loso, -a *ag* touchy

perma'nente *ag* permanent ▷ *sf* permanent wave, perm; **perma'nenza** *sf* permanence; *(soggiorno)* stay

perme'are /72/ *vt* to permeate

per'messo, -a *pp di* **permettere** ▷ *sm* *(autorizzazione)* permission, leave; *(dato a militare, impiegato)* leave; *(licenza)* licence, permit; *(Mil: foglio)* pass; **~?, è ~?** *(posso entrare?)* may I come in?; *(posso passare?)* excuse me; **~ di lavoro/pesca** work/fishing permit; **~ di soggiorno** residence permit

per'mettere /63/ *vt* to allow, permit; **~ a qn qc/di fare qc** to allow sb sth/to do sth; **permettersi** *vpr*: **permettersi qc/di fare qc** to allow o.s. sth/to do sth; *(avere la possibilità)* to afford sth/to do sth

per'misi *ecc vb vedi* **permettere**

per'nacchia [per'nakkja] *sf (fam)*: **fare una ~** to blow a raspberry

per'nice [per'nitʃe] *sf* partridge

'perno *sm* pivot

pernot'tare /72/ *vi* to spend the night, stay overnight

'pero *sm* pear tree

però *cong (ma)* but; *(tuttavia)* however, nevertheless

perpendico'lare *ag, sf* perpendicular

per'plesso, -a *ag* perplexed, puzzled; uncertain

perqui'sire /55/ *vt* to search; **perquisizi'one** *sf (police)* search

'perse *ecc vb vedi* **perdere**

persecuzi'one [persekut'tsjone] *sf* persecution

persegui'tare /72/ *vt* to persecute

perseve'rante *ag* persevering

'persi *ecc vb vedi* **perdere**

persi'ano, -a *ag* Persian ▷ *sf* shutter; **persiana avvolgibile** roller blind

per'sino *av* = **perfino**

persis'tente *ag* persistent

'perso, -a *pp di* **perdere**

per'sona *sf* person; *(qualcuno)*: **una ~** someone, somebody; *(espressione)* anyone *o* anybody

perso'naggio [perso'naddʒo] *sm* *(persona ragguardevole)* personality, figure; *(tipo)* character, individual; *(Letteratura)* character

perso'nale *ag* personal ▷ *sm* staff; personnel; *(figura fisica)* build

personalità *sf inv* personality

perspi'cace [perspi'katʃe] *ag* shrewd, discerning

persu'adere /88/ *vt*: **~ qn (di qc/a fare)** to persuade sb (of sth/to do)

per'tanto *cong (quindi)* so, therefore

per'tica, -che *sf* pole

perti'nente *ag*: **~ (a)** relevant (to), pertinent (to)

per'tosse *sf* whooping cough

perturbazi'one [perturbat'tsjone] *sf* disruption; disturbance; **~ atmosferica** atmospheric disturbance

per'vadere /52/ *vt* to pervade

per'verso, -a *ag* perverted; perverse

perver'tito, -a *sm/f* pervert

p.es. *abbr* (= *per esempio*) e.g.

pe'sante *ag* heavy

pe'sare /72/ *vt* to weigh ▷ *vi (avere un peso)* to weigh; *(essere pesante)* to be heavy; (fig) to carry weight; **~ su** (fig) to lie heavy on; to influence; to hang over; **tutta la responsabilità pesa su di lui** all the responsibility rests on his shoulders; **è una situazione che mi pesa** it's a difficult situation for me; **il suo parere pesa molto** his opinion counts for a lot

'pesca (pl **pesche**) sf (frutto) peach; (il pescare) fishing; **andare a ~** to go fishing; **~ di beneficenza** (lotteria) lucky dip; **~ con la lenza** angling

pes'care /20/ vt (pesce) to fish for; to catch; (qc nell'acqua) to fish out; (fig: trovare) to get hold of, find

pesca'tore sm fisherman; (con lenza) angler

'pesce ['peʃʃe] sm fish (gen inv); **Pesci** (dello zodiaco) Pisces; **~ d'aprile!** April Fool!; **~ rosso** goldfish; **~ spada** swordfish; **pesce'cane** sm shark

pesche'reccio [peske'rettʃo] sm fishing boat

pesche'ria [peske'ria] sf fishmonger's (shop) (BRIT), fish store (US)

pesche'rò ecc [peske'rɔ] vb vedi **pescare**

'peso sm weight; (Sport) shot; **essere di ~ a qn** (fig) to be a burden to sb; **rubare sul ~** to give short weight; **~ lordo/netto** gross/net weight; **~ piuma/mosca/gallo/medio/ massimo** (Pugilato) feather/fly/ bantam/middle/heavyweight

pessi'mismo sm pessimism; **pessi'mista, -i, -e** ag pessimistic ▷ smf pessimist

'pessimo, -a ag very bad, awful

pes'tare /72/ vt to tread on, trample on; (sale, pepe) to grind; (uva, aglio) to crush; (fig: picchiare): **~ qn** to beat sb up

'peste sf plague; (persona) nuisance, pest

pes'tello sm pestle

'petalo sm (Bot) petal

pe'tardo sm firecracker, banger (BRIT)

petizi'one [petit'tsjone] sf petition

petroli'era sf (nave) oil tanker

pe'trolio sm oil, petroleum; (per lampada, fornello) paraffin

> Attenzione! In inglese esiste la parola *petrol*, che però significa *benzina*.

pette'golare /72/ vi to gossip

pette'golezzo [pette'leddzo] sm gossip no pl; **fare pettegolezzi** to gossip

pet'tegolo, -a ag gossipy ▷ sm/f gossip

petti'nare /72/ vt to comb (the hair of); **pettinarsi** vpr to comb one's hair; **pettina'tura** sf (acconciatura) hairstyle

'pettine sm comb; (Zool) scallop

petti'rosso sm robin

'petto sm chest; (seno) breast, bust; (Cuc: di carne bovina) brisket; (di pollo ecc) breast; **a doppio ~** (abito) double-breasted

petu'lante ag insolent

'pezza ['pɛttsa] sf piece of cloth; (toppa) patch; (cencio) rag, cloth

pez'zente [pet'tsɛnte] smf beggar

'pezzo ['pɛttso] sm (gen) piece; (brandello, frammento) piece, bit; (di macchina, arnese ecc) part; (Stampa) article; **aspettare un ~** to wait quite a while o some time; **in** o **a pezzi** in pieces; **andare a pezzi** to break into pieces; **un bel ~ d'uomo** a fine figure of a man; **abito a due pezzi** two-piece suit; **~ di cronaca** (Stampa) report; **~ grosso** (fig) bigwig; **~ di ricambio** spare part

pi'accio ecc ['pjattʃo] vb vedi **piacere**

pia'cente [pja'tʃɛnte] ag attractive

pia'cere [pja'tʃere] /74/ vi to please ▷ sm pleasure; (favore) favour (BRIT), favor (US); **una ragazza che piace** a likeable girl; (attraente) an attractive girl; **mi piace** I like it; **quei ragazzi non mi piacciono** I don't like those boys; **gli ~bbe andare al cinema** he would like to go to the cinema;

il suo discorso è piaciuto molto his speech was well received; **"~!"** (*nelle presentazioni*) "pleased to meet you!"; **~ (di conoscerla)** nice to meet you; **con ~** certainly, with pleasure; **per ~** please; **fare un ~ a qn** to do sb a favour; **pia'cevole** *ag* pleasant, agreeable

pi'acqui *ecc vb vedi* **piacere**

pi'aga, -ghe *sf* (*lesione*) sore; (*ferita: anche fig*) wound; (*fig: flagello*) scourge, curse; (: *persona*) pest, nuisance

piagnuco'lare [pjaɲɲuko'lare] /72/ *vi* to whimper

pianeggi'ante [pjaned'dʒante] *ag* flat, level

piane'rottolo *sm* landing

pia'neta *sm* (*Astr*) planet

pi'angere ['pjandʒere] /75/ *vi* to cry, weep; (*occhi*) to water ▷ *vt* to cry, weep; (*lamentare*) to bewail, lament; **~ la morte di qn** to mourn sb's death

pianifi'care /20/ *vt* to plan

pia'nista, -i, -e *smf* pianist

pi'ano, -a *ag* (*piatto*) flat, level; (*Mat*) plane; (*chiaro*) clear, plain ▷ *av* (*adagio*) slowly; (*a bassa voce*) softly; (*con cautela*) slowly, carefully ▷ *sm* (*Mat*) plane; (*Geo*) plain; (*livello*) level, plane; (*di edificio*) floor; (*programma*) plan; (*Mus*) piano; **pian ~** very slowly; (*poco a poco*) little by little; **al ~ terra** on the ground floor; **in primo/ secondo ~** in the foreground/ background; **di primo ~** (*fig*) prominent, high-ranking

piano'forte *sm* piano, pianoforte

piano'terra *sm inv* = **piano terra**

pi'ansi *ecc vb vedi* **piangere**

pi'anta *sf* (*Bot*) plant; (*Anat: anche:* **~ del piede**) sole (of the foot); (*grafico*) plan; (*cartina topografica*) map; **in ~ stabile** on the permanent staff; **pian'tare** /72/ *vt* to plant; (*conficcare*) to drive o hammer in; (*tenda*) to put up, pitch; (*fig: lasciare*) to leave, desert; **piantarsi** *vpr*: **piantarsi**

davanti a qn to plant o.s. in front of sb; **piantala!** (*fam*) cut it out!

pianter'reno *sm* ground floor

pian'tina *sf* (*di edificio, città*) (small) map; (*Bot*) (small) plant

pia'nura *sf* plain

pi'astra *sf* plate; (*di pietra*) slab; (*di fornello*) hotplate; **panino alla ~** ≈ toasted sandwich; **~ di registrazione** tape deck

pias'trella *sf* tile

pias'trina *sf* (*Mil*) identity disc (*BRIT*) o tag (*US*)

piatta'forma *sf* (*anche fig*) platform

piat'tino *sm* saucer

pi'atto, -a *ag* flat; (*fig: scialbo*) dull ▷ *sm* (*recipiente, vivanda*) dish; (*portata*) course; (*parte piana*) flat (part); **piatti** *smpl* (*Mus*) cymbals; **~ fondo** soup dish; **~ forte** main course; **~ del giorno** dish of the day, plat du jour; **~ del giradischi** turntable; **~ piano** dinner plate

pi'azza ['pjattsa] *sf* square; (*Comm*) market; **far ~ pulita** to make a clean sweep; **~ d'armi** (*Mil*) parade ground; **piaz'zale** *sm* (large) square

piaz'zola [pjat'tsɔla] *sf* (*Aut*) lay-by; (*di tenda*) pitch

pic'cante *ag* hot, pungent; (*fig*) racy; biting

pic'chetto [pik'ketto] *sm* (*Mil, di scioperanti*) picket; (*di tenda*) peg

picchi'are [pik'kjare] /19/ *vt* (*persona: colpire*) to hit, strike; (: *prendere a botte*) to beat (up); (*battere*) to beat; (*sbattere*) to bang ▷ *vi* (*bussare*) to knock; (: *con forza*) to bang; (*colpire*) to hit, strike; (*sole*) to beat down; **picchi'ata** *sf* (*Aer*) dive

'picchio ['pikkjo] *sm* woodpecker

pic'cino, -a [pit'tʃino] *ag* tiny, very small

picci'one [pit'tʃone] *sm* pigeon

'picco, -chi *sm* peak; **a ~** vertically

'piccolo, -a *ag* small; (*oggetto, mano, di età: bambino*) small, little; (*dav sostantivo: di breve durata, viaggio*) short; (fig) mean, petty ▷ sm/f child, little one

pic'cone sm pick(-axe)

pic'cozza [pik'kɔttsa] sf ice-axe

pic'nic sm inv picnic

pi'docchio [pi'dokkjo] sm louse

pi'ede sm foot; (di mobile) leg; **in piedi** standing; **a piedi** on foot; **a piedi nudi** barefoot; **su due piedi** (fig) at once; **prendere ~** (fig) to gain ground, catch on; **sul ~ di guerra** (Mil) ready for action; **~ di porco** crowbar

pi'ega, -ghe sf (piegatura, Geo) fold; (di gonna) pleat; (di pantaloni) crease; (grinza) wrinkle, crease; **prendere una brutta** o **cattiva ~** (fig) to take a turn for the worse

pie'gare /80/ vt to fold; (braccia, gambe, testa) to bend ▷ vi to bend; **piegarsi** vpr to bend; (fig): **piegarsi (a)** to yield (to), submit (to)

piegherò ecc [pjege'rɔ] vb vedi **piegare**

pie'ghevole ag pliable, flexible; (porta) folding

Pie'monte sm: **il ~** Piedmont

pi'ena sf vedi **pieno**

pi'eno, -a ag full; (muro, mattone) solid ▷ sm (colmo) height, peak; (carico) full load ▷ sf (di fiume) flood, spate; **~ di** full of; **in ~ giorno** in broad daylight; **fare il ~ (di benzina)** to fill up (with petrol)

'piercing ['pirsing] sm: **farsi il ~ all'ombelico** to have one's navel pierced

pietà sf pity; (Rel) piety; **senza ~** pitiless, ruthless; **avere ~ di** (compassione) to pity, feel sorry for; (misericordia) to have pity o mercy on

pie'tanza [pje'tantsa] sf dish, course

pie'toso, -a ag (compassionevole) pitying, compassionate; (che desta pietà) pitiful

pi'etra sf stone; **~ preziosa** precious stone, gem

'piffero sm (Mus) pipe

pigi'ama [pi'dʒama] sm pyjamas pl

pigli'are [piʎ'ʎare] /27/ vt to take, grab; (afferrare) to catch

'pigna ['piɲɲa] sf pine cone

pi'gnolo, -a ag pernickety

pi'grizia [pi'grittsja] sf laziness

'pigro, -a ag lazy

PIL sigla m (= prodotto interno lordo) GDP

'pila sf (catasta, di ponte) pile; (Elettr) battery; (torcia) torch (BRIT), flashlight

pi'lastro sm pillar

'pile ['pail] sm inv fleece

'pillola sf pill; **prendere la ~** to be on the pill

pi'lone sm (di ponte) pier; (di linea elettrica) pylon

pi'lota, -i, -e smf pilot; (Aut) driver ▷ ag inv pilot cpd; **~ automatico** automatic pilot

pinaco'teca, -che sf art gallery

pi'neta sf pinewood

ping-'pong [piŋ'pɔŋ] sm table tennis

'pinna sf fin; (di cetaceo, per nuotare) flipper

'pino sm pine (tree); **pi'nolo** sm pine kernel

'pinza ['pintsa] sf pliers pl; (Med) forceps pl; (Zool) pincer

pin'zette [pin'tsette] sfpl tweezers

pi'oggia, -ge ['pjɔddʒa] sf rain; **~ acida** acid rain

pi'olo sm peg; (di scala) rung

piom'bare /72/ vi to fall heavily; (gettarsi con impeto): **~ su** to fall upon, assail ▷ vt (dente) to fill; **piomba'tura** sf (di dente) filling

piom'bino sm (sigillo) (lead) seal; (del filo a piombo) plummet; (Pesca) sinker

pi'ombo sm (Chim) lead; **a ~** (cadere) straight down; **senza ~** (benzina) unleaded

pioni'ere, -a sm/f pioneer

pi'oppo sm poplar

pi'overe /76/ vb impers to rain ▷ vi (fig: scendere dall'alto) to rain down;

(*affluire in gran numero*): **~ in** to pour into; **pioviggi'nare** /72/ *vb impers* to drizzle; **pio'voso, -a** *ag* rainy

pi'ovra *sf* octopus

pi'ovve *ecc vb vedi* **piovere**

'pipa *sf* pipe

pipì *sf (fam)*: **fare ~** to have a wee (wee)

pipis'trello *sm (Zool)* bat

pi'ramide *sf* pyramid

pi'rata, -i *sm* pirate; **~ informatico** hacker; **~ della strada** hit-and-run driver

Pire'nei *smpl*: **i ~** the Pyrenees

pi'romane *smf* pyromaniac; arsonist

pi'roscafo *sm* steamer, steamship

pisci'are [piʃʃare] /14/ *vi (fam!)* to piss (!), pee (!)

pi'scina [piʃʃina] *sf* (swimming) pool

pi'sello *sm* pea

piso'lino *sm* nap

'pista *sf (traccia)* track, trail; *(di stadio)* track; *(di pattinaggio)* rink; *(da sci)* run; *(Aer)* runway; *(di circo)* ring; **~ da ballo** dance floor

pis'tacchio [pis'takkjo] *sm* pistachio (tree); pistachio (nut)

pis'tola *sf* pistol, gun

pis'tone *sm* piston

pi'tone *sm* python

pit'tore, -'trice *sm/f* painter; **pitto'resco, -a, -schi, -sche** *ag* picturesque

pit'tura *sf* painting; **pittu'rare** /72/ *vt* to paint

PAROLA CHIAVE

più *av* **1** *(in maggiore quantità)* more; **più del solito** more than usual; **in più, di più** more; **ne voglio di più** I want some more; **ci sono 3 persone in *o* di più** there are 3 more *o* extra people; **più o meno** more or less; **per di più** *(inoltre)* what's more, moreover

2 *(comparativo)* more; (: *se monosillabo, spesso)* + ...er; **più ... di/che** more ...

than; **lavoro più di te/di Paola** I work harder than you/than Paola; **è più intelligente che ricco** he's more intelligent than rich

3 *(superlativo)* most; (: *se monosillabo, spesso)* + ...est; **il più grande/intelligente** the biggest/most intelligent; **è quello che compro più spesso** that's the one I buy most often; **al più presto** as soon as possible; **al più tardi** at the latest

4 *(negazione)*: **non ... più** no more, no longer; **non ho più soldi** I've got no more money, I don't have any more money; **non lavoro più** I'm no longer working, I don't work any more; **a più non posso** *(gridare)* at the top of one's voice; *(correre)* as fast as one can

5 *(Mat)* plus; **4 più 5 fa 9** 4 plus 5 equals 9; **più 5 gradi** 5 degrees above freezing, plus 5

▶ *prep* plus

▶ *ag inv* **1**: **più ... (di)** more ... (than); **più denaro/tempo** more money/time; **più persone di quante ci aspettassimo** more people than we expected

2 *(numerosi, diversi)* several; **l'aspettai per più giorni** I waited for it for several days

▶ *sm* **1** *(la maggior parte)*: **il più è fatto** most of it is done

2 *(Mat)* plus (sign)

3: **i più** the majority

pi'uma *sf* feather; **piu'mino** *sm* (eider)down; *(per letto)* eiderdown; (: *tipo danese*) duvet, continental quilt; *(giacca)* quilted jacket *(with goose-feather padding)*; *(per cipria)* powder puff; *(per spolverare)* feather duster

piut'tosto *av* rather; **~ che** *(anziché)* rather than

'pizza ['pittsa] *sf* pizza; **pizze'ria** *sf* place where pizzas are made, sold or eaten

pizzi'care [pittsi'kare] /20/ vt
(stringere) to nip, pinch; (pungere)
to sting; to bite; (Mus) to pluck ▷ vi
(prudere) to itch, be itchy; (cibo) to be
hot o spicy

'pizzico ['pittsiko] sm (pizzicotto)
pinch, nip; (piccola quantità) pinch,
dash; (d'insetto) sting; bite

pizzi'cotto [pittsi'kotto] sm
pinch, nip

'pizzo ['pittso] sm (merletto) lace;
(barbetta) goatee beard

plagi'are [pla'dʒare] /62/ vt (copiare)
to plagiarize

plaid [plɛd] sm inv (travelling) rug
(BRIT), lap robe (US)

pla'nare /72/ vi (Aer) to glide

'plasma sm plasma

plas'mare /72/ vt to mould , shape

'plastico, -a, -ci, -che ag plastic
▷ sf (arte) plastic arts pl; (Med) plastic
surgery; (sostanza) plastic; **plastica
facciale** face lift

'platano sm plane tree

pla'tea sf (Teat) stalls pl

pla'tino sm platinum

plau'sibile ag plausible

pleni'lunio sm full moon

'plettro sm plectrum

pleu'rite sf pleurisy

'plico, -chi sm (pacco) parcel; **in ~ a
parte** (Comm) under separate cover

plo'tone sm (Mil) platoon; **~
d'esecuzione** firing squad

plu'rale ag, sm plural

P.M. abbr (Pol) = **Pubblico Ministero**;
(= Polizia Militare) MP

PMI sigla fpl (= Piccole e Medie Imprese)
SME

pneu'matico, -a, -ci, -che ag
inflatable; (Tecn) pneumatic ▷ sm
(Aut) tyre (BRIT), tire (US)

po' av, sm vedi **poco**

○ **PAROLA CHIAVE**

poco, -a, -chi, -che ag (quantità)
little, not much; (numero) few, not

many; **poco pane/denaro/spazio**
little o not much bread/money/space;
poche persone/idee few o not many
people/ideas; **ci vediamo tra poco**
(sottinteso: tempo) see you soon
▷ av 1 (in piccola quantità) little, not
much; (: numero limitato) few, not
many; **guadagna poco** he doesn't
earn much, he earns little
2 (con ag, av) (a) little, not very; **è
poco più vecchia di lui** she's a little
o slightly older than him; **sta poco
bene** he isn't very well
3 (tempo): **poco dopo/prima** shortly
afterwards/before; **il film dura
poco** the film doesn't last very long;
ci vediamo molto poco we don't see
each other very often, we hardly ever
see each other
4: **un po'** a little, a bit; **è un po'
corto** it's a little o a bit short;
arriverà fra un po' he'll arrive
shortly o in a little while
5: **a dir poco** to say the least; **a
poco a poco** little by little; **per poco
non cadevo** I nearly fell; **è una
cosa da poco** it's nothing, it's of no
importance; **una persona da poco**
a worthless person
▷ pron (a) little

podcast ['podkast] sm podcast

po'dere sm (Agr) farm

'podio sm dais, platform; (Mus)
podium

po'dismo sm (Sport: marcia) walking;
(: corsa) running

poe'sia sf (arte) poetry;
(componimento) poem

po'eta, -'essa sm/f poet/poetess

poggi'are [pod'dʒare] /62/ vt to
lean, rest; (posare) to lay, place;
poggia'testa sm inv (Aut) headrest

'poggio ['poddʒo] sm hillock, knoll

'poi av then; (alla fine) finally, at last; **e
~** (inoltre) and besides; **questa ~ (è
bella)!** (ironico) that's a good one!

poiché [poi'ke] cong since, as

'**poker** sm poker
po'lacco, -a, -chi, -che ag Polish
▷ sm/f Pole
po'lare ag polar
po'lemico, -a, -ci, -che ag
polemical, controversial ▷ sf
controversy
po'lenta sf (Cuc) sort of thick porridge
made with maize flour
'**polipo** sm polyp
polisti'rolo sm polystyrene
po'litica, -che sf vedi **politico**;
politica'mente av politically;
politicamente corretto politically
correct
po'litico, -a, -ci, -che ag political
▷ sm/f politician ▷ sf politics sg; (linea
di condotta) policy
poli'zia [polit'tsia] sf police;
~ giudiziaria ≈ Criminal Investigation
Department (CID) (BRIT), Federal
Bureau of Investigation (FBI) (US);
~ stradale traffic police; **polizi'esco,
-a, -schi, -sche** ag police cpd; (film,
romanzo) detective cpd; **polizi'otto**
sm policeman; **cane poliziotto**
police dog; **donna poliziotto**
policewoman; **poliziotto di
quartiere** local police officer

○ **POLIZIA DI STATO**
○
○
○ The remit of the polizia di stato
○ is to maintain public order, to
○ uphold the law, and to prevent and
○ investigate crime. This is a civilian
○ branch of the police force; male
○ and female officers perform similar
○ duties. The polizia di stato reports to
○ the Minister of the Interior.

'**polizza** ['polittsa] sf (Comm) bill; **~ di
assicurazione** insurance policy; **~ di
carico** bill of lading
pol'laio sm henhouse
'**pollice** ['pollitʃe] sm thumb
'**polline** sm pollen
'**pollo** sm chicken

pol'mone sm lung; **~ d'acciaio** (Med)
iron lung; **polmo'nite** sf pneumonia;
polmonite atipica SARS
'**polo** sm (Geo, Fisica) pole; (gioco) polo;
il ~ sud/nord the South/North Pole
Po'lonia sf: **la ~** Poland
'**polpa** sf flesh, pulp; (carne) lean meat
pol'paccio [pol'pattʃo] sm (Anat) calf
polpas'trello sm fingertip
pol'petta sf (Cuc) meatball
'**polpo** sm octopus
pol'sino sm cuff
'**polso** sm (Anat) wrist; (pulsazione)
pulse; (fig: forza) drive, vigour
pol'trire /55/ vi to laze about
pol'trona sf armchair; (Teat: posto)
seat in the front stalls (BRIT) o the
orchestra (US)
'**polvere** sf dust; (sostanza ridotta
minutissima) powder, dust; **caffè
in ~** instant coffee; **latte in ~** dried
o powdered milk; **sapone in ~**
soap powder; **~ pirica** o **da sparo**
gunpowder
po'mata sf ointment, cream
po'mello sm knob
pome'riggio [pome'riddʒo] sm
afternoon
'**pomice** ['pomitʃe] sf pumice
'**pomo** sm (mela) apple; (ornamentale)
knob; (di sella) pommel; **~ d'Adamo**
(Anat) Adam's apple
pomo'doro sm tomato; **pomodori
pelati** skinned tomatoes
'**pompa** sf pump; (sfarzo) pomp (and
ceremony); **~ antincendio** fire hose;
~ di benzina petrol (BRIT) o gas (US)
pump; (distributore) filling o gas (US)
station; **impresa di pompe funebri**
funeral parlour sg (BRIT), undertaker's
sg; **pom'pare** /72/ vt to pump;
(trarre) to pump out; (gonfiare d'aria)
to pump up
pom'pelmo sm grapefruit
pompi'ere sm fireman
po'nente sm west
'**pongo** vb vedi **porre**
'**poni** vb vedi **porre**

'**ponte** sm bridge; (di nave) deck; (anche: **~ di comando**) bridge; (impalcatura) scaffold; **fare il ~** (fig) to take the extra day off; (between 2 public holidays): **governo ~** interim government; **~ aereo** airlift; **~ levatoio** drawbridge; **~ sospeso** suspension bridge

pon'**tefice** sm (Rel) pontiff

'**popcorn** ['pɔpkɔːn] sm inv popcorn

popo'**lare** /72/ ag popular; (quartiere, clientela) working-class ▷ vt (rendere abitato) to populate; **popolarsi** vpr to fill with people, get crowded; **popolazi'one** sf population

'**popolo** sm people

'**poppa** sf (di nave) stern; (fam: mammella) breast

porcel'**lana** [portʃel'lana] sf porcelain, china; (oggetto) piece of porcelain

porcel'**lino, -a** [portʃel'lino] sm/f piglet; **~ d'India** guinea pig

porche'**ria** [porke'ria] sf filth, muck; (fig: oscenità) obscenity; (: azione disonesta) dirty trick; (: cosa mal fatta) rubbish

por'**cile** [por'tʃile] sm pigsty

por'**cino, -a** [por'tʃino] ag of pigs, pork cpd ▷ sm (fungo) type of edible mushroom

'**porco, -ci** sm pig; (carne) pork

porcos'**pino** sm porcupine

'**porgere** ['pɔrdʒere] /115/ vt to hand, give; (tendere) to hold out

pornogra'**fia** sf pornography; **porno'grafico, -a, -ci, -che** ag pornographic

'**poro** sm pore

'**porpora** sf purple

'**porre** /77/ vt (mettere) to put; (collocare) to place; (posare) to lay (down), put (down); (fig: supporre): **poniamo (il caso) che .:.** let's suppose that ...

'**porro** sm (Bot) leek; (Med) wart

'**porsi** ecc vb vedi **porgere**

'**porta** sf door; (Sport) goal

porta...: portaba'gagli sm inv (facchino) porter; (Aut, Ferr) luggage rack; **porta-'CD** sm inv (mobile) CD rack; (astuccio) CD holder; **porta'cenere** sm inv ashtray; **portachi'avi** sm inv keyring; **porta'erei** sf inv (nave) aircraft carrier; **portafi'nestra** (pl **portefinestre**) sf French window; **porta'foglio** sm wallet; (Pol, Borsa) portfolio; **portafor'tuna** sm inv lucky charm; mascot

por'**tale** sm (di chiesa, Inform) portal

porta'**mento** sm carriage, bearing

portamo'**nete** sm inv purse

por'**tante** ag (muro ecc) supporting, load-bearing

portan'**tina** sf sedan chair; (per ammalati) stretcher

portaom'**brelli** sm inv umbrella stand

porta'**pacchi** [porta'pakki] sm inv (di moto, bicicletta) luggage rack

porta'**penne** [porta'penne] sm inv pen holder; (astuccio) pencil case

por'**tare** /72/ vt (sostenere, sorreggere: peso, bambino, pacco) to carry; (indossare: abito, occhiali) to wear; (: capelli lunghi) to have; (avere: nome, titolo) to have, bear; (recare): **~ qc a qn** to take (o bring) sth to sb; (fig: sentimenti) to bear

portasiga'**rette** sm inv cigarette case

por'**tata** sf (vivanda) course; (Aut) carrying (o loading) capacity; (di arma) range; (volume d'acqua) (rate of) flow; (fig: limite) scope, capability; (: importanza) impact, import; **alla ~ di tutti** (conoscenza) within everybody's capabilities; (prezzo) within everybody's means; **a/fuori ~ (di)** within/out of reach (of); **a ~ di mano** within (arm's) reach

por'**tatile** ag portable

por'**tato, -a** ag (incline): **~ a** inclined o apt to

p

portau'ovo *sm inv* eggcup
porta'voce [porta'votʃe] *smf inv* spokesman/woman
por'tento *sm* wonder, marvel
porti'era *sf* (Aut) door
porti'ere *sm* (portinaio) concierge, caretaker; (di hotel) porter; (nel calcio) goalkeeper
porti'naio, -a *sm/f* concierge, caretaker
portine'ria *sf* caretaker's lodge
'porto, -a *pp di* **porgere** ▷ *sm* (Naut) harbour , port ▷ *sm inv* port (wine); **~ d'armi** gun licence (BRIT) o license (US)
Porto'gallo *sm*: **il ~** Portugal; **porto'ghese** *ag, smf, sm* Portuguese *inv*
por'tone *sm* main entrance, main door
portu'ale *ag* harbour *cpd*, port *cpd* ▷ *sm* dock worker
porzi'one [por'tsjone] *sf* portion, share; (di cibo) portion, helping
'posa *sf* (Fot) exposure; (atteggiamento, di modello) pose
po'sare /72/ *vt* to put (down), lay (down) ▷ *vi* (ponte, edificio, teoria): **~ su** to rest on; (fig: atteggiarsi) to pose; **posarsi** *vpr* (ape, aereo) to land; (uccello) to alight; (sguardo) to settle
po'sata *sf* piece of cutlery
pos'critto *sm* postscript
'posi *ecc vb vedi* **porre**
posi'tivo, -a *ag* positive
posizi'one [pozit'tsjone] *sf* position; **prendere ~** (fig) to take a stand; **luci di ~** (Aut) sidelights
pos'porre /77/ *vt* to place after; (differire) to postpone, defer
posse'dere /107/ *vt* to own, possess; (qualità, virtù) to have, possess
posses'sivo, -a *ag* possessive
pos'sesso *sm* ownership *no pl*; possession
posses'sore *sm* owner
pos'sibile *ag* possible ▷ *sm*: **fare tutto il ~** to do everything possible;

nei limiti del ~ as far as possible; **al più tardi ~** as late as possible; **possibilità** *sf inv* possibility ▷ *sf pl* (mezzi) means; **aver la possibilità di fare** to be in a position to do; to have the opportunity to do
possi'dente *smf* landowner
possi'edo *ecc vb vedi* **possedere**
'posso *ecc vb vedi* **potere**
'posta *sf* (servizio) post, postal service; (corrispondenza) post, mail; (ufficio postale) post office; (nei giochi d'azzardo) stake; **poste** *sf pl* (amministrazione) post office; **~ aerea** airmail; **~ elettronica** E-mail, e-mail, electronic mail; **~ ordinaria** ≈ second-class mail; **~ prioritaria** first class (post); **ministro delle Poste e Telecomunicazioni** Postmaster General; **pos'tale** *ag* postal, post office *cpd*
posteggi'are [posted'dʒare] /62/ *vt, vi* to park; **pos'teggio** *sm* car park (BRIT), parking lot (US); (di taxi) rank (BRIT), stand (US)
'poster *sm inv* poster
posteri'ore *ag* (dietro) back; (dopo) later ▷ *sm* (fam: sedere) behind
postici'pare [postitʃi'pare] /72/ *vt* to defer, postpone
pos'tino *sm* postman (BRIT), mailman (US)
'posto, -a *pp di* **porre** ▷ *sm* (sito, posizione) place; (impiego) job; (spazio libero) room, space; (di parcheggio) space; (sedile: al teatro, in treno ecc) seat; (Mil) post; **a ~** (in ordine) in place, tidy; (fig) settled; (persona) reliable; **mettere a ~** to tidy (up), put in order; (faccende) to straighten out; **al ~ di** in place of; **sul ~** on the spot; **~ di blocco** roadblock; **~ di lavoro** job; **~ di polizia** police station; **posti in piedi** (Teat, in autobus) standing room
po'tabile *ag* drinkable; **acqua ~** drinking water
po'tare /72/ *vt* to prune

po'tassio sm potassium

po'tente ag (nazione) strong, powerful; (veleno, farmaco) potent, strong; **po'tenza** sf power; (forza) strength

potenzi'ale [poten'tsjale] ag, sm potential

PAROLA CHIAVE

po'tere /78/ sm power; **al potere** (partito ecc) in power; **potere d'acquisto** purchasing power
▶ vb aus **1** (essere in grado di) can, be able to; **non ha potuto ripararlo** he couldn't o he wasn't able to repair it; **non è potuto venire** he couldn't o he wasn't able to come; **spiacente di non poter aiutare** sorry not to be able to help
2 (avere il permesso) can, may, be allowed to; **posso entrare?** can o may I come in?; **posso chiederti, dove sei stato?** where, may I ask, have you been?
3 (eventualità) may, might, could; **potrebbe essere vero** it might o could be true; **può aver avuto un incidente** he may o might o could have had an accident; **può darsi** perhaps; **può darsi** o **può essere che non venga** he may o might not come
4 (augurio): **potessi almeno parlargli!** if only I could speak to him!
5 (suggerimento): **potresti almeno scusarti!** you could at least apologize!
▶ vt can, be able to; **può molto per noi** he can do a lot for us; **non ne posso più** (per stanchezza) I'm exhausted; (per rabbia) I can't take any more

potrò ecc vb vedi **potere**

povero, -a ag poor; (disadorno) plain, bare ▷ sm/f poor man/woman; **i poveri** the poor; **~ di** lacking in,

having little; **povertà** sf poverty; **povertà energetica** fuel poverty

poz'zanghera [pot'tsangera] sf puddle

pozzo ['pottso] sm well; (cava: di carbone) pit; (di miniera) shaft; **~ petrolifero** oil well

P.R.A. [pra] sigla m (= Pubblico Registro Automobilistico) ≈ DVLA

pran'zare [pran'dzare] /72/ vi to dine, have dinner, to lunch, have lunch

pranzo ['prandzo] sm dinner; (a mezzogiorno) lunch

prassi sf usual procedure

pratica, -che sf practice; (esperienza) experience; (conoscenza) knowledge, familiarity; (tirocinio) training, practice; (Amm: affare) matter, case; (: incartamento) file, dossier; **in ~** (praticamente) in practice; **mettere in ~** to put into practice

prati'cabile ag (progetto) practicable, feasible; (luogo) passable, practicable

pratica'mente av (in modo pratico) in a practical way, practically; (quasi) practically, almost

prati'care /20/ vt to practise; (Sport: tennis ecc) to play; (: nuoto, scherma ecc) to go in for; (eseguire: apertura, buco) to make; **~ uno sconto** to give a discount

pratico, -a, -ci, -che ag practical; **~ di** (esperto) experienced o skilled in; (familiare) familiar with

prato sm meadow; (di giardino) lawn

preav'viso sm notice; **telefonata con ~** personal o person to person call

pre'cario, -a ag precarious; (Ins) temporary

precauzi'one [prekaut'tsjone] sf caution, care; (misura) precaution

prece'dente [pretʃe'dente] ag previous ▷ sm precedent; **il discorso/film ~** the previous o preceding speech/film; **senza precedenti** unprecedented;

precedenti penali criminal record *sg*; **prece'denza** *sf* priority, precedence; (*Aut*) right of way
pre'cedere [pre'tʃɛdere] /29/ *vt* to precede, go *o* (come) before
precipi'tare [pretʃipi'tare] /72/ *vi* (*cadere*) to fall headlong; (*fig: situazione*) to get out of control ▷ *vt* (*gettare dall'alto in basso*) to hurl, fling; (*fig: affrettare*) to rush; **precipitarsi** *vpr* (*gettarsi*) to hurl *o* fling o.s.; (*affrettarsi*) to rush; **precipi'toso, -a** *ag* (*caduta, fuga*) headlong; (*fig: avventato*) rash, reckless; (: *affrettato*) hasty, rushed
preci'pizio [pretʃi'pittsjo] *sm* precipice; **a ~** (*fig*) (*correre*) headlong
precisa'mente [pretʃiza'mente] *av* (*gen*) precisely; (*con esattezza*) exactly
preci'sare [pretʃi'zare] /72/ *vt* to state, specify; (*spiegare*) to explain (in detail)
precisi'one [pretʃi'zjone] *sf* precision; accuracy
pre'ciso, -a [pre'tʃizo] *ag* (*esatto*) precise; (*accurato*) accurate, precise; (*deciso: idea*) precise, definite; (*uguale*): **2 vestiti precisi** 2 dresses exactly the same; **sono le 9 precise** it's exactly 9 o'clock
pre'cludere /3/ *vt* to block, obstruct
pre'coce [pre'kɔtʃe] *ag* early; (*bambino*) precocious; (*vecchiaia*) premature
precon'cetto, -a [prekon'tʃetto] *sm* preconceived idea, prejudice
precur'sore *sm* forerunner, precursor
'preda *sf* (*bottino*) booty; (*animale, fig*) prey; **essere ~ di** to fall prey to; **essere in ~ a** to be prey to
'predica, -che *sf* sermon; (*fig*) lecture, talking-to
predi'care /20/ *vt, vi* to preach
predi'cato *sm* (*Ling*) predicate
predi'letto, -a *pp di* **prediligere** ▷ *ag, sm/f* favourite
predi'ligere [predi'lidʒere] /117/ *vt* to prefer, have a preference for

pre'dire /38/ *vt* to foretell, predict
predis'porre /77/ *vt* to get ready, prepare; **~ qn a qc** to predispose sb to sth
predizi'one [predit'tsjone] *sf* prediction
prefazi'one [prefat'tsjone] *sf* preface, foreword
prefe'renza [prefe'rɛntsa] *sf* preference
prefe'rire /55/ *vt* to prefer, like better; **~ il caffè al tè** to prefer coffee to tea, like coffee better than tea
pre'figgersi [pre'fiddʒersi] /79/ *vpr*: **~ uno scopo** to set o.s. a goal
pre'fisso, -a *pp di* **prefiggersi** ▷ *sm* (*Ling*) prefix; (*Tel*) dialling (BRIT) *o* dial (US) code
pre'gevole [pre'dʒevole] *ag* valuable
pregherò *ecc* [prege'rɔ] *vb vedi* **pregare**
preghi'era [pre'gjɛra] *sf* (*Rel*) prayer; (*domanda*) request
pregi'ato, -a [pre'dʒato] *ag* (*opera*) valuable; **vino ~** vintage wine
'pregio ['prɛdʒo] *sm* (*stima*) esteem, regard; (*qualità*) (good) quality, merit; (*valore*) value, worth
pregiudi'care [predʒudi'kare] /20/ *vt* to prejudice, harm, be detrimental to
pregiu'dizio [predʒu'dittsjo] *sm* (*idea errata*) prejudice; (*danno*) harm *no pl*
'prego *escl* (*a chi ringrazia*) don't mention it!; (*invitando qn ad accomodarsi*) please sit down!; (*invitando qn ad andare prima*) after you!
pregus'tare /72/ *vt* to look forward to
prele'vare /72/ *vt* (*denaro*) to withdraw; (*campione*) to take; (*polizia*) to take, capture

preli'evo sm (Banca) withdrawal; (Med): **fare un ~ (di)** to take a sample (of); **fare un ~ di sangue** to take a blood sample

prelimi'nare ag preliminary

premere /29/ vt to press ▷ vi: **~ su** to press down on; (fig) to put pressure on; **~ a** (fig) (importare) to matter to

pre'mettere /63/ vt to put before; (dire prima) to start by saying, state first

premi'are /19/ vt to give a prize to; (fig: merito, onestà) to reward

premiazi'one [premjat'tsjone] sf prize giving

premio sm prize; (ricompensa) reward; (Comm) premium; (Amm: indennità) bonus

pre'misi ecc vb vedi **premettere**

premu'nirsi /55/ vpr: **~ di** to provide o.s. with; **~ contro** to protect o.s. from, guard o.s. against

pre'mura sf (fretta) haste, hurry; (riguardo) attention, care; **premure** sfpl (attenzioni, cure) care sg: **aver ~** to be in a hurry; **far ~ a qn** to hurry sb; **usare ogni ~ nei riguardi di qn** to be very attentive to sb; **premu'roso, -a** ag thoughtful, considerate

prendere /81/ vt to take; (andare a prendere) to get, fetch; (ottenere) to get; (guadagnare) to get, earn; (catturare: ladro, pesce) to catch; (collaboratore, dipendente) to take on; (passeggero) to pick up; (chiedere: somma, prezzo) to charge, ask; (trattare: persona) to handle ▷ vi (colla, cemento) to set; (pianta) to take; (fuoco: nel camino) to catch; (voltare): **~ a destra** to turn (to the) right; **prendersi** vpr (azzuffarsi): **prendersi a pugni** to come to blows; **prende qualcosa?** (da bere, da mangiare) would you like something to eat (o drink)?; **prendo un caffè** I'll have a coffee; **~ qn/qc per** (scambiare) to take sb/sth for; **~ fuoco** to catch fire; **~ parte a** to take part in;

prendersi cura di qn/qc to look after sb/sth; **prendersela** (adirarsi) to get annoyed; (preoccuparsi) to get upset, worry

preno'tare /72/ vt to book, reserve; **prenotazi'one** [prenotat'tsjone] sf booking, reservation

preoccu'pare /72/ vt to worry; to preoccupy; **preoccuparsi** vpr: **preoccuparsi di qn/qc** to worry about sb/sth; **preoccuparsi per qn** to be anxious for sb; **preoccupazi'one** sf worry, anxiety

prepa'rare /72/ vt to prepare; (esame, concorso) to prepare for; **prepararsi** vpr (vestirsi) to get ready; **prepararsi a qc/a fare** to get ready o prepare (o.s.) for sth/to do; **~ da mangiare** to prepare a meal; **prepara'tivi** smpl preparations

preposizi'one [prepozit'tsjone] sf (Ling) preposition

prepo'tente ag (persona) domineering, arrogant; (bisogno, desiderio) overwhelming, pressing ▷ smf bully

'presa sf taking no pl; catching no pl; (di città) capture; (indurimento: di cemento) setting; (appiglio, Sport) hold; (di acqua, gas) (supply) point; (piccola quantità: di sale ecc) pinch; (Carte) trick; **~ (di corrente)** socket; (al muro) point; **far ~** (colla) to set; **ha fatto ~ sul pubblico** (fig) it caught the public's imagination; **essere alle prese con qc** (fig) to be struggling with sth; **~ d'aria** air inlet

pre'sagio [pre'zadʒo] sm omen

'presbite ag long-sighted

pres'crivere /105/ vt to prescribe

'prese ecc vb vedi **prendere**

presen'tare /72/ vt to present; (Amm: inoltrare) to submit; (far conoscere): **~ qn (a)** to introduce sb (to); **presentarsi** vpr (recarsi, farsi vedere) to present o.s., appear; (farsi conoscere) to introduce o.s.; (occasione) to arise; **presentarsi**

P

come candidato (*Pol*) to stand (*BRIT*) o run (*US*) as a candidate; **presentarsi bene/male** to have a good/poor appearance

pre'sente *ag* present; (*questo*) this ▷ *sm* present; **i presenti** those present; **aver ~ qc/qn** to remember sth/sb; **tener ~ qn/qc** to keep sb/sth in mind

presenti'mento *sm* premonition

pre'senza [pre'zɛntsa] *sf* presence; (*aspetto esteriore*) appearance; **~ di spirito** presence of mind

pre'sepe, pre'sepio *sm* crib

preser'vare /72/ *vt* to protect; to save; **preserva'tivo** *sm* sheath, condom

'presi *ecc vb vedi* **prendere**

'preside *smf* (*Ins*) head (teacher) (*BRIT*), principal (*US*); (*di facoltà universitaria*) dean; **~ di facoltà** (*Università*) dean of faculty

presi'dente *sm* (*Pol*) president; (*di assemblea, Comm*) chairman; **P~ del Consiglio (dei Ministri)** ≈ Prime Minister

presi'edere /29/ *vt* to preside over ▷ *vi*: **~ a** to direct, be in charge of

pressap'poco *av* about, roughly

pres'sare /72/ *vt* to press

pressi'one *sf* pressure; **far ~ su qn** to put pressure on sb; **~ sanguigna** blood pressure; **~ atmosferica** atmospheric pressure

'presso *av* (*vicino*) nearby, close at hand ▷ *prep* (*vicino a*) near; (*accanto a*) beside, next to; (*in casa di*): **~ qn** at sb's home; (*nelle lettere*) care of, c/o; (*alle dipendenze di*): **lavora ~ di noi** he works for o with us ▷ *smpl*: **nei pressi di** near, in the vicinity of

pres'tante *ag* good-looking

pres'tare /72/ *vt*: **~ (qc a qn)** to lend (sb sth o sth to sb); **prestarsi** *vpr* (*offrirsi*): **prestarsi a fare** to offer to do; (*essere adatto*): **prestarsi a** to lend itself to, be suitable for; **~ aiuto** to lend a hand; **~ ascolto** o **orecchio** to listen; **~ attenzione** to pay attention; **~ fede a qc/qn** to give credence to sth/sb; **prestazi'one** *sf* (*Tecn, Sport*) performance

prestigia'tore, -'trice [prestidʒa'tore] *sm/f* conjurer

pres'tigio [pres'tidʒo] *sm* (*potere*) prestige; (*illusione*): **gioco di ~** conjuring trick

'prestito *sm* lending *no pl*; loan; **dar in ~** to lend; **prendere in ~** to borrow

'presto *av* (*tra poco*) soon; (*in fretta*) quickly; (*di buon'ora*) early; **a ~** see you soon; **fare ~ a fare qc** to hurry up and do sth; (*non costare fatica*) to have no trouble doing sth; **si fa ~ a criticare** it's easy to criticize

pre'sumere /12/ *vt* to presume, assume

pre'sunsi *ecc vb vedi* **presumere**

presuntu'oso, -a *ag* presumptuous

presunzi'one [prezun'tsjone] *sf* presumption

'prete *sm* priest

preten'dente *smf* pretender ▷ *sm* (*corteggiatore*) suitor

pre'tendere /120/ *vt* (*esigere*) to demand, require; (*sostenere*): **~ che** to claim that; **pretende di aver sempre ragione** he thinks he's always right

> Attenzione! In inglese esiste il verbo *to pretend*, che però significa *far finta*.

pre'teso, -a *pp di* **pretendere** ▷ *sf* (*esigenza*) claim, demand; (*presunzione, sfarzo*) pretentiousness; **senza pretese** unpretentious

pre'testo *sm* pretext, excuse

preva'lere /126/ *vi* to prevail

preve'dere /82/ *vt* (*indovinare*) to foresee; (*presagire*) to foretell; (*considerare*) to make provision for

preve'nire /128/ *vt* (*anticipare*) to forestall; (: *domanda*) to anticipate; (*evitare*) to avoid, prevent

preven'tivo, -a ag preventive ▷ sm (Comm) estimate

prevenzi'one [preven'tsjone] sf prevention; (preconcetto) prejudice

previ'dente ag showing foresight; prudent; **previ'denza** sf foresight; **istituto di previdenza** provident institution; **previdenza sociale** social security (BRIT), welfare (US)

pre'vidi ecc vb vedi **prevedere**

previsi'one sf forecast, prediction; **previsioni meteorologiche** o **del tempo** weather forecast sg

pre'visto, -a pp di **prevedere** ▷ sm: **piú/meno del ~** more/less than expected

prezi'oso, -a [pret'tsjoso] ag precious; (aiuto, consiglio) invaluable ▷ sm jewel; valuable

prez'zemolo [pret'tsemolo] sm parsley

'prezzo ['prettso] sm price; **~ d'acquisto/di vendita** purchase/ selling price

prigi'one [pri'dʒone] sf prison; **prigioni'ero, -a** ag captive ▷ sm/f prisoner

'prima sf vedi **primo** ▷ av before; (in anticipo) in advance, beforehand; (per l'addietro) at one time, formerly; (più presto) sooner, earlier; (in primo luogo) first ▷ cong: **~ di fare/che parta** before doing/he leaves; **~ di** before; **~ o poi** sooner or later

pri'mario, -a ag primary; (principale) chief, leading, primary ▷ sm/f (medico) chief physician

prima'tista, -i, -e smf (Sport) record holder

pri'mato sm supremacy; (Sport) record

prima'vera sf spring

primi'tivo, -a ag primitive; (significato) original

pri'mizie [pri'mittsje] sfpl early produce sg

'primo, -a ag first; (fig) initial; basic; prime ▷ sm/f first (one) ▷ sm (Cuc) first course; (in date): **il ~ luglio** the first of July ▷ sf (Teat) first night; (Cine) première; (Aut) first (gear); **le prime ore del mattino** the early hours of the morning; **ai primi di maggio** at the beginning of May; **viaggiare in prima** to travel first-class; **in ~ luogo** first of all, in the first place; **di prim'ordine** o **di prima qualità** first-class, first-rate; **in un ~ tempo** o **momento** at first; **prima donna** leading lady; (di opera lirica) prima donna

primordi'ale ag primordial

'primula sf primrose

princi'pale [printʃi'pale] ag main, principal ▷ sm manager, boss

principal'mente [printʃipal'mente] av mainly, principally

'principe ['printʃipe] sm prince; **~ ereditario** crown prince; **princi'pessa** sf princess

principi'ante [printʃi'pjante] smf beginner

prin'cipio [prin'tʃipjo] sm (inizio) beginning, start; (origine) origin, cause; (concetto, norma) principle; **principi** smpl (concetti fondamentali) principles; **al** o **in ~** at first; **per ~** on principle; **una questione di ~** a matter of principle

priorità sf priority

priori'tario, -a ag of utmost importance; (interesse) overriding

pri'vare /72/ vt: **~ qn di** to deprive sb of; **privarsi** vpr: **privarsi di** to go o do without

pri'vato, -a ag private ▷ sm/f private citizen; **in ~** in private

privilegi'are [privile'dʒare] /62/ vt to grant a privilege to

privilegi'ato, -a [privile'dʒato] ag (individuo, classe) privileged; (trattamento, Comm: credito) preferential; **azioni privilegiate** preference shares (BRIT), preferred stock (US)

P

privi'legio [priviˈlɛdʒo] *sm* privilege
'privo, -a *ag*: **~ di** without, lacking
pro *prep* for, on behalf of ▷ *sm inv*
 (*utilità*) advantage, benefit; **a che ~?**
 what's the use?; **il ~ e il contro** the
 pros and cons
pro'babile *ag* probable, likely;
 probabilità *sf inv* probability
probabil'mente *av* probably
pro'blema, -i *sm* problem
pro'boscide [proˈbɔʃʃide] *sf* (*di*
 elefante) trunk
pro'cedere [proˈtʃɛdere] /29/ *vi* to
 proceed; (*comportarsi*) to behave;
 (*iniziare*): **~ a** to start; **~ contro** (*Dir*)
 to start legal proceedings against;
 proce'dura *sf* (*Dir*) procedure
proces'sare [protʃesˈsare] /72/ *vt*
 (*Dir*) to try
processi'one [protʃesˈsjone] *sf*
 procession
pro'cesso [proˈtʃɛsso] *sm* (*Dir*) trial;
 proceedings *pl*; (*metodo*) process
pro'cinto [proˈtʃinto] *sm*: **in ~ di fare**
 about to do, on the point of doing
procla'mare /72/ *vt* to proclaim
procre'are /72/ *vt* to procreate
procu'rare /72/ *vt*: **~ qc a qn** (*fornire*)
 to get o obtain sth for sb; (*causare*:
 noie ecc) to bring o give sb sth
pro'digio [proˈdidʒo] *sm* marvel,
 wonder; (*persona*) prodigy
pro'dotto, -a *pp di* **produrre** ▷ *sm*
 product; **prodotti agricoli** farm
 produce *sg*
pro'duco *ecc vb vedi* **produrre**
pro'durre /90/ *vt* to produce
pro'dussi *ecc vb vedi* **produrre**
produzi'one *sf* production;
 (*rendimento*) output
Prof. *abbr* (= *professore*) Prof
profa'nare /72/ *vt* to desecrate
profes'sare /72/ *vt* to profess;
 (*medicina ecc*) to practise
professio'nale *ag* professional
professi'one *sf* profession;
 professio'nista, -i, -e *smf*
 professional

profes'sore, -'essa *sm/f* (*Ins*)
 teacher; (: *di università*) lecturer;
 (: *titolare di cattedra*) professor
pro'filo *sm* profile; (*breve descrizione*)
 sketch, outline; **di ~** in profile
pro'fitto *sm* advantage, profit,
 benefit; (*fig*: *progresso*) progress;
 (*Comm*) profit
profondità *sf inv* depth
pro'fondo, -a *ag* deep; (*rancore,*
 meditazione) profound ▷ *sm* depth(s),
 bottom; **~ 8 metri** 8 metres deep
'profugo, -a, -ghi, -ghe *sm/f*
 refugee
profu'mare /72/ *vt* to perfume ▷ *vi* to
 be fragrant; **profumarsi** *vpr* to put on
 perfume o scent
profu'mato, -a *ag* (*fiore, aria*)
 fragrant; (*fazzoletto, saponetta*)
 scented; (*pelle*) sweet-smelling;
 (*persona*) with perfume on
profume'ria *sf* perfumery; (*negozio*)
 perfume shop
pro'fumo *sm* (*prodotto*) perfume,
 scent; (*fragranza*) scent, fragrance
proget'tare [prodʒetˈtare] /72/ *vt*
 to plan; (*edificio*) to plan, design;
 pro'getto *sm* plan; (*idea*) plan,
 project; **progetto di legge** bill
pro'gramma, -i *sm* programme; (*TV,*
 Radio) programmes *pl*; (*Ins*) syllabus,
 curriculum; (*Inform*) program;
 program'mare /72/ *vt* (*TV, Radio*) to
 put on; (*Inform*) to program; (*Econ*)
 to plan; **programma'tore, -'trice**
 sm/f (*Inform*) computer programmer
 (*BRIT*) o programer (*US*)
progre'dire /55/ *vi* to progress, make
 progress
pro'gresso *sm* progress *no pl*; **fare**
 progressi to make progress
proi'bire /55/ *vt* to forbid, prohibit
proiet'tare /72/ *vt* (*gen, Geom, Cine*)
 to project; (: *presentare*) to show,
 screen; (*luce, ombra*) to throw, cast,
 project; **proi'ettile** *sm* projectile,
 bullet, shell *etc*; **proiet'tore** *sm* (*Cine*)
 projector; (*Aut*) headlamp; (*Mil*)

searchlight; **proiezi'one** *sf* (Cine) projection; showing

prolife'rare /72/ *vi* (fig) to proliferate

pro'lunga, -ghe *sf* (di cavo elettrico ecc) extension

prolun'gare /80/ *vt* (discorso, attesa) to prolong; (linea, termine) to extend

prome'moria *sm inv* memorandum

pro'messa *sf* promise

pro'mettere /63/ *vt* to promise ▷ *vi* to be o look promising; **~ a qn di fare** to promise sb that one will do

promi'nente *ag* prominent

pro'misi *ecc vb vedi* **promettere**

promon'torio *sm* promontory, headland

promozi'one [promot'tsjone] *sf* promotion

promu'overe /66/ *vt* to promote

proni'pote *smf* (di nonni) great-grandchild, great-grandson/granddaughter; (di zii) great-nephew/niece

pro'nome *sm* (Ling) pronoun

pron'tezza [pron'tettsa] *sf* readiness; quickness, promptness

'pronto, -a *ag* ready; (rapido) fast, quick, prompt; **~!** (Tel) hello!; **~ all'ira** quick-tempered; **~ soccorso** (trattamento) first aid; (reparto) A&E (BRIT), ER (US)

prontu'ario *sm* manual, handbook

pro'nuncia [pro'nuntʃa] *sf* pronunciation

pronunci'are [pronun'tʃare] /14/ *vt* (parola, sentenza) to pronounce; (dire) to utter; (discorso) to deliver

propa'ganda *sf* propaganda

pro'pendere /8/ *vi*: **~ per** to favour, lean towards

propi'nare /72/ *vt* to administer

pro'porre /77/ *vt* (suggerire): **~ qc (a qn)** to suggest sth (to sb); (candidato) to put forward; (legge, brindisi) to propose; **~ di fare** to suggest o propose doing; **proporsi di fare** to propose o intend to do; **proporsi una meta** to set o.s. a goal

proporzio'nale [proportsjo'nale] *ag* proportional

proporzi'one [propor'tsjone] *sf* proportion; **in ~ a** in proportion to; **proporzioni** *sfpl* (dimensioni) proportions; **di vaste proporzioni** huge

pro'posito *sm* (intenzione) intention, aim; (argomento) subject, matter; **a ~ di** regarding, with regard to; **di ~** (apposta) deliberately, on purpose; **a ~** by the way; **capitare a ~** (cosa, persona) to turn up at the right time

proposizi'one [propozit'tsjone] *sf* (Ling) clause; (: periodo) sentence

pro'posto, -a *pp di* **proporre** ▷ *sf* proposal; (suggerimento) suggestion; **proposta di legge** bill

proprietà *sf inv* (ciò che si possiede) property, estate; (caratteristica) property; (correttezza) correctness; **~ privata** private property; **proprie'tario, -a** *sm/f* owner; (di albergo ecc) proprietor, owner; (per l'inquilino) landlord/lady

'proprio, -a *ag* (possessivo) own; (: impersonale) one's; (esatto) exact, correct, proper; (senso, significato) literal; (Ling: nome) proper; (particolare): **~ di** characteristic of, peculiar to ▷ *av* (precisamente) just, exactly; (davvero) really; (affatto): **non ... ~** not ... at all; **l'ha visto con i (suoi) propri occhi** he saw it with his own eyes

proro'gare /80/ *vt* to extend; (differire) to postpone, defer

'prosa *sf* prose

pro'sciogliere [proʃ'ʃoʎʎere] /103/ *vt* to release; (Dir) to acquit

prosciu'gare [proʃʃu'gare] /80/ *vt* (terreni) to drain, reclaim; **prosciugarsi** *vpr* to dry up

prosci'utto [proʃ'ʃutto] *sm* ham; **~ cotto/crudo** cooked/cured ham

prosegui'mento *sm* continuation; **buon ~!** all the best!; (a chi viaggia) enjoy the rest of your journey!

prosegu'ire /45/ vt to carry on with, continue ▷ vi to carry on, go on

prospe'rare /72/ vi to thrive

prospet'tare /72/ vt (esporre) to point out, show; **prospettarsi** vpr to look, appear

prospet'tiva sf (Arte) perspective; (veduta) view; (fig: previsione, possibilità) prospect

pros'petto sm (Disegno) elevation; (veduta) view, prospect; (facciata) façade, front; (tabella) table; (sommario) summary

prossimità sf nearness, proximity; **in ~ di** near (to), close to

'prossimo, -a ag (che viene subito dopo) next; (parente) close; (vicino): **~ a** near (to), close to ▷ sm neighbour, fellow man

prostitu'irsi /55/ vpr to prostitute o.s.

prosti'tuta sf prostitute

protago'nista, -i, -e smf protagonist

pro'teggere [pro'tɛddʒere] /83/ vt to protect

prote'ina sf protein

pro'tendere /120/ vt to stretch out

pro'testa sf protest

protes'tante ag, smf Protestant

protes'tare /72/ vt, vi to protest

pro'tetto, -a pp di **proteggere**

protezi'one [protet'tsjone] sf protection; (patrocinio) patronage

pro'totipo sm prototype

pro'trarre /123/ vt (prolungare) to prolong; **protrarsi** vpr to go on, continue

protube'ranza [protube'rantsa] sf protuberance, bulge

'prova sf (esperimento, cimento) test, trial; (tentativo) attempt, try; (Mat) proof no pl; (Dir) evidence no pl, proof no pl; (Ins) exam, test; (Teat) rehearsal; (di abito) fitting; **a ~ di** (in testimonianza di) as proof of; **a ~ di fuoco** fireproof; **mettere alla ~** to put to the test; **giro di ~** test o trial

run; **fino a ~ contraria** until (it's) proved otherwise; **~ generale** (Teat) dress rehearsal

pro'vare /72/ vt (sperimentare) to test; (tentare) to try, attempt; (assaggiare) to try, taste; (sperimentare in sé) to experience; (sentire) to feel; (cimentare) to put to the test; (dimostrare) to prove; (abito) to try on; **~ a fare** to try o attempt to do

proveni'enza [prove'njɛntsa] sf origin, source

prove'nire /128/ vi: **~ da** to come from

pro'venti smpl revenue sg

pro'verbio sm proverb

pro'vetta sf test tube; **bambino in ~** test-tube baby

pro'vider [pro'vaider] sm inv (Inform) service provider

pro'vincia [pro'vintʃa], **-ce** o **-cie** sf province

pro'vino sm (Cine) screen test; (campione) specimen

provo'cante ag (attraente) provocative

provo'care /20/ vt (causare) to cause, bring about; (eccitare: riso, pietà) to arouse; (irritare, sfidare) to provoke; **provocazi'one** sf provocation

provve'dere /82/ vi (prendere un provvedimento) to take steps, act; (disporre): **~ (a)** to provide (for); **provvedi'mento** sm measure; (di previdenza) precaution

provvi'denza [provvi'dɛntsa] sf: **la ~** providence

provvigi'one [provvi'dʒone] sf (Comm) commission

provvi'sorio, -a ag temporary

prov'vista sf supply

'prua sf (Naut) bow(s), prow

pru'dente ag cautious, prudent; (assennato) sensible, wise; **pru'denza** sf prudence, caution; wisdom

'prudere /29/ vi to itch, be itchy

'prugna ['pruɲɲa] sf plum; **~ secca** prune

pru'rito *sm* itchiness *no pl*; itch
P.S. *abbr* (= *postscriptum*) PS ▷ *sigla f*
(*Polizia*) = **Pubblica Sicurezza**
pseu'donimo *sm* pseudonym
psica'nalisi *sf* psychoanalysis
psicana'lista, -i, -e *smf*
psychoanalyst
'psiche ['psike] *sf* (*Psic*) psyche
psichi'atra, -i, -e [psi'kjatra] *smf*
psychiatrist; **psichi'atrico, -a, -ci,
-che** *ag* psychiatric
psicolo'gia [psikolo'dʒia] *sf*
psychology; **psico'logico, -a, -ci,
-che** *ag* psychological; **psi'cologo,
-a, -gi, -ghe** *sm/f* psychologist
psico'patico, -a, -ci, -che *ag*
psychopathic ▷ *sm/f* psychopath
pubbli'care /20/ *vt* to publish
pubblicazi'one [pubblikat'tsjone]
sf publication
pubblicità [pubblitʃi'ta] *sf*
(*diffusione*) publicity; (*attività*)
advertising; (*annunci nei giornali*)
advertisements *pl*
'pubblico, -a, -ci, -che *ag* public;
(*statale, scuola ecc*) state *cpd* ▷ *sm*
public; (*spettatori*) audience; **in ~** in
public; **~ funzionario** civil servant;
P~ Ministero Public Prosecutor's
Office; **la Pubblica Sicurezza** the
police
'pube *sm* (*Anat*) pubis
pubertà *sf* puberty
'pudico, -a, -ci, -che *ag* modest
pu'dore *sm* modesty
pue'rile *ag* childish
pugi'lato [pudʒi'lato] *sm* boxing
'pugile ['pudʒile] *sm* boxer
pugna'lare [puɲɲa'lare] /72/ *vt*
to stab
pu'gnale [puɲ'ɲale] *sm* dagger
'pugno ['puɲɲo] *sm* fist; (*colpo*)
punch; (*quantità*) fistful
'pulce ['pultʃe] *sf* flea
pul'cino [pul'tʃino] *sm* chick
pu'lire /55/ *vt* to clean; (*lucidare*)
to polish; **pu'lito, -a** *ag* (*anche fig*)
clean; (*ordinato*) neat, tidy; **puli'tura**

sf cleaning; **pulitura a secco**
dry-cleaning; **puli'zia** *sf* cleaning;
(*condizione*) cleanness; **fare le
pulizie** to do the cleaning, do the
housework; **pulizia etnica** ethnic
cleansing
'pullman *sm inv* coach
pul'lover *sm inv* pullover, jumper
pullu'lare /72/ *vi* to swarm, teem
pul'mino *sm* minibus
'pulpito *sm* pulpit
pul'sante *sm* (push-)button
pul'sare /72/ *vi* to pulsate, beat
pul'viscolo *sm* fine dust;
~ atmosferico specks *pl* of dust
'puma *sm inv* puma
pun'gente [pun'dʒente] *ag* prickly;
stinging; (*anche fig*) biting
'pungere ['pundʒere] /84/ *vt* to
prick; (*insetto, ortica*) to sting; (*freddo*)
to bite
pungigli'one [pundʒiʎ'ʎone] *sm*
sting
pu'nire /55/ *vt* to punish;
puni'zione *sf* punishment; (*Sport*)
penalty
'punsi *ecc vb vedi* **pungere**
'punta *sf* point; (*parte terminale*)
tip, end; (*di monte*) peak; (*di costa*)
promontory; (*minima parte*) touch,
trace; **in ~ di piedi** on tiptoe; **ore di
~** peak hours; **uomo di ~** front-rank
o leading man
pun'tare /72/ *vt* (*piedi a terra, gomiti
sul tavolo*) to plant; (*dirigere: pistola*)
to point; (*scommettere*): **~ su** to bet on
▷ *vi* (*mirare*): **~ a** to aim at; (*avviarsi*):
~ su to head *o* make for; (*fig: contare*):
~ su to count *o* rely on
pun'tata *sf* (*gita*) short trip;
(*scommessa*) bet; (*di opera*)
instalment; **romanzo a puntate**
serial
punteggia'tura [punteddʒa'tura]
sf (*Ling*) punctuation
pun'teggio [pun'teddʒo] *sm* score
puntel'lare /72/ *vt* to support
pun'tello *sm* prop, support

pun'tina *sf*: ~ **da disegno** drawing pin

pun'tino *sm* dot; **fare qc a ~** to do sth properly

'**punto, -a** *pp di* **pungere** ▷ *sm* point; (*segno, macchiolina*) dot; (*Ling*) full stop; (*di indirizzo e-mail*) dot; (*posto*) spot; (*a scuola*) mark; (*nel cucire, nella maglia, Med*) stitch ▷ *av*: **non ... ~** not ... at all; **~ cardinale** point of the compass, cardinal point; **~ debole** weak point; **~ esclamativo/interrogativo** exclamation/question mark; **~ nero** (*comedone*) blackhead; **~ di partenza** (*anche fig*) starting point; **~ di riferimento** landmark; (*fig*) point of reference; **~ di vendita** retail outlet; **~ e virgola** semicolon; **~ di vista** (*fig*) point of view

puntu'ale *ag* punctual

pun'tura *sf* (*di ago*) prick; (*di insetto*) sting, bite; (*Med*) puncture; (: *iniezione*) injection; (*dolore*) sharp pain

> Attenzione! In inglese esiste la parola *puncture*, che si usa per indicare la foratura di una gomma.

punzecchi'are [puntsek'kjare] /19/ *vt* to prick; (*fig*) to tease

può *vb vedi* **potere**

pu'pazzo [pu'pattso] *sm* puppet

pu'pillo, -a *sm/f* (*Dir*) ward ▷ *sf* (*Anat*) pupil

purché [pur'ke] *cong* provided that, on condition that

'**pure** *cong* (*tuttavia*) and yet, nevertheless; (*anche se*) even if ▷ *av* (*anche*) too, also; **pur di** (*al fine di*) just to; **faccia ~!** go ahead!, please do!

purè *sm*, **pu'rea** *sf* (*Cuc*) purée; (*di patate*) mashed potatoes *pl*

pu'rezza [pu'rettsa] *sf* purity

pur'gante *sm* (*Med*) purgative, purge

purga'torio *sm* purgatory

purifi'care /20/ *vt* to purify; (*metallo*) to refine

'**puro, -a** *ag* pure; (*acqua*) clear, limpid; (*vino*) undiluted; **puro'sangue** *sm inv*, *f inv* thoroughbred

pur'troppo *av* unfortunately

pus *sm* pus

'**pustola** *sf* pimple

puti'ferio *sm* rumpus, row

put'tana *sf* (*fam!*) whore (!)

puz'zare [put'tsare] /72/ *vi* to stink

'**puzzo** ['puttso] *sm* stink, foul smell

'**puzzola** ['puttsola] *sf* polecat

puzzo'lente [puttso'lɛnte] *ag* stinking

P.V.C. [pivi'tʃi] *sigla m* (= *polyvinyl chloride*) PVC

q

q *abbr* (= *quintale*) q

qua *av* here; **in ~** (*verso questa parte*) this way; **da un anno in ~** for a year now; **da quando in ~?** since when?; **per di ~** (*passare*) this way; **al di ~ di** (*fiume, strada*) on this side of; **~ dentro/fuori** *ecc* in/out here *ecc*; *vedi anche* **questo**

qua'derno *sm* notebook; (*per scuola*) exercise book

qua'drante *sm* quadrant; (*di orologio*) face

qua'drare /72/ *vi* (*bilancio*) to balance, tally; **~ (con)** to correspond (with) ▷ *vt* (*Mat*) to square; **non mi quadra** I don't like it; **qua'drato, -a** *ag* square; (*fig: equilibrato*) level-headed, sensible; (*: peg*) square ▷ *sm* (*Mat*) square; (*Pugilato*) ring; **5 al quadrato** 5 squared

quadri'foglio [kwadri'fɔʎʎo] *sm* four-leaf clover

quadri'mestre *sm* (*periodo*) four-month period; (*Ins*) term

'quadro *sm* (*pittura*) painting, picture; (*quadrato*) square; (*tabella*) table, chart; (*Tecn*) board, panel; (*Teat*) scene; (*fig: scena, spettacolo*) sight; (*: descrizione*) outline, description; **quadri** *smpl* (*Pol*) party organizers; (*Comm*) managerial staff; (*Mil*) cadres; (*Carte*) diamonds

'quadruplo, -a *ag, sm* quadruple

quaggiù [kwad'dʒu] *av* down here

'quaglia ['kwaʎʎa] *sf* quail

PAROLA CHIAVE

'qualche ['kwalke] *det* **1** some, a few; (*in interrogative*) any; **ho comprato qualche libro** I've bought some *o* a few books; **qualche volta** sometimes; **hai qualche sigaretta?** have you any cigarettes?
2 (*uno*): **c'è qualche medico?** is there a doctor?; **in qualche modo** somehow
3 (*un certo, parecchio*) some; **un personaggio di qualche rilievo** a figure of some importance
4: **qualche cosa** = **qualcosa**

qual'cosa *pron* something; (*in espressioni interrogative*) anything; **qualcos'altro** something else; anything else; **~ di nuovo** something new; anything new; **~ da mangiare** something to eat; anything to eat; **c'è ~ che non va?** is there something *o* anything wrong?

qual'cuno *pron* (*persona*) someone, somebody; (*: in espressioni interrogative*) anyone, anybody; (*alcuni*) some; **~ è favorevole a noi** some are on our side; **qualcun altro** someone *o* somebody else; anyone *o* anybody else

PAROLA CHIAVE

'quale (*spesso troncato in* **qual**) *det* **1** (*interrogativo*) what; (*: scegliendo tra*

due o più cose o persone) which; **quale uomo/denaro?** what man/money?; which man/money?; **quali sono i tuoi programmi?** what are your plans?; **quale stanza preferisci?** which room do you prefer?
2 (*relativo, come*): **il risultato fu quale ci si aspettava** the result was as expected
3 (*in elenchi*) such as, like; **piante quali l'edera** plants such as *o* like ivy
4 (*esclamativo*) what; **quale disgrazia!** what bad luck!
▶ *pron* **1** (*interrogativo*) which; **quale dei due scegli?** which of the two do you want?
2 (*relativo*): **il (la) quale** (*persona*) (*soggetto*) who; (*oggetto, con preposizione*) whom; (*cosa*) which; (*possessivo*) whose; **suo padre, il quale è avvocato, ...** his father, who is a lawyer, ...; **il signore con il quale parlavo** the gentleman to whom I was speaking; **l'albergo al quale ci siamo fermati** the hotel where we stayed *o* which we stayed at; **la signora della quale ammiriamo la bellezza** the lady whose beauty we admire
▶ *av* as; **quale sindaco di questa città** as mayor of this town

qua'lifica, -che *sf* qualification; (*titolo*) title
qualifi'cato, -a *ag* (*dotato di qualifica*) qualified; (*esperto, abile*) skilled; **non mi ritengo ~ per questo lavoro** I don't think I'm qualified for this job; **è un medico molto ~** he is a very distinguished doctor
qualificazi'one *sf*: **gara di ~** (*Sport*) qualifying event
qualità *sf inv* quality; **in ~ di** in one's capacity as
qua'lora *cong* in case, if
qual'siasi, qua'lunque *det* (*inv*) any; (*quale che sia*) whatever; (*discriminativo*) whichever; (*posposto,*

mediocre) poor, indifferent; ordinary; **mettiti un vestito ~** put on any old dress; **~ cosa** anything; **~ cosa accada** whatever happens; **a ~ costo** at any cost, whatever the cost; **l'uomo ~** the man in the street; **~ persona** anyone, anybody

'quando *cong, av* when; **~ sarò ricco** when I'm rich; **da ~** (*dacché*) since; (*interrogativo*): **da ~ sei qui?** how long have you been here?; **quand'anche** even if

quantità *sf inv* quantity; **una ~ di** (*gran numero*) a great deal of; a lot of; **in grande ~** in large quantities

PAROLA CHIAVE

'quanto, -a *det* **1** (*interrogativo: quantità*) how much; (*: numero*) how many; **quanto pane/denaro?** how much bread/money?; **quanti libri/ragazzi?** how many books/boys?; **quanto tempo?** how long?; **quanti anni hai?** how old are you?
2 (*esclamativo*): **quante storie!** what a lot of nonsense!; **quanto tempo sprecato!** what a waste of time!
3 (*relativo: quantità*) as much ... as; (*: numero*) as many ... as; **ho quanto denaro mi occorre** I have as much money as I need; **prendi quanti libri vuoi** take as many books as you like
▶ *pron* **1** (*interrogativo: quantità*) how much; (*: numero*) how many; (*: tempo*) how long; **quanto mi dai?** how much will you give me?; **quanti me ne hai portati?** how many did you bring me?; **da quanto sei qui?** how long have you been here?; **quanti ne abbiamo oggi?** what's the date today?
2 (*relativo: quantità*) as much as; (*: numero*) as many as; **farò quanto posso** I'll do as much as I can; **possono venire quanti sono stati invitati** all those who have been invited can come

▸ *av* **1** (*interrogativo: con ag, av*) how; (: *con vb*) how much; **quanto stanco ti sembrava?** how tired did he seem to you?; **quanto corre la tua moto?** how fast can your motorbike go?; **quanto costa?** how much does it cost?; **quant'è?** how much is it?
2 (*esclamativo: con ag, av*) how; (: *con vb*) how much; **quanto sono felice!** how happy I am!; **sapessi quanto abbiamo camminato!** if you knew how far we've walked!; **studierò quanto posso** I'll study as much as o all I can; **quanto prima** as soon as possible
3: in quanto (*in qualità di*) as; (*perché, per il fatto che*) as, since; **(in) quanto a** (*per ciò che riguarda*) as for, as regards
4: per quanto (*nonostante, anche se*) however; **per quanto si sforzi, non ce la farà** try as he may, he won't manage it; **per quanto sia brava, fa degli errori** however good she may be, she makes mistakes

qua'ranta *num* forty
quaran'tena *sf* quarantine
quaran'tesimo, -a *num* fortieth
quaran'tina *sf*: **una ~ (di)** about forty
'**quarta** *sf vedi* **quarto**
quar'tetto *sm* quartet(te)
quarti'ere *sm* district, area; (*Mil*) quarters *pl*: **~ generale** headquarters *pl*
'**quarto, -a** *ag* fourth ▸ *sm* fourth; (*quarta parte*) quarter ▸ *sf* (*Aut*) fourth (gear); **le 6 e un ~** a quarter past (BRIT) o after (US) 6; **~ d'ora** quarter of an hour; **quarti di finale** quarter finals
'**quarzo** ['kwartso] *sm* quartz
'**quasi** *av* almost, nearly ▸ *cong* (*anche*: **~ che**) as if; **(non) ... ~ mai** hardly ever; **~ ~ me ne andrei** I've half a mind to leave
quas'sù *av* up here

quat'tordici [kwat'torditʃi] *num* fourteen
quat'trini *smpl* money *sg*, cash *sg*
'**quattro** *num* four; **in ~ e quattr'otto** in less than no time; **quattro'cento** *num* four hundred ▸ *sm*: **il Quattrocento** the fifteenth century

PAROLA CHIAVE

'**quello, -a** (*dav sm* **quel** + *C,* **quell'** + *V,* **quello** + *s impura, gn, pn, ps, x, z; pl* **quei** + *C,* **quegli** + *V o s impura, gn, pn, ps, x, z; dav sf* **quella** + *C,* **quell'** + *V; pl* **quelle**) *det* that; (*pl*) those; **quella casa** that house; **quegli uomini** those men; **voglio quella camicia (lì o là)** I want that shirt
▸ *pron* **1** (*dimostrativo*) that one; (: *pl*) those ones; (: *ciò*) that; **conosci quella?** do you know her?; **prendo quello bianco** I'll take the white one; **chi è quello?** who's that?; **prendiamo quello (lì o là)** let's take that one (there)
2 (*relativo*): **quello(a) che** (*persona*) the one (who); (*cosa*) the one (which), the one (that); **quelli(e) che** (*persone*) those who; (*cose*) those which; **è lui quello che non voleva venire** he's the one who didn't want to come; **ho fatto quello che potevo** I did what I could

'**quercia, -ce** ['kwertʃa] *sf* oak (tree); (*legno*) oak
que'rela *sf* (*Dir*) (legal) action
que'sito *sm* question, query; problem
questio'nario *sm* questionnaire
questi'one *sf* problem, question; (*controversia*) issue; (*litigio*) quarrel; **in ~** in question; **è ~ di tempo** it's a matter o question of time

PAROLA CHIAVE

'**questo, -a** *det* **1** (*dimostrativo*) this; (: *pl*) these; **questo libro (qui o**

q

qua) this book; **io prendo questo cappotto, tu quello** I'll take this coat, you take that one; **quest'oggi** today; **questa sera** this evening **2** (*enfatico*): **non fatemi più prendere di queste paure** don't frighten me like that again ▶ *pron* (*dimostrativo*) this (one); (: *pl*) these (ones); (: *ciò*) this; **prendo questo (qui** *o* **qua)** I'll take this one; **preferisci questi o quelli?** do you prefer these (ones) or those (ones)?; **questo intendevo io** this is what I meant; **vengono Paolo e Luca: questo da Roma, quello da Palermo** Paolo and Luca are coming: the former from Palermo, the latter from Rome

ques'tura *sf* police headquarters *pl*
qui *av* here; **da** *o* **di ~** from here; **di ~ in avanti** from now on; **di ~ a poco/ una settimana** in a little while/a week's time; **~ dentro/sopra/ vicino** in/up/near here; *vedi anche* **questo**
quie'tanza [kwje'tantsa] *sf* receipt
qui'ete *sf* quiet, quietness; calmness; stillness; peace
qui'eto, -a *ag* quiet; (*notte*) calm, still; (*mare*) calm
'**quindi** *av* then ▷ *cong* therefore, so
'**quindici** ['kwinditʃi] *num* fifteen; **~ giorni** a fortnight (BRIT), two weeks
quindi'cina [kwindi'tʃina] *sf* (*serie*): **una ~ (di)** about fifteen; **fra una ~ di giorni** in a fortnight (BRIT) *o* two weeks
quinta *sf vedi* **quinto**
quin'tale *sm* quintal (100 kg)
'**quinto, -a** *num* fifth ▷ *sf* (*Aut*) fifth (gear)
quiz [kwidz] *sm inv* (*domanda*) question; (*anche*: **gioco a ~**) quiz game
'**quota** *sf* (*parte*) quota, share; (*Aer*) height, altitude; (*Ippica*) odds *pl*:

prendere/perdere ~ (*Aer*) to gain/ lose height *o* altitude; **~ d'iscrizione** enrolment fee; (*ad un club*) membership fee
quotidi'ano, -a *ag* daily; (*banale*) everyday ▷ *sm* (*giornale*) daily (paper)
quozi'ente [kwot'tsjɛnte] *sm* (*Mat*) quotient; **~ d'intelligenza** intelligence quotient, IQ

r

R, r ['ɛrre] *sm o f (lettera)* R, r; **R come Roma** ≈ R for Robert (*BRIT*), R for Roger (*US*)

'**rabbia** *sf (ira)* anger, rage; *(accanimento, furia)* fury; *(Med: idrofobia)* rabies *sg*

rab'bino *sm* rabbi

rabbi'oso, -a *ag* angry, furious; *(facile all'ira)* quick-tempered; *(forze, acqua ecc)* furious, raging; *(Med)* rabid, mad

rabbo'nire /55/ *vt* to calm down

rabbrivi'dire /55/ *vi* to shudder, shiver

raccapez'zarsi [rakkapet'tsarsi] /72/ *vpr:* **non ~** to be at a loss

raccapricci'ante [rakkaprit'tʃante] *ag* horrifying

raccatta'palle *sm inv (Sport)* ballboy

raccat'tare /72/ *vt* to pick up

rac'chetta [rak'ketta] *sf (per tennis)* racket; *(per ping-pong)* bat; **~ da neve** snowshoe; **~ da sci** ski stick

racchi'udere [rak'kjudere] /22/ *vt* to contain

rac'cogliere [rak'kɔʎʎere] /23/ *vt* to collect; *(raccattare)* to pick up; *(frutti, fiori)* to pick, pluck; *(Agr)* to harvest; *(approvazione, voti)* to win

raccogli'tore [rakkoʎʎi'tore] *sm (cartella)* folder, binder

rac'colta *sf vedi* **raccolto**

rac'colto, -a *pp di* **raccogliere** ▷ *ag (persona: pensoso)* thoughtful; *(luogo: appartato)* secluded, quiet ▷ *sm (Agr)* crop, harvest ▷ *sf* collecting *no pl*; collection; *(Agr)* harvesting *no pl*, gathering *no pl*; harvest, crop; *(adunata)* gathering; **raccolta differenziata** *(dei rifiuti)* separate collection of different kinds of household waste

raccoman'dabile *ag (highly)* commendable; **è un tipo poco ~** he is not to be trusted

raccoman'dare /72/ *vt* to recommend; *(affidare)* to entrust; **~ a qn di fare qc** to recommend that sb does sth

raccoman'dato, -a *ag (lettera, pacco)* recorded-delivery ▷ *sf (anche:* **lettera raccomandata**) recorded-delivery letter

raccon'tare /72/ *vt:* **~ (a qn)** *(dire)* to tell (sb); *(narrare)* to relate (to sb), tell (sb) about; **rac'conto** *sm* telling *no pl*, relating *no pl*; *(fatto raccontato)* story, tale; **racconti per bambini** children's stories

rac'cordo *sm (Tecn: giunzione)* connection, joint; **~ anulare** *(Aut)* ring road (*BRIT*), beltway (*US*); **~ autostradale** slip road (*BRIT*), entrance *(o exit)* ramp (*US*); **~ ferroviario** siding; **~ stradale** link road

racimo'lare [ratʃimo'lare] /72/ *vt (fig)* to scrape together, glean

'**rada** *sf (natural)* harbour (*BRIT*) *o* harbor (*US*)

'**radar** *sm inv* radar

raddoppi'are /19/ *vt*, *vi* to double

raddriz'zare [raddrit'tsare] /72/ *vt* to straighten; (*fig: correggere*) to put straight, correct

'**radere** /85/ *vt* (*barba*) to shave off; (*mento*) to shave; (*fig: rasentare*) to graze; to skim; **radersi** *vpr* to shave (o.s.); **~ al suolo** to raze to the ground

radi'are /19/ *vt* to strike off

radia'tore *sm* radiator

radiazi'one [radjat'tsjone] *sf* (*Fisica*) radiation; (*cancellazione*) striking off

radi'cale *ag* radical ▷ *sm* (*Ling*) root; **radicali liberi** free radicals

ra'dicchio [ra'dikkjo] *sm* variety of chicory

ra'dice [ra'ditʃe] *sf* root

'**radio** *sf inv* radio ▷ *sm* (*Chim*) radium; **radioat'tivo, -a** *ag* radioactive; **radio'cronaca, -che** *sf* radio commentary; **radiogra'fia** *sf* radiography; (*foto*) X-ray photograph

radi'oso, -a *ag* radiant

radios'veglia [radjoz'veʎʎa] *sf* radio alarm

'**rado, -a** *ag* (*capelli*) sparse, thin; (*visite*) infrequent; **di ~** rarely

radu'nare /72/ *vt*, **radu'narsi** *vpr* to gather, assemble

ra'dura *sf* clearing

raf'fermo, -a *ag* stale

'**raffica, -che** *sf* (*Meteor*) gust (of wind); **~ di colpi** (*di fucile*) burst of gunfire

raffigu'rare /72/ *vt* to represent

raffi'nato, -a *ag* refined

raffor'zare [raffor'tsare] /72/ *vt* to reinforce

raffredda'mento *sm* cooling

raffred'dare /72/ *vt* (*fig*) to dampen, have a cooling effect on; **raffreddarsi** *vpr* to grow cool o cold; (*prendere un raffreddore*) to catch a cold; (*fig*) to cool (off)

raffred'dato, -a *ag* (*Med*): **essere ~** to have a cold

raffred'dore *sm* (*Med*) cold

raf'fronto *sm* comparison

'**rafia** *sf* (*fibra*) raffia

rafting ['rafting] *sm* white-water rafting

ra'gazzo, -a [ra'gattso] *sm/f* boy/ girl; (*fam: fidanzato*) boyfriend/ girlfriend; **ragazzi** *smpl* (*figli*) kids; **ragazza madre** unmarried mother; **ciao ragazzi!** (*gruppo*) hi guys!

raggi'ante [rad'dʒante] *ag* radiant, shining

'**raggio** ['raddʒo] *sm* (*di sole ecc*) ray; (*Mat, distanza*) radius; (*di ruota ecc*) spoke; **~ d'azione** range; **raggi X** X-rays

raggi'rare [raddʒi'rare] /72/ *vt* to take in, trick

raggi'ungere [rad'dʒundʒere] /5/ *vt* to reach; (*persona: riprendere*) to catch up (with); (*bersaglio*) to hit; (*fig: meta*) to achieve

raggomito'larsi /72/ *vpr* to curl up

raggranel'lare /72/ *vt* to scrape together

raggrup'pare /72/ *vt* to group (together)

ragiona'mento [radʒona'mento] *sm* reasoning *no pl*; arguing *no pl*; argument

ragio'nare [radʒo'nare] /72/ *vi* to reason; (*discorrere*): **~ (di)** to argue (about)

ragi'one [ra'dʒone] *sf* reason; (*dimostrazione, prova*) argument, reason; (*diritto*) right; **aver ~** to be right; **aver ~ di qn** to get the better of sb; (*fatto*) to prove sb right; **in ~ di** at the rate of; to the amount of; according to; **a o con ~** rightly, justly; **perdere la ~** to become insane; (*fig*) to take leave of one's senses; **a ragion veduta** after due consideration; **~ sociale** (*Comm*) corporate name

ragione'ria [radʒone'ria] *sf* accountancy; (*ufficio*) accounts department

ragio'nevole [radʒo'nevole] *ag*
reasonable

ragioni'ere, -a [radʒo'njɛre] *sm/f*
accountant

ragli'are [raʎ'ʎare] /27/ *vi* to bray

ragna'tela [raɲɲa'tela] *sf* cobweb,
spider's web

'ragno ['raɲɲo] *sm* spider

ragù *sm inv* (*Cuc*) meat sauce (*for
pasta*); stew

RAI-TV [raiti'vu] *sigla f* (= *Radio
televisione italiana*) Italian Broadcasting
Company

ralle'grare /72/ *vt* to cheer up;
rallegrarsi *vpr* to cheer up; (*provare
allegrezza*) to rejoice; **rallegrarsi con
qn** to congratulate sb

rallen'tare /72/ *vt* to slow down; (*fig*)
to lessen, slacken ▷ *vi* to slow down

rallenta'tore *sm* (*Cine*) slow-motion
camera; **al ~** (*anche fig*) in slow
motion

raman'zina [raman'dzina] *sf*
lecture, telling-off

'rame *sm* (*Chim*) copper

rammari'carsi /20/ *vpr*: **~ (di)**
(*rincrescersi*) to be sorry (about),
regret; (*lamentarsi*) to complain
(about)

rammen'dare /72/ *vt* to mend;
(*calza*) to darn

'ramo *sm* branch

ramo'scello [ramoʃ'ʃɛllo] *sm* twig

'rampa *sf* flight (of stairs); **~ di lancio**
launching pad

rampi'cante *ag* (*Bot*) climbing

'rana *sf* frog

'rancido, -a ['rantʃido] *ag* rancid

ran'core *sm* rancour, resentment

ran'dagio, -a, -gi, -gie *o* **-ge**
[ran'dadʒo] *ag* (*gatto, cane*) stray

ran'dello *sm* club, cudgel

'rango, -ghi *sm* (*grado*) rank;
(*condizione sociale*) station

rannicchi'arsi [rannik'kjarsi] /19/
vpr to crouch, huddle

rannuvo'larsi /72/ *vpr* to cloud over,
become overcast

'rapa *sf* (*Bot*) turnip

ra'pace [ra'patʃe] *ag* (*animale*)
predatory; (*fig*) rapacious, grasping
▷ *sm* bird of prey

ra'pare /72/ *vt* (*capelli*) to crop, cut
very short

rapida'mente *av* quickly, rapidly

rapidità *sf* speed

'rapido, -a *ag* fast; (*esame, occhiata*)
quick, rapid ▷ *sm* (*Ferr*) express
(train)

rapi'mento *sm* kidnapping; (*fig*)
rapture

ra'pina *sf* robbery; **~ in banca** bank
robbery; **~ a mano armata** armed
robbery; **rapi'nare** /72/ *vt* to rob;
rapina'tore, -'trice *sm/f* robber

ra'pire /55/ *vt* (*cose*) to steal;
(*persone*) to kidnap; (*fig*) to enrapture,
delight; **rapi'tore, -'trice** *sm/f*
kidnapper

rap'porto *sm* (*resoconto*) report;
(*legame*) relationship; (*Mat, Tecn*)
ratio; **rapporti sessuali** sexual
intercourse *sg*

rappre'saglia [rappre'saʎʎa] *sf*
reprisal, retaliation

rappresen'tante *smf* representative

rappresen'tare /72/ *vt* to represent;
(*Teat*) to perform; **rappresentazi'one**
sf representation; performing *no pl*;
(*spettacolo*) performance

rara'mente *av* seldom, rarely

rare'fatto, -a *ag* rarefied

'raro, -a *ag* rare

ra'sare /72/ *vt* (*barba ecc*) to shave off;
(*siepi, erba*) to trim, cut; **rasarsi** *vpr* to
shave (o.s.)

raschi'are [ras'kjare] /19/ *vt* to
scrape; (*macchia, fango*) to scrape off
▷ *vi* to clear one's throat

ra'sente *prep*: **~ (a)** close to, very near

'raso, -a *pp di* **radere** ▷ *ag* (*barba*)
shaved; (*capelli*) cropped; (*con misure
di capacità*) level; (*pieno: bicchiere*)
full to the brim ▷ *sm* (*tessuto*) satin;
~ terra close to the ground; **un
cucchiaio ~** a level spoonful

ra'soio *sm* razor; **~ elettrico** electric shaver *o* razor

ras'segna [ras'seɲɲa] *sf* (*Mil*) inspection, review; (*esame*) inspection; (*resoconto*) review, survey; (*pubblicazione letteraria ecc*) review; (*mostra*) exhibition, show; **passare in ~** (*Mil: fig*) to review

rasse'gnare [rasseɲ'ɲare] /15/ *vt*: **~ le dimissioni** to resign; **rassegnarsi** *vpr* (*accettare*): **rassegnarsi (a qc/a fare)** to resign o.s. (to sth/to doing)

rassicu'rare /72/ *vt* to reassure

rasso'dare /72/ *vt* to harden, stiffen; **rassodarsi** *vpr* to harden, to strengthen

rassomigli'anza [rassomiʎ'ʎantsa] *sf* resemblance

rassomigli'are [rassomiʎ'ʎare] /27/ *vi*: **~ a** to resemble, look like

rastrel'lare /72/ *vt* to rake; (*fig: perlustrare*) to comb

ras'trello *sm* rake

'rata *sf* (*quota*) instalment; **pagare a rate** to pay by instal(l)ments *o* on hire purchase (BRIT)

ratifi'care /20/ *vt* (*Dir*) to ratify

'ratto *sm* (*Dir*) abduction; (*Zool*) rat

rattop'pare /72/ *vt* to patch

rattris'tare /72/ *vt* to sadden; **rattristarsi** *vpr* to become sad

'rauco, -a, -chi, -che *ag* hoarse

rava'nello *sm* radish

ravi'oli *smpl* ravioli *sg*

ravvi'vare /72/ *vt* to revive; (*fig*) to brighten up, enliven

razio'nale [rattsjo'nale] *ag* rational

razio'nare [rattsjo'nare] /72/ *vt* to ration

razi'one [rat'tsjone] *sf* ration; (*porzione*) portion, share

'razza ['rattsa] *sf* race; (*Zool*) breed; (*discendenza, stirpe*) stock, race; (*sorta*) sort, kind

razzi'ale [rat'tsjale] *ag* racial

raz'zismo [rat'tsizmo] *sm* racism, racialism

raz'zista, -i, -e [rat'tsista] *ag, smf* racist, racialist

'razzo ['raddzo] *sm* rocket

RC *sigla* = **Reggio Calabria**; (= *partito della Rifondazione Comunista*) left-wing Italian political party

re *sm inv* king; (*Mus*) D; (: *solfeggiando la scala*) re; **i Re Magi** the Three Wise Men, the Magi

rea'gire [rea'dʒire] /55/ *vi* to react

re'ale *ag* real; (*di, da re*) royal ▷ *sm*: **il ~** reality

reality [ri'aliti] *sm inv* reality show

realiz'zare [realid'dzare] /72/ *vt* (*progetto ecc*) to realize, carry out; (*sogno, desiderio*) to realize, fulfil; (*scopo*) to achieve; (*Comm: titoli ecc*) to realize; (*Calcio: ecc*) to score; **realizzarsi** *vpr* to be realized

real'mente *av* really, actually

realtà *sf inv* reality

re'ato *sm* offence

reat'tore *sm* (*Fisica*) reactor; (*Aer: aereo*) jet; (: *motore*) jet engine

reazio'nario, -a [reattsjo'narjo] *ag* (*Pol*) reactionary

reazi'one [reat'tsjone] *sf* reaction

'rebus *sm inv* rebus; (*fig*) puzzle; enigma

recapi'tare /72/ *vt* to deliver

re'capito *sm* (*indirizzo*) address; (*consegna*) delivery; **~ telefonico** phone number; **~ a domicilio** home delivery (service)

re'care /20/ *vt* (*portare*) to bring; **recarsi** *vpr*: **recarsi in città/a scuola** to go into town/to school

re'cedere [re'tʃedere] /29/ *vi* to withdraw

recensi'one [retʃen'sjone] *sf* review

re'cente [re'tʃɛnte] *ag* recent; **di ~** recently; **recente'mente** *av* recently

re'cidere [re'tʃidere] /34/ *vt* to cut off, chop off

recin'tare [retʃin'tare] /72/ *vt* to enclose, fence off

re'cinto [re'tʃinto] *sm* enclosure; (*ciò che recinge*) fence; surrounding wall

recipi'ente [retʃi'pjɛnte] *sm* container

re'ciproco, -a, -ci, -che [re'tʃiproko] *ag* reciprocal

'recita ['rɛtʃita] *sf* performance

reci'tare [retʃi'tare] /72/ *vt* (*poesia, lezione*) to recite; (*dramma*) to perform; (*ruolo*) to play o act (the part of)

recla'mare /72/ *vi* to complain ▷ *vt* (*richiedere*) to demand

re'clamo *sm* complaint

recli'nabile *ag* (*sedile*) reclining

reclusi'one *sf* (*Dir*) imprisonment

re'cluta *sf* recruit

re'condito, -a *ag* secluded; (*fig*) secret, hidden

'record *ag inv* record *cpd* ▷ *sm inv* record; **in tempo ~, a tempo di ~** in record time; **detenere il ~ di** to hold the record for; **~ mondiale** world record

recriminazi'one [rekriminat'tsjone] *sf* recrimination

recupe'rare *ecc* = **ricuperare** *ecc*

redargu'ire /55/ *vt* to rebuke

re'dassi *ecc vb vedi* **redigere**

reddi'tizio, -a [reddi'tittsjo] *ag* profitable

'reddito *sm* income; (*dello Stato*) revenue; (*di un capitale*) yield

re'densi *ecc vb vedi* **redimere**

re'dento, -a *pp di* **redimere**

re'digere [re'didʒere] /47/ *vt* to write; (*contratto*) to draw up

re'dimere /86/ *vt* to deliver; (*Rel*) to redeem

'redini *sfpl* reins

'reduce ['rɛdutʃe] *ag*: **~ da** returning from, back from ▷ *smf* survivor

refe'rendum *sm inv* referendum

refe'renza [refe'rɛntsa] *sf* reference

re'ferto *sm* medical report

rega'lare /72/ *vt* to give (as a present), make a present of

re'galo *sm* gift, present

re'gata *sf* regatta

'reggere ['rɛddʒere] /87/ *vt* (*tenere*) to hold; (*sostenere*) to support, bear, hold up; (*portare*) to carry, bear; (*resistere*) to withstand; (*dirigere: impresa*) to manage, run; (*governare*) to rule, govern; (*Ling*) to take, be followed by ▷ *vi* (*resistere*): **~ a** to stand up to, hold out against; (*sopportare*): **~ a** to stand; (*durare*) to last; (*fig: teoria ecc*) to hold water; **reggersi** *vpr* (*stare ritto*) to stand

'reggia, -ge ['rɛddʒa] *sf* royal palace

reggi'calze [reddʒi'kaltse] *sm inv* suspender belt

reggi'mento [reddʒi'mento] *sm* (*Mil*) regiment

reggi'seno [reddʒi'seno] *sm* bra

re'gia, -gie [re'dʒia] *sf* (*TV, Cine: ecc*) direction

re'gime [re'dʒime] *sm* (*Pol*) regime; (*Dir: aureo, patrimoniale ecc*) system; (*Med*) diet; (*Tecn*) (engine) speed

re'gina [re'dʒina] *sf* queen

regio'nale [redʒo'nale] *ag* regional ▷ *sm* local train (*stopping frequently*)

regi'one [re'dʒone] *sf* (*gen*) region; (*territorio*) region, district, area; *see note* **"regione"**

re'gista, -i, -e [re'dʒista] *smf* (*TV, Cine ecc*) director

regis'trare [redʒis'trare] /72/ *vt* (*Amm*) to register; (*Comm*) to enter; (*notare*) to report, note; (*canzone, conversazione: strumento di misura*) to record; (*mettere a punto*) to adjust, regulate; **~ i bagagli** to check in one's luggage; **registra'tore** *sm* (*strumento*) recorder, register; (*magnetofono*) tape recorder; **registratore di cassa** cash register; **registratore a cassette** cassette recorder

re'gistro [re'dʒistro] *sm* register; (*Dir*) registry; (*Comm*): **~ (di cassa)** ledger; **~ di bordo** logbook

re'gnare [reɲ'ɲare] /15/ *vi* to reign, rule

regno ['reɲɲo] *sm* kingdom; (*periodo*) reign; (*fig*) realm; **il ~ animale/ vegetale** the animal/vegetable kingdom; **il R~ Unito** the United Kingdom

regola *sf* rule; **a ~ d'arte** duly; perfectly; **avere le carte in ~** to have one's papers in order

rego'labile *ag* adjustable

regola'mento *sm* (*complesso di norme*) regulations *pl*; (*di debito*) settlement; **~ di conti** (*fig*) settling of scores

rego'lare /72/ *ag* regular; (*in regola: documento*) in order ▷ *vt* to regulate, control; (*apparecchio*) to adjust, regulate; (*questione, conto, debito*) to settle; **regolarsi** *vpr* (*comportarsi*) to behave, act; **regolarsi nel bere/ nello spendere** (*moderarsi*) to control one's drinking/spending

rela'tivo, -a *ag* relative

relazi'one [relat'tsjone] *sf* (*fra cose, persone*) relation(ship); (*resoconto*) report, account

rele'gare /80/ *vt* to banish; (*fig*) to relegate

religi'one [reli'dʒone] *sf* religion

religi'oso, -a [reli'dʒoso] *ag* religious

re'liquia *sf* relic

re'litto *sm* wreck; (*fig*) down-and-out

re'mare /72/ *vi* to row

remini'scenze [reminiʃʃɛntse] *sfpl* reminiscences

remis'sivo, -a *ag* submissive, compliant

'remo *sm* oar

re'moto, -a *ag* remote

'rendere /88/ *vt* (*ridare*) to return, give back; (*: saluto ecc*) to return; (*produrre*) to yield, bring in; (*esprimere, tradurre*) to render; **~ qc possibile** to make sth possible; **~ grazie a qn** to thank sb; **~ omaggio a qn** to honour sb; **~ un servizio a qn** to do sb a service; **~ una testimonianza** to give evidence; **~ la visita** to pay a return visit; **non so se rendo l'idea** I don't know whether I'm making myself clear

rendi'mento *sm* (*reddito*) yield; (*di manodopera, Tecn*) efficiency; (*capacità*) output; (*di studenti*) performance

rendita *sf* (*di individuo*) private *o* unearned income; (*Comm*) revenue; **~ annua** annuity

'rene *sm* kidney

'renna *sf* reindeer *inv*

re'parto *sm* department, section; (*Mil*) detachment

repel'lente *ag* repulsive

repen'taglio [repen'taʎʎo] *sm*: **mettere a ~** to jeopardize, risk

repen'tino, -a *ag* sudden, unexpected

reper'torio *sm* (*Teat*) repertory; (*elenco*) index, (alphabetical) list

'replica, -che *sf* repetition; reply, answer; (*obiezione*) objection; (*Teat, Cine*) repeat performance; (*copia*) replica

repli'care /20/ *vt* (*ripetere*) to repeat; (*rispondere*) to answer, reply

repressi'one *sf* repression

re'presso, -a *pp di* **reprimere**

re'primere /50/ *vt* to suppress, repress

re'pubblica, -che *sf* republic

reputazi'one [reputat'tsjone] *sf* · reputation

requi'sire /55/ *vt* to requisition

requi'sito *sm* requirement

'resa *sf* (*l'arrendersi*) surrender; (*restituzione, rendimento*) return; **~ dei conti** rendering of accounts; (*fig*) day of reckoning

'resi *ecc vb vedi* **rendere**

resi'dente *ag* resident; **residenzi'ale** *ag* residential

re'siduo, -a *ag* residual, remaining ▷ *sm* remainder; (*Chim*) residue

'resina *sf* resin

resis'tente *ag* (*che resiste*): **~ a** resistant to; (*forte*) strong; (*duraturo*) long-lasting, durable; **~ al caldo**

heat-resistant; **resis'tenza** *sf* resistance; (*di persona: fisica*) stamina, endurance; (: *mentale*) endurance, resistance

○ **RESISTENZA**
○
○
○ The Italian *Resistenza* fought
○ against both the Nazis and
○ the Fascists during the Second
○ World War. It was particularly
○ active after the fall of the
○ Fascist government on 25 July
○ 1943, throughout the German
○ occupation and during the period
○ of Mussolini's Republic of Salò
○ in northern Italy. Resistance
○ members spanned the whole
○ political spectrum and played a
○ vital role in the Liberation and
○ in the formation of the new
○ democratic government.

re'sistere /11/ *vi* to resist; **~ a** (*assalto, tentazioni*) to resist; (*dolore*) to withstand; (*non patir danno*) to be resistant to

reso'conto *sm* report, account

res'pingere [res'pindʒere] /114/ *vt* to drive back, repel; (*rifiutare*) to reject; (*Ins: bocciare*) to fail

respi'rare /72/ *vi* to breathe; (*fig*) to get one's breath; to breathe again ▷ *vt* to breathe (in), inhale; **respirazi'one** *sf* breathing; **respirazione artificiale** artificial respiration; **res'piro** *sm* breathing *no pl*; (*singolo atto*) breath; (*fig*) respite, rest; **mandare un respiro di sollievo** to give a sigh of relief

respon'sabile *ag* responsible ▷ *smf* person responsible; (*capo*) person in charge; **~ di** responsible for; (*Dir*) liable for; **responsabilità** *sf inv* responsibility; (*legale*) liability

res'ponso *sm* answer

'ressa *sf* crowd, throng

'ressi *ecc vb vedi* **reggere**

res'tare /72/ *vi* (*rimanere*) to remain, stay; (*avanzare*) to be left, remain; **~ orfano/cieco** to become o be left an orphan/become blind; **~ d'accordo** to agree; **non resta più niente** there's nothing left; **restano pochi giorni** there are only a few days left

restau'rare /72/ *vt* to restore

res'tio, -a, -'tii, -'tie *ag*: **~ a** reluctant to

restitu'ire /55/ *vt* to return, give back; (*energie, forze*) to restore

'resto *sm* remainder, rest; (*denaro*) change; (*Mat*) remainder; **resti** *smpl* leftovers; (*di città*) remains; **del ~** moreover, besides; **tenga pure il ~** keep the change; **resti mortali** (mortal) remains

res'tringere [res'trindʒere] /117/ *vt* to reduce; (*vestito*) to take in; (*stoffa*) to shrink; (*fig*) to restrict, limit; **restringersi** *vpr* (*strada*) to narrow; (*stoffa*) to shrink

'rete *sf* net; (*di recinzione*) wire netting; (*Aut, Ferr, di spionaggio ecc*) network; (*fig*) trap, snare; **segnare una ~** (*Calcio*) to score a goal; **~ ferroviaria/stradale/ di distribuzione** railway/road/ distribution network; **~ del letto** (sprung) bed base; **~ sociale** social network; **~ (televisiva)** (*sistema*) network; (*canale*) channel; **la R~** the web

reti'cente [reti'tʃɛnte] *ag* reticent

retico'lato *sm* grid; (*rete metallica*) wire netting; (*di filo spinato*) barbed wire fence

'retina *sf* (*Anat*) retina

re'torico, -a, -ci, -che *ag* rhetorical

retribu'ire /55/ *vt* to pay

'retro *sm inv* back ▷ *av* (*dietro*): **vedi ~** see over(leaf)

retro'cedere [retro'tʃɛdere] /29/ *vi* to withdraw ▷ *vt* (*Calcio*) to relegate; (*Mil*) to degrade

re'trogrado, -a *ag* (*fig*) reactionary, backward-looking

retro'marcia [retro'martʃa] sf (Aut) reverse; (: dispositivo) reverse gear

retro'scena [retroʃ'ʃɛna] sf inv (Teat) backstage ▷ sm inv: **i ~** (fig) the behind-the-scenes activities

retrovi'sore sm (Aut) (rear-view) mirror

'retta sf (Mat) straight line; (di convitto) charge for bed and board; (fig: ascolto): **dar ~ a** to listen to, pay attention to

rettango'lare ag rectangular

ret'tangolo, -a ag right-angled ▷ sm rectangle

ret'tifica, -che sf rectification, correction

'rettile sm reptile

retti'lineo, -a ag rectilinear

'retto, -a pp di **reggere** ▷ ag straight; (onesto) honest, upright; (giusto, esatto) correct, proper, right; **angolo ~** (Mat) right angle

ret'tore sm (Rel) rector; (di università) ≈ chancellor

reuma'tismo sm rheumatism

revisi'one sf auditing no pl; audit; servicing no pl; overhaul; review; revision; **~ contabile interna** internal audit

revi'sore sm: **~ di conti/bozze** auditor/proofreader

re'vival [ri'vaivəl] sm inv revival

'revoca sf revocation

revo'care /20/ vt to revoke

re'volver sm inv revolver

ri'abbia ecc vb vedi **riavere**

riabili'tare /72/ vt to rehabilitate

riabilitazi'one [riabilitat'tsjone] sf rehabilitation

rianimazi'one [rianimat'tsjone] sf (Med) resuscitation; **centro di ~** intensive care unit

ria'prire /9/ vt, **ria'prirsi** vpr to reopen, open again

ri'armo sm (Mil) rearmament

rias'sumere /12/ vt (riprendere) to resume; (impiegare di nuovo) to re-employ; (sintetizzare) to summarize;

rias'sunto, -a pp di **riassumere** ▷ sm summary

riattac'care /20/ vt (attaccare di nuovo): **~ (a)** (manifesto, francobollo) to stick back (on); (bottone) to sew back (on); (quadro, chiavi) to hang back up (on); **~ (il telefono o il ricevitore)** to hang up (the receiver)

ria'vere /13/ vt to have again; (avere indietro) to get back; (riacquistare) to recover; **riaversi** vpr to recover

riba'dire /55/ vt (fig) to confirm

ri'balta sf flap; (Teat: proscenio) front of the stage; **luci della ~** footlights pl; (fig) limelight

ribal'tabile ag (sedile) tip-up

ribal'tare /72/ vt, vi (anche: **ribaltarsi**) to turn over, tip over

ribas'sare /72/ vt to lower, bring down ▷ vi to come down, fall

ri'battere /1/ vt to return, hit back; (confutare) to refute; **~ che** to retort that

ribel'larsi /72/ vpr: **~ (a)** to rebel (against); **ri'belle** ag (soldati) rebel; (ragazzo) rebellious ▷ smf rebel

'ribes sm inv currant; **~ nero** blackcurrant; **~ rosso** redcurrant

ri'brezzo [ri'breddzo] sm disgust, loathing; **far ~ a** to disgust

ribut'tante ag disgusting, revolting

rica'dere /18/ vi to fall again; (scendere a terra: fig: nel peccato ecc) to fall back; (vestiti, capelli ecc) to hang (down); (riversarsi: fatiche, colpe): **~ su** to fall on; **rica'duta** sf (Med) relapse

rica'mare /72/ vt to embroider

ricambi'are /19/ vt to change again; (contraccambiare) to return, repay; **ri'cambio** sm exchange, return; (Fisiol) metabolism

ri'camo sm embroidery

ricapito'lare /72/ vt to recapitulate, sum up

ricari'care /20/ vt (arma, macchina fotografica) to reload; (penna, pipa) to refill; (orologio, giocattolo) to rewind; (Elettr) to recharge

ricat'tare /72/ *vt* to blackmail;
ri'catto *sm* blackmail

rica'vare /72/ *vt* (*estrarre*) to draw
out, extract; (*ottenere*) to obtain, gain

ric'chezza [rik'kettsa] *sf* wealth;
(*fig*) richness

'**riccio, -a, -ci, -ce** ['rittʃo] *ag* curly
▷ *sm* (*Zool*) hedgehog; (*anche:* ~ **di
mare**) sea urchin; '**ricciolo** *sm* curl

'**ricco, -a, -chi, -che** *ag* rich; (*persona,
paese*) rich, wealthy ▷ *sm/f* rich man/
woman; **i ricchi** the rich; ~ **di** full of;
(*risorse, fauna ecc*) rich in

ri'cerca, -che [ri'tʃerka] *sf* search;
(*indagine*) investigation, inquiry;
(*studio*): **la ~** research; **una ~** a piece
of research; ~ **di mercato** market
research

ricer'care [ritʃer'kare] /20/ *vt*
(*motivi, cause*) to look for, try to
determine; (*successo, piacere*) to
pursue; (*onore, gloria*) to seek;
ricer'cato, -a *ag* (*apprezzato*) much
sought-after; (*affettato*) studied,
affected ▷ *sm/f* (*Polizia*) wanted
man/woman

ricerca'tore, -'trice [ritʃerka'tore]
sm/f (*Ins*) researcher

ri'cetta [ri'tʃetta] *sf* (*Med*)
prescription; (*Cuc*) recipe

ricettazi'one [ritʃettat'tsjone] *sf*
(*Dir*) receiving (stolen goods)

ri'cevere [ri'tʃevere] /29/ *vt* to
receive; (*stipendio, lettera*) to
get, receive; (*accogliere: ospite*)
to welcome; (*vedere: cliente,
rappresentante ecc*) to see;
ricevi'mento *sm* receiving *no pl*;
(*trattenimento*) reception; **ricevi'tore**
sm (*Tecn*) receiver; **rice'vuta** *sf*
receipt; **accusare ricevuta di qc**
(*Comm*) to acknowledge receipt of
sth; **ricevuta fiscale** official receipt
(for tax purposes); **ricevuta di
ritorno** (*Posta*) advice of receipt

richia'mare [rikja'mare] /72/ *vt*
(*chiamare indietro, ritelefonare*) to call
back; (*ambasciatore, truppe*) to recall;

(*rimproverare*) to reprimand; (*attirare*)
to attract, draw; **richiamarsi** *vpr*:
richiamarsi a (*riferirsi a*) to refer to

richi'edere [ri'kjɛdere] /21/ *vt* to
ask again for; (*chiedere: per sapere*)
to ask; (: *per avere*) to ask for; (*Amm:
documenti*) to apply for; (*esigere*) to
need, require; (*chiedere indietro*): ~ **qc**
to ask for sth back

richi'esto, -a [ri'kjɛsto] *pp di*
richiedere ▷ *sf* (*domanda*) request;
(*Amm*) application, request; (*esigenza*)
demand, request; **a richiesta** on
request

rici'claggio [ritʃi'kladdʒo] *sm*
recycling

rici'clare [ritʃi'klare] /72/ *vt* to recycle

'**ricino** ['ritʃino] *sm*: **olio di ~**
castor oil

ricognizi'one [rikoɲɲit'tsjone]
sf (*Mil*) reconnaissance; (*Dir*)
recognition, acknowledgment

ricominci'are [rikomin'tʃare] /14/
vt, vi to start again, begin again

ricom'pensa *sf* reward

ricompen'sare /72/ *vt* to reward

riconcili'are [rikontʃi'ljare] /19/ *vt*
to reconcile; **riconciliarsi** *vpr* to be
reconciled

ricono'scente [rikonoʃ'ʃɛnte] *ag*
grateful

rico'noscere [riko'noʃʃere] /26/ *vt*
to recognize; (*Dir: figlio, debito*) to
acknowledge; (*ammettere: errore*) to
admit, acknowledge

rico'perto, -a *pp di* **ricoprire**

ricopi'are /19/ *vt* to copy

rico'prire /9/ *vt* (*coprire*) to cover;
(*occupare: carica*) to hold

ricor'dare /72/ *vt* to remember,
recall; (*richiamare alla memoria*): ~ **qc
a qn** to remind sb of sth; **ricordarsi**
vpr: **ricordarsi (di)** to remember;
ricordarsi di qc/di aver fatto to
remember sth/having done

ri'cordo *sm* memory; (*regalo*)
keepsake, souvenir; (*di viaggio*)
souvenir

ricor'rente *ag* recurrent, recurring; **ricor'renza** *sf* recurrence; (*festività*) anniversary

ri'correre /28/ *vi* (*ripetersi*) to recur; **~ a** (*rivolgersi*) to turn to; (*Dir*) to appeal to; (*servirsi di*) to have recourse to

ricostitu'ente *ag* (*Med*): **cura ~** tonic

ricostru'ire /55/ *vt* (*casa*) to rebuild; (*fatti*) to reconstruct

ri'cotta *sf* soft white unsalted cheese made from sheep's milk

ricove'rare /72/ *vt* to give shelter to; **~ qn in ospedale** to admit sb to hospital

ri'covero *sm* shelter, refuge; (*Mil*) shelter; (*Med*) admission (to hospital)

ricreazi'one [rikreat'tsjone] *sf* recreation, entertainment; (*Ins*) break

ri'credersi /29/ *vpr* to change one's mind

ricupe'rare /72/ *vt* (*rientrare in possesso di*) to recover, get back; (*tempo perduto*) to make up for; (*Naut*) to salvage; (: *naufraghi*) to rescue; (*delinquente*) to rehabilitate; **~ lo svantaggio** (*Sport*) to close the gap

ridacchi'are [ridak'kjare] /19/ *vi* to snigger

ri'dare /33/ *vt* to return, give back

'ridere /89/ *vi* to laugh; (*deridere, beffare*): **~ di** to laugh at, make fun of

ri'dicolo, -a *ag* ridiculous, absurd

ridimensio'nare /72/ *vt* to reorganize; (*fig*) to see in the right perspective

ri'dire /38/ *vt* to repeat; (*criticare*) to find fault with; to object to; **trova sempre qualcosa da ~** he always manages to find fault

ridon'dante *ag* redundant

ri'dotto, -a *pp di* **ridurre** ▷ *ag* (*biglietto*) reduced; (*formato*) small

ri'duco *ecc vb vedi* **ridurre**

ri'durre /90/ *vt* (*anche Chim, Mat*) to reduce; (*prezzo, spese*) to cut, reduce; (*accorciare: opera letteraria*) to abridge; (: *Radio, TV*) to adapt; **ridursi** *vpr*

(*diminuirsi*) to be reduced, shrink; **ridursi a** to be reduced to; **ridursi a pelle e ossa** to be reduced to skin and bone; **ri'dussi** *ecc vb vedi* **ridurre**; **ridut'tore** *sm* (*Tecn, Chim*) reducer; (*Elettr*) adaptor; **riduzi'one** *sf* reduction; abridgement; adaptation

ri'ebbi *ecc vb vedi* **riavere**

riem'pire /91/ *vt* to fill (up); (*modulo*) to fill in *o* out; **riempirsi** *vpr* to fill (up); **~ qc di** to fill sth (up) with

rien'tranza [rien'trantsa] *sf* recess; indentation

rien'trare /72/ *vi* (*entrare di nuovo*) to go (*o* come) back in; (*tornare*) to return; (*fare una rientranza*) to go in, curve inwards; to be indented; (*riguardare*): **~ in** to be included among, form part of

riepilo'gare /80/ *vt* to summarize ▷ *vi* to recapitulate

ri'esco *ecc vb vedi* **riuscire**

ri'fare /53/ *vt* to do again; (*ricostruire*) to make again; (*nodo*) to tie again, do up again; (*imitare*) to imitate, copy; **rifarsi** *vpr* (*risarcirsi*): **rifarsi di** to make up for; (*vendicarsi*): **rifarsi di qc su qn** to get one's own back on sb for sth; (*riferirsi*): **rifarsi a** to go back to; to follow; **~ il letto** to make the bed; **rifarsi una vita** to make a new life for o.s

riferi'mento *sm* reference; **in** *o* **con ~ a** with reference to

rife'rire /55/ *vt* (*riportare*) to report ▷ *vi* to do a report; **riferirsi** *vpr*: **riferirsi a** to refer to

rifi'nire /55/ *vt* to finish off, put the finishing touches to

rifiu'tare /72/ *vt* to refuse; **~ di fare** to refuse to do; **rifi'uto** *sm* refusal; **rifiuti** *smpl* (*spazzatura*) rubbish *sg*, refuse *sg*

riflessi'one *sf* (*Fisica, meditazione*) reflection; (*il pensare*) thought, reflection; (*osservazione*) remark

rifles'sivo, -a *ag* (*persona*) thoughtful, reflective; (*Ling*) reflexive

ri'flesso, -a *pp di* **riflettere** ▷ *sm (di luce, allo specchio)* reflection; *(Fisiol)* reflex; **di** *o* **per ~** indirectly

riflessolo'gia [riflessolo'dʒia] *sf:* reflexology

ri'flettere /92/ *vt* to reflect ▷ *vi* to think; **riflettersi** *vpr* to be reflected; **~ su** to think over

riflet'tore *sm* reflector; *(proiettore)* floodlight; *(Mil)* searchlight

ri'flusso *sm* flowing back; *(della marea)* ebb; **un'epoca di ~** an era of nostalgia

ri'forma *sf* reform; **la R~** *(Rel)* the Reformation

riforma'torio *sm (Dir)* community home (BRIT), reformatory (US)

riforni'mento *sm* supplying, providing; restocking; *(di carburante)* refuelling; **rifornimenti** *smpl (provviste)* supplies, provisions

rifor'nire /55/ *vt (fornire di nuovo: casa ecc)* to restock; *(provvedere)*: **~ di** to supply *o* provide with; **rifornirsi** *vpr*: **rifornirsi di qc** to stock up on sth

rifugi'arsi [rifu'dʒarsi] /62/ *vpr* to take refuge; **rifugi'ato, -a** *sm/f* refugee

ri'fugio [ri'fudʒo] *sm* refuge, shelter; *(in montagna)* shelter; **~ antiaereo** air-raid shelter

'riga, -ghe *sf* line; *(striscia)* stripe; *(di persone, cose)* line, row; *(regolo)* ruler; *(scriminatura)* parting; **mettersi in ~** to line up; **a righe** *(foglio)* lined; *(vestito)* striped

ri'gare /80/ *vt (foglio)* to rule ▷ *vi*: **~ diritto** *(fig)* to toe the line

rigatti'ere *sm* junk dealer

ri'ghello [ri'gεllo] *sm* ruler

righerò *ecc* [rige'rɔ] *vb vedi* **rigare**

'rigido, -a ['ridʒido] *ag* rigid, stiff; *(membra ecc, indurite)* stiff; *(Meteor)* harsh, severe; *(fig)* strict

rigogli'oso, -a [rigoʎ'ʎoso] *ag (pianta)* luxuriant; *(fig: commercio, sviluppo)* thriving

ri'gore *sm (Meteor)* harshness, rigours *pl*; *(fig)* severity, strictness; *(anche: calcio di ~)* penalty; **di ~** compulsory; **a rigor di termini** strictly speaking

riguar'dare /72/ *vt* to look at again; *(considerare)* to regard, consider; *(concernere)* to regard, concern; **riguardarsi** *vpr (aver cura di sé)* to look after o.s.

rigu'ardo *sm (attenzione)* care; *(considerazione)* regard, respect; **~ a** concerning, with regard to; **non aver riguardi nell'agire/nel parlare** to act/speak freely

rilasci'are [rilaʃ'ʃare] /14/ *vt (rimettere in libertà)* to release; *(Amm: documenti)* to issue

rilas'sare /72/ *vt* to relax; **rilassarsi** *vpr* to relax; *(fig: disciplina)* to become slack

rile'gare /80/ *vt (libro)* to bind

ri'leggere [ri'lεddʒere] /61/ *vt* to reread, read again; *(rivedere)* to read over

ri'lento: a ~ *av* slowly

rile'vante *ag* considerable; important

rile'vare /72/ *vt (ricavare)* to find; *(notare)* to notice; *(mettere in evidenza)* to point out; *(venire a conoscere: notizia)* to learn; *(raccogliere: dati)* to gather, collect; *(Topografia)* to survey; *(Mil)* to relieve; *(Comm)* to take over

rili'evo *sm (Arte, Geo)* relief; *(fig: rilevanza)* importance; *(osservazione)* point, remark; *(Topografia)* survey; **dar ~ a** *o* **mettere in ~ qc** *(fig)* to bring sth out, highlight sth

rilut'tante *ag* reluctant

'rima *sf* rhyme; *(verso)* verse; **far ~ con** to rhyme with; **rispondere a qn per le rime** to give sb tit for tat

riman'dare /72/ *vt* to send again; *(restituire, rinviare)* to send back, return; **~ qc (a)** *(differire)* to postpone sth *o* put sth off (till); **~ qn a** *(fare* *riferimento*) to refer sb to; **essere rimandato** (*Ins*) to have to resit one's exams

ri'mando *sm* (*rinvio*) return; (*dilazione*) postponement; (*riferimento*) cross-reference

rima'nente *ag* remaining ▷ *sm* rest, remainder; **i rimanenti** (*persone*) the rest of them, the others

rima'nere /93/ *vi* (*restare*) to remain, stay; (*avanzare*) to be left, remain; (*restare stupito*) to be amazed; **rimangono poche settimane a Pasqua** there are only a few weeks left till Easter; **~ vedovo** to be left a widower; **~ confuso/sorpreso** to be confused/surprised; **rimane da vedere se** it remains to be seen whether

rimangi'are [riman'dʒare] /62/ *vt* to eat again; **rimangiarsi la parola/una promessa** (*fig*) to go back on one's word/one's promise

ri'mango *ecc vb vedi* **rimanere**

rimargi'nare [rimardʒi'nare] /72/ *vt, vi,* **rimarginarsi** *vpr* to heal

rimbal'zare [rimbal'tsare] /72/ *vi* to bounce back, rebound; (*proiettile*) to ricochet

rimbam'bito, -a *ag* senile, in one's dotage

rimboc'care /20/ *vt* (*coperta*) to tuck in; (*maniche, pantaloni*) to turn *o* roll up

rimbom'bare /72/ *vi* to resound

rimbor'sare /72/ *vt* to pay back, repay

rimedi'are /19/ *vi*: **~ a** to remedy ▷ *vt* (*fam: procurarsi*) to get *o* scrape together

ri'medio *sm* (*medicina*) medicine; (*cura, fig*) remedy, cure

ri'mettere /63/ *vt* (*mettere di nuovo*) to put back; (*Comm: merci*) to deliver; (*: denaro*) to remit; (*vomitare*) to bring up; (*perdere: anche:* **rimetterci**) to lose; (*indossare di nuovo*): **~ qc** to put sth back on, put sth on again;

(*affidare*) to entrust; (*decisione*) to refer; (*condonare*) to remit; **rimettersi al bello** (*tempo*) to clear up; **rimettersi in salute** to get better, recover one's health

ri'misi *ecc vb vedi* **rimettere**

'rimmel® *sm inv* mascara

rimoder'nare /72/ *vt* to modernize

rimorchi'are [rimor'kjare] /19/ *vt* to tow; (*fig: ragazza*) to pick up

ri'morchio [ri'mɔrkjo] *sm* tow; (*veicolo*) trailer

ri'morso *sm* remorse

rimozi'one [rimot'tsjone] *sf* removal; (*da un impiego*) dismissal; (*Psic*) repression

rimpatri'are /19/ *vi* to return home ▷ *vt* to repatriate

rimpi'angere [rim'pjandʒere] /75/ *vt* to regret; (*persona*) to miss; **rimpi'anto, -a** *pp di* **rimpiangere** ▷ *sm* regret

rimpiaz'zare [rimpjat'tsare] /72/ *vt* to replace

rimpicco'lire [rimpittʃo'lire] /55/ *vt* to make smaller ▷ *vi* (*anche:* **rimpicciolirsi**) to become smaller

rimpin'zare [rimpin'tsare] /72/ *vt*: **~ di** to cram *o* stuff with; **rimpinzarsi** *vpr*: **rimpinzarsi (di qc)** to stuff o.s. (with sth)

rimprove'rare /72/ *vt* to rebuke, reprimand

rimu'overe /66/ *vt* to remove; (*destituire*) to dismiss

Rinasci'mento [rinaʃʃi'mento] *sm*: **il ~** the Renaissance

ri'nascita [ri'naʃʃita] *sf* rebirth, revival

rinca'rare /72/ *vt* to increase the price *o* ▷ *vi* to go up, become more expensive

rinca'sare /72/ *vi* to go home

rinchi'udere [rin'kjudere] /22/ *vt* to shut (*o* lock) up; **rinchiudersi** *vpr*: **rinchiudersi in** to shut o.s. up in; **rinchiudersi in se stesso** to withdraw into o.s.

rin'correre /28/ *vt* to chase, run after

rin'corso, -a *pp di* **rincorrere** ▷ *sf* short run

rin'crescere [rin'kreʃʃere] /30/ *vb impers*: **mi rincresce che/di non poter fare** I'm sorry that/I can't do, I regret that/being unable to do

rinfacci'are [rinfat'tʃare] /14/ *vt* (*fig*): **~ qc a qn** to throw sth in sb's face

rinfor'zare [rinfor'tsare] /72/ *vt* to reinforce, strengthen ▷ *vi* (*anche*: **rinforzarsi**) to grow stronger

rinfres'care /20/ *vt* (*atmosfera, temperatura*) to cool (down); (*abito, pareti*) to freshen up ▷ *vi* (*tempo*) to grow cooler; **rinfrescarsi** *vpr* (*ristorarsi*) to refresh o.s.; (*lavarsi*) to freshen up; **rin'fresco, -schi** *sm* (*festa*) party; **rinfreschi** *smpl* refreshments

rin'fusa *sf*: **alla ~** in confusion, higgledy-piggledy

ringhi'are [rin'gjare] /19/ *vi* to growl, snarl

ringhi'era [rin'gjɛra] *sf* railing; (*delle scale*) banister(s)

ringiova'nire [rindʒova'nire] /55/ *vt*: **~ qn** (*vestito, acconciatura ecc*) to make sb look younger; (*vacanze ecc*) to rejuvenate sb ▷ *vi* (*anche*: **ringiovanirsi**) to become (*o* look) younger

ringrazia'mento [ringrattsja'mento] *sm* thanks *pl*

ringrazi'are [ringrat'tsjare] /19/ *vt* to thank; **~ qn di qc** to thank sb for sth

rinne'gare /80/ *vt* (*fede*) to renounce; (*figlio*) to disown, repudiate

rinno'vabile *ag* (*contratto, energia*) renewable

rinnova'mento *sm* renewal; (*economico*) revival

rinno'vare /72/ *vt* to renew; (*ripetere*) to repeat, renew

rinoce'ronte [rinotʃe'ronte] *sm* rhinoceros

rino'mato, -a *ag* renowned, celebrated

rintracci'are [rintrat'tʃare] /14/ *vt* to track down

rintro'nare /72/ *vi* to boom, roar ▷ *vt* (*assordare*) to deafen; (*stordire*) to stun

rinunci'are [rinun'tʃare] /14/ *vi*: **~ a** to give up, renounce; **~ a fare qc** to give up doing sth

rinvi'are /60/ *vt* (*rimandare indietro*) to send back, return; **~ qc (a)** (*differire*) to postpone sth *o* put sth off (till); (*seduta*) to adjourn sth (till); **~ qn a** (*fare un rimando*) to refer sb to

rin'vio, -'vii *sm* (*rimando*) return; (*differimento*) postponement; (: *di seduta*) adjournment; (*in un testo*) cross-reference; **~ a giudizio** (*Dir*) indictment

riò *ecc vb vedi* **riavere**

ri'one *sm* district, quarter

riordi'nare /72/ *vt* (*rimettere in ordine*) to tidy; (*riorganizzare*) to reorganize

riorganiz'zare [riorganid'dzare] /72/ *vt* to reorganize

ripa'gare /80/ *vt* to repay

ripa'rare /72/ *vt* (*proteggere*) to protect, defend; (*correggere: male, torto*) to make up for; (: *errore*) to put right; (*aggiustare*) to repair ▷ *vi* (*mettere rimedio*): **~ a** to make up for; **ripararsi** *vpr* (*rifugiarsi*) to take refuge *o* shelter; **riparazi'one** *sf* (*di un torto*) reparation; (*di guasto, scarpe*) repairing *no pl*; repair; (*risarcimento*) compensation

ri'paro *sm* (*protezione*) shelter, protection; (*rimedio*) remedy

ripar'tire /45/ *vt* (*dividere*) to divide up; (*distribuire*) to share out ▷ *vi* to set off again; to leave again

ripas'sare /72/ *vi* to come (*o* go) back ▷ *vt* (*scritto, lezione*) to go over (again)

ripen'sare /72/ *vi* to think; (*cambiare idea*) to change one's mind; (*tornare col pensiero*): **~ a** to recall

ripercu'otersi /106/ *vpr*: **~ su** (*fig*) to have repercussions on

ripercussi'one *sf* (*fig*): **avere una ~ o delle ripercussioni su** to have repercussions on

ripes'care /20/ *vt* (*pesce*) to catch again; (*persona, cosa*) to fish out; (*fig*: *ritrovare*) to dig out

ri'petere /1/ *vt* to repeat; (*ripassare*) to go over; **ripetizi'one** *sf* repetition; (*di lezione*) revision; **ripetizi'oni** *sfpl* (*Ins*) private tutoring *o* coaching *sg*

ripi'ano *sm* (*di mobile*) shelf

ri'picca *sf*: **per ~** out of spite

'ripido, -a *ag* steep

ripie'gare /80/ *vt* to refold; (*piegare più volte*) to fold (up) ▷ *vi* (*Mil*) to retreat, fall back; (*fig*: *accontentarsi*): **~ su** to make do with

ripi'eno, -a *ag* full; (*Cuc*) stuffed; (: *panino*) filled ▷ *sm* (*Cuc*) stuffing

ri'pone *vb vedi* **riporre**

ri'pongo *ecc vb vedi* **riporre**

ri'porre /77/ *vt* (*porre al suo posto*) to put back, replace; (*mettere via*) to put away; (*fiducia, speranza*): **~ qc in qn** to place *o* put sth in sb

ripor'tare /72/ *vt* (*portare indietro*) to bring (*o* take) back; (*riferire*) to report; (*citare*) to quote; (*vittoria*) to gain; (*successo*) to have; (*Mat*) to carry; **riportarsi** *vpr*: **riportarsi a** (*anche fig*) to go back to; (*riferirsi a*) to refer to; **~ danni** to suffer damage

ripo'sare /72/ *vt* to rest ▷ *vi* to rest; **riposarsi** *vpr* to rest

ri'posi *ecc vb vedi* **riporre**

ri'poso *sm* rest; (*Mil*): **~!** at ease!; **a ~** (*in pensione*) retired; **giorno di ~** day off

ripos'tiglio [ripos'tiλλo] *sm* lumber room

ri'prendere /81/ *vt* (*prigioniero, fortezza*) to recapture; (*prendere indietro*) to take back; (*ricominciare: lavoro*) to resume; (*andare a prendere*) to fetch, come back for; (*assumere di nuovo: impiegati*) to take on again, re-employ; (*rimproverare*) to tell off; (*restringere: abito*) to take in; (*Cine*) to shoot; **riprendersi** *vpr* to recover; (*correggersi*) to correct o.s.

ri'preso, -a *pp di* **riprendere** ▷ *sf* recapture; resumption; (*economica, da malattia, emozione*) recovery; (*Aut*) acceleration *no pl*; (*Teat, Cine*) rerun; (*Cine*: *presa*) shooting *no pl*; shot; (*Sport*) second half; (*Pugilato*) round; **a più riprese** on several occasions, several times; **ripresa cinematografica** shot

ripristi'nare /72/ *vt* to restore

ripro'durre /90/ *vt* to reproduce; **riprodursi** *vpr* (*Biol*) to reproduce; (*riformarsi*) to form again

ripro'vare /72/ *vt* (*provare di nuovo: gen*) to try again; (: *vestito*) to try on again; (: *sensazione*) to experience again ▷ *vi* (*tentare*): **~ (a fare qc)** to try (to do sth) again; **riproverò più tardi** I'll try again later

ripudi'are /19/ *vt* to repudiate, disown

ripu'gnante [ripuɲ'ɲante] *ag* disgusting, repulsive

ri'quadro *sm* square; (*Archit*) panel

ri'saia *sf* paddy field

risa'lire /98/ *vi* (*ritornare in su*) to go back up; **~ a** (*ritornare con la mente*) to go back to; (*datare da*) to date back to, go back to

risal'tare /72/ *vi* (*fig*: *distinguersi*) to stand out; (*Archit*) to project, jut out

risa'puto, -a *ag*: **è ~ che ...** everyone knows that ..., it's common knowledge that ...

risarci'mento [risartʃi'mento] *sm*: **~ (di)** compensation (for); **aver diritto al ~ dei danni** to be entitled to damages

risar'cire [risar'tʃire] /55/ *vt* (*cose*) to pay compensation for; (*persona*): **~ qn di qc** to compensate sb for sth

ri'sata *sf* laugh

riscalda'mento *sm* heating; **~ centrale** central heating

riscal'dare /72/ *vt* (*scaldare*) to heat; (: *mani, persona*) to warm; (*minestra*) to reheat; **riscaldarsi** *vpr* to warm up

ris'catto sm ransom; redemption
rischia'rare [riskja'rare] /72/ vt
(illuminare) to light up; (colore) to
make lighter; **rischiararsi** vpr (tempo)
to clear up; (cielo) to clear; (fig: volto)
to brighten up; **rischiararsi la voce**
to clear one's throat
rischi'are [ris'kjare] /19/ vt to risk
▷ vi: **~ di fare qc** to risk o run the risk
of doing sth
'rischio ['riskjo] sm risk; **rischi'oso,
-a** ag risky, dangerous
risciac'quare /72/ vt to rinse
riscon'trare /72/ vt (rilevare) to find
riscri'vibile ag (CD, DVD) rewritable
riscu'otere /106/ vt (ritirare una
somma dovuta) to collect; (: stipendio)
to draw, collect; (assegno) to cash;
(fig: successo ecc) to win, earn
'rise ecc vb vedi **ridere**
risenti'mento sm resentment
risen'tire /45/ vt to hear again;
(provare) to feel ▷ vi: **~ di** to feel (o
show) the effects of; **risentirsi** vpr:
risentirsi di o per to take offence
(BRIT) o offense (US) at, resent;
risen'tito, -a ag resentful
ri'serbo sm reserve
ri'serva sf reserve; (di caccia, pesca)
preserve; (restrizione, di indigeni)
reservation; **tenere di ~** to keep
in reserve
riser'vare /72/ vt (tenere in serbo) to
keep, put aside; (prenotare) to book,
reserve; **riser'vato, -a** ag (prenotato:
fig: persona) reserved; (confidenziale)
confidential
'risi ecc vb vedi **ridere**
risi'edere /29/ vi: **~ a o in** to reside in
'risma sf (di carta) ream; (fig) kind,
sort
'riso¹, -a pp di **ridere** ▷ sm (il ridere): **un
~** a laugh; **il ~** laughter
'riso² sm (pianta) rice
riso'lino sm snigger
ri'solsi ecc vb vedi **risolvere**
ri'solto, -a pp di **risolvere**
riso'luto, -a ag determined, resolute

risoluzi'one [risolut'tsjone] sf
solving no pl; (Mat) solution;
(decisione, di schermo, immagine)
resolution
ri'solvere /94/ vt (difficoltà,
controversia) to resolve; (problema) to
solve; (decidere) **~ di fare** to resolve
to do; **risolversi** vpr (decidersi):
risolversi a fare to make up
one's mind to do; (andare a finire):
risolversi in to end up, turn out;
risolversi in nulla to come to
nothing
riso'nanza [riso'nantsa] sf
resonance; **aver vasta ~** (fig) (fatto
ecc) to be known far and wide
ri'sorgere [ri'sordʒere] /109/ vi
to rise again; **risorgi'mento** sm
revival; **il Risorgimento** (Storia) the
Risorgimento

⊛ **RISORGIMENTO**
⊛
⊛ The Risorgimento, the period
⊛ stretching from the early
⊛ nineteenth century to 1861 and the
⊛ proclamation of the Kingdom of
⊛ Italy, saw considerable upheaval
⊛ and change. Political and
⊛ personal freedom took on new
⊛ importance as the events of the
⊛ French Revolution unfolded. The
⊛ Risorgimento paved the way for the
⊛ unification of Italy in 1871.

ri'sorsa sf expedient, resort; **risorse
umane** human resources
ri'sorsi ecc vb vedi **risorgere**
ri'sotto sm (Cuc) risotto
risparmi'are /19/ vt to save; (non
uccidere) to spare ▷ vi to save; **~ qc a
qn** to spare sb sth
ris'parmio sm saving no pl; (denaro)
savings pl; **risparmi** smpl (denaro)
savings
rispecchi'are [rispek'kjare] /19/ vt
to reflect
rispet'tabile ag respectable

rispet'tare /72/ vt to respect; **farsi ~**
to command respect

rispet'tivo, -a ag respective

ris'petto sm respect; **rispetti** smpl
(saluti) respects, regards; **~ a** (in
paragone a) compared to; (in relazione
a) as regards, as for

ris'pondere /95/ vi to answer, reply;
(freni) to respond; **~ a** (domanda) to
answer, reply to; (persona) to answer;
(invito) to reply to; (provocazione,
veicolo, apparecchio) to respond to;
(corrispondere a) to correspond to;
(speranze, bisogno) to answer; **~ a**
qn di qc (essere responsabile) to be
answerable to sb for sth

ris'posto, -a pp di **rispondere** ▷ sf
answer, reply; **in risposta a** in reply to

'rissa sf brawl

ris'tampa sf reprinting no pl; reprint

risto'rante sm restaurant

ris'tretto, -a pp di **restringere** ▷ ag
(racchiuso) enclosed, hemmed in;
(angusto) narrow; (Cuc: brodo) thick;
(: caffè) extra strong; **~ (a)** (limitato)
restricted o limited (to)

ristruttu'rare /72/ vt (azienda) to
reorganize; (edificio) to restore;
(appartamento) to alter; (crema,
balsamo) to repair

risucchi'are [risuk'kjare] /19/ vt
to suck in

risul'tare /72/ vi (dimostrarsi) to prove
(to be), turn out (to be); (riuscire): **~**
vincitore to emerge as the winner;
~ da (provenire) to result from, be
the result of; **mi risulta che ...** I
understand that ...; **non mi risulta**
not as far as I know; **risul'tato** sm
result

risuo'nare /72/ vi (rimbombare) to
resound

risurrezi'one [risurret'tsjone] sf
(Rel) resurrection

risusci'tare [risuʃʃi'tare] /72/ vt to
resuscitate, restore to life; (fig) to
revive, bring back ▷ vi to rise (from
the dead)

ris'veglio [riz'veʎʎo] sm waking up;
(fig) revival

ris'volto sm (di giacca) lapel; (di
pantaloni) turn-up; (di manica) cuff;
(di tasca) flap; (di libro) inside flap; (fig)
implication

ritagli'are [ritaʎ'ʎare] /27/ vt (tagliar
via) to cut out

ritar'dare /72/ vi (persona, treno)
to be late; (orologio) to be slow ▷ vt
(rallentare) to slow down; (impedire) to
delay, hold up; (differire) to postpone,
delay

ri'tardo sm delay; (di persona
aspettata) lateness no pl; (fig: mentale)
backwardness; **in ~** late

ri'tegno [ri'teɲɲo] sm restraint

rite'nere /121/ vt (trattenere) to hold
back; (: somma) to deduct; (giudicare)
to consider, believe

ri'tengo ecc vb vedi **ritenere**

ri'tenni ecc vb vedi **ritenere**

riter'rò ecc vb vedi **ritenere**

ritiene ecc vb vedi **ritenere**

riti'rare /72/ vt to withdraw; (Pol:
richiamare) to recall; (andare a
prendere: pacco ecc) to collect, pick
up; **ritirarsi** vpr to withdraw; (da
un'attività) to retire; (stoffa) to shrink;
(marea) to recede

'ritmo sm rhythm; (fig) rate; (: della
vita) pace, tempo

'rito sm rite; **di ~** usual, customary

ritoc'care /20/ vt (disegno,
fotografia) to touch up; (testo)
to alter

ritor'nare /72/ vi to return, go (o
come) back, get back; (ripresentarsi)
to recur; (ridiventare): **~ ricco** to
become rich again ▷ vt (restituire) to
return, give back

ritor'nello sm refrain

ri'torno sm return; **essere di ~** to be
back; **avere un ~ di fiamma** (Aut)
to backfire; (fig: persona) to be back
in love again

ri'trarre /123/ vt (trarre indietro, via)
to withdraw; (distogliere: sguardo) to

turn away; (*rappresentare*) to portray, depict; (*ricavare*) to get, obtain

ritrat'tare /72/ *vt* (*disdire*) to retract, take back; (*trattare nuovamente*) to deal with again

ri'tratto, -a *pp di* **ritrarre** ▷ *sm* portrait

ritro'vare /72/ *vt* to find; (*salute*) to regain; (*persona*) to find; to meet again; **ritrovarsi** *vpr* (*essere, capitare*) to find o.s.; (*raccapezzarsi*) to find one's way; (*con senso reciproco*) to meet (again)

'ritto, -a *ag* (*in piedi*) standing, on one's feet; (*levato in alto*) erect, raised; (: *capelli*) standing on end; (*posto verticalmente*) upright

ritu'ale *ag, sm* ritual

riuni'one *sf* (*adunanza*) meeting; (*riconciliazione*) reunion

riu'nire /55/ *vt* (*ricongiungere*) to join (together); (*riconciliare*) to reunite, bring together (again); **riunirsi** *vpr* (*adunarsi*) to meet; (*tornare a stare insieme*) to be reunited

riu'scire [riuʃˈʃire] /125/ *vi* (*uscire di nuovo*) to go out again, go back out; (*aver esito: fatti, azioni*) to go, turn out; (*aver successo*) to succeed, be successful; (*essere, apparire*) to be, prove; (*raggiungere il fine*) to manage, succeed; **~ a fare qc** to manage *o* be able to do sth

'riva *sf* (*di fiume*) bank; (*di lago, mare*) shore

ri'vale *smf* rival; **rivalità** *sf* rivalry

rivalu'tare /72/ *vt* (*Econ*) to revalue

rive'dere /127/ *vt* to see again; (*ripassare*) to revise; (*verificare*) to check

rivedrò *ecc vb vedi* **rivedere**

rive'lare /72/ *vt* to reveal; (*divulgare*) to reveal, disclose; (*dare indizio*) to reveal, show; **rivelarsi** *vpr* (*manifestarsi*) to be revealed; **rivelarsi onesto** *ecc* to prove to be honest *etc*; **rivelazi'one** *sf* revelation

rivendi'care /20/ *vt* to claim, demand

rivendi'tore, -'trice *smf* retailer; **~ autorizzato** (*Comm*) authorized dealer

ri'verbero *sm* (*di luce, calore*) reflection; (*di suono*) reverberation

rivesti'mento *sm* covering; coating

rives'tire /45/ *vt* to dress again; (*ricoprire*) to cover; (*con vernice*) to coat; (*fig: carica*) to hold

ri'vidi *ecc vb vedi* **rivedere**

ri'vincita [riˈvintʃita] *sf* (*Sport*) return match; (*fig*) revenge

ri'vista *sf* review; (*periodico*) magazine, review; (*Teat*) revue; variety show

ri'volgere [riˈvɔldʒere] /96/ *vt* (*attenzione, sguardo*) to turn, direct; (*parole*) to address; **rivolgersi** *vpr* to turn round; **rivolgersi a** (*fig*) (*dirigersi per informazioni*) to go and see, go and speak to; (*ufficio*) to enquire at

ri'volsi *ecc vb vedi* **rivolgere**

ri'volta *sf* revolt, rebellion

rivol'tella *sf* revolver

rivoluzio'nare [rivoluttsjoˈnare] /72/ *vt* to revolutionize

rivoluzio'nario, -a [rivoluttsjoˈnarjo] *ag, sm/f* revolutionary

rivoluzi'one [rivolutˈtsjone] *sf* revolution

riz'zare [ritˈtsare] /72/ *vt* to raise, erect; **rizzarsi** *vpr* to stand up; (*capelli*) to stand on end

'roba *sf* stuff, things *pl*; (*possessi, beni*) belongings *pl*, things *pl*, possessions *pl*; **~ da mangiare** things to eat, food; **~ da matti!** it's sheer madness *o* lunacy!

'robot *sm inv* robot

ro'busto, -a *ag* robust, sturdy; (*solido: catena*) strong

roc'chetto [rokˈketto] *sm* reel, spool

'roccia, -ce [ˈrɔttʃa] *sf* rock; **fare ~** (*Sport*) to go rock climbing

'roco, -a, -chi, -che *ag* hoarse

ro'daggio [ro'daddʒo] sm running (BRIT) o breaking (US) in; **in ~** running o breaking in

rodi'tore sm (Zool) rodent

rodo'dendro sm rhododendron

ro'gnone [roɲ'ɲone] sm (Cuc) kidney

'rogo, -ghi sm (per cadaveri) (funeral) pyre; (supplizio): **il ~** the stake

rol'lio sm roll(ing)

'Roma sf Rome

Roma'nia sf: **la ~** Romania

ro'manico, -a, -ci, -che ag Romanesque

ro'mano, -a ag, sm/f Roman

ro'mantico, -a, -ci, -che ag romantic

romanzi'ere [roman'dzjɛre] sm novelist

ro'manzo, -a [ro'mandzo] ag (Ling) romance cpd ▷ sm novel; **~ d'appendice** serial (story); **~ poliziesco, ~ giallo** detective story; **~ rosa** romantic novel

'rombo sm rumble, thunder, roar; (Mat) rhombus; (Zool) turbot; brill

'rompere /97/ vt to break; (conversazione, fidanzamento) to break off ▷ vi to break; **rompersi** vpr to break; **mi rompe le scatole** (fam) he (o she) is a pain in the neck; **rompersi un braccio** to break an arm; **rompis'catole** smf inv (fam) pest, pain in the neck

'rondine sf (Zool) swallow

ron'zare [ron'dzare] /72/ vi to buzz, hum

ron'zio, -ii [ron'dzio] sm buzzing

'rosa sf rose ▷ ag inv, sm pink; **ro'sato, -a** ag pink, rosy ▷ sm (vino) rosé (wine)

rosicchi'are [rosik'kjare] /19/ vt to gnaw (at); (mangiucchiare) to nibble (at)

rosma'rino sm rosemary

roso'lare /72/ vt (Cuc) to brown

roso'lia sf (Med) German measles sg, rubella

ro'sone sm rosette; (vetrata) rose window

'rospo sm (Zool) toad

ros'setto sm (per labbra) lipstick

'rosso, -a ag, sm, sm/f red; **il mar R~** the Red Sea; **~ d'uovo** egg yolk

rosticce'ria [rostittʃe'ria] sf shop selling roast meat and other cooked food

ro'taia sf rut, track; (Ferr) rail

ro'tella sf small wheel; (di mobile) castor

roto'lare /72/ vt, vi to roll; **rotolarsi** vpr to roll (about)

'rotolo sm roll; **andare a rotoli** (fig) to go to rack and ruin

ro'tondo, -a ag round

'rotta sf (Aer, Naut) course, route; (Mil) rout; **a ~ di collo** at breakneck speed; **essere in ~ con qn** to be on bad terms with sb

rotta'mare /72/ vt to scrap old vehicles in return for incentives

rottama'zione [rottamat'tsjone] sf (come incentivo) the scrapping of old vehicles in return for incentives

rot'tame sm fragment, scrap, broken bit; **rottami** smpl (di nave aereo ecc) wreckage sg

'rotto, -a pp di rompere ▷ ag broken; (calzoni) torn, split ▷ sm: **per il ~ della cuffia** by the skin of one's teeth

rot'tura sf breaking no pl; break; (di rapporti) breaking off; (Med) fracture, break

rou'lotte [ru'lɔt] sf inv caravan

ro'vente ag red-hot

'rovere sm oak

ro'vescia [ro'veʃʃa] sf: **alla ~** upside-down; inside-out; **oggi mi va tutto alla ~** everything is going wrong (for me) today

rovesci'are [roveʃ'ʃare] /14/ vt (versare in giù) to pour; (: accidentalmente) to spill; (capovolgere) to turn upside down; (gettare a terra) to knock down; (fig: governo) to overthrow; (piegare all'indietro: testa) to throw back;

rovesciarsi vpr (sedia, macchina) to overturn; (barca) to capsize; (liquido) to spill; (fig: situazione) to be reversed

ro'vescio [ro'veʃʃo] sm other side, wrong side; (della mano) back; (di moneta) reverse; (pioggia) sudden downpour; (fig) setback; (Maglia: anche: **punto ~**) purl (stitch); (Tennis) backhand (stroke); **a ~** upside-down; (con l'esterno all'interno) inside-out; **capire qc a ~** to misunderstand sth

ro'vina sf ruin; **rovine** sfpl (ruderi) ruins; **andare in ~** (andare a pezzi) to collapse; (fig) to go to rack and ruin; **mandare qc/qn in ~** to ruin sth/sb

rovi'nare /72/ vi to collapse, fall down ▷ vt (danneggiare: fig) to ruin; **rovinarsi** vpr (persona) to ruin o.s.; (oggetto, vestito) to be ruined

rovis'tare /72/ vt (casa) to ransack; (tasche) to rummage in (o through)

rovo sm (Bot) blackberry o bramble bush

rozzo, -a ['roddzo] ag rough, coarse

ru'bare /72/ vt to steal; **~ qc a qn** to steal sth from sb

rubi'netto sm tap, faucet (US)

ru'bino sm ruby

ru'brica, -che sf (di giornale) column; (quadernetto) index book; address book; **~ d'indirizzi** address book; **~ telefonica** list of telephone numbers

rudere sm (rovina) ruins pl

rudimen'tale ag rudimentary, basic

rudi'menti smpl rudiments; basic principles; basic knowledge sg

ruffi'ano sm pimp

ruga, -ghe sf wrinkle

ruggine ['ruddʒine] sf rust

rug'gire [rud'dʒire] /55/ vi to roar

rugi'ada [ru'dʒada] sf dew

ru'goso, -a ag wrinkled

rul'lino sm (Fot) (roll of) film, spool

rullo sm (di tamburi) roll; (arnese cilindrico, Tip) roller; **~ compressore** steam roller; **~ di pellicola** roll of film

rum sm rum

ru'meno, -a ag, sm/f, sm Romanian

rumi'nare /72/ vt (Zool) to ruminate

ru'more sm: **un ~** a noise, a sound; **il ~** noise; **rumo'roso, -a** ag noisy

> Attenzione! In inglese esiste la parola *rumour*, che però significa *voce* nel senso *diceria*.

ru'olo sm (Teat, fig) role, part; (elenco) roll, register, list; **di ~** permanent, on the permanent staff

ru'ota sf wheel; **~ anteriore/posteriore** front/back wheel; **~ di scorta** spare wheel

ruo'tare /72/ vt, vi to rotate

'rupe sf cliff

'ruppi ecc vb vedi **rompere**

ru'rale ag rural, country cpd

ru'scello [ruʃʃello] sm stream

'ruspa sf excavator

rus'sare /72/ vi to snore

'Russia sf: **la ~** Russia; **'russo, -a** ag, sm/f, sm Russian

'rustico, -a, -ci, -che ag rustic; (fig) rough, unrefined

rut'tare /72/ vi to belch; **'rutto** sm belch

'ruvido, -a ag rough, coarse

S

S. *abbr* (= *sud*) S; (= *santo*) St
sa *vb vedi* **sapere**
'sabato *sm* Saturday; **di** *o* **il ~** on Saturdays
'sabbia *sf* sand; **sabbie mobili** quicksand(s *pl*); **sabbi'oso, -a** *ag* sandy
'sacca, -che *sf* bag; (*bisaccia*) haversack; **~ da viaggio** travelling bag
sacca'rina *sf* saccharin(e)
saccheggi'are [sakked'dʒare] /62/ *vt* to sack, plunder
sac'chetto [sak'ketto] *sm* (small) bag; (small) sack; **~ di carta/di plastica** paper/plastic bag
'sacco, -chi *sm* bag; (*per carbone ecc*) sack; (*Anat, Biol*) sac; (*tela*) sacking; (*saccheggio*) sack(ing); (*fig: grande quantità*) **un ~ di** lots of, heaps of; **~ a pelo** sleeping bag; **~ per i rifiuti** bin bag
sacer'dote [satʃer'dɔte] *sm* priest

sacrifi'care /20/ *vt* to sacrifice; **sacrificarsi** *vpr* to sacrifice o.s.; (*privarsi di qc*) to make sacrifices
sacri'ficio [sakri'fitʃo] *sm* sacrifice
'sacro, -a *ag* sacred
'sadico, -a, -ci, -che *ag* sadistic ▷ *sm/f* sadist
sa'etta *sf* arrow; (*fulmine*) thunderbolt; flash of lightning
sa'fari *sm inv* safari
sag'gezza [sad'dʒettsa] *sf* wisdom
'saggio, -a, -gi, -ge ['sadd ʒo] *ag* wise ▷ *sm* (*persona*) sage; (*operazione sperimentale*) test; (*fig: prova*) proof; (*campione indicativo*) sample; (*scritto*) essay
Sagit'tario [sadʒit'tarjo] *sm* Sagittarius
'sagoma *sf* (*profilo*) outline, profile; (*forma*) form, shape; (*Tecn*) template; (*bersaglio*) target; (*fig: persona*) character
'sagra *sf* festival
sagres'tano *sm* sacristan; sexton
sagres'tia *sf* sacristy
Sa'hara [sa'ara] *sm*: **il (Deserto del) ~** the Sahara (Desert)
'sai *vb vedi* **sapere**
'sala *sf* hall; (*stanza*) room; (*Cine: di proiezione*) cinema; **~ d'aspetto** waiting room; **~ da ballo** ballroom; **~ per concerti** concert hall; **~ giochi** amusement arcade; **~ operatoria** operating theatre (*BRIT*) *o* room (*US*); **~ da pranzo** dining room
sa'lame *sm* salami *no pl*, salami sausage
sala'moia *sf* (*Cuc*) brine
sa'lato, -a *ag* (*sapore*) salty; (*Cuc*) salted, salt *cpd*; (*fig: prezzi*) steep, stiff
sal'dare /72/ *vt* (*congiungere*) to join, bind; (*parti metalliche*) to solder; (: *con saldatura autogena*) to weld; (*conto*) to settle, pay
'saldo, -a *ag* (*resistente, forte*) strong, firm; (*fermo*) firm, steady, stable; (*fig*) firm, steadfast ▷ *sm* (*svendita*) sale; (*di conto*) settlement; (*Econ*) balance;

saldi smpl (Comm) sales; **essere ~ nella propria fede** (fig) to stick to one's guns

'**sale** sm salt; **ha poco ~ in zucca** he doesn't have much sense; **~ grosso** cooking salt; **~ fino** table salt

'**salgo** ecc vb vedi **salire**

'**salice** ['salitʃe] sm willow; **~ piangente** weeping willow

sali'ente ag (fig) salient, main

sali'era sf salt cellar

sa'lire /98/ vi to go (o come) up; (aereo ecc) to climb, go up; (passeggero) to get on; (sentiero, prezzi, livello) to go up, rise ▷ vt (scale, gradini) to go (o come) up; **~ su** to climb (up); **~ sul treno/sull'autobus** to board the train/the bus; **~ in macchina** to get into the car; **sa'lita** sf climb, ascent; (erta) hill, slope; **in salita** ag, av uphill

sa'liva sf saliva

'**salma** sf corpse

'**salmo** sm psalm

sal'mone sm salmon

sa'lone sm (stanza) sitting room, lounge; (in albergo) lounge; (su nave) lounge, saloon; (mostra) show, exhibition; **~ di bellezza** beauty salon

sa'lotto sm lounge, sitting room; (mobilio) lounge suite

sal'pare /72/ vi (Naut) to set sail; (anche: **~ l'ancora**) to weigh anchor

'**salsa** sf (Cuc) sauce; **~ di pomodoro** tomato sauce

sal'siccia, -ce [sal'sittʃa] sf pork sausage

sal'tare /72/ vi to jump, leap; (esplodere) to blow up, explode; (: valvola) to blow; (venir via) to pop off; (non aver luogo: corso ecc) to be cancelled ▷ vt to jump (over), leap (over); (fig: pranzo, capitolo) to skip, miss (out); (Cuc) to sauté; **far ~** to blow up; to burst open; **~ fuori** to turn up

saltel'lare /72/ vi to skip; to hop

'**salto** sm jump; (Sport) jumping; **fare un ~** to jump, leap; **fare un ~ da qn** to pop over to sb's (place); **~ in alto/ lungo** high/long jump; **~ con l'asta** pole vaulting; **~ mortale** somersault

saltu'ario, -a ag occasional, irregular

sa'lubre ag healthy, salubrious

sa'lume sm (Cuc) cured pork; **salumi** smpl cured pork meats

salume'ria sf delicatessen

salu'tare /72/ ag healthy; (fig) salutary, beneficial ▷ vt (per dire buon giorno, fig) to greet; (per dire addio) to say goodbye to; (Mil) to salute

sa'lute sf health; **~!** (a chi starnutisce) bless you!; (nei brindisi) cheers!; **bere alla ~ di qn** to drink (to) sb's health

sa'luto sm (gesto) wave; (parola) greeting; (Mil) salute

salvada'naio sm moneybox, piggy bank

salva'gente [salva'dʒɛnte] sm (Naut) lifebuoy; (stradale: pl inv) traffic island; **~ a ciambella** lifebelt; **~ a giubbotto** lifejacket (BRIT), life preserver (US)

salvaguar'dare /72/ vt to safeguard

sal'vare /72/ vt to save; (trarre da un pericolo) to rescue; (proteggere) to protect; **salvarsi** vpr to save o.s.; to escape; **salvas'chermo** sm (Inform) screen saver; **salva'slip** sm inv panty liner; **salva'taggio** sm rescue

'**salve** escl (fam) hi!

'**salvia** sf (Bot) sage

salvi'etta sf napkin; **~ umidificata** baby wipe

'**salvo, -a** ag safe, unhurt, unharmed; (fuori pericolo) safe, out of danger ▷ sm: **in ~** safe ▷ prep (eccetto) except; **~ che** (a meno che) unless; (eccetto che) except (that); **mettere qc in ~** to put sth in a safe place; **~ imprevisti** barring accidents

sam'buco sm elder (tree)

'**sandalo** sm (Bot) sandalwood; (calzatura) sandal

'**sangue** sm blood; **farsi cattivo ~** to fret, get worked up; **~ freddo** (fig)

s

sang-froid, calm; **a ~ freddo** in cold blood; **sangui'nare** /72/ *vi* to bleed

sanità *sf* health; (*salubrità*) healthiness; **Ministero della S~** Department of Health; **~ mentale** sanity

sani'tario, -a *ag* health *cpd*; (*condizioni*) sanitary ▷ *sm* (*Amm*) doctor; **sanitari** (*impianti*) bathroom o sanitary fittings

'sanno *vb vedi* **sapere**

'sano, -a *ag* healthy; (*denti, costituzione*) healthy, sound; (*integro*) whole, unbroken; (*fig: politica, consigli*) sound; **~ di mente** sane; **di sana pianta** completely, entirely; **~ e salvo** safe and sound

San Silvestro [san sil'vestro] *sm* (*giorno*) New Year's Eve

'santo, -a *ag* holy; (*fig*) saintly; (*seguito da nome proprio: dav sm* **san** *+ C,* **sant'** *+ V,* **santo** *+ s impura, gn, pn, ps, x, z; dav sf* **santa** *+ C,* **sant'** *+ V*) saint ▷ *sm/f* saint; **la Santa Sede** the Holy See

santu'ario *sm* sanctuary

sanzi'one [san'tsjone] *sf* sanction; (*penale, civile*) sanction, penalty

sa'pere /99/ *vt* to know; (*essere capace di*): **so nuotare** I know how to swim, I can swim ▷ *vi*: **~ di** (*aver sapore*) to taste of; (*aver odore*) to smell of ▷ *sm* knowledge; **far ~ qc a qn** to inform sb about sth, let sb know sth; **mi sa che non sia vero** I don't think that's true; **non lo so** I don't know; **non so l'inglese** I don't speak English

sa'pone *sm* soap; **~ da bucato** washing soap

sa'pore *sm* taste, flavour; **sapo'rito, -a** *ag* tasty

sappi'amo *vb vedi* **sapere**

saprò *ecc vb vedi* **sapere**

sarà *ecc vb vedi* **essere**

saraci'nesca, -sche [sarat∫i'neska] *sf* (*serranda*) rolling shutter

sar'castico, -a, -ci, -che *ag* sarcastic

Sar'degna [sar'deɲɲa] *sf*: **la ~** Sardinia

sar'dina *sf* sardine

'sardo, -a *ag, sm/f* Sardinian

sa'rei *ecc vb vedi* **essere**

SARS *sf* (= *severe acute respiratory syndrome*) SARS

'sarta *sf vedi* **sarto**

'sarto, -a *sm/f* tailor/dressmaker

'sasso *sm* stone; (*ciottolo*) pebble; (*masso*) rock

sas'sofono *sm* saxophone

sas'soso, -a *ag* stony; pebbly

'Satana *sm* Satan

satelli'tare *ag* satellite *cpd*

sa'tellite *sm, ag* satellite

'satira *sf* satire

'sauna *sf* sauna

sazi'are [sat'tsjare] /19/ *vt* to satisfy, satiate; **saziarsi** *vpr*: **saziarsi (di)** to eat one's fill (of); (*fig*): **saziarsi di** to grow tired o weary of

'sazio, -a ['sattsjo] *ag*: **~ (di)** sated (with), full (of); (*fig: stufo*) fed up (with), sick (of); **sono ~** I'm full (up)

sba'dato, -a *ag* careless, inattentive

sbadigli'are [zbadiʎ'ʎare] /27/ *vi* to yawn; **sba'diglio** *sm* yawn

sbagli'are [zbaʎ'ʎare] /27/ *vt* to make a mistake in, get wrong ▷ *vi* to make a mistake (o mistakes), be mistaken; (*ingannarsi*) to be wrong; (*operare in modo non giusto*) to err; **sbagliarsi** *vpr* to make a mistake, be mistaken, be wrong; **~ la mira/strada** to miss one's target/take the wrong road

sbagli'ato, -a [zbaʎ'ʎato] *ag* (*gen*) wrong; (*compito*) full of mistakes; (*conclusione*) erroneous

'sbaglio *sm* mistake, error; (*morale*) error; **fare uno ~** to make a mistake

sbalor'dire /55/ *vt* to stun, amaze ▷ *vi* to be stunned, be amazed

sbal'zare [zbal'tsare] /72/ *vt* to throw, hurl ▷ *vi* (*balzare*) to bounce; (*saltare*) to leap, bound

sban'dare /72/ *vi* (*Naut*) to list; (*Aut*) to skid; (*Aer*) to bank

sba'raglio [zba'raʎʎo] *sm* rout; defeat; **gettarsi allo ~** to risk everything

sbaraz'zarsi [zbarat'tsarsi] /72/ *vpr*: **~ di** to get rid of, rid o.s. of

sbar'care /20/ *vt* (*passeggeri*) to disembark; (*merci*) to unload ▷ *vi* to disembark

'sbarra *sf* bar; (*di passaggio a livello*) barrier; (*Dir*): **mettere/presentarsi alla ~** to bring/appear before the court

sbar'rare /72/ *vt* (*strada ecc*) to block, bar; (*assegno*) to cross; **~ il passo** to bar the way; **~ gli occhi** to open one's eyes wide

'sbattere /1/ *vt* (*porta*) to bang, slam; (*tappeti, ali, Cuc*) to beat; (*urtare*) to knock, hit ▷ *vi* (*porta, finestra*) to bang; (*agitarsi: ali, vele ecc*) to flap; **me ne sbatto!** (*fam*) I don't give a damn!

sba'vare /72/ *vi* to dribble; (*colore*) to smear, smudge

'sberla *sf* slap

sbia'dire /55/ *vi* to fade ▷ *vt* to fade; **sbia'dito, -a** *ag* faded; (*fig*) colourless, dull

sbian'care /20/ *vt* to whiten; (*tessuto*) to bleach ▷ *vi* (*impallidire*) to grow pale *o* white

sbirci'ata [zbir'tʃata] *sf*: **dare una ~ a qc** to glance at sth, have a look at sth

sbloc'care /20/ *vt* to unblock, free; (*freno*) to release; (*prezzi, affitti*) to free from controls; **sbloccarsi** *vpr* (*gen*) to become unblocked; (*passaggio, strada*) to clear, become unblocked

sboc'care /20/ *vi*: **~ in** (*fiume*) to flow into; (*strada*) to lead into; (*persona*) to come (out) into; (*fig: concludersi*) to end (up) in

sboc'cato, -a *ag* (*persona*) foul-mouthed; (*linguaggio*) foul

sbocci'are [zbot'tʃare] /14/ *vi* (*fiore*) to bloom, open (out)

sbol'lire /55/ *vi* (*fig*) to cool down, calm down

'sbornia *sf* (*fam*): **prendersi una ~** to get plastered

sbor'sare /72/ *vt* (*denaro*) to pay out

sbot'tare /72/ *vi*: **~ in una risata/ per la collera** to burst out laughing/ explode with anger

sbotto'nare /72/ *vt* to unbutton, undo

sbrai'tare /72/ *vi* to yell, bawl

sbra'nare /72/ *vt* to tear to pieces

sbricio'lare [zbritʃo'lare] /72/ *vt*, **sbricio'larsi** *vpr* to crumble

sbri'gare /80/ *vt* to deal with; **sbrigarsi** *vpr* to hurry (up)

'sbronza ['zbrontsa] (*fam*) *sf* (*ubriaco*): **prendersi una ~** to get plastered

sbron'zarsi [zbron'tsarsi] /72/ *vpr* (*fam*) to get plastered

'sbronzo, -a ['zbrontso] *ag* (*fam*) plastered

sbruf'fone, -a *sm/f* boaster

sbu'care /20/ *vi* to come out, emerge; (*improvvisamente*) to pop out (*o* up)

sbucci'are [zbut'tʃare] /14/ *vt* (*arancia, patata*) to peel; (*piselli*) to shell; **sbucciarsi un ginocchio** to graze one's knee

sbucherò *ecc* [zbuke'rɔ] *vb vedi* **sbucare**

sbuf'fare /72/ *vi* (*persona, cavallo*) to snort; (*: ansimare*) to puff, pant; (*treno*) to puff

sca'broso, -a *ag* (*fig: difficile*) difficult, thorny; (*: imbarazzante*) embarrassing; (*: sconcio*) indecent

scacchi'era [skak'kjɛra] *sf* chessboard

scacci'are [skat'tʃare] /14/ *vt* to chase away *o* out, drive away *o* out

'scaddi *ecc vb vedi* **scadere**

sca'dente *ag* shoddy, of poor quality

sca'denza [ska'dentsa] *sf* (*di cambiale, contratto*) maturity; (*di passaporto*) expiry date; **a breve/ lunga ~** short-/long-term; **data di ~** expiry date

sca'dere /18/ vi (contratto ecc) to expire; (debito) to fall due; (valore, forze, peso) to decline, go down

sca'fandro sm (di palombaro) diving suit; (di astronauta) spacesuit

scaf'fale sm shelf; (mobile) set of shelves

'**scafo** sm (Naut, Aer) hull

scagio'nare [skadʒo'nare] /72/ vt to exonerate, free from blame

'**scaglia** ['skaʎʎa] sf (Zool) scale; (scheggia) chip, flake

scagli'are [skaʎ'ʎare] /27/ vt (lanciare: anche fig) to hurl, fling; **scagliarsi** vpr: **scagliarsi su** o **contro** to hurl o fling o.s. at; (fig) to rail at

'**scala** sf (a gradini ecc) staircase, stairs pl; (a pioli, di corda) ladder; (Mus, Geo, di colori, valori, fig) scale; **scale** sfpl (scalinata) stairs; **su larga** o **vasta ~** on a large scale; **su ~ ridotta** on a small scale; **~ a libretto** stepladder; **~ mobile** escalator; (Econ) sliding scale; **~ mobile (dei salari)** index-linked pay scale

sca'lare /72/ vt (Alpinismo, muro) to climb, scale; (debito) to scale down, reduce

scalda'bagno [skalda'baɲɲo] sm water heater

scal'dare /72/ vt to heat; **scaldarsi** vpr to warm up, heat up; (al fuoco, al sole) to warm o.s.; (fig) to get excited

scal'fire /55/ vt to scratch

scali'nata sf staircase

sca'lino sm (anche fig) step; (di scala a pioli) rung

'**scalo** sm (Naut) slipway; (: porto d'approdo) port of call; (Aer) stopover; **fare ~ (a)** (Naut) to call (at), put in (at); (Aer) to land (at), make a stop (at); **~ merci** (Ferr) goods (BRIT) o freight yard

scalop'pina sf (Cuc) escalope

scal'pello sm chisel

scal'pore sm noise, row; **far ~** (notizia) to cause a sensation o a stir

'**scaltro, -a** ag cunning, shrewd

'**scalzo, -a** ['skaltso] ag barefoot

scambi'are /19/ vt to exchange; (confondere): **~ qn/qc per** to take o mistake sb/sth for; **mi hanno scambiato il cappello** they've given me the wrong hat; **scambiarsi** vpr (auguri, confidenze, visite) to exchange

'**scambio** sm exchange; (Ferr) points pl: **fare (uno) ~** to make a swap

scampa'gnata [skampaɲ'ɲata] sf trip to the country

scam'pare /72/ vt (salvare) to rescue, save; (evitare: morte, prigione) to escape ▷ vi: **~ (a qc)** to survive (sth), escape (sth); **scamparla bella** to have a narrow escape

'**scampo** sm (salvezza) escape; (Zool) prawn; **cercare ~ nella fuga** to seek safety in flight

'**scampolo** sm remnant

scanala'tura sf (incavo) channel, groove

scandagli'are [skandaʎ'ʎare] /27/ vt (Naut) to sound; (fig) to sound out; to probe

scandaliz'zare [skandalid'dzare] /72/ vt to shock, scandalize; **scandalizzarsi** vpr to be shocked

'**scandalo** sm scandal

Scandi'navia sf: **la ~** Scandinavia; **scandi'navo, -a** ag, sm/f Scandinavian

'**scanner** ['skanner] sm inv scanner

scansafa'tiche [skansafa'tike] smf inv idler, loafer

scan'sare /72/ vt (rimuovere) to move (aside), shift; (schivare: schiaffo) to dodge; (sfuggire) to avoid; **scansarsi** vpr to move aside

scan'sia sf shelves pl; (per libri) bookcase

'**scanso** sm: **a ~ di** in order to avoid, as a precaution against

scanti'nato sm basement

scapacci'one [skapat'tʃone] sm clout

scapes'trato, -a ag dissolute

'scapola *sf* shoulder blade

'scapolo *sm* bachelor

scappa'mento *sm* (Aut) exhaust

scap'pare /72/ *vi* (fuggire) to escape; (andare via in fretta) to rush off; **~ di prigione** to escape from prison; **~ di mano** (oggetto) to slip out of one's hands; **~ di mente a qn** to slip sb's mind; **lasciarsi ~** (occasione, affare) to let go by; **mi scappò detto** I let it slip; **scappa'toia** *sf* way out

scara'beo *sm* beetle

scarabocchi'are [skarabok'kjare] /19/ *vt* to scribble, scrawl; **scara'bocchio** *sm* scribble, scrawl

scara'faggio [skara'faddʒo] *sm* cockroach

scaraman'zia [skaraman'tsia] *sf*: **per ~** for luck

scaraven'tare /72/ *vt* to fling, hurl; **scaraventarsi** *vpr* to fling o.s.

scarce'rare [skartʃe'rare] /72/ *vt* to release (from prison)

scardi'nare /72/ *vt*: **~ una porta** to take a door off its hinges

scari'care /20/ *vt* (merci, camion ecc) to unload; (passeggeri) to set down, put off; (da Internet) to download; (arma) to unload; (: sparare, anche Elettr) to discharge; (corso d'acqua) to empty, pour; (fig: liberare da un peso) to unburden, relieve; **scaricarsi** *vpr* (orologio) to run o wind down; (batteria, accumulatore) to go flat o dead; (fig: rilassarsi) to unwind; (: sfogarsi) to let off steam

'scarico, -a, -chi, -che *ag* unloaded; (orologio) run down; (batteria, accumulatore) dead, flat ▷ *sm* (di merci, materiali) unloading; (di immondizie) dumping, tipping (BRIT); (Tecn: deflusso) draining; (: dispositivo) drain; (Aut) exhaust

scarlat'tina *sf* scarlet fever

scar'latto, -a *ag* scarlet

'scarpa *sf* shoe; **scarpe da ginnastica** gym shoes; **scarpe da tennis** tennis shoes

scar'pata *sf* escarpment

scarpi'era *sf* shoe rack

scar'pone *sm* boot; **scarponi da montagna** climbing boots; **scarponi da sci** ski-boots

scarseggi'are [skarsed'dʒare] /62/ *vi* to be scarce; **~ di** to be short of, lack

'scarso, -a *ag* (insufficiente) insufficient, meagre; (povero: annata) poor, lean; (Ins: voto) poor; **~ di** lacking in; **3 chili scarsi** just under 3 kilos, barely 3 kilos

scar'tare /72/ *vt* (pacco) to unwrap; (idea) to reject; (Mil) to declare unfit for military service; (carte da gioco) to discard; (Calcio) to dodge (past) ▷ *vi* to swerve

'scarto *sm* (cosa scartata, anche Comm) reject; (di veicolo) swerve; (differenza) gap, difference

scassi'nare /72/ *vt* to break, force

scate'nare /72/ *vt* (fig) to incite, stir up; **scatenarsi** *vpr* (temporale) to break; (rivolta) to break out; (persona: infuriarsi) to rage

'scatola *sf* box; (di latta) tin (BRIT), can; **cibi in ~** tinned (BRIT) o canned foods; **~ cranica** cranium; **scato'lone** *sm* (big) box

scat'tare /72/ *vt* (fotografia) to take ▷ *vi* (congegno, molla ecc) to be released; (balzare) to spring up; (Sport) to put on a spurt; (fig: per l'ira) to fly into a rage; **~ in piedi** to spring to one's feet

'scatto *sm* (dispositivo) release; (: di arma da fuoco) trigger mechanism; (rumore) click; (balzo) jump, start; (Sport) spurt; (fig: di ira ecc) fit; (: di stipendio) increment; **di ~** suddenly

scaval'care /20/ *vt* (ostacolo) to pass (o climb) over; (fig) to get ahead of, overtake

sca'vare /72/ *vt* (terreno) to dig; (legno) to hollow out; (pozzo, galleria) to bore; (città sepolta ecc) to excavate

'scavo *sm* excavating *no pl*; excavation

'sce'gliere [ʃeʎʎere] /100/ vt to choose, select

sce'icco, -chi [ʃeikko] sm sheik

'scelgo ecc [ʃelgo] vb vedi **scegliere**

scel'lino [ʃelˈlino] sm shilling

'scelto, -a [ʃelto] pp di **scegliere** ▷ ag (gruppo) carefully selected; (frutta, verdura) choice, top quality; (Mil: specializzato) crack cpd, highly skilled ▷ sf choice; (selezione) selection, choice; **frutta o formaggi a scelta** choice of fruit or cheese; **di prima scelta** top grade o quality

'scemo, -a [ʃemo] ag stupid, silly

'scena [ʃɛna] sf (gen) scene; (palcoscenico) stage; **le scene** (fig) (teatro) the stage; **andare in ~** to be staged o put on o performed; **mettere in ~** to stage; **fare una ~** to make a scene

sce'nario [ʃeˈnarjo] sm scenery; (di film) scenario

sce'nata [ʃeˈnata] sf row, scene

'scendere [ʃendere] /101/ vi to go (o come) down; (strada, sole) to go down; (notte) to fall; (passeggero: fermarsi) to get out, alight; (fig: temperatura, prezzi) to fall, drop ▷ vt (scale, pendio) to go (o come) down; **~ dalle scale** to go (o come) down the stairs; **~ dal treno** to get off o out of the train; **~ dalla macchina** to get out of the car; **~ da cavallo** to dismount, get off one's horse

sceneggi'ato [ʃenedˈdʒato] sm television drama

'scettico, -a, -ci, -che [ʃɛttiko] ag sceptical

'scettro [ʃɛttro] sm sceptre

'scheda [ˈskɛda] sf (index) card; **~ elettorale** ballot paper; **~ di memoria** (Inform) memory card; **~ ricaricabile** (Tel) top-up card; **~ telefonica** phone card; **sche'dario** sm file; (mobile) filing cabinet

sche'dina [skeˈdina] sf ≈ pools coupon (BRIT)

'scheggia, -ge [ˈskeddʒa] sf splinter, sliver

'scheletro [ˈskɛletro] sm skeleton

'schema, -i [ˈskɛma] sm (diagramma) diagram, sketch; (progetto, abbozzo) outline, plan

'scherma [ˈskerma] sf fencing

scher'maglia [skerˈmaʎʎa] sf (fig) skirmish

'schermo [ˈskermo] sm shield, screen; (Cine, TV) screen; **a ~ panoramico** (TV) widescreen

scher'nire [skerˈnire] /55/ vt to mock, sneer at

scher'zare [skerˈtsare] /72/ vi to joke

'scherzo [ˈskertso] sm joke; (tiro) trick; (Mus) scherzo; **è uno ~!** (una cosa facile) it's child's play!, it's easy!; **per ~** in jest; for a joke o a laugh; **fare un brutto ~ a qn** to play a nasty trick on sb

schiaccia'noci [skjattʃaˈnotʃi] sm inv nutcracker

schiacci'are [skjatˈtʃare] /14/ vt (dito) to crush; (noci) to crack; **~ un pisolino** to have a nap; **schiacciarsi** vpr (appiattirsi) to get squashed; (frantumarsi) to get crushed

schiaffeggi'are [skjaffedˈdʒare] /62/ vt to slap

schi'affo [ˈskjaffo] sm slap

schian'tare [skjanˈtare] /72/ vt to break; **schiantarsi** vpr to break (up), shatter

schia'rire [skjaˈrire] /55/ vt to lighten, make lighter ▷ vi (anche: **schiarirsi**) to grow lighter; (tornar sereno) to clear, brighten up; **schiarirsi la voce** to clear one's throat

schiavitù [skjaviˈtu] sf slavery

schi'avo, -a [ˈskjavo] sm/f slave

schi'ena [ˈskjɛna] sf (Anat) back; **schie'nale** sm (di sedia) back

schi'era [ˈskjɛra] sf (Mil) rank; (gruppo) group, band

schiera'mento [skjeraˈmento] sm (Mil, Sport) formation; (fig) alliance

schie'rare [skje'rare] /72/ vt (esercito) to line up, draw up, marshal; **schierarsi** vpr to line up; (fig): **schierarsi con** o **dalla parte di/contro qn** to side with/oppose sb

'**schifo** ['skifo] sm disgust; **fare ~** (essere fatto male, dare pessimi risultati) to be awful; **mi fa ~** it makes me sick, it's disgusting; **quel libro è uno ~** that book's rotten; **schi'foso, -a** ag disgusting, revolting; (molto scadente) rotten, lousy

schioc'care /20/ vt (frusta) to crack; (dita) to snap; (lingua) to click; **~ le labbra** to smack one's lips

schi'udere ['skjudere] /22/ vt, **schi'udersi** vpr to open

schi'uma ['skjuma] sf foam; (di sapone) lather; (di latte) froth; (fig: feccia) scum

schi'vare [ski'vare] /72/ vt to dodge, avoid

'**schivo, -a** ['skivo] ag (ritroso) stand-offish, reserved; (timido) shy

schiz'zare [skit'tsare] /72/ vt (spruzzare) to spurt, squirt; (sporcare) to splash, spatter; (fig: abbozzare) to sketch ▷ vi to spurt, squirt; (saltar fuori) to dart up (o off ecc)

schizzi'noso, -a [skittsi'noso] ag fussy, finicky

'**schizzo** ['skittso] sm (di liquido) spurt; splash, spatter; (abbozzo) sketch

sci [ʃi] sm inv (attrezzo) ski; (attività) skiing; **~ di fondo** cross-country skiing, ski touring (US); **~ d'acqua** o **nautico** water-skiing

'**scia** ['ʃia] (pl **scie**) sf (di imbarcazione) wake; (di profumo) trail

scià [ʃa] sm inv shah

sci'abola ['ʃabola] sf sabre

scia'callo [ʃa'kallo] sm jackal

sciac'quare [ʃak'kware] /72/ vt to rinse

scia'gura [ʃa'gura] sf disaster, calamity; misfortune

scialac'quare [ʃalak'kware] /72/ vt to squander

sci'albo, -a ['ʃalbo] ag pale, dull; (fig) dull, colourless

sci'alle ['ʃalle] sm shawl

scia'luppa [ʃa'luppa] sf (anche: **~ di salvataggio**) lifeboat

sci'ame ['ʃame] sm swarm

sci'are [ʃi'are] /60/ vi to ski

sci'arpa ['ʃarpa] sf scarf; (fascia) sash

scia'tore, -'trice [ʃia'tore] sm/f skier

sci'atto, -a ['ʃatto] ag (persona) slovenly, unkempt

scien'tifico, -a, -ci, -che [ʃen'tifiko] ag scientific

sci'enza ['ʃɛntsa] sf science; (sapere) knowledge; **scienze** sfpl (Ins) science sg: **scienze naturali** natural sciences; **scienzi'ato, -a** sm/f scientist

'**scimmia** ['ʃimmja] sf monkey

scimpanzé [ʃimpan'tse] sm inv chimpanzee

'**scindere** ['ʃindere] /102/, '**scindersi** vpr to split (up)

scin'tilla [ʃin'tilla] sf spark; **scintil'lare** /72/ vi to spark; (acqua, occhi) to sparkle

scioc'chezza [ʃok'kettsa] sf stupidity no pl; stupid o foolish thing; **dire sciocchezze** to talk nonsense

sci'occo, -a, -chi, -che ['ʃokko] ag stupid, foolish

sci'ogliere [ʃ'ɔʎʎere] /103/ vt (nodo) to untie; (capelli) to loosen; (persona, animale) to untie, release; (nell'acqua: zucchero ecc) to dissolve; (fig: mistero) to solve; (porre fine a: contratto) to cancel; (: società, matrimonio) to dissolve; (: riunione) to bring to an end; (fig: persona): **~ da** to release from; (neve) to melt; **sciogliersi** vpr to loosen, come untied; to melt; to dissolve; (assemblea, corteo, duo) to break up; **~ i muscoli** to limber up; **scioglilingua** [ʃoʎʎi'lingwa] sm inv tongue-twister

sci'olgo ecc ['ʃɔlgo] vb vedi **sciogliere**

sci'olto, -a ['ʃɔlto] pp di **sciogliere**
▷ ag loose; (agile) agile, nimble;
supple; (disinvolto) free and easy;
versi sciolti (Poesia) blank verse

sciope'rare [ʃope'rare] /72/ vi to
strike, go on strike

sci'opero ['ʃɔpero] sm strike; **fare
~** to strike; **~ bianco** work-to-rule
(BRIT), slowdown (US); **~ selvaggio**
wildcat strike; **~ a singhiozzo**
on-off strike

scio'via [ʃio'via] sf ski lift

scip'pare [ʃip'pare] /72/ vt: **~ qn** to
snatch sb's bag

sci'rocco [ʃi'rɔkko] sm sirocco

sci'roppo [ʃi'rɔppo] sm syrup

'scisma, -i ['ʃizma] sm (Rel) schism

scissi'one [ʃis'sjone] sf (anche fig)
split, division; (Fisica) fission

'scisso, -a ['ʃisso] pp di **scindere**

sciu'pare [ʃu'pare] /72/ vt (abito,
libro, appetito) to spoil, ruin; (tempo,
denaro) to waste

scivo'lare [ʃivo'lare] /72/ vi to slide
o glide along; (involontariamente) to
slip, slide; **'scivolo** sm slide; (Tecn)
chute; **scivo'loso, -a** ag slippery

scle'rosi sf sclerosis

scoc'care /20/ vt (freccia) to shoot
▷ vi (guizzare) to shoot up; (battere:
ora) to strike

scocche'rò ecc [skokke'rɔ] vb vedi
scoccare

scocci'are [skot'tʃare] /14/ vt to
bother, annoy; **scocciarsi** vpr to be
bothered o annoyed

sco'della sf bowl

scodinzo'lare [skodintso'lare] /72/
vi to wag its tail

scogli'era [skoʎ'ʎɛra] sf reef;
(rupe) cliff

'scoglio ['skɔʎʎo] sm (al mare) rock

scoi'attolo sm squirrel

scola'pasta sm inv colander

scolapi'atti sm inv drainer (for
plates)

sco'lare /72/ ag: **età ~** school age ▷ vt
to drain ▷ vi to drip

scola'resca sf schoolchildren pl,
pupils pl

sco'laro, -a sm/f pupil, schoolboy/
girl

> Attenzione! In inglese esiste la
> parola scholar, che però significa
> studioso.

sco'lastico, -a, -ci, -che ag (gen)
scholastic; (libro, anno, divisa)
school cpd

scol'lato, -a ag (vestito) low-cut, low-
necked; (donna) wearing a low-cut
dress (o blouse ecc)

scolla'tura sf neckline

scolle'gare /80/ vt (fili, apparecchi)
to disconnect; **scollegarsi** vpr (da
Internet) to disconnect; (da chat-line)
to log off

'scolo sm drainage

scolo'rire /55/ vt to fade; to discolour
(BRIT), discolor (US) ▷ vi (anche:
scolorirsi) to fade; to become
discoloured; (impallidire) to turn pale

scol'pire /55/ vt to carve, sculpt

scombus'solare /72/ vt to upset

scom'messo, -a pp di **scommettere**
▷ sf bet, wager

scom'mettere /63/ vt, vi to bet

scomo'dare /72/ vt to trouble,
bother, disturb; **scomodarsi** vpr to
put o.s. out; **scomodarsi a fare** to
go to the bother o trouble of doing

'scomodo, -a ag uncomfortable;
(sistemazione, posto) awkward,
inconvenient

scompa'rire /7/ vi (sparire) to
disappear, vanish; (fig) to be
insignificant

scomparti'mento sm
compartment

scompigli'are [skompiʎ'ʎare]
/27/ vt (cassetto, capelli) to mess up,
disarrange; (fig: piani) to upset

scomuni'care /20/ vt to
excommunicate

'sconcio, -a, -ci, -ce ['skontʃo] ag
(osceno) indecent, obscene ▷ sm
disgrace

scon'figgere [skon'fiddʒere] /104/ vt to defeat, overcome

sconfi'nare /72/ vi to cross the border; (*in proprietà privata*) to trespass; (*fig*): **~ da** to stray o digress from

scon'fitto, -a pp di **sconfiggere** ▷ sf defeat

scon'forto sm despondency

sconge'lare [skondʒe'lare] /72/ vt to defrost

scongiu'rare [skondʒu'rare] /72/ vt (*implorare*) to beseech, entreat, implore; (*eludere: pericolo*) to ward off, avert; **scongiuro** sm (*esorcismo*) exorcism; **fare gli scongiuri** to touch wood (BRIT), knock on wood (US)

scon'nesso, -a ag incoherent

sconosci'uto, -a [skonoʃ'ʃuto] ag unknown; new, strange ▷ sm/f stranger; unknown person

sconsigli'are [skonsiʎ'ʎare] /27/ vt: **~ qc a qn** to advise sb against sth; **~ qn dal fare qc** to advise sb not to do o against doing sth

sconso'lato, -a ag inconsolable; desolate

scon'tare /72/ vt (*Comm: detrarre*) to deduct; (: *debito*) to pay off; (: *cambiale*) to discount; (*pena*) to serve; (*colpa, errori*) to pay for, suffer for

scon'tato, -a ag (*previsto*) foreseen, taken for granted; **dare per ~ che** to take it for granted that

scon'tento, -a ag: **~ (di)** discontented o dissatisfied (with) ▷ sm dissatisfaction

'sconto sm discount; **fare** o **concedere uno ~** to give a discount; **uno ~ del 10%** a 10% discount

scon'trarsi /72/ vpr (*treni ecc*) to crash, collide; (*venire ad uno scontro*: *fig*) to clash; **~ con** to crash into, collide with

scon'trino sm ticket; (*di cassa*) receipt

'scontro sm clash, encounter; (*di veicoli*) crash, collision

scon'troso, -a ag sullen, surly; (*permaloso*) touchy

sconveni'ente ag unseemly, improper

scon'volgere [skon'vɔldʒere] /96/ vt to throw into confusion, upset; (*turbare*) to shake, disturb, upset; **scon'volto, -a** pp di **sconvolgere**

'scooter ['skuter] sm inv scooter

'scopa sf broom; (*Carte*) Italian card game; **sco'pare** /72/ vt to sweep

sco'perto, -a pp di **scoprire** ▷ ag uncovered; (*capo*) uncovered, bare; (*macchina*) open; (*Mil*) exposed, without cover; (*conto*) overdrawn ▷ sf discovery

'scopo sm aim, purpose; **a che ~?** what for?

scoppi'are /19/ vi (*spaccarsi*) to burst; (*esplodere*) to explode; (*fig*) to break out; **~ in pianto** o **a piangere** to burst out crying; **~ dalle risa** o **dal ridere** to split one's sides laughing

scoppiet'tare /72/ vi to crackle

'scoppio sm explosion; (*di tuono, arma ecc*) crash, bang; (*fig: di risa, ira*) fit; (*di pneumatico*) bang; (*fig: di guerra*) outbreak; **a ~ ritardato** delayed-action

sco'prire /9/ vt to discover; (*liberare da ciò che copre*) to uncover; (: *monumento*) to unveil; **scoprirsi** vpr to put on lighter clothes; (*fig*) to give o.s. away

scoraggi'are [skorad'dʒare] /62/ vt to discourage; **scoraggiarsi** vpr to become discouraged, lose heart

scorcia'toia [skortʃa'toja] sf short cut

'scorcio ['skortʃo] sm (*Arte*) foreshortening; (*di secolo, periodo*) end, close; **~ panoramico** vista

scor'dare /72/ vt to forget; **scordarsi** vpr: **scordarsi di qc/di fare** to forget sth/to do

s

'**scorgere** ['skɔrdʒere] /59/ vt to make out, distinguish, see

scorpacci'ata [skorpat'tʃata] sf: **fare una ~ (di)** to stuff o.s. (with), eat one's fill (of)

scorpi'one sm scorpion; **S~** Scorpio

'**scorrere** /28/ vt (giornale, lettera) to run o skim through ▷ vi (liquido, fiume) to run, flow; (fune) to run; (cassetto, porta) to slide easily; (tempo) to pass (by)

scor'retto, -a ag incorrect; (sgarbato) impolite; (sconveniente) improper

scor'revole ag (porta) sliding; (fig: stile) fluent, flowing

'**scorsi** ecc vb vedi **scorgere**

'**scorso, -a** pp di **scorrere** ▷ ag last

scor'soio, -a ag: **nodo ~** noose

'**scorta** sf (di personalità, convoglio) escort; (provvista) supply, stock

scor'tese ag discourteous, rude

'**scorza** ['skɔrdza] sf (di albero) bark; (di agrumi) peel, skin

sco'sceso, -a [skoʃ'ʃeso] ag steep

'**scosso, -a** pp di **scuotere** ▷ ag (turbato) shaken, upset ▷ sf jerk, jolt, shake; (Elettr, fig) shock; **scossa di terremoto** earth tremor

scos'tante ag (fig) off-putting (BRIT), unpleasant

scotch [skɔtʃ] sm inv (whisky) Scotch®; (nastro adesivo) Scotch tape®, Sellotape®

scot'tare /72/ vt (ustionare) to burn; (: con liquido bollente) to scald ▷ vi to burn; (caffè) to be too hot; **scottarsi** vpr to burn/scald o.s.; (fig) to have one's fingers burnt; **scotta'tura** sf burn; scald

'**scotto, -a** ag overcooked ▷ sm (fig): **pagare lo ~ (di)** to pay the penalty (for)

sco'vare /72/ vt to drive out, flush out; (fig) to discover

'**Scozia** ['skɔttsja] sf: **la ~** Scotland; **scoz'zese** ag Scottish ▷ smf Scot

scredi'tare /72/ vt to discredit

'**screen saver** ['skriin'seɪvər] sm inv (Inform) screen saver

scre'mato, -a ag skimmed; **parzialmente ~** semi-skimmed

screpo'lato, -a ag (labbra) chapped; (muro) cracked

'**screzio** ['skrɛttsjo] sm disagreement

scricchio'lare [skrikkjo'lare] /72/ vi to creak, squeak

'**scrigno** ['skriɲɲo] sm casket

scrimina'tura sf parting

'**scrissi** ecc vb vedi **scrivere**

'**scritto, -a** pp di **scrivere** ▷ ag written ▷ sm writing; (lettera) letter, note ▷ sf inscription

scrit'toio sm writing desk

scrit'tore, -'trice sm/f writer

scrit'tura sf writing; (Comm) entry; (contratto) contract; (Rel): **la Sacra S~** the Scriptures pl

scrittu'rare /72/ vt (Teat, Cine) to sign up, engage; (Comm) to enter

scriva'nia sf desk

'**scrivere** /105/ vt to write; **come si scrive?** how is it spelt?, how do you write it?

scroc'cone, -a sm/f scrounger

'**scrofa** sf (Zool) sow

scrol'lare /72/ vt to shake; **scrollarsi** vpr (anche fig) to give o.s. a shake; **~ le spalle/il capo** to shrug one's shoulders/shake one's head

'**scrupolo** sm scruple; (meticolosità) care, conscientiousness

scrupo'loso, -a ag scrupulous; conscientious

scru'tare /72/ vt to scrutinize; (intenzioni, causa) to examine, scrutinize

scu'cire [sku'tʃire] /31/ vt (orlo ecc) to unpick, undo; **scucirsi** vpr to come unstitched

scude'ria sf stable

scu'detto sm (Sport) (championship) shield; (distintivo) badge

'**scudo** sm shield

sculacci'are [skulat'tʃare] /14/ vt to spank

scul'tore, -'trice sm/f sculptor
scul'tura sf sculpture
scu'ola sf school; **~ elementare** o
primaria primary (BRIT) o grade (US)
school (for children from 6 to 11 years
of age); **~ guida** driving school; **~
media** secondary (BRIT) o high (US)
school; **~ dell'obbligo** compulsory
education; **scuole serali** evening
classes, night school sg: **~ tecnica**
technical college
scu'otere /106/ vt to shake
'**scure** sf axe
'**scuro, -a** ag dark; (fig: espressione)
grim ▷ sm darkness; dark colour
(BRIT) o color (US); (imposta)
(window) shutter; **verde/rosso** ecc
~ dark green/red etc
'**scusa** sf excuse; **scuse** sfpl apology
sg, apologies; **chiedere ~ a qn (per)**
to apologize to sb (for); **chiedo ~** I'm
sorry; (disturbando ecc) excuse me
scu'sare /72/ vt to excuse; **scusarsi**
vpr: **scusarsi (di)** to apologize (for);
(mi) scusi I'm sorry; (per richiamare
l'attenzione) excuse me
sde'gnato, -a [zdeɲ'ɲato] ag
indignant, angry
'**sdegno** ['zdeɲɲo] sm scorn, disdain
sdolci'nato, -a [zdoltʃi'nato] ag
mawkish, oversentimental
sdrai'arsi /19/ vpr to stretch out,
lie down
'**sdraio** sm: **sedia a ~** deck chair
sdruccio'levole [zdruttʃo'levole]
ag slippery

PAROLA CHIAVE

se pron vedi **si**
▷ cong **1** (condizionale, ipotetica) if; **se
nevica non vengo** I won't come
if it snows; **sarei rimasto se me
l'avessero chiesto** I would have
stayed if they'd asked me; **non puoi
fare altro se non telefonare** all you
can do is phone; **se mai** if, if ever;
siamo noi se mai che le siamo
grati it is we who should be grateful
to you; **se no** (altrimenti) or (else),
otherwise
2 (in frasi dubitative, interrogative
indirette) if, whether; **non so se
scrivere o telefonare** I don't know
whether o if I should write or phone

sé pron (gen) oneself; (esso, essa,
lui, lei, loro) itself; himself; herself;
themselves; **sé stesso(a)** pron
oneself; itself; himself; herself
seb'bene cong although, though
sec. abbr (= secolo) c.
'**secca** sf vedi **secco**
sec'care /20/ vt to dry; (prosciugare)
to dry up; (fig: importunare) to annoy,
bother ▷ vi to dry; to dry up; **seccarsi**
vpr to dry; to dry up; (fig) to grow
annoyed
sec'cato, -a ag (fig: infastidito)
bothered, annoyed; (: stufo) fed up
secca'tura sf (fig) bother no pl,
trouble no pl
seccherò ecc [sekke'rɔ] vb vedi
seccare
secchi'ello sm bucket; **~ del
ghiaccio** ice bucket
'**secchio** ['sekkjo] sm bucket, pail
'**secco, -a, -chi, -che** ag dry; (fichi,
pesce) dried; (foglie, ramo) withered;
(magro: persona) thin, skinny; (fig:
risposta, modo di fare) curt, abrupt;
(: colpo) clean, sharp ▷ sm (siccità)
drought ▷ sf (del mare) shallows
pl: **restarci ~** (morire sul colpo) to
drop dead; **tirare a ~** (barca) to
beach; **rimanere a ~** (fig) to be left
in the lurch
seco'lare ag age-old, centuries-old;
(laico, mondano) secular
'**secolo** sm century; (epoca) age
se'conda sf vedi **secondo**
secon'dario, -a ag secondary
se'condo, -a ag second ▷ sm second;
(di pranzo) main course ▷ sf (Aut)
second (gear) ▷ prep according to;
(nel modo prescritto) in accordance

with; **seconda classe** second-class; **di seconda mano** second-hand; **viaggiare in seconda** to travel second-class; **a seconda di** according to; in accordance with; **~ me** in my opinion, to my mind

'**sedano** *sm* celery

seda'tivo, -a *ag, sm* sedative

'**sede** *sf (di ditta: principale)* head office; *(di organizzazione)* headquarters *pl*: **~ centrale** head office; **~ sociale** registered office

seden'tario, -a *ag* sedentary

se'dere /107/ *vi* to sit, be seated

'**sedia** *sf* chair; **~ elettrica** electric chair; **~ a rotelle** wheelchair

'**sedici** ['seditʃi] *num* sixteen

se'dile *sm* seat; *(panchina)* bench

sedu'cente [sedu'tʃɛnte] *ag* seductive; *(proposta)* very attractive

se'durre /90/ *vt* to seduce

se'duta *sf* session, sitting; *(riunione)* meeting; **~ stante** *(fig)* immediately; **~ spiritica** seance

seduzi'one [sedut'tsjone] *sf* seduction; *(fascino)* charm, appeal

SEeO *abbr (= salvo errori e omissioni)* E & OE

'**sega, -ghe** *sf* saw

'**segale** *sf* rye

se'gare /80/ *vt* to saw; *(recidere)* to saw off

'**seggio** ['sɛddʒo] *sm* seat; **~ elettorale** polling station

seggi'ola ['sɛddʒola] *sf* chair; **seggio'lone** *sm (per bambini)* highchair

seggio'via [sɛddʒo'via] *sf* chairlift

segherò *ecc* [sege'rɔ] *vb vedi* **segare**

segna'lare [seɲɲa'lare] /72/ *vt (avvertire)* to signal; *(menzionare)* to indicate; *(: fatto, risultato, aumento)* to report; *(: errore, dettaglio)* to point out; *(persona)* to single out

se'gnale [seɲ'ɲale] *sm* signal; *(cartello)*: **~ stradale** road sign; **~ acustico** acoustic *o* sound signal; **~ d'allarme** alarm; *(Ferr)*

communication cord; **~ orario** *(Radio)* time signal

segna'libro [seɲɲa'libro] *sm (anche Inform)* bookmark

se'gnare [seɲ'ɲare] /15/ *vt* to mark; *(prendere nota)* to note; *(indicare)* to indicate, mark; *(Sport: goal)* to score

'**segno** ['seɲɲo] *sm* sign; *(impronta, contrassegno)* mark; *(limite)* limit, bounds *pl*; *(bersaglio)* target; **fare ~ di sì/no** to nod (one's head)/shake one's head; **fare ~ a qn di fermarsi** to motion (to) sb to stop; **cogliere** *o* **colpire nel ~** *(fig)* to hit the mark; **~ zodiacale** star sign

segre'tario, -a *sm/f* secretary; **~ comunale** town clerk; **S~ di Stato** Secretary of State

segrete'ria *sf (di ditta, scuola)* (secretary's) office; *(d'organizzazione internazionale)* secretariat; *(Pol: ecc: carica)* office of Secretary; **~ telefonica** answering machine

se'greto, -a *ag* secret ▷ *sm* secret; secrecy *no pl* ▷ *sf* dungeon; **in ~** in secret, secretly

segu'ace [se'gwatʃe] *smf* follower, disciple

segu'ente *ag* following, next

segu'ire /45/ *vt* to follow; *(frequentare: corso)* to attend ▷ *vi* to follow; *(continuare: testo)* to continue

segui'tare /72/ *vt* to continue, carry on with ▷ *vi* to continue, carry on

'**seguito** *sm (scorta)* suite, retinue; *(discepoli)* followers *pl*; *(favore)* following; *(continuazione)* continuation; *(conseguenza)* result; **di ~** at a stretch, on end; **in ~** later on; **in ~ a, a ~ di** following; *(a causa di)* as a result of, owing to

'**sei** *vb vedi* **essere** ▷ *num* six

sei'cento [sei'tʃɛnto] *num* six hundred ▷ *sm*: **il S~** the seventeenth century

selci'ato [sel'tʃato] *sm* cobbled surface

selezio'nare [selettsjo'nare] /72/ *vt* to select

selezi'one [selet'tsjone] *sf* selection
'sella *sf* saddle
sel'lino *sm* saddle
selvag'gina [selvad'dʒina] *sf* (*animali*) game
sel'vaggio, -a, -gi, -ge [sel'vaddʒo] *ag* wild; (*tribù*) savage, uncivilized; (*fig*) savage, brutal ▷ *sm/f* savage
sel'vatico, -a, -ci, -che *ag* wild
se'maforo *sm* (*Aut*) traffic lights *pl*
sem'brare /72/ *vi* to seem ▷ *vb impers*: **sembra che** it seems that; **mi sembra che** it seems to me that; I think (that); **~ di essere** to seem to be
'seme *sm* seed; (*sperma*) semen; (*Carte*) suit
se'mestre *sm* half-year, six-month period
semifi'nale *sf* semifinal
semi'freddo *sm* ice-cream dessert
semi'nare /72/ *vt* to sow
semi'nario *sm* seminar; (*Rel*) seminary
seminter'rato *sm* basement; (*appartamento*) basement flat (*BRIT*) o apartment (*US*)
'semola *sf*: **~ di grano duro** durum wheat
semo'lino *sm* semolina
'semplice ['semplitʃe] *ag* simple; (*di un solo elemento*) single
'sempre *av* always; (*ancora*) still; **posso ~ tentare** I can always o still try; **da ~** always; **per ~** forever; **una volta per ~** once and for all; **~ che** provided (that); **~ più** more and more; **~ meno** less and less
sempre'verde *ag, sm o f* (*Bot*) evergreen
'senape *sf* (*Cuc*) mustard
se'nato *sm* senate; **sena'tore, -'trice** *sm/f* senator
'senno *sm* judgment, (*common*) sense; **col ~ di poi** with hindsight
'seno *sm* (*Anat: petto, mammella*) breast; (: *grembo, anche fig*) womb; (: *cavità*) sinus

sen'sato, -a *ag* sensible
sensazio'nale [sensattsjo'nale] *ag* sensational
sensazi'one [sensat'tsjone] *sf* feeling, sensation; **fare ~** to cause a sensation, create a stir; **avere la ~ che** to have a feeling that
sen'sibile *ag* sensitive; (*ai sensi*) perceptible; (*rilevante, notevole*) appreciable; noticeable; **~ a** sensitive to

> Attenzione! In inglese esiste la parola *sensible*, che però significa *ragionevole*.

sensibiliz'zare [sensibilid'dzare] /72/ *vt* (*fig*) to make aware, awaken
'senso *sm* (*Fisiol, istinto*) sense; (*impressione, sensazione*) feeling, sensation; (*significato*) meaning, sense; (*direzione*) direction; **sensi** *smpl* (*coscienza*) consciousness *sg*; (*sensualità*) senses; **fare ~ a** (*ripugnare*) to disgust, repel; **ciò non ha ~** that doesn't make sense; **~ comune** common sense; **in ~ orario/antiorario** clockwise/anticlockwise; **~ di colpa** sense of guilt; **a ~ unico** one-way; **"~ vietato"** (*Aut*) "no entry"
sensu'ale *ag* sensual; sensuous
sen'tenza [sen'tentsa] *sf* (*Dir*) sentence; (*massima*) maxim
senti'ero *sm* path
sentimen'tale *ag* sentimental; (*vita, avventura*) love *cpd*
senti'mento *sm* feeling
senti'nella *sf* sentry
sen'tire /45/ *vt* (*percepire al tatto, fig*) to feel; (*udire*) to hear; (*ascoltare*) to listen to; (*odore*) to smell; (*avvertire con il gusto, assaggiare*) to taste ▷ *vi*: **~ di** (*avere sapore*) to taste of; (*avere odore*) to smell of; **sentirsi** *vpr* (*uso reciproco*) to be in touch; **sentirsi bene/male** to feel well/unwell o ill; **sentirsi di fare qc** (*essere disposto*) to feel like doing sth
sen'tito, -a *ag* (*sincero*) sincere, warm; **per ~ dire** by hearsay

'senza ['sɛntsa] *prep, cong* without;
~ dir nulla without saying a word;
fare ~ qc to do without sth; **~ di me**
without me; **~ che io lo sapessi**
without me *o* my knowing; **~ amici**
friendless; **senz'altro** of course,
certainly; **~ dubbio** no doubt;
~ scrupoli unscrupulous

sepa'rare /72/ *vt* to separate;
(*dividere*) to divide; (*tenere distinto*) to
distinguish; **separarsi** *vpr* (*coniugi*)
to separate, part; (*amici*) to part,
leave each other; **separarsi da**
(*coniuge*) to separate *o* part from;
(*amico, socio*) to part company with;
(*oggetto*) to part with; **sepa'rato, -a**
ag (*letti, conto ecc*) separate; (*coniugi*)
separated

seppel'lire /55/ *vt* to bury

'seppi *ecc vb vedi* **sapere**

'seppia *sf* cuttlefish ⊳ *ag inv* sepia

se'quenza [se'kwɛntsa] *sf* sequence

seques'trare /72/ *vt* (*Dir*) to
impound; (*rapire*) to kidnap;
se'questro *sm* (*Dir*) impoundment;
sequestro di persona kidnapping

'sera *sf* evening; **di ~** in the evening;
domani ~ tomorrow evening,
tomorrow night; **se'rale** *ag* evening
cpd; **se'rata** *sf* evening; (*ricevimento*)
party

ser'bare /72/ *vt* to keep; (*mettere da
parte*) to put aside; **~ rancore/odio
verso qn** to bear sb a grudge/hate sb

serba'toio *sm* tank; (*cisterna*) cistern

'Serbia *sf*: **la ~** Serbia

'serbo, -a *ag* Serbian ⊳ *sm/f* Serbian,
Serb ⊳ *sm* (*Ling*) Serbian; (*il serbare*):
mettere/tenere *o* **avere in ~ qc** to
put/keep sth aside

se'reno, -a *ag* (*tempo, cielo*) clear; (*fig*)
serene, calm

ser'gente [ser'dʒɛnte] *sm* (*Mil*)
sergeant

'serie *sf inv* (*successione*) series *inv*;
(*gruppo, collezione di chiavi ecc*) set;
(*Sport*) division; league; (*Comm*):
modello di ~/fuori ~ standard/

custom-built model; **in ~** in quick
succession; (*Comm*) mass *cpd*

serietà *sf* seriousness; reliability

'serio, -a *ag* serious; (*impiegato*)
responsible, reliable; (*ditta, cliente*)
reliable, dependable; **sul ~** (*davvero*)
really, truly; (*seriamente*) seriously,
in earnest

ser'pente *sm* snake; **~ a sonagli**
rattlesnake

'serra *sf* greenhouse; hothouse

ser'randa *sf* roller shutter

serra'tura *sf* lock

'server ['server] *sm inv* (*Inform*) server

ser'vire /45/ *vt* to serve; (*clienti: al
ristorante*) to wait on; (: *al negozio*) to
serve, attend to; (*fig: giovare*) to aid,
help; (*Carte*) to deal ⊳ *vi* (*Tennis*) to
serve; (*essere utile*): **~ a qn** to be of use
to sb; **servirsi** *vpr* (*usare*): **servirsi di**
to use; (*prendere: cibo*): **servirsi (di)** to
help o.s. (to); (*essere cliente abituale*):
servirsi da to be a regular customer
at, go to; **~ a qc/a fare** (*utensile ecc*)
to be used for sth/for doing; **~ (a qn)
da** to serve as (for sb); **serviti pure!**
help yourself!

servizi'evole [servit'tsjevole] *ag*
obliging, willing to help

ser'vizio [ser'vittsjo] *sm* service; (*al
ristorante, sul conto*) service (charge);
(*Stampa, TV, Radio*) report; (*da tè,
caffè ecc*) set, service; (*di casa*) kitchen and bathroom;
(*Econ*) services; **essere di ~** to be
on duty; **fuori ~** (*telefono ecc*) out
of order; **~ compreso/escluso**
service included/not included; **~
assistenza clienti** customer service;
~ di posate set of cutlery; **~ militare**
military service; **servizi segreti**
secret service *sg*

ses'santa *num* sixty; **sessan'tesimo,
-a** *num* sixtieth

sessi'one *sf* session

'sesso *sm* sex; **sessu'ale** *ag* sexual,
sex *cpd*

ses'tante *sm* sextant

'**sesto, -a** *num* sixth
'**seta** *sf* silk
'**sete** *sf* thirst; **avere ~** to be thirsty
'**setola** *sf* bristle
'**setta** *sf* sect
set'tanta *num* seventy;
  settan'tesimo, -a *num* seventieth
set'tare /72/ *vt* (*Inform*) to set up
'**sette** *num* seven
sette'cento [sette'tʃɛnto] *num* seven
  hundred ▷ *sm*: **il S~** the eighteenth
  century
set'tembre *sm* September
settentrio'nale *ag* northern
settentri'one *sm* north
setti'mana *sf* week; **settima'nale**
  ag, *sm* weekly

  ○ **SETTIMANA BIANCA**
  ○
  ○ *Settimana bianca* is the name given
  ○ to a week-long winter-sports
  ○ holiday taken by many Italians
  ○ some time in the skiing season.

'**settimo, -a** *num* seventh
set'tore *sm* sector
severità *sf* severity
se'vero, -a *ag* severe
sevizi'are [sevit'tsjare] /19/ *vt* to
  torture
sezio'nare [settsjo'nare] /72/ *vt* to
  divide into sections; (*Med*) to dissect
sezi'one [set'tsjone] *sf* section
sfacchi'nata [sfakki'nata] *sf* (*fam*)
  chore, drudgery *no pl*
sfacci'ato, -a [sfat'tʃato] *ag*
  (*maleducato*) cheeky, impudent;
  (*vistoso*) gaudy
sfa'mare /72/ *vt* to feed; (*cibo*) to fill;
  sfamarsi *vpr* to satisfy one's hunger,
  fill o.s. up
sfasci'are [sfaʃ'ʃare] /14/ *vt* (*ferita*) to
  unbandage; (*distruggere*) to smash,
  shatter; **sfasciarsi** *vpr* (*rompersi*) to
  smash, shatter
sfavo'revole *ag* unfavourable
'**sfera** *sf* sphere

sfer'rare /72/ *vt* (*fig*: *colpo*) to land,
  deal; (: *attacco*) to launch
'**sfida** *sf* challenge
sfi'dare /72/ *vt* to challenge; (*fig*) to
  defy, brave
sfi'ducia [sfi'dutʃa] *sf* distrust,
  mistrust
sfi'gato, -a (*fam*) *ag*: **essere ~**
  (*sfortunato*) to be unlucky
sfigu'rare /72/ *vt* (*persona*) to
  disfigure; (*quadro*, *statua*) to deface
  ▷ *vi* (*far cattiva figura*) to make a bad
  impression
sfi'lare /72/ *vt* (*ago*) to unthread;
  (*abito*, *scarpe*) to slip off ▷ *vi* (*truppe*)
  to march past, parade; (*atleti*) to
  parade; **sfilarsi** *vpr* (*perle ecc*) to come
  unstrung; (*orlo*, *tessuto*) to fray; (*calza*)
  to run, ladder; **sfi'lata** *sf* (*Mil*) parade;
  (*di manifestanti*) march; **sfilata di
  moda** fashion show
'**sfinge** ['sfindʒe] *sf* sphinx
sfi'nito, -a *ag* exhausted
sfio'rare /72/ *vt* to brush (against);
  (*argomento*) to touch upon
sfio'rire /55/ *vi* to wither, fade
sfo'cato, -a *ag* (*Fot*) out of focus
sfoci'are [sfo'tʃare] /14/ *vi*: **~ in**
  to flow into; (*fig*: *malcontento*) to
  develop into
sfode'rato, -a *ag* (*vestito*) unlined
sfo'gare /80/ *vt* to vent; **sfogarsi** *vpr*
  (*sfogare la propria rabbia*) to give vent
  to one's anger; (*confidarsi*): **sfogarsi
  (con)** to pour out one's feelings (to);
  non sfogarti su di me! don't take
  your bad temper out on me!
sfoggi'are [sfod'dʒare] /62/ *vt*, *vi*
  to show off
'**sfoglia** *sf* sheet of pasta dough;
  pasta ~ (*Cuc*) puff pastry
sfogli'are /27/ *vt* (*libro*) to leaf
  through
'**sfogo, -ghi** *sm* (*eruzione cutanea*)
  rash; (*fig*) outburst; **dare ~ a** (*fig*) to
  give vent to
sfon'dare /72/ *vt* (*porta*) to break
  down; (*scarpe*) to wear a hole in;

s

(*cesto*, *scatola*) to burst, knock the bottom out of; (*Mil*) to break through ▷ *vi* (*riuscire*) to make a name for o.s.

'**sfondo** *sm* background

sfor'mato *sm* (*Cuc*) type of soufflé

sfor'tuna *sf* misfortune, ill luck *no pl*; **avere ~** to be unlucky; **sfortu'nato, -a** *ag* unlucky; (*impresa*, *film*) unsuccessful

sfor'zare [sfor'tsare] /72/ *vt* to force; **sforzarsi** *vpr*: **sforzarsi di** *o* **a** *o* **per fare** to try hard to do

'**sforzo** ['sfɔrtso] *sm* effort; (*tensione eccessiva*, *Tecn*) strain; **fare uno ~** to make an effort

sfrat'tare /72/ *vt* to evict; '**sfratto** *sm* eviction

sfrecci'are [sfret'tʃare] /14/ *vi* to shoot *o* flash past

sfre'gare /80/ *vt* (*strofinare*) to rub; (*graffiare*) to scratch; **sfregarsi le mani** to rub one's hands; **~ un fiammifero** to strike a match

sfregi'are [sfre'dʒare] /62/ *vt* to slash, gash; (*persona*) to disfigure; (*quadro*) to deface

sfre'nato, -a *ag* (*fig*) unrestrained, unbridled

sfron'tato, -a *ag* shameless

sfrutta'mento *sm* exploitation

sfrut'tare /72/ *vt* (*terreno*) to overwork, exhaust; (*miniera*) to exploit, work; (*fig*: *operai*, *occasione*, *potere*) to exploit

sfug'gire [sfud'dʒire] /31/ *vi* to escape; **~ a** (*custode*) to escape (from); (*morte*) to escape; **~ a qn** (*dettaglio*, *nome*) to escape sb; **~ di mano a qn** to slip out of sb's hand (*o* hands)

sfu'mare /72/ *vt* (*colori*, *contorni*) to soften, shade off ▷ *vi* to shade (off), fade; (*fig*: *svanire*) to vanish, disappear; (: *speranze*) to come to nothing

sfuma'tura *sf* shading off *no pl*; (*tonalità*) shade, tone; (*fig*) touch, hint

sfuri'ata *sf* (*scatto di collera*) fit of anger; (*rimprovero*) sharp rebuke

sga'bello *sm* stool

sgabuz'zino [zgabud'dzino] *sm* lumber room

sgambet'tare /72/ *vi* to kick one's legs about

sgam'betto *sm*: **far lo ~ a qn** to trip sb up; (*fig*) to oust sb

sganci'are [zgan'tʃare] /14/ *vt* to unhook; (*Ferr*) to uncouple; (*bombe*: *da aereo*) to release, drop; (*fig*: *fam*: *soldi*) to fork out; **sganciarsi** *vpr* (*fig*): **sganciarsi (da)** to get away (from)

sganghe'rato, -a [zgange'rato] *ag* (*porta*) off its hinges; (*auto*) ramshackle; (*riso*) wild, boisterous

sgar'bato, -a *ag* rude, impolite

'**sgarbo** *sm*: **fare uno ~ a qn** to be rude to sb

sgargi'ante [zgar'dʒante] *ag* gaudy, showy

sgattaio'lare /72/ *vi* to sneak away *o* off

sge'lare [zdʒe'lare] /72/ *vi*, *vt* to thaw

sghignaz'zare [zgiɲɲat'tsare] /72/ *vi* to laugh scornfully

sgob'bare /72/ *vi* (*scolaro*) to swot; (*operaio*) to slog

sgombe'rare /72/, **sgomb'rare** *vt* (*tavolo*, *stanza*) to clear; (*evacuare*: *piazza*, *città*) to evacuate ▷ *vi* to move

'**sgombro, -a** *ag*: **~ (di)** clear (of), free (from) ▷ *sm* (*Zool*) mackerel; (*anche*: **sgombero**) clearing; vacating; evacuation; (*trasloco*) removal

sgonfi'are /19/ *vt* to let down, deflate; **sgonfiarsi** *vpr* to go down

'**sgonfio, -a** *ag* (*pneumatico*, *pallone*) flat

'**sgorbio** *sm* blot; scribble

sgra'devole *ag* unpleasant, disagreeable

sgra'dito, -a *ag* unpleasant, unwelcome

sgra'nare /72/ *vt* (*piselli*) to shell; **~ gli occhi** to open one's eyes wide

sgran'chire [zgran'kire] /55/ vt, **sgranchirsi** [zgran'kirsi]vpr to stretch; **sgranchirsi le gambe** to stretch one's legs

sgranocchi'are [zgranok'kjare] /19/ vt to munch

'sgravio sm: ~ **fiscale** o **contributivo** tax relief

sgrazi'ato, -a [zgrat'tsjato] ag clumsy, ungainly

sgri'dare /72/ vt to scold

sgual'cire [zgwal'tʃire] /55/ vt to crumple (up), crease

sgual'drina sf(peg) slut

sgu'ardo sm (occhiata) look, glance; (espressione) look (in one's eye)

sguaz'zare [zgwat'tsare] /72/ vi (nell'acqua) to splash about; (nella melma) to wallow; ~ **nell'oro** to be rolling in money

sguinzagli'are [zgwintsaʎ'ʎare] /27/ vt to let off the leash; (fig: persona): ~ **qn dietro a qn** to set sb on sb

sgusci'are [zguʃ'ʃare] /14/ vt to shell ▷ vi (sfuggire di mano) to slip; ~ **via** to slip o slink away

'shampoo ['ʃampo] sm inv shampoo

'shiatzu ['tʃiatsu] sm inv shiatsu

shock [ʃɔk] sm inv shock

PAROLA CHIAVE

si (dav lo, la, li, le, ne diventa **se**) pron 1 (riflessivo: maschile) himself; (: femminile) herself; (: neutro) itself; (: impersonale) oneself; (: pl) themselves; **lavarsi** to wash (oneself); **si è tagliato** he has cut himself; **si credono importanti** they think a lot of themselves

2 (riflessivo, con complemento oggetto): **lavarsi le mani** to wash one's hands; **si sta lavando i capelli** he (o she) is washing his (o her) hair

3 (reciproco) one another, each other; **si amano** they love one another o each other

4 (passivo): **si ripara facilmente** it is easily repaired

5 (impersonale): **si dice che ...** they o people say that ...; **si vede che è vecchio** one o you can see that it's old

6 (noi) we; **tra poco si parte** we're leaving soon

sì av yes; **un giorno sì e uno no** every other day

'sia ecc vb vedi **essere**

si'amo vb vedi **essere**

si'cario sm hired killer

sicché [sik'ke] cong (perciò) so (that), therefore; (e quindi) (and) so

siccità [sittʃi'ta] sf drought

sic'come cong since, as

Si'cilia [si'tʃilja] sf: **la ~** Sicily; **sicili'ano, -a** [sitʃi'ljano] ag, sm/f Sicilian

si'cura sf safety catch; (Aut) safety lock

sicu'rezza [siku'rettsa] sf safety; security; confidence; certainty; **di ~** safety cpd; **la ~ stradale** road safety

si'curo, -a ag safe; (ben difeso) secure; (fiducioso) confident; (certo) sure, certain; (notizia, amico) reliable; (esperto) skilled ▷ av (anche: **di ~**) certainly; **essere/mettere al ~** to be safe/put in a safe place; **~ di sé** self-confident, sure of o.s.; **sentirsi ~** to feel safe o secure

si'edo ecc vb vedi **sedere**

si'epe sf hedge

si'ero sm (Med) serum; **sieronega'tivo, -a** ag HIV-negative; **sieroposi'tivo, -a** ag HIV-positive

si'ete vb vedi **essere**

si'filide sf syphilis

Sig. abbr (= signore) Mr

siga'retta sf cigarette

'sigaro sm cigar

Sigg. abbr (= signori) Messrs

sigil'lare [sidʒil'lare] /72/ vt to seal

si'gillo [si'dʒillo] sm seal

'sigla sf initials pl; (abbreviazione) acronym, abbreviation;

s

~ automobilistica abbreviation of province on vehicle number plate; **~ musicale** signature tune

Sig.na abbr (= signorina) Miss

signifi'care [siɲɲifi'kare] /20/ vt to mean; **signi'cato** sm meaning

si'gnora [siɲ'ɲora] sf lady; **la ~ X** Mrs X; **buon giorno S~/Signore/ Signorina** good morning; (deferente) good morning Madam/Sir/Madam; (quando si conosce il nome) good morning Mrs/Mr/Miss X; **Gentile S~/Signore/Signorina** (in una lettera) Dear Madam/Sir/Madam; **il signor Rossi e ~** Mr Rossi and his wife; **signore e signori** ladies and gentlemen

si'gnore [siɲ'ɲore] sm gentleman; (padrone) lord, master; (Rel): **il S~** the Lord; **il signor X** Mr X; **i signori Bianchi** (coniugi) Mr and Mrs Bianchi; vedi anche **signora**

signo'rile [siɲɲo'rile] ag refined

signo'rina [siɲɲo'rina] sf young lady; **la ~ X** Miss X; vedi anche **signora**

Sig.ra abbr (= signora) Mrs

silenzia'tore [silentsja'tore] sm silencer

si'lenzio [si'lentsjo] sm silence; **fare ~** to be quiet, stop talking; **silenzi'oso, -a** ag silent, quiet

si'licio [si'litʃo] sm silicon

sili'cone sm silicone

'sillaba sf syllable

si'luro sm torpedo

SIM [sim] sigla f inv (Tel): **~ card** SIM card

simboleggi'are [simboled'dʒare] /62/ vt to symbolize

'simbolo sm symbol

'simile ag (analogo) similar; (di questo tipo): **un uomo ~** such a man, a man like this; **libri simili** such books; **~ a** similar to; **i suoi simili** one's fellow men; one's peers

simme'tria sf symmetry

simpa'tia sf (qualità) pleasantness; (inclinazione) liking; **avere ~ per**

qn to like sb, have a liking for sb; **sim'patico, -a, -ci, -che** ag (persona) nice, pleasant, likeable; (casa, albergo ecc) nice, pleasant

> Attenzione! In inglese esiste la parola sympathetic, che però significa comprensivo.

simpatiz'zare [simpatid'dzare] /72/ vi: **~ con** to take a liking to

simu'lare /72/ vt to sham, simulate; (Tecn) to simulate

simul'taneo, -a ag simultaneous

sina'goga, -ghe sf synagogue

sincerità [sintʃeri'ta] sf sincerity

sin'cero, -a [sin'tʃero] ag sincere; (onesto) genuine; heartfelt

sinda'cale ag (trade-)union cpd

sinda'cato sm (di lavoratori) (trade) union; (Amm, Econ, Dir) syndicate, trust, pool

'sindaco, -ci sm mayor

sinfo'nia sf (Mus) symphony

singhioz'zare [singjot'tsare] /72/ vi to sob; to hiccup

singhi'ozzo [sin'gjottso] sm sob; (Med) hiccup; **avere il ~** to have the hiccups; **a ~** (fig) by fits and starts

'single ['siŋgol] ag inv, smf inv single

singo'lare ag (insolito) remarkable, singular; (Ling) singular ▷ sm (Ling) singular; (Tennis): **~ maschile/ femminile** men's/women's singles

'singolo, -a ag single, individual ▷ sm (persona) individual; (Tennis); = **singolare**

si'nistro, -a ag left, left-hand; (fig) sinister ▷ sm (incidente) accident ▷ sf (Pol) left (wing); **a sinistra** on the left; (direzione) to the left

si'nonimo sm synonym; **~ di** synonymous with

sin'tassi sf syntax

'sintesi sf synthesis; (riassunto) summary, résumé

sin'tetico, -a, -ci, -che ag synthetic

sintetiz'zare [sintetid'dzare] /72/ vt to synthesize; (riassumere) to summarize

sinto'matico, -a, -ci, -che *ag* symptomatic

'sintomo *sm* symptom

sintoniz'zare [sintonid'dzare] /72/ *vt* to tune (in); **sintonizzarsi** *vpr*: **sintonizzarsi su** to tune in to

si'pario *sm* (*Teat*) curtain

si'rena *sf* (*apparecchio*) siren; (*nella mitologia, fig*) siren, mermaid

'Siria *sf*: **la ~** Syria

si'ringa, -ghe *sf* syringe

'sismico, -a, -ci, -che *ag* seismic

sis'tema, -i *sm* system; (*metodo*) method, way; **~ nervoso** nervous system; **~ operativo** (*Inform*) operating system; **~ solare** solar system

siste'mare /72/ *vt* (*mettere a posto*) to tidy, put in order; (*risolvere: questione*) to sort out, settle; (*procurare un lavoro a*) to find a job for; (*dare un alloggio a*) to settle, find accommodation (*BRIT*) *o* accommodations (*US*) for; **sistemarsi** *vpr* (*problema*) to be settled; (*persona: trovare alloggio*) to find accommodation(s); (: *trovarsi un lavoro*) to get fixed up with a job; **ti sistemo io!** I'll soon sort you out!

siste'matico, -a, -ci, -che *ag* systematic

sistemazi'one [sistemat'tsjone] *sf* arrangement, order; settlement; employment; accommodation (*BRIT*), accommodations (*US*)

'sito *sm*: **~ Internet** website

situ'ato, -a *ag*: **~ a/su** situated at/on

situazi'one [situat'tsjone] *sf* situation

ski-lift [ski'lift] *sm inv* ski tow

slacci'are [zlat'tʃare] /14/ *vt* to undo, unfasten

slanci'ato, -a [zlan'tʃato] *ag* slender

'slancio *sm* dash, leap; (*fig*) surge; **di ~** impetuously

'slavo, -a *ag* Slav(onic), Slavic

sle'ale *ag* disloyal; (*concorrenza ecc*) unfair

sle'gare /80/ *vt* to untie

slip [zlip] *sm inv* briefs *pl*

'slitta *sf* sledge; (*trainata*) sleigh

slit'tare /72/ *vi* to slip, slide; (*Aut*) to skid

s.l.m. *abbr* (= *sul livello del mare*) a.s.l.

slo'gare /80/ *vt* (*Med*) to dislocate

sloggi'are [zlod'dʒare] /62/ *vt* (*inquilino*) to turn out ▷ *vi* to move out

Slo'vacchia [zlo'vakkja] *sf* Slovakia

slo'vacco, -a, -ci, -che *ag, sm/f* Slovak

Slo'venia *sf* Slovenia

slo'veno, -a *ag, sm/f* Slovene, Slovenian ▷ *sm* (*Ling*) Slovene

smacchi'are [zmak'kjare] /19/ *vt* to remove stains from; **smacchia'tore** *sm* stain remover

'smacco, -chi *sm* humiliating defeat

smagli'ante [zmaʎ'ʎante] *ag* brilliant, dazzling

smaglia'tura [zmaʎʎa'tura] *sf* (*su maglia, calza*) ladder; (*sulla pelle*) stretch mark

smalizi'ato, -a [smalit'tsjato] *ag* shrewd, cunning

smalti'mento *sm* (*di rifiuti*) disposal

smal'tire /55/ *vt* (*merce*) to sell off; (*rifiuti*) to dispose of; (*cibo*) to digest; (*peso*) to lose; (*rabbia*) to get over; **~ la sbornia** to sober up

'smalto *sm* (*anche di denti*) enamel; (*per ceramica*) glaze; **~ per unghie** nail varnish

smantel'lare /72/ *vt* to dismantle

smarri'mento *sm* loss; (*fig*) bewilderment; dismay

smar'rire /55/ *vt* to lose; (*non riuscire a trovare*) to mislay; **smarrirsi** *vpr* (*perdersi*) to lose one's way, get lost; (: *oggetto*) to go astray

smasche'rare [zmaske'rare] /72/ *vt* to unmask

SME *abbr* = **Stato Maggiore Esercito** ▷ *sigla m* (= *Sistema Monetario Europeo*) EMS

smen'tire /55/ vt (negare) to deny; (testimonianza) to refute; **smentirsi** vpr to be inconsistent

sme'raldo sm emerald

'smesso, -a pp di **smettere**

'smettere /63/ vt to stop; (vestiti) to stop wearing ▷ vi to stop, cease; **~ di fare** to stop doing

'smilzo, -a ['zmiltso] ag thin, lean

sminu'ire /72/ vt to diminish, lessen; (fig) to belittle

sminuz'zare [zminut'tsare] /72/ vt to break into small pieces; to crumble

'smisi ecc vb vedi **smettere**

smis'tare /72/ vt (pacchi ecc) to sort; (Ferr) to shunt

smisu'rato, -a ag boundless, immeasurable; (grandissimo) immense, enormous

'smoking ['smoukɪŋ] sm inv dinner jacket

smon'tare /72/ vt (mobile, macchina ecc) to take to pieces, dismantle; (fig: scoraggiare) to dishearten ▷ vi (scendere: da cavallo) to dismount; (: da treno) to get off; (terminare il lavoro) to stop (work); **smontarsi** vpr to lose heart; to lose one's enthusiasm

'smorfia sf grimace; (atteggiamento lezioso) simpering; **fare smorfie** to make faces; to simper

'smorto, -a ag (viso) pale, wan; (colore) dull

smor'zare [zmor'tsare] /72/ vt (suoni) to deaden; (colori) to tone down; (luce) to dim; (sete) to quench; (entusiasmo) to dampen; **smorzarsi** vpr (suono, luce) to fade; (entusiasmo) to dampen

sms ['esse'emme'esse] sm inv text (message)

smu'overe /66/ vt to move, shift; (fig: commuovere) to move; (: dall'inerzia) to rouse, stir

snatu'rato, -a ag inhuman, heartless

'snello, -a ag (agile) agile; (svelto) slender, slim

sner'vante ag (attesa, lavoro) exasperating

sniffare [znif'fare] /72/ vt (fam: cocaina) to snort

snob'bare /72/ vt to snub

sno'dare /72/ vt (rendere agile, mobile) to loosen; **snodarsi** vpr to come loose; (articolarsi) to bend; (strada, fiume) to wind

sno'dato, -a ag (articolazione, persona) flexible; (fune ecc) undone

so vb vedi **sapere**

sobbar'carsi /20/ vpr: **~ a** to take on, undertake

'sobrio, -a ag sober

socchi'udere [sok'kjudere] /22/ vt (porta) to leave ajar; (occhi) to half-close; **socchi'uso, -a** pp di **socchiudere**

soc'correre /28/ vt to help, assist

soccorri'tore, -'trice sm/f rescuer

soc'corso, -a pp di **soccorrere** ▷ sm help, aid, assistance; **~ stradale** breakdown service

soci'ale [so'tʃale] ag social; (di associazione) club cpd, association cpd

socia'lismo [sotʃa'lizmo] sm socialism; **socia'lista, -i, -e** ag, smf socialist; **socializ'zare** [sotʃalid'dzare] /72/ vi to socialize

società [sotʃe'ta] sf inv society; (sportiva) club; (Comm) company; **~ per azioni** joint-stock company; **~ a responsabilità limitata** type of limited liability company

soci'evole [so'tʃevole] ag sociable

'socio ['sɔtʃo] sm (Dir, Comm) partner; (membro di associazione) member

'soda sf (Chim) soda; (acqua gassata) soda (water)

soddisfa'cente [soddisfa'tʃɛnte] ag satisfactory

soddis'fare /41/ vt, vi: **~ (a)** to satisfy; (impegno) to fulfil; (debito) to pay off; (richiesta) to meet, comply with; **soddis'fatto, -a** pp di **soddisfare** ▷ ag satisfied; **essere soddisfatto di** to be satisfied o pleased with; **soddisfazi'one** sf satisfaction

'**sodo, -a** ag firm, hard; (uovo) hard-boiled ▷ av (picchiare, lavorare) hard; **dormire ~** to sleep soundly

sofà sm inv sofa

soffe'renza [soffe'rɛntsa] sf suffering

sof'ferto, -a pp di **soffrire**

soffi'are /19/ vt to blow; (notizia, segreto) to whisper ▷ vi to blow; (sbuffare) to puff (and blow); **soffiarsi il naso** to blow one's nose; **~ qc/qn a qn** (fig) to pinch o steal sth/sb from sb; **~ via qc** to blow sth away

soffi'ata sf (fam) tip-off; **fare una ~ alla polizia** to tip off the police

'**soffice** ['sɔffitʃe] ag soft

'**soffio** sm (di vento) breath; (Med) murmur

soffitta sf attic

soffitto sm ceiling

soffo'cante ag suffocating, stifling

soffo'care /20/ vi (anche: **soffocarsi**) to suffocate, choke ▷ vt to suffocate, choke; (fig) to stifle, suppress

soff'rire /70/ vt to suffer, endure; (sopportare) to bear, stand ▷ vi to suffer; to be in pain; **~ (di) qc** (Med) to suffer from sth

soff'ritto, -a pp di **soffriggere** ▷ sm (Cuc) fried mixture of herbs, bacon and onions

sofisti'cato, -a ag sophisticated; (vino) adulterated

'**software** ['sɔftwɛə] sm: **~ applicativo** applications package

sogget'tivo, -a [soddʒet'tivo] ag subjective

sog'getto, -a [sod'dʒɛtto] ag: **~ a** (sottomesso) subject to; (esposto) (a variazioni, danni ecc) subject o liable to ▷ sm subject

soggezi'one [soddʒet'tsjone] sf subjection; (timidezza) awe; **avere ~ di qn** to stand in awe of sb; to be ill at ease in sb's presence

soggi'orno [sod'dʒorno] sm (permanenza) stay; (stanza) living room

'**soglia** ['sɔʎʎa] sf doorstep; (anche fig) threshold

sogli'ola ['sɔʎʎola] sf (Zool) sole

so'gnare [soɲ'ɲare] /15/ vt, vi to dream; **~ a occhi aperti** to daydream

'**sogno** ['soɲɲo] sm dream

'**soia** sf (Bot) soya

sol sm (Mus) G; (: solfeggiando la scala) so(h)

so'laio sm (soffitta) attic

sola'mente av only, just

so'lare ag solar, sun cpd

'**solco, -chi** sm (scavo, fig: ruga) furrow; (incavo) rut, track; (di disco) groove

sol'dato sm soldier; **~ semplice** private

'**soldo** sm (fig): **non vale un ~** it's not worth a penny; **soldi** smpl (denaro) money sg: **non ho soldi** I haven't got any money

'**sole** sm sun; (luce) sun(light); (tempo assolato) sun(shine); **prendere il ~** to sunbathe

soleggi'ato, -a [soled'dʒato] ag sunny

so'lenne ag solemn

so'lere /108/ vb impers: **come suole accadere** as is usually the case, as usually happens

soli'dale ag: **essere ~ con qn** to be in agreement with sb

solidarietà sf solidarity

'**solido, -a** ag solid; (forte, robusto) sturdy, solid; (fig: ditta) sound, solid ▷ sm (Mat) solid

so'lista, -i, -e ag solo ▷ smf soloist

solita'mente av usually, as a rule

soli'tario, -a ag (senza compagnia) solitary, lonely; (solo, isolato) solitary, lone; (deserto) lonely ▷ sm (gioiello, gioco) solitaire

'**solito, -a** ag usual; **essere ~ fare** to be in the habit of doing; **di ~** usually;

più tardi del ~ later than usual;
come al ~ as usual
soli'tudine *sf* solitude
sol'letico *sm* tickling; **soffrire il ~** to
be ticklish
solleva'mento *sm* raising; lifting;
(*ribellione*) revolt; **~ pesi** (*Sport*)
weight-lifting
solle'vare /72/ *vt* to lift, raise; (*fig:
persona: alleggerire*): **~ (da)** to relieve
(of); (: *dar conforto*) to comfort,
relieve; (: *questione*) to raise; (: *far
insorgere*) to stir (to revolt); **sollevarsi**
vpr to rise; (*fig: riprendersi*) to recover;
(: *ribellarsi*) to rise up
solli'evo *sm* relief; (*conforto*) comfort
'solo, -a *ag* alone; (*in senso spirituale:
isolato*): *allegerire*; (*unico*): **un ~ libro**
only one book, a single book; (*con ag
numerale*): **veniamo noi tre soli** just
o only the three of us are coming ▷ *av*
(*soltanto*) only, just; **non ~ ... ma
anche** not only ... but also; **fare qc
da ~** to do sth (all) by oneself
sol'tanto *av* only
so'lubile *ag* (*sostanza*) soluble
soluzi'one [solut'tsjone] *sf* solution
sol'vente *ag*, *sm* solvent
so'maro *sm* ass, donkey
somigli'anza [somiʎ'ʎantsa] *sf*
resemblance
somigli'are [somiʎ'ʎare] /27/ *vi*:
~ a to be like, resemble; (*nell'aspetto
fisico*) to look like; **somigliarsi** *vpr* to
be (*o* look) alike
'somma *sf* (*Mat*) sum; (*di denaro*) sum
(of money)
som'mare /72/ *vt* to add up;
(*aggiungere*) to add; **tutto sommato**
all things considered
som'mario, -a *ag* (*racconto, indagine*)
brief; (*giustizia*) summary ▷ *sm*
summary
sommer'gibile [sommer'dʒibile]
sm submarine
som'merso, -a *pp di* **sommergere**
sommità *sf inv* summit, top; (*fig*)
height

som'mossa *sf* uprising
'sonda *sf* (*Med, Meteor, Aer*) probe;
(*Mineralogia*) drill ▷ *ag inv*: **pallone** *m*
~ weather balloon
son'daggio [son'daddʒo] *sm*
sounding; probe; boring, drilling;
(*indagine*) survey; **~ d'opinioni**
opinion poll
son'dare /72/ *vt* (*Naut*) to sound;
(*atmosfera, piaga*) to probe;
(*Mineralogia*) to bore, drill; (*fig:
opinione ecc*) to survey, poll
so'netto *sm* sonnet
son'nambulo, -a *sm/f* sleepwalker
sonnel'lino *sm* nap
son'nifero *sm* sleeping drug (*o* pill)
'sonno *sm* sleep; **aver ~** to be sleepy;
prendere ~ to fall asleep
'sono *vb vedi* **essere**
so'noro, -a *ag* (*ambiente*) resonant;
(*voce*) sonorous, ringing; (*onde: Cine*)
sound *cpd*
sontu'oso, -a *ag* sumptuous; lavish
sop'palco, -chi *sm* mezzanine
soppor'tare /72/ *vt* (*subire: perdita,
spese*) to bear, sustain; (*soffrire: dolore*)
to bear, endure; (*cosa: freddo*) to
withstand; (*persona: freddo, vino*) to
take; (*tollerare*) to put up with, tolerate

> Attenzione! In inglese esiste il
> verbo *to support*, che però non
> significa *sopportare*.

sop'primere /50/ *vt* (*carica, privilegi
ecc*) to do away with; (*pubblicazione*)
to suppress; (*parola, frase*) to delete
'sopra *prep* (*gen*) on; (*al di sopra di, più
in alto di*) above; over; (*riguardo a*) on,
about ▷ *av* on top; (*attaccato, scritto*)
on it; (*al di sopra*) above; (*al piano
superiore*) upstairs; **donne ~ i 30 anni**
women over 30 (years of age); **abito
di ~** I live upstairs; **dormirci ~** (*fig*)
to sleep on it
so'prabito *sm* overcoat
soprac'ciglio [soprat'tʃiʎʎo] (*pl f*
sopracciglia) *sm* eyebrow
sopraf'fare /41/ *vt* to overcome,
overwhelm

soprallu'ogo, -ghi sm (di esperti) inspection; (di polizia) on-the-spot investigation

sopram'mobile sm ornament

soprannatu'rale ag supernatural

sopran'nome sm nickname

so'prano, -a sm/f (persona) soprano ▷ sm (voce) soprano

soprappensi'ero av lost in thought

sopras'salto sm: **di ~** with a start; suddenly

soprasse'dere /107/ vi: **~ a** to delay, put off

soprat'tutto av (anzitutto) above all; (specialmente) especially

sopravvalu'tare /72/ vt to overestimate

soprav'vento sm: **avere/prendere il ~ su qn** to have/get the upper hand over sb

sopravvis'suto, -a pp di **sopravvivere**

soprav'vivere /130/ vi to survive; (continuare a vivere): **~ (in)** to live on (in); **~ a** (incidente ecc) to survive; (persona) to outlive

so'pruso sm abuse of power; **subire un ~** to be abused

soq'quadro sm: **mettere a ~** to turn upside-down

sor'betto sm sorbet, water ice

sor'dina sf: **in ~** softly; (fig) on the sly

'sordo, -a ag deaf; (rumore) muffled; (dolore) dull; (odio, rancore) veiled ▷ sm/f deaf person; **sordo'muto, -a** ag deaf-and-dumb ▷ sm/f deaf-mute

so'rella sf sister; **sorel'lastra** sf stepsister; (con genitore in comune) half sister

sor'gente [sor'dʒɛnte] sf (acqua che sgorga) spring; (di fiume, Fisica, fig) source

'sorgere ['sordʒere] /109/ vi to rise; (scaturire) to spring, rise; (fig: difficoltà) to arise

sorni'one, -a ag sly

sorpas'sare /72/ vt (Aut) to overtake; (fig) to surpass; (: eccedere) to exceed,

go beyond; **~ in altezza** to be higher than; (persona) to be taller than

sorpren'dente ag surprising

sor'prendere /81/ vt (cogliere: in flagrante ecc) to catch; (stupire) to surprise; **sorprendersi** vpr: **sorprendersi (di)** to be surprised (at); **sor'preso, -a** pp di **sorprendere** ▷ sf surprise; **fare una sorpresa a qn** to give sb a surprise

sor'reggere [sor'rɛddʒere] /87/ vt to support, hold up; (fig) to sustain; **sorreggersi** vpr (tenersi ritto) to stay upright

sor'ridere /89/ vi to smile; **sor'riso, -a** pp di **sorridere** ▷ sm smile

'sorsi ecc vb vedi **sorgere**

'sorso sm sip

'sorta sf sort, kind; **di ~** whatever, of any kind at all

'sorte sf (fato) fate, destiny; (evento fortuito) chance; **tirare a ~** to draw lots

sor'teggio [sor'teddʒo] sm draw

sorvegli'ante [sorveʎ'ʎante] smf (di carcere) guard, warder (BRIT); (di fabbrica ecc) supervisor

sorvegli'anza [sorveʎ'ʎantsa] sf watch; supervision; (Polizia, Mil) surveillance

sorvegli'are [sorveʎ'ʎare] /27/ vt (bambino, bagagli, prigioniero) to watch, keep an eye on; (malato) to watch over; (territorio, casa) to watch o keep watch over; (lavori) to supervise

sorvo'lare /72/ vt (territorio) to fly over ▷ vi: **~ su** (fig) to skim over

S.O.S. sigla m mayday, SOS

'sosia sm inv double

sos'pendere /8/ vt (appendere) to hang (up); (interrompere, privare di una carica) to suspend; (rimandare) to defer; (appendere) to hang

sospet'tare /72/ vt to suspect ▷ vi: **~ di** to suspect; (diffidare) to be suspicious of

S

sos'petto, -a *ag* suspicious ▷ *sm* suspicion; **sospet'toso, -a** *ag* suspicious

sospi'rare /72/ *vi* to sigh ▷ *vt* to long for, yearn for; **sos'piro** *sm* sigh

'**sosta** *sf* (*fermata*) stop, halt; (*pausa*) pause, break; **senza ~** non-stop, without a break

sostan'tivo *sm* noun, substantive

sos'tanza [sos'tantsa] *sf* substance; **sostanze** *sfpl* (*ricchezze*) wealth *sg*, possessions; **in ~** in short, to sum up

sos'tare /72/ *vi* (*fermarsi*) to stop (for a while), stay; (*fare una pausa*) to take a break

sos'tegno [sos'teɲɲo] *sm* support

soste'nere /121/ *vt* to support; (*prendere su di sé*) to take on, bear; (*resistere*) to withstand, stand up to; (*affermare*): **~ che** to maintain that; **sostenersi** *vpr* to hold o.s. up, support o.s.; (*fig*) to keep up one's strength; **~ gli esami** to sit exams

sostenta'mento *sm* maintenance, support

sostitu'ire /55/ *vt* (*mettere al posto di*): **~ qn/qc a** to substitute sb/sth for; (*prendere il posto di*) to replace, take the place of

sosti'tuto, -a *sm/f* substitute

sostituzi'one [sostitut'tsjone] *sf* substitution; **in ~ di** as a substitute for, in place of

sotta'ceti [sotta'tʃeti] *smpl* pickles

sot'tana *sf* (*sottoveste*) underskirt; (*gonna*) skirt; (*Rel*) soutane, cassock

sotter'fugio [sotter'fudʒo] *sm* subterfuge

sotter'raneo, -a *ag* underground ▷ *sm* cellar

sotter'rare /72/ *vt* to bury

sot'tile *ag* thin; (*figura, caviglia*) thin, slim, slender; (*fine: polvere, capelli*) fine; (*fig: leggero*) light; (: *vista*) sharp, keen; (: *olfatto*) fine, discriminating; (: *mente*) subtle; shrewd ▷ *sm*: **non andare per il ~** not to mince matters

sottin'teso, -a *pp di* **sottintendere** ▷ *sm* allusion; **parlare senza sottintesi** to speak plainly

'**sotto** *prep* (*gen*) under; (*più in basso di*) below ▷ *av* underneath, beneath; below; **(al piano) di ~** downstairs; **~ il monte** at the foot of the mountain; **~ la pioggia/il sole** in the rain/sun(shine); **siamo ~ Natale/Pasqua** it's nearly Christmas/Easter; **~ forma di** in the form of; **~ terra** underground; **chiuso ~ vuoto** vacuum packed

sotto'fondo *sm* background; **~ musicale** background music

sottoline'are /72/ *vt* to underline; (*fig*) to emphasize, stress

sottoma'rino, -a *ag* (*flora*) submarine; (*cavo, navigazione*) underwater ▷ *sm* (*Naut*) submarine

sottopas'saggio [sottopas'saddʒo] *sm* (*Aut*) underpass; (*pedonale*) subway, underpass

sotto'porre /77/ *vt* (*costringere*) to subject; (*fig: presentare*) to submit; **sottoporsi** *vpr* to submit; **sottoporsi a** (*subire*) to undergo

sotto'sopra *av* upside-down

sotto'terra *av* underground

sotto'titolo *sm* subtitle

sottovalu'tare /72/ *vt* to underestimate

sotto'veste *sf* underskirt

sotto'voce [sotto'votʃe] *av* in a low voice

sottovu'oto *av*: **confezionare ~** to vacuum-pack ▷ *ag*: **confezione** *f* **~** vacuum pack

sot'trarre /123/ *vt* (*Mat*) to subtract, take away; **sottrarsi** *vpr*: **sottrarsi a** (*sfuggire*) to escape; (*evitare*) to avoid; **~ qn/qc a** (*togliere*) to remove sb/sth from; (*salvare*) to save *o* rescue sb/sth from; **~ qc a qn** (*rubare*) to steal sth from sb; **sottrazi'one** *sf* subtraction; (*furto*) removal

souve'nir [suv(ə)'nir] *sm inv* souvenir

sovi'etico, -a, -ci, -che *ag* Soviet ▷ *sm/f* Soviet citizen

sovrac'carico, -a, -chi, -che *ag*: **~ (di)** overloaded (with) ▷ *sm* excess load; **~ di lavoro** extra work

sovraffol'lato, -a *ag* overcrowded

sovrannatu'rale *ag* = **soprannaturale**

so'vrano, -a *ag* sovereign; *(fig: sommo)* supreme ▷ *sm/f* sovereign, monarch

sovrap'porre /77/ *vt* to place on top of, put on top of

sovvenzi'one [sovven'tsjone] *sf* subsidy, grant

'sozzo, -a ['sottso] *ag* filthy, dirty

S.p.A. *abbr vedi* **società per azioni**

spac'care /20/ *vt* to split, break; *(legna)* to chop; **spaccarsi** *vpr* to split, break; **spacca'tura** *sf* split

spaccherò *ecc* [spakke'rɔ] *vb vedi* **spaccare**

spacci'are /14/ *vt (vendere)* to sell (off); *(mettere in circolazione)* to circulate; *(droga)* to peddle, push; **spacciarsi** *vpr*: **spacciarsi per** *(farsi credere)* to pass o.s. off as, pretend to be; **spaccia'tore, -'trice** [spattʃa'tore] *sm/f (di droga)* pusher; *(di denaro falso)* dealer; **'spaccio** *sm*: **spaccio (di)** *(di merce rubata, droga)* trafficking (in); *(di denaro falso)* passing (of); *(vendita)* sale; *(bottega)* shop

'spacco, -chi *sm (fenditura)* split, crack; *(strappo)* tear; *(di gonna)* slit

spac'cone *smf* boaster, braggart

'spada *sf* sword

spae'sato, -a *ag* disorientated, lost

spa'ghetti [spa'getti] *smpl (Cuc)* spaghetti *sg*

'Spagna ['spaɲɲa] *sf*: **la ~** Spain; **spa'gnolo, -a** *ag* Spanish ▷ *sm/f* Spaniard ▷ *sm (Ling)* Spanish; **gli Spagnoli** the Spanish

'spago, -ghi *sm* string, twine

spai'ato, -a *ag (calza, guanto)* odd

spalan'care /20/ *vt*, **spalan'carsi** *vpr* to open wide

spa'lare /72/ *vt* to shovel

'spalla *sf* shoulder; *(fig: Teat)* stooge; **spalle** *sfpl (dorso)* back

spalli'era *sf (di sedia ecc)* back; *(di letto: da capo)* head(board); *(: da piedi)* foot(board); *(Ginnastica)* wall bars *pl*

spal'lina *sf (di sottoveste, maglietta)* strap; *(imbottitura)* shoulder pad

spal'mare /72/ *vt* to spread

'spalti *smpl (di stadio)* terraces

spamming ['spammiŋ] *sm (Internet)* spamming

'spandere /110/ *vt* to spread; *(versare)* to pour (out)

spa'rare /72/ *vt* to fire ▷ *vi (far fuoco)* to fire; *(tirare)* to shoot; **spara'toria** *sf* exchange of shots

sparecchi'are [sparek'kjare] /19/ *vt*: **~ (la tavola)** to clear the table

spa'reggio [spa'reddʒo] *sm (Sport)* play-off

'spargere ['spardʒere] /111/ *vt* *(sparpagliare)* to scatter; *(versare: vino)* to spill; *(: lacrime, sangue)* to shed; *(diffondere)* to spread; *(emanare)* to give off (*o* out); **spargersi** *vpr* to spread

spa'rire /112/ *vi* to disappear, vanish

spar'lare /72/ *vi*: **~ di** to run down, speak ill of

'sparo *sm* shot

spar'tire /55/ *vt (eredità, bottino)* to share out; *(avversari)* to separate

spar'tito *sm (Mus)* score

sparti'traffico *sm inv (Aut)* central reservation (BRIT), median (strip) (US)

sparvi'ero *sm (Zool)* sparrowhawk

spasi'mante *sm* suitor

spassio'nato, -a *ag* dispassionate, impartial

'spasso *sm (divertimento)* amusement, enjoyment; **andare a ~** to go out for a walk; **essere a ~** *(fig)* to be out of work; **mandare qn a ~** *(fig)* to give sb the sack

'spatola *sf* spatula; *(di muratore)* trowel

S

spa'valdo, -a *ag* arrogant, bold
spaventa'passeri *sm inv* scarecrow
spaven'tare /72/ *vt* to frighten, scare; **spaventarsi** *vpr* to become frightened, become scared; to get a fright; **spa'vento** *sm* fear, fright; **far spavento a qn** to give sb a fright; **spaven'toso, -a** *ag* frightening, terrible; (*fig: fam*) tremendous, fantastic
spazien'tirsi [spattsjen'tirsi] /55/ *vpr* to lose one's patience
'spazio ['spattsjo] *sm* space; **~ aereo** airspace; **spazi'oso, -a** *ag* spacious
spazzaca'mino [spattsaka'mino] *sm* chimney sweep
spazza'neve [spattsa'neve] *sm inv* snowplough
spaz'zare [spat'tsare] /72/ *vt* to sweep; (*foglie ecc*) to sweep up; (*cacciare*) to sweep away; **spazza'tura** *sf* sweepings *pl*; (*immondizia*) rubbish; **spaz'zino** *sm* street sweeper
'spazzola ['spattsola] *sf* brush; **~ per abiti** clothesbrush; **~ da capelli** hairbrush; **spazzo'lare** /72/ *vt* to brush; **spazzo'lino** *sm* (small) brush; **spazzolino da denti** toothbrush
specchi'arsi [spek'kjarsi] /19/ *vpr* to look at o.s. in a mirror; (*riflettersi*) to be mirrored, be reflected
specchi'etto [spek'kjetto] *sm* (*tabella*) table, chart; **~ da borsetta** pocket mirror; **~ retrovisore** (*Aut*) rear-view mirror
'specchio ['spekkjo] *sm* mirror
speci'ale [spe'tʃale] *ag* special; **specia'lista, -i, -e** *smf* specialist; **specialità** *sf inv* speciality; (*branca di studio*) special field, speciality; **specializzazi'one** *sf* specialization; **special'mente** *av* especially, particularly
'specie ['spetʃe] *sf inv* (*Biol, Bot, Zool*) species *inv*; (*tipo*) kind, sort ▷ *av* especially, particularly; **una ~ di** a kind of; **fare ~ a qn** to surprise sb; **la ~ umana** mankind

specifi'care [spetʃifi'kare] /20/ *vt* to specify, state
spe'cifico, -a, -ci, -che [spe'tʃifiko] *ag* specific
specu'lare /72/ *vi*: **~ su** (*Comm*) to speculate in; (*sfruttare*) to exploit; (*meditare*) to speculate on; **speculazi'one** *sf* speculation
spe'dire /55/ *vt* to send
'spegnere ['spɛɲɲere] /113/ *vt* (*fuoco, sigaretta*) to put out, extinguish; (*apparecchio elettrico*) to turn o switch off; (*gas*) to turn off; (*fig: suoni, passioni*) to stifle; (*debito*) to cancel; **spegnersi** *vpr* to go out; to go off; (*morire*) to pass away; **puoi ~ la luce?** could you switch off the light?
spel'lare /72/ *vt* (*scuoiare*) to skin; **spellarsi** *vpr* to peel
'spendere /8/ *vt* to spend
'spengo *ecc vb vedi* **spegnere**
'spensi *ecc vb vedi* **spegnere**
spensie'rato, -a *ag* carefree
'spento, -a *pp di* **spegnere** ▷ *ag* (*suono*) muffled; (*colore*) dull; (*sigaretta*) out; (*civiltà, vulcano*) extinct
spe'ranza [spe'rantsa] *sf* hope
spe'rare /72/ *vt* to hope for ▷ *vi*: **~ in** to trust in; **~ che/di fare** to hope that/to do; **lo spero, spero di sì** I hope so
sper'duto, -a *ag* (*isolato*) out-of-the-way; (*persona: smarrita, a disagio*) lost
sperimen'tale *ag* experimental
sperimen'tare /72/ *vt* to experiment with, test; (*fig*) to test, put to the test
'sperma, -i *sm* sperm
spe'rone *sm* spur
sperpe'rare /72/ *vt* to squander
'spesa *sf* (*soldi spesi*) expense; (*costo*) cost; (*acquisto*) purchase; (*fam: acquisto del cibo quotidiano*) shopping; **spese postali** postage *sg*; **spese di viaggio** travelling (BRIT) o traveling (US) expenses

'spesso, -a ag (fitto) thick; (frequente) frequent ▷ av often; **spesse volte** frequently, often

spes'sore sm thickness

Spett. abbr vedi **spettabile**

spet'tabile ag (in lettere, abbr Spett.): **~ ditta X** Messrs X and Co

spet'tacolo sm (rappresentazione) performance, show; (vista, scena) sight; **dare ~ di sé** to make an exhibition o a spectacle of o.s.

spet'tare /72/ vi: **~ a** (decisione) to be up to; (stipendio) to be due to; **spetta a lei decidere** it's up to you to decide

spetta'tore, -'trice sm/f (Cine, Teat) member of the audience; (di avvenimento) onlooker, witness

spettego'lare /72/ vi to gossip

spetti'nato, -a ag dishevelled

'spettro sm (fantasma) spectre; (Fisica) spectrum

'spezie ['spɛttsje] sfpl (Cuc) spices

spez'zare [spet'tsare] /72/ vt (rompere) to break; (fig: interrompere) to break up; **spezzarsi** vpr to break

spezza'tino [spettsa'tino] sm (Cuc) stew

spezzet'tare [spettset'tare] /72/ vt to break up (o chop) into small pieces

'spia sf spy; (confidente della polizia) informer; (Elettr) indicating light; warning light; (fessura) peephole; (fig: sintomo) sign, indication

spia'cente [spja'tʃɛnte] ag sorry; **essere ~ di qc/di fare qc** to be sorry about sth/for doing sth

spia'cevole [spja'tʃevole] ag unpleasant, disagreeable

spi'aggia, -ge ['spjaddʒa] sf beach; **~ libera** public beach

spia'nare /72/ vt (terreno) to level, make level; (edificio) to raze to the ground; (pasta) to roll out; (rendere liscio) to smooth (out)

spi'are /60/ vt to spy on

spi'azzo ['spjattso] sm open space; (radura) clearing

'spicchio ['spikkjo] sm (di agrumi) segment; (di aglio) clove; (parte) piece, slice

spicci'are [spit'tʃare] /14/ vt to finish off; **spicciarsi** vpr to hurry up

'spicciolo, -a ['spittʃolo] ag: **moneta spicciola** (small) change; **spiccioli** smpl (small) change

'spicco, -chi sm: **fare ~** to stand out; **di ~** outstanding; (tema) main, principal

spie'dino sm (utensile) skewer; (cibo) kebab

spi'edo sm (Cuc) spit

spie'gare /80/ vt (far capire) to explain; (tovaglia) to unfold; (vele) to unfurl; **spiegarsi** vpr to explain o.s., make o.s. clear; **~ qc a qn** to explain sth to sb; **spiegazi'one** sf explanation

spieghe'rò ecc [spjege'rɔ] vb vedi **spiegare**

spie'tato, -a ag ruthless, pitiless

spiffe'rare /72/ vt (fam) to blurt out, blab

'spiffero sm draught (BRIT), draft (US)

'spiga, -ghe sf (Bot) ear

spigli'ato, -a [spiʎ'ʎato] ag self-possessed, self-confident

'spigolo sm corner; (Geom) edge

'spilla sf brooch; (da cravatta, cappello) pin; **~ di sicurezza** o **da balia** safety pin

'spillo sm pin; **~ di sicurezza** o **da balia** safety pin; **~ di sicurezza** (Mil) (safety) pin

spi'lorcio, -a, -ci, -ce [spi'lortʃo] ag mean, stingy

'spina sf (Bot) thorn; (Zool) spine, prickle; (di pesce) bone; (Elettr) plug; (di botte) bunghole; **birra alla ~** draught beer; **~ dorsale** (Anat) backbone

spi'nacio [spi'natʃo] sm spinach no pl; (Cuc): **spinaci** spinach sg

spi'nello sm (Droga: gergo) joint

'spingere ['spindʒere] /114/ vt to push; (condurre: anche fig) to drive;

s

(*stimolare*): **~ qn a fare** to urge o press sb to do

spi'noso, -a *ag* thorny, prickly

'spinsi *ecc vb vedi* **spingere**

'spinto, -a *pp di* **spingere** ▷ *sf* (*urto*) push; (*Fisica*) thrust; (*fig: stimolo*) incentive, spur; (: *appoggio*) string-pulling *no pl*; **dare una spinta a qn** (*fig*) to pull strings for sb

spio'naggio [spio'naddʒo] *sm* espionage, spying

spion'cino [spion'tʃino] *sm* peephole

spi'raglio [spi'raʎʎo] *sm* (*fessura*) chink, narrow opening; (*raggio di luce, fig*) glimmer, gleam

spi'rale *sf* spiral; (*contraccettivo*) coil; **a ~** spiral(-shaped)

spiri'tato, -a *ag* possessed; (*fig: persona, espressione*) wild

spiri'tismo *sm* spiritualism

'spirito *sm* (*Rel, Chim, disposizione d'animo, di legge ecc, fantasma*) spirit; (*pensieri, intelletto*) mind; (*arguzia*) wit; (*umorismo*) humour, wit; **lo S~ Santo** the Holy Spirit o Ghost

spirito'saggine [spirito'saddʒine] *sf* witticism; (*peg*) wisecrack

spiri'toso, -a *ag* witty

spiritu'ale *ag* spiritual

'splendere /29/ *vi* to shine

'splendido, -a *ag* splendid; (*splendente*) shining; (*sfarzoso*) magnificent, splendid

splen'dore *sm* splendour; (*luce intensa*) brilliance, brightness

spogli'are [spoʎ'ʎare] /27/ *vt* (*svestire*) to undress; (*privare, fig: depredare*): **~ qn di qc** to deprive sb of sth; (*togliere ornamenti: anche fig*): **~ qn/qc di** to strip sb/sth of; **spogliarsi** *vpr* to undress, strip; **spogliarsi di** (*ricchezze ecc*) to deprive o.s. of, give up; (*pregiudizi*) to rid o.s. of; **spoglia'rello** *sm* striptease; **spoglia'toio** *sm* dressing room; (*di scuola ecc*) cloakroom; (*Sport*) changing room

'spola *sf* (*bobina*) spool; **fare la ~ (fra)** to go to and fro o shuttle (between)

spolve'rare /72/ *vt* (*anche Cuc*) to dust; (*con spazzola*) to brush; (*con battipanni*) to beat; (*fig*) to polish off ▷ *vi* to dust

spon'taneo, -a *ag* spontaneous; (*persona*) unaffected, natural

spor'care /20/ *vt* to dirty, make dirty; (*fig*) to sully, soil; **sporcarsi** *vpr* to get dirty

spor'cizia [spor'tʃittsja] *sf* (*stato*) dirtiness; (*sudiciume*) dirt, filth; (*cosa sporca*) dirt *no pl*, something dirty

'sporco, -a, -chi, -che *ag* dirty, filthy

spor'genza [spor'dʒentsa] *sf* projection

'sporgere ['spordʒere] /115/ *vt* to put out, stretch out ▷ *vi* (*venire in fuori*) to stick out; **sporgersi** *vpr* to lean out; **~ querela contro qn** (*Dir*) to take legal action against sb

'sporsi *ecc vb vedi* **sporgere**

sport *sm inv* sport

spor'tello *sm* (*di treno, auto ecc*) door; (*di banca, ufficio*) window, counter; **~ automatico** (*Banca*) cash dispenser, automated telling machine

spor'tivo, -a *ag* (*gara, giornale*) sports *cpd*; (*persona*) sporty; (*abito*) casual; (*spirito, atteggiamento*) sporting

'sposa *sf* bride; (*moglie*) wife

sposa'lizio [spoza'littsjo] *sm* wedding

spo'sare /72/ *vt* to marry; (*fig: idea, fede*) to espouse; **sposarsi** *vpr* to get married, marry; **sposarsi con qn** to marry sb, get married to sb; **spo'sato, -a** *ag* married

'sposo *sm* (*bride*)groom; (*marito*) husband

spos'sato, -a *ag* exhausted, weary

spos'tare /72/ *vt* to move, shift; (*cambiare: orario*) to change; **spostarsi** *vpr* to move

'spranga, -ghe *sf* (*sbarra*) bar

spre'care /20/ *vt* to waste

spre'gevole [spre'dʒevole] *ag* contemptible, despicable

'spremere /62/ *vt* to squeeze

spremia'grumi *sm inv* lemon squeezer

spre'muta *sf* fresh fruit juice; **~ d'arancia** fresh orange juice

sprez'zante [spret'tsante] *ag* scornful, contemptuous

sprofon'dare /72/ *vi* to sink; (*casa*) to collapse; (*suolo*) to give way, subside

spro'nare /72/ *vt* to spur (on)

sproporzio'nato, -a [sproportsjo'nato] *ag* disproportionate, out of all proportion

sproporzi'one [spropor'tsjone] *sf* disproportion

spro'posito *sm* blunder; **a ~** at the wrong time; (*rispondere, parlare*) irrelevantly

sprovve'duto, -a *ag* inexperienced, naïve

sprov'visto, -a *ag* (*mancante*): **~ di** lacking in, without; **alla sprovvista** unawares

spruz'zare [sprut'tsare] /72/ *vt* (*a nebulizzazione*) to spray; (*aspergere*) to sprinkle; (*inzaccherare*) to splash

'spugna ['spuɲɲa] *sf* (*Zool*) sponge; (*tessuto*) towelling

'spuma *sf* (*schiuma*) foam; (*bibita*) fizzy drink

spu'mante *sm* sparkling wine

spun'tare /72/ *vt* (*coltello*) to break the point of; (*capelli*) to trim ▷ *vi* (*uscire: germogli*) to sprout; (*: capelli*) to begin to grow; (*: denti*) to come through; (*apparire*) to appear (suddenly)

spun'tino *sm* snack

'spunto *sm* (*Teat, Mus*) cue; (*fig*) starting point; **dare lo ~ a** (*fig*) to give rise to

spu'tare /72/ *vt* to spit out; (*fig*) to belch (out) ▷ *vi* to spit

'squadra *sf* (*strumento*) (set) square; (*gruppo*) team, squad; (*di operai*) gang, squad; (*Mil*) squad; (*: Aer, Naut*) squadron; (*Sport*) team; **lavoro a squadre** teamwork

squagli'arsi [skwaʎ'ʎarsi] /27/ *vpr* to melt; (*fig*) to sneak off

squa'lifica, -che *sf* disqualification

squalifi'care /20/ *vt* to disqualify

'squallido, -a *ag* wretched, bleak

'squalo *sm* shark

'squama *sf* scale

squarcia'gola [skwartʃa'gola]: **a ~ av** at the top of one's voice

squattri'nato, -a *ag* penniless

squili'brato, -a *ag* (*Psic*) unbalanced

squil'lante *ag* shrill, sharp

squil'lare /72/ *vi* (*campanello, telefono*) to ring (out); (*tromba*) to blare; **'squillo** *sm* ring, ringing *no pl*; blare ▷ *sf inv* (*anche*: **ragazza squillo**) call girl

squi'sito, -a *ag* exquisite; (*cibo*) delicious; (*persona*) delightful

squit'tire /55/ *vi* (*uccello*) to squawk; (*topo*) to squeak

sradi'care /20/ *vt* to uproot; (*fig*) to eradicate

srego'lato, -a *ag* (*senza ordine: vita*) disorderly; (*smodato*) immoderate; (*dissoluto*) dissolute

S.r.l. *abbr vedi* **società a responsabilità limitata**

sroto'lare /72/ *vt*, **sroto'larsi** *vpr* to unroll

SS *sigla* = **Sassari**

S.S.N. *abbr* (= *Servizio Sanitario Nazionale*) ≈ NHS

sta *ecc vb vedi* **stare**

'stabile *ag* stable, steady; (*tempo: non variabile*) settled; (*Teat: compagnia*) resident ▷ *sm* (*edificio*) building

stabili'mento *sm* (*edificio*) establishment; (*fabbrica*) plant, factory

stabi'lire /55/ *vt* to establish; (*fissare: prezzi, data*) to fix; (*decidere*) to decide; **stabilirsi** *vpr* (*prendere dimora*) to settle

stac'care /20/ *vt* (*levare*) to detach, remove; (*separare: anche fig*) to separate, divide; (*strappare*) to tear off (o out); (*scandire: parole*) to pronounce clearly; (*Sport*) to leave behind; **staccarsi** *vpr* (*bottone ecc*) to come off; (*scostarsi*): **staccarsi (da)** to move away (from); (*fig: separarsi*): **staccarsi da** to leave; **non ~ gli occhi da qn** not to take one's eyes off sb

'**stadio** *sm* (*Sport*) stadium; (*periodo, fase*) phase, stage

'**staffa** *sf* (*di sella, Tecn*) stirrup; **perdere le staffe** (*fig*) to fly off the handle

staf'fetta *sf* (*messo*) dispatch rider; (*Sport*) relay race

stagio'nale [stadʒo'nale] *ag* seasonal

stagio'nato, -a [stadʒo'nato] *ag* seasoned matured; (*scherzoso: attempato*) getting on in years

stagi'one [sta'dʒone] *sf* season; **alta/bassa ~** high/low season

sta'gista, -i, -e [sta'dʒista] *smf* trainee, intern (*US*)

'**stagno, -a** ['staɲɲo] *ag* watertight; (*a tenuta d'aria*) airtight ▷ *sm* (*acquitrino*) pond; (*Chim*) tin

sta'gnola [staɲ'ɲɔla] *sf* tinfoil

'**stalla** *sf* (*per bovini*) cowshed; (*per cavalli*) stable

stal'lone *sm* stallion

stamat'tina *av* this morning

stam'becco, -chi *sm* ibex

stami'nale *ag*: **cellula ~** stem cell

'**stampa** *sf* (*Tip, Fot: tecnica*) printing; (*impressione, copia fotografica*) print; (*insieme di quotidiani, giornalisti ecc*): **la ~** the press

stam'pante *sf* (*Inform*) printer

stam'pare /72/ *vt* to print; (*pubblicare*) to publish; (*coniare*) to strike, coin; (*imprimere: anche fig*) to impress

stampa'tello *sm* block letters *pl*

stam'pella *sf* crutch

'**stampo** *sm* mould; (*fig: indole*) type, kind, sort

sta'nare /72/ *vt* to drive out

stan'care /20/ *vt* to tire, make tired; (*annoiare*) to bore; (*infastidire*) to annoy; **stancarsi** *vpr* to get tired, tire o.s. out; **stancarsi (di)** to grow weary (of), grow tired (of)

stan'chezza [stan'kettsa] *sf* tiredness, fatigue

'**stanco, -a, -chi, -che** *ag* tired; **~ di** tired of, fed up with

stan'ghetta [stan'getta] *sf* (*di occhiali*) leg; (*Mus, di scrittura*) bar

'**stanno** *vb vedi* **stare**

sta'notte *av* tonight; (*notte passata*) last night

'**stante** *prep*: **a sé ~** (*appartamento, casa*) independent, separate

stan'tio, -a, -'tii, -'tie *ag* stale; (*burro*) rancid; (*fig*) old

stan'tuffo *sm* piston

'**stanza** ['stantsa] *sf* room; (*Poesia*) stanza; **~ da bagno** bathroom; **~ da letto** bedroom

stap'pare /72/ *vt* to uncork; (*tappo a corona*) to uncap

'**stare** /116/ *vi* (*restare in un luogo*) to stay, remain; (*abitare*) to stay, live; (*essere situato*) to be, be situated; (*anche*: **~ in piedi**) to stand; (*essere, trovarsi*) to be; (*seguito da gerundio*): **sta studiando** he's studying; **se stesse in me** if it were up to me, if it depended on me; **~ per fare qc** to be about to do sth; **starci** (*esserci spazio*): **nel baule non ci sta più niente** there's no more room in the boot; (*accettare*) to accept; **ci stai?** is that okay with you?; **~ a** (*attenersi a*) to follow, stick to; (*seguito dall'infinito*): **stiamo a discutere** we're talking; (*toccare a*): **sta a te a giocare** it's your turn to play; **~ a qn** (*abiti ecc*) to fit sb; **queste scarpe mi stanno strette** these shoes are tight for me; **il rosso ti sta bene** red suits you; **come sta?** how are you?; **io sto bene/male** I'm very well/not very well

starnu'tire /55/ *vi* to sneeze; **star'nuto** *sm* sneeze

sta'sera *av* this evening, tonight

sta'tale *ag* state *cpd*, government *cpd* ▷ *smf* state employee, local authority employee; (*nell'amministrazione*) ≈ civil servant; **strada ~** ≈ trunk (BRIT) o main road

sta'tista, -i *sm* statesman

sta'tistico, -a, -ci, -che *ag* statistical ▷ *sf* statistics *sg*

'stato, -a *pp di* **essere**; **stare** ▷ *sm* (*condizione*) state, condition; (*Pol*) state; (*Dir*) status; **essere in ~ d'accusa** (*Dir*) to be committed for trial; **~ d'assedio/d'emergenza** state of siege/emergency; **~ civile** (*Amm*) marital status; **~ d'animo** mood; **~ maggiore** (*Mil*) general staff; **gli Stati Uniti (d'America)** the United States (of America)

'statua *sf* statue

statuni'tense *ag* United States *cpd*, of the United States

sta'tura *sf* (*Anat*) height, stature; (*fig*) stature

sta'tuto *sm* (*Dir*) statute; constitution

sta'volta *av* this time

stazio'nario, -a [stattsjo'narjo] *ag* stationary; (*fig*) unchanged

stazi'one [stat'tsjone] *sf* station; (*balneare, invernale ecc*) resort; **~ degli autobus** bus station; **~ balneare** seaside resort; **~ ferroviaria** railway (BRIT) o railroad (US) station; **~ invernale** winter sports resort; **~ di polizia** police station (*in small town*); **~ di servizio** service o petrol (BRIT) o filling station

stecca, -che *sf* stick; (*di ombrello*) rib; (*di sigarette*) carton; (*Med*) splint; (*stonatura*): **fare una ~** to sing (o play) a wrong note

stec'cato *sm* fence

'stella *sf* star; **~ alpina** (*Bot*) edelweiss; **~ cadente** o **filante**

shooting star; **~ di mare** (*Zool*) starfish

'stelo *sm* stem; (*asta*) rod; **lampada a ~** standard lamp

'stemma, -i *sm* coat of arms

'stemmo *vb vedi* **stare**

stempi'ato, -a *ag* with a receding hairline

'stendere /120/ *vt* (*braccia, gambe*) to stretch (out); (*tovaglia*) to spread (out); (*bucato*) to hang out; (*mettere a giacere*) to lay (down); (*spalmare: colore*) to spread; (*mettere per iscritto*) to draw up; **stendersi** *vpr* (*coricarsi*) to stretch out, lie down; (*estendersi*) to extend, stretch

stenogra'fia *sf* shorthand

sten'tare /72/ *vi*: **~ a fare** to find it hard to do, have difficulty doing

'stento *sm* (*fatica*) difficulty; **stenti** *smpl* (*privazioni*) hardship *sg*, privation *sg*: **a ~** with difficulty, barely

'sterco *sm* dung

'stereo *ag inv* stereo ▷ *sm inv* (*impianto*) stereo

'sterile *ag* sterile; (*terra*) barren; (*fig*) futile, fruitless

steriliz'zare [sterilid'dzare] /72/ *vt* to sterilize

ster'lina *sf* pound (sterling)

stermi'nare /72/ *vt* to exterminate, wipe out

stermi'nato, -a *ag* immense; endless

ster'minio *sm* extermination, destruction

'sterno *sm* (*Anat*) breastbone

ste'roide *sm* steroid

ster'zare [ster'tsare] /72/ *vt, vi* (*Aut*) to steer; **'sterzo** *sm* steering; (*volante*) steering wheel

'stessi *ecc vb vedi* **stare**

'stesso, -a *ag* same; (*rafforzativo: in persona, proprio*): **il re ~** the king himself o in person ▷ *pron*: **lo(la) ~(a)** the same (one); **i suoi stessi avversari lo ammirano** even his enemies admire him; **fa lo ~** it doesn't matter; **per me è lo ~** it's all the same to me, it doesn't matter to me; *vedi* **io; tu** *ecc*

ste'sura *sf* drafting *no pl*, drawing up *no pl*; (*documento*) draft

'stetti *ecc vb vedi* **stare**

'stia *ecc vb vedi* **stare**

sti'lare /72/ *vt* to draw up, draft

'stile *sm* style; **~ libero** freestyle; **sti'lista, -i, -e** *smf* designer

stilo'grafica, -che *sf* (*anche*: **penna ~**) fountain pen

'stima *sf* esteem; valuation; assessment, estimate

sti'mare /72/ *vt* (*persona*) to esteem, hold in high regard; (*terreno, casa ecc*) to value; (*stabilire in misura approssimativa*) to estimate, assess; (*ritenere*): **~ che** to consider that; **stimarsi fortunato** to consider o.s. (to be) lucky

stimo'lare /72/ *vt* to stimulate; (*incitare*): **~ qn (a fare)** to spur sb on (to do)

'stimolo *sm* (*anche fig*) stimulus

'stingere ['stindʒere] /37/ *vt, vi* (*anche*: **stingersi**) to fade; **'stinto, -a** *pp di* **stingere**

sti'pare /72/ *vt* to cram, pack; **stiparsi** *vpr* (*accalcarsi*) to crowd, throng

sti'pendio *sm* salary

'stipite *sm* (*di porta, finestra*) jamb

stipu'lare /72/ *vt* (*redigere*) to draw up

sti'rare /72/ *vt* (*abito*) to iron; (*distendere*) to stretch; (*strappare: muscolo*) to strain; **stirarsi** *vpr* to stretch (o.s.)

stiti'chezza [stiti'kettsa] *sf* constipation

'stitico, -a, -ci, -che *ag* constipated

'stiva *sf* (*di nave*) hold

sti'vale *sm* boot

'stizza ['stittsa] *sf* anger, vexation

'stoffa *sf* material, fabric; (*fig*): **aver la ~ di** to have the makings of

'stomaco, -chi *sm* stomach; **dare di ~** to vomit, be sick

sto'nato, -a *ag* (*persona*) off-key; (*strumento*) off-key, out of tune

stop *sm inv* (*Telegrafia*) stop; (*Aut: cartello*) stop sign; (: *fanalino d'arresto*) brake-light

'storcere ['stɔrtʃere] /106/ *vt* to twist; **storcersi** *vpr* to writhe, twist; **~ il naso** (*fig*) to turn up one's nose; **storcersi la caviglia** to twist one's ankle

stor'dire /55/ *vt* (*intontire*) to stun, daze; **stor'dito, -a** *ag* stunned

'storia *sf* (*scienza, avvenimenti*) history; (*racconto, bugia*) story; (*faccenda, questione*) business *no pl*; (*pretesto*) excuse, pretext; **storie** *sfpl* (*smancerie*) fuss *sg*; **'storico, -a, -ci, -che** *ag* historic(al) ▷ *sm/f* historian

stori'one *sm* (*Zool*) sturgeon

'stormo *sm* (*di uccelli*) flock

'storpio, -a *ag* crippled, maimed

'storsi *ecc vb vedi* **storcere**

'storto, -a *pp di* **storcere** ▷ *ag* (*chiodo*) twisted, bent; (*gamba, quadro*) crooked ▷ *sf* (*distorsione*) sprain, twist

sto'viglie [sto'viλλe] *sfpl* dishes *pl*, crockery *sg*

'strabico, -a, -ci, -che *ag* squint-eyed; (*occhi*) squint

strac'chino [strak'kino] *sm* type of soft cheese

stracci'are [strat'tʃare] /14/ *vt* to tear; **stracciarsi** *vpr* to tear

'straccio, -a, -ci, -ce ['strattʃo] *ag*: **carta straccia** waste paper ▷ *sm* rag; (*per pulire*) cloth, duster; **stracci** *smpl* (*indumenti*) rags; **si è ridotto a uno ~** he's worn himself out; **non ha uno ~ di lavoro** he's not got a job of any sort

'strada *sf* road; (*di città*) street; (*cammino, via, fig*) way; **~ facendo** on the way; **essere fuori ~** (*fig*) to be on the wrong track; **fare o farsi ~** (*fig*) to get on in life; **~ senza uscita** dead end; **stra'dale** *ag* road *cpd*

trafalci'one [strafal'tʃone] sm blunder, howler

tra'fare/53/ vi to overdo it

trafot'tente ag: **è ~** he doesn't give a damn, he couldn't care less

strage ['stradʒe] sf massacre, slaughter

tralu'nato, -a ag (occhi) rolling; (persona) beside o.s., very upset

strambo, -a ag strange, queer

trampa'lato, -a ag odd, eccentric

tra'nezza [stra'nettsa] sf strangeness

strango'lare/72/ vt to strangle

trani'ero, -a ag foreign ▷ sm/f foreigner

> Attenzione! In inglese esiste la parola *stranger*, che però significa *sconosciuto* oppure *estraneo*.

strano, -a ag strange, odd

straordi'nario, -a ag extraordinary; (treno ecc) special ▷ sm (lavoro) overtime

strapi'ombo sm overhanging rock; **a ~** overhanging

strap'pare/72/ vt (gen) to tear, rip; (pagina ecc) to tear off, tear out; (sradicare) to pull up; (fig) to wrest sth from sb; (togliere): **~ qc a qn** to snatch sth from sb; **strapparsi** vpr (lacerarsi) to rip, tear; (rompersi) to break; **strapparsi un muscolo** to tear a muscle; **'strappo** sm pull, tug; (lacerazione) tear, rip; **fare uno strappo alla regola** to make an exception to the rule; **strappo muscolare** torn muscle

strari'pare/72/ vi to overflow

strascico, -chi ['straʃʃiko] sm (di abito) train; (conseguenza) after-effect

strata'gemma, -i [strata'dʒemma] sm stratagem

strate'gia, -'gie [strate'dʒia] sf strategy; **stra'tegico, -a, -ci, -che** ag strategic

strato sm layer; (rivestimento) coat, coating; (Geo, fig) stratum; (Meteor) stratus; **~ d'ozono** ozone layer

strat'tone sm tug, jerk; **dare uno ~ a qc** to tug o jerk sth, give sth a tug o jerk

strava'gante ag odd, eccentric

'strazio ['strattsjo] sm torture; (fig: cosa fatta male): **essere uno ~** to be appalling

strega, -ghe sf witch

stre'gare/80/ vt to bewitch

stre'gone sm (mago) wizard; (di tribù) witch doctor

strepi'toso, -a ag clamorous, deafening; (fig: successo) resounding

stres'sante ag stressful

stres'sato, -a ag under stress

stretch [stretʃ] ag inv stretch

'stretta sf vedi **stretto**

stretta'mente av tightly; (rigorosamente) strictly

'stretto, -a pp di **stringere** ▷ ag (corridoio, limiti) narrow; (gonna, scarpe, nodo, curva) tight; (intimo: parente, amico) close; (rigoroso: osservanza) strict; (preciso: significato) precise, exact ▷ sm (braccio di mare) strait ▷ sf (di mano) grasp; (finanziaria) squeeze; (fig: dolore, turbamento) pang; **a denti stretti** with clenched teeth; **lo ~ necessario** the bare minimum; **una stretta di mano** a handshake; **essere alle strette** to have one's back to the wall; **stret'toia** sf bottleneck; (fig) tricky situation

stri'ato, -a ag streaked

'stridulo, -a ag shrill

stril'lare/72/ vt, vi to scream, shriek; **'strillo** sm scream, shriek

strimin'zito, -a [strimin'tsito] ag (misero) shabby; (molto magro) skinny

strimpel'lare/72/ vt (Mus) to strum

'stringa, -ghe sf lace

strin'gato, -a ag (fig) concise

'stringere ['strindʒere] /117/ vt (avvicinare due cose) to press (together), squeeze (together); (tenere stretto) to hold tight, clasp, clutch; (pugno, mascella, denti)

S

to clench; (*labbra*) to compress; (*avvitare*) to tighten; (*abito*) to take in; (*scarpe*) to pinch, be tight for; (*fig: concludere: patto*) to make; (: *accelerare: passo*) to quicken ▷ *vi* (*essere stretto*) to be tight; (*tempo: incalzare*) to be pressing

'**strinsi** *ecc vb vedi* **stringere**

'**striscia, -sce** ['striʃʃa] *sf* (*di carta, tessuto ecc*) strip; (*riga*) stripe; **strisce (pedonali)** zebra crossing *sg*

strisci'are [striʃ'ʃare] /14/ *vt* (*piedi*) to drag; (*muro, macchina*) to graze ▷ *vi* to crawl, creep

'**striscio** ['striʃʃo] *sm* graze; (*Med*) smear; **colpire di ~** to graze

strisci'one [striʃ'ʃone] *sm* banner

strito'lare /72/ *vt* to grind

striz'zare [strit'tsare] /72/ *vt* (*panni*) to wring (out); **~ l'occhio** to wink

'**strofa** *sf* strophe

strofi'naccio [strofi'nattʃo] *sm* duster, cloth; (*per piatti*) dishcloth; (*per pavimenti*) floorcloth

strofi'nare /72/ *vt* to rub

stron'care /20/ *vt* to break off; (*fig: ribellione*) to suppress, put down; (: *film, libro*) to tear to pieces

'**stronzo** ['strontso] *sm* (*sterco*) turd; (*fam!: persona*) shit (!)

stroz'zare [strot'tsare] /72/ *vt* (*soffocare*) to choke, strangle

struc'care /20/ *vt* to remove make-up from; **struccarsi** *vpr* to remove one's make-up

strumen'tale *ag* (*Mus*) instrumental

strumentaliz'zare [strumentalid'dzare] /72/ *vt* to exploit, use to one's own ends

stru'mento *sm* (*arnese, fig*) instrument, tool; (*Mus*) instrument; **~ a corda** *o* **ad arco/a fiato** string(ed)/wind instrument

'**strutto** *sm* lard

strut'tura *sf* structure

'**struzzo** ['struttso] *sm* ostrich

stuc'care /20/ *vt* (*muro*) to plaster; (*vetro*) to putty; (*decorare con stucchi*) to stucco

'**stucco, -chi** *sm* plaster; (*da vetri*) putty; (*ornamentale*) stucco; **rimanere di ~** (*fig*) to be dumbfounded

stu'dente, -'essa *sm/f* student; (*scolaro*) pupil, schoolboy/girl

studi'are /19/ *vt* to study

'**studio** *sm* studying; (*ricerca, saggio, stanza*) study; (*di professionista*) office (*di artista, Cine, TV, Radio*) studio; (*di medico*) surgery (BRIT), office (US); **studi** *smpl* (*Ins*) studies

studi'oso, -a *ag* studious, hardworking ▷ *sm/f* scholar

'**stufa** *sf* stove; **~ elettrica** electric fire *o* heater

stu'fare /72/ *vt* (*Cuc*) to stew; (*fig: fam*) to bore; **stufarsi** *vpr* (*fam*): **stufarsi (di)** (*fig*) to get fed up (with); '**stufo, -a** *ag* (*fam*): **essere stufo di** to be fed up with, be sick and tired of

stu'oia *sf* mat

stupefa'cente [stupefa'tʃɛnte] *ag* stunning, astounding ▷ *sm* drug, narcotic

stu'pendo, -a *ag* marvellous, wonderful

stupi'daggine [stupi'daddʒine] *sf* stupid thing (to do *o* say)

stupidità *sf* stupidity

'**stupido, -a** *ag* stupid

stu'pire /55/ *vt* to amaze, stun ▷ *vi* (*anche*: **stupirsi**): **~ (di)** to be amazed (at), be stunned (by)

stu'pore *sm* amazement, astonishment

stu'prare /72/ *vt* to rape

'**stupro** *sm* rape

stu'rare /72/ *vt* (*lavandino*) to clear

stuzzica'denti [stuttsika'dɛnti] *sm* toothpick

stuzzi'care [stuttsi'kare] /20/ *vt* (*ferita ecc*) to poke (at), prod (at); (*fig*) to tease; (: *appetito*) to whet;

(: *curiosità*) to stimulate; **~ i denti** to pick one's teeth

PAROLA CHIAVE

su (*su* + *il* = **sul**, *su* + *lo* = **sullo**, *su* + *l'* = **sull'**, *su* + *la* = **sulla**, *su* + *i* = **sui**, *su* + *gli* = **sugli**, *su* + *le* = **sulle**) *prep* **1** (*gen*) on; (*moto*) on(to); (*in cima a*) on (top of); **mettilo sul tavolo** put it on the table; **un paesino sul mare** a village by the sea

2 (*argomento*) about, on; **un libro su Cesare** a book on *o* about Caesar

3 (*circa*) about; **costerà sui 3 milioni** it will cost about 3 million; **una ragazza sui 17 anni** a girl of about 17 (years of age)

4: **su misura** made to measure; **su richiesta** on request; **3 casi su dieci** 3 cases out of 10

▷ *av* **1** (*in alto, verso l'alto*) up; **vieni su** come on up; **guarda su** look up; **su le mani!** hands up!; **in su** (*verso l'alto*) up(wards); (*in poi*) onwards; **dai 20 anni in su** from the age of 20 onwards

2 (*addosso*) on; **cos'hai su?** what have you got on?

▷ *escl* come on!; **su coraggio!** come on, cheer up!

su'bacqueo, -a *ag* underwater ▷ *sm* skin-diver

sub'buglio [sub'buʎʎo] *sm* confusion, turmoil

'subdolo, -a *ag* underhand, sneaky

suben'trare /72/ *vi*: **~ a qn in qc** to take over sth from sb

su'bire /55/ *vt* to suffer, endure

'subito *av* immediately, at once, straight away

subodo'rare /72/ *vt* (*insidia ecc*) to smell, suspect

subordi'nato, -a *ag* subordinate; (*dipendente*): **~ a** dependent on, subject to

suc'cedere [sut'tʃɛdere] /118/ *vi* (*accadere*) to happen; **~ a** (*prendere*

il posto di) to succeed; (*venire dopo*) to follow; **cos'è successo?** what happened?; **succes'sivo, -a** *ag* successive; **suc'cesso, -a** *pp di* **succedere** ▷ *sm* (*esito*) outcome; (*buona riuscita*) success; **di successo** (*libro, personaggio*) successful

succhi'are [suk'kjare] /19/ *vt* to suck (up)

succhi'otto [suk'kjɔtto] *sm* dummy (BRIT), pacifier (US), comforter (US)

suc'cinto, -a [sut'tʃinto] *ag* (*discorso*) succinct; (*abito*) brief

'succo, -chi *sm* juice; (*fig*) essence, gist; **~ di frutta/pomodoro** fruit/ tomato juice

succur'sale *sf* branch (office)

sud *sm* south ▷ *ag inv* south; (*regione*) southern

Su'dafrica *sm*: **il ~** South Africa; **sudafri'cano, -a** *ag, sm/f* South African

Suda'merica *sm*: **il ~** South America

su'dare /72/ *vi* to perspire, sweat; **~ freddo** to come out in a cold sweat

su'dato, -a *ag* (*persona, mani*) sweaty; (*fig: denaro*) hard-earned ▷ *sf* (*anche fig*) sweat; **una vittoria sudata** a hard-won victory; **ho fatto una bella sudata per finirlo in tempo** it was a real sweat to get it finished in time

suddi'videre /43/ *vt* to subdivide

su'dest *sm* south-east

'sudicio, -a, -ci, -ce ['suditʃo] *ag* dirty, filthy

su'doku *sm inv* sudoku

su'dore *sm* perspiration, sweat

su'dovest *sm* south-west

suffici'ente [suffi'tʃɛnte] *ag* enough, sufficient; (*borioso*) self-important; (*Ins*) satisfactory; **suffici'enza** *sf* self-importance; (*Ins*) pass mark; **a sufficienza** enough; **ne ho avuto a sufficienza!** I've had enough of this!

suf'fisso *sm* (*Ling*) suffix

S

suggeri'mento [suddʒeri'mento] *sm* suggestion; (*consiglio*) piece of advice, advice *no pl*

sugge'rire [suddʒe'rire] /55/ *vt* (*risposta*) to tell; (*consigliare*) to advise; (*proporre*) to suggest; (*Teat*) to prompt

suggestio'nare [suddʒestjo'nare] /72/ *vt* to influence

sugges'tivo, -a [suddʒes'tivo] *ag* (*paesaggio*) evocative; (*teoria*) interesting, attractive

'sughero ['sugero] *sm* cork

'sugo, -ghi *sm* (*succo*) juice; (*di carne*) gravy; (*condimento*) sauce; (*fig*) gist, essence

sui'cida, -i, -e [sui't∫ida] *ag* suicidal ▷ *smf* suicide

suici'darsi [suit∫i'darsi] /72/ *vpr* to commit suicide

sui'cidio [sui't∫idjo] *sm* suicide

su'ino, -a *ag*: **carne suina** pork ▷ *sm* pig

sul'tano, -a *sm/f* sultan (sultana)

'suo (*f* **'sua**, *pl* **'sue, su'oi**) *det*: **il ~, la sua** *ecc* (*di lui*) his; (*di lei*) her; (*di esso*) its; (*con valore indefinito*) one's, his/her; (*forma di cortesia: anche*: **S~**) your ▷ *pron*: **il ~, la sua** *ecc* his; hers; yours; **i ~i** his (*o* her *ecc*) family

su'ocero, -a ['swɔt∫ero] *sm/f* father/mother-in-law

su'ola *sf* (*di scarpa*) sole

su'olo *sm* (*terreno*) ground; (*terra*) soil

suo'nare /72/ *vt* (*Mus*) to play; (*campana*) to ring; (*ore*) to strike; (*clacson, allarme*) to sound ▷ *vi* to play; (*telefono, campana*) to ring; (*ore*) to strike; (*clacson, fig: parole*) to sound

suone'ria *sf* alarm

su'ono *sm* sound

su'ora *sf* (*Rel*) nun; **Suor Maria** Sister Maria

'super *ag inv*: (*benzina*) **~** ≈ four-star (petrol) (*BRIT*), ≈ premium (*US*)

supe'rare /72/ *vt* (*oltrepassare: limite*) to exceed, surpass; (*percorrere*) to cover; (*attraversare: fiume*) to cross; (*sorpassare: veicolo*) to overtake; (*fig:*

essere più bravo di) to surpass, outdo; (*: difficoltà*) to overcome; (*: esame*) to get through; **~ qn in altezza/peso** to be taller/heavier than sb; **ha superato la cinquantina** he's over fifty (years of age)

su'perbia *sf* pride; **su'perbo, -a** *ag* proud; (*fig*) magnificent, superb

superfici'ale [superfi't∫ale] *ag* superficial

super'ficie, -ci [super'fit∫e] *sf* surface

su'perfluo, -a *ag* superfluous

superi'ore *ag* (*piano, arto, classi*) upper; (*più elevato: temperatura, livello*): **~ (a)** higher (than); (*migliore*): **~ (a)** superior (to)

superla'tivo, -a *ag, sm* superlative

supermer'cato *sm* supermarket

su'perstite *ag* surviving ▷ *smf* survivor

superstizi'one [superstit'tsjone] *sf* superstition; **superstizi'oso, -a** *ag* superstitious

super'strada *sf* ≈ expressway

su'pino, -a *ag* supine

supplemen'tare *ag* extra; (*treno*) relief *cpd*; (*entrate*) additional

supple'mento *sm* supplement

sup'plente *smf* temporary member of staff; supply (*o* substitute) teacher

'supplica, -che *sf* (*preghiera*) plea; (*domanda scritta*) petition, request

suppli'care /20/ *vt* to implore, beseech

sup'plizio [sup'plittsjo] *sm* torture

sup'pongo, sup'poni *ecc vb vedi* **supporre**

sup'porre /77/ *vt* to suppose; **supponiamo che ...** let's *o* just suppose that ...

sup'porto *sm* (*sostegno*) support

sup'posta *sf* (*Med*) suppository

su'premo, -a *ag* supreme

surge'lare [surdʒe'lare] /72/ *vt* to (deep-)freeze

surge'lato, -a [surdʒe'lato] *ag* (deep-)frozen ▷ *smpl*: **i surgelati** frozen food *sg*

sur'plus *sm inv* (Econ) surplus

surriscal'dare /72/ *vt* to overheat

suscet'tibile [suʃʃet'tibile] *ag* (sensibile) touchy, sensitive

susci'tare [suʃʃi'tare] /72/ *vt* to provoke, arouse

su'sina *sf* plum

susse'gui re /45/ *vt* to follow; **susseguirsi** *vpr* to follow one another

sus'sidio *sm* subsidy; **sussidi didattici/audiovisivi** teaching/audiovisual aids

sussul'tare /72/ *vi* to shudder

sussur'rare /72/ *vt, vi* to whisper, murmur; **sus'surro** *sm* whisper, murmur

sva'gare /80/ *vt* (divertire) to amuse; **svagarsi** *vpr* to amuse o.s.

'svago, -ghi *sm* (riposo) relaxation; (ricreazione) amusement; (passatempo) pastime

svaligi'are [zvali'dʒare] /62/ *vt* to rob, burgle (BRIT), burglarize (US)

svalu'tare /72/ *vt* (Econ) to devalue; **svalutarsi** *vpr* (Econ) to be devalued

svalutazi'one *sf* devaluation

sva'nire /55/ *vi* to disappear, vanish

svantaggi'ato, -a [zvantad'dʒato] *ag* at a disadvantage

svan'taggio [zvan'taddʒo] *sm* disadvantage; (inconveniente) drawback, disadvantage

svari'ato, -a *ag* varied; (numeroso) various

svastica, -che *sf* swastika

sve'dese *ag* Swedish ▷ *smf* Swede ▷ *sm* (Ling) Swedish

'sveglia ['zveʎʎa] *sf* waking up; (orologio) alarm (clock); **~ telefonica** alarm call

svegli'are [zveʎ'ʎare] /27/ *vt* to wake up; (fig) to awaken, arouse; **svegliarsi** *vpr* to wake up; (fig) to be revived, reawaken

'sveglio, -a ['zveʎʎo] *ag* awake; (fig) quick-witted

sve'lare /72/ *vt* to reveal

'svelto, -a *ag* (passo) quick; (mente) quick, alert; **alla svelta** quickly

'svendere /29/ *vt* to sell off, clear

'svendita *sf* (Comm) (clearance) sale

'svengo *ecc vb vedi* **svenire**

sveni'mento *sm* fainting fit, faint

sve'nire /128/ *vi* to faint

sven'tare /72/ *vt* to foil, thwart

sven'tato, -a *ag* (distratto) scatterbrained; (imprudente) rash

svento'lare /72/ *vt, vi* to wave, flutter

sven'tura *sf* misfortune

sverrò *ecc vb vedi* **svenire**

sves'tire /45/ *vt* to undress; **svestirsi** *vpr* to get undressed

'Svezia ['zvɛttsja] *sf*: **la ~** Sweden

svi'are /60/ *vt* to divert; (fig) to lead astray

svi'gnarsela [zviɲ'ɲarsela] /72/ *vpr* to slip away, sneak off

svilup'pare /72/ *vt*, **svilup'parsi** *vpr* to develop

sviluppa'tore, -trice *sm/f* (Inform) developer

svi'luppo *sm* development

'svincolo *sm* (stradale) motorway (BRIT) o expressway (US) intersection

'svista *sf* oversight

svi'tare /72/ *vt* to unscrew

'Svizzera ['zvittsera] *sf*: **la ~** Switzerland; **svizzero, -a** ['zvittsero] *ag, sm/f* Swiss

svogli'ato, -a [zvoʎ'ʎato] *ag* listless; (pigro) lazy

'svolgere ['zvɔldʒere] /96/ *vt* to unwind; (srotolare) to unroll; (fig: argomento) to develop; (: piano, programma) to carry out; **svolgersi** *vpr* to unwind; to unroll; (fig: aver luogo) to take place; (: procedere) to go on

'svolsi *ecc vb vedi* **svolgere**

'svolta *sf* (atto) turning *no pl*; (curva) turn, bend; (fig) turning-point

svol'tare /72/ *vi* to turn

svuo'tare /72/ *vt* to empty (out)

T, t [ti] *sf o m inv (lettera)* T, t; **T come Taranto** ≈ T for Tommy

t *abbr* = **tonnellata**

tabacche'ria [tabakke'ria] *sf* tobacconist's (shop)

ta'bacco, -chi *sm* tobacco

ta'bella *sf (tavola)* table; *(elenco)* list

tabel'lone *sm (per pubblicità)* billboard; *(in stazione)* timetable board

TAC *sigla f (Med)* (= *Tomografia Assiale Computerizzata*) CAT

tac'chino [tak'kino] *sm* turkey

'tacco, -chi *sm* heel; **tacchi a spillo** stiletto heels

taccu'ino *sm* notebook

ta'cere [ta'tʃere] /119/ *vi* to be silent *o* quiet; *(smettere di parlare)* to fall silent ▷ *vt* to keep to oneself, say nothing about; **far ~ qn** to make sb be quiet; *(fig)* to silence sb

ta'chimetro [ta'kimetro] *sm* speedometer

'tacqui *ecc vb vedi* **tacere**

ta'fano *sm* horsefly

'taglia ['taʎʎa] *sf (statura)* height; *(misura)* size; *(riscatto)* ransom; *(ricompensa)* reward; **taglie forti** *(Abbigliamento)* outsize

taglia'carte [taʎʎa'karte] *sm inv* paperknife

tagli'ando [taʎ'ʎando] *sm* coupon

tagli'are [taʎ'ʎare] /27/ *vt* to cut; *(recidere, interrompere)* to cut off; *(intersecare)* to cut across, intersect; *(carne)* to carve; *(vini)* to blend ▷ *vi* to cut; *(prendere una scorciatoia)* to take a short-cut; **tagliarsi** *vpr* to cut o.s.; **~ la strada a qn** to cut across in front of sb; **~ corto** *(fig)* to cut short; **~ la corda** *(fig)* to sneak off; **~ i ponti (con)** *(fig)* to break off relations (with); **mi sono tagliato** I've cut myself

taglia'telle [taʎʎa'tɛlle] *sfpl* tagliatelle *pl*

taglia'unghie [taʎʎa'ungje] *sm inv* nail clippers *pl*

tagli'ente [taʎ'ʎɛnte] *ag* sharp

'taglio ['taʎʎo] *sm (anche fig)* cut; cutting *no pl*; *(parte tagliente)* cutting edge; *(di abito)* cut, style; *(di stoffa)* length; *(di vini)* blending; **di ~** on edge, edgeways; **banconote di piccolo/grosso ~** notes of small/large denomination; **~ cesareo** Caesarean section

tailan'dese *ag, smf, sm* Thai

Tai'landia *sf*: **la ~** Thailand

'talco *sm* talcum powder

 PAROLA CHIAVE

'tale *det* **1** *(simile, così grande)* such; **un(a) tale …** such a …; **non accetto tali discorsi** I won't allow such talk; **è di una tale arroganza** he is so arrogant; **fa una tale confusione!** he makes such a mess!
2 *(persona o cosa indeterminata)* such-and-such; **il giorno tale**

all'ora tale on such-and-such a day at such-and-such a time; **la tal persona** that person; **ha telefonato una tale Giovanna** somebody called Giovanna phoned
3 (*nelle similitudini*): **tale ... tale** like ... like; **tale padre tale figlio** like father, like son; **hai il vestito tale quale il mio** your dress is just *o* exactly like mine
▶ *pron* (*indefinito, persona*): **un(a) tale** someone; **quel (*o* quella) tale** that person, that man (*o* woman); **il tal dei tali** what's-his-name

tale'bano *sm* Taliban
ta'lento *sm* talent
talis'mano *sm* talisman
tallon'cino [tallon'tʃino] *sm* counterfoil
tal'lone *sm* heel
tal'mente *av* so
'talpa *sf* (*Zool: anche fig*) mole
tal'volta *av* sometimes, at times
tambu'rello *sm* tambourine
tam'buro *sm* drum
Ta'migi [ta'midʒi] *sm*: **il ~** the Thames
tampo'nare /72/ *vt* (*otturare*) to plug; (*urtare: macchina*) to crash *o* ram into
tam'pone *sm* (*Med*) wad, pad; (*per timbri*) ink-pad; (*respingente*) buffer; **~ assorbente** tampon
'tana *sf* lair, den
'tanga *sm inv* G-string
tan'gente [tan'dʒɛnte] *ag* (*Mat*): **~ a** tangential to ▶ *sf* tangent; (*quota*) share
tangenzi'ale [tandʒen'tsjale] *sf* (*strada*) bypass
'tanica *sf* (*contenitore*) jerry can

PAROLA CHIAVE

'tanto, -a *det* **1** (*molto: quantità*) a lot of, much; (*: numero*) a lot of, many; **tanto tempo** a lot of time, a long time; **tanti auguri!** all the best!;

tante grazie many thanks; **tante volte** many times, often; **ogni tanti chilometri** every so many kilometres
2 (*così tanto: quantità*) so much, such a lot of; (*: numero*) so many, such a lot of; **ho aspettato per tanto tempo** I waited so long *o* for such a long time
3: **tanto ... quanto** (*quantità*) as much ... as; (*numero*) as many ... as; **ho tanta pazienza quanta ne hai tu** I have as much patience as you have *o* as you; **ha tanti amici quanti nemici** he has as many friends as he has enemies
▶ *pron* **1** (*molto*) much, a lot; (*così tanto*) so much, such a lot; **tanti, -e** many, a lot; so many; such a lot; **credevo ce ne fosse tanto** I thought there was (such) a lot, I thought there was plenty
2: **tanto quanto** (*denaro*) as much as; (*cioccolatini*) as many as; **ne ho tanto quanto basta** I have as much as I need; **due volte tanto** twice as much
3 (*indeterminato*) so much; **tanto per l'affitto, tanto per il gas** so much for the rent, so much for the gas; **costa un tanto al metro** it costs so much per metre; **di tanto in tanto, ogni tanto** every so often; **tanto vale che ...** I (*o* we *ecc*) may as well ...; **tanto meglio!** so much the better!; **tanto peggio per lui!** so much the worse for him!
▶ *av* **1** (*molto*) very; **vengo tanto volentieri** I'd be very glad to come; **non ci vuole tanto a capirlo** it doesn't take much to understand it
2 (*così tanto: con ag, av*) so; (*: con vb*) so much, such a lot; **è tanto bella!** she's so beautiful!; **non urlare tanto (forte)** don't shout so much; **sto tanto meglio adesso** I'm so much better now; **tanto ... che ...** so ... (that); **tanto ... da** so ... as
3: **tanto ... quanto** as ... as; **conosco tanto Carlo quanto suo**

padre I know both Carlo and his father; **non è poi tanto complicato quanto sembra** it's not as difficult as it seems; **tanto più insisti, tanto più non mollerà** the more you insist, the more stubborn he'll be; **quanto più … tanto meno** the more … the less

4 (*solamente*) just; **tanto per cambiare/scherzare** just for a change/a joke; **una volta tanto** for once

5 (*a lungo*) (for) long

▶ *cong* after all

'**tappa** *sf* (*luogo di sosta, fermata*) stop, halt; (*parte di un percorso*) stage, leg; (*Sport*) lap; **a tappe** in stages

tap'pare /72/ *vt* to plug, stop up; (*bottiglia*) to cork; **tapparsi** *vpr*: **tapparsi in casa** to shut o.s. up at home; **tapparsi la bocca** to shut up; **tapparsi le orecchie** to turn a deaf ear

tappa'rella *sf* rolling shutter

tappe'tino *sm* (*per auto*) car mat; **~ antiscivolo** (*da bagno*) non-slip mat; **~ del mouse** mouse mat

tap'peto *sm* carpet; (*anche*: **tappetino**) rug; (*Sport*): **andare al ~** to go down for the count; **mettere sul ~** (*fig*) to bring up for discussion

tappez'zare [tappet'tsare] /72/ *vt* (*con carta*) to paper; (*rivestire*): **~ qc (di)** to cover sth (with); **tappezze'ria** *sf* (*tessuto*) tapestry; (*carta da parati*) wallpaper; (*arte*) upholstery; **far da tappezzeria** (*fig*) to be a wallflower

'**tappo** *sm* stopper; (*in sughero*) cork

tar'dare /72/ *vi* to be late ▷ *vt* to delay; **~ a fare** to delay doing

'**tardi** *av* late; **più ~** later (on); **al più ~** at the latest; **sul ~** (*verso sera*) late in the day; **far ~** to be late; (*restare alzato*) to stay up late; **è troppo ~** it's too late

'**targa, -ghe** *sf* plate; (*Aut*) number (BRIT) o license (US) plate; **targ'hetta**

sf (*con nome: su porta*) nameplate; (: *su bagaglio*) name tag

ta'riffa *sf* (*gen*) rate, tariff; (*di trasporti*) fare; (*elenco*) price list; tariff

'**tarlo** *sm* woodworm

'**tarma** *sf* moth

ta'rocco, -chi *sm* tarot card; **tarocchi** *smpl* (*gioco*) tarot *sg*

tarta'ruga *sf* tortoise; (*di mare*) turtle; (*materiale*) tortoiseshell

tar'tina *sf* canapé

tar'tufo *sm* (*Bot*) truffle

'**tasca, -sche** *sf* pocket; **tas'cabile** *ag* (*libro*) pocket *cpd*

'**tassa** *sf* (*imposta*) tax; (*doganale*) duty; (*per iscrizione, a scuola ecc*) fee; **~ di circolazione/di soggiorno** road/tourist tax

tas'sare /72/ *vt* to tax; to levy a duty on

tas'sello *sm* plug; (*assaggio*) wedge

tassì *sm inv* = **taxi**; **tas'sista, -i, -e** *smf* taxi driver

'**tasso** *sm* (*di natalità, d'interesse ecc*) rate; (*Bot*) yew; (*Zool*) badger; **~ di cambio/d'interesse** rate of exchange/interest

tas'tare /72/ *vt* to feel; **~ il terreno** (*fig*) to see how the land lies

tasti'era *sf* keyboard

'**tasto** *sm* key; (*tatto*) touch, feel

tas'toni *av*: **procedere (a) ~** to grope one's way forward

'**tatto** *sm* (*senso*) touch; (*fig*) tact; **duro al ~** hard to the touch; **aver ~** to be tactful, have tact

tatu'aggio [tatu'addʒo] *sm* tattooing; (*disegno*) tattoo

tatu'are /72/ *vt* to tattoo

TAV [tav] *sigla m* (*inv*), *sigla f* (*inv*) (= *treno alta velocità*) high-speed train; (*sistema*) high-speed rail system

'**tavola** *sf* table; (*asse*) plank, board; (*lastra*) tablet; (*quadro*) panel (*painting*); (*illustrazione*) plate; **~ calda** snack bar; **~ rotonda** (*fig*) round table; **~ a vela** windsurfer

tavo'letta *sf* tablet, bar; **a ~** (*Aut*) flat out

tavo'lino *sm* small table; (*scrivania*) desk

'tavolo *sm* table

'taxi *sm inv* taxi

'tazza ['tattsa] *sf* cup; **~ da caffè/tè** coffee/tea cup; **una ~ di caffè/tè** a cup of coffee/tea

TBC *abbr f* (= *tubercolosi*) TB

te *pron* (*soggetto: in forme comparative, oggetto*) you

tè *sm inv* tea; (*trattenimento*) tea party

tea'trale *ag* theatrical

te'atro *sm* theatre

techno ['tɛkno] *ag inv* (*musica*) techno

'tecnico, -a, -ci, -che *ag* technical ▷ *sm/f* technician ▷ *sf* technique; (*tecnologia*) technology

tecnolo'gia [teknolo'dʒia] *sf* technology

te'desco, -a, -schi, -sche *ag, sm/f, sm* German

te'game *sm* (*Cuc*) pan

'tegola *sf* tile

tei'era *sf* teapot

tel. *abbr* (= *telefono*) tel.

'tela *sf* (*tessuto*) cloth; (*per vele, quadri*) canvas; (*dipinto*) canvas, painting; **di ~** (*calzoni*) (heavy) cotton *cpd*; (*scarpe, borsa*) canvas *cpd*; **~ cerata** oilcloth

te'laio *sm* (*apparecchio*) loom; (*struttura*) frame

tele'camera *sf* television camera

teleco'mando *sm* remote control

tele'cronaca, -che *sf* television report

telefo'nare /72/ *vi* to telephone, ring; (*fare una chiamata*) to make a phone call ▷ *vt* to telephone; **~ a qn** to phone *o* ring *o* call sb (up)

telefo'nata *sf* (telephone) call; **~ a carico del destinatario** reverse charge (BRIT), collect (US) call

tele'fonico, -a, -ci, -che *ag* (tele) phone *cpd*

telefo'nino *sm* mobile phone

te'lefono *sm* telephone; **~ a gettoni** ≈ pay phone; **~ fisso** landline

telegior'nale [teledʒor'nale] *sm* television news (programme)

tele'gramma, -i *sm* telegram

tela'voro *sm* teleworking

teleno'vela *sf* soap opera

Tele'pass® *sm inv* *automatic payment card for use on Italian motorways*

telepa'tia *sf* telepathy

teles'copio *sm* telescope

teleselezi'one [teleselet'tsjone] *sf* direct dialling

telespetta'tore, -'trice *sm/f* (television) viewer

tele'vendita *sf* teleshopping

televisi'one *sf* television

televi'sore *sm* television set

'tema, -i *sm* theme; (*Ins*) essay, composition

te'mere /29/ *vt* to fear, be afraid of; (*essere sensibile a: freddo, calore*) to be sensitive to ▷ *vi* to be afraid; (*essere preoccupato*) **~ per** to worry about, fear for; **~ di/che** to be afraid of/that

temperama'tite *sm inv* pencil sharpener

tempera'mento *sm* temperament

tempera'tura *sf* temperature

tempe'rino *sm* penknife

tem'pesta *sf* storm; **~ di sabbia/ neve** sand/snowstorm

'tempia *sf* (*Anat*) temple

'tempio *sm* (*edificio*) temple

'tempo *sm* (*Meteor*) weather; (*cronologico*) time; (*epoca*) time, times *pl*; (*di film, gioco: parte*) part; (*Mus*) time; (: *battuta*) beat; (*Ling*) tense; **che ~ fa?** what's the weather like?; **un ~** once; **~ fa** some time ago; **al ~ stesso** *o* **a un ~** at the same time; **per ~** early; **aver fatto il proprio ~** to have had its (*o* his *ecc*) day; **primo/ secondo ~** (*Teat*) first/second part; (*Sport*) first/second half; **in ~ utile** in due time *o* course; **a ~ pieno** full-time; **~ libero** free time

tempo'rale *ag* temporal ▷ *sm* (*Meteor*) (thunder)storm

tempo'raneo, -a *ag* temporary

te'nace [te'natʃe] *ag* strong, tough; (*fig*) tenacious

te'naglie [te'naʎʎe] *sfpl* pincers *pl*

'**tenda** *sf* (*riparo*) awning; (*di finestra*) curtain; (*per campeggio ecc*) tent

ten'denza [ten'dɛntsa] *sf* tendency; (*orientamento*) trend; **avere ~ a** o **per qc** to have a bent for sth

'**tendere** /120/ *vt* (*allungare al massimo*) to stretch, draw tight; (*porgere: mano*) to hold out; (*fig: trappola*) to lay, set ▷ *vi*: **~ a qc/a fare** to tend towards sth/to do; **~ l'orecchio** to prick up one's ears; **il tempo tende al caldo** the weather is getting hot; **un blu che tende al verde** a greenish blue

'**tendine** *sm* tendon, sinew

ten'done *sm* (*da circo*) big top

'**tenebre** *sfpl* darkness *sg*

te'nente *sm* lieutenant

te'nere /121/ *vt* to hold; (*conservare, mantenere*) to keep; (*ritenere, considerare*) to consider; (*occupare: spazio*) to take up, occupy; (*seguire: strada*) to keep to ▷ *vi* to hold; (*colori*) to be fast; (*dare importanza*): **~ a** to care about; **~ a fare** to want to do, be keen to do; **tenersi** *vpr* (*stare in una determinata posizione*) to stand; (*stimarsi*) to consider o.s.; (*aggrapparsi*): **tenersi a** to hold on to; (*attenersi*): **tenersi a** to stick to; **~ una conferenza** to give a lecture; **~ conto di qc** to take sth into consideration; **~ presente qc** to bear sth in mind

'**tenero, -a** *ag* tender; (*pietra, cera, colore*) soft; (*fig*) tender, loving

'**tengo** *ecc vb vedi* **tenere**

'**tenni** *ecc vb vedi* **tenere**

'**tennis** *sm* tennis

ten'nista, -i, -e *smf* tennis player

te'nore *sm* (*tono*) tone; (*Mus*) tenor; **~ di vita** (*livello*) standard of living

tensi'one *sf* tension

ten'tare /72/ *vt* (*indurre*) to tempt; (*provare*): **~ qc/di fare** to attempt o try sth/to do; **tenta'tivo** *sm* attempt; **tentazi'one** *sf* temptation

tenten'nare /72/ *vi* to shake, be unsteady; (*fig*) to hesitate, waver

ten'toni *av*: **andare a ~** (*anche fig*) to grope one's way

'**tenue** *ag* (*sottile*) fine; (*colore*) soft; (*fig*) slender, slight

te'nuta *sf* (*capacità*) capacity; (*divisa*) uniform; (*abito*) dress; (*Agr*) estate; **a ~ d'aria** airtight; **~ di strada** roadholding power

teolo'gia [teolo'dʒia] *sf* theology

teo'ria *sf* theory

te'pore *sm* warmth

tep'pista, -i *sm* hooligan

tera'pia *sf* therapy; **~ intensiva** intensive care

tergicris'tallo [terdʒikris'tallo] *sm* windscreen (*BRIT*) o windshield (*US*) wiper

tergiver'sare [terdʒiver'sare] /72/ *vi* to shilly-shally

ter'male *ag* thermal; **stazione** *sf* **~ spa**

'**terme** *sfpl* thermal baths

termi'nale *ag, sm* terminal

termi'nare /72/ *vt* to end; (*lavoro*) to finish ▷ *vi* to end

'**termine** *sm* term; (*fine, estremità*) end; (*di territorio*) boundary, limit; **contratto a ~** (*Comm*) forward contract; **a breve/lungo ~** short-/long-term; **parlare senza mezzi termini** to talk frankly, not to mince one's words

ter'mometro *sm* thermometer

'**termos** *sm inv* = **thermos**

termosi'fone *sm* radiator

ter'mostato *sm* thermostat

'**terra** *sf* (*gen, Elettr*) earth; (*sostanza*) soil, earth; (*opposto al mare*) land *no pl*; (*regione, paese*) land; (*argilla*) clay; **terre** *sfpl* (*possedimento*) lands, land *sg*: **a** o **per ~** (*stato*) on the ground (o floor); (*moto*) to the ground, down; **mettere a ~** to earth

terra'cotta *sf* terracotta; **vasellame** *sm* **di ~** earthenware

terra'ferma *sf* dry land, terra firma; (*continente*) mainland

ter'razza [ter'rattsa] *sf*, **ter'razzo** [ter'rattso] *sm* terrace

terre'moto *sm* earthquake

ter'reno, -a *ag* (*vita, beni*) earthly ▷ *sm* (*suolo, fig*) ground; (*Comm*) land *no pl*, plot (of land); site; (*Sport, Mil*) field

ter'restre *ag* (*superficie*) of the earth, earth's; (*di terra: battaglia, animale*) land *cpd*; (*Rel*) earthly, worldly

ter'ribile *ag* terrible, dreadful

terrifi'cante *ag* terrifying

ter'rina *sf* tureen

territori'ale *ag* territorial

terri'torio *sm* territory

ter'rore *sm* terror; **terro'rismo** *sm* terrorism; **terro'rista, -i, -e** *smf* terrorist

terroriz'zare [terrorid'dzare] /72/ *vt* to terrorize

terza ['tɛrtsa] *sf vedi* **terzo**

ter'zino [ter'tsino] *sm* (*Calcio*) fullback, back

terzo, -a ['tɛrtso] *ag* third ▷ *sm* (*frazione*) third; (*Dir*) third party ▷ *sf* (*Aut*) third (gear); (*Ins: elementare*) third year at primary school; (: *media*) third year at secondary school; (: *superiore*) sixth year at secondary school; **terzi** *smpl* (*altri*) others, other people; **la terza pagina** (*Stampa*) the Arts page

teschio ['tɛskjo] *sm* skull

tesi *ecc vb vedi* **tendere**

teso, -a *pp di* **tendere** ▷ *ag* (*tirato*) taut, tight; (*fig*) tense

te'soro *sm* treasure; **il Ministero del T~** the Treasury

tessera *sf* (*documento*) card

tes'suto *sm* fabric, material; (*Biol*) tissue

test ['tɛst] *sm inv* test

testa *sf* head; (*di cose: estremità, parte anteriore*) front, head; **di ~** (*vettura ecc*) front; **fare di ~ propria** to go one's own way; **in ~** (*Sport*) in the lead; **tenere ~ a qn** (*nemico ecc*) to stand up to sb; **una ~ d'aglio** a bulb of garlic; **~ o croce?** heads or tails?; **avere la ~ dura** to be stubborn; **~ di serie** (*Tennis*) seed, seeded player

testa'mento *sm* (*atto*) will; **l'Antico/ il Nuovo T~** (*Rel*) the Old/New Testament

tes'tardo, -a *ag* stubborn, pig-headed

tes'tata *sf* (*parte anteriore*) head; (*intestazione*) heading

tes'ticolo *sm* testicle

testi'mone *smf* (*Dir*) witness; **~ oculare** eye witness

testimoni'are /19/ *vt* to testify; (*fig*) to bear witness to, testify to ▷ *vi* to give evidence, testify

testo *sm* text; **fare ~** (*opera, autore*) to be authoritative; **questo libro non fa ~** this book is not essential reading

tes'tuggine [tes'tuddʒine] *sf* tortoise; (*di mare*) turtle

tetano (*Med*) tetanus

tetto *sm* roof; **tet'toia** *sf* roofing; canopy

tet'tuccio [tet'tuttʃo] *sm*: **~ apribile** (*Aut*) sunroof

Tevere *sm*: **il ~** the Tiber

TG [tid'dʒi], **tg** *abbr m* (= *telegiornale*) TV news *sg*

thermos® ['tɛrmos] *sm inv* vacuum *o* Thermos® flask

ti *pron* (*dav lo, la, li, le, ne diventa* **te**, *oggetto*) you; (*complemento di termine*) (to) you; (*riflessivo*) yourself

Tibet *sm*: **il ~** Tibet

tibia *sf* tibia, shinbone

tic *sm inv* tic, (nervous) twitch; (*fig*) mannerism

ticchet'tio [tikket'tio] *sm* (*di macchina da scrivere*) clatter; (*di orologio*) ticking; (*della pioggia*) patter

'ticket *sm inv* (*Med*) prescription charge (*BRIT*)

ti'ene *ecc vb vedi* **tenere**

ti'epido, -a *ag* lukewarm, tepid

'tifo *sm* (*Med*) typhus; (*fig*): **fare il ~ per** to be a fan of

ti'fone *sm* typhoon

ti'foso, -a *sm/f* (*Sport: ecc*) fan

tigì [ti'dʒi] *sm inv* TV news

'tiglio ['tiʎʎo] *sm* lime (tree), linden (tree)

'tigre *sf* tiger

tim'brare /72/ *vt* to stamp; (*annullare: francobolli*) to postmark; **~ il cartellino** to clock in

'timbro *sm* stamp; (*Mus*) timbre, tone

'timido, -a *ag* shy; timid

'timo *sm* thyme

ti'mone *sm* (*Naut*) rudder

ti'more *sm* (*paura*) fear; (*rispetto*) awe

'timpano *sm* (*Anat*) eardrum

'tingere ['tindʒere] /37/ *vt* to dye

'tinsi *ecc vb vedi* **tingere**

'tinta *sf* (*materia colorante*) dye; (*colore*) shade

tintin'nare /72/ *vi* to tinkle

tinto'ria *sf* (*lavasecco*) dry cleaner's (shop)

tin'tura *sf* (*operazione*) dyeing; (*colorante*) dye; **~ di iodio** tincture of iodine

'tipico, -a, -ci, -che *ag* typical

'tipo *sm* type; (*genere*) kind, type; (*fam*) chap, fellow; **che ~ di...?** what kind of ...?

tipogra'fia *sf* typography; (*procedimento*) letterpress (printing); (*officina*) printing house

T.I.R. *sigla m* (= *Transports Internationaux Routiers*) International Heavy Goods Vehicle

ti'rare /72/ *vt* (*gen*) to pull; (*chiudere: tenda ecc*) to draw, pull; (*tracciare, disegnare*) to draw, trace; (*lanciare: sasso, palla*) to throw; (*stampare*) to print; (*pistola, freccia*) to fire; (*estrarre*): **~ qc da** to take o pull sth out of; to get sth out of; to extract sth from

▷ *vi* (*pipa, camino*) to draw; (*vento*) to blow; (*abito*) to be tight; (*fare fuoco*) to fire; (*fare del tiro, Calcio*) to shoot; **~ a indovinare** to take a guess; **~ sul prezzo** to bargain; **~ avanti** *vi* to struggle on; *vt* to keep going; **~ fuori** (*estrarre*) to take out, pull out; **~ giù** (*abbassare*) to bring down, to lower; (*da scaffale ecc*) to take down; **~ su** to pull up; (*capelli*) to put up; (*fig: bambino*) to bring up; **tirar dritto** to keep right on going; **~ via** (*togliere*) to take off; **tirarsi indietro** to move back; (*fig*) to back out; **tirati su!** cheer up!

tira'tura *sf* (*azione*) printing; (*di libro*) (print) run; (*di giornale*) circulation

'tirchio, -a ['tirkjo] *ag* mean, stingy

'tiro *sm* shooting *no pl*, firing *no pl*; (*colpo, sparo*) shot; (*di palla: lancio*) throwing *no pl*; throw; (*fig*) trick; **cavallo da ~** draught (*BRIT*) o draft (*US*) horse; **~ a segno** target shooting; (*luogo*) shooting range; **~ con l'arco** archery

tiro'cinio [tiro'tʃinjo] *sm* apprenticeship; (*professionale*) training

ti'roide *sf* thyroid (gland)

Tir'reno *sm*: **il (mar) ~** the Tyrrhenian Sea

ti'sana *sf* herb tea

tito'lare *smf* incumbent; (*proprietario*) owner; (*Calcio*) regular player

'titolo *sm* title; (*di giornale*) headline; (*diploma*) qualification; (*Comm*) security; (*: azione*) share; **a che ~?** for what reason?; **a ~ di amicizia** out of friendship; **a ~ di premio** as a prize; **~ di credito** share; **titoli di stato** government securities; **titoli di testa** (*Cine*) credits

titu'bante *ag* hesitant, irresolute

toast [toust] *sm inv* toasted sandwich (*generally with ham and cheese*)

toc'cante *ag* touching

toc'care /20/ vt to touch; (*tastare*) to feel; (*fig: riguardare*) to concern; (: *commuovere*) to touch, move; (: *pungere*) to hurt, wound; (: *far cenno a: argomento*) to touch on, mention ▷ vi: ~ **a** (*accadere*) to happen to; (*spettare*) to be up to; **tocca a te difenderci** it's up to you to defend us; **a chi tocca?** whose turn is it?; **mi toccò pagare** I had to pay; ~ **il fondo** (*in acqua*) to touch the bottom

toccherò ecc [tokke'rɔ] vb vedi **toccare**

togliere ['tɔʎʎere] /122/ vt (*rimuovere*) to take away (o off), remove; (*riprendere, non concedere più*) to take away, remove; (*Mat*) to take away, subtract; ~ **qc a qn** to take sth (away) from sb; **ciò non toglie che ...** nevertheless ..., be that as it may ...; **togliersi il cappello** to take off one's hat

toilette [twa'lɛt] sf inv toilet; (*mobile*) dressing table

Tokyo sf Tokyo

tolgo ecc vb vedi **togliere**

tolle'rare /72/ vt to tolerate

tolsi ecc vb vedi **togliere**

tomba sf tomb

tom'bino sm manhole cover

tombola sf (*gioco*) tombola; (*ruzzolone*) tumble

tondo, -a ag round

tonfo sm splash; (*rumore sordo*) thud; (*caduta*): **fare un ~** to take a tumble

tonifi'care /20/ vt (*muscoli, pelle*) to tone up; (*irrobustire*) to invigorate, brace

tonnel'lata sf ton

tonno sm tuna (fish)

tono sm (*gen, Mus*) tone; (*di pezzo*) key; (*di colore*) shade, tone

ton'silla sf tonsil

tonto, -a ag dull, stupid

to'pazio [to'pattsjo] sm topaz

topo sm mouse

toppa sf (*serratura*) keyhole; (*pezza*) patch

to'race [to'ratʃe] sm chest

torba sf peat

torcere ['tɔrtʃere] /106/ vt to twist; **torcersi** vpr to twist, writhe

torcia, -ce ['tɔrtʃa] sf torch; ~ **elettrica** torch (BRIT), flashlight (US)

torci'collo [tortʃi'kɔllo] sm stiff neck

tordo sm thrush

To'rino sf Turin

tor'menta sf snowstorm

tormen'tare /72/ vt to torment; **tormentarsi** vpr to fret, worry o.s.

tor'nado sm tornado

tor'nante sm hairpin bend (BRIT) o curve (US)

tor'nare /72/ vi to return, go (o come) back; (*ridiventare: anche fig*) to become (again); (*riuscire giusto, esatto: conto*) to work out; (*risultare*) to turn out (to be), prove (to be); ~ **a casa** to go (o come) home; ~ **utile** to prove o turn out (to be) useful; **torno a casa martedì** I'm going home on Tuesday

tor'neo sm tournament

tornio sm lathe

toro sm bull; **T~** Taurus

torre sf tower; (*Scacchi*) rook, castle; ~ **di controllo** (*Aer*) control tower

tor'rente sm torrent

torri'one sm keep

tor'rone sm nougat

torsi ecc vb vedi **torcere**

torsi'one sf twisting; (*Tecn*) torsion

torso sm torso, trunk; (*Arte*) torso

torsolo sm (*di cavolo ecc*) stump; (*di frutta*) core

torta sf cake

tortel'lini smpl (*Cuc*) tortellini

torto, -a pp di **torcere** ▷ ag (*ritorto*) twisted; (*storto*) twisted, crooked ▷ sm (*ingiustizia*) wrong; (*colpa*) fault; **a ~** wrongly; **aver ~** to be wrong

tortora sf turtle dove

tor'tura sf torture; **tortu'rare** /72/ vt to torture

to'sare /72/ vt (*pecora*) to shear; (*siepe*) to clip

Tos'cana *sf*: **la ~** Tuscany

'tosse *sf* cough; **ho la ~** I've got a cough

'tossico, -a, -ci, -che *ag* toxic; *(Econ)*: **titolo ~** toxic asset

tossicodipen'dente *smf* drug addict

tos'sire /55/ *vi* to cough

tosta'pane *sm inv* toaster

to'tale *ag, sm* total

toto'calcio [toto'kaltʃo] *sm* gambling pool *betting on football results* ≈ (football) pools *pl (BRIT)*

to'vaglia [to'vaλλa] *sf* tablecloth; **tovagli'olo** *sm* napkin

tra *prep (di due persone, cose)* between; *(di più persone, cose)* among(st); *(tempo: entro)* within, in; **litigano ~ (di) loro** they're fighting amongst themselves; **~ 5 giorni** in 5 days' time; **~ breve** *o* **poco** soon; **~ sé e sé** *(parlare ecc)* to oneself; **sia detto ~ noi ...** between you and me ...

traboc'care /20/ *vi* to overflow

traboc'chetto [trabok'ketto] *sm (fig)* trap

'traccia, -ce ['trattʃa] *sf (segno, striscia)* trail, track; *(orma)* tracks *pl*; *(residuo, testimonianza)* trace, sign; *(abbozzo)* outline

tracci'are [trat'tʃare] /14/ *vt* to trace, mark (out); *(disegnare)* to draw; *(fig: abbozzare)* to outline

tra'chea [tra'kɛa] *sf* windpipe, trachea

tra'colla *sf* shoulder strap; **borsa a ~** shoulder bag

tradi'mento *sm* betrayal; *(Dir, Mil)* treason

tra'dire /55/ *vt* to betray; *(coniuge)* to be unfaithful to; *(doveri: mancare)* to fail in; *(rivelare)* to give away, reveal

tradizio'nale [tradittsjo'nale] *ag* traditional

tradizi'one [tradit'tsjone] *sf* tradition

tra'durre /90/ *vt* to translate; *(spiegare)* to render, convey;

tradut'tore, -'trice *sm/f* translator; **traduzi'one** *sf* translation

'trae *vb vedi* **trarre**

traffi'cante *smf* dealer; *(peg)* trafficker

traffi'care /20/ *vi (affaccendarsi)* to busy o.s.; *(commerciare)*: **~ (in)** to trade (in), deal (in) ▷ *vt (peg)* to traffic in

'traffico, -ci *sm* traffic; *(commercio)* trade, traffic; **~ di armi/droga** arms/drug trafficking

tra'gedia [tra'dʒedja] *sf* tragedy

'traggo *ecc vb vedi* **trarre**

tra'ghetto [tra'getto] *sm* ferry(boat)

'tragico, -a, -ci, -che ['tradʒiko] *ag* tragic

tra'gitto [tra'dʒitto] *sm (passaggio)* crossing; *(viaggio)* journey

tragu'ardo *sm (Sport)* finishing line; *(fig)* goal, aim

'trai *ecc vb vedi* **trarre**

traiet'toria *sf* trajectory

trai'nare /72/ *vt* to drag, haul; *(rimorchiare)* to tow

tralasci'are [tralaʃ'ʃare] /14/ *vt (studi)* to neglect; *(dettagli)* to leave out, omit

tra'liccio [tra'littʃo] *sm (Elettr)* pylon

tram *sm inv* tram

'trama *sf (filo)* weft, woof; *(fig: argomento, maneggio)* plot

traman'dare /72/ *vt* to pass on, hand down

tram'busto *sm* turmoil

tramez'zino [tramed'dzino] *sm* sandwich

'tramite *prep* through

tramon'tare /72/ *vi* to set, go down; **tra'monto** *sm* setting; *(del sole)* sunset

trampo'lino *sm (per tuffi)* springboard, diving board; *(per lo sci)* ski-jump

tra'nello *sm* trap

'tranne *prep* except (for), but (for); **~ che** unless

tranquil'lante *sm (Med)* tranquillizer

tranquillità *sf* calm, stillness; quietness; peace of mind

tranquilliz'zare [trankwillid'dzare] /72/ *vt* to reassure

> Attenzione! In inglese esiste il verbo *to tranquillize*, che però significa "calmare con un tranquillante".

tran'quillo, -a *ag* calm, quiet; (*bambino, scolaro*) quiet; (*sereno*) with one's mind at rest; **sta' ~** don't worry

transazi'one [transat'tsjone] *sf* compromise; (*Dir*) settlement; (*Comm*) transaction, deal

tran'senna *sf* barrier

trans'genico, -a, -ci, -che [trans'dʒɛniko] *ag* genetically modified

tran'sigere [tran'sidʒere] /47/ *vi* (*venire a patti*) to compromise, come to an agreement

transi'tabile *ag* passable

transi'tare /72/ *vi* to pass

transi'tivo, -a *ag* transitive

'transito *sm* transit; **di ~** (*merci*) in transit; (*stazione*) transit *cpd*; **"divieto di ~"** "no entry"

'trapano *sm* (*utensile*) drill; (*Med*) trepan

trape'lare /72/ *vi* to leak, drip; (*fig*) to leak out

tra'pezio [tra'pɛttsjo] *sm* (*Mat*) trapezium; (*attrezzo ginnico*) trapeze

trapian'tare /72/ *vt* to transplant; **trapi'anto** *sm* transplanting; (*Med*) transplant; **trapianto cardiaco** heart transplant

'trappola *sf* trap

tra'punta *sf* quilt

'trarre /123/ *vt* to draw, pull; (*portare*) to take; (*prendere, tirare fuori*) to take (out), draw; (*derivare*) to obtain; **~ origine da qc** to have its origins o originate in sth

trasa'lire /55/ *vi* to start, jump

trasan'dato, -a *ag* shabby

trasci'nare [traʃʃi'nare] /72/ *vt* to drag; **trascinarsi** *vpr* to drag o.s. along; (*fig*) to drag on

tras'correre /28/ *vt* (*tempo*) to spend, pass ▷ *vi* to pass

tras'crivere /105/ *vt* to transcribe

trascu'rare /72/ *vt* to neglect; (*non considerare*) to disregard

trasferi'mento *sm* transfer; (*trasloco*) removal, move; **~ di chiamata** (*Tel*) call forwarding

trasfe'rire /55/ *vt* to transfer; **trasferirsi** *vpr* to move; **tras'ferta** *sf* transfer; (*indennità*) travelling expenses *pl*; (*Sport*) away game

trasfor'mare /72/ *vt* to transform, change; **trasformarsi** *vpr* to be transformed; **trasformarsi in qc** to turn into sth; **trasforma'tore** *sm* (*Elettr*) transformer

trasfusi'one *sf* (*Med*) transfusion

trasgre'dire /55/ *vt* to disobey, contravene

traslo'care /20/ *vt* to move, transfer; **tras'loco, -chi** *sm* removal

tras'mettere /63/ *vt* (*passare*): **~ qc a qn** to pass sth on to sb; (*mandare*) to send; (*Tecn, Tel, Med*) to transmit; (*TV, Radio*) to broadcast; **trasmissi'one** *sf* (*gen, Fisica, Tecn*) transmission; (*passaggio*) transmission, passing on; (*TV, Radio*) broadcast

traspa'rente *ag* transparent

traspor'tare /72/ *vt* to carry, move; (*merce*) to transport, convey; **lasciarsi ~ (da qc)** (*fig*) to let o.s. be carried away (by sth); **tras'porto** *sm* transport

'trassi *ecc vb vedi* **trarre**

trasver'sale *ag* cross(-); (*retta*) transverse; running at right angles

'tratta *sf* (*Econ*) draft; **la ~ delle bianche** the white slave trade

tratta'mento *sm* treatment; (*servizio*) service

trat'tare /72/ *vt* (*gen*) to treat; (*commerciare*) to deal in; (*svolgere: argomento*) to discuss, deal with;

(*negoziare*) to negotiate ▷ vi: **~ di** to deal with; **~ con** (*persona*) to deal with; **si tratta di ...** it's about ...

tratte'nere /121/ vt (*far rimanere: persona*) to detain; (*intrattenere: ospiti*) to entertain; (*tenere, frenare, reprimere*) to hold back, keep back; (*astenersi dal consegnare*) to hold, keep; (*detrarre: somma*) to deduct; **trattenersi** vpr (*astenersi*) to restrain o.s., stop o.s.; (*soffermarsi*) to stay, remain

trat'tino sm dash; (*in parole composte*) hyphen

'tratto, -a pp di **trarre** ▷ sm (*di penna, matita*) stroke; (*parte*) part, piece; (*di strada*) stretch; (*di mare, cielo*) expanse; (*di tempo*) period (of time)

trat'tore sm tractor

tratto'ria sf (*small*) restaurant

'trauma, -i sm trauma

tra'vaglio [tra'vaʎʎo] sm (*angoscia*) pain, suffering; (*Med*) pains pl

trava'sare /72/ vt to decant

tra'versa sf (*trave*) crosspiece; (*via*) sidestreet; (*Ferr*) sleeper (BRIT), (railroad) tie (US); (*Calcio*) crossbar

traver'sata sf crossing; (*Aer*) flight, trip

traver'sie sfpl mishaps, misfortunes

tra'verso, -a ag oblique; **di ~** ag askew ▷ av sideways; **andare di ~** (*cibo*) to go down the wrong way; **guardare di ~** to look askance at

travesti'mento sm disguise

traves'tire /45/ vt to disguise; **travestirsi** vpr to disguise o.s.

tra'volgere [tra'vɔldʒere] /96/ vt to sweep away, carry away; (*fig*) to overwhelm

tre num three

'treccia, -ce ['trettʃa] sf plait, braid

tre'cento [tre'tʃento] num three hundred ▷ sm: **il T~** the fourteenth century

'tredici ['treditʃi] num thirteen

'tregua sf truce; (*fig*) respite

tre'mare /72/ vi: **~ di** (*freddo ecc*) to shiver o tremble with; (*paura, rabbia*) to shake o tremble with

tre'mendo, -a ag terrible, awful

> Attenzione! In inglese esiste la parola *tremendous*, che però significa *enorme* oppure *fantastico, strepitoso*.

'tremito sm trembling no pl; shaking no pl; shivering no pl

'treno sm train; **~ di gomme** set of tyres o (BRIT) o tires (US); **~ merci** goods (BRIT) o freight train; **~ viaggiatori** passenger train

TRENI

There are several different types of train in Italy. "Regionali" and "interregionali" are local trains which stop at every small town and village; the former operate within regional boundaries, while the latter may cross them. "Diretti" are ordinary trains for which passengers do not pay a supplement; the main difference from "espressi" is that the latter are long-distance and mainly run at night. "Intercity" and "eurocity" are faster and entail a supplement. "Rapidi" only contain first-class seats, and the high-speed "pendolino", which offers both first- and second-class travel, runs between the major cities.

'trenta num thirty; **tren'tesimo, -a** num thirtieth; **tren'tina** sf: **una trentina (di)** thirty or so, about thirty

trepi'dante ag anxious

triango'lare ag triangular

tri'angolo sm triangle

tri'bù sf inv tribe

tri'buna sf (*podio*) platform; (*in aule ecc*) gallery; (*di stadio*) stand

tribu'nale sm court

tri'ciclo [tri'tʃiklo] *sm* tricycle
tri'foglio [tri'fɔʎʎo] *sm* clover
'triglia ['triʎʎa] *sf* red mullet
tri'mestre *sm* period of three months; (*Ins*) term, quarter (*US*); (*Comm*) quarter
trin'cea [trin'tʃea] *sf* trench
trion'fare /72/ *vi* to triumph, win; **~ su** to triumph over, overcome; **tri'onfo** *sm* triumph
tripli'care /20/ *vt* to triple
'triplo, -a *ag* triple; treble ▷ *sm*: **il ~ (di)** three times as much (as); **la spesa è tripla** it costs three times as much
'trippa *sf* (*Cuc*) tripe
'triste *ag* sad; (*luogo*) dreary, gloomy
tri'tare /72/ *vt* to mince, grind (*US*)
trivi'ale *ag* vulgar, low
tro'feo *sm* trophy
'tromba *sf* (*Mus*) trumpet; (*Aut*) horn; **~ d'aria** whirlwind; **~ delle scale** stairwell
trom'bone *sm* trombone
trom'bosi *sf* thrombosis
tron'care /20/ *vt* to cut off; (*spezzare*) to break off
'tronco, -a, -chi, -che *ag* cut off; broken off; (*Ling*) truncated; (*fig*) cut short ▷ *sm* (*Bot, Anat*) trunk; (*fig: tratto*) section; **licenziare qn in ~** to fire sb on the spot
'trono *sm* throne
tropi'cale *ag* tropical

PAROLA CHIAVE

'troppo, -a *det* (*in eccesso: quantità*) too much; (: *numero*) too many; **c'era troppa gente** there were too many people; **fa troppo caldo** it's too hot
▶ *pron* (*in eccesso: quantità*) too much; (: *numero*) too many; **ne hai messo troppo** you've put in too much; **meglio troppi che pochi** better too many than too few
▶ *av* (*eccessivamente: con ag, av*) too; (: *con vb*) too much; **troppo amaro/tardi** too bitter/late; **lavora troppo** he works too much; **costa troppo** it costs too much; **di troppo** too much; too many; **qualche tazza di troppo** a few cups too many; **5 euro di troppo** 5 euros too much; **essere di troppo** to be in the way

'trota *sf* trout
'trottola *sf* spinning top
tro'vare /72/ *vt* to find; (*giudicare*): **trovo che** I find o think that; **trovarsi** *vpr* (*reciproco: incontrarsi*) to meet; (*essere, stare*) to be; (*arrivare, capitare*) to find o.s.; **andare a ~ qn** to go and see sb; **~ qn colpevole** to find sb guilty; **trovarsi bene/male** (*in un luogo, con qn*) to get on well/badly
truc'care /20/ *vt* (*falsare*) to fake; (*attore ecc*) to make up; (*travestire*) to disguise; (*Sport*) to fix; (*Aut*) to soup up; **truccarsi** *vpr* to make up (one's face)
'trucco, -chi *sm* trick; (*cosmesi*) make-up
'truffa *sf* fraud, swindle; **truffare** /72/ *vt* to swindle, cheat
truffa'tore, -'trice *sm/f* swindler, cheat
'truppa *sf* troop
tu *pron* you; **tu stesso(a)** you yourself; **dare del tu a qn** to address sb as "tu"
'tubo *sm* tube; (*per conduttore*) pipe; **~ digerente** (*Anat*) alimentary canal, digestive tract; **~ di scappamento** (*Aut*) exhaust pipe
tuf'fare /72/ *vt* to plunge; **tuffarsi** *vpr* to plunge, dive
'tuffo *sm* dive; (*breve bagno*) dip
tuli'pano *sm* tulip
tu'more *sm* (*Med*) tumour
Tuni'sia *sf*: **la ~** Tunisia
'tuo (*f* **'tua**, *pl* **'tuoi**, **'tue**) *det*: **il ~, la tua** *ecc* your ▷ *pron*: **il ~, la tua** *ecc* yours
tuo'nare /72/ *vi* to thunder; **tuona** it is thundering, there's some thunder
tu'ono *sm* thunder

tu'orlo sm yolk

tur'bante sm turban

tur'bare /72/ vt to disturb, trouble

tur'bato, -a ag upset; (preoccupato, ansioso) anxious

turbo'lenza [turbo'lɛntsa] sf turbulence

tur'chese [tur'kese] sf turquoise

Tur'chia [tur'kia] sf: **la ~** Turkey

'turco, -a, -chi, -che ag Turkish ▷ sm/f Turk (Turkish woman) ▷ sm (Ling) Turkish; **parlare ~** (fig) to talk double Dutch

tu'rismo sm tourism; tourist industry; **~ sessuale** sex tourism; **tu'rista, -i, -e** smf tourist; **tu'ristico, -a, -ci, -che** ag tourist cpd

'turno sm turn; (di lavoro) shift; **di ~** (soldato, medico, custode) on duty; **a ~** (rispondere) in turn; (lavorare) in shifts; **fare a ~ a fare qc** to take turns to do sth; **è il suo ~** it's your (o his ecc) turn

'turpe ag filthy, vile

'tuta sf overalls pl; (Sport) tracksuit

tu'tela sf (Dir: di minore) guardianship; (: protezione) protection; (difesa) defence

tutor ['tiutor] sm inv (Aut) speed monitoring system

tutta'via cong nevertheless, yet

PAROLA CHIAVE

'tutto, -a det 1 (intero) all; **tutto il latte** all the milk; **tutta la notte** all night, the whole night; **tutto il libro** the whole book; **tutta una bottiglia** a whole bottle

2 (pl, collettivo) all; every; **tutti i libri** all the books; **tutte le notti** every night; **tutti i venerdì** every Friday; **tutti gli uomini** all the men; (collettivo) all men; **tutto l'anno** all year long; **tutti e due** both o each of us (o them o you); **tutti e cinque** all five of us (o them o you)

3 (completamente): **era tutta sporca** she was all dirty; **tremava tutto** he was trembling all over; **è tutta sua madre** she's just o exactly like her mother

4: **a tutt'oggi** so far, up till now; **a tutta velocità** at full o top speed

▷ pron 1 (ogni cosa) everything, all; (qualsiasi cosa) anything; **ha mangiato tutto** he's eaten everything; **tutto considerato** all things considered; **100 euro in tutto** 100 euros in all; **in tutto eravamo 50** there were 50 of us in all

2: **tutti, e** (ognuno) all, everybody; **vengono tutti** they are all coming, everybody's coming; **tutti quanti** all and sundry

▷ av (completamente) entirely, quite; **è tutto il contrario** it's quite o exactly the opposite; **tutt'al più: saranno stati tutt'al più una cinquantina** there were about fifty of them at (the very) most; **tutt'al più possiamo prendere un treno** if the worst comes to the worst we can take a train; **tutt'altro** on the contrary; **è tutt'altro che felice** he's anything but happy; **tutt'a un tratto** suddenly

▷ sm: **il tutto** the whole lot, all of it

tut'tora av still

TV [ti'vu] sf inv (= televisione) TV ▷ sigla = **Treviso**

u

ubbidi'ente ag obedient
ubbi'dire /55/ vi to obey; **~ a** to obey;
(veicolo, macchina) to respond to
ubria'care /20/ vt: **~ qn** to get sb
drunk; (alcool) to make sb drunk; (fig) to
make sb's head spin o reel; **ubriacarsi**
vpr to get drunk; **ubriacarsi di** (fig) to
become intoxicated with
ubri'aco, -a, -chi, -che ag, sm/f
drunk
uc'cello [ut'tʃello] sm bird
uc'cidere [ut'tʃidere] /34/ vt to kill;
uccidersi vpr (suicidarsi) to kill o.s.;
(perdere la vita) to be killed
u'dire /124/ vt to hear
u'dito sm (sense of) hearing
UE sigla f (= Unione Europea) EU
UEM sigla f (= Unione economica e
monetaria) EMU
'uffa escl tut!
uffici'ale [uffi'tʃale] ag official ▷ sm
(Amm) official, officer; (Mil) officer;
~ di stato civile registrar

uf'ficio [uffitʃo] sm (gen) office;
(dovere) duty; (mansione) task,
function, job; (agenzia) agency,
bureau; (Rel) service; **d'~** ag office
cpd; official ▷ av officially; **~ di
collocamento** employment office;
~ informazioni information bureau;
~ oggetti smarriti lost property
office (BRIT), lost and found (US);
~ postale post office; **~ vendite/
del personale** sales/personnel
department
uffici'oso, -a [uffi'tʃoso] ag unofficial
uguagli'anza [ugwaʎ'ʎantsa] sf
equality
uguagli'are [ugwaʎ'ʎare] /27/ vt
to make equal; (essere uguale) to
equal, be equal to; (livellare) to level;
uguagliarsi vpr: **uguagliarsi a** o **con
qn** (paragonarsi) to compare o.s. to sb
ugu'ale ag equal; (identico) identical,
the same; (uniforme) level, even ▷ av:
costano ~ they cost the same; **sono
bravi ~** they're equally good
UIL sigla f (= Unione Italiana del Lavoro)
trade union federation
'ulcera ['ultʃera] sf ulcer
U'livo sm (Pol) centre-left coalition
ulteri'ore ag further
ultima'mente av lately, of late
ulti'mare /72/ vt to finish, complete
'ultimo, -a ag (finale) last; (estremo)
farthest, utmost; (recente:
notizia, moda) latest; (fig: sommo,
fondamentale) ultimate ▷ sm/f last
(one); **fino all'~** to the last, until
the end; **da ~, in ~** in the end; **per ~**
(entrare, arrivare) last; **abitare all'~
piano** to live on the top floor
ultravio'letto, -a ag ultraviolet
ulu'lare /72/ vi to howl
umanità sf humanity
u'mano, -a ag human; (comprensivo)
humane
umidità sf dampness; humidity
'umido, -a ag damp; (mano, occhi)
moist; (clima) humid ▷ sm dampness,
damp; **carne in ~** stew

'**umile** *ag* humble
umili'are /19/ *vt* to humiliate;
umiliarsi *vpr* to humble o.s.
u'more *sm* (*disposizione d'animo*)
mood; (*carattere*) temper; **di buon/
cattivo ~** in a good/bad mood
umo'rismo *sm* humour (BRIT),
humor (US); **avere il senso dell'~** to
have a sense of humour; **umo'ristico,
-a, -ci, -che** *ag* humorous, funny
u'nanime *ag* unanimous
unci'netto [untʃi'netto] *sm* crochet
hook
un'cino [un'tʃino] *sm* hook
undi'cenne [undi'tʃɛnne] *ag*, *smf*
eleven-year-old
undi'cesimo, -a [undi'tʃɛzimo] *ag*
eleventh
'**undici** ['unditʃi] *num* eleven
'**ungere** ['undʒere] /5/ *vt* to grease,
oil; (*Rel*) to anoint; (*fig*) to flatter,
butter up
unghe'rese [unge'rese] *ag*, *smf*, *sm*
Hungarian
Unghe'ria [unge'ria] *sf*: **l'~** Hungary
'**unghia** ['ungja] *sf* (*Anat*) nail; (*di
animale*) claw; (*di rapace*) talon; (*di
cavallo*) hoof
ungu'ento *sm* ointment
'**unico, -a, -ci, -che** *ag* (*solo*) only;
(*ineguagliabile*) unique; (*singolo:
binario*) single; **è figlio ~** he's an
only child
unifi'care /20/ *vt* to unite,
unify; (*sistemi*) to standardize;
unificazi'one *sf* uniting; unification;
standardization
uni'forme *ag* uniform; (*superficie*)
even ▷ *sf* (*divisa*) uniform
uni'one *sf* union; (*fig: concordia*) unity,
harmony; **U~ Europea** European
Union; **ex U~ Sovietica** former
Soviet Union
u'nire /55/ *vt* to unite; (*congiungere*)
to join, connect; (: *ingredienti, colori*)
to combine; (*in matrimonio*) to unite,
join together; **unirsi** *vpr* to unite; (*in
matrimonio*) to be joined together;

~ qc a to unite sth with; to join *o*
connect sth with; to combine sth
with; **unirsi a** (*gruppo, società*) to join
unità *sf inv* (*unione, concordia*) unity;
(*Mat, Mil, Comm, di misura*) unit; **~ di
misura** unit of measurement
u'nito, -a *ag* (*paese*) united; (*amici,
famiglia*) close; **in tinta unita** plain,
self-coloured
univer'sale *ag* universal; general
università *sf inv* university
uni'verso *sm* universe

PAROLA CHIAVE

'**uno, -a** (*dav sm* **un** + C, V, **uno** + *s
impura, gn, pn, ps, x, z; dav sf* **un'** +
V,* **una** + C) *det* **1** *a*; (*dav vocale*) an;
un bambino a child; **una strada** a
street; **uno zingaro** a gypsy
2 (*intensivo*): **ho avuto una paura!** I
got such a fright!
▶ *pron* **1** one; **prendine uno** take one
(of them); **l'uno o l'altro** either (of
them); **l'uno e l'altro** both (of them);
aiutarsi l'un l'altro to help one
another *o* each other; **sono entrati
l'uno dopo l'altro** they came in one
after the other
2 (*un tale*) someone, somebody
3 (*con valore impersonale*) one, you; **se
uno vuole** if one wants, if you want
▶ *num* one; **una mela e due pere** one
apple and two pears; **uno più uno
fa due** one plus one equals two, one
and one are two
▶ *sf*: **è l'una** it's one (o'clock)

'**unsi** *ecc vb vedi* **ungere**
'**unto, -a** *pp di* **ungere** ▷ *ag* greasy,
oily ▷ *sm* grease
u'omo (*pl* **uomini**) *sm* man; **da ~** (*abito,
scarpe*) men's, for men; **~ d'affari**
businessman; **~ di paglia** stooge;
~ politico politician; **~ rana** frogman
u'ovo (*pl f* **uova**) *sm* egg; **~ affogato
o in camicia** poached egg; **~
bazzotto/sodo** soft-/hard-boiled

egg; **~ alla coque** boiled egg; **~ di Pasqua** Easter egg; **~ al tegame** o **all'occhio di bue** fried egg; **uova strapazzate** scrambled eggs

ura'gano *sm* hurricane

urba'nistica *sf* town planning

ur'bano, -a *ag* urban, city *cpd*, town *cpd*; (*Tel: chiamata*) local; (*fig*) urbane

ur'gente [ur'dʒɛnte] *ag* urgent; ur'genza *sf* urgency; **in caso d'urgenza** in (case of) an emergency; **d'urgenza** *av* emergency; *av* urgently, as a matter of urgency

ur'lare /72/ *vi* (*persona*) to scream, yell; (*animale, vento*) to howl ▷ *vt* to scream, yell

'urlo (*pl m* **urli** o *pl f* **urla**) *sm* scream, yell; howl

URP *sigla m* (= *Ufficio Relazioni con il Pubblico*) PR Office

urrà *escl* hurrah!

U.R.S.S. *sigla f* = **Unione delle Repubbliche Socialiste Sovietiche**; **l'~** the USSR

ur'tare /72/ *vt* to bump into, knock against, crash into; (*fig: irritare*) to annoy ▷ *vi*: **~ contro** o **in** to bump into, knock against; (*fig: imbattersi*) to come up against; **urtarsi** *vpr* (*reciproco: scontrarsi*) to collide; (: *fig*) to clash; (*irritarsi*) to get annoyed

'USA *smpl*: **gli ~** the USA

u'sanza [u'zantsa] *sf* custom; (*moda*) fashion

u'sare /72/ *vt* to use, employ ▷ *vi* (*essere di moda*) to be fashionable; (*servirsi*): **~ di** to use; (*diritto*) to exercise; (*essere solito*): **~ fare** to be in the habit of doing, be accustomed to doing ▷ *vb impers*: **qui usa così** it's the custom round here; u'sato, -a *ag* used; (*consumato*) worn; (*di seconda mano*) used, second-hand ▷ *sm* second-hand goods *pl*

u'scire [uʃʃire] /125/ *vi* (*gen*) to come out; (*partire, andare a passeggio, a uno spettacolo ecc*) to go out; (*essere sorteggiato: numero*) to come up;

~ da (*gen*) to leave; (*posto*) to go (*o* come) out of, leave; (*solco, vasca ecc*) to come out of; (*muro*) to stick out of; (*competenza ecc*) to be outside of; (*infanzia, adolescenza*) to leave behind; (*famiglia nobile ecc*) to come from; **~ da** o **di casa** to go out; (*fig*) to leave home; **~ in automobile** to go out in the car, go for a drive; **~ di strada** (*Aut*) to go off o leave the road

u'scita [uʃʃita] *sf* (*passaggio, varco*) exit, way out; (*per divertimento*) outing; (*Econ: somma*) expenditure; (*Teat*) entrance; (*fig: battuta*) witty remark; **~ di sicurezza** emergency exit

usi'gnolo [uziɲ'nɔlo] *sm* nightingale

'uso *sm* (*utilizzazione*) use; (*esercizio*) practice; (*abitudine*) custom; **a ~ di** for (the use of); **d'~** (*corrente*) in use; **fuori ~** out of use; **per ~ esterno** for external use only

usti'one *sf* burn

usu'ale *ag* common, everyday

u'sura *sf* usury; (*logoramento*) wear (and tear)

uten'sile *sm* tool, implement; **utensili da cucina** kitchen utensils

u'tente *smf* user

'utero *sm* uterus

'utile *ag* useful ▷ *sm* (*vantaggio*) advantage, benefit; (*Econ: profitto*) profit

utiliz'zare [utilid'dzare] /72/ *vt* to use, make use of, utilize

UVA *abbr* (= *ultravioletto prossimo*) UVA

'uva *sf* grapes *pl*: **~ passa** raisins *pl*: **~ spina** gooseberry

UVB *abbr* (= *ultravioletto lontano*) UVB

u

V

v. *abbr* (= *vedi*) v.

va, va' *vb vedi* **andare**

va'cante *ag* vacant

va'canza [va'kantsa] *sf* (*riposo, ferie*) holiday(s *pl*) (BRIT), vacation (US); (*giorno di permesso*) day off, holiday; **vacanze** *sfpl* (*periodo di ferie*) holidays, vacation *sg*: **essere/andare in ~** to be/go on holiday *o* vacation; **vacanze estive** summer holiday(s) *o* vacation; **vacanze natalizie** Christmas holidays *o* vacation

> Attenzione! In inglese esiste la parola *vacancy* che però indica un posto vacante o una camera disponibile.

'vacca, -che *sf* cow

vacci'nare [vattʃi'nare] /72/ *vt* to vaccinate

vac'cino [vat'tʃino] *sm* (*Med*) vaccine

vacil'lare [vatʃil'lare] /72/ *vi* to sway, wobble; (*fiamma, luce*) to flicker; (*fig: memoria, coraggio*) to be failing, falter

'vacuo, -a *ag* (*fig*) empty, vacuous

'vado *ecc vb vedi* **andare**

vaga'bondo, -a *sm/f* tramp, vagrant

va'gare /80/ *vi* to wander

vagherò *ecc* [vage'rɔ] *vb vedi* **vagare**

va'gina [va'dʒina] *sf* vagina

'vaglia ['vaʎʎa] *sm inv* money order; **~ postale** postal order

vagli'are [vaʎ'ʎare] /27/ *vt* to sift; (*fig*) to weigh up

'vago, -a, -ghi, -ghe *ag* vague

va'gone *sm* (*Ferr: per passeggeri*) coach; (*: per merci*) truck, wagon; **~ letto** sleeper, sleeping car; **~ ristorante** dining *o* restaurant car

'vai *vb vedi* **andare**

vai'olo *sm* smallpox

va'langa, -ghe *sf* avalanche

va'lere /126/ *vi* (*avere forza, potenza*) to have influence; (*essere valido*) to be valid; (*avere vigore, autorità*) to hold, apply; (*essere capace: poeta, studente*) to be good, be able ▷ *vt* (*prezzo, sforzo*) to be worth; (*corrispondere*) to correspond to; (*procurare*): **~ qc a qn** to earn sb sth; **valersi** *vpr*: **valersi di** to make use of, take advantage of; **far ~** (*autorità ecc*) to assert; **vale a dire** that is to say; **~ la pena** to be worth the effort *o* worth it

'valgo *ecc vb vedi* **valere**

vali'care /20/ *vt* to cross

'valico, -chi *sm* (*passo*) pass

'valido, -a *ag* valid; (*rimedio*) effective; (*aiuto*) real; (*persona*) worthwhile

vali'getta *sf* briefcase; **~ ventiquattrore** overnight bag *o* case

va'ligia, -gie *o* **-ge** [va'lidʒa] *sf* (*suit*) case; **fare le valigie** to pack (up)

'valle *sf* valley; **a ~** (*di fiume*) downstream; **scendere a ~** to go downhill

va'lore *sm* (*gen*) value; (*merito*) merit, worth; (*coraggio*) valour , courage; (*Finanza: titolo*) security; **valori** *smpl* (*oggetti preziosi*) valuables

valoriz'zare [valorid'dzare] /72/ vt (terreno) to develop; (fig) to make the most of

va'luta sf currency, money; (Banca): **~ 15 gennaio** interest to run from January 15th

valu'tare /72/ vt (casa, gioiello, fig) to value; (stabilire: peso, entrate, fig) to estimate

'valvola sf (Tecn, Anat) valve; (Elettr) fuse

'valzer ['valtser] sm inv waltz

vam'pata sf (di fiamma) blaze; (di calore) blast; (: al viso) flush

vam'piro sm vampire

vanda'lismo sm vandalism

'vandalo sm vandal

vaneggi'are [vaned'dʒare] /62/ vi to rave

'vanga, -ghe sf spade

van'gelo [van'dʒɛlo] sm gospel

va'niglia [va'niʎʎa] sf vanilla

vanità sf vanity; (di promessa) emptiness; (di sforzo) futility; **vani'toso, -a** ag vain, conceited

'vanno vb vedi **andare**

'vano, -a ag vain ▷ sm (spazio) space; (apertura) opening; (stanza) room

van'taggio [van'taddʒo] sm advantage; **essere/portarsi in ~** (Sport) to be in/take the lead; **vantaggi'oso, -a** ag advantageous, favourable

van'tare /72/ vt to praise, speak highly of; **vantarsi** vpr: **vantarsi (di/di aver fatto)** to boast o brag (about/about having done)

'vanvera sf: **a ~** haphazardly; **parlare a ~** to talk nonsense

va'pore sm vapour; (anche: **~ acqueo**) steam; (nave) steamer; **a ~** (turbina ecc) steam cpd; **al ~** (Cuc) steamed

va'rare /72/ vt (Naut, fig) to launch; (Dir) to pass

var'care /20/ vt to cross

'varco, -chi sm passage; **aprirsi un ~ tra la folla** to push one's way through the crowd

vare'china [vare'kina] sf bleach

vari'abile ag variable; (tempo, umore) changeable, variable ▷ sf (Mat) variable

vari'cella [vari'tʃɛlla] sf chickenpox

vari'coso, -a ag varicose

varietà sf inv variety ▷ sm inv variety show

'vario, -a ag varied; (parecchi: col sostantivo al pl) various; (mutevole: umore) changeable

'varo sm (Naut, fig) launch; (di leggi) passing

varrò ecc vb vedi **valere**

Var'savia sf Warsaw

va'saio sm potter

'vasca, -sche sf basin; (anche: **~ da bagno**) bathtub, bath

vas'chetta [vas'ketta] sf (per gelato) tub; (per sviluppare fotografie) dish

vase'lina sf vaseline

'vaso sm (recipiente) pot; (: barattolo) jar; (: decorativo) vase; (Anat) vessel; **~ da fiori** vase; (per piante) flowerpot

vas'soio sm tray

'vasto, -a ag vast, immense

Vati'cano sm: **il ~** the Vatican

ve pron, av vedi **vi**

vecchi'aia [vek'kjaja] sf old age

'vecchio, -a ['vɛkkjo] ag old ▷ sm/f old man/woman; **i vecchi** the old

ve'dere /127/ vt, vi to see; **vedersi** vpr to meet, see one another; **avere a che ~ con** to have to do with; **far ~ qc a qn** to show sb sth; **farsi ~** to show o.s.; (farsi vivo) to show one's face; **vedi di non farlo** make sure o see you don't do it; **non (ci) si vede** (è buio ecc) you can't see a thing; **non lo posso ~** (fig) I can't stand him

ve'detta sf (sentinella, posto) look-out; (Naut) patrol boat

'vedovo, -a sm/f widower (widow)

vedrò ecc vb vedi **vedere**

ve'duta sf view; **vedute** sfpl (fig: opinioni) views; **di larghe o ampie vedute** broad-minded; **di vedute limitate** narrow-minded

vege'tale [vedʒe'tale] *ag, sm* vegetable

vegetari'ano, -a [vedʒeta'rjano] *ag, sm/f* vegetarian

vegetazi'one [vedʒetat'tsjone] *sf* vegetation

'vegeto, -a ['vɛdʒeto] *ag (pianta)* thriving; *(persona)* strong, vigorous

'veglia ['veʎʎa] *sf* wakefulness; *(sorveglianza)* watch; *(trattenimento)* evening gathering; **fare la ~ a un malato** to watch over a sick person

vegli'one [veʎ'ʎone] *sm* ball, dance; **~ di Capodanno** New Year's Eve party

ve'icolo *sm* vehicle

'vela *sf (Naut: tela)* sail; *(: sport)* sailing

ve'leno *sm* poison; **vele'noso, -a** *ag* poisonous

veli'ero *sm* sailing ship

vel'luto *sm* velvet; **~ a coste** cord

'velo *sm* veil; *(tessuto)* voile

ve'loce [ve'lotʃe] *ag* fast, quick ▷ *av* fast, quickly; **velocità** *sf* speed; **a forte velocità** at high speed; **velocità di crociera** cruising speed

'vena *sf (gen)* vein; *(filone)* vein, seam; *(fig: ispirazione)* inspiration; *(: umore)* mood; **essere in ~ di qc** to be in the mood for sth

ve'nale *ag (prezzo, valore)* market *cpd*; *(fig)* venal; mercenary

ven'demmia *sf (raccolta)* grape harvest; *(quantità d'uva)* grape crop, grapes *pl*; *(vino ottenuto)* vintage

'vendere /29/ *vt* to sell; **"vendesi"** "for sale"

ven'detta *sf* revenge

vendi'care /20/ *vt* to avenge; **vendicarsi** *vpr*: **vendicarsi (di)** to avenge o.s. (for); *(per rancore)* to take one's revenge (for); **vendicarsi su qn** to revenge o.s. on sb

'vendita *sf* sale; **la ~** *(attività)* selling; *(smercio)* sales *pl*; **in ~** on sale; **~ all'asta** sale by auction; **~ per telefono** telesales *sg*

vene'rare /72/ *vt* to venerate

venerdì *sm inv* Friday; **di** *o* **il ~** on Fridays; **V~ Santo** Good Friday

ve'nereo, -a *ag* venereal

Ve'nezia [ve'nɛttsja] *sf* Venice

'vengo *ecc vb vedi* **venire**

veni'ale *ag* venial

ve'nire /128/ *vi* to come; *(riuscire: dolce, fotografia)* to turn out; *(come ausiliare: essere)*: **viene ammirato da tutti** he is admired by everyone; **~ da** to come from; **quanto viene?** how much does it cost?; **far ~** *(mandare a chiamare)* to send for; **~ giù** to come down; **~ meno** *(svenire)* to faint; **~ meno a qc** not to fulfil sth; **~ su** to come up; **~ via** to come away; **~ a trovare qn** to come and see sb

'venni *ecc vb vedi* **venire**

ven'taglio [ven'taʎʎo] *sm* fan

ven'tata *sf* gust (of wind)

ven'tenne *ag*: **una ragazza ~** a twenty-year-old girl, a girl of twenty

ven'tesimo, -a *num* twentieth

'venti *num* twenty

venti'lare /72/ *vt (stanza)* to air, ventilate; *(fig: idea, proposta)* to air; **ventila'tore** *sm* ventilator, fan

ven'tina *sf*: **una ~ (di)** around twenty, twenty or so

'vento *sm* wind

'ventola *sf (Aut, Tecn)* fan

ven'tosa *sf (Zool)* sucker; *(di gomma)* suction pad

ven'toso, -a *ag* windy

'ventre *sm* stomach

'vera *sf* wedding ring

vera'mente *av* really

ve'randa *sf* veranda(h)

ver'bale *ag* verbal ▷ *sm (di riunione)* minutes *pl*

'verbo *sm (Ling)* verb; *(parola)* word; *(Rel)*: **il V~** the Word

'verde *ag, sm* green; **~ bottiglia/ oliva** bottle/olive green; **essere al ~** to be broke

ver'detto *sm* verdict

ver'dura *sf* vegetables *pl*

'vergine ['verdʒine] *sf* virgin; **V~** Virgo ▷ *ag* virgin; (*ragazza*): **essere ~** to be a virgin

ver'gogna [ver'goɲɲa] *sf* shame; (*timidezza*) shyness, embarrassment; **vergo'gnarsi** /15/ *vpr*: **vergognarsi (di)** to be *o* feel ashamed (of); to be shy (about), be embarrassed (about); **vergo'gnoso, -a** *ag* ashamed; (*timido*) shy, embarrassed; (*causa di vergogna: azione*) shameful

ve'rifica, -che *sf* checking *no pl*; check

verifi'care /20/ *vt* (*controllare*) to check; (*confermare*) to confirm, bear out

verità *sf inv* truth

'verme *sm* worm

ver'miglio [ver'miʎʎo] *sm* vermilion, scarlet

ver'nice [ver'nitʃe] *sf* (*colorazione*) paint; (*trasparente*) varnish; (*pelle*) patent leather; **"~ fresca"** "wet paint"; **vernici'are** /19/ *vt* to paint; to varnish

'vero, -a *ag* (*veridico: fatti, testimonianza*) true; (*autentico*) real ▷ *sm* (*verità*) truth; (*realtà*) (real) life; **un ~ e proprio delinquente** a real criminal, an out and out criminal

vero'simile *ag* likely, probable

verrò *ecc vb vedi* **venire**

ver'ruca, -che *sf* wart

versa'mento *sm* (*pagamento*) payment; (*deposito di denaro*) deposit

ver'sante *sm* slopes *pl*, side

ver'sare /72/ *vt* (*fare uscire: vino, farina*) to pour (out); (*spargere: lacrime, sangue*) to shed; (*rovesciare*) to spill; (*Econ*) to pay; (*: depositare*) to deposit, pay in

versa'tile *ag* versatile

versi'one *sf* version; (*traduzione*) translation

'verso *sm* (*di poesia*) verse, line; (*di animale, uccello, venditore ambulante*) cry; (*direzione*) direction; (*modo*) way; (*di foglio di carta*) verso; (*di moneta*) reverse; **versi** *smpl* (*poesia*) verse *sg* ▷ *prep* (*in direzione di*) toward(s); (*nei pressi di*) near, around (about); (*in senso temporale*) about, around; (*nei confronti di*) for; **non c'è ~ di persuaderlo** there's no way of persuading him, he can't be persuaded; **~ di me** towards me; **~ sera** towards evening

'vertebra *sf* vertebra

verte'brale *ag* vertebral; **colonna ~** spinal column, spine

verti'cale *ag, sf* vertical

'vertice ['vɛrtitʃe] *sm* summit, top; (*Mat*) vertex; **conferenza al ~** (*Pol*) summit conference

ver'tigine [ver'tidʒine] *sf* dizziness *no pl*; dizzy spell; (*Med*) vertigo; **avere le vertigini** to feel dizzy

ve'scica, -che [veʃʃika] *sf* (*Anat*) bladder; (*Med*) blister

'vescovo *sm* bishop

'vespa *sf* wasp

ves'taglia [ves'taʎʎa] *sf* dressing gown

ves'tire /45/ *vt* (*bambino, malato*) to dress; (*avere indosso*) to have on, wear; **vestirsi** *vpr* to dress, get dressed; **ves'tito, -a** *ag* dressed ▷ *sm* garment; (*da donna*) dress; (*da uomo*) suit; **vestiti** *smpl* (*indumenti*) clothes; **vestito di bianco** dressed in white

veteri'nario, -a *ag* veterinary ▷ *sm* veterinary surgeon (*BRIT*), veterinarian (*US*), vet

'veto *sm inv* veto

ve'traio *sm* glassmaker; (*per finestre*) glazier

ve'trato, -a *ag* (*porta, finestra*) glazed; (*che contiene vetro*) glass *cpd* ▷ *sf* glass door (*o* window); (*di chiesa*) stained glass window; **carta vetrata** sandpaper

ve'trina *sf* (*di negozio*) (shop) window; (*armadio*) display cabinet; **vetri'nista, -i, -e** *smf* window dresser

'vetro *sm* glass; (*per finestra, porta*) pane (of glass)

'vetta *sf* peak, summit, top

vet'tura *sf* (*carrozza*) carriage; (*Ferr*) carriage (*BRIT*), car (*US*); (*auto*) car (*BRIT*), automobile (*US*)

vezzeggia'tivo [vettseddʒa'tivo]
  sm (*Ling*) term of endearment
vi (*dav lo, la, li, le, ne diventa* **ve**) *pron*
  (*oggetto*) you; (*complemento di termine*)
  (to) you; (*riflessivo*) yourselves;
  (*reciproco*) each other ▷ *av* (*lì*) there;
  (*qui*) here; (*per questo/quel luogo*)
  through here/there; **vi è/sono**
  there is/are
'**via** *sf* (*gen*) way; (*strada*) street;
  (*sentiero, pista*) path, track; (*Amm:
  procedimento*) channels *pl* ▷ *prep*
  (*passando per*) via, by way of ▷ *av*
  away ▷ *escl* go away!; (*suvvia*) come
  on!; (*Sport*) go! ▷ *sm* (*Sport*) starting
  signal; **per ~ di** (*a causa di*) because
  of, on account of; **in** *o* **per ~** on the
  way; **in ~ di guarigione** on the
  road to recovery; **per ~ aerea** by
  air; (*lettere*) by airmail; **andare/
  essere ~** to go/be away; **~ ~ che** (*a
  mano a mano*) as; **dare il ~** (*Sport*)
  to give the starting signal; **dare il
  ~ a** (*fig*) to start; **in ~ provvisoria**
  provisionally; **V~ lattea** (*Astr*) Milky
  Way; **~ di mezzo** middle course; **non
  c'è ~ di scampo** *o* **d'uscita** there's
  no way out
via'dotto *sm* viaduct
viaggi'are [viad'dʒare] /62/ *vi*
  to travel; **viaggia'tore, -'trice** *ag*
  travelling ▷ *sm* traveller, passenger
vi'aggio *sm* travel(ling); (*tragitto*)
  journey, trip; **buon ~!** have a good
  trip!; **~ di nozze** honeymoon
vi'ale *sm* avenue
via'vai *sm* coming and going, bustle
vi'brare /72/ *vi* to vibrate
'**vice** ['vitʃe] *sm/f* deputy
vi'cenda [vi'tʃenda] *sf* event; **a ~**
  in turn
vice'versa [vitʃe'vɛrsa] *av* vice versa;
  da Roma a Pisa e ~ from Rome to
  Pisa and back
vici'nanza [vitʃi'nantsa] *sf*
  nearness, closeness
vi'cino, -a [vi'tʃino] *ag* (*gen*) near;
  (*nello spazio*) near, nearby; (*accanto*)

next; (*nel tempo*) near, close at hand
  ▷ *sm/f* neighbour (BRIT), neighbor
  (US) ▷ *av* near, close; **da ~** (*guardare*)
  close up; (*esaminare, seguire*) closely;
  (*conoscere*) well, intimately; **~ a** near
  (to), close to; (*accanto a*) beside; **~ di
  casa** neighbour
'**vicolo** *sm* alley; **~ cieco** blind alley
'**video** *sm inv* (*TV: schermo*) screen;
  video'camera *sf* camcorder;
  videocas'setta *sf* videocassette
videochia'mare [videokja'mare]
  /72/ *vt* to video call
video: video'clip [video'klip] *sm
  inv* videoclip; **videogi'oco, -chi**
  [video'dʒɔko] *sm* video game;
  videoregistra'tore *sm* video
  (recorder); **videote'lefono** *sm*
  videophone
'**vidi** *ecc vb vedi* **vedere**
vie'tare /72/ *vt* to forbid; (*Amm*) to
  prohibit; **~ a qn di fare** to forbid sb to
  do; to prohibit sb from doing
vie'tato, -a *ag* (*vedi vb*) forbidden;
  prohibited; banned; **"~
  fumare/l'ingresso"** "no smoking/
  admittance"; **~ ai minori di 14/18
  anni** prohibited to children under
  14/18; **"senso ~"** (*Aut*) "no entry";
  "sosta vietata" (*Aut*) "no parking"
Viet'nam *sm*: **il ~** Vietnam;
  vietna'mita, -i, -e *ag, smf, sm*
  Vietnamese *inv*
vi'gente [vi'dʒɛnte] *ag* in force
'**vigile** ['vidʒile] *ag* watchful ▷ *sm*
  (*anche*: **~ urbano**) policeman (*in
  towns*); **~ del fuoco** fireman
vi'gilia [vi'dʒilja] *sf* (*giorno
  antecedente*) eve; **la ~ di Natale**
  Christmas Eve
vigli'acco, -a, -chi, -che
  [viʎ'ʎakko] *ag* cowardly ▷ *sm/f*
  coward
'**vigna** ['viɲɲa] *sf*, **vi'gneto**
  [viɲ'ɲeto] *sm* vineyard
vi'gnetta [viɲ'ɲetta] *sf* cartoon;
  (*Aut: anche*: **~ autostradale**) (: *tassa*)
  car tax (*for motorways*); (: *adesivo*)

sticker showing that this tax has been paid

vi'gore sm vigour; (Dir): **essere/ entrare in ~** to be in/come into force

'vile ag (spregevole) low, mean, base; (codardo) cowardly

'villa sf villa

vil'laggio [vil'laddʒo] sm village; **~ turistico** holiday village

vil'lano, -a ag rude, ill-mannered

villeggia'tura [villeddʒa'tura] sf holiday; (giuramento, legge) to violate

vil'letta sf, **vil'lino** sm small house (with a garden), cottage

'vimini smpl wicker; **mobili di ~** wicker furniture sg

'vincere ['vintʃere] /129/ vt (in guerra, al gioco, a una gara) to defeat, beat; (premio, guerra, partita) to win; (fig) to overcome, conquer ▷ vi to win; **~ qn in** (abilità, bellezza) to surpass sb in; **vinci'tore, -'trice** sm/f winner; (Mil) victor

vi'nicolo, -a ag wine cpd

'vino sm wine; **~ bianco/rosato/ rosso** white/rosé/red wine; **~ da pasto** table wine

'vinsi ecc vb vedi **vincere**

vi'ola sf (Bot) violet; (Mus) viola ▷ ag, sm inv (colore) purple

vio'lare /72/ vt (chiesa) to desecrate, violate; (giuramento, legge) to violate

violen'tare /72/ vt to use violence on; (donna) to rape

vio'lento, -a ag violent; **vio'lenza** sf violence; **violenza carnale** rape

vio'letto, -a ag, sm (colore) violet ▷ sf (Bot) violet

violi'nista, -i, -e smf violinist

vio'lino sm violin

violon'cello [violon'tʃɛllo] sm cello

vi'ottolo sm path, track

VIP [vip] sm inv, f inv (= Very Important Person) VIP

'vipera sf viper, adder

vi'rare /72/ vi (Naut, Aer) to turn; (Fot) to tone; **~ di bordo** to change course; (Naut) to tack

'virgola sf (Ling) comma; (Mat) point; **virgo'lette** sfpl inverted commas, quotation marks

vi'rile ag (proprio dell'uomo) masculine; (non puerile, da uomo) manly, virile

virtù sf inv virtue; **in o per ~ di** by virtue of, by

virtu'ale ag virtual

'virus sm inv (anche Inform) virus

'viscere ['viʃʃere] sfpl (di animale) entrails pl; (fig) bowels pl

'vischio ['viskjo] sm (Bot) mistletoe; (pania) birdlime

'viscido, -a ['viʃʃido] ag slimy

vi'sibile ag visible

visibilità sf visibility

visi'era sf (di elmo) visor; (di berretto) peak

visi'one sf vision; **prendere ~ di qc** to examine sth, look sth over; **prima/seconda ~** (Cine) first/second showing

'visita sf visit; (Med) visit, call; (: esame) examination; **~ medica** medical examination; **~ guidata** guided tour; **visi'tare** /72/ vt to visit; (Med) to visit, call on; (: esaminare) to examine; **visita'tore, -'trice** sm/f visitor

vi'sivo, -a ag visual

'viso sm face

vi'sone sm mink

'vispo, -a ag quick, lively

'vissi ecc vb vedi **vivere**

'vista sf (facoltà) (eye)sight; (veduta) view; (fatto di vedere): **la ~ di** the sight of; **sparare a ~** to shoot on sight; **in ~** in sight; **perdere qn di ~** to lose sight of sb; (fig) to lose touch with sb; **far ~ di fare** to pretend to do; **a ~ d'occhio** as far as the eye can see; (fig) before one's very eyes

'visto, -a pp di **vedere** ▷ sm visa; **~ che** seeing (that)

vis'toso, -a ag gaudy, garish; (ingente) considerable

visu'ale ag visual

'vita sf life; (Anat) waist; **a ~** for life

vi'tale ag vital

vita'mina sf vitamin

'vite sf (Bot) vine; (Tecn) screw

vi'tello sm (Zool) calf; (carne) veal; (pelle) calfskin

'vittima sf victim

'vitto sm food; (in un albergo ecc) board; **~ e alloggio** board and lodging

vit'toria sf victory

'viva escl: **~ il re!** long live the king!

vi'vace [vi'vatʃe] ag (vivo, animato) lively; (: mente) lively, sharp; (colore) bright

vi'vaio sm (di pesci) hatchery; (Agr) nursery

viva'voce [viva'votʃe] sm inv (dispositivo) loudspeaker; **mettere in ~** to switch on the loudspeaker

vi'vente ag living, alive; **i viventi** the living

'vivere /130/ vi to live ▷ vt to live; (passare: brutto momento) to live through, go through; (sentire: gioie, pene di qn) to share ▷ sm life; (anche: modo di ~) way of life; **viveri** smpl (cibo) food sg, provisions; **~ di** to live on

'vivido, -a ag (colore) vivid, bright

vivisezi'one [viviset'tsjone] sf vivisection

'vivo, -a ag (vivente) alive, living; (: animale) live; (fig) lively; (: colore) bright, brilliant; **i vivi** the living; **~ e vegeto** hale and hearty; **farsi ~** to show one's face; to keep in touch; **ritrarre dal ~** to paint from life; **pungere qn nel ~** (fig) to cut sb to the quick

vivrò ecc vb vedi **vivere**

vizi'are [vit'tsjare] /19/ vt (bambino) to spoil; (corrompere moralmente) to corrupt; **vizi'ato, -a** ag spoilt; (aria, acqua) polluted

'vizio ['vittsjo] sm (morale) vice; (cattiva abitudine) bad habit; (imperfezione) flaw, defect; (errore) fault, mistake

V.le abbr = **viale**

vocabo'lario sm (dizionario) dictionary; (lessico) vocabulary

vo'cabolo sm word

vo'cale ag vocal ▷ sf vowel

vocazi'one [vokat'tsjone] sf vocation; (fig) natural bent

'voce ['votʃe] sf voice; (diceria) rumour; (di un elenco: in bilancio) item; **aver ~ in capitolo** (fig) to have a say in the matter

'voga sf (Naut) rowing; (usanza): **essere in ~** to be in fashion o in vogue

vo'gare /80/ vi to row

vogherò ecc [voge'rɔ] vb vedi **vogare**

'voglia ['vɔʎʎa] sf desire, wish; (macchia) birthmark; **aver ~ di qc/ di fare** to feel like sth/like doing; (più forte) to want sth/to do

'voglio ecc ['vɔʎʎo] vb vedi **volere**

'voi pron you; **voi'altri** pron you

vo'lante ag flying ▷ sm (steering) wheel

volan'tino sm leaflet

vo'lare /72/ vi (uccello, aereo, fig) to fly; (cappello) to blow away o off, fly away o off; **~ via** to fly away o off

vo'latile ag (Chim) volatile ▷ sm (Zool) bird

volente'roso, -a ag willing

volenti'eri av willingly; **"~"** "with pleasure", "I'd be glad to"

 PAROLA CHIAVE

vo'lere /131/ sm will, wish(es); **contro il volere di** against the wishes of; **per volere di qn** in obedience to sb's will o wishes

▷ vt **1** (esigere, desiderare) to want; **volere fare qc** to want to do sth; **volere che qn faccia qc** to want sb to do sth; **vorrei questo/fare** I would o I'd like this/to do; **come vuoi** as you like; **vuoi un caffè?** would you like a coffee?; **senza volere** (inavvertitamente) without meaning to, unintentionally

2 (consentire): **vogliate attendere, per piacere** please wait; **vogliamo andare?** shall we go?; **vuole essere così gentile da …?** would you be so kind as to …?; **non ha voluto ricevermi** he wouldn't see me

3: **volerci** (essere necessario) (materiale, attenzione) to be needed; (tempo) to take; **quanta farina ci vuole per questa torta?** how much flour do you need for this cake?; **ci vuole un'ora per arrivare a Venezia** it takes an hour to get to Venice

4: **voler bene a qn** (amore) to love sb; (affetto) to be fond of sb, like sb very much; **voler male a qn** to dislike sb; **volerne a qn** to bear sb a grudge; **voler dire** to mean

vol'gare ag vulgar

voli'era sf aviary

voli'tivo, -a ag strong-willed

'volli ecc vb vedi **volere**

'volo sm flight; **colpire qc al ~** to hit sth as it flies past; **capire al ~** to understand straight away; **~ charter** charter flight; **~ di linea** scheduled flight

volontà sf inv will; **a ~** (mangiare, bere) as much as one likes; **buona/cattiva ~** goodwill/lack of goodwill

volontari'ato sm (lavoro) voluntary work

volon'tario, -a ag voluntary ▷ sm (Mil) volunteer

'volpe sf fox

'volta sf (momento, circostanza) time; (turno, giro) turn; (curva) turn, bend; (Archit) vault; (direzione): **partire alla ~ di** to set off for; **a mia** (o **tua** ecc) **~** in turn; **una ~** once; **una ~ sola** only once; **due volte** twice; **una cosa per ~** one thing at a time; **una ~ per tutte** once and for all; **a volte** at times, sometimes; **una ~ che** (temporale) once; (causale) since; **3 volte 4** 3 times 4

volta'faccia [volta'fattʃa] sm inv (fig) volte-face

vol'taggio [vol'taddʒo] sm (Elettr) voltage

vol'tare /72/ vt to turn; (girare: moneta) to turn over; (rigirare) to turn round ▷ vi to turn; **voltarsi** vpr to turn; to turn over; to turn round

voltas'tomaco sm nausea; (fig) disgust

'volto, -a pp di **volgere** ▷ sm face

vo'lubile ag changeable, fickle

vo'lume sm volume

vomi'tare /72/ vt, vi to vomit; **'vomito** sm vomiting no pl; vomit

'vongola sf clam

vo'race [vo'ratʃe] ag voracious, greedy

vo'ragine [vo'radʒine] sf abyss, chasm

vorrò ecc vb vedi **volere**

'vortice ['vortitʃe] sm whirlwind; whirlpool; (fig) whirl

'vostro, -a det: **il (la) ~(a)** ecc your ▷ pron: **il (la) ~(a)** ecc yours

vo'tante smf voter

vo'tare /72/ vi to vote ▷ vt (sottoporre a votazione) to take a vote on; (approvare) to vote for; (Rel): **~ qc a** to dedicate sth to

'voto sm (Pol) vote; (Ins) mark (BRIT), grade (US); (Rel) vow; (: offerta) votive offering; **aver voti belli/brutti** (Ins) to get good/bad marks o grades

vs. abbr (= vostro) yr

vul'cano sm volcano

vulne'rabile ag vulnerable

vu'oi, vu'ole vb vedi **volere**

vuo'tare /72/ vt, **vuo'tarsi** vpr to empty

vu'oto, -a ag empty; (fig: privo): **~ di** (senso ecc) devoid of ▷ sm empty space, gap; (spazio in bianco) blank; (Fisica) vacuum; (fig: mancanza) gap, void; **a mani vuote** empty-handed; **~ d'aria** air pocket; **"~ a rendere"** "returnable bottle"

W X

'wafer ['vafer] *sm inv* (*Cuc, Elettr*) wafer
'water ['wɔːtəʳ] *sm inv* toilet
watt [vat] *sm inv* watt
WC *sm inv* WC
web [uɛb] *sm*: **il ~** the web ▷ *ag inv*: **pagina ~** webpage; **cercare nel ~** to search the web; **webcam** [web'kam] *sf inv* (*Inform*) webcam
'weekend ['wiːkɛnd] *sm inv* weekend
'western ['wɛstern] *ag* (*Cine*) cowboy *cpd* ▷ *sm inv* western, cowboy film; **~ all'italiana** spaghetti western
'whisky ['wiski] *sm inv* whisky
Wi-Fi [uai'fai] (*Inform*) *sm* Wi-Fi ▷ *ag inv* Wi-Fi
'windsurf ['windsəːf] *sm inv* (*tavola*) windsurfer; (*sport*) windsurfing
'würstel ['vyrstəl] *sm inv* frankfurter

xe'nofobo, -a [kse'nɔfobo] *ag* xenophobic ▷ *sm/f* xenophobe
xi'lofono [ksi'lɔfono] *sm* xylophone

Y   Z

yacht [jɔt] *sm inv* yacht
yoga ['jɔga] *ag inv, sm* yoga (*cpd*)
yogurt ['jɔgurt] *sm inv* yog(h)urt

zabaione [dzaba'jone] *sm dessert made of egg yolks, sugar and marsala*
zaffata [tsaf'fata] *sf (tanfo)* stench
zafferano [dzaffe'rano] *sm* saffron
zaffiro [dzaf'firo] *sm* sapphire
zainetto [dzai'netto] *sm* (small) rucksack
zaino ['dzaino] *sm* rucksack
zampa ['tsampa] *sf (di animale: gamba)* leg; (: *piede)* paw; **a quattro zampe** on all fours
zampillare [tsampil'lare] /72/ *vi* to gush, spurt
zanzara [dzan'dzara] *sf* mosquito; **zanzariera** *sf* mosquito net
zappa ['tsappa] *sf* hoe
zapping ['tsapiŋ] *sm* (*TV*) channel-hopping
zar, zarina [tsar, tsa'rina] *sm/f* tsar (tsarina)
zattera ['dzattera] *sf* raft

z

'zebra ['dzɛbra] *sf* zebra; **zebre**
sfpl (*Aut*) zebra crossing *sg* (BRIT),
crosswalk *sg* (US)
'zecca, -che ['tsekka] *sf* (*Zool*) tick;
(*officina di monete*) mint
'zelo ['dzɛlo] *sm* zeal
zen'zero [dzen'dzero] *sm* ginger
'zeppa ['tseppa] *sf* wedge
'zeppo, -a ['tseppo] *ag*: **~ di**
crammed o packed with
zer'bino [dzer'bino] *sm* doormat
'zero ['dzɛro] *sm* zero, nought;
vincere per tre a ~ (*Sport*) to win
three-nil
'zia ['tsia] *sf* aunt
zibel'lino [dzibel'lino] *sm* sable
'zigomo ['dzigomo] *sm* cheekbone
zig'zag [dzig'dzag] *sm inv* zigzag;
andare a ~ to zigzag
Zim'babwe [tsim'babwe] *sm*: **lo ~**
Zimbabwe
'zinco ['dzinko] *sm* zinc
'zingaro, -a ['dzingaro] *sm/f* gipsy
'zio ['tsio] (*pl* **zii**) *sm* uncle
zip'pare /72/ *vt* (*Inform: file*) to zip
zi'tella [dzi'tɛlla] *sf* spinster; (*peg*)
old maid
'zitto, -a ['tsitto] *ag* quiet, silent; **sta'
~!** be quiet!
'zoccolo ['tsɔkkolo] *sm* (*calzatura*)
clog; (*di cavallo ecc*) hoof; (*Archit*)
plinth; (*di armadio*) base
zodia'cale [dzodia'kale] *ag* zodiac
cpd; **segno ~** sign of the zodiac
zo'diaco [dzo'diako] *sm* zodiac
'zolfo ['tsolfo] *sm* sulphur
'zolla ['dzolla] *sf* clod (of earth)

zol'letta [dzol'letta] *sf* sugar lump
'zona ['dzɔna] *sf* zone, area; **~ di
depressione** (*Meteor*) trough of
low pressure; **~ disco** (*Aut*) ≈ meter
zone; **~ industriale** industrial
estate; **~ pedonale** pedestrian
precinct; **~ verde** (*di abitato*)
green area
'zonzo ['dzondzo]: **a ~** *av* **andare a ~**
to wander about, stroll about
'zoo ['dzɔo] *sm inv* zoo
zoolo'gia [dzoolo'dʒia] *sf* zoology
zoppi'care [tsoppi'kare] /20/ *vi* to
limp; (*fig: mobile*) rickety
'zoppo, -a ['tsɔppo] *ag* lame; (*fig:
mobile*) shaky, rickety
ZTL *sigla f* (= *Zona a Traffico Limitato*)
controlled traffic zone
'zucca, -che ['tsukka] *sf* (*Bot*)
marrow; pumpkin
zucche'rare [tsukke'rare] /72/ *vt*
to put sugar in; **zucche'rato, -a** *ag*
sweet, sweetened
zuccheri'era [tsukke'rjɛra] *sf*
sugar bowl
'zucchero ['tsukkero] *sm* sugar; **~ di
canna** cane sugar; **~ filato** candy
floss, cotton candy (US)
zuc'china [tsuk'kina] *sf* courgette
(BRIT), zucchini (US)
'zuffa ['tsuffa] *sf* brawl
'zuppa ['tsuppa] *sf* soup; (*fig*)
mixture, muddle; **~ inglese** (*Cuc*)
*dessert made with sponge cake, custard
and chocolate* ≈ trifle (BRIT)
'zuppo, -a ['tsuppo] *ag*: **~ (di)**
drenched (with), soaked (with)

Italian in focus

Introduction	2
Italy and its regions	3
A snapshot of Italy	5
The Italian-speaking world	6
The Italian State	8
Italian words that have travelled the world	9
Italian words used in English	10
English words used in Italian	11
Improving your pronunciation	12
Improving your fluency	14
Correspondence	16
Text messaging	16
Writing an email	17
Writing a personal letter	19
Writing a formal letter	21
Making a call	23
Italian phrases and sayings	24
Some common translation difficulties	27

Introduction

Italian in focus gives you an introduction to various aspects of Italy and the Italian language. The following pages help you get to know the country where the language is spoken and the people who speak it.

Practical language tips and helpful notes on common translation difficulties will enable you to become a more confident Italian speaker. A useful correspondence section gives you all the information you need to be able to communicate effectively.

We've also included a number of links to useful websites, which will give you the opportunity to read more about Italy and the Italian language.

We hope you will enjoy using your *Italian in focus* supplement. We are sure it will help you find out more about Italy and Italians and become more confident in writing and speaking Italian.

Cominciamo!

Italy and its regions

Italy's neighbours

Italian is an official language in two Swiss cantons, Ticino and Grigioni, in the republic of San Marino and in Vatican City. Italian is also spoken in Malta, part of Croatia, and part of Slovenia.

Italy and its regions

The six biggest Italian cities

City	Name of inhabitants	Population
Roma	i romani	2,542,003
Milano	i milanesi	1,272,898
Napoli	i napoletani	1,000,449
Torino	i torinesi	867,857
Palermo	i palermitani	679,430
Genova	i genovesi	601,338

Italy consists of the mainland and two large islands, Sardegna and Sicilia, together with smaller islands such as Elba and Capri.

There are 20 administrative regions, five of which are *regioni autonome*, which have more decision-making powers than the others. Three of the 'autonomous regions' are in the north – Valle d'Aosta, Friuli-Venezia Giulia and Trentino-Alto Adige. The other two are the islands of Sardegna and Sicilia. Central government retains jurisdiction for matters such as defence, foreign affairs and the legal system, which affect the country as a whole.

Italy has only been a unified country since 1870. Before then parts of the peninsula were under the control of various countries, such as Spain, Austria and France. There was, and still is, a strong regional identity, with many people speaking one of the diverse local dialects. Nowadays everyone learns standard Italian at school; however many people speak *dialetto* with neighbours, friends and family.

As is often the case in areas bordering other countries, there are some bilingual communities. For example, in the Trentino-Alto Adige area in the far north of Italy, the majority language is German.

A snapshot of Italy

In area, Italy (301, 323 km²) is somewhat bigger than the UK (244,110 km²).

The Po (652 km) is Italy's longest river. It rises in the Alps and flows into the Adriatic near Venice.

The population of Italy is about 58.4 million, which is slightly less than that of the UK. The birth rate is very low (1.2 children per woman). Deaths outnumber births.

The Italian economy is the fourth biggest in the EU and seventh biggest in the world.

Italy is the world's biggest wine-producing country.

- Gran Paradiso (4061) is Italy's highest peak.

- About 37 million tourists visit Italy every year, making it the 5th most popular tourist destination in the world.

- Italy has four active volcanoes: Etna, Vesuvius, Stromboli and Vulcano. Etna erupts frequently and is Europe's most active volcano.

Some useful links are:
www.governo.it
Website of the Italian government.
www.istat.it
The Italian statistics office.
www.enit.it
Italian state tourist board.

The Italian-speaking world

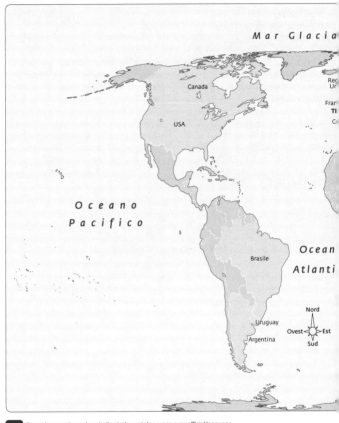

Countries or regions where Italian is the main language or an official language

Countries or regions where many of the population speak Italian

rtico

Belgio
Germania
IGIONI
Slovenia
Croazia
SAN MARINO
Albania
ITALIA
MALTA

Somalia

Oceano
Pacifico

Oceano
Indiano

Australia

Many Italians went to the Americas – particularly to the US and Argentina – and to Australia. There are 1 ½ million Italian speakers in Argentina and nearly a milion in the US. Italian has had a major influence on the way Spanish is spoken in Argentina

7

The Italian State

- Italy has dozens of political parties. The two main political groupings are the centre-right and the centre-left. The government tends to be formed by a coalition consisting of several parties.

- Italy has two houses of parliament: the Senate (*il Senato*) and the Chamber of Deputies (*la Camera dei Deputati*). The President of the Republic (*il Presidente della Repubblica*), who is the head of state, has a tenure of seven years.

- The Prime Minister (*il Presidente del Consiglio*) is the head of government.

- Inside Italy there are two tiny independent states: San Marino and Vatican City.

- San Marino is the smallest republic in Europe.

- Vatican City is the spiritual and administrative centre of the Roman Catholic Church. It has two official languages, Italian and Latin.

Italian words that have travelled the world

An important part of the language Italians took to foreign countries was to do with food – many immigrants opened cafés and restaurants. These days people all over the world drink cappuccinos and espressos, and eat ciabatta, spaghetti, minestrone and pizza.

While everyone is familiar with these food items, they may not realize that the Italian words themselves have interesting, highly descriptive meanings. Here are just a few:

- cappuccino
  This comes from the word capuchin. Capuchins are friars whose habits are brown – the colour of cappuccino coffee.

- ciabatta
  This means 'slipper'. The bread has this name because of its shape.

- macchiato
  macchiato means 'stained' and describes the look of a dark coffee with a little spot of milk on it.

- spaghetti
  spago means 'string' – so *spaghetti* are 'little strings'. There's another pasta called *orecchiette*. If you bear in mind that *un orecchio* is an ear, you can probably guess what this pasta looks like.

- tiramisù
  This word doesn't describe the appearance of the dessert, but the effect it has, as it means 'pick-me-up' (a reference to the stimulating effect of the coffee it contains).

- vermicelli
  This kind of pasta is very, very thin, and its name means 'little worms'.

Italian words used in English

Apart from lots of words to do with food, there are other Italian words that are very often used in English. Here are a few interesting examples:

• solo
This means 'alone' in Italian and was originally borrowed as a musical term – but it's now used in all kinds of contexts.

• fiasco
English has borrowed only one of this word's two senses: the other one is 'wine bottle'!

• piano
This is the Italian for 'soft'. When the pianoforte was invented it was so called because it could be played either soft (*piano*), or loud (*forte*), unlike its predecessor, the harpsichord.

• prima donna
This word for leading lady means 'first woman'. This is another musical term which has come to be used more generally.

• bimbo
Unlike in English, in Italian this is not a derogatory word for a woman – it just means 'little boy'. *Una bimba* is a little girl.

• al fresco
In Italian this doesn't mean 'outside' but 'in the cool', and in a figurative sense, 'in jail'.

English words used in Italian

Italians have as great an appetite for English words as other people have for Italian food. Words from every conceivable field are borrowed; daily life, popular culture, science, computing, sport, business and so on.

- Countless words are borrowed in their original form:

lo stress	*la privacy*
lo shopping	*il gay*
il fast food	*il blues*
il jazz	*lo show*
il talk show	*il computer*
il mouse	*il golf*
lo sport	*il supporter*
il record	*il training*
il manager	*il target*

In the plural, these words get a plural article (*i*, *gli* or *le*) but no final 's':

Singular	Plural
il talk show	*i talk show*
lo sport	*gli sport*
la star	*le star*

- Other words are Italianized, but still recognizably English:

chattare	to chat
craccare	to crack
dribblare	to dribble
sprintare	to sprint
scrollare	to scroll
standardizzare	to standardize
interfaccia	interface
reality	reality show

- Some words look English, but have taken on a different meaning:

un box	a garage
un golf	a cardigan (it also means the sport)
un ticket	a prescription charge
uno smoking	a dinner jacket
uno spot	a tv or radio advert

Improving your pronunciation

Italian sounds

Vowels

Each English vowel can be pronounced in several quite different ways – think of the sound the letter **i** has, for example, in the words m**i**lk, k**i**nd and c**i**rcus. Italian vowels vary much less in their pronunciation:

a – is like the *a* in father
e – is like the *e* in set
i – is like the *ee* in sheep OR is pronounced like *y* in yard
o – is like the *o* in orange
u – is like the *oo* in soon

Avoid saying Italian words like their English lookalikes: the *i* in *Milano* and in *aprile*, for example is the long ee sound, not the short i used in Milan and April.

Unlike English, Italian is pronounced exactly as it is written, so *interessante*, for example, has five syllables, with a clearly pronounced vowel in each one: *in-te-res-san-te*.

• Italian vowels never disappear as they do in English words like interesting (int-res-ting) and camera (cam-ra). Always pronounce them fully.

• Italian vowels never have the indistinct 'uh' sound to be heard at the end of many English words, for example, hos<u>tel</u>, hospi<u>tal</u> and cir<u>cus</u>. Always pronounce Italian vowels clearly.

• When *i* is pronounced **y**, make sure that it's **y** as in yard, not **y** as in very:

andiamo   an-dya-mo
(not an-dy-a-mo)
ravioli   rav-yo-lee
(not ra-vee-o-lee)
stazione   sta-zyo-ne
(not sta-zee-o-ne)

Improving your pronunciation

Consonants

- The presence of a double consonant in Italian makes the consonant sound longer: *cat-ti-vo*, *inte-res-san-te*, *An-na*.

- *c* followed by *e* or *i* is pronounced **tch**, as in *centro* and *facile*.

- *ch* is pronounced **k**, as in *fuochi* and *chiuso*.

- *g* followed by *e* and *i* is pronounced **j**, as in *leggero* and *giardino*.

- *gh* is pronounced like *g* in get, as in *lunghi* and *spaghetti*.

- *gl* followed by *e* and *i* is normally pronounced like the **lli** in million, for example *luglio*, *bagagli*.

- *gn* is pronounced **ny**, for example *gnocchi*, *giugno*.

- *sc* followed by *e* and *i* is pronounced **sh**, as in *lasciare* and *sciare*.

Stress

- Italian words are usually stressed on the next to the last syllable, for example *cucina*, *studente*, *straniero*, *diciassette*, *parlare*, *avere*.

- If a word is spelled with an accent on the last vowel, for example, *fedeltà*, *università*, *però*, *così*, *caffè*, put the stress on this vowel.

- Some words are stressed on other syllables; the 'they' form of verbs, for example, usually stresses the third to last syllable: *capiscono* (= they understand); *parlano* (= they speak).

- Other words, such as *subito*, *macchina*, *vendere* and *camera* stress the first syllable. Be aware that words aren't always stressed as you'd expect and when in doubt look in the dictionary: you'll see that in each headword there's a mark that looks like an apostrophe. The syllable immediately following this apostrophe is the one you stress.

A useful link is:
www.accademiadellacrusca.it
National language academy of Italy.

Improving your fluency

Conversational words and phrases

In English we insert lots of words and phrases, such as *so, then, by the way*, into our conversation, to give our thoughts a structure and often to show our attitude. The Italian words below do the same thing. If you use them you'll sound more fluent and natural.

- *allora*
  Allora, *che facciamo stasera?* (= so)

- *va bene*
  Va bene, *ho capito.* (= okay)

- *ecco*
  Ecco *perché non sono venuti.*
  (= that's)
  Ecco *Mario!* (= here's)
  Eccolo! (= there ... is)

- *forse*
  Sì, ma **forse** *hanno ragione.*
  (= maybe)

- *certo*
  Certo *che puoi.* (= of course)

- *dunque*
  Dunque, *come dicevo ...* (= well)
  Dunque *ha ragione lui.* (= so)

- *può darsi*
  Sì, lo so, ma **può darsi** *che ...*
  (= perhaps)

- *purtroppo*
  Sì, **purtroppo**. (= unfortunately)

- *sinceramente*
  Sinceramente, *non m'importa niente.*
  (= really)

- *comunque*
  Comunque, *non è sempre così.*
  (= however)

- *senz'altro*
  Mi scriverai? – **Senz'altro**!
  (= of course)
  È **senz'altro** *meglio lui.* (= definitely)

- *davvero*
  Ha pagato lui. – **Davvero**? (= really)

Improving your fluency

Varying the words you use to get your message across will also make you sound more fluent in Italian. For example, instead of *Mi piace molto il calcio*, you could say *Il calcio è la mia passione*. Here are some other suggestions.

Saying what you like or dislike

Adoro le ciliege.	I love ...
Mi è piaciuto molto il tuo regalo.	I (really) liked ...
Non mi piace il tennis.	I don't like ...
Il suo ultimo film *non mi piace per niente.*	I don't like ... (at all).
Detesto mentire.	I hate ...

Expressing your opinion

Credo che sia giusto.	I think ...
Penso che costino di più.	I think ...
Sono sicuro/sicura che ti piacerà.	I'm sure ...
Secondo me è stato un errore.	In my opinion ...
A mio parere vincerà lui.	In my opinion ...
A me sembra che qualche volta ...	It seems to me ...

Agreeing or disagreeing

Ha ragione.	You're right.
Giusto!	Quite right!
(Non) sono d'accordo.	I (don't) agree.
Non direi.	I wouldn't say so.
Certo!	Of course!

Correspondence

The following section on correspondence has been designed to help you communicate confidently in written as well as spoken Italian. Sample letters, emails and sections on text messaging and making telephone calls will ensure that you have all the vocabulary you need to correspond successfully.

Text messaging

un sms (*esse emme esse*) = text message
mandare un sms a qualcuno = to text somebody

Abbreviation	Italian	English
+ tardi	più tardi	later
+o-	più o meno	more or less
ba	bacio	kiss
bn	bene	well
C6?	ci sei?	are you there?
cs	cosa	what
c ved	ci vediamo	see you soon
dv	dove	where
k6?	chi sei?	who are you?
ke cs?	che cosa?	what?
tu6	tu sei	you are
k	che	that, what
qd	quando	when
nn	non	not
k fai?	che fai?	what are you doing?
qnd	quando	when
TVB	ti voglio bene	I love you
TVTB	ti voglio tanto bene	I love you so much
x	per	for
xke	perché	because
xke?	perché?	why?
TAT	ti amo tanto	love you loads

Writing an email

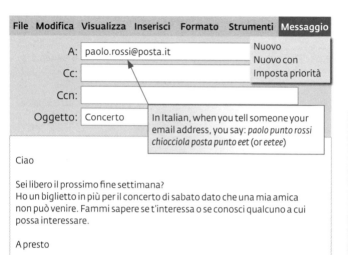

file	file
modifica	edit
visualizza	view
formato	format
inserisci	insert
?	help
strumenti	tools
scrivere	to compose
help	help
invia	send
crea messaggio	new message

rispondi	reply
rispondi a tutti	reply to all
inoltrare	to forward
allega	attachment
A	to
Cc (copia carbone)	cc (carbon copy)
Ccn (copia carbone nascosta)	bcc (blind carbon copy)
oggetto	subject
da	from
dat	date

Here is some additional useful Internet vocabulary:

ADSL	broadband	*Internet*	the Internet
avanti	forward	*la Rete*	the (World-Wide) Web
cartella	folder	*motore di recerca*	search engine
cercare	to search	*navigare in Internet*	to surf the Net
cliccare	to click	*pagina iniziale*	home page
collegamenti	links	*pagina web*	web page
collegarsi	to log on	*prefereti*	favourites
copiare	to copy	*programma*	program
cronologia	history	*provider*	Internet Service Provider
domande frequenti	FAQs	*salvare*	to save
fare doppio click	to double-click	*scaricare*	to download
finestra	window	*scollegarsi*	to log off
foglio di calcolo	spreadsheet	*sito Internet*	website
icona	icon	*stampare*	print
impostazioni	settings	*tagliare*	to cut
incollare	to paste	*tartiera*	keyboard
indietro	back	*visualizzare*	to view

Writing a personal letter

Town/city you are writing from, and the date → *Siena, 5 giugno 2012*

Cara Maria,

No capital for start of letter

ti ringrazio moltissimo del biglietto che mi hai mandato per il mio compleanno, che è arrivato proprio il giorno della mia festa!

Mi dispiace che tu non sia potuta venire a Milano per il mio compleanno e spero che ti sia ripresa dopo l'influenza. Mi piacerebbe poterti incontrare presto perché ho molte novità da raccontarti. Forse tra due settimane verrò a Torino con degli amici. Pensi di essere libera il giorno 12? Ti telefono la prossima settimana, così ci mettiamo d'accordo.

Baci,

Anna

Writing a personal letter

Other ways of starting a personal letter	Other ways of ending a personal letter
Carissima Maria Mia cara Maria Cari Luigi e Silvia	Un abbraccio Bacioni Con affetto A presto

Some useful phrases

Ti ringrazio per la tua lettera.	Thank you for your letter.
Mi ha fatto piacere ricevere tue notizie.	It was lovely to hear from you.
Scusami se non ti ho scritto prima.	I'm sorry I didn't reply sooner.
Salutami tanto Lucia.	Give my love to Lucia.
Tanti saluti anche da Paolo.	Paolo sends his best wishes.
Scrivi presto!	Write soon!

Writing a formal letter

Your own name and address   ⟶   Paola Rossotti
Via San Francesco, 28
10100 Torino

19 settembre 2012   ⟵   Date

Agenzia immobiliare
Il giardino   ⟵   Name and address of the person or company you are writing to
Via Roma, 18
47900 Rimini

OGGETTO: Richiesta di rimborso

Egr. signori,
vi scrivo per presentare reclamo in merito all'appartamento che ho affittato nel condominio Le Torri per il periodo 5-12 agosto. Avevo espressamente richiesto un appartamento con due camere e invece mi è stato assegnato un appartamento con una camera sola; mancava inoltre il condizionatore d'aria di cui il contratto di locazione fa specifica menzione.
Chiedo quindi un rimborso di 1000 euro comprensivo della differenza tra la tariffa che ho pagato per un appartamento con due camere e aria condizionata e quella per un appartamento con una camera sola senza aria condizionata, e di un risarcimento per i disagi subiti.

Allego fotocopia del contratto di locazione.

Distinti saluti

Paola Rossotti

Writing a formal letter

Other ways of starting a formal letter	Other ways of ending a formal letter
Egregio signore, *Gentile signora,* *Egregio Signor Paolozzo,* *Gentile Signora Paolozzo,* *Spett. Ditta,* (when writing to a firm)	*Distinti saluti* *La prego di accettare i miei più distinti saluti* *Cordiali saluti*

Some useful phrases

La ringrazio della sua lettera del ...	Thank you for your letter of ...
In riferimento a ...	With reference to ...
Vi prego di inviarmi ...	Please send me ...
In attesa di una sua risposta la ringrazio per l'attenzione.	I look forward to hearing from you.
La ringrazio in anticipo per ...	Thank you in advance for ...

Agenzia immobiliare
Il giardino
Via Roma, 18 ◄——— The house number comes
47900 Rimini   after the street name, and
                   the postcode comes before
                   the name of the town.

Making a call

Asking for information

Qual è il prefisso di Livorno?	What's the code for Livorno?
Cosa devo fare per ottenere la linea esterna?	How do I get an outside line?
Può darmi il numero dell'interno della Signora Busi?	Could you give me Ms Busi's extension number?

When your number answers

Buongiorno, c'è Andrea?	Hello! Is Andrea there?
Potrei parlare con Lucia, per favore?	Could I speak to Lucia, please?
Parla la Signora de Maggio?	Is that Mrs de Maggio?
Può chiedergli/chiederle di richiamarmi?	Could you ask him/her to call me back?
Richiamo fra mezz'ora.	I'll call back in half an hour.
Posso lasciare un messaggio, per favore?	Could I leave a message, please?

When you answer the telephone

Pronto!	Hello!
Chi parla?	Who's speaking?
Sono Marco.	It's Marco speaking.
Sì, sono io.	Speaking.
Vuole lasciare un messaggio?	Would you like to leave a message?

What you may hear

Chi devo dire?	Who shall I say is calling?
Le passo la comunicazione.	I'm putting you through now.
Attenda in linea.	Please hold.
Non risponde nessuno.	There's no reply.
La linea è occupata.	The line is engaged (*Brit*)/busy (*US*).
Vuole lasciare un messaggio?	Would you like to leave a message?

If you have a problem

Scusi, ho sbagliato numero.	Sorry, I dialled the wrong number.
La linea è molto disturbata.	This is a very bad line.
Qui non c'è campo.	There's no signal here.
Ho la batteria quasi scarica.	My battery's low.
Non ti sento.	I can't hear you.

Italian phrases and sayings

In Italian, as in many languages, people use vivid expressions based on images from their experience of real life. We've grouped the common expressions below according to the type of image they use. For fun, we have given you the word-for-word translation as well as the English equivalent.

Food and drink

dire pane al pane e vino al vino
word for word:
→ to call a spade a spade
to call bread bread and wine wine

Se non è zuppa è pan bagnato.
word for word:
→ It's much of a muchness.
if it's not soup it's wet bread

rendere pan per focaccia
word for word:
→ to give as good as you get
to give bread for focaccia

avere le mani in pasta
word for word:
→ to have a finger in the pie
to have your hands in the dough

lavorare per la pagnotta
word for word:
→ to earn your living
to work for your loaf

Ormai la frittata è fatta.
word for word:
→ The damage is done.
the omelette is made now

Weather

fare il bello e il cattivo tempo
word for word:
→ to do as one pleases
to make the good and bad weather

una tempesta in un bicchier d'acqua
word for word:
→ a storm in a teacup
a storm in a glass of water

sposa bagnata sposa fortunata
word for word:
→ rain on your wedding day is lucky
wet bride, lucky bride

Italian phrases and sayings

prendere due piccioni con una fava → to kill two birds with one stone
    word for word: *to get two pigeons with one broad bean*

Quando il gatto non c'è i topi ballano. → When the cat's away the mice will play.
    word for word: *when the cat's not there the mice dance*

Chi dorme non piglia pesci. → The early bird catches the worm.
    word for word: *if you're asleep you don't catch any fish*

In bocca al lupo! → Break a leg!
    word for word: *into the wolf's mouth!*

Meglio un uovo oggi che una gallina domani. → A bird in the hand is worth two in the bush.
    word for word: *better an egg today than a hen tomorrow*

L'ospite è come il pesce, dopo tre giorni puzza. → It's nice when they come and it's nice when they go.
    word for word: *guests are like fish – after three days they start to smell*

Parts of the body

essere un pugno in un occhio → to be an eyesore
    word for word: *to be a punch in the eye*

Chi non ha testa ha gambe. → Use your head to save your legs.
    word for word: *people who have no head have legs*

rimanere a bocca aperta → to be amazed
    word for word: *to be left open-mouthed*

avere le mani bucate → to spend money like water
    word for word: *to have holes in your hands*

Italian phrases and sayings

nascere con la camicia

    word for word:

→ to be born with a silver spoon in your mouth
to be born with with a shirt on

sudare sette camicie
    word for word:

→ to work like a dog
to sweat seven shirts

tirare qualcuno per la giacca
    word for word:

→ to twist someone's arm
to pull someone by the coat

Plants

Se sono rose fioriranno.

    word for word:

→ The proof of the pudding is in the eating.
if they're roses they'll bloom

fare di ogni erba un fascio
    word for word:

→ to lump everything together
to put all the grasses into one bundle

Non sono tutte rose e fiori.
    word for word:

→ It's not all a bed of roses.
it's not all roses and flowers

Colours

Rosso di sera, bel tempo si spera.
    word for word:

→ Red sky at night, shepherd's delight.
(if the sky's) red at night you can hope for good weather

vedere tutto nero
    word for word:

→ to look on the black side
to see everything as black

Al buio tutti i gatti sono neri.
    word for word:

→ At night all cats are grey.
in the dark all cats are black

Some common translation difficulties

On the following pages we have shown some of the translation difficulties you are most likely to come across. We hope that the tips we have given will help you to avoid these common pitfalls when writing or speaking Italian.

How to say 'you' in Italian

There are three ways of saying *you* in Italian: **tu** and **lei** are used to speak to one person, and **voi** is used to speak to more than one person.

- Use **tu** when you are speaking to a person you know well, or to a child.
  If you are a student you can call another student **tu**.

> And how old are you, Roberto? → *E **tu**, Roberto, quanti anni hai?*

- Use **lei** when speaking to strangers, or anyone you're not on familiar terms with. As you get to know someone better they may suggest that you call each other **tu** instead of **lei**. In shops, hotels and restaurants customers are always addressed as **lei**.

> Would you like a coffee too, madam? → *Vuole un caffè anche **lei**, signora?*

It may seem potentially confusing that **lei** also means 'she', but in practice it's quite obvious that if someone speaks directly to you using **lei**, the meaning is *you*.

- Use **voi** when you are speaking to more than one person.

> Where are you boys from? → ***Voi** ragazzi, di dove siete?*

'You' has to go with the verb in English, but in Italian you often use the verb alone:

> How old are you? → *Quanti anni hai?*
> You speak good Italian, madam. → *Parla bene l'italiano, signora.*
> You're young. → *Siete giovani.*

Some common translation difficulties

You use the words **tu**, **lei** and **voi** to attract someone's attention, or for the sake of emphasis.

> _Tu cosa pensi?_ → What do <u>you</u> think?
>
> _Lei quale preferisce?_ → Which one do <u>you</u> prefer?

Showing possession

In English -'s is a common way of showing who or what something belongs to. In Italian you have to use **di**:

> my brother**'s** car → _la macchina **di** mio fratello_
>
> Maria**'s** house → _la casa **di** Maria_

Translating 'to like'

There are two ways of saying you like something, depending on whether it is singular or plural:

> I like Italy. → **Mi piace** _l'Italia._
>
> word-for-word meaning of Italian: _to me is pleasing Italy_

> I like dogs. → **Mi piacciono** _i cani._
>
> word-for-word meaning of Italian: _to me are pleasing dogs_

If you bear in mind the word-for-word meaning of the Italian you'll have no trouble deciding whether to use **piace** or **piacciono**.

To say 'we like', change **mi** to **ci**.

> We like the sea. → **Ci piace** _il mare._
>
> We like his films. → **Ci piacciono** _i suoi film._

Some common translation difficulties

If you want to ask someone if they like something:

• Use **ti** when asking someone you know well.

Do you like my shoes? → **Ti piacciono** le mie scarpe?

• Use **le** when speaking politely

Do you like Italian food, madam? → **Le piace** la cucina italiana, signora?

• Use **vi** when talking to more than one person.

Do you like football, boys? → **Vi piace** il calcio, ragazzi?

Translating *-ing*

The English *-ing* form is used to talk about something you are doing or were doing. This can be translated into Italian by using the Italian present continuous tense (the verb form that ends **-ando** or **-endo**).

They were gett**ing** bored. → *Si stavano annoi**ando**.*
He's read**ing** the paper. → *Sta legg**endo** il giornale.*
She's talk**ing** to Mum. → *Sta parl**ando** con la mamma.*

It is, however, just as common to translate the *–ing* form in English with the present simple tense in Italian.

He's read**ing** the paper. → ***Legge*** *il giornale.*
She's talk**ing** to Mum. → ***Parla*** *con la mamma.*

In other cases the Italian infinitive (the verb form that ends in **-are**, **-ere**, or **-ire**) is often used where the *-ing* form is used in English.

• Use the infinitive when talking about activities:

I love **reading**. → *Mi piace moltissimo **leggere**.*
We don't like **walking**. → *Non ci piace **camminare**.*
Smoking is bad for you. → ***Fumare** fa male.*

Some common translation difficulties

Use the infinitive to translate prepositions such as *without* + *-ing* (**senza** + infinitive), *before* + *-ing* (**prima di** + infinitive), *after* + *-ing* (**dopo aver** + past participle).

He went away **without saying** anything.	→ *È andato via **senza dire** niente.*
Before opening the packet, read the instructions.	→ ***Prima di aprire** il pacchetto, leggi le istruzioni.*
After making a phone call she went out.	→ ***Dopo aver** telefonato è uscita.*

More on prepositions

Sentences that have no preposition in English may contain a preposition in Italian. The dictionary can help you with these. For example:

They started **laughing**.	→ *Hanno cominciato **a ridere**.*
Have you finished **eating**?	→ *Hai finito **di mangiare**?*
When did you stop **smoking**?	→ *Quando hai smesso **di fumare**?*

Saying Sorry

- To apologize about something, use **scusi** to someone you're on formal terms with, and **scusa** to a friend. Use **scusate** to more than one person.

Sorry.	→ *Scusi.*
Sorry I'm late.	→ *Scusi il ritardo.*
Sorry, Paola, I've got to go.	→ *Scusa, Paola, devo andare.*
Sorry to disturb you.	→ *Scusate il disturbo.*

- **Scusi** is also used to mean '*excuse me*' when you stop somebody to ask something.

Excuse me, where is the station?	→ *Scusi, dov'è la stazione?*

Some common translation difficulties

When you haven't heard what someone said, say **come, scusi**?

• To express regret use **mi dispiace**:

My grandfather has died. –
    Oh, **I'm sorry**.
	→	*È morto mio nonno. –*
		    Oh, mi dispiace.

I haven't got time, **sorry**.	→	*Non ho tempo, mi dispiace.*
I'm sorry but I can't come.	→	*Mi dispiace ma non posso venire.*
I'm sorry for them.	→	*Mi dispiace per loro.*

Translating 'to be'

'To be' usually corresponds to **essere**, but remember:

• In phrases describing how you feel, use **avere**:

I **am** hot/cold	→	*ho caldo/freddo*
they **are** hungry/thirsty	→	*hanno fame/sete*
he **is** scared	→	*ha paura*

• To describe the weather, use **fare**:

It**'s** nice weather today.	→	*Fa bel tempo oggi.*

• To say your age, use **avere**:

I**'m** fifteen.	→	*Ho quindici anni.*

• To talk about your health, use **stare**:

I**'m** fine, thanks.	→	*Sto bene, grazie*

Some common translation difficulties

'Have' or 'have got' usually correspond to **avere**:

I've **got** two brothers.	→ **Ho** due fratelli.
Have you **got** a bike?	→ **Hai** una bici?
I**'ve** spent a lot of money.	→ **Ho** speso molti soldi.
What **have** you done?	→ Cos'**hai** fatto?

Remember, though that 'have' and 'has' are translated by **essere**:

• In the perfect tense of some common verbs such as to go (*andare*), to come (*venire*) and to arrive (*arrivare*):

Where **have** they gone?	→ Dove **sono** andati?
She **has** come too.	→ **È** venuta anche lei.
We**'ve** arrived.	→ **Siamo** arrivati.

• In the perfect tense of all reflexive verbs:

I**'ve** hurt myself.	→ Mi **sono** fatto male.
Has she had a good time?	→ Si **è** divertita?

A [eɪ] n (Mus) la m; **A road** n (BRIT Aut) ≈ strada statale; **A to Z®** n stradario

KEYWORD

a [ə] (before vowel or silent h: an) indef art
1 un, uno (+ s impure, gn, pn, ps, x, z), una f, un' + vowel; **a book** un libro; **a mirror** uno specchio; **an apple** una mela; **she's a doctor** è medico
2 (instead of the number "one") un(o), una f; **a year ago** un anno fa; **a hundred/thousand pounds** cento/mille sterline
3 (in expressing ratios, prices etc) a, per; **3 a day/week** 3 al giorno/alla settimana; **10 km an hour** 10 km all'ora; **£5 a person** 5 sterline a persona or per persona

A2 n abbr (BRIT Scol) seconda parte del diploma di studi superiori chiamato "A level"

AA n abbr (BRIT: = Automobile Association) ≈ A.C.I. m; (= Alcoholics Anonymous) A.A. f
AAA n abbr (= American Automobile Association) ≈ A.C.I. m
aback [ə'bæk] adv: **to be taken ~** essere sbalordito/a
abandon [ə'bændən] vt abbandonare ▷ n abbandono; **with ~** sfrenatamente, spensieratamente
abattoir ['æbətwɑː'] n (BRIT) mattatoio
abbey ['æbɪ] n abbazia, badia
abbreviation [əbriːvɪ'eɪʃən] n abbreviazione f
abdomen ['æbdəmən] n addome m
abduct [æb'dʌkt] vt rapire
abide [ə'baɪd] vt sopportare; **I can't ~ it/him** non lo posso soffrire or sopportare; **abide by** vt fus conformarsi a
ability [ə'bɪlɪtɪ] n abilità f inv
able ['eɪbl] adj capace; **to be ~ to do sth** essere capace di fare qc, poter fare qc
abnormal [æb'nɔːməl] adj anormale
aboard [ə'bɔːd] adv a bordo ▷ prep a bordo di
abolish [ə'bɔlɪʃ] vt abolire
abolition [æbəu'lɪʃən] n abolizione f
abort [ə'bɔːt] vt abortire; **abortion** [ə'bɔːʃən] n aborto; **to have an abortion** abortire

KEYWORD

about [ə'baut] adv **1** (approximately) circa, quasi; **about a hundred/thousand** un centinaio/migliaio, circa cento/mille; **it takes about 10 hours** ci vogliono circa 10 ore; **at about 2 o'clock** verso le 2; **I've just about finished** ho quasi finito
2 (referring to place) qua e là, in giro; **to leave things lying about** lasciare delle cose in giro; **to run about** correre qua e là; **to walk about** camminare

3: **to be about to do sth** stare per fare qc
▶ *prep* **1** *(relating to)* su, di; **a book about London** un libro su Londra; **what is it about?** di che si tratta?; *(book, film etc)* di cosa tratta?; **we talked about it** ne abbiamo parlato; **what** *or* **how about doing this?** che ne dici di fare questo?
2 *(referring to place)*: **to walk about the town** camminare per la città; **her clothes were scattered about the room** i suoi vestiti erano sparsi *or* in giro per tutta la stanza

above [ə'bʌv] *adv, prep* sopra; **mentioned ~** suddetto; **~ all** soprattutto
abroad [ə'brɔːd] *adv* all'estero
abrupt [ə'brʌpt] *adj (sudden)* improvviso/a; *(gruff, blunt)* brusco/a
abscess [ˈæbsɪs] *n* ascesso
absence [ˈæbsəns] *n* assenza
absent [ˈæbsənt] *adj* assente; **absent-minded** *adj* distratto/a
absolute [ˈæbsəluːt] *adj* assoluto/a; **absolutely** [-'luːtlɪ] *adv* assolutamente
absorb [əb'sɔːb] *vt* assorbire; **to be ~ed in a book** essere immerso in un libro; **absorbent cotton** [əb'zɔːbənt-] *n (US)* cotone *m* idrofilo; **absorbing** *adj* avvincente, molto interessante
abstain [əb'steɪn] *vi*: **to ~ (from)** astenersi (da)
abstract [ˈæbstrækt] *adj* astratto/a
absurd [əb'sɜːd] *adj* assurdo/a
abundance [ə'bʌndəns] *n* abbondanza
abundant [ə'bʌndənt] *adj* abbondante
abuse *n* [ə'bjuːs] abuso; *(insults)* ingiurie *fpl* ▷ *vt* [ə'bjuːz] abusare di; **abusive** *adj* ingiurioso/a
abysmal [ə'bɪzməl] *adj* spaventoso/a
academic [ækə'dɛmɪk] *adj* accademico/a; *(pej: issue)* puramente

formale ▷ *n* universitario/a; **academic year** *n* anno accademico
academy [ə'kædəmɪ] *n (learned body)* accademia; *(school)* scuola privata; **~ of music** conservatorio
accelerate [æk'sɛləreɪt] *vt, vi* accelerare; **acceleration** *n* accelerazione *f*; **accelerator** *n* acceleratore *m*
accent [ˈæksɛnt] *n* accento
accept [ək'sɛpt] *vt* accettare; **acceptable** *adj* accettabile; **acceptance** *n* accettazione *f*
access [ˈæksɛs] *n* accesso; **accessible** [æk'sɛsəbl] *adj* accessibile
accessory [æk'sɛsərɪ] *n* accessorio; *(Law)*: **~ to** complice *m/f* di
accident [ˈæksɪdənt] *n* incidente *m*; *(chance)* caso; **I've had an ~** ho avuto un incidente; **by ~** per caso; **accidental** [-'dɛntl] *adj* accidentale; **accidentally** [-'dɛntəlɪ] *adv* per caso; **Accident and Emergency Department** *n (BRIT)* pronto soccorso; **accident insurance** *n* assicurazione *f* contro gli infortuni
acclaim [ə'kleɪm] *n* acclamazione *f*
accommodate [ə'kɔmədeɪt] *vt* alloggiare; *(oblige, help)* favorire
accommodation [əkɔmə'deɪʃən] *n*, *(US)* **accommodations** *n pl* alloggio
accompaniment [ə'kʌmpənɪmənt] *n* accompagnamento
accompany [ə'kʌmpənɪ] *vt* accompagnare
accomplice [ə'kʌmplɪs] *n* complice *m/f*
accomplish [ə'kʌmplɪʃ] *vt* compiere; *(goal)* raggiungere; **accomplishment** *n* compimento; realizzazione *f*
accord [ə'kɔːd] *n* accordo ▷ *vt* accordare; **of his own ~** di propria iniziativa; **accordance** *n*: **in accordance with** in conformità con; **according**: **according to**

prep secondo; **accordingly** *adv* in conformità

account [əˈkaʊnt] *n* (*Comm*) conto; (*report*) descrizione *f*; **accounts** *npl* (*Comm*) conti *mpl*; **of little ~** di poca importanza; **on ~** in acconto; **on no ~** per nessun motivo; **on ~ of** a causa di; **to take into ~, take ~ of** tener conto di; **account for** *vt fus* (*explain*) spiegare; giustificare; **accountable** *adj*: **accountable (to)** responsabile (verso); **accountant** [əˈkaʊntənt] *n* ragioniere/a; **account number** *n* numero di conto

accumulate [əˈkjuːmjuleɪt] *vt* accumulare ▷ *vi* accumularsi

accuracy [ˈækjurəsɪ] *n* precisione *f*

accurate [ˈækjurɪt] *adj* preciso/a; **accurately** *adv* precisamente

accusation [ækjuˈzeɪʃən] *n* accusa

accuse [əˈkjuːz] *vt* accusare; **accused** *n* accusato/a

accustomed [əˈkʌstəmd] *adj*: **~ to** abituato/a a

ace [eɪs] *n* asso

ache [eɪk] *n* male *m*, dolore *m* ▷ *vi* (*be sore*) far male, dolere; **my head ~s** mi fa male la testa

achieve [əˈtʃiːv] *vt* (*aim*) raggiungere; (*victory, success*) ottenere; **achievement** *n* compimento; successo

acid [ˈæsɪd] *adj* acido/a ▷ *n* acido

acknowledge [əkˈnɒlɪdʒ] *vt* (*fact*) riconoscere; (*letter: also*: **~ receipt of**) accusare ricevuta di; **acknowledgement** *n* riconoscimento; (*of letter*) conferma

acne [ˈæknɪ] *n* acne *f*

acorn [ˈeɪkɔːn] *n* ghianda

acoustic [əˈkuːstɪk] *adj* acustico/a

acquaintance [əˈkweɪntəns] *n* conoscenza; (*person*) conoscente *m/f*

acquire [əˈkwaɪəʳ] *vt* acquistare; **acquisition** [ækwɪˈzɪʃən] *n* acquisto

acquit [əˈkwɪt] *vt* assolvere; **to ~ o.s. well** comportarsi bene

acre [ˈeɪkəʳ] *n* acro (= 4047 *m*²)

acronym [ˈækrənɪm] *n* acronimo

across [əˈkrɒs] *prep* (*on the other side*) dall'altra parte di; (*crosswise*) attraverso ▷ *adv* dall'altra parte; in larghezza; **to run/swim ~** attraversare di corsa/a nuoto; **~ from** di fronte a

acrylic [əˈkrɪlɪk] *adj* acrilico/a

act [ækt] *n* atto; (*in music-hall etc*) numero; (*Law*) decreto ▷ *vi* agire; (*Theat*) recitare; (*pretend*) fingere ▷ *vt* (*part*) recitare; **to ~ as** agire da; **act up** (*col*) *vi* (*person*) comportarsi male; (*knee, back, injury*) fare male; (*machine*) non funzionare; **acting** *adj* che fa le funzioni di ▷ *n* (*of actor*) recitazione *f*; **to do some acting** fare del teatro (*or* del cinema)

action [ˈækʃən] *n* azione *f*; (*Mil*) combattimento; (*Law*) processo ▷ *vt* (*Comm: request*) evadere; (*tasks*) portare a termine; **to take ~** agire; **out of ~** fuori combattimento; (*machine etc*) fuori servizio; **action replay** *n* (*TV*) replay *m inv*

activate [ˈæktɪveɪt] *vt* (*mechanism*) fare funzionare, attivare

active [ˈæktɪv] *adj* attivo/a; **actively** *adv* (*participate*) attivamente; (*discourage, dislike*) vivamente

activist [ˈæktɪvɪst] *n* attivista *m/f*

activity [ækˈtɪvɪtɪ] *n* attività *f inv*; **activity holiday** *n* vacanza attiva (*in bici, a cavallo, in barca, a vela ecc.*)

actor [ˈæktəʳ] *n* attore *m*

actress [ˈæktrɪs] *n* attrice *f*

actual [ˈæktjuəl] *adj* reale, vero/a

■ Be careful not to translate *actual* by the Italian word *attuale*.

actually [ˈæktjuəlɪ] *adv* veramente; (*even*) addirittura

■ Be careful not to translate *actually* by the Italian word *attualmente*.

acupuncture [ˈækjupʌŋktʃəʳ] *n* agopuntura

acute [əˈkjuːt] *adj* acuto/a; (*mind, person*) perspicace

AD adv abbr (= Anno Domini) d. C.

ad [æd] n abbr = **advertisement**

adamant ['ædəmənt] adj irremovibile

adapt [ə'dæpt] vt adattare ▷ vi: **to ~ (to)** adattarsi (a); **adapter, adaptor** n (Elec) adattatore m

add [æd] vt aggiungere ▷ vi: **to ~ to** (increase) aumentare ▷ n (Internet): **thanks for the ~** grazie per avermi aggiunto (come amico); **add up** vt (figures) addizionare ▷ vi (fig): **it doesn't ~ up** non ha senso; **it doesn't ~ up to much** non è un granché

addict ['ædıkt] n tossicomane m/f; (fig) fanatico/a; **addicted** [ə'dıktıd] adj: **to be addicted to** (drink etc) essere dedito/a a; (fig: football etc) essere tifoso/a di; **addiction** [ə'dıkʃən] n (Med) tossicodipendenza; **addictive** [ə'dıktıv] adj che dà assuefazione

addition [ə'dıʃən] n addizione f; (thing added) aggiunta; **in ~** inoltre; **in ~ to** oltre; **additional** adj supplementare

additive ['ædıtıv] n additivo

address [ə'drɛs] n indirizzo; (talk) discorso ▷ vt indirizzare; (speak to) fare un discorso a; (issue) affrontare; **my ~ is ...** il mio indirizzo è...; **address book** n rubrica

adequate ['ædıkwıt] adj adeguato/a; sufficiente

adhere [əd'hıə'] vi: **to ~ to** aderire a; (fig: rule, decision) seguire

adhesive [əd'hiːzıv] n adesivo; **~ tape** (BRIT: for parcels etc) nastro adesivo; (US Med) cerotto adesivo

adjacent [ə'dʒeısənt] adj adiacente; **~ to** accanto a

adjective ['ædʒɛktıv] n aggettivo

adjoining [ə'dʒɔınıŋ] adj accanto inv, adiacente

adjourn [ə'dʒəːn] vt rimandare ▷ vi essere aggiornato/a

adjust [ə'dʒʌst] vt aggiustare; (Comm: change) rettificare ▷ vi: **to**

~ (to) adattarsi (a); **adjustable** adj regolabile; **adjustment** n (Psych) adattamento; (of machine) regolazione f; (of prices, wages) aggiustamento

administer [əd'mınıstə'] vt amministrare; (justice) somministrare; **administration** [ədmınıs'treıʃən] n amministrazione f; **administrative** [əd'mınıstrətıv] adj amministrativo/a

administrator [əd'mınıstreıtə'] n amministratore/trice

admiral ['ædmərəl] n ammiraglio

admiration [ædmə'reıʃən] n ammirazione f

admire [əd'maıə'] vt ammirare; **admirer** n ammiratore/trice

admission [əd'mıʃən] n ammissione f; (to exhibition, nightclub etc) ingresso; (confession) confessione f

admit [əd'mıt] vt ammettere; far entrare; (agree) riconoscere; **admit to** vt fus riconoscere; **admittance** n ingresso; **admittedly** adv bisogna pur riconoscere (che)

adolescent [ædəu'lɛsnt] adj, n adolescente m/f

adopt [ə'dɔpt] vt adottare; **adopted** adj adottivo/a; **adoption** [ə'dɔpʃən] n adozione f

adore [ə'dɔː'] vt adorare

adorn [ə'dɔːn] vt ornare

Adriatic [eıdrı'ætık] n: **the ~ (Sea)** il mare Adriatico, l'Adriatico

adrift [ə'drıft] adv alla deriva

ADSL n abbr (= asymmetric digital subscriber line) ADSL m

adult ['ædʌlt] n adulto/a ▷ adj adulto/a; (work, education) per adulti; **adult education** n scuola per adulti

adultery [ə'dʌltərı] n adulterio

advance [əd'vɑːns] n avanzamento; (money) anticipo ▷ adj (booking etc) in anticipo ▷ vt (date, money) anticipare ▷ vi avanzare; **in ~** in anticipo; **do I need to book in ~?** occorre che prenoti in anticipo?; **advanced** adj avanzato/a; (Scol: studies) superiore

advantage [əd'vɑ:ntɪdʒ] n (also Tennis) vantaggio; **to take ~ of** approfittarsi di

advent [ˈædvənt] n avvento; **A~** (Rel) Avvento

adventure [əd'vɛntʃər] n avventura; **adventurous** [əd'vɛntʃərəs] adj avventuroso/a

adverb [ˈædvə:b] n avverbio

adversary [ˈædvəsərɪ] n avversario/a

adverse [ˈædvə:s] adj avverso/a

advert [ˈædvə:t] n abbr (BRIT) = **advertisement**

advertise [ˈædvətaɪz] vi, vt fare pubblicità or réclame (a), fare un'inserzione (per vendere); **to ~ for** (staff) cercare tramite annuncio; **advertisement** [əd'və:tɪsmənt] n (Comm) réclame f inv, pubblicità f inv; (in classified ads) inserzione f; **advertiser** n azienda che reclamizza un prodotto; (in newspaper) inserzionista m/f; **advertising** [ˈædvətaɪzɪŋ] n pubblicità

advice [əd'vaɪs] n consigli mpl; **piece of ~** consiglio; **to take legal ~** consultare un avvocato

advisable [əd'vaɪzəbl] adj consigliabile

advise [əd'vaɪz] vt consigliare; **to ~ sb of sth** informare qn di qc; **to ~ sb against sth/against doing sth** sconsigliare qc a qn/a qn di fare qc; **adviser** n consigliere/a; (in business) consulente m/f, consigliere/a; **advisory** [-ərɪ] adj consultivo/a

advocate n [ˈædvəkɪt] (upholder) sostenitore/trice; (Law) avvocato (difensore) ▷ vt [ˈædvəkeɪt] propugnare

Aegean (Sea) [iːˈdʒiːən-] n (mare m) Egeo

aerial [ˈɛərɪəl] n antenna ▷ adj aereo/a

aerobics [ɛəˈrəubɪks] n aerobica

aeroplane [ˈɛərəpleɪn] (BRIT) n aeroplano

aerosol [ˈɛərəsɔl] (BRIT) n aerosol m inv

affair [əˈfɛər] n affare m; (also: **love ~**) relazione f amorosa; **affairs** (business) affari

affect [əˈfɛkt] vt toccare; (influence) influire su, incidere su; (feign) fingere; **affected** adj affettato/a; **affection** [əˈfɛkʃən] n affetto; **affectionate** adj affettuoso/a

afflict [əˈflɪkt] vt affliggere

affluent [ˈæfluənt] adj ricco/a; **the ~ society** la società del benessere

afford [əˈfɔːd] vt permettersi; (provide) fornire; **affordable** adj (che ha un prezzo) abbordabile

Afghanistan [æfˈgænɪstɑːn] n Afganistan m

afraid [əˈfreɪd] adj impaurito/a; **to be ~ of** aver paura di; **to be ~ of doing** or **to do** aver paura di fare; **to be ~ that** aver paura che; **I'm ~ so!** ho paura di sì!; **I'm ~ not** no, mi dispiace

Africa [ˈæfrɪkə] n Africa; **African** adj, n africano/a; **African-American** adj, n afroamericano/a

after [ˈɑːftər] prep, adv dopo ▷ conj dopo che; **what/who are you ~?** che/chi cerca?; **~ he left/having done** dopo che se ne fu andato/dopo aver fatto; **to name sb ~ sb** dare a qn il nome di qn; **it's twenty ~ eight** (US) sono le otto e venti; **to ask ~ sb** chiedere di qn; **~ you!** dopo di lei!; **~ all** dopo tutto; **after-effects** npl conseguenze fpl; (of illness) postumi mpl; **aftermath** n conseguenze fpl; **in the aftermath of** nel periodo dopo; **afternoon** n pomeriggio; **after-shave (lotion)** [ˈɑːftəʃeɪv-] n dopobarba m inv; **aftersun** [ˈɑːftəsʌn] adj; **aftersun (lotion/cream)** (lozione f/crema) doposole m inv; **afterwards**, (US) **afterward** adv dopo

again [əˈgɛn] *adv* di nuovo; **to begin/ see ~** ricominciare/rivedere; **not ... ~** non ... più; **~ and ~** ripetutamente
against [əˈgɛnst] *prep* contro
age [eɪdʒ] *n* età *f inv* ▷ *vt*, *vi* invecchiare; **he is 20 years of ~** ha 20 anni; **~d 10** di 10 anni; **to come of ~** diventare maggiorenne; **it's been ~s since ...** sono secoli che ...; **the ~d** gli anziani; **age group** *n* generazione *f*; **age limit** *n* limite *m* d'età
agency [ˈeɪdʒənsɪ] *n* agenzia
agenda [əˈdʒɛndə] *n* ordine *m* del giorno
agent [ˈeɪdʒənt] *n* agente *m*
aggravate [ˈægrəveɪt] *vt* aggravare; (*annoy*) esasperare
aggression [əˈgrɛʃən] *n* aggressione *f*
aggressive [əˈgrɛsɪv] *adj* aggressivo/a
agile [ˈædʒaɪl] *adj* agile
agitated [ˈædʒɪteɪtɪd] *adj* agitato/a, turbato/a
AGM *n abbr* = **annual general meeting**
ago [əˈgəu] *adv*: **2 days ~** 2 giorni fa; **not long ~** poco tempo fa; **how long ~?** quanto tempo fa?
agony [ˈægənɪ] *n* dolore *m* atroce; **I was in ~** avevo dei dolori atroci
agree [əˈgriː] *vt* (*price*) pattuire ▷ *vi*: **to ~ (with)** essere d'accordo (con); (*Ling*) concordare (con); **to ~ to sth/ to do sth** accettare qc/di fare qc; **to ~ that** (*admit*) ammettere che; **to ~ on sth** accordarsi su qc; **garlic doesn't ~ with me** l'aglio non mi va; **agreeable** *adj* gradevole; (*willing*) disposto/a; **agreed** *adj* (*time*, *place*) stabilito/a; **agreement** *n* accordo; **in agreement** d'accordo
agricultural [ægrɪˈkʌltʃərəl] *adj* agricolo/a
agriculture [ˈægrɪkʌltʃəʳ] *n* agricoltura
ahead [əˈhɛd] *adv* avanti; davanti; **~ of** davanti a; (*fig: schedule etc*) in

anticipo su; **~ of time** in anticipo; **go right** *or* **straight ~** tiri diritto
aid [eɪd] *n* aiuto ▷ *vt* aiutare; **in ~ of** a favore di
aide [eɪd] *n* (*person*) aiutante *m/f*
AIDS [eɪdz] *n abbr* (= *acquired immune deficiency* or *immunodeficiency syndrome*) AIDS *f*
ailing [ˈeɪlɪŋ] *adj* sofferente; (*fig: economy, industry etc*) in difficoltà
ailment [ˈeɪlmənt] *n* indisposizione *f*
aim [eɪm] *vt*: **to ~ sth at** (*gun*) mirare qc a, puntare qc a; (*camera*, *remark*) rivolgere qc a; (*missile*) lanciare qc contro ▷ *vi* (*also*: **take ~**) prendere la mira ▷ *n* mira; **to ~ at** mirare; **to ~ to do** aver l'intenzione di fare
ain't [eɪnt] (*col*) = **am not; aren't; isn't**
air [ɛəʳ] *n* aria ▷ *vt* (*room*, *bed*) arieggiare; (*clothes*) far prendere aria a; (*idea*, *grievance*) esprimere pubblicamente ▷ *cpd* (*currents*) d'aria; (*attack*) aereo/a; **to throw sth into the ~** lanciare qc in aria; **by ~** (*travel*) in aereo; **to be on the ~** (*Radio, TV*) (*programme*) essere in onda; **airbag** *n* airbag *m inv*; **airbed** *n* (BRIT) materassino; **airborne** [ˈɛəbɔːn] *adj* (*plane*) in volo; (*troops*) aerotrasportato/a; **as soon as the plane was airborne** appena l'aereo ebbe decollato; **air-conditioned** *adj* con o ad aria condizionata; **air conditioning** *n* condizionamento d'aria; **aircraft** *n* (*pl inv*) apparecchio; **airfield** *n* campo d'aviazione; **Air Force** *n* aviazione *f* militare; **air hostess** *n* (BRIT) hostess *f inv*; **airing cupboard** [ˈɛərɪŋ-] *n* armadio riscaldato per asciugare panni; **airlift** *n* ponte *m* aereo; **airline** *n* linea aerea; **airliner** *n* aereo di linea; **airmail** *n* posta aerea; **by airmail** per via *or* posta aerea; **airplane** *n* (US) aeroplano; **airport** *n* aeroporto; **air raid** *n* incursione *f* aerea; **airsick** *adj*: **to be airsick** soffrire di mal d'aereo;

airspace n spazio aereo; **airstrip** n pista d'atterraggio; **air terminal** n air-terminal m inv; **airtight** adj ermetico/a; **air traffic controller** n controllore m del traffico aereo; **airy** adj arioso/a; (manners) noncurante

aisle [aɪl] n (of church) navata laterale; navata centrale; (of plane) corridoio; **aisle seat** n (on plane) posto sul corridoio

ajar [ə'dʒɑːʳ] adj socchiuso/a

à la carte [ɑ:lɑ:'kɑ:t] adv alla carta

alarm [ə'lɑːm] n allarme m ▷ vt allarmare; **alarm call** n (in hotel etc) sveglia; **could I have an alarm call at 7 am, please?** vorrei essere svegliato alle 7, per favore; **alarm clock** n sveglia; **alarmed** adj (person) allarmato/a; (house, car etc) dotato/a di allarme; **alarming** adj allarmante, preoccupante

Albania [æl'beɪnɪə] n Albania

albeit [ɔːl'biːɪt] conj sebbene + sub, benché + sub

album ['ælbəm] n album m inv

alcohol ['ælkəhɔl] n alcool m; **alcohol-free** adj analcolico/a; **alcoholic** [-'hɔlɪk] adj alcolico/a ▷ n alcolizzato/a

alcove ['ælkəʊv] n alcova

ale [eɪl] n birra

alert [ə'lɜːt] adj vigile ▷ n allarme m ▷ vt: **to ~ sb (to sth)** avvertire qn (di qc); **to ~ sb to the dangers of sth** mettere qn in guardia contro qc

algebra ['ældʒɪbrə] n algebra

Algeria [æl'dʒɪərɪə] n Algeria

alias ['eɪlɪəs] adv alias ▷ n pseudonimo, falso nome m

alibi ['ælɪbaɪ] n alibi m inv

alien ['eɪlɪən] n straniero/a; (extraterrestrial) alieno/a ▷ adj: **~ (to)** estraneo/a (a); **alienate** vt alienare

alight [ə'laɪt] adj acceso/a ▷ vi scendere; (bird) posarsi

align [ə'laɪn] vt allineare

alike [ə'laɪk] adj simile ▷ adv allo stesso modo; **to look ~** assomigliarsi

alive [ə'laɪv] adj vivo/a; (active) attivo/a

all [ɔːl] adj tutto/a; **all day** tutto il giorno; **all night** tutta la notte; **all men** tutti gli uomini; **all five came** sono venuti tutti e cinque; **all the books** tutti i libri; **all the food** tutto il cibo; **all the time** tutto il tempo; (always) sempre; **all his life** tutta la vita

▷ pron 1 tutto/a; **I ate it all, I ate all of it** l'ho mangiato tutto; **all of us went** tutti noi siamo andati; **all of the boys went** tutti i ragazzi sono andati

2 (in phrases): **above all** soprattutto; **after all** dopotutto; **at all: not at all** (in answer to question) niente affatto; (in answer to thanks) prego!, di niente!, s'immagini!; **I'm not at all tired** non sono affatto stanco; **anything at all will do** andrà bene qualsiasi cosa; **all in all** tutto sommato

▷ adv: **all alone** tutto/a solo/a; **it's not as hard as all that** non è poi così difficile; **all the more/the better** tanto più/meglio; **all but** quasi; **the score is two all** il punteggio è di due a due or è due pari

Allah ['ælə] n Allah m

allegation [ælɪ'geɪʃən] n asserzione f

alleged [ə'lɛdʒd] adj presunto/a; **allegedly** [ə'lɛdʒɪdlɪ] adv secondo quanto si asserisce

allegiance [ə'liːdʒəns] n fedeltà

allergic [ə'lɜːdʒɪk] adj: **~ to** allergico/a a

allergy ['ælədʒɪ] n allergia

alleviate [ə'liːvɪeɪt] vt sollevare

alley ['ælɪ] n vicolo

alliance [ə'laɪəns] n alleanza

allied ['ælaɪd] adj alleato/a

alligator ['ælɪgeɪtəʳ] n alligatore m

all-in ['ɔːlɪn] *adj*, *adv* (BRIT: *charge*)
tutto compreso
allocate ['æləkeɪt] *vt*: **to ~ sth to**
assegnare qc a
allot [ə'lɒt] *vt*: **to ~ sth to** (*duties*)
assegnare qc a
all-out ['ɔːlaut] *adj* (*effort etc*) totale
▷ *adv*: **to go all out for** mettercela
tutta per
allow [ə'lau] *vt* (*practice, behaviour*)
permettere; (*sum to spend etc*)
accordare; (*sum, time estimated*) dare;
(*concede*): **to ~ that** ammettere che;
to ~ sb to permettere a qn di fare;
he is ~ed to (do it) lo può fare; **allow
for** *vt fus* tener conto di; **allowance**
n (*money received*) assegno; (*for
travelling, accommodation*) indennità
f inv; (*Tax*) detrazione *f* di imposta;
to make allowance(s) for tener
conto di
all right *adv* (*feel, work*) bene; (*as
answer*) va bene
ally *n* ['ælaɪ] alleato
almighty [ɔːl'maɪtɪ] *adj*
onnipotente; (*row etc*) colossale
almond ['ɑːmənd] *n* mandorla
almost ['ɔːlməust] *adv* quasi
alone [ə'ləun] *adj*, *adv* solo/a; **to
leave sb ~** lasciare qn in pace; **to
leave sth ~** lasciare stare qc; **let ~ ...**
figuriamoci poi ..., tanto meno ...
along [ə'lɒŋ] *prep* lungo ▷ *adv*: **is
he coming ~?** viene con noi?; **he
was hopping/limping ~** veniva
saltellando/zoppicando; **~ with**
insieme con; **all ~** (*all the time*)
sempre, fin dall'inizio; **alongside**
prep accanto a; lungo ▷ *adv* accanto
aloof [ə'luːf] *adj* distaccato/a ▷ *adv*
a distanza, in disparte; **to stand ~**
tenersi a distanza *or* in disparte
aloud [ə'laud] *adv* ad alta voce
alphabet ['ælfəbɛt] *n* alfabeto
Alps [ælps] *npl*: **the ~** le Alpi
already [ɔːl'rɛdɪ] *adv* già
alright ['ɔːl'raɪt] *adv* (BRIT) = **all right**
also ['ɔːlsəu] *adv* anche

altar ['ɔltər] *n* altare *m*
alter ['ɔltər] *vt*, *vi* alterare; **alteration**
[ɔltə'reɪʃən] *n* modificazione *f*,
alterazione *f*; **alterations** (*Sewing*,
Archit) modifiche *fpl*; **timetable
subject to alteration** orario
soggetto a variazioni
alternate *adj* [ɔl'təːnɪt] alterno/a;
(US: *plan etc*) alternativo/a ▷ *vi*
['ɔltəneɪt]: **to ~ (with)** alternarsi
(a); **on ~ days** ogni due giorni
alternative [ɔl'təːnətɪv] *adj*
alternativo/a ▷ *n* (*choice*)
alternativa; **alternatively** *adv* come
alternativa
although [ɔːl'ðəu] *conj* benché + *sub*,
sebbene + *sub*
altitude ['æltɪtjuːd] *n* altitudine *f*
altogether [ɔːltə'gɛðər] *adv* del
tutto, completamente; (*on the whole*)
tutto considerato; (*in all*) in tutto
aluminium [æljuˈmɪnɪəm], (US)
aluminum [ə'luːmɪnəm] *n*
alluminio
always ['ɔːlweɪz] *adv* sempre
Alzheimer's ['æltshaɪməz] *n* (*also*:
~ disease) morbo di Alzheimer
am [æm] *vb see* **be**
amalgamate [ə'mælgəmeɪt] *vt*
amalgamare ▷ *vi* amalgamarsi
amass [ə'mæs] *vt* ammassare
amateur ['æmətər] *n* dilettante *m/f*
▷ *adj* (*Sport*) dilettante
amaze [ə'meɪz] *vt* stupire; **amazed**
adj sbalordito/a; **to be amazed
(at)** essere sbalordito/a (da);
amazement *n* stupore *m*; **amazing**
adj sorprendente, sbalorditivo/a
Amazon ['æməzən] *n* (*Mythology*)
Amazzone *f*; **the ~** il Rio delle
Amazzoni ▷ *cpd* (*basin, jungle*)
amazzonico/a
ambassador [æm'bæsədər] *n*
ambasciatore/trice
amber ['æmbər] *n* ambra; **at ~** (BRIT
Aut) giallo
ambiguous [æm'bɪgjuəs] *adj*
ambiguo/a

ambition [æm'bɪʃən] *n* ambizione *f*; **ambitious** [æm'bɪʃəs] *adj* ambizioso/a

ambulance ['æmbjuləns] *n* ambulanza

ambush ['æmbuʃ] *n* imboscata

amen ['ɑː'mɛn] *excl* così sia, amen

amend [ə'mɛnd] *vt* (*law*) emendare; (*text*) correggere; **to make ~s** fare ammenda; **amendment** *n* emendamento; correzione *f*

amenities [ə'miːnɪtɪz] *npl* attrezzature *fpl* ricreative e culturali

America [ə'mɛrɪkə] *n* America; **American** *adj, n* americano/a; **American football** *n* (BRIT) football *m* americano

amicable ['æmɪkəbl] *adj* amichevole

amid(st) [ə'mɪd(st)] *prep* in mezzo a

ammunition [æmju'nɪʃən] *n* munizioni *fpl*

amnesty ['æmnɪstɪ] *n* amnistia; **to grant an ~ to** concedere l'amnistia a, amnistiare

among(st) [ə'mʌŋ(st)] *prep* fra, tra, in mezzo a

amount [ə'maunt] *n* somma; ammontare *m*; (*quantity*) quantità *f inv* ▷ *vi*: **to ~ to** (*total*) ammontare a; (*be same as*) essere come

amp(ère) ['æmp(εər)] *n* ampere *m inv*

ample ['æmpl] *adj* ampio/a; spazioso/a; (*enough*): **this is ~** questo è più che sufficiente

amplifier ['æmplɪfaɪər] *n* amplificatore *m*

amputate ['æmpjuteɪt] *vt* amputare

Amtrak ['æmtræk] (US) *n* società ferroviaria americana

amuse [ə'mjuːz] *vt* divertire; **amusement** *n* divertimento; **amusement arcade** *n* sala giochi; **amusement park** *n* luna park *m inv*

amusing [ə'mjuːzɪŋ] *adj* divertente

an [æn, ən, n] *indef art see* **a**

anaemia [ə'niːmɪə] *n* anemia

anaemic [ə'niːmɪk] *adj* anemico/a

anaesthetic [ænɪs'θɛtɪk] *adj* anestetico/a ▷ *n* anestetico

analog(ue) ['ænələg] *adj* (*watch, computer*) analogico/a

analogy [ə'nælədʒɪ] *n* analogia; **to draw an ~ between** fare un'analogia tra

analyse, (US) **analyze** ['ænəlaɪz] *vt* analizzare; **analysis** (*pl* **analyses**) [ə'næləsɪs, -siːz] *n* analisi *f inv*; **analyst** ['ænəlɪst] *n* (*political analyst etc*) analista *m/f*; (US) (*psic*) analista *m/f*

analyze ['ænəlaɪz] *vt* (US) = **analyse**

anarchy ['ænəkɪ] *n* anarchia

anatomy [ə'nætəmɪ] *n* anatomia

ancestor ['ænsɪstər] *n* antenato/a

anchor ['æŋkər] *n* ancora ▷ *vi* (*also*: **to drop ~**) gettare l'ancora ▷ *vt* ancorare; **to weigh ~** salpare *or* levare l'ancora

anchovy ['æntʃəvɪ] *n* acciuga

ancient ['eɪnʃənt] *adj* antico/a; (*person, car*) vecchissimo/a

and [ænd] *conj* e (*often 'ed' before vowel*); **~ so on** e così via; **try ~ come** cerca di venire; **he talked ~ talked** non la finiva di parlare; **better ~ better** sempre meglio

Andes ['ændiːz] *npl*: **the ~** le Ande

anemia *etc* [ə'niːmɪə] (US) = **anaemia** *etc*

anesthetic [ænɪs'θɛtɪk] (US) = **anaesthetic**

angel ['eɪndʒəl] *n* angelo

anger ['æŋɡər] *n* rabbia

angina [æn'dʒaɪnə] *n* angina pectoris

angle ['æŋɡl] *n* angolo; **from their ~** dal loro punto di vista

angler ['æŋɡlər] *n* pescatore *m* con la lenza

Anglican ['æŋɡlɪkən] *adj, n* anglicano/a

angling ['æŋɡlɪŋ] *n* pesca con la lenza

angrily ['æŋɡrɪlɪ] *adv* con rabbia

angry ['æŋgrɪ] adj arrabbiato/a, furioso/a; (wound) infiammato/a; **to be ~ with sb/at sth** essere in collera con qn/per qc; **to get ~** arrabbiarsi; **to make sb ~** fare arrabbiare qn

anguish ['æŋgwɪʃ] n angoscia

animal ['ænɪməl] adj animale ▷ n animale m

animated ['ænɪmeɪtɪd] adj animato/a

animation [ænɪ'meɪʃən] n animazione f

aniseed ['ænɪsi:d] n semi mpl di anice

ankle ['æŋkl] n caviglia

annex n ['æneks] (BRIT: also: **~e**) edificio annesso ▷ vt [ə'neks] annettere

anniversary [ænɪ'və:sərɪ] n anniversario

announce [ə'nauns] vt annunciare; **announcement** n annuncio; (letter, card) partecipazione f; **announcer** n (Radio, TV: between programmes) annunciatore/trice; (: in a programme) presentatore/trice

annoy [ə'nɔɪ] vt dare fastidio a; **don't get ~ed!** non irritarti!; **annoying** adj irritante

annual ['ænjuəl] adj annuale ▷ n (Bot) pianta annua; (book) annuario; **annually** adv annualmente

anonymous [ə'nɔnɪməs] adj anonimo/a

anorak ['ænəræk] n giacca a vento

anorexia [ænə'rɛksɪə] n (Med: also: **~ nervosa**) anoressia

anorexic [ænə'rɛksɪk] adj, n anoressico/a

another [ə'nʌðə*] adj: **~ book** (one more) un altro libro, ancora un libro; (a different one) un altro libro ▷ pron un altro (un'altra), ancora uno/a; see also **one**

answer ['ɑːnsə*] n risposta; soluzione f ▷ vi rispondere ▷ vt (reply to) rispondere a; (problem) risolvere; (prayer) esaudire; **in ~**

to your letter in risposta alla sua lettera; **to ~ the phone** rispondere (al telefono); **to ~ the bell** rispondere al campanello; **to ~ the door** aprire la porta; **answer back** vi ribattere; **answerphone** n (esp BRIT) segreteria telefonica

ant [ænt] n formica

Antarctic [ænt'ɑːktɪk] n: **the ~** l'Antartide f

antelope ['æntɪləup] n antilope f

antenatal ['æntɪ'neɪtl] adj prenatale

antenna (pl **antennae**) [æn'tɛnə, -niː] n antenna

anthem ['ænθəm] n: **national ~** inno nazionale

anthology [æn'θɔlədʒɪ] n antologia

anthrax ['ænθræks] n antrace m

anthropology [ænθrə'pɔlədʒɪ] n antropologia

anti- ['æntɪ] prefix anti...; **antibiotic** ['æntɪbaɪ'ɔtɪk] n antibiotico; **antibody** ['æntɪbɔdɪ] n anticorpo

anticipate [æn'tɪsɪpeɪt] vt prevedere; pregustare; (wishes, request) prevenire; **anticipation** [æntɪsɪ'peɪʃən] n anticipazione f; (expectation) aspettativa fpl

anticlimax ['æntɪ'klaɪmæks] n: **it was an ~** fu una completa delusione

anticlockwise ['æntɪ'klɔkwaɪz] adj, adv in senso antiorario

antics ['æntɪks] npl buffonerie fpl

anti: antidote ['æntɪdəut] n antidoto; **antifreeze** ['æntɪfriːz] n anticongelante m; **anti-globalization** [æntɪgləubəlaɪ'zeɪʃən] n antiglobalizzazione f; **antihistamine** [æntɪ'hɪstəmiːn] n antistaminico; **antiperspirant** ['æntɪ'pə:spərənt] adj antitraspirante

antique [æn'tiːk] n antichità f inv ▷ adj antico/a; **antique shop** n negozio d'antichità

antiseptic [æntɪ'sɛptɪk] n antisettico

antisocial ['æntɪ'səuʃəl] adj asociale

antiviral [æntɪ'vaɪərəl] *adj* (Med) antivirale

antivirus [æntɪ'vaɪərəs] *adj* (Comput) antivirus *inv*; **antivirus software** *n* antivirus *m inv*

antlers ['æntləz] *npl* palchi *mpl*

anxiety [æŋ'zaɪətɪ] *n* ansia; (*keenness*): **~ to do** smania di fare

anxious ['æŋkʃəs] *adj* ansioso/a, inquieto/a; (*worrying*) angosciante; (*keen*): **~ to do/that** impaziente di fare/che + *sub*

KEYWORD

any ['ɛnɪ] *adj* **1** (*in questions etc*): **have you any butter?** hai del burro?, hai un po' di burro?; **have you any children?** hai bambini?; **if there are any tickets left** se ci sono ancora (dei) biglietti, se c'è ancora qualche biglietto
2 (*with negative*): **I haven't any money/books** non ho soldi/libri
3 (*no matter which*) qualsiasi, qualunque; **choose any book you like** scegli un libro qualsiasi
4 (*in phrases*): **in any case** in ogni caso; **any day now** da un giorno all'altro; **at any moment** in qualsiasi momento, da un momento all'altro; **at any rate** ad ogni modo
▶ *pron* **1** (*in questions, with negative*): **have you got any?** ne hai?; **can any of you sing?** qualcuno di voi sa cantare?; **I haven't any (of them)** non ne ho
2 (*no matter which one(s)*): **take any of those books (you like)** prendi uno qualsiasi di quei libri
▶ *adv* **1** (*in questions etc*): **do you want any more soup/sandwiches?** vuoi ancora un po' di minestra/degli altri panini?; **are you feeling any better?** ti senti meglio?
2 (*with negative*): **I can't hear him any more** non lo sento più; **don't wait any longer** non aspettare più

anybody ['ɛnɪbɒdɪ] *pron* (*in interrogative sentences*) qualcuno; (*in negative sentences*) nessuno; (*no matter who*) chiunque; **can you see ~?** vedi qualcuno or nessuno?; **if ~ should phone ...** se telefona qualcuno ...; **I don't see ~** non vedo nessuno; **~ could do it** chiunque potrebbe farlo

anyhow ['ɛnɪhaʊ] *adv* (*at any rate*) ad ogni modo, comunque; (*haphazard*): **do it ~ you like** fallo come ti pare; **I shall go ~** ci andrò lo stesso or comunque; **she leaves things just ~** lascia tutto come capita

anyone ['ɛnɪwʌn] *pron* = **anybody**

anything ['ɛnɪθɪŋ] *pron* (*in interrogative sentences*) qualcosa, niente; (*with negative*) niente; **you can say ~ you like** (*no matter what*) puoi dire quello che ti pare; **can you see ~?** vedi niente or qualcosa?; **if ~ happens to me ...** se mi dovesse succedere qualcosa ...; **I can't see ~** non vedo niente; **~ will do** va bene qualsiasi cosa or tutto; **~ else?** (*in shop*) basta (così)?; **it can cost ~ between £15 and £20** può costare qualcosa come 15 o 20 sterline

anytime ['ɛnɪtaɪm] *adv* in qualunque momento; quando vuole

anyway ['ɛnɪweɪ] *adv* (*at any rate*) ad ogni modo, comunque; (*besides*) ad ogni modo

anywhere ['ɛnɪwɛəʳ] *adv* (*in interrogative sentences*) da qualche parte; (*with negative*) da nessuna parte; (*no matter where*) da qualsiasi or qualunque parte, dovunque; **can you see him ~?** lo vedi da qualche parte?; **I don't see him ~** non lo vedo da nessuna parte; **~ in the world** dovunque nel mondo

apart [ə'pɑːt] *adv* (*to one side*) a parte; (*separately*) separatamente; **with one's legs ~** con le gambe divaricate; **10 miles/a long way ~** a 10 miglia di distanza/molto lontani

l'uno dall'altro; **to take ~** smontare;
~ from a parte, eccetto
apartment [ə'pɑːtmənt] n (US)
appartamento; (room) locale m;
apartment building n (US) stabile
m, caseggiato
apathy ['æpəθɪ] n apatia
ape [eɪp] n scimmia ▷ vt
scimmiottare
aperitif [ə'pɛrɪtiːf] n aperitivo
aperture ['æpətʃjʊəʳ] n apertura
APEX n abbr (= advance purchase
excursion) APEX m inv
apologize [ə'pɒlədʒaɪz] vi: **to ~
(for sth to sb)** scusarsi (di qc a qn),
chiedere scusa (a qn per qc)
apology [ə'pɒlədʒɪ] n scuse fpl
apostrophe [ə'pɒstrəfɪ] n (sign)
apostrofo
app n abbr (col: Comput) = **application**
applicazione f
appal, (US) **appall** [ə'pɔːl] vt
atterrire; sconvolgere; **appalling** adj
spaventoso/a
apparatus [æpə'reɪtəs] n apparato;
(in gymnasium) attrezzatura
apparent [ə'pærənt] adj evidente;
apparently adv evidentemente
appeal [ə'piːl] vi (Law) appellarsi
alla legge ▷ n (Law) appello; (request)
richiesta; (charm) attrattiva; **to ~ for**
chiedere (con insistenza); **to ~ to**
(person) appellarsi a; (thing) piacere
a; **it doesn't ~ to me** mi dice poco;
appealing adj (attractive) attraente
appear [ə'pɪəʳ] vi apparire; (Law)
comparire; (publication) essere
pubblicato/a; (seem) sembrare;
it would ~ that sembra che;
appearance n apparizione f;
apparenza; (look, aspect) aspetto
appendicitis [əpɛndɪ'saɪtɪs] n
appendicite f
appendix (pl **appendices**)
[ə'pɛndɪks, -siːz] n appendice f
appetite ['æpɪtaɪt] n appetito
appetizer ['æpɪtaɪzəʳ] n stuzzichino
applaud [ə'plɔːd] vt, vi applaudire

applause [ə'plɔːz] n applauso
apple ['æpl] n mela; **apple pie** n
torta di mele
appliance [ə'plaɪəns] n apparecchio
applicable [ə'plɪkəbl] adj
applicabile; **to be ~ to** essere valido
per; **the law is ~ from January** la
legge entrerà in vigore in gennaio
applicant ['æplɪkənt] n candidato/a
application [æplɪ'keɪʃən] n
applicazione f; (for a job, a grant etc)
domanda; (Comput) applicazione f;
application form n modulo per la
domanda
apply [ə'plaɪ] vt: **to ~ (to)** (paint,
ointment) dare (a); (theory, technique)
applicare (a) ▷ vi: **to ~ to** (ask)
rivolgersi a; (be suitable for, relevant
to) riguardare, riferirsi a; **to ~ (for)**
(permit, grant, job) fare domanda
(per); **to ~ o.s. to** dedicarsi a
appoint [ə'pɔɪnt] vt nominare;
appointment n nomina;
(arrangement to meet) appuntamento;
to make an appointment with sb
prendere un appuntamento con qn; **I
have an appointment (with) ...** ho
un appuntamento (con) ...
appraisal [ə'preɪzl] n valutazione f
appreciate [ə'priːʃɪeɪt] vt (like)
apprezzare; (be grateful for) essere
riconoscente di; (be aware of) rendersi
conto di ▷ vi (Comm) aumentare;
I'd ~ your help ti sono grato per
l'aiuto; **appreciation** [əpriːʃɪ'eɪʃən]
n apprezzamento; (Finance) aumento
del valore
apprehension [æprɪ'hɛnʃən] n
(fear) inquietudine f
apprehensive [æprɪ'hɛnsɪv] adj
apprensivo/a
apprentice [ə'prɛntɪs] n
apprendista m/f
approach [ə'prəʊtʃ] vi avvicinarsi
▷ vt (come near) avvicinarsi a; (ask,
apply to) rivolgersi a; (subject, passer-
by) avvicinare ▷ n approccio; accesso;
(to problem) modo di affrontare

appropriate vt [ə'prəuprɪeɪt] (take) appropriarsi di ▷ adj [ə'prəuprɪɪt] appropriato/a, adatto/a
approval [ə'pruːvəl] n approvazione f; **on ~** (Comm) in prova, in esame
approve [ə'pruːv] vt, vi approvare; **approve of** vt fus approvare
approximate adj [ə'prɒksɪmɪt] approssimativo/a; **approximately** adv circa
Apr. abbr (= April) apr.
apricot ['eɪprɪkɒt] n albicocca
April ['eɪprəl] n aprile m; **~ fool!** pesce d'aprile!; **April Fools' Day** n vedi nota "**April Fools' Day**"

- APRIL FOOLS' DAY
-
- April Fools' Day è il primo aprile, il
- giorno degli scherzi e delle burle.
- Il nome deriva dal fatto che, se
- una persona cade nella trappola
- che gli è stata tesa, fa la figura del
- fool, cioè dello sciocco. Di recente
- gli scherzi stanno diventando
- sempre più elaborati, e persino
- i giornalisti a volte inventano
- vicende incredibili per burlarsi
- dei lettori.

apron ['eɪprən] n grembiule m
apt [æpt] adj (suitable) adatto/a; (able) capace; (likely): **to be ~ to do** avere tendenza a fare
aquarium [ə'kwɛərɪəm] n acquario
Aquarius [ə'kwɛərɪəs] n Acquario
Arab ['ærəb] adj, n arabo/a
Arabia [ə'reɪbɪə] n Arabia; **Arabian** [ə'reɪbɪən] adj arabo/a; **Arabic** ['ærəbɪk] adj arabico/a, arabo/a ▷ n arabo; **Arabic numerals** npl numeri mpl arabi, numerazione f araba
arbitrary ['ɑːbɪtrərɪ] adj arbitrario/a
arbitration [ɑːbɪ'treɪʃən] n (Law) arbitrato; (Industry) arbitraggio
arc [ɑːk] n arco
arcade [ɑː'keɪd] n portico; (passage with shops) galleria

arch [ɑːtʃ] n arco; (of foot) arco plantare ▷ vt inarcare
archaeology [ɑːkɪ'ɒlədʒɪ] n archeologia
archbishop [ɑːtʃ'bɪʃəp] n arcivescovo
archeology [ɑːkɪ'ɒlədʒɪ] = **archaeology**
architect ['ɑːkɪtɛkt] n architetto; **architectural** [ɑːkɪ'tɛktʃərəl] adj architettonico/a; **architecture** ['ɑːkɪtɛktʃəʳ] n architettura
archive ['ɑːkaɪv] n (also Comput) archivio; **archives** npl archivi mpl
Arctic ['ɑːktɪk] adj artico/a ▷ n: **the ~** l'Artico
are [ɑːʳ] vb see **be**
area ['ɛərɪə] n (Geom) area; (zone) zona; (: smaller) settore m; **area code** n (US Tel) prefisso
arena [ə'riːnə] n arena
aren't [ɑːnt] = **are not**
Argentina [ɑːdʒən'tiːnə] n Argentina; **Argentinian** [-'tɪnɪən] adj, n argentino/a
arguably ['ɑːgjuəblɪ] adv: **it is ~ ...** si può sostenere che sia ...
argue ['ɑːgjuː] vi (quarrel) litigare; (reason) ragionare; **to ~ that** sostenere che
argument ['ɑːgjumənt] n (reasons) argomento; (quarrel) lite f
Aries ['ɛərɪz] n Ariete m
arise (pt **arose**, pp **arisen**) [ə'raɪz, ə'rəuz, ə'rɪzn] vi (opportunity, problem) presentarsi
arithmetic [ə'rɪθmətɪk] n aritmetica
arm [ɑːm] n braccio ▷ vt armare; **~ in ~** a braccetto; see also **arms**; **armchair** n poltrona
armed [ɑːmd] adj armato/a; **armed robbery** n rapina a mano armata
armour, (US) **armor** ['ɑːməʳ] n armatura; (Mil: tanks) mezzi mpl blindati
armpit ['ɑːmpɪt] n ascella
armrest ['ɑːmrɛst] n bracciolo

arms [ɑːmz] *npl* (*weapons*) armi *fpl*
army ['ɑːmɪ] *n* esercito
aroma [ə'rəʊmə] *n* aroma;
  aromatherapy *n* aromaterapia
arose [ə'rəʊz] *pt of* **arise**
around [ə'raʊnd] *adv* attorno,
  intorno ▷ *prep* intorno a; (*fig: about*):
  ~ £5/3 o'clock circa 5 sterline/le 3; **is
  he ~?** è in giro?
arouse [ə'raʊz] *vt* (*sleeper*) svegliare;
  (*curiosity, passions*) suscitare
arrange [ə'reɪndʒ] *vt* sistemare;
  (*programme*) preparare; **to ~ to do
  sth** mettersi d'accordo per fare qc;
  arrangement *n* sistemazione *f*;
  (*agreement*) accordo; **arrangements**
  npl (*plans etc*) progetti *mpl*, piani *mpl*
array [ə'reɪ] *n*: **~ of** fila di
arrears [ə'rɪəz] *npl* arretrati *mpl*; **to
  be in ~ with one's rent** essere in
  arretrato con l'affitto
arrest [ə'rɛst] *vt* arrestare; (*sb's
  attention*) attirare ▷ *n* arresto; **under
  ~** in arresto
arrival [ə'raɪvəl] *n* arrivo; (*person*)
  arrivato/a; **a new ~** un nuovo
  venuto; (*baby*) un neonato
arrive [ə'raɪv] *vi* arrivare; **arrive at** *vt
  fus* arrivare a
arrogance ['ærəgəns] *n* arroganza
arrogant ['ærəgənt] *adj* arrogante
arrow ['ærəʊ] *n* freccia
arse [ɑːs] *n* (*col!*) culo (!)
arson ['ɑːsn] *n* incendio doloso
art [ɑːt] *n* arte *f*; (*craft*) mestiere *m*;
  see also **arts**; **art college** *n* scuola
  di belle arti
artery ['ɑːtərɪ] *n* arteria
art gallery *n* galleria d'arte
arthritis [ɑː'θraɪtɪs] *n* artrite *f*
artichoke ['ɑːtɪtʃəʊk] *n* carciofo;
  Jerusalem ~ topinambur *m inv*
article ['ɑːtɪkl] *n* articolo; **articles**
  npl (BRIT Law: *training*) contratto di
  tirocinio; **~s of clothing** indumenti
  mpl
articulate *adj* [ɑː'tɪkjʊlɪt] (*person*)
  che si esprime forbitamente; (*speech*)

articolato/a ▷ *vi* [ɑː'tɪkjʊleɪt]
  articolare
artificial [ɑːtɪ'fɪʃəl] *adj* artificiale
artist ['ɑːtɪst] *n* artista *m/f*; **artistic**
  [ɑː'tɪstɪk] *adj* artistico/a
arts [ɑːts] *npl* (*Scol*) lettere *fpl*
art school *n* scuola d'arte

KEYWORD

as [æz] *conj* 1 (*referring to time*)
  mentre; **as the years went by** col
  passare degli anni; **he came in as
  I was leaving** arrivò mentre stavo
  uscendo; **as from tomorrow** da
  domani
  2 (*in comparisons*): **as big as** grande
  come; **twice as big as** due volte più
  grande di; **as much/many as** tanto
  quanto/tanti quanti; **as soon as
  possible** prima possibile
  3 (*since, because*) dal momento che,
  siccome
  4 (*referring to manner, way*) come; **do
  as you wish** fa' come vuoi; **as she
  said** come ha detto lei
  5 (*concerning*): **as for** *or* **to that** per
  quanto riguarda *or* quanto a quello
  6: **as if** *or* **though** come se; **he
  looked as if he was ill** sembrava
  stare male; *see also* **long; such; well**
  ▷ *prep*: **he works as a driver** fa
  l'autista; **as chairman of the
  company, he …** come presidente
  della compagnia, lui …; **he gave me
  it as a present** me lo ha regalato

a.s.a.p. *abbr* (= *as soon as possible*)
  prima possibile
asbestos [æz'bɛstəs] *n* asbesto,
  amianto
ASBO *n abbr* (BRIT: = *antisocial
  behaviour order*) provvedimento
  restrittivo per comportamento
  antisociale
ascent [ə'sɛnt] *n* salita
ash [æʃ] *n* (*dust*) cenere *f*; **~ (tree)**
  frassino

ashamed [əˈʃeɪmd] *adj* vergognoso/a; **to be ~ of** vergognarsi di

ashore [əˈʃɔːʳ] *adv* a terra

ashtray [ˈæʃtreɪ] *n* portacenere *m*

Ash Wednesday *n* Mercoledì *m inv* delle Ceneri

Asia [ˈeɪʃə] *n* Asia; **Asian** *adj, n* asiatico/a

aside [əˈsaɪd] *adv* da parte ▷ *n* a parte *m*

ask [ɑːsk] *vt* (*question*) domandare; (*invite*) invitare; **to ~ sb sth/sb to do sth** chiedere qc a qn/a qn di fare qc; **to ~ sb about sth** chiedere a qn di qc; **to ~ (sb) a question** fare una domanda (a qn); **to ~ sb out to dinner** invitare qn a mangiare fuori; **ask for** *vt fus* chiedere; **it's just ~ing for trouble** *or* **for it** è proprio (come) andarsele a cercare

asleep [əˈsliːp] *adj* addormentato/a; **to be ~** dormire; **to fall ~** addormentarsi

AS level *n abbr* (= *Advanced Subsidiary level*) prima parte del diploma di studi superiori chiamato "A level"

asparagus [əsˈpærəgəs] *n* asparagi *mpl*

aspect [ˈæspɛkt] *n* aspetto

aspiration [æspəˈreɪʃən] *n* aspirazione *f*; **aspirations** *npl* aspirazioni *fpl*

aspire [əsˈpaɪəʳ] *vi*: **to ~ to** aspirare a

aspirin [ˈæsprɪn] *n* aspirina

ass [æs] *n* asino; (*col*) scemo/a; (*us col!*) culo (*!*)

assassin [əˈsæsɪn] *n* assassino; **assassinate** [əˈsæsɪneɪt] *vt* assassinare

assault [əˈsɔːlt] *n* (*Mil*) assalto; (*gen: attack*) aggressione *f* ▷ *vt* assaltare; aggredire; (*sexually*) violentare

assemble [əˈsɛmbl] *vt* riunire; (*Tech*) montare ▷ *vi* riunirsi

assembly [əˈsɛmblɪ] *n* (*meeting*) assemblea; (*construction*) montaggio

assert [əˈsəːt] *vt* asserire; (*insist on*) far valere; **assertion** [əˈsəːʃən] *n* asserzione *f*

assess [əˈsɛs] *vt* valutare; **assessment** *n* valutazione *f*

asset [ˈæsɛt] *n* vantaggio; **assets** *npl* (*Comm: of individual*) beni *mpl*; (: *of company*) attivo

assign [əˈsaɪn] *vt*: **to ~ (to)** (*task*) assegnare (a); (*resources*) riservare (a); (*cause, meaning*) attribuire (a); **to ~ a date to sth** fissare la data di qc; **assignment** *n* compito

assist [əˈsɪst] *vt* assistere, aiutare; **assistance** *n* assistenza, aiuto; **assistant** *n* assistente *m/f*; (BRIT: *also*: **shop assistant**) commesso/a

associate *adj* [əˈsəʊʃɪɪt] associato/a; (*member*) aggiunto/a ▷ *n* [əˈsəʊʃɪɪt] collega *m/f* ▷ *vt* [əˈsəʊʃɪeɪt] associare ▷ *vi* [əˈsəʊʃɪeɪt]: **to ~ with sb** frequentare qn

association [əsəʊsɪˈeɪʃən] *n* associazione *f*

assorted [əˈsɔːtɪd] *adj* assortito/a

assortment [əˈsɔːtmənt] *n* assortimento

assume [əˈsjuːm] *vt* supporre; (*responsibilities etc*) assumere; (*attitude, name*) prendere

assumption [əˈsʌmpʃən] *n* supposizione *f*, ipotesi *f inv*; (*of power*) assunzione *f*

assurance [əˈʃuərəns] *n* assicurazione *f*; (*self-confidence*) fiducia in se stesso

assure [əˈʃuəʳ] *vt* assicurare

asterisk [ˈæstərɪsk] *n* asterisco

asthma [ˈæsmə] *n* asma

astonish [əˈstɒnɪʃ] *vt* stupire; **astonished** *adj* stupito/a, sorpreso/a; **to be astonished (at)** essere stupito/a (da); **astonishing** *adj* sorprendente, stupefacente; **I find it astonishing that ...** mi stupisce che ...; **astonishment** *n* stupore *m*

astound [əˈstaund] *vt* sbalordire

astray [əˈstreɪ] *adv*: **to go ~** smarrirsi; **to lead ~** portare sulla cattiva strada

astrology [əsˈtrɒlədʒɪ] *n* astrologia

astronaut [ˈæstrənɔːt] *n* astronauta *m/f*

astronomer [əsˈtrɒnəməʳ] *n* astronomo/a

astronomical [æstrəˈnɒmɪkl] *adj* astronomico/a

astronomy [əsˈtrɒnəmɪ] *n* astronomia

astute [əsˈtjuːt] *adj* astuto/a

asylum [əˈsaɪləm] *n* asilo; (*lunatic asylum*) manicomio

 KEYWORD

at [æt] *prep* **1** (*referring to position, direction*) a; **at the top** in cima; **at the desk** al banco, alla scrivania; **at home/school** a casa/scuola; **at the baker's** dal panettiere; **to look at sth** guardare qc; **to throw sth at sb** lanciare qc a qn
2 (*referring to time*) a; **at 4 o'clock** alle 4; **at night** di notte; **at Christmas** a Natale; **at times** a volte
3 (*referring to rates, speed etc*) a; **at £1 a kilo** a 1 sterlina al chilo; **two at a time** due alla volta, due per volta; **at 50 km/h** a 50 km/h
4 (*referring to manner*): **at a stroke** d'un solo colpo; **at peace** in pace
5 (*referring to activity*): **to be at work** essere al lavoro; **to play at cowboys** giocare ai cowboy; **to be good at sth/doing sth** essere bravo in qc/a fare qc
6 (*referring to cause*): **shocked/surprised/annoyed at sth** colpito da/sorpreso da/arrabbiato per qc; **I went at his suggestion** ci sono andato dietro suo consiglio *n*
▸ *n* (@ *symbol*) chiocciola

ate [eɪt] *pt of* **eat**

atheist [ˈeɪθɪɪst] *n* ateo/a

Athens [ˈæθɪnz] *n* Atene *f*

athlete [ˈæθliːt] *n* atleta *m/f*

athletic [æθˈlɛtɪk] *adj* atletico/a; **athletics** *n* atletica

Atlantic [ətˈlæntɪk] *adj* atlantico/a ▸ *n*: **the ~ (Ocean)** l'Atlantico, l'Oceano Atlantico

atlas [ˈætləs] *n* atlante *m*

ATM *abbr* (= *automated telling machine*) (sportello) Bancomat® *m inv*

atmosphere [ˈætməsfɪəʳ] *n* atmosfera

atom [ˈætəm] *n* atomo; **atomic** [əˈtɒmɪk] *adj* atomico/a; **atom(ic) bomb** *n* bomba atomica

atrocity [əˈtrɒsɪtɪ] *n* atrocità *f inv*

attach [əˈtætʃ] *vt* attaccare; (*document, letter*) allegare; (*importance etc*) attribuire; **to be ~ed to sb/sth** (*to like*) essere affezionato/a a qn/qc; **attachment** [əˈtætʃmənt] *n* (*tool*) accessorio; (*love*): **attachment (to)** affetto (per)

attack [əˈtæk] *vt* attaccare; (*person*) aggredire; (*task etc*) iniziare; (*problem*) affrontare ▸ *n* attacco; (*also*: **heart ~**) infarto; **attacker** *n* aggressore *m*

attain [əˈteɪn] *vt* (*also*: **~ to**) arrivare a, raggiungere

attempt [əˈtɛmpt] *n* tentativo ▸ *vt* tentare; **to make an ~ on sb's life** attentare alla vita di qn

attend [əˈtɛnd] *vt* frequentare; (*meeting, talk*) andare a; (*patient*) assistere; **attend to** *vt fus* (*needs, affairs etc*) prendersi cura di; (*customer*) occuparsi di; **attendance** *n* (*being present*) presenza; (*people present*) gente *f* presente; **attendant** *n* custode *m/f*; persona di servizio ▸ *adj* concomitante

Be careful not to translate *attend* by the Italian word *attendere*.

attention [əˈtɛnʃən] *n* attenzione *f*; (*Mil*) attenti!; **for the ~ of** (*Admin*) per l'attenzione di

attic [ˈætɪk] *n* soffitta

attitude [ˈætɪtjuːd] n
atteggiamento; (posture) posa
attorney [əˈtəːnɪ] n (lawyer)
avvocato; (having proxy) mandatario;
Attorney General (BRIT)
Procuratore m Generale; (US)
Ministro della Giustizia
attract [əˈtrækt] vt attirare;
attraction [əˈtrækʃən] n (gen pl:
pleasant things) attrattiva; (Physics,
fig: towards sth) attrazione f;
attractive adj attraente
attribute n [ˈætrɪbjuːt] attributo ▷ vt
[əˈtrɪbjuːt]: **to ~ sth to** attribuire qc a
aubergine [ˈəubəʒiːn] n melanzana
auburn [ˈɔːbən] adj tizianesco/a
auction [ˈɔːkʃən] n (also: **sale by ~**)
asta ▷ vt (also: **sell by ~**) vendere
all'asta; (also: **put up for ~**) mettere
all'asta
audible [ˈɔːdɪbl] adj udibile
audience [ˈɔːdɪəns] n (people)
pubblico; spettatori mpl; ascoltatori
mpl; (interview) udienza
audit [ˈɔːdɪt] vt rivedere, verificare
audition [ɔːˈdɪʃən] n audizione f
auditor [ˈɔːdɪtəʳ] n revisore m
auditorium [ɔːdɪˈtɔːrɪəm] n sala,
auditorio
Aug. abbr (= August) ago., ag.
August [ˈɔːɡəst] n agosto
aunt [ɑːnt] n zia; **auntie, aunty**
[ˈɑːntɪ] n zietta
au pair [ˈəuˈpɛəʳ] n (also: **~ girl**)
(ragazza f) alla pari inv
aura [ˈɔːrə] n aura
austerity [ɔsˈtɛrɪtɪ] n austerità f inv
Australia [ɔsˈtreɪlɪə] n Australia;
Australian adj, n australiano/a
Austria [ˈɔstrɪə] n Austria; **Austrian**
adj, n austriaco/a
authentic [ɔːˈθɛntɪk] adj
autentico/a
author [ˈɔːθəʳ] n autore/trice
authority [ɔːˈθɔrɪtɪ] n autorità f inv;
(permission) autorizzazione f; **the
authorities** npl (government etc) le
autorità

authorize [ˈɔːθəraɪz] vt autorizzare
auto [ˈɔːtəu] n (US) auto f inv;
autobiography [ɔːtəbaɪˈɔɡrəfɪ]
n autobiografia; **autograph**
[ˈɔːtəɡrɑːf] n autografo ▷ vt
firmare; **automatic** [ɔːtəˈmætɪk]
adj automatico/a ▷ n (gun) arma
automatica; (car) automobile
f con cambio automatico;
(washing machine) lavatrice f
automatica; **automatically** adv
automaticamente; **automobile**
[ˈɔːtəməbiːl] n (US) automobile
f; **autonomous** [ɔːˈtɔnəməs]
adj autonomo/a; **autonomy**
[ɔːˈtɔnəmɪ] n autonomia
autumn [ˈɔːtəm] n autunno
auxiliary [ɔːɡˈzɪlɪərɪ] adj ausiliario/a
▷ n ausiliare m/f
avail [əˈveɪl] vt: **to ~ o.s. of** servirsi
di; approfittarsi di ▷ n: **to no ~**
inutilmente
availability [əveɪləˈbɪlɪtɪ] n
disponibilità
available [əˈveɪləbl] adj disponibile
avalanche [ˈævəlɑːnʃ] n valanga
Ave. abbr = **avenue**
avenue [ˈævənjuː] n viale m; (fig)
strada, via
average [ˈævərɪdʒ] n media ▷ adj
medio/a ▷ vt (also: **~ out at**) essere in
media di; **on ~** in media
avert [əˈvəːt] vt evitare, prevenire;
(one's eyes) distogliere
avid [ˈævɪd] adj (supporter etc)
accanito/a
avocado [ævəˈkɑːdəu] n (BRIT: also:
~ pear) avocado m inv
avoid [əˈvɔɪd] vt evitare
await [əˈweɪt] vt aspettare
awake [əˈweɪk] (pt **awoke**, pp
awoken or **awaked**) vt svegliare ▷ vi
svegliarsi ▷ adj sveglio/a
award [əˈwɔːd] n premio; (Law)
decreto; (sum) risarcimento ▷ vt
assegnare; (Law: damages) decretare
aware [əˈwɛəʳ] adj: **~ of** (conscious)
conscio/a di; (informed) informato/a

di; **to become ~ of** accorgersi di;
awareness n consapevolezza
away [ə'weɪ] adj, adv via; lontano/a;
two kilometres ~ a due chilometri
di distanza; **two hours ~ by car**
a due ore di distanza in macchina;
the holiday was two weeks ~
mancavano due settimane alle
vacanze; **he's ~ for a week** è andato
via per una settimana; **to take
~** portare via; **he was working/
pedalling ~** lavorava/pedalava più
che poteva; **to fade ~** scomparire
awe [ɔ:] n timore m
awe-inspiring ['ɔ:ɪnspaɪərɪŋ],
awesome ['ɔ:səm] adj imponente
awful ['ɔ:fəl] adj terribile; **an ~ lot
of** (people, cars, dogs) un numero
incredibile di; (jam, flowers) una
quantità incredibile di; **awfully** adv
(very) terribilmente
awkward ['ɔ:kwəd] adj (clumsy)
goffo/a; (inconvenient) scomodo/a;
(embarrassing) imbarazzante
awoke [ə'wəuk] pt of **awake**
awoken [ə'wəukən] pp of **awake**
axe, (US) **ax** [æks] n scure f ▷ vt
(project etc) abolire; (jobs) sopprimere
axle ['æksl] n (also: **~-tree**) asse m
ay(e) [aɪ] excl (yes) sì
azalea [ə'zeɪlɪə] n azalea

b

B [bi:] n (Mus) si m; **B road** n (BRIT Aut)
≈ strada secondaria
BA n abbr = **Bachelor of Arts**
baby ['beɪbɪ] n bambino/a; **baby
carriage** n (US) carrozzina; **baby-sit**
vi fare il (or la) babysitter; **baby-sitter**
n baby-sitter mf inv; **baby wipe** n
salvietta umidificata
bachelor ['bætʃələʳ] n scapolo;
B~ of Arts/Science (BA/BSc) ≈
laureato/a in lettere/scienze
back [bæk] n (of person, horse) dorso,
schiena; (as opposed to front) dietro;
(of hand) dorso; (of train) coda; (of
chair) schienale m; (of page) rovescio;
(of book) retro; (Football) difensore m
▷ vt (candidate) appoggiare; (horse:
at races) puntare su; (car) guidare a
marcia indietro ▷ vi indietreggiare;
(car etc) fare marcia indietro ▷ adj
(in compounds) posteriore, di dietro
▷ adv (not forward) indietro; (returned):
he's ~ è tornato; **he ran ~** tornò

indietro di corsa; **throw the ball ~** (restitution) ritira la palla; **can I have it ~?** posso riaverlo?; **he called ~** (again) ha richiamato; **~ seats/wheels** (Aut) sedili mpl/ruote fpl posteriori; **back down** vi (fig) fare marcia indietro; **back out** vi (of promise) tirarsi indietro; **back up** vt (support) appoggiare, sostenere; (Comput) fare una copia di riserva di; **backache** n mal m di schiena; **backbencher** n (BRIT) parlamentare che non ha incarichi né al governo né all'opposizione; **backbone** n spina dorsale; **back door** n porta sul retro; **backfire** vi (Aut) dar ritorni di fiamma; (plans) fallire; **backgammon** n tavola reale; **background** n sfondo; (of events) background m inv; (basic knowledge) base f; (experience) esperienza; **family background** ambiente m familiare; **backing** n (fig) appoggio; **backlog** n: **backlog of work** lavoro arretrato; **backpack** n zaino; **backpacker** n chi viaggia con zaino e sacco a pelo; **backslash** n backslash m inv, barra obliqua inversa; **backstage** adv nel retroscena; **backstroke** n nuoto sul dorso; **backup** adj (train, plane) supplementare; (Comput) di riserva ▷ n (support) appoggio, sostegno; (also: **backup file**) file m inv di riserva; **backward** adj (movement) indietro inv; (person) tardivo/a; (country) arretrato/a; **backwards** adv indietro; (fall, walk) all'indietro; **back yard** n cortile m sul retro

bacon ['beɪkən] n pancetta

bacteria [bæk'tɪərɪə] npl batteri mpl

bad [bæd] adj cattivo/a; (child) cattivello/a; (meat, food) andato/a a male; **his ~ leg** la sua gamba malata; **to go ~** andare a male

badge [bædʒ] n insegna; (of policeman) stemma m

badger ['bædʒəʳ] n tasso

badly ['bædlɪ] adv (work, dress etc) male; **~ wounded** gravemente ferito; **he needs it ~** ne ha gran bisogno

bad-mannered [bæd'mænəd] adj maleducato/a, sgarbato/a

badminton ['bædmɪntən] n badminton m

bad-tempered [bæd'tempəd] adj irritabile; (in bad mood) di malumore

bag [bæg] n sacco; (handbag etc) borsa; **~s of** (col) (lots of) un sacco di

baggage n bagagli mpl; **baggage allowance** n peso bagaglio consentito; **baggage claim, baggage reclaim** n ritiro m bagaglio inv

baggy adj largo/a, sformato/a

bagpipes npl cornamusa

bail [beɪl] n cauzione f ▷ vt (prisoner: also: **grant ~ to**) concedere la libertà provvisoria su cauzione a; (Naut: also: **~ out**) aggottare; **on ~** in libertà provvisoria su cauzione

bait [beɪt] n esca ▷ vt (hook) innescare; (trap) munire di esca; (fig) tormentare

bake [beɪk] vt cuocere al forno ▷ vi cuocersi al forno; **baked beans** [-biːnz] npl fagioli mpl in salsa di pomodoro; **baked potato** n patata (con la buccia) cotta al forno; **baker** n fornaio/a, panettiere/a; **bakery** n panetteria; **baking** n cottura (al forno); **baking powder** n lievito in polvere

balance ['bæləns] n equilibrio; (Comm: sum) bilancio; (remainder) resto; (scales) bilancia ▷ vt tenere in equilibrio; (budget) far quadrare; (account) pareggiare; (compensate) contrappesare; **~ of trade/payments** bilancia commerciale/dei pagamenti; **balanced** adj (personality, diet) equilibrato/a; **balance sheet** n bilancio

balcony ['bælkənɪ] n balcone m; (in theatre) balconata

bald [bɔːld] *adj* calvo/a; (*tyre*) liscio/a
Balearics [bælɪˈærɪks], **Balearic Islands** *npl*: **the ~** le Baleari *fpl*
ball [bɔːl] *n* palla; (*football*) pallone *m*; (*for golf*) pallina; (*of wool, string*) gomitolo; (*dance*) ballo; **to play ~ (with sb)** (*fig*) stare al gioco (di qn)
ballerina [bæləˈriːnə] *n* ballerina
ballet [ˈbæleɪ] *n* balletto; **ballet dancer** *n* ballerino/a classico/a
balloon [bəˈluːn] *n* pallone *m*
ballot [ˈbælət] *n* scrutinio
ball-point pen [ˈbɔːlpɔɪnt-] *n* penna a sfera
ballroom [ˈbɔːlrum] *n* sala da ballo
Baltic [ˈbɔːltɪk] *adj, n*: **the ~ Sea** il (mar) Baltico
bamboo [bæmˈbuː] *n* bambù *m*
ban [bæn] *n* interdizione *f* ▷ *vt* interdire
banana [bəˈnɑːnə] *n* banana
band [bænd] *n* banda; (*at a dance*) orchestra; (*Mil*) fanfara
bandage [ˈbændɪdʒ] *n* benda, fascia
Band-Aid® [ˈbændeɪd] *n* (*US*) cerotto
B & B *n abbr* = **bed and breakfast**
bandit [ˈbændɪt] *n* bandito
bang [bæŋ] *n* (*of door*) lo sbattere; (*blow*) colpo ▷ *vt* battere (violentemente); (*door*) sbattere ▷ *vi* scoppiare; sbattere
Bangladesh [bɑːŋɡləˈdɛʃ] *n* Bangladesh *m*
bangle [ˈbæŋɡl] *n* braccialetto
bangs [bæŋz] *npl* (*US: fringe*) frangia, frangetta
banish [ˈbænɪʃ] *vt* bandire
banister(s) [ˈbænɪstə(z)] *n(pl)* ringhiera
banjo [ˈbændʒəʊ] (*pl* **banjoes** or **banjos**) *n* banjo *m inv*
bank [bæŋk] *n* banca, banco; (*of river, lake*) riva, sponda; (*of earth*) banco ▷ *vi* (*Aviat*) inclinarsi in virata; **bank on** *vt fus* contare su; **bank account** *n* conto in banca; **bank balance** *n* saldo; **a healthy bank balance** un

solido conto in banca; **bank card** *n* carta *f* assegni *inv*; **bank charges** *npl* (*BRIT*) spese *fpl* bancarie; **banker** *n* banchiere *m*; **bank holiday** *n* (*BRIT*) giorno di festa; *vedi nota* **"bank holiday"**; **banking** *n* attività bancaria; professione *f* di banchiere; **bank manager** *n* direttore *m* di banca; **banknote** *n* banconota

○ **BANK HOLIDAY**
○
○
○ Una *bank holiday*, in Gran
○ Bretagna, è una giornata in cui
○ le banche e molti negozi sono
○ chiusi. Generalmente le banche
○ *holiday* cadono di lunedì e molti
○ ne approfittano per fare una
○ breve vacanza fuori città. Di
○ conseguenza, durante questi fine
○ settimana lunghi ("*bank holiday*
○ *weekend*") si verifica un notevole
○ aumento del traffico sulle strade,
○ negli aeroporti e nelle stazioni e
○ molte località turistiche registrano
○ il tutto esaurito.

bankrupt [ˈbæŋkrʌpt] *adj* fallito/a; **to go ~** fallire; **bankruptcy** *n* fallimento
bank statement *n* estratto conto
banner [ˈbænəʳ] *n* striscione *m*
bannister(s) [ˈbænɪstə(z)] *n(pl) see* **banister(s)**
banquet [ˈbæŋkwɪt] *n* banchetto
baptism [ˈbæptɪzəm] *n* battesimo
baptize [bæpˈtaɪz] *vt* battezzare
bar [bɑːʳ] *n* (*rod*) barra; (*of window etc*) sbarra; (*of chocolate*) tavoletta; (*fig*) ostacolo; restrizione *f*; (*pub*) bar *m inv*; (*counter*) banco; (*Mus*) battuta ▷ *vt* (*road, window*) sbarrare; (*person*) escludere; (*activity*) interdire; **~ of soap** saponetta; **the B~** (*Law*) l'Ordine *m* degli avvocati; **behind ~s** (*prisoner*) dietro le sbarre; **~ none** senza eccezione
barbaric [bɑːˈbærɪk] *adj* barbarico/a

barbecue ['bɑːbɪkjuː] n barbecue m inv

barbed wire ['bɑːbd-] n filo spinato

barber ['bɑːbəʳ] n barbiere m; **barber's (shop)**, (US) **barber shop** n barbiere m

bar code n codice m a barre

bare [bɛəʳ] adj nudo/a ▷ vt scoprire, denudare; (teeth) mostrare; **the ~ essentials, the ~ necessities** lo stretto necessario; **barefoot** adj, adv scalzo/a; **barely** adv appena

bargain ['bɑːgɪn] n (transaction) contratto; (good buy) affare m ▷ vi contrattare; **into the ~** per giunta; **bargain for** vt fus (col): **to ~ for sth** aspettarsi qc; **he got more than he ~ed for** gli è andata peggio di quel che si aspettasse

barge [bɑːdʒ] n chiatta; **barge in** vi (walk in) piombare dentro; (interrupt talk) intromettersi a sproposito

bark [bɑːk] n (of tree) corteccia; (of dog) abbaio ▷ vi abbaiare

barley ['bɑːlɪ] n orzo

barmaid ['bɑːmeɪd] n cameriera al banco

barman ['bɑːmən] n (irreg) barista m

barn [bɑːn] n granaio

barometer [bəˈrɔmɪtəʳ] n barometro

baron ['bærən] n barone m; **baroness** n baronessa

barracks ['bærəks] npl caserma

barrage ['bærɑːʒ] n (Mil, dam) sbarramento; (fig) fiume m

barrel ['bærəl] n barile m; (of gun) canna

barren ['bærən] adj sterile; (soil) arido/a

barrette [bəˈrɛt] n (US) fermaglio per capelli

barricade [bærɪˈkeɪd] n barricata

barrier ['bærɪəʳ] n barriera

barring ['bɑːrɪŋ] prep salvo

barrister ['bærɪstəʳ] n (BRIT) avvocato/essa

barrow ['bærəu] n (cart) carriola

bartender ['bɑːtɛndəʳ] n (US) barista m

base [beɪs] n base f ▷ adj vile ▷ vt: **to ~ sth on** basare qc su

baseball ['beɪsbɔːl] n baseball m; **baseball cap** n berretto da baseball

basement ['beɪsmənt] n seminterrato; (of shop) piano interrato

bases ['beɪsiːz] npl of **basis**

bash [bæʃ] vt (col) picchiare

basic ['beɪsɪk] adj (principles, precautions, rules) elementare; **basically** ['beɪsɪklɪ] adv fondamentalmente, sostanzialmente; **basics** npl: **the basics** l'essenziale m

basil ['bæzl] n basilico

basin ['beɪsn] n (vessel, also Geo) bacino; (also: **wash~**) lavabo

basis (pl **bases**) ['beɪsɪs, -siːz] n base f; **on a part-time ~** part-time; **on a trial ~** in prova

basket ['bɑːskɪt] n cesta; (smaller) cestino; (with handle) paniere m; **basketball** n pallacanestro f

bass [beɪs] n (Mus) basso

bastard ['bɑːstəd] n bastardo/a; (col!) stronzo (!)

bat [bæt] n pipistrello; (for baseball etc) mazza; (BRIT: for table tennis) racchetta ▷ vt: **he didn't ~ an eyelid** non battè ciglio

batch [bætʃ] n (of bread) infornata; (of papers) cumulo

bath (pl **baths**) [bɑːθ, bɑːðz] n bagno; (bathtub) vasca da bagno ▷ vt far fare il bagno a; **to have a ~** fare un bagno; see also **baths**

bathe [beɪð] vi fare il bagno ▷ vt (wound etc) lavare

bathing ['beɪðɪŋ] n bagni mpl; **bathing costume**, (US) **bathing suit** n costume m da bagno

bath: **bathrobe** ['bɑːθrəub] n accappatoio; **bathroom** ['bɑːθrum] n stanza da bagno; **baths** [bɑːðz] npl bagni mpl pubblici; **bath towel** n

asciugamano da bagno; **bathtub** n
(vasca da) bagno
baton ['bætən] n (Mus) bacchetta;
(Athletics) testimone m; (club)
manganello
batter ['bætə^r] vt battere ▷ n
pastetta; **battered** adj (hat)
sformato/a; (pan) ammaccato/a
battery ['bætərɪ] n batteria; (of torch)
pila; **battery farming** n allevamento
in batteria
battle ['bætl] n battaglia ▷ vi
battagliare, lottare; **battlefield** n
campo di battaglia
bay [beɪ] n (of sea) baia; **to hold sb at
~** tenere qn a bada
bazaar [bə'zɑː^r] n bazar m inv; vendita
di beneficenza
BBC n abbr = **British Broadcasting
Corporation**

- **BBC**
-
- La BBC è l'azienda statale che
- fornisce il servizio radiofonico e
- televisivo in Gran Bretagna. Pur
- dovendo rispondere al Parlamento
- del proprio operato, la BBC non
- è soggetta al controllo dello
- stato per scelte e programmi,
- anche perché si autofinanzia
- con il ricavato dei canoni
- d'abbonamento. La BBC ha canali
- televisivi digitali e terrestri, oltre
- a diverse emittenti radiofoniche
- nazionali e locali. Fornisce
- un servizio di informazione
- internazionale, il "BBC World
- Service", trasmesso in tutto il
- mondo.

BC adv abbr (= before Christ) a.C.

 KEYWORD

be [biː] (pt **was**, **were**, pp **been**) aux
vb **1** (with present participle, forming
continuous tenses): **what are you
doing?** che fai?, che stai facendo?;
they're coming tomorrow vengono
domani; **I've been waiting for her
for hours** sono ore che l'aspetto
2 (with pp, forming passives) essere; **to
be killed** essere or venire ucciso/a;
the box had been opened la scatola
era stata aperta; **the thief was
nowhere to be seen** il ladro non si
trovava da nessuna parte
3 (in tag questions): **it was fun,
wasn't it?** è stato divertente, no?;
he's good-looking, isn't he? è un
bell'uomo, vero?; **she's back, is she?**
così è tornata, eh?
4 (+ to + infinitive): **the house is
to be sold** abbiamo (or hanno etc)
intenzione di vendere casa; **you're
to be congratulated for all your
work** dovremo farvi i complimenti
per tutto il vostro lavoro; **he's not to
open it** non deve aprirlo
▷ vb + complement **1** (gen) essere; **I'm
English** sono inglese; **I'm tired** sono
stanco/a; **I'm hot/cold** ho caldo/
freddo; **he's a doctor** è medico; **2
and 2 are 4** 2 più 2 fa 4; **be careful!**
sta attento/a!; **be good** sii buono/a
2 (of health) stare; **how are you?**
come sta?; **he's very ill** sta molto
male
3 (of age): **how old are you?** quanti
anni hai?; **I'm sixteen (years old)**
ho sedici anni
4 (cost) costare; **how much was the
meal?** quant'era or quanto costava il
pranzo?; **that'll be £5, please** (sono)
5 sterline, per favore
▷ vi **1** (exist, occur etc) essere, esistere;
the best singer that ever was il
migliore cantante mai esistito or
di tutti tempi; **be that as it may**
comunque sia, sia come sia; **so be it**
sia pure, e sia
2 (referring to place) essere, trovarsi; **I
won't be here tomorrow** non ci sarò
domani; **Edinburgh is in Scotland**
Edimburgo si trova in Scozia

3 (*referring to movement*): **where have you been?** dove sei stato?; **I've been to China** sono stato in Cina
▶ *impers vb* 1 (*referring to time, distance*) essere; **it's 5 o'clock** sono le 5; **it's the 28th of April** è il 28 aprile; **it's 10 km to the village** di qui al paese sono 10 km

2 (*referring to the weather*) fare; **it's too hot/cold** fa troppo caldo/freddo; **it's windy** c'è vento

3 (*emphatic*): **it's me** sono io; **it was Maria who paid the bill** è stata Maria che ha pagato il conto

beach [biːtʃ] *n* spiaggia ▷ *vt* tirare in secco
beacon ['biːkən] *n* (*lighthouse*) faro; (*marker*) segnale *m*
bead [biːd] *n* perlina; **beads** *npl* (*necklace*) collana
beak [biːk] *n* becco
beam [biːm] *n* trave *f*; (*of light*) raggio ▷ *vi* brillare
bean [biːn] *n* fagiolo; (*coffee bean*) chicco; **runner ~** fagiolino; **beansprouts** *npl* germogli *mpl* di soia
bear [bɛəʳ] (*pt* **bore**, *pp* **borne**) *n* orso ▷ *vt* portare; (*produce*) generare; (*endure*) sopportare ▷ *vi*: **to ~ right/left** piegare a destra/sinistra
beard [bɪəd] *n* barba
bearer ['bɛərəʳ] *n* portatore *m*
bearing ['bɛərɪŋ] *n* portamento; (*connection*) rapporto; **bearings** *npl* (*also*: **ball ~s**) cuscinetti *mpl* a sfere; **to take a ~** fare un rilevamento; **to find one's ~** orientarsi
beast [biːst] *n* bestia
beat [biːt] *n* colpo; (*of heart*) battito; (*Mus*) tempo, battuta; (*of policeman*) giro ▷ *vt* (*pt* **beat**, *pp* **beaten**) battere; (*eggs, cream*) sbattere; **off the ~ en track** fuori mano; **~ it!** (*col*) fila!, fuori dai piedi!; **beat up** *vt* (*col*: *person*) picchiare; (*eggs*) sbattere; **beating** *n* botte *fpl*

beautiful ['bjuːtɪful] *adj* bello/a; **beautifully** *adv* splendidamente
beauty ['bjuːtɪ] *n* bellezza; **beauty parlour** [-'pɑːləʳ], (*US*) **beauty parlor** *n* salone *m* di bellezza; **beauty salon** *n* istituto di bellezza; **beauty spot** *n* (*BRIT Tourism*) luogo pittoresco
beaver ['biːvəʳ] *n* castoro
became [bɪ'keɪm] *pt of* **become**
because [bɪ'kɔz] *conj* perché; **~ of** a causa di
beckon ['bɛkən] *vt* (*also*: **~ to**) chiamare con un cenno
become [bɪ'kʌm] *vt* (*irreg: like* **come**) diventare; **to ~ fat/thin** ingrassarsi/dimagrire
bed [bɛd] *n* letto; (*of flowers*) aiuola; (*of coal, clay*) strato; **bed and breakfast** *n* (*terms*) camera con colazione; (*place*) ≈ pensione *f* familiare; *vedi nota* **"bed and breakfast (B & B)"**; **bedclothes** ['bɛdkləuðz] *npl* coperte *fpl* e lenzuola *fpl*; **bedding** *n* coperte e lenzuola *fpl*; **bed linen** *n* biancheria da letto; **bedroom** *n* camera da letto; **bedside** *n*: **at sb's bedside** al capezzale di qn; **bedside lamp** *n* lampada da comodino; **bedside table** *n* comodino; **bedsit(ter)** ['bɛdsɪt(əʳ)] *n* (*BRIT*) monolocale *m*; **bedspread** *n* copriletto; **bedtime** *n*: **it's bedtime** è ora di andare a letto

○ **BED AND BREAKFAST (B & B)**
○
○ I *bed and breakfasts*, anche *B & Bs*,
○ sono piccole pensioni a conduzione
○ familiare, in case private o fattorie,
○ dove si affittano camere e viene
○ servita al mattino la tradizionale
○ colazione all'inglese. Queste
○ pensioni offrono un servizio di
○ camera con prima colazione,
○ appunto *bed and breakfast*, a
○ prezzi più contenuti rispetto agli
○ alberghi.

bee [biː] n ape f
beech [biːtʃ] n faggio
beef [biːf] n manzo; **roast ~** arrosto di manzo; **beefburger** n hamburger m inv; **Beefeater** n guardia della Torre di Londra
been [biːn] pp of **be**
beer [bɪəʳ] n birra; **beer garden** n (BRIT) giardino (di pub)
beet [biːt] (US) n (also: **red ~**) barbabietola rossa
beetle ['biːtl] n scarafaggio; coleottero
beetroot ['biːtruːt] n (BRIT) barbabietola
before [bɪ'fɔːʳ] prep (in time) prima di; (in space) davanti a ▷ conj prima che + sub; prima di ▷ adv prima; **~ going** prima di andare; **~ she goes** prima che vada; **the week ~** la settimana prima; **I've seen it ~** l'ho già visto; **I've never seen it ~** è la prima volta che lo vedo; **beforehand** adv in anticipo
beg [bɛg] vi chiedere l'elemosina ▷ vt (also: **~ for**) chiedere in elemosina; (favour) chiedere; **to ~ sb to do** pregare qn di fare
began [bɪ'gæn] pt of **begin**
beggar ['bɛgəʳ] n mendicante m/f
begin (pt **began**, pp **begun**) [bɪ'gɪn, bɪ'gæn, bɪ'gʌn] vt, vi cominciare; **to ~ doing** or **to do sth** incominciare or iniziare a fare qc; **beginner** n principiante m/f; **beginning** n inizio, principio
begun [bɪ'gʌn] pp of **begin**
behalf [bɪ'hɑːf] n: **on ~ of** per conto di; a nome di
behave [bɪ'heɪv] vi comportarsi; (well: also: **~ o.s.**) comportarsi bene; **behaviour**, (US) **behavior** [bɪ'heɪvjəʳ] n comportamento, condotta
behind [bɪ'haɪnd] prep dietro; (followed by pronoun) dietro di; (time) in ritardo con ▷ adv dietro; (leave, stay) indietro ▷ n didietro; **~ the scenes**

dietro le quinte; **to be ~ (schedule) with sth** essere indietro con qc
beige [beɪʒ] adj beige inv
Beijing [beɪ'dʒɪŋ] n Pechino f
being ['biːɪŋ] n essere m
belated [bɪ'leɪtɪd] adj tardo/a
belch [bɛltʃ] vi ruttare ▷ vt (gen: also: **~ out**: smoke etc) eruttare
Belgian ['bɛldʒən] adj, n belga m/f
Belgium ['bɛldʒəm] n Belgio m
belief [bɪ'liːf] n (opinion) opinione f, convinzione f; (trust, faith) fede f
believe [bɪ'liːv] vt, vi credere; **to ~ in** (God) credere in; (ghosts) credere a; (method) avere fiducia in; **believer** n (Rel) credente m/f; (in idea, activity): **to be a believer in** credere in
bell [bɛl] n campana; (small, on door, electric) campanello
bellboy ['bɛlbɔɪ], (US) **bellhop** ['bɛlhɔp] n ragazzo d'albergo, fattorino d'albergo
bellow ['bɛləʊ] vi muggire
bell pepper (esp US) n peperone m
belly ['bɛlɪ] n pancia; **bellybutton** n ombelico
belong [bɪ'lɔŋ] vi: **to ~ to** appartenere a; (club etc) essere socio di; **this book ~s here** questo libro va qui; **belongings** npl cose fpl, roba
beloved [bɪ'lʌvɪd] adj adorato/a
below [bɪ'ləʊ] prep sotto, al di sotto di ▷ adv di sotto; giù; **see ~** vedi sotto or oltre
belt [bɛlt] n cintura; (Tech) cinghia ▷ vt (thrash) picchiare ▷ vi (col) filarsela; **beltway** n (US: Aut: ring road) circonvallazione f; (: motorway) autostrada
bemused [bɪ'mjuːzd] adj perplesso/a, stupito/a
bench [bɛntʃ] n panca; (in workshop, Pol) banco; **the B~** (Law) la Corte
bend [bɛnd] (pt, pp **bent**) vt curvare; (leg, arm) piegare ▷ vi curvarsi; piegarsi ▷ n (in road) curva; (in pipe, river) gomito; **bend down** vi chinarsi; **bend over** vi piegarsi

beneath [bɪ'ni:θ] *prep* sotto, al di sotto di; (*unworthy of*) indegno/a di ▷ *adv* sotto, di sotto

beneficial [benɪ'fɪʃəl] *adj* che fa bene; vantaggioso/a

benefit ['benɪfɪt] *n* beneficio, vantaggio; (*allowance of money*) indennità *f inv* ▷ *vt* far bene a ▷ *vi*: **he'll ~ from it** ne trarrà beneficio or profitto

benign [bɪ'naɪn] *adj* (*person, smile*) benevolo/a; (*Med*) benigno/a

bent [bent] *pt, pp of* **bend** ▷ *n* inclinazione *f* ▷ *adj* (*col: dishonest*) losco/a; **to be ~ on** essere deciso/a a

bereaved [bɪ'ri:vd] *npl*: **the ~** i familiari in lutto

beret ['bereɪ] *n* berretto

Berlin [bə:'lɪn] *n* Berlino *f*

Bermuda [bə:'mju:də] *n* le Bermude

berry ['berɪ] *n* bacca

berth [bə:θ] *n* (*bed*) cuccetta; (*for ship*) ormeggio ▷ *vi* (*in harbour*) entrare in porto; (*at anchor*) gettare l'ancora

beside [bɪ'saɪd] *prep* accanto a; **to be ~ o.s. (with anger)** essere fuori di sé; **that's ~ the point** non c'entra; **besides** [bɪ'saɪdz] *adv* inoltre, per di più ▷ *prep* oltre a; (*except*) a parte

best [best] *adj* migliore ▷ *adv* meglio; **the ~ part of** (*quantity*) la maggior parte di; **at ~** tutt'al più; **to make the ~ of sth** cavare il meglio possibile da qc; **to do one's ~** fare del proprio meglio; **to the ~ of my knowledge** per quel che ne so; **to the ~ of my ability** al massimo delle mie capacità; **best-before date** *n* (*Comm*): **"best-before date: ..."** da consumarsi preferibilmente entro il...; **best man** *n* (*irreg*) testimone *m* dello sposo; **bestseller** *n* bestseller *m inv*

bet [bet] *n* scommessa ▷ *vt, vi* (*pt, pp* **bet** *or* **betted**) scommettere; **to ~ sb sth** scommettere qc con qn

betray [bɪ'treɪ] *vt* tradire

better ['betə'] *adj* migliore ▷ *adv* meglio ▷ *vt* migliorare ▷ *n*: **to get**

the ~ avere la meglio su; **you had ~ do it** è meglio che lo faccia; **he thought ~ of it** cambiò idea; **to get ~** migliorare

betting ['betɪŋ] *n* scommesse *fpl*; **betting shop** *n* (*BRIT*) ufficio dell'allibratore

between [bɪ'twi:n] *prep* tra ▷ *adv* in mezzo, nel mezzo

beverage ['bevərɪdʒ] *n* bevanda

beware [bɪ'weə'] *vt, vi*: **to ~ (of)** stare attento/a (a); **"~ of the dog"** "attenti al cane"

bewildered [bɪ'wɪldəd] *adj* sconcertato/a, confuso/a

beyond [bɪ'jɔnd] *prep* (*in space*) oltre; (*exceeding*) al di sopra di ▷ *adv* di là; **~ doubt** senza dubbio; **~ repair** irreparabile

bias ['baɪəs] *n* (*prejudice*) pregiudizio; (*preference*) preferenza; **bias(s)ed** *adj* parziale

bib [bɪb] *n* bavaglino

Bible ['baɪbl] *n* Bibbia

bicarbonate of soda [baɪ'kɑːbənɪt-] *n* bicarbonato (di sodio)

biceps ['baɪseps] *n* bicipite *m*

bicycle ['baɪsɪkl] *n* bicicletta; **bicycle pump** *n* pompa della bicicletta

bid [bɪd] (*pt* **bade** *or* **bid**, *pp* **bidden** *or* **bid**) *n* offerta; (*attempt*) tentativo ▷ *vi* fare un'offerta ▷ *vt* fare un'offerta; **to ~ sb good day** dire buon giorno a qn; **bidder** *n*: **the highest bidder** il maggior offerente

bidet ['bi:deɪ] *n* bidè *m inv*

big [bɪg] *adj* grande; grosso/a; **Big Apple** *n vedi nota* **"Big Apple"**; **bigheaded** ['bɪg'hedɪd] *adj* presuntuoso/a; **big toe** *n* alluce *m*

- **BIG APPLE**
-
- Tutti sanno che *The Big Apple*, la
- Grande Mela, è New York ("*apple*"
- in gergo significa grande città),
- ma sicuramente i soprannomi

di altre città americane non
sono così conosciuti. Chicago è
soprannominata "the Windy City"
perché è ventosa, New Orleans si
chiama "the Big Easy" per il modo
di vivere tranquillo e rilassato
dei suoi abitanti, e l'industria
automobilistica ha fatto sì che
Detroit fosse soprannominata
"Motown".

bike [baɪk] n bici f inv; **bike lane** n
pista ciclabile
bikini [bɪˈkiːnɪ] n bikini m inv
bilateral [baɪˈlætərl] adj bilaterale
bilingual [baɪˈlɪŋgwəl] adj bilingue
bill [bɪl] n conto; (Pol) atto; (US:
banknote) banconota; (of bird) becco;
(of show) locandina; **may I have
the ~ please?** posso avere il conto
per piacere?; **"stick or post no ~s"**
"divieto di affissione"; **to fit or fill
the ~** (fig) fare al caso; **billboard** n
tabellone m; **billfold** [ˈbɪlfəuld] n
(US) portafoglio
billiards [ˈbɪljədz] n biliardo
billion [ˈbɪljən] n (BRIT) bilione m;
(US) miliardo
bin [bɪn] n (for coal, rubbish) bidone m;
(for bread) cassetta; (BRIT: also: **dust~**)
pattumiera; (:also: **litter ~**) cestino
bind (pt, pp **bound**) [baɪnd, baund]
vt legare; (oblige) obbligare ▷ n (col)
scocciatura
binge [bɪndʒ] n (col): **to go on a ~** fare
baldoria; **binge drinker** n persona che
di norma beve troppo
bingo [ˈbɪŋgəu] n gioco simile alla
tombola
binoculars [bɪˈnɔkjuləz] npl
binocolo
bio… [baɪə…] prefix bio;
biochemistry [baɪəuˈkɛmɪstrɪ]
n biochimica; **biodegradable**
[ˈbaɪəudɪˈgreɪdəbl] adj
biodegradabile; **biofuel**
[ˈbaɪəufjuəl] n biocarburante;
biography [baɪˈɔgrəfɪ] n biografia;

biological adj biologico/a; **biology**
[baɪˈɔlədʒɪ] n biologia; **biometric**
[baɪəuˈmɛtrɪk] adj biometrico/a
birch [bəːtʃ] n betulla
bird [bəːd] n uccello; (BRIT col: girl)
bambola; **bird flu** n influenza aviaria;
bird of prey n (uccello) rapace m;
birdwatching n birdwatching m
Biro® [ˈbaɪrəu] n biro® f inv
birth [bəːθ] n nascita; **to give ~
to** dare alla luce, partorire; **birth
certificate** n certificato di nascita;
birth control n controllo delle
nascite; contraccezione f; **birthday**
n compleanno ▷ cpd di compleanno;
birthmark n voglia; **birthplace** n
luogo di nascita
biscuit [ˈbɪskɪt] n (BRIT) biscotto
bishop [ˈbɪʃəp] n vescovo
bistro [ˈbiːstrəu] n bistrò m inv
bit [bɪt] pt of **bite** ▷ n pezzo; (of horse)
morso; (Comput) bit m inv; **a ~** un
po' di; **a ~ mad/dangerous** un po'
matto/pericoloso; **~ by ~** a poco
a poco
bitch [bɪtʃ] n (dog) cagna; (col!)
puttana (!)
bite [baɪt] vt, vi (pt **bit**, pp **bitten**)
mordere; (insect) pungere ▷ n morso;
(insect bite) puntura; (mouthful)
boccone m; **let's have a ~ to eat**
mangiamo un boccone; **to ~ one's
nails** mangiarsi le unghie
bitten [ˈbɪtn] pp of **bite**
bitter [ˈbɪtə*] adj amaro/a; (wind,
criticism) pungente ▷ n (BRIT: beer)
birra amara
bizarre [bɪˈzɑː*] adj bizzarro/a
black [blæk] adj nero/a ▷ n nero ▷ vt
(BRIT Industry) boicottare; **B~** negro/a;
~ coffee caffè m inv nero; **to give sb
a ~ eye** fare un occhio nero a qn; **in
the ~** (in credit) in attivo; **black out** vi
(faint) svenire; **blackberry** n mora;
blackbird n merlo; **blackboard** n
lavagna; **blackcurrant** n ribes m
inv; **black ice** n strato trasparente
di ghiaccio; **blackmail** n ricatto

▷ vt ricattare; **black market** n mercato nero; **blackout** n oscuramento; (*fainting*) svenimento; (*TV*) interruzione f delle trasmissioni; **black pepper** n pepe m nero; **black pudding** n sanguinaccio; **Black Sea** n: **the Black Sea** il mar Nero

bladder ['blædə^r] n vescica

blade [bleɪd] n lama; (*of oar*) pala; **~ of grass** filo d'erba

blame [bleɪm] n colpa ▷ vt: **to ~ sb/ sth for sth** dare la colpa di qc a qn/ qc; **who's to ~?** chi è colpevole?

bland [blænd] adj mite; (*taste*) blando/a

blank [blæŋk] adj bianco/a; (*look*) distratto/a ▷ n spazio vuoto; (*cartridge*) cartuccia a salve

blanket ['blæŋkɪt] n coperta

blast [blɑ:st] n (*of wind*) raffica; (*bomb blast*) esplosione f ▷ vt far saltare

blatant ['bleɪtənt] adj flagrante

blaze [bleɪz] n (*fire*) incendio; (*fig*) vampata; splendore m ▷ vi (*fire*) ardere, fiammeggiare; (*guns*) sparare senza sosta; (*fig: eyes*) ardere ▷ vt: **to ~ a trail** (*fig*) tracciare una via nuova; **in a ~ of publicity** circondato da grande pubblicità

blazer ['bleɪzə^r] n blazer m inv

bleach [bli:tʃ] n (*also*: **household ~**) varechina ▷ vt (*material*) candeggiare; **bleachers** npl (*us Sport*) posti mpl di gradinata

bleak [bli:k] adj tetro/a

bled [blɛd] pt, pp of **bleed**

bleed (*pt, pp* **bled**) [bli:d, blɛd] vi sanguinare; **my nose is ~ing** mi viene fuori sangue dal naso

blemish ['blɛmɪʃ] n macchia

blend [blɛnd] n miscela ▷ vt mescolare ▷ vi (*colours etc: also*: **~ in**) armonizzare; **blender** n (*Culin*) frullatore m

bless (*pt, pp* **blessed** or **blest**) [blɛs, blɛst] vt benedire; **~ you!** (*sneezing*) salute!; **blessing** n benedizione f; fortuna

blew [blu:] pt of **blow**

blight [blaɪt] vt (*hopes etc*) deludere; (*life*) rovinare

blind [blaɪnd] adj cieco/a ▷ n (*for window*) avvolgibile m; (*Venetian blind*) veneziana ▷ vt accecare; **the blind** npl i ciechi; **blind alley** n vicolo cieco; **blindfold** n benda ▷ adj, adv bendato/a ▷ vt bendare gli occhi a

blink [blɪŋk] vi battere gli occhi; (*light*) lampeggiare

bliss [blɪs] n estasi f

blister ['blɪstə^r] n (*on skin*) vescica; (*on paintwork*) bolla ▷ vi (*paint*) coprirsi di bolle

blizzard ['blɪzəd] n bufera di neve

bloated ['bləʊtɪd] adj gonfio/a

blob [blɔb] n (*drop*) goccia; (*stain, spot*) macchia

block [blɔk] n blocco; (*in pipes*) ingombro; (*toy*) cubo; (*of buildings*) isolato ▷ vt bloccare; **the sink is ~ed** il lavandino è otturato; **block up** vt bloccare; (*pipe*) ingorgare, intasare; **blockade** [blɔ'keɪd] n blocco; **blockage** n ostacolo; **blockbuster** n grande successo; **block capitals** npl stampatello; **block letters** npl stampatello

blog [blɔg] n blog m inv ▷ vi scrivere blog, bloggare

blogger ['blɔgə^r] n (*Comput*) blogger mf inv

blogging ['blɔgɪŋ] n blogging m ▷ adj: **~ website** sito di blogging

bloke [bləʊk] n (*BRIT col*) tizio

blond(e) [blɔnd] n ▷ adj biondo/a

blood [blʌd] n sangue m; **blood donor** n donatore/trice di sangue; **blood group** n gruppo sanguigno; **blood poisoning** n setticemia; **blood pressure** n pressione f sanguigna; **bloodshed** n spargimento di sangue; **bloodshot** adj: **bloodshot eyes** occhi iniettati di sangue; **bloodstream** n flusso del sangue; **blood test** n analisi f inv del sangue; **blood transfusion** n trasfusione f di sangue; **blood type** n gruppo sanguigno; **blood vessel** n vaso sanguigno; **bloody** adj (fight) sanguinoso/a; (nose) sanguinante; (BRIT col!): **this bloody ...** questo maledetto ...; **bloody awful/good** (col!) veramente terribile/buono; **a bloody awful day** (col!) una giornata di merda (!)

bloom [blu:m] n fiore m ▷ vi essere in fiore

blossom ['blɔsəm] n fiore m; (with pl sense) fiori mpl ▷ vi essere in fiore

blot [blɔt] n macchia ▷ vt macchiare

blouse [blauz] n camicetta

blow [bləu] (pt **blew**, pp **blown**) n colpo ▷ vi soffiare ▷ vt (fuse) far saltare; (wind) spingere; (instrument) suonare; **to ~ one's nose** soffiarsi il naso; **to ~ a whistle** fischiare; **blow away** vi volare via ▷ vt portare via; **blow out** vi scoppiare; **blow up** vi saltare in aria ▷ vt far saltare in aria; (tyre) gonfiare; (Phot) ingrandire; **blow-dry** n messa in piega a föhn

blown [bləun] pp of **blow**

blue [blu:] adj azzurro/a; (depressed) giù inv; **~ film/joke** film/barzelletta pornografico(a); **out of the ~** (fig) all'improvviso; **bluebell** n giacinto di bosco; **blueberry** n mirtillo; **blue cheese** n formaggio tipo gorgonzola; **blues** npl: **the blues** (Mus) il blues; **to have the blues** (col) (feeling) essere a terra; **bluetit** n cinciarella

bluff [blʌf] vi bluffare ▷ n bluff m inv ▷ adj (person) brusco/a; **to call sb's ~** mettere alla prova il bluff di qn

blunder ['blʌndə'] n abbaglio ▷ vi prendere un abbaglio

blunt [blʌnt] adj smussato/a; (point) spuntato/a; (person) brusco/a

blur [blə:'] n forma indistinta ▷ vt offuscare; **blurred** adj (photo) mosso/a; (TV) sfuocato/a

blush [blʌʃ] vi arrossire ▷ n rossore m; **blusher** n fard m inv

board [bɔ:d] n tavola; (on wall) tabellone m; (committee) consiglio,

comitato; (in firm) consiglio d'amministrazione; (Naut, Aviat): **on ~** a bordo ▷ vt (ship) salire a bordo di; (train) salire su; **full ~** (BRIT) pensione f completa; **half ~** (BRIT) mezza pensione; **~ and lodging** vitto e alloggio; **to go by the ~** venir messo/a da parte; **board game** n gioco da tavolo; **boarding card** n (Aviat, Naut) carta d'imbarco; **boarding pass** n (BRIT) = **boarding card**; **boarding school** n collegio; **board room** n sala del consiglio

boast [bəust] vi: **to ~ (about** or **of)** vantarsi (di)

boat [bəut] n nave f; (small) barca

bob [bɔb] vi (boat, cork on water: also: **~ up and down**) andare su e giù

bobby pin ['bɔbɪ-] (us) n fermaglio per capelli

body ['bɔdɪ] n corpo; (of car) carrozzeria; (of plane) fusoliera; (fig: group) gruppo; (: organization) associazione f, organizzazione f; (quantity) quantità f inv; **body-building** n culturismo; **bodyguard** n guardia del corpo; **bodywork** n carrozzeria

bog [bɔg] n palude f ▷ vt: **to get ~ged down** (fig) impantanarsi

bogus ['bəugəs] adj falso/a; finto/a

boil [bɔɪl] vt, vi bollire ▷ n (Med) foruncolo; **to come to the** or (US) **a ~** raggiungere l'ebollizione; **~ed egg** uovo alla coque; **~ed potatoes** patate fpl bollite or lesse; **boil over** vi traboccare (bollendo); **boiler** n caldaia; **boiling** adj bollente; **I'm boiling (hot)** (col) sto morendo di caldo; **boiling point** n punto di ebollizione

bold [bəuld] adj audace; (child) impudente; (colour) deciso/a

Bolivia [bə'lɪvɪə] n Bolivia

Bolivian [bə'lɪvɪən] adj, n boliviano/a

bollard ['bɔləd] n (Aut) colonnina luminosa

Bollywood ['bɔlɪwud] n Bollywood f

bolt [bəult] n chiavistello; (with nut) bullone m ▷ adv: **~ upright** diritto/a come un fuso ▷ vt serrare; (also: **~ together**) imbullonare; (food) mangiare in fretta ▷ vi scappare via

bomb [bɔm] n bomba ▷ vt bombardare; **bombard** [bɔm'bɑːd] vt bombardare; **bomber** n (Aviat) bombardiere m; (terrorist) dinamitardo/a; **bomb scare** n stato di allarme (per sospetta presenza di una bomba)

bond [bɔnd] n legame m; (binding promise, Finance) obbligazione f; (Comm): **in ~** in attesa di sdoganamento

bone [bəun] n osso; (of fish) spina, lisca ▷ vt disossare; togliere le spine a

bonfire ['bɔnfaɪə'] n falò m inv

bonnet ['bɔnɪt] n cuffia; (BRIT: of car) cofano

bonus ['bəunəs] n premio; (fig) sovrappiù m inv

boo [buː] excl ba! ▷ vt fischiare

book [buk] n libro; (of stamps etc) blocchetto ▷ vt (ticket, seat, room) prenotare; (driver) multare; (football player) ammonire; **books** npl (Comm) conti mpl ▷ vt (BRIT: at hotel) prendere una camera; **book up** vt riservare, prenotare; **the hotel is ~ed up** l'albergo è al completo; **all seats are ~ed up** è tutto esaurito; **bookcase** n libreria; **booking** n (BRIT) prenotazione f; **booking office** n (BRIT: Rail) biglietteria; (Theat) botteghino; **book-keeping** n contabilità; **booklet** n opuscolo, libriccino; **bookmaker** n allibratore m; **bookmark** n segnalibro ▷ vt (Comput) mettere un segnalibro a; (Internet) aggiungere a "Preferiti"; **bookseller** n libraio; **bookshelf** n mensola (per libri); **bookshop** n libreria

boom [buːm] n (noise) rimbombo; (busy period) boom m inv ▷ vi rimbombare; andare a gonfie vele

boost [buːst] n spinta ▷ vt spingere

boot [buːt] n stivale m; (for hiking) scarpone m da montagna; (for football etc) scarpa; (BRIT: of car) portabagagli m inv ▷ vt (Comput) inizializzare; **to ~** (in addition) per giunta, in più

booth [buːð] n (at fair) baraccone m; (of cinema, telephone etc) cabina

booze [buːz] (col) n alcool m

border ['bɔːdə'] n orlo; margine m; (of a country) frontiera; (for flowers) aiuola (laterale) ▷ vt (road) costeggiare; **the B~s** la zona di confine tra l'Inghilterra e la Scozia; **border on** vt fus confinare con; **borderline** n: **on the borderline** incerto/a

bore [bɔː'] pt of **bear** ▷ vt (hole) scavare; (person) annoiare ▷ n (person) seccatore/trice; (of gun) calibro; **bored** adj annoiato/a; **to be bored** annoiarsi; **he's bored to tears** or **bored to death** or **bored stiff** è annoiato a morte; **boredom** n noia

boring ['bɔːrɪŋ] adj noioso/a

born [bɔːn] adj: **to be ~** nascere; **I was ~ in 1960** sono nato nel 1960

borne [bɔːn] pp of **bear**

borough ['bʌrə] n comune m

borrow ['bɔrəu] vt: **to ~ sth (from sb)** prendere in prestito qc (da qn)

Bosnia-Herzegovina ['bɔznɪəhɜːrzə'gəuviːnə] n Bosnia-Erzegovina; **Bosnian** ['bɔznɪən] adj, n bosniaco/a

bosom ['buzəm] n petto; (fig) seno

boss [bɔs] n capo ▷ vt (also: **~ about** or **around**) comandare a bacchetta; **bossy** adj prepotente

both [bəuθ] adj entrambi/e, tutt'e due ▷ pron: **~ of them** entrambi/e ▷ adv: **they sell ~ meat and poultry** vendono insieme la carne ed il pollame; **~ of us went, we ~ went** ci siamo andati tutt'e due

bother ['bɔðə'] vt (worry) preoccupare; (annoy) infastidire ▷ vi (also: **~ o.s.**) preoccuparsi ▷ n: **it is a ~ to have to do** è una seccatura dover fare; **it was no ~** non c'era problema; **to ~ doing sth** darsi la pena di fare qc

bottle ['bɒtl] n bottiglia; (baby's) biberon m inv ▷ vt imbottigliare; **bottle bank** n contenitore m per la raccolta del vetro; **bottle-opener** n apribottiglie m inv

bottom ['bɒtəm] n fondo; (buttocks) sedere m ▷ adj più basso/a, ultimo/a; **at the ~ of** in fondo a

bought [bɔːt] pt, pp of **buy**

boulder ['bəʊldəʳ] n masso (tondeggiante)

bounce [baʊns] vi (ball) rimbalzare; (cheque) essere restituito/a ▷ vt far rimbalzare ▷ n (rebound) rimbalzo; **bouncer** (col) n buttafuori m inv

bound [baʊnd] pt, pp of **bind** ▷ n (gen pl) limite m; (leap) salto ▷ vi saltare ▷ vt (limit) delimitare ▷ adj: **~ by law** obbligato/a per legge; **to be ~ to do sth** (obliged) essere costretto/a a fare qc; **he's ~ to fail** (likely) fallirà di certo; **~ for** diretto/a a; **out of ~s** il cui accesso è vietato

boundary ['baʊndrɪ] n confine m

bouquet ['bʊkeɪ] n bouquet m inv

bourbon ['bʊəbən] n (US: also: **~ whiskey**) bourbon m inv

bout [baʊt] n periodo; (of malaria etc) attacco; (Boxing etc) incontro

boutique [buːˈtiːk] n boutique f inv

bow¹ [bəʊ] n nodo; (weapon) arco; (Mus) archetto

bow² [baʊ] n (with body) inchino; (Naut: also: **~s**) prua ▷ vi inchinarsi; (yield): **to ~ to** or **before** sottomettersi a

bowels [baʊəlz] npl intestini mpl; (fig) viscere fpl

bowl [bəʊl] n (for eating) scodella; (for washing) bacino; (ball) boccia ▷ vi (Cricket) servire (la palla); **bowler** ['bəʊləʳ] n (Cricket) lanciatore m; (BRIT: also: **bowler hat**) bombetta; **bowling** ['bəʊlɪŋ] n (game) gioco delle bocce; **bowling alley** n pista da

bowling; **bowling green** n campo di bocce; **bowls** [bəʊlz] n gioco delle bocce

bow tie n cravatta a farfalla

box [bɒks] n scatola; (also: **cardboard ~**) (scatola di) cartone m; (Theat) palco ▷ vi fare pugilato ▷ vt mettere in (una) scatola, inscatolare; **boxer** n (person) pugile m; **boxer shorts** ['bɒksəʃɔːts] npl boxer; **a pair of boxer shorts** un paio di boxer; **boxing** n (Sport) pugilato; **Boxing Day** n (BRIT) ≈ Santo Stefano; vedi nota **"Boxing Day"**; **boxing gloves** npl guantoni mpl da pugile; **boxing ring** n ring m inv; **box office** n biglietteria

> ● **BOXING DAY**
> ●
> ● Il Boxing Day è un giorno di festa
> ● e cade in genere il 26 dicembre.
> ● Prende il nome dall'usanza di
> ● donare pacchi regalo natalizi, un
> ● tempo chiamati "Christmas boxes", a
> ● fornitori e dipendenti.

boy [bɔɪ] n ragazzo

boycott ['bɔɪkɒt] n boicottaggio ▷ vt boicottare

boyfriend ['bɔɪfrɛnd] n ragazzo

bra [brɑː] n reggipetto, reggiseno

brace [breɪs] n (on teeth) apparecchio correttore; (tool) trapano ▷ vt rinforzare, sostenere; **to ~ o.s.** (fig) farsi coraggio; see also **braces**

bracelet ['breɪslɪt] n braccialetto

braces ['breɪsɪz] npl (BRIT) bretelle fpl

bracket ['brækɪt] n (Tech) mensola; (group) gruppo; (Typ) parentesi f inv ▷ vt mettere fra parentesi

brag [bræg] vi vantarsi

braid [breɪd] n (trimming) passamano; (of hair) treccia

brain [breɪn] n cervello; **brains** npl (intelligence) cervella fpl; **he's got ~s** è intelligente

braise [breɪz] vt brasare

brake [breɪk] n (on vehicle) freno ▷ vi frenare; **brake light** n (fanalino dello) stop m inv

bran [bræn] n crusca

branch [brɑːntʃ] n ramo; (Comm) succursale f; **branch off** vi diramarsi; **branch out** vi: **to ~ out into** intraprendere una nuova attività nel ramo di

brand [brænd] n marca; (fig) tipo ▷ vt (cattle) marcare (a ferro rovente); **brand name** n marca; **brand-new** adj nuovo/a di zecca

brandy ['brændɪ] n brandy m inv

brash [bræʃ] adj sfacciato/a

brass [brɑːs] n ottone m; **the ~** (Mus) gli ottoni; **brass band** n fanfara

brat [bræt] n (pej) marmocchio, monello/a

brave [breɪv] adj coraggioso/a ▷ vt affrontare; **bravery** n coraggio

brawl [brɔːl] n rissa

Brazil [brə'zɪl] n Brasile m; **Brazilian** adj, n brasiliano/a

breach [briːtʃ] vt aprire una breccia in ▷ n (gap) breccia, varco; (breaking): **~ of contract** rottura di contratto; **~ of the peace** violazione f dell'ordine pubblico

bread [brɛd] n pane m; **breadbin** n cassetta f portapane inv; **breadbox** n (US) cassetta f portapane inv; **breadcrumbs** npl briciole fpl; (Culin) pangrattato

breadth [brɛtθ] n larghezza; (fig: of knowledge etc) ampiezza

break [breɪk] (pt **broke**, pp **broken**) vt rompere; (law) violare ▷ vi rompersi; (storm) scoppiare; (weather) cambiare; (dawn) spuntare; (news) saltare fuori ▷ n (gap) breccia; (fracture) rottura; (rest, also Scol) intervallo; (: short) pausa; (chance) possibilità f inv; **to ~ one's leg** etc rompersi la gamba etc; **to ~ a record** battere un primato; **to ~ the news to sb** comunicare per primo la notizia a qn; **to ~ even** coprire le spese; **to ~ free** or **loose** liberarsi; **break down** vt (figures, data) analizzare; (door etc) buttare giù, abbattere; (resistance) stroncare ▷ vi crollare; (Med) avere un esaurimento (nervoso); (Aut) guastarsi; **break in** vt (horse etc) domare ▷ vi (burglar) fare irruzione; **break into** vt fus (house) fare irruzione in; **break off** vi (speaker) interrompersi; (branch) troncarsi ▷ vt (talks, engagement) rompere; **break out** vi evadere; **to ~ out in spots** coprirsi di macchie; **break up** vi (partnership) sciogliersi; (friends) separarsi; **the line's** or **you're ~ing up** la linea è disturbata ▷ vt fare in pezzi, spaccare; (fight etc) interrompere, far cessare; (marriage) finire; **breakdown** n (Aut) guasto; (in communications) interruzione f; (of marriage) rottura; (Med: also: **nervous breakdown**) esaurimento nervoso; (of payments, statistics etc) resoconto; **breakdown truck, breakdown van** n carro m attrezzi inv

breakfast ['brɛkfəst] n colazione f

break: break-in n irruzione f; **breakthrough** n (fig) passo avanti

breast [brɛst] n (of woman) seno; (chest, Culin) petto; **breast-feed** vt, vi (irreg: like **feed**) allattare (al seno); **breast-stroke** n nuoto a rana

breath [brɛθ] n respiro; **out of ~** senza fiato

Breathalyser® ['brɛθəlaɪzə'] (BRIT) n alcoltest m inv

breathe [briːð] vt, vi respirare; **breathe in** vi inspirare ▷ vt respirare; **breathe out** vt, vi espirare; **breathing** n respiro, respirazione f

breath: breathless ['brɛθlɪs] adj senza fiato; **breathtaking** ['brɛθteɪkɪŋ] adj mozzafiato inv; **breath test** n ≈ prova del palloncino

bred [brɛd] pt, pp of **breed**

breed [briːd] (pt, pp **bred**) vt allevare ▷ vi riprodursi ▷ n razza; (type, class) varietà f inv

breeze [briːz] n brezza
breezy ['briːzɪ] adj allegro/a
brew [bruː] vt (tea) fare un infuso di; (beer) fare ▷ vi (storm, fig: trouble etc) prepararsi; **brewery** n fabbrica di birra
bribe [braɪb] n bustarella ▷ vt comprare; **bribery** n corruzione f
bric-a-brac ['brɪkəbræk] n bric-a-brac m
brick [brɪk] n mattone m; **bricklayer** n muratore m
bride [braɪd] n sposa; **bridegroom** n sposo; **bridesmaid** n damigella d'onore
bridge [brɪdʒ] n ponte m; (Naut) ponte di comando; (of nose) dorso; (Cards, Dentistry) bridge m inv ▷ vt (fig: gap) colmare
bridle ['braɪdl] n briglia
brief [briːf] adj breve ▷ n (Law) comparsa; (gen) istruzioni fpl ▷ vt: **to ~ sb (about sth)** mettere qn al corrente (di qc); see also **briefs**; **briefcase** n cartella; **briefing** n istruzioni fpl, briefing m inv; **briefly** adv (speak, visit, explain, say) brevemente; (glimpse, glance) di sfuggita
brigadier [brɪgə'dɪə{}^r] n generale m di brigata
bright [braɪt] adj luminoso/a; (person) sveglio/a; (colour) vivace
brilliant ['brɪljənt] adj brillante; (light, smile) radioso/a; (col) splendido/a
brim [brɪm] n orlo
brine [braɪn] n (Culin) salamoia
bring (pt, pp **brought**) [brɪŋ, brɔːt] vt portare; **bring about** vt causare; **bring back** vt riportare; **bring down** vt (lower) far scendere; (shoot down) abbattere; (government) far cadere; **bring in** vt (person) fare entrare; (object) portare; (Pol: bill) presentare; (: legislation) introdurre; (Law: verdict) emettere; (produce: income) rendere; **bring on** vt (illness, attack) causare,

provocare; (player, substitute) far scendere in campo; **bring out** vt (meaning) mettere in evidenza; (new product) lanciare; (book) pubblicare, fare uscire; **bring up** vt allevare; (question) introdurre
brink [brɪŋk] n orlo
brisk [brɪsk] adj (person, tone) spiccio/a; (trade etc) vivace; (pace) svelto/a
bristle ['brɪsl] n setola ▷ vi rizzarsi; **bristling with** irto/a di
Brit [brɪt] n abbr (col) (= British person) britannico/a
Britain ['brɪtən] n (also: **Great ~**) Gran Bretagna
British ['brɪtɪʃ] adj britannico/a; **the ~ Isles** n pl le Isole Britanniche
Briton ['brɪtən] n britannico/a
brittle ['brɪtl] adj fragile
broad [brɔːd] adj largo/a; (distinction) generale; (accent) spiccato/a; **in ~ daylight** in pieno giorno; **broadband** adj (Comput) a banda larga, ADSL ▷ n banda larga, ADSL m inv; **broad bean** n fava; **broadcast** (pt, pp **broadcast**) n trasmissione f ▷ vt trasmettere per radio (or per televisione) ▷ vi fare una trasmissione; **broaden** vt allargare ▷ vi allargarsi; **broadly** adv (fig) in generale; **broad-minded** adj di mente aperta
broccoli ['brɔkəlɪ] n broccoli mpl
brochure ['brəʊʃjuə{}^r] n dépliant m inv
broil [brɔɪl] vt cuocere a fuoco vivo
broiler ['brɔɪlə{}^r] (us) n (grill) griglia
broke [brəʊk] pt of **break** ▷ adj (col) squattrinato/a
broken ['brəʊkən] pp of **break** ▷ adj rotto/a; **a ~ leg** una gamba rotta; **in ~ French/English** in un francese/inglese stentato
broker ['brəʊkə{}^r] n agente m
bronchitis [brɔŋ'kaɪtɪs] n bronchite f
bronze [brɔnz] n bronzo

brooch [brəʊtʃ] n spilla
brood [bruːd] n covata ▷ vi (person) rimuginare
broom [brum] n scopa; (Bot) ginestra
Bros. abbr (= brothers) F.lli
broth [brɒθ] n brodo
brothel ['brɒθl] n bordello
brother ['brʌðəʳ] n fratello; **brother-in-law** n cognato
brought [brɔːt] pt, pp of **bring**
brow [braʊ] n fronte f; (rare, gen: also: **eye~**) sopracciglio; (of hill) cima
brown [braʊn] adj bruno/a, marrone; (tanned) abbronzato/a ▷ n (colour) color m bruno or marrone ▷ vt (Culin) rosolare; **brown bread** n pane m integrale, pane nero
Brownie ['braʊnɪ] n giovane esploratrice f
brown rice n riso greggio
brown sugar n zucchero greggio
browse [braʊz] vi (in bookshop etc) curiosare; **to ~ through a book** sfogliare un libro; **browser** n (Comput) browser m inv
bruise [bruːz] n (on person) livido ▷ vt farsi un livido a
brunette [bruːˈnɛt] n bruna
brush [brʌʃ] n spazzola; (for painting, shaving) pennello; (quarrel) schermaglia ▷ vt spazzolare; (also: ~ **past**, ~ **against**) sfiorare
Brussels ['brʌslz] n Bruxelles f; **Brussels sprout** [spraʊt] n cavolo di Bruxelles
brutal ['bruːtl] adj brutale
BSc n abbr (Univ) = **Bachelor of Science**
BSE n abbr (= bovine spongiform encephalopathy) encefalite f bovina spongiforme
bubble ['bʌbl] n bolla ▷ vi ribollire; (sparkle, fig) essere effervescente; **bubble bath** n bagno m schiuma inv; **bubble gum** n gomma americana
buck [bʌk] n maschio (di camoscio, caprone, coniglio ecc); (us col) dollaro ▷ vi sgroppare; **to pass the ~ (to sb)** scaricare (su di qn) la propria responsabilità
bucket ['bʌkɪt] n secchio
buckle ['bʌkl] n fibbia ▷ vt allacciare ▷ vi (wheel etc) piegarsi
bud [bʌd] n gemma; (of flower) bocciolo ▷ vi germogliare; (flower) sbocciare
Buddhism ['bʊdɪzəm] n buddismo
Buddhist ['bʊdɪst] adj, n buddista (m/f)
buddy ['bʌdɪ] n (us) compagno
budge [bʌdʒ] vt scostare; (fig) smuovere ▷ vi spostarsi; smuoversi
budgerigar ['bʌdʒərɪgɑːʳ] n pappagallino
budget ['bʌdʒɪt] n bilancio preventivo ▷ vi: **to ~ for sth** fare il bilancio per qc
budgie ['bʌdʒɪ] n = **budgerigar**
buff [bʌf] adj color camoscio inv ▷ n (col: enthusiast) appassionato/a
buffalo ['bʌfələʊ] (pl **buffalo** or **buffaloes**) n bufalo; (us) bisonte m
buffer ['bʌfəʳ] n respingente m; (Comput) memoria tampone, buffer m inv ▷ vi (Comput) fare il buffering, trasferire nella memoria tampone; **buffering** n buffering m inv, trasferimento nella memoria tampone
buffet n ['bufeɪ] (food, BRIT: bar) buffet m inv ▷ vt ['bʌfɪt] sferzare; **buffet car** n (BRIT Rail) ≈ servizio ristoro
bug [bʌg] n (insect) insetto; (fig: germ) virus m inv; (spy device) microfono spia; (Comput) bug m inv ▷ vt mettere sotto controllo; (annoy) scocciare
buggy ['bʌgɪ] n (baby buggy) passeggino
build [bɪld] n (of person) corporatura ▷ vt (pt, pp **built**) costruire; **build up** vt (reputation) consolidare; (increase) incrementare; **builder** n costruttore m; **building** n costruzione f; edificio; (also: **building trade**) edilizia; **building site** n cantiere m

di costruzione; **building society** *n* società immobiliare e finanziaria

built [bɪlt] *pt, pp of* **build**; **built-in** *adj* (*cupboard*) a muro; (*device*) incorporato/a; **built-up area** ['bɪltʌp-] *n* abitato

bulb [bʌlb] *n* (*Bot*) bulbo; (*Elec*) lampadina

Bulgaria [bʌl'gɛərɪə] *n* Bulgaria; **Bulgarian** *adj* bulgaro/a ▷ *n* bulgaro/a; (*Ling*) bulgaro

bulge [bʌldʒ] *n* rigonfiamento ▷ *vi* essere protuberante *or* rigonfio/a; **to be bulging with** essere pieno/*aor* zeppo/a di

bulimia [bə'lɪmɪə] *n* bulimia

bulimic [bju:'lɪmɪk] *adj, n* bulimico/a

bulk [bʌlk] *n* massa, volume *m*; **the ~ of** il grosso di; **(to buy) in ~** (comprare) in grande quantità; (*Comm*) (comprare) all'ingrosso; **bulky** *adj* grosso/a; voluminoso/a

bull [bul] *n* toro; (*male elephant, whale*) maschio

bulldozer ['buldəuzəʳ] *n* bulldozer *m inv*

bullet ['bulɪt] *n* pallottola

bulletin ['bulɪtɪn] *n* bollettino; **bulletin board** *n* (*Comput*) bulletin board *m inv*

bullfight ['bulfaɪt] *n* corrida; **bullfighter** *n* torero; **bullfighting** *n* tauromachia

bully ['bulɪ] *n* prepotente *m* ▷ *vt* angariare; (*frighten*) intimidire

bum [bʌm] *n* (*col: backside*) culo; (*tramp*) vagabondo/a

bumblebee ['bʌmblbi:] *n* bombo

bump [bʌmp] *n* (*in car*) piccolo tamponamento; (*jolt*) scossa; (*on road etc*) protuberanza; (*on head*) bernoccolo ▷ *vt* battere; **bump into** *vt fus* scontrarsi con; (*meet*) imbattersi in; **bumper** *n* paraurti *m inv* ▷ *adj*: **bumper harvest** raccolto eccezionale; **bumpy** ['bʌmpɪ] *adj* (*road*) dissestato/a

bun [bʌn] *n* focaccia; (*of hair*) crocchia

bunch [bʌntʃ] *n* (*of flowers, keys*) mazzo; (*of bananas*) casco; (*of people*) gruppo; **~ of grapes** grappolo d'uva; **bunches** *npl* (*in hair*) codine *fpl*

bundle ['bʌndl] *n* fascio ▷ *vt* (*also: ~ up*) legare in un fascio; (*put*): **to ~ sth/sb into** spingere qc/qn in

bungalow ['bʌŋgələu] *n* bungalow *m inv*

bungee jumping ['bʌndʒi:'dʒʌmpɪŋ] *n* salto nel vuoto da ponti, grattacieli ecc con un cavo fissato alla caviglia

bunion ['bʌnjən] *n* callo (al piede)

bunk [bʌŋk] *n* cuccetta; **bunk beds** *npl* letti *mpl* a castello

bunker ['bʌŋkəʳ] *n* (*coal store*) ripostiglio per il carbone; (*Mil, Golf*) bunker *m inv*

bunny ['bʌnɪ] *n* (*also: ~ rabbit*) coniglietto

buoy [bɔɪ] *n* boa; **buoyant** *adj* galleggiante; (*fig*) vivace

burden ['bə:dn] *n* carico, fardello ▷ *vt* caricare; **to ~ sb with** caricare qn di

bureau (*pl* **bureaux**) ['bjuərəu, -z] *n* (BRIT: *writing desk*) scrivania; (US: *chest of drawers*) cassettone *m*; (*office*) ufficio, agenzia

bureaucracy [bjuə'rɔkrəsɪ] *n* burocrazia

bureaucrat ['bjuərəkræt] *n* burocrate *m/f*

bureau de change [-də'ʃɑ̃ʒ] (*pl* **bureaux de change**) *n* cambiavalute *inv*

bureaux [bjuə'rəuz] *npl of* **bureau**

burger ['bə:gəʳ] *n* hamburger *m inv*

burglar ['bə:gləʳ] *n* scassinatore *m*; **burglar alarm** *n* (allarme *m*) antifurto *m inv*; **burglary** *n* furto con scasso

burial ['berɪəl] *n* sepoltura

burn [bə:n] *vt, vi* (*pt, pp* **burned** *or* **burnt**) bruciare ▷ *n* bruciatura, scottatura; **burn down** *vt* distruggere col fuoco; **burn out** *vt* (*writer etc*): **to ~ o.s. out** esaurirsi;

burning *adj* in fiamme; (*sand*) che scotta; (*ambition*) bruciante

Burns Night *n vedi nota* **"Burns Night"**

burnt [bə:nt] *pt, pp of* **burn**

burp [bə:p] (*col*) *n* rutto ▷ *vi* ruttare

burrow ['bʌrəu] *n* tana ▷ *vt* scavare

burst [bə:st] (*pt, pp* **burst**) *vt* far scoppiare *or* esplodere ▷ *vi* esplodere; (*tyre*) scoppiare ▷ *n* scoppio; (*also: ~ pipe*) rottura nel tubo, perdita; **a ~ of speed** uno scatto (di velocità); **to ~ into flames/tears** scoppiare in fiamme/lacrime; **to be ~ing with** essere pronto a scoppiare di; **to ~ out laughing** scoppiare a ridere; **burst into** *vt fus* (*room etc*) irrompere in

bury ['bɛrɪ] *vt* seppellire

bus [bʌs] (*pl* **buses**) *n* autobus *m inv*; **bus conductor** *n* autista *m/f* (dell'autobus)

bush [buʃ] *n* cespuglio; (*scrub land*) macchia; **to beat about the ~** menare il cane per l'aia

business ['bɪznɪs] *n* (*matter*) affare *m*; (*trading*) affari *mpl*; (*firm*) azienda; (*job, duty*) lavoro; **to be away on ~** essere andato via per affari; **it's none of my ~** questo non mi riguarda; **he means ~** non scherza; **business class** *n* (*Aviat*) business class *f*; **businesslike** *adj* serio/a; efficiente; **businessman** *n* (*irreg*) uomo d'affari; **business trip** *n*

viaggio d'affari; **businesswoman** *n* (*irreg*) donna d'affari

busker ['bʌskə^r] *n* (BRIT) suonatore/ trice ambulante

bus: bus pass *n* tessera dell'autobus; **bus shelter** *n* pensilina (*alla fermata dell'autobus*); **bus station** *n* stazione *f* delle corriere, autostazione *f*; **bus stop** *n* fermata d'autobus

bust [bʌst] *n* busto; (*Anat*) seno ▷ *adj* (*col: broken*) rotto/a; **to go ~** fallire

bustling ['bʌslɪŋ] *adj* animato/a

busy ['bɪzɪ] *adj* occupato/a; (*shop, street*) molto frequentato/a ▷ *vt*: **to ~ o.s.** darsi da fare; **busy signal** *n* (US Tel) segnale *m* di occupato

 KEYWORD

but [bʌt] *conj* ma; **I'd love to come, but I'm busy** vorrei tanto venire, ma ho da fare

▶ *prep* (*apart from, except*) eccetto, tranne, meno; **he was nothing but trouble** non dava altro che guai; **no-one but him can do it** nessuno può farlo tranne lui; **but for you/ your help** se non fosse per te/per il tuo aiuto; **anything but that** tutto ma non questo

▶ *adv* (*just, only*) solo, soltanto; **she's but a child** è solo una bambina; **had I but known** se solo avessi saputo; **I can but try** tentar non nuoce; **all but finished** quasi finito

butcher ['butʃə^r] *n* macellaio ▷ *vt* macellare; **~'s (shop)** macelleria

butler ['bʌtlə^r] *n* maggiordomo

butt [bʌt] *n* (*cask*) grossa botte *f*; (*of gun*) calcio; (*of cigarette*) mozzicone *m*; (BRIT fig: *target*) oggetto ▷ *vt* cozzare

butter ['bʌtə^r] *n* burro ▷ *vt* imburrare; **buttercup** *n* ranuncolo

butterfly ['bʌtəflaɪ] *n* farfalla; (*Swimming: also: ~ stroke*) (nuoto a) farfalla

buttocks [ˈbʌtəks] *npl* natiche *fpl*
button [ˈbʌtn] *n* bottone *m*; (*us: badge*) distintivo ▷ *vt* (*also:* **~ up**) abbottonare ▷ *vi* abbottonarsi
buy [baɪ] *vt* (*pt, pp* **bought**) comprare ▷ *n* acquisto; **to ~ sb sth/sth from sb** comprare qc per qn/qc da qn; **to ~ sb a drink** offrire da bere a qn; **buy out** *vt* (*business*) rilevare; **buy up** *vt* accaparrare; **buyer** *n* compratore/trice
buzz [bʌz] *n* ronzio; (*col: phone call*) colpo di telefono ▷ *vi* ronzare; **buzzer** [ˈbʌzəʳ] *n* cicalino

KEYWORD

by [baɪ] *prep* **1** (*referring to cause, agent*) da; **killed by lightning** ucciso da un fulmine; **surrounded by a fence** circondato da uno steccato; **a painting by Picasso** un quadro di Picasso
2 (*referring to method, manner, means*): **by bus/car/train** in autobus/macchina/treno, con l'autobus/la macchina/il treno; **to pay by cheque** pagare con (un) assegno; **by moonlight** al chiaro di luna; **by saving hard, he ...** risparmiando molto, lui ...
3 (*via, through*) per; **we came by Dover** siamo venuti via Dover
4 (*close to, past*) accanto a; **the house by the river** la casa sul fiume; **a holiday by the sea** una vacanza al mare; **she sat by his bed** si sedette accanto al suo letto; **she rushed by me** mi è passata accanto correndo; **I go by the post office every day** passo davanti all'ufficio postale ogni giorno
5 (*not later than*) per, entro; **by 4 o'clock** per *or* entro le 4; **by this time tomorrow** domani a quest'ora; **by the time I got here it was too late** quando sono arrivato era ormai troppo tardi

6 (*during*): **by day/night** di giorno/notte
7 (*amount*) a; **by the kilo** a chili; **paid by the hour** pagato all'ora; **one by one** uno per uno; **little by little** a poco a poco
8 (*Math: measure*): **to divide/multiply by 3** dividere/moltiplicare per 3; **it's broader by a metre** è un metro più largo, è più largo di un metro
9 (*according to*) per; **to play by the rules** attenersi alle regole; **it's all right by me** per me va bene
10: **(all) by oneself** (tutto/a) solo/a; **he did it (all) by himself** lo ha fatto (tutto) da solo
11: **by the way** a proposito; **this wasn't my idea by the way** tra l'altro l'idea non è stata mia
▷ *adv* **1** *see* **go; pass** *etc*
2: **by and by** (*in past*) poco dopo; (*in future*) fra breve; **by and large** nel complesso

bye(-bye) [ˈbaɪ(ˈbaɪ)] *excl* ciao!, arrivederci!
by-election [ˈbaɪɪlɛkʃən] *n* (BRIT) elezione *f* straordinaria
bypass [ˈbaɪpɑːs] *n* circonvallazione *f*; (*Med*) by-pass *m inv* ▷ *vt* fare una deviazione intorno a
byte [baɪt] *n* (*Comput*) byte *m inv*, bicarattere *m*

C

C [siː] *n* (*Mus*) do

cab [kæb] *n* taxi *m inv*; (*of train, truck*) cabina

cabaret ['kæbəreɪ] *n* cabaret *m inv*

cabbage ['kæbɪdʒ] *n* cavolo

cabin ['kæbɪn] *n* capanna; (*on ship*) cabina; **cabin crew** *n* equipaggio

cabinet ['kæbɪnɪt] *n* (*Pol*) consiglio dei ministri; (*furniture*) armadietto; (*also*: **display ~**) vetrinetta; **cabinet minister** *n* ministro (*membro del Consiglio*)

cable ['keɪbl] *n* cavo; fune *f*; (*Tel*) cablogramma *m* ⊳ *vt* telegrafare; **cable-car** *n* funivia; **cable television** *n* televisione *f* via cavo

cactus (*pl* **cacti**) ['kæktəs, -taɪ] *n* cactus *m inv*

café ['kæfeɪ] *n* caffè *m inv*

cafeteria [kæfɪ'tɪərɪə] *n* self-service *m inv*

caffein(e) ['kæfiːn] *n* caffeina

cage [keɪdʒ] *n* gabbia

cagoule [kə'guːl] *n* K-way® *m inv*

cake [keɪk] *n* (*large*) torta; (*small*) pasticcino; **~ of soap** saponetta

calcium ['kælsɪəm] *n* calcio

calculate ['kælkjuleɪt] *vt* calcolare; **calculation** [kælkju'leɪʃən] *n* calcolo; **calculator** *n* calcolatrice *f*

calendar ['kæləndə^r] *n* calendario

calf (*pl* **calves**) [kɑːf, kɑːvz] *n* (*of cow*) vitello; (*of other animals*) piccolo; (*also*: **~skin**) (*pelle f di*) vitello; (*Anat*) polpaccio

calibre, (*US*) **caliber** ['kælɪbə^r] *n* calibro

call [kɔːl] *vt* (*gen, also Tel*) chiamare; (*meeting, strike*) indire ⊳ *vi* chiamare; (*visit: also*: **~ in, ~ round**) passare ⊳ *n* (*shout*) grido, urlo; (*also*: **telephone ~**) telefonata; **to be ~ed** (*person, object*) chiamarsi; **to be on ~** essere a disposizione; **call back** *vi* (*return*) ritornare; (*Tel*) ritelefonare, richiamare; **can you ~ back later?** può richiamare più tardi?; **call for** *vt fus* richiedere; (*collect*) passare a prendere; **call in** *vt* (*doctor, expert, police*) chiamare, far venire; **call off** *vt* disdire; **call on** *vt fus* (*visit*) passare da; (*request*): **to ~ on sb to do** chiedere a qn di fare; **call out** *vi* (*in pain*) urlare; (*to person*) chiamare; **call up** *vt* (*Mil*) richiamare; (*Tel*) telefonare a; **callbox** *n* (*BRIT*) cabina telefonica; **call centre**, (*US*) **call center** *n* centro informazioni telefoniche; **caller** *n* persona che chiama; visitatore/trice

callous ['kæləs] *adj* indurito/a, insensibile

calm [kɑːm] *adj* calmo/a ⊳ *n* calma ⊳ *vt* calmare; **calm down** *vi* calmarsi ⊳ *vt* calmare; **calmly** *adv* con calma

Calor gas® ['kælə^r-] *n* butano

calorie ['kælərɪ] *n* caloria

calves [kɑːvz] *npl of* **calf**

camcorder ['kæmkɔːdə^r] *n* videocamera

came [keɪm] *pt of* **come**

camel ['kæməl] n cammello

camera ['kæmərə] n macchina fotografica; (Cine, TV) cinepresa; **in ~** a porte chiuse; **cameraman** n (irreg) cameraman m inv; **camera phone** n telefono cellulare con fotocamera integrata

camouflage ['kæməflɑːʒ] n (Mil, Zool) mimetizzazione f ▷ vt mimetizzare

camp [kæmp] n campeggio; (Mil) campo ▷ vi accamparsi ▷ adj effeminato/a

campaign [kæm'peɪn] n (Mil, Pol etc) campagna ▷ vi: **to ~ (for/against)** (also fig) fare una campagna (per/contro); **campaigner** n: **campaigner for** fautore/trice di; **campaigner against** oppositore/trice di

camp: campbed n (BRIT) brandina; **camper** ['kæmpəʳ] n campeggiatore/trice; (vehicle) camper m inv; **campground** n (US) campeggio; **camping** ['kæmpɪŋ] n campeggio; **to go camping** andare in campeggio; **camp site** ['kæmpsaɪt] n campeggio

campus ['kæmpəs] n campus m inv

can¹ [kæn] n (of milk) scatola; (of oil) bidone m; (of water) tanica; (tin) scatola ▷ vt mettere in scatola

 KEYWORD

can² [kæn] (negative **cannot**, **can't**, conditional, pt **could**) aux vb **1** (be able to) potere; **I can't go any further** non posso andare oltre; **you can do it if you try** sei in grado di farlo - basta provarci; **I'll help you all I can** ti aiuterò come potrò; **I can't see you** non ti vedo

2 (know how to) sapere, essere capace di; **I can swim** so nuotare; **can you speak French?** parla francese?

3 (may) potere; **could I have a word with you?** posso parlarle un momento?

4 (expressing disbelief, puzzlement etc): **it can't be true!** non può essere vero!; **what CAN he want?** cosa può mai volere?

5 (expressing possibility, suggestion etc): **he could be in the library** può darsi che sia in biblioteca; **she could have been delayed** può aver avuto un contrattempo

Canada ['kænədə] n Canada m; **Canadian** [kə'neɪdɪən] adj, n canadese (m/f)

canal [kə'næl] n canale m

canary [kə'nɛərɪ] n canarino

Canary Islands, Canaries [kə'nɛərɪz] npl: **the ~ le** (isole) Canarie

cancel ['kænsəl] vt annullare; (train) sopprimere; (cross out) cancellare; **cancellation** [kænsə'leɪʃən] n annullamento; soppressione f; cancellazione f; (Tourism) prenotazione f annullata

cancer ['kænsəʳ] n cancro; **C~** (sign) Cancro

candidate ['kændɪdeɪt] n candidato/a

candle ['kændl] n candela; (in church) cero; **candlestick** n bugia; (bigger, ornate) candeliere m

candy ['kændɪ] n zucchero candito; (US) caramella; caramelle fpl; **candy bar** (US) n lungo biscotto, in genere ricoperto di cioccolata; **candy-floss** ['kændɪflɒs] n (BRIT) zucchero filato

cane [keɪn] n canna; (for baskets, chairs etc) bambù m; (Scol) verga ▷ vt (BRIT Scol) punire a colpi di verga

canister ['kænɪstəʳ] n scatola metallica

cannabis ['kænəbɪs] n canapa indiana

canned ['kænd] adj (food) in scatola

cannon ['kænən] (pl **cannon** or **cannons**) n (gun) cannone m

cannot ['kænɒt] = **can not**

canoe [kə'nu:] n canoa; **canoeing** n
canottaggio

canon ['kænən] n (clergyman)
canonico; (standard) canone m

can opener [-əupnə^r] n apriscatole
m inv

can't [kænt] = **can not**

canteen [kæn'ti:n] n mensa; (BRIT:
of cutlery) portaposate m inv

> Be careful not to translate
> canteen by the Italian word
> cantina.

canter ['kæntə^r] vi andare al piccolo
galoppo

canvas ['kænvəs] n tela

canvass ['kænvəs] vi (Pol): **to ~
for** raccogliere voti per ▷ vt fare un
sondaggio di

canyon ['kænjən] n canyon m inv

cap [kæp] n (also BRIT Football: hat)
berretto; (of pen) coperchio; (of bottle)
tappo; (contraceptive) diaframma m
▷ vt (outdo) superare; (limit) fissare
un tetto (a)

capability [keɪpə'bɪlɪtɪ] n capacità f
inv, abilità f inv

capable ['keɪpəbl] adj capace

capacity [kə'pæsɪtɪ] n capacità f inv;
(of lift etc) capienza

cape [keɪp] n (garment) cappa;
(Geo) capo

caper ['keɪpə^r] n (Culin) cappero;
(prank) scherzetto

capital ['kæpɪtl] n (also: ~ **city**)
capitale f; (money) capitale m;
(also: ~ **letter**) (lettera) maiuscola;
capitalism n capitalismo; **capitalist**
adj, n capitalista (m/f); **capital
punishment** n pena capitale

Capitol ['kæpɪtl] n: **the ~** il
Campidoglio

Capricorn ['kæprɪkɔ:n] n
Capricorno

capsize [kæp'saɪz] vt capovolgere
▷ vi capovolgersi

capsule ['kæpsju:l] n capsula

captain ['kæptɪn] n capitano

caption ['kæpʃən] n leggenda

captivity [kæp'tɪvɪtɪ] n prigionia

capture ['kæptʃə^r] vt catturare;
(Comput) registrare ▷ n cattura; (data
capture) registrazione f or rilevazione
f di dati

car [kɑ:^r] n macchina, automobile f;
(Rail) vagone m

carafe [kə'ræf] n caraffa

caramel ['kærəməl] n caramello

carat ['kærət] n carato; **18 ~ gold** oro
a 18 carati

caravan ['kærəvæn] n (BRIT)
roulotte f inv; (of camels) carovana;
caravan site n (BRIT) campeggio
per roulotte

carbohydrate [kɑ:bəu'haɪdreɪt] n
carboidrato

carbon ['kɑ:bən] n carbonio;
carbon copy n copia f carbone
inv; **carbon dioxide** [-daɪ'ɔksaɪd]
n diossido di carbonio; **carbon
footprint** n impronta di carbonio;
carbon monoxide [-mɔ'nɔksaɪd] n
monossido di carbonio

car boot sale n vedi nota "**car boot
sale**"

- **CAR BOOT SALE**
-
- Il car boot sale è un mercatino
- dell'usato molto popolare in Gran
- Bretagna. Normalmente ha luogo
- in un parcheggio o in un grande
- spiazzo, e la merce viene in genere
- esposta nei bagagliai, in inglese
- appunto "boots", aperti delle
- macchine.

carburettor, (US) **carburetor**
[kɑ:bju'rɛtə^r] n carburatore m

card [kɑ:d] n carta; (visiting card
etc) biglietto; (Christmas card etc)
cartolina; **cardboard** n cartone m;
card game n gioco di carte

cardigan ['kɑ:dɪgən] n cardigan
m inv

cardinal ['kɑ:dɪnl] adj, n cardinale
(m)

cardphone ['kɑːdfəun] n telefono a scheda (magnetica)

care [keəʳ] n cura, attenzione f; (*worry*) preoccupazione f ▷ vi: **to ~ about** curarsi di; (*thing, idea*) interessarsi di; **in sb's ~** alle cure di qn; **to take ~** fare attenzione; **to take ~ of** curarsi di; (*details, arrangements, bill, problem*) occuparsi di; **I don't ~** non me ne importa; **I couldn't ~ less** non me ne importa un bel niente; **~ of (c/o)** presso; **care for** vt fus aver cura di; (*like*) voler bene a

career [kə'rɪəʳ] n carriera ▷ vi (*also*: **~ along**) andare di (gran) carriera

care: **carefree** ['keəfriː] adj sgombro/a di preoccupazioni; **careful** ['keəful] adj attento/a; (*cautious*) cauto/a; **(be) careful!** attenzione!; **carefully** adv con cura; cautamente; **caregiver** (*US*) n (*professional*) badante m/f; (*unpaid*) persona che si prende cura di un parente malato o anziano; **careless** ['keəlɪs] adj negligente; (*heedless*) spensierato/a; **carelessness** n negligenza; mancanza di tatto; **carer** ['keərəʳ] n chi si occupa di un familiare anziano o invalido; **caretaker** ['keəteɪkəʳ] n custode m

car-ferry ['kɑːfɛrɪ] n traghetto

cargo ['kɑːgəu] (pl **cargoes**) n carico

car hire n autonoleggio

Caribbean [kærɪ'biːən] adj: **the ~ (Sea)** il Mar dei Caraibi

caring ['keərɪŋ] adj (*person*) premuroso/a; (*society, organization*) umanitario/a

carnation [kɑː'neɪʃən] n garofano

carnival ['kɑːnɪvəl] n (*public celebration*) carnevale m; (*US: funfair*) luna park m inv

carol ['kærəl] n: **(Christmas) ~** canto di Natale

carousel [kærə'sɛl] n (*US*) giostra

car park n (*BRIT*) parcheggio

carpenter ['kɑːpɪntəʳ] n carpentiere m

carpet ['kɑːpɪt] n tappeto ▷ vt coprire con tappeto

car rental n (*US*) autonoleggio

carriage ['kærɪdʒ] n vettura; (*of goods*) trasporto; **carriageway** n (*BRIT: part of road*) carreggiata

carrier ['kærɪəʳ] n (*of disease*) portatore/trice; (*Comm*) impresa di trasporti; **carrier bag** n (*BRIT*) sacchetto

carrot ['kærət] n carota

carry ['kærɪ] vt (*person*) portare; (*vehicle*) trasportare; (*involve: responsibilities etc*) comportare; (*Med*) essere portatore/trice di ▷ vi (*sound*) farsi sentire; **to be** or **get carried away** (*fig*) farsi trascinare; **carry on** vi: **to ~ on with sth/doing** continuare qc/a fare ▷ vt mandare avanti; **carry out** vt (*orders*) eseguire; (*investigation*) svolgere

cart [kɑːt] n carro ▷ vt (*col*) trascinare

carton ['kɑːtən] n (*box*) scatola di cartone; (*of yogurt*) cartone m; (*of cigarettes*) stecca

cartoon [kɑː'tuːn] n (*in newspaper etc*) vignetta; (*comic strip*) fumetto; (*Cine, TV*) cartone m animato

cartridge ['kɑːtrɪdʒ] n (*for gun, pen*) cartuccia; (*music tape*) cassetta

carve [kɑːv] vt (*meat*) trinciare; (*wood, stone*) intagliare; **carving** n (*in wood etc*) scultura

car wash n lavaggio auto

case [keɪs] n caso; (*Law*) causa, processo; (*box*) scatola; (*BRIT: also*: **suit~**) valigia; **in ~ of** in caso di; **in ~ he** caso mai lui; **in any ~** in ogni caso; **just in ~** in caso di bisogno

cash [kæʃ] n (*coins, notes*) soldi mpl, denaro ▷ vt incassare; **I haven't got any ~** non ho contanti; **to pay (in) ~** pagare in contanti; **~ with order/on delivery (COD)** pagamento all'ordinazione/alla consegna; **cashback** n (*discount*) sconto; (*at supermarket etc*) anticipo di contanti ottenuto presso la cassa di un negozio tramite una carta di debito; **cash card** n (*BRIT*) carta per prelievi automatici; **cash desk** n (*BRIT*) cassa; **cash dispenser** n (*BRIT*) sportello automatico

cashew [kæ'ʃuː] n (*also*: **~ nut**) anacardio

cashier [kæ'ʃɪə^r] n cassiere/a

cashmere ['kæʃmɪə^r] n cachemire m

cash point n sportello bancario automatico, Bancomat® m inv

cash register n registratore m di cassa

casino [kə'siːnəu] n casinò m inv

casket ['kɑːskɪt] n cofanetto; (*US*: *coffin*) bara

casserole ['kæsərəul] n casseruola; **chicken ~** n pollo in casseruola

cassette [kæ'sɛt] n cassetta; **cassette player** n riproduttore m a cassette

cast [kɑːst] vt (*pt, pp* **cast**) (*throw*) gettare; (*metal*) gettare, fondere; (*Theat*): **to ~ sb as Hamlet** scegliere qn per la parte di Amleto ▷ n (*Theat*) cast m inv; (*also*: **plaster ~**) ingessatura; **to ~ one's vote** votare, dare il voto; **cast off** vi (*Naut*) salpare

castanets [kæstə'nɛts] npl castagnette fpl

caster sugar ['kɑːstə-] n (*BRIT*) zucchero semolato

cast iron n ghisa ▷ adj: **cast-iron** (*lit*) di ghisa; (*fig*: *will, alibi*) di ferro

castle ['kɑːsl] n castello

casual ['kæʒjul] adj (*chance*) casuale, fortuito/a; (*irregular*: *work etc*) avventizio/a; (*unconcerned*) noncurante, indifferente; **~ wear** casual m

casualty ['kæʒjultɪ] n ferito/a; (*dead*) morto/a, vittima; (*Med*: *department*) pronto soccorso

cat [kæt] n gatto

catalogue, (*US*) **catalog** ['kætələg] n catalogo ▷ vt catalogare

catalytic converter [kætə'lɪtɪk kən'vəːtə^r] n marmitta catalitica, catalizzatore m

cataract ['kætərækt] n (*also Med*) cateratta

catarrh [kə'tɑː^r] n catarro

catastrophe [kə'tæstrəfɪ] n catastrofe f

catch [kætʃ] (*pt, pp* **caught**) vt prendere; (*ball*) afferrare; (*person*: *by surprise*) sorprendere; (*attention*) attirare; (*comment, whisper*) cogliere; (*person*) raggiungere ▷ vi (*fire*) prendere ▷ n (*fish etc caught*) retata, (*of ball*) presa; (*trick*) inganno; (*Tech*) gancio; (*game*) catch m inv; **to ~ fire** prendere fuoco; **to ~ sight of** scorgere; **catch up** vi mettersi in pari ▷ vt (*also*: **~ up with**) raggiungere; **catching** ['kætʃɪŋ] adj (*Med*) contagioso/a

category ['kætɪgərɪ] n categoria

cater ['keɪtə^r]; **cater for** vt fus (*BRIT*: *needs*) provvedere a; (: *readers, consumers*) incontrare i gusti di; (*Comm*: *provide food*) provvedere alla ristorazione di

caterpillar ['kætəpɪlə^r] n bruco

cathedral [kə'θiːdrəl] n cattedrale f, duomo

Catholic ['kæθəlɪk] adj, n (*Rel*) cattolico/a

Catseye® ['kæts'aɪ] n (*BRIT Aut*) catarifrangente m

cattle ['kætl] npl bestiame m, bestie fpl

catwalk ['kætwɔːk] n passerella

caught [kɔːt] pt, pp of **catch**

cauliflower ['kɔlɪflauə^r] n cavolfiore m

cause [kɔːz] n causa ▷ vt causare

caution ['kɔːʃən] n prudenza; (*warning*) avvertimento ▷ vt avvertire; ammonire; **cautious** ['kɔːʃəs] adj cauto/a, prudente

cave [keɪv] n caverna, grotta; **cave in** vi (*roof etc*) crollare

caviar(e) ['kævɪɑː^r] n caviale m

cavity ['kævɪtɪ] n cavità f inv
cc abbr (= cubic centimetre) cc; (on letter etc) = **carbon copy**
CCTV n abbr (= closed-circuit television) televisione f a circuito chiuso
CD n abbr (= compact disk) CD m inv; (player) lettore m CD inv; **CD burner** n masterizzatore m (di) CD; **CD player** n lettore m CD; **CD-ROM** ['si:'di:'rɔm] n abbr (= compact disc read-only memory) CD-ROM m inv
cease [si:s] vt, vi cessare; **ceasefire** n cessate il fuoco m inv
cedar ['si:də'] n cedro
ceilidh ['keɪlɪ] n festa con musiche e danze popolari scozzesi o irlandesi
ceiling ['si:lɪŋ] n soffitto; (fig: upper limit) tetto
celebrate ['sɛlɪbreɪt] vt, vi celebrare; **celebration** [sɛlɪ'breɪʃən] n celebrazione f
celebrity [sɪ'lɛbrɪtɪ] n celebrità f inv
celery ['sɛlərɪ] n sedano
cell [sɛl] n cella; (of revolutionaries, Biol) cellula; (Elec) elemento (di batteria)
cellar ['sɛlə'] n sottosuolo; cantina
cello ['tʃɛləu] n violoncello
cellophane® ['sɛləfeɪn] n cellophane® m
cellphone ['sɛlfəun] n cellulare m
Celsius ['sɛlsɪəs] adj Celsius inv
Celtic ['kɛltɪk, 'sɛltɪk] adj celtico/a
cement [sə'mɛnt] n cemento
cemetery ['sɛmɪtrɪ] n cimitero
censor ['sɛnsə'] n censore m ▷ vt censurare; **censorship** n censura
census ['sɛnsəs] n censimento
cent [sɛnt] n (of dollar, euro) centesimo; see also **per cent**
centenary [sɛn'ti:nərɪ], (US) **centennial** [sɛn'tɛnɪəl] n centenario
center ['sɛntə'] n, vt (US) = **centre**
centi...: **centigrade** ['sɛntɪgreɪd] adj centigrado/a; **centimetre**, (US) **centimeter** ['sɛntɪmi:tə'] n

centimetro; **centipede** ['sɛntɪpi:d] n centopiedi m inv
central ['sɛntrəl] adj centrale; **Central America** n America centrale; **central heating** n riscaldamento centrale; **central reservation** n (BRIT Aut) banchina f spartitraffico inv
centre, (US) **center** ['sɛntə'] n centro ▷ vt centrare; (concentrate): **to ~ (on)** concentrare (su); **centre-forward** n (Sport) centroavanti m inv; **centre-half** n (Sport) centromediano
century ['sɛntjurɪ] n secolo; **in the twentieth ~** nel ventesimo secolo
CEO n abbr = **chief executive officer**
ceramic [sɪ'ræmɪk] adj ceramico/a
cereal ['si:rɪəl] n cereale m
ceremony ['sɛrɪmənɪ] n cerimonia; **to stand on ~** fare complimenti
certain ['sə:tən] adj certo/a; **to make ~ of** assicurarsi di; **for ~** per certo, di sicuro; **certainly** adv certamente, certo; **certainty** n certezza
certificate [sə'tɪfɪkɪt] n certificato; diploma m
certify ['sə:tɪfaɪ] vt certificare; (award diploma to) conferire un diploma a; (declare insane) dichiarare pazzo/a
cf. abbr (= compare) cfr
CFC n abbr (= chlorofluorocarbon) CFC m inv
chain [tʃeɪn] n catena ▷ vt (also: ~ up) incatenare; **chain-smoke** vi fumare una sigaretta dopo l'altra
chair [tʃɛə'] n sedia; (armchair) poltrona; (of university) cattedra; (of meeting) presidenza ▷ vt (meeting) presiedere; **chairlift** n seggiovia; **chairman** n (irreg) presidente m; **chairperson** n presidente/essa; **chairwoman** n (irreg) presidentessa
chalet ['ʃæleɪ] n chalet m inv
chalk [tʃɔ:k] n gesso; **chalkboard** (US) n lavagna
challenge ['tʃælɪndʒ] n sfida ▷ vt sfidare; (statement, right)

mettere in dubbio; **to ~ sb to do** sfidare qn a fare; **challenging** adj (task) impegnativo/a; (remark) provocatorio/a; (look) di sfida

chamber ['tʃeɪmbə^r] n camera; **chambermaid** n cameriera

champagne [ʃæm'peɪn] n champagne m inv

champion ['tʃæmpɪən] n campione/essa; **championship** n campionato

chance [tʃɑːns] n caso; (opportunity) occasione f; (likelihood) possibilità f inv ▷ vt: **to ~ it** rischiare, provarci ▷ adj fortuito/a; **to take a ~** rischiare; **by ~** per caso

chancellor ['tʃɑːnsələ^r] n cancelliere m; **C~ of the Exchequer** (BRIT) Cancelliere m dello Scacchiere

chandelier [ʃændə'lɪə^r] n lampadario

change [tʃeɪndʒ] vt cambiare; (transform): **to ~ sb into** trasformare qn in ▷ vi cambiare; (change one's clothes) cambiarsi; (be transformed): **to ~ into** trasformarsi in ▷ n cambiamento; (money) resto; **to ~ one's mind** cambiare idea; **a ~ of clothes** un cambio (di vestiti); **for a ~** tanto per cambiare; **small ~** spiccioli mpl; **keep the ~** tenga il resto; **sorry, I don't have any ~** mi dispiace, non ho spiccioli; **change over** vi (from sth to sth) passare; (players etc) scambiarsi (di posto o di campo) ▷ vt cambiare; **changeable** adj (weather) variabile; **change machine** n distributore m automatico di monete; **changing room** n (BRIT: in shop) camerino; (Sport) spogliatoio

channel ['tʃænl] n canale m; (of river, sea) alveo ▷ vt canalizzare; **Channel Tunnel** n: **the Channel Tunnel** il tunnel sotto la Manica

chant [tʃɑːnt] n canto; salmodia ▷ vt cantare; salmodiare

chaos ['keɪɔs] n caos m

chaotic [keɪ'ɔtɪk] adj caotico/a

chap [tʃæp] n (BRIT col: man) tipo

chapel ['tʃæpl] n cappella

chapped [tʃæpt] adj (skin, lips) screpolato/a

chapter ['tʃæptə^r] n capitolo

character ['kærɪktə^r] n carattere m; (in novel, film) personaggio; **characteristic** ['kærɪktə'rɪstɪk] adj caratteristico/a ▷ n caratteristica; **characterize** ['kærɪktəraɪz] vt caratterizzare; (describe): **to characterize (as)** descrivere (come)

charcoal ['tʃɑːkəul] n carbone m di legna

charge [tʃɑːdʒ] n accusa; (cost) prezzo; (responsibility) responsabilità ▷ vt (gun, battery, Mil: enemy) caricare; (customer) fare pagare a; (sum) fare pagare; (Law): **to ~ sb (with)** accusare qn (di) ▷ vi (gen with, up, along etc) lanciarsi; **charges** npl: **bank ~s** commissioni fpl bancarie; **to reverse the ~s** (Tel) fare una telefonata a carico del destinatario; **to take ~ of** incaricarsi di; **to be in ~ of** essere responsabile per; **how much do you ~ for this repair?** quanto chiede per la riparazione?; **to ~ an expense (up) to sb** addebitare una spesa a qn; **charge card** n (of shop) carta f clienti inv; **charger** n (also: **battery charger**) caricabatterie m inv; (old: warhorse) destriero

charismatic [kærɪz'mætɪk] adj carismatico/a

charity ['tʃærɪtɪ] n carità; (organization) opera pia; **charity shop** n (BRIT) negozi che vendono articoli di seconda mano e devolvono il ricavato in beneficenza

charm [tʃɑːm] n fascino; (on bracelet) ciondolo ▷ vt affascinare, incantare; **charming** adj affascinante

chart [tʃɑːt] n tabella; grafico; (map) carta nautica ▷ vt fare una carta nautica di; **charts** npl (Mus) hit parade f

charter ['tʃɑːtə^r] vt (plane) noleggiare ▷ n (document) carta; **chartered accountant** ['tʃɑːtəd-] n (BRIT) ragioniere/a professionista; **charter flight** n volo m charter inv

chase [tʃeɪs] vt inseguire; (also: **~ away**) cacciare ▷ n caccia

chat [tʃæt] vi (also: **have a ~**) chiacchierare; (on the internet) chattare ▷ n chiacchierata; (on the internet) chat f inv; **chat up** vt (BRIT col: girl, boy) abbordare; **chat room** n (Internet) chat f inv; **chat show** n (BRIT) talk show m inv

chatter ['tʃætə^r] vi (person) ciarlare; (bird) cinguettare; (teeth) battere ▷ n ciarle fpl; cinguettio

chauffeur ['ʃəʊfə^r] n autista m

chauvinist ['ʃəʊvɪnɪst] n (also: **male ~**) maschilista m; (nationalist) sciovinista m/f

cheap [tʃiːp] adj a buon mercato, economico/a; (joke) grossolano/a; (poor quality) di cattiva qualità ▷ adv a buon mercato; **cheap day return** n biglietto ridotto di andata e ritorno valido in giornata; **cheaply** adv a buon prezzo, a buon mercato

cheat [tʃiːt] vi imbrogliare; (at school) copiare ▷ vt ingannare ▷ n imbroglione m; **to ~ sb out of sth** defraudare qn di qc; **cheat on** vt fus (husband, wife) tradire

Chechnya [tʃɪtʃˈnjɑː] n Cecenia

check [tʃɛk] vt verificare; (passport, ticket) controllare; (halt) fermare; (restrain) contenere ▷ n verifica; controllo; (curb) freno; (US: bill) conto; (pattern: gen pl) quadretti mpl; (US) = **cheque** ▷ adj (pattern, cloth) a quadretti; **check in** vi (in hotel) registrare; (at airport) presentarsi all'accettazione ▷ vt (luggage) depositare; **check off** vt segnare; **check out** vi (from hotel) saldare il conto; **check up** vi: **to ~ up (on sth)** investigare (qc); **to ~ up on sb** informarsi sul conto di qn

checkbook n (US) = **chequebook**; **checkers** n (US) dama; **check-in** n (also: **check-in desk**) (at airport) check-in m inv, accettazione f (bagagli inv); **checking account** n (US) conto corrente; **checklist** n lista di controllo; **checkmate** n scaccomatto; **checkout** n (in supermarket) cassa; **checkpoint** n posto di blocco; **checkroom** n (US) deposito m bagagli inv; **checkup** n (Med) controllo medico

cheddar ['tʃedə^r] n formaggio duro di latte di mucca di colore bianco o arancione

cheek [tʃiːk] n guancia; (impudence) faccia tosta; **cheekbone** n zigomo; **cheeky** adj sfacciato/a

cheer [tʃɪə^r] vt applaudire; (gladden) rallegrare ▷ vi applaudire ▷ n grido (di incoraggiamento); **cheers** npl (of approval, encouragement) applausi mpl; evviva mpl; **~s!** salute!; **cheer up** vi rallegrarsi, farsi animo ▷ vt rallegrare; **cheerful** adj allegro/a

cheerio ['tʃɪərɪˈəʊ] excl (BRIT) ciao!

cheerleader ['tʃɪəliːdə^r] n cheerleader f inv

cheese [tʃiːz] n formaggio; **cheeseburger** n cheeseburger m inv; **cheesecake** n specie di torta di ricotta, a volte con frutta

chef [ʃɛf] n capocuoco

chemical ['kemɪkl] adj chimico/a ▷ n prodotto chimico

chemist ['kemɪst] n (BRIT: pharmacist) farmacista m/f; (scientist) chimico/a; **~'s shop** n (BRIT) farmacia; **chemistry** n chimica

cheque, (US) **check** [tʃɛk] n assegno; **chequebook** n libretto degli assegni; **cheque card** n carta f assegni inv

cherry ['tʃerɪ] n ciliegia; (also: **~ tree**) ciliegio

chess [tʃes] n scacchi mpl

chest [tʃest] n petto; (box) cassa

chestnut ['tʃesnʌt] n castagna; (also: **~ tree**) castagno

chest of drawers n cassettone m
chew [tʃuː] vt masticare; **chewing gum** n chewing gum m
chic [ʃiːk] adj elegante
chick [tʃɪk] n pulcino; (col) pollastrella
chicken ['tʃɪkɪn] n pollo; (col: coward) coniglio; **chicken out** vi (col) avere fifa; **chickenpox** n varicella
chickpea ['tʃɪkpiː] n cece m
chief [tʃiːf] n capo ▷ adj principale; **chief executive**, (US) **chief executive officer** n direttore m generale; **chiefly** adv per lo più, soprattutto
child (pl **children**) [tʃaɪld, 'tʃɪldrən] n bambino/a; **child abuse** n molestie fpl a minori; **child benefit** n (BRIT) ≈ assegni mpl familiari; **childbirth** n parto; **child-care** n il badare ai bambini; **childhood** n infanzia; **childish** adj puerile; **child minder** [-'maɪndə'] n (BRIT) bambinaia; **children** ['tʃɪldrən] npl of **child**
Chile ['tʃɪlɪ] n Cile m
Chilean ['tʃɪlɪən] adj, n cileno/a
chill [tʃɪl] n freddo; (Med) infreddatura ▷ vt raffreddare; **chill out** vi (esp US col) darsi una calmata
chilli, (US) **chili** ['tʃɪlɪ] n peperoncino
chilly ['tʃɪlɪ] adj freddo/a, fresco/a; **to feel ~** sentirsi infreddolito/a
chimney ['tʃɪmnɪ] n camino
chimpanzee [tʃɪmpæn'ziː] n scimpanzé m inv
chin [tʃɪn] n mento
China ['tʃaɪnə] n Cina
china ['tʃaɪnə] n porcellana
Chinese [tʃaɪ'niːz] adj cinese ▷ n (pl inv) cinese m/f; (Ling) cinese m
chip [tʃɪp] n (gen pl: Culin) patatina fritta; (: US: also: **potato ~**) patatina; (of wood, glass, stone) scheggia; (microchip) chip m inv ▷ vt (cup, plate) scheggiare; **chip and PIN** n sistema m chip e PIN; **chip and PIN machine** lettore m di carte chip e PIN; **chip and PIN card** carta chip e PIN; **chip shop** n (BRIT) vedi nota **"chip shop"**

○ **CHIP SHOP**

○ I chip shops, anche chiamati fish-
○ and-chip shops, sono friggitorie che
○ vendono principalmente filetti di
○ pesce impanati e patatine fritte
○ che un tempo venivano serviti
○ ai clienti avvolti in carta di giornale.

chiropodist [kɪ'rɔpədɪst] n (BRIT) pedicure mf inv
chisel ['tʃɪzl] n cesello
chives [tʃaɪvz] npl erba cipollina
chlorine ['klɔːriːn] n cloro
choc-ice ['tʃɔkaɪs] n (BRIT) gelato ricoperto al cioccolato
chocolate ['tʃɔklɪt] n (substance) cioccolato, cioccolata; (drink) cioccolata; (a sweet) cioccolatino
choice [tʃɔɪs] n scelta ▷ adj scelto/a
choir ['kwaɪə'] n coro
choke [tʃəuk] vi soffocare ▷ vt soffocare; (block) ingombrare ▷ n (Aut) valvola dell'aria; **to be ~d with** essere intasato/a
cholesterol [kə'lɛstərɔl] n colesterolo
chook [tʃuk] n (AUST, NZ col) gallina
choose (pt **chose**, pp **chosen**) [tʃuːz, tʃəuz, 'tʃəuzn] vt scegliere; **to ~ to do** decidere di fare; preferire fare
chop [tʃɔp] vt (wood) spaccare; (Culin: also: **~ up**) tritare ▷ n (Culin) costoletta; **chop down** vt (tree) abbattere; **chop off** vt tagliare; **chopsticks** ['tʃɔpstɪks] npl bastoncini mpl cinesi
chord [kɔːd] n (Mus) accordo
chore [tʃɔː'] n faccenda; **household ~s** faccende fpl domestiche
chorus ['kɔːrəs] n coro; (repeated part of song, also fig) ritornello
chose [tʃəuz] pt of **choose**
chosen ['tʃəuzn] pp of **choose**
Christ [kraɪst] n Cristo
christen ['krɪsn] vt battezzare; **christening** n battesimo

Christian ['krɪstɪən] *adj, n*
cristiano/a; **Christianity**
[krɪstɪ'ænɪtɪ] *n* cristianesimo;
Christian name *n* nome *m* di
battesimo

Christmas ['krɪsməs] *n* Natale *m*;
happy *or* **merry ~!** Buon Natale!;
Christmas card *n* cartolina di
Natale; **Christmas carol** *n* canto
natalizio; **Christmas Day** *n* il giorno
di Natale; **Christmas Eve** *n* la vigilia
di Natale; **Christmas pudding** *n* (*esp*
BRIT) specie di budino con frutta secca,
spezie e brandy; **Christmas tree** *n*
albero di Natale

chrome [krəum] *n* cromo

chronic ['krɒnɪk] *adj* cronico/a

chrysanthemum [krɪ'sænθəməm]
n crisantemo

chubby ['tʃʌbɪ] *adj* paffuto/a

chuck [tʃʌk] *vt* buttare, gettare; **to ~
(up** *or* **in)** (BRIT) piantare; **chuck out**
vt buttar fuori

chuckle ['tʃʌkl] *vi* ridere
sommessamente

chum [tʃʌm] *n* compagno/a

chunk [tʃʌŋk] *n* pezzo

church [tʃə:tʃ] *n* chiesa; **churchyard**
n sagrato

churn [tʃə:n] *n* (*for butter*) zangola;
(*also:* **milk ~**) bidone *m*

chute [ʃu:t] *n* (*also:* **rubbish ~**) canale
m di scarico; (BRIT: *children's slide*)
scivolo

chutney ['tʃʌtnɪ] *n* salsa piccante (di
frutta, zucchero e spezie)

CIA *n abbr* (US: = *Central Intelligence
Agency*) C.I.A. *f*

CID *n abbr* (BRIT: = *Criminal Investigation
Department*) ≈ polizia giudiziaria

cider ['saɪdə^r] *n* sidro

cigar [sɪ'gɑː^r] *n* sigaro

cigarette [sɪgə'rɛt] *n* sigaretta;
cigarette lighter *n* accendino

cinema ['sɪnəmə] *n* cinema *m inv*

cinnamon ['sɪnəmən] *n* cannella

circle ['sə:kl] *n* cerchio; (*of friends etc*)
circolo; (*in cinema*) galleria ▷ *vi* girare

in circolo ▷ *vt* (*surround*) circondare;
(*move round*) girare intorno a

circuit ['sə:kɪt] *n* circuito

circular ['sə:kjulə^r] *adj* circolare ▷ *n*
circolare *f*

circulate ['sə:kjuleɪt] *vi* circolare
▷ *vt* far circolare; **circulation**
[sə:kju'leɪʃən] *n* circolazione *f*; (*of
newspaper*) tiratura

circumstances ['sə:kəmstənsɪz]
npl circostanze *fpl*; (*financial condition*)
condizioni *fpl* finanziarie

circus ['sə:kəs] *n* circo

cite [saɪt] *vt* citare

citizen ['sɪtɪzn] *n* (*of country*)
cittadino/a; (*of town*) abitante *m/f*;
citizenship *n* cittadinanza

citrus fruit ['sɪtrəs-] *n* agrume *m*

city ['sɪtɪ] *n* città *f inv*; **the C~** la
Città di Londra (*centro commerciale*);
city centre *n* centro della città;
City Technology College *n* (BRIT)
istituto tecnico superiore (*finanziato
dall'industria*)

civic ['sɪvɪk] *adj* civico/a

civil ['sɪvɪl] *adj* civile; **civilian**
[sɪ'vɪlɪən] *adj, n* borghese (*m/f*)

civilization [sɪvɪlaɪ'zeɪʃən] *n*
civiltà *f inv*

civilized ['sɪvɪlaɪzd] *adj* civilizzato/a;
(*fig*) cortese

civil: civil law *n* codice *m* civile;
(*study*) diritto civile; **civil rights**
npl diritti *mpl* civili; **civil servant** *n*
impiegato/a statale; **Civil Service** *n*
amministrazione *f* statale; **civil war**
n guerra civile

CJD *n abbr* (= *Creutzfeld-Jakob disease*)
malattia di Creutzfeldt-Jakob

claim [kleɪm] *vt* (*rights etc*)
rivendicare; (*damages*) richiedere;
(*assert*) sostenere ▷ *vi* (*for insurance*)
fare una domanda d'indennizzo ▷ *n*
rivendicazione *f*; pretesa; richiesta;
claim form *n* (*gen*) modulo di
richiesta; (*for expenses*) modulo di
rimborso spese

clam [klæm] *n* vongola

clamp [klæmp] *n* pinza; morsa ▷ *vt* stringere con una morsa; (*Aut: wheel*) applicare le ganasce a

clan [klæn] *n* clan *m inv*

clap [klæp] *vi* applaudire

claret ['klærət] *n* vino di Bordeaux

clarify ['klærɪfaɪ] *vt* chiarificare, chiarire

clarinet [klærɪ'nɛt] *n* clarinetto

clarity ['klærɪtɪ] *n* chiarezza

clash [klæʃ] *n* frastuono; (*fig*) scontro ▷ *vi* scontrarsi; cozzare

clasp [klɑːsp] *n* (*hold*) stretta; (*of necklace, bag*) fermaglio, fibbia ▷ *vt* stringere

class [klɑːs] *n* classe *f* ▷ *vt* classificare

classic ['klæsɪk] *adj* classico/a ▷ *n* classico; **classical** *adj* classico/a

classification [klæsɪfɪ'keɪʃən] *n* classificazione *f*

classify ['klæsɪfaɪ] *vt* classificare

classmate ['klɑːsmeɪt] *n* compagno/a di classe

classroom ['klɑːsrʊm] *n* aula

classy ['klɑːsɪ] *adj* (*col*) chic *inv*, elegante

clatter ['klætəʳ] *n* tintinnio; scalpitio ▷ *vi* tintinnare; scalpitare

clause [klɔːz] *n* clausola; (*Ling*) proposizione *f*

claustrophobic [klɔːstrə'fəʊbɪk] *adj* claustrofobico/a

claw [klɔː] *n* (*of bird of prey*) artiglio; (*of lobster*) pinza

clay [kleɪ] *n* argilla

clean [kliːn] *adj* pulito/a; (*outline, break, movement*) netto/a ▷ *vt* pulire; **clean up** *vt* (*also fig*) ripulire; **cleaner** *n* (*person*) uomo (donna) delle pulizie; **cleaner's** *n* (*also:* **dry cleaner's**) tintoria; **cleaning** *n* pulizia

cleanser ['klɛnzəʳ] *n* detergente *m*

clear [klɪəʳ] *adj* chiaro/a; (*glass etc*) trasparente; (*road, way*) libero/a; (*conscience*) pulito/a ▷ *vt* sgombrare; liberare; (*table*) sparecchiare; (*Law: suspect*) discolpare; (*obstacle*) superare; (*cheque*) fare la compensazione di ▷ *vi* (*weather*) rasserenarsi; (*fog*) andarsene ▷ *adv*: **~ of** distante da; **clear away** *vt* (*things, clothes, etc*) mettere a posto; **to ~ away the dishes** sparecchiare la tavola; **clear up** *vt* mettere in ordine; (*mystery*) risolvere; **clearance** *n* (*removal*) sgombro; (*permission*) autorizzazione *f*, permesso; **clear-cut** *adj* ben delineato/a, distinto/a; **clearing** *n* radura; **clearly** *adv* chiaramente; **clearway** *n* (*BRIT*) strada con divieto di sosta

clench [klɛntʃ] *vt* stringere

clergy ['klə:dʒɪ] *n* clero

clerk [klɑːk, *US* kləːrk] *n* (*BRIT*) impiegato/a; (*US*) commesso/a

clever ['klɛvəʳ] *adj* (*mentally*) intelligente; (*deft, skilful*) abile; (*device, arrangement*) ingegnoso/a

cliché ['kliːʃeɪ] *n* cliché *m inv*

click [klɪk] *vi* scattare ▷ *vt*: **to ~ one's tongue** schioccare la lingua; **to ~ one's heels** battere i tacchi

client ['klaɪənt] *n* cliente *m/f*

cliff [klɪf] *n* scogliera scoscesa, rupe *f*

climate ['klaɪmɪt] *n* clima *m*; **climate change** *n* cambiamenti *mpl* climatici

climax ['klaɪmæks] *n* culmine *m*; (*sexual*) orgasmo

climb [klaɪm] *vi* salire; (*clamber*) arrampicarsi ▷ *vt* salire; (*Climbing*) scalare ▷ *n* salita; arrampicata; scalata; **climb down** *vi* scendere; (*BRIT fig*) far marcia indietro; **climber** *n* rocciatore/trice; alpinista *m/f*; **climbing** *n* alpinismo

clinch [klɪntʃ] *vt* (*deal*) concludere

cling (*pt, pp* **clung**) [klɪŋ, klʌŋ] *vi*: **to ~ (to)** tenersi stretto/a (a), aggrapparsi (a); (*clothes*) aderire strettamente (a)

clingfilm® ['klɪŋfɪlm] *n* pellicola trasparente (*per alimenti*)

clinic ['klɪnɪk] *n* clinica

clip [klɪp] *n* (*for hair*) forcina; (*also:* **paper ~**) graffetta; (*TV, Cine*) sequenza ▷ vt attaccare insieme; (hair, nails) tagliare; (hedge) tosare; **clipping** n (from newspaper) ritaglio

cloak [kləuk] n mantello ▷ vt avvolgere; **cloakroom** n (for coats etc) guardaroba m inv; (BRIT: W.C.) gabinetti mpl

clock [klɔk] n orologio; **clock in, clock on** vi timbrare il cartellino (all'entrata); **clock off, clock out** vi timbrare il cartellino (all'uscita); **clockwise** adv in senso orario; **clockwork** n movimento or meccanismo a orologeria ▷ adj a molla

clog [klɔg] n zoccolo ▷ vt intasare ▷ vi (also: ~ **up**) intasarsi, bloccarsi

clone [kləun] n clone m

close¹ [kləus] adj vicino/a; (watch) stretto/a; (examination) attento/a; (contest) combattuto/a; (weather) afoso/a ▷ adv vicino, dappresso; **to** ~ vicino/a; ~ **by**, ~ **at hand** qui (or lì) vicino; **a** ~ **friend** un amico intimo; **to have a** ~ **shave** (fig) scamparla bella

close² [kləuz] vt chiudere ▷ vi (shop etc) chiudere; (lid, door etc) chiudersi; (end) finire ▷ n (end) fine f; **close down** vi cessare (definitivamente); **closed** adj chiuso/a

closely ['kləuslɪ] adv (examine, watch) da vicino; **we are ~ related** siamo parenti stretti

closet ['klɔzɪt] n (cupboard) armadio

close-up ['kləusʌp] n primo piano

closing time n orario di chiusura

closure ['kləuʒər] n chiusura

clot [klɔt] n (also: **blood ~**) coagulo; (col: idiot) scemo/a ▷ vi coagularsi

cloth [klɔθ] n (material) tessuto, stoffa; (BRIT: also: **tea~**) strofinaccio

clothes [kləuðz] npl abiti mpl, vestiti mpl; **clothes line** n corda (per stendere il bucato); **clothes peg**, (US) **clothes pin** n molletta

clothing ['kləuðɪŋ] n = **clothes**

cloud [klaud] n nuvola; **cloud over** vi rannuvolarsi; (fig) offuscarsi; **cloudy** adj nuvoloso/a; (liquid) torbido/a

clove [kləuv] n chiodo di garofano; **clove of garlic** n spicchio d'aglio

clown [klaun] n pagliaccio ▷ vi (also: ~ **about**, ~ **around**) fare il pagliaccio

club [klʌb] n (society) club m inv, circolo; (weapon, Golf) mazza ▷ vt bastonare ▷ vi: **to** ~ **together** associarsi; **clubs** npl (Cards) fiori mpl; **club class** n (Aviat) classe f club inv

clue [klu:] n indizio; (in crosswords) definizione f; **I haven't a** ~ non ho la minima idea

clump [klʌmp] n (of flowers, trees) gruppo; (of grass) ciuffo

clumsy ['klʌmzɪ] adj goffo/a

clung [klʌŋ] pt, pp of **cling**

cluster ['klʌstər] n gruppo ▷ vi raggrupparsi

clutch [klʌtʃ] n (grip, grasp) presa, stretta; (Aut) frizione f ▷ vt afferrare, stringere forte

cm abbr (= centimetre) cm

Co. abbr = **county**; (= company) C., C.ia

c/o abbr (= care of) presso

coach [kəutʃ] n (bus) pullman m inv; (horse-drawn, of train) carrozza; (Sport) allenatore/trice; (tutor) chi dà ripetizioni ▷ vt allenare; dare ripetizioni a; **coach station** (BRIT) n stazione f delle corriere; **coach trip** n viaggio in pullman

coal [kəul] n carbone m

coalition [kəuə'lɪʃən] n coalizione f

coarse [kɔːs] adj (salt, sand etc) grosso/a; (cloth, person) rozzo/a

coast [kəust] n costa ▷ vi (with cycle etc) scendere a ruota libera; **coastal** adj costiero/a; **coastguard** n guardia costiera; **coastline** n linea costiera

coat [kəut] n cappotto; (of animal) pelo; (of paint) mano f ▷ vt coprire; **coat hanger** n attaccapanni m inv; **coating** n rivestimento

coax [kəuks] vt indurre (con moine)

cob [kɔb] n see **corn**

cobbled ['kɔbld] adj: ~ **street** strada pavimentata a ciottoli

cobweb ['kɔbwɛb] n ragnatela

cocaine [kə'keɪn] n cocaina

cock [kɔk] n (rooster) gallo; (male bird) maschio ▷ vt (gun) armare; **cockerel** n galletto

cockney ['kɔknɪ] n cockney mf inv (abitante dei quartieri popolari dell'East End di Londra)

cockpit ['kɔkpɪt] n abitacolo

cockroach ['kɔkrəʊtʃ] n blatta

cocktail ['kɔkteɪl] n cocktail m inv

cocoa ['kəʊkəʊ] n cacao

coconut ['kəʊkənʌt] n noce f di cocco

cod [kɔd] n merluzzo

C.O.D. abbr = **cash on delivery**

code [kəʊd] n codice m

coeducational ['kəʊɛdjʊ'keɪʃənl] adj misto/a

coffee ['kɔfɪ] n caffè m inv; **coffee bar** n (BRIT) caffè m inv; **coffee bean** n grano or chicco di caffè; **coffee break** n pausa per il caffè; **coffee maker** n bollitore m per il caffè; **coffeepot** n caffettiera; **coffee shop** n ≈ caffè m inv; **coffee table** n tavolino

coffin ['kɔfɪn] n bara

cog [kɔg] n dente m

cognac ['kɔnjæk] n cognac m inv

coherent [kəʊ'hɪərənt] adj coerente

coil [kɔɪl] n rotolo; (Aut, Elec) bobina; (contraceptive) spirale f ▷ vt avvolgere

coin [kɔɪn] n moneta ▷ vt (word) coniare

coincide [kəʊɪn'saɪd] vi coincidere; **coincidence** [kəʊ'ɪnsɪdəns] n combinazione f

Coke® [kəʊk] n coca f inv

coke [kəʊk] n coke m

colander ['kɔləndər] n colino

cold [kəʊld] adj freddo/a ▷ n freddo; (Med) raffreddore m; **it's** ~ fa freddo; **to be** ~ (person) aver freddo; (object) essere freddo/a; **to catch** ~ prendere freddo; **to catch a** ~ prendere un raffreddore; **in** ~ **blood** a sangue freddo; **cold sore** n erpete m

coleslaw ['kəʊlslɔː] n insalata di cavolo bianco

colic ['kɔlɪk] n colica

collaborate [kə'læbəreɪt] vi collaborare

collapse [kə'læps] vi crollare ▷ n crollo; (Med) collasso

collar ['kɔlər] n (of coat, shirt) colletto; (for dog) collare m; **collarbone** n clavicola

colleague ['kɔliːg] n collega m/f

collect [kə'lɛkt] vt (gen) raccogliere; (as a hobby) fare collezione di; (BRIT: call for) prendere; (money owed, pension) riscuotere; (donations, subscriptions) fare una colletta di ▷ vi adunarsi, riunirsi; (rubbish etc) ammucchiarsi ▷ (US Tel): **to call** ~ fare una chiamata a carico del destinatario; **collection** [kə'lɛkʃən] n collezione f; raccolta; (for money) colletta; **collective** adj collettivo/a ▷ n collettivo; **collector** [kə'lɛktər] n collezionista m/f

college ['kɔlɪdʒ] n college m inv; (of technology, agriculture etc) istituto superiore

collide [kə'laɪd] vi: **to** ~ **(with)** scontrarsi (con)

collision [kə'lɪʒən] n collisione f, scontro

cologne [kə'ləʊn] n (also: **eau de** ~) acqua di colonia

Colombia [kə'lɔmbɪə] n Colombia; **Colombian** adj, n colombiano/a

colon ['kəʊlən] n (sign) due punti mpl; (Med) colon m inv

colonel ['kəːnl] n colonnello

colonial [kə'ləʊnɪəl] adj coloniale

colony ['kɔlənɪ] n colonia

colour, (US) **color** ['kʌlər] n colore m ▷ vt colorare; (tint, dye) tingere; (fig: affect) influenzare ▷ vi (blush) arrossire; **colour in** vt colorare; **colour-blind** adj daltonico/a; **coloured** adj (photo) a colori; (person) di colore; **colour film** n (for camera) pellicola a colori; **colourful** adj pieno/a di colore, a vivaci colori; (personality) colorato/a; **colouring** n (substance) colorante m; (complexion) colorito; **colour television** n televisione f a colori

column ['kɔləm] n colonna

coma ['kəumə] n coma m inv

comb [kəum] n pettine m ▷ vt (hair) pettinare; (area) battere a tappeto

combat ['kɔmbæt] n combattimento ▷ vt combattere, lottare contro

combination [kɔmbɪ'neɪʃən] n combinazione f

combine [kəm'baɪn] vt: **to ~ (with)** combinare (con); (one quality with another): **to ~ sth with sth** unire qc a qc ▷ vi unirsi; (Chem) combinarsi ▷ n ['kɔmbaɪn] (Econ) associazione f

come (pt **came**, pp **come**) [kʌm, keɪm] vi venire; arrivare; **to ~ to** (decision etc) raggiungere; **I've ~ to like him** ha cominciato a piacermi; **to ~ undone/loose** slacciarsi/ allentarsi; **come across** vt fus trovare per caso; **come along** vi (pupil, work) fare progressi; **~ along!** avanti!, andiamo!, forza!; **come back** vi ritornare; **come down** vi scendere; (prices) calare; (buildings) essere demolito/a; **come from** vt fus venire da; provenire da; **come in** vi entrare; **come off** vi (button) staccarsi; (stain) andar via; (attempt) riuscire; **come on** vi (lights) accendersi; (electricity) entrare in funzione; (pupil, undertaking) fare progressi; **~ on!** avanti!, andiamo!, forza!; **come out** vi uscire; (stain) andare via; **come round** vi (after faint, operation) riprendere conoscenza, rinvenire; **come to** vi rinvenire; **come up** vi (sun) salire; (problem) sorgere; (event) essere in arrivo; (in conversation) saltar fuori; **come up with** vt fus: **he**

came up with an idea venne fuori con un'idea

comeback ['kʌmbæk] n (Theat etc) ritorno

comedian [kə'miːdɪən] n comico

comedy ['kɔmɪdɪ] n commedia

comet ['kɔmɪt] n cometa

comfort ['kʌmfət] n comodità f inv, benessere m; (relief) consolazione f, conforto ▷ vt consolare, confortare; **comfortable** adj comodo/a; (financially) agiato/a; **comfort station** n (us) gabinetti mpl

comic ['kɔmɪk] adj (also: **~al**) comico/a ▷ n comico; (BRIT: magazine) giornaletto; **comic book** n (us) giornalino (a fumetti); **comic strip** n fumetto

comma ['kɔmə] n virgola

command [kə'mɑːnd] n ordine m, comando; (Mil: authority) comando; (mastery) padronanza ▷ vt comandare; **to ~ sb to do** ordinare a qn di fare; **commander** n capo; (Mil) comandante m

commemorate [kə'meməreɪt] vt commemorare

commence [kə'mens] vt, vi cominciare; **commencement** n (us Univ) cerimonia di consegna dei diplomi

commend [kə'mend] vt lodare; raccomandare

comment ['kɔment] n commento ▷ vi: **to ~ (on)** fare commenti (su); **commentary** ['kɔmentərɪ] n commentario; (Sport) radiocronaca; telecronaca; **commentator** ['kɔmenteɪtər] n commentatore/ trice; (Sport) radiocronista m/f; telecronista m/f

commerce ['kɔməːs] n commercio

commercial [kə'məːʃəl] adj commerciale ▷ n (TV, Radio) pubblicità f inv; **commercial break** n intervallo pubblicitario

commission [kə'mɪʃən] n commissione f ▷ vt (work of art) commissionare; **out of ~** (*Naut*) in disarmo; **commissioner** n (*Police*) questore m

commit [kə'mɪt] vt (*act*) commettere; (*to sb's care*) affidare; **to ~ o.s. (to do)** impegnarsi (a fare); **to ~ suicide** suicidarsi; **commitment** n impegno; promessa

committee [kə'mɪtɪ] n comitato, commissione f

commodity [kə'mɔdɪtɪ] n prodotto, articolo

common ['kɔmən] adj comune; (*pej*) volgare; (*usual*) normale ▷ n terreno comune; **in ~** in comune; *see also* **Commons**; **commonly** adv comunemente, usualmente; **commonplace** adj banale, ordinario/a; **Commons** npl (*BRIT Pol*): **the (House of) Commons** la Camera dei Comuni; **common sense** n buon senso; **Commonwealth** n: **the Commonwealth** il Commonwealth

- **COMMONWEALTH**
- Il *Commonwealth* è un'associazione
- di stati sovrani indipendenti e
- di alcuni territori annessi che
- facevano parte dell'antico Impero
- Britannico. Ancora oggi molti stati
- del *Commonwealth* riconoscono
- simbolicamente il sovrano
- brittanico come capo di stato, e i
- loro rappresentanti si riuniscono
- per discutere questioni di comune
- interesse.

communal ['kɔmjuːnl] adj (*for common use*) pubblico/a

commune n ['kɔmjuːn] (*group*) comune f ▷ vi [kə'mjuːn]: **to ~ with** mettersi in comunione con

communicate [kə'mjuːnɪkeɪt] vt comunicare, trasmettere ▷ vi: **to ~ (with)** comunicare (con)

communication [kəmjuːnɪ'keɪʃən] n comunicazione f

communion [kə'mjuːnɪən] n (*also*: **Holy C~**) comunione f

communism ['kɔmjunɪzəm] n comunismo; **communist** adj, n comunista (m/f)

community [kə'mjuːnɪtɪ] n comunità f inv; **community centre**, (*US*) **community center** n circolo ricreativo; **community service** n (*BRIT*) ≈ lavoro sostitutivo

commute [kə'mjuːt] vi fare il pendolare ▷ vt (*Law*) commutare; **commuter** n pendolare m/f

compact adj [kəm'pækt] compatto/a ▷ n ['kɔmpækt] (*also*: **powder ~**) portacipria m inv; **compact disc** n compact disc m inv; **compact disc player** n lettore m CD inv

companion [kəm'pænjən] n compagno/a

company ['kʌmpənɪ] n (*also Comm, Mil, Theat*) compagnia; **to keep sb ~** tenere compagnia a qn; **company car** n macchina (di proprietà) della ditta; **company director** n amministratore m, consigliere m di amministrazione

comparable ['kɔmpərəbl] adj simile; **~ to** or **with** paragonabile a

comparative [kəm'pærətɪv] adj relativo/a; (*adjective, adverb etc*) comparativo/a; **comparatively** adv relativamente

compare [kəm'pɛəʳ] vt: **to ~ sth/ sb with/to** confrontare qc/qn con/a ▷ vi: **to ~ (with)** reggere il confronto (con); **comparison** [kəm'pærɪsn] n confronto; **in comparison with** confronto a

compartment [kəm'pɑːtmənt] n compartimento; (*Rail*) scompartimento

compass ['kʌmpəs] n bussola; **(a pair of) ~es** (*Math*) compasso; **within the ~ of** entro i limiti di

compassion [kəm'pæʃən] n compassione f

compatible [kəmˈpætɪbl] *adj*
compatibile

compel [kəmˈpɛl] *vt* costringere,
obbligare; **compelling** *adj* (*fig:*
argument) irresistibile

compensate [ˈkɔmpənseɪt] *vt*
risarcire ▷ *vi:* **to ~ for** compensare;
compensation [kɔmpənˈseɪʃən]
n compensazione *f;* (*money*)
risarcimento

compete [kəmˈpiːt] *vi* (*take part*)
concorrere; (*vie*): **to ~ (with)** fare
concorrenza (a)

competent [ˈkɔmpɪtənt] *adj*
competente

competition [kɔmpɪˈtɪʃən] *n* gara;
concorso; (*Econ*) concorrenza

competitive [kəmˈpɛtɪtɪv] *adj*
(*sports*) agonistico/a; (*person*)
che ha spirito di competizione;
che ha spirito di agonismo; (*Econ*)
concorrenziale

competitor [kəmˈpɛtɪtəʳ] *n*
concorrente *m/f*

complacent [kəmˈpleɪsnt] *adj*
compiaciuto/a di sé

complain [kəmˈpleɪn] *vi* lagnarsi,
lamentarsi; **complaint** *n* lamento;
(*in shop etc*) reclamo; (*Med*) malattia

complement *n* [ˈkɔmplɪmənt]
complemento; (*especially of ship's crew*
etc) effettivo ▷ *vt* [ˈkɔmplɪmɛnt]
(*enhance*) accompagnarsi bene a;
complementary [kɔmplɪˈmɛntərɪ]
adj complementare

complete [kəmˈpliːt] *adj*
completo/a ▷ *vt* completare;
(*form*) riempire; **completely** *adv*
completamente; **completion** *n*
completamento

complex [ˈkɔmplɛks] *adj*
complesso/a ▷ *n* (*Psych, buildings etc*)
complesso

complexion [kəmˈplɛkʃən] *n* (*of*
face) carnagione *f*

compliance [kəmˈplaɪəns] *n*
acquiescenza; **in ~ with** (*orders,*
wishes etc) in conformità con

complicate [ˈkɔmplɪkeɪt] *vt*
complicare; **complicated** *adj*
complicato/a; **complication**
[kɔmplɪˈkeɪʃən] *n* complicazione *f*

compliment *n* [ˈkɔmplɪmənt]
complimento ▷ *vt* [ˈkɔmplɪmɛnt]
fare un complimento a;
complimentary [kɔmplɪˈmɛntərɪ]
adj complimentoso/a, elogiativo/a;
(*free*) in omaggio

comply [kəmˈplaɪ] *vi:* **to ~ with**
assentire a; conformarsi a

component [kəmˈpəʊnənt] *adj, n*
componente (*m*)

compose [kəmˈpəʊz] *vt* (*music,*
poem etc) comporre; **to ~ o.s.**
ricomporsi; **~d of** composto/a di;
composer *n* (*Mus*) compositore/
trice; **composition** [kɔmpəˈzɪʃən] *n*
composizione *f*

composure [kəmˈpəʊʒəʳ] *n* calma

compound [ˈkɔmpaʊnd] *n* (*Chem,*
Ling) composto; (*enclosure*) recinto
▷ *adj* composto/a

comprehension [kɔmprɪˈhɛnʃən]
n comprensione *f*

comprehensive [kɔmprɪˈhɛnsɪv]
adj completo/a; **comprehensive**
(school) *n* (BRIT) scuola secondaria
aperta a tutti

> Be careful not to translate
> *comprehensive* by the Italian word
> *comprensivo.*

compress *vt* [kəmˈprɛs] comprimere
▷ *n* [ˈkɔmprɛs] (*Med*) compressa

comprise [kəmˈpraɪz] *vt* (*also:* **be ~d**
of) comprendere

compromise [ˈkɔmprəmaɪz] *n*
compromesso ▷ *vt* compromettere
▷ *vi* venire a un compromesso

compulsive [kəmˈpʌlsɪv] *adj* (*liar,*
gambler) che non riesce a controllarsi;
(*viewing, reading*) cui non si può fare
a meno

compulsory [kəmˈpʌlsərɪ] *adj*
obbligatorio/a

computer [kəmˈpjuːtəʳ] *n* computer
m inv, elaboratore *m* elettronico;

computer game n gioco per computer; **computer-generated** adj realizzato/a al computer; **computerize** vt computerizzare; **computer programmer** n programmatore/trice; **computer programming** n programmazione f di computer; **computer science** n informatica; **computer studies** npl informatica; **computing** n informatica

con [kɔn] vt (col) truffare ▷ n truffa

conceal [kən'siːl] vt nascondere

concede [kən'siːd] vt concedere; (admit) ammettere

conceited [kən'siːtɪd] adj presuntuoso/a, vanitoso/a

conceive [kən'siːv] vt concepire ▷ vi concepire un bambino

concentrate ['kɔnsəntreɪt] vi concentrarsi ▷ vt concentrare

concentration [kɔnsən'treɪʃən] n concentrazione f

concept ['kɔnsɛpt] n concetto

concern [kən'səːn] n affare m; (Comm) azienda, ditta; (anxiety) preoccupazione f ▷ vt riguardare; **to be ~ed (about)** preoccuparsi (di); **concerning** prep riguardo a, circa

concert ['kɔnsət] n concerto; **concert hall** n sala da concerti

concerto [kən'tʃəːtəu] n concerto

concession [kən'sɛʃən] n concessione f

concise [kən'saɪs] adj conciso/a

conclude [kən'kluːd] vt concludere; **conclusion** [kən'kluːʒən] n conclusione f

concrete ['kɔnkriːt] n calcestruzzo ▷ adj concreto/a; di calcestruzzo

concussion [kən'kʌʃən] n commozione f cerebrale

condemn [kən'dɛm] vt condannare; (building) dichiarare pericoloso/a

condensation [kɔndɛn'seɪʃən] n condensazione f

condense [kən'dɛns] vi condensarsi ▷ vt condensare

condition [kən'dɪʃən] n condizione f; (disease) malattia ▷ vt condizionare; **on ~ that** a condizione che + sub, a condizione di; **conditional** adj condizionale; **to be conditional upon** dipendere da; **conditioner** n (for hair) balsamo; (for fabrics) ammorbidente m

condo ['kɔndəu] n abbr (US col) = **condominium**

condom ['kɔndəm] n preservativo

condominium [kɔndə'mɪnɪəm] n (US) condominio

condone [kən'dəun] vt condonare

conduct n ['kɔndʌkt] condotta ▷ vt [kən'dʌkt] condurre; (manage) dirigere; amministrare; (Mus) dirigere; **to ~ o.s.** comportarsi; **conducted tour** [kən'dʌktɪd-] n gita accompagnata; **conductor** n (of orchestra) direttore m d'orchestra; (on bus) bigliettaio; (US Rail) controllore m; (Elec) conduttore m

cone [kəun] n cono; (Bot) pigna; (traffic cone) birillo

confectionery [kən'fɛkʃənərɪ] n dolciumi mpl

confer [kən'fəːʳ] vt: **to ~ sth on** conferire qc a ▷ vi conferire

conference ['kɔnfərns] n congresso

confess [kən'fɛs] vt confessare, ammettere ▷ vi confessarsi; **confession** [kən'fɛʃən] n confessione f

confide [kən'faɪd] vi: **to ~ in** confidarsi con

confidence ['kɔnfɪdns] n confidenza; (trust) fiducia; (also: **self-~**) sicurezza di sé; **in ~** (speak, write) in confidenza, confidenzialmente; **confident** adj sicuro/a; sicuro/a di sé; **confidential** [kɔnfɪ'dɛnʃəl] adj riservato/a, confidenziale

confine [kən'faɪn] vt limitare; (shut up) rinchiudere; **confined** adj (space) ristretto/a

confirm [kənˈfəːm] *vt* confermare; **confirmation** [kɒnfəˈmeɪʃən] *n* conferma; (*Rel*) cresima

confiscate [ˈkɒnfɪskeɪt] *vt* confiscare

conflict *n* [ˈkɒnflɪkt] conflitto ▷ *vi* [kənˈflɪkt] essere in conflitto

conform [kənˈfɔːm] *vi*: **to ~ (to)** conformarsi (a)

confront [kənˈfrʌnt] *vt* (*enemy, danger*) affrontare; **confrontation** [kɒnfrənˈteɪʃən] *n* scontro

confuse [kənˈfjuːz] *vt* (*one thing with another*) confondere; **confused** *adj* confuso/a; **confusing** *adj* che fa confondere; **confusion** [kənˈfjuːʒən] *n* confusione *f*

congestion [kənˈdʒɛstʃən] *n* congestione *f*

congratulate [kənˈɡrætjuleɪt] *vt*: **to ~ sb (on)** congratularsi con qn (per *or* di); **congratulations** [kənɡrætjuˈleɪʃənz] *npl* auguri *mpl*; (*on success*) complimenti *mpl*; **congratulations (on)** congratulazioni *fpl* (per)

congregation [kɒnɡrɪˈɡeɪʃən] *n* congregazione *f*

congress [ˈkɒnɡrɛs] *n* congresso; **congressman** [ˈkɒnɡrɛsmən] *n* (*irreg*: US) membro del Congresso; **congresswoman** [ˈkɒnɡrɛswumən] *n* (*irreg*: US) (donna) membro del Congresso

conifer [ˈkɒnɪfər] *n* conifero

conjugate [ˈkɒndʒugeɪt] *vt* coniugare

conjugation [kɒndʒəˈɡeɪʃən] *n* coniugazione *f*

conjunction [kənˈdʒʌŋkʃən] *n* congiunzione *f*

conjure [ˈkʌndʒər] *vi* fare giochi di prestigio

connect [kəˈnɛkt] *vt* connettere, collegare; (*Elec*) collegare; (*fig*) associare ▷ *vi* (*train*): **to ~ with** essere in coincidenza con; **to be ~ed with** (*associated*) aver rapporti con; **connecting flight** *n* volo in coincidenza; **connection** [kəˈnɛkʃən] *n* relazione *f*, rapporto; (*Elec*) connessione *f*; (*Tel*) collegamento; (*train, plane etc*) coincidenza

conquer [ˈkɒŋkər] *vt* conquistare; (*feelings*) vincere

conquest [ˈkɒŋkwɛst] *n* conquista

cons [kɒnz] *npl see* **pro**; **convenience**

conscience [ˈkɒnʃəns] *n* coscienza

conscientious [kɒnʃɪˈɛnʃəs] *adj* coscienzioso/a

conscious [ˈkɒnʃəs] *adj* consapevole; (*Med*) cosciente; **consciousness** *n* consapevolezza; (*Med*) coscienza

consecutive [kənˈsɛkjutɪv] *adj* consecutivo/a; **on 3 ~ occasions** 3 volte di fila

consensus [kənˈsɛnsəs] *n* consenso; **the ~ of opinion** l'opinione *f* unanime *or* comune

consent [kənˈsɛnt] *n* consenso ▷ *vi*: **to ~ (to)** acconsentire (a)

consequence [ˈkɒnsɪkwəns] *n* conseguenza, risultato; importanza

consequently [ˈkɒnsɪkwəntlɪ] *adv* di conseguenza, dunque

conservation [kɒnsəˈveɪʃən] *n* conservazione *f*

conservative [kənˈsəːvətɪv] *adj*, *n* conservatore/trice; (*cautious*) cauto/a; **C~** *adj*, *n* (BRIT *Pol*) conservatore/trice

conservatory [kənˈsəːvətrɪ] *n* (*greenhouse*) serra; (*Mus*) conservatorio

consider [kənˈsɪdər] *vt* considerare; (*take into account*) tener conto di; **to ~ doing sth** considerare la possibilità di fare qc; **considerable** [kənˈsɪdərəbl] *adj* considerevole, notevole; **considerably** *adv* notevolmente, decisamente; **considerate** [kənˈsɪdərɪt] *adj* premuroso/a; **consideration** [kənsɪdəˈreɪʃən] *n* considerazione *f* f; **considering** [kənˈsɪdərɪŋ] prep in considerazione di

consignment [kənˈsaɪnmənt] n (of goods) consegna; spedizione f

consist [kənˈsɪst] vi: **to ~ of** constare di, essere composto/a di

consistency [kənˈsɪstənsɪ] n consistenza; (fig) coerenza

consistent [kənˈsɪstənt] adj coerente

consolation [kɒnsəˈleɪʃən] n consolazione f

console vt [kənˈsəʊl] consolare ▷ n [ˈkɒnsəʊl] quadro di comando

consonant [ˈkɒnsənənt] n consonante f

conspicuous [kənˈspɪkjʊəs] adj cospicuo/a

conspiracy [kənˈspɪrəsɪ] n congiura, cospirazione f

constable [ˈkʌnstəbl] n (BRIT) ≈ poliziotto, agente m di polizia; **chief ~** ≈ questore m

constant [ˈkɒnstənt] adj costante; continuo/a; **constantly** adv costantemente; continuamente

constipated [ˈkɒnstɪpeɪtɪd] adj stitico/a; **constipation** [kɒnstɪˈpeɪʃən] n stitichezza

constituency [kənˈstɪtjʊənsɪ] n collegio elettorale

constitute [ˈkɒnstɪtjuːt] vt costituire

constitution [kɒnstɪˈtjuːʃən] n costituzione f

constraint [kənˈstreɪnt] n costrizione f

construct [kənˈstrʌkt] vt costruire; **construction** [kənˈstrʌkʃən] n costruzione f; **constructive** adj costruttivo/a

consul [ˈkɒnsl] n console m; **consulate** [ˈkɒnsjʊlɪt] n consolato

consult [kənˈsʌlt] vt: **to ~ sb (about sth)** consultare qn (su or riguardo a qc); **consultant** n (Med) consulente m medico; (other specialist) consulente; **consultation** [kɒnsəlˈteɪʃən] n (discussion) consultazione f; (Med, Law) consulto; **consulting room** [kənˈsʌltɪŋ-] n (BRIT) ambulatorio

consume [kənˈsjuːm] vt consumare; **consumer** n consumatore/trice

consumption [kənˈsʌmpʃən] n consumo

cont. abbr (= continued) segue

contact [ˈkɒntækt] n contatto; (person) conoscenza ▷ vt mettersi in contatto con; **contact lenses** npl lenti fpl a contatto

contagious [kənˈteɪdʒəs] adj (also fig) contagioso/a

contain [kənˈteɪn] vt contenere; **to ~ o.s.** contenersi; **container** n recipiente m; (for shipping etc) container m inv

contaminate [kənˈtæmɪneɪt] vt contaminare

cont'd abbr (= continued) segue

contemplate [ˈkɒntəmpleɪt] vt contemplare; (consider) pensare a (or di)

contemporary [kənˈtempərərɪ] adj, n contemporaneo/a

contempt [kənˈtempt] n disprezzo; **~ of court** (Law) oltraggio alla Corte

contend [kənˈtend] vt: **to ~ that** sostenere che ▷ vi: **to ~ with** lottare contro

content¹ [ˈkɒntent] n contenuto; **contents** npl (of box, case etc) contenuto; **(table of) ~s** indice m

content² [kənˈtent] adj contento/a, soddisfatto/a ▷ vt contentare, soddisfare; **contented** [kənˈtentɪd] adj contento/a, soddisfatto/a

contest n [ˈkɒntest] lotta; (competition) gara, concorso ▷ vt [kənˈtest] contestare; (Law) impugnare; (compete for) contendersi; **contestant** [kənˈtestənt] n concorrente m/f; (in fight) avversario/a

context [ˈkɒntekst] n contesto

continent ['kɒntɪnənt] n
continente m; **the C~** (BRIT)
l'Europa continentale; **continental**
[kɒntɪ'nɛntl] adj continentale;
continental breakfast n colazione
f all'europea (senza piatti caldi);
continental quilt n (BRIT) piumino

continual [kən'tɪnjuəl] adj
continuo/a; **continually** adv di
continuo

continue [kən'tɪnju:] vi continuare
▷ vt continuare; (start again)
riprendere

continuity [kɒntɪ'nju:ɪtɪ] n
continuità; (Cine) (ordine m della)
sceneggiatura

continuous [kən'tɪnjuəs] adj
continuo/a, ininterrotto/a;
continuous assessment n
(BRIT) valutazione f continua;
continuously adv (repeatedly)
continuamente; (uninterruptedly)
ininterrottamente

contour ['kɒntuər] n contorno,
profilo; (also: **~ line**) curva di livello

contraception [kɒntrə'sɛpʃən] n
contraccezione f

contraceptive [kɒntrə'sɛptɪv]
adj contraccettivo/a ▷ n
contraccettivo

contract n ['kɒntrækt] contratto
▷ vi [kən'trækt] (become smaller)
contrarsi; (Comm): **to ~ to do sth**
fare un contratto per fare qc ▷ vt
[kən'trækt] (illness) contrarre;
contractor n imprenditore m

contradict [kɒntrə'dɪkt] vt
contraddire; **contradiction**
[kɒntrə'dɪkʃən] n contraddizione
f; **to be in contradiction with**
discordare con

contrary¹ ['kɒntrərɪ] adj
contrario/a; (unfavourable) avverso/a,
contrario/a ▷ n contrario; **on the ~**
al contrario; **unless you hear to the
~** salvo contrordine

contrary² [kən'trɛərɪ] adj (perverse)
bisbetico/a

contrast n ['kɒntrɑ:st] contrasto
▷ vt ['kɒntrɑ:st] mettere in
contrasto; **in ~ to** or **with**
contrariamente a

contribute [kən'trɪbju:t] vi
contribuire ▷ vt: **to ~ £10/an article
to** dare 10 sterline/un articolo a; **to ~
to** contribuire a; (newspaper) scrivere
per; **contribution** [kɒntrɪ'bju:ʃən]
n contributo; **contributor**
[kən'trɪbjutər] n (to newspaper)
collaboratore/trice

control [kən'trəul] vt (firm,
operation etc) dirigere; (check)
controllare ▷ n controllo; **controls**
npl (of vehicle etc) comandi mpl; **to
be in ~ of** avere il controllo di; **to
go out of ~** (car) non rispondere
ai comandi; (situation) sfuggire di
mano; **control tower** n (Aviat) torre
f di controllo

controversial [kɒntrə'və:ʃl] adj
controverso/a, polemico/a

controversy ['kɒntrəvə:sɪ] n
controversia, polemica

convenience [kən'vi:nɪəns] n
comodità f inv; **at your ~** a suo
comodo; **all modern ~s,** (BRIT)
all mod cons tutte le comodità
moderne

convenient [kən'vi:nɪənt] adj
comodo/a

▎ Be careful not to translate
convenient by the Italian word
conveniente.

convent ['kɒnvənt] n convento

convention [kən'vɛnʃən] n
convenzione f; (meeting) convegno;
conventional adj convenzionale

conversation [kɒnvə'seɪʃən] n
conversazione f

conversely [kɒn'və:slɪ] adv al
contrario, per contro

conversion [kən'və:ʃən] n
conversione f; (BRIT: of house)
trasformazione f, rimodernamento

convert vt [kən'və:t] (Rel, Comm)
convertire; (alter) trasformare ▷ n

['kɔnvə:t] convertito/a; **convertible** n macchina decappottabile

convey [kən'veɪ] vt trasportare; (*thanks*) comunicare; (*idea*) dare; **conveyor belt** [kən'veɪəʳ-] n nastro trasportatore

convict vt [kən'vɪkt] dichiarare colpevole ▷ n ['kɔnvɪkt] carcerato/a; **conviction** [kən'vɪkʃən] n condanna; (*belief*) convinzione f

convince [kən'vɪns] vt: **to ~ sb (of sth/that)** convincere qn (di qc/ che), persuadere qn (di qc/che); **convinced** adj: **convinced of/that** convinto/a di/che; **convincing** adj convincente

convoy ['kɔnvɔɪ] n convoglio

cook [kuk] vt cucinare, cuocere ▷ vi cuocere; (*person*) cucinare ▷ n cuoco/a; **cookbook** ['kukbuk] n = **cookery book**; **cooker** n fornello, cucina; **cookery** n cucina; **cookery book** n (BRIT) libro di cucina; **cookie** n (US) biscotto; (*Comput*) cookie m inv; **cooking** n cucina

cool [ku:l] adj fresco/a; (*not afraid*) calmo/a; (*unfriendly*) freddo/a ▷ vt raffreddare; (*room*) rinfrescare ▷ vi (*water*) raffreddarsi; (*air*) rinfrescarsi; **cool down** vi raffreddarsi; (*fig: person, situation*) calmarsi; **cool off** vi (*become calmer*) calmarsi; (*lose enthusiasm*) perdere interesse

cop [kɔp] n (col) sbirro

cope [kəup] vi: **to ~ with** (*problems*) far fronte a

copper ['kɔpəʳ] n rame m; (col: *policeman*) sbirro

copy ['kɔpɪ] n copia ▷ vt copiare; **copyright** n diritto d'autore

coral ['kɔrəl] n corallo

cord [kɔ:d] n corda; (*Elec*) filo; **cords** npl (*trousers*) calzoni mpl (di velluto) a coste; **cordless** adj senza cavo

corduroy ['kɔ:dərɔɪ] n fustagno

core [kɔ:ʳ] n (*of fruit*) torsolo; (*of organization etc*) cuore m ▷ vt estrarre il torsolo da

coriander [kɔrɪ'ændəʳ] n coriandolo

cork [kɔ:k] n sughero; (*of bottle*) tappo; **corkscrew** n cavatappi m inv

corn [kɔ:n] n (BRIT: *wheat*) grano; (US: *maize*) granturco; (*on foot*) callo; **~ on the cob** (*Culin*) pannocchia cotta

corned beef ['kɔ:nd-] n carne f di manzo in scatola

corner ['kɔ:nəʳ] n angolo; (*Aut*) curva ▷ vt intrappolare; mettere con le spalle al muro; (*Comm: market*) accaparrare ▷ vi prendere una curva

corner shop n (BRIT) piccolo negozio di generi alimentari

cornflakes ['kɔ:nfleɪks] npl fiocchi mpl di granturco

cornflour ['kɔ:nflauəʳ] n (BRIT) farina finissima di granturco

cornstarch ['kɔ:nstɑ:tʃ] n (US) = **cornflour**

Cornwall ['kɔ:nwəl] n Cornovaglia

coronary ['kɔrənərɪ] n: **~ (thrombosis)** trombosi f coronaria

coronation [kɔrə'neɪʃən] n incoronazione f

coroner ['kɔrənəʳ] n magistrato incaricato di indagare la causa di morte in circostanze sospette

corporal ['kɔ:prəl] n caporalmaggiore m ▷ adj: **~ punishment** pena corporale

corporate ['kɔ:pərɪt] adj comune; (*Comm*) costituito/a (in corporazione)

corporation [kɔ:pə'reɪʃən] n (*of town*) consiglio comunale; (*Comm*) ente m

corps (pl **corps**) [kɔ:, kɔ:z] n corpo

corpse [kɔ:ps] n cadavere m

correct [kə'rɛkt] adj (*accurate*) corretto/a, esatto/a; (*proper*) corretto/a ▷ vt correggere; **correction** [kə'rɛkʃən] n correzione f

correspond [kɔrɪs'pɔnd] vi corrispondere; **correspondence** n corrispondenza; **correspondent** n corrispondente m/f; **corresponding** adj corrispondente

corridor [ˈkɔrɪdɔːʳ] n corridoio

corrode [kəˈrəud] vt corrodere ▷ vi corrodersi

corrupt [kəˈrʌpt] adj corrotto/a; (*Comput*) alterato/a ▷ vt corrompere; **corruption** n corruzione f

Corsica [ˈkɔːsɪkə] n Corsica

cosmetic [kɔzˈmɛtɪk] n cosmetico; **cosmetic surgery** n chirurgia plastica

cosmopolitan [kɔzməˈpɔlɪtn] adj cosmopolita

cost [kɔst] (*pt, pp* **cost**) n costo ▷ vi costare ▷ vt stabilire il prezzo di; **costs** npl (*Law*) spese fpl; **how much does it ~?** quanto costa?

co-star [ˈkəustɑːʳ] n attore/trice della stessa importanza del protagonista

Costa Rica [ˈkɔstəˈriːkə] n Costa Rica

costly [ˈkɔstlɪ] adj costoso/a, caro/a

cost-of-living [ˈkɔstəvˈlɪvɪŋ] adj: **~ allowance** indennità f inv di contingenza

costume [ˈkɔstjuːm] n costume m; (*lady's suit*) tailleur m inv; (*BRIT: also*: **swimming ~**) costume da bagno

cosy, (*US*) **cozy** [ˈkəuzɪ] adj intimo/a; **I'm very ~ here** sto proprio bene qui

cot [kɔt] n (*BRIT: child's*) lettino; (*US: folding bed*) brandina

cottage [ˈkɔtɪdʒ] n cottage m inv; **cottage cheese** n fiocchi mpl di latte magro

cotton [ˈkɔtn] n cotone m; **~ dress** etc vestito etc di cotone; **cotton on** vi (*col*): **to ~ on (to sth)** afferrare (qc); **cotton bud** n (*BRIT*) cotton fioc® m inv; **cotton candy** (*US*) n zucchero filato; **cotton wool** n (*BRIT*) cotone m idrofilo

couch [kautʃ] n sofà m inv

cough [kɔf] vi tossire ▷ n tosse f; **I've got a ~** ho la tosse; **cough mixture**, **cough syrup** n sciroppo per la tosse

could [kud] pt of **can²**

couldn't [ˈkudnt] = **could not**

council [ˈkaunsl] n consiglio; **city** or **town ~** consiglio comunale; **council estate** n (*BRIT*) quartiere m di case popolari; **council house** n (*BRIT*) casa popolare; **councillor**, (*US*) **councilor** n consigliere/a; **council tax** n (*BRIT*) tassa comunale sulla proprietà

counsel [ˈkaunsl] n avvocato; consultazione f ▷ vt: **to ~ sth/sb to do sth** consigliare qc/a qn di fare qc; **counselling**, (*US*) **counseling** n (*Psych*) assistenza psicologica; **counsellor**, (*US*) **counselor** n consigliere/a; (*US*) avvocato

count [kaunt] vt, vi contare ▷ n conto; (*nobleman*) conte m; **count in** vt (*col*) includere; **~ me in** ci sto anch'io; **count on** vt fus contare su; **countdown** n conto alla rovescia

counter [ˈkauntəʳ] n banco ▷ vt opporsi a ▷ adv: **~ to** contro; in opposizione a; **counter-clockwise** [ˈkauntəˈklɔkwaɪz] (*US*) adv in senso antiorario

counterfeit [ˈkauntəfɪt] n contraffazione f, falso ▷ vt contraffare, falsificare ▷ adj falso/a

counterpart [ˈkauntəpɑːt] n (*of document etc*) copia; (*of person*) corrispondente m/f

counterterrorism [ˈkauntəˈterərɪzəm] n antiterrorismo

countess [ˈkauntɪs] n contessa

countless [ˈkauntlɪs] adj innumerevole

country [ˈkʌntrɪ] n paese m; (*native land*) patria; (*as opposed to town*) campagna; (*region*) regione f; **country and western (music)** n musica country e western, country m; **country house** n villa in campagna; **countryside** n campagna

county [ˈkauntɪ] n contea

coup (*pl* **coups**) [kuː, kuːz] n colpo; (*also*: **~ d'état**) colpo di Stato

couple ['kʌpl] n coppia; **a ~ of** un paio di

coupon ['ku:pɔn] n buono; (*Comm*) coupon m inv

courage ['kʌrɪdʒ] n coraggio; **courageous** adj coraggioso/a

courgette [kuə'ʒet] n (*BRIT*) zucchina

courier ['kurɪər] n corriere m; (*for tourists*) guida

course [kɔ:s] n corso; (*of ship*) rotta; (*for golf*) campo; (*part of meal*) piatto; **of ~** senz'altro, naturalmente; **~ (of action)** modo d'agire; **a ~ of treatment** (*Med*) una cura

court [kɔ:t] n corte f; (*Tennis*) campo ▷ vt (*woman*) fare la corte a; **to take to ~** citare in tribunale

courtesy ['kɔ:təsɪ] n cortesia; **by ~ of** per gentile concessione di; **courtesy bus, courtesy coach** n navetta gratuita (*di hotel, aeroporto*)

court: court-house n (*US*) palazzo di giustizia; **courtroom** ['kɔ:trum] n tribunale m; **courtyard** ['kɔ:tjɑ:d] n cortile m

cousin ['kʌzn] n cugino/a; **first ~** cugino di primo grado

cover ['kʌvər] vt coprire; (*book, table*) rivestire; (*include*) comprendere; (*Press*) fare un servizio su ▷ n (*of pan*) coperchio; (*over furniture*) fodera; (*of bed*) copriletto; (*of book*) copertina; (*shelter*) riparo; (*Comm, Insurance, of spy*) copertura; **covers** npl (*on bed*) lenzuola fpl e coperte fpl; **to take ~** mettersi al riparo; **under ~** al riparo; **under ~ of darkness** protetto dall'oscurità; **under separate ~** (*Comm*) a parte, in plico separato; **cover up** vi: **to ~ up for sb** (*fig*) coprire qn; **coverage** n (*Press, TV, Radio*): **to give full coverage to** fare un ampio servizio su; **cover charge** n coperto; **cover-up** n occultamento (di informazioni)

cow [kau] n vacca ▷ vt (*person*) intimidire

coward ['kauəd] n vigliacco/a; **cowardly** adj vigliacco/a

cowboy ['kaubɔɪ] n cow-boy m inv

cozy ['kəuzɪ] adj (*US*) = **cosy**

crab [kræb] n granchio

crack [kræk] n fessura, crepa; incrinatura; (*noise*) schiocco; (: *of gun*) scoppio; (*Drugs*) crack m inv ▷ vt spaccare; incrinare; (*whip*) schioccare; (*nut*) schiacciare; (*solve: problem, case*) risolvere; (: *code*) decifrare ▷ cpd (*troops*) fuori classe; **to ~ jokes** dire battute, scherzare; **to get ~ing** (*col*) darsi una mossa; **crack down on** vt fus prendere serie misure contro, porre freno a; **cracked** adj (*col*) matto/a; **cracker** ['krækər] n cracker m inv; (*firework*) petardo

crackle ['krækl] vi crepitare

cradle ['kreɪdl] n culla

craft [krɑ:ft] n mestiere m; (*cunning*) astuzia; (*boat*) naviglio; **craftsman** n artigiano; **craftsmanship** n abilità

cram [kræm] vi (*for exams*) prepararsi (in gran fretta) ▷ vt (*fill*): **to ~ sth with** riempire qc di; (*put*): **to ~ sth into** stipare qc in

cramp [kræmp] n crampo; **I've got ~ in my leg** ho un crampo alla gamba; **cramped** adj ristretto/a

cranberry ['krænbərɪ] n mirtillo

crane [kreɪn] n gru f inv

crap [kræp] n (*col!*) fesserie fpl; **to have a ~** cacare (!)

crash [kræʃ] n fragore m; (*of car*) incidente m; (*of plane*) caduta; (*Stock Exchange*) crollo ▷ vt fracassare ▷ vi (*plane*) fracassarsi; (*car*) avere un incidente; (*two cars*) scontrarsi; (*business etc*) fallire, andare in rovina; **crash course** n corso intensivo; **crash helmet** n casco

crate [kreɪt] n cassa

crave [kreɪv] vt, vi: **to ~ (for)** desiderare ardentemente

crawl [krɔ:l] vi strisciare carponi; (*vehicle*) avanzare lentamente ▷ n (*Swimming*) crawl m

crayfish ['kreɪfɪʃ] *n inv* (*freshwater*) gambero (d'acqua dolce); (*saltwater*) gambero

crayon ['kreɪən] *n* matita colorata

craze [kreɪz] *n* mania

crazy ['kreɪzɪ] *adj* matto/a; (*col: keen*): **to be ~ about sb** essere pazzo di qn; **to be ~ about sth** andare matto per qc

creak [kriːk] *vi* cigolare, scricchiolare

cream [kriːm] *n* crema; (*fresh*) panna ▷ *adj* (*colour*) color crema *inv*; **cream cheese** *n* formaggio fresco; **creamy** *adj* cremoso/a

crease [kriːs] *n* grinza; (*deliberate*) piega ▷ *vt* sgualcire ▷ *vi* sgualcirsi

create [kriːˈeɪt] *vt* creare; **creation** [kriːˈeɪʃən] *n* creazione *f*; **creative** *adj* creativo/a; **creator** *n* creatore/trice

creature ['kriːtʃəʳ] *n* creatura

crèche [krɛʃ] *n* asilo infantile

credentials [krɪˈdɛnʃlz] *npl* credenziali *fpl*

credibility [krɛdɪˈbɪlɪtɪ] *n* credibilità

credible ['krɛdɪbl] *adj* credibile; (*witness, source*) attendibile

credit ['krɛdɪt] *n* credito; onore *m* ▷ *vt* (*Comm*) accreditare; (*believe: also:* **give ~ to**) credere, prestar fede a; **to ~ sb with sth** (*fig*) attribuire qc a qn; **to be in ~** (*person*) essere creditore/trice; (*bank account*) essere coperto/a; *see also* **credits**; **credit card** *n* carta di credito; **credit crunch** *n* improvvisa stretta di credito

credits ['krɛdɪts] *npl* (*Cine*) titoli *mpl*

creek [kriːk] *n* insenatura; (*US*) piccolo fiume *m*

creep (*pt, pp* **crept**) [kriːp, krɛpt] *vi* avanzare furtivamente (*or* pian piano)

cremate [krɪˈmeɪt] *vt* cremare

crematorium (*pl* **crematoria**) [krɛməˈtɔːrɪəm, -ˈtɔːrɪə] *n* forno crematorio

crept [krɛpt] *pt, pp of* **creep**

crescent ['krɛsnt] *n* (*shape*) mezzaluna; (*street*) strada semicircolare

cress [krɛs] *n* crescione *m*

crest [krɛst] *n* cresta; (*of coat of arms*) cimiero

crew [kruː] *n* equipaggio; **crew-neck** *n* girocollo

crib [krɪb] *n* culla ▷ *vt* (*col*) copiare

cricket ['krɪkɪt] *n* (*insect*) grillo; (*game*) cricket *m*; **cricketer** *n* giocatore *m* di cricket

crime [kraɪm] *n* crimine *m*; **criminal** ['krɪmɪnl] *adj, n* criminale (*m/f*)

crimson ['krɪmzn] *adj* color cremisi *inv*

cringe [krɪndʒ] *vi* acquattarsi; (*in embarrassment*) sentirsi sprofondare

cripple ['krɪpl] *n* zoppo/a ▷ *vt* azzoppare

crisis (*pl* **crises**) ['kraɪsɪs, -siːz] *n* crisi *f inv*

crisp [krɪsp] *adj* croccante; (*fig*) frizzante; vivace; deciso/a; **crispy** *adj* croccante

criterion (*pl* **criteria**) [kraɪˈtɪərɪən, -ˈtɪərɪə] *n* criterio

critic ['krɪtɪk] *n* critico/a; **critical** *adj* critico/a; **criticism** ['krɪtɪsɪzəm] *n* critica; **criticize** ['krɪtɪsaɪz] *vt* criticare

Croat ['krəuæt] *adj, n* = **Croatian**

Croatia [krəuˈeɪʃə] *n* Croazia; **Croatian** *adj* croato/a ▷ *n* croato/a; (*Ling*) croato

crockery ['krɔkərɪ] *n* vasellame *m*

crocodile ['krɔkədaɪl] *n* coccodrillo

crocus ['krəukəs] *n* croco

croissant ['krwasã] *n* brioche *f inv*, croissant *m inv*

crook [kruk] *n* (*col*) truffatore *m*; (*of shepherd*) bastone *m*; **crooked** ['krukɪd] *adj* curvo/a, storto/a; (*person, action*) disonesto/a

crop [krɔp] *n* (*produce*) coltivazione *f*; (*amount produced*) raccolto; (*riding crop*) frustino ▷ *vt* (*hair*) rapare; **crop up** *vi* presentarsi

cross [krɔs] n croce f; (Biol) incrocio
▷ vt (street etc) attraversare; (arms, legs, Biol) incrociare; (cheque) sbarrare ▷ adj di cattivo umore; **cross off** vt cancellare (tirando una riga con la penna); **cross out** vt cancellare; **cross over** vi attraversare; **cross-Channel ferry** ['krɔs'tʃænl-] n traghetto che attraversa la Manica; **crosscountry (race)** n cross-country m inv; **crossing** n incrocio; (sea-passage) traversata; (also: **pedestrian crossing**) passaggio pedonale; **crossing guard** (US) n dipendente comunale che aiuta i bambini ad attraversare la strada; **crossroads** n incrocio; **crosswalk** n (US) strisce fpl pedonali, passaggio pedonale; **crossword** n cruciverba m inv

crotch [krɔtʃ] n (Anat) inforcatura; (of garment) pattina

crouch [krautʃ] vi acquattarsi; rannicchiarsi

crouton ['kru:tɔn] n crostino

crow [krəu] n (bird) cornacchia; (of cock) canto del gallo ▷ vi (cock) cantare

crowd [kraud] n folla ▷ vt affollare, stipare ▷ vi: **to ~ round/in** affollarsi intorno a/in; **crowded** adj affollato/a; **crowded with** stipato/a di

crown [kraun] n corona; (of head) calotta cranica; (of hat) cocuzzolo; (of hill) cima ▷ vt incoronare; (fig: career) coronare; **crown jewels** npl gioielli mpl della Corona

crucial ['kru:ʃl] adj cruciale, decisivo/a

crucifix ['kru:sıfıks] n crocifisso

crude [kru:d] adj (materials) greggio/a; non raffinato/a; (fig: basic) crudo/a, primitivo/a; (: vulgar) rozzo/a, grossolano/a ▷ n (also: **~ oil**) (petrolio) greggio

cruel ['kruəl] adj crudele; **cruelty** n crudeltà f inv

cruise [kru:z] n crociera ▷ vi andare a velocità di crociera; (taxi) circolare

crumb [krʌm] n briciola

crumble ['krʌmbl] vt sbriciolare ▷ vi sbriciolarsi; (plaster etc) sgretolarsi; (land, earth) franare; (building, fig) crollare

crumpet ['krʌmpıt] n specie di frittella

crumple ['krʌmpl] vt raggrinzare, spiegazzare

crunch [krʌntʃ] vt sgranocchiare; (underfoot) scricchiolare ▷ n (fig) punto or momento cruciale; **crunchy** adj croccante

crush [krʌʃ] n folla; (love): **to have a ~ on sb** avere una cotta per qn; (drink): **lemon ~** spremuta di limone ▷ vt schiacciare; (crumple) sgualcire

crust [krʌst] n crosta; **crusty** adj (bread) croccante; (person) brontolone/a; (remark) brusco/a

crutch [krʌtʃ] n gruccia

cry [kraı] vi piangere; (shout) urlare ▷ n urlo, grido; **cry out** vi, vt gridare

crystal ['krıstl] n cristallo

cub [kʌb] n cucciolo; (also: **~ scout**) lupetto

Cuba ['kju:bə] n Cuba

Cuban ['kju:bən] adj, n cubano/a

cube [kju:b] n cubo ▷ vt (Math) elevare al cubo; **cubic** adj cubico/a; **cubic metre** etc metro etc cubo

cubicle ['kju:bıkl] n scompartimento separato; cabina

cuckoo ['kuku:] n cucù m inv

cucumber ['kju:kʌmbəʳ] n cetriolo

cuddle ['kʌdl] vt abbracciare, coccolare ▷ vi abbracciarsi

cue [kju:] n stecca; (Theat etc) segnale m

cuff [kʌf] n (BRIT: of shirt, coat etc) polsino; (US: on trousers) risvolto; **off the ~** improvvisando; **cufflink** ['kʌflıŋk] n gemello

cuisine [kwı'zi:n] n cucina

cul-de-sac ['kʌldəsæk] n vicolo cieco

cull [kʌl] vt (ideas etc) scegliere ▷ n (of animals) abbattimento selettivo

culminate ['kʌlmıneıt] vi: **to ~ in** culminare con

culprit [ˈkʌlprɪt] n colpevole m/f
cult [kʌlt] n culto
cultivate [ˈkʌltɪveɪt] vt (also fig) coltivare
cultural [ˈkʌltʃərəl] adj culturale
culture [ˈkʌltʃəʳ] n (also fig) cultura
cumin [ˈkʌmɪn] n (spice) cumino
cunning [ˈkʌnɪŋ] n astuzia, furberia ▷ adj astuto/a, furbo/a
cup [kʌp] n tazza; (prize, of bra) coppa
cupboard [ˈkʌbəd] n armadio
cup final n (BRIT Football) finale f di coppa
curator [kjuəˈreɪtəʳ] n direttore m (di museo ecc)
curb [kə:b] vt tenere a freno ▷ n freno; (US) bordo del marciapiede
curdle [ˈkə:dl] vi cagliare
cure [kjuəʳ] vt guarire; (Culin) trattare; affumicare; essiccare ▷ n rimedio
curfew [ˈkə:fju:] n coprifuoco
curiosity [kjuərɪˈɒsɪtɪ] n curiosità
curious [ˈkjuərɪəs] adj curioso/a
curl [kə:l] n riccio ▷ vt ondulare; (tightly) arricciare ▷ vi arricciarsi; **curl up** vi rannicchiarsi; **curler** n bigodino; **curly** [ˈkə:lɪ] adj ricciuto/a
currant [ˈkʌrnt] n (dried) uvetta; (bush, fruit) ribes m inv
currency [ˈkʌrnsɪ] n moneta; **to gain ~** (fig) acquistare larga diffusione
current [ˈkʌrnt] adj corrente ▷ n corrente f; **current account** n (BRIT) conto corrente; **current affairs** npl attualità fpl; **currently** adv attualmente
curriculum (pl **curriculums** or **curricula**) [kəˈrɪkjuləm, -lə] n curriculum m inv; **curriculum vitae** [-ˈvi:taɪ] n curriculum vitae m inv
curry [ˈkʌrɪ] n curry m inv ▷ vt: **to ~ favour with** cercare di attirarsi i favori di; **curry powder** n curry m
curse [kə:s] vt maledire ▷ vi bestemmiare ▷ n maledizione f; bestemmia

cursor [ˈkə:səʳ] n (Comput) cursore m
curt [kə:t] adj secco/a
curtain [ˈkə:tn] n tenda; (Theat) sipario
curve [kə:v] n curva ▷ vi curvarsi; **curved** adj curvo/a
cushion [ˈkuʃən] n cuscino ▷ vt (shock) fare da cuscinetto a
custard [ˈkʌstəd] n (for pouring) crema
custody [ˈkʌstədɪ] n (of child) custodia; **to take sb into ~** mettere qn in detenzione preventiva
custom [ˈkʌstəm] n costume m; consuetudine f; (Comm) clientela
customer [ˈkʌstəməʳ] n cliente m/f
customized [ˈkʌstəmaɪzd] adj (car) fuoriserie inv
customs [ˈkʌstəmz] npl dogana; **customs officer** n doganiere m
cut [kʌt] (pt, pp **cut**) vt tagliare; (shape, make) intagliare; (reduce) ridurre ▷ vi tagliare ▷ n taglio; (in salary etc) riduzione f; **I've ~ myself** mi sono tagliato; **to ~ a tooth** mettere un dente; **cut back** vt (plants) tagliare; (production, expenditure) ridurre; **cut down** vt (tree) abbattere; **cut down on** vt fus ridurre; **cut off** vt tagliare; (fig) isolare; **cut out** vt tagliare; eliminare; (picture) ritagliare; **cut up** vt tagliare a pezzi; **cutback** n riduzione f
cute [kju:t] adj carino/a
cutlery [ˈkʌtlərɪ] n posate fpl
cutlet [ˈkʌtlɪt] n costoletta; (nut cutlet) cotoletta vegetariana
cut: cut-price, (US) **cut-rate** adj a prezzo ridotto; **cutting** [ˈkʌtɪŋ] adj tagliente ▷ n taglio (di giornale); (from plant) talea
CV n abbr = **curriculum vitae**
cwt. abbr = **hundredweight**
cyberbullying [ˈsaɪbəbulɪɪŋ] n bullismo informatico
cybercafé [ˈsaɪbəkæfeɪ] n cybercaffè m inv

cybercrime ['saɪbəkraɪm] *n* delinquenza informatica

cyberspace ['saɪbəspeɪs] *n* ciberspazio

cycle ['saɪkl] *n* ciclo; (*bicycle*) bicicletta ⊳ *vi* andare in bicicletta; **cycle hire** *n* noleggio *m* biciclette *inv*; **cycle lane** *n* pista ciclabile; **cycle path** *n* pista ciclabile; **cycling** ['saɪklɪŋ] *n* ciclismo; **to go on a cycling holiday** (*BRIT*) fare una vacanza in bicicletta; **cyclist** ['saɪklɪst] *n* ciclista *m/f*

cyclone ['saɪkləun] *n* ciclone *m*

cylinder ['sɪlɪndər] *n* cilindro

cymbals ['sɪmblz] *npl* piatti *mpl*

cynical ['sɪnɪkl] *adj* cinico/a

Cypriot ['sɪprɪət] *adj*, *n* cipriota (*m/f*)

Cyprus ['saɪprəs] *n* Cipro

cyst [sɪst] *n* cisti *f inv*; **cystitis** [sɪ'staɪtɪs] *n* cistite *f*

czar [zɑːr] *n* zar *m inv*

Czech [tʃɛk] *adj* ceco/a ⊳ *n* ceco/a; (*Ling*) ceco; **Czech Republic** *n*: **the Czech Republic** la Repubblica Ceca

D [diː] *n* (*Mus*) re *m*

dab [dæb] *vt* (*eyes, wound*) tamponare; (*paint, cream*) applicare (con leggeri colpetti)

dad [dæd], **daddy** ['dædɪ] *n* babbo, papà *m inv*

daffodil ['dæfədɪl] *n* trombone *m*, giunchiglia

daft [dɑːft] *adj* sciocco/a

dagger ['dægər] *n* pugnale *m*

daily ['deɪlɪ] *adj* quotidiano/a, giornaliero/a ⊳ *n* quotidiano ⊳ *adv* tutti i giorni

dairy ['dɛərɪ] *n* (*shop*) latteria; (*on farm*) caseificio ⊳ *cpd* caseario/a; **dairy produce** *n* latticini *mpl*

daisy ['deɪzɪ] *n* margherita

dam [dæm] *n* diga ⊳ *vt* sbarrare; costruire dighe su

damage ['dæmɪdʒ] *n* danno, danni *mpl*; (*fig*) danno ⊳ *vt* danneggiare; **damages** *npl* (*Law*) danni *mpl*

damn [dæm] vt condannare; (curse) maledire ▷ n (col): **I don't give a ~** non me ne frega niente ▷ adj (col: also: **~ed**): **this ~ ...** questo maledetto ...; **~ (it)!** accidenti!

damp [dæmp] adj umido/a ▷ n umidità, umido ▷ vt (also: **~en**: cloth, rag) inumidire, bagnare; (: enthusiasm etc) spegnere

dance [dɑːns] n danza, ballo; (ball) ballo ▷ vi ballare; **dance floor** n pista da ballo; **dancer** n danzatore/trice; (professional) ballerino/a; **dancing** ['dɑːnsɪŋ] n danza, ballo

dandelion ['dændɪlaɪən] n dente m di leone

dandruff ['dændrəf] n forfora

Dane [deɪn] n danese m/f

danger ['deɪndʒəʳ] n pericolo; **there is a ~ of fire** c'è pericolo di incendio; **in ~** in pericolo; **he was in ~ of falling** rischiava di cadere; **dangerous** adj pericoloso/a

dangle ['dæŋgl] vt dondolare; (fig) far balenare ▷ vi pendolare

Danish ['deɪnɪʃ] adj danese ▷ n (Ling) danese m

dare [dɛəʳ] vt: **to ~ sb to do** sfidare qn a fare ▷ vi: **to ~ (to) do sth** osare fare qc; **I ~ say** (I suppose) immagino (che); **daring** adj audace, ardito/a ▷ n audacia

dark [dɑːk] adj (night, room) buio/a, scuro/a; (colour, complexion) scuro/a; (fig) cupo/a, tetro/a, nero/a ▷ n: **in the ~** al buio; **in the ~ about** (fig) all'oscuro di; **after ~** a notte fatta; **darken** vt (colour) scurire ▷ vi (sky, room) oscurarsi; **darkness** n oscurità, buio; **darkroom** n camera oscura

darling ['dɑːlɪŋ] adj caro/a ▷ n tesoro

dart [dɑːt] n freccetta; (Sewing) pince f inv ▷ vi: **to ~ towards** precipitarsi verso; **to ~ along** passare come un razzo; **to ~ away/along** sfrecciare via/lungo; **dartboard** n bersaglio (per freccette); **darts** n tiro al bersaglio (con freccette)

dash [dæʃ] n (sign) lineetta; (small quantity: of liquid) goccio, goccino ▷ vt (missile) gettare; (hopes) infrangere ▷ vi: **to ~ towards** precipitarsi verso

dashboard ['dæʃbɔːd] n (Aut) cruscotto

data ['deɪtə] npl dati mpl; **database** n database m inv, base f di dati; **data processing** n elaborazione f (elettronica) dei dati

date [deɪt] n data; (appointment) appuntamento; (fruit) dattero ▷ vt datare; (person) uscire con; **what's the ~ today?** quanti ne abbiamo oggi?; **~ of birth** data di nascita; **to ~** (until now) fino a oggi; **dated** adj passato/a di moda

daughter ['dɔːtəʳ] n figlia; **daughter-in-law** n nuora

daunting ['dɔːntɪŋ] adj non invidiabile

dawn [dɔːn] n alba ▷ vi (day) spuntare; **it ~ed on him that ...** gli è venuto in mente che ...

day [deɪ] n giorno; (as duration) giornata; (period of time, age) tempo, epoca; **the ~ before** il giorno avanti or prima; **the ~ after, the following ~** il giorno dopo, il giorno seguente; **the ~ before yesterday** l'altroieri; **the ~ after tomorrow** dopodomani; **by ~** di giorno; **day care centre** n scuola materna; **daydream** vi sognare a occhi aperti; **daylight** n luce f del giorno; **day return** n (BRIT) biglietto giornaliero di andata e ritorno; **daytime** n giorno; **day-to-day** adj (routine, life, organization) quotidiano/a; **day trip** n gita (di un giorno)

dazed [deɪzd] adj stordito/a

dazzle ['dæzl] vt abbagliare; **dazzling** adj (light) abbagliante; (colour) violento/a; (smile) smagliante

DC abbr (= direct current) c.c.

dead [dɛd] adj morto/a; (numb) intirizzito/a; (telephone) muto/a; (battery) scarico/a ▷ adv assolutamente, perfettamente; **the dead** npl i morti; **he was shot ~** fu colpito a morte; **~ tired** stanco/a morto/a; **to stop ~** fermarsi di colpo; **dead end** n vicolo cieco; **deadline** n scadenza; **deadly** adj mortale; (weapon, poison) micidiale; **Dead Sea** n: **the Dead Sea** il mar Morto

deaf [dɛf] adj sordo/a; **deafen** vt assordare; **deafening** adj fragoroso/a, assordante

deal [diːl] n accordo; (business deal) affare m ▷ vt (pt, pp **dealt** [dɛlt]) (blow, cards) dare; **a great ~ of** molto/a; **deal with** vt fus (Comm) fare affari con, trattare con; (handle) occuparsi di; (be about: book etc) trattare di; **dealer** n commerciante m/f; **dealings** npl (Comm) relazioni fpl; (relations) rapporti mpl

dealt [dɛlt] pt, pp of **deal**

dean [diːn] n (Rel) decano; (Scol) preside m di facoltà (or di collegio)

dear [dɪəʳ] adj caro/a ▷ n: **my ~** caro mio/cara mia ▷ excl: **~ me!** Dio mio!; **D~ Sir/Madam** (in letter) Egregio Signore/Egregia Signora; **D~ Mr/Mrs X** Gentile Signor/Signora X; **dearly** adv (love) moltissimo; (pay) a caro prezzo

death [dɛθ] n morte f; (Admin) decesso; **death penalty** n pena di morte; **death sentence** n condanna a morte

debate [dɪˈbeɪt] n dibattito ▷ vt dibattere; discutere

debit [ˈdɛbɪt] n debito ▷ vt: **to ~ a sum to sb** or **to sb's account** addebitare una somma a qn; **debit card** n carta di debito

debris [ˈdɛbriː] n detriti mpl

debt [dɛt] n debito; **to be in ~** essere indebitato/a

debug [diːˈbʌg] vt (Comput) localizzare e rimuovere errori in

debut [ˈdeɪbjuː] n debutto

Dec. abbr (= December) dic.

decade [ˈdɛkeɪd] n decennio

decaffeinated [dɪˈkæfɪneɪtɪd] adj decaffeinato/a

decay [dɪˈkeɪ] n decadimento; (also: **tooth ~**) carie f ▷ vi (rot) imputridire

deceased [dɪˈsiːst] n: **the ~** il (la) defunto(a)

deceit [dɪˈsiːt] n inganno; **deceive** [dɪˈsiːv] vt ingannare

December [dɪˈsɛmbəʳ] n dicembre m

decency [ˈdiːsənsɪ] n decenza

decent [ˈdiːsənt] adj decente; (respectable) per bene; (kind) gentile

deception [dɪˈsɛpʃən] n inganno

deceptive [dɪˈsɛptɪv] adj ingannevole

decide [dɪˈsaɪd] vt (person) far prendere una decisione a; (question, argument) risolvere, decidere ▷ vi decidere, decidersi; **to ~ to do/ that** decidere di fare/che; **to ~ on** decidere per

decimal [ˈdɛsɪməl] adj, n decimale (m)

decision [dɪˈsɪʒən] n decisione f

decisive [dɪˈsaɪsɪv] adj decisivo/a; (manner, person) deciso/a

deck [dɛk] n (Naut) ponte m; **top ~** imperiale m; **record ~** piatto (giradischi); (of cards) mazzo; **deckchair** n sedia a sdraio

declaration [dɛkləˈreɪʃən] n dichiarazione f

declare [dɪˈklɛəʳ] vt dichiarare

decline [dɪˈklaɪn] n (decay) declino; (lessening) ribasso ▷ vt declinare; rifiutare ▷ vi declinare; diminuire

decorate [ˈdɛkəreɪt] vt (adorn, give a medal to) decorare; (paint and paper) tinteggiare e tappezzare; **decoration** [dɛkəˈreɪʃən] n (medal etc, adornment) decorazione f; **decorator** n decoratore/trice

decrease n [ˈdiːkriːs] diminuzione f ▷ vt, vi [diːˈkriːs] diminuire

decree [dɪˈkriː] n decreto

dedicate [ˈdɛdɪkeɪt] vt consacrare; (book etc) dedicare; **dedicated** adj coscienzioso/a; (Comput)

specializzato/a, dedicato/a;
dedication [dɛdɪ'keɪʃən] n (*devotion*)
dedizione f; (*in book*) dedica
deduce [dɪ'djuːs] vt dedurre
deduct [dɪ'dʌkt] vt: **to ~ sth
(from)** dedurre qc (da); **deduction**
[dɪ'dʌkʃən] n deduzione f
deed [diːd] n azione f, atto; (*Law*) atto
deem [diːm] vt (*formal*) giudicare,
ritenere; **to ~ it wise to do** ritenere
prudente fare
deep [diːp] adj profondo/a ▷ adv:
spectators stood 20 ~ c'erano
20 file di spettatori; **4 metres ~**
profondo(a) 4 metri; **how ~ is
the water?** quanto è profonda
l'acqua?; **deep-fry** vt friggere
in olio abbondante; **deeply** adv
profondamente
deer [dɪə^r] n (pl inv): **the ~** i cervidi
(*Zool*); **(red) ~** cervo; **(fallow) ~**
daino; **(roe) ~** capriolo
default [dɪ'fɔːlt] n (*Comput: also:* **~
value**) default m inv; **by ~** (*Sport*) per
abbandono
defeat [dɪ'fiːt] n sconfitta ▷ vt (*team,
opponents*) sconfiggere
defect n ['diːfɛkt] difetto ▷ vi
[dɪ'fɛkt]: **to ~ to the enemy/the
West** passare al nemico/all'Ovest;
defective [dɪ'fɛktɪv] adj difettoso/a
defence, (*US*) **defense** [dɪ'fɛns]
n difesa
defend [dɪ'fɛnd] vt difendere;
defendant n imputato/a; **defender**
n difensore/a
defense [dɪ'fɛns] n (*US*) = **defence**
defensive [dɪ'fɛnsɪv] adj difensivo/a
▷ n: **on the ~** sulla difensiva
defer [dɪ'fəː^r] vt (*postpone*) differire,
rinviare
defiance [dɪ'faɪəns] n sfida; **in ~ of**
a dispetto di; **defiant** [dɪ'faɪənt] adj
(*attitude*) di sfida; (*person*) ribelle
deficiency [dɪ'fɪʃənsɪ] n deficienza;
carenza; **deficient** adj deficiente;
insufficiente; **to be deficient in**
mancare di

deficit ['dɛfɪsɪt] n disavanzo, deficit
m inv
define [dɪ'faɪn] vt definire
definite ['dɛfɪnɪt] adj (*fixed*)
definito/a, preciso/a; (*clear, obvious*)
ben definito/a, esatto/a; (*Ling*)
determinativo/a; **he was ~ about
it** ne era sicuro; **definitely** adv
indubbiamente
definition [dɛfɪ'nɪʃən] n definizione f
deflate [diː'fleɪt] vt sgonfiare
deflect [dɪ'flɛkt] vt deflettere,
deviare
defraud [dɪ'frɔːd] vt: **to ~ (of)**
defraudare (di)
defriend [diː'frɛnd] vt (*Internet*)
cancellare dagli amici
defrost [diː'frɔst] vt (*fridge*)
disgelare
defuse [diː'fjuːz] vt disinnescare; (*fig*)
distendere
defy [dɪ'faɪ] vt sfidare; (*efforts etc*)
resistere a; **it defies description**
supera ogni descrizione
degree [dɪ'griː] n grado; (*Scol*) laurea
(universitaria); **a (first) ~ in maths**
una laurea in matematica; **by ~s**
(*gradually*) gradualmente, a poco
a poco; **to some ~** fino a un certo
punto, in certa misura
dehydrated [diːhaɪ'dreɪtɪd] adj
disidratato/a; (*milk, eggs*) in polvere
de-icer ['diːaɪsə^r] n sbrinatore m
delay [dɪ'leɪ] vt ritardare ▷ vi: **to ~ (in
doing sth)** ritardare (a fare qc) ▷ n
ritardo; **to be ~ed** subire un ritardo;
(*person*) essere trattenuto/a
delegate n ['dɛlɪgɪt] delegato/a ▷ vt
['dɛlɪgeɪt] delegare
delete [dɪ'liːt] vt cancellare
deli ['dɛlɪ] n = **delicatessen**
deliberate adj [dɪ'lɪbərɪt]
(*intentional*) intenzionale; (*slow*)
misurato/a ▷ vi [dɪ'lɪbəreɪt]
deliberare, riflettere; **deliberately**
adv (*on purpose*) deliberatamente
delicacy ['dɛlɪkəsɪ] n delicatezza
delicate ['dɛlɪkɪt] adj delicato/a

delicatessen [dɛlɪkə'tɛsn] *n* ≈ salumeria

delicious [dɪ'lɪʃəs] *adj* delizioso/a, squisito/a

delight [dɪ'laɪt] *n* delizia, gran piacere *m* ▷ *vt* dilettare; **to take ~ in** divertirsi a; **delighted** *adj*: **delighted (at** *or* **with sth)** contentissimo/a (di qc), felice (di qc); **to be delighted to do sth/ that** essere felice di fare qc/che + *sub*; **delightful** *adj* delizioso/a; incantevole

delinquent [dɪ'lɪŋkwənt] *adj, n* delinquente (*m/f*)

deliver [dɪ'lɪvə'] *vt* (*mail*) distribuire; (*goods*) consegnare; (*speech*) pronunciare; (*Med*) far partorire; **delivery** *n* distribuzione *f*; consegna; (*of speaker*) dizione *f*; (*Med*) parto

delusion [dɪ'luːʒən] *n* illusione *f*

de luxe [də'lʌks] *adj* di lusso

delve [dɛlv] *vi*: **to ~ into** frugare in; (*subject*) far ricerche in

demand [dɪ'mɑːnd] *vt* richiedere; (*rights*) rivendicare ▷ *n* richiesta; (*Econ*) domanda; (*claim*) rivendicazione *f*; **in ~** ricercato/a, richiesto/a; **on ~** a richiesta; **demanding** *adj* (*boss*) esigente; (*work*) impegnativo/a

demise [dɪ'maɪz] *n* decesso

demo [ˈdɛməu] *n abbr* (*col*) (= *demonstration*) manifestazione *f*

democracy [dɪ'mɔkrəsɪ] *n* democrazia; **democrat** [ˈdɛməkræt] *n* democratico/a; **democratic** [dɛmə'krætɪk] *adj* democratico/a

demolish [dɪ'mɔlɪʃ] *vt* demolire

demolition [dɛmə'lɪʃən] *n* demolizione *f*

demon [ˈdiːmən] *n* (*also fig*) demonio ▷ *cpd*: **a ~ squash player** un mago dello squash; **a ~ driver** un guidatore folle

demonstrate [ˈdɛmənstreɪt] *vt* dimostrare, provare ▷ *vi*: **to ~ (for/against)** dimostrare (per/contro), manifestare (per/contro); **demonstration** [dɛmən'streɪʃən] *n* dimostrazione *f*; (*Pol*) manifestazione *f*, dimostrazione; **demonstrator** *n* (*Pol*) dimostrante *m/f*; (*Comm*) dimostratore/trice

demote [dɪ'məut] *vt* far retrocedere

den [dɛn] *n* tana, covo; (*room*) buco

denial [dɪ'naɪəl] *n* diniego; rifiuto

denim [ˈdɛnɪm] *n* tessuto di cotone ritorto; *see also* **denims**

denims [ˈdɛnɪmz] *npl* blue jeans *mpl*

Denmark [ˈdɛnmɑːk] *n* Danimarca

denomination [dɪnɔmɪ'neɪʃən] *n* (*of money*) valore *m*; (*Rel*) confessione *f*

denounce [dɪ'nauns] *vt* denunciare

dense [dɛns] *adj* fitto/a; (*smoke*) denso/a; (*col: stupid*) ottuso/a, duro/a

density [ˈdɛnsɪtɪ] *n* densità *f inv*

dent [dɛnt] *n* ammaccatura ▷ *vt* (*also*: **make a ~ in**) ammaccare

dental [ˈdɛntl] *adj* dentale; **dental floss** [-flɔs] *n* filo interdentale; **dental surgery** *n* studio dentistico

dentist [ˈdɛntɪst] *n* dentista *m/f*

denture(s) [ˈdɛntʃə(z)] *n(pl)* dentiera

deny [dɪ'naɪ] *vt* negare; (*refuse*) rifiutare

deodorant [diː'əudərənt] *n* deodorante *m*

depart [dɪ'pɑːt] *vi* partire; **to ~ from** (*fig*) deviare da

department [dɪ'pɑːtmənt] *n* (*Comm*) reparto; (*Scol*) sezione *f*, dipartimento; (*Pol*) ministero; **department store** *n* grande magazzino

departure [dɪ'pɑːtʃə'] *n* partenza; (*fig*): **~ from** deviazione *f* da; **a new ~** una svolta (decisiva); **departure lounge** *n* sala d'attesa

depend [dɪ'pɛnd] *vi*: **to ~ (up)on** dipendere da; (*rely on*) contare su; **it ~s** dipende; **~ing on the result ...** a seconda del risultato ...; **dependant** *n* persona a carico; **dependent** *adj*: **to be dependent (on)** dipendere

(da); (*child, relative*) essere a carico (di)
▷ *n* = **dependant**

depict [dɪ'pɪkt] *vt* (*in picture*)
dipingere; (*in words*) descrivere

deport [dɪ'pɔːt] *vt* deportare;
espellere

deposit [dɪ'pozɪt] *n* (*Comm, Geo*)
deposito; (*of ore, oil*) giacimento;
(*Chem*) sedimento; (*part payment*)
acconto; (*for hired goods etc*) cauzione
f ▷ *vt* depositare; dare in acconto;
(*luggage etc*) mettere *or* lasciare in
deposito; **deposit account** *n* conto
vincolato

depot ['dɛpəʊ] *n* deposito; (*us*)
stazione *f* ferroviaria

depreciate [dɪ'priːʃɪeɪt] *vi* svalutarsi

depress [dɪ'prɛs] *vt* deprimere;
(*price, wages*) abbassare; (*press
down*) premere; **depressed** *adj*
(*person*) depresso/a, abbattuto/a;
(*market, trade*) in ribasso; (*industry*)
in crisi; **depressing** *adj* deprimente;
depression [dɪ'prɛʃən] *n*
depressione *f*

deprive [dɪ'praɪv] *vt*: **to ~ sb
of** privare qn di; **deprived** *adj*
disgraziato/a

dept. *abbr* = **department**

depth [dɛpθ] *n* profondità *f inv*; **in
the ~s of** nel profondo di; nel cuore
di; **to be out of one's ~** (*BRIT*)
(*swimmer*) essere dove non si tocca;
(*fig*) non sentirsi all'altezza della
situazione

deputy ['dɛpjʊtɪ] *n* (*second in
command*) vice *m/f*; (*us: also: ~
sheriff*) vice-sceriffo ▷ *cpd*: **~ head**
(*BRIT*) (*Scol*) vicepreside *m/f*

derail [dɪ'reɪl] *vt*: **to be ~ed**
deragliare

derelict ['dɛrɪlɪkt] *adj*
abbandonato/a

derive [dɪ'raɪv] *vt*: **to ~ sth from**
derivare qc da; trarre qc da ▷ *vi*: **to ~
from** derivare da

descend [dɪ'sɛnd] *vt, vi* discendere,
scendere; **to ~ from** discendere da;

to ~ to (*lying, begging*) abbassarsi
a; **descendant** *n* discendente *m/f*;
descent [dɪ'sɛnt] *n* discesa; (*origin*)
discendenza, famiglia

describe [dɪs'kraɪb] *vt* descrivere;
description [dɪs'krɪpʃən] *n*
descrizione *f*; (*sort*) genere *m*, specie *f*

desert *n* ['dɛzət] deserto ▷ *vt* [dɪ'zəːt]
lasciare, abbandonare ▷ *vi* [dɪ'zəːt]
(*Mil*) disertare; **deserted** [dɪ'zəːtɪd]
adj deserto/a

deserve [dɪ'zəːv] *vt* meritare

design [dɪ'zaɪn] *n* (*sketch*) disegno;
(*layout, shape*) linea; (*pattern*)
fantasia; (*intention*) intenzione *f*
▷ *vt* disegnare; progettare; **design
and technology** *n* (*BRIT Scol*)
progettazione *f* e tecnologie *fpl*

designate *vt* ['dɛzɪgneɪt] designare
▷ *adj* ['dɛzɪgnɪt] designato/a

designer [dɪ'zaɪnəʳ] *n* (*Tech*)
disegnatore/trice; (*fashion designer*)
disegnatore/trice di moda

desirable [dɪ'zaɪərəbl] *adj*
desiderabile; **it is ~ that** è opportuno
che + *sub*

desire [dɪ'zaɪəʳ] *n* desiderio, voglia
▷ *vt* desiderare, volere

desk [dɛsk] *n* (*in office*) scrivania; (*for
pupil*) banco; (*BRIT: in shop, restaurant*)
cassa; (*in hotel*) ricevimento; (*at
airport*) accettazione *f*; **desktop
publishing** *n* desktop publishing *m*

despair [dɪs'pɛəʳ] *n* disperazione *f*
▷ *vi*: **to ~ of** disperare di

despatch [dɪs'pætʃ] *n, vt* = **dispatch**

desperate ['dɛspərɪt] *adj*
disperato/a; (*fugitive*) capace
di tutto; **to be ~ for sth/to do**
volere disperatamente qc/fare;
desperately *adv* disperatamente;
(*very*) terribilmente, estremamente;
desperation [dɛspə'reɪʃən] *n*
disperazione *f*

despise [dɪs'paɪz] *vt* disprezzare,
sdegnare

despite [dɪs'paɪt] *prep* malgrado, a
dispetto di, nonostante

dessert [dɪ'zə:t] n dolce m; frutta; **dessertspoon** n cucchiaio da dolci

destination [dɛstɪ'neɪʃən] n destinazione f

destined ['dɛstɪnd] adj: **to be ~ to do sth** essere destinato(a) a fare qc; **~ for London** diretto a Londra

destiny ['dɛstɪnɪ] n destino

destroy [dɪs'trɔɪ] vt distruggere

destruction [dɪs'trʌkʃən] n distruzione f

destructive [dɪs'trʌktɪv] adj distruttivo/a

detach [dɪ'tætʃ] vt staccare, distaccare; **detached** adj (attitude) distante; **detached house** n villa

detail ['di:teɪl] n particolare m, dettaglio ▷ vt dettagliare, particolareggiare; **in ~** nei particolari; **detailed** adj particolareggiato/a

detain [dɪ'teɪn] vt trattenere; (in captivity) detenere

detect [dɪ'tɛkt] vt scoprire, scorgere; (Med, Police, Radar etc) individuare; **detection** [dɪ'tɛkʃən] n scoperta; individuazione f; **detective** n investigatore/trice; **detective story** n giallo

detention [dɪ'tɛnʃən] n detenzione f; (Scol) permanenza forzata per punizione

deter [dɪ'tə:ʳ] vt dissuadere

detergent [dɪ'tə:dʒənt] n detersivo

deteriorate [dɪ'tɪərɪəreɪt] vi deteriorarsi

determination [dɪtə:mɪ'neɪʃən] n determinazione f

determine [dɪ'tə:mɪn] vt determinare; **determined** adj (person) risoluto/a, deciso/a; **to be determined to do sth** essere determinato or deciso a fare qc

deterrent [dɪ'tɛrənt] n deterrente m; **to act as a ~** fungere da deterrente

detest [dɪ'tɛst] vt detestare

detour ['di:tuəʳ] n deviazione f

detract [dɪ'trækt] vi: **to ~ from** detrarre da

detrimental [dɛtrɪ'mɛntl] adj: **~ to** dannoso/a a, nocivo/a a

devastating ['dɛvəsteɪtɪŋ] adj devastatore/trice, sconvolgente

develop [dɪ'vɛləp] vt sviluppare; (habit) prendere (gradualmente) ▷ vi svilupparsi; (facts, symptoms: appear) manifestarsi, rivelarsi; **developing country** n paese m in via di sviluppo; **development** n sviluppo

device [dɪ'vaɪs] n (apparatus) congegno

devil ['dɛvl] n diavolo; demonio

devious ['di:vɪəs] adj (person) subdolo/a

devise [dɪ'vaɪz] vt escogitare, concepire

devote [dɪ'vəut] vt: **to ~ sth to** dedicare qc a; **devoted** adj devoto/a; **to be devoted to** essere molto affezionato/a a; **devotion** [dɪ'vəuʃən] n devozione f, attaccamento; (Rel) atto di devozione, preghiera

devour [dɪ'vauəʳ] vt divorare

devout [dɪ'vaut] adj pio/a, devoto/a

dew [dju:] n rugiada

diabetes [daɪə'bi:ti:z] n diabete m

diabetic [daɪə'bɛtɪk] adj, n diabetico/a

diagnose [daɪəg'nəuz] vt diagnosticare

diagnosis (pl **diagnoses**) [daɪəg'nəusɪs, -si:z] n diagnosi f inv

diagonal [daɪ'ægənl] adj, n diagonale (f)

diagram ['daɪəgræm] n diagramma m

dial ['daɪəl] n quadrante m; (on radio) lancetta; (on telephone) disco combinatore ▷ vt (number) fare

dialect ['daɪəlɛkt] n dialetto

dialling code ['daɪəlɪŋ-], (US) **area code** n prefisso

dialling tone ['daɪəlɪŋ-], (US) **dial tone** n segnale m di linea libera

dialogue ['daɪəlɒg], (US) **dialog** n dialogo

diameter [daɪ'æmɪtəʳ] n diametro

diamond ['daɪəmənd] n diamante m; (shape) rombo; **diamonds** npl (Cards) quadri mpl

diaper ['daɪəpəʳ] n (US) pannolino

diarrhoea, (US) **diarrhea** [daɪə'riːə] n diarrea

diary ['daɪərɪ] n (daily account) diario; (book) agenda

dice [daɪs] n (pl inv) dado ▷ vt (Culin) tagliare a dadini

dictate vt [dɪk'teɪt] dettare; **dictation** [dɪk'teɪʃən] n (to secretary etc) dettatura; (Scol) dettato

dictator [dɪk'teɪtəʳ] n dittatore m

dictionary [dɪkʃənrɪ] n dizionario

did [dɪd] pt of **do**

didn't [dɪdnt] = **did not**

die [daɪ] vi morire; **to be dying for sth/to do sth** morire dalla voglia di qc/di fare qc; **die down** vi abbassarsi; **die out** vi estinguersi

diesel ['diːzl] n (vehicle) diesel m inv

diet ['daɪət] n alimentazione f; (restricted food) dieta ▷ vi (also: **be on a ~**) stare a dieta

differ ['dɪfəʳ] vi: **to ~ from sth** differire da qc; essere diverso/a da qc; **to ~ from sb over sth** essere in disaccordo con qn su qc; **difference** n differenza; (quarrel) screzio; **different** adj diverso/a; **differentiate** [dɪfə'renʃɪeɪt] vi differenziarsi; **to differentiate between** discriminare fra, fare differenza fra; **differently** adv diversamente

difficult ['dɪfɪkəlt] adj difficile; **difficulty** n difficoltà f inv

dig [dɪg] (pt, pp **dug**) vt (hole) scavare; (garden) vangare ▷ n (prod) gomitata; (fig) frecciata; (Archaeology) scavo; **dig up** vt (tree etc) sradicare; (information) scavare fuori

digest vt [daɪ'dʒɛst] digerire ▷ n ['daɪdʒɛst] compendio; **digestion** [dɪ'dʒɛstʃən] n digestione f

digit ['dɪdʒɪt] n cifra; (finger) dito; **digital** adj digitale; **digital camera** n fotocamera digitale; **digital TV** n televisione f digitale

dignified ['dɪgnɪfaɪd] adj dignitoso/a

dignity ['dɪgnɪtɪ] n dignità

digs [dɪgz] npl (BRIT col) camera ammobiliata

dilemma [daɪ'lɛmə] n dilemma m

dill [dɪl] n aneto

dilute [daɪ'luːt] vt diluire; (with water) annacquare

dim [dɪm] adj (light, eyesight) debole; (memory, outline) vago/a; (room) in penombra; (col: stupid) ottuso/a, tonto/a ▷ vt (light) abbassare

dime [daɪm] n (US) = **10 cents**

dimension [dɪ'mɛnʃən] n dimensione f

diminish [dɪ'mɪnɪʃ] vt, vi diminuire

din [dɪn] n chiasso, fracasso

dine [daɪn] vi pranzare; **diner** n (person) cliente m/f; (US: eating place) tavola calda

dinghy ['dɪŋɡɪ] n gommone m; (also: **sailing ~**) dinghy m inv

dingy ['dɪndʒɪ] adj grigio/a

dining car ['daɪnɪŋ-] (BRIT) n vagone m ristorante

dining room n sala da pranzo

dining table n tavolo da pranzo

dinkum ['dɪŋkʌm] adj (AUST, NZ col) genuino/a

dinner ['dɪnəʳ] n (lunch) pranzo; (evening meal) cena; (public) banchetto; **dinner jacket** n smoking m inv; **dinner party** n cena; **dinner time** n ora di pranzo (or cena)

dinosaur ['daɪnəsɔːʳ] n dinosauro

dip [dɪp] n discesa; (in sea) bagno; (Culin) salsetta ▷ vt immergere; bagnare; (BRIT Aut: lights) abbassare ▷ vi abbassarsi

diploma [dɪ'pləumə] n diploma m

diplomacy [dɪ'pləuməsɪ] n diplomazia

diplomat ['dɪpləmæt] n diplomatico; **diplomatic** [dɪplə'mætɪk] adj diplomatico/a

dipstick ['dɪpstɪk] n (Aut) indicatore m di livello dell'olio

dire [daɪə^r] adj terribile; estremo/a

direct [daɪ'rɛkt] adj diretto/a ▷ vt dirigere; (order): **to ~ sb to do sth** dare direttive a qn di fare qc ▷ adv direttamente; **can you ~ me to …?** mi può indicare la strada per …?; **direct debit** n (Banking) addebito effettuato per ordine di un cliente di banca

direction [dɪ'rɛkʃən] n direzione f; **directions** npl (advice) chiarimenti mpl; **~s for use** istruzioni fpl; **sense of ~** senso dell'orientamento

directly [dɪ'rɛktlɪ] adv (in straight line) direttamente; (at once) subito

director [dɪ'rɛktə^r] n direttore/trice, amministratore/trice; (Theat, Cine, TV) regista m/f

directory [dɪ'rɛktərɪ] n elenco; **directory enquiries**, (US) **directory assistance** n (Tel) informazioni fpl; elenco abbonati

dirt [də:t] n sporcizia; immondizia; (earth) terra; **dirty** adj sporco/a ▷ vt sporcare

disability [dɪsə'bɪlɪtɪ] n invalidità f inv; (Law) incapacità f inv

disabled [dɪs'eɪbld] adj (mentally) ritardato/a ▷ npl: **the ~** gli invalidi

disadvantage [dɪsəd'vɑːntɪdʒ] n svantaggio

disagree [dɪsə'griː] vi (differ) discordare; (be against, think otherwise): **to ~ (with)** essere in disaccordo (con), dissentire (da); **disagreeable** adj sgradevole; (person) antipatico/a; **disagreement** n disaccordo; (quarrel) dissapore m

disappear [dɪsə'pɪə^r] vi scomparire; **disappearance** n scomparsa

disappoint [dɪsə'pɔɪnt] vt deludere; **disappointed** adj deluso/a; **disappointing** adj deludente; **disappointment** n delusione f

disapproval [dɪsə'pruːvəl] n disapprovazione f

disapprove [dɪsə'pruːv] vi: **to ~ of** disapprovare

disarm [dɪs'ɑːm] vt disarmare; **disarmament** n disarmo

disaster [dɪ'zɑːstə^r] n disastro; **disastrous** [dɪ'zɑːstrəs] adj disastroso/a

disbelief ['dɪsbə'liːf] n incredulità

disc [dɪsk] n disco; (Comput) = **disk**

discard [dɪs'kɑːd] vt (old things) scartare; (fig) abbandonare

discharge vt [dɪs'tʃɑːdʒ] (duties) compiere; (Elec, waste etc) scaricare; (Med) emettere; (patient) dimettere; (employee) licenziare; (soldier) congedare; (defendant) liberare ▷ n ['dɪstʃɑːdʒ] (Elec) scarica; (Med) emissione f; licenziamento; congedo; liberazione f

discipline ['dɪsɪplɪn] n disciplina ▷ vt disciplinare; (punish) punire

disc jockey n disc jockey m inv

disclose [dɪs'kləuz] vt rivelare, svelare

disco ['dɪskəu] n abbr discoteca

discoloured, (US) **discolored** [dɪs'kʌləd] adj scolorito/a, ingiallito/a

discomfort [dɪs'kʌmfət] n disagio; (lack of comfort) scomodità f inv

disconnect [dɪskə'nɛkt] vt sconnettere, staccare; (Elec, Radio) staccare; (gas, water) chiudere

discontent [dɪskən'tɛnt] n scontentezza

discontinue [dɪskən'tɪnjuː] vt smettere, cessare; **"~d"** (Comm) "fuori produzione"

discount n ['dɪskaunt] sconto ▷ vt [dɪs'kaunt] scontare; (report, idea etc) non badare a

discourage [dɪs'kʌrɪdʒ] vt scoraggiare

discover [dɪs'kʌvə^r] vt scoprire; **discovery** n scoperta

discredit [dɪs'krɛdɪt] vt screditare; mettere in dubbio

discreet [dɪˈskriːt] *adj* discreto/a

discrepancy [dɪˈskrɛpənsɪ] *n* discrepanza

discretion [dɪˈskrɛʃən] *n* discrezione *f*; **use your own ~** giudichi lei

discriminate [dɪˈskrɪmɪneɪt] *vi*: **to ~ between** distinguere tra; **to ~ against** discriminare contro; **discrimination** [dɪskrɪmɪˈneɪʃən] *n* discriminazione *f*; (*judgement*) discernimento

discuss [dɪˈskʌs] *vt* discutere; (*debate*) dibattere; **discussion** [dɪˈskʌʃən] *n* discussione *f*; **discussion forum** *n* (*Comput*) forum *m inv* di discussione

disease [dɪˈziːz] *n* malattia

disembark [dɪsɪmˈbɑːk] *vt, vi* sbarcare

disgrace [dɪsˈɡreɪs] *n* vergogna; (*disfavour*) disgrazia ▷ *vt* disonorare, far cadere in disgrazia; **disgraceful** *adj* scandaloso/a, vergognoso/a

disgruntled [dɪsˈɡrʌntld] *adj* scontento/a, di cattivo umore

disguise [dɪsˈɡaɪz] *n* travestimento ▷ *vt*: **to ~ o.s. as** travestirsi da; **in ~** travestito/a

disgust [dɪsˈɡʌst] *n* disgusto, nausea ▷ *vt* disgustare, far schifo a; **disgusted** [dɪsˈɡʌstɪd] *adj* indignato/a; **disgusting** [dɪsˈɡʌstɪŋ] *adj* disgustoso/a, ripugnante

dish [dɪʃ] *n* piatto; **to do** *or* **wash the ~es** fare i piatti; **dishcloth** *n* strofinaccio dei piatti

dishonest [dɪsˈɔnɪst] *adj* disonesto/a

dishtowel [ˈdɪʃtaʊəl] *n* strofinaccio dei piatti

dishwasher [ˈdɪʃwɔʃəʳ] *n* lavastoviglie *f inv*

disillusion [dɪsɪˈluːʒən] *vt* disilludere, disingannare

disinfectant [dɪsɪnˈfɛktənt] *n* disinfettante *m*

disintegrate [dɪsˈɪntɪɡreɪt] *vi* disintegrarsi

disk [dɪsk] *n* (*Comput*) disco; **double-sided ~** disco a doppia faccia; **disk drive** *n* disk drive *m inv*; **diskette** *n* (*Comput*) dischetto

dislike [dɪsˈlaɪk] *n* antipatia, avversione *f*; (*gen pl*) cosa che non piace ▷ *vt*: **he ~s it** non gli piace

dislocate [ˈdɪsləkeɪt] *vt* slogare

disloyal [dɪsˈlɔɪəl] *adj* sleale

dismal [ˈdɪzml] *adj* triste, cupo/a

dismantle [dɪsˈmæntl] *vt* (*machine*) smontare

dismay [dɪsˈmeɪ] *n* costernazione *f* ▷ *vt* sgomentare

dismiss [dɪsˈmɪs] *vt* congedare; (*employee*) licenziare; (*idea*) scacciare; (*Law*) respingere; **dismissal** *n* congedo; licenziamento

disobedient [dɪsəˈbiːdɪənt] *adj* disubbidiente

disobey [dɪsəˈbeɪ] *vt* disubbidire a

disorder [dɪsˈɔːdəʳ] *n* disordine *m*; (*rioting*) tumulto; (*Med*) disturbo

disorganized [dɪsˈɔːɡənaɪzd] *adj* (*person, life*) disorganizzato/a; (*system, meeting*) male organizzato/a

disown [dɪsˈəun] *vt* rinnegare, disconoscere

dispatch [dɪsˈpætʃ] *vt* spedire, inviare ▷ *n* spedizione *f*, invio; (*Mil, Press*) dispaccio

dispel [dɪsˈpɛl] *vt* dissipare, scacciare

dispense [dɪsˈpɛns] *vt* distribuire, amministrare; **dispenser** *n* (*container*) distributore *m*

disperse [dɪsˈpəːs] *vt* disperdere; (*knowledge*) disseminare ▷ *vi* disperdersi

display [dɪsˈpleɪ] *n* esposizione *f*; (*of feeling etc*) manifestazione *f*; (*screen*) schermo ▷ *vt* mostrare; (*goods*) esporre; (*pej*) ostentare

displease [dɪsˈpliːz] *vt* dispiacere a, scontentare; **~d with** scontento/a di

disposable [dɪsˈpəuzəbl] *adj* (*pack etc*) a perdere; (*income*) disponibile

disposal [dɪsˈpəuzl] *n* (*of rubbish*) smaltimento; (*of property etc*) cessione *f*; **at one's ~** alla sua disposizione

dispose [dɪs'pəuz] *vt* disporre; **dispose of** *vt fus* sbarazzarsi di; **disposition** [dɪspə'zɪʃən] *n* disposizione *f*; *(temperament)* carattere *m*

disproportionate [dɪsprə'pɔːʃənət] *adj* sproporzionato/a

dispute [dɪs'pjuːt] *n* disputa; *(also:* **industrial ~**) controversia (sindacale) ▷ *vt* contestare; *(matter)* discutere; *(victory)* disputare

disqualify [dɪs'kwɔlɪfaɪ] *vt (Sport)* squalificare; **to ~ sb from sth/ from doing** rendere qn incapace a qc/a fare; squalificare qn da qc/da fare; **to ~ sb from driving** ritirare la patente a qn

disregard [dɪsrɪ'gɑːd] *vt* non far caso a, non badare a

disrupt [dɪs'rʌpt] *vt* disturbare; *(public transport)* creare scompiglio in; **disruption** [dɪs'rʌpʃən] *n* disordine *m*; interruzione *f*

dissatisfaction [dɪssætɪs'fækʃən] *n* scontentezza, insoddisfazione *f*

dissatisfied [dɪs'sætɪsfaɪd] *adj*: **~ (with)** scontento/a *or* insoddisfatto/a (di)

dissect [dɪ'sɛkt] *vt* sezionare

dissent [dɪ'sɛnt] *n* dissenso

dissertation [dɪsə'teɪʃən] *n* tesi *f inv*, dissertazione *f*

dissolve [dɪ'zɔlv] *vt* dissolvere, sciogliere; *(Comm, Pol, marriage)* sciogliere ▷ *vi* dissolversi, sciogliersi

distance [ˈdɪstns] *n* distanza; **in the ~** in lontananza

distant [ˈdɪstnt] *adj* lontano/a, distante; *(manner)* riservato/a, freddo/a

distil, *(us)* **distill** [dɪs'tɪl] *vt* distillare; **distillery** *n* distilleria

distinct [dɪs'tɪŋkt] *adj* distinto/a; **as ~ from** a differenza di; **distinction** [dɪs'tɪŋkʃən] *n* distinzione *f*; *(in exam)* lode *f*; **distinctive** *adj* distintivo/a

distinguish [dɪs'tɪŋgwɪʃ] *vt* distinguere; discernere; **distinguished** *adj (eminent)* eminente

distort [dɪs'tɔːt] *vt* distorcere; *(Tech)* deformare

distract [dɪs'trækt] *vt* distrarre; **distracted** *adj* distratto/a; **distraction** [dɪs'trækʃən] *n* distrazione *f*

distraught [dɪs'trɔːt] *adj* stravolto/a

distress [dɪs'trɛs] *n* angoscia ▷ *vt* affliggere; **distressing** *adj* doloroso/a

distribute [dɪs'trɪbjuːt] *vt* distribuire; **distribution** [dɪstrɪ'bjuːʃən] *n* distribuzione *f*; **distributor** *n* distributore *m*

district [ˈdɪstrɪkt] *n (of country)* regione *f*; *(of town)* quartiere *m*; *(Admin)* distretto; **district attorney** *n (us)* ≈ sostituto procuratore *m* della Repubblica

distrust [dɪs'trʌst] *n* diffidenza, sfiducia ▷ *vt* non aver fiducia in

disturb [dɪs'təːb] *vt* disturbare; **disturbance** *n* disturbo; *(by drunks etc)* disordini *mpl*; **disturbed** *adj (worried, upset)* turbato/a; **to be emotionally disturbed** avere turbe emotive; **disturbing** *adj* sconvolgente

ditch [dɪtʃ] *n* fossa ▷ *vt (col)* piantare in asso

ditto [ˈdɪtəu] *adv* idem

dive [daɪv] *n* tuffo; *(of submarine)* immersione *f* ▷ *vi* tuffarsi; immergersi; **diver** *n* tuffatore/trice; palombaro

diverse [daɪ'vəːs] *adj* vario/a

diversion [daɪ'vəːʃən] *n (BRIT Aut)* deviazione *f*; *(distraction)* divertimento

diversity [daɪ'vəːsɪtɪ] *n* diversità *f inv*, varietà *f inv*

divert [daɪ'vəːt] *vt* deviare

divide [dɪ'vaɪd] *vt* dividere; *(separate)* separare ▷ *vi* dividersi; **divided**

highway *n* (US) strada a doppia carreggiata

divine [dɪ'vaɪn] *adj* divino/a

diving ['daɪvɪŋ] *n* tuffo; **diving board** *n* trampolino

division [dɪ'vɪʒən] *n* divisione *f*; separazione *f*; (*Football*) serie *f inv*

divorce [dɪ'vɔːs] *n* divorzio ▷ *vt* divorziare da; (*dissociate*) separare; **divorced** *adj* divorziato/a; **divorcee** [dɪvɔː'siː] *n* divorziato/a

D.I.Y. *n abbr* (BRIT) = **do-it-yourself**

dizzy ['dɪzɪ] *adj*: **to feel ~** avere il capogiro

DJ *n abbr* = **disc jockey**

DNA *n abbr* (= *deoxyribonucleic acid*) DNA *m*; **DNA test** *n* test *m inv* del DNA

KEYWORD

do [duː] (*pt* **did**, *pp* **done**) *aux vb* **1** (*in negative constructions*) non tradotto; **I don't understand** non capisco

2 (*to form questions*) non tradotto; **didn't you know?** non lo sapevi?; **why didn't you come?** perché non sei venuto?

3 (*for emphasis, in polite expressions*): **she does seem rather late** sembra essere piuttosto in ritardo; **do sit down** si accomodi la prego, prego si sieda; **do take care!** mi raccomando, stai attento!

4 (*used to avoid repeating vb*): **she swims better than I do** lei nuota meglio di me; **do you agree? — yes, I do/no, I don't** sei d'accordo? — sì/no; **she lives in Glasgow — so do I** lei vive a Glasgow — anch'io; **he asked me to help him and I did** mi ha chiesto di aiutarlo ed io l'ho fatto

5 (*in question tags*): **you like him, don't you?** ti piace, vero?; **I don't know him, do I?** non lo conosco, vero?

▷ *vt* (*gen: carry out, perform etc*) fare; **what are you doing tonight?** che

fai stasera?; **to do the cooking** cucinare; **to do the washing-up** fare i piatti; **to do one's teeth** lavarsi i denti; **to do one's hair/nails** farsi i capelli/le unghie; **the car was doing 100** la macchina faceva i 100 all'ora

▷ *vi* **1** (*act, behave*) fare; **do as I do** faccia come me, faccia come faccio io

2 (*get on, fare*) andare; **he's doing well/badly at school** va bene/male a scuola; **how do you do?** piacere!

3 (*suit*) andare bene; **this room will do** questa stanza va bene

4 (*be sufficient*) bastare; **will £10 do?** basteranno 10 sterline?; **that'll do** basta così; **that'll do!** (*in annoyance*) ora basta!; **to make do (with)** arrangiarsi (con)

▷ *n* (*col: party etc*) festa; **it was rather a grand do** è stato un ricevimento piuttosto importante

do away with *vt fus* (*col: kill*) far fuori; (*abolish*) abolire

do up *vt* (*laces*) allacciare; (*dress, buttons*) abbottonare; (*renovate: room, house*) rimettere a nuovo, rifare

do with *vt fus* (*need*) aver bisogno di; (*be connected*): **what has it got to do with you?** e tu che c'entri?; **I won't have anything to do with it** non voglio avere niente a che farci; **it has to do with money** si tratta di soldi

do without *vi* fare senza ▷ *vt fus* fare a meno di

dock [dɔk] *n* (Naut) bacino; (Law) banco degli imputati ▷ *vi* entrare in bacino; (Space) agganciarsi; **docks** *npl* (Naut) dock *m inv*

doctor ['dɔktə^r] *n* medico/a; (PhD etc) dottore/essa ▷ *vt* (*food, drink*) adulterare; **Doctor of Philosophy, PhD** *n* dottorato di ricerca; (*person*) titolare *m/f* di un dottorato di ricerca

document *n* ['dɔkjumənt] documento; **documentary** [dɔkju'mɛntərɪ] *adj* (*evidence*) documentato/a ▷ *n* documentario;

documentation [dɔkjumən'teɪʃən] n documentazione f
dodge [dɔdʒ] n trucco; schivata ▷ vt schivare, eludere
dodgy ['dɔdʒɪ] adj (BRIT col: uncertain) rischioso/a; (untrustworthy) sospetto/a
does [dʌz] see **do**
doesn't ['dʌznt] = **does not**
dog [dɔg] n cane m ▷ vt (follow closely) pedinare; (fig: memory etc) perseguitare; **doggy bag** n sacchetto per gli avanzi (da portare a casa)
do-it-yourself ['du:ɪtjɔ:'sɛlf] n il far da sé
dole [dəul] n (BRIT) sussidio di disoccupazione; **to be on the ~** vivere del sussidio
doll [dɔl] n bambola
dollar ['dɔlər] n dollaro
dolphin ['dɔlfɪn] n delfino
dome [dəum] n cupola
domestic [də'mɛstɪk] adj (duty, happiness, animal) domestico/a; (policy, affairs, flights) nazionale; **domestic appliance** n elettrodomestico
dominant ['dɔmɪnənt] adj dominante
dominate ['dɔmɪneɪt] vt dominare
domino ['dɔmɪnəu] (pl **dominoes**) n domino; **dominoes** npl (game) gioco del domino
donate [də'neɪt] vt donare; **donation** [də'neɪʃən] n donazione f
done [dʌn] pp of **do**
donkey ['dɔŋkɪ] n asino
donor ['dəunər] n donatore/trice; **donor card** n tessera di donatore di organi
don't [dəunt] = **do not**
donut ['dəunʌt] n (US) = **doughnut**
doodle ['du:dl] vi scarabocchiare
doom [du:m] n destino; rovina ▷ vt: **to be ~ed (to failure)** essere predestinato/a (a fallire)
door [dɔ:r] n porta; **doorbell** n campanello; **door handle** n maniglia;

doorknob ['dɔ:nɔb] n pomello, maniglia; **doorstep** n gradino della porta; **doorway** n porta
dope [dəup] n (col: drugs) roba ▷ vt (horse etc) drogare
dormitory ['dɔ:mɪtrɪ] n dormitorio; (US) casa dello studente
DOS [dɔs] n abbr (= disk operating system) DOS m
dosage ['dəusɪdʒ] n posologia
dose [dəus] n dose f; (bout) attacco
dot [dɔt] n punto; macchiolina ▷ vt: **~ted with** punteggiato(a) di; **on the ~** in punto; **dotcom** [dɔt'kɔm] n azienda che opera in Internet; **dotted line** ['dɔtɪd-] n linea punteggiata
double ['dʌbl] adj doppio/a ▷ adv (twice): **to cost ~ sth** costare il doppio (di qc) ▷ n sosia m inv ▷ vt raddoppiare; (fold) piegare doppio or in due ▷ vi raddoppiarsi; **on the ~, (BRIT) at the ~** a passo di corsa; **double back** vi (person) tornare sui propri passi; **double bass** n contrabbasso; **double bed** n letto matrimoniale; **double-check** vt, vi ricontrollare; **double-click** vi (Comput) fare doppio click; **double-cross** ['dʌbl'krɔs] vt fare il doppio gioco con; **doubledecker** n autobus m inv a due piani; **double glazing** n (BRIT) doppi vetri mpl; **double room** n camera matrimoniale; **doubles** n (Tennis) doppio; **double yellow lines** npl (BRIT Aut) linea gialla doppia continua che segnala il divieto di sosta
doubt [daut] n dubbio ▷ vt dubitare di; **to ~ that** dubitare che + sub; **doubtful** adj dubbioso/a, incerto/a; (person) equivoco/a; **doubtless** adv indubbiamente
dough [dəu] n pasta, impasto; **doughnut, (US) donut** n bombolone m
dove [dʌv] n colombo/a
down [daun] n piumino ▷ adv giù, di sotto ▷ prep giù per ▷ vt (col: drink)

scolarsi; **~ with X!** abbasso X!;
down-and-out n barbone m;
downfall n caduta; rovina; **downhill**
adv: **to go downhill** andare in
discesa; (business) lasciarsi andare;
andare a rotoli

Downing Street ['daunɪŋ-] n:
10 ~ residenza del primo ministro
inglese

down: download vt (Comput)
scaricare; **downloadable** adj
(Comput) scaricabile; **downright** adj
franco/a; (refusal) assoluto/a

Down's syndrome n sindrome f
di Down

down: downstairs adv di sotto; al
piano inferiore; **down-to-earth** adj
pratico/a; **downtown** adv in città;
down under adv (Australia etc) agli
antipodi; **downward** adj ▷ adv in giù,
in discesa; **downwards** ['daunwədz]
adv in giù, in discesa

doz. abbr = **dozen**

doze [dəuz] vi sonnecchiare

dozen ['dʌzn] n dozzina; **a ~ books**
una dozzina di libri; **8op a ~** 8o pence
la dozzina; **~s of times** centinaia or
migliaia di volte

Dr, Dr. abbr (= doctor) Dr, Dott./
Dott.ssa; (in street names) = **drive**

drab [dræb] adj tetro/a, grigio/a

draft [drɑːft] n abbozzo; (Pol) bozza;
(Comm) tratta; (US Mil: call-up) leva
▷ vt abbozzare; see also **draught**

drag [dræg] vt trascinare; (river)
dragare ▷ vi trascinarsi ▷ n (col)
noioso/a; (: task) noia; (women's
clothing): **in ~** travestito (da donna)

dragon ['drægən] n drago

dragonfly ['drægənflaɪ] n libellula

drain [dreɪn] n (for sewage) fogna;
(on resources) salasso ▷ vt (land,
marshes) prosciugare; (vegetables)
scolare ▷ vi (water) defluire; **drainage**
n prosciugamento; fognatura;
drainpipe n tubo di scarico

drama ['drɑːmə] n (art) dramma
m, teatro; (play) commedia; (event)
dramma; **dramatic** [drə'mætɪk] adj
drammatico/a

drank [dræŋk] pt of **drink**

drape [dreɪp] vt drappeggiare; see
also **drapes**; **drapes** [dreɪps] npl (US:
curtains) tende fpl

drastic ['dræstɪk] adj drastico/a

draught, (US) **draft** [drɑːft] n
corrente f d'aria; (Naut) pescaggio;
on ~ (beer) alla spina; **draught beer**
n birra alla spina; **draughts** n (BRIT)
(gioco della) dama

draw [drɔː] (pt **drew**, pp **drawn**) vt
tirare; (take out) estrarre; (attract)
attirare; (picture) disegnare; (line,
circle) tracciare; (money) ritirare ▷ vi
(Sport) pareggiare ▷ n pareggio;
(in lottery) estrazione f; **to ~ near**
avvicinarsi; **draw out** vi (lengthen)
allungarsi ▷ vt (money) ritirare; **draw
up** vi (stop) arrestarsi, fermarsi
▷ vt (chair) avvicinare; (document)
compilare; **drawback** n svantaggio,
inconveniente m

drawer [drɔːr] n cassetto

drawing ['drɔːɪŋ] n disegno;
drawing pin n (BRIT) puntina da
disegno; **drawing room** n salotto

drawn [drɔːn] pp of **draw**

dread [drɛd] n terrore m ▷ vt tremare
all'idea di; **dreadful** adj terribile

dream [driːm] n sogno ▷ vt, vi (pt,
pp **dreamed** or **dreamt** [drɛmt])
sognare; **dreamer** n sognatore/trice

dreamt [drɛmt] *pt, pp of* **dream**

dreary ['drɪərɪ] *adj* tetro/a; monotono/a

drench [drɛntʃ] *vt* inzuppare

dress [drɛs] *n* vestito; (*no pl: clothing*) abbigliamento ▷ *vt* vestire; (*wound*) fasciare ▷ *vi* vestirsi; **to get ~ed** vestirsi; **dress up** *vi* vestirsi a festa; (*in fancy dress*) vestirsi in costume; **dress circle** (BRIT) *n* prima galleria; **dresser** *n* (*furniture*) credenza; (*US*) cassettone *m*; **dressing** *n* (*Med*) benda; (*Culin*) condimento; **dressing gown** *n* (BRIT) vestaglia; **dressing room** *n* (*Theat*) camerino; (*Sport*) spogliatoio; **dressing table** *n* toilette *f inv*; **dressmaker** *n* sarta

drew [druː] *pt of* **draw**

dribble ['drɪbl] *vi* (*baby*) sbavare ▷ *vt* (*ball*) dribblare

dried [draɪd] *adj* (*fruit, beans*) secco/a; (*eggs, milk*) in polvere

drier ['draɪəʳ] *n* = **dryer**

drift [drɪft] *n* (*of current etc*) direzione *f*; forza; (*of sand, snow*) cumulo; turbine *m*; (*general meaning*) senso ▷ *vi* (*boat*) essere trasportato/a dalla corrente; (*sand, snow*) ammucchiarsi

drill [drɪl] *n* trapano; (*Mil*) esercitazione *f* ▷ *vt* trapanare; (*soldiers*) addestrare ▷ *vi* (*for oil*) fare trivellazioni

drink [drɪŋk] *n* bevanda, bibita; (*alcoholic drink*) bicchierino; (*sip*) sorso ▷ *vt, vi* (*pt* **drank**, *pp* **drunk**) bere; **to have a ~** bere qualcosa; **a ~ of water** un po' d'acqua; **drink-driving** *n* guida in stato di ebbrezza; **drinker** *n* bevitore/trice; **drinking water** *n* acqua potabile

drip [drɪp] *n* goccia; (*dripping*) sgocciolio; (*Med*) fleboclisi *f inv* ▷ *vi* gocciolare; (*washing, tap*) sgocciolare

drive (*pt* **drove**, *pp* **driven**) [draɪv, drəuv, 'drɪvn] *n* passeggiata *or* giro in macchina; (*also:* **~way**) viale *m* d'accesso; (*energy*) energia; (*campaign*) campagna; (*also:* **disk ~**) disk drive *m inv* ▷ *vt* guidare; (*nail*) piantare; (*push*) cacciare, spingere; (*Tech: motor*) azionare; far funzionare ▷ *vi* (*Aut: at controls*) guidare; (*: travel*) andare in macchina; **left-/right-hand ~** guida a sinistra/destra; **to ~ sb mad** far impazzire qn; **drive out** *vt* (*force out*) cacciare, mandare via; **drive-in** *adj, n* (*esp US*) drive-in (*m inv*)

driven ['drɪvn] *pp of* **drive**

driver ['draɪvəʳ] *n* conducente *m/f*; (*of taxi*) tassista *m*; (*chauffeur: of bus*) autista *m/f*; **driver's license** *n* (*US*) patente *f* di guida

driveway ['draɪvweɪ] *n* viale *m* d'accesso

driving ['draɪvɪŋ] *n* guida; **driving instructor** *n* istruttore/trice di scuola guida; **driving lesson** *n* lezione *f* di guida; **driving licence** *n* (BRIT) patente *f* di guida; **driving test** *n* esame *m* di guida

drizzle ['drɪzl] *n* pioggerella

droop [druːp] *vi* (*flower*) appassire; (*head, shoulders*) chinarsi

drop [drɔp] *n* (*of water*) goccia; (*lessening*) diminuzione *f*; (*fall*) caduta ▷ *vt* lasciar cadere; (*name from list*) lasciare fuori ▷ *vi* cascare; (*wind, temperature, price*) calare, abbassarsi; (*voice*) abbassarsi; **drops** *npl* (*Med*) gocce *fpl*; **drop in** *vi* (*col: visit*): **to ~ in (on)** fare un salto (da), passare (da); **drop off** *vi* (*sleep*) addormentarsi ▷ *vt*: **to ~ sb off** far scendere qn; **drop out** *vi* (*withdraw*) ritirarsi; (*student etc*) smettere di studiare

drought [draut] *n* siccità *f inv*

drove [drəuv] *pt of* **drive**

drown [draun] *vt* affogare; (*fig: noise*) soffocare

drowsy ['drauzɪ] *adj* sonnolento/a, assonnato/a

drug [drʌg] *n* farmaco; (*narcotic*) droga ▷ *vt* drogare; **to be on ~s** drogarsi; (*Med*) prendere medicinali; **hard/soft ~s** droghe pesanti/leggere; **drug addict** *n* tossicomane *m/f*; **drug dealer** *n* trafficante *m/f* di droga; **druggist** *n* (*US*) farmacista *m/f*; **drugstore** ['drʌgstɔːʳ] *n* (*US*) negozio di generi vari e di articoli di farmacia con un bar

drum [drʌm] *n* tamburo; (*for oil, petrol*) fusto ▷ *vi* tamburellare; **drums** *npl* (*set of drums*) batteria; **drummer** *n* batterista *m/f*

drunk [drʌŋk] *pp of* **drink** ▷ *adj* ubriaco/a, ebbro/a ▷ *n* ubriacone/a; **drunken** *adj* ubriaco/a, da ubriaco

dry [draɪ] *adj* secco/a; (*day, clothes*) asciutto/a ▷ *vt* seccare; (*clothes, hair, hands*) asciugare ▷ *vi* asciugarsi; **dry off** *vi* asciugarsi ▷ *vt* asciugare; **dry up** *vi* seccarsi; **dry-cleaner's** *n* lavasecco *m inv*; **dry-cleaning** *n* pulitura a secco; **dryer** *n* (*for hair*) föhn *m inv*, asciugacapelli *m inv*; (*for clothes*) asciugabiancheria *m inv*; (*US: spin-dryer*) centrifuga

DSS *n abbr* (*BRIT: = Department of Social Security*) ministero della Previdenza sociale

DTP *n abbr* (= *desk-top publishing*) desktop publishing *m inv*

dual ['djuəl] *adj* doppio/a; **dual carriageway** *n* (*BRIT*) strada a doppia carreggiata

dubious ['djuːbɪəs] *adj* dubbio/a

Dublin ['dʌblɪn] *n* Dublino *f*

duck [dʌk] *n* anatra ▷ *vi* abbassare la testa

due [djuː] *adj* dovuto/a; (*expected*) atteso/a; (*fitting*) giusto/a ▷ *n* dovuto ▷ *adv*: **~ north** diritto verso nord

duel ['djuəl] *n* duello

duet [djuː'ɛt] *n* duetto

dug [dʌg] *pt, pp of* **dig**

duke [djuːk] *n* duca *m*

dull [dʌl] *adj* (*light*) debole; (*boring*) noioso/a; (*slow-witted*) ottuso/a; (*sound, pain*) sordo/a; (*weather, day*) fosco/a, scuro/a ▷ *vt* (*pain, grief*) attutire; (*mind, senses*) intorpidire

dumb [dʌm] *adj* muto/a; (*stupid*) stupido/a

dummy ['dʌmɪ] *n* (*tailor's model*) manichino; (*Tech, Comm*) riproduzione *f*; (*BRIT: for baby*) tettarella ▷ *adj* falso/a, finto/a

dump [dʌmp] *n* (*also*: **rubbish ~**) mucchio di rifiuti (*place*) discarica ▷ *vt* (*put down*) scaricare; mettere giù; (*get rid of*) buttar via

dumpling ['dʌmplɪŋ] *n* specie di gnocco

dune [djuːn] *n* duna

dungarees [dʌŋgə'riːz] *npl* tuta

dungeon ['dʌndʒən] *n* prigione *f* sotterranea

duplex ['djuːplɛks] *n* (*US: house*) casa con muro divisorio in comune con un'altra; (: *also*: **~ apartment**) appartamento su due piani

duplicate *n* ['djuːplɪkət] doppio ▷ *vt* ['djuːplɪkeɪt] duplicare; **in ~** in duplice copia

durable ['djuərəbl] *adj* durevole; (*clothes, metal*) resistente

duration [djuə'reɪʃən] *n* durata

during ['djuərɪŋ] *prep* durante, nel corso di

dusk [dʌsk] *n* crepuscolo

dust [dʌst] *n* polvere *f* ▷ *vt* (*furniture*) spolverare; (*cake etc*) **to ~ with** cospargere con; **dustbin** *n* (*BRIT*) pattumiera; **duster** *n* straccio per la polvere; **dustman** *n* (*irreg: BRIT*) netturbino; **dustpan** *n* pattumiera; **dusty** *adj* polveroso/a

Dutch [dʌtʃ] *adj* olandese ▷ *n* (*Ling*) olandese *m* ▷ *adv*: **to go ~** *or* **d~** (*col*) fare alla romana; **the ~** gli Olandesi; **Dutchman** (**Dutchwoman**) *n* (*irreg*) olandese *m/f*

duty ['djuːtɪ] *n* dovere *m*; (*tax*) dazio, tassa; **on ~** di servizio; **off ~** libero(a), fuori servizio; **duty-free** *adj* esente da dazio

duvet ['duːveɪ] (*BRIT*) *n* piumino, piumone *m*

DVD *n abbr* (= *digital versatile or video disc*) DVD *m inv*; **DVD burner** *n* masterizzatore *m* (di) DVD; **DVD player** *n* lettore *m* DVD

DVD writer *n* masterizzatore *m* (di) DVD

dwarf [dwɔːf] *n* nano/a ▷ *vt* far apparire piccolo

dwell (*pt, pp* **dwelt**) [dwɛl, dwɛlt] *vi* dimorare; **dwell on** *vt fus* indugiare su

dwelt [dwɛlt] *pt, pp of* **dwell**

dwindle ['dwɪndl] *vi* diminuire

dye [daɪ] *n* tintura ▷ *vt* tingere

dying ['daɪɪŋ] *adj* morente, moribondo/a

dynamic [daɪ'næmɪk] *adj* dinamico/a

dynamite ['daɪnəmaɪt] *n* dinamite *f*

dyslexia [dɪs'lɛksɪə] *n* dislessia

dyslexic [dɪs'lɛksɪk] *adj, n* dislessico/a

E [iː] *n (Mus)* mi *m*

E111 *n abbr (formerly) (also:* **form ~**) E111 *(modulo UE per rimborso spese mediche)*

each [iːtʃ] *adj* ogni, ciascuno/a ▷ *pron* ciascuno/a, ognuno/a; **~ one** ognuno(a); **~ other** si (*or* ci *etc*); **they hate ~ other** si odiano (l'un l'altro); **you are jealous of ~ other** siete gelosi l'uno dell'altro; **they have 2 books ~** hanno 2 libri ciascuno

eager ['iːgəʳ] *adj* impaziente; desideroso/a; ardente; **to be ~ for** essere desideroso di, aver gran voglia di

eagle ['iːgl] *n* aquila

ear [ɪəʳ] *n* orecchio; (*of corn*) pannocchia; **earache** *n* mal *m* d'orecchi; **eardrum** *n* timpano

earl [əːl] (*BRIT*) *n* conte *m*

earlier ['əːlɪəʳ] *adj* precedente ▷ *adv* prima

early ['əːlɪ] *adv* presto, di buon'ora; (*ahead of time*) in anticipo ▷ *adj* primo/a; (*quick: reply*) veloce; **at an ~ hour** di buon'ora; **have an ~ night/start** vada a letto/parta presto; **in the ~** *or* **in the spring/19th century** all'inizio della primavera/dell'Ottocento; **early retirement** *n* prepensionamento

earmark ['ɪəmɑːk] *vt*: **to ~ sth for** destinare qc a

earn [əːn] *vt* guadagnare; (*rest, reward*) meritare

earnest ['əːnɪst] *adj* serio/a; **in ~** sul serio

earnings ['əːnɪŋz] *npl* guadagni *mpl*; (*salary*) stipendio

ear: earphones ['ɪəfəʊnz] *npl* cuffia; **earplugs** *npl* tappi *mpl* per le orecchie; **earring** *n* orecchino

earth [əːθ] *n* terra ▷ *vt* (*BRIT Elec*) mettere a terra; **earthquake** *n* terremoto

ease [iːz] *n* agio, comodo ▷ *vt* (*soothe*) calmare; (*loosen*) allentare; **at ~** a proprio agio; (*Mil*) a riposo; **to ~ sth out/in** tirare fuori/infilare qc con delicatezza; facilitare l'uscita/l'entrata di qc

easily ['iːzɪlɪ] *adv* facilmente

east [iːst] *n* est *m* ▷ *adj* dell'est ▷ *adv* a oriente; **the E~** l'Oriente *m*; (*Pol*) i Paesi dell'Est; **eastbound** ['iːstbaʊnd] *adj* (*traffic*) diretto/a a est; (*carriageway*) che porta a est

Easter ['iːstə^r] *n* Pasqua; **Easter egg** *n* uovo di Pasqua

eastern ['iːstən] *adj* orientale, d'oriente; (*Pol*) dell'est

Easter Sunday *n* domenica di Pasqua

easy ['iːzɪ] *adj* facile; (*manner*) disinvolto/a ▷ *adv*: **to take it** *or* **things ~** prendersela con calma; **easy-going** *adj* accomodante

eat (*pt* **ate**, *pp* **eaten**) [iːt, eɪt, 'iːtn] *vt* mangiare; **eat out** *vi* mangiare fuori

eavesdrop ['iːvzdrɔp] *vi*: **to ~ (on a conversation)** origliare (una conversazione)

e-book ['iːbuk] *n* libro elettronico

e-business ['iːbɪznɪs] *n* (*company*) azienda che opera in Internet; (*commerce*) commercio elettronico

EC *n abbr* (= European Community) CE *f*

eccentric [ɪk'sɛntrɪk] *adj*, *n* eccentrico/a

echo ['ɛkəʊ] (*pl* **echoes**) *n* eco *m or f* ▷ *vt* ripetere; fare eco a ▷ *vi* echeggiare; dare un eco

eclipse [ɪ'klɪps] *n* eclissi *f inv*

eco-friendly [iːkəʊ'frɛndlɪ] *adj* ecologico/a

ecological [iːkə'lɔdʒɪkəl] *adj* ecologico/a

ecology [ɪ'kɔlədʒɪ] *n* ecologia

e-commerce [iːˈkɔməːs] *n* commercio elettronico

economic [iːkə'nɔmɪk] *adj* economico/a; **economical** *adj* economico/a; (*person*) economo/a; **economics** *n* economia ▷ *npl* (*financial aspect*) lato finanziario

economist [ɪ'kɔnəmɪst] *n* economista *m/f*

economize [ɪ'kɔnəmaɪz] *vi* risparmiare, fare economia

economy [ɪ'kɔnəmɪ] *n* economia; **economy class** *n* (*Aviat etc*) classe *f* turistica; **economy class syndrome** *n* sindrome *f* della classe economica

ecstasy ['ɛkstəsɪ] *n* estasi *f inv*; **ecstatic** [ɛks'tætɪk] *adj* estatico/a, in estasi

eczema ['ɛksɪmə] *n* eczema *m*

edge [ɛdʒ] *n* margine *m*; (*of table, plate, cup*) orlo; (*of knife etc*) taglio ▷ *vt* bordare; **on ~** (*fig*) = **edgy**; **to ~ away from** sgattaiolare da

edgy ['ɛdʒɪ] *adj* nervoso/a

edible ['ɛdɪbl] *adj* commestibile; (*meal*) mangiabile

Edinburgh ['ɛdɪnbərə] *n* Edimburgo *f*

edit ['ɛdɪt] *vt* curare; **edition** [ɪ'dɪʃən] *n* edizione *f*; **editor** *n* (*in newspaper*) redattore/trice;

redattore/trice capo; (of sb's work)
curatore/trice; **editorial** [ɛdɪˈtɔːrɪəl]
adj redazionale, editoriale ▷ n
editoriale m

> Be careful not to translate editor
by the Italian word editore.

educate [ˈɛdjukeɪt] vt istruire;
educare; **educated** adj istruito/a
education [ɛdjuˈkeɪʃən] n (teaching)
insegnamento; (schooling) istruzione
f; **educational** adj pedagogico/a;
scolastico/a; istruttivo/a
eel [iːl] n anguilla
eerie [ˈɪərɪ] adj che fa accapponare
la pelle
effect [ɪˈfɛkt] n effetto ▷ vt
effettuare; (law) entrare
in vigore; (drug) fare effetto; **in
~** effettivamente; **effective** adj
efficace; (actual) effettivo/a;
effectively adv efficacemente;
effettivamente; **effects** npl (Theat)
effetti mpl scenici; (property) effetti
mpl
efficiency [ɪˈfɪʃənsɪ] n efficienza;
rendimento effettivo
efficient [ɪˈfɪʃənt] adj efficiente;
efficiently adv efficientemente;
efficacemente
effort [ˈɛfət] n sforzo; **effortless** adj
senza sforzo, facile
e.g. adv abbr (= exempli gratia) per
esempio, p.es.
egg [ɛg] n uovo; **hard-boiled/
soft-boiled ~** uovo sodo/alla coque;
eggcup n portauovo m inv; **eggplant**
n (esp us) melanzana; **eggshell** n
guscio d'uovo; **egg white** n albume
m, bianco d'uovo; **egg yolk** n tuorlo,
rosso (d'uovo)
ego [ˈiːgəu] n ego m inv
Egypt [ˈiːdʒɪpt] n Egitto; **Egyptian**
[ɪˈdʒɪpʃən] adj, n egiziano/a
eight [eɪt] num otto; **eighteen**
num diciotto; **eighteenth** num
diciottesimo/a; **eighth** [eɪtθ] num
ottavo/a; **eightieth** [ˈeɪtɪɪθ] num
ottantesimo/a; **eighty** num ottanta

Eire [ˈɛərə] n Repubblica d'Irlanda
either [ˈaɪðəʳ] adj l'uno o l'altro/a;
(both, each) ciascuno/a; **on ~ side**
su ciascun lato ▷ pron: **~ (of them)**
(o) l'uno o l'altro/a; **I don't like ~**
non mi piace né l'uno né l'altro ▷ adv
neanche; **no, I don't ~** no, neanch'io
▷ conj: **~ good or bad** o buono o
cattivo
eject [ɪˈdʒɛkt] vt espellere; lanciare
elaborate adj [ɪˈlæbərɪt]
elaborato/a, minuzioso/a
▷ vt [ɪˈlæbəreɪt] elaborare ▷ vi
[ɪˈlæbəreɪt] fornire i dettagli
elastic [ɪˈlæstɪk] adj elastico/a
▷ n elastico; **elastic band** n (BRIT)
elastico
elbow [ˈɛlbəu] n gomito
elder [ˈɛldəʳ] adj maggiore, più
vecchio/a ▷ n (tree) sambuco;
one's ~s i più anziani; **elderly** adj
anziano/a ▷ npl: **the elderly** gli
anziani
eldest [ˈɛldɪst] adj, n: **the ~ (child)** il
(la) maggiore (dei bambini)
elect [ɪˈlɛkt] vt eleggere; **to ~ to do**
decidere di fare ▷ adj: **the president
~** il presidente designato; **election**
[ɪˈlɛkʃən] n elezione f; **electoral**
[ɪˈlɛktərəl] adj elettorale; **electorate**
n elettorato
electric [ɪˈlɛktrɪk] adj elettrico/a;
electrical adj elettrico/a; **electric
blanket** n coperta elettrica; **electric
fire** n stufa elettrica; **electrician**
[ɪlɛkˈtrɪʃən] n elettricista m;
electricity [ɪlɛkˈtrɪsɪtɪ] n elettricità;
electric shock n scossa (elettrica);
electrify [ɪˈlɛktrɪfaɪ] vt (Rail)
elettrificare; (audience) elettrizzare
electronic [ɪlɛkˈtrɔnɪk] adj
elettronico/a; **electronic mail** n
posta elettronica; **electronics** n
elettronica
elegance [ˈɛlɪgəns] n eleganza
elegant [ˈɛlɪgənt] adj elegante
element [ˈɛlɪmənt] n elemento; (of
heater, kettle etc) resistenza

elementary [ɛlɪˈmɛntərɪ] *adj* elementare; **elementary school** *n* (*US*) scuola elementare

elephant [ˈɛlɪfənt] *n* elefante/essa

elevate [ˈɛlɪveɪt] *vt* elevare

elevator [ˈɛlɪveɪtəʳ] *n* elevatore *m*; (*US*: lift) ascensore *m*

eleven [ɪˈlɛvn] *num* undici; **eleventh** *adj* undicesimo/a

eligible [ˈɛlɪdʒəbl] *adj* eleggibile; (*for membership*) che ha i requisiti

eliminate [ɪˈlɪmɪneɪt] *vt* eliminare

elm [ɛlm] *n* olmo

eloquent [ˈɛləkwənt] *adj* eloquente

else [ɛls] *adv* altro; **something ~** qualcos'altro; **somewhere ~** altrove; **everywhere ~** in qualsiasi altro luogo; **nobody ~** nessun altro; **where ~?** in quale altro luogo?; **little ~** poco altro; **elsewhere** *adv* altrove

elusive [ɪˈluːsɪv] *adj* elusivo/a

email [ˈiːmeɪl] *n abbr* (= *electronic mail*) posta elettronica, e-mail *m or f inv* ▷ *vt* mandare un messaggio di posta elettronica *or* un e-mail a; **email address** *n* indirizzo di posta elettronica

embankment [ɪmˈbæŋkmənt] *n* (*of road, railway*) massicciata

embargo [ɪmˈbɑːɡəu] *n* (*pl* **embargoes**) (*Comm, Naut*) embargo ▷ *vt* mettere l'embargo su; **to put an ~ on sth** mettere l'embargo su qc

embark [ɪmˈbɑːk] *vi*: **to ~ (on)** imbarcarsi (su) ▷ *vt* imbarcare; **to ~ on** (*fig*) imbarcarsi in

embarrass [ɪmˈbærəs] *vt* imbarazzare; **embarrassed** *adj* imbarazzato/a; **embarrassing** *adj* imbarazzante; **embarrassment** *n* imbarazzo

embassy [ˈɛmbəsɪ] *n* ambasciata

embrace [ɪmˈbreɪs] *vt* abbracciare ▷ *vi* abbracciarsi ▷ *n* abbraccio

embroider [ɪmˈbrɔɪdəʳ] *vt* ricamare; **embroidery** *n* ricamo

embryo [ˈɛmbrɪəu] *n* embrione *m*

emerald [ˈɛmərəld] *n* smeraldo

emerge [ɪˈməːdʒ] *vi* emergere

emergency [ɪˈməːdʒənsɪ] *n* emergenza; **in an ~** in caso di emergenza; **emergency brake** (*US*) *n* freno a mano; **emergency exit** *n* uscita di sicurezza; **emergency landing** *n* atterraggio forzato; **emergency room** (*US Med*) *n* pronto soccorso

emergency service *n* servizio di pronto intervento

emigrate [ˈɛmɪɡreɪt] *vi* emigrare; **emigration** [ɛmɪˈɡreɪʃən] *n* emigrazione *f*

eminent [ˈɛmɪnənt] *adj* eminente

emission [ɪˈmɪʃən] *n* (*of gas, radiation*) emissione *f*

emit [ɪˈmɪt] *vt* emettere

emoticon [ɪˈməutɪkən] *n* (*Comput*) faccina

emotion [ɪˈməuʃən] *n* emozione *f*; **emotional** *adj* (*person*) emotivo/a; (*scene*) commovente; (*tone, speech*) carico/a d'emozione

emperor [ˈɛmpərəʳ] *n* imperatore *m*

emphasis (*pl* **emphases**) [ˈɛmfəsɪs, -siːz] *n* enfasi *f inv*; importanza

emphasize [ˈɛmfəsaɪz] *vt* (*word, point*) sottolineare; (*feature*) mettere in evidenza

empire [ˈɛmpaɪəʳ] *n* impero

employ [ɪmˈplɔɪ] *vt* impiegare; **employee** [ɪmplɔɪˈiː] *n* impiegato/a; **employer** *n* principale *m/f*, datore *m* di lavoro; **employment** *n* impiego; **employment agency** *n* agenzia di collocamento

empower [ɪmˈpauəʳ] *vt*: **to ~ sb to do** concedere autorità a qn di fare

empress [ˈɛmprɪs] *n* imperatrice *f*

emptiness [ˈɛmptɪnɪs] *n* vuoto

empty [ˈɛmptɪ] *adj* vuoto/a; (*threat, promise*) vano/a ▷ *vt* vuotare ▷ *vi* vuotarsi; (*liquid*) scaricarsi; **empty-handed** *adj* a mani vuote

EMU *n abbr* (= *economic and monetary union*) UEM *f*

emulsion [ɪˈmʌlʃən] *n* emulsione *f*

enable [ɪ'neɪbl] *vt*: **to ~ sb to do** permettere a qn di fare

enamel [ɪ'næməl] *n* smalto; **enamel paint** *n* vernice *f* a smalto

enchanting [ɪn'tʃɑːntɪŋ] *adj* incantevole, affascinante

encl. *abbr* (*on letters etc* = *enclosed*, *enclosure*) all., alleg.

enclose [ɪn'kləuz] *vt* (*land*) circondare, recingere; (*letter etc*): **to ~ (with)** allegare (con); **please find ~d** trovi qui accluso

enclosure [ɪn'kləuʒə^r] *n* recinto

encore [ɔŋ'kɔː^r] *excl*, *n* bis (*m inv*)

encounter [ɪn'kauntə^r] *n* incontro ▷ *vt* incontrare

encourage [ɪn'kʌrɪdʒ] *vt* incoraggiare; **encouragement** *n* incoraggiamento

encouraging [ɪn'kʌrɪdʒɪŋ] *adj* incoraggiante

encyclop(a)edia [ɛnsaɪkləu'piːdɪə] *n* enciclopedia

end [ɛnd] *n* fine *f*; (*aim*) fine *m*; (*of table*) bordo estremo; (*of pointed object*) punta ▷ *vt* finire; (*also*: **bring to an ~, put an ~ to**) mettere fine a ▷ *vi* finire; **in the ~** alla fine; **on ~** (*object*) ritto/a; **to stand on ~** (*hair*) rizzarsi; **for hours on ~** per ore e ore; **end up** *vi*: **to ~ up in** finire in

endanger [ɪn'deɪndʒə^r] *vt* mettere in pericolo

endearing [ɪn'dɪərɪŋ] *adj* accattivante

endeavour, (*US*) **endeavor** [ɪn'dɛvə^r] *n* sforzo, tentativo ▷ *vi*: **to ~ to do** cercare *or* sforzarsi di fare

ending ['ɛndɪŋ] *n* fine *f*, conclusione *f*; (*Ling*) desinenza

endless ['ɛndlɪs] *adj* senza fine

endorse [ɪn'dɔːs] *vt* (*cheque*) girare; (*approve*) approvare, appoggiare; **endorsement** *n* approvazione *f*; (*on driving licence*) contravvenzione registrata sulla patente

endurance [ɪn'djuərəns] *n* resistenza; pazienza

endure [ɪn'djuə^r] *vt* sopportare, resistere a ▷ *vi* durare

enemy ['ɛnəmɪ] *adj*, *n* nemico/a

energetic [ɛnə'dʒɛtɪk] *adj* energico/a, attivo/a

energy ['ɛnədʒɪ] *n* energia

enforce [ɪn'fɔːs] *vt* (*Law*) applicare, far osservare

engaged [ɪn'geɪdʒd] *adj* (*BRIT*: *busy, in use*) occupato/a; (*betrothed*) fidanzato/a; **the line's ~** (*BRIT*) la linea è occupata; **to get ~** fidanzarsi; **engaged tone** *n* (*BRIT Tel*) segnale *m* di occupato

engagement [ɪn'geɪdʒmənt] *n* impegno, obbligo; appuntamento; (*to marry*) fidanzamento; **engagement ring** *n* anello di fidanzamento

engaging [ɪn'geɪdʒɪŋ] *adj* attraente

engine ['ɛndʒɪn] *n* (*Aut*) motore *m*; (*Rail*) locomotiva

engineer [ɛndʒɪ'nɪə^r] *n* ingegnere *m*; (*BRIT*: *for domestic appliances*) tecnico; (*US Rail*) macchinista *m*; **engineering** *n* ingegneria

England ['ɪŋglənd] *n* Inghilterra

English ['ɪŋglɪʃ] *adj* inglese ▷ *n* (*Ling*) inglese *m*; **the English** *npl* gli Inglesi; **English Channel** *n*: **the English Channel** il Canale della Manica; **Englishman** *n* (*irreg*) inglese *m*; **Englishwoman** *n* (*irreg*) inglese *f*

engrave [ɪn'greɪv] *vt* incidere

engraving [ɪn'greɪvɪŋ] *n* incisione *f*

enhance [ɪn'hɑːns] *vt* accrescere

enjoy [ɪn'dʒɔɪ] *vt* godere; (*have*: *success, fortune*) avere; **to ~ o.s.** godersela, divertirsi; **enjoyable** *adj* piacevole; **enjoyment** *n* piacere *m*, godimento

enlarge [ɪn'lɑːdʒ] *vt* ingrandire ▷ *vi*: **to ~ on** (*subject*) dilungarsi su; **enlargement** *n* (*Phot*) ingrandimento

enlist [ɪn'lɪst] *vt* arruolare; (*support*) procurare ▷ *vi* arruolarsi

enormous [ɪ'nɔːməs] *adj* enorme

enough [ɪˈnʌf] *adj, n*: **~ time/books** assai tempo/libri; **have you got ~?** ne ha abbastanza *or* a sufficienza? ▷ *adv*: **big ~** abbastanza grande; **he has not worked ~** non ha lavorato abbastanza; **~!** basta!; **that's ~, thanks** basta così, grazie; **I've had ~ of him** ne ho abbastanza di lui; **... which, funnily ~** ... che, strano a dirsi

enquire [ɪnˈkwaɪəʳ] *vt, vi* (*esp BRIT*) = **inquire**

enquiry [ɪnˈkwaɪərɪ] *n* (*esp BRIT*) = **inquiry**

enrage [ɪnˈreɪdʒ] *vt* fare arrabbiare

enrich [ɪnˈrɪtʃ] *vt* arricchire

enrol, (*us*) **enroll** [ɪnˈrəul] *vt* iscrivere ▷ *vi* iscriversi; **enrolment**, (*us*) **enrollment** *n* iscrizione *f*

en route [ɔnˈruːt] *adv*: **~ for/from/to** in viaggio per/da/a

en suite [ɔnˈswiːt] *adj*: **room with ~ bathroom** camera con bagno

ensure [ɪnˈʃuəʳ] *vt* assicurare; garantire

entail [ɪnˈteɪl] *vt* comportare

enter [ˈɛntəʳ] *vt* entrare in; (*army*) arruolarsi in; (*competition*) partecipare a; (*sb for a competition*) iscrivere; (*write down*) registrare; (*Comput*) inserire ▷ *vi* entrare

enterprise [ˈɛntəpraɪz] *n* (*undertaking, company*) impresa; (*spirit*) iniziativa; **free ~** liberalismo economico; **private ~** iniziativa privata; **enterprising** [ˈɛntəpraɪzɪŋ] *adj* intraprendente

entertain [ɛntəˈteɪn] *vt* divertire; (*invite*) ricevere; (*idea, plan*) nutrire; **entertainer** *n* comico/a; **entertaining** *adj* divertente; **entertainment** *n* (*amusement*) divertimento; (*show*) spettacolo

enthusiasm [ɪnˈθuːzɪæzəm] *n* entusiasmo

enthusiast [ɪnˈθuːzɪæst] *n* entusiasta *m/f*; **enthusiastic** [ɪnθuːzɪˈæstɪk] *adj* entusiasta, entusiastico/a; **to be enthusiastic about sth/sb** essere appassionato di qc/entusiasta di qn

entire [ɪnˈtaɪəʳ] *adj* intero/a; **entirely** *adv* completamente, interamente

entitle [ɪnˈtaɪtl] *vt* (*give right*) **to ~ sb to sth/to do** dare diritto a qn a qc/a fare; **entitled** *adj* (*book*) che si intitola; **to be entitled to sth** avere diritto a qc; **to be entitled to do sth** avere il diritto di fare qc

entrance *n* [ˈɛntrns] entrata, ingresso; (*of person*) entrata ▷ *vt* [ɪnˈtraːns] incantare, rapire; **to gain ~ to** (*university etc*) essere ammesso a; **entrance examination** *n* esame *m* di ammissione; **entrance fee** *n* tassa d'iscrizione; (*to museum etc*) prezzo d'ingresso; **entrance ramp** *n* (*us Aut*) rampa di accesso; **entrant** [ˈɛntrnt] *n* partecipante *m/f*; concorrente *m/f*

entrepreneur [ˈɔntrəprəˈnəːʳ] *n* imprenditore *m*

entrust [ɪnˈtrʌst] *vt*: **to ~ sth to** affidare qc a

entry [ˈɛntrɪ] *n* entrata; (*way in*) entrata, ingresso; (*item: on list*) iscrizione *f*; (*in dictionary*) voce *f*; **"no ~"** "vietato l'ingresso"; (*Aut*) "divieto di accesso"; **entry phone** *n* citofono

envelope [ˈɛnvələup] *n* busta

envious [ˈɛnvɪəs] *adj* invidioso/a

environment [ɪnˈvaɪərənmənt] *n* ambiente *m*; **environmental** [ɪnvaɪərənˈmɛntl] *adj* ecologico/a; ambientale; **environmentally** [ɪnvaɪərənˈmɛntəlɪ] *adv*: **environmentally sound/friendly** che rispetta l'ambiente

envisage [ɪnˈvɪzɪdʒ] *vt* immaginare; prevedere

envoy [ˈɛnvɔɪ] *n* inviato/a

envy [ˈɛnvɪ] *n* invidia ▷ *vt* invidiare; **to ~ sb sth** invidiare qn per qc

epic [ˈɛpɪk] *n* poema *m* epico ▷ *adj* epico/a

epidemic [ɛpɪˈdɛmɪk] *n* epidemia

epilepsy [ˈɛpɪlɛpsɪ] *n* epilessia

epileptic [ɛpɪˈlɛptɪk] *adj*, *n* epilettico/a; **epileptic fit** *n* attacco epilettico

episode [ˈɛpɪsəud] *n* episodio

equal [ˈiːkwl] *adj*, *n* pari *(m/f)* ▷ *vt* uguagliare; **~ to** *(task)* all'altezza di; **equality** [iːˈkwɔlɪtɪ] *n* uguaglianza; **equalize** *vi* pareggiare; **equally** *adv* ugualmente

equation [ɪˈkweɪʃən] *n (Math)* equazione *f*

equator [ɪˈkweɪtəʳ] *n* equatore *m*

equip [ɪˈkwɪp] *vt* equipaggiare, attrezzare; **to ~ sb/sth with** fornire qn/qc di; **to be well ~ped** *(office etc)* essere ben attrezzato/a; **he is well ~ped for the job** ha i requisiti necessari per quel lavoro; **equipment** *n* attrezzatura; *(electrical etc)* apparecchiatura

equivalent [ɪˈkwɪvələnt] *adj*, *n* equivalente *(m)*; **to be ~ to** equivalere a

ER *abbr (BRIT)* = **Elizabeth Regina**; *(US Med)* = **emergency room**

era [ˈɪərə] *n* era, età *f inv*

erase [ɪˈreɪz] *vt* cancellare; **eraser** *n* gomma

erect [ɪˈrɛkt] *adj* eretto/a ▷ *vt* costruire; *(assemble)* montare; **erection** [ɪˈrɛkʃən] *n (also Physiol)* erezione *f*; *(of building)* costruzione *f*; *(of machinery)* montaggio

ERM *n abbr (= Exchange Rate Mechanism)* ERM *m*, meccanismo dei tassi di cambio

erode [ɪˈrəud] *vt* erodere; *(metal)* corrodere

erosion [ɪˈrəuʒən] *n* erosione *f*

erotic [ɪˈrɔtɪk] *adj* erotico/a

errand [ˈɛrənd] *n* commissione *f*

erratic [ɪˈrætɪk] *adj* imprevedibile; *(person, mood)* incostante

error [ˈɛrəʳ] *n* errore *m*

erupt [ɪˈrʌpt] *vi (volcano)* mettersi *(or* essere*)* in eruzione; *(war, crisis)* scoppiare; **eruption** [ɪˈrʌpʃən] *n* eruzione *f*; scoppio

escalate [ˈɛskəleɪt] *vi* intensificarsi

escalator [ˈɛskəleɪtəʳ] *n* scala mobile

escape [ɪˈskeɪp] *n* evasione *f*; fuga; *(of gas etc)* fuga, fuoriuscita ▷ *vi* fuggire; *(from jail)* evadere, scappare; *(leak)* uscire ▷ *vt* sfuggire a; **to ~ from** *(place)* fuggire da; *(person)* sfuggire a

escort *n* [ˈɛskɔːt] scorta; *(to dance etc)*: **her ~** il suo cavaliere ▷ *vt* [ɪˈskɔːt] scortare; accompagnare

especially [ɪˈspɛʃlɪ] *adv* specialmente; *(above all)* soprattutto; *(specifically)* espressamente

espionage [ˈɛspɪənɑːʒ] *n* spionaggio

essay [ˈɛseɪ] *n (Scol)* composizione *f*; *(Literature)* saggio

essence [ˈɛsns] *n* essenza

essential [ɪˈsɛnʃəl] *adj* essenziale ▷ *n* elemento essenziale; **essentially** *adv* essenzialmente; **essentials** *npl*: **the essentials** l'essenziale *msg*

establish [ɪˈstæblɪʃ] *vt* stabilire; *(business)* mettere su; *(one's power etc)* affermare; **establishment** *n* stabilimento; **the Establishment** la classe dirigente; l'establishment *m*

estate [ɪˈsteɪt] *n* proprietà *f inv*; *(Law)* beni *mpl*, patrimonio; *(BRIT: also: **housing ~**)* complesso edilizio; **estate agent** *n (BRIT)* agente *m* immobiliare; **estate car** *n (BRIT)* giardiniera

estimate *n* [ˈɛstɪmət] stima; *(Comm)* preventivo ▷ *vt* [ˈɛstɪmeɪt] stimare, valutare

etc. *abbr (= et cetera)* ecc., etc.

eternal [ɪˈtəːnl] *adj* eterno/a

eternity [ɪˈtəːnɪtɪ] *n* eternità *f*

ethical [ˈɛθɪkl] *adj* etico/a, morale; **ethics** [ˈɛθɪks] *n* etica ▷ *npl* morale *f*

Ethiopia [iːθɪˈəupɪə] *n* Etiopia

ethnic [ˈɛθnɪk] *adj* etnico/a; **ethnic minority** *n* minoranza etnica

e-ticket [ˈiːtɪkɪt] *n* biglietto elettronico

etiquette [ˈɛtɪkɛt] *n* etichetta

EU *n abbr (= European Union)* UE *f*

euro [ˈjuərəu] *n (currency)* euro *m inv*

e

Europe ['jʊərəp] n Europa; **European** [jʊərə'piːən] adj, n europeo/a; **European Community** n Comunità Europea; **European Union** n Unione f europea

Eurostar® ['jʊərəʊstɑːʳ] n Eurostar® m inv

evacuate [ɪ'vækjʊeɪt] vt evacuare

evade [ɪ'veɪd] vt (tax) evadere; (duties etc) sottrarsi a; (person) schivare

evaluate [ɪ'væljʊeɪt] vt valutare

evaporate [ɪ'væpəreɪt] vi evaporare

eve [iːv] n: **on the ~ of** alla vigilia di

even ['iːvn] adj regolare; (number) pari inv ▷ adv anche, perfino; **~ if, ~ though** anche se; **~ more** ancora di più; **~ so** ciò nonostante; **not ~ ...** nemmeno ...; **to get ~ with sb** dare la pari a qn

evening ['iːvnɪŋ] n sera; (as duration, event) serata; **in the ~** la sera; **evening class** n corso serale; **evening dress** n (woman's) abito da sera; **in evening dress** (man) in abito scuro; (woman) in abito lungo

event [ɪ'vɛnt] n avvenimento; (Sport) gara; **in the ~ of** in caso di; **eventful** adj denso/a di eventi

eventual [ɪ'vɛntʃʊəl] adj finale
> Be careful not to translate eventual by the Italian word eventuale.

eventually [ɪ'vɛntʃʊəlɪ] adv alla fine
> Be careful not to translate eventually by the Italian word eventualmente.

ever ['ɛvəʳ] adv mai; (at all times) sempre; **the best ~** il migliore che ci sia mai stato; **have you ~ seen it?** l'ha mai visto?; **~ so pretty** così bello(a); **~ since** adv da allora; conj sin da quando; **evergreen** n sempreverde m

every ['ɛvrɪ] adj ogni; **~ day** tutti i giorni, ogni giorno; **~ other/third day** ogni due/tre giorni; **~ other car** una macchina su due; **~ now and then** ogni tanto, di quando in

quando; **everybody** pron ognuno, tutti pl; **everyday** adj quotidiano/a; di ogni giorno; **everyone** ['ɛvrɪwʌn] = **everybody**; **everything** pron tutto, ogni cosa; **everywhere** adv dappertutto; (wherever) ovunque

evict [ɪ'vɪkt] vt sfrattare

evidence ['ɛvɪdəns] n (proof) prova; (of witness) testimonianza; **to show ~ of** (sign) dare segni di; **to give ~** deporre

evident ['ɛvɪdənt] adj evidente; **evidently** adv evidentemente

evil ['iːvl] adj cattivo/a, maligno/a ▷ n male m

evoke [ɪ'vəuk] vt evocare

evolution [iːvə'luːʃən] n evoluzione f

evolve [ɪ'vɔlv] vt elaborare ▷ vi svilupparsi, evolversi

ewe [juː] n pecora

ex (col) [ɛks] n: **my ex** il (la) mio/a ex

ex- [ɛks] prefix ex

exact [ɪg'zækt] adj esatto/a ▷ vt: **to ~ sth (from)** estorcere qc (da); esigere qc (da); **exactly** adv esattamente

exaggerate [ɪg'zædʒəreɪt] vt, vi esagerare; **exaggeration** [ɪgzædʒə'reɪʃən] n esagerazione f

exam [ɪg'zæm] n abbr (Scol) = **examination**

examination [ɪgzæmɪ'neɪʃən] n (Scol) esame m; (Med) controllo

examine [ɪg'zæmɪn] vt esaminare; **examiner** n esaminatore/trice

example [ɪg'zɑːmpl] n esempio; **for ~** ad or per esempio

exasperated [ɪg'zɑːspəreɪtɪd] adj esasperato/a

excavate ['ɛkskəveɪt] vt scavare

exceed [ɪk'siːd] vt superare; (one's powers, time limit) oltrepassare; **exceedingly** adv eccessivamente

excel [ɪk'sɛl] vi eccellere ▷ vt sorpassare; **to ~ o.s.** (BRIT) superare se stesso

excellence ['ɛksələns] n eccellenza

excellent ['ɛksələnt] adj eccellente

except [ɪkˈsɛpt] prep (also: **~ for, ~ing**) salvo, all'infuori di, eccetto ▷ vt escludere; **~ if/when** salvo se/quando; **~ that** salvo che; **exception** [ɪkˈsɛpʃən] n eccezione f; **to take exception to** trovare a ridire su; **exceptional** [ɪkˈsɛpʃənl] adj eccezionale; **exceptionally** [ɪkˈsɛpʃənəlɪ] adv eccezionalmente

excerpt [ˈɛksəːpt] n estratto

excess [ɪkˈsɛs] n eccesso; **excess baggage** n bagaglio in eccedenza; **excessive** adj eccessivo/a

exchange [ɪksˈtʃeɪndʒ] n scambio; (also: **telephone ~**) centralino ▷ vt: **to ~ (for)** scambiare (con); **exchange rate** n tasso di cambio

excite [ɪkˈsaɪt] vt eccitare; **to get ~d** eccitarsi; **excited** adj: **to get excited** essere elettrizzato/a; **excitement** n eccitazione f; agitazione f; **exciting** adj avventuroso/a; (film, book) appassionante

exclaim [ɪkˈskleɪm] vi esclamare; **exclamation** [ɛkskləˈmeɪʃən] n esclamazione f; **exclamation mark**, (US) **exclamation point** n punto esclamativo

exclude [ɪkˈskluːd] vt escludere

excluding [ɪkˈskluːdɪŋ] prep: **~ VAT** IVA esclusa

exclusion [ɪkˈskluːʒən] n esclusione f; **to the ~ of** escludendo

exclusive [ɪkˈskluːsɪv] adj esclusivo/a; **~ of VAT** IVA esclusa; **exclusively** adv esclusivamente

excruciating [ɪkˈskruːʃɪeɪtɪŋ] adj straziante, atroce

excursion [ɪkˈskəːʃən] n escursione f, gita

excuse n [ɪkˈskjuːs] scusa ▷ vt [ɪkˈskjuːz] scusare; **to ~ sb from** (activity) dispensare qn da; **~ me!** mi scusi!; **now if you will ~ me, ...** ora, mi scusi ma ...

ex-directory [ˈɛksdɪˈrɛktərɪ] adj (BRIT): **to be ~** non essere sull'elenco

execute [ˈɛksɪkjuːt] vt (prisoner) giustiziare; (plan etc) eseguire; **execution** [ɛksɪˈkjuːʃən] n esecuzione f

executive [ɪgˈzɛkjutɪv] n (Comm) dirigente m; (Pol) esecutivo ▷ adj esecutivo/a

exempt [ɪgˈzɛmpt] adj: **~ (from)** esentato/a (da) ▷ vt: **to ~ sb from** esentare qn da

exercise [ˈɛksəsaɪz] n (keep fit) moto; (Scol, Mil etc) esercizio ▷ vt esercitare; (patience) usare; (dog) portar fuori ▷ vi (also: **take ~**) fare del movimento or moto; **exercise book** n quaderno

exert [ɪgˈzəːt] vt esercitare; **to ~ o.s.** sforzarsi; **exertion** [ɪgˈzəːʃən] n sforzo

exhale [ɛksˈheɪl] vt, vi espirare

exhaust [ɪgˈzɔːst] n (also: **~ fumes**) scappamento; (also: **~ pipe**) tubo di scappamento ▷ vt esaurire; **exhausted** adj esaurito/a; **exhaustion** [ɪgˈzɔːstʃən] n esaurimento; **nervous exhaustion** sovraffaticamento mentale

exhibit [ɪgˈzɪbɪt] n (Art) oggetto esposto; (Law) documento or oggetto esibito ▷ vt esporre; (courage, skill) dimostrare; **exhibition** [ɛksɪˈbɪʃən] n mostra, esposizione f

exhilarating [ɪgˈzɪləreɪtɪŋ] adj esilarante; stimolante

exile [ˈɛksaɪl] n esilio; (person) esiliato/a ▷ vt esiliare

exist [ɪgˈzɪst] vi esistere; **existence** n esistenza; **existing** adj esistente; attuale

exit [ˈɛksɪt] n uscita ▷ vi (Comput, Theat) uscire; **exit ramp** n (US Aut) rampa di uscita

exotic [ɪgˈzɔtɪk] adj esotico/a

expand [ɪkˈspænd] vt espandere; (influence) estendere; (horizons) allargare ▷ vi (gas) espandersi; (metal) dilatarsi

expansion [ɪk'spænʃən] n (gen) espansione f; (of town, economy) sviluppo; (of metal) dilatazione f

expect [ɪk'spɛkt] vt (anticipate) prevedere, aspettarsi, prevedere or aspettarsi che + sub; (require) richiedere, esigere; (suppose) supporre; (await, also baby) aspettare ▷ vi: **to be ~ing** essere in stato interessante; **to ~ sb to do** aspettarsi che qn faccia; **expectation** [ɛkspɛk'teɪʃən] n aspettativa; speranza

expedition [ɛkspə'dɪʃən] n spedizione f

expel [ɪk'spɛl] vt espellere

expenditure [ɪk'spɛndɪtʃər] n spesa

expense [ɪk'spɛns] n spesa; (high cost) costo; **expenses** npl (Comm) spese fpl, indennità fpl; **at the ~ of** a spese di; **expense account** n conto m spese inv

expensive [ɪk'spɛnsɪv] adj caro/a, costoso/a

experience [ɪk'spɪərɪəns] n esperienza ▷ vt (pleasure) provare; (hardship) soffrire; **experienced** adj esperto/a

experiment n [ɪk'spɛrɪmənt] esperimento, esperienza ▷ vi [ɪk'spɛrɪmɛnt] fare esperimenti; **experimental** [ɪkspɛrɪ'mɛntl] adj sperimentale; **at the experimental stage** in via di sperimentazione

expert ['ɛkspəːt] adj, n esperto/a; **expertise** [ɛkspəː'tiːz] n competenza

expire [ɪk'spaɪər] vi (period of time, licence) scadere; **expiry** n scadenza; **expiry date** n (of medicine, food item) data di scadenza

explain [ɪk'spleɪn] vt spiegare; **explanation** [ɛksplə'neɪʃən] n spiegazione f

explicit [ɪk'splɪsɪt] adj esplicito/a

explode [ɪk'spləud] vi esplodere

exploit n ['ɛksplɔɪt] impresa ▷ vt [ɪk'splɔɪt] sfruttare; **exploitation** [ɛksplɔɪ'teɪʃən] n sfruttamento

explore [ɪk'splɔːr] vt esplorare; (possibilities) esaminare; **explorer** n esploratore/trice

explosion [ɪk'spləuʒən] n esplosione f; **explosive** [ɪk'spləusɪv] adj esplosivo/a ▷ n esplosivo

export vt [ɛk'spɔːt] esportare ▷ n ['ɛkspɔːt] esportazione f; articolo di esportazione ▷ cpd d'esportazione; **exporter** n esportatore m

expose [ɪk'spəuz] vt esporre; (unmask) smascherare; **exposed** adj (land, house) esposto/a; **exposure** [ɪk'spəuʒər] n esposizione f; (Phot) posa; (Med) assideramento

express [ɪk'sprɛs] adj (definite) chiaro/a, espresso/a; (BRIT: letter etc) espresso inv ▷ n (train) espresso ▷ vt esprimere; **expression** [ɪk'sprɛʃən] n espressione f; **expressway** n (US: urban motorway) autostrada che attraversa la città

exquisite [ɛk'skwɪzɪt] adj squisito/a

extend [ɪk'stɛnd] vt (visit) protrarre; (road, deadline) prolungare; (building) ampliare; (offer) offrire, porgere ▷ vi (land) estendersi; **extension** [ɪk'stɛnʃən] n (of road, term) prolungamento; (of contract, deadline) proroga; (of building) annesso; (to wire, table) prolunga; (telephone) interno; (: in private house) apparecchio supplementare; **extension cable** or **lead** n (Elec) prolunga

extensive [ɪk'stɛnsɪv] adj esteso/a, ampio/a; (damage) su larga scala; (inquiries, coverage, discussion) esauriente; (use) grande

extent [ɪk'stɛnt] n estensione f; **to some ~** fino a un certo punto; **to what ~?** fino a che punto?; **to such an ~ that ...** a tal punto che ...; **to the ~ of ...** fino al punto di ...

exterior [ɛk'stɪərɪər] adj esteriore, esterno/a ▷ n esteriore m, esterno; aspetto (esteriore)

external [ɛk'stəːnl] adj esterno/a, esteriore

extinct [ɪk'stɪŋkt] *adj* estinto/a; **extinction** [ɪk'stɪŋkʃən] *n* estinzione *f*

extinguish [ɪk'stɪŋgwɪʃ] *vt* estinguere

extra ['ɛkstrə] *adj* extra *inv*, supplementare ▷ *adv* (*in addition*) di più ▷ *n* extra *m inv*; (*surcharge*) supplemento; (*Theat*) comparso

extract *vt* [ɪk'strækt] estrarre; (*money, promise*) strappare ▷ *n* ['ɛkstrækt] estratto; (*passage*) brano

extradite ['ɛkstrədaɪt] *vt* estradare

extraordinary [ɪk'strɔ:dnrɪ] *adj* straordinario/a

extravagance [ɪk'strævəgəns] *n* sperpero; (*thing bought*) stravaganza

extravagant [ɪk'strævəgənt] *adj* (*in spending*) prodigo/a; (: *tastes*) dispendioso/a; esagerato/a

> Be careful not to translate *extravagant* by the Italian word *stravagante*.

extreme [ɪk'stri:m] *adj* estremo/a ▷ *n* estremo; **extremely** *adv* estremamente

extremist [ɪk'stri:mɪst] *adj*, *n* estremista (*m/f*)

extrovert ['ɛkstrəvə:t] *n* estroverso/a

eye [aɪ] *n* occhio; (*of needle*) cruna ▷ *vt* osservare; **to keep an ~ on** tenere d'occhio; **eyeball** *n* globo dell'occhio; **eyebrow** *n* sopracciglio; **eyedrops** *npl* gocce *fpl* oculari, collirio; **eyelash** *n* ciglio; **eyelid** *n* palpebra; **eyeliner** *n* eye-liner *m inv*; **eyeshadow** *n* ombretto; **eyesight** *n* vista; **eye witness** *n* testimone *m/f* oculare

F [ɛf] *n* (*Mus*) fa *m*

fabric ['fæbrɪk] *n* stoffa, tessuto

fabulous ['fæbjuləs] *adj* favoloso/a; (*super*) favoloso/a, fantastico/a

face [feɪs] *n* faccia, viso, volto; (*expression*) faccia; (*of clock*) quadrante *m*; (*of building*) facciata ▷ *vt* fronteggiare; (*fig*) affrontare; **~ down** (*person*) bocconi; (*object*) a faccia in giù; **to pull a ~** fare una smorfia; **in the ~ of** (*difficulties etc*) di fronte a; **on the ~ of it** a prima vista; **~ to ~** faccia a faccia; **face up to** *vt fus* affrontare, far fronte a; **face cloth** *n* (*BRIT*) guanto di spugna; **face pack** *n* (*BRIT*) maschera di bellezza

facial ['feɪʃəl] *adj* facciale, del viso ▷ *n* trattamento del viso

facilitate [fə'sɪlɪteɪt] *vt* facilitare

facility [fə'sɪlɪtɪ] *n* facilità; **facilities** *npl* attrezzature *fpl*; **credit facilities** facilitazioni *fpl* di credito

fact [fækt] *n* fatto; **in ~** in effetti

faction ['fækʃən] n fazione f

factor ['fæktə'] n fattore m

factory ['fæktərɪ] n fabbrica, stabilimento

> Be careful not to translate *factory* by the Italian word *fattoria*.

factual ['fæktjuəl] adj che si attiene ai fatti

faculty ['fækəltɪ] n facoltà f inv; (US) corpo insegnante

fad [fæd] n mania; capriccio

fade [feɪd] vi sbiadire, sbiadirsi; (light, sound, hope) attenuarsi, affievolirsi; (flower) appassire; **fade away** vi (sound) affievolirsi

fag [fæg] n (BRIT: col: cigarette) cicca

Fahrenheit ['fɑːrənhaɪt] n Fahrenheit m inv

fail [feɪl] vt (exam) non superare; (candidate) bocciare; (courage, memory) mancare a ▷ vi fallire; (student) essere respinto/a; (eyesight, health, light) venire a mancare; **to ~ to do sth** (neglect) mancare di fare qc; (be unable) non riuscire a fare qc; **without ~** senza fallo; certamente; **failing** n difetto ▷ prep in mancanza di; **failure** ['feɪljə'] n fallimento; (person) fallito/a; (mechanical etc) guasto

faint [feɪnt] adj debole; (recollection) vago/a; (mark) indistinto/a ▷ n (Med) svenimento ▷ vi svenire; **to feel ~** sentirsi svenire; **faintest** adj: **I haven't the faintest idea** non ho la più pallida idea; **faintly** adv debolmente; vagamente

fair [fɛə'] adj (person, decision) giusto/a, equo/a; (quite large, quite good) discreto/a; (hair etc) biondo/a; (skin, complexion) chiaro/a; (weather) bello/a, clemente ▷ adv: **to play ~** giocare correttamente ▷ n fiera; (BRIT: funfair) luna park m inv; **fairground** n luna park m inv; **fair-haired** [fɛə'hɛəd] adj (person) biondo/a; **fairly** adv equamente; (quite) abbastanza; **fair trade** n

commercio equo e solidale; **fairway** n (Golf) fairway m inv

fairy ['fɛərɪ] n fata; **fairy tale** n fiaba

faith [feɪθ] n fede f; (trust) fiducia; (sect) religione f, fede f; **faithful** adj fedele; (person) impostore/a adv fedelmente; **yours faithfully** (BRIT) (in letters) distinti saluti

fake [feɪk] n imitazione f; (picture) falso; (person) impostore/a ▷ adj falso/a ▷ vt (accounts) falsificare; (illness) fingere; (painting) contraffare

falcon ['fɔːlkən] n falco, falcone m

fall [fɔːl] n caduta; (in temperature) abbassamento; (in price) ribasso; (US: autumn) autunno ▷ vi (pt **fell**, pp **fallen**) cadere; (temperature, price) scendere; **to ~ flat** (on one's face) cadere bocconi; (joke) fare cilecca; (plan) fallire; **fall apart** vi cadere a pezzi; **fall down** vi (person) cadere; (building, hopes) crollare; **fall for** vt fus (person) prendere una cotta per; **to ~ for a trick** (or a story etc) cascarci; **fall off** vi cadere; (diminish) diminuire, abbassarsi; **fall out** vi (hair, teeth) cadere; (friends etc) litigare; **fall through** vi (plan, project) fallire

fallen ['fɔːlən] pp of **fall**

fallout ['fɔːlaut] n fall-out m

falls npl (waterfall) cascate fpl

false [fɔːls] adj falso/a; **under ~ pretences** con l'inganno; **false alarm** n falso allarme m; **false teeth** npl (BRIT) denti mpl finti

fame [feɪm] n fama, celebrità

familiar [fə'mɪlɪə'] adj familiare; (close) intimo/a; **to be ~ with** conoscere; **familiarize** [fə'mɪlɪəraɪz] vt: **to familiarize o.s. with** familiarizzare con

family ['fæmɪlɪ] n famiglia; **family doctor** n medico di famiglia; **family planning** n pianificazione f familiare

famine ['fæmɪn] n carestia

famous ['feɪməs] adj famoso/a

fan [fæn] n (folding) ventaglio; (machine) ventilatore m; (person) ammiratore/trice; tifoso/a ▷ vt far vento a; (fire, quarrel) alimentare

fanatic [fə'nætɪk] n fanatico/a

fan belt n cinghia del ventilatore

fan club n fan club m inv

fancy ['fænsɪ] n immaginazione f, fantasia; (whim) capriccio ▷ adj (hat) stravagante; (hotel, food) speciale ▷ vt (feel like, want) aver voglia di; (imagine) immaginare; **to take a ~ to** incapricciarsi di; **he fancies her** gli piace; **fancy dress** n costume m (per maschera)

fan heater n (BRIT) stufa ad aria calda

fantasize ['fæntəsaɪz] vi fantasticare, sognare

fantastic [fæn'tæstɪk] adj fantastico/a

fantasy ['fæntəsɪ] n fantasia, immaginazione f; fantasticheria; chimera

fanzine ['fænzi:n] n rivista specialistica (per appassionati)

FAQ abbr (= frequently asked question(s)) FAQ

far [fɑː^r] adj lontano/a ▷ adv lontano; (much, greatly) molto; **is it ~ from here?** è molto lontano da qui?; **how ~?** quanto lontano?; (referring to activity etc) fino a dove?; **how ~ is the town centre?** quanto dista il centro da qui?; **~ away, ~ off** lontano, distante; **~ better** assai migliore; **~ from** lontano da; **by ~** di gran lunga; **go as ~ as the farm** vada fino alla fattoria; **as ~ as I know** per quel che so

farce [fɑːs] n farsa

fare [fɛə^r] n (on trains, buses) tariffa; (in taxi) prezzo della corsa; (food) vitto, cibo; **half ~** metà tariffa; **full ~** tariffa intera

Far East n: **the ~** l'Estremo Oriente m

farewell [fɛə'wɛl] excl, n addio

farm [fɑːm] n fattoria, podere m ▷ vt coltivare; **farmer** n coltivatore/trice, agricoltore/trice; **farmhouse** n fattoria; **farming** n (gen) agricoltura; (of crops) coltivazione f; (of animals) allevamento; **farmyard** n aia

far-reaching [fɑː'riːtʃɪŋ] adj di vasta portata

fart [fɑːt] (col!) n scoreggia (!) ▷ vi scoreggiare (!)

farther ['fɑːðə^r] adv più lontano ▷ adj più lontano/a

farthest ['fɑːðɪst] adv superlative of **far**

fascinate ['fæsɪneɪt] vt affascinare; **fascinated** adj affascinato/a; **fascinating** adj affascinante; **fascination** [fæsɪ'neɪʃən] n fascino

fascist ['fæʃɪst] adj, n fascista (m/f)

fashion ['fæʃən] n moda; (manner) maniera, modo ▷ vt foggiare, formare; **in ~** alla moda; **out of ~** passato/a di moda; **fashionable** adj alla moda, di moda; **fashionista** [fæʃə'nɪstə] n fashionista m/f, maniaco/a della moda; **fashion show** n sfilata di moda

fast [fɑːst] adj rapido/a, svelto/a, veloce; (clock): **to be ~** andare avanti; (dye, colour) solido/a ▷ adv rapidamente; (stuck, held) saldamente ▷ n digiuno ▷ vi digiunare; **~ asleep** profondamente addormentato

fasten ['fɑːsn] vt chiudere, fissare; (coat) abbottonare, allacciare ▷ vi chiudersi, fissarsi; abbottonarsi, allacciarsi

fast food n fast food m inv

fat [fæt] adj grasso/a; (book, profit etc) grosso/a ▷ n grasso

fatal ['feɪtl] adj fatale; mortale; disastroso/a; **fatality** [fə'tælɪtɪ] n (road death etc) morto/a, vittima; **fatally** adv a morte

fate [feɪt] n destino; (of person) sorte f

father ['fɑːðə^r] n padre m; **Father Christmas** n Babbo Natale; **father-in-law** n suocero

fatigue [fəˈtiːg] n stanchezza
fattening [ˈfætnɪŋ] adj (food) che fa ingrassare
fatty [ˈfætɪ] adj (food) grasso/a ▷ n (col) ciccione/a
faucet [ˈfɔːsɪt] n (US) rubinetto
fault [fɔːlt] n colpa; (Tennis) fallo; (defect) difetto; (Geo) faglia ▷ vt criticare; **it's my ~** è colpa mia; **to find ~ with** trovare da ridire su; **at ~** in fallo; **faulty** adj difettoso/a
fauna [ˈfɔːnə] n fauna
favour, (US) **favor** [ˈfeɪvəʳ] n favore m ▷ vt (proposition) essere favorevole a; (pupil etc) favorire; (team, horse) dare per vincente; **to do sb a ~** fare un favore or una cortesia a qn; **in ~ of** in favore di; **to find ~ with sb** (person) entrare nelle buone grazie di qn; (suggestion) avere l'approvazione di qn; **favourable** adj favorevole; **favourite** [ˈfeɪvrɪt] adj, n favorito/a
fawn [fɔːn] n daino ▷ adj (also: ~-coloured) marrone chiaro inv ▷ vi: **to ~ (up)on** adulare servilmente
fax [fæks] n (document, machine) facsimile m inv, telecopia; (machine) telecopiatrice f ▷ vt teletrasmettere, spedire via fax
FBI n abbr (US: = Federal Bureau of Investigation) FBI f
fear [fɪəʳ] n paura, timore m ▷ vt aver paura di, temere; **for ~ of** per paura di; **fearful** adj pauroso/a; (sight, noise) terribile, spaventoso/a; **fearless** adj intrepido/a, senza paura
feasible [ˈfiːzəbl] adj fattibile, realizzabile
feast [fiːst] n festa, banchetto; (Rel: also: ~ day) festa ▷ vi banchettare
feat [fiːt] n impresa, fatto insigne
feather [ˈfɛðəʳ] n penna
feature [ˈfiːtʃəʳ] n caratteristica; (article) articolo ▷ vt (film) avere come protagonista ▷ vi figurare; **features** npl (of face) fisionomia; **feature film** n film m inv principale

Feb. [fɛb] abbr (= February) feb.
February [ˈfɛbruərɪ] n febbraio
fed [fɛd] pt, pp of **feed**
federal [ˈfɛdərəl] adj federale
federation [fɛdəˈreɪʃən] n federazione f
fed up adj: **to be ~** essere stufo/a
fee [fiː] n pagamento; (of doctor, lawyer) onorario; (for examination) tassa d'esame; **school ~s** tasse fpl scolastiche
feeble [ˈfiːbl] adj debole
feed [fiːd] n (of baby) pappa; (of animal) mangime m; (on printer) meccanismo di alimentazione ▷ vt (pt, pp **fed**) nutrire; (baby) allattare; (horse etc) dare da mangiare a; (fire, machine) alimentare ▷ vi (baby, animal) mangiare; **to ~ data/ information into sth** inserire dati/ informazioni in qc; **feedback** n feed-back m
feel [fiːl] n (sense of touch) tatto; (of substance) consistenza ▷ vt (pt, pp **felt**) toccare; palpare; tastare; (cold, pain, anger) sentire; (think, believe): **to ~ that** pensare che; **to ~ hungry/ cold** aver fame/freddo; **to ~ lonely/ better** sentirsi solo/meglio; **I don't ~ well** non mi sento bene; **it ~s soft** è morbido al tatto; **to ~ like** (want) aver voglia di; **to ~ about** or **around for** cercare a tastoni; **feeling** n sensazione f; (emotion) sentimento
feet [fiːt] npl of **foot**
fell [fɛl] pt of **fall** ▷ vt (tree) abbattere
fellow [ˈfɛləu] n individuo, tipo; (comrade) compagno; (of learned society) membro cpd; **fellow citizen** n concittadino/a; **fellow countryman** n (irreg) compatriota m; **fellow men** npl simili mpl; **fellowship** n associazione f; compagnia; (Scol) specie di borsa di studio universitaria
felony [ˈfɛlənɪ] n reato, crimine m
felt [fɛlt] pt, pp of **feel** ▷ n feltro
female [ˈfiːmeɪl] n (Zool) femmina; (pej: woman) donna, femmina ▷ adj

(*sex, character*) femminile; (*Biol, Elec*) femmina *inv*; (*vote etc*) di donne

feminine ['fɛmɪnɪn] *adj, n* femminile (*m*)

feminist ['fɛmɪnɪst] *n* femminista *m/f*

fence [fɛns] *n* recinto ▷ *vt* (*also*: **~ in**) recingere ▷ *vi*; (*Sport*) tirare di scherma; **fencing** *n* (*Sport*) scherma

fend [fɛnd] *vi*: **to ~ for o.s.** arrangiarsi; **fend off** *vt* (*attack, attacker*) respingere, difendersi da

fender ['fɛndər] *n* parafuoco; (*on boat*) parabordo; (*US*) parafango; paraurti *m inv*

fennel ['fɛnl] *n* finocchio

ferment *vi* [fə'mɛnt] fermentare ▷ *n* ['fə:mɛnt] (*fig*) agitazione *f*, eccitazione *f*

fern [fə:n] *n* felce *f*

ferocious [fə'rəuʃəs] *adj* feroce

ferret ['fɛrɪt] *n* furetto

ferry ['fɛrɪ] *n* (*small*) traghetto; (*large: also*: **~boat**) nave *f* traghetto *inv* ▷ *vt* traghettare

fertile ['fə:taɪl] *adj* fertile; (*Biol*) fecondo/a; **fertilize** ['fə:tɪlaɪz] *vt* fertilizzare; fecondare; **fertilizer** ['fə:tɪlaɪzər] *n* fertilizzante *m*

festival ['fɛstɪvəl] *n* (*Rel*) festa; (*Art, Mus*) festival *m inv*

festive ['fɛstɪv] *adj* di festa; **the ~ season** (*BRIT: Christmas*) il periodo delle feste

fetch [fɛtʃ] *vt* andare a prendere; (*sell for*) essere venduto/a per

fête [feɪt] *n* festa

fetus ['fi:təs] *n* (*US*) = **foetus**

feud [fju:d] *n* contesa, lotta

fever ['fi:vər] *n* febbre *f*; **feverish** *adj* febbrile

few [fju:] *adj* pochi/e ▷ *pron* alcuni/e; **a ~ ...** qualche ...; **fewer** *adj* meno *inv*; meno numerosi/e; **fewest** *adj* il minor numero di

fiancé [fɪ'ɑ̃:ŋseɪ] *n* fidanzato; **fiancée** *n* fidanzata

fiasco [fɪ'æskəu] *n* fiasco

fib [fɪb] *n* piccola bugia

fibre, (*US*) **fiber** ['faɪbər] *n* fibra; **fibreglass**, (*US*) **fiberglass** *n* fibra di vetro

fickle ['fɪkl] *adj* incostante, capriccioso/a

fiction ['fɪkʃən] *n* narrativa, romanzi *mpl*; (*sth made up*) finzione *f*; **fictional** *adj* immaginario/a

fiddle ['fɪdl] *n* (*Mus*) violino; (*cheating*) imbroglio; truffa ▷ *vt* (*BRIT: accounts*) falsificare, falsare; **fiddle with** *vt fus* gingillarsi con

fidelity [fɪ'dɛlɪtɪ] *n* fedeltà; (*accuracy*) esattezza

field [fi:ld] *n* campo; **field marshal** *n* feldmaresciallo

fierce [fɪəs] *adj* (*look*) fiero/a; (*fighting*) accanito/a; (*wind*) furioso/a; (*heat*) intenso/a; (*animal, person, attack*) feroce

fifteen [fɪf'ti:n] *num* quindici; **fifteenth** *num* quindicesimo/a

fifth [fɪfθ] *num* quinto/a

fiftieth ['fɪftɪɪθ] *num* cinquantesimo/a

fifty ['fɪftɪ] *num* cinquanta; **fifty-fifty** *adj*: **a fifty-fifty chance** una possibilità su due ▷ *adv*: **to go fifty-fifty with sb** fare a metà con qn

fig [fɪg] *n* fico

fight (*pt, pp* **fought**) [faɪt, fɔːt] *n* zuffa, rissa; (*Mil*) battaglia, combattimento; (*against cancer etc*) lotta ▷ *vt* (*person*) azzuffarsi con; (*enemy: also Mil*) combattere; (*cancer, alcoholism, emotion*) lottare contro, combattere; (*election*) partecipare a ▷ *vi* combattere; **fight off** *vt* (*attack, attacker*) respingere; (*disease, sleep, urge*) lottare contro; **fighting** *n* combattimento

figure ['fɪgər] *n* figura; (*number, cipher*) cifra ▷ *vt* (*think: esp US*) pensare ▷ *vi* (*appear*) figurare; **figure out** *vt* riuscire a capire; calcolare

file [faɪl] *n* (*tool*) lima; (*dossier*) incartamento; (*folder*) cartellina;

(row) fila; (Comput) archivio ▷ vt (nails, wood) limare; (papers) archiviare; (Law: claim) presentare; passare agli atti; **filing cabinet** ['faɪlɪŋ-] n casellario

Filipino [fɪlɪ'pi:nəʊ] n filippino/a; (Ling) tagal m

fill [fɪl] vt riempire; (job) coprire ▷ n: **to eat one's ~** mangiare a sazietà; **fill in** vt (hole) riempire; (form) compilare; **fill out** vt (form, receipt) riempire; **fill up** vt riempire; **~ it up, please** (Aut) il pieno, per favore

fillet ['fɪlɪt] n filetto; **fillet steak** n bistecca di filetto

filling ['fɪlɪŋ] n (Culin) impasto, ripieno, (for tooth) otturazione f; **filling station** n stazione f di rifornimento

film [fɪlm] n (Cine) film m inv; (Phot) pellicola, rullino; (of powder, liquid) sottile strato ▷ vt (scene) filmare ▷ vi girare; **film star** n divo/a dello schermo

filter ['fɪltər] n filtro ▷ vt filtrare; **filter lane** n (BRIT Aut) corsia di svincolo

filth [fɪlθ] n sporcizia; **filthy** adj lordo/a, sozzo/a; (language) osceno/a

fin [fɪn] n (of fish) pinna

final ['faɪnl] adj finale, ultimo/a; definitivo/a ▷ n (Sport) finale f; **finals** npl (Scol) esami mpl finali; **finale** [fɪ'nɑ:lɪ] n finale m; **finalist** ['faɪnəlɪst] n (Sport) finalista m/f; **finalize** ['faɪnəlaɪz] vt mettere a punto; **finally** ['faɪnəlɪ] adv (lastly) alla fine; (eventually) finalmente

finance [faɪ'næns] n finanza; (capital) capitale m ▷ vt finanziare; **finances** npl (funds) finanze fpl; **financial** [faɪ'nænʃəl] adj finanziario/a; **financial year** n anno finanziario, esercizio finanziario

find [faɪnd] vt (pt, pp **found**) trovare; (lost object) ritrovare ▷ n trovata, scoperta; **to ~ sb guilty** (Law) giudicare qn colpevole; **find out**

vt (truth, secret) scoprire; (person) cogliere in fallo ▷ vi: **to ~ out about** informarsi su; (by chance) venire a sapere; **findings** npl (Law) sentenza, conclusioni fpl; (of report) conclusioni

fine [faɪn] adj bello/a; ottimo/a; (thin, subtle) fine ▷ adv (well) molto bene ▷ n (Law) multa ▷ vt (Law) multare; **to be ~** (person) stare bene; (weather) far bello; **fine arts** npl belle arti fpl

finger ['fɪŋgər] n dito ▷ vt toccare, tastare; **little/index ~** mignolo/ (dito) indice m; **fingernail** n unghia; **fingerprint** n impronta digitale; **fingertip** n punta del dito

finish ['fɪnɪʃ] n fine f; (polish etc) finitura ▷ vt, vi finire; **to ~ doing sth** finire di fare qc; **to ~ first/second** arrivare primo/secondo; **finish off** vt compiere; (kill) uccidere; **finish up** vi, vt finire

Finland ['fɪnlənd] n Finlandia; **Finn** [fɪn] n finlandese m/f; **Finnish** adj finlandese ▷ n (Ling) finlandese m

fir [fə:r] n abete m

fire [faɪər] n fuoco; (destructive) incendio; (gas fire, electric fire) stufa ▷ vt (discharge): **to ~ a gun** fare fuoco; (arrow) sparare; (fig) infiammare; (dismiss) licenziare ▷ vi sparare, far fuoco; **~!** al fuoco!; **on ~** in fiamme; **fire alarm** n allarme m d'incendio; **firearm** n arma da fuoco; **fire brigade** [-brɪ'geɪd], (US) **fire department** n (corpo dei) pompieri mpl; **fire engine** n autopompa; **fire escape** n scala di sicurezza; **fire exit** n uscita di sicurezza; **fire extinguisher** [-ɪk'stɪŋgwɪʃər] n estintore m; **fireman** n (irreg) pompiere m; **fireplace** n focolare m; **fire station** n caserma dei pompieri; **firetruck** (US) n = **fire engine**; **firewall** n (Internet) firewall m inv; **firewood** ['faɪəwʊd] n legna; **fireworks** npl fuochi mpl d'artificio

firm [fə:m] adj fermo/a ▷ n ditta, azienda; **firmly** adv fermamente

first [fəːst] adj primo/a ▷ adv (before others) il primo, la prima; (before other things) per primo; (when listing reasons etc) per prima cosa ▷ n (person: in race) primo/a; (BRIT Scol) laurea con lode; (Aut) prima; **at ~** dapprima, all'inizio; **~ of all** prima di tutto; **first aid** n pronto soccorso; **first-aid kit** n cassetta pronto soccorso; **first-class** adj di prima classe; **first-hand** adj di prima mano; **first lady** n (US) moglie f del presidente; **firstly** adv in primo luogo; **first name** n prenome m; **first-rate** adj di prima qualità, ottimo/a

fiscal ['fɪskəl] adj fiscale; **~ year** anno fiscale

fish [fɪʃ] n pesce m ▷ vt (river, area) pescare in ▷ vi pescare; **to go ~ing** andare a pesca; **fish-and-chip shop** [fɪʃən'tʃɪp-] n ≈ friggitoria; see **chip shop**; **fisherman** n (irreg) pescatore m; **fish fingers** npl (BRIT) bastoncini mpl di pesce (surgelati); **fishing** n pesca; **fishing boat** n barca da pesca; **fishing line** n lenza; **fishmonger** n pescivendolo; **fishmonger's (shop)** pescheria; **fish sticks** npl (US) = **fish fingers**; **fishy** ['fɪʃɪ] adj (tale, story) sospetto/a

fist [fɪst] n pugno

fit [fɪt] adj (Med, Sport) in forma; (proper) adatto/a, appropriato/a; conveniente ▷ vt (clothes) stare bene a; (put in, attach) mettere; installare; (equip) fornire, equipaggiare ▷ vi (clothes) stare bene; (parts) andare bene, adattarsi; (in space, gap) entrare ▷ n (Med) accesso, attacco; **~ to** in grado di; **~ for** adatto(a) a; degno(a) di; **this dress is a tight/ good ~** questo vestito è stretto/ sta bene; **~ of anger/enthusiasm** accesso d'ira/d'entusiasmo; **fit in** vi accordarsi; adattarsi; **fitness** n (Med) forma fisica; **fitted** adj: **fitted carpet** moquette f inv; **fitted cupboards** armadi mpl

a muro; **fitted kitchen** (BRIT) cucina componibile; **fitting** adj appropriato/a ▷ n (of dress) prova; (of piece of equipment) montaggio, aggiustaggio; **fitting room** n (in shop) camerino; **fittings** ['fɪtɪŋz] npl (in building) impianti mpl

five [faɪv] num cinque; **fiver** n (col: BRIT) biglietto da cinque sterline; (: US) biglietto da cinque dollari

fix [fɪks] vt fissare; (mend) riparare; (meal, drink) preparare ▷ n: **to be in a ~** essere nei guai; **fix up** vt (date, meeting) fissare; **to ~ sb up with sth** procurare qc a qn; **fixed** [fɪkst] adj (prices etc) fisso/a; **fixture** ['fɪkstʃər] n impianto (fisso); (Sport) incontro (del calendario sportivo)

fizzy ['fɪzɪ] adj frizzante; gassato/a

flag [flæg] n bandiera; (also: **~stone**) pietra da lastricare ▷ vi stancarsi; affievolirsi; **flagpole** ['flægpəʊl] n albero

flair [flɛər] n (for business etc) fiuto; (for languages etc) facilità; (style) stile m

flak [flæk] n (Mil) fuoco d'artiglieria; (col: criticism) critiche fpl

flake [fleɪk] n (of rust, paint) scaglia; (of snow, soap powder) fiocco ▷ vi (also: **~ off**) sfaldarsi

flamboyant [flæm'bɔɪənt] adj sgargiante

flame [fleɪm] n fiamma

flamingo [flə'mɪŋɡəʊ] n fenicottero, fiammingo

flammable ['flæməbl] adj infiammabile

flan [flæn] n (BRIT) flan m inv

flank [flæŋk] n fianco ▷ vt fiancheggiare

flannel ['flænl] n (BRIT: also: **face ~**) guanto di spugna; (fabric) flanella

flap [flæp] n (of pocket) patta; (of envelope) lembo ▷ vt (wings) battere ▷ vi (sail, flag) sbattere; (col: also: **be in a ~**) essere in agitazione

flare [flɛər] n razzo; (in skirt etc) svasatura; **flares** (trousers) pantaloni *mpl* a zampa d'elefante; **flare up** *vi* andare in fiamme; (*fig: person*) infiammarsi di rabbia; (: *revolt*) scoppiare

flash [flæʃ] *n* vampata; (*also:* **news ~**) notizia *f* lampo *inv*; (*Phot*) flash *m inv* ▷ *vt* accendere e spegnere; (*send: message*) trasmettere; (: *look, smile*) lanciare ▷ *vi* brillare; (*light on ambulance, eyes etc*) lampeggiare; **in a ~** in un lampo; **to ~ one's headlights** lampeggiare; **he ~ed by** *or* **past** ci passò davanti come un lampo; **flashback** *n* flashback *m inv*; **flashbulb** *n* cubo *m* flash *inv*; **flashlight** *n* lampadina tascabile

flask [flɑ:sk] *n* fiasco; (*also:* **vacuum ~**) thermos® *m inv*

flat [flæt] *adj* piatto/a; (*tyre*) sgonfio/a, a terra; (*battery*) scarico/a; (*beer*) svampito/a; (*denial*) netto/a; (*Mus*) bemolle *inv*; (: *voice*) stonato/a ▷ *n* (*BRIT: rooms*) appartamento; (*Mus*) bemolle *m*; (*Aut*) pneumatico sgonfio ▷ *adv*: **(to work) ~ out** (lavorare) a tutta; **I'm busy ~ out** non posso; **~ rate of pay** tariffa unica di pagamento; **flatten** *vt* (*also:* **flatten out**) appiattire; (*house, city*) abbattere

flatter ['flætə'] *vt* lusingare; **flattering** *adj* lusinghiero/a; (*clothes etc*) che dona

flaunt [flɔ:nt] *vt* fare mostra di

flavour, (*US*) **flavor** ['fleɪvə'] *n* gusto ▷ *vt* insaporire, aggiungere sapore a; **what ~s do you have?** che gusti avete?; **vanilla-~ed** al gusto di vaniglia; **flavouring** *n* essenza (artificiale)

flaw [flɔ:] *n* difetto; **flawless** *adj* senza difetti

flea [fli:] *n* pulce *f*; **flea market** *n* mercato delle pulci

flee (*pt, pp* **fled**) [fli:, flɛd] *vt* fuggire da ▷ *vi* fuggire, scappare

fleece [fli:s] *n* vello ▷ *vt* (*col*) pelare

fleet [fli:t] *n* flotta; (*of lorries etc*) convoglio; (*of cars*) parco

fleeting ['fli:tɪŋ] *adj* fugace, fuggitivo/a; (*visit*) volante

Flemish ['flɛmɪʃ] *adj* fiammingo/a

flesh [flɛʃ] *n* carne *f*; (*of fruit*) polpa

flew [flu:] *pt* of **fly**

flex [flɛks] *n* filo (flessibile) ▷ *vt* flettere; (*muscles*) contrarre; **flexibility** *n* flessibilità; **flexible** *adj* flessibile; **flexitime** ['flɛksɪtaɪm] *n* orario flessibile

flick [flɪk] *n* colpetto; scarto ▷ *vt* dare un colpetto a; **flick through** *vt fus* sfogliare

flicker ['flɪkə'] *vi* tremolare

flies [flaɪz] *npl* of **fly**

flight [flaɪt] *n* volo; (*escape*) fuga; (*also:* **~ of steps**) scalinata; **flight attendant** *n* (*US*) steward *m*, hostess *f inv*

flimsy ['flɪmzɪ] *adj* (*fabric*) leggero/a; (*building*) poco solido/a; (*excuse*) debole

flinch [flɪntʃ] *vi* ritirarsi; **to ~ from** tirarsi indietro di fronte a

fling (*pt, pp* **flung**) [flɪŋ, flʌŋ] *vt* lanciare, gettare

flint [flɪnt] *n* selce *f*; (*in lighter*) pietrina

flip [flɪp] *vt* (*switch*) far scattare; (*coin*) lanciare in aria

flip-flops ['flɪpflɔps] *npl* (*esp BRIT: sandals*) infradito *mpl*

flipper ['flɪpə'] *n* pinna

flirt [flə:t] *vi* flirtare ▷ *n* civetta

float [fləʊt] *n* galleggiante *m*; (*in procession*) carro; (*sum of money*) somma ▷ *vi* galleggiare

flock [flɔk] *n* (*of sheep, Rel*) gregge *m*; (*of birds*) stormo ▷ *vi*: **to ~ to** accorrere in massa a

flood [flʌd] *n* alluvione *f*; (*of letters etc*) marea ▷ *vt* allagare; (*fig*) invadere ▷ *vi* (*place*) allagarsi; (*people*): **to ~ into** riversarsi in; **flooding** *n* inondazione *f*; **floodlight** *n* riflettore *m* ▷ *vt* illuminare a giorno

floor [flɔ:'] *n* pavimento; (*storey*) piano; (*of sea, valley*) fondo ▷ *vt* (*knock down*) atterrare; (*silence*) far tacere; **on the ~** sul pavimento, per terra; **ground ~**, (US) **first ~** pianterreno; **first ~**, (US) **second ~** primo piano; **floorboard** n tavellone m di legno; **flooring** n (*floor*) pavimento; (*material*) materiale m per pavimentazioni; **floor show** n spettacolo di varietà

flop [flɔp] n fiasco ▷ vi far fiasco; (*fall*) lasciarsi cadere; **floppy** ['flɔpi] adj floscio/a, molle

flora ['flɔːrə] n flora

floral ['flɔːrl] adj floreale

Florence ['flɔrəns] n Firenze f

Florentine ['flɔrəntaɪn] adj fiorentino/a

florist ['flɔrɪst] n fioraio/a; **florist's (shop)** n fioraio/a

flotation [fləu'teɪʃən] n (Comm) lancio

flour ['flauər] n farina

flourish ['flʌrɪʃ] vi fiorire ▷ n (*bold gesture*): **with a ~** con ostentazione

flow [fləu] n flusso; circolazione f ▷ vi fluire; (*traffic, blood in veins*) circolare; (*hair*) scendere

flower ['flauər] n fiore m ▷ vi fiorire; **flower bed** n aiuola; **flowerpot** n vaso da fiori

flown [fləun] pp of **fly**

fl. oz. abbr = **fluid ounce**

flu [fluː] n influenza

fluctuate ['flʌktjueɪt] vi fluttuare, oscillare

fluent ['fluːənt] adj (*speech*) facile, sciolto/a; corrente; **he speaks ~ Italian, he's ~ in Italian** parla l'italiano correntemente

fluff [flʌf] n lanugine f; **fluffy** adj lanuginoso/a; (*toy*) di peluche

fluid ['fluːɪd] adj fluido/a ▷ n fluido; **fluid ounce** n (BRIT) = 0.028 l; 0.05 pints

fluke [fluːk] n (col) colpo di fortuna

flung [flʌŋ] pt, pp of **fling**

fluorescent [fluə'rɛsnt] adj fluorescente

fluoride ['fluəraɪd] n fluoruro

flurry ['flʌrɪ] n (*of snow*) tempesta; **a ~ of activity/excitement** un'intensa attività/un'improvvisa agitazione

flush [flʌʃ] n rossore m; (*fig: of youth, beauty etc*) rigoglio, pieno vigore ▷ vt ripulire con un getto d'acqua ▷ vi arrossire ▷ adj: **~ with** a livello di, pari a; **to ~ the toilet** tirare l'acqua

flute [fluːt] n flauto

flutter ['flʌtər] n agitazione f; (*of wings*) battito ▷ vi (*bird*) battere le ali

fly (pt **flew**, pp **flown**) [flaɪ, fluː, fləun] n (*insect*) mosca; (*on trousers: also:* **flies**) patta ▷ vt pilotare; (*passengers, cargo*) trasportare (in aereo); (*distances*) percorrere ▷ vi volare; (*passengers*) andare in aereo; (*escape*) fuggire; (*flag*) sventolare; **fly away** vi volar via; **fly-drive** n: **fly-drive holiday** fly and drive inv; **flying** n (*activity*) aviazione f; (*action*) volo ▷ adj: **flying visit** visita volante; **with flying colours** con risultati brillanti; **flying saucer** n disco volante; **flyover** n (BRIT: *bridge*) cavalcavia m inv

FM abbr = **frequency modulation**

foal [fəul] n puledro

foam [fəum] n schiuma; (*also:* **~ rubber**) gommapiuma® ▷ vi schiumare; (*soapy water*) fare la schiuma

focus ['fəukəs] n (pl **focuses**) fuoco; (*of interest*) centro ▷ vt (*field glasses etc*) mettere a fuoco ▷ vi: **to ~ on** (*with camera*) mettere a fuoco; (*person*) fissare lo sguardo su; **in ~** a fuoco; **out of ~** sfocato/a

foetus, (US) **fetus** ['fiːtəs] n feto

fog [fɔg] n nebbia; **foggy** adj: **it's foggy** c'è nebbia; **fog lamp**, (US) **fog light** n (Aut) faro m antinebbia inv

foil [fɔɪl] vt confondere, frustrare ▷ n lamina di metallo; (*also:* **kitchen ~**) foglio di alluminio; (*Fencing*) fioretto; **to act as a ~ to** (*fig*) far risaltare

fold [fəʊld] n (bend, crease) piega; (Agr) ovile m; (fig) gregge m ▷ vt piegare; **to ~ one's arms** incrociare le braccia; **fold up** vi (map etc) piegarsi; (business) crollare ▷ vt (map etc) piegare, ripiegare; **folder** n (for papers) cartella; cartellina; **folding** adj (chair, bed) pieghevole

foliage [ˈfəʊlɪɪdʒ] n fogliame m

folk [fəʊk] npl gente f ▷ cpd popolare; **folks** npl: **my ~s** i miei; **folklore** [ˈfəʊklɔːʳ] n folclore m; **folk music** n musica folk inv; **folksong** n canto popolare

follow [ˈfɒləʊ] vt seguire ▷ vi seguire; (result) conseguire, risultare; **he ~ed suit** lui ha fatto lo stesso; **follow up** vt (letter, offer) fare seguito a; (case) seguire; **follower** n seguace m/f; **following** adj seguente ▷ n seguito, discepoli mpl; **follow-up** n seguito

fond [fɒnd] adj (memory, look) tenero/a, affettuoso/a; **to be ~ of** volere bene a; **she's ~ of swimming** le piace nuotare

food [fuːd] n cibo; **food mixer** n frullatore m; **food poisoning** n intossicazione f alimentare; **food processor** [-ˈprəʊsesə] n tritatutto m inv elettrico; **food stamp** n (US) buono alimentare dato agli indigenti

fool [fuːl] n sciocco/a; (Culin) frullato ▷ vt ingannare ▷ vi (gen): **~ around** fare lo sciocco; **fool about, fool around** vi (waste time) perdere tempo; **foolish** adj scemo/a, stupido/a; imprudente; **foolproof** adj (plan etc) sicurissimo/a

foot [fʊt] n (pl **feet** [fiːt]) piede m; (measure) piede (=304 mm; =12 inches); (of animal) zampa ▷ vt (bill) pagare; **on ~** a piedi; **footage** n (Cine: length) ≈ metraggio; (: material) sequenza; **foot and mouth (disease)** n afta epizootica; **football** n pallone m; (sport: BRIT) calcio; (: US) football m americano; **footballer** n (BRIT) = **football player**; **football match** n

(BRIT) partita di calcio; **football player** n (BRIT: also: **footballer**) calciatore m; (US) giocatore m di football americano; **footbridge** n passerella; **foothills** npl contrafforti fpl; **foothold** n punto d'appoggio; **footing** n (fig) posizione f; **to lose one's footing** mettere un piede in fallo; **footnote** n nota (a piè di pagina); **footpath** n sentiero; (in street) marciapiede m; **footprint** n orma, impronta; **footstep** n passo; **footwear** n calzatura

KEYWORD

for [fɔːʳ] prep **1** (indicating destination, intention, purpose) per; **the train for London** il treno per Londra; **he went for the paper** è andato a prendere il giornale; **it's time for lunch** è ora di pranzo; **what's it for?** a che serve?; **what for?** (why) perché?

2 (on behalf of, representing) per; **to work for sb/sth** lavorare per qn/qc; **I'll ask him for you** glielo chiederò a nome tuo; **G for George** ≈ G come George

3 (because of) per, a causa di; **for this reason** per questo motivo

4 (with regard to) per; **it's cold for July** è freddo per luglio; **for everyone who voted yes, 50 voted no** per ogni voto a favore ce n'erano 50 contro

5 (in exchange for) per; **I sold it for £5** l'ho venduto per 5 sterline

6 (in favour of) per, a favore di; **are you for or against us?** sei con noi o contro di noi?; **I'm all for it** sono completamente a favore

7 (referring to distance, time) per; **there are roadworks for 5 km** ci sono lavori in corso per 5 km; **he was away for 2 years** è stato via per 2 anni; **she will be away for a month** starà via un mese; **it hasn't rained for 3 weeks** non piove da

3 settimane; **can you do it for tomorrow?** può farlo per domani? **8** (*with infinitive clauses*): **it is not for me to decide** non sta a me decidere; **it would be best for you to leave** sarebbe meglio che lei se ne andasse; **there is still time for you to do it** ha ancora tempo per farlo; **for this to be possible ...** perché ciò sia possibile ...
9 (*in spite of*) nonostante; **for all his complaints, he's very fond of her** nonostante tutte le sue lamentele, le vuole molto bene
▶ *conj* (*since, as: formal*) dal momento che, poiché

forbid (*pt* **forbad(e)**, *pp* **forbidden**) [fə'bɪd, -'bæd, -'bɪdn] *vt* vietare, interdire; **to ~ sb to do sth** proibire a qn di fare qc; **forbidden** *pt of* **forbid** ▷ *adj* (*food*) proibito/a; (*area, territory*) vietato/a; (*word, subject*) tabù *inv*
force [fɔːs] *n* forza ▷ *vt* forzare; **forced** *adj* forzato/a; **forceful** *adj* forte, vigoroso/a
ford [fɔːd] *n* guado
fore [fɔː*ʳ*] *n*: **to come to the ~** mettersi in evidenza; **forearm** ['fɔːrɑːm] *n* avambraccio; **forecast** ['fɔːkɑːst] *n* (*irreg: like* **cast**) previsione *f* ▷ *vt* prevedere; **forecourt** ['fɔːkɔːt] *n* (*of garage*) corte *f* esterna; **forefinger** ['fɔːfɪŋɡə*ʳ*] *n* (dito) indice *m*; **forefront** ['fɔːfrʌnt] *n*: **in the forefront of** all'avanguardia di; **foreground** ['fɔːɡraʊnd] *n* primo piano; **forehead** ['fɔrɪd] *n* fronte *f*
foreign ['fɔrən] *adj* straniero/a; (*trade*) estero/a; (*object, matter*) estraneo/a; **foreign currency** *n* valuta estera; **foreigner** *n* straniero/a; **foreign exchange** *n* cambio di valuta; (*currency*) valuta estera; **Foreign Office** *n* (BRIT) Ministero degli Esteri; **foreign**

secretary *n* (BRIT) ministro degli Affari esteri
fore: foreman ['fɔːmən] *n* (*irreg*) caposquadra *m*; **foremost** ['fɔːməust] *adj* principale; più in vista ▷ *adv*: **first and foremost** innanzitutto; **forename** *n* nome *m* di battesimo
forensic [fə'rɛnsɪk] *adj*: **~ medicine** medicina legale
foresee [fɔː'siː] *vt* (*irreg: like* **see**) prevedere; **foreseeable** *adj* prevedibile
forest ['fɔrɪst] *n* foresta; **forestry** ['fɔrɪstrɪ] *n* silvicoltura
forever [fə'rɛvə*ʳ*] *adv* per sempre; (*endlessly*) sempre, di continuo
foreword ['fɔːwəːd] *n* prefazione *f*
forfeit ['fɔːfɪt] *vt* perdere; (*one's happiness, health*) giocarsi
forgave [fə'ɡeɪv] *pt of* **forgive**
forge [fɔːdʒ] *n* fucina ▷ *vt* (*signature*) contraffare, falsificare; (*wrought iron*) fucinare, foggiare; **forger** *n* contraffattore *m*; **forgery** *n* falso; (*activity*) contraffazione *f*
forget (*pt* **forgot**, *pp* **forgotten**) [fə'ɡɛt, -'ɡɔt, -'ɡɔtn] *vt*, *vi* dimenticare; **forgetful** *adj* di corta memoria; **forgetful of** dimentico(a) di
forgive (*pt* **forgave**, *pp* **forgiven**) [fə'ɡɪv, -'ɡeɪv, -'ɡɪvn] *vt* perdonare; **to ~ sb for sth/for doing sth** perdonare qc a qn/a qn di aver fatto qc
forgot [fə'ɡɔt] *pt of* **forget**
forgotten [fə'ɡɔtn] *pp of* **forget**
fork [fɔːk] *n* (*for eating*) forchetta; (*for gardening*) forca; (*of roads, railways*) bivio, biforcazione *f* ▷ *vi* (*road*) biforcarsi
forlorn [fə'lɔːn] *adj* (*person*) sconsolato/a; (*cottage*) abbandonato/a; (*attempt*) disperato/a; (*hope*) vano/a
form [fɔːm] *n* forma; (*Scol*) classe *f*; (*questionnaire*) modulo ▷ *vt* formare; **in top ~** in gran forma

formal ['fɔ:məl] adj formale;
(gardens) simmetrico/a, regolare;
formality [fɔ:'mælɪti] n formalità
f inv

format ['fɔ:mæt] n formato ▷ vt
(Comput) formattare

formation [fɔ:'meɪʃən] n
formazione f

former ['fɔ:məʳ] adj vecchio/a (before
n), ex inv (before n); **the ~ ... the
latter** quello ... questo; **formerly** adv
in passato

formidable ['fɔ:mɪdəbl] adj
formidabile

formula ['fɔ:mjulə] n formula

fort [fɔ:t] n forte m

forthcoming [fɔ:θ'kʌmɪŋ]
adj (event) prossimo/a; (help)
disponibile; (character) aperto/a,
comunicativo/a

fortieth ['fɔ:tɪɪθ] num
quarantesimo/a

fortify ['fɔ:tɪfaɪ] vt (city) fortificare;
(person) armare

fortnight ['fɔ:tnaɪt] n (BRIT) quindici
giorni mpl, due settimane fpl;
fortnightly adj bimensile ▷ adv ogni
quindici giorni

fortress ['fɔ:trɪs] n fortezza, rocca

fortunate ['fɔ:tʃənɪt] adj
fortunato/a; **it is ~ that** è una
fortuna che + sub; **fortunately** adv
fortunatamente

fortune ['fɔ:tʃən] n fortuna; **fortune-
teller** ['fɔ:tʃənteləʳ] n indovino/a

forty ['fɔ:tɪ] num quaranta

forum ['fɔ:rəm] n foro

forward ['fɔ:wəd] adj (ahead of
schedule) in anticipo; (movement,
position) in avanti; (not shy)
sfacciato/a ▷ n (Sport) avanti m inv
▷ vt (letter) inoltrare; (parcel, goods)
spedire; (career, plans) promuovere,
appoggiare; **to move ~** avanzare;
forwarding address n nuovo recapito
cui spedire la posta; **forwards** adv
avanti; **forward slash** n barra
obliqua

fossick ['fɔsɪk] vi (AUST, NZ col)
cercare; **to ~ in a drawer** rovistare
in un cassetto

fossil ['fɔsl] adj, n fossile (m)

foster ['fɔstəʳ] vt incoraggiare,
nutrire; (child) avere in affidamento;
foster child n bambino/a preso/a
in affidamento; **foster mother** n
madre f affidataria

fought [fɔ:t] pt, pp of **fight**

foul [faul] adj (smell, food) cattivo/a;
(weather) brutto/a; (language)
osceno/a ▷ n (Football) fallo ▷ vt
sporcare; **foul play is
not suspected** si è scartata l'ipotesi
dell'atto criminale

found [faund] pt, pp of **find** ▷ vt
(establish) fondare; **foundation**
[faun'deɪʃən] n (act) fondazione
f; (base) base f; (also: **foundation
cream**) fondo tinta; **foundations** npl
(of building) fondamenta fpl

founder ['faundəʳ] n fondatore/trice
▷ vi affondare

fountain ['fauntɪn] n fontana;
fountain pen n penna stilografica

four [fɔ:ʳ] num quattro; **on all ~s**
a carponi; **four-letter word** n
parolaccia; **four-poster** n (also:
four-poster bed) letto a quattro
colonne; **fourteen** num quattordici;
fourteenth num quattordicesimo/a;
fourth num quarto/a; **four-wheel
drive** ['fɔ:wi:l-] n (Aut): **with
four-wheel drive** con quattro ruote
motrici

fowl [faul] n pollame m; volatile m

fox [fɔks] n volpe f ▷ vt confondere

foyer ['fɔɪeɪ] n atrio; (Theat) ridotto

fraction ['frækʃən] n frazione f

fracture ['fræktʃəʳ] n frattura

fragile ['frædʒaɪl] adj fragile

fragment ['frægmənt] n frammento

fragrance ['freɪgrəns] n fragranza,
profumo

frail [freɪl] adj debole, delicato/a

frame [freɪm] n (of building)
armatura; (of human, animal)

ossatura, corpo; (of picture) cornice f; (of door, window) telaio; (of spectacles: also: **~s**) montatura ▷ vt (picture) incorniciare; **framework** n struttura
France [frɑːns] n Francia
franchise ['fræntʃaɪz] n (Pol) diritto di voto; (Comm) concessione f
frank [fræŋk] adj franco/a, aperto/a ▷ vt (letter) affrancare; **frankly** adv francamente, sinceramente
frantic ['fræntɪk] adj frenetico/a
fraud [frɔːd] n truffa; (Law) frode f; (person) impostore/a
fraught [frɔːt] adj: **~ with** pieno(a) di, intriso(a) da
fray [freɪ] vt logorare ▷ vi logorarsi
freak [friːk] n fenomeno, mostro
freckle ['frɛkl] n lentiggine f
free [friː] adj libero/a; (gratis) gratuito/a ▷ vt (prisoner, jammed person) liberare; (jammed object) districare; **~ (of charge)** gratuitamente; **freedom** ['friːdəm] n libertà; **Freefone®** n ≈ numero verde; **free gift** n regalo, omaggio; **free kick** n calcio libero; **freelance** adj indipendente; **freely** adv liberamente; (liberally) liberamente; **Freepost®** n affrancatura a carica del destinatario; **free-range** adj (hen) ruspante; (eggs) di gallina ruspante; **freeway** n (US) superstrada; **free will** n libero arbitrio; **of one's own free will** di spontanea volontà
freeze (pt **froze**, pp **frozen**) [friːz, frəuz, 'frəuzn] vi gelare ▷ vt gelare; (food) congelare; (prices, salaries) bloccare ▷ n gelo; blocco; **freezer** n congelatore m; **freezing** ['friːzɪŋ] adj (wind, weather) gelido/a ▷ n (also: **freezing point**) punto di congelamento; **3 degrees below freezing** 3 gradi sotto zero
freight [freɪt] n (goods) merce f, merci fpl; (money charged) spese fpl di trasporto; **freight train** n (US) treno m merci inv

French [frɛntʃ] adj francese ▷ n (Ling) francese m; **the French** npl i Francesi; **French bean** n fagiolino; **French bread** n baguette f inv; **French dressing** n (Culin) condimento per insalata; **French fried potatoes**, (US) **French fries** npl patate fpl fritte; **Frenchman** n (irreg) francese m; **French stick** n baguette f inv; **French window** n portafinestra; **Frenchwoman** n (irreg) francese f
frenzy ['frɛnzɪ] n frenesia
frequency ['friːkwənsɪ] n frequenza
frequent adj ['friːkwənt] frequente ▷ vt [frɪ'kwɛnt] frequentare; **frequently** adv frequentemente, spesso
fresh [frɛʃ] adj fresco/a; (new) nuovo/a; (cheeky) sfacciato/a; **freshen** vi (wind, air) rinfrescare; **freshen up** vi rinfrescarsi; **fresher** n (BRIT Scol: col) = **freshman**; **freshly** adv di recente, di fresco; **freshman** n (irreg) (Scol) matricola; **freshwater** adj (fish) d'acqua dolce
fret [frɛt] vi agitarsi, affliggersi
Fri. abbr (= Friday) ven.
friction ['frɪkʃən] n frizione f, attrito
Friday ['fraɪdɪ] n venerdì m inv
fridge [frɪdʒ] n (BRIT) frigo, frigorifero
fried [fraɪd] pt, pp of **fry** ▷ adj fritto/a
friend [frɛnd] n amico/a ▷ vt (Internet) aggiungere tra gli amici; **friendly** adj amichevole; **friendship** n amicizia
fries [fraɪz] npl (esp US) patate fpl fritte
frigate ['frɪgɪt] n (Naut: modern) fregata
fright [fraɪt] n paura, spavento; **to take ~** spaventarsi; **frighten** vt spaventare, far paura a; **frightened** adj spaventato/a; **frightening** adj spaventoso/a, pauroso/a; **frightful** adj orribile
frill [frɪl] n balza
fringe [frɪndʒ] n (BRIT: of hair) frangia; (edge: of forest etc) margine m

Frisbee® ['frɪzbɪ] n frisbee® m inv
fritter ['frɪtə'] n frittella
frivolous ['frɪvələs] adj frivolo/a
fro [frəʊ] adv: **to and ~** avanti e
indietro
frock [frɔk] n vestito
frog [frɔg] n rana; **frogman**
['frɔgmən] n (irreg) uomo m rana inv

KEYWORD

from [frɔm] prep 1 (indicating starting
place, origin etc) da; **where do you
come from?, where are you from?**
da dove viene?, di dov'è?; **from
London to Glasgow** da Londra a
Glasgow; **a letter from my sister**
una lettera da mia sorella; **tell him
from me that ...** gli dica da parte
mia che ...
2 (indicating time) da; **from one
o'clock to** or **until** or **till two** dall'una
alle due; **from January (on)** da
gennaio, a partire da gennaio
3 (indicating distance) da; **the hotel is
1 km from the beach** l'albergo è a 1
km dalla spiaggia
4 (indicating price, number etc) da;
prices range from £10 to £50 i
prezzi vanno dalle 10 alle 50 sterline
5 (indicating difference) da; **he
can't tell red from green** non sa
distinguere il rosso dal verde
6 (because of, on the basis of): **from
what he says** da quanto dice lui;
weak from hunger debole per
la fame

front [frʌnt] n (of house, dress)
davanti m inv; (of train) testa; (of book)
copertina; (promenade: also: **sea ~**)
lungomare m; (Mil, Pol, Meteor) fronte
m; (fig: appearances) fronte f ▷ adj
primo/a; anteriore, davanti inv; **in ~
(of)** davanti (a); **front door** n porta
d'entrata; (of car) sportello anteriore;
frontier ['frʌntɪə'] n frontiera; **front
page** n prima pagina; **front-wheel**

drive ['frʌntwiːl-] n trasmissione
f anteriore
frost [frɔst] n gelo; (also: **hoar~**)
brina; **frostbite** n congelamento;
frosting n (us: on cake) glassa; **frosty**
adj (weather, look, welcome) gelido/a
froth ['frɔθ] n spuma; schiuma
frown [fraun] vi accigliarsi
froze [frəʊz] pt of **freeze**
frozen ['frəʊzn] pp of **freeze**
fruit [fruːt] n (pl inv) frutto;
(collectively) frutta; **fruit juice** n
succo di frutta; **fruit machine** n
(brit) macchina f mangiasoldi inv;
fruit salad n macedonia
frustrate [frʌs'treɪt] vt frustrare;
frustrated adj frustrato/a
fry (pt, pp **fried**) [fraɪ, -d] vt friggere
▷ npl: **the small ~** i pesci piccoli;
frying pan n padella
ft. abbr = **foot; feet**
fudge [fʌdʒ] n (Culin) specie di
caramella a base di latte, burro e
zucchero
fuel [fjuəl] n (for heating) combustibile
m; (for propelling) carburante m; **fuel
poverty** n povertà energetica; **fuel
tank** n deposito m nafta inv; (on
vehicle) serbatoio (della benzina)
fulfil [ful'fɪl] vt (function) compiere;
(order) eseguire; (wish, desire)
soddisfare, appagare
full [ful] adj pieno/a; (details, skirt)
ampio/a ▷ adv: **to know ~ well that**
sapere benissimo che; **I'm ~ (up)**
sono sazio; **a ~ two hours** due ore
intere; **at ~ speed** a tutta velocità; **in
~** per intero; **full-length** adj (portrait)
in piedi; (film) a lungometraggio;
(coat, novel) lungo/a; **full moon** n
luna piena; **full-scale** adj (plan, model)
in grandezza naturale; (attack, search,
retreat) su vasta scala; **full stop** n
punto; **full-time** adj, adv (work) a
tempo pieno; **fully** adv interamente,
pienamente, completamente
fumble ['fʌmbl] vi brancolare;
fumble with vt fus trafficare con

fume [fjuːm] vi essere furioso/a; **fumes** npl esalazioni fpl, vapori mpl

fun [fʌn] n divertimento, spasso; **to have ~** divertirsi; **for ~** per scherzo; **to make ~ of** prendersi gioco di

function ['fʌŋkʃən] n funzione f; cerimonia, ricevimento ▷ vi funzionare

fund [fʌnd] n fondo, cassa; (source) fondo, (store) riserva; **funds** npl (money) fondi mpl

fundamental [fʌndə'mɛntl] adj fondamentale

funeral ['fjuːnərəl] n funerale m; **funeral director** n impresario di pompe funebri; **funeral parlour** [-'pɑːlər] n impresa di pompe funebri

fun fair ['fʌnfɛər] n luna park m inv

fungus (pl **fungi**) ['fʌŋgəs, -gaɪ] n fungo; (mould) muffa

funnel ['fʌnl] n imbuto; (of ship) ciminiera

funny ['fʌnɪ] adj divertente, buffo/a; (strange) strano/a, bizzarro/a

fur [fəːʳ] n pelo; pelliccia; (BRIT: in kettle etc) deposito calcare; **fur coat** n pelliccia

furious ['fjuərɪəs] adj furioso/a; (effort) accanito/a

furnish ['fəːnɪʃ] vt ammobiliare; (supply) fornire; **furnishings** npl mobili mpl, mobilia

furniture ['fəːnɪtʃər] n mobili mpl; **piece of ~** mobile m

furry ['fəːrɪ] adj (animal) peloso/a

further ['fəːðər] adj supplementare, altro/a; nuovo/a; più lontano/a ▷ adv più lontano; (more) di più; (moreover) inoltre ▷ vt favorire, promuovere; **further education** n ≈ corsi mpl di formazione; **college of further education** istituto statale con corsi specializzati (di formazione professionale, aggiornamento professionale ecc); **furthermore** [fəːðə'mɔːr] adv inoltre, per di più

furthest ['fəːðɪst] adv superlative of **far**

fury ['fjuərɪ] n furore m

fuse, (US) **fuze** [fjuːz] n fusibile m; (for bomb etc) miccia, spoletta ▷ vt fondere; (Elec): **to ~ the lights** far saltare i fusibili ▷ vi fondersi; **fuse box** n cassetta dei fusibili

fusion ['fjuːʒən] n fusione f

fuss [fʌs] n agitazione f; (complaining) storie fpl; **to make a ~** fare delle storie; **fussy** adj (person) puntiglioso/a, esigente; che fa le storie; (dress) carico/a di fronzoli; (style) elaborato/a

future ['fjuːtʃər] adj futuro/a ▷ n futuro, avvenire m; (Ling) futuro; **futures** npl (Comm) operazioni fpl a termine; **in ~** in futuro

fuze [fjuːz] n, vt, vi (US) = **fuse**

fuzzy ['fʌzɪ] adj (Phot) indistinto/a, sfocato/a; (hair) crespo/a

g

G [dʒiː] n (Mus) sol m

g abbr (= gram, gravity) g

G8 n abbr (Pol: = Group of Eight) G8 m

G20 n abbr (Pol: = Group of Twenty) G20 m

gadget ['gædʒɪt] n aggeggio

Gaelic ['geɪlɪk] adj gaelico/a ▷ n (language) gaelico

gag [gæg] n bavaglio; (joke) facezia, scherzo ▷ vt imbavagliare

gain [geɪn] n guadagno, profitto ▷ vt guadagnare ▷ vi (watch) andare avanti; (benefit): **to ~ (from)** trarre beneficio (da); **to ~ 3lbs (in weight)** aumentare di 3 libbre; **gain (up)on** vt fus guadagnare terreno su

gal. abbr = **gallon**

gala ['gɑːlə] n gala; **swimming ~** manifestazione f di nuoto

galaxy ['gæləksɪ] n galàssia

gale [geɪl] n vento forte; burrasca

gall bladder ['gɔːl-] n cistifellea

gallery ['gælərɪ] n galleria

gallon ['gælən] n gallone m (Brit = 4.543 l; 8 pints; US = 3.785 l)

gallop ['gæləp] n galoppo ▷ vi galoppare

gallstone ['gɔːlstəun] n calcolo biliare

gamble ['gæmbl] n azzardo, rischio calcolato ▷ vt, vi giocare; **to ~ on** (fig) giocare su; **gambler** n giocatore/trice d'azzardo; **gambling** ['gæmblɪŋ] n gioco d'azzardo

game [geɪm] n gioco; (event) partita; (Tennis) game m inv; (Hunting, Culin) selvaggina ▷ adj (ready): **to be ~ (for sth/to do)** essere pronto/a (a qc/a fare); **games** npl (Scol) attività fpl sportive; **big ~** selvaggina grossa; **gamer** ['geɪmə'] n chi gioca con i videogame; **games console** n console f inv dei videogame; **gameshow** ['geɪmʃəu] n gioco a premi; **gaming** ['geɪmɪŋ] n (Comput) il giocare con i videogame

gammon ['gæmən] n (bacon) quarto di maiale; (ham) prosciutto affumicato

gang [gæŋ] n banda, squadra ▷ vi: **to ~ up on sb** far combutta contro qn

gangster ['gæŋstə'] n gangster m inv

gap [gæp] n (space) buco; (in time) intervallo; (difference): **~ (between)** divario (tra)

gape [geɪp] vi (person) restare a bocca aperta; (shirt, hole) essere spalancato/a

gap year n (Scol) anno di pausa preso prima di iniziare l'università, per lavorare o viaggiare

garage ['gærɑːʒ] n garage m inv; **garage sale** n vendita di oggetti usati nel garage di un privato

garbage ['gɑːbɪdʒ] (US) n immondizie fpl, rifiuti mpl; (col) sciocchezze fpl; **garbage can** n (US) bidone m della spazzatura; **garbage collector** n (US) spazzino/a

garden ['gɑːdn] n giardino; **gardens** npl (public) giardini pubblici;

garden centre n vivaio; **gardener** n giardiniere/a; **gardening** n giardinaggio

garlic ['gɑːlɪk] n aglio

garment ['gɑːmənt] n indumento

garnish ['gɑːnɪʃ] vt (food) guarnire

garrison ['gærɪsn] n guarnigione f ▷ vt guarnire

gas [gæs] n gas m inv; (US: gasoline) benzina ▷ vt asfissiare con il gas; **gas cooker** n (BRIT) cucina a gas; **gas cylinder** n bombola del gas; **gas fire** n (BRIT) radiatore m a gas

gasket ['gæskɪt] n (Aut) guarnizione f

gasoline ['gæsəliːn] n (US) benzina

gasp [gɑːsp] n respiro affannoso, ansito ▷ vi ansimare, boccheggiare; (in surprise) restare senza fiato

gas: gas pedal (esp US) n pedale m dell'accelleratore; **gas station** n (US) distributore m di benzina; **gas tank** n (US Aut) serbatoio (di benzina)

gate [geɪt] n cancello; (at airport) uscita

gâteau (pl **gâteaux**) ['gætəu, -z] n torta

gatecrash ['geɪtkræʃ] (BRIT) vt partecipare senza invito a

gateway ['geɪtweɪ] n porta

gather ['gæðər] vt (flowers, fruit) cogliere; (pick up) raccogliere; (assemble) radunare; raccogliere; (understand) capire; (Sewing) increspare ▷ vi (assemble) radunarsi; **to ~ speed** acquistare velocità; **gathering** n adunanza

gauge [geɪdʒ] n (instrument) indicatore m ▷ vt misurare; (fig) valutare

gave [geɪv] pt of **give**

gay [geɪ] adj (homosexual) omosessuale; (cheerful) gaio/a, allegro/a; (colour) vivace, vivo/a

gaze [geɪz] n sguardo fisso ▷ vi: **to ~ at** guardare fisso

GB abbr (= Great Britain) GB

GCSE n abbr (BRIT: = General Certificate of Secondary Education) diploma di istruzione secondaria conseguito a 16 anni in Inghilterra e Galles

gear [gɪər] n attrezzi mpl, equipaggiamento; (Tech) ingranaggio; (Aut) marcia ▷ vt (fig: adapt): **to ~ sth to** adattare qc a; **top** or **high/low/bottom ~** (US) quinta (or sesta)/seconda/prima; **in ~** in marcia; **gear up** vi: **to ~ up (to do)** prepararsi (a fare); **gear box** n scatola del cambio; **gear lever**, (US) **gear shift** n leva del cambio

geese [giːs] npl of **goose**

gel [dʒɛl] n gel m inv

gem [dʒɛm] n gemma

Gemini ['dʒɛmɪnaɪ] n Gemelli mpl

gender ['dʒɛndər] n genere m

gene [dʒiːn] n (Biol) gene m

general ['dʒɛnərl] n generale m ▷ adj generale; **in ~** in genere; **general anaesthetic**, (US) **general anesthetic** n anestesia totale; **general election** n elezioni fpl generali; **generalize** vi generalizzare; **generally** adv generalmente; **general practitioner** n medico generico; **general store** n emporio

generate ['dʒɛnəreɪt] vt generare

generation [dʒɛnə'reɪʃən] n generazione f

generator ['dʒɛnəreɪtər] n generatore m

generosity [dʒɛnə'rɔsɪtɪ] n generosità

generous ['dʒɛnərəs] adj generoso/a; (copious) abbondante

genetic [dʒɪ'nɛtɪk] adj genetico/a; **~ engineering** ingegneria genetica; **genetically modified** adj geneticamente modificato/a, transgenico/a; **genetics** [dʒɪ'nɛtɪks] n genetica

Geneva [dʒɪ'niːvə] n Ginevra

genitals ['dʒɛnɪtlz] npl genitali mpl

genius ['dʒiːnɪəs] n genio

Genoa ['dʒɛnəuə] n Genova

gent [dʒɛnt] n abbr = **gentleman**

g

gentle ['dʒɛntl] *adj* delicato/a;
(*person*) dolce

▪ Be careful not to translate *gentle*
by the Italian word *gentile*.

gentleman ['dʒɛntlmən] *n*
(*irreg*) signore *m*; (*well-bred man*)
gentiluomo

gently ['dʒɛntlɪ] *adv* delicatamente

gents [dʒɛnts] *n* W.C. *m* (per signori)

genuine ['dʒɛnjuɪn] *adj* autentico/a;
sincero/a; **genuinely** *adv*
genuinamente

geographic(al) [dʒɪə'græfɪk(l)] *adj*
geografico/a

geography [dʒɪ'ɔgrəfɪ] *n* geografia

geology [dʒɪ'ɔlədʒɪ] *n* geologia

geometry [dʒɪ'ɔmətrɪ] *n* geometria

geranium [dʒɪ'reɪnɪəm] *n* geranio

geriatric [dʒɛrɪ'ætrɪk] *adj*
geriatrico/a

germ [dʒə:m] *n* (*Med*) microbo; (*Biol,
fig*) germe *m*

German ['dʒə:mən] *adj* tedesco/a
▷ *n* tedesco/a; (*Ling*) tedesco;
German measles (BRIT) *n* rosolia

Germany ['dʒə:mənɪ] *n* Germania

gesture ['dʒɛstjə'] *n* gesto

KEYWORD

get [gɛt] (*pt, pp* **got**, (US) *pp* **gotten**) *vi*
1 (*become, be*) diventare, farsi; **to get
drunk** ubriacarsi; **to get killed** venire
or rimanere ucciso/a; **it's getting
late** si sta facendo tardi; **to get old**
invecchiare; **when do I get paid?**
quando mi pagate?; **to get tired**
stancarsi

2 (*go*): **to get to/from** andare a/da;
to get home arrivare *or* tornare a
casa; **how did you get here?** come
sei venuto?

3 (*begin*) mettersi a, cominciare a;
to get to know sb incominciare a
conoscere qn; **let's get going** *or*
started muoviamoci

4 (*modal aux vb*): **you've got to do
it** devi farlo

▶ *vt* **1**: **to get sth done** (*do*) fare qc;
(*have done*) far fare qc; **to get one's
hair cut** tagliarsi *or* farsi tagliare i
capelli; **to get sb to do sth** far fare
qc a qn

2 (*obtain*: *money, permission, results*)
ottenere; (*find*: *job, flat*) trovare; (*fetch*:
person, doctor) chiamare; (*object*)
prendere; **get me Mr Jones, please**
(*Tel*) mi passi il signor Jones, per
favore; **to get sth for sb** prendere
or procurare qc a qn; **can I get you a
drink?** le posso offrire da bere?

3 (*receive*: *present, letter, prize*) ricevere;
(*acquire*: *reputation*) farsi; **how much
did you get for the painting?**
quanto le hanno dato per il quadro?

4 (*catch*) prendere; **to get sb by
the arm/throat** afferrare qn per
un braccio/alla gola; **get him!**
prendetelo!

5 (*hit*: *target etc*) colpire

6 (*take, move*) portare; **to get sth to
sb** far avere qc a qn; **do you think
we'll get it through the door?** pensi
che riusciremo a farlo passare per
la porta?

7 (*catch, take*: *plane, bus etc*) prendere;
where do we get the ferry to …?
dove si prende il traghetto per …?

8 (*understand*) afferrare; **I've got it!** ci
sono arrivato!, ci sono!

9 (*hear*) sentire; **I'm sorry, I didn't
get your name** scusi, non ho capito
(*or* sentito) come si chiama

10 (*have, possess*): **to have got** avere;
how many have you got? quanti
ne ha?

get along *vi* (*agree*) andare d'accordo;
(*depart*) andarsene; (*manage*) = **get by**

get at *vt fus* (*attack*) prendersela con;
(*reach*) raggiungere, arrivare a

get away *vi* partire, andarsene;
(*escape*) scappare

get away with *vt fus* cavarsela;
farla franca

get back *vi* (*return*) ritornare, tornare
▷ *vt* riottenere, riavere; **when do we**

get back? quando ritorniamo?
get by vi (pass) passare; (manage) farcela
get down vi, vt fus scendere ▷ vt far scendere; (depress) buttare giù
get down to vt fus (work) mettersi a (fare)
get in vi entrare; (train) arrivare; (arrive home) tornare
get into vt fus entrare in; **to get into a rage** incavolarsi
get off vi (from train etc) scendere; (depart: person, car) andare via; (escape) cavarsela ▷ vt (remove: clothes, stain) levare ▷ vt fus (train, bus) scendere da
get on vi: **how did you get on?** com'è andata?; **to get on (with sb)** andare d'accordo (con qn) ▷ vt fus montare in; (horse) montare su
get out vi uscire; (of vehicle) scendere ▷ vt tirar fuori, far uscire
get out of vt fus uscire da; (duty etc) evitare
get over vt fus (illness) riaversi da
get round vt fus aggirare; (fig: person) rigirare
get through vi (Tel) avere la linea
get through to vt fus (Tel) parlare a
get together vi riunirsi ▷ vt raccogliere; (people) adunare
get up vi (rise) alzarsi ▷ vt fus salire su per
get up to vt fus (reach) raggiungere; (prank etc) fare

getaway ['gɛtəweɪ] n fuga
Ghana ['gɑːnə] n Ghana m
ghastly ['gɑːstlɪ] adj orribile, orrendo/a; (pale) spettrale
ghetto ['gɛtəu] n ghetto
ghost [gəust] n fantasma m, spettro
giant ['dʒaɪənt] n gigante/essa ▷ adj gigantesco/a, enorme
gift [gɪft] n regalo; (donation, ability) dono; **gifted** adj dotato/a; **gift shop**, (us) **gift store** n negozio di souvenir; **gift token, gift voucher** n buono (acquisto)

gig [gɪg] n (col: of musician) serata
gigabyte [gi:gəbaɪt] n gigabyte m inv
gigantic [dʒaɪˈgæntɪk] adj gigantesco/a
giggle ['gɪgl] vi ridere scioccamente
gills [gɪlz] npl (of fish) branchie fpl
gilt [gɪlt] n doratura ▷ adj dorato/a
gimmick ['gɪmɪk] n trucco
gin [dʒɪn] n (liquor) gin m inv
ginger ['dʒɪndʒəʳ] n zenzero
gipsy ['dʒɪpsɪ] n zingaro/a
giraffe [dʒɪˈrɑːf] n giraffa
girl [gəːl] n ragazza; (young unmarried woman) signorina; (daughter) figlia, figliola; **girlfriend** n (of girl) amica; (of boy) ragazza; **Girl Scout** n (us) Giovane Esploratrice f
gist [dʒɪst] n succo
give [gɪv] (pt **gave**, pp **given**) vt dare ▷ vi cedere; **to ~ sb sth, ~ sth to sb** dare qc a qn; **I'll ~ you £5 for it** te lo pago 5 sterline; **to ~ a cry/ sigh** emettere un grido/sospiro; **to ~ a speech** fare un discorso; **give away** vt dare via; (disclose) rivelare; (bride) condurre all'altare; **give back** vt rendere; **give in** vi cedere ▷ vt consegnare; **give out** vt distribuire; annunciare; **give up** vi rinunciare ▷ vt rinunciare a; **to ~ up smoking** smettere di fumare; **to ~ o.s. up** arrendersi
given ['gɪvn] pp of **give** ▷ adj (fixed: time, amount) dato/a, determinato/a ▷ conj: **~ (that) …** dato che …; **~ the circumstances …** date le circostanze …
glacier ['glæsɪəʳ] n ghiacciaio
glad [glæd] adj lieto/a, contento/a; **gladly** ['glædlɪ] adv volentieri
glamorous ['glæmərəs] adj affascinante, seducente
glamour, (us) **glamor** ['glæməʳ] n fascino
glance [glɑːns] n occhiata, sguardo ▷ vi: **to ~ at** dare un'occhiata a; **glance off** vt fus (bullet) rimbalzare su
gland [glænd] n ghiandola

g

glare [glɛəʳ] n (of anger) sguardo furioso; (of light) riverbero, luce f abbagliante; (of publicity) chiasso ▷ vi abbagliare; **to ~ at** guardare male; **glaring** adj (mistake) madornale

glass [glɑːs] n (substance) vetro; (tumbler) bicchiere m; **glasses** ['glɑːsɪz] npl (spectacles) occhiali mpl

glaze [gleɪz] vt (door) fornire di vetri; (pottery) smaltare ▷ n smalto

gleam [gliːm] vi luccicare

glen [glɛn] n valletta

glide [glaɪd] vi scivolare; (Aviat, birds) planare; **glider** n (Aviat) aliante m

glimmer ['glɪməʳ] n barlume m

glimpse [glɪmps] n impressione f fugace ▷ vt vedere di sfuggita

glint [glɪnt] vi luccicare

glisten ['glɪsn] vi luccicare

glitter ['glɪtəʳ] vi scintillare

global ['gləʊbl] adj globale; **globalization** [gləʊbəlaɪ'zeɪʃən] n globalizzazione f; **global warming** n riscaldamento globale

globe [gləʊb] n globo, sfera

gloom [gluːm] n oscurità, buio; (sadness) tristezza, malinconia; **gloomy** adj scuro/a, fosco/a, triste

glorious ['glɔːrɪəs] adj glorioso/a, magnifico/a

glory ['glɔːrɪ] n gloria; splendore m

gloss [glɒs] n (shine) lucentezza; (also: **~ paint**) vernice f a olio

glossary ['glɒsərɪ] n glossario

glossy ['glɒsɪ] adj lucente

glove [glʌv] n guanto; **glove compartment** n (Aut) vano portaoggetti

glow [gləʊ] vi ardere; (face) essere luminoso/a

glucose ['gluːkəʊs] n glucosio

glue [gluː] n colla ▷ vt incollare

GM adj abbr (= genetically modified) geneticamente modificato/a

gm abbr = **gram**

GM-free [dʒiːɛm'friː] adj privo/a di OGM

GMO n abbr (= genetically modified organism) OGM m inv

GMT abbr (= Greenwich Mean Time) T.M.G.

gnaw [nɔː] vt rodere

go [gəʊ] vi (pt **went**, pp **gone**) andare; (depart) partire, andarsene; (work) funzionare; (time) passare; (break etc) cedere; (be sold): **to go for £10** essere venduto per 10 sterline; (fit, suit): **to go with** andare bene con; (become): **to go pale** diventare pallido/a; **to go mouldy** ammuffire ▷ n (pl **goes**): **to have a go (at)** provare; **to be on the go** essere in moto; **whose go is it?** a chi tocca?; **he's going to do** sta per fare; **to go for a walk** andare a fare una passeggiata; **to go dancing/ shopping** andare a ballare/fare la spesa; **just then the bell went** proprio allora suonò il campanello; **how did it go?** com'è andato?; **to go round the back/by the shop** passare da dietro/davanti al negozio; **go ahead** vi andare avanti; **go away** vi partire, andarsene; **go back** vi tornare, ritornare; **go by** vi (years, time) scorrere ▷ vt fus attenersi a, seguire (alla lettera); prestar fede a; **go down** vi scendere; (ship) affondare; (sun) tramontare ▷ vt fus scendere; **go for** vt fus (fetch) andare a prendere; (like) andar matto/a per; (attack) attaccare; saltare addosso a; **go in** vi entrare; **go into** vt fus entrare in; (investigate) indagare, esaminare; (embark on) lanciarsi in; **go off** vi partire, andar via; (food) guastarsi; (explode) esplodere, scoppiare; (event) passare ▷ vt fus: **I've gone off chocolate** la cioccolata non mi piace più; **the gun went off** il fucile si scaricò; **go on** vi continuare; (happen) succedere; **to go on doing** continuare a fare; **go out** vi uscire; (fire, light) spegnersi; **they went out for 3 years** (couple) sono stati insieme per 3 anni; **go over** vi (ship) ribaltarsi ▷ vt fus (*check*) esaminare; **go past** *vi* passare ▷ *vt fus* passare davanti a; **go round** *vi* (*circulate: news, rumour*) circolare; (*revolve*) girare; (*suffice*) bastare (per tutti); **to go round (to sb's)** (*visit*) passare (da qn); **to go round (by)** (*make a detour*) passare (per); **go through** *vt fus* (*town etc*) attraversare; (*files, papers*) vagliare attentamente; (*examine: list, book*) leggere da cima a fondo; **go up** *vi* salire; **go with** *vt fus* (*accompany*) accompagnare; **go without** *vt fus* fare a meno di

go-ahead ['gəʊəhɛd] *adj* intraprendente ▷ *n*: **to give sb/sth the ~** dare il via libera a qn/qc

goal [gəʊl] *n* (*Sport*) gol *m*, rete *f*; (: *place*) porta; (*fig: aim*) fine *m*, scopo; **goalkeeper** *n* portiere *m*; **goalpost** ['gəʊlpəʊst] *n* palo (della porta)

goat [gəʊt] *n* capra

gobble ['gɔbl] *vt* (*also: ~ down, ~ up*) ingoiare

god [gɔd] *n* dio; **G~** Dio; **godchild** *n* figlioccio/a; **goddaughter** *n* figlioccia; **goddess** *n* dea; **godfather** *n* padrino; **godmother** *n* madrina; **godson** *n* figlioccio

goggles ['gɔglz] *npl* occhiali *mpl* (di protezione)

going ['gəʊɪŋ] *n* (*conditions*) andare *m*, stato del terreno ▷ *adj*: **the ~ rate** la tariffa in vigore

gold [gəʊld] *n* oro ▷ *adj* d'oro; **golden** *adj* (*made of gold*) d'oro; (*gold in colour*) dorato/a; **goldfish** *n* pesce *m* dorato o rosso; **goldmine** *n* (*also fig*) miniera d'oro; **gold-plated** *adj* placcato/a a oro *inv*

golf [gɔlf] *n* golf *m*; **golf ball** *n* (*for game*) pallina da golf; (*on typewriter*) pallina; **golf club** *n* circolo di golf; (*stick*) bastone *m* or mazza da golf; **golf course** *n* campo di golf; **golfer** *n* giocatore/trice di golf

gone [gɔn] *pp of* **go** ▷ *adj* partito/a

gong [gɔŋ] *n* gong *m inv*

good [gʊd] *adj* buono/a; (*kind*) buono/a, gentile; (*child*) bravo/a ▷ *n* bene *m*; **~!** bene!, ottimo!; **to be ~ at** essere bravo/a in; **to be ~ for** andare bene per; **it's ~ for you** fa bene; **to make ~** (*loss, damage*) compensare; **it's no ~ complaining** brontolare non serve a niente; **for ~** per sempre, definitivamente; **would you be ~ enough to …?** avrebbe la gentilezza di …?; **a ~ deal (of)** molto/a, una buona quantità (di); **a ~ many** molti/e; **~ morning!** buon giorno!; **~ afternoon/evening!** buona sera!; **~ night!** buona notte!; **goodbye** *excl* arrivederci!; **Good Friday** *n* Venerdì Santo; **good-looking** *adj* bello/a; **good-natured** *adj* affabile; **goodness** *n* (*of person*) bontà; **for goodness sake!** per amor di Dio!; **goodness gracious!** santo cielo!, mamma mia!; **goods** *npl* (*Comm etc*) merci *fpl*, articoli *mpl*; **goods train** *n* (*BRIT*) treno *m* merci *inv*; **goodwill** *n* amicizia, benevolenza

google ['guːgl] *vt, vi* cercare con Google®

goose (*pl* **geese**) [guːs, giːs] *n* oca

gooseberry ['guzbərɪ] *n* uva spina; **to play ~** (*BRIT*) tenere la candela

goose bumps ['guːsbʌmpz] *n*, **gooseflesh** ['guːsflɛʃ] *n*, **goosepimples** ['guːspɪmplz] *npl* pelle *f* d'oca

gorge [gɔːdʒ] *n* gola ▷ *vt*: **to ~ o.s. (on)** ingozzarsi (di)

gorgeous ['gɔːdʒəs] *adj* magnifico/a

gorilla [gə'rɪlə] *n* gorilla *m inv*

gosh [gɔʃ] *excl* (*col*) perdinci!

gospel ['gɔspl] *n* vangelo

gossip ['gɔsɪp] *n* chiacchiere *fpl*; pettegolezzi *mpl*; (*person*) pettegolo/a ▷ *vi* chiacchierare; **gossip column** *n* cronaca mondana

got [gɔt] *pt, pp of* **get**

gotten ['gɔtn] (*US*) *pp of* **get**

gourmet ['guəmeɪ] *n* buongustaio/a

govern ['gʌvən] vt governare;
government n governo; **governor**
['gʌvənər] n (of state, bank) governatore
m; (of school, hospital) amministratore
m; (BRIT: of prison) direttore/trice
gown [gaun] n vestito lungo; (of
teacher, judge: BRIT) toga
GP n abbr = **general practitioner**
GPS n abbr (= global positioning system)
GPS m
grab [græb] vt afferrare, arraffare;
(property, power) impadronirsi di ▷ vi:
to ~ at cercare di afferrare
grace [greɪs] n grazia ▷ vt onorare;
5 days' ~ dilazione f di 5 giorni;
graceful adj elegante, aggraziato/a;
gracious ['greɪʃəs] adj grazioso/a,
misericordioso/a
grade [greɪd] n (Comm) qualità f
inv; classe f; categoria; (in hierarchy)
grado; (us Scol: mark) voto; (: school
class) classe ▷ vt classificare;
ordinare; graduare; **grade crossing**
n (US) passaggio a livello; **grade
school** n (US) scuola elementare or
primaria
gradient ['greɪdɪənt] n pendenza,
inclinazione m
gradual ['grædjuəl] adj graduale;
gradually adv man mano, a poco
a poco
graduate n ['grædjuɪt] laureato/a;
(us Scol: mark) diplomato/a ▷ vi ['grædjueɪt]
laurearsi; diplomarsi; **graduation**
[grædju'eɪʃən] n cerimonia del
conferimento della laurea
graffiti [grə'fiːti] npl graffiti mpl
graft [grɑːft] n (Agr, Med) innesto;
(col: bribery) corruzione f ▷ vt
innestare; **it's hard ~** (BRIT col) è un
lavoraccio
grain [greɪn] n grano; (of sand)
granello; (of wood) venatura
gram [græm] n grammo
grammar ['græmər] n grammatica;
grammar school n (BRIT) ≈ liceo
gramme [græm] n = **gram**
gran (col) [græn] n (BRIT) nonna

grand [grænd] adj grande,
magnifico/a; grandioso/a; **grandad**
(col) n = **granddad**; **grandchild** (pl
-children) n nipote m; **granddad**
n (col) nonno; **granddaughter**
n nipote f; **grandfather** n
nonno; **grandma** n (col) nonna;
grandmother n nonna; **grandpa** n
(col); = **granddad**; **grandparent** n
nonno/a; **grand piano** n pianoforte
m a coda; **Grand Prix** ['grɑ̃:'priː] n
(Aut) Gran Premio, Grand Prix m inv;
grandson n nipote m
granite ['grænɪt] n granito
granny ['grænɪ] n (col) nonna
grant [grɑːnt] vt accordare;
(a request) accogliere; (admit)
ammettere, concedere ▷ n (Scol)
borsa; (Admin) sussidio, sovvenzione
f; **to take sth for ~ed** dare qc per
scontato; **to take sb for ~ed** dare
per scontata la presenza di qn
grape [greɪp] n chicco d'uva, acino
grapefruit ['greɪpfruːt] n pompelmo
graph [grɑːf] n grafico; **graphic**
adj grafico/a; (vivid) vivido/a;
graphics n (art, process) grafica ▷ npl
illustrazioni fpl
grasp [grɑːsp] vt afferrare ▷ n (grip)
presa; (fig) potere m; comprensione f
grass [grɑːs] n erba; **grasshopper** n
cavalletta
grate [greɪt] n graticola (del focolare)
▷ vi cigolare, stridere ▷ vt (Culin)
grattugiare
grateful ['greɪtful] adj grato/a,
riconoscente
grater ['greɪtər] n grattugia
gratitude ['grætɪtjuːd] n gratitudine f
grave [greɪv] n tomba ▷ adj grave,
serio/a
gravel ['grævl] n ghiaia
gravestone ['greɪvstəun] n pietra
tombale
graveyard ['greɪvjɑːd] n cimitero
gravity ['grævɪtɪ] n (Physics) gravità;
pesantezza; (seriousness) gravità,
serietà

gravy ['greɪvɪ] n intingolo della carne; salsa

gray [greɪ] adj (US) = **grey**

graze [greɪz] vi pascolare, pascere ▷ vt (touch lightly) sfiorare; (scrape) escoriare ▷ n (Med) escoriazione f

grease [gri:s] n (fat) grasso; (lubricant) lubrificante m ▷ vt ingrassare; lubrificare; **greasy** adj grasso/a, untuoso/a

great [greɪt] adj grande; (col) magnifico/a, meraviglioso/a; **Great Britain** n Gran Bretagna; **great-grandfather** n bisnonno; **great-grandmother** n bisnonna; **greatly** adv molto

Greece [gri:s] n Grecia

greed [gri:d] n (also: **~iness**) avarizia; (for food) golosità, ghiottoneria; **greedy** adj avido/a; goloso/a, ghiotto/a

Greek [gri:k] adj greco/a ▷ n greco/a; (Ling) greco

green [gri:n] adj verde; (inexperienced) inesperto/a, ingenuo/a ▷ n verde m; (stretch of grass) prato; (of golf course) green m inv; **greens** npl (vegetables) verdura; **green card** n (BRIT Aut) carta verde; (US Admin) permesso di soggiorno e di lavoro; **greengage** ['gri:ngeɪdʒ] n susina Regina Claudia; **greengrocer** n (BRIT) fruttivendolo/a, erbivendolo/a; **greenhouse** n serra; **greenhouse effect** n: **the greenhouse effect** l'effetto serra

Greenland ['gri:nlənd] n Groenlandia

green salad n insalata verde

greet [gri:t] vt salutare; **greeting** n saluto; **greeting(s) card** n cartolina d'auguri

grew [gru:] pt of **grow**

grey, (US) **gray** [greɪ] adj grigio/a; **grey-haired** adj dai capelli grigi; **greyhound** n levriere m

grid [grɪd] n grata; (Elec) rete f; **gridlock** ['grɪdlɔk] n (traffic jam) paralisi f inv del traffico; **gridlocked** adj paralizzato/a dal traffico; (talks etc) in fase di stallo

grief [gri:f] n dolore m

grievance ['gri:vəns] n lagnanza

grieve [gri:v] vi affliggersi ▷ vt addolorare; **to ~ for sb** (dead person) piangere qn

grill [grɪl] n (on cooker) griglia; (also: **mixed ~**) grigliata mista ▷ vt (BRIT) cuocere ai ferri; (col: question) interrogare senza sosta

grille [grɪl] n grata; (Aut) griglia

grim [grɪm] adj sinistro/a, brutto/a

grime [graɪm] n sudiciume m

grin [grɪn] n sorriso smagliante ▷ vi: **to ~ (at)** fare un gran sorriso (a)

grind [graɪnd] (pt, pp **ground**) vt macinare; (make sharp) arrotare ▷ n (work) sgobbata

grip [grɪp] n impugnatura; presa; (holdall) borsa da viaggio ▷ vt (object) afferrare; (attention) catturare; **to come to ~s with** affrontare; cercare di risolvere; **gripping** ['grɪpɪŋ] adj avvincente

grit [grɪt] n ghiaia; (courage) fegato ▷ vt (road) coprire di sabbia; **to ~ one's teeth** stringere i denti

grits [grɪts] npl (US) macinato grosso (di avena etc)

groan [grəun] n gemito ▷ vi gemere

grocer ['grəusər] n negoziante m di generi alimentari; **~'s (shop)** negozio di alimentari; **grocery** ['grəusərɪ] n (shop) (negozio di) alimentari; **groceries** npl provviste fpl

groin [grɔɪn] n inguine m

groom [gru:m] n palafreniere m; (also: **bride~**) sposo ▷ vt (horse) strigliare; **to ~ sb for** avviare qn a; **well-~ed** (person) curato/a

groove [gru:v] n scanalatura, solco

grope [grəup] vi: **to ~ for sth** cercare qc a tastoni

gross [grəus] adj grossolano/a; (Comm) lordo/a; **grossly** adv (greatly) molto

grotesque [grəʊˈtɛsk] *adj* grottesco/a

ground [graʊnd] *pt, pp of* **grind** ▷ *n* suolo, terra; (*land*) terreno; (*Sport*) campo; (*reason: gen pl*) ragione *f*; (*US: also:* **~ wire**) (presa a) terra ▷ *vt* (*plane*) tenere a terra; (*US Elec*) mettere la presa a terra a; **grounds** *npl* (*of coffee etc*) fondi *mpl*; (*gardens etc*) terreno, giardini *mpl*; **on/to the ~** per/a terra; **to gain/lose ~** guadagnare/perdere terreno; **ground floor** *n* pianterreno; **groundsheet** *n* (*BRIT*) telone *m* impermeabile; **groundwork** *n* preparazione *f*

group [gruːp] *n* gruppo ▷ *vt* (*also:* **~ together**) raggruppare ▷ *vi* (*also:* **~ together**) raggrupparsi

grouse [graʊs] *n* (*pl inv: bird*) tetraone *m* ▷ *vi* (*complain*) brontolare

grovel [ˈgrɒvl] *vi* (*fig*): **to ~ (before)** strisciare (di fronte a)

grow (*pt* **grew**, *pp* **grown**) [grəʊ, gruː, grəʊn] *vi* crescere; (*increase*) aumentare; (*develop*) svilupparsi; (*become*): **to ~ rich/weak** arricchirsi/ indebolirsi ▷ *vt* coltivare, far crescere; **grow on** *vt fus*: **that painting is ~ing on me** quel quadro più lo guardo più mi piace; **grow up** *vi* farsi grande, crescere

growl [graʊl] *vi* ringhiare

grown [grəʊn] *pp of* **grow**; **grown-up** *n* adulto/a, grande *m/f*

growth [grəʊθ] *n* crescita, sviluppo; (*what has grown*) crescita; (*Med*) escrescenza, tumore *m*

grub [grʌb] *n* larva; (*col: food*) roba (da mangiare)

grubby [ˈgrʌbɪ] *adj* sporco/a

grudge [grʌdʒ] *n* rancore *m* ▷ *vt*: **to ~ sb sth** dare qc a qn di malavoglia; invidiare qc a qn; **to bear sb a ~ (for)** serbar rancore a qn (per)

gruelling, (*US*) **grueling** [ˈgruəlɪŋ] *adj* estenuante

gruesome [ˈgruːsəm] *adj* orribile

grumble [ˈgrʌmbl] *vi* brontolare, lagnarsi

grumpy [ˈgrʌmpɪ] *adj* scorbutico/a

grunt [grʌnt] *vi* grugnire

guarantee [gærənˈtiː] *n* garanzia ▷ *vt* garantire

guard [gɑːd] *n* guardia; (*one man*) guardia, sentinella; (*BRIT Rail*) capotreno; (*on machine*) schermo protettivo; (*also:* **fire-~**) parafuoco ▷ *vt* fare la guardia a; **to ~ (against** *or* **from)** proteggere (da); **to be on one's ~** stare in guardia; **guardian** *n* custode *m*; (*of minor*) tutore/trice

guerrilla [gəˈrɪlə] *n* guerrigliero

guess [gɛs] *vi* indovinare ▷ *vt* indovinare; (*US*) credere, pensare ▷ *n* congettura; **to take** *or* **have a ~** provare a indovinare

guest [gɛst] *n* ospite *m/f*; (*in hotel*) cliente *m/f*; **guest-house** *n* pensione *f*; **guest room** *n* camera degli ospiti

guidance [ˈgaɪdəns] *n* guida, direzione *f*

guide [gaɪd] *n* guida; (*BRIT: also:* **girl ~**) giovane esploratrice *f* ▷ *vt* guidare; **guidebook** *n* guida; **guide dog** *n* cane *m* guida *inv*; **guided tour** *n* visita guidata; **what time does the guided tour start?** a che ora comincia la visita guidata?; **guidelines** *npl* (*fig*) indicazioni *fpl*, linee *fpl* direttive

guild [gɪld] *n* arte *f*, corporazione *f*; associazione *f*

guilt [gɪlt] *n* colpevolezza; **guilty** *adj* colpevole

guinea pig [ˈgɪnɪ-] *n* cavia

guitar [gɪˈtɑːʳ] *n* chitarra; **guitarist** *n* chitarrista *m/f*

gulf [gʌlf] *n* golfo; (*abyss*) abisso

gull [gʌl] *n* gabbiano

gulp [gʌlp] *vi* deglutire; (*from emotion*) avere il nodo in gola ▷ *vt* (*also:* **~ down**) tracannare, inghiottire

gum [gʌm] *n* (*Anat*) gengiva; (*glue*) colla; (*sweet*) caramella gommosa; (*also:* **chewing-~**) chewing-gum *m* ▷ *vt* incollare

gun [gʌn] *n* fucile *m*; (*small*) pistola, rivoltella; (*rifle*) carabina; (*shotgun*) fucile da caccia; (*cannon*) cannone *m*; **gunfire** *n* spari *mpl*; **gunman** *n* (*irreg*) bandito armato; **gunpoint** *n*: **at gunpoint** sotto minaccia di fucile; **gunpowder** *n* polvere *f* da sparo; **gunshot** *n* sparo

gush [gʌʃ] *vi* sgorgare; (*fig*) abbandonarsi ad effusioni

gust [gʌst] *n* (*of wind*) raffica; (*of smoke*) buffata

gut [gʌt] *n* intestino, budello; **guts** *npl* (*of animals*) interiora *fpl*; (*courage*) fegato

gutter ['gʌtəʳ] *n* (*of roof*) grondaia; (*in street*) cunetta

guy [gaɪ] *n* (*also*: **~rope**) cavo *or* corda di fissaggio; (*col: man*) tipo, elemento; (*figure*) effigie di Guy Fawkes

Guy Fawkes Night [-'fɔːks-] *n* (BRIT) *vedi nota* **"Guy Fawkes Night"**

gym [dʒɪm] *n* (*also*: **~nasium**) palestra; (*also*: **~nastics**) ginnastica; **gymnasium** [dʒɪm'neɪzɪəm] *n* palestra; **gymnast** ['dʒɪmnæst] *n* ginnasta *m/f*; **gymnastics** [dʒɪm'næstɪks] *n*, *npl* ginnastica; **gym shoes** *npl* scarpe *fpl* da ginnastica

gynaecologist, (US) **gynecologist** [gaɪnɪ'kɔlədʒɪst] *n* ginecologo/a

gypsy ['dʒɪpsɪ] *n* = **gipsy**

haberdashery ['hæbədæʃərɪ] (BRIT) *n* merceria

habit ['hæbɪt] *n* abitudine *f*; (*costume*) abito; (*Rel*) tonaca

habitat ['hæbɪtæt] *n* habitat *m inv*

hack [hæk] *vt* tagliare, fare a pezzi ▷ *n* (*pej: writer*) scribacchino/a; **hacker** ['hækəʳ] *n* (*Comput*) pirata *m* informatico

had [hæd] *pt*, *pp of* **have**

haddock ['hædək] (*pl* **haddock** *or* **haddocks**) *n* eglefino

hadn't ['hædnt] = **had not**

haemorrhage, (US) **hemorrhage** ['hɛmərɪdʒ] *n* emorragia

haemorrhoids, (US) **hemorrhoids** ['hɛmərɔɪdz] *npl* emorroidi *fpl*

haggle ['hægl] *vi* mercanteggiare

Hague [heɪg] *n*: **The ~** L'Aia

hail [heɪl] *n* grandine *f*; (*of criticism etc*) pioggia ▷ *vt* (*call*) chiamare; (*flag down: taxi*) fermare; (*greet*) salutare

▷ vi grandinare; **hailstone** n chicco di grandine

hair [hɛəʳ] n capelli mpl; (single hair: on head) capello; (: on body) pelo; **to do one's ~** pettinarsi; **hairband** ['hɛəbænd] n (elastic) fascia per i capelli; (rigid) cerchietto; **hairbrush** n spazzola per capelli; **haircut** n taglio di capelli; **hairdo** ['hɛəduː] n acconciatura, pettinatura; **hairdresser** n parrucchiere/a; **hairdresser's** n parrucchiere/a; **hair-dryer** ['hɛədraɪəʳ] n asciugacapelli m inv; **hair gel** n gel m inv per capelli; **hair spray** n lacca per capelli; **hairstyle** n pettinatura, acconciatura; **hairy** adj irsuto/a; peloso/a; (col: frightening) spaventoso/a

haka ['hɑːkə] n (NZ) danza eseguita dai giocatori prima di una partita

hake [heɪk] (pl **hake** or **hakes**) n nasello

half [hɑːf] n (pl **halves**) mezzo, metà f inv ▷ adj mezzo/a ▷ adv a mezzo, a metà; **~ an hour** mezz'ora; **~ a dozen** mezza dozzina; **~ a pound** mezza libbra; **two and a ~** due e mezzo; **a week and a ~** una settimana e mezza; **~ (of it)** la metà; **~ (of)** la metà di; **to cut sth in ~** tagliare qc in due; **~ asleep** mezzo/a addormentato/a; **half board** (BRIT) n mezza pensione; **half-brother** n fratellastro; **half day** n mezza giornata; **half fare** n tariffa a metà prezzo; **half-hearted** adj tiepido/a; **half-hour** n mezz'ora; **half-price** adj ▷ adv a metà prezzo; **half term** n (BRIT Scol) vacanza a or di metà trimestre; **half-time** n (Sport) intervallo; **halfway** adv a metà strada

hall [hɔːl] n sala, salone m; (entrance way) entrata; **~ of residence** n (BRIT) casa dello studente

hallmark ['hɔːlmɑːk] n marchio di garanzia; (fig) caratteristica

hallo [həˈləʊ] excl = **hello**

hall of residence (BRIT) n casa dello studente

Halloween ['hæləʊ'iːn] n vigilia d'Ognissanti

hallucination [həluːsɪ'neɪʃən] n allucinazione f

hallway ['hɔːlweɪ] n ingresso; corridoio

halo ['heɪləʊ] n (of saint etc) aureola

halt [hɔːlt] n fermata ▷ vt fermare ▷ vi fermarsi

halve [hɑːv] vt (apple etc) dividere a metà; (expense) ridurre di metà

halves [hɑːvz] npl of **half**

ham [hæm] n prosciutto

hamburger ['hæmbəːgəʳ] n hamburger m inv

hamlet ['hæmlɪt] n paesetto

hammer ['hæməʳ] n martello ▷ vt martellare ▷ vi: **to ~ on** or **at the door** picchiare alla porta

hammock ['hæmək] n amaca

hamper ['hæmpəʳ] vt impedire ▷ n cesta

hamster ['hæmstəʳ] n criceto

hamstring ['hæmstrɪŋ] n (Anat) tendine m del ginocchio

hand [hænd] n mano f; (of clock) lancetta; (handwriting) scrittura; (at cards) mano; (: game) partita; (worker) operaio/a ▷ vt dare, passare; **to give sb a ~** dare una mano a qn; **at ~** a portata di mano; **in ~** a disposizione; (work) in corso; **to be on ~** (person) essere disponibile;

(*emergency services*) essere pronto/a a intervenire; **to ~** (*information etc*) a portata di mano; **on the one ~ ..., on the other ~** da un lato ..., dall'altro; **hand down** *vt* passare giù; (*tradition, heirloom*) tramandare; (*US: sentence, verdict*) emettere; **hand in** *vt* consegnare; **hand out** *vt* distribuire; **hand over** *vt* passare; cedere; **handbag** *n* borsetta; **hand baggage** *n* bagaglio a mano; **handbook** *n* manuale *m*; **handbrake** *n* freno a mano; **handcuffs** *npl* manette *fpl*; **handful** *n* manciata, pugno

handicap ['hændɪkæp] *n* handicap *m inv* ▷ *vt* handicappare; **to be mentally ~ped** essere un handicappato mentale; **to be physically ~ped** essere handicappato

handkerchief ['hæŋkətʃɪf] *n* fazzoletto

handle ['hændl] *n* (*of door etc*) maniglia; (*of cup etc*) ansa; (*of knife etc*) impugnatura; (*of saucepan*) manico; (*for winding*) manovella ▷ *vt* toccare, maneggiare; (*deal with*) occuparsi di; (*treat: people*) trattare; **"~ with care"** "fragile"; **to fly off the ~** (*fig*) perdere le staffe, uscire dai gangheri

handlebar(s) ['hændlbɑː(z)] *n(pl)* manubrio

hand: hand luggage ['hændlʌɡɪdʒ] *n* bagagli *mpl* a mano; **handmade** *adj* fatto/a a mano; **handout** *n* (*money, food*) elemosina; (*leaflet*) volantino; (*at lecture*) prospetto; **hands-free** *n, adj* (*telephone*) con auricolare; (*microphone*) vivavoce *inv*

handsome ['hænsəm] *adj* bello/a; (*profit, fortune*) considerevole

handwriting ['hændraɪtɪŋ] *n* scrittura

handy ['hændɪ] *adj* (*person*) bravo/a; (*close at hand*) a portata di mano; (*convenient*) comodo/a

hang (*pt, pp* **hung**) [hæŋ, hʌŋ] *vt* appendere; (*criminal*) impiccare ▷ *vi* (*painting*) essere appeso/a; (*hair*) scendere; (*drapery*) cadere; **to get the ~ of (doing) sth** (*col*) cominciare a capire (come si fa) qc; **hang about** *vi* bighellonare, ciondolare; **hang down** *vi* ricadere; **hang on** *vi* (*wait*) aspettare; **hang out** *vt* (*washing*) stendere (fuori); (*col: live*) stare ▷ *vi* penzolare, pendere; **hang round** *vi* = **hang around**; **hang up** *vi* (*Tel*) riattaccare ▷ *vt* appendere

hanger ['hæŋər] *n* gruccia

hang-gliding ['hæŋɡlaɪdɪŋ] *n* volo col deltaplano

hangover ['hæŋəʊvər] *n* (*after drinking*) postumi *mpl* di sbornia

hankie ['hæŋkɪ] *n abbr* = **handkerchief**

happen ['hæpən] *vi* accadere, succedere; **to ~ to do sth** fare qc per caso; **as it ~s** guarda caso; **what's ~ing?** cosa succede?

happily ['hæpɪlɪ] *adv* felicemente; fortunatamente

happiness ['hæpɪnɪs] *n* felicità, contentezza

happy ['hæpɪ] *adj* felice, contento/a; **~ with** (*arrangements etc*) soddisfatto/a di; **to be ~ to do** (*willing*) fare volentieri; **~ birthday!** buon compleanno!

harass ['hærəs] *vt* molestare; **harassment** *n* molestia

harbour, (*US*) **harbor** ['hɑːbər] *n* porto ▷ *vt* (*hope*) nutrire; (*fear*) avere; (*grudge*) covare; (*criminal*) dare rifugio a

hard [hɑːd] *adj* duro/a ▷ *adv* (*work*) sodo; (*think, try*) bene; **to look ~ at** guardare fissamente; esaminare attentamente; **no ~ feelings!** senza rancore!; **to be ~ of hearing** essere duro/a d'orecchio; **to be ~ done by** essere trattato/a ingiustamente; **hardback** *n* libro rilegato; **hardboard** *n* legno precompresso;

hard disk n (Comput) disco rigido;
harden vt indurire
hardly ['hɑːdlɪ] adv (scarcely) appena;
it's ~ the case non è proprio il caso; **~
anyone/anywhere** quasi nessuno/
da nessuna parte; **~ ever** quasi mai
hard: hardship ['hɑːdʃɪp] n avversità
f inv; privazioni fpl; **hard shoulder**
n (BRIT Aut) corsia d'emergenza;
hard-up adj (col) al verde; **hardware**
['hɑːdwɛəʳ] n ferramenta fpl;
(Comput) hardware m; (Mil)
armamenti mpl; **hardware shop**,
(US) **hardware store** n (negozio
di) ferramenta fpl; **hard-working**
[hɑːd'wəːkɪŋ] adj lavoratore/trice
hardy ['hɑːdɪ] adj robusto/a; (plant)
resistente al gelo
hare [hɛəʳ] n lepre f
harm [hɑːm] n male m; (wrong)
danno ▷ vt (person) fare male a;
(thing) danneggiare; **out of ~'s way**
al sicuro; **harmful** adj dannoso/a;
harmless adj innocuo/a;
inoffensivo/a
harmony ['hɑːmənɪ] n armonia
harness ['hɑːnɪs] n (for horse)
bardatura, finimenti mpl; (for
child) briglie fpl; (safety harness)
imbracatura ▷ vt (horse) bardare;
(resources) sfruttare
harp [hɑːp] n arpa ▷ vi: **to ~ on
about** insistere tediosamente su
harsh [hɑːʃ] adj (life, winter) duro/a;
(judge, criticism) severo/a; (sound)
rauco/a; (colour) chiassoso/a; (light)
violento/a
harvest ['hɑːvɪst] n raccolto;
(of grapes) vendemmia ▷ vt
fare il raccolto di, raccogliere;
vendemmiare
has [hæz] see **have**
hasn't ['hæznt] = **has not**
hassle ['hæsl] n (col) sacco di
problemi
haste [heɪst] n fretta; precipitazione
f; **hasten** ['heɪsn] vt affrettare ▷ vi:
to hasten (to) affrettarsi (a); **hastily**

adv in fretta, precipitosamente;
hasty adj affrettato/a, precipitoso/a
hat [hæt] n cappello
hatch [hætʃ] n (Naut: also: **~way**)
boccaporto; (also: **service ~**) portello
di servizio ▷ vi (bird) uscire dal guscio;
(egg) schiudersi
hatchback ['hætʃbæk] n (Aut) tre (or
cinque) porte f inv
hate [heɪt] vt odiare, detestare
▷ n odio; **hater** ['heɪtəʳ] n: **cop-~**
persona che odia i poliziotti; **woman-~**
misogino/a; **hatred** ['heɪtrɪd] n odio
haul [hɔːl] vt trascinare, tirare ▷ n
(of fish) pescata; (of stolen goods etc)
bottino
haunt [hɔːnt] vt (fear) pervadere;
(person) frequentare ▷ n rifugio; **this
house is ~ed** questa casa è abitata
da un fantasma; **haunted** adj
(castle etc) abitato/a dai fantasmi or
dagli spiriti; (look) ossessionato/a,
tormentato/a

KEYWORD

have [hæv] (pt, pp **had**) aux vb 1 (gen)
avere; essere; **to have arrived/
gone** essere arrivato/a/andato/a;
to have eaten/slept avere
mangiato/dormito; **he has been
kind/promoted** è stato gentile/
promosso; **having finished** or **when
he had finished, he left** dopo aver
finito, se n'è andato
2 (in tag questions): **you've done
it, haven't you?** l'hai fatto, (non è)
vero?; **he hasn't done it, has he?**
non l'ha fatto, vero?
3 (in short answers and questions):
**you've made a mistake — no
I haven't/so I have** ha fatto un
errore — ma no, niente affatto/sì,
è vero; **we haven't paid — yes we
have!** non abbiamo pagato — ma
sì che abbiamo pagato!; **I've been
there before, have you?** ci sono già
stato, e lei?

▶modal aux vb (be obliged): **to have (got) to do sth** dover fare qc; **I haven't got** or **I don't have to wear glasses** non ho bisogno di portare gli occhiali

▶vt 1 (possess, obtain) avere; **he has (got) blue eyes/dark hair** ha gli occhi azzurri/i capelli scuri; **have you got** or **do you have a car/phone?** ha la macchina/il telefono?; **may I have your address?** potrebbe darmi il suo indirizzo?; **you can have it for £5** te lo do per 5 sterline 2 (+ noun: take, hold etc): **to have breakfast/a swim/a bath** fare colazione/una nuotata/un bagno; **to have a cigarette** fumare una sigaretta; **to have dinner** cenare; **to have a drink** bere qualcosa; **to have lunch** pranzare 3: **to have sth done** far fare qc; **to have one's hair cut** tagliarsi or farsi tagliare i capelli; **to have sb do sth** far fare qc a qn 4 (experience, suffer) avere; **to have a cold/flu** avere il raffreddore/l'influenza; **she had her bag stolen** le hanno rubato la borsa 5 (phrases: col): **you've been had!** ci sei cascato!

have out vt: **to have it out with sb** (settle a problem etc) mettere le cose in chiaro con qn

haven ['heɪvn] n porto; (fig) rifugio
haven't ['hævnt] = **have not**
havoc ['hævək] n gran subbuglio; **to play ~ with sth** scombussolare qc
Hawaii [hə'waɪ:] n le Hawaii
hawk [hɔːk] n falco
hawthorn ['hɔːθɔːn] n biancospino
hay [heɪ] n fieno; **hay fever** n febbre f da fieno; **haystack** n pagliaio
hazard ['hæzəd] n azzardo, ventura; (risk) pericolo, rischio ▷ vt (guess, remark) azzardare; **hazardous** adj pericoloso/a; **hazard warning lights** npl (Aut) luci fpl di emergenza

haze [heɪz] n foschia
hazel ['heɪzl] n (tree) nocciolo ▷ adj (eyes) (color) nocciola inv; **hazelnut** ['heɪzlnʌt] n nocciola
hazy ['heɪzɪ] adj fosco/a; (idea) vago/a
HD abbr (= high definition) HD, alta definizione
HDTV n abbr (= high definition television) televisore m HD, TV f inv ad alta definizione
he [hi:] pron lui, egli; **it is he who ...** è lui che ...
head [hɛd] n testa; (leader) capo; (of school) preside m/f ▷ vt (list) essere in testa a; (group) essere a capo di; **~s (or tails)** testa (o croce), pari (o dispari); **~ first** a capofitto, di testa; **~ over heels in love** pazzamente innamorato/a; **to ~ the ball** dare di testa alla palla; **head for** vt fus dirigersi verso; **head off** vt (threat, danger) sventare; **headache** n mal di testa; **heading** n titolo; intestazione f; **headlamp** ['hɛdlæmp] (BRIT) = **headlight**; **headlight** n fanale m; **headline** n titolo; **head office** n sede f (centrale); **headphones** npl cuffia; **headquarters** npl ufficio centrale; (Mil) quartiere m generale; **headroom** n (in car) altezza dell'abitacolo; (under bridge) altezza limite; **headscarf** n foulard m inv; **headset** n = **headphones**; **headteacher** n (of primary school) direttore/trice; (of secondary school) preside m/f; **head waiter** n capocameriere m
heal [hi:l] vt, vi guarire
health [hɛlθ] n salute f; **health care** n assistenza sanitaria; **health centre** n (BRIT) poliambulatorio; **health food** n alimenti mpl macrobiotici; **Health Service** n: **the Health Service** (BRIT) ≈ il Servizio Sanitario Statale; **healthy** adj (person) sano/a, in buona salute; (climate) salubre;

(appetite, attitude etc) sano/a; (economy) florido/a; (bank balance) solido/a

heap [hi:p] n mucchio ▷ vt (stones, sand): **to ~ (up)** ammucchiare; **~s (of)** (col) (lots) un mucchio (di)

hear (pt, pp **heard**) [hɪəʳ, hə:d] vt sentire; (news) ascoltare ▷ vi sentire; **to ~ about** avere notizie di; sentire parlare di

hearing ['hɪərɪŋ] n (sense) udito; (of witnesses) audizione f; (of a case) udienza; **hearing aid** n apparecchio acustico

hearse [hə:s] n carro funebre

heart [hɑ:t] n cuore m; **hearts** npl (Cards) cuori mpl; **at ~** in fondo; **by ~** (learn, know) a memoria; **to take ~** farsi coraggio or animo; **to lose ~** perdere coraggio, scoraggiarsi; **heart attack** n attacco di cuore; **heartbeat** n battito del cuore; **heartbroken** adj: **to be heartbroken** avere il cuore spezzato; **heartburn** n bruciore m di stomaco; **heart disease** n malattia di cuore

hearth [hɑ:θ] n focolare m

heartless ['hɑ:tlɪs] adj senza cuore

hearty ['hɑ:tɪ] adj caloroso/a; robusto/a, sano/a; vigoroso/a

heat [hi:t] n calore m; (fig) ardore m; fuoco; (Sport: also: **qualifying ~**) prova eliminatoria ▷ vt scaldare; **heat up** vi (liquids) scaldarsi; (room) riscaldarsi ▷ vt riscaldare; **heated** adj riscaldato/a; (argument) acceso/a; **heater** n radiatore m; (stove) stufa

heather ['hɛðəʳ] n erica

heating ['hi:tɪŋ] n riscaldamento

heatwave ['hi:tweɪv] n ondata di caldo

heaven ['hɛvn] n paradiso, cielo; **heavenly** adj divino/a, celeste

heavily ['hɛvɪlɪ] adv pesantemente; (drink, smoke) molto

heavy ['hɛvɪ] adj pesante; (sea) grosso/a; (rain) forte; (weather)

afoso/a; (drinker, smoker) gran (before noun)

Hebrew ['hi:bru:] adj ebreo/a ▷ n (Ling) ebraico

hectare ['hɛktɑ:ʳ] n (BRIT) ettaro

hectic ['hɛktɪk] adj movimentato/a

he'd [hi:d] = **he would; he had**

hedge [hɛdʒ] n siepe f ▷ vi essere elusivo/a; **to ~ one's bets** (fig) coprirsi dai rischi

hedgehog ['hɛdʒhɔg] n riccio

heed [hi:d] vt (also: **take ~ of**) badare a, far conto di

heel [hi:l] n (Anat) calcagno; (of shoe) tacco ▷ vt (shoe) rifare i tacchi a

hefty ['hɛftɪ] adj (person) solido/a; (parcel) pesante; (piece, price, profit) grosso/a

height [haɪt] n altezza; (high ground) altura; (fig: of glory) apice m; (: of stupidity) colmo; **heighten** vt (fig) accrescere

heir [ɛəʳ] n erede m; **heiress** n erede f

held [hɛld] pt, pp of **hold**

helicopter ['hɛlɪkɔptəʳ] n elicottero

hell [hɛl] n inferno; **oh ~!** (col) porca miseria!, accidenti!

he'll [hi:l] = **he will; he shall**

hello [hə'ləu] excl buon giorno!; ciao! (to sb one addresses as "tu"); (surprise) ma guarda!

helmet ['hɛlmɪt] n casco

help [hɛlp] n aiuto; (charwoman) donna di servizio ▷ vt aiutare; **~!** aiuto!; **can you ~ me?** può aiutarmi?; **~ yourself (to bread)** si serva (del pane); **he can't ~ it** non ci può far niente; **help out** vi aiutare ▷ vt: **to ~ sb out** aiutare qn; **helper** n aiutante m/f, assistente m/f; **helpful** adj di grande aiuto; (useful) utile; **helping** n porzione f; **helpless** adj impotente; debole; **helpline** n ≈ telefono amico; (Comm) servizio m informazioni inv (a pagamento)

hem [hɛm] n orlo ▷ vt fare l'orlo a

hemisphere ['hɛmɪsfɪəʳ] n emisfero

hemorrhage ['hɛmərɪdʒ] n (US)
= **haemorrhage**
hemorrhoids ['hɛmərɔɪdz] npl (US)
= **haemorrhoids**
hen [hɛn] n gallina; (female bird)
femmina
hence [hɛns] adv (therefore) dunque;
2 years ~ di qui a 2 anni
hen night n (col) addio al nubilato
hepatitis [hɛpə'taɪtɪs] n epatite f
her [hə:ʳ] pron (direct) la, l' + vowel;
(indirect) le; (stressed, after prep) lei
▷ adj il (la) suo/a, i (le) suoi (sue); see
also **me; my**
herb [hə:b] n erba; **herbal** adj di erbe;
herbal tea tisana
herd [hə:d] n mandria
here [hɪəʳ] adv qui, qua ▷ excl ehi! **~!**
(at roll call) presente!; **~ is, ~ are** ecco;
~ he/she is eccolo/eccola
hereditary [hɪ'rɛdɪtrɪ] adj
ereditario/a
heritage ['hɛrɪtɪdʒ] n eredità; (of
country, nation) retaggio
hernia ['hə:nɪə] n ernia
hero ['hɪərəu] (pl **heroes**) n eroe m;
heroic [hɪ'rəuɪk] adj eroico/a
heroin ['hɛrəuɪn] n eroina (droga)
heroine ['hɛrəuɪn] n eroina (donna)
heron ['hɛrən] n airone m
herring ['hɛrɪŋ] n aringa
hers [hə:z] pron il (la) suo/a, i (le) suoi
(sue); see also **mine¹**
herself [hə:'sɛlf] pron (reflexive) si;
(emphatic) lei stessa; (after prep) se
stessa, sé; see also **oneself**
he's [hi:z] = **he is; he has**
hesitant ['hɛzɪtənt] adj esitante,
indeciso/a
hesitate ['hɛzɪteɪt] vi: **to ~ (about/
to do)** esitare (su/a fare); **hesitation**
[hɛzɪ'teɪʃən] n esitazione f
heterosexual [hɛtərəu'sɛksjuəl]
adj, n eterosessuale (m/f)
hexagon ['hɛksəgən] n esagono
hey [heɪ] excl ehi!
heyday ['heɪdeɪ] n: **the ~ of** i bei
giorni di, l'età d'oro di

HGV n abbr = **heavy goods vehicle**
hi [haɪ] excl ciao!
hibernate ['haɪbəneɪt] vi ibernare
hiccough, hiccup ['hɪkʌp] vi
singhiozzare
hid [hɪd] pt of **hide**
hidden ['hɪdn] pp of **hide**
hide [haɪd] (pt **hid**, pp **hidden**) n
(skin) pelle f ▷ vt: **to ~ sth (from sb)**
nascondere qc (a qn) ▷ vi: **to ~ (from
sb)** nascondersi (da qn)
hideous ['hɪdɪəs] adj laido/a;
orribile
hiding ['haɪdɪŋ] n (beating)
bastonata; **to be in ~** (concealed)
tenersi nascosto/a
hi-fi ['haɪ'faɪ] adj, n abbr (= high fidelity)
hi-fi (m) inv
high [haɪ] adj alto/a; (speed, respect,
number) grande; (wind) forte;
(voice) acuto/a ▷ adv alto, in alto;
20m ~ alto/a 20m; **highchair** n
seggiolone m; **high-class** adj
(neighbourhood) elegante; (hotel)
di prim'ordine; (person) di gran
classe; (food) raffinato/a; **higher
education** n istruzione f superiore
or universitaria; **high heels** npl
(heels) tacchi mpl alti; (shoes) scarpe
fpl con i tacchi alti; **high jump** n
(Sport) salto in alto; **highlands** npl
zona montuosa; **the Highlands**
le Highlands scozzesi; **highlight** n
(fig: of event) momento culminante;
(in hair) colpo di sole ▷ vt mettere
in evidenza; **highlights** npl (in hair)
colpi mpl di sole; **highlighter** n (pen)
evidenziatore m; **highly** adv molto;
to speak highly of parlare molto
bene di; **highness** n: **Her Highness**
Sua Altezza; **high-rise** n (also:
high-rise block, high-rise building)
palazzone m; **high school** n scuola
secondaria; (US) istituto d'istruzione
secondaria; **high season** n (BRIT)
alta stagione; **high street** n (BRIT)
strada principale; **high-tech** (col) adj
high-tech inv; **highway** ['haɪweɪ] n

strada maestra; **Highway Code** n
(BRIT) codice m della strada
hijack ['haɪdʒæk] vt dirottare;
hijacker n dirottatore/trice
hike [haɪk] vi fare un'escursione
a piedi ⊳ n escursione f a piedi;
hiker n escursionista m/f; **hiking** n
escursioni fpl a piedi
hilarious [hɪ'lɛərɪəs] adj (behaviour,
event) spassosissimo/a
hill [hɪl] n collina, colle m; (fairly high)
montagna; (on road) salita; **hillside**
n fianco della collina; **hill walking** n
escursioni fpl in collina; **hilly** ['hɪlɪ]
adj collinoso/a
him [hɪm] pron (direct) lo, l' + vowel;
(indirect) gli; (stressed, after prep) lui;
himself pron (reflexive) si; (emphatic)
lui stesso; (after prep) se stesso, sé; see
also **oneself**
hind [haɪnd] adj posteriore ⊳ n cerva
hinder ['hɪndə'] vt ostacolare
hindsight ['haɪndsaɪt] n: **with (the
benefit of) ~** con il senno di poi
Hindu ['hɪnduː] n indù mf inv;
Hinduism n (Rel) induismo
hinge [hɪndʒ] n cardine m ⊳ vi (fig): **to
~ on** dipendere da
hint [hɪnt] n (suggestion) allusione f;
(advice) consiglio; (sign) accenno ⊳ vt:
to ~ that lasciar capire che ⊳ vi: **to ~
at** accennare a, alludere a
hip [hɪp] n anca, fianco
hippie ['hɪpɪ] n hippy mf inv
hippo ['hɪpəu] (pl **hippos**) n
ippopotamo
hippopotamus (pl
hippopotamuses or **hippopotami**)
[hɪpə'pɔtəməs, -'pɔtəmaɪ] n
ippopotamo
hippy ['hɪpɪ] n = **hippie**
hire ['haɪə'] vt (BRIT: car, equipment)
noleggiare; (worker) assumere, dare
lavoro a ⊳ n nolo, noleggio; **for
~** da nolo; (taxi) libero/a; **hire(d)
car** n (BRIT) macchina a nolo; **hire
purchase** n (BRIT) acquisto (or
vendita) rateale

his [hɪz] adj, pron il (la) suo (sua), i (le)
suoi (sue); see also **my; mine¹**
Hispanic [hɪs'pænɪk] adj ispanico/a
hiss [hɪs] vi fischiare; (cat, snake)
sibilare
historian [hɪ'stɔːrɪən] n storico/a
historic(al) [hɪ'stɔrɪk(l)] adj
storico/a
history ['hɪstərɪ] n storia
hit [hɪt] vt (pt, pp **hit**) colpire,
picchiare; (knock against) battere;
(reach: target) raggiungere; (collide
with: car) urtare contro; (fig: affect)
colpire; (find: problem) incontrare ⊳ n
colpo; (success, song) successo; **to ~ it
off with sb** andare molto d'accordo
con qn; **hit back** vi: **to ~ back at sb**
restituire il colpo a qn
hitch [hɪtʃ] vt (fasten) attaccare;
(also: ~ **up**) tirare su ⊳ n (difficulty)
intoppo, difficoltà f inv; **to ~ a
lift** fare l'autostop; **hitch-hike** vi
fare l'autostop; **hitch-hiker** n
autostoppista m/f; **hitch-hiking** n
autostop m
hi-tech ['haɪ'tɛk] adj high-tech inv
hitman ['hɪtmæn] n (col) sicario
HIV n abbr: **~-negative/-positive** adj
sieronegativo/a/sieropositivo/a
hive [haɪv] n alveare m
hoard [hɔːd] n (of food) provviste fpl;
(of money) gruzzolo ⊳ vt ammassare
hoarse [hɔːs] adj rauco/a
hoax [həuks] n scherzo; falso
allarme
hob [hɔb] n piastra (con fornelli)
hobble ['hɔbl] vi zoppicare
hobby ['hɔbɪ] n hobby m inv,
passatempo
hobo ['həubəu] n (US) vagabondo
hockey ['hɔkɪ] n hockey m; **hockey
stick** n bastone m da hockey
hog [hɔg] n maiale m ⊳ vt (fig)
arraffare; **to go the whole ~** farlo
fino in fondo
Hogmanay [hɔgmə'neɪ] n
(SCOTTISH) ≈ San Silvestro
hoist [hɔɪst] n paranco ⊳ vt issare

hold [həuld] (*pt, pp* **held**) *vt* tenere; (*contain*) contenere; (*keep back*) trattenere; (*believe*) mantenere; considerare; (*possess*) avere, possedere; detenere ▷ *vi* (*withstand pressure*) tenere; (*be valid*) essere valido/a ▷ *n* presa; (*control*): **to have a ~ over** avere controllo su; (*Naut*) stiva; **~ the line!** (*Tel*) resti in linea!; **to ~ one's own** (*fig*) difendersi bene; **to catch** *or* **get (a) ~ of** afferrare; **hold back** *vt* trattenere; (*secret*) tenere celato/a; **hold on** *vi* tener fermo; (*wait*) aspettare; **~ on!** (*Tel*) resti in linea!; **hold out** *vt* offrire ▷ *vi* (*resist*): **to ~ out (against)** resistere (a); **hold up** *vt* (*raise*) alzare; (*support*) sostenere; (*delay*) ritardare; (*rob*) assaltare; **holdall** *n* (*BRIT*) borsone *m*; **holder** *n* (*container*) contenitore *m*; (*of ticket, title*) possessore (posseditrice); (*of office etc*) incaricato/a; (*of record*) detentore/trice

hole [həul] *n* buco, buca

holiday ['hɔlədɪ] *n* vacanza; (*day off*) giorno di vacanza; (*public*) giorno festivo; **to be on ~** essere in vacanza; **holiday camp** *n* (*BRIT*) (*also:* **holiday centre**) ≈ villaggio (di vacanze); **holiday home** *n* seconda casa (*per le vacanze*); **holiday job** *n* (*BRIT*) ≈ lavoro estivo; **holiday-maker** *n* (*BRIT*) villeggiante *m/f*; **holiday resort** *n* luogo di villeggiatura

Holland ['hɔlənd] *n* Olanda

hollow ['hɔləu] *adj* cavo/a; (*container, claim*) vuoto/a; (*laugh*) forzato/a; (*sound*) cavernoso/a ▷ *n* cavità *f inv*; (*in land*) valletta, depressione *f*; **hollow out** *vt* scavare

holly ['hɔlɪ] *n* agrifoglio

Hollywood ['hɔlɪwud] *n* Hollywood *f*

holocaust ['hɔləkɔːst] *n* olocausto

holy ['həulɪ] *adj* santo/a; (*bread*) benedetto/a, consacrato/a

home [həum] *n* casa; (*country*) patria; (*institution*) casa, ricovero ▷ *cpd* familiare; (*cooking etc*) casalingo/a; (*Econ, Pol*) nazionale, interno/a; (*Sport*) di casa ▷ *adv* a casa; in patria; (*right in: nail etc*) fino in fondo; **at ~** a casa; (*in situation*) a proprio agio; **to go** (*or* **come**) **~** tornare a casa (*or* in patria); **make yourself at ~** si metta a suo agio; **home address** *n* indirizzo di casa; **homeland** *n* patria; **homeless** *adj* senza tetto; spatriato/a; **homely** ['həumlɪ] *adj* semplice, alla buona; accogliente; **home-made** *adj* casalingo/a; **home match** *n* partita in casa; **Home Office** *n* (*BRIT*) ministero degli Interni; **home owner** *n* proprietario/a di casa; **home page** *n* (*Comput*) home page *f inv*; **Home Secretary** *n* (*BRIT*) ministro degli Interni; **homesick** *adj*: **to be homesick** avere la nostalgia; **home town** *n* città *f inv* natale; **homework** *n* compiti *mpl* (*per casa*)

homicide ['hɔmɪsaɪd] *n* (*US*) omicidio

homoeopathic, (*US*) **homeopathic** ['həumɪəu'pæθɪk] *adj* omeopatico/a

homoeopathy, (*US*) **homeopathy** [həumɪ'ɔpəθɪ] *n* omeopatia

homosexual [hɔməu'sɛksjuəl] *adj*, *n* omosessuale (*m/f*)

honest ['ɔnɪst] *adj* onesto/a; sincero/a; **honestly** *adv* onestamente; sinceramente; **honesty** *n* onestà

honey ['hʌnɪ] *n* miele *m*; **honeymoon** *n* luna di miele, viaggio di nozze; **honeysuckle** ['hʌnɪsʌkl] *n* (*Bot*) caprifoglio

Hong Kong ['hɔŋ'kɔŋ] *n* Hong Kong *f*

honorary ['ɔnərərɪ] *adj* onorario/a; (*duty, title*) onorifico/a

honour, (*US*) **honor** ['ɔnər] *vt* onorare ▷ *n* onore *m*; **honourable**, (*US*) **honorable** *adj* onorevole; **honours degree** *n* (*Scol*) laurea (con corso di studi di 4 o 5 anni)

hood [hud] n cappuccio; (on cooker) cappa; (BRIT Aut) capote f; (US Aut) cofano

hoof (pl **hoofs** or **hooves**) [hu:f, hu:vz] n zoccolo

hook [huk] n gancio; (for fishing) amo ▷ vt uncinare; (dress) agganciare

hooligan ['hu:lɪgən] n giovinastro, teppista m

hoop [hu:p] n cerchio

hooray [hu:'reɪ] excl = **hurrah**

hoot [hu:t] vi (Aut) suonare il clacson; (siren) ululare; (owl) gufare

hoover® ['hu:vəʳ] n (BRIT) aspirapolvere m inv ▷ vt pulire con l'aspirapolvere

hooves [hu:vz] npl of **hoof**

hop [hɒp] vi saltellare, saltare; (on one foot) saltare su una gamba

hope [həup] vt: **to ~ that/to do** sperare che/di fare ▷ vi sperare ▷ n speranza; **I ~ so/not** spero di sì/no; **hopeful** adj (person) pieno/a di speranza; (situation) promettente; **hopefully** adv con speranza; **hopefully he will recover** speriamo che si riprenda; **hopeless** adj senza speranza, disperato/a; (useless) inutile

hops [hɒps] npl luppoli mpl

horizon [hə'raɪzn] n orizzonte m; **horizontal** [hɒrɪ'zɒntl] adj orizzontale

hormone ['hɔ:məun] n ormone m

horn [hɔ:n] n (Zool, Mus) corno; (Aut) clacson m inv

horoscope ['hɒrəskəup] n oroscopo

horrendous [hɒ'rɛndəs] adj orrendo/a

horrible ['hɒrɪbl] adj orribile, tremendo/a

horrid ['hɒrɪd] adj orrido/a; (person) odioso/a

horrific [hɒ'rɪfɪk] adj (accident) spaventoso/a; (film) orripilante

horrifying ['hɒrɪfaɪɪŋ] adj terrificante

horror ['hɒrəʳ] n orrore m; **horror film** n film m inv dell'orrore

hors d'œuvre [ɔ:'də:vrə] n antipasto

horse [hɔ:s] n cavallo; **horseback**: **on horseback** adj, adv a cavallo; **horse chestnut** n ippocastano; **horsepower** n cavallo (vapore); **horse-racing** n ippica; **horseradish** n rafano; **horse riding** n (BRIT) equitazione f

hose [həuz] n (also: **~pipe**) tubo; (also: **garden ~**) tubo per annaffiare

hospital ['hɒspɪtl] n ospedale m

hospitality [hɒspɪ'tælɪtɪ] n ospitalità

host [həust] n ospite m; (Rel) ostia; (large number): **a ~ of** una schiera di

hostage ['hɒstɪdʒ] n ostaggio/a

hostel ['hɒstl] n ostello; (also: **youth ~**) ostello della gioventù

hostess ['həustɪs] n ospite f; (BRIT Aviat) hostess f inv

hostile ['hɒstaɪl] adj ostile

hostility [hɒ'stɪlɪtɪ] n ostilità f inv

hot [hɒt] adj caldo/a; (as opposed to only warm) molto caldo/a; (spicy) piccante; (fig) accanito/a; ardente; violento/a, focoso/a, **to be ~** (person) aver caldo; (thing) essere caldo/a; (Meteor) far caldo; **hot dog** n hot dog m inv

hotel [həu'tɛl] n albergo

hotspot ['hɒtspɒt] n (Comput: also: **wireless ~**) hotspot m inv Wi-Fi

hot-water bottle [hɒt'wɔ:tə-] n borsa dell'acqua calda

hound [haund] vt perseguitare ▷ n segugio

hour ['auəʳ] n ora; **hourly** adj (ad) ogni ora

house n [haus, 'hauzɪz] casa; (Pol) camera; (Theat) sala; pubblico; spettacolo ▷ vt [hauz] (person) ospitare, alloggiare; **on the ~** (fig) offerto/a dalla casa; **household** n famiglia; casa; **householder** n padrone/a di casa; (head of house) capofamiglia m/f; **housekeeper** n governante f; **housekeeping** n

(*work*) governo della casa; (*also:*
housekeeping money) soldi *mpl*
per le spese di casa; **housewife** *n*
(*irreg*) massaia, casalinga; **house
wine** *n* vino della casa; **housework** *n*
faccende *fpl* domestiche

housing ['hauzɪŋ] *n* alloggio;
housing development, (*BRIT*)
housing estate *n* zona residenziale
con case popolari e/o private

hover ['hɔvər] *vi* (*bird*) librarsi;
hovercraft *n* hovercraft *m inv*

how [hau] *adv* come; **~ are you?**
come stai?; **~ do you do?**
piacere!; **~ far is it to …?** quanto è lontano
…?; **~ long have you been here?** da
quanto tempo è qui?; **~ lovely!** che
bello!; **~ many?** quanti/e?; **~ much?**
quanto/a?; **~ many people/much
milk?** quante persone/quanto latte?;
~ old are you? quanti anni ha?

however [hau'ɛvər] *adv* in qualsiasi
modo *or* maniera che; (+ *adjective*)
per quanto + *sub*; (*in questions*) come
▷ *conj* comunque, però

howl [haul] *vi* ululare; (*baby, person*)
urlare

HP *n abbr* (*BRIT*) = **hire purchase**

hp *abbr* (*Aut*) = **horsepower**

HQ *abbr* (= *headquarters*) Q.G.

hr *abbr* (= *hour*) h

hrs *abbr* (= *hours*) h

HTML *n abbr* (= *hypertext markup
language*) HTML *m inv*

hubcap ['hʌbkæp] *n* coprimozzo

huddle ['hʌdl] *vi*: **to ~ together**
rannicchiarsi l'uno contro l'altro

huff [hʌf] *n*: **in a ~** stizzito/a

hug [hʌg] *vt* abbracciare; (*shore, kerb*)
stringere

huge [hju:dʒ] *adj* enorme,
immenso/a

hull [hʌl] *n* (*of ship*) scafo

hum [hʌm] *vt* (*tune*) canticchiare
▷ *vi* canticchiare; (*insect, plane, tool*)
ronzare

human ['hju:mən] *adj* (*irreg*)
umano/a ▷ *n* essere *m* umano

humane [hju:'meɪn] *adj*
umanitario/a

humanitarian [hju:mænɪ'tɛərɪən]
adj umanitario/a

humanity [hju:'mænɪtɪ] *n* umanità

human rights *npl* diritti *mpl*
dell'uomo

humble ['hʌmbl] *adj* umile,
modesto/a ▷ *vt* umiliare

humid ['hju:mɪd] *adj* umido/a;
humidity [hju:'mɪdɪtɪ] *n* umidità

humiliate [hju:'mɪlɪeɪt] *vt*
umiliare; **humiliating** *adj* umiliante;
humiliation [hju:mɪlɪ'eɪʃən] *n*
umiliazione *f*

hummus ['huməs] *n* purè di ceci

humorous ['hju:mərəs] *adj*
umoristico/a; (*person*) buffo/a

humour, (*US*) **humor** ['hju:mər] *n*
umore *m* ▷ *vt* assecondare

hump [hʌmp] *n* gobba

hunch [hʌntʃ] *n* (*premonition*)
intuizione *f*

hundred ['hʌndrəd] *num* cento;
~s of people centinaia *fpl* di
persone; **hundredth** [-ɪdθ] *num*
centesimo/a

hung [hʌŋ] *pt, pp of* **hang**

Hungarian [hʌŋ'gɛərɪən] *adj*
ungherese ▷ *n* ungherese *m/f*; (*Ling*)
ungherese *m*

Hungary ['hʌŋgərɪ] *n* Ungheria

hunger ['hʌŋgər] *n* fame *f* ▷ *vi*: **to ~
for** desiderare ardentemente

hungry ['hʌŋgrɪ] *adj* affamato/a; **to
be ~** aver fame

hunt [hʌnt] *vt* (*seek*) cercare; (*Sport*)
cacciare ▷ *vi*: **to ~ (for)** andare a
caccia (di) ▷ *n* caccia; **hunter** *n*
cacciatore *m*; **hunting** *n* caccia

hurdle ['hə:dl] *n* (*Sport, fig*) ostacolo

hurl [hə:l] *vt* lanciare con violenza

hurrah [hu'rɑː], **hurray** [hu'reɪ]
excl urra!, evviva!

hurricane ['hʌrɪkən] *n* uragano

hurry ['hʌrɪ] *n* fretta ▷ *vi* (*also:* **~ up**)
affrettarsi ▷ *vt* (*also:* **~ up**: *person*)
affrettare; (: *work*) far in fretta; **to**

be in a ~ aver fretta; **hurry up** vi sbrigarsi

hurt [həːt] (pt, pp **hurt**) vt (cause pain to) far male a; (injure, fig) ferire ▷ vi far male

husband ['hʌzbənd] n marito

hush [hʌʃ] n silenzio, calma ▷ vt zittire

husky ['hʌskɪ] adj roco/a ▷ n cane m eschimese

hut [hʌt] n rifugio; (shed) ripostiglio

hyacinth ['haɪəsɪnθ] n giacinto

hydrangea [haɪ'dreɪnʒə] n ortensia

hydrofoil ['haɪdrəfɔɪl] n aliscafo

hydrogen ['haɪdrədʒən] n idrogeno

hygiene ['haɪdʒiːn] n igiene f; **hygienic** [haɪ'dʒiːnɪk] adj igienico/a

hymn [hɪm] n inno; cantica

hype [haɪp] n (col) battage m inv pubblicitario

hyperlink ['haɪpəlɪŋk] n link m inv ipertestuale

hyphen ['haɪfn] n trattino

hypnotize ['hɪpnətaɪz] vt ipnotizzare

hypocrite ['hɪpəkrɪt] n ipocrita m/f

hypocritical [hɪpə'krɪtɪkl] adj ipocrita

hypothesis (pl **hypotheses**) [haɪ'pɔθɪsɪs, -siːz] n ipotesi f inv

hysterical [hɪ'stɛrɪkl] adj isterico/a

hysterics [hɪ'stɛrɪks] npl accesso di isteria; (laughter) attacco di riso

I [aɪ] pron io

ice [aɪs] n ghiaccio; (on road) gelo ▷ vt (cake) glassare ▷ vi (also: **~ over**) ghiacciare; (also: **~ up**) gelare; **iceberg** n iceberg m inv; **ice cream** n gelato; **ice cube** n cubetto di ghiaccio; **ice hockey** n hockey m su ghiaccio

Iceland ['aɪslənd] n Islanda; **Icelander** n islandese m/f; **Icelandic** [aɪs'lændɪk] adj islandese ▷ n (Ling) islandese m

ice: ice lolly n (BRIT) ghiacciolo; **ice rink** n pista di pattinaggio; **ice skating** n pattinaggio sul ghiaccio

icing ['aɪsɪŋ] n (Culin) glassa; **icing sugar** (BRIT) n zucchero a velo

icon ['aɪkɔn] n icona

icy ['aɪsɪ] adj ghiacciato/a; (weather, temperature) gelido/a

I'd [aɪd] = **I would**; **I had**

ID card n = **identity card**

idea [aɪ'dɪə] n idea

ideal [aɪˈdɪəl] *adj, n* ideale (*m*);
ideally [aɪˈdɪəlɪ] *adv* perfettamente,
assolutamente; **ideally the book
should have ...** l'ideale sarebbe che il
libro avesse ...
identical [aɪˈdɛntɪkl] *adj* identico/a
identification [aɪdɛntɪfɪˈkeɪʃən] *n*
identificazione *f*; **means of ~** carta
d'identità
identify [aɪˈdɛntɪfaɪ] *vt* identificare
identity [aɪˈdɛntɪtɪ] *n* identità *f inv*;
identity card *n* carta d'identità;
identity theft *n* furto d'identità
ideology [aɪdɪˈɔlədʒɪ] *n* ideologia
idiom [ˈɪdɪəm] *n* idioma *m*; (*phrase*)
espressione *f* idiomatica
idiot [ˈɪdɪət] *n* idiota *m/f*
idle [ˈaɪdl] *adj* inattivo/a, (*lazy*)
pigro/a, ozioso/a; (*unemployed*)
disoccupato/a; (*question, pleasures*)
ozioso/a ▷ *vi* (*engine*) girare al
minimo
idol [ˈaɪdl] *n* idolo
idyllic [ɪˈdɪlɪk] *adj* idillico/a
i.e. *abbr* (*that is*) cioè
if [ɪf] *conj* se; **if I were you ...** se fossi
in te ..., io al tuo posto ...; **if so** se è
così; **if not** se no; **if only** se solo *or*
soltanto
ignite [ɪgˈnaɪt] *vt* accendere ▷ *vi*
accendersi
ignition [ɪgˈnɪʃən] *n* (*Aut*) accensione
f; **to switch on/off the ~** accendere/
spegnere il motore
ignorance [ˈɪgnərəns] *n* ignoranza;
to keep sb in ~ of sth tenere qn
all'oscuro di qc
ignorant [ˈɪgnərənt] *adj* ignorante;
to be ~ of (*subject*) essere ignorante
in; (*events*) essere ignaro/a di
ignore [ɪgˈnɔːˈ] *vt* non tener conto di;
(*person, fact*) ignorare
ill [ɪl] *adj* (*sick*) malato/a; (*bad*)
cattivo/a ▷ *n* male *m*; **to take** *or* **be
taken ~** ammalarsi; **to speak/think
~ of sb** parlar/pensar male di qn
I'll [aɪl] = **I will; I shall**
illegal [ɪˈliːgl] *adj* illegale

illegible [ɪˈlɛdʒɪbl] *adj* illeggibile
illegitimate [ɪlɪˈdʒɪtɪmət] *adj*
illegittimo/a
ill health *n* problemi *mpl* di salute
illiterate [ɪˈlɪtərət] *adj* analfabeta,
illetterato/a; (*letter*) scorretto/a
illness [ˈɪlnɪs] *n* malattia
illuminate [ɪˈluːmɪneɪt] *vt*
illuminare
illusion [ɪˈluːʒən] *n* illusione *f*
illustrate [ˈɪləstreɪt] *vt* illustrare
illustration [ɪləˈstreɪʃən] *n*
illustrazione *f*
IM *n* (= *instant messaging*) messaggeria
istantanea
I'm [aɪm] = **I am**
image [ˈɪmɪdʒ] *n* immagine *f*; (*public
face*) immagine (pubblica)
imaginary [ɪˈmædʒɪnərɪ] *adj*
immaginario/a
imagination [ɪmædʒɪˈneɪʃən] *n*
immaginazione *f*, fantasia
imaginative [ɪˈmædʒɪnətɪv] *adj*
immaginoso/a
imagine [ɪˈmædʒɪn] *vt* immaginare
imbalance [ɪmˈbæləns] *n* squilibrio
imitate [ˈɪmɪteɪt] *vt* imitare
imitation [ɪmɪˈteɪʃən] *n* imitazione *f*
immaculate [ɪˈmækjulət] *adj*
immacolato/a; (*dress, appearance*)
impeccabile
immature [ɪməˈtjuəˈ] *adj*
immaturo/a
immediate [ɪˈmiːdɪət] *adj*
immediato/a; **immediately** *adv*
(*at once*) subito, immediatamente;
immediately next to proprio
accanto a
immense [ɪˈmɛns] *adj* immenso/a;
enorme; **immensely** *adv*
immensamente
immerse [ɪˈməːs] *vt* immergere
immigrant [ˈɪmɪgrənt] *n*
immigrante *m/f*; (*already established*)
immigrato/a; **immigration**
[ɪmɪˈgreɪʃən] *n* immigrazione *f*
imminent [ˈɪmɪnənt] *adj* imminente
immoral [ɪˈmɔrl] *adj* immorale

immortal [ɪˈmɔːtl] *adj, n* immortale *(m/f)*

immune [ɪˈmjuːn] *adj*: **~ (to)** immune (da); **immune system** *n* sistema *m* immunitario

immunize [ˈɪmjunaɪz] *vt* immunizzare

impact [ˈɪmpækt] *n* impatto

impair [ɪmˈpɛəʳ] *vt* danneggiare

impartial [ɪmˈpɑːʃl] *adj* imparziale

impatience [ɪmˈpeɪʃəns] *n* impazienza

impatient [ɪmˈpeɪʃənt] *adj* impaziente; **to get** *or* **grow ~** perdere la pazienza

impeccable [ɪmˈpɛkəbl] *adj* impeccabile

impending [ɪmˈpɛndɪŋ] *adj* imminente

imperative [ɪmˈpɛrətɪv] *adj* imperativo/a; necessario/a, urgente; *(voice)* imperioso/a

imperfect [ɪmˈpəːfɪkt] *adj* imperfetto/a; *(goods etc)* difettoso/a ▷ *n (Ling: also:* **~ tense)** imperfetto

imperial [ɪmˈpɪərɪəl] *adj* imperiale; *(measure)* legale

impersonal [ɪmˈpəːsənl] *adj* impersonale

impersonate [ɪmˈpəːsəneɪt] *vt* spacciarsi per, fingersi; *(Theat)* imitare

impetus [ˈɪmpətəs] *n* impeto

implant [ɪmˈplɑːnt] *vt (Med)* innestare; *(fig: idea, principle)* inculcare

implement *n* [ˈɪmplɪmənt] attrezzo; *(for cooking)* utensile *m* ▷ *vt* [ˈɪmplɪmɛnt] effettuare

implicate [ˈɪmplɪkeɪt] *vt* implicare

implication [ɪmplɪˈkeɪʃən] *n* implicazione *f*; **by ~** implicitamente

implicit [ɪmˈplɪsɪt] *adj* implicito/a; *(complete)* completo/a

imply [ɪmˈplaɪ] *vt* insinuare; suggerire

impolite [ɪmpəˈlaɪt] *adj* scortese

import *vt* [ɪmˈpɔːt] importare ▷ *n* [ˈɪmpɔːt] *(Comm)* importazione *f*

importance [ɪmˈpɔːtns] *n* importanza

important [ɪmˈpɔːtnt] *adj* importante; **it's not ~** non ha importanza

importer [ɪmˈpɔːtəʳ] *n* importatore/ trice

impose [ɪmˈpəuz] *vt* imporre ▷ *vi*: **to ~ on sb** sfruttare la bontà di qn; **imposing** [ɪmˈpəuzɪŋ] *adj* imponente

impossible [ɪmˈpɔsɪbl] *adj* impossibile

impotent [ˈɪmpətnt] *adj* impotente

impoverished [ɪmˈpɔvərɪʃt] *adj* impoverito/a

impractical [ɪmˈpræktɪkl] *adj* non pratico/a

impress [ɪmˈprɛs] *vt* impressionare; *(mark)* imprimere, stampare; **to ~ sth on sb** far capire qc a qn

impression [ɪmˈprɛʃən] *n* impressione *f*; **to be under the ~ that** avere l'impressione che

impressive [ɪmˈprɛsɪv] *adj* notevole

imprison [ɪmˈprɪzn] *vt* imprigionare; **imprisonment** *n* imprigionamento

improbable [ɪmˈprɔbəbl] *adj* improbabile; *(excuse)* inverosimile

improper [ɪmˈprɔpəʳ] *adj* scorretto/a; *(unsuitable)* inadatto/a, improprio/a; sconveniente, indecente

improve [ɪmˈpruːv] *vt* migliorare ▷ *vi* migliorare; *(pupil etc)* fare progressi; **improvement** *n* miglioramento; progresso

improvise [ˈɪmprəvaɪz] *vt, vi* improvvisare

impulse [ˈɪmpʌls] *n* impulso; **to act on ~** agire d'impulso *or* impulsivamente; **impulsive** [ɪmˈpʌlsɪv] *adj* impulsivo/a

 KEYWORD

in [ɪn] *prep* **1** *(indicating place, position)* in; **in the house/garden** in casa/

giardino; **in the box** nella scatola; **in the fridge** nel frigorifero; **I have it in my hand** ce l'ho in mano; **in town/ the country** in città/campagna; **in school** a scuola; **in here/there** qui/lì dentro

2 (*with place names, of town, region, country*): **in London** a Londra; **in England** in Inghilterra; **in the United States** negli Stati Uniti; **in Yorkshire** nello Yorkshire

3 (*indicating time: during, in the space of*) in; **in spring/summer** in primavera/estate; **in 1988** nel 1988; **in May** in *or* a maggio; **I'll see you in July** ci vediamo a luglio; **in the afternoon** nel pomeriggio; **at 4 o'clock in the afternoon** alle 4 del pomeriggio; **I did it in 3 hours/days** l'ho fatto in 3 ore/giorni; **I'll see you in 2 weeks** *or* **in 2 weeks' time** ci vediamo tra 2 settimane

4 (*indicating manner etc*) a; **in a loud/ soft voice** a voce alta/bassa; **in pencil** a matita; **in English/French** in inglese/francese; **the boy in the blue shirt** il ragazzo con la camicia blu

5 (*indicating circumstances*): **in the sun** al sole; **in the shade** all'ombra; **in the rain** sotto la pioggia; **a rise in prices** un aumento dei prezzi

6 (*indicating mood, state*): **in tears** in lacrime; **in anger** per la rabbia; **in despair** disperato/a; **in good condition** in buono stato, in buone condizioni; **to live in luxury** vivere nel lusso

7 (*with ratios, numbers*): **1 in 10** 1 su 10; **20 pence in the pound** 20 pence per sterlina; **they lined up in twos** si misero in fila per due

8 (*referring to people, works*) in; **the disease is common in children** la malattia è comune nei bambini; **in (the works of) Dickens** in Dickens

9 (*indicating profession etc*) in; **to be in teaching** fare l'insegnante, insegnare; **to be in publishing** lavorare nell'editoria

10 (*after superlative*) di; **the best in the class** il migliore della classe

11 (*with present participle*): **in saying this** dicendo questo, nel dire questo

▸ *adv*: **to be in** (*person: at home, work*) esserci; (*train, ship, plane*) essere arrivato/a; (*in fashion*) essere di moda; **to ask sb in** invitare qn ad entrare; **to run/limp** *etc* **in** entrare di corsa/zoppicando *etc*

▸ *n*: **the ins and outs of the problem** tutti gli aspetti del problema

inability [ɪnəˈbɪlɪtɪ] *n* incapacità
inaccurate [ɪnˈækjurət] *adj* inesatto/a; impreciso/a
inadequate [ɪnˈædɪkwət] *adj* insufficiente
inadvertently [ɪnədˈvɜːtntlɪ] *adv* senza volerlo
inappropriate [ɪnəˈprəuprɪət] *adj* non adatto/a; (*word, expression*) improprio/a
inaugurate [ɪˈnɔːgjureɪt] *vt* inaugurare; (*president, official*) insediare
Inc. *abbr* (*us*: = *incorporated*) S.A.
incapable [ɪnˈkeɪpəbl] *adj*: **~ (of doing sth)** incapace (di fare qc)
incense *n* [ˈɪnsɛns] incenso ▷ *vt* [ɪnˈsɛns] (*anger*) infuriare
incentive [ɪnˈsɛntɪv] *n* incentivo
inch [ɪntʃ] *n* pollice *m* (= *25 mm; 12 in a foot*); **within an ~ of** a un pelo da; **he wouldn't give an ~** (*fig*) non ha ceduto di un millimetro
incidence [ˈɪnsɪdns] *n* (*of crime, disease*) incidenza
incident [ˈɪnsɪdnt] *n* incidente *m*; (*in book*) episodio
incidentally [ɪnsɪˈdɛntəlɪ] *adv* (*by the way*) a proposito
inclination [ɪnklɪˈneɪʃən] *n* inclinazione *f*

incline *n* ['ɪnklaɪn] pendenza, pendio ▷ *vt* [ɪn'klaɪn] inclinare ▷ *vi* (*surface*) essere inclinato/a; **to be ~d to do** tendere a fare; essere propenso/a a fare

include [ɪn'kluːd] *vt* includere, comprendere; **including** *prep* compreso/a, incluso/a; **inclusion** [ɪn'kluːʒən] *n* inclusione *f*; **inclusive** [ɪn'kluːsɪv] *adj* incluso/a, compreso/a; **inclusive of tax** *etc* tasse *etc* comprese

income ['ɪnkʌm] *n* reddito; **income support** *n* (BRIT) sussidio di indigenza *or* povertà; **income tax** *n* imposta sul reddito

incoming ['ɪnkʌmɪŋ] *adj* (*passengers, flight, mail*) in arrivo; (*government, tenant*) subentrante; **~ tide** marea montante

incompatible [ɪnkəm'pætɪbl] *adj* incompatibile

incompetence [ɪn'kɔmpɪtns] *n* incompetenza, incapacità

incompetent [ɪn'kɔmpɪtnt] *adj* incompetente, incapace

incomplete [ɪnkəm'pliːt] *adj* incompleto/a

inconsistent [ɪnkən'sɪstnt] *adj* incoerente; **~ with** in contraddizione con

inconvenience [ɪnkən'viːnjəns] *n* inconveniente *m*; (*trouble*) disturbo ▷ *vt* disturbare

inconvenient [ɪnkən'viːnjənt] *adj* scomodo/a

incorporate [ɪn'kɔːpəreɪt] *vt* incorporare; (*contain*) contenere

incorrect [ɪnkə'rɛkt] *adj* scorretto/a; (*statement*) inesatto/a

increase *n* ['ɪnkriːs] aumento ▷ *vi* [ɪn'kriːs] aumentare; **increasingly** *adv* sempre più

incredible [ɪn'krɛdɪbl] *adj* incredibile; **incredibly** *adv* incredibilmente

incur [ɪn'kəːʳ] *vt* (*expenses*) incorrere; (*debt*) contrarre; (*loss*) subire; (*anger, risk*) esporsi a

indecent [ɪn'diːsnt] *adj* indecente

indeed [ɪn'diːd] *adv* infatti; veramente; **yes ~!** certamente!

indefinitely [ɪn'dɛfɪnɪtlɪ] *adv* (*wait*) indefinitamente

independence [ɪndɪ'pɛndns] *n* indipendenza; **Independence Day** *n* (US) *vedi nota* **"Independence Day"**

independent [ɪndɪ'pɛndnt] *adj* indipendente; **independent school** *n* (BRIT) istituto scolastico indipendente che si autofinanzia

index ['ɪndɛks] *n* (*pl* **indexes**: *in book*) indice *m*; (: *in library etc*) catalogo; (*pl* **indices**: *ratio, sign*) indice *m*

India ['ɪndɪə] *n* India; **Indian** *adj, n* indiano/a

indicate ['ɪndɪkeɪt] *vt* indicare; **indication** [ɪndɪ'keɪʃən] *n* indicazione *f*, segno; **indicative** [ɪn'dɪkətɪv] *adj*: **indicative of** indicativo/a di ▷ *n* (*Ling*) indicativo; **to be indicative of sth** essere indicativo/aor un indice di qc; **indicator** ['ɪndɪkeɪtəʳ] *n* (*Aut*) indicatore *m* di direzione, freccia

indices ['ɪndɪsiːz] *npl of* **index**

indict [ɪn'daɪt] *vt* accusare; **indictment** [ɪn'daɪtmənt] *n* accusa

indifference [ɪn'dɪfrəns] *n* indifferenza

indifferent [ɪn'dɪfrənt] *adj* indifferente; (*poor*) mediocre

indigenous [ɪnˈdɪdʒɪnəs] *adj*
indigeno/a

indigestion [ɪndɪˈdʒɛstʃən] *n*
indigestione *f*

indignant [ɪnˈdɪgnənt] *adj*: **~ (at
sth/with sb)** indignato/a (per qc/
contro qn)

indirect [ɪndɪˈrɛkt] *adj* indiretto/a

indispensable [ɪndɪˈspɛnsəbl] *adj*
indispensabile

individual [ɪndɪˈvɪdjuəl] *n* individuo
▷ *adj* individuale; (*characteristic*)
particolare, originale; **individually**
adv singolarmente, uno/a per uno/a

Indonesia [ɪndəʊˈniːzɪə] *n*
Indonesia

indoor [ˈɪndɔːʳ] *adj* da interno; (*plant*)
d'appartamento; (*swimming pool*)
coperto/a; (*sport, games*) fatto/a
al coperto; **indoors** [ɪnˈdɔːz] *adv*
all'interno

induce [ɪnˈdjuːs] *vt* persuadere;
(*bring about, Med*) provocare

indulge [ɪnˈdʌldʒ] *vt* (*whim*)
compiacere, soddisfare; (*child*)
viziare ▷ *vi*: **to ~ in sth** concedersi
qc; abbandonarsi a qc; **indulgent** *adj*
indulgente

industrial [ɪnˈdʌstrɪəl] *adj*
industriale; (*injury*) sul lavoro;
industrial estate (BRIT) *n*
zona industriale; **industrialist**
[ɪnˈdʌstrɪəlɪst] *n* industriale
m; **industrial park** *n* (US) zona
industriale

industry [ˈɪndəstrɪ] *n* industria;
(*diligence*) operosità

inefficient [ɪnɪˈfɪʃənt] *adj*
inefficiente

inequality [ɪnɪˈkwɔlɪtɪ] *n*
ineguaglianza

inevitable [ɪnˈɛvɪtəbl] *adj*
inevitabile; **inevitably** *adv*
inevitabilmente

inexpensive [ɪnɪkˈspɛnsɪv] *adj* poco
costoso/a

inexperienced [ɪnɪkˈspɪərɪənst] *adj*
inesperto/a, senza esperienza

inexplicable [ɪnɪkˈsplɪkəbl] *adj*
inesplicabile

infamous [ˈɪnfəməs] *adj* infame

infant [ˈɪnfənt] *n* bambino/a

infantry [ˈɪnfəntrɪ] *n* fanteria

infant school *n* (BRIT) scuola
elementare (*per bambini dall'età di
5 a 7 anni*)

infect [ɪnˈfɛkt] *vt* infettare;
infection [ɪnˈfɛkʃən] *n* infezione
f; **infectious** [ɪnˈfɛkʃəs] *adj*
(*disease*) infettivo/a, contagioso/a;
(*person, laughter, enthusiasm*)
contagioso/a

infer [ɪnˈfəːʳ] *vt*: **to ~ (from)** dedurre
(da), concludere (da)

inferior [ɪnˈfɪərɪəʳ] *adj* inferiore;
(*goods*) di qualità scadente ▷ *n*
inferiore *m/f*; (*in rank*) subalterno/a

infertile [ɪnˈfəːtaɪl] *adj* sterile

infertility [ɪnfəˈtɪlɪtɪ] *n* sterilità

infested [ɪnˈfɛstɪd] *adj*: **~ (with)**
infestato/a (di)

infinite [ˈɪnfɪnɪt] *adj* infinito/a;
infinitely *adv* infinitamente

infirmary [ɪnˈfəːmərɪ] *n* ospedale *m*;
(*in school, factory*) infermeria

inflamed [ɪnˈfleɪmd] *adj*
infiammato/a

inflammation [ɪnfləˈmeɪʃən] *n*
infiammazione *f*

inflatable [ɪnˈfleɪtəbl] *adj*
gonfiabile

inflate [ɪnˈfleɪt] *vt* (*tyre, balloon*)
gonfiare; (*fig*) esagerare; gonfiare;
inflation [ɪnˈfleɪʃən] *n* (*Econ*)
inflazione *f*

inflexible [ɪnˈflɛksɪbl] *adj*
inflessibile, rigido/a

inflict [ɪnˈflɪkt] *vt*: **to ~ on**
infliggere a

influence [ˈɪnfluəns] *n* influenza
▷ *vt* influenzare; **under the ~ of
alcohol** sotto l'influenza or l'effetto
dell'alcool; **influential** [ɪnfluˈɛnʃl]
adj influente

influx [ˈɪnflʌks] *n* afflusso

info [ˈɪnfəʊ] *n* (*col*) = **information**

inform [ɪn'fɔːm] vt: **to ~ sb (of)** informare qn (di) ▷ vi: **to ~ on sb** denunciare qn

informal [ɪn'fɔːml] adj informale; (announcement, invitation) non ufficiale

information [ɪnfə'meɪʃən] n informazioni fpl; particolari mpl; **a piece of ~** un'informazione; **information office** n ufficio m informazioni inv; **information technology** n informatica

informative [ɪn'fɔːmətɪv] adj istruttivo/a

infra-red [ɪnfrə'rɛd] adj infrarosso/a

infrastructure ['ɪnfrəstrʌktʃər] n infrastruttura

infrequent [ɪn'friːkwənt] adj infrequente, raro/a

infuriate [ɪn'fjuərɪeɪt] vt rendere furioso/a

infuriating [ɪn'fjuərɪeɪtɪŋ] adj molto irritante

ingenious [ɪn'dʒiːnjəs] adj ingegnoso/a

ingredient [ɪn'griːdɪənt] n ingrediente m; elemento

inhabit [ɪn'hæbɪt] vt abitare; **inhabitant** [ɪn'hæbɪtnt] n abitante m/f

inhale [ɪn'heɪl] vt inalare ▷ vi (in smoking) aspirare; **inhaler** n inalatore m

inherent [ɪn'hɪərənt] adj: **~ (in or to)** inerente (a)

inherit [ɪn'hɛrɪt] vt ereditare; **inheritance** n eredità

inhibit [ɪn'hɪbɪt] vt (Psych) inibire; **inhibition** [ɪnhɪ'bɪʃən] n inibizione f

initial [ɪ'nɪʃl] adj iniziale ▷ n iniziale f ▷ vt siglare; **initials** npl (of name) iniziali fpl; (as signature) sigla; **initially** adv inizialmente, all'inizio

initiate [ɪ'nɪʃɪeɪt] vt (start) avviare; intraprendere; iniziare; (person) iniziare; **to ~ sb into a secret** mettere qn a parte di un segreto; **to**

~ proceedings against sb (Law) intentare causa a or contro qn

initiative [ɪ'nɪʃətɪv] n iniziativa

inject [ɪn'dʒɛkt] vt (liquid) iniettare; (person) fare un'iniezione a; (money): **to ~ sb with sth** fare a qn un'iniezione di qc; **to ~ into** immettere in; **injection** [ɪn'dʒɛkʃən] n iniezione f, puntura

injure ['ɪndʒər] vt ferire; (damage: reputation etc) nuocere a; **injured** adj ferito/a; **injury** ['ɪndʒərɪ] n ferita

injustice [ɪn'dʒʌstɪs] n ingiustizia

ink [ɪŋk] n inchiostro; **ink-jet printer** ['ɪŋkdʒɛt-] n stampante f a getto d'inchiostro

inland adj ['ɪnlənd] interno/a ▷ adv [ɪn'lænd] all'interno; **Inland Revenue** n (BRIT) Fisco

in-laws ['ɪnlɔːz] npl suoceri mpl; famiglia del marito (or della moglie)

inmate ['ɪnmeɪt] n (in prison) carcerato/a; (in asylum) ricoverato/a

inn [ɪn] n locanda

inner ['ɪnər] adj interno/a, interiore; **inner city** n centro di una zona urbana

inning ['ɪnɪŋ] n (US Baseball) ripresa; **~s** (Cricket) turno di battuta

innocence ['ɪnəsns] n innocenza

innocent ['ɪnəsnt] adj innocente

innovation [ɪnəu'veɪʃən] n innovazione f

innovative ['ɪnəu'veɪtɪv] adj innovativo/a

in-patient ['ɪnpeɪʃənt] n ricoverato/a

input ['ɪnput] n input m

inquest ['ɪnkwɛst] n inchiesta

inquire [ɪn'kwaɪər] vi informarsi ▷ vt domandare, informarsi di or su; **inquiry** n domanda; (Law) indagine f, investigazione f; **"inquiries"** "informazioni"

ins. abbr = **inches**

insane [ɪn'seɪn] adj matto/a, pazzo/a; (Med) alienato/a

insanity [ɪnˈsænɪtɪ] *n* follia; (*Med*) alienazione *f* mentale

insect [ˈɪnsɛkt] *n* insetto; **insect repellent** *n* insettifugo

insecure [ɪnsɪˈkjuəʳ] *adj* malsicuro/a; (*person*) insicuro/a

insecurity [ɪnsɪˈkjuərɪtɪ] *n* mancanza di sicurezza

insensitive [ɪnˈsɛnsɪtɪv] *adj* insensibile

insert [ɪnˈsəːt] *vt* inserire, introdurre

inside [ˈɪnsaɪd] *n* interno, parte *f* interiore ▷ *adj* interno/a, interiore ▷ *adv* dentro, all'interno ▷ *prep* dentro, all'interno di; (*of time*): **~ 10 minutes** entro 10 minuti; **insides** *npl* (*col*) ventre *m*; **~ out** *adv* alla rovescia; **to turn sth ~ out** rivoltare qc; **to know sth ~ out** conoscere qc a fondo; **inside lane** *n* (*Aut*) corsia di marcia

insight [ˈɪnsaɪt] *n* acume *m*, perspicacia; (*glimpse, idea*) percezione *f*

insignificant [ɪnsɪɡˈnɪfɪkənt] *adj* insignificante

insincere [ɪnsɪnˈsɪəʳ] *adj* insincero/a

insist [ɪnˈsɪst] *vi* insistere; **to ~ on doing** insistere per fare; **to ~ that** insistere perché + *sub*; (*claim*) sostenere che; **insistent** *adj* insistente

insomnia [ɪnˈsɒmnɪə] *n* insonnia

inspect [ɪnˈspɛkt] *vt* ispezionare; (*BRIT: ticket*) controllare; **inspection** [ɪnˈspɛkʃən] *n* ispezione *f*; controllo; **inspector** *n* ispettore/trice; (*BRIT: on buses, trains*) controllore *m*

inspiration [ɪnspəˈreɪʃən] *n* ispirazione *f*; **inspire** [ɪnˈspaɪəʳ] *vt* ispirare; **inspiring** *adj* stimolante

instability [ɪnstəˈbɪlɪtɪ] *n* instabilità

install [ɪnˈstɔːl], (*US*) **instal** *vt* installare; **installation** [ɪnstəˈleɪʃən] *n* installazione *f*

instalment, (*US*) **installment** [ɪnˈstɔːlmənt] *n* rata; (*of TV serial etc*)

puntata; **in ~s** (*pay*) a rate; (*receive*) una parte per volta; (*publication*) a fascicoli

instance [ˈɪnstəns] *n* esempio, caso; **for ~** per *or* ad esempio; **in the first ~** in primo luogo

instant [ˈɪnstənt] *n* istante *m*, attimo ▷ *adj* immediato/a; urgente; (*coffee, food*) in polvere; **instantly** *adv* immediatamente, subito; **instant messaging** *n* messaggeria istantanea

instead [ɪnˈstɛd] *adv* invece; **~ of** invece di

instinct [ˈɪnstɪŋkt] *n* istinto; **instinctive** *adj* istintivo/a

institute [ˈɪnstɪtjuːt] *n* istituto ▷ *vt* istituire, stabilire; (*inquiry*) avviare; (*proceedings*) iniziare

institution [ɪnstɪˈtjuːʃən] *n* istituzione *f*; istituto (d'istruzione); istituto (psichiatrico)

instruct [ɪnˈstrʌkt] *vt*: **to ~ sb in sth** insegnare qc a qn; **to ~ sb to do** dare ordini a qn di fare; **instruction** [ɪnˈstrʌkʃən] *n* istruzione *f*; **instructions (for use)** istruzioni per l'uso; **instructor** *n* istruttore/trice; (*for skiing*) maestro/a

instrument [ˈɪnstrumənt] *n* strumento; **instrumental** [ɪnstruˈmɛntl] *adj* (*Mus*) strumentale; **to be instrumental in sth/in doing sth** contribuire fattivamente a qc/a fare qc

insufficient [ɪnsəˈfɪʃənt] *adj* insufficiente

insulate [ˈɪnsjuleɪt] *vt* isolare; **insulation** [ɪnsjuˈleɪʃən] *n* isolamento

insulin [ˈɪnsjulɪn] *n* insulina

insult *n* [ˈɪnsʌlt] insulto, affronto ▷ *vt* [ɪnˈsʌlt] insultare; **insulting** *adj* offensivo/a, ingiurioso/a

insurance [ɪnˈʃuərəns] *n* assicurazione *f*; **fire/life ~** assicurazione contro gli incendi/sulla vita; **insurance company** *n* società di assicurazioni; **insurance policy** *n* polizza d'assicurazione

insure [ɪnˈʃuəʳ] *vt* assicurare

intact [ɪnˈtækt] *adj* intatto/a

intake [ˈɪnteɪk] *n* (*Tech*) immissione *f*; (*of food*) consumo; (BRIT: *of pupils etc*) afflusso

integral [ˈɪntɪɡrəl] *adj* integrale; (*part*) integrante

integrate [ˈɪntɪɡreɪt] *vt* integrare ▷ *vi* integrarsi

integrity [ɪnˈtɛɡrɪtɪ] *n* integrità

intellect [ˈɪntəlɛkt] *n* intelletto; **intellectual** [ɪntəˈlɛktjuəl] *adj*, *n* intellettuale (*m/f*)

intelligence [ɪnˈtɛlɪdʒəns] *n* intelligenza; (*Mil etc*) informazioni *fpl*

intelligent [ɪnˈtɛlɪdʒənt] *adj* intelligente

intend [ɪnˈtɛnd] *vt* (*gift etc*): **to ~ sth for** destinare qc a; **to ~ to do** aver l'intenzione di fare

intense [ɪnˈtɛns] *adj* intenso/a; (*person*) di forti sentimenti

intensify [ɪnˈtɛnsɪfaɪ] *vt* intensificare

intensity [ɪnˈtɛnsɪtɪ] *n* intensità

intensive [ɪnˈtɛnsɪv] *adj* intensivo/a; **intensive care** *n* terapia intensiva; **intensive care unit** *n* reparto terapia intensiva

intent [ɪnˈtɛnt] *n* intenzione *f* ▷ *adj*: **~ (on)** intento/a (a), immerso/a (in); **to all ~s and purposes** a tutti gli effetti; **to be ~ on doing sth** essere deciso a fare qc

intention [ɪnˈtɛnʃən] *n* intenzione *f*; **intentional** *adj* intenzionale, deliberato/a

interact [ɪntərˈækt] *vi* interagire; **interaction** [ɪntərˈækʃən] *n* azione *f* reciproca, interazione *f*; **interactive** *adj* (*Comput*) interattivo/a

intercept [ɪntəˈsɛpt] *vt* intercettare; (*person*) fermare

interchange *n* [ˈɪntətʃeɪndʒ] (*exchange*) scambio; (*on motorway*) incrocio pluridirezionale

intercourse [ˈɪntəkɔːs] *n* rapporti *mpl*

interest [ˈɪntrɪst] *n* interesse *m*; (*Comm: stake, share*) interessi *mpl* ▷ *vt* interessare; **interested** *adj* interessato/a; **to be interested in** interessarsi di; **interesting** *adj* interessante; **interest rate** *n* tasso di interesse

interface [ˈɪntəfeɪs] *n* (*Comput*) interfaccia

interfere [ɪntəˈfɪəʳ] *vi*: **to ~ (in)** (*quarrel, other people's business*) immischiarsi (in); **to ~ with** (*object*) toccare; (*plans, duty*) interferire con; **interference** [ɪntəˈfɪərəns] *n* interferenza

interim [ˈɪntərɪm] *adj* provvisorio/a ▷ *n*: **in the ~** nel frattempo

interior [ɪnˈtɪərɪəʳ] *n* interno; (*of country*) entroterra ▷ *adj* interno/a; (*minister*) degli Interni; **interior design** *n* architettura d'interni

intermediate [ɪntəˈmiːdɪət] *adj* intermedio/a

intermission [ɪntəˈmɪʃən] *n* pausa; (*Theat, Cine*) intermissione *f*, intervallo

intern *vt* [ɪnˈtəːn] internare ▷ *n* [ˈɪntəːn] (*US*) medico interno

internal [ɪnˈtəːnl] *adj* interno/a; **Internal Revenue, Internal Revenue Service** *n* (*US*) Fisco

international [ɪntəˈnæʃənl] *adj* internazionale ▷ *n* (BRIT *Sport*) incontro internazionale

Internet [ˈɪntənɛt] *n*: **the ~** Internet *f*; **Internet café** *n* cybercaffè *m* *inv*; **Internet Service Provider** *n* Provider *m* *inv*; **Internet user** *n* utente *m/f* Internet

interpret [ɪnˈtəːprɪt] *vt* interpretare ▷ *vi* fare da interprete; **interpretation** [ɪntəːprɪˈteɪʃən] *n* interpretazione *f*; **interpreter** *n* interprete *m/f*

interrogate [ɪnˈtɛrəʊɡeɪt] *vt* interrogare; **interrogation**

[ɪntɛrəʊ'geɪʃən] n interrogazione f; (of suspect etc) interrogatorio

interrogative [ɪntə'rɒgətɪv] adj interrogativo/a ▷ n (Ling) interrogativo

interrupt [ɪntə'rʌpt] vt, vi interrompere; **interruption** [ɪntə'rʌpʃən] n interruzione f

intersection [ɪntə'sɛkʃən] n intersezione f; (of roads) incrocio

interstate ['ɪntərsteɪt] (US) n fra stati

interval ['ɪntəvl] n intervallo; **at ~s** a intervalli

intervene [ɪntə'viːn] vi (time) intercorrere; (event, person) intervenire

interview ['ɪntəvjuː] n (Radio, TV etc) intervista; (for job) colloquio ▷ vt intervistare; avere un colloquio con; **interviewer** n intervistatore/trice

intimate adj ['ɪntɪmət] intimo/a; (knowledge) profondo/a ▷ vt ['ɪntɪmeɪt] lasciar capire

intimidate [ɪn'tɪmɪdeɪt] vt intimidire, intimorire

intimidating [ɪn'tɪmɪdeɪtɪŋ] adj (sight) spaventoso/a; (appearance, figure) minaccioso/a

into ['ɪntu] prep dentro, in; **come ~ the house** entra in casa; **he worked late ~ the night** lavorò fino a tarda notte; **~ Italian** in italiano

intolerant [ɪn'tɒlərnt] adj: **~ (of)** intollerante (di)

intranet ['ɪntrənɛt] n Intranet f

intransitive [ɪn'trænsɪtɪv] adj intransitivo/a

intricate ['ɪntrɪkət] adj intricato/a, complicato/a

intrigue [ɪn'triːg] n intrigo ▷ vt affascinare; **intriguing** adj affascinante

introduce [ɪntrə'djuːs] vt introdurre; **to ~ sb (to sb)** presentare qn (a qn); **to ~ sb to** (pastime, technique) iniziare qn a; **introduction** [ɪntrə'dʌkʃən] n introduzione f; (of person)

presentazione f; (to new experience) iniziazione f; **introductory** adj introduttivo/a

intrude [ɪn'truːd] vi (person) intromettersi; **to ~ on**; intromettersi in; **intruder** n intruso/a

intuition [ɪntjuː'ɪʃən] n intuizione f

inundate ['ɪnʌndeɪt] vt: **to ~ with** inondare di

invade [ɪn'veɪd] vt invadere

invalid n ['ɪnvəlɪd] malato/a; (with disability) invalido/a ▷ adj [ɪn'vælɪd] (not valid) invalido/a, non valido/a

invaluable [ɪn'væljuəbl] adj prezioso/a; inestimabile

invariably [ɪn'vɛərɪəblɪ] adv invariabilmente; sempre

invasion [ɪn'veɪʒən] n invasione f

invent [ɪn'vɛnt] vt inventare; **invention** [ɪn'vɛnʃən] n invenzione f; **inventor** n inventore m

inventory ['ɪnvəntrɪ] n inventario m

inverted commas [ɪn'və:tɪd-] npl (BRIT) virgolette fpl

invest [ɪn'vɛst] vt investire ▷ vi: **to ~ in** investire in

investigate [ɪn'vɛstɪgeɪt] vt investigare, indagare; (crime) fare indagini su; **investigation** [ɪnvɛstɪ'geɪʃən] n investigazione f; (of crime) indagine f

investigator [ɪn'vɛstɪgeɪtər] n investigatore/trice; **a private ~** un investigatore privato, un detective

investment [ɪn'vɛstmənt] n investimento

investor [ɪn'vɛstər] n investitore/trice; (shareholder) azionista m/f

invisible [ɪn'vɪzɪbl] adj invisibile

invitation [ɪnvɪ'teɪʃən] n invito

invite [ɪn'vaɪt] vt invitare; (opinions etc) sollecitare; **inviting** adj invitante, attraente

invoice ['ɪnvɔɪs] n fattura ▷ vt fatturare

involve [ɪn'vɒlv] vt (entail) richiedere, comportare; (associate): **to ~ sb (in)** implicare qn (in); coinvolgere qn (in); **involved** adj involuto/a, complesso/a; **to be involved in** essere coinvolto/a in; **involvement** n implicazione f; coinvolgimento

inward ['ɪnwəd] adj (movement) verso l'interno; (thought, feeling) interiore, intimo/a ▷ adv verso l'interno

iPod® ['aɪpɒd] n iPod® m inv

IQ n abbr (= intelligence quotient) quoziente m d'intelligenza

IRA n abbr (= Irish Republican Army) I.R.A. f

Iran [ɪ'rɑːn] n Iran m; **Iranian** [ɪ'reɪnɪən] adj, n iraniano/a

Iraq [ɪ'rɑːk] n Iraq m; **Iraqi** adj, n iracheno/a

Ireland ['aɪələnd] n Irlanda

iris ['aɪrɪs, -ɪz] n (pl **irises**) iride f; (Bot) giaggiolo, iride

Irish ['aɪrɪʃ] adj irlandese ▷ npl: **the ~** gli Irlandesi; **Irishman** n (irreg) irlandese m; **Irish Sea** n: **the Irish Sea** il mar d'Irlanda; **Irishwoman** n (irreg) irlandese f

iron ['aɪən] n ferro; (for clothes) ferro da stiro ▷ adj di or in ferro ▷ vt (clothes) stirare

ironic(al) [aɪ'rɒnɪk(l)] adj ironico/a; **ironically** adv ironicamente

ironing ['aɪənɪŋ] n (act) stirare m; (clothes) roba da stirare; **ironing board** n asse f da stiro

irony ['aɪrənɪ] n ironia

irrational [ɪ'ræʃənl] adj irrazionale

irregular [ɪ'rɛgjulə'] adj irregolare

irrelevant [ɪ'rɛləvənt] adj non pertinente

irresistible [ɪrɪ'zɪstɪbl] adj irresistibile

irresponsible [ɪrɪ'spɒnsɪbl] adj irresponsabile

irrigation [ɪrɪ'geɪʃən] n irrigazione f

irritable ['ɪrɪtəbl] adj irritabile

irritate ['ɪrɪteɪt] vt irritare; **irritating** adj (person, sound etc) irritante; **irritation** [ɪrɪ'teɪʃən] n irritazione f

IRS n abbr (US) = **Internal Revenue Service**

is [ɪz] vb see **be**

ISDN n abbr (= Integrated Services Digital Network) ISDN f

Islam ['ɪzlɑːm] n Islam m; **Islamic** [ɪz'læmɪk] adj islamico/a

island ['aɪlənd] n isola; **islander** n isolano/a

isle [aɪl] n isola

isn't ['ɪznt] = **is not**

isolated ['aɪsəleɪtɪd] adj isolato/a

isolation [aɪsə'leɪʃən] n isolamento

ISP n abbr (Comput: = internet service provider) provider m inv

Israel ['ɪzreɪl] n Israele m; **Israeli** [ɪz'reɪlɪ] adj, n israeliano/a

issue ['ɪʃjuː] n questione f, problema m; (of banknotes etc) emissione f; (of newspaper etc) numero ▷ vt (statement) rilasciare; (rations, equipment) distribuire; (book) pubblicare; (banknotes, cheques, stamps) emettere; **at ~** in gioco, in discussione; **to take ~ with sb (over sth)** prendere posizione contro qn (riguardo a qc); **to make an ~ of sth** fare un problema di qc

IT n abbr = **information technology**

KEYWORD

it [ɪt] pron **1** (specific: subject) esso/a; (: direct object) lo (la), l'; (: indirect object) gli (le); **where's my book? — it's on the table** dov'è il mio libro? — è sulla tavola; **I can't find it** non lo (or la) trovo; **give it to me** dammelo (or dammela); **about/ from/of it** ne; **I spoke to him about it** gliene ho parlato; **what did you learn from it?** quale insegnamento ne hai tratto?; **I'm proud of it** ne sono fiero; **put the book in it** mettici il libro; **did you go to it?** ci sei andato?

2 (impers): **it's raining** piove; **it's Friday tomorrow** domani è venerdì; **it's 6 o'clock** sono le 6; **who is it? — it's me** chi è? — sono io

Italian [ɪˈtæljən] *adj* italiano/a ▷ *n*
italiano/a; (*Ling*) italiano; **the ~s**
gli Italiani

italic [ɪˈtælɪk] *adj* corsivo/a; **italics**
npl corsivo

Italy [ˈɪtəlɪ] *n* Italia

ITC *n abbr* (BRIT: = Independent Television
Commission) organo di controllo sulle
reti televisive

itch [ɪtʃ] *n* prurito ▷ *vi* (*person*) avere il
prurito; (*part of body*) prudere; **to be
~ing to do** avere una gran voglia di
fare; **itchy** *adj* che prude; **my back is
itchy** ho prurito alla schiena

it'd [ˈɪtd] = **it would; it had**

item [ˈaɪtəm] *n* articolo; (*on agenda*)
punto; (*also*: **news ~**) notizia

itinerary [aɪˈtɪnərərɪ] *n* itinerario

it'll [ˈɪtl] = **it will; it shall**

its [ɪts] *adj* il (la) suo/a, i (le) suoi (sue)

it's [ɪts] = **it is; it has**

itself [ɪtˈsɛlf] *pron* (*emphatic*) esso/a
stesso/a; (*reflexive*) si

ITV *n abbr* (BRIT: = Independent
Television) rete televisiva indipendente

I've [aɪv] = **I have**

ivory [ˈaɪvərɪ] *n* avorio

ivy [ˈaɪvɪ] *n* edera

jab [dʒæb] *vt* dare colpetti a; **to ~ sth
into** affondare *or* piantare qc dentro
▷ *n* (*Med*: *col*) puntura

jack [dʒæk] *n* (*Aut*) cricco; (*Cards*)
fante *m*

jacket [ˈdʒækɪt] *n* giacca; (*of book*)
copertura; **jacket potato** *n* patata
cotta al forno con la buccia

jackpot [ˈdʒækpɔt] *n* primo premio
(in denaro)

Jacuzzi® [dʒəˈkuːzɪ] *n* vasca per
idromassaggio Jacuzzi®

jagged [ˈdʒægɪd] *adj* seghettato/a;
(*cliffs etc*) frastagliato/a

jail [dʒeɪl] *n* prigione *f* ▷ *vt* mandare in
prigione; **jail sentence** *n* condanna
al carcere

jam [dʒæm] *n* marmellata; (*also*:
traffic ~) ingorgo; (*col*) pasticcio
▷ *vt* (*passage etc*) ingombrare,
ostacolare; (*mechanism, drawer etc*)
bloccare; (*Radio*) disturbare con
interferenze ▷ *vi* incepparsi; **to ~**

sth into forzare qc dentro; infilare qc a forza dentro

Jamaica [dʒəˈmeɪkə] n Giamaica

jammed [dʒæmd] adj (door) bloccato/a; (rifle, printer) inceppato/a

Jan. abbr (= January) gen., genn.

janitor [ˈdʒænɪtə^r] n (caretaker) portiere m; (: Scol) bidello

January [ˈdʒænjʊərɪ] n gennaio

Japan [dʒəˈpæn] n Giappone m; **Japanese** [dʒæpəˈniːz] adj giapponese ▷ n (pl inv) giapponese m/f; (Ling) giapponese m

jar [dʒɑː^r] n (container) barattolo, vasetto ▷ vi (sound) stridere; (colours etc) stonare

jargon [ˈdʒɑːgən] n gergo

javelin [ˈdʒævlɪn] n giavellotto

jaw [dʒɔː] n mascella

jazz [dʒæz] n jazz m

jealous [ˈdʒɛləs] adj geloso/a; **jealousy** n gelosia

jeans [dʒiːnz] npl (blue-)jeans mpl

Jello® [ˈdʒɛləʊ] n (US) gelatina di frutta

jelly [ˈdʒɛlɪ] n gelatina; **jellyfish** n medusa

jeopardize [ˈdʒɛpədaɪz] vt mettere in pericolo

jerk [dʒəːk] n sobbalzo, scossa; sussulto; (col) povero/a scemo/a ▷ vt dare una scossa a ▷ vi (vehicles) sobbalzare

Jersey [ˈdʒəːzɪ] n Jersey m

jersey [ˈdʒəːzɪ] n maglia; (fabric) jersey m

Jesus [ˈdʒiːzəs] n Gesù m

jet [dʒɛt] n (of gas, liquid) getto; (Aviat) aviogetto; **jet lag** n (problemi mpl dovuti allo) sbalzo dei fusi orari; **jet-ski** vi acquascooter m inv

jetty [ˈdʒɛtɪ] n molo

Jew [dʒuː] n ebreo

jewel [ˈdʒuːəl] n gioiello; **jeweller**, (US) **jeweler** n orefice m, gioielliere/a; **jeweller's shop** oreficeria, gioielleria; **jewellery**, (US) **jewelry** n gioielli mpl; **jewelry store** (US) oreficeria, gioielleria

Jewish [ˈdʒuːɪʃ] adj ebreo/a, ebraico/a

jigsaw [ˈdʒɪgsɔː] n (also: ~ **puzzle**) puzzle m inv

job [dʒɔb] n lavoro; (employment) impiego, posto; **that's not my ~** non è compito mio; **it's a good ~ that ...** meno male che ...; **just the ~!** proprio quello che ci vuole!; **job centre** (BRIT) n ufficio di collocamento; **jobless** adj senza lavoro, disoccupato/a

jockey [ˈdʒɔkɪ] n fantino, jockey m inv ▷ vi: **to ~ for position** manovrare per una posizione di vantaggio

jog [dʒɔg] vt urtare ▷ vi (Sport) fare footing, fare jogging; **to ~ along** trottare; (fig) andare avanti pian piano; **to ~ sb's memory** rinfrescare la memoria di qn; **jogging** n footing m, jogging m

join [dʒɔɪn] vt unire, congiungere; (become member of) iscriversi a; (meet) raggiungere; riunirsi a ▷ vi (roads, rivers) confluire ▷ n giuntura; **join in** vt fus unirsi a ▷ vi partecipare; **join up** vi incontrarsi; (Mil) arruolarsi

joiner [ˈdʒɔɪnə^r] n (BRIT) falegname m

joint [dʒɔɪnt] n (Tech) giuntura; giunto; (Anat) articolazione f, giuntura; (BRIT Culin) arrosto; (col: place) locale m; (: of cannabis) spinello ▷ adj comune; **joint account** n (at bank etc) conto comune; **jointly** adv in comune, insieme

joke [dʒəʊk] n scherzo; (funny story) barzelletta; (also: **practical ~**) beffa ▷ vi scherzare; **to play a ~ on** fare uno scherzo a; **joker** n (Cards) matta, jolly m inv

jolly [ˈdʒɔlɪ] adj allegro/a, gioioso/a ▷ adv (BRIT col) veramente, proprio

jolt [dʒəʊlt] n scossa, sobbalzo ▷ vt urtare

Jordan [ˈdʒɔːdən] n (country) Giordania; (river) Giordano

journal [ˈdʒəːnl] n giornale m; (periodical) rivista; (diary) diario;

journalism n giornalismo;
journalist n giornalista m/f
journey ['dʒəːnɪ] n viaggio; (distance covered) tragitto; **how was your ~?** com'è andato il viaggio?; **the ~ takes two hours** il viaggio dura due ore
joy [dʒɔɪ] n gioia; **joyrider** ['dʒɔɪraɪdə^r] n chi ruba una macchina per andare a farsi un giro; **joy stick** ['dʒɔɪstɪk] n (Aviat) barra di comando; (Comput) joystick m inv
Jr. abbr = **junior**
judge [dʒʌdʒ] n giudice m/f ▷ vt giudicare
judo ['dʒuːdəu] n judo
jug [dʒʌg] n brocca, bricco
juggle ['dʒʌgl] vi fare giochi di destrezza; **juggler** n giocoliere/a
juice [dʒuːs] n succo; **juicy** ['dʒuːsɪ] adj succoso/a
Jul. abbr (= July) lug., lu.
July [dʒuːˈlaɪ] n luglio
jumble ['dʒʌmbl] n miscuglio ▷ vt (also: ~ **up, ~ together**) mischiare; **jumble sale** (BRIT) n ≈ vendita di beneficenza

○ **JUMBLE SALE**
○
○ La jumble sale è un mercatino dove
○ vengono venduti vari oggetti,
○ per lo più di seconda mano; viene
○ organizzata in chiese, scuole o
○ circoli ricreativi. I proventi delle
○ vendite vengono devoluti in
○ beneficenza o usati per una giusta
○ causa.

jumbo ['dʒʌmbəu] adj: ~ **jet** jumbo-jet m inv; **~ size** formato gigante
jump [dʒʌmp] vi saltare, balzare; (start) sobbalzare; (increase) rincarare ▷ vt saltare ▷ n salto, balzo; sobbalzo
jumper ['dʒʌmpə^r] n (BRIT: pullover) maglione m; (US: pinafore dress) scamiciato
jump leads, (US) **jumper cables** npl cavi mpl per batteria

Jun. abbr = **junior**
junction ['dʒʌŋkʃən] n (BRIT: of roads) incrocio; (of rails) nodo ferroviario
June [dʒuːn] n giugno
jungle ['dʒʌŋgl] n giungla
junior ['dʒuːnɪə^r] adj, n: **he's ~ to me (by 2 years), he's my ~ (by 2 years)** è più giovane di me (di 2 anni); **he's ~ to me** (seniority) è al di sotto di me, ho più anzianità di lui; **junior high school** n (US) scuola media (da 12 a 15 anni); **junior school** n (BRIT) scuola elementare (da 8 a 11 anni)
junk [dʒʌŋk] n cianfrusaglie fpl; (cheap goods) robaccia; **junk food** n porcherie fpl
junkie ['dʒʌŋkɪ] n (col) drogato/a
junk mail n pubblicità f inv in cassetta
Jupiter ['dʒuːpɪtə^r] n (planet) Giove m
jurisdiction [dʒuərɪsˈdɪkʃən] n giurisdizione f; **it falls** or **comes within/outside our ~** è/non è di nostra competenza
jury ['dʒuərɪ] n giuria
just [dʒʌst] adj giusto/a ▷ adv: **he's ~ done it/left** lo ha appena fatto/è appena partito; **~ right** proprio giusto; **~ 2 o'clock** le 2 precise; **she's ~ as clever as you** è in gamba proprio quanto te; **~ as I arrived** proprio mentre arrivavo; **it was ~ before/enough/here** era poco prima/appena assai/proprio qui; **it's ~ me** sono solo io; **~ missed/caught** appena perso/preso; **~ listen to this!** senta un po' questo!; **it's ~ as well you didn't go** meno male che non ci sei andato
justice ['dʒʌstɪs] n giustizia
justification [dʒʌstɪfɪˈkeɪʃən] n giustificazione f; (Typ) giustezza
justify ['dʒʌstɪfaɪ] vt giustificare
jut [dʒʌt] vi (also: ~ **out**) sporgersi
juvenile ['dʒuːvənaɪl] adj giovane, giovanile; (court) dei minorenni; (books) per ragazzi ▷ n giovane m/f, minorenne m/f

K *n abbr* (= *one thousand*) mille ▷ *abbr* (= *kilobyte*) K

kangaroo [kæŋɡəˈruː] *n* canguro

karaoke [kɑːrəˈəʊkɪ] *n* karaoke *m inv*

karate [kəˈrɑːtɪ] *n* karate *m*

kebab [kəˈbæb] *n* spiedino

keel [kiːl] *n* chiglia; **on an even ~** (*fig*) in uno stato normale

keen [kiːn] *adj* (*interest, desire*) vivo/a; (*eye, intelligence*) acuto/a; (*competition*) serrato/a; (*edge*) affilato/a; (*eager*) entusiasta; **to be ~ to do** *or* **on doing sth** avere una gran voglia di fare qc; **to be ~ on sth** essere appassionato/a di qc; **to be ~ on sb** avere un debole per qn

keep (*pt, pp* **kept**) [kiːp, kɛpt] *vt* tenere; (*hold back*) trattenere; (*feed: one's family etc*) mantenere, sostentare; (*a promise*) mantenere; (*chickens, bees, pigs etc*) allevare ▷ *vi* (*food*) mantenersi; (*remain: in a certain state or place*) restare ▷ *n* (*of castle*) maschio; (*food etc*): **enough for his ~** abbastanza per vitto e alloggio; **to ~ doing sth** continuare a fare qc; fare qc di continuo; **to ~ sb from doing/sth from happening** impedire a qn di fare/che qc succeda; **to ~ sb busy/a place tidy** tenere qn occupato/a/un luogo in ordine; **to ~ sth to o.s.** tenere qc per sé; **to ~ sth (back) from sb** celare qc a qn; **to ~ time** (*clock*) andar bene; **keep away** *vt*: **to ~ sth/sb away from sb** tenere qc/qn lontano da qn ▷ *vi*: **to ~ away (from)** stare lontano (da); **keep back** *vt* (*crowds, tears, money*) trattenere ▷ *vi* tenersi indietro; **keep off** *vt* (*dog, person*) tenere lontano da ▷ *vi* stare alla larga; **~ your hands off!** non toccare!, giù le mani!; **"~ off the grass"** "non calpestare l'erba"; **keep on** *vi*: **to ~ on doing** continuare a fare; **to ~ on (about sth)** continuare a insistere (su qc); **keep out** *vt* tener fuori; **"~ out"** "vietato l'accesso"; **keep up** *vt* continuare, mantenere ▷ *vi*: **to ~ up with** tener dietro a, andare di pari passo con; (*work etc*) farcela a seguire; **keeper** *n* custode *m/f*, guardiano/a; **keeping** *n* (*care*) custodia; **in keeping with** in armonia con; in accordo con; **keeps** *n*: **for keeps** (*col*) per sempre

kennel [ˈkɛnl] *n* canile *m*; **kennels** *npl* canile *m*; **to put a dog in ~s** mettere un cane al canile

Kenya [ˈkɛnjə] *n* Kenia *m*

kept [kɛpt] *pt, pp of* **keep**

kerb [kəːb] *n* (*BRIT*) orlo del marciapiede

kerosene [ˈkɛrəsiːn] *n* cherosene *m*

ketchup [ˈkɛtʃəp] *n* ketchup *m inv*

kettle [ˈkɛtl] *n* bollitore *m*

key [kiː] *n* (*gen, Mus*) chiave *f*; (*of piano, typewriter*) tasto ▷ *cpd* chiave *inv*; **key in** *vt* (*text*) digitare; **keyboard** *n* tastiera; **keyhole** *n* buco della serratura; **key ring** *n* portachiavi *m inv*

kg *abbr* (= kilogram) Kg

khaki ['kɑːkɪ] *adj*, *n* cachi (*m*)

kick [kɪk] *vt* calciare, dare calci a; (*col: habit etc*) liberarsi di ▷ *vi* (*horse*) tirar calci ▷ *n* calcio; (*col: thrill*): **he does it for ~s** lo fa giusto per il piacere di farlo; **kick off** *vi* (*Sport*) dare il primo calcio; **kick-off** *n* (*Sport*) calcio d'inizio

kid [kɪd] *n* (*col: child*) ragazzino/a; (*animal, leather*) capretto ▷ *vi* (*col*) scherzare

kidnap ['kɪdnæp] *vt* rapire, sequestrare; **kidnapping** *n* sequestro (di persona)

kidney ['kɪdnɪ] *n* (*Anat*) rene *m*; (*Culin*) rognone *m*; **kidney bean** *n* fagiolo borlotto

kill [kɪl] *vt* uccidere, ammazzare ▷ *n* uccisione *f*; **killer** *n* uccisore *m*, killer *m* *inv*; assassino/a; **killing** *n* assassinio; (*col*): **to make a killing** fare un bel colpo

kiln [kɪln] *n* forno

kilo ['kiːləu] *n* abbr chilo; **kilobyte** *n* (*Comput*) kilobyte *m* *inv*; **kilogram(me)** ['kɪləugræm] *n* chilogrammo; **kilometre**, (US) **kilometer** ['kɪləmiːtə'] *n* chilometro; **kilowatt** ['kɪləuwɔt] *n* chilowatt *m* *inv*

kilt [kɪlt] *n* gonnellino scozzese

kin [kɪn] *n see* **next of kin**

kind [kaɪnd] *adj* gentile, buono/a ▷ *n* sorta, specie *f*; (*species*) genere *m*; **what ~ of ...?** che tipo di ...?; **to be two of a ~** essere molto simili; **in ~** (*Comm*) in natura

kindergarten ['kɪndəgɑːtn] *n* giardino d'infanzia

kindly ['kaɪndlɪ] *adj* pieno/a di bontà, benevolo/a ▷ *adv* con bontà, gentilmente; **will you ~ ...** vuole ... per favore

kindness ['kaɪndnɪs] *n* bontà, gentilezza

king [kɪŋ] *n* re *m* *inv*; **kingdom** *n* regno, reame *m*; **kingfisher** *n* martin *m* *inv* pescatore

king-size(d) ['kɪŋsaɪz(d)] *adj* super *inv*; **king-size(d) bed** *n* letto king-size

kiosk ['kiːɔsk] *n* edicola, chiosco; (BRIT: *also*: **telephone ~**) cabina (telefonica)

kipper ['kɪpə'] *n* aringa affumicata

kiss [kɪs] *n* bacio ▷ *vt* baciare; **to ~ (each other)** baciarsi; **~ of life** respirazione *f* bocca a bocca

kit [kɪt] *n* equipaggiamento, corredo; (*set of tools etc*) attrezzi *mpl*; (*for assembly*) scatola di montaggio

kitchen ['kɪtʃɪn] *n* cucina

kite [kaɪt] *n* (*toy*) aquilone *m*

kitten ['kɪtn] *n* gattino/a, micino/a

kiwi ['kiːwiː], **kiwi fruit** *n* kiwi *m* *inv*

km *abbr* (= kilometre) km

km/h *abbr* (= kilometres per hour) km/h

knack [næk] *n*: **to have the ~ of** avere l'abilità di

knee [niː] *n* ginocchio; **kneecap** *n* rotula

kneel [niːl] *vi* (*pt*, *pp* **knelt** [nɛlt]) (*also*: **~ down**) inginocchiarsi

knelt [nɛlt] *pt*, *pp of* **kneel**

knew [njuː] *pt of* **know**

knickers ['nɪkəz] *npl* (BRIT) mutandine *fpl*

knife [naɪf] *n* (*pl* **knives**) coltello ▷ *vt* accoltellare, dare una coltellata a

knight [naɪt] *n* cavaliere *m*; (*Chess*) cavallo

knit [nɪt] *vt* fare a maglia ▷ *vi* lavorare a maglia; (*broken bones*) saldarsi; **to ~ one's brows** aggrottare le sopracciglia; **knitting** *n* lavoro a maglia; **knitting needle** *n* ferro (da calza); **knitwear** *n* maglieria

knives [naɪvz] *npl of* **knife**

knob [nɔb] *n* bottone *m*; manopola

knock [nɔk] *vt* colpire; urtare; (*fig: col*) criticare ▷ *vi* (*at door etc*): **to ~ at/on** bussare a ▷ *n* bussata; colpo, botta; **knock down** *vt* abbattere; **knock off** *vi* (*col: finish*) smettere (di lavorare) ▷ *vt* (*from price*) far abbassare; (*col: steal*) sgraffignare;

knock out *vt* stendere; (*Boxing*) mettere K.O.; (*defeat*) battere; **knock over** *vt* (*object*) far cadere; (*pedestrian*) investire; **knockout** *n* (*Boxing*) knock out *m inv* ▷ *cpd* a eliminazione

knot [nɔt] *n* nodo ▷ *vt* annodare

know [nəu] *vt* (*pt* **knew** [njuː], *pp* **known** [nəun]) sapere; (*person, author, place*) conoscere; **to ~ how to do** sapere fare; **I don't ~** non lo so; **to ~ about** *or* **of sth/sb** conoscere qc/qn; **know-all** *n* sapientone/a; **know-how** *n* tecnica; pratica; **knowing** *adj* (*look etc*) d'intesa; **knowingly** *adv* (*purposely*) consapevolmente; (*smile, look*) con aria d'intesa; **know-it-all** *n* (*us*) = **know-all**

knowledge ['nɔlɪdʒ] *n* consapevolezza; (*learning*) conoscenza, sapere *m*; **knowledgeable** *adj* ben informato/a

known [nəun] *pp of* **know**

knuckle ['nʌkl] *n* nocca

koala [kəu'ɑːlə] *n* (*also:* **~ bear**) koala *m inv*

Koran [kɔ'rɑːn] *n* Corano

Korea [kə'rɪə] *n* Corea; **Korean** *adj, n* coreano/a

kosher ['kəuʃəʳ] *adj* kasher *inv*

Kosovar, Kosovan ['kɔsəvaʳ, 'kɔsəvən] *adj* kosovaro/a

Kosovo ['kusəvəu] *n* Kosovo

Kremlin ['krɛmlɪn] *n*: **the ~** il Cremlino

Kuwait [ku'weɪt] *n* Kuwait *m*

L *abbr* (BRIT) = **learner**

l *abbr* (= *litre*) l

lab [læb] *n abbr* (= *laboratory*) laboratorio

label ['leɪbl] *n* etichetta, cartellino; (*brand: of record*) casa ▷ *vt* etichettare

labor *etc* ['leɪbəʳ] (*us*) = **labour** *etc*

laboratory [lə'bɔrətərɪ] *n* laboratorio

Labor Day *n* (*us*) festa del lavoro

> **LABOR DAY**
>
> Negli Stati Uniti e nel Canada
> il *Labor Day*, la festa del lavoro,
> cade il primo lunedì di settembre,
> contrariamente a quanto accade
> nella maggior parte dei paesi
> europei dove tale celebrazione ha
> luogo il primo maggio.

labor union *n* (*us*) sindacato

Labour ['leɪbə'] *n* (BRIT Pol: *also*: **the ~ Party**) il partito laburista, i laburisti

labour, (US) **labor** ['leɪbə'] *n* (*task*) lavoro; (*workmen*) manodopera ▷ *vi*: **to ~ (at)** lavorare duro(a); **to be in ~** (*Med*) avere le doglie; **hard ~** lavori *mpl* forzati; **labourer**, (US) **laborer** ['leɪbərə'] *n* manovale *m*; **farm labourer** lavoratore *m* agricolo

lace [leɪs] *n* merletto, pizzo; (*of shoe etc*) laccio ▷ *vt* (*shoe: also*: **~ up**) allacciare

lack [læk] *n* mancanza ▷ *vt* mancare di; **through** *or* **for ~ of** per mancanza di; **to be ~ing** mancare; **to be ~ing in** mancare di

lacquer ['lækə'] *n* lacca

lacy ['leɪsɪ] *adj* (*like lace*) che sembra un pizzo

lad [læd] *n* ragazzo, giovanotto

ladder ['lædə'] *n* scala; (BRIT: *in tights*) smagliatura

ladle ['leɪdl] *n* mestolo

lady ['leɪdɪ] *n* signora; dama; **L~ Smith** lady Smith; **the ladies' (toilets)** i gabinetti per signore; **ladybird** ['leɪdɪbəːd], (US) **ladybug** ['leɪdɪbʌg] *n* coccinella

lag [læg] *n* (*of time*) lasso, intervallo ▷ *vi* (*also*: **~ behind**) trascinarsi ▷ *vt* (*pipes*) rivestire di materiale isolante

lager ['lɑːgə'] *n* lager *m inv*

lagoon [lə'guːn] *n* laguna

laid [leɪd] *pt*, *pp of* **lay**

laid-back [leɪd'bæk] *adj* (*col*) rilassato/a, tranquillo/a

lain [leɪn] *pp of* **lie**

lake [leɪk] *n* lago

lamb [læm] *n* agnello

lame [leɪm] *adj* zoppo/a; (*excuse etc*) zoppicante

lament [lə'mɛnt] *n* lamento ▷ *vt* lamentare, piangere

lamp [læmp] *n* lampada; **lamppost** ['læmppəʊst] (BRIT) *n* lampione *m*; **lampshade** ['læmpʃeɪd] *n* paralume *m*

land [lænd] *n* (*as opposed to sea*) terra (ferma); (*country*) paese *m*; (*soil*) terreno; suolo; (*estate*) terreni *mpl*, terre *fpl* ▷ *vi* (*from ship*) sbarcare; (*Aviat*) atterrare; (*fig: fall*) cadere ▷ *vt* (*passengers*) sbarcare; (*goods*) scaricare; **to ~ sb with sth** affibbiare qc a qn; **landing** *n* atterraggio; (*of staircase*) pianerottolo; **landing card** *n* carta di sbarco; **landlady** *n* padrona *or* proprietaria di casa; **landline** *n* telefono fisso; **landlord** *n* padrone *m or* proprietario di casa; (*of pub etc*) padrone *m*; **landmark** *n* punto di riferimento; (*fig*) pietra miliare; **landowner** ['lændəʊnə'] *n* proprietario/a terriero/a; **landscape** *n* paesaggio; **landslide** *n* (*Geo*) frana; (*fig: Pol*) valanga

lane [leɪn] *n* (*in town*) stradina; (*Aut, in race*) corsia; **"get in ~"** "immettersi in corsia"

language ['læŋgwɪdʒ] *n* lingua; (*way one speaks*) linguaggio; **bad ~** linguaggio volgare; **language laboratory** *n* laboratorio linguistico

lantern ['læntn] *n* lanterna

lap [læp] *n* (*of track*) giro; **in** *or* **on one's ~** in grembo ▷ *vt* (*also*: **~ up**) papparsi, leccare ▷ *vi* (*waves*) sciabordare

lapel [lə'pɛl] *n* risvolto

lapse [læps] *n* lapsus *m inv*; (*longer*) caduta ▷ *vi* (*law, act*) cadere; (*ticket, passport, membership, contract*) scadere; **to ~ into bad habits** pigliare cattive abitudini; **~ of time** spazio di tempo

laptop ['læptɔp] *n* (*also*: **~ computer**) laptop *m inv*

lard [lɑːd] *n* lardo

larder ['lɑːdə'] *n* dispensa

large [lɑːdʒ] *adj* grande; (*person, animal*) grosso/a; **at ~** (*free*) in libertà; (*generally*) in generale; nell'insieme; **largely** *adv* in gran parte; **large-scale** *adj* (*map, drawing etc*) in grande scala; (*reforms, business activities*) su vasta scala

lark [lɑːk] *n* (*bird*) allodola; (*joke*) scherzo, gioco

larrikin ['lærɪkɪn] *n* (AUST, NZ *col*) furfante *m/f*

laryngitis [lærɪn'dʒaɪtɪs] *n* laringite *f*

lasagne [lə'zænjə] *n* lasagne *fpl*

laser ['leɪzər] *n* laser *m*; **laser printer** *n* stampante *f* laser *inv*

lash [læʃ] *n* frustata; (*also:* **eye~**) ciglio ▷ *vt* frustare; (*tie*) legare; **to ~ to/together** legare a insieme; **lash out** *vi*: **to ~ out (at** *or* **against sb/sth)** attaccare violentemente (qn/qc)

lass [læs] *n* ragazza

last [lɑːst] *adj* ultimo/a; (*week, month, year*) scorso/a, passato/a ▷ *adv* per ultimo ▷ *vi* durare; **~ week** la settimana scorsa; **~ night** ieri sera, la notte scorsa; **at ~** finalmente, alla fine; **~ but one** penultimo/a; **lastly** *adv* infine, per finire; **last-minute** *adj* fatto/a (*or* preso/a *etc*) all'ultimo momento

latch [lætʃ] *n* chiavistello; (*automatic lock*) serratura a scatto; **latch on to** *vt fus* (*cling to: person*) attaccarsi a, appiccicarsi a; (: *idea*) afferrare, capire

late [leɪt] *adj* (*not on time*) in ritardo; (*far on in day etc*) tardi; tardo/a; (*former*) ex; (*dead*) defunto/a ▷ *adv* tardi; (*behind time, schedule*) in ritardo; **sorry I'm ~** scusi il ritardo; **the flight is two hours ~** il volo ha due ore di ritardo; **it's too ~** è troppo tardi; **of ~** di recente; **in the ~ afternoon** nel tardo pomeriggio; **in ~ May** verso la fine di maggio; **latecomer** *n* ritardatario/a; **lately** *adv* recentemente; **later** ['leɪtər] *adj* (*date etc*) posteriore; (*version etc*) successivo/a ▷ *adv* più tardi; **later on today** oggi più tardi; **latest** ['leɪtɪst] *adj* ultimo/a, più recente; **at the latest** al più tardi

lather ['lɑːðər] *n* schiuma di sapone ▷ *vt* insaponare

Latin ['lætɪn] *n* latino ▷ *adj* latino/a; **Latin America** *n* America Latina; **Latin American** *adj* sudamericano/a

latitude ['lætɪtjuːd] *n* latitudine *f*; (*fig*) libertà d'azione

latter ['lætər] *adj* secondo/a; più recente ▷ *n*: **the ~** quest'ultimo, il secondo

laugh [lɑːf] *n* risata ▷ *vi* ridere; **laugh at** *vt fus* (*misfortune etc*) ridere di; **laughter** *n* riso; risate *fpl*

launch [lɔːntʃ] *n* (*of rocket, product etc*) lancio; (*of new ship*) varo; (*also:* **motor ~**) lancia ▷ *vt* (*rocket, product*) lanciare; (*ship, plan*) varare; **launch into** *vt fus* lanciarsi in

launder ['lɔːndər] *vt* lavare e stirare

Launderette® [lɔːn'drɛt], (US) **Laundromat®** ['lɔːndrəmæt] *n* lavanderia (automatica)

laundry ['lɔːndrɪ] *n* lavanderia; (*clothes*) biancheria; (: *dirty*) panni *mpl* da lavare

lava ['lɑːvə] *n* lava

lavatory ['lævətərɪ] *n* gabinetto

lavender ['lævəndər] *n* lavanda

lavish ['lævɪʃ] *adj* copioso/a, abbondante; (*giving freely*): **~ with** prodigo/a di, largo/a in ▷ *vt*: **to ~ sth on sb/sth** colmare qn/qc di qc

law [lɔː] *n* legge *f*; **civil/criminal ~** diritto civile/penale; **lawful** *adj* legale, lecito/a; **lawless** *adj* senza legge

lawn [lɔːn] *n* tappeto erboso; **lawnmower** *n* tosaerba *m inv or f inv*

lawsuit ['lɔːsuːt] *n* processo, causa

lawyer ['lɔːjər] *n* (*for sales, wills etc*) ≈ notaio; (*partner, in court*) ≈ avvocato/essa

lax [læks] *adj* rilassato/a; negligente

laxative ['læksətɪv] *n* lassativo

lay [leɪ] *pt of* **lie** *adj* laico/a; (*not expert*) profano/a ▷ *vt* (*pt, pp* **laid** [leɪd]) posare, mettere; (*eggs*) fare; (*trap*) tendere; (*plans*) fare, elaborare;

to ~ the table apparecchiare la tavola; **lay down** vt mettere giù; (rules etc) formulare, fissare; **to ~ down the law** dettar legge; **to ~ down one's life** dare la propria vita; **lay off** vt (workers) licenziare; **lay on** vt (provide) fornire; **lay out** vt (display) presentare; **lay-by** n (BRIT) piazzola (di sosta)

layer ['leɪəʳ] n strato

layman ['leɪmən] n (irreg) laico; profano

layout ['leɪaut] n lay-out m inv, disposizione f; (Press) impaginazione f

lazy ['leɪzɪ] adj pigro/a

lb. abbr (= pound (weight)) lb.

lead¹ (pt, pp **led**) [liːd, lɛd] n (front position) posizione f di testa; (distance, time ahead) vantaggio; (clue) indizio; (Elec) filo (elettrico); (for dog) guinzaglio; (Theat) parte f principale ▷ vt guidare, condurre; (induce) indurre; (be leader of) essere a capo di ▷ vi condurre; (Sport) essere in testa; **in the ~** in testa; **to ~ the way** far strada; **lead up to** vt fus portare a

lead² [lɛd] n (metal) piombo; (in pencil) mina

leader ['liːdəʳ] n capo; leader m inv; (in newspaper) articolo di fondo; (Sport) chi è in testa; **leadership** n direzione f; capacità di comando

lead-free ['lɛdfriː] adj senza piombo

leading ['liːdɪŋ] adj primo/a, principale

lead singer n cantante alla testa di un gruppo

leaf [liːf] n (pl **leaves**) foglia; **to turn over a new ~** cambiar vita; **leaf through** vt sfogliare

leaflet ['liːflɪt] n dépliant m inv; (Pol, Rel) volantino

league [liːg] n lega; (Football) campionato; **to be in ~ with** essere in lega con

leak [liːk] n (out) fuga; (in) infiltrazione f; (security leak) fuga d'informazioni ▷ vi (roof, bucket) perdere; (liquid) uscire; (shoes) lasciar passare l'acqua ▷ vt (information) divulgare

lean (pt, pp **leaned** or **leant**) [liːn, lɛnt] adj magro/a ▷ vt: **to ~ sth on** appoggiare qc su ▷ vi (slope) pendere; (rest): **to ~ against** appoggiarsi contro; essere appoggiato/a a; **to ~ on** appoggiarsi a; **lean forward** vi sporgersi in avanti; **lean over** vi inclinarsi; **leaning** n: **leaning (towards)** propensione f (per)

leant [lɛnt] pt, pp of **lean**

leap [liːp] n salto, balzo ▷ vi (pt, pp **leaped** or **leapt** [lɛpt]) saltare, balzare

leapt [lɛpt] pt, pp of **leap**

leap year n anno bisestile

learn (pt, pp **learned** or **learnt**) [ləːn, -t] vt, vi imparare; **to ~ (how) to do sth** imparare a fare qc; **to ~ about sth** (hear) apprendere qc; **learner** n principiante m/f; apprendista m/f; **he's a learner (driver)** (BRIT) sta imparando a guidare; **learning** n erudizione f, sapienza

learnt [ləːnt] pt, pp of **learn**

lease [liːs] n contratto d'affitto ▷ vt affittare

leash [liːʃ] n guinzaglio

least [liːst] adj: **the ~** (+ noun) il (la) più piccolo/a, il (la) minimo/a; (smallest amount of) il (la) meno ▷ adv (+ verb) meno; **the ~** (+ adjective): **the ~ beautiful girl** la ragazza meno bella; **the ~ possible effort** il minimo sforzo possibile; **I have the ~ money** ho meno denaro di tutti; **at ~** almeno; **not in the ~** affatto, per nulla

leather ['lɛðəʳ] n cuoio

leave (pt, pp **left**) [liːv, lɛft] vt lasciare; (go away from) partire da ▷ vi partire, andarsene; (bus, train) partire ▷ n (time off) congedo; (Mil, consent) licenza; **to be left** rimanere; **there's some milk left over** c'è rimasto del latte; **on ~** in congedo; **leave**

behind vt (also fig) lasciare; (forget) dimenticare; **leave out** vt omettere, tralasciare
leaves [li:vz] npl of **leaf**
Lebanon ['lɛbənən] n Libano
lecture ['lɛktʃəʳ] n conferenza; (Scol) lezione f ▷ vi fare conferenze; fare lezioni ▷ vt (scold): **to ~ sb on** or **about sth** rimproverare qn or fare una ramanzina a qn per qc; **to give a ~ (on)** fare una conferenza (su); **lecture hall** n aula magna; **lecturer** ['lɛktʃərəʳ] n (BRIT: at university) professore/essa, docente m/f; **lecture theatre** n = **lecture hall**
led [lɛd] pt, pp of **lead**¹
ledge [lɛdʒ] n (of window) davanzale m; (on wall etc) sporgenza; (of mountain) cornice f, cengia
leek [li:k] n porro
left [lɛft] pt, pp of **leave** ▷ adj sinistro/a ▷ adv a sinistra ▷ n sinistra; **on the ~, to the ~** a sinistra; **the L~** (Pol) la sinistra; **left-hand** adj: **the left-hand side** il lato sinistro; **left-hand drive** adj guida a sinistra; **left-handed** adj mancino/a; **left-luggage locker** n armadietto per deposito bagagli; **left-luggage (office)** n deposito m bagagli inv; **left-overs** npl avanzi mpl, resti mpl; **left wing** n (Pol) sinistra ▷ adj: **left-wing** (Pol) di sinistra
leg [lɛg] n gamba; (of animal) zampa; (of furniture) piede m; (Culin: of chicken) coscia; (of journey) tappa; **1st/2nd ~** (Sport) partita di andata/ritorno
legacy ['lɛgəsɪ] n eredità f inv
legal ['li:gl] adj legale; **legal holiday** n (US) giorno festivo, festa nazionale; **legalize** vt legalizzare; **legally** adv legalmente; **legally binding** legalmente vincolante
legend ['lɛdʒənd] n leggenda; **legendary** ['lɛdʒəndərɪ] adj leggendario/a
leggings ['lɛgɪŋz] npl ghette fpl
legible ['lɛdʒəbl] adj leggibile

legislation [lɛdʒɪs'leɪʃən] n legislazione f
legislative ['lɛdʒɪslətɪv] adj legislativo/a
legitimate [lɪ'dʒɪtɪmət] adj legittimo/a
leisure ['lɛʒəʳ] n agio, tempo libero; ricreazioni fpl; **at ~** con comodo; **leisure centre** n centro di ricreazione; **leisurely** adj tranquillo/a, fatto/a con comodo or senza fretta
lemon ['lɛmən] n limone m; **lemonade** [lɛmə'neɪd] n limonata; **lemon tea** n tè m inv al limone
lend (pt, pp **lent**) [lɛnd, lɛnt] vt: **to ~ sth (to sb)** prestare qc (a qn)
length [lɛŋθ] n lunghezza; (distance) distanza; (section: of road, pipe etc) pezzo, tratto; **~ of time** periodo (di tempo); **at ~** (at last) finalmente, alla fine; (lengthily) a lungo; **lengthen** vt allungare, prolungare ▷ vi allungarsi; **lengthways** adv per il lungo; **lengthy** adj molto lungo/a
lens [lɛnz] n lente f; (of camera) obiettivo
Lent [lɛnt] n Quaresima
lent [lɛnt] pt, pp of **lend**
lentil ['lɛntl] n lenticchia
Leo ['li:əu] n Leone m
leopard ['lɛpəd] n leopardo
leotard ['li:ətɑ:d] n calzamaglia
leprosy ['lɛprəsɪ] n lebbra
lesbian ['lɛzbɪən] n lesbica
less [lɛs] adj, pron, adv, prep meno; **~ tax/10% discount** meno tasse/ il 10% di sconto; **~ than you/ever** meno di lei/che mai; **~ than half** meno della metà; **~ and ~** sempre meno; **the ~ he works ...** meno lavora ...; **lessen** ['lɛsn] vi diminuire, attenuarsi ▷ vt diminuire, ridurre; **lesser** ['lɛsəʳ] adj minore, più piccolo/a; **to a lesser extent** or **degree** in grado or misura minore
lesson ['lɛsn] n lezione f; **to teach sb a ~** dare una lezione a qn

let (*pt, pp* **let**) [lɛt] *vt* lasciare; (*BRIT: lease*) dare in affitto; **to ~ sb do sth** lasciar fare qc a qn, lasciare che qn faccia qc; **to ~ sb know sth** far sapere qc a qn; **~'s go** andiamo; **~ him come** lo lasci venire; **"to ~"** "affittasi"; **let down** *vt* (*lower*) abbassare; (*dress*) allungare; (*hair*) sciogliere; (*disappoint*) deludere; (*BRIT: tyre*) sgonfiare; **let in** *vt* lasciare entrare; (*visitor etc*) far entrare; **let off** *vt* (*allow to go*) lasciare andare; (*firework etc*) far partire; **let out** *vt* lasciare uscire; (*scream*) emettere

lethal ['liːθl] *adj* letale, mortale

letter ['lɛtə'] *n* lettera; **letterbox** (*BRIT*) *n* buca delle lettere

lettuce ['lɛtɪs] *n* lattuga, insalata

leukaemia, (*US*) **leukemia** [luːˈkiːmɪə] *n* leucemia

level ['lɛvl] *adj* piatto/a, piano/a; orizzontale ▷ *n* livello ▷ *vt* livellare, spianare; **to be ~ with** essere alla pari di; **to draw ~ with** mettersi alla pari di; **level crossing** *n* (*BRIT*) passaggio a livello

lever ['liːvə'] *n* leva; **leverage** *n*: **leverage (on** *or* **with)** forza (su); (*fig*) ascendente *m* (su)

levy ['lɛvɪ] *n* tassa, imposta ▷ *vt* imporre

liability [laɪəˈbɪlətɪ] *n* responsabilità *f inv*; (*handicap*) peso

liable ['laɪəbl] *adj* (*subject*): **~ to** soggetto/a a; passibile di; (*responsible*): **~ (for)** responsabile (di); (*likely*): **~ to do** propenso/a a fare

liaise [liːˈeɪz] *vi*: **to ~ (with)** mantenere i contatti (con)

liar ['laɪə'] *n* bugiardo/a

liberal ['lɪbərl] *adj* liberale; (*generous*): **to be ~ with** distribuire liberamente; **Liberal Democrat** *n* liberaldemocratico/a

liberate ['lɪbəreɪt] *vt* liberare

liberation [lɪbəˈreɪʃən] *n* liberazione *f*

liberty ['lɪbətɪ] *n* libertà *f inv*; **at ~** (*criminal*) in libertà; **at ~ to do** libero/a di fare

Libra ['liːbrə] *n* Bilancia

librarian [laɪˈbrɛərɪən] *n* bibliotecario/a

library ['laɪbrərɪ] *n* biblioteca

Libya ['lɪbɪə] *n* Libia

lice [laɪs] *npl of* **louse**

licence, (*US*) **license** ['laɪsns] *n* autorizzazione *f*, permesso; (*Comm*) licenza; (*Radio, TV*) canone *m*, abbonamento; (*also:* **driving ~**, (*US*) **driver's license**) patente *f* di guida; (*excessive freedom*) licenza

license ['laɪsns] *n* (*US*) = **licence** ▷ *vt* dare una licenza a; **licensed** *adj* (*for alcohol*) che ha la licenza di vendere bibite alcoliche; **license plate** *n* (*esp US Aut*) targa (automobilistica); **licensing hours** (*BRIT*) *npl* orario d'apertura (*di un pub*)

lick [lɪk] *vt* leccare; (*col: defeat*) stracciare; **to ~ one's lips** (*fig*) leccarsi i baffi

lid [lɪd] *n* coperchio; (*eyelid*) palpebra

lie [laɪ] *n* bugia, menzogna ▷ *vi* mentire, dire bugie; (*rest*) giacere, star disteso/a; (*object: be situated*) trovarsi, essere; **to tell ~s** raccontare *or* dire bugie; **to ~ low** (*fig*) latitare; **lie about, lie around** *vi* (*things*) essere in giro; (*person*) bighellonare; **lie down** *vi* stendersi, sdraiarsi

Liechtenstein ['lɪktənstaɪn] *n* Liechtenstein *m*

lie-in ['laɪɪn] *n* (*BRIT*): **to have a ~** rimanere a letto

lieutenant [lɛfˈtɛnənt, *US* luːˈtɛnənt] *n* tenente *m*

life [laɪf] *n* (*pl* **lives**) vita ▷ *cpd* di vita; della vita; a vita; **to come to ~** rianimarsi; **life assurance** *n* (*BRIT*) = **life insurance**; **lifeboat** *n* scialuppa di salvataggio; **lifeguard** *n* bagnino; **life insurance** *n* assicurazione *f* sulla vita; **life jacket** *n* giubbotto di salvataggio;

lifelike adj che sembra vero/a; rassomigliante; **life preserver** [-prɪˈzəːvəʳ] n (US) salvagente m; giubbotto di salvataggio; **life sentence** n (condanna all')ergastolo; **life style** n stile m di vita; **lifetime** [ˈlaɪftaɪm] n: **in his lifetime** durante la sua vita; **in a lifetime** nell'arco della vita; **in tutta la vita; the chance of a lifetime** un'occasione unica

lift [lɪft] vt sollevare; (ban, rule) levare ▷ vi (fog) alzarsi ▷ n (BRIT: elevator) ascensore m; **to give sb a ~** (BRIT) dare un passaggio a qn; **lift up** vt sollevare, alzare; **lift-off** n decollo

light (pt, pp **lighted**, pt, pp **lit**) [laɪt, lɪt] n luce f, lume m; (daylight) luce, giorno; (lamp) lampada; (Aut: rear light) luce f di posizione; (: headlamp) fanale m; (for cigarette etc): **have you got a ~?** ha da accendere? ▷ vt (candle, cigarette, fire) accendere; (room) illuminare ▷ adj (room, colour) chiaro/a; (not heavy, also fig) leggero/a; **lights** npl (Aut: traffic lights) semaforo; **to come to ~** venire alla luce, emergere; **to be lit by** essere illuminato/a da; **light up** vi illuminarsi ▷ vt illuminare; **light bulb** n lampadina; **lighten** vt (make less heavy) alleggerire; **lighter** n (also: **cigarette lighter**) accendino; **light-hearted** adj gioioso/a, gaio/a; **lighthouse** n faro; **lighting** n illuminazione f; **lightly** [ˈlaɪtlɪ] adv leggermente; **to get off lightly** cavarsela a buon mercato

lightning [ˈlaɪtnɪŋ] n lampo, fulmine m

lightweight [ˈlaɪtweɪt] adj (suit) leggero/a ▷ n (Boxing) peso leggero

like [laɪk] vt (person) volere bene a; (activity, object, food): **I ~ swimming/ that book/chocolate** mi piace nuotare/quel libro/il cioccolato ▷ prep come ▷ adj simile, uguale ▷ n: **the ~** uno/a uguale; **I would ~, I'd ~** mi piacerebbe, vorrei; **would you ~ a coffee?** gradirebbe un caffè?; **to be/look ~ sb/sth** somigliare a qn/ qc; **what does it look/taste ~?** che aspetto/gusto ha?; **what does it sound ~?** come fa?; **that's just ~ him** è proprio da lui; **do it ~ this** fallo così; **it is nothing ~ ...** non è affatto come ...; **his ~s and dislikes** i suoi gusti; **likeable** adj simpatico/a

likelihood [ˈlaɪklɪhud] n probabilità

likely [ˈlaɪklɪ] adj probabile; plausibile; **he's ~ to leave** probabilmente partirà, è probabile che parta; **not ~!** neanche per sogno!

likewise [ˈlaɪkwaɪz] adv similmente, nello stesso modo

liking [ˈlaɪkɪŋ] n: **~ (for)** debole m (per); **to be to sb's ~** piacere a qn

lilac [ˈlaɪlək] n lilla m inv

Lilo® [ˈlaɪləu] n materassino gonfiabile

lily [ˈlɪlɪ] n giglio

limb [lɪm] n arto

limbo [ˈlɪmbəu] n: **to be in ~** (fig) essere lasciato/a nel dimenticatoio

lime [laɪm] n (tree) tiglio; (fruit) limetta; (Geo) calce f

limelight [ˈlaɪmlaɪt] n: **in the ~** (fig) alla ribalta, in vista

limestone [ˈlaɪmstəun] n pietra calcarea; (Geo) calcare m

limit [ˈlɪmɪt] n limite m ▷ vt limitare; **limited** adj limitato/a, ristretto/a; **to be limited to** limitarsi a

limousine [ˈlɪməziːn] n limousine f inv

limp [lɪmp] n: **to have a ~** zoppicare ▷ vi zoppicare ▷ adj floscio/a, flaccido/a

line [laɪn] n linea; (rope) corda; (for fishing) lenza; (wire) filo; (of poem) verso; (row, series) fila, riga; coda; (on face) ruga ▷ vt (trees, crowd) fiancheggiare; **to ~ (with)** (clothes) foderare (di); (box) rivestire or foderare (di); **in his ~ of business** nel suo ramo; **in ~ with** in linea con; **line up** vi allinearsi, mettersi in fila

▷ vt mettere in fila; (event, celebration) preparare

linear ['lɪnɪə'] adj lineare

linen ['lɪnɪn] n biancheria, panni mpl; (cloth) tela di lino

liner ['laɪnə'] n nave f di linea; **dustbin ~** sacchetto per la pattumiera

line-up ['laɪnʌp] n allineamento, fila; (Sport) formazione f di gioco

linger ['lɪŋgə'] vi attardarsi; indugiare; (smell, tradition) persistere

lingerie ['lænʒəri:] n biancheria intima (femminile)

linguist ['lɪŋgwɪst] n linguista m/f; poliglotta m/f; **linguistic** adj linguistico/a

lining ['laɪnɪŋ] n fodera

link [lɪŋk] n (of a chain) anello; (relationship) legame m; (connection) collegamento ▷ vt collegare, unire, congiungere; (associate): **to ~ with** or **to** collegare a; **link up** vt collegare, unire ▷ vi riunirsi; associarsi; **links** [lɪŋks] npl pista or terreno da golf

lion ['laɪən] n leone m; **lioness** n leonessa

lip [lɪp] n labbro; (of cup etc) orlo; **lipread** ['lɪpriːd] vi leggere sulle labbra; **lip salve** [-sælv] n burro di cacao; **lipstick** n rossetto

liqueur [lɪ'kjuə'] n liquore m

liquid ['lɪkwɪd] n liquido ▷ adj liquido/a; **liquidizer** n frullatore m (a brocca)

liquor ['lɪkə'] n alcool m; **liquor store** n (us) negozio di liquori

Lisbon ['lɪzbən] n Lisbona

lisp [lɪsp] n pronuncia blesa della "s"

list [lɪst] n lista, elenco ▷ vt (write down) mettere in lista; fare una lista di; (enumerate) elencare

listen ['lɪsn] vi ascoltare; **to ~ to** ascoltare; **listener** n ascoltatore/ trice

lit [lɪt] pt, pp of **light**

liter ['liːtə'] n (us) = **litre**

literacy ['lɪtərəsɪ] n il sapere leggere e scrivere

literal ['lɪtərl] adj letterale; **literally** adv alla lettera, letteralmente

literary ['lɪtərərɪ] adj letterario/a

literate ['lɪtərɪt] adj che sa leggere e scrivere

literature ['lɪtərɪtʃə'] n letteratura; (brochures etc) materiale m

litre, (us) **liter** ['liːtə'] n litro

litter ['lɪtə'] n (rubbish) rifiuti mpl; (young animals) figliata; **litter bin** n (BRIT) cestino per rifiuti; **littered** adj: **littered with** coperto di

little ['lɪtl] adj (small) piccolo/a; (not much) poco/a ▷ adv poco; **a ~** un po' (di); **a ~ bit** un pochino; **~ by ~** a poco a poco; **little finger** n mignolo

live¹ [lɪv] vi vivere; (reside) vivere, abitare; **where do you ~?** dove abita?; **live together** vi vivere insieme, convivere; **live up to** vt fus tener fede a, non venir meno a

live² [laɪv] adj (animal) vivo/a; (wire) sotto tensione; (broadcast) diretto/a; (ammunition) inesploso/a; (performance) dal vivo

livelihood ['laɪvlɪhud] n mezzi mpl di sostentamento

lively ['laɪvlɪ] adj vivace, vivo/a

liven up ['laɪvn-] vt (discussion, evening) animare ▷ vi ravvivarsi

liver ['lɪvə'] n fegato

lives [laɪvz] npl of **life**

livestock ['laɪvstɔk] n bestiame m

living ['lɪvɪŋ] adj vivo/a, vivente ▷ n: **to earn** or **make a ~** guadagnarsi la vita; **living room** n soggiorno

lizard ['lɪzəd] n lucertola

load [ləud] n (weight) peso; (thing carried) carico ▷ vt (also: **~ up**): **to ~ (with)** (lorry, ship) caricare (di); (gun, camera) caricare (con); **a ~ of**, **~s of** (fig) un sacco di; **to ~ a program** (Comput) caricare un programma; **loaded** adj (question, word) capzioso/a; (col: rich) pieno/a di soldi; **loaded (with)** (vehicle) carico/a (di)

loaf [ləuf] n (pl **loaves**) pane m, pagnotta
loan [ləun] n prestito ▷ vt dare in prestito; **on ~** in prestito
loathe [ləuð] vt detestare, aborrire
loaves [ləuvz] npl of **loaf**
lobby ['lɔbɪ] n atrio, vestibolo; (Pol: pressure group) gruppo di pressione ▷ vt fare pressione su
lobster ['lɔbstə^r] n aragosta
local ['ləukl] adj locale ▷ n (BRIT: pub) ≈ bar m inv all'angolo; **the locals** npl la gente della zona; **local anaesthetic** n anestesia locale; **local authority** n ente m locale; **local government** n amministrazione f locale; **locally** ['ləukəlɪ] adv da queste parti; nel vicinato
locate [ləu'keɪt] vt (find) trovare; (situate) situare; **location** [ləu'keɪʃən] n posizione f; **on ~** (Cine) all'esterno
loch [lɔx] n lago
lock [lɔk] n (of door, box) serratura; (of canal) chiusa; (of hair) ciocca, riccio ▷ vt (with key) chiudere a chiave ▷ vi (door etc) chiudersi; (wheels) bloccarsi, incepparsi; **lock in** vt chiudere dentro (a chiave); **lock out** vt chiudere fuori; **lock up** vt (criminal, mental patient) rinchiudere; (house) chiudere (a chiave) ▷ vi chiudere tutto (a chiave)
locker ['lɔkə^r] n armadietto; **locker-room** n (US Sport) spogliatoio
locksmith ['lɔksmɪθ] n magnano
locomotive [ləukə'məutɪv] n locomotiva
lodge [lɔdʒ] n casetta, portineria; (hunting lodge) casino di caccia ▷ vi (person): **to ~ (with)** essere a pensione (presso or da); (bullet etc) conficcarsi ▷ vt (appeal etc) presentare, fare; **to ~ a complaint** presentare un reclamo; **lodger** n affittuario/a; (with room and meals) pensionante m/f

lodging ['lɔdʒɪŋ] n alloggio; see also **board**
loft [lɔft] n solaio, soffitta
log [lɔg] n (of wood) ceppo; (also: **~book**) (Naut, Aviat) diario di bordo; (Aut) libretto di circolazione ▷ vt registrare; **log in, log on** vi (Comput) aprire una sessione (con codice di riconoscimento); **log off, log out** vi (Comput) terminare una sessione
logic ['lɔdʒɪk] n logica; **logical** adj logico/a
login ['lɔgɪn] n (Comput) nome m utente inv
logo ['ləugəu] n logo m inv
lol abbr (Internet, Tel: = laugh out loud) lol (morto dal ridere)
lollipop ['lɔlɪpɔp] n lecca lecca m inv
lolly ['lɔlɪ] n (col) lecca lecca m inv; (also: **ice ~**) ghiacciolo; (money) grana
London ['lʌndən] n Londra; **Londoner** n londinese m/f
lone [ləun] adj solitario/a
loneliness ['ləunlɪnɪs] n solitudine f, isolamento
lonely ['ləunlɪ] adj solo/a; solitario/a; isolato/a
long [lɔŋ] adj lungo/a ▷ adv a lungo, per molto tempo ▷ vi: **to ~ for sth/ to do** desiderare qc/di fare; non veder l'ora di aver qc/di fare; **how ~ is this river/course?** quanto è lungo questo fiume/corso?; **6 metres ~** lungo 6 metri; **6 months ~** che dura 6 mesi, di 6 mesi; **all night ~** tutta la notte; **he no ~er comes** non viene più; **~ before** molto tempo prima; **before ~** (+ future) presto, fra poco; (+ past) poco tempo dopo; **don't be ~!** faccia presto!; **at ~ last** finalmente; **so** or **as ~ as** (while) finché; (provided that) sempre che + sub; **long-distance** adj (race) di fondo; (call) interurbano/a; **long-haul** ['lɔŋ,hɔ:l] adj (flight) a lunga percorrenza inv; **longing** n desiderio, voglia, brama
longitude ['lɔŋgɪtjuːd] n longitudine f

long: long jump n salto in lungo; **long-life** adj (milk) a lunga conservazione; (batteries) di lunga durata; **long-sighted** adj presbite; **long-standing** adj di vecchia data; **long-term** adj a lungo termine

loo [luː] n (BRIT col) W.C. m inv, cesso

look [luk] vi guardare; (seem) sembrare, parere; (building etc): **to ~ south/on to the sea** dare a sud/sul mare ▷ n sguardo; (appearance) aspetto, aria; **looks** npl (good looks) bellezza; **look after** vt fus occuparsi di, prendersi cura di; (keep an eye on) guardare, badare a; **look around** vi guardarsi intorno; **look at** vt fus guardare; **look back** vi: **to ~ back on** (event, period) ripensare a; **look down on** vt fus (fig) guardare dall'alto, disprezzare; **look for** vt fus cercare; **look forward to** vt fus non veder l'ora di; **~ing forward to hearing from you** (in letter) in attesa di una vostra gentile risposta; **look into** vt fus esaminare; **look out** vi (beware): **to ~ out (for)** stare in guardia (per); **look out for** vt fus cercare; **look round** vi (turn) girarsi, voltarsi; (in shops) dare un'occhiata; **look through** vt fus (papers, book) scorrere; (telescope) guardare attraverso; **look up** vi alzare gli occhi; (improve) migliorare ▷ vt (word) cercare; (friend) andare a trovare; **look up to** vt fus avere rispetto per; **lookout** n posto d'osservazione; guardia; **to be on the lookout (for)** stare in guardia (per)

loom [luːm] n telaio ▷ vi sorgere; (fig) incombere

loony ['luːnɪ] n (col) pazzo/a

loop [luːp] n cappio ▷ vt: **to ~ sth round sth** passare qc intorno a qc; **loophole** n via d'uscita; scappatoia

loose [luːs] adj (knot) sciolto/a; (screw) allentato/a; (stone) cadente; (clothes) ampio/a, largo/a; (animal) in libertà, scappato/a; (life, morals) dissoluto/a ▷ n: **to be on the ~** essere in libertà; **loosely** adv senza stringere; approssimativamente; **loosen** ['luːsn] vt sciogliere; (belt etc) allentare

loot [luːt] n bottino ▷ vt saccheggiare

lop-sided ['lɒp'saɪdɪd] adj non equilibrato/a, asimmetrico/a

lord [lɔːd] n signore m; **L~ Smith** lord Smith; **the L~** il Signore; **good L~!** buon Dio!; **the (House of) L~s** (BRIT) la Camera dei Lord

lorry ['lɒrɪ] n (BRIT) camion m inv; **lorry driver** n (BRIT) camionista m

lose (pt, pp **lost**) [luːz, lɒst] vt perdere ▷ vi perdere; **to ~ (time)** (clock) ritardare; **lose out** vi rimetterci; **loser** n perdente m/f

loss [lɒs] n perdita; **to be at a ~** essere perplesso/a

lost [lɒst] pt, pp of **lose** ▷ adj perduto/a; **lost property**, (US) **lost and found** n oggetti mpl smarriti

lot [lɒt] n (at auctions) lotto; (destiny) destino, sorte f; **the ~** tutto/a quanto/a; tutti/e quanti/e; **a ~** molto; **a ~ of** una gran quantità di, un sacco di; **~s of** molto/a; **to draw ~s (for sth)** tirare a sorte (per qc)

lotion ['ləʊʃən] n lozione f

lottery ['lɒtərɪ] n lotteria

loud [laʊd] adj forte, alto/a; (gaudy) vistoso/a, sgargiante ▷ adv (speak etc) forte; **out ~** (read etc) ad alta voce; **loudly** adv fortemente, ad alta voce; **loudspeaker** n altoparlante m

lounge [laʊndʒ] n salotto, soggiorno; (of airport) sala d'attesa; (BRIT: also: **~ bar**) bar m inv con servizio a tavolino ▷ vi oziare

louse [laʊs] n (pl **lice**) pidocchio

lousy ['laʊzɪ] adj (col: fig) orrendo/a, schifoso/a; **to feel ~** stare da cani

love [lʌv] n amore m ▷ vt amare; voler bene a; **I ~ you** ti amo; **to ~ to do: I ~ to do** mi piace fare; **to be in ~ with** essere innamorato/a di; **to fall in ~ with** innamorarsi di; **to make ~** fare l'amore; **"15 ~"** (Tennis) "15 a zero";

love affair n relazione f; **love life** n vita sentimentale

lovely ['lʌvlɪ] adj bello/a; (delicious: smell, meal) buono/a

lover ['lʌvər] n amante m/f; (person in love) innamorato/a; (amateur): **a ~ of** un (un') amante di; un (un') appassionato/a di

loving ['lʌvɪŋ] adj affettuoso/a

low [ləʊ] adj basso/a ▷ adv in basso ▷ n (Meteor) depressione f; **to be ~ on** (supplies etc) avere scarsità di; **to feel ~** sentirsi giù; **low-alcohol** adj a basso contenuto alcolico; **low-calorie** adj a basso contenuto calorico

lower ['ləʊər] adj, adv comparative (bottom: of 2 things) più basso; (less important) meno importante ▷ vt calare; (price, eyes, voice) abbassare

low-fat ['ləʊ'fæt] adj magro/a

loyal ['lɔɪəl] adj fedele, leale; **loyalty** n fedeltà, lealtà; **loyalty card** n carta che offre sconti a clienti abituali

LP n abbr (= long-playing record) LP m

L-plate ['ɛlpleɪt] n ≈ contrassegno P principiante

Lt. abbr (= lieutenant) Ten.

Ltd abbr (= limited) ≈ S.r.l.

luck [lʌk] n fortuna, sorte f; **bad ~** sfortuna, mala sorte; **good ~** (buona) fortuna; **luckily** adv fortunatamente, per fortuna; **lucky** adj fortunato/a; (number etc) che porta fortuna

lucrative ['lu:krətɪv] adj lucrativo/a, lucroso/a, profittevole

ludicrous ['lu:dɪkrəs] adj ridicolo/a

luggage ['lʌgɪdʒ] n bagagli mpl; **luggage rack** n portabagagli m inv

lukewarm ['lu:kwɔ:m] adj tiepido/a

lull [lʌl] n intervallo di calma ▷ vt: **to ~ sb to sleep** cullare qn finché si addormenta

lullaby ['lʌləbaɪ] n ninnananna

lumber ['lʌmbər] n (wood) legname m; (junk) roba vecchia

luminous ['lu:mɪnəs] adj luminoso/a

lump [lʌmp] n pezzo; (in sauce) grumo; (swelling) gonfiore m; (also: **sugar ~**) zolletta ▷ vt (also: **~ together**) riunire, mettere insieme; **lump sum** n somma globale; **lumpy** adj (sauce) pieno/a di grumi; (bed) bitorzoluto/a

lunatic ['lu:nətɪk] adj pazzo/a, matto/a

lunch [lʌntʃ] n pranzo, colazione f; **lunch break** n intervallo del pranzo; **lunchtime** n ora di pranzo

lung [lʌŋ] n polmone m

lure [luər] n richiamo; lusinga ▷ vt attirare (con l'inganno)

lurk [lə:k] vi stare in agguato

lush [lʌʃ] adj lussureggiante

lust [lʌst] n lussuria; cupidigia; desiderio; (fig): **~ for** sete f di

Luxembourg ['lʌksəmbə:g] n (state) Lussemburgo m; (city) Lussemburgo f

luxurious [lʌg'zjuərɪəs] adj sontuoso/a, di lusso

luxury ['lʌkʃərɪ] n lusso ▷ cpd di lusso

Be careful not to translate luxury by the Italian word lussuria.

Lycra® ['laɪkrə] n lycra® f inv

lying ['laɪɪŋ] n bugie fpl, menzogne fpl ▷ adj bugiardo/a

lyric ['lɪrɪk] adj lirico/a; **lyrics** npl (of song) parole fpl

m *abbr* (= metre) m; = **mile; million**

MA *n abbr* = **Master of Arts**

ma [mɑ:] *n* (*col*) mamma

mac [mæk] *n* (BRIT) impermeabile *m*

macaroni [mækə'rəʊnɪ] *n* maccheroni *mpl*

Macedonia [mæsɪ'dəʊnɪə] *n* Macedonia; **Macedonian** [mæsɪ'dəʊnɪən] *adj* macedone ▷ *n* macedone *m/f*; (*Ling*) macedone *m*

machine [mə'ʃi:n] *n* macchina ▷ *vt* (*dress etc*) cucire a macchina; (*Tech*) lavorare (a macchina); **machine gun** *n* mitragliatrice *f*; **machinery** *n* macchinario, macchine *fpl*; (*fig*) macchina; **machine washable** *adj* lavabile in lavatrice

macho ['mætʃəʊ] *adj* macho *inv*

mackerel ['mækrəl] *n* (*pl inv*) sgombro

mackintosh ['mækɪntɒʃ] *n* (BRIT) impermeabile *m*

mad [mæd] *adj* matto/a, pazzo/a; (*foolish*) sciocco/a; (*angry*) furioso/a; **to be ~ (keen) about** *or* **on sth** (*col*) andar matto/a per qc

Madagascar [mædə'gæskəʳ] *n* Madagascar *m*

madam ['mædəm] *n* signora

mad cow disease *n* encefalite *f* bovina spongiforme

made [meɪd] *pt, pp of* **make**; **made-to-measure** *adj* (BRIT) fatto/a su misura; **made-up** ['meɪdʌp] *adj* (*story*) inventato/a

madly ['mædlɪ] *adv* follemente

madman ['mædmən] *n* (*irreg*) pazzo, alienato

madness ['mædnɪs] *n* pazzia

Madrid [mə'drɪd] *n* Madrid *f*

Mafia ['mæfɪə] *n* mafia *f*

mag. [mæg] *n abbr* (BRIT col: Press); = **magazine**

magazine [mægə'zi:n] *n* (*Press*) rivista; (*Radio, TV*) rubrica

> Be careful not to translate *magazine* by the Italian word *magazzino*.

maggot ['mægət] *n* baco, verme *m*

magic ['mædʒɪk] *n* magia ▷ *adj* magico/a; **magical** *adj* magico/a; **magician** [mə'dʒɪʃən] *n* mago/a

magistrate ['mædʒɪstreɪt] *n* magistrato; giudice *m/f*

magnet ['mægnɪt] *n* magnete *m*, calamita; **magnetic** [mæg'nɛtɪk] *adj* magnetico/a

magnificent [mæg'nɪfɪsnt] *adj* magnifico/a

magnify ['mægnɪfaɪ] *vt* ingrandire; **magnifying glass** *n* lente *f* d'ingrandimento

magpie ['mægpaɪ] *n* gazza

mahogany [mə'hɒgənɪ] *n* mogano

maid [meɪd] *n* domestica; (*in hotel*) cameriera

maiden name ['meɪdn-] *n* nome da *m* nubile *or* da ragazza

mail [meɪl] *n* posta ▷ *vt* spedire (per posta); **mailbox** *n* (US) cassetta delle lettere; **mailing list** *n* elenco d'indirizzi; **mailman** *n* (*irreg: US*) portalettere *m inv*, postino; **mail-order** *n* vendita (*or* acquisto) per corrispondenza

main [meɪn] *adj* principale ▷ *n* (*pipe*) conduttura principale; **the ~s** (*Elec*) la linea principale; **in the ~** nel complesso, nell'insieme; **main course** *n* (*Culin*) piatto principale, piatto forte; **mainland** *n* continente *m*; **mainly** *adv* principalmente, soprattutto; **main road** *n* strada principale; **mainstream** *n* (*fig*) corrente *f* principale; **main street** *n* strada principale

maintain [meɪn'teɪn] *vt* mantenere; (*affirm*) sostenere; **maintenance** ['meɪntənəns] *n* manutenzione *f*; (*alimony*) alimenti *mpl*

maisonette [meɪzə'nɛt] *n* (BRIT) appartamento a due piani

maize [meɪz] *n* granturco, mais *m*

majesty ['mædʒɪstɪ] *n* maestà *f inv*

major ['meɪdʒə'] *n* (*Mil*) maggiore *m* ▷ *adj* (*greater, Mus*) maggiore; (*in importance*) principale, importante

Majorca [mə'jɔːkə] *n* Maiorca

majority [mə'dʒɔrɪtɪ] *n* maggioranza

make [meɪk] *vt* (*pt, pp* **made**) fare; (*manufacture*) fare, fabbricare; (*cause to be*): **to ~ sb sad** *etc* rendere qn triste *etc*; (*force*): **to ~ sb do sth** costringere qn a fare qc, far fare qc a qn; (*equal*): **2 and 2 ~ 4** 2 più 2 fa 4 ▷ *n* fabbricazione *f*; (*brand*) marca; **to ~ a fool of sb** far fare a qn la figura dello scemo; **to ~ a profit** realizzare un profitto; **to ~ a loss** subire una perdita; **to ~ it** (*in time etc*) arrivare; (*succeed*) farcela; **what time do you ~ it?** che ora fai?; **to ~ do with** arrangiarsi con; **make off** *vi* svignarsela; **make out** *vt* (*write out*) scrivere; (: *cheque*) emettere; (*understand*) capire; (*see*) distinguere; (: *numbers*) decifrare; **make up** *vt* (*constitute*) formare; (*invent*) inventare; (*parcel*) fare ▷ *vi* conciliarsi; (*with cosmetics*) truccarsi; **make up**

for *vt fus* compensare; ricuperare; **makeover** ['meɪkəʊvə'] *n* cambio di immagine; **to give sb a makeover** far cambiare immagine a qn; **maker** *n* (*of programme etc*) creatore/trice; (*manufacturer*) fabbricante *m*; **makeshift** *adj* improvvisato/a; **make-up** *n* trucco

making ['meɪkɪŋ] *n* (*fig*): **in the ~** in formazione; **he has the ~s of an actor** ha la stoffa dell'attore

malaria [mə'lɛərɪə] *n* malaria

Malaysia [mə'leɪzɪə] *n* Malaysia

male [meɪl] *n* (*Biol, Elec*) maschio ▷ *adj* maschile; (*animal, child*) maschio/a

malicious [mə'lɪʃəs] *adj* malevolo/a; (*Law*) doloso/a

malignant [mə'lɪgnənt] *adj* (*Med*) maligno/a

mall [mɔːl] *n* (*also*: **shopping ~**) centro commerciale

mallet ['mælɪt] *n* maglio

malnutrition [mælnjuː'trɪʃən] *n* denutrizione *f*

malpractice [mæl'præktɪs] *n* prevaricazione *f*; negligenza

malt [mɔːlt] *n* malto

Malta ['mɔːltə] *n* Malta; **Maltese** [mɔːl'tiːz] *adj, n* (*pl inv*) maltese (*m/f*); (*Ling*) maltese *m*

mammal ['mæml] *n* mammifero

mammoth ['mæməθ] *adj* enorme, gigantesco/a

man [mæn] *n* (*pl* **men**) uomo ▷ *vt* fornire d'uomini; stare a; **an old ~** un vecchio; **~ and wife** marito e moglie

manage ['mænɪdʒ] *vi* farcela ▷ *vt* (*be in charge of*) occuparsi di; (*shop, restaurant*) gestire; **to ~ to do sth** riuscire a far qc; **manageable** *adj* maneggevole; (*task etc*) fattibile; **management** *n* amministrazione *f*, direzione *f*; **manager** *n* direttore *m*; (*of shop, restaurant*) gerente *m*; (*of artist, Sport*) manager *m inv*; **manageress** [mænɪdʒə'rɛs] *n* direttrice *f*; gerente *f*;

managerial [mænə'dʒɪərɪəl] *adj*
dirigenziale; **managing director**
['mænɪdʒɪŋ-] *n* amministratore *m*
delegato

mandarin ['mændərɪn] *n* (*person,
fruit*) mandarino

mandate ['mændeɪt] *n* mandato

mandatory ['mændətərɪ] *adj*
obbligatorio/a; ingiuntivo/a

mane [meɪn] *n* criniera

mangetout ['mɔnʒ'tuː] *n* pisello
dolce, taccola

mango ['mæŋgəu] (*pl* **mangoes**)
n mango

man: manhole ['mænhəul] *n* botola
stradale; **manhood** ['mænhud] *n*
età virile; virilità

mania [meɪnɪə] *n* mania; **maniac**
['meɪnɪæk] *n* maniaco/a

manic ['mænɪk] *adj* (*behaviour,
activity*) maniacale

manicure ['mænɪkjuəʳ] *n* manicure
f inv

manifest ['mænɪfɛst] *vt* manifestare
▷ *adj* manifesto/a, palese

manifesto [mænɪ'fɛstəu] *n*
manifesto

manipulate [mə'nɪpjuleɪt] *vt*
manipolare

man: mankind [mæn'kaɪnd] *n*
umanità, genere *m* umano; **manly**
['mænlɪ] *adj* virile; coraggioso/a;
man-made *adj* sintetico/a;
artificiale

manner ['mænəʳ] *n* maniera, modo;
(*behaviour*) modo di fare; (*type, sort*):
all ~ of things ogni genere di cosa;
manners *npl* (*conduct*) maniere *fpl*;
bad ~s maleducazione *f*; **all ~ of**
ogni sorta di

manoeuvre, (*us*) **maneuver**
[mə'nuːvəʳ] *vt* manovrare ▷ *vi* far
manovre ▷ *n* manovra

manpower ['mænpauəʳ] *n*
manodopera

mansion ['mænʃən] *n* casa signorile

manslaughter ['mænslɔːtəʳ] *n*
omicidio preterintenzionale

mantelpiece ['mæntlpiːs] *n*
mensola del caminetto

manual ['mænjuəl] *adj*, *n*
manuale (*m*)

manufacture [mænju'fæktʃəʳ]
vt fabbricare ▷ *n* fabbricazione *f*,
manifattura; **manufacturer** *n*
fabbricante *m*

manure [mə'njuəʳ] *n* concime *m*

manuscript ['mænjuskrɪpt] *n*
manoscritto

many ['mɛnɪ] *adj* molti/e ▷ *pron*
molti/e; **a great ~** moltissimi/e,
un gran numero (di); **~ a ...**
molti/e ...

map [mæp] *n* carta (geografica); (*of
city*) cartina

maple ['meɪpl] *n* acero

mar [mɑːʳ] *vt* sciupare

Mar. *abbr* (= *March*) mar.

marathon ['mærəθən] *n* maratona

marble ['mɑːbl] *n* marmo; (*toy*)
pallina, bilia

March [mɑːtʃ] *n* marzo

march [mɑːtʃ] *vi* marciare; sfilare
▷ *n* marcia

mare [mɛəʳ] *n* giumenta

margarine [mɑːdʒə'riːn] *n*
margarina

margin ['mɑːdʒɪn] *n* margine *m*;
marginal *adj* marginale; **marginal
seat** (*Pol*) seggio elettorale ottenuto con
una stretta maggioranza; **marginally**
adv (*bigger, better*) lievemente, di
poco; (*different*) un po'

marigold ['mærɪgəuld] *n* calendola

marijuana [mærɪ'wɑːnə] *n*
marijuana

marina [mə'riːnə] *n* marina

marinade *n* [mærɪ'neɪd] marinata
▷ *vt* ['mærɪneɪd] = **marinate**

marinate ['mærɪneɪt] *vt* marinare

marine [mə'riːn] *adj* (*animal, plant*)
marino/a; (*forces, engineering*)
marittimo/a ▷ *n* (*brit*) fante *m* di
marina; (*us*) marine *m inv*

marital ['mærɪtl] *adj* maritale,
coniugale; **~ status** stato coniugale

m

maritime ['mærɪtaɪm] *adj*
marittimo/a

marjoram ['mɑːdʒərəm] *n*
maggiorana

mark [mɑːk] *n* segno; (*stain*)
macchia; (*of skid etc*) traccia;
(*BRIT Scol*) voto; (*Sport*) bersaglio;
(*currency*) marco ▷ *vt* segnare; (*stain*)
macchiare; (*indicate*) indicare; (*BRIT
Scol*) dare un voto a; correggere; **to
~ time** segnare il passo; **marked** *adj*
spiccato/a, chiaro/a; **marker** *n* (*sign*)
segno; (*bookmark*) segnalibro

market ['mɑːkɪt] *n* mercato
▷ *vt* (*Comm*) mettere in vendita;
marketing *n* marketing *m*;
marketplace *n* (piazza del) mercato;
(*world of trade*) piazza, mercato;
market research *n* indagine *f* or
ricerca di mercato

marmalade ['mɑːməleɪd] *n*
marmellata d'arance

maroon [mə'ruːn] *vt* (*fig*): **to be ~ed
(in** *or* **at)** essere abbandonato/a (in)
▷ *adj* bordeaux *inv*

marquee [mɑː'kiː] *n* padiglione *m*

marriage ['mærɪdʒ] *n* matrimonio;
marriage certificate *n* certificato di
matrimonio

married ['mærɪd] *adj* sposato/a; (*life,
love*) coniugale, matrimoniale

marrow ['mærəu] *n* midollo;
(*vegetable*) zucca

marry ['mærɪ] *vt* sposare, sposarsi
con; (*father, priest etc*) dare in
matrimonio ▷ *vi* (*also:* **get married**)
sposarsi

Mars [mɑːz] *n* (*planet*) Marte *m*

marsh [mɑːʃ] *n* palude *f*

marshal ['mɑːʃl] *n* maresciallo; (*us:
fire marshal*) capo; (*: police marshal*)
capitano ▷ *vt* (*thoughts, support*)
ordinare; (*soldiers*) adunare

martyr ['mɑːtəʳ] *n* martire *m/f*

marvel ['mɑːvl] *n* meraviglia ▷ *vi*: **to
~ (at)** meravigliarsi (di); **marvellous**,
(*us*) **marvelous** *adj* meraviglioso/a

Marxism ['mɑːksɪzəm] *n* marxismo

Marxist ['mɑːksɪst] *adj*, *n* marxista
(*m/f*)

marzipan ['mɑːzɪpæn] *n* marzapane
m

mascara [mæs'kɑːrə] *n* mascara
m inv

mascot ['mæskət] *n* mascotte *f inv*

masculine ['mæskjulɪn] *adj*
maschile; (*woman*) mascolino/a

mash [mæʃ] *vt* passare, schiacciare

mashed [mæʃt] *adj*: **~ potatoes**
purè *m* di patate

mask [mɑːsk] *n* maschera ▷ *vt*
mascherare

mason ['meɪsn] *n* (*also:* **stone~**)
scalpellino; (*also:* **free~**) massone *m*;
masonry *n* muratura

mass [mæs] *n* moltitudine *f*, massa;
(*Physics*) massa; (*Rel*) messa ▷ *cpd*
di massa ▷ *vi* ammassarsi; **the ~es**
(*ordinary people*) le masse; **~es of** (*col*)
una montagna di

massacre ['mæsəkəʳ] *n* massacro

massage ['mæsɑːʒ] *n* massaggio

massive ['mæsɪv] *adj* enorme,
massiccio/a

mass media *npl* mass media *mpl*

mass-produce ['mæsprə'djuːs] *vt*
produrre in serie

mast [mɑːst] *n* albero

master ['mɑːstəʳ] *n* padrone *m*;
(*teacher: in primary school, Art etc*)
maestro; (*: in secondary school*)
professore *m*; (*title for boys*): **M~ X**
Signorino X ▷ *vt* domare; (*learn*)
imparare a fondo; (*understand*)
conoscere a fondo; **mastermind**
n mente *f* superiore ▷ *vt* essere il
cervello di; **Master of Arts/Science**
n Master *m inv* in lettere/scienze;
masterpiece *n* capolavoro

masturbate ['mæstəbeɪt] *vi*
masturbare

mat [mæt] *n* stuoia; (*also:* **door~**)
stoino, zerbino; (*also:* **table ~**)
sottopiatto ▷ *adj* = **matt**

match [mætʃ] *n* fiammifero; (*game*)
partita, incontro; (*fig*) uguale *m/f*;

matrimonio; partito ▷ *vt* intonare; (*go well with*) andare benissimo con; (*equal*) uguagliare; (*correspond to*) corrispondere a; (*pair: also:* **~ up**) accoppiare ▷ *vi* intonarsi; **to be a good ~** andare bene; **matchbox** *n* scatola per fiammiferi; **matching** *adj* ben assortito/a

mate [meɪt] *n* compagno/a di lavoro; (*col: friend*) amico/a; (*animal*) compagno/a; (*in merchant navy*) secondo ▷ *vi* accoppiarsi

material [mə'tɪərɪəl] *n* (*substance*) materiale *m*, materia; (*cloth*) stoffa ▷ *adj* materiale; **materials** *npl* (*equipment etc*) materiali *mpl*

materialize [mə'tɪərɪəlaɪz] *vi* materializzarsi, realizzarsi

maternal [mə'tə:nl] *adj* materno/a

maternity [mə'tə:nɪtɪ] *n* maternità; **maternity hospital** *n* ≈ clinica ostetrica; **maternity leave** *n* congedo di maternità

math [mæθ] *n abbr* (US) = **mathematics**

mathematical [mæθə'mætɪkl] *adj* matematico/a

mathematician [mæθəmə'tɪʃən] *n* matematico/a

mathematics [mæθə'mætɪks] *n* matematica

maths [mæθs] *n abbr* (BRIT) = **mathematics**

matinée ['mætɪneɪ] *n* matinée *f inv*

matron ['meɪtrən] *n* (*in hospital*) capoinfermiera; (*in school*) infermiera

matt [mæt] *adj* opaco/a

matter ['mætə'] *n* questione *f*; (*Physics*) materia, sostanza; (*content*) contenuto; (*Med: pus*) pus *m* ▷ *vi* importare; **matters** *npl* (*affairs*) questioni; **it doesn't ~** non importa; (*I don't mind*) non fa niente; **what's the ~?** che cosa c'è?; **no ~ what** qualsiasi cosa accada; **as a ~ of course** come cosa naturale; **as a ~ of fact** in verità

mattress ['mætrɪs] *n* materasso

mature [mə'tjuə'] *adj* maturo/a; (*cheese*) stagionato/a ▷ *vi* maturare; stagionare; **mature student** *n* studente universitario che ha più di 25 anni; **maturity** *n* maturità

maul [mɔ:l] *vt* lacerare

mauve [məuv] *adj* malva *inv*

max. *abbr* = **maximum**

maximize ['mæksɪmaɪz] *vt* (*profits etc*) massimizzare; (*chances*) aumentare al massimo

maximum ['mæksɪməm] *adj* massimo/a ▷ *n* (*pl* **maxima**) massimo

May [meɪ] *n* maggio

may [meɪ] *vi* (*conditional* **might**) (*indicating possibility*): **he ~ come** può darsi che venga; (*be allowed to*): **~ I smoke?** posso fumare?; (*wishes*): **~ God bless you!** Dio la benedica!; **I might as well go** potrei anche andarmene

maybe ['meɪbi:] *adv* forse, può darsi; **~ he'll ...** può darsi che lui ... + *sub*, forse lui ...

May Day *n* il primo maggio

mayhem ['meɪhɛm] *n* cagnara

mayonnaise [meɪə'neɪz] *n* maionese *f*

mayor [mɛə'] *n* sindaco; **mayoress** *n* sindaco (*donna*); moglie *f* del sindaco

maze [meɪz] *n* labirinto, dedalo

MD *n abbr* (= *Doctor of Medicine*) titolo di studio; (*Comm*) = **managing director**

me [mi:] *pron* mi, m' + *vowel or silent* "*h*"; (*stressed, after prep*) me; **he heard me** mi ha *or* m'ha sentito; **give me a book** dammi (*or* mi dia) un libro; **it's me** sono io; **with me** con me; **without me** senza di me

meadow ['mɛdəu] *n* prato

meagre [*(US)* **meager** ['mi:gə'] *adj* magro/a

meal [mi:l] *n* pasto; (*flour*) farina; **mealtime** *n* l'ora di mangiare

mean [mi:n] *adj* (*with money*) avaro/a, gretto/a; (*unkind*) meschino/a, maligno/a; (*shabby*)

misero/a; (*average*) medio/a ▷ *vt*
(*pt, pp* **meant**) (*signify*) significare,
voler dire; (*intend*): **to ~ to do** aver
l'intenzione di fare ▷ *n* mezzo;
(*Math*) media; **to be ~t for** essere
destinato/a a; **do you ~ it?** dice sul
serio?; **what do you ~?** che cosa vuol
dire?; *see also* **means**

meaning ['mi:nɪŋ] *n* significato,
senso; **meaningful** *adj*
significativo/a; **meaningless** *adj*
senza senso

means [mi:nz] *npl* (*way, money*) mezzi
mpl; **by means of** per mezzo di; **by
all means** ma certo, prego

meant [mɛnt] *pt, pp of* **mean**

meantime ['mi:ntaɪm],
meanwhile ['mi:nwaɪl] *adv* (*also:*
in the ~) nel frattempo

measles ['mi:zlz] *n* morbillo

measure ['mɛʒəʳ] *vt, vi* misurare ▷ *n*
misura; (*ruler*) metro

measurement ['mɛʒəmənt] *n*
(*act*) misurazione *f*; (*measure*)
misura; **chest/hip ~** giro petto/
fianchi; **to take sb's ~s** prendere le
misure di qn

meat [mi:t] *n* carne *f*; **cold ~s**
affettati *mpl*; **meatball** *n* polpetta
di carne

Mecca ['mɛkə] *n* La Mecca; (*fig*): **a ~
(for)** la Mecca (di)

mechanic [mɪ'kænɪk] *n* meccanico;
mechanical *adj* meccanico/a

mechanism ['mɛkənɪzəm] *n*
meccanismo

medal ['mɛdl] *n* medaglia;
medallist, (*US*) **medalist** *n* (*Sport*):
to be a gold medallist essere
medaglia d'oro

meddle ['mɛdl] *vi*: **to ~ in**
immischiarsi in, mettere le mani in;
to ~ with toccare

media ['mi:dɪə] *npl* media *mpl*

mediaeval [mɛdɪ'i:vl] *adj*
= **medieval**

mediate ['mi:dɪeɪt] *vi* fare da
mediatore/trice

medical ['mɛdɪkl] *adj* medico/a;
~ (examination) *n* visita medica;
medical certificate *n* certificato
medico

medicated ['mɛdɪkeɪtɪd] *adj*
medicato/a

medication [mɛdɪ'keɪʃən] *n*
medicinali *mpl*, farmaci *mpl*

medicine ['mɛdsɪn] *n* medicina

medieval [mɛdɪ'i:vl] *adj* medievale

mediocre [mi:dɪ'əʊkəʳ] *adj* mediocre

meditate ['mɛdɪteɪt] *vi*: **to ~ (on)**
meditare (su)

meditation [mɛdɪ'teɪʃən] *n*
meditazione *f*

Mediterranean [mɛdɪtə'reɪnɪən]
adj mediterraneo/a; **the ~ (Sea)** il
(mare) Mediterraneo

medium ['mi:dɪəm] *adj* medio/a
▷ *n* (*pl* **media**: *means*) mezzo; (*pl*
mediums: *person*) medium *m*
inv; **medium-sized** *adj* (*tin etc*) di
grandezza media; (*clothes*) di taglia
media; **medium wave** *n* onde *fpl*
medie

meek [mi:k] *adj* dolce, umile

meet (*pt, pp* **met**) [mi:t, mɛt] *vt*
incontrare; (*for the first time*) fare la
conoscenza di; (*go and fetch*) andare a
prendere; (*fig*) affrontare; soddisfare;
raggiungere ▷ *vi* incontrarsi; (*in
session*) riunirsi; (*join: objects*) unirsi
▷ *n* (*BRIT Hunting*) raduno (dei
partecipanti alla caccia alla volpe);
(*US Sport*) raduno (sportivo); **I'll ~
you at the station** verrò a prenderla
alla stazione; **pleased to ~ you!**
piacere (di conoscerla)!; **meet up** *vi*:
to ~ up with sb incontrare qn; **meet
with** *vt fus* incontrare; **meeting** *n*
incontro; (*session: of club etc*) riunione
f; (*interview*) intervista; **she's at
a meeting** (*Comm*) è in riunione;
meeting place *n* luogo d'incontro

megabyte ['mɛgəbaɪt] *n* (*Comput*)
megabyte *m inv*

megaphone ['mɛgəfəʊn] *n*
megafono

megapixel ['mɛgəpɪksl] *n*
megapixel *m inv*
melancholy ['mɛlənkəlɪ] *n*
malinconia ▷ *adj* malinconico/a
melody ['mɛlədɪ] *n* melodia
melon ['mɛlən] *n* melone *m*
melt [mɛlt] *vi* (*gen*) sciogliersi,
struggersi; (*metals*) fondersi ▷ *vt*
sciogliere, struggere; fondere
member ['mɛmbər] *n* membro;
Member of Congress (*us*) *n*
membro del Congresso; **Member
of Parliament** (*BRIT*) *n* deputato/a;
**Member of the European
Parliament** (*BRIT*) *n* eurodeputato/a;
**Member of the House of
Representatives** (*us*) *n* membro
della Camera dei Rappresentanti;
**Member of the Scottish
Parliament** (*BRIT*) *n* deputato/a del
Parlamento scozzese; **membership**
n iscrizione *f*; (*numero d'*)iscritti *mpl*,
membri *mpl*; **membership card** *n*
tessera (di iscrizione)
memento [mə'mɛntəu] *n* ricordo,
souvenir *m inv*
memo ['mɛməu] *n* appunto; (*Comm
etc*) comunicazione *f* di servizio
memorable ['mɛmərəbl] *adj*
memorabile
memorandum (*pl* **memoranda**)
[mɛmə'rændəm, -də] *n* appunto;
(*Comm etc*) comunicazione *f* di servizio
memorial [mɪ'mɔːrɪəl] *n*
monumento commemorativo ▷ *adj*
commemorativo/a
memorize ['mɛməraɪz] *vt*
memorizzare
memory ['mɛmərɪ] *n* (*gen, Comput*)
memoria; (*recollection*) ricordo;
memory stick *n* (*Comput*) stick *m inv*
di memoria
men [mɛn] *npl of* **man**
menace ['mɛnɪs] *n* minaccia ▷ *vt*
minacciare
mend [mɛnd] *vt* aggiustare, riparare;
(*darn*) rammendare ▷ *n*: **on the ~** in
via di guarigione

meningitis [mɛnɪn'dʒaɪtɪs] *n*
meningite *f*
menopause ['mɛnəupɔːz] *n*
menopausa
men's room *n*: **the ~** (*esp us*) la
toilette degli uomini
menstruation [mɛnstru'eɪʃən] *n*
mestruazione *f*
menswear ['mɛnzwɛər] *n*
abbigliamento maschile
mental ['mɛntl] *adj* mentale;
mental hospital *n* ospedale
m psichiatrico; **mentality**
[mɛn'tælɪt] *n* mentalità *f inv*;
mentally *adv*: **to be mentally
handicapped** essere minorato
psichico
menthol ['mɛnθɔl] *n* mentolo
mention ['mɛnʃən] *n* menzione *f* ▷ *vt*
menzionare, far menzione di; **don't
~ it!** non c'è di che!, prego!
menu ['mɛnjuː] *n* (*set menu, Comput*)
menù *m inv*; (*printed*) carta
MEP *n abbr* = **Member of the
European Parliament**
mercenary ['məːsɪnərɪ] *adj* venale
▷ *n* mercenario
merchandise ['məːtʃəndaɪz] *n*
merci *fpl*
merchant ['məːtʃənt] *n* mercante *m*,
commerciante *m*; **merchant navy**,
(*us*) **merchant marine** *n* marina
mercantile
merciless ['məːsɪlɪs] *adj* spietato/a
mercury ['məːkjurɪ] *n* mercurio
mercy ['məːsɪ] *n* pietà; (*Rel*)
misericordia; **at the ~ of** alla
mercè di
mere [mɪər] *adj* semplice; **by a ~
chance** per mero caso; **merely** *adv*
semplicemente, non ... che
merge [məːdʒ] *vt* unire ▷ *vi* fondersi,
unirsi; (*Comm*) fondersi; **merger** *n*
(*Comm*) fusione *f*
meringue [mə'ræŋ] *n* meringa
merit ['mɛrɪt] *n* merito, valore *m* ▷ *vt*
meritare
mermaid ['məːmeɪd] *n* sirena

m

merry ['mɛrɪ] *adj* gaio/a, allegro/a;
M~ Christmas! Buon Natale!;
merry-go-round *n* carosello

mesh [mɛʃ] *n* maglia; rete *f*

mess [mɛs] *n* confusione *f*, disordine
m; (*fig*) pasticcio; (*dirt*) sporcizia; (*Mil*)
mensa; **mess about, mess around**
vi (*col*) trastullarsi; **mess with** *vt fus*
(*col: challenge, confront*) litigare con;
(: *drugs, drinks*) abusare di; **mess up**
vt (*col*) sporcare; fare un pasticcio
di; rovinare

message ['mɛsɪdʒ] *n* messaggio;
message board *n* (*Comput*) bacheca
elettronica

messenger ['mɛsɪndʒər] *n*
messaggero/a

Messrs, Messrs. ['mɛsəz] *abbr* (*on
letters*: = *messieurs*) Spett.

messy ['mɛsɪ] *adj* sporco/a;
disordinato/a

met [mɛt] *pt, pp of* **meet**

metabolism [mɛ'tæbəlɪzəm] *n*
metabolismo

metal ['mɛtl] *n* metallo; **metallic**
[mɛ'tælɪk] *adj* metallico/a

metaphor ['mɛtəfər] *n* metafora

meteor ['miːtɪər] *n* meteora;
meteorite ['miːtɪəraɪt] *n* meteorite
m

meteorology [miːtɪə'rɒlədʒɪ] *n*
meteorologia

meter ['miːtər] *n* (*instrument*)
contatore *m*; (*parking meter*)
parchimetro; (*us: unit*) = **metre**

method ['mɛθəd] *n* metodo;
methodical [mɪ'θɒdɪkl] *adj*
metodico/a

meths [mɛθs] (*BRIT*) *n* = **methylated
spirits**

methylated spirits ['mɛθɪleɪtɪd-]
n (*BRIT: also:* **meths**) alcool *m*
denaturato

meticulous [mɛ'tɪkjuləs] *adj*
meticoloso/a

metre, (US) meter ['miːtər] *n* metro

metric ['mɛtrɪk] *adj* metrico/a

metro ['mɛtrəu] *n* metro *m inv*

metropolitan [mɛtrə'pɒlɪtən] *adj*
metropolitano/a

Mexican ['mɛksɪkən] *adj, n*
messicano/a

Mexico ['mɛksɪkəu] *n* Messico

mg *abbr* (= *milligram*) mg

mice [maɪs] *npl of* **mouse**

micro... ['maɪkrəu] *prefix* micro...;
microchip *n* microcircuito
integrato; **microphone** *n* microfono;
microscope *n* microscopio;
microwave *n* (*also:* **microwave
oven**) forno a microonde

mid [mɪd] *adj:* ~ **May** metà maggio;
~ **afternoon** metà pomeriggio;
in ~ air a mezz'aria; **midday** *n*
mezzogiorno

middle ['mɪdl] *n* mezzo; centro;
(*waist*) vita ▷ *adj* di mezzo; **in the ~
of the night** nel cuore della notte;
middle-aged *adj* di mezza età;
Middle Ages *npl:* **the Middle Ages**
il Medioevo; **middle class** *adj* (*also:*
middle-class) ≈ borghese; **Middle
East** *n:* **the Middle East** il Medio
Oriente; **middle name** *n* secondo
nome *m*; **middle school** *n* (*US*) *scuola
media per ragazzi dagli 11 ai 14 anni;*
(*BRIT*) *scuola media per ragazzi dagli 8 o
9 ai 12 o 13 anni*

midge [mɪdʒ] *n* moscerino

midget ['mɪdʒɪt] *n* nano/a

midnight ['mɪdnaɪt] *n* mezzanotte *f*

midst [mɪdst] *n:* **in the ~ of** in
mezzo a

midsummer [mɪd'sʌmər] *n* mezza
or piena estate *f*

midway [mɪd'weɪ] *adj, adv:* ~
(between) a mezza strada (fra); ~
(through) a metà (di)

midweek [mɪd'wiːk] *adv* a metà
settimana

midwife (*pl* **midwives**) ['mɪdwaɪf,
-vz] *n* levatrice *f*

midwinter [mɪd'wɪntər] *n* pieno
inverno

might [maɪt] *vb see* **may** ▷ *n* potere
m, forza; **mighty** *adj* forte, potente

migraine ['miːgreɪn] n emicrania
migrant ['maɪgrənt] adj (bird)
migratore/trice; (worker)
emigrato/a
migrate [maɪ'greɪt] vi (bird) migrare;
(person) emigrare
migration [maɪ'greɪʃən] n
migrazione f
mike [maɪk] n abbr (= microphone)
microfono
Milan [mɪ'læn] n Milano f
mild [maɪld] adj mite; (person, voice)
dolce; (flavour) delicato/a; (illness)
leggero/a; (interest) blando/a ▷ n
(beer) birra leggera; **mildly** ['maɪldlɪ]
adv mitemente; dolcemente;
delicatamente; leggermente;
blandamente; **to put it mildly** a
dire poco
mile [maɪl] n miglio; **mileage** n
distanza in miglia, ≈ chilometraggio;
mileometer [maɪ'lɔmɪtəʳ] n
(BRIT) = **milometer**; **milestone**
['maɪlstəʊn] n pietra miliare
military ['mɪlɪtərɪ] adj militare
militia [mɪ'lɪʃə] n milizia
milk [mɪlk] n latte m ▷ vt (cow)
mungere; (fig) sfruttare; **milk
chocolate** n cioccolato al latte;
milkman n (irreg) lattaio; **milky** adj
lattiginoso/a; (colour) latteo/a
mill [mɪl] n mulino; (small, for coffee,
pepper etc) macinino; (factory)
fabbrica; (spinning mill) filatura
▷ vt macinare ▷ vi (also: **~ about**)
brulicare
millennium (pl **millenniums** or
millennia) [mɪ'lɛnɪəm, -'lɛnɪə] n
millennio
milli... ['mɪlɪ] prefix milli...;
milligram(me) n milligrammo;
millilitre, (US) **milliliter** ['mɪlɪliːtəʳ]
n millilitro; **millimetre**, (US)
millimeter n millimetro
million ['mɪljən] num milione
m; **millionaire** n milionario,
≈ miliardario; **millionth** num
milionesimo/a

milometer [maɪ'lɔmɪtəʳ] n ≈
contachilometri m inv
mime [maɪm] n mimo ▷ vt, vi
mimare
mimic ['mɪmɪk] n imitatore/trice
▷ vt imitare
min. abbr = **minute**; (= minimum) min.
mince [mɪns] vt tritare, macinare
▷ n (BRIT Culin) carne f tritata or
macinata; **mincemeat** n frutta secca
tritata per uso in pasticceria; (US) carne
f tritata or macinata; **mince pie** n
specie di torta con frutta secca
mind [maɪnd] n mente f ▷ vt (attend
to, look after) badare a, occuparsi di;
(be careful) fare attenzione a, stare
attento/a a; (object to): **I don't ~
the noise** il rumore non mi dà alcun
fastidio; **do you ~ if ...?** le dispiace se
...?; **I don't ~** non m'importa; **~ you,
...** sì, però va detto che ...; **never ~**
non importa, non fa niente; (don't
worry) non preoccuparti; **it is on my
~** mi preoccupa; **to my ~** secondo
me, a mio parere; **to be out of one's
~** essere uscito/a di mente; **to keep
sth in ~** non dimenticare qc; **to bear
sth in ~** tener presente qc; **to make
up one's ~** decidersi; **"~ the step"**
"attenzione allo scalino"; **mindless**
adj idiota
mine¹ [maɪn] pron il (la) mio/a; (pl) i
(le) miei (mie); **this book is ~** questo
libro è mio; **yours is red, ~ is green** il
tuo è rosso, il mio è verde; **a friend of
~** un mio amico
mine² [maɪn] n miniera; (explosive)
mina ▷ vt (coal) estrarre; (ship, beach)
minare; **minefield** ['maɪnfiːld] n
campo minato; **miner** ['maɪnəʳ] n
minatore m
mineral ['mɪnərəl] adj minerale ▷ n
minerale m; **mineral water** n acqua
minerale
mingle ['mɪŋgl] vi: **to ~ with**
mescolarsi a, mischiarsi con
miniature ['mɪnətʃəʳ] adj in
miniatura ▷ n miniatura

m

minibar ['mɪnɪbɑːʳ] n minibar m inv

minibus ['mɪnɪbʌs] n minibus m inv

minicab ['mɪnɪkæb] n (BRIT) ≈ taxi m inv

minimal ['mɪnɪml] adj minimo/a

minimize ['mɪnɪmaɪz] vt minimizzare

minimum ['mɪnɪməm] n (pl **minima**) minimo ▷ adj minimo/a

mining ['maɪnɪŋ] n industria mineraria

miniskirt ['mɪnɪskəːt] n minigonna

minister ['mɪnɪstəʳ] n (BRIT Pol) ministro; (Rel) pastore m

ministry ['mɪnɪstrɪ] n ministero

minor ['maɪnəʳ] adj minore, di poca importanza; (Mus) minore ▷ n (Law) minorenne m/f

Minorca [mɪ'nɔːkə] n Minorca

minority [maɪ'nɔrɪtɪ] n minoranza

mint [mɪnt] n (plant) menta; (sweet) pasticca di menta ▷ vt (coins) battere; **the (Royal) M~** (BRIT), **the (US) M~** (US) la Zecca; **in ~ condition** come nuovo/a di zecca

minus ['maɪnəs] n (also: **~ sign**) segno meno ▷ prep meno

minute¹ ['mɪnɪt] n minuto; **minutes** npl (of meeting) verbale m

minute² [maɪ'njuːt] adj minuscolo/a; (detail) minuzioso/a

miracle ['mɪrəkl] n miracolo

miraculous [mɪ'rækjuləs] adj miracoloso/a

mirage ['mɪrɑːʒ] n miraggio

mirror ['mɪrəʳ] n specchio; (in car) specchietto

misbehave [mɪsbɪ'heɪv] vi comportarsi male

misc. abbr = **miscellaneous**

miscarriage ['mɪskærɪdʒ] n (Med) aborto spontaneo; **~ of justice** errore m giudiziario

miscellaneous [mɪsɪ'leɪnɪəs] adj (items) vario/a; (selection) misto/a

mischief ['mɪstʃɪf] n (naughtiness) birichineria; (maliciousness) malizia; **mischievous** adj birichino/a

misconception [mɪskən'sɛpʃən] n idea sbagliata

misconduct [mɪs'kɔndʌkt] n cattiva condotta; **professional ~** reato professionale

miser ['maɪzəʳ] n avaro

miserable ['mɪzərəbl] adj infelice; (wretched) miserabile; (weather) deprimente; (offer, failure) misero/a

misery ['mɪzərɪ] n (unhappiness) tristezza; (wretchedness) miseria

misfortune [mɪs'fɔːtʃən] n sfortuna

misgiving [mɪs'gɪvɪŋ] n dubbi mpl; **to have ~s about sth** essere diffidente or avere dei dubbi per quanto riguarda qc

misguided [mɪs'gaɪdɪd] adj sbagliato/a; poco giudizioso/a

mishap ['mɪshæp] n disgrazia

misinterpret [mɪsɪn'təːprɪt] vt interpretare male

misjudge [mɪs'dʒʌdʒ] vt giudicare male

mislay [mɪs'leɪ] vt (irreg) smarrire

mislead [mɪs'liːd] vt (irreg) sviare; **misleading** adj ingannevole

misplace [mɪs'pleɪs] vt smarrire

misprint ['mɪsprɪnt] n errore m di stampa

misrepresent [mɪsrɛprɪ'zɛnt] vt travisare

Miss [mɪs] n Signorina

miss [mɪs] vt (fail to get) perdere; (fail to hit) mancare; (fail to see): **you can't ~ it** non puoi non vederlo; (regret the absence of): **I ~ him/it** sento la sua mancanza ▷ vi mancare ▷ n (shot) colpo mancato; **we ~ed our train** abbiamo perso il treno; **miss out** vt (BRIT) omettere; **miss out on** vt fus (fun, party) perdersi; (chance, bargain) lasciarsi sfuggire

missile ['mɪsaɪl] n (Aviat) missile m; (object thrown) proiettile m

missing ['mɪsɪŋ] adj perso/a, smarrito/a; (removed) mancante; **~ person** scomparso/a; (after *disaster*) disperso/a; **~ in action** (*Mil*) disperso/a; **to be ~** mancare

mission ['mɪʃən] *n* missione *f*; **missionary** *n* missionario/a

misspell [mɪs'spɛl] *vt* (*irreg: like* **spell**) sbagliare l'ortografia di

mist [mɪst] *n* nebbia, foschia ▷ *vi* (*also:* **~ over, ~ up**) annebbiarsi; (*BRIT: windows*) appannarsi

mistake [mɪs'teɪk] *n* sbaglio, errore *m* ▷ *vt* (*irreg: like* **take**) sbagliarsi di; fraintendere; **to ~ for** prendere per; **by ~** per sbaglio; **to make a ~** fare uno sbaglio *or* un errore, sbagliare; **there must be some ~** ci dev'essere un errore; **mistaken** *pp of* **mistake** ▷ *adj* (*idea etc*) sbagliato/a; **to be mistaken** sbagliarsi

mister ['mɪstə'] *n* (*col*) signore *m*; *see* **Mr**

mistletoe ['mɪsltəʊ] *n* vischio

mistook [mɪs'tʊk] *pt of* **mistake**

mistress ['mɪstrɪs] *n* padrona; (*lover*) amante *f*; (*BRIT Scol*) insegnante *f*

mistrust [mɪs'trʌst] *vt* diffidare di

misty ['mɪstɪ] *adj* nebbioso/a, brumoso/a

misunderstand [mɪsʌndə'stænd] *vt, vi* (*irreg*) capire male, fraintendere; **misunderstanding** *n* malinteso, equivoco; **there's been a misunderstanding** c'è stato un malinteso

misunderstood [mɪsʌndə'stʊd] *pt, pp of* **misunderstand**

misuse *n* [mɪs'juːs] cattivo uso; (*of power*) abuso ▷ *vt* [mɪs'juːz] far cattivo uso di; abusare di

mitt(en) ['mɪt(n)] *n* mezzo guanto; manopola

mix [mɪks] *vt* mescolare ▷ *vi* (*people*): **to ~ with** avere a che fare con ▷ *n* mescolanza; preparato; **mix up** *vt* mescolare; (*confuse*) confondere; **mixed** *adj* misto/a; **mixed grill** *n* (*BRIT*) misto alla griglia; **mixed salad** *n* insalata mista; **mixed-up** *adj* (*confused*) confuso/a; **mixer** *n*

(*for food: electric*) frullatore *m*; (: *hand*) frullino; **he is a good mixer** è molto socievole; **mixture** *n* mescolanza; (*blend: of tobacco etc*) miscela; (*Med*) sciroppo; **mix-up** *n* confusione *f*

ml *abbr* (= *millilitre(s)*) ml

mm *abbr* (= *millimetre*) mm

moan [məʊn] *n* gemito ▷ *vi* (*col: complain*): **to ~ (about)** lamentarsi (di)

moat [məʊt] *n* fossato

mob [mɔb] *n* calca ▷ *vt* accalcarsi intorno a

mobile ['məʊbaɪl] *adj* mobile ▷ *n* (*phone*) telefonino, cellulare *m*; (*Art*) mobile *m inv*; **mobile home** *n* grande roulotte *f inv* (*utilizzata come domicilio*); **mobile phone** *n* telefono portatile, telefonino

mobility [məʊ'bɪlɪtɪ] *n* mobilità; (*of applicant*) disponibilità a viaggiare

mobilize ['məʊbɪlaɪz] *vt* mobilitare ▷ *vi* mobilitarsi

mock [mɔk] *vt* deridere, burlarsi di ▷ *adj* falso/a; **mocks** *npl* (*BRIT col: Scol*) simulazione *f* degli esami; **mockery** *n* derisione *f*; **to make a mockery of** burlarsi di; (*exam*) rendere una farsa

mod cons ['mɔd'kɔnz] *npl abbr* (*BRIT*) = **modern conveniences**

mode [məʊd] *n* modo

model ['mɔdl] *n* modello; (*person: for fashion*) indossatore/trice; (: *for artist*) modello/a ▷ *vt* modellare ▷ *vi* fare l'indossatore (*or* l'indossatrice) ▷ *adj* (*small-scale: railway etc*) in miniatura; (*child, factory*) modello *inv*; **to ~ clothes** presentare degli abiti; **to ~ sb/sth on** modellare qn/qc su

modem ['məʊdɛm] *n* modem *m inv*

moderate *adj* ['mɔdərɪt] moderato/a ▷ *vi* ['mɔdəreɪt] moderarsi, placarsi ▷ *vt* moderare

moderation [mɔdə'reɪʃən] *n* moderazione *f*, misura; **in ~** in quantità moderata, con moderazione

modern ['mɔdən] *adj* moderno/a;
~ **conveniences** comodità *fpl*
moderne; ~ **languages** lingue
fpl moderne; **modernize** *vt*
modernizzare

modest ['mɔdɪst] *adj* modesto/a;
modesty *n* modestia

modification [mɔdɪfɪ'keɪʃən] *n*
modificazione *f*; **to make ~s** fare *or*
apportare delle modifiche

modify ['mɔdɪfaɪ] *vt* modificare

module ['mɔdjuːl] *n* modulo

mohair ['məuhɛəʳ] *n* mohair *m*

Mohammed [məu'hæmɪd] *n*
Maometto

moist [mɔɪst] *adj* umido/a;
moisture ['mɔɪstʃəʳ] *n* umidità;
(*on glass*) goccioline *fpl* di vapore;
moisturizer ['mɔɪstʃəraɪzəʳ] *n*
idratante *f*

mold *etc* [məuld] (*US*) = **mould** *etc*

mole [məul] *n* (*animal, fig*) talpa;
(*spot*) neo

molecule ['mɔlɪkjuːl] *n* molecola

molest [məu'lɛst] *vt* molestare

molten ['məultən] *adj* fuso/a

mom [mɔm] *n* (*US*) = **mum**

moment ['məumənt] *n* momento,
istante *m*; **at that ~** in quel
momento; **at the ~** al momento,
in questo momento; **momentarily**
['məuməntərɪlɪ] *adv* per un
momento; (*US: very soon*) da un
momento all'altro; **momentary**
adj momentaneo/a, passeggero/a;
momentous [məu'mɛntəs] *adj* di
grande importanza

momentum [məu'mɛntəm] *n*
(*Physics*) momento; (*fig*) impeto; **to
gather ~** aumentare di velocità

mommy ['mɔmɪ] *n* (*US*) mamma

Mon. *abbr* (= *Monday*) lun.

Monaco ['mɔnəkəu] *n* Monaco *f*

monarch ['mɔnək] *n* monarca *m*;
monarchy *n* monarchia

monastery ['mɔnəstərɪ] *n*
monastero

Monday ['mʌndɪ] *n* lunedì *m inv*

monetary ['mʌnɪtərɪ] *adj*
monetario/a

money ['mʌnɪ] *n* denaro, soldi *mpl*;
money belt *n* marsupio (*per soldi*);
money order *n* vaglia *m inv*

mongrel ['mʌŋgrəl] *n* (*dog*) cane *m*
bastardo

monitor ['mɔnɪtəʳ] *n* (*TV, Comput*)
monitor *m inv* ▷ *vt* controllare

monk [mʌŋk] *n* monaco

monkey ['mʌŋkɪ] *n* scimmia

monologue ['mɔnəlɔg] *n* monologo

monopoly [mə'nɔpəlɪ] *n* monopolio

monosodium glutamate
[mɔnə'səudɪəm'gluːtəmeɪt] *n*
glutammato di sodio

monotonous [mə'nɔtənəs] *adj*
monotono/a

monsoon [mɔn'suːn] *n* monsone *m*

monster ['mɔnstəʳ] *n* mostro

month [mʌnθ] *n* mese *m*; **monthly**
adj mensile ▷ *adv* al mese; ogni mese

monument ['mɔnjumənt] *n*
monumento

mood [muːd] *n* umore *m*; **to be
in a good/bad ~** essere di buon/
cattivo umore; **moody** *adj* (*variable*)
capriccioso/a, lunatico/a; (*sullen*)
imbronciato/a

moon [muːn] *n* luna; **moonlight** *n*
chiaro di luna

moor [muəʳ] *n* brughiera ▷ *vt* (*ship*)
ormeggiare ▷ *vi* ormeggiarsi

moose [muːs] *n* (*pl inv*) alce *m*

mop [mɔp] *n* lavapavimenti *m inv*;
(*also*: ~ **of hair**) zazzera ▷ *vt* lavare
con lo straccio; (*face*) asciugare;
mop up *vt* asciugare con uno
straccio

mope [məup] *vi* fare il broncio

moped ['məupɛd] *n* (*BRIT*)
ciclomotore *m*

moral ['mɔrəl] *adj* morale ▷ *n*
morale *f*; **morals** *npl* (*principles*)
moralità

morale [mɔ'rɑːl] *n* morale *m*

morality [mə'rælɪtɪ] *n* moralità

morbid ['mɔːbɪd] *adj* morboso/a

○ **KEYWORD**

more [mɔː^r] *adj* **1** (*greater in number etc*) più; **more people/letters than we expected** più persone/lettere di quante ne aspettavamo; **I have more wine/money than you** ho più vino/soldi di te; **I have more wine than beer** ho più vino che birra **2** (*additional*) altro/a, ancora; **do you want (some) more tea?** vuole dell'altro tè?, vuole ancora del tè?; **I have no** *or* **I don't have any more money** non ho più soldi
▸ *pron* **1** (*greater amount*) più; **more than 10** più di 10; **it cost more than we expected** è costato più di quanto ci aspettassimo
2 (*further or additional amount*) ancora; **is there any more?** ce n'è ancora?; **there's no more** non ce n'è più; **a little more** ancora un po'; **many/much more** molti/e/ molto/a di più
▸ *adv*: **more dangerous/easily (than)** più pericoloso/facilmente (di); **more and more** sempre di più; **more and more difficult** sempre più difficile; **more or less** più o meno; **more than ever** più che mai

moreover [mɔːˈrəuvə^r] *adv* inoltre, di più
morgue [mɔːɡ] *n* obitorio
morning [ˈmɔːnɪŋ] *n* mattina, mattino; (*duration*) mattinata ▸ *cpd* del mattino; **in the ~** la mattina; **7 o'clock in the ~** le 7 di *or* della mattina; **morning sickness** *n* nausee *fpl* mattutine
Moroccan [məˈrɔkən] *adj, n* marocchino/a
Morocco [məˈrɔkəu] *n* Marocco
moron [ˈmɔːrɔn] *n* (*col*) deficiente *m/f*
morphine [ˈmɔːfiːn] *n* morfina
morris dancing [ˈmɔrɪs-] *n vedi nota* **"morris dancing"**

● **MORRIS DANCING**
●
● Il *morris dancing* è una
● danza folcloristica inglese
● tradizionalmente riservata agli
● uomini. Vestiti di bianco e con dei
● campanelli attaccati alle caviglie,
● i ballerini eseguono una danza
● tenendo in mano dei fazzoletti
● bianchi e lunghi bastoni. Questa
● danza è molto popolare nelle feste
● paesane.

Morse [mɔːs] *n* (*also*: **~ code**) alfabeto Morse
mortal [ˈmɔːtl] *adj, n* mortale (*m*)
mortar [ˈmɔːtə^r] *n* (*Constr*) malta; (*dish*) mortaio
mortgage [ˈmɔːɡɪdʒ] *n* ipoteca; (*loan*) prestito ipotecario ▸ *vt* ipotecare
mortician [mɔːˈtɪʃən] *n* (*US*) impresario di pompe funebri
mortified [ˈmɔːtɪfaɪd] *adj* umiliato/a
mortuary [ˈmɔːtjuərɪ] *n* camera mortuaria; obitorio
mosaic [məuˈzeɪɪk] *n* mosaico
Moscow [ˈmɔskəu] *n* Mosca
Moslem [ˈmɔzləm] *adj, n* = **Muslim**
mosque [mɔsk] *n* moschea
mosquito [mɔsˈkiːtəu] (*pl* **mosquitoes**) *n* zanzara
moss [mɔs] *n* muschio
most [məust] *adj* (*almost all*) la maggior parte di; (*largest, greatest*): **who has (the) ~ money?** chi ha più soldi di tutti? ▸ *pron* la maggior parte ▸ *adv* più; (*work, sleep etc*) di più; (*very*) molto, estremamente; **the ~** (*also* + *adjective*) il (la) più; **~ of** la maggior parte di; **~ of them** quasi tutti; **I saw ~** ho visto più io; **at the (very) ~** al massimo; **to make the ~ of** trarre il massimo vantaggio da; **a ~ interesting book** un libro estremamente interessante; **mostly** *adv* per lo più

MOT n abbr (BRIT) = **Ministry of Transport**; **the ~ (test)** revisione obbligatoria degli autoveicoli

motel [məu'tɛl] n motel m inv

moth [mɔθ] n farfalla notturna; tarma

mother ['mʌðəʳ] n madre f ▷ vt (care for) fare da madre a; **motherhood** n maternità; **mother-in-law** n suocera; **mother-of-pearl** [mʌðərəv'pəːl] n madreperla; **Mother's Day** n la festa della mamma; **mother-to-be** [mʌðətə'biː] n futura mamma; **mother tongue** n madrelingua

motif [məu'tiːf] n motivo

motion ['məuʃən] n movimento, moto; (gesture) gesto; (at meeting) mozione f ▷ vt, vi: **to ~ (to) sb to do** fare cenno a qn di fare; **motionless** adj immobile; **motion picture** n film m inv

motivate ['məutiveit] vt (act, decision) dare origine a, motivare; (person) spingere

motivation [məuti'veiʃən] n motivazione f

motive ['məutiv] n motivo

motor ['məutəʳ] n motore m; (BRIT col: vehicle) macchina ▷ adj (industry, accident) automobilistico/a; autoveicolo; **motorbike** n moto f inv; **motorboat** n motoscafo; **motorcar** n (BRIT) automobile f; **motorcycle** n motocicletta; **motorcyclist** n motociclista m/f; **motoring** n (BRIT) turismo automobilistico; **motorist** n automobilista m/f; **motor racing** n (BRIT) corse fpl automobilistiche; **motorway** n (BRIT) autostrada

motto ['mɔtəu] (pl **mottoes**) n motto

mould, (US) **mold** [məuld] n forma, stampo; (mildew) muffa ▷ vt formare; (fig) foggiare; **mouldy**, (US) **moldy** adj ammuffito/a; (smell) di muffa

mound [maund] n rialzo, collinetta; (heap) mucchio

mount [maunt] n (Geo) monte m ▷ vt montare; (horse) montare a ▷ vi salire; **mount up** vi (build up) accumularsi

mountain ['mauntin] n montagna ▷ cpd di montagna; **mountain bike** n mountain bike f inv; **mountaineer** [maunti'niəʳ] n alpinista m/f; **mountaineering** [maunti'niəriŋ] n alpinismo; **mountainous** adj montagnoso/a; **mountain range** n catena montuosa

mourn [mɔːn] vt piangere, lamentare ▷ vi: **to ~ (for sb)** piangere (la morte di qn); **mourner** n parente m/f (or amico/a) del defunto; **mourning** n lutto; **in mourning** in lutto

mouse (pl **mice**) [maus, mais] n topo; (Comput) mouse m inv; **mouse mat, mouse pad** n (Comput) tappetino del mouse

moussaka [mu'saːkə] n moussaka

mousse [muːs] n mousse f inv

moustache [məs'taːʃ], (US) **mustache** n baffi mpl

mouth [mauθ] n bocca; (of river) bocca, foce f; (opening) orifizio; **mouthful** n boccata; **mouth organ** n armonica; **mouthpiece** n (Mus) imboccatura, bocchino; (person) portavoce m/f inv; **mouthwash** n collutorio

move [muːv] n (movement) movimento; (in game) mossa; (: turn to play) turno; (change: of house) trasloco; (: of job) cambiamento ▷ vt muovere; (change position of) spostare; (emotionally) commuovere; (Pol: resolution etc) proporre ▷ vi (gen) muoversi, spostarsi; (also: **~ house**) cambiar casa, traslocare; **to ~ towards** andare verso; **to ~ sb to do sth** indurre or spingere qn a fare qc; **to get a ~ on** affrettarsi, sbrigarsi; **move back** vi (return) ritornare; **move in** vi (to a house) entrare (in una nuova casa); (police etc) intervenire; **move off** vi partire; **move on** vi riprendere la strada; **move out** vi (of house) sgombrare; **move over** vi spostarsi; **move up** vi avanzare; **movement** ['mu:vmənt] n (gen) movimento; (gesture) gesto; (of stars, water, physical) moto

movie ['mu:vɪ] n film m inv; **the ~s** il cinema; **movie theater** (us) n cinema m inv

moving ['mu:vɪŋ] adj mobile; (causing emotion) commovente

mow (pt **mowed**, pp **mowed** or **mown**) [məu, -n] vt (grass) tagliare; (corn) mietere; **mower** n (also: **lawn mower**) tagliaerba m inv

Mozambique [məuzəm'bi:k] n Mozambico

MP n abbr = **Member of Parliament**

MP3 n MP3 m inv; **MP3 player** n lettore m MP3

mpg n abbr = **miles per gallon**

mph n abbr = **miles per hour**

Mr, (us) **Mr.** ['mɪstəʳ] n: **Mr X** Signor X, Sig. X

Mrs, (us) **Mrs.** ['mɪsɪz] n: **~ X** Signora X, Sig.ra X

Ms, (us) **Ms.** [mɪz] n = **Miss**; **Mrs**; **Ms X** ≈ Signora X, ≈ Sig.ra X

MSP n abbr = **Member of the Scottish Parliament**

Mt abbr (Geo: = mount) M

KEYWORD

much [mʌtʃ] adj, pron molto/a; **he's done so much work** ha lavorato così tanto; **I have as much money as you** ho tanti soldi quanti ne hai tu; **how much is it?** quant'è?; **it costs too much** costa troppo; **as much as you want** quanto vuoi

▶adv **1** (greatly) molto, tanto; **thank you very much** molte grazie; **he's very much the gentleman** è il vero gentiluomo; **I read as much as I can** leggo quanto posso; **as much as you** tanto quanto te

2 (by far) molto; **it's much the biggest company in Europe** è di gran lunga la più grossa società in Europa

3 (almost) grossomodo, praticamente; **they're much the same** sono praticamente uguali

muck [mʌk] n (dirt) sporcizia; **muck up** vt (col: spoil) rovinare; **mucky** adj (dirty) sporco/a, lordo/a

mucus ['mju:kəs] n muco

mud [mʌd] n fango

muddle ['mʌdl] n confusione f, disordine m; pasticcio ▷ vt (also: **~ up**) confondere

muddy ['mʌdɪ] adj fangoso/a

mudguard ['mʌdgɑ:d] n parafango

muesli ['mju:zlɪ] n muesli m inv

muffin ['mʌfɪn] n specie di pasticcino soffice da tè

muffled ['mʌfld] adj smorzato/a, attutito/a

muffler ['mʌfləʳ] n (us: Aut) marmitta; (: on motorbike) silenziatore m

mug [mʌg] n (cup) tazzone m; (for beer) boccale m; (col: face) muso; (: fool) scemo/a ▷ vt (assault) assalire; **mugger** ['mʌgəʳ] n aggressore m; **mugging** n aggressione f (a scopo di rapina)

muggy ['mʌgɪ] adj afoso/a

mule [mju:l] n mulo

multicoloured, (us) **multicolored** ['mʌltɪkʌləd] adj multicolore, variopinto/a

multimedia ['mʌltɪ'mi:dɪə] adj multimedia inv

multinational [mʌltɪ'næʃənl] adj, n multinazionale (f)

m

multiple ['mʌltɪpl] *adj* multiplo/a; molteplice ▷ *n* multiplo; **multiple choice (test)** *n* esercizi *mpl* a scelta multipla; **multiple sclerosis** [-sklɪ'rəusɪs] *n* sclerosi *f* a placche

multiplex ['mʌltɪplɛks] *n* (*also:* **~ cinema**) cinema *m inv* multisale *inv*

multiplication [mʌltɪplɪ'keɪʃən] *n* moltiplicazione *f*

multiply ['mʌltɪplaɪ] *vt* moltiplicare ▷ *vi* moltiplicarsi

multistorey ['mʌltɪ'stɔːrɪ] *adj* (BRIT: *building, car park*) a più piani

mum [mʌm] *n* (BRIT *col*) mamma ▷ *adj*: **to keep ~** non aprire bocca

mumble ['mʌmbl] *vt, vi* borbottare

mummy ['mʌmɪ] *n* (BRIT: *mother*) mamma; (*embalmed*) mummia

mumps [mʌmps] *n* orecchioni *mpl*

munch [mʌntʃ] *vt, vi* sgranocchiare

municipal [mjuː'nɪsɪpl] *adj* municipale

mural ['mjuərəl] *n* dipinto murale

murder ['mɜːdəʳ] *n* assassinio, omicidio ▷ *vt* assassinare; **to commit ~** commettere un omicidio; **murderer** *n* omicida *m*, assassino

murky ['mɜːkɪ] *adj* tenebroso/a

murmur ['mɜːməʳ] *n* mormorio ▷ *vt, vi* mormorare

muscle ['mʌsl] *n* muscolo; (*fig*) forza; **muscular** ['mʌskjuləʳ] *adj* muscolare; (*person, arm*) muscoloso/a

museum [mjuː'zɪəm] *n* museo

mushroom ['mʌʃrum] *n* fungo ▷ *vi* svilupparsi rapidamente

music ['mjuːzɪk] *n* musica; **musical** *adj* musicale; (*person*) portato/a per la musica ▷ *n* (*show*) commedia musicale; **musical instrument** *n* strumento musicale; **musician** [mjuː'zɪʃən] *n* musicista *m/f*

Muslim ['mʌzlɪm] *adj, n* musulmano/a

muslin ['mʌzlɪn] *n* mussola

mussel ['mʌsl] *n* cozza

must [mʌst] *aux vb* (*obligation*): **I ~ do it** devo farlo; (*probability*): **he ~ be there by now** dovrebbe essere arrivato ormai; **I ~ have made a mistake** devo essermi sbagliato ▷ *n*: **this programme/trip is a ~** è un programma/viaggio da non perdersi

mustache ['mʌstæʃ] *n* (US) = **moustache**

mustard ['mʌstəd] *n* senape *f*, mostarda

mustn't ['mʌsnt] = **must not**

mute [mjuːt] *adj, n* muto/a

mutilate ['mjuːtɪleɪt] *vt* mutilare

mutiny ['mjuːtɪnɪ] *n* ammutinamento

mutter ['mʌtəʳ] *vt, vi* borbottare, brontolare

mutton ['mʌtn] *n* carne *f* di montone

mutual ['mjuːtʃuəl] *adj* mutuo/a, reciproco/a

muzzle ['mʌzl] *n* muso; (*protective device*) museruola; (*of gun*) bocca ▷ *vt* mettere la museruola a

my [maɪ] *adj* il (la) mio/a; (*pl*) i (le) miei (mie); **my house** la mia casa; **my books** i miei libri; **my brother** mio fratello; **I've washed my hair/ cut my finger** mi sono lavato i capelli/tagliato

myself [maɪ'sɛlf] *pron* (*reflexive*) mi; (*emphatic*) io stesso/a; (*after prep*) me; *see also* **oneself**

mysterious [mɪs'tɪərɪəs] *adj* misterioso/a

mystery ['mɪstərɪ] *n* mistero

mystical ['mɪstɪkəl] *adj* mistico/a

mystify ['mɪstɪfaɪ] *vt* mistificare; (*puzzle*) confondere

myth [mɪθ] *n* mito; **mythology** [mɪ'θɔlədʒɪ] *n* mitologia

n

n/a abbr (= not applicable) non pertinente

nag [næg] vt tormentare ▷ vi brontolare in continuazione

nail [neɪl] n (human) unghia; (metal) chiodo ▷ vt inchiodare; **to ~ sb down to a date/price** costringere qn a un appuntamento/ad accettare un prezzo; **nailbrush** n spazzolino da or per unghie; **nailfile** n lima da or per unghie; **nail polish** n smalto da or per unghie; **nail polish remover** n acetone m, solvente m; **nail scissors** npl forbici fpl da or per unghie; **nail varnish** n (BRIT) = **nail polish**

naïve [naɪ'iːv] adj ingenuo/a

naked ['neɪkɪd] adj nudo/a

name [neɪm] n nome m; (reputation) nome, reputazione f ▷ vt (baby etc) chiamare; (plant, illness) nominare; (person, object) identificare; (price, date) fissare; **by ~** di nome; **she knows them all by ~** li conosce tutti per nome; **what's your ~?** come si chiama?; **namely** adv cioè

nanny ['nænɪ] n bambinaia

nap [næp] n (sleep) pisolino; (of cloth) peluria ▷ vi: **to be caught ~ping** essere preso alla sprovvista

napkin ['næpkɪn] n tovagliolo

nappy ['næpɪ] n (BRIT) pannolino

narcotic [nɑː'kɔtɪk] n (Med) narcotico; **narcotics** npl (drugs) narcotici, stupefacenti mpl

narrative ['nærətɪv] n narrativa

narrator [nə'reɪtəʳ] n narratore/trice

narrow ['nærəu] adj stretto/a; (resources, means) limitato/a, modesto/a ▷ vi restringersi; **to have a ~ escape** farcela per un pelo; **narrow down** vt (search, investigation, possibilities) restringere; (list) ridurre; **narrowly** adv per un pelo; (time) per poco; **narrow-minded** adj meschino/a

nasal ['neɪzl] adj nasale

nasty ['nɑːstɪ] adj (unpleasant: person, remark) cattivo/a; (rude) villano/a; (smell, wound, situation) brutto/a

nation ['neɪʃən] n nazione f

national ['næʃənl] adj nazionale ▷ n cittadino/a; **national anthem** n inno nazionale; **national dress** n costume m nazionale; **National Health Service** n (BRIT) ≈ Servizio sanitario nazionale; **National Insurance** n (BRIT) ≈ Previdenza Sociale; **nationalist** adj, n nazionalista (m/f); **nationality** [næʃə'nælɪtɪ] n nazionalità f inv; **nationalize** vt nazionalizzare; **national park** n parco nazionale; **National Trust** n sovrintendenza ai beni culturali e ambientali

- **NATIONAL TRUST**

- Fondato nel 1895, il *National Trust*
- è un'organizzazione che si occupa
- della tutela e salvaguardia di edifici
- e monumenti di interesse storico e

● di territori di interesse ambientale
● nel Regno Unito.

nationwide ['neɪʃənwaɪd] *adj*
diffuso/a in tutto il paese ▷ *adv* in
tutto il paese

native ['neɪtɪv] *n* abitante *m/f* del
paese ▷ *adj* indigeno/a; (*country*)
natio/a; (*ability*) innato/a; **a ~ of
Russia** un nativo della Russia; **a ~
speaker of French** una persona
di madrelingua francese; **Native
American** *n* discendente *di tribù*
dell'America settentrionale

NATO ['neɪtəʊ] *n abbr* (= *North Atlantic
Treaty Organization*) N.A.T.O. *f*

natural ['nætʃrəl] *adj* naturale;
(*ability*) innato/a; (*manner*) semplice;
natural gas *n* gas *m* metano;
natural history *n* storia naturale;
naturally *adv* naturalmente; (*by
nature: gifted*) di natura; **natural
resources** *npl* risorse *fpl* naturali

nature ['neɪtʃə^r] *n* natura; (*character*)
natura, indole *f*; **by ~** di natura; **nature
reserve** *n* (BRIT) parco naturale

naughty ['nɔːtɪ] *adj* (*child*)
birichino/a, cattivello/a; (*story, film*)
spinto/a

nausea ['nɔːsɪə] *n* (*Med*) nausea; (*fig:
disgust*) schifo

naval ['neɪvl] *adj* navale

navel ['neɪvl] *n* ombelico

navigate ['nævɪgeɪt] *vt* percorrere
navigando ▷ *vi* navigare; (*Aut*)
fare da navigatore; **navigation**
[nævɪ'geɪʃən] *n* navigazione *f*

navy ['neɪvɪ] *n* marina

Nazi ['nɑːtsɪ] *n* nazista (*m/f*)

NB *abbr* (= *nota bene*) N.B.

near [nɪə^r] *adj* vicino/a; (*relation*)
prossimo/a ▷ *adv* vicino ▷ *prep* (*also:
~ to*) vicino a, presso; (*in time*) verso
▷ *vt* avvicinarsi a; **nearby** [nɪə'baɪ]
adj vicino/a ▷ *adv* vicino; **nearly** *adv*
quasi; **I nearly lost it** per poco non lo
perdevo; **near-sighted** [nɪə'saɪtɪd]
adj miope

neat [niːt] *adj* (*person, room*)
ordinato/a; (*work*) pulito/a; (*solution,
plan*) ben indovinato/a, azzeccato/a;
(*spirits*) liscio/a; **neatly** *adv* con
ordine; (*skilfully*) abilmente

necessarily ['nɛsɪsrɪlɪ] *adv*
necessariamente

necessary ['nɛsɪsrɪ] *adj*
necessario/a

necessity [nɪ'sɛsɪtɪ] *n* necessità *f inv*

neck [nɛk] *n* collo; (*of garment*)
colletto ▷ *vi* (*col*) pomiciare,
sbaciucchiarsi; **~ and ~** testa a
testa; **necklace** ['nɛklɪs] *n* collana;
necktie ['nɛktaɪ] *n* cravatta

nectarine ['nɛktərɪn] *n* nocepesca

need [niːd] *n* bisogno ▷ *vt* aver
bisogno di; **do you ~ anything?** ha
bisogno di qualcosa?; **I ~ to do it** lo
devo fare, bisogna che io lo faccia;
you don't ~ to go non deve andare,
non c'è bisogno che lei vada

needle ['niːdl] *n* ago; (*on record player*)
puntina ▷ *vt* punzecchiare

needless ['niːdlɪs] *adj* inutile

needlework ['niːdlwəːk] *n* cucito

needn't ['niːdnt] = **need not**

needy ['niːdɪ] *adj* bisognoso/a

negative ['nɛgətɪv] *n* (*Phot*)
negativo; (*Ling*) negazione *f* ▷ *adj*
negativo/a

neglect [nɪ'glɛkt] *vt* trascurare ▷ *n*
(*of person, duty*) negligenza; (*of child,
house etc*) scarsa cura; **state of ~**
stato di abbandono

negotiate [nɪ'gəʊʃɪeɪt] *vi*
negoziare ▷ *vt* (*Comm*) negoziare;
(*obstacle*) superare; **negotiation**
[nɪgəʊʃɪ'eɪʃən] *n* trattativa; (*Pol*)
negoziato

negotiator [nɪ'gəʊʃɪeɪtə^r] *n*
negoziatore/trice

neighbour, (US) **neighbor** ['neɪbə^r]
n vicino/a; **neighbourhood** *n*
vicinato; **neighbouring** *adj* vicino/a

neither ['naɪðə^r] *adj, pron* né l'uno/a
né l'altro/a, nessuno/a dei (delle) due
▷ *conj* neanche, nemmeno, neppure

▷ *adv*: **~ good nor bad** né buono né cattivo; **I didn't move and ~ did Claude** io non mi mossi e nemmeno Claude; **… ~ did I refuse** …, ma non ho nemmeno rifiutato

neon ['niːɔn] *n* neon *m*

Nepal [nɪ'pɔːl] *n* Nepal *m*

nephew ['nɛvjuː] *n* nipote *m*

nerve [nəːv] *n* nervo; (*fig*) coraggio; (*impudence*) faccia tosta; **he gets on my ~s** mi dà ai nervi; **a fit of ~s** una crisi di nervi

nervous ['nəːvəs] *adj* nervoso/a; (*anxious*) agitato/a, in apprensione; **nervous breakdown** *n* esaurimento nervoso

nest [nɛst] *n* nido ▷ *vi* fare il nido, nidificare

net [nɛt] *n* rete *f* ▷ *adj* netto/a ▷ *vt* (*person, profit*) ricavare un utile netto di; (*fish etc*) prendere con la rete; **the N~** (*Internet*) Internet *f*; **netball** *n* specie di pallacanestro

Netherlands ['nɛðələndz] *npl*: **the ~** i Paesi Bassi

netiquette ['nɛtɪkɛt] *n* netiquette *f inv*

nett [nɛt] *adj* = **net**

nettle ['nɛtl] *n* ortica

network ['nɛtwəːk] *n* rete *f*

neurotic [njuə'rɔtɪk] *adj*, *n* nevrotico/a

neuter ['njuːtəʳ] *adj* neutro/a ▷ *vt* (*cat etc*) castrare

neutral ['njuːtrəl] *adj* neutro/a; (*person, nation*) neutrale ▷ *n* (*Aut*): **in ~** in folle

never ['nɛvəʳ] *adv* (non…) mai; **~ again** mai più; **I'll ~ go there again** non ci vado più; **~ in my life** mai in vita mia; *see also* **mind**; **never-ending** *adj* interminabile; **nevertheless** [nɛvəðə'lɛs] *adv* tuttavia, ciò nonostante, ciò nondimeno

new [njuː] *adj* nuovo/a; (*brand new*) nuovo/a di zecca; **New Age** *n* New Age *f inv*; **newbie** ['njuːbɪ] *n* (*Comput, Tech*) utilizzatore/trice inesperto/a; (*to a job or group*) nuovo/a arrivato/a; (*to a hobby or experience*) neofita *m/f*; **newborn** *adj* neonato/a; **newcomer** ['njuːkʌməʳ] *n* nuovo/a venuto/a; **newly** *adv* di recente

news [njuːz] *n* notizie *fpl*; (*Radio*) giornale *m* radio; (*TV*) telegiornale *m*: **a piece of ~** una notizia; **news agency** *n* agenzia di stampa; **newsagent** *n* (*BRIT*) giornalaio; **newscaster** *n* (*Radio, TV*) annunciatore/trice; **newsdealer** ['njuːzdiːləʳ] *n* (*US*) = **newsagent**; **newsletter** *n* bollettino; **newspaper** *n* giornale *m*; **newsreader** *n* = **newscaster**

newt [njuːt] *n* tritone *m*

New Year *n* Anno Nuovo; **New Year's Day** *n* il Capodanno; **New Year's Eve** *n* la vigilia di Capodanno

New York [-'jɔːk] *n* New York *f*

New Zealand [-'ziːlənd] *n* Nuova Zelanda; **New Zealander** *n* neozelandese *m/f*

next [nɛkst] *adj* prossimo/a ▷ *adv* accanto; (*in time*) dopo; **~ to** accanto a; **~ to nothing** quasi niente; **~ please!** (*avanti*) il prossimo!; **~ time** la prossima volta; **the ~ day** il giorno dopo, l'indomani; **~ year** l'anno prossimo *or* venturo; **when do we meet ~?** quando ci rincontriamo?; **next door** *adv*, *adj* accanto *inv*; **next of kin** *n* parente *m/f* prossimo/a

NHS *n abbr* = **National Health Service**

nibble ['nɪbl] *vt* mordicchiare

nice [naɪs] *adj* (*holiday, trip*) piacevole; (*flat, picture*) bello/a; (*person*) simpatico/a, gentile; **nicely** *adv* bene

niche [niːʃ] *n* (*Archit*) nicchia

nick [nɪk] *n* taglietto; tacca ▷ *vt* (*col*) rubare; **in the ~ of time** appena in tempo

nickel ['nɪkl] *n* nichel *m*; (*US*) *moneta da cinque centesimi di dollaro*

nickname ['nɪkneɪm] *n* soprannome *m*

n

nicotine ['nɪkəti:n] *n* nicotina
niece [ni:s] *n* nipote *f*
Nigeria [naɪ'dʒɪərɪə] *n* Nigeria
night [naɪt] *n* notte *f*; (*evening*) sera;
at ~ la sera; **by ~** di notte; **the ~
before last** l'altro ieri notte; l'altro
ieri sera; **night club** *n* locale *m*
notturno; **nightdress** *n* camicia da
notte; **nightie** ['naɪtɪ] *n* camicia da
notte; **night life** ['naɪtlaɪf] *n* vita
notturna; **nightly** ['naɪtlɪ] *adj* di ogni
notte *or* sera; (*by night*) notturno/a
▷ *adv* ogni notte *or* sera; **nightmare**
['naɪtmɛəʳ] *n* incubo; **night school** *n*
scuola serale; **nightshift** ['naɪtʃɪft] *n*
turno di notte; **night-time** *n* notte *f*
nil [nɪl] *n* nulla *m*; (*BRIT Sport*) zero
nine [naɪn] *num* nove; **nineteen** *num*
diciannove; **nineteenth** [naɪn'ti:nθ]
num diciannovesimo/a; **ninetieth**
['naɪntɪɪθ] *num* novantesimo/a;
ninety *num* novanta; **ninth** [naɪnθ]
num nono/a
nip [nɪp] *vt* pizzicare; (*bite*) mordere
nipple ['nɪpl] *n* (*Anat*) capezzolo
nitrogen ['naɪtrədʒən] *n* azoto

◯ **KEYWORD**

no [nəu] *adv* (*opposite of "yes"*) no; **are
you coming? — no (I'm not)** viene?
— no (non vengo); **would you like
some more? — no thank you** ne
vuole ancora un po'? — no, grazie
▶ *adj* (*not any*) nessuno/a; **I have no
money/time/books** non ho soldi/
tempo/libri; **no student would
have done it** nessuno studente lo
avrebbe fatto; **"no parking"** "divieto
di sosta"; **"no smoking"** "vietato
fumare"
▶ *n* (*pl* **noes**) no *m inv*

nobility [nəu'bɪlɪtɪ] *n* nobiltà
noble ['nəubl] *adj* nobile
nobody ['nəubədɪ] *pron* nessuno
nod [nɔd] *vi* accennare col capo, fare
un cenno; (*in agreement*) annuire

con un cenno del capo; (*sleep*)
sonnecchiare ▷ *vt*: **to ~ one's head**
fare di sì col capo ▷ *n* cenno; **nod off**
vi assopirsi
noise [nɔɪz] *n* rumore *m*; (*din, racket*)
chiasso; **noisy** *adj* (*street, car*)
rumoroso/a; (*person*) chiassoso/a
nominal ['nɔmɪnl] *adj* nominale;
(*rent*) simbolico/a
nominate ['nɔmɪneɪt] *vt* (*propose*)
proporre come candidato;
(*elect*) nominare; **nomination**
[nɔmɪ'neɪʃən] *n* nomina,
candidatura; **nominee** [nɔmɪ'ni:] *n*
persona nominata; candidato/a
none [nʌn] *pron* (*not one thing*) niente;
(*not one person*) nessuno; **~ of you**
nessuno/a di voi; **I have ~ left** non ne
ho più; **he's ~ the worse for it** non
ne ha risentito
nonetheless ['nʌnðə'lɛs] *adv*
nondimeno
non-fiction [nɔn'fɪkʃən] *n*
saggistica
nonsense ['nɔnsəns] *n* sciocchezze *fpl*
non: **non-smoker** *n* non fumatore/
trice; **non-smoking** *adj* (*person*)
che non fuma; (*area, section*) per
non fumatori; **non-stick** *adj*
antiaderente, antiadesivo/a
noodles ['nu:dlz] *npl* taglierini *mpl*
noon [nu:n] *n* mezzogiorno
no one ['nəuwʌn] *pron* = **nobody**
nor [nɔ:ʳ] *conj* = **neither** ▷ *adv* see
neither
norm [nɔ:m] *n* norma
normal ['nɔ:ml] *adj* normale;
normally *adv* normalmente
north [nɔ:θ] *n* nord *m*, settentrione *m*
▷ *adj* nord *inv*, del nord, settentrionale
▷ *adv* verso nord; **North America**
n America del Nord; **North
American** *adj*, *n* nordamericano/a;
northbound ['nɔ:θbaund] *adj*
(*traffic*) diretto/a a nord; (*carriageway*)
nord *inv*; **north-east** *n* nord-est *m*;
northeastern *adj* nordorientale;
northern ['nɔ:ðən] *adj* del nord,

settentrionale; **Northern Ireland** n Irlanda del Nord; **North Korea** n Corea del Nord; **North Pole** n: **the North Pole** il Polo Nord; **North Sea** n: **the North Sea** il mare del Nord; **north-west** n nord-ovest m; **northwestern** adj nordoccidentale

Norway ['nɔːweɪ] n Norvegia; **Norwegian** [nɔː'wiːdʒən] adj norvegese ▷ n norvegese m/f; (Ling) norvegese m

nose [nəuz] n naso; (of animal) muso; **nose about** vi aggirarsi; **nosebleed** n emorragia nasale; **nosey** ['nəuzɪ] adj curioso/a

nostalgia [nɔs'tældʒɪə] n nostalgia

nostalgic [nɔs'tældʒɪk] adj nostalgico/a

nostril ['nɔstrɪl] n narice f; (of horse) froqia

nosy ['nəuzɪ] adj = **nosey**

not [nɔt] adv non; **you must ~ or mustn't do this** non deve fare questo; **it's too late, isn't it** or **is it ~?** è troppo tardi, vero?; **he is ~ or isn't here** non è qui, non c'è; **~ that I don't like him** non che (lui) non mi piaccia; **~ yet/now** non ancora/ora

notable ['nəutəbl] adj notevole; **notably** ['nəutəblɪ] adv notevolmente; (in particular) in particolare

notch [nɔtʃ] n tacca; (in saw) dente m

note [nəut] n nota; (letter, banknote) biglietto ▷ vt: **to take ~ of** prendere nota di; **to take ~s** prendere appunti; **notebook** n taccuino; **noted** ['nəutɪd] adj celebre; **notepad** n bloc-notes m inv; **notepaper** n carta da lettere

nothing ['nʌθɪŋ] n nulla m, niente m; (zero) zero; **he does ~** non fa niente; **~ new** niente di nuovo; **for ~** per niente

notice ['nəutɪs] n avviso; (of leaving) preavviso ▷ vt notare, accorgersi di; **to take ~ of** fare attenzione a; **to bring sth to sb's ~** far notare qc a qn; **to hand in one's ~** licenziarsi;

at short ~ con un breve preavviso; **until further ~** fino a nuovo avviso; **noticeable** adj evidente

notify ['nəutɪfaɪ] vt: **to ~ sth to sb** notificare qc a qn; **to ~ sb of sth** avvisare qn di qc

notion ['nəuʃən] n idea; (concept) nozione f; **notions** ['nəuʃənz] npl (US: haberdashery) merceria

notorious [nəu'tɔːrɪəs] adj famigerato/a

notwithstanding [nɔtwɪθ'stændɪŋ] adv nondimeno ▷ prep nonostante, malgrado

nought [nɔːt] n zero

noun [naun] n nome m, sostantivo

nourish ['nʌrɪʃ] vt nutrire; **nourishment** n nutrimento

Nov. abbr (= November) nov.

novel ['nɔvl] n romanzo ▷ adj nuovo/a; **novelist** n romanziere/a; **novelty** n novità f inv

November [nəu'vɛmbər] n novembre m

novice ['nɔvɪs] n principiante m/f; (Rel) novizio/a

now [nau] adv ora, adesso ▷ conj: **~ (that)** adesso che, ora che; **right ~** subito; **by ~** ormai; **just ~** proprio ora; **that's the fashion just ~** è la moda del momento; **I saw her just ~** l'ho vista proprio adesso; **~ and then, ~ and again** ogni tanto; **from ~ on** da ora in poi; **nowadays** ['nauədeɪz] adv oggidì

nowhere ['nəuwɛər] adv in nessun luogo, da nessuna parte

nozzle ['nɔzl] n (of hose etc) boccaglio; (of fire extinguisher) lancia

nr abbr (BRIT) = **near**

nuclear ['njuːklɪər] adj nucleare

nucleus (pl **nuclei**) ['njuːklɪəs, 'njuːklɪaɪ] n nucleo

nude [njuːd] adj nudo/a ▷ n (Art) nudo; **in the ~** tutto/a nudo/a

nudge [nʌdʒ] vt dare una gomitata a

nudist ['njuːdɪst] n nudista m/f

nudity ['njuːdɪtɪ] n nudità

nuisance ['nju:sns] *n*: **it's a ~** è una seccatura; **he's a ~** dà fastidio

numb [nʌm] *adj* intorpidito/a; **~ with** (*fear, grief*) paralizzato/a da; **~ with cold** intirizzito/a (dal freddo)

number ['nʌmbəʳ] *n* numero ▷ *vt* numerare; (*include*) contare; **a ~ of** un certo numero di; **to be ~ed among** venire annoverato/a tra; **they were 10 in ~** erano in tutto 10; **number plate** *n* (BRIT Aut) targa; **Number Ten** *n* (BRIT: = 10 Downing Street) residenza del Primo Ministro del Regno Unito

numerical [nju:'mɛrɪkl] *adj* numerico/a

numerous ['nju:mərəs] *adj* numeroso/a

nun [nʌn] *n* suora, monaca

nurse [nə:s] *n* infermiere/a; (*also:* **~maid**) bambinaia ▷ *vt* (*patient, cold*) curare; (*baby:* BRIT) cullare; (: US) allattare, dare il latte a

nursery ['nə:sərɪ] *n* (*room*) camera dei bambini; (*institution*) asilo; (*for plants*) vivaio; **nursery rhyme** *n* filastrocca; **nursery school** *n* scuola materna; **nursery slope** *n* (BRIT Ski) pista per principianti

nursing ['nə:sɪŋ] *n* (*profession*) professione *f* di infermiere (*or* di infermiera); (*care*) cura; **nursing home** *n* casa di cura

nurture ['nə:tʃəʳ] *vt* allevare; nutrire

nut [nʌt] *n* (*of metal*) dado; (*fruit*) noce *f* (*or* nocciola *or* mandorla *etc*); **he's ~s** (*col*) è matto

nutmeg ['nʌtmɛg] *n* noce *f* moscata

nutrient ['nju:trɪənt] *adj* nutriente ▷ *n* sostanza nutritiva

nutrition [nju:'trɪʃən] *n* nutrizione *f*

nutritious [nju:'trɪʃəs] *adj* nutriente

NVQ *n abbr* (BRIT) = **National Vocational Qualification**

nylon ['naɪlɔn] *n* nailon *m* ▷ *adj* di nailon

O

oak [əuk] *n* quercia ▷ *cpd* di quercia

OAP *n abbr* (BRIT) = **old-age pensioner**

oar [ɔːʳ] *n* remo

oasis (*pl* **oases**) [əu'eɪsɪs, əu'eɪsi:z] *n* oasi *f inv*

oath [əuθ] *n* giuramento; (*swear word*) bestemmia

oatmeal ['əutmi:l] *n* farina d'avena

oats [əuts] *npl* avena

obedience [ə'bi:dɪəns] *n* ubbidienza

obedient [ə'bi:dɪənt] *adj* ubbidiente

obese [əu'bi:s] *adj* obeso/a

obesity [əu'bi:sɪtɪ] *n* obesità

obey [ə'beɪ] *vt* ubbidire a; (*instructions, regulations*) osservare

obituary [ə'bɪtjuərɪ] *n* necrologia

object *n* ['ɔbdʒɪkt] oggetto; (*purpose*) scopo, intento; (*Ling*) complemento oggetto ▷ *vi* [əb'dʒɛkt]: **to ~ to** (*attitude*) disapprovare; (*proposal*) protestare contro, sollevare delle obiezioni contro; **I ~!** mi oppongo!;

he **~ed that ...** obiettò che ...;
expense is no ~ non si bada a spese;
objection [əbˈdʒɛkʃən] n obiezione
f; **objective** n obiettivo

obligation [ɔblɪˈɡeɪʃən] n obbligo,
dovere m; **"without ~"** "senza
impegno"

obligatory [əˈblɪɡətərɪ] adj
obbligatorio/a

oblige [əˈblaɪdʒ] vt (do a favour) fare
una cortesia a; (force): **to ~ sb to do**
costringere qn a fare; **to be ~d to sb
for sth** essere grato a qn per qc

oblique [əˈbliːk] adj obliquo/a;
(allusion) indiretto/a

obliterate [əˈblɪtəreɪt] vt cancellare

oblivious [əˈblɪvɪəs] adj: **~ of**
incurante di; inconscio/a di

oblong [ˈɔblɔŋ] adj oblungo/a ▷ n
rettangolo

obnoxious [əbˈnɔkʃəs] adj odioso/a;
(smell) disgustoso/a, ripugnante

oboe [ˈəʊbəʊ] n oboe m

obscene [əbˈsiːn] adj osceno/a

obscure [əbˈskjuəʳ] adj oscuro/a ▷ vt
oscurare; (hide: sun) nascondere

observant [əbˈzɜːvnt] adj attento/a

> Be careful not to translate
> observant by the Italian word
> osservante.

observation [ɔbzəˈveɪʃən] n
osservazione f; (by police etc)
sorveglianza

observatory [əbˈzɜːvətrɪ] n
osservatorio

observe [əbˈzɜːv] vt osservare;
(remark) fare osservare; **observer** n
osservatore/trice

obsess [əbˈsɛs] vt ossessionare;
obsession [əbˈsɛʃən] n ossessione f;
obsessive adj ossessivo/a

obsolete [ˈɔbsəliːt] adj obsoleto/a

obstacle [ˈɔbstəkl] n ostacolo

obstinate [ˈɔbstɪnɪt] adj ostinato/a

obstruct [əbˈstrʌkt] vt (block)
ostruire, ostacolare; (halt) fermare;
(hinder) impedire; **obstruction**
[əbˈstrʌkʃən] n ostruzione f; ostacolo

obtain [əbˈteɪn] vt ottenere

obvious [ˈɔbvɪəs] adj ovvio/a,
evidente; **obviously** adv
ovviamente; **obviously!** certo!

occasion [əˈkeɪʒən] n occasione f;
(event) avvenimento; **occasional**
adj occasionale; **occasionally** adv
ogni tanto

occult [ɔˈkʌlt] adj occulto/a ▷ n: **the
~** l'occulto

occupant [ˈɔkjupənt] n occupante
m/f; (of boat, car etc) persona a bordo

occupation [ɔkjuˈpeɪʃən] n
occupazione f; (job) mestiere m,
professione f

occupy [ˈɔkjupaɪ] vt occupare; **to ~
o.s. by doing** occuparsi a fare

occur [əˈkəːʳ] vi accadere; (difficulty,
opportunity) capitare; **to ~ to sb**
venire in mente a qn; **occurrence** n
caso, fatto; presenza

> Be careful not to translate occur
> by the Italian word occorrere.

ocean [ˈəʊʃən] n oceano

o'clock [əˈklɔk] adv: **it is 5 ~** sono le 5

Oct. abbr (= October) ott.

October [ɔkˈtəʊbəʳ] n ottobre m

octopus [ˈɔktəpəs] n polpo, piovra

odd [ɔd] adj (strange) strano/a,
bizzarro/a; (number) dispari inv; (not
of a set) spaiato/a; **60-~** 60 e oltre;
at ~ times di tanto in tanto; **the
~ one out** l'eccezione f; **oddly** adv
stranamente; **odds** npl (in betting)
quota

odometer [ɔˈdɔmɪtəʳ] n odometro

odour, (US) **odor** [ˈəʊdəʳ] n odore m;
(unpleasant) cattivo odore

 KEYWORD

of [ɔv, əv] prep **1** (gen) di; **a boy of 10**
un ragazzo di 10 anni; **a friend of
ours** un nostro amico; **that was
kind of you** è stato molto gentile
da parte sua

2 (expressing quantity, amount, dates
etc) di; **a kilo of flour** un chilo di

farina; **how much of this do you need?** quanto gliene serve?; **there were four of them** (*people*) erano in quattro; (*objects*) ce n'erano quattro; **three of us went** tre di noi sono andati; **the 5th of July** il 5 luglio
3 (*from, out of*) di, in; **made of wood** (fatto) di *or* in legno

KEYWORD

off [ɔf] *adv* **1** (*distance, time*): **it's a long way off** è lontano; **the game is 3 days off** la partita è tra 3 giorni
2 (*departure, removal*) via; **to go off to Paris** andarsene a Parigi; **I must be off** devo andare via; **to take off one's coat** togliersi il cappotto; **the button came off** il bottone è venuto via *or* si è staccato; **10% off** con lo sconto del 10%
3 (*not at work*): **to have a day off** avere un giorno libero; **to be off sick** essere assente per malattia
▶ *adj* (*engine*) spento/a; (*tap*) chiuso/a; (*cancelled*) sospeso/a; (*BRIT: food*) andato/a a male; **on the off chance** nel caso; **to have an off day** non essere in forma
▶ *prep* **1** (*motion, removal etc*) da; (*distant from*) a poca distanza da; **a street off the square** una strada che parte dalla piazza
2: **to be off meat** non mangiare più la carne

offence, (*US*) **offense** [ə'fɛns] *n* (*Law*) contravvenzione *f*; (*: more serious*) reato; **to take ~ at** offendersi per

offend [ə'fɛnd] *vt* (*person*) offendere; **offender** *n* delinquente *m/f*; (*against regulations*) contravventore/trice

offense [ə'fɛns] *n* (*US*) = **offence**

offensive [ə'fɛnsɪv] *adj* offensivo/a; (*smell etc*) sgradevole, ripugnante ▶ *n* (*Mil*) offensiva

offer ['ɔfə'] *n* offerta, proposta ▶ *vt* offrire; **"on ~"** (*Comm*) "in offerta speciale"

offhand [ɔf'hænd] *adj* disinvolto/a, noncurante ▶ *adv*: **I can't tell you ~** non posso dirglielo su due piedi

office ['ɔfɪs] *n* (*place*) ufficio; (*position*) carica; **doctor's ~** (*US*) ambulatorio; **to take ~** entrare in carica; **office block**, (*US*) **office building** *n* complesso di uffici; **office hours** *npl* orario d'ufficio; (*US Med*) orario di visite

officer ['ɔfɪsə'] *n* (*Mil etc*) ufficiale *m*; (*of organization*) funzionario; (*also*: **police ~**) agente *m* di polizia

office worker *n* impiegato/a d'ufficio

official [ə'fɪʃl] *adj* (*authorized*) ufficiale ▶ *n* ufficiale *m*; (*civil servant*) impiegato/a statale; funzionario

off: off-licence *n* (*BRIT*) spaccio di bevande alcoliche; **off-line** *adj, adv* (*Comput*) off-line *inv*, non in linea; (*: switched off*) spento/a; **off-peak** *adj* (*ticket etc*) a tariffa ridotta; (*time*) non di punta; **off-putting** *adj* (*BRIT*) sgradevole; **off-season** *adj, adv* fuori stagione; **offset** ['ɔfsɛt] *vt* (*irreg: counteract*) controbilanciare, compensare; **offshore** [ɔf'ʃɔːʳ] *adj* (*breeze*) di terra; (*island*) vicino alla costa; (*fishing*) costiero/a; **offside** ['ɔf'saɪd] *adj* (*Sport*) fuori gioco; (*Aut: with right-hand drive*) destro/a; (*: with left-hand drive*) sinistro/a; **offspring** ['ɔfsprɪŋ] *n* prole *f*, discendenza

often ['ɔfn] *adv* spesso; **how ~ do you go?** quanto spesso ci va?

oh [əu] *excl* oh!

oil [ɔɪl] *n* olio; (*petroleum*) petrolio; (*for central heating*) nafta ▶ *vt* (*machine*) lubrificare; **oil filter** *n* (*Aut*) filtro dell'olio; **oil painting** *n* quadro a olio; **oil refinery** *n* raffineria di petrolio; **oil rig** *n* derrick *m inv*; (*at* *sea*) piattaforma per trivellazioni subacquee; **oil slick** *n* chiazza d'olio; **oil tanker** *n* (*ship*) petroliera; (*truck*) autocisterna per petrolio; **oil well** *n* pozzo petrolifero; **oily** *adj* unto/a, oleoso/a; (*food*) grasso/a

ointment ['ɔɪntmənt] *n* unguento

O.K. [əu'keɪ] *excl* d'accordo! ▷ *vt* approvare ▷ *adj* non male *inv*; **is it ~?, are you ~?** tutto bene?

old [əuld] *adj* vecchio/a; (*ancient*) antico/a, vecchio/a; (*person*) vecchio/a, anziano/a; **how ~ are you?** quanti anni ha?; **he's 10 years ~** ha 10 anni; **~er brother/sister** fratello/sorella maggiore; **old age** *n* vecchiaia; **old-age pension** ['əuldeɪdʒ-] *n* (BRIT) pensione *f* di vecchiaia; **old-age pensioner** *n* (BRIT) pensionato/a; **old-fashioned** *adj* antiquato/a, fuori moda; (*person*) all'antica; **old people's home** *n* ricovero per anziani

olive ['ɔlɪv] *n* (*fruit*) oliva; (*tree*) olivo ▷ *adj* (*also*: **~-green**) verde oliva *inv*; **olive oil** *n* olio d'oliva

Olympic [əu'lɪmpɪk] *adj* olimpico/a; **the ~ Games, the ~s** i giochi olimpici, le Olimpiadi

omelet(te) ['ɔmlɪt] *n* omelette *f inv*

omen ['əumən] *n* presagio, augurio

ominous ['ɔmɪnəs] *adj* minaccioso/a; (*event*) di malaugurio

omit [əu'mɪt] *vt* omettere

KEYWORD

on [ɔn] *prep* **1** (*indicating position*) su; **on the wall** sulla parete; **on the left** a *or* sulla sinistra
2 (*indicating means, method, condition etc*): **on foot** a piedi; **on the train/plane** in treno/aereo; **on the telephone** al telefono; **on the radio/television** alla radio/televisione; **to be on drugs** drogarsi; **on holiday** in vacanza
3 (*referring to time*): **on Friday** venerdì;

on Fridays il *or* di venerdì; **on June 20th** il 20 giugno; **on Friday, June 20th** venerdì, 20 giugno; **a week on Friday** venerdì a otto; **on his arrival** al suo arrivo; **on seeing this** vedendo ciò
4 (*about, concerning*) su, di; **information on train services** informazioni sui collegamenti ferroviari; **a book on Goldoni/physics** un libro su Goldoni/di *or* sulla fisica

▶ *adv* **1** (*referring to dress, covering*): **to have one's coat on** avere indosso il cappotto; **to put one's coat on** mettersi il cappotto; **what's she got on?** cosa indossa?; **she put her boots/gloves/hat on** si mise gli stivali/i guanti/il cappello; **screw the lid on tightly** avvita bene il coperchio
2 (*further, continuously*): **to walk on, go on** *etc* continuare, proseguire; **to read on** continuare a leggere; **on and off** ogni tanto

▶ *adj* **1** (*in operation: machine, TV, light*) acceso/a; (*tap*) aperto/a; (*brake*) inserito/a; **is the meeting still on?** (*in progress*) la riunione è ancora in corso?; (*not cancelled*) è confermato l'incontro?; **there's a good film on at the cinema** danno un buon film al cinema
2 (*col*): **that's not on!** (*not acceptable*) non si fa così!; (*not possible*) non se ne parla neanche!

once [wʌns] *adv* una volta ▷ *conj* non appena, quando; **~ he had left/it was done** dopo che se n'era andato/fu fatto; **at ~** subito; (*simultaneously*) a un tempo; **~ a week** una volta alla settimana; **~ more** ancora una volta; **~ and for all** una volta per sempre; **~ upon a time there was ...** c'era una volta ...

oncoming ['ɔnkʌmɪŋ] *adj* (*traffic*) che viene in senso opposto

KEYWORD

one [wʌn] *num* uno/a; **one hundred and fifty** centocinquanta; **one day** un giorno
▶ *adj* **1** (*sole*) unico/a; **the one book which** l'unico libro che; **the one man who** l'unico che
2 (*same*) stesso/a; **they came in the one car** sono venuti nella stessa macchina
▶ *pron* **1**: **this one** questo/a; **that one** quello/a; **I've already got one/a red one** ne ho già uno/uno rosso; **one by one** uno per uno
2: **one another** l'un l'altro; **to look at one another** guardarsi; **to help one another** aiutarsi l'un l'altro *or* a vicenda
3 (*impersonal*) si; **one never knows** non si sa mai; **to cut one's finger** tagliarsi un dito; **one needs to eat** bisogna mangiare; **one-off** (*BRIT col*) *n* fatto eccezionale

oneself [wʌn'sɛlf] *pron* (*reflexive*) si; (*after prep*) sé, se stesso/a; **to do sth (by) ~** fare qc da sé; **to hurt ~** farsi male; **to keep sth for ~** tenere qc per sé; **to talk to ~** parlare da solo
one: **one-shot** [wʌn'ʃɔt] *n* (*US*) = **one-off**; **one-sided** *adj* (*decision, view, argument*) unilaterale; **one-to-one** *adj* (*relationship*) univoco/a; **one-way** *adj* (*street, traffic*) a senso unico
ongoing ['ɔngəuɪŋ] *adj* in corso; in attuazione
onion ['ʌnjən] *n* cipolla
on-line ['ɔnlaɪn] *adj, adv* (*Comput*) on-line *inv*
onlooker ['ɔnlukər] *n* spettatore/trice
only ['əunlɪ] *adv* solo, soltanto ▶ *adj* solo/a, unico/a ▶ *conj* solo che, ma; **an ~ child** un figlio unico; **not ~ non** solo
on-screen [ɔn'skriːn] *adj* sullo schermo *inv*
onset ['ɔnsɛt] *n* inizio

onto ['ɔntu] *prep* su, sopra
onward(s) ['ɔnwəd(z)] *adv* (*move*) in avanti; **from this time onward(s)** d'ora in poi
oops [ups] *excl* ops! (*esprime rincrescimento per un piccolo contrattempo*); **~-a-daisy!** oplà!
ooze [uːz] *vi* stillare
opaque [əu'peɪk] *adj* opaco/a
open ['əupn] *adj* aperto/a; (*road*) libero/a; (*meeting*) pubblico/a ▶ *vt* aprire ▶ *vi* (*eyes, door, debate*) aprirsi; (*flower*) sbocciare; (*shop, bank, museum*) aprire; (*book etc: commence*) cominciare; **in the ~ (air)** all'aperto; **is it ~ to the public?** è aperto al pubblico?; **what time do you ~?** a che ora aprite?; **open up** *vt* aprire; (*blocked road*) sgombrare ▶ *vi* (*shop, business*) aprire; **open-air** *adj* all'aperto; **opening** *n* apertura; (*opportunity*) occasione *f*, opportunità *f inv*; sbocco ▶ *adj* (*speech*) di apertura; **opening hours** *npl* orario d'apertura; **open learning** *n* sistema educativo secondo il quale lo studente ha maggior controllo e gestione delle modalità di apprendimento; **openly** *adv* apertamente; **open-minded** *adj* che ha la mente aperta; **open-necked** *adj* col collo slacciato; **open-plan** *adj* senza pareti divisorie; **Open University** *n* (*BRIT*) vedi nota **"Open University"**

⬡ **OPEN UNIVERSITY**

⬡
⬡ La *Open University* (*OU*), fondata
⬡ in Gran Bretagna nel 1969,
⬡ organizza corsi universitari per
⬡ corrispondenza o via Internet,
⬡ basati anche su lezioni che
⬡ vengono trasmesse dalla *BBC*
⬡ per radio e per televisione e su
⬡ corsi estivi.

opera ['ɔpərə] *n* opera; **opera house** *n* opera; **opera singer** *n* cantante *m/f* d'opera *or* lirico/a

operate ['ɔpəreɪt] *vt* (*machine*) azionare, far funzionare; (*system*) usare ▷ *vi* funzionare; (*drug, person*) agire; **to ~ on sb (for)** (*Med*) operare qn (di)

operating room *n* (*US*) = **operating theatre**

operating theatre *n* (*Med*) sala operatoria

operation [ɔpə'reɪʃən] *n* operazione *f*; **to be in ~** (*machine*) essere in azione *or* funzionamento; (*system*) essere in vigore; **to have an ~ (for)** (*Med*) essere operato/a (di); **operational** *adj* d'esercizio; (*ready for use or action*) in funzione

operative ['ɔpərətɪv] *adj* (*measure*) operativo/a

operator ['ɔpəreɪtə^r] *n* (*of machine*) operatore/trice; (*Tel*) centralinista *m/f*

opinion [ə'pɪnjən] *n* opinione *f*, parere *m*; **in my ~** secondo me, a mio avviso; **opinion poll** *n* sondaggio di opinioni

opponent [ə'pəunənt] *n* avversario/a

opportunity [ɔpə'tjuːnɪtɪ] *n* opportunità *f inv*, occasione *f*; **to take the ~ to do** *or* **of doing** cogliere l'occasione per fare

oppose [ə'pəuz] *vt* opporsi a; **~d to** contrario/a a; **as ~d to** in contrasto con

opposite ['ɔpəzɪt] *adj* opposto/a; (*house etc*) di fronte ▷ *adv* di fronte, dirimpetto ▷ *prep* di fronte a ▷ *n* opposto, contrario; **the ~ sex** l'altro sesso

opposition [ɔpə'zɪʃən] *n* opposizione *f*

oppress [ə'prɛs] *vt* opprimere

opt [ɔpt] *vi*: **to ~ for** optare per; **to ~ to do** scegliere di fare; **opt out** *vi*: **to ~ out of** ritirarsi da

optician [ɔp'tɪʃən] *n* ottico

optimism ['ɔptɪmɪzəm] *n* ottimismo

optimist ['ɔptɪmɪst] *n* ottimista *m/f*; **optimistic** [ɔptɪ'mɪstɪk] *adj* ottimistico/a

optimum ['ɔptɪməm] *adj* ottimale

option ['ɔpʃən] *n* scelta *f*; (*Scol*) materia facoltativa; (*Comm*) opzione *f*; **optional** *adj* facoltativo/a; (*Comm*) a scelta

or [ɔː^r] *conj* o, oppure; (*with negative*): **he hasn't seen or heard anything** non ha visto né sentito niente; **or else** se no, altrimenti; oppure

oral ['ɔːrəl] *adj* orale ▷ *n* esame *m* orale

orange ['ɔrɪndʒ] *n* (*fruit*) arancia ▷ *adj* arancione; **orange juice** *n* succo d'arancia; **orange squash** *n* succo d'arancia (*da diluire con l'acqua*)

orbit ['ɔːbɪt] *n* orbita ▷ *vt* orbitare intorno a

orchard ['ɔːtʃəd] *n* frutteto

orchestra ['ɔːkɪstrə] *n* orchestra; (*US: seating*) platea

orchid ['ɔːkɪd] *n* orchidea

ordeal [ɔː'diːl] *n* prova, travaglio

order ['ɔːdə^r] *n* ordine *m*; (*Comm*) ordinazione *f* ▷ *vt* ordinare; **to ~ sb to do** ordinare a qn di fare; **in ~** in ordine; (*document*) in regola; **in ~ to do** per fare; **in ~ that** affinché + *sub*; **a machine in working ~** una macchina che funziona bene; **out of ~** non in ordine; **to be out of ~** (*machine, toilets*) essere guasto/a; **to be on ~** essere stato ordinato; **order form** *n* modulo d'ordinazione; **orderly** *n* (*Mil*) attendente *m*; (*Med*) inserviente *m* ▷ *adj* (*room*) in ordine; (*mind*) metodico/a; (*person*) ordinato/a, metodico/a

ordinary ['ɔːdnrɪ] *adj* normale, comune; (*pej*) mediocre ▷ *n*: **out of the ~** diverso dal solito, fuori dell'ordinario

ore [ɔː^r] *n* minerale *m* grezzo

oregano [ɔrɪ'gɑːnəu] *n* origano

organ ['ɔːgən] *n* organo; **organic** [ɔː'gænɪk] *adj* organico/a; (*food,* *produce*) biologico/a; **organism** *n* organismo

organization [ɔːɡənaɪˈzeɪʃən] *n* organizzazione *f*

organize [ˈɔːɡənaɪz] *vt* organizzare; **to get ~d** organizzarsi; **organized** [ˈɔːɡənaɪzd] *adj* organizzato/a; **organizer** *n* organizzatore/trice

orgasm [ˈɔːɡæzəm] *n* orgasmo

orgy [ˈɔːdʒɪ] *n* orgia

oriental [ɔːrɪˈentl] *adj, n* orientale (*m/f*)

orientation [ɔːrɪenˈteɪʃən] *n* orientamento

origin [ˈɒrɪdʒɪn] *n* origine *f*

original [əˈrɪdʒɪnl] *adj* originale; (*earliest*) originario/a ⊳ *n* originale *m*; **originally** *adv* (*at first*) all'inizio

originate [əˈrɪdʒɪneɪt] *vi*: **to ~ from** essere originario/a di; (*suggestion*) provenire da; **to ~ in** avere origine in

Orkneys [ˈɔːknɪz] *npl*: **the ~** (*also:* **the Orkney Islands**) le (isole) Orcadi

ornament [ˈɔːnəmənt] *n* ornamento; (*trinket*) ninnolo; **ornamental** [ɔːnəˈmentl] *adj* ornamentale

ornate [ɔːˈneɪt] *adj* molto ornato/a

orphan [ˈɔːfn] *n* orfano/a

orthodox [ˈɔːθədɒks] *adj* ortodosso/a

orthopaedic, (*US*) **orthopedic** [ɔːθəˈpiːdɪk] *adj* ortopedico/a

osteopath [ˈɒstɪəpæθ] *n* specialista *m/f* di osteopatia

ostrich [ˈɒstrɪtʃ] *n* struzzo

other [ˈʌðər] *adj* altro/a ⊳ *pron*: **the ~** l'altro/a; **the ~s** gli altri; **~ than** altro che; a parte; **otherwise** *adv, conj* altrimenti

otter [ˈɒtər] *n* lontra

ouch [autʃ] *excl* ohi!, ahi!

ought [ɔːt] *aux vb*: **I ~ to do it** dovrei farlo; **this ~ to have been corrected** questo avrebbe dovuto essere corretto; **he ~ to win** dovrebbe vincere

ounce [auns] *n* oncia (= *28.35 g; 16 in a pound*)

our [auər] *adj* il (la) nostro/a; (*pl*) i (le) nostri/e; **ours** *pron* il (la) nostro/a; (*pl*) i (le) nostri/e; *see also* **mine¹**; **ourselves** *pl pron* (*reflexive*) ci; (*after preposition*) noi; (*emphatic*) noi stessi/e; *see also* **oneself**

oust [aust] *vt* cacciare, espellere

KEYWORD

out [aut] *adv* (*gen*) fuori; **out here/ there** qui/là fuori; **to speak out loud** parlare forte; **to have a night out** uscire una sera; **the boat was 10 km out** la barca era a 10 km dalla costa; **3 days out from Plymouth** a 3 giorni da Plymouth
▶ *prep*: **out of** (*outside, beyond*) fuori di; (*because of*) per; **out of 10** su 10; **out of petrol** senza benzina

out: outback [ˈautbæk] *n* (*in Australia*) interno, entroterra; **outbound** *adj*: **outbound (for or from)** in partenza (per or da); **outbreak** *n* scoppio; epidemia; **outburst** *n* scoppio; **outcast** [ˈautkɑːst] *n* esule *m/f*; (*socially*) paria *m inv*; **outcome** [ˈautkʌm] *n* esito, risultato; **outcry** [ˈautkraɪ] *n* protesta, clamore *m*; **outdated** [autˈdeɪtɪd] *adj* (*custom, clothes*) fuori moda; (*idea*) sorpassato/a; **outdoor** [autˈdɔːr] *adj* all'aperto; **outdoors** *adv* fuori; all'aria aperta

outer [ˈautər] *adj* esteriore; **outer space** *n* spazio cosmico

outfit [ˈautfɪt] *n* (*clothes*) completo; (: *for sport*) tenuta

out: outgoing [ˈautɡəʊɪŋ] *adj* (*character*) socievole; **outgoings** *npl* (*BRIT: expenses*) spese *fpl*, uscite *fpl*; **outhouse** [ˈauthaus] *n* costruzione *f* annessa

outing [ˈautɪŋ] *n* gita; escursione *f*

out: outlaw [ˈautlɔː] *n* fuorilegge *m/f* ⊳ *vt* bandire; **outlay** [ˈautleɪ] *n* spese *fpl*; (*investment*) sborsa, spesa;

outlet ['autlɛt] n (for liquid etc) sbocco, scarico; (also: **retail outlet**) punto di vendita; (us Elec) presa di corrente;

outline ['autlaɪn] n contorno, profilo; (summary) abbozzo, grandi linee fpl ▷ vt (fig) descrivere a grandi linee;

outlook ['autluk] n prospettiva, vista; **outnumber** [aut'nʌmbər] vt superare in numero; **out-of-date** adj (passport, ticket) scaduto/a; (clothes) fuori moda inv; **out-of-doors** [autəv'dɔːz] adv all'aperto; **out-of-the-way** (remote) fuori mano; **out-of-town** [ˌautəv'taun] adj (shopping centre etc) inv uori città; **outpatient** ['autpeɪʃənt] n paziente m/f esterno/a; **outpost** ['autpəust] n avamposto; **output** ['autput] n produzione f; (Comput) output m inv

outrage ['autreɪdʒ] n oltraggio; scandalo ▷ vt oltraggiare; **outrageous** [aut'reɪdʒəs] adj oltraggioso/a; scandaloso/a

outright adv [aut'raɪt] completamente; schiettamente; apertamente; sul colpo ▷ adj ['autraɪt] completo/a; schietto/a e netto/a

outset ['autsɛt] n inizio

outside [aut'saɪd] n esterno, esteriore m ▷ adj esterno/a, esteriore ▷ adv fuori, all'esterno ▷ prep fuori di, all'esterno di; **at the ~** (fig) al massimo; **outside lane** n (Aut) corsia di sorpasso; **outside line** n (Tel) linea esterna; **outsider** n (in race etc) outsider m inv; (stranger) straniero/a

out: outsize ['autsaɪz] adj (clothes) per taglie forti; **outskirts** ['autskəːts] npl sobborghi mpl; **outspoken** [aut'spəukən] adj molto franco/a; **outstanding** [aut'stændɪŋ] adj eccezionale, di rilievo; (unfinished) non completo/a; non evaso/a; non regolato/a

outward ['autwəd] adj (sign, appearances) esteriore; (journey) d'andata; **outwards** ['autwədz] adv (esp BRIT) = **outward**

outweigh [aut'weɪ] vt avere maggior peso di

oval ['əuvl] adj, n ovale (m)

ovary ['əuvərɪ] n ovaia

oven ['ʌvn] n forno; **oven glove** n guanto da forno; **ovenproof** adj da forno; **oven-ready** adj pronto/a da infornare

over ['əuvər] adv al di sopra ▷ adj, adv (finished) finito/a, terminato/a; (too much) troppo; (remaining) che avanza ▷ prep su; sopra; (above) al di sopra di; (on the other side of) di là di; (more than) più di; (during) durante; **~ here** qui; **~ there** là; **all ~** (everywhere) dappertutto; (finished) tutto/a finito/a; **~ and ~ (again)** più e più volte; **~ and above** oltre (a); **to ask ~** invitare qn (a passare)

overall adj ['əuvərɔːl] totale ▷ n ['əuvərɔːl] (BRIT) grembiule m ▷ adv [əuvər'ɔːl] nell'insieme, complessivamente; **overalls** npl tuta (da lavoro)

overboard ['əuvəbɔːd] adv (Naut) fuori bordo, in acqua

overcame [əuvə'keɪm] pt of **overcome**

overcast ['əuvəkɑːst] adj (sky) coperto/a

overcharge [əuvə'tʃɑːdʒ] vt: **to ~ sb for sth** far pagare troppo caro a qn per qc

overcoat ['əuvəkəut] n soprabito, cappotto

overcome [əuvə'kʌm] vt (irreg) superare; sopraffare

over: overcrowded [əuvə'kraudɪd] adj sovraffollato/a; **overdo** [əuvə'duː] vt (irreg) esagerare; (overcook) cuocere troppo; **overdone** [əuvə'dʌn] adj troppo cotto/a; **overdose** ['əuvədəus] n dose f eccessiva; **overdraft** ['əuvədrɑːft] n scoperto (di conto); **overdrawn** [əuvə'drɔːn] adj (account) scoperto/a; **overdue** [əuvə'djuː]

adj in ritardo; **overestimate** [əʊvərˈɛstɪmeɪt] vt sopravvalutare

overflow vi [əʊvəˈfləʊ] traboccare ▷ n [ˈəʊvəfləʊ] (also: **~ pipe**) troppopieno

overgrown [əʊvəˈgrəʊn] adj (garden) ricoperto/a di vegetazione

overhaul vt [əʊvəˈhɔːl] revisionare ▷ n [ˈəʊvəhɔːl] revisione f

overhead adv [əʊvəˈhɛd] di sopra ▷ adj [ˈəʊvəhɛd] aereo/a; (lighting) verticale ▷ n [ˈəʊvəhɛd] (US) = **overheads**; **overhead projector** n lavagna luminosa; **overheads** npl spese fpl generali

over: overhear [əʊvəˈhɪər] vt (irreg) sentire (per caso); **overheat** [əʊvəˈhiːt] vi surriscaldarsi; **overland** adj, adv per via di terra; **overlap** vi [əʊvəˈlæp] sovrapporsi; **overleaf** [əʊvəˈliːf] adv a tergo; **overload** [əʊvəˈləʊd] vt sovraccaricare; **overlook** [əʊvəˈlʊk] vt (have view of) dare su; (miss) trascurare; (forgive) passare sopra a

overnight adv [əʊvəˈnaɪt] (happen) durante la notte; (fig) tutto ad un tratto ▷ adj [ˈəʊvənaɪt] (stay): **he stayed there ~** ci ha passato la notte; **overnight bag** n borsa da viaggio

overpass [ˈəʊvəpɑːs] n cavalcavia m inv

overpower [əʊvəˈpaʊər] vt sopraffare; **overpowering** adj irresistibile; (heat, stench) soffocante

over: overreact [əʊvəriːˈækt] vi reagire in modo esagerato; **overrule** [əʊvəˈruːl] vt (decision) annullare; (claim) respingere; **overrun** [əʊvəˈrʌn] vt (irreg: like **run**) (country etc) invadere; (time limit etc) superare

overseas [əʊvəˈsiːz] adv oltremare; (abroad) all'estero ▷ adj (trade) estero/a; (visitor) straniero/a

oversee [əʊvəˈsiː] vt (irreg) sorvegliare

overshadow [əʊvəˈʃædəʊ] vt far ombra su; (fig) eclissare

oversight [ˈəʊvəsaɪt] n omissione f, svista

oversleep [əʊvəˈsliːp] vi (irreg) dormire troppo a lungo

overspend [əʊvəˈspɛnd] vi (irreg) spendere troppo; **we have overspent by 5000 dollars** abbiamo speso 5000 dollari di troppo

overt [əʊˈvəːt] adj palese

overtake [əʊvəˈteɪk] vt (irreg) sorpassare

over: overthrow [əʊvəˈθrəʊ] vt (irreg: government) rovesciare; **overtime** [ˈəʊvətaɪm] n (lavoro) straordinario

overtook [əʊvəˈtʊk] pt of **overtake**

over: overturn [əʊvəˈtəːn] vt rovesciare ▷ vi rovesciarsi; **overweight** [əʊvəˈweɪt] adj (person) troppo grasso/a; **overwhelm** [əʊvəˈwɛlm] vt sopraffare; sommergere; schiacciare; **overwhelming** adj (victory, defeat) schiacciante; (heat, desire) intenso/a

ow [aʊ] excl ahi!

owe [əʊ] vt: **to ~ sb sth, to ~ sth to sb** dovere qc a qn; **owing to** prep a causa di

owl [aʊl] n gufo

own [əʊn] adj proprio/a ▷ vt possedere; **a room of my ~** la mia propria camera; **to get one's ~ back** vendicarsi; **on one's ~** tutto/a solo/a; **own up** vi confessare; **owner** n proprietario/a; **ownership** n possesso

ox (pl **oxen**) [ɔks, ˈɔksn] n bue m

Oxbridge [ˈɔksbrɪdʒ] n le università di Oxford e/o Cambridge

oxen [ˈɔksn] npl of **ox**

oxygen [ˈɔksɪdʒən] n ossigeno

oyster [ˈɔɪstər] n ostrica

oz. abbr = **ounce**

ozone [ˈəʊzəʊn] n ozono; **ozone-friendly** adj che non danneggia lo strato d'ozono; **ozone layer** n fascia d'ozono

P

p [piː] *abbr* = **penny; pence**
PA *n abbr* = **personal assistant; public address system**
p.a. *abbr* = **per annum**
pace [peɪs] *n* passo; (*speed*) passo; velocità ▷ *vi*: **to ~ up and down** camminare su e giù; **to keep ~ with** camminare di pari passo a; (*events*) tenersi al corrente di; **pacemaker** *n* (*Med*) pacemaker *m inv*, stimolatore *m* cardiaco; (*Sport*) chi fa l'andatura
Pacific [pə'sɪfɪk] *n*: **the ~ (Ocean)** il Pacifico, l'Oceano Pacifico
pacifier ['pæsɪfaɪəʳ] *n* (*US: dummy*) succhiotto, ciuccio (*col*)
pack [pæk] *n* pacco; (*US: of cigarettes*) pacchetto; (*of hounds*) muta; (*of thieves etc*) banda; (*of cards*) mazzo ▷ *vt* (*in suitcase etc*) mettere; (*box*) riempire; (*cram*) stipare, pigiare ▷ *vi*: **to ~ one's bags** fare la valigia; **to send sb ~ing** spedire via qn; **pack in** (*BRIT col*) *vi* (*watch, car*) guastarsi ▷ *vt*

mollare, piantare; **~ it in!** piantala!, dacci un taglio!; **pack off** *vt* (*person*) spedire; **to ~ sb off** spedire via qn; **pack up** *vi* (*BRIT col: machine*) guastarsi; (*person*) far fagotto ▷ *vt* (*belongings, clothes*) mettere in una valigia; (*goods, presents*) imballare
package ['pækɪdʒ] *n* pacco; balla; (*also: ~ deal*) pacchetto; forfait *m inv*; **package holiday** *n* vacanza organizzata; **package tour** *n* viaggio organizzato
packaging ['pækɪdʒɪŋ] *n* confezione *f*, imballo
packed [pækt] *adj* (*crowded*) affollato/a; **~ lunch** (*BRIT*) pranzo al sacco
packet ['pækɪt] *n* pacchetto
packing ['pækɪŋ] *n* imballaggio
pact [pækt] *n* patto, accordo; trattato
pad [pæd] *n* blocco; (*to prevent friction*) cuscinetto; (*col: flat*) appartamentino ▷ *vt* imbottire; **padded** *adj* imbottito/a
paddle ['pædl] *n* (*oar*) pagaia; (*US: for table tennis*) racchetta da ping-pong ▷ *vi* sguazzare ▷ *vt* (*boat*) fare andare a colpi di pagaia; **paddling pool** *n* (*BRIT*) piscina per bambini
paddock ['pædək] *n* prato recintato; (*at racecourse*) paddock *m inv*
padlock ['pædlɒk] *n* lucchetto
paedophile, (*US*) **pedophile** ['piːdəʊfaɪl] *adj*, *n* pedofilo/a
page [peɪdʒ] *n* pagina; (*also: ~ boy*) paggio ▷ *vt* (*in hotel etc*) (far) chiamare
pager ['peɪdʒəʳ] *n* (*Tel*) cercapersone *m inv*
paid [peɪd] *pt*, *pp of* **pay** ▷ *adj* (*work, official*) rimunerato/a; **to put ~ to** (*BRIT*) mettere fine a
pain [peɪn] *n* dolore *m*; **to be in ~** soffrire, aver male; **to take ~s to do** mettercela tutta per fare; **painful** *adj* doloroso/a, che fa male; (*difficult*) difficile, penoso/a; **painkiller**

n antalgico, antidolorifico;
painstaking ['peɪnzteɪkɪŋ]
adj (*person*) sollecito/a; (*work*)
accurato/a

paint [peɪnt] *n* vernice *f*; colore *m*
▷ *vt* dipingere; (*door etc*) verniciare;
to ~ the door blue verniciare la
porta di azzurro; **paintbrush** *n*
pennello; **painter** *n* (*artist*) pittore
m; (*decorator*) imbianchino; **painting**
n pittura; verniciatura; (*picture*)
dipinto, quadro

pair [pεər] *n* (*of shoes, gloves etc*) paio
m; (*of people*) coppia; duo *m inv*; **a ~ of
scissors/trousers** un paio di forbici/
pantaloni

pajamas [pəˈdʒɑːməz] *npl* (*US*)
pigiama *m*

Pakistan [pɑːkɪˈstɑːn] *n* Pakistan *m*;
Pakistani *adj*, *n* pakistano/a

pal [pæl] *n* (*col*) amico/a,
compagno/a

palace ['pæləs] *n* palazzo

pale [peɪl] *adj* pallido/a ▷ *n*: **to be
beyond the ~** aver oltrepassato
ogni limite

Palestine ['pælɪstaɪn] *n* Palestina;
Palestinian [pælɪsˈtɪnɪən] *adj*, *n*
palestinese (*m/f*)

palm [pɑːm] *n* (*Anat*) palma, palmo;
(*also: ~ tree*) palma ▷ *vt*: **to ~ sth off
on sb** (*col*) rifilare qc a qn

pamper ['pæmpər] *vt* viziare,
coccolare

pamphlet ['pæmflət] *n* dépliant
m inv

pan [pæn] *n* (*also: sauce~*)
casseruola; (*also: frying ~*) padella

pancake ['pænkeɪk] *n* frittella

panda ['pændə] *n* panda *m inv*

pandemic [pænˈdɛmɪk] *n* pandemia

pane [peɪn] *n* vetro

panel ['pænl] *n* (*of wood, cloth etc*)
pannello; (*Radio, TV*) giuria

panhandler ['pænhændlər] *n* (*US
col*) accattone/a

panic ['pænɪk] *n* panico ▷ *vi* perdere il
sangue freddo

panorama [pænəˈrɑːmə] *n*
panorama *m*

pansy ['pænzɪ] *n* (*Bot*) viola del
pensiero, pensée *f inv*; (*col, pej*)
femminuccia

pant [pænt] *vi* ansare

panther ['pænθər] *n* pantera

panties ['pæntɪz] *npl* slip *m*,
mutandine *fpl*

pantomime ['pæntəmaɪm] *n* (*BRIT*:
at Christmas) spettacolo natalizio;
(*tecnica*) pantomima

> ● **PANTOMIME**
> ●
> ● In Gran Bretagna la *pantomime*
> ● (abbreviata in *panto*) è una
> ● sorta di libera interpretazione
> ● delle favole più conosciute che
> ● vengono messe in scena nei teatri
> ● durante il periodo natalizio. Gli
> ● attori principali sono la dama,
> ● "*dame*", che è un uomo vestito da
> ● donna, il protagonista, "*principal
> ● boy*", che è una donna travestita da
> ● uomo, e il cattivo, "*villain*". È uno
> ● spettacolo per tutta la famiglia,
> ● che prevede la partecipazione del
> ● pubblico.

pants [pænts] *npl* mutande *fpl*, slip
m; (*US: trousers*) pantaloni *mpl*

paper ['peɪpər] *n* carta; (*also: wall~*)
carta da parati, tappezzeria; (*also:
news~*) giornale *m*; (*study, article*)
saggio; (*exam*) prova scritta ▷ *adj*
di carta ▷ *vt* tappezzare; *see also*
papers; **paperback** *n* tascabile *m*;
edizione *f* economica; **paper bag**
n sacchetto di carta; **paper clip**
n graffetta, clip *f inv*; **papers** *npl*
(*also: identity papers*) carte *fpl*,
documenti *mpl*; **paper shop** *n* (*BRIT*)
giornalaio (*negozio*); **paperwork** *n*
lavoro amministrativo

paprika ['pæprɪkə] *n* paprica

par [pɑːr] *n* parità, pari *f*; (*Golf*) norma;
on a ~ with alla pari con

paracetamol [pærə'si:təmɔl] *n*
(BRIT) paracetamolo
parachute ['pærəʃu:t] *n* paracadute
m inv
parade [pə'reɪd] *n* parata ▷ *vt* (fig)
fare sfoggio di ▷ *vi* sfilare in parata
paradise ['pærədaɪs] *n* paradiso
paradox ['pærədɔks] *n* paradosso
paraffin ['pærəfɪn] *n* (BRIT): **~ (oil)**
paraffina
paragraph ['pærəgrɑ:f] *n*
paragrafo
parallel ['pærəlɛl] *adj* parallelo/a;
(fig) analogo/a ▷ *n* (line) parallela;
(fig, Geo) parallelo
paralysed ['pærəlaɪzd] *adj*
paralizzato/a
paralysis (*pl* **paralyses**) [pə'rælɪsɪs,
-si:z] *n* paralisi *f inv*
paramedic [pærə'mɛdɪk] *n*
paramedico
paranoid ['pærənɔɪd] *adj*
paranoico/a
parasite ['pærəsaɪt] *n* parassita *m*
parcel ['pɑ:sl] *n* pacco, pacchetto
▷ *vt* (also: **~ up**) impaccare
pardon ['pɑ:dn] *n* perdono; grazia
▷ *vt* perdonare; (Law) graziare; **~ me!**
mi scusi!; **I beg your ~!** scusi!; **(I beg
your) ~?**, (US) **~ me?** prego?
parent ['pɛərənt] *n* padre *m* (*or*
madre *f*); **parents** *npl* genitori *mpl*;
parental [pə'rɛntl] *adj* dei genitori
   Be careful not to translate *parent*
   by the Italian word *parente*.
Paris ['pærɪs] *n* Parigi *f*
parish ['pærɪʃ] *n* parrocchia; (BRIT:
civil) ≈ municipio
Parisian [pə'rɪzɪən] *adj, n*
parigino/a
park [pɑ:k] *n* parco ▷ *vt, vi*
parcheggiare
parking ['pɑ:kɪŋ] *n* parcheggio; **"no
~"** "sosta vietata"; **parking lot** *n* (US)
posteggio, parcheggio; **parking
meter** *n* parchimetro; **parking
ticket** *n* multa per sosta vietata
parkway ['pɑ:kweɪ] *n* (US) viale *m*

parliament ['pɑ:ləmənt] *n*
parlamento; **parliamentary**
[pɑ:lə'mɛntərɪ] *adj* parlamentare
Parmesan [pɑ:mɪ'zæn] *n* (also: **~
cheese**) parmigiano
parole [pə'rəul] *n*: **on ~** in libertà per
buona condotta
parrot ['pærət] *n* pappagallo
parsley ['pɑ:slɪ] *n* prezzemolo
parsnip ['pɑ:snɪp] *n* pastinaca
parson ['pɑ:sn] *n* prete *m*; (Church of
England) parroco
part [pɑ:t] *n* parte *f*; (of machine)
pezzo; (US: in hair) scriminatura
▷ *adj* in parte ▷ *adv* = **partly** ▷ *vt*
separare ▷ *vi* (people) separarsi; **to
take ~ in** prendere parte a; **to take
sb's ~** parteggiare per qn, prendere
le parti di qn; **for my ~** per parte
mia; **for the most ~** in generale;
nella maggior parte dei casi; **to
take sth in good/bad ~** prendere
bene/male qc; **~ of speech** parte del
discorso; **part with** *vt fus* separarsi
da; rinunciare a
partial ['pɑ:ʃl] *adj* parziale; **to be ~ to**
avere un debole per
participant [pɑ:'tɪsɪpənt] *n*: **~ (in)**
partecipante *m/f* (a)
participate [pɑ:'tɪsɪpeɪt] *vi*: **to ~
(in)** prendere parte (a), partecipare
(a)
particle ['pɑ:tɪkl] *n* particella
particular [pə'tɪkjulə'] *adj*
particolare; speciale; (fussy)
difficile; meticoloso/a; **particulars**
npl particolari *mpl*, dettagli *mpl*;
(information) informazioni *fpl*; **in
~** in particolare, particolarmente;
particularly *adv* particolarmente;
in particolare
parting ['pɑ:tɪŋ] *n* separazione *f*;
(BRIT: in hair) scriminatura ▷ *adj*
d'addio
partition [pɑ:'tɪʃən] *n* (Pol)
partizione *f*; (wall) tramezzo
partly ['pɑ:tlɪ] *adv* parzialmente;
in parte

P

partner ['pɑːtnə^r] n (Comm) socio/a; (wife, husband etc, Sport) compagno/a; (at dance) cavaliere (dama); **partnership** n associazione f; (Comm) società f inv

partridge ['pɑːtrɪdʒ] n pernice f

part-time ['pɑːt'taɪm] adj, adv a orario ridotto

party ['pɑːtɪ] n (Pol) partito; (team) squadra; (Law) parte f; (celebration) ricevimento; serata; festa ▷ adj (Pol) del partito, di partito

pass [pɑːs] vt (gen) passare; (place) passare davanti a; (exam) passare, superare; (candidate) promuovere; (overtake, surpass) sorpassare, superare; (approve) approvare ▷ vi passare ▷ n (permit) lasciapassare m inv; permesso; (in mountains) passo, gola; (Sport) passaggio; (Scol): **to get a ~** prendere la sufficienza; **could you ~ the vegetables round?** potrebbe far passare i contorni?; **to ~ sth through a hole** etc far passare qc attraverso un buco etc; **to make a ~ at sb** (col) fare delle proposte or delle avances a qn; **pass away** vi morire; **pass by** vi passare ▷ vt trascurare; **pass on** vt: **to ~ on (to)** passare (a); **pass out** vi svenire; **pass over** vi (die) spirare ▷ vt lasciare da parte; **pass up** vt (opportunity) lasciarsi sfuggire, perdere; **passable** adj (road) praticabile; (work) accettabile

passage ['pæsɪdʒ] n (gen) passaggio; (also: **~way**) corridoio; (in book) brano, passo; (by boat) traversata

passenger ['pæsɪndʒə^r] n passeggero/a

passer-by [pɑːsə'baɪ] n passante m/f

passing place n (Aut) piazzola (di sosta)

passion ['pæʃən] n passione f; amore m; **passionate** adj appassionato/a; **passion fruit** n frutto della passione

passive ['pæsɪv] adj (also Ling) passivo/a

passport ['pɑːspɔːt] n passaporto; **passport control** n controllo m passaporti inv; **passport office** n ufficio m passaporti inv

password ['pɑːswəːd] n parola d'ordine

past [pɑːst] prep (further than) oltre, di là di; dopo; (later than) dopo ▷ adv: **to run ~** passare di corsa ▷ adj passato/a; (president etc) ex inv ▷ n passato; **he's ~ forty** ha più di quarant'anni; **ten ~ eight** le otto e dieci; **for the ~ few days** da qualche giorno; in questi ultimi giorni

pasta ['pæstə] n pasta

paste [peɪst] n (glue) colla; (Culin) pâté m inv; pasta ▷ vt collare

pastel ['pæstl] adj pastello inv

pasteurized ['pæstəraɪzd] adj pastorizzato/a

pastime ['pɑːstaɪm] n passatempo

pastor ['pɑːstə^r] n pastore m

past participle [-'pɑːtɪsɪpl] n (Ling) participio passato

pastry ['peɪstrɪ] n pasta

pasture ['pɑːstʃə^r] n pascolo

pasty¹ ['pæstɪ] n pasticcio di carne

pasty² ['peɪstɪ] adj (complexion) pallido/a, smorto/a

pat [pæt] vt accarezzare, dare un colpetto (affettuoso) a

patch [pætʃ] n (of material) toppa; (eye patch) benda; (spot) macchia ▷ vt (clothes) rattoppare; **a bad ~** un brutto periodo; **patchy** adj irregolare

pâté ['pæteɪ] n pâté m inv

patent ['peɪtnt] n brevetto ▷ vt brevettare ▷ adj patente, manifesto/a

paternal [pə'təːnl] adj paterno/a

paternity leave [pə'təːnɪtɪ-] n congedo di paternità

path [pɑːθ] n sentiero, viottolo; viale m; (fig) via, strada; (of planet, missile) traiettoria

pathetic [pə'θɛtɪk] adj (pitiful) patetico/a; (very bad) penoso/a

pathway ['pɑːθweɪ] n sentiero

patience ['peɪʃns] n pazienza; (BRIT Cards) solitario

patient ['peɪʃnt] n paziente m/f; malato/a ▷ adj paziente

patio ['pætɪəu] n terrazza

patriotic [pætrɪ'ɔtɪk] adj patriottico/a

patrol [pə'trəul] n pattuglia ▷ vt pattugliare; **patrol car** n autoradio f inv (della polizia)

patron ['peɪtrən] n (in shop) cliente m/f; (of charity) benefattore/trice; **~ of the arts** mecenate m/f

patronizing ['pætrənaɪzɪŋ] adj condiscendente

pattern ['pætən] n modello; (design) disegno, motivo; **patterned** adj a disegni, a motivi; (material) fantasia inv

pause [pɔːz] n pausa ▷ vi fare una pausa, arrestarsi

pave [peɪv] vt pavimentare; **to ~ the way for** aprire la via a

pavement ['peɪvmənt] n (BRIT) marciapiede m

> Be careful not to translate
> pavement by the Italian word
> pavimento.

pavilion [pə'vɪlɪən] n (Sport) edificio annesso ad un campo sportivo

paving ['peɪvɪŋ] n pavimentazione f

paw [pɔː] n zampa

pawn [pɔːn] n (Chess) pedone m; (fig) pedina ▷ vt dare in pegno; **pawnbroker** n prestatore m su pegno

pay [peɪ] (pt, pp **paid**) n stipendio, paga ▷ vt pagare ▷ vi (be profitable) rendere; **to ~ attention (to)** fare attenzione (a); **to ~ sb a visit** far visita a qn; **to ~ one's respects to sb** porgere i propri rispetti a qn; **pay back** vt rimborsare; **pay for** vt fus pagare; **pay in** vt versare; **pay off** vt (debts) saldare; (creditor) pagare; (workers) licenziare ▷ vi (scheme) funzionare; (patience) dare dei frutti; **pay out** vt (money) sborsare, tirar

fuori; (rope) far allentare; **pay up** vt saldare; **payable** adj pagabile; **pay-as-you-go** ['peɪəzjə'gəu] adj (mobile phone) con scheda prepagata; **pay day** n giorno di paga; **pay envelope** n (US) busta f paga inv; **payment** n pagamento; versamento; saldo; **payout** n pagamento; (in competition) premio; **pay packet** n (BRIT) busta f paga inv; **payphone** n cabina telefonica; **payroll** n ruolo (organico); **pay slip** n foglio m paga inv; **pay television** n televisione f a pagamento, pay-tv f inv

PC n abbr = **personal computer** ▷ adj abbr = **politically correct**

pc abbr = **per cent**

PDA n abbr (= personal digital assistant) PDA m inv

PE n abbr (= physical education) ed. fisica

pea [piː] n pisello

peace [piːs] n pace f; **peaceful** adj pacifico/a, calmo/a

peach [piːtʃ] n pesca

peacock ['piːkɔk] n pavone m

peak [piːk] n (of mountain) cima, vetta; (mountain itself) picco; (of cap) visiera; (fig) apice m; **peak hours** npl ore fpl di punta

peanut ['piːnʌt] n arachide f, nocciolina americana; **peanut butter** n burro di arachidi

pear [pɛər] n pera

pearl [pəːl] n perla

peasant ['pɛznt] n contadino/a

peat [piːt] n torba

pebble ['pɛbl] n ciottolo

peck [pɛk] vt (also: ~ at) beccare ▷ n colpo di becco; (kiss) bacetto; **peckish** adj (BRIT col): **I feel peckish** ho un languorino

peculiar [pɪ'kjuːlɪər] adj strano/a, bizzarro/a; (particular) particolare; **~ to** tipico/a di

pedal ['pɛdl] n pedale m ▷ vi pedalare

pedalo ['pɛdələu] n pedalò m inv

pedestal ['pɛdəstl] n piedestallo

pedestrian [pɪ'dɛstrɪən] n
pedone/a ▷ adj pedonale; (fig)
prosaico/a, pedestre; **pedestrian
crossing** n (BRIT) passaggio
pedonale; **pedestrianized** adj:
a pedestrianized street una
zona pedonalizzata; **pedestrian
precinct,** (US) **pedestrian zone** n
zona pedonale

pedigree ['pɛdɪgriː] n (of animal)
pedigree m inv; (fig) background m inv
▷ cpd (animal) di razza

pedophile ['piːdəʊfaɪl] (US) n
= **paedophile**

pee [piː] vi (col) pisciare

peek [piːk] vi guardare
furtivamente

peel [piːl] n buccia; (of orange, lemon)
scorza ▷ vt sbucciare ▷ vi (paint etc)
staccarsi

peep [piːp] n (look) sguardo furtivo,
sbirciata; (sound) pigolio ▷ vi
guardare furtivamente

peer [pɪə^r] vi: **to ~ at** scrutare ▷ n
(noble) pari m inv; (equal) pari mf
inv, uguale m/f; (contemporary)
contemporaneo/a

peg [pɛg] n caviglia; (for coat etc)
attaccapanni m inv; (BRIT: also:
clothes ~) molletta

pelican ['pɛlɪkən] n pellicano;
pelican crossing n (BRIT Aut)
attraversamento pedonale con semaforo
a controllo manuale

pelt [pɛlt] vt: **to ~ sb (with)**
bombardare qn (con) ▷ vi (rain)
piovere a dirotto; (col: run) filare
▷ n pelle f

pelvis ['pɛlvɪs] n pelvi f inv, bacino

pen [pɛn] n penna; (for sheep) recinto

penalty ['pɛnltɪ] n penalità f inv;
sanzione f penale; (fine) ammenda;
(Sport) penalizzazione f

pence [pɛns] npl (BRIT) of **penny**

pencil ['pɛnsl] n matita ▷ vt (also:
~ in) scrivere a matita; **pencil
case** n astuccio per matite; **pencil
sharpener** n temperamatite m inv

pendant ['pɛndnt] n pendaglio

pending ['pɛndɪŋ] prep in attesa di
▷ adj in sospeso

penetrate ['pɛnɪtreɪt] vt penetrare

penfriend ['pɛnfrɛnd] n (BRIT)
corrispondente m/f

penguin ['pɛŋgwɪn] n pinguino

penicillin [pɛnɪ'sɪlɪn] n penicillina

peninsula [pə'nɪnsjʊlə] n penisola

penis ['piːnɪs] n pene m

penitentiary [pɛnɪ'tɛnʃərɪ] n (US)
carcere m

penknife ['pɛnnaɪf] n temperino

penniless ['pɛnɪlɪs] adj senza un
soldo

penny (pl **pennies** or **pence**) ['pɛnɪ,
'pɛnɪz, pɛns] n (BRIT) penny m; (US)
centesimo

penpal ['pɛnpæl] n corrispondente
m/f

pension ['pɛnʃən] n pensione f;
pensioner n (BRIT) pensionato/a

pentagon ['pɛntəgən] n
pentagono; **the P~** (US Pol) il
Pentagono

penthouse ['pɛnthaʊs] n
appartamento (di lusso) nell'attico

penultimate [pɪ'nʌltɪmət] adj
penultimo/a

people ['piːpl] npl gente f; persone
fpl; (citizens) popolo ▷ n (nation,
race) popolo; **4/several ~ came** 4/
parecchie persone sono venute; **~
say that ...** si dice or la gente dice
che ...

pepper ['pɛpə^r] n pepe m; (vegetable)
peperone m ▷ vt (fig): **to ~ with**
spruzzare di; **peppermint** n (sweet)
pasticca di menta

per [pə^r] prep per; a; **~ hour** all'ora;
~ kilo etc il chilo etc; **~ day** al giorno

perceive [pə'siːv] vt percepire;
(notice) accorgersi di

per cent adv per cento

percentage [pə'sɛntɪdʒ] n
percentuale f

perception [pə'sɛpʃən] n percezione
f; sensibilità; perspicacia

perch [pəːtʃ] n (fish) pesce m persico; (for bird) sostegno, ramo ▷ vi appollaiarsi

percussion [pəˈkʌʃən] n percussione f; (Mus) strumenti mpl a percussione

perfect ['pəːfɪkt] adj perfetto/a ▷ n (also: ~ tense) perfetto, passato prossimo ▷ vt [pəˈfɛkt] perfezionare; mettere a punto; **perfection** [pəˈfɛkʃən] n perfezione f; **perfectly** adv perfettamente, alla perfezione

perform [pəˈfɔːm] vt (carry out) eseguire, fare; (symphony etc) suonare; (play, ballet) dare; (opera) fare ▷ vi suonare; recitare; **performance** n esecuzione f; (at theatre etc) rappresentazione f, spettacolo; (of an artist) interpretazione f; (of player etc) performance f; (of car, engine) prestazione f; **performer** n artista m/f

perfume ['pəːfjuːm] n profumo

perhaps [pəˈhæps] adv forse

perimeter [pəˈrɪmɪtəʳ] n perimetro

period ['pɪərɪəd] n (length of time) epoca; (Scol) lezione f; (full stop) punto; (Med) mestruazioni fpl ▷ adj (costume, furniture) d'epoca; **periodical** [pɪərɪˈɔdɪkl] n periodico; **periodically** adv periodicamente

perish ['pɛrɪʃ] vi perire, morire; (decay) deteriorarsi

perjury ['pəːdʒərɪ] n spergiuro

perk [pəːk] n (col) vantaggio

perm [pəːm] n (for hair) permanente f

permanent ['pəːmənənt] adj permanente; **permanently** adv definitivamente

permission [pəˈmɪʃən] n permesso

permit n ['pəːmɪt] permesso ▷ vt [pəˈmɪt] permettere; **to ~ sb to do** permettere a qn di fare

perplex [pəˈplɛks] vt lasciare perplesso/a

persecute ['pəːsɪkjuːt] vt perseguitare

persecution [pəːsɪˈkjuːʃən] n persecuzione f

persevere [pəːsɪˈvɪəʳ] vi perseverare

Persian ['pəːʃən] adj persiano/a ▷ n (Ling) persiano; **the ~ Gulf** n il Golfo Persico

persist [pəˈsɪst] vi: **to ~ (in doing)** persistere (nel fare); ostinarsi (a fare); **persistent** adj persistente; ostinato/a

person ['pəːsn] n persona; **in ~** di or in persona, personalmente; **personal** adj personale; individuale; **personal assistant** n segretaria personale; **personal computer** n personal computer m inv; **personality** [pəːsəˈnælɪtɪ] n personalità f inv; **personally** adv personalmente; **to take sth personally** prendere qc come una critica personale; **personal organizer** n agenda; (electronic) agenda elettronica; **personal stereo** n walkman® m inv

personnel [pəːsəˈnɛl] n personale m

perspective [pəˈspɛktɪv] n prospettiva

perspiration [pəːspɪˈreɪʃən] n traspirazione f, sudore m

persuade [pəˈsweɪd] vt: **to ~ sb to do sth** persuadere qn a fare qc

persuasion [pəˈsweɪʒən] n persuasione f; (creed) convinzione f, credo

persuasive [pəˈsweɪsɪv] adj persuasivo/a

perverse [pəˈvəːs] adj perverso/a

pervert n ['pəːvəːt] pervertito/a ▷ vt [pəˈvəːt] pervertire

pessimism ['pɛsɪmɪzəm] n pessimismo

pessimist ['pɛsɪmɪst] n pessimista m/f; **pessimistic** [pɛsɪˈmɪstɪk] adj pessimistico/a

pest [pɛst] n animale m (or insetto) pestifero; (fig) peste f

pester ['pɛstəʳ] vt tormentare, molestare

pesticide ['pɛstɪsaɪd] n pesticida m

pet [pɛt] n animale m domestico; (favourite) favorito/a ▷ vt accarezzare; **teacher's ~** favorito/a del maestro

petal ['pɛtl] n petalo

petite [pə'ti:t] adj piccolo/a e aggraziato/a

petition [pə'tɪʃən] n petizione f

petrified ['pɛtrɪfaɪd] adj (fig) morto/a di paura

petrol ['pɛtrəl] n (BRIT) benzina; **two/four-star ~** ≈ benzina normale/super

Be careful not to translate petrol by the Italian word petrolio.

petroleum [pə'trəʊlɪəm] n petrolio

petrol: petrol pump n (BRIT: in car, at garage) pompa di benzina; **petrol station** n (BRIT) stazione f di rifornimento; **petrol tank** n (BRIT) serbatoio della benzina

petticoat ['pɛtɪkəʊt] n sottana

petty ['pɛtɪ] adj (mean) meschino/a; (unimportant) insignificante

pew [pju:] n panca (di chiesa)

pewter ['pju:təʳ] n peltro

phantom ['fæntəm] n fantasma m

pharmacist ['fɑ:məsɪst] n farmacista m/f

pharmacy ['fɑ:məsɪ] n farmacia

phase [feɪz] n fase f, periodo; **phase in** vt introdurre gradualmente; **phase out** vt (machinery) eliminare gradualmente; (product) ritirare gradualmente; (job, subsidy) abolire gradualmente

PhD n abbr = **Doctor of Philosophy**

pheasant ['fɛznt] n fagiano

phenomena [fə'nɔmɪnə] npl of **phenomenon**

phenomenal [fɪ'nɔmɪnl] adj fenomenale

phenomenon (pl **phenomena**) [fə'nɔmɪnən, -nə] n fenomeno

Philippines ['fɪlɪpi:nz] npl: **the ~** le Filippine

philosopher [fɪ'lɔsəfəʳ] n filosofo/a

philosophical [fɪlə'sɔfɪkl] adj filosofico/a

philosophy [fɪ'lɔsəfɪ] n filosofia

phlegm [flɛm] n flemma

phobia ['fəʊbjə] n fobia

phone [fəʊn] n telefono ▷ vt telefonare a ▷ vi telefonare; **to be on the ~** avere il telefono; (be calling) essere al telefono; **phone back** vt, vi richiamare; **phone up** vt telefonare a ▷ vi telefonare; **phone book** n guida del telefono, elenco telefonico; **phone box**, (US) **phone booth** n cabina telefonica; **phone call** n telefonata; **phonecard** n scheda telefonica; **phone number** n numero di telefono

phonetics [fə'nɛtɪks] n fonetica

phoney ['fəʊnɪ] adj falso/a, fasullo/a

photo ['fəʊtəʊ] n foto f inv; **photo album** n (new) album m inv per fotografie; (containing photos) album m inv delle fotografie; **photocopier** n fotocopiatrice f; **photocopy** n fotocopia ▷ vt fotocopiare

photograph ['fəʊtəgræf] n fotografia ▷ vt fotografare; **photographer** [fə'tɔgrəfəʳ] n fotografo; **photography** [fə'tɔgrəfɪ] n fotografia

phrase [freɪz] n espressione f; (Ling) locuzione f; (Mus) frase f ▷ vt esprimere

phrasebook ['freɪzbʊk] n vocabolarietto

physical ['fɪzɪkl] adj fisico/a; **~ education** n educazione f fisica; **physically** adv fisicamente

physician [fɪ'zɪʃən] n medico

physicist ['fɪzɪsɪst] n fisico

physics ['fɪzɪks] n fisica

physiotherapist [fɪzɪəʊ'θɛrəpɪst] n fisioterapista m/f

physiotherapy [fɪzɪəʊ'θɛrəpɪ] n fisioterapia

physique [fɪ'zi:k] n fisico; costituzione f

pianist ['pi:ənɪst] n pianista m/f

piano [pɪ'ænəʊ] n pianoforte m

pick [pɪk] n (tool: also: **~-axe**) piccone m ▷ vt scegliere; (gather) cogliere;

(remove) togliere; (lock) far scattare; **take your** ~ scegliere; **the ~ of** il fior fiore di; **to ~ one's nose** mettersi le dita nel naso; **to ~ one's teeth** pulirsi i denti con lo stuzzicadenti; **to ~ a fight/quarrel with sb** attaccar rissa/briga con qn; **pick on** vt fus (person) avercela con; **pick out** vt scegliere; (distinguish) distinguere; **pick up** vi (improve) migliorarsi ▷ vt raccogliere; (Police) prendere; (collect) passare a prendere; (Aut: give lift to) far salire; (person: for sexual encounter) rimorchiare; (learn) imparare; (Radio, TV, Tel) ricevere; **to ~ o.s. up** rialzarsi; **to ~ up speed** acquistare velocità

pickle ['pɪkl] n (also: **~s**) (as condiment) sottaceti mpl; (fig): **in a ~** nei pasticci ▷ vt mettere sottaceto; mettere in salamoia

pickpocket ['pɪkpɔkɪt] n borsaiolo

pickup ['pɪkʌp] n (BRIT: on record player) pick-up m inv; (small truck: also: **~ truck, ~ van**) camioncino

picnic ['pɪknɪk] n picnic m inv; **picnic area** n area per il picnic

picture ['pɪktʃə'] n quadro; (painting) pittura; (photograph) foto(grafia); (drawing) disegno; (film) film m inv ▷ vt raffigurarsi; **the ~s** (BRIT) il cinema; **to take a ~ of sb/sth** fare una foto a qn/di qc; **picture frame** n cornice f inv; **picture messaging** n picture messaging m, invio di messaggini con immagini

picturesque [pɪktʃə'rɛsk] adj pittoresco/a

pie [paɪ] n torta; (of meat) pasticcio

piece [piːs] n pezzo; (of land) appezzamento; (item): **a ~ of furniture/advice** un mobile/ consiglio ▷ vt: **to ~ together** mettere insieme; **to take to ~s** smontare

pie chart n grafico a torta

pier [pɪə'] n molo; (of bridge etc) pila

pierce [pɪəs] vt forare; (with arrow etc) trafiggere; **pierced** adj: **I've got pierced ears** ho i buchi per gli orecchini

pig [pɪg] n maiale m, porco

pigeon ['pɪdʒən] n piccione m

piggy bank ['pɪgɪ-] n salvadanaio

pigsty ['pɪgstaɪ] n porcile m

pigtail ['pɪgteɪl] n treccina

pike [paɪk] n (fish) luccio

pilchard ['pɪltʃəd] n specie di sardina

pile [paɪl] n (pillar, of books) pila; (heap) mucchio; (of carpet) pelo; **to ~ into** (car) stiparsi or ammucchiarsi in; **pile up** vt ammucchiare; **piles** [paɪlz] npl emorroidi fpl; **pileup** ['paɪlʌp] n (Aut) tamponamento a catena

pilgrimage ['pɪlgrɪmɪdʒ] n pellegrinaggio

pill [pɪl] n pillola; **to be on the ~** prendere la pillola

pillar ['pɪlə'] n colonna

pillow ['pɪləu] n guanciale m; **pillowcase** n federa

pilot ['paɪlət] n pilota m/f ▷ cpd (scheme etc) pilota inv ▷ vt pilotare; **pilot light** n fiamma pilota

pimple ['pɪmpl] n foruncolo

PIN n abbr (= personal identification number) codice m segreto, PIN m inv

pin [pɪn] n spillo; (Tech) perno ▷ vt attaccare con uno spillo; **~s and needles** formicolìo; **to ~ sth on sb** (fig) addossare la colpa di qc a qn; **pin down** vt (fig): **to ~ sb down** obbligare qn a pronunziarsi

pinafore ['pɪnəfɔː'] n (also: **~ dress**) scamiciato

pinch [pɪntʃ] n pizzicotto, pizzico ▷ vt pizzicare; (col: steal) grattare; **at a ~** in caso di bisogno

pine [paɪn] n (also: **~ tree**) pino ▷ vi: **to ~ for** struggersi dal desiderio di

pineapple ['paɪnæpl] n ananas m inv

ping [pɪŋ] n (noise) tintinnio; **Ping-Pong®** ['pɪŋpɔn] n ping-pong® m

pink [pɪŋk] adj rosa inv ▷ n (colour) rosa m inv; (Bot) garofano

pinpoint ['pɪnpɔɪnt] vt indicare con precisione

pint [paɪnt] *n* pinta (*Brit* = 0.57 l; *US* = 0.47 l); (*Brit col: of beer*) ≈ birra grande

pioneer [paɪə'nɪəʳ] *n* pioniere/a

pious ['paɪəs] *adj* pio/a

pip [pɪp] *n* (*seed*) seme *m*; (*Brit*: *time signal on radio*) segnale *m* orario

pipe [paɪp] *n* tubo; (*for smoking*) pipa ▷ *vt* portare per mezzo di tubazione; **pipeline** *n* conduttura; (*for oil*) oleodotto; **piper** *n* piffero; suonatore/trice di cornamusa

pirate ['paɪərət] *n* pirata *m* ▷ *vt* riprodurre abusivamente

Pisces ['paɪsiːz] *n* Pesci *mpl*

piss [pɪs] *vi* (*col!*) pisciare; **pissed** *adj* (*Brit col: drunk*) ubriaco/a fradicio/a

pistol ['pɪstl] *n* pistola

piston ['pɪstən] *n* pistone *m*

pit [pɪt] *n* buca, fossa; (*also:* **coal ~**) miniera; (*quarry*) cava ▷ *vt:* **to ~ sb against sb** opporre qn a qn

pitch [pɪtʃ] *n* (*Mus*) tono; (*fig*) grado, punto; (*Brit Sport*) campo; (*tar*) pece *f* ▷ *vt* (*throw*) lanciare ▷ *vi* (*fall*) cascare; **to ~ a tent** piantare una tenda; **pitch-black** *adj* nero/a come la pece

pitfall ['pɪtfɔːl] *n* trappola

pith [pɪθ] *n* (*of plant*) midollo; (*of orange*) parte *f* interna della scorza; (*fig*) essenza, succo; vigore *m*

pitiful ['pɪtɪful] *adj* (*touching*) pietoso/a

pity ['pɪtɪ] *n* pietà ▷ *vt* aver pietà di; **what a ~!** che peccato!

pizza ['piːtsə] *n* pizza

placard ['plækɑːd] *n* affisso

place [pleɪs] *n* posto, luogo; (*proper position, rank, seat*) posto; (*house*) casa, alloggio; (*home*): **at/to his ~** casa sua ▷ *vt* (*object*) posare, mettere; (*identify*) riconoscere; individuare; **to take ~** aver luogo; succedere; **out of ~** (*not suitable*) inopportuno/a; **in the first ~** in primo luogo; **to change ~s with sb** scambiare il posto con qn; **to ~ an order with sb (for)** fare un'ordinazione a qn (di); **to be ~d** (*in race, exam*) classificarsi; **place mat** *n*

sottopiatto; (*in linen etc*) tovaglietta; **placement** *n* collocamento; (*job*) lavoro

placid ['plæsɪd] *adj* placido/a, calmo/a

plague [pleɪg] *n* peste *f* ▷ *vt* tormentare

plaice [pleɪs] *n* (*pl inv*) pianuzza

plain [pleɪn] *adj* (*clear*) chiaro/a, palese; (*simple*) semplice; (*frank*) franco/a, aperto/a; (*not handsome*) bruttino/a; (*without seasoning etc*) scondito/a; naturale; (*in one colour*) tinta unita *inv* ▷ *adv* francamente, chiaramente ▷ *n* pianura; **plain chocolate** *n* cioccolato fondente; **plainly** *adv* chiaramente; (*frankly*) francamente

plaintiff ['pleɪntɪf] *n* attore/trice

plait [plæt] *n* treccia

plan [plæn] *n* pianta; (*scheme*) progetto, piano ▷ *vt* (*think in advance*) progettare; (*prepare*) organizzare ▷ *vi:* **to ~ (for)** far piani *or* progetti (per); **to ~ to do** progettare di fare

plane [pleɪn] *n* (*Aviat*) aereo; (*tree*) platano; (*tool*) pialla; (*Art, Math etc*) piano ▷ *adj* piano/a, piatto/a ▷ *vt* (*with tool*) piallare

planet ['plænɪt] *n* pianeta *m*

plank [plæŋk] *n* tavola, asse *f*

planning ['plænɪŋ] *n* progettazione *f*; **family ~** pianificazione delle nascite

plant [plɑːnt] *n* pianta; (*machinery*) impianto; (*factory*) fabbrica ▷ *vt* piantare; (*bomb*) mettere

plantation [plæn'teɪʃən] *n* piantagione *f*

plaque [plæk] *n* placca

plaster ['plɑːstəʳ] *n* intonaco; (*also:* **~ of Paris**) gesso; (*Brit: also:* **sticking ~**) cerotto ▷ *vt* intonacare; ingessare; (*cover*): **to ~ with** coprire di; **plaster cast** *n* (*Med*) ingessatura, gesso; (*model, statue*) modello in gesso

plastic ['plæstɪk] *n* plastica ▷ *adj* (*made of plastic*) di *or* in plastica;

plastic bag n sacchetto di plastica;
plastic surgery n chirurgia plastica
plate [pleɪt] n (dish) piatto; (in book)
tavola; (dental plate) dentiera; **gold/
silver ~** vasellame m d'oro/d'argento
plateau (pl **plateaus** or **plateaux**)
['plætəu, -z] n altipiano
platform ['plætfɔːm] n (stage,
at meeting) palco; (BRIT: on bus)
piattaforma; (Rail) marciapiede m;
the train leaves from ~ 7 il treno
parte dal binario 7
platinum ['plætɪnəm] n platino
platoon [plə'tuːn] n plotone m
platter ['plætər] n piatto
plausible ['plɔːzɪbl] adj plausibile,
credibile; (person) convincente
play [pleɪ] n gioco; (Theat)
commedia ▷ vt (game) giocare a;
(team, opponent) giocare contro;
(instrument, piece of music) suonare;
(record, tape) ascoltare; (play, part)
interpretare ▷ vi giocare; suonare;
recitare; **to ~ safe** giocare sul
sicuro; **play back** vt riascoltare,
risentire; **play up** vi (cause trouble)
fare i capricci; **player** n giocatore/
trice; (Theat) attore/trice; (Mus)
musicista m/f; **playful** adj
giocoso/a; **playground** n (in school)
cortile m per la ricreazione; (in park)
parco m giochi inv; **playgroup** n
giardino d'infanzia; **playing card**
n carta da gioco; **playing field** n
campo sportivo; **playschool** n
= **playgroup**; **playtime** n (Scol)
ricreazione f; **playwright** n
drammaturgo/a
plc abbr (BRIT: = public limited company)
società per azioni a responsabilità
limitata quotata in borsa
plea [pliː] n (request) preghiera,
domanda; (Law) (argomento di)
difesa
plead [pliːd] vt patrocinare; (give as
excuse) addurre a pretesto ▷ vi (Law)
perorare la causa; (beg): **to ~ with sb**
implorare qn

pleasant ['plɛznt] adj piacevole,
gradevole
please [pliːz] vt piacere a ▷ vi (think
fit): **do as you ~** faccia come le pare; **~!**
per piacere!, per favore!; (acceptance):
yes, ~ sì, grazie; **~ yourself!** come
ti (or le) pare!; **pleased** adj: **pleased
(with)** contento/a (di); **pleased to
meet you!** piacere!
pleasure ['plɛʒər] n piacere m; **"it's
a ~"** "prego"
pleat [pliːt] n piega
pledge [plɛdʒ] n pegno; (promise)
promessa ▷ vt impegnare;
promettere
plentiful ['plɛntɪful] adj
abbondante, copioso/a
plenty ['plɛntɪ] n: **~ of** tanto/a,
molto/a; un'abbondanza di
pliers ['plaɪəz] npl pinza
plight [plaɪt] n situazione f critica
plod [plɔd] vi camminare a stento;
(fig) sgobbare
plonk [plɔŋk] (col) n (BRIT: wine) vino
da poco ▷ vt: **to ~ sth down** buttare
giù qc bruscamente
plot [plɔt] n congiura, cospirazione
f; (of story, play) trama; (of land)
lotto ▷ vt (mark out) fare la pianta
di; rilevare; (: diagram etc) tracciare;
(conspire) congiurare, cospirare ▷ vi
congiurare
plough, (US) **plow** [plau] n aratro
▷ vt (earth) arare; **to ~ money
into** (company etc) investire
danaro in; **ploughman**, (US)
plowman ['plaumən] n aratore m;
ploughman's lunch n (BRIT) semplice
pasto a base di pane e formaggio
plow etc [plau] (US) = **plough** etc
ploy [plɔɪ] n stratagemma m
pluck [plʌk] vt (fruit) cogliere;
(musical instrument) pizzicare;
(bird) spennare; (hairs) togliere ▷ n
coraggio, fegato; **to ~ up courage**
farsi coraggio
plug [plʌg] n tappo; (Elec) spina; (Aut:
also: **spark(ing) ~**) candela ▷ vt (hole)

P

tappare; (col: advertise) spingere; **plug in** (Elec) vt attaccare a una presa; **plughole** n (BRIT) scarico

plum [plʌm] n (fruit) susina

plumber ['plʌmə'] n idraulico

plumbing ['plʌmɪŋ] n (trade) lavoro di idraulico; (piping) tubature fpl

plummet ['plʌmɪt] vi: **to ~ (down)** cadere a piombo

plump [plʌmp] adj grassoccio/a; **plump for** vt fus (col: choose) decidersi per

plunge [plʌndʒ] n tuffo; (fig) caduta ▷ vt immergere ▷ vi (dive) tuffarsi; (fall) cadere, precipitare; **to take the ~** saltare il fosso

plural ['pluərl] adj, n plurale (m)

plus [plʌs] n (also: ~ sign) segno più ▷ prep più; **ten/twenty ~** più di dieci/venti

ply [plaɪ] n (of wool) capo ▷ vt (a trade) esercitare ▷ vi (ship) fare il servizio; **three ~ (wool)** lana a tre capi; **to ~ sb with drink** dare da bere continuamente a qn; **plywood** n legno compensato

PM n abbr = **prime minister**

p.m. adv abbr (= post meridiem) del pomeriggio

PMS n abbr (= premenstrual syndrome) sindrome f premestruale

PMT n abbr (= premenstrual tension) sindrome f premestruale

pneumatic [nju:'mætɪk] adj pneumatico/a; **~ drill** martello pneumatico

pneumonia [nju:'məunɪə] n polmonite f

poach [pəutʃ] vt (cook: egg) affogare; (: fish) cuocere in bianco; (steal) cacciare (or pescare) di frodo ▷ vi fare il bracconiere; **poached** adj (egg) affogato/a

PO box n abbr = **post office box**

pocket ['pɔkɪt] n tasca ▷ vt intascare; **to be out of ~** (BRIT) rimetterci; **pocketbook** n (US:

wallet) portafoglio; **pocket money** n paghetta, settimana

pod [pɔd] n guscio

podcast ['pɔdkɑːst] n podcast m inv

podiatrist [pɔ'di:ətrɪst] n (US) callista m/f, pedicure m/f

podium ['pəudɪəm] n podio

poem ['pəuɪm] n poesia

poet ['pəuɪt] n poeta/essa; **poetic** [pəu'ɛtɪk] adj poetico/a; **poetry** n poesia

poignant ['pɔɪnjənt] adj struggente

point [pɔɪnt] n (gen) punto; (tip: of needle etc) punta; (Elec) presa (di corrente); (in time) punto, momento; (Scol) voto; (main idea, important part) nocciolo; (also: **decimal ~**): **2 ~ 3 (2.3)** 2 virgola 3 (2,3) ▷ vt (show) indicare; (gun etc): **to ~ sth at** puntare qc contro ▷ vi: **to ~ at** mostrare a dito; **points** npl (Aut) puntine fpl; (Rail) scambio; **to make a ~** fare un'osservazione; **to get/miss the ~** capire/non capire; **to come to the ~** venire al fatto; **to be on the ~ of doing sth** essere sul punto di or stare (proprio) per fare qc; **there's no ~ (in doing)** è inutile (fare); **~ of view** punto di vista; **point out** vt far notare; **point-blank** adv (also: **at point-blank range**) a bruciapelo; (fig) categoricamente; **pointed** adj (shape) aguzzo/a, appuntito/a; (remark) specifico/a; **pointer** n (needle) lancetta; (clue) indicazione f; (advice) consiglio; **pointless** adj inutile, vano/a

poison ['pɔɪzn] n veleno ▷ vt avvelenare; **poisonous** adj velenoso/a

poke [pəuk] vt (fire) attizzare; (jab with finger, stick etc) punzecchiare; (put): **to ~ sth in(to)** spingere qc dentro; **poke about, poke around** vi frugare; **poke out** vi (stick out) sporger fuori

poker ['pəukə'] n attizzatoio; (Cards) poker m

Poland ['pəulənd] n Polonia

polar ['pəulə'] adj polare; **polar bear** n orso bianco

Pole [pəul] n polacco/a

pole [pəul] n (of wood) palo; (Elec, Geo) polo; **pole bean** n (US: runner bean) fagiolino; **pole vault** n salto con l'asta

police [pə'li:s] n polizia ▷ vt mantenere l'ordine in; **police car** n macchina della polizia; **police constable** n (BRIT) agente m di polizia; **police force** n corpo di polizia, polizia; **policeman** n (irreg) poliziotto, agente m di polizia; **police officer** n = **police constable**; **police station** n posto di polizia; **policewoman** n (irreg) donna f poliziotto inv

policy ['pɔlɪsɪ] n politica; (also: **insurance ~**) polizza (d'assicurazione)

polio ['pəulɪəu] n polio f

Polish ['pəulɪʃ] adj polacco/a ▷ n (Ling) polacco

polish ['pɔlɪʃ] n (for shoes) lucido; (for floor) cera; (for nails) smalto; (shine) lucentezza, lustro; (fig: refinement) raffinatezza ▷ vt lucidare; (fig: improve) raffinare; **polish off** vt (food) mangiarsi; **polished** adj (fig) raffinato/a

polite [pə'laɪt] adj cortese; **politeness** n cortesia

political [pə'lɪtɪkl] adj politico/a; **politically** adv politicamente; **politically correct** adj politicamente corretto/a

politician [pɔlɪ'tɪʃən] n politico

politics ['pɔlɪtɪks] n politica ▷ npl (views, policies) idee fpl politiche

poll [pəul] n scrutinio; (votes cast) voti mpl; (also: **opinion ~**) sondaggio (d'opinioni) ▷ vt ottenere

pollen ['pɔlən] n polline m

polling station ['pəulɪŋ-] n (BRIT) sezione f elettorale

pollute [pə'lu:t] vt inquinare

pollution [pə'lu:ʃən] n inquinamento

polo ['pəuləu] n polo; **polo neck** n collo alto; (also: **polo neck sweater**) dolcevita ▷ adj a collo alto; **polo shirt** n polo f inv

polyester [pɔlɪ'ɛstə'] n poliestere m

polystyrene [pɔlɪ'staɪri:n] n polistirolo

polythene ['pɔlɪθi:n] n politene m; **polythene bag** n sacchetto di plastica

pomegranate ['pɔmɪgrænɪt] n melagrana

pompous ['pɔmpəs] adj pomposo/a

pond [pɔnd] n pozza; stagno

ponder ['pɔndə'] vt ponderare, riflettere su

pony ['pəunɪ] n pony m inv; **ponytail** n coda di cavallo; **pony trekking** [-trɛkɪŋ] n (BRIT) escursione f a cavallo

poodle ['pu:dl] n barboncino, barbone m

pool [pu:l] n (of rain) pozza; (pond) stagno; (also: **swimming ~**) piscina; (fig: of light) cerchio; (billiards) specie di biliardo a buca ▷ vt mettere in comune; **typing ~** servizio comune di dattilografia; **to do the (football) ~s** ≈ giocare al totocalcio

poor [puə'] adj povero/a; (mediocre) mediocre, cattivo/a ▷ npl: **the ~** i poveri; **~ in** povero/a di; **poorly** adv poveramente; (badly) male ▷ adj indisposto/a, malato/a

pop [pɔp] n (noise) schiocco; (Mus) musica pop; (US col: father) babbo; (col: drink) bevanda gasata ▷ vt (put) mettere (in fretta) ▷ vi scoppiare; (cork) schioccare; **pop in** vi passare; **pop out** vi fare un salto fuori; **popcorn** n pop-corn m

poplar ['pɔplə'] n pioppo

popper ['pɔpə'] n bottone m a pressione

poppy ['pɔpɪ] n papavero

Popsicle® ['popsɪkl] n (US: ice lolly) ghiacciolo

pop star n pop star f inv

popular ['pɒpjuləʳ] adj popolare; (fashionable) in voga; **popularity** [pɒpju'lærɪtɪ] n popolarità

population [pɒpju'leɪʃən] n popolazione f

pop-up adj (Comput: menu, window) a comparsa

porcelain ['pɔːslɪn] n porcellana

porch [pɔːtʃ] n veranda

pore [pɔːʳ] n poro ▷ vi: **to ~ over** essere immerso/a in

pork [pɔːk] n carne f di maiale; **pork chop** n braciola or costoletta di maiale; **pork pie** n (BRIT Culin) pasticcio di maiale in crosta

porn [pɔːn] (col) n pornografia ▷ adj porno inv; **pornographic** [pɔːnə'græfɪk] adj pornografico/a; **pornography** [pɔː'nɔgrəfɪ] n pornografia

porridge ['pɒrɪdʒ] n porridge m

port¹ [pɔːt] n porto; (Naut: left side) babordo; **~ of call** (porto di) scalo

port² [pɔːt] n (wine) porto

portable ['pɔːtəbl] adj portatile

porter ['pɔːtəʳ] n (for luggage) facchino, portabagagli m inv; (doorkeeper) portiere m, portinaio

portfolio [pɔːt'fəulɪəu] n (case) cartella; (Pol, Econ) portafoglio; (of artist) raccolta dei propri lavori

portion ['pɔːʃən] n porzione f

portrait ['pɔːtreɪt] n ritratto

portray [pɔː'treɪ] vt fare il ritratto di; (character on stage) rappresentare; (in writing) ritrarre

Portugal ['pɔːtjugl] n Portogallo

Portuguese [pɔːtju'giːz] adj portoghese ▷ n (pl inv) portoghese m/f; (Ling) portoghese m

pose [pəuz] n posa ▷ vi posare; (pretend): **to ~ as** atteggiarsi a, posare a ▷ vt porre

posh [pɒʃ] adj (col) elegante; (family) per bene

position [pə'zɪʃən] n posizione f; (job) posto ▷ vt sistemare

positive ['pɒzɪtɪv] adj positivo/a; (certain) sicuro/a, certo/a; (definite) preciso/a; definitivo/a; **positively** adv (affirmatively, enthusiastically) positivamente; (decisively) decisamente; (really) assolutamente

possess [pə'zɛs] vt possedere; **possession** [pə'zɛʃən] n possesso; **possessions** npl (belongings) beni mpl; **possessive** adj possessivo/a

possibility [pɒsɪ'bɪlɪtɪ] n possibilità f inv

possible ['pɒsɪbl] adj possibile; **as big as ~** il più grande possibile; **possibly** adv (perhaps) forse; **if you possibly can** se le è possibile; **I cannot possibly come** proprio non posso venire

post [pəust] n (BRIT) posta; (: collection) levata; (job, situation) posto; (Mil) postazione f; (pole) palo; (on blog, social network) post m inv, commento ▷ vt (BRIT: send by post) impostare; (Mil) appostare; (notice) affiggere; (to internet: video) caricare; (: comment) mandare; (BRIT: appoint): **to ~ to** assegnare a; **postage** n affrancatura; **postal** adj postale; **postal order** n vaglia m inv postale; **postbox** (BRIT) n cassetta delle lettere; **postcard** n cartolina; **postcode** n (BRIT) codice m (di avviamento) postale

poster ['pəustəʳ] n manifesto, affisso

postgraduate ['pəust'grædjuət] n laureato/a che continua gli studi

postman ['pəustmən] n (irreg) postino

postmark ['pəustmɑːk] n bollo or timbro postale

post-mortem [pəust'mɔːtəm] n autopsia

post office n (building) ufficio postale; **the Post Office** ≈ le Poste e Telecomunicazioni

postpone [pəust'pəun] vt rinviare

posture ['pɒstʃə^r] n portamento; (pose) posa, atteggiamento

postwoman ['pəustwumən] (BRIT: irreg) n postina

pot [pɒt] n (for cooking) pentola; casseruola; (teapot) teiera; (coffeepot) caffettiera; (for plants, jam) vaso; (col: marijuana) erba ▷ vt (plant) piantare in vaso; **a ~ of tea for two** tè per due; **to go to ~** (col: work, performance) andare in malora

potato [pə'teɪtəu] (pl **potatoes**) n patata; **potato peeler** n sbucciapatate m inv

potent ['pəutnt] adj potente, forte

potential [pə'tɛnʃl] adj potenziale ▷ n possibilità fpl

pothole ['pɒthəul] n (in road) buca; (BRIT: underground) caverna

pot plant n pianta in vaso

potter ['pɒtə^r] n vasaio ▷ vi (BRIT: to **~ around, ~ about** lavoracchiare; **pottery** n ceramiche fpl; (factory) fabbrica di ceramiche

potty ['pɒtɪ] adj (col: mad) tocco/a ▷ n (child's) vasino

pouch [pautʃ] n borsa; (Zool) marsupio

poultry ['pəultrɪ] n pollame m

pounce [pauns] vi: **to ~ (on)** piombare (su)

pound [paund] n (weight) libbra; (money) (lira) sterlina ▷ vt (beat) battere; (crush) pestare, polverizzare ▷ vi (beat) battere, martellare; **pound sterling** n lira sterlina

pour [pɔː^r] vt versare ▷ vi riversarsi; (rain) piovere a dirotto; **pour in** vi affluire in gran quantità; **pour out** vi (people) riversarsi fuori ▷ vt vuotare; versare; (fig) sfogare; **pouring** adj: **pouring rain** pioggia torrenziale

pout [paut] vi sporgere le labbra; fare il broncio

poverty ['pɒvətɪ] n povertà, miseria

powder ['paudə^r] n polvere f ▷ vt: **~ed milk** latte m in polvere; **to ~ one's nose** incipriarsi il naso

power ['pauə^r] n (strength) potenza, forza; (ability, Pol: of party, leader) potere m; (Elec) corrente f; **to be in ~** essere al potere; **power cut** n (BRIT) interruzione f or mancanza di corrente; **power failure** n interruzione f della corrente elettrica; **powerful** adj potente, forte; **powerless** adj impotente; **powerless to do** impossibilitato/a a fare; **power point** n (BRIT) presa di corrente; **power station** n centrale f elettrica

pp abbr (= pages) pp; (= per procurationem): **pp J. Smith** per il Signor J. Smith

PR n abbr = **public relations**

practical ['præktɪkl] adj pratico/a; **practical joke** n beffa; **practically** adv praticamente

practice ['præktɪs] n pratica; (of profession) esercizio; (at football etc) allenamento; (business) gabinetto; clientela ▷ vt, vi (US) = **practise**; **in ~** (in reality) in pratica; **out of ~** fuori esercizio

practise, (US) **practice** ['præktɪs] vt (work at: piano, one's backhand etc) esercitarsi a; (train for: skiing, running etc) allenarsi a; (a sport, religion) praticare; (method) usare; (profession) esercitare ▷ vi esercitarsi; (train) allenarsi; (lawyer, doctor) esercitare; **practising** adj (Christian etc) praticante; (lawyer) che esercita la professione

practitioner [præk'tɪʃənə^r] n professionista m/f

pragmatic [præg'mætɪk] adj pragmatico/a

prairie ['prɛərɪ] n prateria

praise [preɪz] n elogio, lode f ▷ vt elogiare, lodare

pram [præm] n (BRIT) carrozzina

prank [præŋk] n burla

prawn [prɔːn] n gamberetto; **prawn cocktail** n cocktail m inv di gamberetti

pray [preɪ] *vi* pregare; **prayer** [prɛər] *n* preghiera

preach [pri:tʃ] *vt, vi* predicare; **preacher** *n* predicatore/trice; (*us: minister*) pastore *m*

precarious [prɪ'kɛərɪəs] *adj* precario/a

precaution [prɪ'kɔ:ʃən] *n* precauzione *f*

precede [prɪ'si:d] *vt* precedere; **precedent** ['prɛsɪdənt] *n* precedente *m*; **preceding** [prɪ'si:dɪŋ] *adj* precedente

precinct ['pri:sɪŋkt] *n* (*us*) circoscrizione *f*

precious ['prɛʃəs] *adj* prezioso/a

precise [prɪ'saɪs] *adj* preciso/a; **precisely** *adv* precisamente

precision [prɪ'sɪʒən] *n* precisione *f*

predator ['prɛdətər] *n* predatore *m*

predecessor ['pri:dɪsɛsər] *n* predecessore/a

predicament [prɪ'dɪkəmənt] *n* situazione *f* difficile

predict [prɪ'dɪkt] *vt* predire; **predictable** *adj* prevedibile; **prediction** [prɪ'dɪkʃən] *n* predizione *f*

predominantly [prɪ'dɔmɪnəntlɪ] *adv* in maggior parte; soprattutto

preface ['prɛfəs] *n* prefazione *f*

prefect ['pri:fɛkt] *n* (BRIT: *in school*) studente/essa con funzioni disciplinari; (*Admin: in Italy*) prefetto

prefer [prɪ'fə:r] *vt* preferire; **to ~ doing** *or* **to do** preferire fare; **preferable** ['prɛfrəbl] *adj* preferibile; **preferably** ['prɛfrəblɪ] *adv* preferibilmente; **preference** ['prɛfrəns] *n* preferenza

prefix ['pri:fɪks] *n* prefisso

pregnancy ['prɛgnənsɪ] *n* gravidanza

pregnant ['prɛgnənt] *adj* incinta *adj f*

prehistoric ['pri:hɪs'tɔrɪk] *adj* preistorico/a

prejudice ['prɛdʒudɪs] *n* pregiudizio; (*harm*) torto, danno; **prejudiced**

adj (*view*) prevenuto/a; **to be prejudiced against sb/sth** essere prevenuto contro qn/qc; **prejudiced (in favour of)** ben disposto/a (verso)

preliminary [prɪ'lɪmɪnərɪ] *adj* preliminare

prelude ['prɛlju:d] *n* preludio

premature ['prɛmətʃuər] *adj* prematuro/a

premier ['prɛmɪər] *adj* primo/a ▷ *n* (*Pol*) primo ministro

première ['prɛmɪɛər] *n* prima

Premier League *n* ≈ serie A

premises ['prɛmɪsɪz] *npl* locale *m*; **on the ~** sul posto; **business ~** locali commerciali

premium ['pri:mɪəm] *n* premio; **to be at a ~** essere ricercatissimo

premonition [prɛmə'nɪʃən] *n* premonizione *f*

preoccupied [prɪ'ɔkjupaɪd] *adj* preoccupato/a

prepaid [pri:'peɪd] *adj* pagato/a in anticipo

preparation [prɛpə'reɪʃən] *n* preparazione *f*; **preparations** *npl* (*for trip, war*) preparativi *mpl*

preparatory school [prɪ'pærətərɪ-] *n* scuola elementare privata

prepare [prɪ'pɛər] *vt* preparare ▷ *vi*: **to ~ for** prepararsi a; **prepared** *adj*: **prepared to** pronto/a a

preposition [prɛpə'zɪʃən] *n* preposizione *f*

prep school ['prɛp-] *n* = **preparatory school**

preschool ['pri:'sku:l] *adj* (*age*) prescolastico/a; (*child*) in età prescolastica

prescribe [prɪ'skraɪb] *vt* (*Med*) prescrivere

prescription [prɪ'skrɪpʃən] *n* prescrizione *f*; (*Med*) ricetta

presence ['prɛzns] *n* presenza; **~ of mind** presenza di spirito

present ['prɛznt] *adj* presente; (*wife, residence, job*) attuale ▷ *n* (*gift*) regalo; **the ~** il presente ▷ *vt* [prɪ'zɛnt] presentare; (*give*): **to ~ sb with sth** offrire qc a qn; **at ~** al momento; **to give sb a ~** fare un regalo a qn; **presentable** [prɪ'zɛntəbl] *adj* presentabile; **presentation** [prɛzn'teɪʃən] *n* presentazione *f*; (*ceremony*) consegna ufficiale; **present-day** *adj* attuale, d'oggigiorno; **presenter** *n* (*Radio, TV*) presentatore/trice; **presently** *adv* (*soon*) fra poco, presto; (*at present*) al momento; **present participle** *n* participio presente

preservation [prɛzə'veɪʃən] *n* preservazione *f*, conservazione *f*

preservative [prɪ'zə:vətɪv] *n* conservante *m*

preserve [prɪ'zə:v] *vt* (*keep safe*) preservare, proteggere; (*maintain*) conservare; (*food*) mettere in conserva ▷ *n* (*often pl: jam*) marmellata; (: *fruit*) frutta sciroppata

preside [prɪ'zaɪd] *vi*: **to ~ (over)** presiedere (a)

president ['prɛzɪdənt] *n* presidente *m*; **presidential** [prɛzɪ'dɛnʃl] *adj* presidenziale

press [prɛs] *n* (*tool, machine*) pressa; (*for wine*) torchio; (*newspapers*) stampa ▷ *vt* (*push*) premere, pigiare; (*squeeze*) spremere; (: *hand*) stringere; (*clothes: iron*) stirare; (*pursue*) incalzare; (*insist*): **to ~ sth on sb** far accettare qc da qn ▷ *vi* premere; accalcare; **we are ~ed for time** ci manca il tempo; **to ~ for sth** insistere per avere qc; **press conference** *n* conferenza stampa; **pressing** *adj* urgente; **press stud** *n* (BRIT) bottone *m* a pressione; **press-up** *n* (BRIT) flessione *f* sulle braccia

pressure ['prɛʃə'] *n* pressione *f* ▷ *vt*: **to put ~ on sb (to do)** mettere qn sotto pressione (affinché faccia); **pressure cooker** *n* pentola a

pressione; **pressure group** *n* gruppo di pressione

prestige [prɛs'ti:ʒ] *n* prestigio

prestigious [prɛs'tɪdʒəs] *adj* prestigioso/a

presumably [prɪ'zju:məblɪ] *adv* presumibilmente

presume [prɪ'zju:m] *vt* supporre

pretence, (US) **pretense** [prɪ'tɛns] *n* (*claim*) pretesa; **to make a ~ of doing** far finta di fare; **under false ~s** con l'inganno

pretend [prɪ'tɛnd] *vt* (*feign*) fingere ▷ *vi* far finta; **to ~ to do** far finta di fare

pretense [prɪ'tɛns] *n* (US) = **pretence**

pretentious [prɪ'tɛnʃəs] *adj* pretenzioso/a

pretext ['pri:tɛkst] *n* pretesto

pretty ['prɪtɪ] *adj* grazioso/a, carino/a ▷ *adv* abbastanza, assai

prevail [prɪ'veɪl] *vi* (*win, be usual*) prevalere; (*persuade*): **to ~ (up) on sb to do** persuadere qn a fare; **prevailing** *adj* dominante

prevalent ['prɛvələnt] *adj* (*belief*) predominante; (*customs*) diffuso/a; (*fashion*) corrente; (*disease*) comune

prevent [prɪ'vɛnt] *vt*: **to ~ sb from doing** impedire a qn di fare; **to ~ sth from happening** impedire che qc succeda; **prevention** [prɪ'vɛnʃən] *n* prevenzione *f*; **preventive** *adj* preventivo/a

preview ['pri:vju:] *n* (*of film*) anteprima

previous ['pri:vɪəs] *adj* precedente; anteriore; **previously** *adv* prima

prey [preɪ] *n* preda ▷ *vi*: **to ~ on** far preda di; **it was ~ing on his mind** lo stava ossessionando

price [praɪs] *n* prezzo ▷ *vt* (*goods*) fissare il prezzo di; valutare; **priceless** *adj* di valore inestimabile; **price list** *n* listino (dei) prezzi

prick [prɪk] *n* puntura ▷ *vt* pungere; **to ~ up one's ears** drizzare gli orecchi

prickly ['prɪklɪ] adj spinoso/a

pride [praɪd] n orgoglio; superbia
▷ vt: **to ~ o.s. on** essere orgoglioso/a
di; vantarsi di

priest [priːst] n prete m, sacerdote m

primarily ['praɪmərɪlɪ] adv
principalmente, essenzialmente

primary ['praɪmərɪ] adj primario/a;
(first in importance) primo/a ▷ n (US:
election) primarie fpl; **primary school**
n (BRIT) scuola elementare

prime [praɪm] adj primario/a,
fondamentale; (excellent) di prima
qualità ▷ n: **in the ~ of life** nel fiore
della vita ▷ vt (wood) preparare; (fig)
mettere al corrente; **prime minister**
n primo ministro

primitive ['prɪmɪtɪv] adj
primitivo/a

primrose ['prɪmrəuz] n primavera

prince [prɪns] n principe m

princess [prɪn'sɛs] n principessa

principal ['prɪnsɪpl] adj principale
▷ n (of school, college etc) preside m/f;
principally adv principalmente

principle ['prɪnsɪpl] n principio;
in ~ in linea di principio; **on ~** per
principio

print [prɪnt] n (mark) impronta;
(letters) caratteri mpl; (fabric) tessuto
stampato; (Art, Phot) stampa ▷ vt
imprimere; (publish) stampare,
pubblicare; (write in capitals) scrivere
in stampatello; **out of ~** esaurito/a;
print out vt (Comput) stampare;
printer n tipografo/a; (machine)
stampante f; **print-out** n tabulato

prior ['praɪə'] adj precedente; (claim
etc) più importante; **~ to doing**
prima di fare

priority [praɪ'ɒrɪtɪ] n priorità f inv;
precedenza

prison ['prɪzn] n prigione f ▷ cpd
(system) carcerario/a; (conditions,
food) nelle or delle prigioni; **prisoner**
n prigioniero/a; **prisoner of war**
prigioniero/a di guerra

pristine ['prɪstiːn] adj originario/a

privacy ['prɪvəsɪ] n solitudine f,
intimità

private ['praɪvɪt] adj privato/a;
personale ▷ n soldato semplice; **"~"**
(on envelope) "riservata"; (on door)
"privato"; **in ~** in privato; **privately**
adv in privato; (within o.s.) dentro di
sé; **private property** n proprietà
privata; **private school** n scuola
privata

privatize ['praɪvɪtaɪz] vt
privatizzare

privilege ['prɪvɪlɪdʒ] n privilegio

prize [praɪz] n premio ▷ adj
(example, idiot) perfetto/a;
(bull, novel) premiato/a ▷ vt
apprezzare, pregiare; **prize giving**
n premiazione f; **prizewinner** n
premiato/a

pro [prəu] n (Sport) professionista
m/f ▷ prep pro; **the ~s and cons** il
pro e il contro

probability [prɒbə'bɪlɪtɪ] n
probabilità f inv; **in all ~** con ogni
probabilità

probable ['prɒbəbl] adj probabile

probably ['prɒbəblɪ] adv
probabilmente

probation [prə'beɪʃən] n: **on ~**
(employee) in prova; (Law) in libertà
vigilata

probe [prəub] n (Med, Space) sonda;
(enquiry) indagine f, investigazione f
▷ vt sondare, esplorare; indagare

problem ['prɒbləm] n problema m

procedure [prə'siːdʒə'] n (Admin,
Law) procedura; (method) metodo,
procedimento

proceed [prə'siːd] vi (go forward)
avanzare, andare avanti; (go about
it) procedere; (continue): **to ~ (with)**
continuare; **to ~ to** andare a;
passare a; **to ~ to do** mettersi a fare;
proceedings npl misure fpl; (Law)
procedimento; (meeting) riunione
f; (records) rendiconti mpl; atti mpl;
proceeds ['prəusiːdz] npl profitto,
incasso

process ['prəʊsɛs] n processo; (method) metodo, sistema m ▷ vt trattare; (information) elaborare

procession [prə'sɛʃən] n processione f, corteo; **funeral ~** corteo funebre

proclaim [prə'kleɪm] vt proclamare, dichiarare

prod [prɒd] vt dare un colpetto a; pungolare ▷ n colpetto

produce n ['prɒdjuːs] (Agr) prodotto, prodotti mpl ◁ vt [prə'djuːs] produrre; (show) esibire, mostrare; (cause) cagionare, causare; **producer** n (Theat, Cine, Agr) produttore m

product ['prɒdʌkt] n prodotto; **production** [prə'dʌkʃən] n produzione f; **productive** [prə'dʌktɪv] adj produttivo/a; **productivity** [prɒdʌk'tɪvɪtɪ] n produttività

Prof. abbr (= professor) Prof.

profession [prə'fɛʃən] n professione f; **professional** n professionista m/f ◁ adj professionale; (work) da professionista

professor [prə'fɛsər] n professore m (titolare di una cattedra); (US) professore/essa

profile ['prəʊfaɪl] n profilo

profit ['prɒfɪt] n profitto; beneficio ▷ vi: **to ~ (by or from)** approfittare (di); **profitable** adj redditizio/a

profound [prə'faʊnd] adj profondo/a

programme, (US) **program** ['prəʊgræm] n programma m ▷ vt programmare; **programmer**, (US) **programer** n programmatore/trice; **programming**, (US) **programing** n programmazione f

progress n ['prəʊgrɛs] progresso ▷ vi [prə'grɛs] avanzare, procedere; (also: **make ~**) far progressi; **in ~** in corso; **progressive** [prə'grɛsɪv] adj progressivo/a; (person) progressista

prohibit [prə'hɪbɪt] vt proibire, vietare

project n ['prɒdʒɛkt] (plan) piano; (venture) progetto; (Scol) studio ▷ vt [prə'dʒɛkt] proiettare ▷ vi (stick out) sporgere; **projection** [prə'dʒɛkʃən] n proiezione f; sporgenza; **projector** [prə'dʒɛktər] n proiettore m

prolific [prə'lɪfɪk] adj (artist etc) fecondo/a

prolong [prə'lɒŋ] vt prolungare

prom [prɒm] n abbr = **promenade**; **promenade concert**; (US: ball) ballo studentesco

○ **PROM**

○
○ In Gran Bretagna i Proms (=
○ promenade concerts) sono concerti
○ di musica classica, i più noti dei
○ quali sono quelli eseguiti nella
○ Royal Albert Hall a Londra.
○ Prendono il nome dal fatto che
○ in origine il pubblico li ascoltava
○ stando in piedi o passeggiando.
○ Negli Stati Uniti, invece, con prom
○ si intende il ballo studentesco di
○ un'università o di un college.

promenade [prɒmə'nɑːd] n (by sea) lungomare m

prominent ['prɒmɪnənt] adj (standing out) prominente; (important) importante

promiscuous [prə'mɪskjuəs] adj (sexually) di facili costumi

promise ['prɒmɪs] n promessa ▷ vt, vi promettere; **to ~ sb sth, to ~ sth to sb** promettere qc a qn; **to ~ (sb) that/to do sth** promettere (a qn) che/di fare qc; **promising** adj promettente

promote [prə'məʊt] vt promuovere; (venture, event) organizzare; **promotion** [prə'məʊʃən] n promozione f

prompt [prɒmpt] adj rapido/a, svelto/a; puntuale; (reply) sollecito/a ▷ adv (punctually) in punto ▷ n (Comput) prompt m inv ▷ vt incitare;

p

provocare; (*Theat*) suggerire a; **to ~ sb to do** spingere qn a fare; **promptly** *adv* prontamente; puntualmente

prone [prəun] *adj* (*lying*) prono/a; **~ to** propenso/a a, incline a

prong [prɔŋ] *n* rebbio, punta

pronoun ['prəunaun] *n* pronome *m*

pronounce [prə'nauns] *vt* pronunciare; **how do you ~ it?** come si pronuncia?

pronunciation [prənʌnsı'eıʃən] *n* pronuncia

proof [pru:f] *n* prova; (*of book*) bozza; (*Phot*) provino ▷ *adj*: **~ against** a prova di

prop [prɔp] *n* sostegno, appoggio ▷ *vt* (*also*: **~ up**) sostenere, appoggiare; (*lean*): **to ~ sth against** appoggiare qc contro *or* a; **props** oggetti *m inv* di scena

propaganda [prɔpə'gændə] *n* propaganda

propeller [prə'pelər] *n* elica

proper ['prɔpər] *adj* (*suited, right*) adatto/a, appropriato/a; (*seemly*) decente; (*authentic*) vero/a; (*col: real*) vero/a e proprio/a; **properly** ['prɔpəlı] *adv* (*eat, study*) bene; (*behave*) come si deve; **proper noun** *n* nome *m* proprio

property ['prɔpətı] *n* (*things owned*) beni *mpl*; (*land, building, Chem etc, quality*) proprietà *f inv*

prophecy ['prɔfısı] *n* profezia

prophet ['prɔfıt] *n* profeta *m*

proportion [prə'pɔ:ʃən] *n* proporzione *f*; (*share*) parte *f*; **proportions** *npl* (*size*) proporzioni *fpl*; **proportional** *adj* proporzionale

proposal [prə'pəuzl] *n* proposta; (*plan*) progetto; (*of marriage*) proposta di matrimonio

propose [prə'pəuz] *vt* proporre, suggerire ▷ *vi* fare una proposta di matrimonio; **to ~ to do** proporsi di fare, aver l'intenzione di fare

proposition [prɔpə'zıʃən] *n* proposizione *f*; (*proposal*) proposta

proprietor [prə'praıətər] *n* proprietario/a

prose [prəuz] *n* prosa

prosecute ['prɔsıkju:t] *vt* (*Law*) perseguire; **prosecution** [prɔsı'kju:ʃən] *n* (*accusing side*) accusa; **prosecutor** *n* (*also*: **public prosecutor**) ≈ procuratore *m* della Repubblica

prospect *n* ['prɔspekt] prospettiva; (*hope*) speranza ▷ *vt* [prə'spekt] esplorare ▷ *vi*: **to ~ for gold** cercare l'oro; **prospective** [prə'spektıv] *adj* (*legislation, son-in-law*) futuro/a; **prospects** ['prɔspekts] *npl* (*for work etc*) prospettive *fpl*

prospectus [prə'spektəs] *n* prospetto, programma *m*

prosper ['prɔspər] *vi* prosperare; **prosperity** [prɔ'sperıtı] *n* prosperità; **prosperous** *adj* prospero/a

prostitute ['prɔstıtju:t] *n* prostituta; **male ~** uomo che si prostituisce

protect [prə'tekt] *vt* proteggere, salvaguardare; **protection** *n* protezione *f*; **protective** *adj* protettivo/a

protein ['prəuti:n] *n* proteina

protest *n* ['prəutest] protesta ▷ *vt, vi* [prə'test] protestare

Protestant ['prɔtıstənt] *adj, n* protestante (*m/f*)

protester [prə'testər] *n* dimostrante *m/f*

protractor [prə'træktər] *n* (*Geom*) goniometro

proud [praud] *adj* fiero/a, orglioso/a; (*pej*) superbo/a

prove [pru:v] *vt* provare, dimostrare ▷ *vi*: **to ~ (to be) correct** *etc* risultare vero/a *etc*; **to ~ o.s.** mostrare le proprie capacità

proverb ['prɔvə:b] *n* proverbio

provide [prə'vaıd] *vt* fornire, provvedere; **to ~ sb with sth** fornire *or* provvedere qn di qc; **provide for**

vt fus provvedere a; *(future event)* prevedere; **provided** *conj*: **provided (that)** purché + *sub*, a condizione che + *sub*; **providing** [prə'vaɪdɪŋ] *conj* purché + *sub*, a condizione che + *sub*

province ['prɒvɪns] *n* provincia; **provincial** [prə'vɪnʃəl] *adj* provinciale

provision [prə'vɪʒən] *n (supply)* riserva; *(supplying)* provvista; rifornimento; *(stipulation)* condizione *f*; **provisions** *npl (food)* provviste *fpl*; **provisional** *adj* provvisorio/a

provocative [prə'vɒkətɪv] *adj (aggressive)* provocatorio/a; *(thought-provoking)* stimolante; *(seductive)* provocante

provoke [prə'vəʊk] *vt* provocare; incitare

prowl [praʊl] *vi (also:* **~ about, ~ around)** aggirarsi furtivamente ▷ *n*: **on the ~** in caccia

proximity [prɒk'sɪmɪtɪ] *n* prossimità

proxy ['prɒksɪ] *n*: **by ~** per procura

prudent ['pruːdnt] *adj* prudente

prune [pruːn] *n* prugna secca ▷ *vt* potare

pry [praɪ] *vi*: **to ~ into** ficcare il naso in

PS *n abbr (= postscript)* P.S.

pseudonym ['sjuːdənɪm] *n* pseudonimo

psychiatric [saɪkɪ'ætrɪk] *adj* psichiatrico/a

psychiatrist [saɪ'kaɪətrɪst] *n* psichiatra *m/f*

psychic ['saɪkɪk] *adj (also:* **~al)** psichico/a; *(person)* dotato/a di qualità telepatiche

psychoanalysis *(pl* **-ses)** [saɪkəʊə'nælɪsɪs, -siːz] *n* psicanalisi *f inv*

psychological [saɪkə'lɒdʒɪkl] *adj* psicologico/a

psychologist [saɪ'kɒlədʒɪst] *n* psicologo/a

psychology [saɪ'kɒlədʒɪ] *n* psicologia

psychotherapy [saɪkəʊ'θɛrəpɪ] *n* psicoterapia

pt *abbr* = **pint**; *(= point)* pt

PTO *abbr (= please turn over)* v.r.

pub [pʌb] *n abbr (= public house)* pub *m inv*

puberty ['pjuːbətɪ] *n* pubertà

public ['pʌblɪk] *adj* pubblico/a ▷ *n* pubblico; **in ~** in pubblico

publication [pʌblɪ'keɪʃən] *n* pubblicazione *f*

public: public company *n* ≈ società *f inv* per azioni *(costituita tramite pubblica sottoscrizione)*; **public convenience** *n (BRIT)* gabinetti *mpl*; **public holiday** *n (BRIT)* giorno festivo, festa nazionale; **public house** *n (BRIT)* pub *m inv*

publicity [pʌb'lɪsɪtɪ] *n* pubblicità

publicize ['pʌblɪsaɪz] *vt* rendere pubblico/a

public: public limited company *n* ≈ società per azioni a responsabilità limitata *(quotata in Borsa)*; **publicly** ['pʌblɪklɪ] *adv* pubblicamente; **public opinion** *n* opinione *f* pubblica; **public relations** *n* pubbliche relazioni *fpl*; **public school** *n (BRIT)* scuola privata; *(US)* scuola statale; **public transport** *n* mezzi *mpl* pubblici

publish ['pʌblɪʃ] *vt* pubblicare; **publisher** *n* editore *m*; **publishing** *n (industry)* editoria; *(of a book)* pubblicazione *f*

pub lunch *n*: **to go for a ~** andare a mangiare al pub

pudding ['pʊdɪŋ] *n* budino; *(BRIT: dessert)* dolce *m*; **black ~,** *(US)* **blood ~** sanguinaccio

puddle ['pʌdl] *n* pozza, pozzanghera

Puerto Rico ['pwɛːtəʊ'riːkəʊ] *n* Portorico

puff [pʌf] *n* sbuffo ▷ *vi (pant)* ansare; **to ~ one's pipe** tirare sboccate di fumo; **puff pastry** *n* pasta sfoglia

pull [pʊl] *n (tug)* strattone *m* ▷ *vt* tirare; *(muscle)* strappare; *(trigger)*

P

premere ▷ *vi* tirare; **to give sth a ~** tirare su qc; **to ~ to pieces** fare a pezzi; **to ~ one's punches** (*Boxing*) risparmiare l'avversario; **to ~ one's weight** dare il proprio contributo; **to ~ o.s. together** ricomporsi, riprendersi; **to ~ sb's leg** prendere in giro qn; **pull apart** *vt* (*break*) fare a pezzi; **pull away** *vi* (*move off: vehicle*) muoversi, partire; (: *boat*) staccarsi dal molo, salpare; (*draw back: person*) indietreggiare; **pull back** *vt* (*lever etc*) tirare indietro; (*curtains*) aprire ▷ *vi* (*from confrontation etc*) tirarsi indietro; (*Mil: withdraw*) ritirarsi; **pull down** *vt* (*house*) demolire; (*tree*) abbattere; **pull in** *vi* (*Aut: at the kerb*) accostarsi; (*Rail*) entrare in stazione; **pull off** *vt* (*clothes*) togliere; (*deal etc*) portare a compimento; **pull out** *vi* partire; (*Aut: come out of line*) spostarsi sulla mezzeria ▷ *vt* staccare; far uscire; (*withdraw*) ritirare; **pull over** *vi* (*Aut*) accostare; **pull up** *vi* (*stop*) fermarsi ▷ *vt* (*uproot*) sradicare; (*raise*) sollevare

pulley ['pulɪ] *n* puleggia, carrucola
pullover ['puləuvər] *n* pullover *m inv*
pulp [pʌlp] *n* (*of fruit*) polpa
pulpit ['pulpɪt] *n* pulpito
pulse [pʌls] *n* polso; (*Bot*) legume *m*; **pulses** *npl* (*Culin*) legumi *mpl*
puma ['pjuːmə] *n* puma *m inv*
pump [pʌmp] *n* pompa; (*shoe*) scarpetta ▷ *vt* pompare; **pump up** *vt* gonfiare
pumpkin ['pʌmpkɪn] *n* zucca
pun [pʌn] *n* gioco di parole
punch [pʌntʃ] *n* (*blow*) pugno; (*tool*) punzone *m*; (*drink*) ponce *m* ▷ *vt* (*hit*): **to ~ sb/sth** dare un pugno a qn/qc; **punch-up** *n* (*BRIT col*) rissa
punctual ['pʌŋktjuəl] *adj* puntuale
punctuation [pʌŋktju'eɪʃən] *n* interpunzione *f*, punteggiatura
puncture ['pʌŋktʃər] *n* foratura ▷ *vt* forare

> Be careful not to translate *puncture* by the Italian word *puntura*.

punish ['pʌnɪʃ] *vt* punire; **punishment** *n* punizione *f*
punk [pʌŋk] *n* (*also*: **~ rocker**) punk *mf inv*; (*also*: **~ rock**) musica punk, punk rock *m*; (*us col: hoodlum*) teppista *m*
pup [pʌp] *n* cucciolo/a
pupil ['pjuːpl] *n* allievo/a; (*Anat*) pupilla
puppet ['pʌpɪt] *n* burattino
puppy ['pʌpɪ] *n* cucciolo/a, cagnolino/a
purchase ['pəːtʃɪs] *n* acquisto, compera ▷ *vt* comprare
pure [pjuər] *adj* puro/a; **purely** ['pjuəlɪ] *adv* puramente
purify ['pjuərɪfaɪ] *vt* purificare
purity ['pjuərɪtɪ] *n* purezza
purple ['pəːpl] *adj* di porpora; viola *inv*
purpose ['pəːpəs] *n* intenzione *f*, scopo; **on ~** apposta
purr [pəːr] *vi* fare le fusa
purse [pəːs] *n* (*BRIT*) borsellino; (*US*) borsetta ▷ *vt* contrarre
pursue [pə'sjuː] *vt* inseguire; (*fig: activity etc*) continuare con; (: *aim etc*) perseguire
pursuit [pə'sjuːt] *n* inseguimento; (*fig*) ricerca; (*pastime*) passatempo
pus [pʌs] *n* pus *m*
push [puʃ] *n* spinta; (*effort*) grande sforzo; (*drive*) energia ▷ *vt* spingere; (*button*) premere; (*fig*) fare pubblicità a; (*thrust*): **to ~ sth (into)** ficcare qc (in) ▷ *vi* spingere; premere; **to ~ for** insistere per ottenere; **push in** *vi* introdursi a forza; **push off** *vi* (*col*) filare; **push on** *vi* (*continue*) continuare; **push over** *vt* far cadere; **push through** *vi* farsi largo spingendo ▷ *vt* (*measure*) far approvare; **pushchair** (*BRIT*) *n* passeggino; **pusher** *n* (*also*: **drug pusher**) spacciatore/trice (di droga);

push-up n (US: press-up) flessione f sulle braccia

puss [pus], **pussy(-cat)** ['pusɪ-] n micio

put (pt, pp **put**) [put] vt mettere, porre; (say) dire, esprimere; (a question) fare; (estimate) stimare; **put aside** vt (lay down: book etc) mettere da una parte, posare; (save) mettere da parte; (in shop) tenere da parte; **put away** vt (return) mettere a posto; **put back** vt (replace) rimettere (a posto); (postpone) rinviare; (delay) ritardare; **put by** vt (money) mettere da parte; **put down** vt (parcel etc) posare, mettere giù; (pay) versare; (in writing) mettere per iscritto; (revolt etc) sopprimere; (attribute) attribuire; **put forward** vt (ideas) avanzare, proporre; **put in** vt (application, complaint) presentare; (time, effort) mettere; **put off** vt (postpone) rimandare, rinviare; (discourage) dissuadere; **put on** vt (clothes, lipstick etc) mettere; (light etc) accendere; (play etc) mettere in scena; (food, meal) mettere su; (brake) mettere; **to ~ on weight** ingrassare; **to ~ on airs** darsi delle arie; **put out** vt mettere fuori; (one's hand) porgere; (light etc) spegnere; (inconvenience: person) scomodare; **put through** vt (Tel: caller) mettere in comunicazione; (: call) passare; (plan) far approvare; **put together** vt mettere insieme, riunire; (assemble: furniture) montare; (: meal) improvvisare; **put up** vt (raise) sollevare, alzare; (: umbrella) aprire; (: tent) montare; (pin up) affiggere; (hang) appendere; (build) costruire, erigere; (increase) aumentare; (accommodate) alloggiare; **put up with** vt fus sopportare

putt [pʌt] n colpo leggero; **putting green** n green m inv; campo da putting

puzzle ['pʌzl] n enigma m, mistero; (jigsaw) puzzle m; (also: **crossword ~**) parole fpl incrociate, cruciverba m inv ▷ vt confondere, rendere perplesso/a ▷ vi scervellarsi; **puzzled** adj perplesso/a; **puzzling** adj (question) poco chiaro/a; (attitude, set of instructions) incomprensibile

pyjamas (BRIT) [pə'dʒɑːməz] npl pigiama m

pylon ['paɪlən] n pilone m

pyramid ['pɪrəmɪd] n piramide f

Pyrenees [pɪrə'niːz] npl: **the ~** i Pirenei

P

q

quack [kwæk] n (of duck) qua qua m inv; (pej: doctor) ciarlatano/a

quadruple [kwɔ'drupl] vt quadruplicare ▷ vi quadruplicarsi

quail [kweɪl] n (Zool) quaglia ▷ vi (person): **to ~ at** or **before** perdersi d'animo davanti a

quaint [kweɪnt] adj bizzarro/a; (old-fashioned) antiquato/a e pittoresco/a

quake [kweɪk] vi tremare ▷ n abbr = **earthquake**

qualification [kwɔlɪfɪ'keɪʃən] n (degree etc) qualifica, titolo; (ability) competenza, qualificazione f; (limitation) riserva, restrizione f

qualified ['kwɔlɪfaɪd] adj qualificato/a; (able) competente, qualificato/a; (limited) condizionato/a; **~ for/to do** qualificato/a per/per fare

qualify ['kwɔlɪfaɪ] vt abilitare; (limit: statement) modificare, precisare ▷ vi: **to ~ (as)** qualificarsi (come); **to ~ (for)** acquistare i requisiti necessari (per); (Sport) qualificarsi (per or a)

quality ['kwɔlɪtɪ] n qualità f inv

qualm [kwɑːm] n dubbio; scrupolo

quantify ['kwɔntɪfaɪ] vt quantificare

quantity ['kwɔntɪtɪ] n quantità f inv

quarantine ['kwɔrntiːn] n quarantena

quarrel ['kwɔrl] n lite f, disputa ▷ vi litigare

quarry ['kwɔrɪ] n (for stone) cava; (animal) preda

quart [kwɔːt] n ≈ litro

quarter ['kwɔːtəʳ] n quarto; (of year) trimestre m; (district) quartiere m; (us: 25 cents) quarto di dollaro ▷ vt dividere in quattro; (Mil) alloggiare; **quarters** npl (living quarters) alloggio; (Mil) alloggi mpl, quadrato; **a ~ of an hour** un quarto d'ora; **quarter final** n quarto di finale; **quarterly** adj trimestrale ▷ adv trimestralmente ▷ n periodico trimestrale

quartet(te) [kwɔː'tɛt] n quartetto

quartz [kwɔːts] n quarzo

quay [kiː] n (also: **~side**) banchina

queasy ['kwiːzɪ] adj (stomach) delicato/a; **to feel ~** aver la nausea

queen [kwiːn] n (gen) regina; (Cards etc) regina, donna

queer [kwɪəʳ] adj strano/a, curioso/a ▷ n (col) finocchio

quench [kwɛntʃ] vt: **to ~ one's thirst** dissetarsi

query ['kwɪərɪ] n domanda, questione f ▷ vt mettere in questione

quest [kwɛst] n cerca, ricerca

question ['kwɛstʃən] n domanda, questione f ▷ vt (person) interrogare; (plan, idea) mettere in questione or in dubbio; **it's a ~ of doing** si tratta di fare; **beyond ~** fuori di dubbio; **out of the ~** fuori discussione, impossibile; **questionable** adj discutibile; **question mark** n punto interrogativo; **questionnaire** [kwɛstʃə'nɛəʳ] n questionario

queue [kjuː] (BRIT) n coda, fila ▷ vi fare la coda

quiche [kiːʃ] n torta salata a base di uova, formaggio, prosciutto o altro

quick [kwɪk] adj rapido/a, veloce; (reply) pronto/a; (mind) pronto/a, acuto/a ▷ n: **cut to the ~** (fig) toccato/a sul vivo; **be ~!** fa presto!; **quickly** adv rapidamente, velocemente

quid [kwɪd] n (pl inv: BRIT col) sterlina

quiet ['kwaɪət] adj tranquillo/a, quieto/a; (ceremony) semplice ▷ n tranquillità, calma ▷ vt, vi (US) = **quieten**; **keep ~!** sta zitto!; **quieten** vi (also: **quieten down**) calmarsi, chetarsi ▷ vt calmare, chetare; **quietly** adv tranquillamente, calmamente; silenziosamente

quilt [kwɪlt] n trapunta; **continental ~** piumino

quirky ['kwəːkɪ] adj stravagante

quit [kwɪt] (pt, pp **quit** or **quitted**) vt mollare; (premises) lasciare, partire da ▷ vi (give up) mollare; (resign) dimettersi

quite [kwaɪt] adv (rather) assai; (entirely) completamente, del tutto; **I ~ understand** capisco perfettamente; **~ a few of them** non pochi di loro; **~ (so)!** esatto!; **that's not ~ right** non è proprio esatto

quits [kwɪts] adj: **~ (with)** pari (con); **let's call it ~** adesso siamo pari

quiver ['kwɪvəʳ] vi tremare, fremere

quiz [kwɪz] n (game) quiz m inv; indovinello ▷ vt interrogare

quota ['kwəʊtə] n quota

quotation [kwəʊ'teɪʃən] n citazione f; (of shares etc) quotazione f; (estimate) preventivo; **quotation marks** npl virgolette fpl

quote [kwəʊt] n citazione f ▷ vt (sentence) citare; (price) dare, fissare; (shares) quotare ▷ vi: **to ~ from** citare; **quotes** npl = **quotation marks**

rabbi ['ræbaɪ] n rabbino

rabbit ['ræbɪt] n coniglio

rabies ['reɪbiːz] n rabbia

RAC n abbr (BRIT: = Royal Automobile Club) ≈ A.C.I. m

raccoon [rə'kuːn], **racoon** n procione m

race [reɪs] n razza; (competition, rush) corsa ▷ vt (horse) far correre ▷ vi correre; (engine) imballarsi; **race car** n (US) = **racing car**; **racecourse** n campo di corse, ippodromo; **racehorse** n cavallo da corsa; **racetrack** n pista

racial ['reɪʃl] adj razziale

racing ['reɪsɪŋ] n corsa; **racing car** n (BRIT) macchina da corsa; **racing driver** n (BRIT) corridore m automobilista

racism ['reɪsɪzəm] n razzismo; **racist** adj, n razzista m/f

rack [ræk] n rastrelliera; (also: **luggage ~**) rete f, portabagagli

m inv; (also: **roof ~***)* portabagagli;
(dish rack) scolapiatti *m inv* ▷ *vt:* **to
~ one's brains** scervellarsi; **~ed by**
torturato/a da
racket ['rækɪt] *n (for tennis)*
racchetta; *(noise)* fracasso; baccano;
(swindle) imbroglio, truffa; *(organized
crime)* racket *m inv*
racquet ['rækɪt] *n* racchetta
radar ['reɪdɑːʳ] *n* radar *m*
radiation [reɪdɪ'eɪʃən] *n*
irradiamento; *(radioactive)*
radiazione *f*
radiator ['reɪdɪeɪtəʳ] *n* radiatore *m*
radical ['rædɪkl] *adj* radicale
radio ['reɪdɪəu] *n* radio *f inv;* **on
the ~** alla radio; **radioactive**
['reɪdɪəu'æktɪv] *adj* radioattivo/a;
radio station *n* stazione *f* radio *inv*
radish ['rædɪʃ] *n* ravanello
RAF *n abbr =* **Royal Air Force**
raffle ['ræfl] *n* lotteria
raft [rɑːft] *n* zattera; *(also:* **life ~***)*
zattera di salvataggio
rag [ræg] *n* straccio, cencio; *(pej:
newspaper)* giornalaccio, bandiera;
(for charity) iniziativa studentesca a
scopo benefico; **rags** *npl (torn clothes)*
stracci *mpl*, brandelli *mpl*
rage [reɪdʒ] *n (fury)* collera, furia
▷ *vi (person)* andare su tutte le furie;
(storm) infuriare; **it's all the ~** fa
furore
ragged ['rægɪd] *adj (edge)* irregolare;
(cuff) logoro/a; *(appearance)* pezzente
raid [reɪd] *n (Mil)* incursione *f;*
(criminal) rapina; *(by police)* irruzione
f ▷ *vt* fare un'incursione in; rapinare;
fare irruzione in
rail [reɪl] *n (on stair)* ringhiera; *(on
bridge, balcony)* parapetto; *(of ship)*
battagliola; **railcard** *n (BRIT)* tessera
di riduzione ferroviaria; **railing(s)**
n(pl) ringhiere *fpl;* **railroad** *(US) n
=* **railway; railway** *(BRIT) n* ferrovia;
railway line *n (BRIT)* linea ferroviaria;
railway station *n (BRIT)* stazione *f*
ferroviaria

rain [reɪn] *n* pioggia ▷ *vi* piovere;
in the ~ sotto la pioggia; **it's ~ing**
piove; **rainbow** *n* arcobaleno;
raincoat *n* impermeabile *m;*
raindrop *n* goccia di pioggia; **rainfall**
n pioggia; *(measurement)* piovosità;
rainforest *n* foresta pluviale *or*
equatoriale; **rainy** *adj* piovoso/a
raise [reɪz] *n* aumento ▷ *vt*
(lift) alzare; sollevare; *(increase)*
aumentare; *(a protest, doubt,
question)* sollevare; *(cattle, family)*
allevare; *(crop)* coltivare; *(army, funds)*
raccogliere; *(loan)* ottenere; **to ~
one's voice** alzare la voce
raisin ['reɪzn] *n* uva secca
rake [reɪk] *n (tool)* rastrello ▷ *vt
(garden)* rastrellare
rally ['rælɪ] *n (Pol etc)* riunione *f;* *(Aut)*
rally *m inv;* *(Tennis)* scambio ▷ *vt*
riunire, radunare ▷ *vi (sick person,
Stock Exchange)* riprendersi
RAM [ræm] *n abbr (Comput: = random
access memory)* RAM *f*
ram [ræm] *n* montone *m*, ariete *m*
▷ *vt* conficcare; *(crash into)* cozzare,
sbattere contro; percuotere;
speronare
Ramadan [ræmə'dæn] *n* Ramadan
m inv
ramble ['ræmbl] *n* escursione *f* ▷ *vi*
(pej: also: **~ on***)* divagare; **rambler**
n escursionista *m/f;* *(Bot)* rosa
rampicante; **rambling** *adj (speech)*
sconnesso/a; *(Bot)* rampicante;
(house) tutto/a nicchie e corridoi
ramp [ræmp] *n* rampa; **on/off ~** *(US
Aut)* raccordo di entrata/uscita
rampage [ræm'peɪdʒ] *n:* **to go on
the ~** scatenarsi in modo violento
ran [ræn] *pt of* **run**
ranch [rɑːntʃ] *n* ranch *m inv*
random ['rændəm] *adj* fatto/a *or*
detto/a per caso; *(Comput, Math)*
casuale ▷ *n:* **at ~** a casaccio
rang [ræŋ] *pt of* **ring**
range [reɪndʒ] *n (of mountains)*
catena; *(of missile, voice)* portata;

(of products) gamma; (Mil: also: **shooting ~**) campo di tiro; (also: **kitchen ~**) fornello, cucina economica ▷ vt disporre ▷ vi: **to ~ over** coprire; **to ~ from ... to** andare da ... a

ranger ['reɪndʒəʳ] n guardia forestale

rank [ræŋk] n fila; (status, Mil) grado; (BRIT: also: **taxi ~**) posteggio di taxi ▷ vi: **to ~ among** essere tra ▷ adj puzzolente; (hypocrisy, injustice) vero/a e proprio/a; **the ~ and file** (fig) la gran massa

ransom ['rænsəm] n riscatto; **to hold sb to ~** (fig) esercitare pressione su qn

rant [rænt] vi vociare

rap [ræp] n (music) rap m inv ▷ vt dare dei colpetti a; bussare a

rape [reɪp] n violenza carnale, stupro; (Bot) ravizzone m ▷ vt violentare

rapid ['ræpɪd] adj rapido/a; **rapidly** adv rapidamente; **rapids** npl (Geo) rapida

rapist ['reɪpɪst] n violentatore m

rapport [ræ'pɔːʳ] n rapporto

rare [rɛəʳ] adj raro/a; (Culin: steak) al sangue; **rarely** ['rɛəlɪ] adv raramente

rash [ræʃ] adj imprudente, sconsiderato/a ▷ n (Med) eruzione f; (of events etc) scoppio

rasher ['ræʃəʳ] n fetta sottile (di lardo or prosciutto)

raspberry ['rɑːzbərɪ] n lampone m

rat [ræt] n ratto

rate [reɪt] n (proportion) tasso, percentuale f; (speed) velocità f inv; (price) tariffa ▷ vt valutare; stimare; **to ~ sb/sth as** valutare qn/qc come; **rates** npl (BRIT: property tax) imposte fpl comunali; (fees) tariffe fpl

rather ['rɑːðəʳ] adv piuttosto; **it's ~ expensive** è piuttosto caro; (too much) è un po' caro; **there's ~ a lot** ce n'è parecchio; **I would** or **I'd ~ go** preferirei andare

rating ['reɪtɪŋ] n (assessment) valutazione f; (score) punteggio di merito; **ratings** npl (Radio, TV) indice m di ascolto

ratio ['reɪʃɪəu] n proporzione f; **in the ~ of 2 to 1** in rapporto di 2 a 1

ration ['ræʃən] n razione f ▷ vt razionare; **rations** npl razioni fpl

rational ['ræʃənl] adj razionale, ragionevole; (solution, reasoning) logico/a

rattle ['rætl] n tintinnio; (louder) rumore m di ferraglia; (of baby) sonaglino ▷ vi risuonare, tintinnare; fare un rumore di ferraglia ▷ vt

rave [reɪv] vi (in anger) infuriarsi; (with enthusiasm) andare in estasi; (Med) delirare ▷ n (BRIT): **a ~ (party)** un rave

raven ['reɪvən] n corvo

ravine [rə'viːn] n burrone m

raw [rɔː] adj (uncooked) crudo/a; (not processed) greggio/a; (sore) vivo/a; (inexperienced) inesperto/a; (weather, day) gelido/a

ray [reɪ] n raggio; **a ~ of hope** un barlume di speranza

razor ['reɪzəʳ] n rasoio; **razor blade** n lama di rasoio

Rd abbr = **road**

RE n abbr (BRIT Mil: = Royal Engineers) ≈ G.M.; (BRIT) = **religious education**

re [riː] prep con riferimento a

reach [riːtʃ] n portata; (of river etc) tratto ▷ vt raggiungere; arrivare a ▷ vi stendersi; **out of/within ~** fuori/a portata di mano; **within easy ~ (of)** vicino (a); **reach out** vt (hand) allungare ▷ vi: **to ~ out for** stendere la mano per prendere

react [riː'ækt] vi reagire; **reaction** [riː'ækʃən] n reazione f; **reactor** [riː'æktəʳ] n reattore m

read (pt, pp **read**) [riːd, rɛd] vi leggere ▷ vt leggere; (understand) intendere, interpretare; (study) studiare; **read out** vt leggere ad alta voce; **reader** n lettore/trice; (BRIT: at university) professore con funzioni preminenti di ricerca

readily ['rɛdɪlɪ] adv volentieri; (easily) facilmente; (quickly) prontamente

reading ['riːdɪŋ] n lettura; (understanding) interpretazione f; (on instrument) indicazione f

ready ['rɛdɪ] adj pronto/a; (willing) pronto/a, disposto/a; (available) disponibile ▷ n: **at the ~** (Mil) pronto a sparare ▷ vt preparare; **to get ~** vi prepararsi; **ready-made** adj prefabbricato/a; (clothes) confezionato/a

real [rɪəl] adj reale; vero/a; **in ~ terms** in realtà; **real ale** n birra ad effervescenza naturale; **real estate** n beni mpl immobili; **realistic** [rɪə'lɪstɪk] adj realistico/a; **reality** [riː'ælɪtɪ] n realtà f inv; **reality TV** n reality TV f

realization [rɪəlaɪ'zeɪʃən] n presa di coscienza; (of hopes, project etc) realizzazione f

realize ['rɪəlaɪz] vt (understand) rendersi conto di

really ['rɪəlɪ] adv veramente, davvero; **~!** (indicating annoyance) oh, insomma!

realm [rɛlm] n reame m, regno

Realtor® ['rɪəltɔːʳ] n (US) agente m immobiliare

reappear [riːə'pɪəʳ] vi ricomparire, riapparire

rear [rɪəʳ] adj di dietro; (Aut: wheel etc) posteriore ▷ n didietro, parte f posteriore ▷ vt (cattle, family) allevare ▷ vi (also: ~ **up**: animal) impennarsi

rearrange [riːə'reɪndʒ] vt riordinare

rear: **rear-view mirror** ['rɪəvjuː-] n (Aut) specchio retrovisivo; **rear-wheel drive** n trazione fpl posteriore

reason ['riːzn] n ragione f; (cause, motive) ragione, motivo ▷ vi: **to ~ with sb** far ragionare qn; **it stands to ~ that** è ovvio che; **reasonable** adj ragionevole; (not bad) accettabile; **reasonably** adv ragionevolmente; **reasoning** n ragionamento

reassurance [riːə'ʃuərəns] n rassicurazione f

reassure [riːə'ʃuəʳ] vt rassicurare; **to ~ sb of** rassicurare qn di or su

rebate ['riːbeɪt] n (on tax etc) sgravio

rebel n ['rɛbl] ribelle m/f ▷ vi [rɪ'bɛl] ribellarsi; **rebellion** n ribellione f; **rebellious** adj ribelle

rebuild [riː'bɪld] vt (irreg) ricostruire

recall vt [rɪ'kɔːl] richiamare; (remember) ricordare, richiamare alla mente ▷ n ['riːkɔl] richiamo

recd. abbr = **received**

receipt [rɪ'siːt] n (document) ricevuta; (act of receiving) ricevimento; **receipts** npl (Comm) introiti mpl

receive [rɪ'siːv] vt ricevere; (guest) ricevere, accogliere; **receiver** [rɪ'siːvəʳ] n (Tel) ricevitore m; (Radio) apparecchio ricevente; (of stolen goods) ricettatore/trice; (Law, Comm) curatore m fallimentare

recent ['riːsnt] adj recente; **recently** adv recentemente

reception [rɪ'sɛpʃən] n ricevimento; (welcome) accoglienza; (TV etc) ricezione f; **reception desk** n (in hotel) reception f inv; (in hospital, at doctor's) accettazione f; (in large building, offices) portineria; **receptionist** n receptionist mf inv

recession [rɪ'sɛʃən] n recessione f; **recessionista** [rɪsɛʃə'nɪstə] n recessionista m/f

recharge [riː'tʃɑːdʒ] vt (battery) ricaricare

recipe ['rɛsɪpɪ] n ricetta

recipient [rɪ'sɪpɪənt] n beneficiario/a; (of letter) destinatario/a

recital [rɪ'saɪtl] n recital m inv

recite [rɪ'saɪt] vt (poem) recitare

reckless ['rɛkləs] adj (driver etc) spericolato/a; (spending) folle

reckon ['rɛkən] vt (count) calcolare; (think): **I ~ that ...** penso che ..

reclaim [rɪ'kleɪm] vt (land) bonificare; (demand back) richiedere, reclamare; (materials) recuperare

recline [rɪ'klaɪn] vi stare sdraiato/a
recognition [rɛkəg'nɪʃən] n
riconoscimento; **transformed
beyond ~** irriconoscibile
recognize ['rɛkəgnaɪz] vt: **to ~ (by/
as)** riconoscere (a or da/come)
recollection [rɛkə'lɛkʃən] n ricordo
recommend [rɛkə'mɛnd]
vt raccomandare; (advise)
consigliare; **recommendation**
[rɛkəmən'deɪʃən] n
raccomandazione f; consiglio
reconcile ['rɛkənsaɪl] vt (two people)
riconciliare; (two facts) conciliare,
quadrare; **to ~ o.s. to** rassegnarsi a
reconsider [ri:kən'sɪdər] vt
riconsiderare
reconstruct [ri:kən'strʌkt] vt
ricostruire
record n ['rɛkɔ:d] ricordo,
documento; (of meeting etc) nota,
verbale m; (register) registro; (file)
pratica, dossier m inv; (Comput)
record m inv; (also: **police ~**) fedina
penale sporca; (Mus: disc) disco;
(Sport) record m inv, primato
▷ vt [rɪ'kɔ:d] (set down) prendere
nota di, registrare; (Comput, Mus:
song etc) registrare; **off the ~** adj
ufficioso/a; adv ufficiosamente; **in
~ time** a tempo di record; **recorded
delivery letter** n (BRIT Post) lettera
raccomandata; **recorder** n (Mus)
flauto diritto; **recording** n (Mus)
registrazione f; **record player** n
giradischi m inv
recount [rɪ'kaunt] vt raccontare,
narrare
recover [rɪ'kʌvər] vt ricuperare
▷ vi: **to ~ (from)** riprendersi (da);
recovery [rɪ'kʌvəri] n ricupero;
ristabilimento; ripresa
> Be careful not to translate recover
by the Italian word ricoverare.
recreate [ri:krɪ'eɪt] vt ricreare
recreation [rɛkrɪ'eɪʃən] n
ricreazione f; svago; **recreational
drug** [rɛkrɪ'eɪʃənl-] n droga usata

saltuariamente; **recreational vehicle**
n (US) camper m inv
recruit [rɪ'kru:t] n recluta; (in
company) nuovo/a assunto/a
▷ vt reclutare; **recruitment** n
reclutamento
rectangle ['rɛktæŋgl] n rettangolo;
rectangular [rɛk'tæŋgjulər] adj
rettangolare
rectify ['rɛktɪfaɪ] vt (error) rettificare;
(omission) riparare
rector ['rɛktər] n (Rel) parroco
(anglicano)
recur [rɪ'kə:r] vi riaccadere;
(symptoms) ripresentarsi; **recurring**
adj (Math) periodico/a
recyclable [ri:'saɪkləbl] adj riciclabile
recycle [ri:'saɪkl] vt riciclare
recycling [ri:'saɪklɪŋ] n riciclaggio
red [rɛd] n rosso; (Pol: pej) rosso/a
▷ adj rosso/a; **in the ~** (account)
scoperto; (business) in deficit; **Red
Cross** n Croce f Rossa; **redcurrant**
n ribes m inv
redeem [rɪ'di:m] vt (debt) riscattare;
(sth in pawn) ritirare; (fig, also Rel)
redimere
red: red-haired [-'hɛəd] adj dai capelli
rossi; **redhead** ['rɛdhɛd] n rosso/a;
red-hot adj arroventato/a; **red light**
n: **to go through a red light** (Aut)
passare col rosso; **red-light district**
[rɛd'laɪt-] n quartiere m a luci rosse;
red meat n carne f rossa
reduce [rɪ'dju:s] vt ridurre; (lower)
ridurre, abbassare; **"~ speed now"**
(Aut) "rallentare"; **at a ~d price**
scontato/a; **reduced** adj (decreased)
ridotto/a; **at a reduced price** a
prezzo ribassato or ridotto; **"greatly
reduced prices"** "grandi ribassi";
reduction [rɪ'dʌkʃən] n riduzione f;
(of price) ribasso; (discount) sconto
redundancy [rɪ'dʌndənsɪ] n;
licenziamento
redundant [rɪ'dʌndnt] adj
(worker) licenziato/a; (detail, object)
superfluo/a; **to be made ~** (BRIT)

essere licenziato (per eccesso di personale)
reed [ri:d] n (Bot) canna; (Mus: of clarinet etc) ancia
reef [ri:f] n (at sea) scogliera
reel [ri:l] n (of cotton) bobina, rocchetto; (Fishing) mulinello; (Cine) rotolo; (dance) danza veloce scozzese ▷ vi (sway) barcollare
ref [rɛf] n abbr (col: = referee) arbitro
refectory [rɪˈfɛktərɪ] n refettorio
refer [rɪˈfəːˈ] vt: **to ~ sth to** (dispute, decision) deferire qc a; **to ~ sb to** (inquirer, Med: patient) indirizzare qn a; (reader: to text) rimandare qn a; **refer to** vt fus (allude to) accennare a; (consult) rivolgersi a
referee [rɛfəˈriː] n arbitro; (BRIT: for job application) referenza ▷ vt arbitrare
reference [ˈrɛfrəns] n riferimento; (mention) menzione f, allusione f; (for job application) referenza; **with ~ to** (Comm: in letter) in or con riferimento a; **reference number** n numero di riferimento
refill vt [riːˈfɪl] riempire di nuovo; (pen, lighter etc) ricaricare ▷ n [ˈriːfɪl] (for pen etc) ricambio
refine [rɪˈfaɪn] vt raffinare; **refined** adj (person, taste) raffinato/a; **refinery** n raffineria
reflect [rɪˈflɛkt] vt (light, image) riflettere; (fig) rispecchiare ▷ vi (think) riflettere, considerare; **it ~s badly/well on him** si ripercuote su di lui in senso negativo/positivo; **reflection** [rɪˈflɛkʃən] n riflessione f; (image) riflesso; (criticism): **reflection on** giudizio su; attacco a; **on reflection** pensandoci sopra
reflex [ˈriːflɛks] adj riflesso/a ▷ n riflesso
reform [rɪˈfɔːm] n (of sinner etc) correzione f; (of law etc) riforma ▷ vt correggere; riformare
refrain [rɪˈfreɪn] vi: **to ~ from doing** trattenersi dal fare ▷ n ritornello

refresh [rɪˈfrɛʃ] vt rinfrescare; (food, sleep) ristorare; **refreshing** adj (drink) rinfrescante; (sleep) riposante, ristoratore/trice
refreshment n ristoro; **~(s)** rinfreschi mpl
refrigerator [rɪˈfrɪdʒəreɪtəˈ] n frigorifero
refuel [riːˈfjuəl] vi far rifornimento (di carburante)
refuge [ˈrɛfjuːdʒ] n rifugio; **to take ~ in** rifugiarsi in; **refugee** [rɛfjuˈdʒiː] n rifugiato/a, profugo/a
refund n [ˈriːfʌnd] rimborso ▷ vt [rɪˈfʌnd] rimborsare
refurbish [riːˈfəːbɪʃ] vt rimettere a nuovo
refusal [rɪˈfjuːzəl] n rifiuto; **to have first ~ on sth** avere il diritto d'opzione su qc
refuse¹ [ˈrɛfjuːs] n rifiuti mpl
refuse² [rɪˈfjuːz] vt, vi rifiutare; **to ~ to do sth** rifiutare or rifiutarsi di fare qc
regain [rɪˈgeɪn] vt riguadagnare; riacquistare, ricuperare
regard [rɪˈgɑːd] n riguardo, stima ▷ vt considerare, stimare; **to give one's ~s to** porgere i suoi saluti a; **(kind) ~s** cordiali saluti; **regarding** prep riguardo a, per quanto riguarda; **regardless** adv lo stesso; **regardless of** a dispetto di, nonostante
regenerate [rɪˈdʒɛnəreɪt] vt rigenerare
reggae [ˈrɛgeɪ] n reggae m
regiment n [ˈrɛdʒɪmənt] reggimento
region [ˈriːdʒən] n regione f; **in the ~ of** (fig) all'incirca di; **regional** adj regionale
register [ˈrɛdʒɪstəˈ] n registro; (also: **electoral ~**) lista elettorale ▷ vt registrare; (vehicle) immatricolare; (letter) assicurare; (instrument) segnare ▷ vi iscriversi; (at hotel) firmare il registro; (make impression) entrare in testa; **registered** adj (BRIT: letter) assicurato/a

registrar [ˈrɛdʒɪstrɑːʳ] n ufficiale m di stato civile; segretario

registration [rɛdʒɪsˈtreɪʃən] n (act) registrazione f; iscrizione f; (Aut: also: **~ number**) numero di targa

registry office n (BRIT) anagrafe f; **to get married in a ~** ≈ sposarsi in municipio

regret [rɪˈɡrɛt] n rimpianto, rincrescimento ▷ vt rimpiangere; **regrettable** adj deplorevole

regular [ˈrɛɡjuləʳ] adj regolare; (usual) abituale, normale; (soldier) dell'esercito regolare ▷ n (client etc) cliente m/f abituale; **regularly** adv regolarmente

regulate [ˈrɛɡjuleɪt] vt regolare; **regulation** [rɛɡjuˈleɪʃən] n (rule) regola, regolamento; (adjustment) regolazione f

rehabilitation [ˈriːəbɪlɪˈteɪʃən] n (of offender) riabilitazione f; (of disabled) riadattamento

rehearsal [rɪˈhəːsəl] n prova

rehearse [rɪˈhəːs] vt provare

reign [reɪn] n regno ▷ vi regnare

reimburse [riːɪmˈbəːs] vt rimborsare

rein [reɪn] n (for horse) briglia

reincarnation [riːɪnkɑːˈneɪʃən] n reincarnazione f

reindeer [ˈreɪndɪəʳ] n (pl inv) renna

reinforce [riːɪnˈfɔːs] vt rinforzare; **reinforcement** n rinforzamento; **reinforcements** npl (Mil) rinforzi mpl

reinstate [riːɪnˈsteɪt] vt reintegrare

reject n [ˈriːdʒɛkt] (Comm) scarto ▷ vt [rɪˈdʒɛkt] rifiutare, respingere; (Comm: goods) scartare; **rejection** [rɪˈdʒɛkʃən] n rifiuto

rejoice [rɪˈdʒɔɪs] vi: **to ~ (at or over)** provare diletto (in)

relate [rɪˈleɪt] vt (tell) raccontare; (connect) collegare ▷ vi: **to ~ to** (refer to) riferirsi a; (get on with) stabilire un rapporto con; **relating to** che riguarda, rispetto a; **related** adj: **related to** imparentato/a con

relation [rɪˈleɪʃən] n (person) parente m/f; (link) rapporto, relazione f;

relations npl (relatives) parenti mpl; **relationship** n rapporto; (personal ties) rapporti mpl, relazioni fpl; (also: **family relationship**) legami mpl di parentela

relative [ˈrɛlətɪv] n parente m/f ▷ adj relativo/a; (respective) rispettivo/a; **relatively** adv relativamente; (fairly, rather) abbastanza

relax [rɪˈlæks] vi rilasciarsi; (person: unwind) rilassarsi ▷ vt rilasciare; (mind, person) rilassare; **relaxation** [riːlækˈseɪʃən] n rilasciamento; rilassamento; (entertainment) ricreazione f, svago; **relaxed** adj rilassato/a; **relaxing** adj rilassante

relay [ˈriːleɪ] n (Sport) corsa a staffetta ▷ vt (message) trasmettere

release [rɪˈliːs] n (from prison) rilascio; (from obligation) liberazione f; (of gas etc) emissione f; (of film etc) distribuzione f; (record) disco; (device) disinnesto ▷ vt (prisoner) rilasciare; (from obligation, wreckage etc) liberare; (book, film) fare uscire; (news) rendere pubblico/a; (gas etc) emettere; (Tech: catch, spring etc) disinnestare

relegate [ˈrɛləɡeɪt] vt relegare; (BRIT Sport): **to be ~d** essere retrocesso/a

relent [rɪˈlɛnt] vi cedere; **relentless** adj implacabile

relevant [ˈrɛləvənt] adj pertinente; (chapter) in questione; **~ to** pertinente a

> Be careful not to translate *relevant* by the Italian word *rilevante*.

reliable [rɪˈlaɪəbl] adj (person, firm) fidato/a, che dà affidamento; (method) sicuro/a; (machine) affidabile

relic [ˈrɛlɪk] n (Rel) reliquia; (of the past) resto

relief [rɪˈliːf] n (from pain, anxiety) sollievo; (help, supplies) soccorsi mpl; (Art, Geo) rilievo

relieve [rɪˈliːv] vt (pain, patient) sollevare; (bring help) soccorrere; (take over from: gen) sostituire;

(: *guard*) rilevare; **to ~ sb of sth** (*load*) alleggerire qn di qc; **to ~ o.s.** fare i propri bisogni; **relieved** *adj* sollevato/a; **to be relieved that ...** essere sollevato/a (dal fatto) che ...; **I'm relieved to hear it** mi hai tolto un peso con questa notizia

religion [rɪˈlɪdʒən] *n* religione *f*

religious [rɪˈlɪdʒəs] *adj* religioso/a; **religious education** *n* religione *f*

relish [ˈrelɪʃ] *n* (*Culin*) condimento; (*enjoyment*) gran piacere *m* ▷ *vt* (*food etc*) godere; **~ doing** adorare fare

relocate [riːləʊˈkeɪt] *vt* trasferire ▷ *vi* trasferirsi

reluctance [rɪˈlʌktəns] *n* riluttanza

reluctant [rɪˈlʌktənt] *adj* riluttante, mal disposto/a; **reluctantly** *adv* di mala voglia, a malincuore

rely [rɪˈlaɪ]: **to ~ on** *vt fus* contare su; (*be dependent*) dipendere da

remain [rɪˈmeɪn] *vi* restare, rimanere; **remainder** *n* resto; (*Comm*) rimanenza; **remaining** *adj* che rimane; **remains** *npl* resti *mpl*

remand [rɪˈmɑːnd] *n*: **on ~** in detenzione preventiva ▷ *vt*: **to ~ in custody** rinviare in carcere; trattenere a disposizione della legge

remark [rɪˈmɑːk] *n* osservazione *f* ▷ *vt* osservare, dire; **remarkable** *adj* notevole; eccezionale

remarry [riːˈmærɪ] *vi* risposarsi

remedy [ˈremədɪ] *n*: **~ (for)** rimedio (per) ▷ *vt* rimediare a

remember [rɪˈmɛmbəʳ] *vt* ricordare, ricordarsi di; **~ me to your wife and children!** saluti sua moglie e i bambini da parte mia!

Remembrance Day (BRIT) **Remembrance Sunday** *n vedi nota* **"Remembrance Day"**

● **REMEMBRANCE DAY**
●
● Nel Regno Unito, la domenica
● più vicina all'11 di novembre, data
● in cui fu firmato l'armistizio con
● la Germania nel 1918, ricorre il
● *Remembrance Day* o *Remembrance*
● *Sunday*, giorno in cui vengono
● commemorati i caduti in guerra.
● In questa occasione molti portano
● un papavero di carta appuntato al
● petto in segno di rispetto.

remind [rɪˈmaɪnd] *vt*: **to ~ sb of sth** ricordare qc a qn; **to ~ sb to do** ricordare a qn di fare; **reminder** *n* richiamo; (*note etc*) promemoria *m inv*

reminiscent [remɪˈnɪsnt] *adj*: **~ of** che fa pensare a, che richiama

remnant [ˈremnənt] *n* resto, avanzo

remorse [rɪˈmɔːs] *n* rimorso

remote [rɪˈməʊt] *adj* remoto/a, lontano/a; (*person*) distaccato/a; **remote control** *n* telecomando; **remotely** *adv* remotamente; (*slightly*) vagamente

removal [rɪˈmuːvəl] *n* (*taking away*) rimozione *f*; soppressione *f*; (BRIT: *from house*) trasloco; (*from office*: *sacking*) destituzione *f*; (*Med*) ablazione *f*; **removal man** *n* (*irreg*: BRIT) addetto ai traslochi; **removal van** *n* (BRIT) furgone *m* per traslochi

remove [rɪˈmuːv] *vt* togliere, rimuovere; (*employee*) destituire; (*stain*) far sparire; (*doubt, abuse*) sopprimere, eliminare

Renaissance [rəˈneɪsəns] *n*: **the ~** il Rinascimento

rename [riːˈneɪm] *vt* ribattezzare

render [ˈrendəʳ] *vt* rendere

rendez-vous [ˈrɒndɪvuː] *n* appuntamento; (*place*) luogo d'incontro; (*meeting*) incontro

renew [rɪˈnjuː] *vt* rinnovare; (*negotiations*) riprendere; **renewable** *adj* riutilizzabile; (*contract*) rinnovabile; **renewable energy, renewables** fonti *mpl* di energia rinnovabile

renovate [ˈrenəveɪt] *vt* rinnovare; (*art work*) restaurare

renowned [rɪ'naund] adj
rinomato/a

rent [rɛnt] n affitto ▷ vt (take for
rent) prendere in affitto; (also: **~ out**)
dare in affitto; **rental** n (cost: on TV,
telephone) abbonamento; (: on car)
noleggio

reorganize [riː'ɔːgənaɪz] vt
riorganizzare

rep [rɛp] n abbr (Comm:
= representative) rappresentante
m/f; (Theat: = repertory) teatro di
repertorio

repair [rɪ'pɛəʳ] n riparazione f ▷ vt
riparare; **in good/bad ~** in buono/
cattivo stato; **repair kit** n kit m inv
per riparazioni

repay [riː'peɪ] vt (irreg: money, creditor)
rimborsare, ripagare; (sb's efforts)
ricompensare; (favour) ricambiare;
repayment n rimborso

repeat [rɪ'piːt] n (Radio, TV) replica
▷ vt ripetere; (pattern) riprodurre;
(promise, attack, also Comm: order)
rinnovare ▷ vi ripetere; **repeatedly**
adv ripetutamente, spesso; **repeat
prescription** n (BRIT) ricetta
ripetibile

repellent [rɪ'pɛlənt] adj repellente
▷ n: **insect ~** prodotto m anti-insetti
inv

repercussion [riːpə'kʌʃən] n
ripercussione f

repetition [rɛpɪ'tɪʃən] n ripetizione f

repetitive [rɪ'pɛtɪtɪv] adj (movement)
che si ripete; (work) monotono/a;
(speech) pieno/a di ripetizioni

replace [rɪ'pleɪs] vt (put back)
rimettere a posto; (take the place of)
sostituire; **replacement** n rimessa;
sostituzione f; (person) sostituto/a

replay ['riːpleɪ] n (of match) partita
ripetuta; (of tape, film) replay m inv

replica ['rɛplɪkə] n replica, copia

reply [rɪ'plaɪ] n risposta ▷ vi
rispondere

report [rɪ'pɔːt] n rapporto; (Press
etc) cronaca; (BRIT: also: **school ~**)

pagella; (of gun) sparo ▷ vt riportare;
(Press etc) fare una cronaca su; (bring
to notice: occurrence) segnalare;
(: person) denunciare ▷ vi (make
a report) fare un rapporto (or una
cronaca); (present o.s.): **to ~ (to sb)**
presentarsi (a qn); **report card** n
(US, SCOTTISH) pagella; **reportedly**
adv stando a quanto si dice; **he
reportedly told them to ...** avrebbe
detto loro di ...; **reporter** n reporter
m inv

represent [rɛprɪ'zɛnt] vt
rappresentare; **representation**
[rɛprɪzɛn'teɪʃən] n rappresentazione
f; (petition) rappresentanza;
representative n rappresentante m
(di commercio); (US Pol) deputato/a
▷ adj: **representative (of)**
rappresentativo/a (di)

repress [rɪ'prɛs] vt reprimere;
repression [rɪ'prɛʃən] n
repressione f

reprimand ['rɛprɪmɑːnd] n
rimprovero ▷ vt rimproverare

reproduce [riːprə'djuːs] vt
riprodurre ▷ vi riprodursi;
reproduction [riːprə'dʌkʃən] n
riproduzione f

reptile ['rɛptaɪl] n rettile m

republic [rɪ'pʌblɪk] n repubblica;
republican adj, n repubblicano/a

reputable ['rɛpjutəbl] adj di buona
reputazione; (occupation) rispettabile

reputation [rɛpju'teɪʃən] n
reputazione f

request [rɪ'kwɛst] n domanda;
(formal) richiesta ▷ vt: **to ~ (of or
from sb)** chiedere (a qn); **request
stop** n (BRIT: for bus) fermata
facoltativa or a richiesta

require [rɪ'kwaɪəʳ] vt (need: person)
aver bisogno di; (: thing, situation)
richiedere; (want) volere; esigere; **to
~ sb to do sth/sth of sb** esigere che
qn faccia qc/qc da qn; **requirement**
n esigenza; bisogno; (condition)
requisito

r

resat [riːˈsæt] pt, pp of **resit**

rescue [ˈrɛskjuː] n salvataggio; (help) soccorso ▷ vt salvare

research [rɪˈsəːtʃ] n ricerca, ricerche fpl ▷ vt fare ricerche su

resemblance [rɪˈzɛmbləns] n somiglianza

resemble [rɪˈzɛmbl] vt assomigliare a

resent [rɪˈzɛnt] vt risentirsi di; **resentful** adj pieno/a di risentimento; **resentment** n risentimento

reservation [rɛzəˈveɪʃən] n (booking) prenotazione f; (doubt) dubbio; (protected area) riserva; (BRIT Aut: also: **central ~**) spartitraffico m inv; **reservation desk** n (US: in hotel) reception f inv

reserve [rɪˈzəːv] n riserva ▷ vt (seats etc) prenotare; **reserved** adj (shy) riservato/a

reservoir [ˈrɛzəvwɑːʳ] n serbatoio

residence [ˈrɛzɪdəns] n residenza; **residence permit** n (BRIT) permesso di soggiorno

resident [ˈrɛzɪdənt] n residente m/f; (in hotel) cliente m/f fisso/a ▷ adj residente; (doctor) fisso/a; (course, college) a tempo pieno con pernottamento; **residential** [rɛzɪˈdɛnʃəl] adj di residenza; (area) residenziale

residue [ˈrɛzɪdjuː] n resto; (Chem, Physics) residuo

resign [rɪˈzaɪn] vt (one's post) dimettersi da ▷ vi: **to ~ (from)** dimettersi (da); **to ~ o.s. to** rassegnarsi a; **resignation** [rɛzɪɡˈneɪʃən] n dimissioni fpl; rassegnazione f

resin [ˈrɛzɪn] n resina

resist [rɪˈzɪst] vt resistere a; **resistance** n resistenza

resit [ˈriːsɪt] (pt, pp **resat**) (BRIT) vt (exam) ripresentarsi a; (subject) ridare l'esame di ▷ n: **he's got his French ~ on Friday** deve ridare l'esame di francese venerdì

resolution [rɛzəˈluːʃən] n risoluzione f

resolve [rɪˈzɔlv] n risoluzione f ▷ vi (decide): **to ~ to do** decidere di fare ▷ vt (problem) risolvere

resort [rɪˈzɔːt] n (town) stazione f; (recourse) ricorso ▷ vi: **to ~ to** far ricorso a; **as a last ~** come ultima risorsa

resource [rɪˈsɔːs] n risorsa; **resourceful** adj pieno/a di risorse, intraprendente

respect [rɪsˈpɛkt] n rispetto ▷ vt rispettare; **respectable** adj rispettabile; **respectful** adj rispettoso/a; **respective** [rɪsˈpɛktɪv] adj rispettivo/a; **respectively** adv rispettivamente

respite [ˈrɛspaɪt] n respiro, tregua

respond [rɪsˈpɔnd] vi rispondere; **response** [rɪsˈpɔns] n risposta

responsibility [rɪspɔnsɪˈbɪlɪtɪ] n responsabilità f inv

responsible [rɪsˈpɔnsɪbl] adj: **~ (for)** responsabile (di); (trustworthy) fidato/a; (job) di (grande) responsabilità; **responsibly** adv responsabilmente

responsive [rɪsˈpɔnsɪv] adj che reagisce

rest [rɛst] n riposo; (stop) sosta, pausa; (Mus) pausa; (support) appoggio, sostegno; (remainder) resto, avanzi mpl ▷ vi riposarsi; (remain) rimanere, restare; (be supported): **to ~ on** appoggiarsi su ▷ vt (far) riposare; (lean): **to ~ sth on/against** appoggiare qc su/ contro; **the ~ of them** gli altri; **it ~s with him to decide** sta a lui decidere

restaurant [ˈrɛstərɔŋ] n ristorante m; **restaurant car** n (BRIT) vagone m ristorante

restless [ˈrɛstlɪs] adj agitato/a, irrequieto/a

restoration [rɛstəˈreɪʃən] n restauro; restituzione f

restore [rɪ'stɔːʳ] *vt* (*building*) restaurare; (*sth stolen*) restituire; (*peace, health*) ristorare
restrain [rɪs'treɪn] *vt* (*feeling*) contenere, frenare; (*person*): **to ~ (from doing)** trattenere (dal fare); **restraint** *n* (*restriction*) limitazione *f*; (*moderation*) ritegno; (*of style*) contenutezza
restrict [rɪs'trɪkt] *vt* restringere, limitare; **restriction** [rɪs'trɪkʃən] *n*: **restriction (on)** restrizione *f* (di), limitazione *f* (di)
rest room *n* (US) toletta
restructure [riː'strʌktʃəʳ] *vt* ristrutturare
result [rɪ'zʌlt] *n* risultato ▷ *vi*: **to ~ in** avere per risultato; **as a ~ (of)** in *or* di conseguenza (a), in seguito (a)
resume [rɪ'zjuːm] *vt, vi* (*work, journey*) riprendere
résumé ['reɪzjuːmeɪ] *n* riassunto; (US) curriculum vitae *m inv*
resuscitate [rɪ'sʌsɪteɪt] *vt* (*Med*) risuscitare
retail ['riːteɪl] *cpd* al minuto ▷ *vt* vendere al minuto; **retailer** *n* commerciante *m/f* al minuto, dettagliante *m/f*
retain [rɪ'teɪn] *vt* (*keep*) tenere, serbare
retaliation [rɪtælɪ'eɪʃən] *n* rappresaglie *fpl*
retarded [rɪ'tɑːdɪd] *adj* ritardato/a
retire [rɪ'taɪəʳ] *vi* (*give up work*) andare in pensione; (*withdraw*) ritirarsi, andarsene; (*go to bed*) andare a letto, ritirarsi; **retired** *adj* (*person*) pensionato/a; **retirement** *n* pensione *f*; (*act*) pensionamento
retort [rɪ'tɔːt] *vi* rimbeccare
retreat [rɪ'triːt] *n* ritirata; (*place*) rifugio ▷ *vi* battere in ritirata
retrieve [rɪ'triːv] *vt* (*sth lost*) ricuperare, ritrovare; (*situation, honour*) salvare; (*error, loss*) rimediare a
retrospect ['rɛtrəspɛkt] *n*: **in ~** guardando indietro; **retrospective** [rɛtrə'spɛktɪv] *adj* retrospettivo/a; (*law*) retroattivo/a
return [rɪ'təːn] *n* (*going or coming back*) ritorno; (*of sth stolen etc*) restituzione *f*; (*Comm: from land, shares*) profitto, reddito; **in ~ (for)** in cambio (di) ▷ *cpd* (*journey, match*) di ritorno; (BRIT: *ticket*) di andata e ritorno ▷ *vi* tornare, ritornare ▷ *vt* rendere, restituire; (*bring back*) riportare; (*send back*) mandare indietro; (*put back*) rimettere; (*Pol: candidate*) eleggere; **returns** *npl* (*Comm*) incassi *mpl*; profitti *mpl*; **by ~ of post** a stretto giro di posta; **many happy ~s (of the day)!** cento di questi giorni!; **return ticket** *n* (*esp* BRIT) biglietto di andata e ritorno
reunion [riː'juːnɪən] *n* riunione *f*
reunite [riːjuː'naɪt] *vt* riunire
revamp ['riː'væmp] *vt* (*firm*) riorganizzare
reveal [rɪ'viːl] *vt* (*make known*) rivelare, svelare; (*display*) rivelare, mostrare; **revealing** *adj* rivelatore/trice; (*dress*) scollato/a
revel ['rɛvl] *vi*: **to ~ in sth/in doing** dilettarsi di qc/a fare
revelation [rɛvə'leɪʃən] *n* rivelazione *f*
revenge [rɪ'vɛndʒ] *n* vendetta ▷ *vt* vendicare; **to take ~ on** vendicarsi di
revenue ['rɛvənjuː] *n* reddito
Reverend ['rɛvərənd] *adj* (*in titles*) reverendo/a
reversal [rɪ'vəːsl] *n* capovolgimento
reverse [rɪ'vəːs] *n* contrario, opposto; (*back*) rovescio; (*Aut: also:* **~ gear**) marcia indietro ▷ *adj* (*order*) inverso/a; (*direction*) opposto/a ▷ *vt* (*turn*) invertire, rivoltare; (*change*) capovolgere, rovesciare; (*Law: judgement*) cassare; (*car*) fare marcia indietro con ▷ *vi* (BRIT *Aut, person etc*) fare marcia indietro; **reverse-charge call** [rɪ'vəːstʃɑːdʒ-] *n* (BRIT *Tel*) telefonata con addebito al ricevente;

reversing lights npl (BRIT Aut) luci fpl per la retromarcia

revert [rɪ'vəːt] vi: **to ~ to** tornare a

review [rɪ'vjuː] n rivista; (of book, film) recensione f; (of situation) esame m ▷ vt passare in rivista; fare la recensione di; fare il punto di

revise [rɪ'vaɪz] vt (manuscript) rivedere, correggere; (opinion) emendare, modificare; (study: subject, notes) ripassare; **revision** [rɪ'vɪʒən] n revisione f; ripasso

revival [rɪ'vaɪvəl] n ripresa; ristabilimento; (of faith) risveglio

revive [rɪ'vaɪv] vt (person) rianimare; (custom) far rivivere; (hope, courage, economy) ravvivare; (play, fashion) riesumare ▷ vi (person) rianimarsi; (hope) ravvivarsi; (activity) riprendersi

revolt [rɪ'vəʊlt] n rivolta, ribellione f ▷ vi rivoltarsi, ribellarsi ▷ vt (far) rivoltare; **revolting** adj ripugnante

revolution [revə'luːʃən] n rivoluzione f; (of wheel etc) rivoluzione, giro; **revolutionary** adj, n rivoluzionario/a

revolve [rɪ'vɔlv] vi girare

revolver [rɪ'vɔlvər] n rivoltella

reward [rɪ'wɔːd] n ricompensa, premio ▷ vt: **to ~ (for)** ricompensare (per); **rewarding** adj (fig) soddisfacente

rewind [riː'waɪnd] vt (irreg: watch) ricaricare; (ribbon etc) riavvolgere

rewritable [riː'raɪtəbl] adj (CD, DVD) riscrivibile

rewrite [riː'raɪt] vt (irreg) riscrivere

rheumatism ['ruːmətɪzəm] n reumatismo

rhinoceros [raɪ'nɔsərəs] n rinoceronte m

rhubarb ['ruːbɑːb] n rabarbaro

rhyme [raɪm] n rima; (verse) poesia

rhythm ['rɪðm] n ritmo

rib [rɪb] n (Anat) costola ▷ vt (tease) punzecchiare

ribbon ['rɪbən] n nastro; **in ~s** (torn) a brandelli

rice [raɪs] n riso; **rice pudding** n budino di riso

rich [rɪtʃ] adj ricco/a; (clothes) sontuoso/a; **to be ~ in sth** essere ricco di qc

rid (pt, pp **rid**) [rɪd] vt: **to ~ sb of** sbarazzare or liberare qn di; **to get ~ of** sbarazzarsi di

riddle ['rɪdl] n (puzzle) indovinello ▷ vt: **to be ~d with** (holes) essere crivellato/a di; (doubts) essere pieno/a di

ride (pt **rode**, pp **ridden**) [raɪd, rəʊd, 'rɪdn] n (on horse) cavalcata; (outing) passeggiata; (distance covered) cavalcata; corsa ▷ vi (as sport) cavalcare; (go somewhere: on horse, bicycle) andare (a cavallo or in bicicletta etc); (journey: on bicycle, motorcycle, bus) andare, viaggiare ▷ vt (a horse) montare, cavalcare; **to ~ a horse/bicycle/camel** montare a cavallo/in bicicletta/in groppa a un cammello; **to take sb for a ~** (fig) prendere in giro qn; fregare qn; **rider** n cavalcatore/trice; (jockey) fantino; (on bicycle) ciclista m/f; (on motorcycle) motociclista m/f

ridge [rɪdʒ] n (of hill) cresta; (of roof) colmo; (on object) riga (in rilievo)

ridicule ['rɪdɪkjuːl] n ridicolo; scherno ▷ vt mettere in ridicolo; **ridiculous** [rɪ'dɪkjuləs] adj ridicolo/a

riding ['raɪdɪŋ] n equitazione f; **riding school** n scuola d'equitazione

rife [raɪf] adj diffuso/a; **to be ~ with** abbondare di

rifle ['raɪfl] n carabina ▷ vt vuotare

rift [rɪft] n fessura, crepatura; (fig: disagreement) incrinatura, disaccordo

rig [rɪg] n (also: **oil ~**: on land) derrick m inv; (: at sea) piattaforma di trivellazione ▷ vt (election etc) truccare

right [raɪt] adj giusto/a; (suitable) appropriato/a; (not left) destro/a ▷ n giusto; (title, claim) diritto;

(*not left*) destra ▷ *adv* (*answer*) correttamente; (*not on the left*) a destra ▷ *vt* raddrizzare; (*fig*) riparare ▷ *excl* bene!; **to be ~** (*person*) aver ragione; (*answer*) essere giusto/aor corretto/a; **~ now** proprio adesso; subito; **~ away** subito; **by ~s** di diritto; **on the ~** a destra; **to be in the ~** aver ragione, essere nel giusto; **right angle** n angolo retto; **rightful** *adj* (*heir*) legittimo/a; **right-hand** *adj*: **right-hand drive** guida a destra; **the right-hand side** il lato destro; **right-handed** *adj* (*person*) che adopera la mano destra; **rightly** *adv* bene, correttamente; (*with reason*) a ragione; **right of way** n diritto di passaggio; (*Aut*) precedenza

right wing n (*Pol*) destra ▷ *adj*: **right-wing** (*Pol*) di destra

rigid ['rɪdʒɪd] *adj* rigido/a; (*principle*) rigoroso/a

rigorous ['rɪɡərəs] *adj* rigoroso/a

rim [rɪm] n orlo; (*of spectacles*) montatura; (*of wheel*) cerchione m

rind [raɪnd] n (*of bacon*) cotenna; (*of lemon etc*) scorza

ring [rɪŋ] (*pt* **rang**, *pp* **rung**) n anello; (*of people, objects*) cerchio; (*of spies*) giro; (*of smoke etc*) spirale f; (*arena*) pista, arena; (*for boxing*) ring m inv; (*sound of bell*) scampanio ▷ *vi* (*person, bell, telephone*) suonare; (*also*: **~ out**: *voice, words*) risuonare; (*Tel*) telefonare; (*ears*) fischiare ▷ *vt* (*BRIT Tel*: *also*: **~ up**) telefonare a; (*bell, doorbell*) suonare; **to give sb a ~** (*BRIT Tel*) dare un colpo di telefono a qn; **ring back** *vt*, *vi* (*Tel*) richiamare; **ring off** *vi* (*BRIT Tel*) mettere giù, riattaccare; **ringing tone** n (*BRIT Tel*) segnale m di libero; **ringleader** n (*of gang*) capobanda m; **ring road** n (*BRIT*) raccordo anulare

ringtone n suoneria

rink [rɪŋk] n (*also*: **ice ~**) pista di pattinaggio

rinse [rɪns] n risciacquatura; (*hair tint*) cachet m inv ▷ *vt* sciacquare

riot ['raɪət] n sommossa, tumulto ▷ *vi* tumultuare; **a ~ of colours** un'orgia di colori; **to run ~** creare disordine

rip [rɪp] n strappo ▷ *vt* strappare ▷ *vi* strapparsi; **rip off** *vt* (*col*: *cheat*) fregare; **rip up** *vt* stracciare

ripe [raɪp] *adj* (*fruit, grain*) maturo/a; (*cheese*) stagionato/a

rip-off ['rɪpɔf] n (*col*): **it's a ~!** è un furto!

ripple ['rɪpl] n increspamento, ondulazione f; mormorio ▷ *vi* incresparsi

rise [raɪz] n (*slope*) salita, pendio; (*hill*) altura; (*increase*: *in wages*: BRIT) aumento; (: *in prices, temperature*) rialzo, aumento; (*fig*: *to power etc*) ascesa ▷ *vi* (*pt* **rose** [rəuz], *pp* **risen** ['rɪzn]) alzarsi, levarsi; (*prices*) aumentare; (*waters, river*) crescere; (*sun, wind, person*: *from chair, bed*) levarsi; (*also*: **~ up**) (*building*) ergersi; (*rebel*) insorgere; ribellarsi; (*in rank*) salire; **to give ~ to** provocare, dare origine a; **to ~ to the occasion** dimostrarsi all'altezza della situazione; **risen** ['rɪzn] *pp* of **rise**; **rising** *adj* (*increasing*: *number*) sempre crescente; (: *prices*) in aumento; (*tide*) montante; (*sun, moon*) nascente, che sorge

risk [rɪsk] n rischio; pericolo ▷ *vt* rischiare; **to take** or **run the ~ of doing** correre il rischio di fare; **at ~** in pericolo; **at one's own ~** a proprio rischio e pericolo; **risky** *adj* rischioso/a

rite [raɪt] n rito; **last ~s** l'estrema unzione

ritual ['rɪtjuəl] *adj*, n rituale (m)

rival ['raɪvl] n rivale m/f; (*in business*) concorrente m/f ▷ *adj* rivale; che fa concorrenza ▷ *vt* essere in concorrenza con; **to ~ sb/sth in** competere con qn/qc in; **rivalry** n rivalità; concorrenza

r

river ['rɪvəʳ] n fiume m ▷ cpd (port, traffic) fluviale; **up/down ~** a monte/valle; **riverbank** n argine m

rivet ['rɪvɪt] n ribattino, rivetto ▷ vt (fig) concentrare, fissare

Riviera [rɪvɪˈɛərə] n: **the (French) ~** la Costa Azzurra; **the Italian ~** la Riviera

road [rəud] n strada; (small) cammino; (in town) via ▷ cpd stradale; **major/minor ~** strada con/senza diritto di precedenza; **roadblock** n blocco stradale; **road map** n carta stradale; **road rage** n comportamento aggressivo al volante; **road safety** n sicurezza sulle strade; **roadside** n margine m della strada; **roadsign** n cartello stradale; **road tax** n (BRIT) tassa di circolazione; **roadworks** npl lavori mpl stradali

roam [rəum] vi errare, vagabondare

roar [rɔːʳ] n ruggito; (of crowd) tumulto; (of thunder, storm) muggito; (of laughter) scoppio ▷ vi ruggire; tumultuare; muggire; **to ~ with laughter** scoppiare dalle risa; **to do a ~ing trade** fare affari d'oro

roast [rəust] n arrosto ▷ vt arrostire; (coffee) tostare, torrefare; **roast beef** n arrosto di manzo

rob [rɔb] vt (person) rubare; (bank) svaligiare; **to ~ sb of sth** derubare qn di qc; (fig: deprive) privare qn di qc; **robber** n ladro; (armed) rapinatore m; **robbery** n furto; rapina

robe [rəub] n (for ceremony etc) abito; (also: **bath~**) accappatoio; (US: also: **lap ~**) coperta

robin ['rɔbɪn] n pettirosso

robot ['rəubɔt] n robot m inv

robust [rəuˈbʌst] adj robusto/a; (material, economy) solido/a

rock [rɔk] n (substance) roccia; (boulder) masso; roccia; (in sea) scoglio; (US: pebble) ciottolo; (BRIT: sweet) zucchero candito ▷ vt (swing gently: cradle) dondolare; (: child) cullare; (shake) scrollare, far tremare ▷ vi dondolarsi; oscillare; **on the ~s** (drink) col ghiaccio; (marriage etc) in crisi; **rock and roll** n rock and roll m; **rock climbing** n roccia

rocket ['rɔkɪt] n razzo

rocking chair n sedia a dondolo

rocky ['rɔkɪ] adj (hill) roccioso/a; (path) sassoso/a; (marriage etc) instabile

rod [rɔd] n (metallic, Tech) asta; (wooden) bacchetta; (also: **fishing ~**) canna da pesca

rode [rəud] pt of **ride**

rodent ['rəudnt] n roditore m

rogue [rəug] n mascalzone m

role [rəul] n ruolo; **role model** n modello (di comportamento)

roll [rəul] n rotolo; (of banknotes) mazzo; (also: **bread ~**) panino; (register) lista; (sound: of drums etc) rullo ▷ vt rotolare; (also: **~ up**: string) aggomitolare; (: sleeves) rimboccare; (cigarettes) arrotolare; (eyes) roteare; (also: **~ out**: pastry) stendere; (: lawn, road etc) spianare ▷ vi rotolare; (wheel) girare; (drum) rullare; (vehicle: also: **~ along**) avanzare; (ship) rollare; **roll over** vi rivoltarsi; **roll up** vi (col: arrive) arrivare ▷ vt (carpet, cloth, map) arrotolare; **roller** n rullo; (wheel) rotella; (for hair) bigodino; **rollerblades®** ['rəuləbleɪdz] npl pattini mpl in linea; **roller coaster** [-ˈkəustəʳ] n montagne fpl russe; **roller skates** npl pattini mpl a rotelle; **roller-skating** n pattinaggio a rotelle; **to go roller-skating** andare a pattinare (con i pattini a rotelle); **rolling pin** n matterello

ROM [rɔm] n abbr (Comput: = read-only memory) ROM f

Roman ['rəumən] adj, n romano/a; **Roman Catholic** adj, n cattolico/a

romance [rəˈmæns] n storia (or avventura or film m in) romantico/a; (charm) poesia; (love affair) idillio

Romania [rəuˈmeɪnɪə] n Romania

Romanian [rəu'meɪnɪən] adj
romeno/a ▷ n romeno/a; (Ling)
romeno

Roman numeral n numero romano

romantic [rə'mæntɪk] adj
romantico/a; sentimentale

Rome [rəum] n Roma

roof [ru:f] n tetto; (of tunnel, cave)
volta ▷ vt coprire (con un tetto); **~ of
the mouth** palato; **roof rack** n (Aut)
portabagagli m inv

rook [ruk] n (bird) corvo nero; (Chess)
torre f

room [ru:m] n (in house) stanza;
(bedroom, in hotel) camera; (in school
etc) sala; (space) posto, spazio;
roommate n compagno/a di stanza;
room service n servizio da camera;
roomy adj spazioso/a; (garment)
ampio/a

rooster ['ru:stər] n gallo

root [ru:t] n radice f ▷ vi (plant, belief)
attecchire

rope [rəup] n corda, fune f; (Naut)
cavo ▷ vt (box) legare; (climbers)
legare in cordata; **to ~ sb in** (fig)
coinvolgere qn; **to know the ~s** (fig)
conoscere i trucchi del mestiere

rort [rɔ:t] n (AUSTR, NZ col) truffa ▷ vt
fregare

rose [rəuz] pt of **rise** ▷ n rosa; (also: **~
bush**) rosaio; (on watering can) rosetta

rosé ['rəuzeɪ] n vino rosato

rosemary ['rəuzmərɪ] n rosmarino

rosy ['rəuzɪ] adj roseo/a

rot [rɔt] n (decay) putrefazione f; (col:
nonsense) stupidaggini fpl ▷ vt, vi
imputridire, marcire

rota ['rəutə] n tabella dei turni

rotate [rəu'teɪt] vt (revolve) far girare;
(change round: jobs) fare a turno ▷ vi
(revolve) girare

rotten ['rɔtn] adj (decayed) putrido/a,
marcio/a; (dishonest) corrotto/a; (col:
bad) brutto/a; (: action) vigliacco/a;
to feel ~ (ill) sentirsi a pezzi

rough [rʌf] adj (skin, surface) ruvido/a;
(terrain, road) accidentato/a;

(voice) rauco/a; (person, manner:
coarse) rozzo/a, aspro/a; (: violent)
brutale; (district) malfamato/a;
(weather) cattivo/a; (sea) mosso/a;
(plan) abbozzato/a; (guess)
approssimativo/a ▷ n (Golf) macchia;
to ~ it far vita dura; **to sleep ~** (BRIT)
dormire all'addiaccio; **roughly** adv
(handle) rudemente, brutalmente;
(make) grossolanamente; (speak)
bruscamente; (approximately)
approssimativamente

roulette [ru:'let] n roulette f

round [raund] adj rotondo/a
▷ n (BRIT: of toast) fetta; (duty: of
policeman, milkman etc) giro; (: of
doctor) visite fpl; (game: of cards, golf,
in competition) partita; (Boxing) round
m inv; (of talks) serie f inv ▷ vt (corner)
girare; (bend) prendere ▷ prep intorno
a ▷ adv: **right ~, all ~** tutt'attorno;
the long way ~ il giro più lungo; **all
the year ~** tutto l'anno; **in ~ figures**
in cifra tonda; **it's just ~ the corner**
(also fig) è dietro l'angolo; **to go ~**
to sb's (house) andare da qn; **go ~**
the back passi da dietro; **enough
to go ~** abbastanza per tutti; **~ the**
clock 24 ore su 24; **~ of ammunition**
cartuccia; **~ of applause** applausi
mpl; **~ of drinks** giro di bibite; **~ of**
sandwiches sandwich m inv; **round**
off vt (speech etc) finire; **round**
up vt radunare; (criminals) fare
una retata di; (prices) arrotondare;
roundabout n (BRIT: Aut) rotatoria;
(: at fair) giostra ▷ adj (route, means)
indiretto/a; **round trip** n (viaggio di)
andata e ritorno; **roundup** n raduno;
(of criminals) retata

rouse [rauz] vt (wake up) svegliare;
(stir up) destare; provocare;
risvegliare

route [ru:t] n itinerario; (of bus)
percorso

routine [ru:'ti:n] adj (work) corrente,
abituale; (procedure) solito/a ▷ n (pej)
routine f, tran tran m; (Theat) numero

row¹ [rəu] *n* (*line*) riga, fila; (*Knitting*) ferro; (*behind one another: of cars, people*) fila; (*in boat*) remata ▷ *vi* (*in boat*) remare; (*as sport*) vogare ▷ *vt* (*boat*) manovrare a remi; **in a ~** (*fig*) di fila

row² [rau] *n* (*noise*) baccano, chiasso; (*dispute*) lite *f*; (*scolding*) sgridata ▷ *vi* (*argue*) litigare

rowboat ['rəubəut] *n* (*US*) barca a remi

rowing ['rəuɪŋ] *n* canottaggio; **rowing boat** *n* (*BRIT*) barca a remi

royal ['rɔɪəl] *adj* reale; **royalty** ['rɔɪəltɪ] *n* (*royal persons*) (membri *mpl* della) famiglia reale; (*payment: to author*) diritti *mpl* d'autore

rpm *abbr* (= *revolutions per minute*) giri/min

RSVP *abbr* (= *répondez s'il vous plaît*) R.S.V.P.

Rt. Hon. *abbr* (*BRIT*: = *Right Honourable*) ≈ On.

rub [rʌb] *n*: **to give sth a ~** strofinare qc; (*sore place*) massaggiare qc ▷ *vt* strofinare; massaggiare; (*hands: also:* **~ together**) sfregarsi; **rub off** *vi* andare via; **rub off** *vi* andare via; **rub out** *vt* cancellare

rubber ['rʌbə*] *n* gomma; **rubber band** *n* elastico; **rubber gloves** *npl* guanti *mpl* di gomma

rubbish ['rʌbɪʃ] *n* (*from household*) immondizie *fpl*, rifiuti *mpl*; (*fig, pej*) cose *fpl* senza valore; robaccia; (*nonsense*) sciocchezze *fpl*; **rubbish bin** *n* (*BRIT*) pattumiera; **rubbish dump** *n* discarica

rubble ['rʌbl] *n* macerie *fpl*; (*smaller*) pietrisco

ruby ['ru:bɪ] *n* rubino

rucksack ['rʌksæk] *n* zaino

rudder ['rʌdə*] *n* timone *m*

rude [ru:d] *adj* (*impolite: person*) scortese, rozzo/a; (*: word, manners*) grossolano/a, rozzo/a; (*shocking*) indecente

ruffle ['rʌfl] *vt* (*hair*) scompigliare; (*clothes, water*) increspare; (*fig: person*) turbare

rug [rʌg] *n* tappeto; (*BRIT: for knees*) coperta

rugby ['rʌgbɪ] *n* (*also:* **~ football**) rugby *m*

rugged ['rʌgɪd] *adj* (*landscape*) aspro/a; (*features, determination*) duro/a; (*character*) brusco/a

ruin ['ru:ɪn] *n* rovina ▷ *vt* rovinare; **ruins** *npl* (*of building, castle etc*) rovine *fpl*, ruderi *mpl*

rule [ru:l] *n* regola; (*regulation*) regolamento, regola; (*government*) governo; (*ruler*) riga ▷ *vt* (*country*) governare; (*person*) dominare ▷ *vi* regnare; decidere; (*Law*) dichiarare; **as a ~** normalmente; **rule out** *vt* escludere; **ruler** *n* (*sovereign*) sovrano/a; (*for measuring*) regolo, riga; **ruling** *adj* (*party*) al potere; (*class*) dirigente ▷ *n* (*Law*) decisione *f*

rum [rʌm] *n* rum *m*

Rumania *etc* [ru:'meɪnɪə] = **Romania** *etc*

rumble ['rʌmbl] *n* rimbombo; brontolio ▷ *vi* rimbombare; (*stomach, pipe*) brontolare

rumour, (*US*) **rumor** ['ru:mə*] *n* voce *f* ▷ *vt*: **it is ~ed that** corre voce che

▌ Be careful not to translate *rumour* by the Italian word *rumore*.

rump steak [rʌmp-] *n* bistecca di girello

run [rʌn] (*pt* **ran**, *pp* **run**) *n* corsa; (*outing*) gita (in macchina) ▷ *vt*; (*distance travelled*) percorso, tragitto; (*series*) serie *f inv*; (*Theat*) periodo di rappresentazione; (*Ski*) pista; (*Cricket, Baseball*) meta; (*in tights, stockings*) smagliatura ▷ *vt* (*distance*) correre; (*operate: business*) gestire, dirigere; (*: competition, course*) organizzare; (*: hotel*) gestire; (*: house*) governare; (*Comput*) eseguire; (*water, bath*) far scorrere; (*force through: rope, pipe*): **to ~ through** far passare qc attraverso; (*pass: hand, finger*): **to ~ sth over** passare qc su; (*Press: feature*) presentare ▷ *vi* correre; (*flee*) scappare; (*pass: road etc*) passare; (*work: machine, factory*) funzionare, andare; (*bus, train: operate*) far servizio; (: *travel*) circolare; (*continue: play, contract*) durare; (*slide: drawer: flow: river, bath*) scorrere; (*colours, washing*) stemperarsi; (*in election*) presentarsi come candidato; (*nose*) colare; **to go for a ~** andare a correre; (*in car*) fare un giro (in macchina); **to break into a ~** mettersi a correre; **a ~ of luck** un periodo di fortuna; **to have the ~ of sb's house** essere libero di andare e venire in casa di qn; **there was a ~ on …** c'era una corsa a …; **in the long ~** a lungo andare; **on the ~** in fuga; **to ~ a race** partecipare ad una gara; **I'll ~ you to the station** la porto alla stazione; **to ~ a risk** correre un rischio; **run after** *vt fus* (*to catch up*) rincorrere; (*chase*) correre dietro a; **run away** *vi* fuggire; **run down** *vi* (*clock*) scaricarsi ▷ *vt* (*Aut*) investire; (*criticize*) criticare; (*production*) ridurre gradualmente; (*factory, shop*) rallentare l'attività di; **to be ~ down** (*person*) essere spossato/a; **run into** *vt fus* (*meet: person*) incontrare per caso; (: *trouble*) incontrare, trovare; (*collide with*) andare a sbattere contro; **run off** *vi* fuggire ▷ *vt* (*water*) far defluire; (*copies*) fare; **run out** *vi* (*person*) uscire di corsa; (*liquid*) colare; (*lease*) scadere; (*money*) esaurirsi; **run out of** *vt fus* rimanere a corto di; **run over** *vt* (*Aut*) investire, mettere sotto ▷ *vt fus* (*revise*) rivedere; **run through** *vt fus* (*instructions*) dare una scorsa a; (*rehearse: play*) riprovare, ripetere; **run up** *vt* (*debt*) lasciar accumulare; **to ~ up against** (*difficulties*) incontrare; **runaway** *adj* (*person*)

fuggiasco/a; (*horse*) in libertà; (*truck*) fuori controllo

rung [rʌŋ] *pp of* **ring** ▷ *n* (*of ladder*) piolo

runner ['rʌnə'] *n* (*in race*) corridore *m*; (: *horse*) partente *m/f*; (*on sledge*) pattino; (*for drawer etc*) guida; **runner bean** *n* (BRIT) fagiolino; **runner-up** *n* secondo/a arrivato/a

running ['rʌnɪŋ] *n* corsa; direzione *f*; organizzazione *f*; funzionamento ▷ *adj* (*water*) corrente; (*commentary*) simultaneo/a; **6 days ~** 6 giorni di seguito; **to be in/out of the ~ for sth** essere/non essere più in lizza per qc

runny ['rʌnɪ] *adj* che cola

run-up ['rʌnʌp] *n* (BRIT): **~ to sth** (*election etc*) periodo che precede qc

runway ['rʌnweɪ] *n* (*Aviat*) pista (di decollo)

rupture ['rʌptʃə'] *n* (*Med*) ernia

rural ['rʊərl] *adj* rurale

rush [rʌʃ] *n* corsa precipitosa; (*hurry*) furia, fretta; (*of emotion*) impeto; (*Bot*) giunco; (*sudden demand*): **~ for** corsa a; (*current*) flusso ▷ *vt* mandare *or* spedire velocemente; (*attack: town etc*) prendere d'assalto ▷ *vi* precipitarsi; **rush hour** *n* ora di punta

Russia ['rʌʃə] *n* Russia; **Russian** *adj* russo/a ▷ *n* russo/a; (*Ling*) russo

rust [rʌst] *n* ruggine *f* ▷ *vi* arrugginirsi

rusty ['rʌstɪ] *adj* arrugginito/a

ruthless ['ruːθlɪs] *adj* spietato/a

RV *abbr* (= *revised version*) versione riveduta della Bibbia ▷ *n abbr* (US) = **recreational vehicle**

rye [raɪ] *n* segale *f*

S

Sabbath ['sæbəθ] *n* (*Jewish*) sabato; (*Christian*) domenica

sabotage ['sæbətɑːʒ] *n* sabotaggio ▷ *vt* sabotare

saccharin(e) ['sækərɪn] *n* saccarina

sachet ['sæʃeɪ] *n* bustina

sack [sæk] *n* (*bag*) sacco ▷ *vt* (*dismiss*) licenziare, mandare a spasso; (*plunder*) saccheggiare; **to get the ~** essere mandato a spasso

sacred ['seɪkrɪd] *adj* sacro/a

sacrifice ['sækrɪfaɪs] *n* sacrificio ▷ *vt* sacrificare

sad [sæd] *adj* triste

saddle ['sædl] *n* sella ▷ *vt* (*horse*) sellare; **to be ~d with sth** (*col*) avere qc sulle spalle

sadistic [sə'dɪstɪk] *adj* sadico/a

sadly ['sædlɪ] *adv* tristemente; (*regrettably*) sfortunatamente; **~ lacking in** penosamente privo di

sadness ['sædnɪs] *n* tristezza

sae *abbr* (= *stamped addressed envelope*) busta affrancata e con indirizzo

safari [sə'fɑːrɪ] *n* safari *m inv*

safe [seɪf] *adj* sicuro/a; (*out of danger*) salvo/a, al sicuro; (*cautious*) prudente ▷ *n* cassaforte *f*; **~ from** al sicuro da; **~ and sound** sano/a e salvo/a; **(just) to be on the ~ side** per non correre rischi; **safely** *adv* sicuramente; sano/a e salvo/a; prudentemente; prudentemente; **safe sex** *n* sesso sicuro

safety ['seɪftɪ] *n* sicurezza; **safety belt** *n* cintura di sicurezza; **safety pin** *n* spilla di sicurezza

saffron ['sæfrən] *n* zafferano

sag [sæg] *vi* incurvarsi; afflosciarsi

sage [seɪdʒ] *n* (*herb*) salvia; (*man*) saggio

Sagittarius [sædʒɪ'tɛərɪəs] *n* Sagittario

Sahara [sə'hɑːrə] *n*: **the ~ Desert** il Deserto del Sahara

said [sɛd] *pt, pp of* **say**

sail [seɪl] *n* (*on boat*) vela; (*trip*): **to go for a ~** fare un giro in barca a vela ▷ *vt* (*boat*) condurre, governare ▷ *vi* (*travel: ship*) navigare; (: *passenger*) viaggiare per mare; (*set off*) salpare; (*Sport*) fare della vela; **they ~ed into Genoa** entrarono nel porto di Genova; **sailboat** ['seɪlbəut] *n* (*US*) barca a vela; **sailing** *n* (*sport*) vela; **to go sailing** fare della vela; **sailing boat** *n* barca a vela; **sailor** *n* marinaio

saint [seɪnt] *n* santo/a

sake [seɪk] *n*: **for the ~ of** per, per amore di

salad ['sæləd] *n* insalata; **salad cream** *n* (*BRIT*) (tipo di) maionese *f*; **salad dressing** *n* condimento per insalata

salami [sə'lɑːmɪ] *n* salame *m*

salary ['sælərɪ] *n* stipendio

sale [seɪl] *n* vendita; (*at reduced prices*) svendita, liquidazione *f*; (*auction*) vendita all'asta; **sales** *npl* (*total* *amount sold*) vendite *fpl*; **"for ~"** "in vendita"; **on ~** in vendita; **on ~ or return** da vendere o rimandare; **sales assistant**, (*US*) **sales clerk** *n* commesso/a; **salesman** *n* (*irreg*) commesso; (*representative*) rappresentante *m*; **salesperson** *n* (*irreg*) (*in shop*) /aommesso; (*representative*) rappresentante *m/f* di commercio; **sales rep** *n* rappresentante *m/f* di commercio; **saleswoman** *n* (*irreg*) commessa; (*representative*) rappresentante *f*

saline ['seɪlaɪn] *adj* salino/a

saliva [sə'laɪvə] *n* saliva

salmon ['sæmən] *n* (*pl inv*) salmone *m*

salon ['sælɒn] *n* (*hairdressing salon*) parrucchiere/a; (*beauty salon*) salone *m* di bellezza

saloon [sə'luːn] *n* (*US*) saloon *m inv*, bar *m inv*; (*BRIT Aut*) berlina; (*ship's lounge*) salone *m*

salt [sɔːlt] *n* sale *m* ▷ *vt* salare; **saltwater** *adj* di mare; **salty** *adj* salato/a

salute [sə'luːt] *n* saluto ▷ *vt* salutare

salvage ['sælvɪdʒ] *n* (*saving*) salvataggio; (*things saved*) beni *mpl* salvati *or* recuperati ▷ *vt* salvare, mettere in salvo

Salvation Army [sæl'veɪʃən-] *n* Esercito della Salvezza

same [seɪm] *adj* stesso/a, medesimo/a ▷ *pron*: **the ~** lo (la) stesso/a, gli (le) stessi/e; **the ~ book as** lo stesso libro di (*or* che); **at the ~ time** allo stesso tempo; **all** *or* **just the ~** tuttavia; **to do the ~ as sb** fare come qn; **and the ~ to you!** altrettanto a lei!

sample ['sɑːmpl] *n* campione *m* ▷ *vt* (*food*) assaggiare; (*wine*) degustare

sanction ['sæŋkʃən] *n* sanzione *f* ▷ *vt* sancire, sanzionare; **sanctions** *npl* (*Pol*) sanzioni *fpl*

sanctuary ['sæŋktjuərɪ] *n* (*holy place*) santuario; (*refuge*) rifugio; (*for wildlife*) riserva

sand [sænd] *n* sabbia ▷ *vt* (*also*: **~ down**) cartavetrare

sandal ['sændl] *n* sandalo

sand: sandbox ['sændbɒks] *n* (*US: for children*) buca di sabbia; **sandcastle** ['sændkɑːsl] *n* castello di sabbia; **sand dune** *n* duna di sabbia; **sandpaper** ['sændpeɪpər] *n* carta vetrata; **sandpit** ['sændpɪt] *n* (*for children*) buca di sabbia; **sands** *npl* spiaggia; **sandstone** ['sændstəʊn] *n* arenaria

sandwich ['sændwɪtʃ] *n* tramezzino, panino, sandwich *m inv* ▷ *vt*: **cheese/ham ~** sandwich al formaggio/prosciutto; **to be ~ed between** essere incastrato/a fra

sandy ['sændɪ] *adj* sabbioso/a; (*colour*) color sabbia *inv*, biondo/a rossiccio/a

sane [seɪn] *adj* (*person*) sano/a di mente; (*outlook*) sensato/a

sang [sæŋ] *pt of* **sing**

sanitary towel ['sænɪtərɪ-], (*US*) **sanitary napkin** *n* assorbente *m* (igienico)

sanity ['sænɪtɪ] *n* sanità mentale; (*common sense*) buon senso

sank [sæŋk] *pt of* **sink**

Santa Claus [sæntə'klɔːz] *n* Babbo Natale

sap [sæp] *n* (*of plants*) linfa ▷ *vt* (*strength*) fiaccare

sapphire ['sæfaɪər] *n* zaffiro

sarcasm ['sɑːkæzm] *n* sarcasmo

sarcastic [sɑː'kæstɪk] *adj* sarcastico/a; **to be ~** fare del sarcasmo

sardine [sɑː'diːn] *n* sardina

Sardinia [sɑː'dɪnɪə] *n* Sardegna

SASE *n abbr* (*US*: = *self-addressed stamped envelope*) busta affrancata e con indirizzo

sat [sæt] *pt, pp of* **sit**

Sat. *abbr* (= *Saturday*) sab.

satchel ['sætʃl] *n* cartella

satellite ['sætəlaɪt] *adj, n* satellite *m*; **satellite dish** *n* antenna parabolica;

s

satellite television n televisione f via satellite
satin ['sætɪn] n raso ▷ adj di or in raso
satire ['sætaɪəʳ] n satira
satisfaction [sætɪs'fækʃən] n soddisfazione f
satisfactory [sætɪs'fæktərɪ] adj soddisfacente
satisfied ['sætɪsfaɪd] adj (customer) soddisfatto/a; **to be ~ (with sth)** essere soddisfatto/a (di qc)
satisfy ['sætɪsfaɪ] vt soddisfare; (convince) convincere
satnav ['sætnæv] n abbr (= satellite navigation) navigatore m satellitare
Saturday ['sætədɪ] n sabato
sauce [sɔːs] n salsa; (containing meat, fish) sugo; **saucepan** n casseruola
saucer ['sɔːsəʳ] n sottocoppa m, piattino
Saudi Arabia ['saudɪ-] n Arabia Saudita
sauna ['sɔːnə] n sauna
sausage ['sɔsɪdʒ] n salsiccia; **sausage roll** n rotolo di pasta sfoglia ripieno di salsiccia
sautéed ['səuteɪd] adj saltato/a
savage ['sævɪdʒ] adj (cruel, fierce) selvaggio/a, feroce; (primitive) primitivo/a ▷ n selvaggio/a ▷ vt attaccare selvaggiamente
save [seɪv] vt (person, belongings, Comput) salvare; (money) risparmiare, mettere da parte; (time) risparmiare; (food) conservare; (avoid: trouble) evitare; (Sport) parare ▷ vi (also: ~ **up**) economizzare ▷ n (Sport) parata ▷ prep salvo, a eccezione di
saving ['seɪvɪŋ] n risparmio; **savings** npl risparmi mpl; **savings account** n libretto di risparmio; **savings and loan association** n (us) ≈ società di credito immobiliare
savoury, (us) **savory** ['seɪvərɪ] adj (dish: not sweet) salato/a
saw [sɔː] pt of **see** ▷ n (tool) sega ▷ vt (pt **sawed**, pp **sawed** or **sawn** [sɔːn]) segare; **sawdust** n segatura

sawn [sɔːn] pp of **saw**
saxophone ['sæksəfəun] n sassofono
say [seɪ] n: **to have one's ~** fare sentire il proprio parere; **to have a** or **some ~** avere voce in capitolo ▷ vt (pt, pp **said**) dire; **could you ~ that again?** potrebbe ripeterlo?; **that goes without ~ing** va da sé; **saying** n proverbio, detto
scab [skæb] n crosta; (pej) crumiro/a
scaffolding ['skæfəldɪŋ] n impalcatura
scald [skɔːld] n scottatura ▷ vt scottare
scale [skeɪl] n scala; (of fish) squama ▷ vt (mountain) scalare; **~ of charges** tariffa; **on a large ~** su vasta scala; **scales** [skeɪlz] npl (for weighing) bilancia
scallion ['skæljən] n cipolla; (us: shallot) scalogna; (: leek) porro
scallop ['skɔləp] n (Zool) pettine m; (Sewing) smerlo
scalp [skælp] n cuoio capelluto ▷ vt scotennare
scalpel ['skælpl] n bisturi m inv
scam [skæm] n (col) truffa
scampi ['skæmpɪ] npl scampi mpl
scan [skæn] vt scrutare; (glance at quickly) scorrere, dare un'occhiata a; (TV) analizzare; (Radar) esplorare ▷ n (Med) ecografia
scandal ['skændl] n scandalo; (gossip) pettegolezzi mpl
Scandinavia [skændɪ'neɪvɪə] n Scandinavia; **Scandinavian** adj, n scandinavo/a
scanner ['skænəʳ] n (Radar, Med) scanner m inv
scapegoat ['skeɪpgəut] n capro espiatorio
scar [skɑːʳ] n cicatrice f ▷ vt sfregiare
scarce [skɛəs] adj scarso/a; (copy, edition) raro/a; **to make o.s. ~** (col) squagliarsela; **scarcely** adv appena
scare [skɛəʳ] n spavento; panico ▷ vt spaventare, atterrire; **to ~ sb**

stiff spaventare a morte qn; **there was a bomb ~ at the bank** hanno evacuato la banca per paura di un attentato dinamitardo; **scarecrow** n spaventapasseri m inv; **scared** adj: **to be scared** aver paura

scarf (pl **scarves**) [skɑːf, skɑːvz] n (long) sciarpa; (square) fazzoletto da testa, foulard m inv

scarlet ['skɑːlɪt] adj scarlatto/a

scarves [skɑːvz] npl of **scarf**

scary ['skɛərɪ] adj (col) che fa paura

scatter ['skætə'] vt spargere; (crowd) disperdere ▷ vi disperdersi

scenario [sɪ'nɑːrɪəu] n (Theat, Cine) copione m; (fig) situazione f

scene [siːn] n (Theat, fig etc) scena; (of crime, accident) scena, luogo; (sight, view) vista, veduta; **scenery** n (Theat) scenario; (landscape) panorama m; **scenic** adj scenico/a; panoramico/a

scent [sɛnt] n profumo; (sense of smell) olfatto, odorato; (fig: track) pista

sceptical, (US) **skeptical** ['skɛptɪkl] adj scettico/a

schedule ['ʃɛdjuːl, US 'skɛdjuːl] n programma m, piano; (of trains) orario; (of prices etc) lista, tabella ▷ vt fissare; **on ~** in orario; **to be ahead of/behind ~** essere in anticipo/ritardo sul previsto; **scheduled flight** n volo di linea

scheme [skiːm] n piano, progetto; (method) sistema m; (dishonest plan, plot) intrigo, trama; (arrangement) disposizione f, sistemazione f; (pension scheme etc) programma m ▷ vi fare progetti; (intrigue) complottare

schizophrenic [skɪtsə'frɛnɪk] adj, n schizofrenico/a

scholar ['skɔlə'] n studioso/a; **scholarship** ['skɔləʃɪp] n erudizione f; (grant) borsa di studio

school [skuːl] n (primary, secondary) scuola; (in university: US) scuola, facoltà f inv ▷ cpd scolare, scolastico/a ▷ vt (animal) addestrare; **schoolbook** n libro scolastico; **schoolboy** n scolaro; **schoolchild** n (pl **-children**) scolaro/a; **schoolgirl** n scolara; **schooling** n istruzione f; **schoolteacher** n insegnante m/f, docente m/f; (primary) maestro/a

science ['saɪəns] n scienza; **science fiction** n fantascienza; **scientific** [saɪən'tɪfɪk] adj scientifico/a; **scientist** n scienziato/a

sci-fi ['saɪfaɪ] n abbr (col) = **science fiction**

scissors ['sɪzəz] npl forbici fpl

scold [skəuld] vt rimproverare

scone [skɔn] n focaccia da tè

scoop [skuːp] n mestolo; (for ice cream) cucchiaio dosatore; (Press) colpo giornalistico, notizia (in) esclusiva

scooter ['skuːtə'] n (motorcycle) motoretta, scooter m inv; (toy) monopattino

scope [skəup] n (capacity: of plan, undertaking) portata; (: of person) capacità fpl; (opportunity) possibilità fpl

scorching ['skɔːtʃɪŋ] adj cocente, scottante

score [skɔːr] n punti mpl, punteggio; (Mus) partitura, spartito; (twenty): **a ~** venti ▷ vt (goal, point) segnare, fare; (success) ottenere ▷ vi segnare; (Football) fare un goal; (keep score) segnare i punti; **on that ~** a questo riguardo; **~s of people** (fig) un sacco di gente; **to ~ 6 out of 10** prendere 6 su 10; **score out** vt cancellare con un segno; **scoreboard** n tabellone m segnapunti; **scorer** n marcatore/trice; (keeping score) segnapunti m inv

scorn [skɔːn] n disprezzo ▷ vt disprezzare

Scorpio ['skɔːpɪəu] n Scorpione m

scorpion ['skɔːpɪən] n scorpione m

Scot [skɔt] n scozzese m/f

Scotch tape® ['skɔtʃ-] n scotch® m

Scotland ['skɔtlənd] n Scozia

Scots [skɔts] *adj* scozzese; **Scotsman** *n* (*irreg*) scozzese *m*; **Scotswoman** *n* (*irreg*) scozzese *f*; **Scottish** ['skɔtɪʃ] *adj* scozzese; **the Scottish Parliament** il Parlamento scozzese

scout [skaut] *n* (*Mil*) esploratore *m*; (*also*: **boy ~**) giovane esploratore, scout *m inv*

scowl [skaul] *vi* accigliarsi, aggrottare le sopracciglia; **to ~ at** guardare torvo

scramble ['skræmbl] *n* arrampicata ▷ *vi* inerpicarsi; **to ~ out** *etc* uscire *etc* in fretta; **to ~ for** azzuffarsi per; **scrambled eggs** *npl* uova *fpl* strapazzate

scrap [skræp] *n* pezzo, pezzetto; (*fight*) zuffa; (*also*: **~ iron**) rottami *mpl* di ferro, ferraglia ▷ *vt* demolire; (*fig*) scartare ▷ *vi*: **to ~ (with sb)** fare a botte (con qn); **scraps** *npl* (*waste*) scarti *mpl*; **scrapbook** *n* album *m inv* di ritagli

scrape [skreɪp] *vt*, *vi* raschiare, grattare ▷ *n*: **to get into a ~** cacciarsi in un guaio

scrap paper *n* cartaccia

scratch [skrætʃ] *n* graffio ▷ *cpd*: **~ team** squadra raccogliticcia ▷ *vt* graffiare, rigare ▷ *vi* grattare; (*paint, car*) graffiare; **to start from ~** cominciare *or* partire da zero; **to be up to ~** essere all'altezza; **scratch card** *n* (*BRIT*) cartolina *f* gratta e vinci

scream [skri:m] *n* grido, urlo ▷ *vi* urlare, gridare

screen [skri:n] *n* schermo; (*fig*) muro, cortina, velo ▷ *vt* schermare, fare schermo a; (*from the wind etc*) riparare; (*film*) proiettare; (*book*) adattare per lo schermo; (*candidates etc*) passare al vaglio; **screening** *n* (*Med*) dépistage *m inv*; **screenplay** *n* sceneggiatura; **screensaver** *n* (*Comput*) screen saver *m inv*

screw [skru:] *n* vite *f* ▷ *vt* avvitare; **screw up** *vt* (*paper, material*) spiegazzare; (*col: ruin*) mandare a

monte; **to ~ up one's eyes** strizzare gli occhi; **screwdriver** *n* cacciavite *m*

scribble ['skrɪbl] *n* scarabocchio ▷ *vt* scribacchiare ▷ *vi* scarabocchiare

script [skrɪpt] *n* (*Cine etc*) copione *m*; (*in exam*) elaborato *or* compito d'esame

scroll [skrəul] *n* rotolo di carta

scrub [skrʌb] *n* (*land*) boscaglia ▷ *vt* pulire strofinando; (*reject*) annullare

scruffy ['skrʌfɪ] *adj* sciatto/a

scrum(mage) ['skrʌm(ɪdʒ)] *n* mischia

scrutiny ['skru:tɪnɪ] *n* esame *m* accurato

scuba diving ['sku:bə-] *n* immersioni *fpl* subacquee

sculptor ['skʌlptər] *n* scultore *m*

sculpture ['skʌlptʃər] *n* scultura

scum [skʌm] *n* schiuma; (*pej: people*) feccia

scurry ['skʌrɪ] *vi* sgambare, affrettarsi

sea [si:] *n* mare *m* ▷ *cpd* marino/a, del mare; (*ship, port, route, transport*) marittimo/a; (*bird, fish*) di mare; **on the ~** (*boat*) in mare; (*town*) di mare; **to go by ~** andare per mare; **out to ~** al largo; **(out) at ~** in mare; **seafood** *n* frutti *mpl* di mare; **sea front** *n* lungomare *m*; **seagull** *n* gabbiano

seal [si:l] *n* (*animal*) foca; (*stamp*) sigillo; (*impression*) impronta del sigillo ▷ *vt* sigillare; **seal off** *vt* (*close*) sigillare; (*forbid entry to*) bloccare l'accesso a

sea level *n* livello del mare

seam [si:m] *n* cucitura; (*of coal*) filone *m*

search [sə:tʃ] *n* ricerca; (*Law: at sb's home*) perquisizione *f* ▷ *vt* frugare ▷ *vi*: **to ~ for** ricercare; **in ~ of** alla ricerca di; **search engine** *n* (*Comput*) motore *m* di ricerca; **search party** *n* squadra di soccorso

sea: seashore ['si:ʃɔ:r] *n* spiaggia; **seasick** ['si:sɪk] *adj* che soffre il mal di mare; **seaside** ['si:saɪd] *n* spiaggia; **seaside resort** n stazione f balneare

season ['siːzn] n stagione f ▷ vt condire, insaporire; **seasonal** adj stagionale; **seasoning** n condimento; **season ticket** n abbonamento

seat [siːt] n sedile m; (in bus, train: place) posto; (Parliament) seggio; (buttocks) didietro; (of trousers) fondo ▷ vt far sedere; (have room for) avere or essere fornito/a di posti a sedere per; **to be ~ed** essere seduto/a; **seat belt** n cintura di sicurezza; **seating** n posti mpl a sedere

sea: sea water n acqua di mare; **seaweed** ['siːwiːd] n alghe fpl

sec. abbr = **second**

secluded [sɪ'kluːdɪd] adj isolato/a, appartato/a

second ['sɛkənd] num secondo/a ▷ adv (in race etc) al secondo posto ▷ n (unit of time) secondo; (BRIT Scol: degree) laurea con punteggio discreto; (Aut: also: **~ gear**) seconda; (Comm: imperfect) scarto ▷ vt (motion) appoggiare; **~ thoughts** ripensamenti mpl; **on ~ thoughts** (BRIT) or **thought** (US) ripensandoci bene; **secondary** adj secondario/a; **secondary school** n scuola secondaria; **second-class** adj di seconda classe ▷ adv: **to travel second-class** viaggiare in seconda (classe); **second-hand** adj di seconda mano, usato/a; **secondly** adv in secondo luogo; **second-rate** adj scadente

secrecy ['siːkrəsɪ] n segretezza

secret ['siːkrɪt] adj segreto/a ▷ n segreto; **in ~** in segreto

secretary ['sɛkrətrɪ] n segretario/a; **S~ of State (for)** (BRIT Pol) ministro (di)

secretive ['siːkrətɪv] adj riservato/a

secret service n servizi mpl segreti

sect [sɛkt] n setta

section ['sɛkʃən] n sezione f

sector ['sɛktər] n settore m

secular ['sɛkjulər] adj secolare

secure [sɪ'kjuər] adj sicuro/a; (firmly fixed) assicurato/a, ben fermato/a; (in safe place) al sicuro ▷ vt (fix) fissare, assicurare; (get) ottenere, assicurarsi

security [sɪ'kjuərɪtɪ] n sicurezza; (for loan) garanzia; **securities** npl (Stock Exchange) titoli mpl; **security guard** n guardia giurata

sedan [sə'dæn] n (US Aut) berlina

sedate [sɪ'deɪt] adj posato/a; calmo/a ▷ vt calmare

sedative ['sɛdɪtɪv] n sedativo, calmante m

seduce [sɪ'djuːs] vt sedurre; **seductive** [sɪ'dʌktɪv] adj seducente

see [siː] (pt **saw**, pp **seen**) vt vedere; (accompany): **to ~ sb to the door** accompagnare qn alla porta ▷ vi vedere; (understand) capire ▷ n sede f vescovile; **to ~ that** (ensure) badare che + sub, fare in modo che + sub; **~ you soon/later/tomorrow!** a presto/più tardi/domani!; **see off** vt salutare alla partenza; **see out** vt (take to the door) accompagnare alla porta, **see through** vt portare a termine ▷ vt fus non lasciarsi ingannare da; **see to** vt fus occuparsi di

seed [siːd] n seme m; (fig) germe m; (Tennis) testa di serie; **to go to ~** fare seme; (fig) scadere

seeing ['siːɪŋ] conj: **~ (that)** visto che

seek [siːk] (pt, pp **sought**) vt cercare

seem [siːm] vi sembrare, parere; **there ~s to be ...** sembra che ci sia ...; **seemingly** adv apparentemente

seen [siːn] pp of **see**

seesaw ['siːsɔː] n altalena a bilico

segment ['sɛgmənt] n segmento

segregate ['sɛgrɪgeɪt] vt segregare, isolare

seize [siːz] vt (grasp) afferrare; (take possession of) impadronirsi di; (Law) sequestrare

seizure ['siːʒər] n (Med) attacco; (Law) confisca, sequestro

S

seldom ['sɛldəm] *adv* raramente
select [sɪ'lɛkt] *adj* scelto/a ▷ *vt*
scegliere, selezionare; **selection** *n*
selezione *f*, scelta; **selective** *adj*
selettivo/a
self [sɛlf] *n*: **the ~** l'io *m* ▷ *prefix*
auto...; **self-assured** *adj* sicuro/a
di sé; **self-catering** *adj* (BRIT) in cui
ci si cucina da sé; **self-centred**, (US)
self-centered *adj* egocentrico/a;
self-confidence *n* sicurezza di sé;
self-confident *adj* sicuro/a di sé;
self-conscious [sɛlf'kɔnʃəs] *adj*
timido/a; **self-contained** *adj* (BRIT:
flat) indipendente; **self-control** *n*
autocontrollo; **self-defence**, (US)
self-defense *n* autodifesa; (*Law*)
legittima difesa; **self-drive** *adj*
(BRIT: *rented car*) senza autista; **self-
employed** *adj* che lavora in proprio;
self-esteem *n* amor proprio *m*;
self-indulgent *adj* indulgente verso
se stesso/a; **self-interest** *n* interesse
m personale; **selfish** *adj* egoista;
self-pity *n* autocommiserazione
f; **self-raising**, (US) **self-rising** *adj*:
self-raising flour miscela di farina
e lievito; **self-respect** *n* rispetto
di sé, amor proprio; **self-service** *n*
autoservizio, self-service *m*
sell (*pt, pp* **sold**) [sɛl, səuld] *vt* vendere
▷ *vi* vendersi; **to ~ at** *or* **for 100 euros**
essere in vendita a 100 euro; **sell off**
vt svendere, liquidare; **sell out** *vt*
esaurire; **the tickets are all sold
out** i biglietti sono esauriti; **sell-by
date** [-baɪ-] *n* data di scadenza;
seller *n* venditore/trice
Sellotape® ['sɛləuteɪp] *n* (BRIT)
nastro adesivo, scotch® *m*
selves [sɛlvz] *npl of* **self**
semester [sɪ'mɛstə[r]] *n* (US)
semestre *m*
semi... ['sɛmɪ] *prefix* semi...;
semicircle *n* semicerchio;
semidetached (house)
[sɛmɪdɪ'tætʃt-] *n* (BRIT) casa gemella;
semifinal *n* semifinale *f*

seminar ['sɛmɪnɑː[r]] *n* seminario
semi-skimmed ['sɛmɪ'skɪmd] *adj*
(*milk*) parzialmente scremato/a
senate ['sɛnɪt] *n* senato; **senator** *n*
senatore/trice
send [sɛnd] (*pt, pp* **sent**) *vt* mandare;
send back *vt* rimandare; **send
for** *vt fus* mandare a chiamare, far
venire; **send in** *vt* (*report, application,
resignation*) presentare; **send off** *vt*
(*goods*) spedire; (BRIT *Sport: player*)
espellere; **send on** *vt* (BRIT: *letter*)
inoltrare; (*luggage etc: in advance*)
spedire in anticipo; **send out** *vt*
(*invitation*) diramare; **send up** *vt*
(*person, price*) far salire; (BRIT: *parody*)
mettere in ridicolo; **sender** *n*
mittente *m/f*; **send-off** *n*: **to give
sb a good send-off** festeggiare la
partenza di qn
senile ['siːnaɪl] *adj* senile
senior ['siːnɪə[r]] *adj* (*older*) più
vecchio/a; (*of higher rank*) di grado più
elevato; **senior citizen** *n* persona
anziana; **senior high school** *n*
(US) ≈ liceo
sensation [sɛn'seɪʃən] *n* sensazione
f; **sensational** *adj* sensazionale;
(*marvellous*) eccezionale
sense [sɛns] *n* senso; (*feeling*)
sensazione *f*, senso; (*meaning*) senso,
significato; (*wisdom*) buonsenso
▷ *vt* sentire, percepire; **it makes ~**
ha senso; **~ of humour** (senso dell')
umorismo; **senseless** *adj* sciocco/a;
(*unconscious*) privo/a di sensi
sensible ['sɛnsɪbl] *adj* sensato/a,
ragionevole

> Be careful not to translate
> *sensible* by the Italian word
> *sensibile*.

sensitive ['sɛnsɪtɪv] *adj* sensibile;
(*skin, question*) delicato/a
sensual ['sɛnsjuəl] *adj* sensuale
sensuous ['sɛnsjuəs] *adj* sensuale
sent [sɛnt] *pt, pp of* **send**
sentence ['sɛntns] *n* (*Ling*) frase *f*;
(*Law: judgement*) sentenza;

(: *punishment*) condanna ⊳ *vt*: **to ~ sb to death/to 5 years** condannare qn a morte/a 5 anni

sentiment ['sɛntɪmənt] *n* sentimento; (*opinion*) opinione *f*; **sentimental** [sɛntɪ'mɛntl] *adj* sentimentale

Sep. *abbr* (= *September*) Sett.

separate *adj* ['sɛprɪt] separato/a ⊳ *vt* ['sɛpəreɪt] separare ⊳ *vi* ['sɛpəreɪt] separarsi; **separately** *adv* separatamente; **separates** *npl* (*clothes*) coordinati *mpl*; **separation** [sɛpə'reɪʃən] *n* separazione *f*

September [sɛp'tɛmbəʳ] *n* settembre *m*

septic ['sɛptɪk] *adj* settico/a; (*wound*) infettato/a; **septic tank** *n* fossa settica

sequel ['si:kwl] *n* conseguenza; (*of story*) seguito; (*of film*) sequenza

sequence ['si:kwəns] *n* (*series*) serie *f inv*; (*order*) ordine *m*

sequin ['si:kwɪn] *n* lustrino, paillette *f inv*

Serb [sə:b] *adj*, *n* = **Serbian**

Serbia ['sə:bɪə] *n* Serbia

Serbian ['sə:bɪən] *adj* serbo/a ⊳ *n* serbo/a; (*Ling*) serbo

sergeant ['sɑ:dʒənt] *n* sergente *m*; (*Police*) brigadiere *m*

serial ['sɪərɪəl] *n* (*Press*) romanzo a puntate; (*Radio, TV*) trasmissione *f* a puntate, serial *m inv*; **serial killer** *n* serial killer *mf inv*; **serial number** *n* numero di serie

series ['sɪərɪːz] *n* (*pl inv*) serie *f inv*; (*Publishing*) collana

serious ['sɪərɪəs] *adj* serio/a, grave; **seriously** *adv* seriamente

sermon ['sə:mən] *n* sermone *m*

servant ['sə:vənt] *n* domestico/a

serve [sə:v] *vt* (*employer etc*) servire, essere a servizio di; (*purpose*) servire a; (*customer, food, meal*) servire; (*apprenticeship*) fare; (*prison term*) scontare ⊳ *vi* (*also Tennis*) servire; (*be useful*): **to ~ as/for/to do** servire da/

per/per fare ⊳ *n* (*Tennis*) servizio; **it ~s him right** ben gli sta, se l'è meritata; **server** *n* (*Comput*) server *m inv*

service ['sə:vɪs] *n* servizio; (*Aut: maintenance*) assistenza, revisione *f* ⊳ *vt* (*car, washing machine*) revisionare; **services** *npl* (BRIT: *on motorway*) stazione *f* di servizio; (*Mil*): **the S~s** le forze armate; **to be of ~ to sb** essere d'aiuto a qn; **~ included/not included** servizio compreso/escluso; **service area** *n* (*on motorway*) area di servizio; **service charge** *n* (BRIT) servizio; **serviceman** *n* (*irreg*) militare *m*; **service station** *n* stazione *f* di servizio

serviette [sə:vɪ'ɛt] *n* (BRIT) tovagliolo

session ['sɛʃən] *n* (*sitting*) seduta, sessione *f*; (*Scol*) anno scolastico (*or* accademico)

set [sɛt] *n* serie *f inv*; (*of cutlery etc*) servizio; (*Radio, TV*) apparecchio; (*Tennis*) set *m inv*; (*group of people*) mondo, ambiente *m*; (*Cine*) scenario; (*Theat: stage*) scene *fpl*; (: *scenery*) scenario; (*Math*) insieme *m*; (*Hairdressing*) messa in piega ⊳ *adj* (*fixed*) stabilito/a, determinato/a; (*ready*) pronto/a ⊳ *vt* (*pt, pp* **set**) (*place*) posare, mettere; (*arrange*) sistemare; (*fix*) fissare; (*adjust*) regolare; (*decide: rules etc*) stabilire, fissare ⊳ *vi* (*pt, pp* **set**) (*sun*) tramontare; (*jam, jelly*) rapprendersi; (*concrete*) fare presa; **to be ~ on doing** essere deciso a fare; **to ~ to music** mettere in musica; **to ~ on fire** dare fuoco a; **to ~ free** liberare; **to ~ sth going** mettere in moto qc; **to ~ sail** prendere il mare; **set aside** *vt* mettere da parte; **set down** *vt* (*bus, train*) lasciare; **set in** *vi* (*infection*) svilupparsi; (*complications*) intervenire; **the rain has ~ in for the day** ormai pioverà tutto il giorno; **set off** *vi* partire ⊳ *vt* (*bomb*) far scoppiare; (*cause to* *start*) mettere in moto; (*show up well*) dare risalto a; **set out** *vi* partire; **to ~ out to do** proporsi di fare ▷ *vt* (*arrange*) disporre; (*state*) esporre, presentare; **set up** *vt* (*organization*) fondare, costituire; **setback** *n* (*hitch*) contrattempo, inconveniente *m*; **set menu** *n* menù *m inv* fisso

settee [sɛˈtiː] *n* divano, sofà *m inv*

setting [ˈsɛtɪŋ] *n* (*background*) ambiente *m*; (*of controls*) posizione *f*; (*of sun*) tramonto; (*of jewel*) montatura

settle [ˈsɛtl] *vt* (*argument, matter*) appianare; (*bill, account*) regolare; (*Med: calm*) calmare ▷ *vi* (*bird, dust etc*) posarsi; (*sediment*) depositarsi; (*also: ~ down*) sistemarsi, stabilirsi; (*become calmer*) calmarsi; **to ~ for sth** accontentarsi di qc; **to ~ on sth** decidersi per qc; **settle in** *vi* sistemarsi; **settle up** *vi*: **to ~ up with sb** regolare i conti con qn; **settlement** *n* (*payment*) pagamento, saldo; (*agreement*) accordo; (*colony*) colonia; (*village etc*) villaggio, comunità *f*

setup [ˈsɛtʌp] *n* (*arrangement*) sistemazione *f*; (*situation*) situazione *f*

seven [ˈsɛvn] *num* sette; **seventeen** *num* diciassette; **seventeenth** [sɛvnˈtiːnθ] *num* diciassettesimo/a; **seventh** *num* settimo/a; **seventieth** [ˈsɛvntɪəθ] *num* settantesimo/a; **seventy** *num* settanta

sever [ˈsɛvə*] *vt* recidere, tagliare; (*relations*) troncare

several [ˈsɛvərl] *adj, pron* alcuni/e, diversi/e; **~ of us** alcuni di noi

severe [sɪˈvɪə*] *adj* severo/a; (*serious*) serio/a, grave; (*hard*) duro/a; (*plain*) semplice, sobrio/a

sew [səu] (*pt* **sewed**, *pp* **sewn**) *vt, vi* cucire

sewage [ˈsuːɪdʒ] *n* acque *fpl* di scolo

sewer [ˈsuːə*] *n* fogna

sewing [ˈsəuɪŋ] *n* cucitura; cucito; **sewing machine** *n* macchina da cucire

sewn [səun] *pp of* **sew**

sex [sɛks] *n* sesso; **to have ~ with** avere rapporti sessuali con; **sexism** [ˈsɛksɪzəm] *n* sessismo; **sexist** *adj, n* sessista (*m/f*); **sexual** [ˈsɛksjuəl] *adj* sessuale; **sexual intercourse** rapporti *mpl* sessuali; **sexuality** [sɛksjuˈælɪtɪ] *n* sessualità; **sexy** [ˈsɛksɪ] *adj* provocante, sexy *inv*

shabby [ˈʃæbɪ] *adj* malandato/a; (*behaviour*) meschino/a

shack [ʃæk] *n* baracca, capanna

shade [ʃeɪd] *n* ombra; (*for lamp*) paralume *m*; (*of colour*) tonalità *f inv*; (*small quantity*): **a ~ (more/too large)** un po' (di più/troppo grande) ▷ *vt* ombreggiare, fare ombra a; **shades** *npl* (*us: sunglasses*) occhiali *mpl* da sole; **in the ~** all'ombra

shadow [ˈʃædəu] *n* ombra ▷ *vt* (*follow*) pedinare; **shadow cabinet** *n* (*BRIT Pol*) governo *m* ombra *inv*

shady [ˈʃeɪdɪ] *adj* ombroso/a; (*fig: dishonest*) losco/a, equivoco/a

shaft [ʃɑːft] *n* (*of arrow, spear*) asta; (*Aut, Tech*) albero; (*of mine*) pozzo; (*of lift*) tromba; (*of light*) raggio

shake [ʃeɪk] (*pt* **shook**, *pp* **shaken**) *vt* scuotere; (*bottle, cocktail*) agitare ▷ *vi* tremare; **to ~ one's head** (*in refusal, dismay*) scuotere la testa; **to ~ hands with sb** stringere *or* dare la mano a qn; **shake off** *vt* scrollare (via); (*fig*) sbarazzarsi di; **shake up** *vt* scuotere; **shaky** *adj* (*hand, voice*) tremante; (*building*) traballante

shall [ʃæl] *aux vb*: **I ~ go** andrò; **~ I open the door?** apro io la porta?; **I'll get some, ~ I?** ne prendo un po', va bene?

shallow [ˈʃæləu] *adj* poco profondo/a; (*fig*) superficiale

sham [ʃæm] *n* finzione *f*, messinscena; (*jewellery, furniture*) imitazione *f*

shambles [ˈʃæmblz] *n* confusione *f*, baraonda, scompiglio

shame [ʃeɪm] *n* vergogna ▷ *vt* far vergognare; **it is a ~ (that/to do)** è un peccato (che + sub/fare); **what a ~!** che peccato!; **shameful** adj vergognoso/a; **shameless** adj sfrontato/a; (immodest) spudorato/a

shampoo [ʃæm'puː] n shampoo m inv ▷ vt fare lo shampoo a

shandy ['ʃændɪ] n birra con gassosa

shan't [ʃɑːnt] = **shall not**

shape [ʃeɪp] n forma ▷ vt formare; (statement) formulare; (sb's ideas) condizionare; **to take ~** prendere forma

share [ʃeəʳ] n (thing received, contribution) parte f; (Comm) azione f ▷ vt dividere; (have in common) condividere, avere in comune; **shareholder** n azionista m/f

shark [ʃɑːk] n squalo, pescecane m

sharp [ʃɑːp] adj (razor, knife) affilato/a; (point) acuto/a, acuminato/a; (nose, chin) aguzzo/a; (outline) netto/a; (cold, pain) pungente; (voice) stridulo/a; (person: quick-witted) sveglio/a; (: unscrupulous) disonesto/a; (Mus): **C ~** do diesis m inv ▷ n (Mus) diesis m inv ▷ adv: **at 2 o'clock ~** alle due in punto; **sharpen** vt affilare; (pencil) fare la punta a; (fig) acuire; **sharpener** n (also: **pencil sharpener**) temperamatite m inv; **sharply** adv (abruptly) bruscamente; (clearly) nettamente; (harshly) duramente, aspramente

shatter ['ʃætəʳ] vt mandare in frantumi, frantumare; (fig: upset) distruggere; (: ruin) rovinare ▷ vi frantumarsi, andare in pezzi; **shattered** adj (grief-stricken) sconvolto/a; (exhausted) a pezzi, distrutto/a

shave [ʃeɪv] vt radere, rasare ▷ vi radersi, farsi la barba ▷ n: **to have a ~** farsi la barba; **shaver** n (also: **electric shaver**) rasoio elettrico

shaving foam n crema da barba

shaving foam n = **shaving cream**

shawl [ʃɔːl] n scialle m

she [ʃiː] pron ella, lei; **~-cat** gatta; **~-elephant** elefantessa

sheath [ʃiːθ] n fodero, guaina; (contraceptive) preservativo

shed [ʃed] n capannone m ▷ vt (pt, pp **shed**) (leaves, fur etc) perdere; (tears, blood) versare; (workers) liberarsi di

she'd [ʃiːd] = **she had; she would**

sheep [ʃiːp] n (pl inv) pecora; **sheepdog** n cane m da pastore; **sheepskin** n pelle f di pecora

sheer [ʃɪəʳ] adj (utter) vero/a (e proprio/a); (steep) a picco, perpendicolare; (almost transparent) sottile ▷ adv a picco

sheet [ʃiːt] n (on bed) lenzuolo; (of paper) foglio; (of glass) lastra; (of metal) foglio, lamina

sheik(h) [ʃeɪk] n sceicco

shelf (pl **shelves**) [ʃelf, ʃelvz] n scaffale m, mensola

shell [ʃel] n (on beach) conchiglia; (of egg, nut etc) guscio; (explosive) granata; (of building) scheletro ▷ vt (peas) sgranare; (Mil) bombardare

she'll [ʃiːl] = **she will; she shall**

shellfish ['ʃelfɪʃ] n (pl inv: crab etc) crostaceo; (scallop etc) mollusco; (as food) crostacei; molluschi

shelter ['ʃeltəʳ] n riparo, rifugio ▷ vt riparare, proteggere; (give lodging to) dare rifugio or asilo a ▷ vi ripararsi, mettersi al riparo; **sheltered** adj riparato/a

shelves [ʃelvz] npl of **shelf**

shelving ['ʃelvɪŋ] n scaffalature fpl

shepherd ['ʃepəd] n pastore m ▷ vt (guide) guidare; **shepherd's pie** (BRIT) n timballo di carne macinata e purè di patate

sheriff ['ʃerɪf] (US) n sceriffo

sherry ['ʃerɪ] n sherry m inv

she's [ʃiːz] = **she is; she has**

Shetland ['ʃetlənd] n (also: **the ~s, the ~ Isles**) le (isole) Shetland

shield [ʃiːld] n scudo; (trophy) scudetto; (protection) schermo ▷ vt: **to ~ (from)** riparare (da), proteggere (da or contro)

S

shift [ʃɪft] n (change) cambiamento; (of workers) turno ▷ vt spostare, muovere; (remove) rimuovere ▷ vi spostarsi, muoversi

shin [ʃɪn] n tibia

shine [ʃaɪn] (pt, pp **shone**) n splendore m, lucentezza ▷ vi (ri) splendere, brillare ▷ vt far brillare, far risplendere; (torch): **to ~ sth on** puntare qc verso

shingles ['ʃɪŋglz] n (Med) herpes zoster m

shiny ['ʃaɪnɪ] adj lucente, lucido/a

ship [ʃɪp] n nave f ▷ vt trasportare (via mare); (send) spedire (via mare); **shipment** n carico; **shipping** n (ships) naviglio; (traffic) navigazione f; **shipwreck** n relitto; (event) naufragio ▷ vt: **to be shipwrecked** naufragare, fare naufragio; **shipyard** n cantiere m navale

shirt [ʃəːt] n camicia; **in ~ sleeves** in maniche di camicia

shit [ʃɪt] excl (col!) merda (!)

shiver ['ʃɪvəʳ] n brivido ▷ vi rabbrividire, tremare

shock [ʃɔk] n (impact) urto, colpo; (Elec) scossa; (emotional) colpo, shock m inv; (Med) shock ▷ vt colpire, scioccare; scandalizzare; **shocking** adj scioccante, traumatizzante; (scandalous) scandaloso/a

shoe [ʃuː] n scarpa; (also: **horse~**) ferro di cavallo ▷ vt (pt, pp **shod** [ʃɔd]) (horse) ferrare; **shoelace** n stringa; **shoe polish** n lucido per scarpe; **shoeshop** n calzoleria

shone [ʃɔn] pt, pp of **shine**

shonky ['ʃɔŋkɪ] adj (AUST, NZ col: untrustworthy) sospetto/a

shook [ʃuk] pt of **shake**

shoot [ʃuːt] (pt, pp **shot**) n (on branch, seedling) germoglio ▷ vt (game) cacciare, andare a caccia di; (person) sparare a; (execute) fucilare; (film) girare ▷ vi (Football) sparare, tirare (forte); **to ~ (at)** (with gun) sparare (a), fare fuoco (su); (with bow)

tirare (su); **shoot down** vt (plane) abbattere; **shoot up** vi (fig) salire alle stelle; **shooting** n (shots) sparatoria; (Hunting) caccia

shop [ʃɔp] n negozio; (workshop) officina ▷ vi (also: **go ~ping**) fare spese; **shop assistant** n (BRIT) commesso/a; **shopkeeper** n negoziante m/f, bottegaio/a; **shoplifting** n taccheggio; **shopping** n (goods) spesa, acquisti mpl; **shopping bag** n borsa per la spesa; **shopping centre**, (US) **shopping center** n centro commerciale; **shopping mall** n centro commerciale; **shopping trolley** n (BRIT) carrello del supermercato; **shop window** n vetrina

shore [ʃɔːʳ] n (of sea) riva, spiaggia; (of lake) riva ▷ vt: **to ~ (up)** puntellare; **on ~** a riva

short [ʃɔːt] adj (not long) corto/a; (soon finished) breve; (person) basso/a; (curt) brusco/a, secco/a; (insufficient) insufficiente ▷ n (also: **~ film**) cortometraggio; **it is ~ for** è l'abbreviazione or il diminutivo di; **to be ~ of sth** essere a corto di or mancare di qc; **to run ~ of sth** rimanere senza qc; **in ~** in breve; **~ of doing** a meno che non si faccia; **everything ~ of** tutto fuorché; **to cut ~** (speech, visit) accorciare, abbreviare; **to fall ~ of** venire meno a; non soddisfare; **to stop ~** fermarsi di colpo; **to stop ~ of** non arrivare fino a; **shortage** n scarsezza, carenza; **shortbread** n biscotto di pasta frolla; **shortcoming** n difetto; **short(crust) pastry** n (BRIT) pasta frolla; **shortcut** n scorciatoia; **shorten** vt accorciare, ridurre; **shortfall** n deficit m inv; **shorthand** n stenografia; **short-lived** adj di breve durata; **shortly** adv fra poco; **shorts** npl (also: **a pair of shorts**) i calzoncini; **short-sighted** adj (BRIT) miope; **short-sleeved** ['ʃɔːtsliːvd] *adj* a maniche corte; **short story** *n* racconto, novella; **short-tempered** *adj* irascibile; **short-term** *adj* (*effect*) di *or* a breve durata; (*borrowing*) a breve scadenza

shot [ʃɔt] *pt, pp of* **shoot** ▷ *n* sparo, colpo; (*try*) prova; (*Football*) tiro; (*injection*) iniezione *f*; (*Phot*) foto *f inv*; **like a ~** come un razzo; (*very readily*) immediatamente; **shotgun** *n* fucile *m* da caccia

should [ʃud] *aux vb*: **I ~ go now** dovrei andare ora; **he ~ be there now** dovrebbe essere arrivato ora; **I ~ go if I were you** se fossi in lei andrei; **I ~ like to** mi piacerebbe

shoulder [ˈʃəuldə^r] *n* spalla; **hard ~** corsia d'emergenza ▷ *vt* (*fig*) addossarsi, prendere sulle proprie spalle; **shoulder blade** *n* scapola

shouldn't [ˈʃudnt] = **should not**

shout [ʃaut] *n* urlo, grido ▷ *vt* gridare ▷ *vi* (*also*: **~ out**) urlare, gridare

shove [ʃʌv] *vt* spingere; (*col: put*): **to ~ sth in** ficcare qc in

shovel [ˈʃʌvl] *n* pala ▷ *vt* spalare

show [ʃəu] (*pt* **showed**, *pp* **shown**) *n* (*of emotion*) dimostrazione *f*, manifestazione *f*; (*semblance*) apparenza; (*exhibition*) mostra, esposizione *f*; (*Theat, Cine*) spettacolo ▷ *vt* far vedere, mostrare; (*courage etc*) dimostrare, dar prova di; (*exhibit*) esporre ▷ *vi* vedersi, essere visibile; **to be on ~** essere esposto; **it's just for ~** è solo per far scena; **show in** *vt* (*person*) far entrare; **show off** *vi* (*pej*) esibirsi, mettersi in mostra ▷ *vt* (*display*) mettere in risalto; (*pej*) mettere in mostra; **show out** *vt* (*person*) accompagnare alla porta; **show up** *vi* (*stand out*) essere ben visibile; (*col: turn up*) farsi vedere ▷ *vt* mettere in risalto; **show business** *n* industria dello spettacolo

shower [ˈʃauə^r] *n* doccia; (*rain*) acquazzone *m*; (*of stones etc*) pioggia ▷ *vi* fare la doccia ▷ *vt*: **to ~ sb**

with (*gifts, abuse etc*) coprire qn di; (*missiles*) lanciare contro qn una pioggia di; **to have** *or* **take a ~** fare la doccia; **shower cap** *n* cuffia da doccia; **shower gel** *n* gel *m* doccia *inv*

showing [ˈʃəuɪŋ] *n* (*of film*) proiezione *f*

show jumping *n* concorso ippico (di salto ad ostacoli)

shown [ʃəun] *pp of* **show**

show: show-off *n* (*col: person*) esibizionista *m/f*; **showroom** *n* sala d'esposizione

shrank [ʃræŋk] *pt of* **shrink**

shred [ʃred] *n* (*gen pl*) brandello ▷ *vt* fare a brandelli; (*Culin*) sminuzzare, tagliuzzare

shrewd [ʃru:d] *adj* astuto/a, scaltro/a

shriek [ʃri:k] *n* strillo ▷ *vi* strillare

shrimp [ʃrɪmp] *n* gamberetto

shrine [ʃraɪn] *n* reliquario; (*place*) santuario

shrink [ʃrɪŋk] (*pt* **shrank**, *pp* **shrunk**) *vi* restringersi; (*fig*) ridursi; (*also*: **~ away**) ritrarsi ▷ *vt* (*wool*) far restringere ▷ *n* (*col, pej*) psicanalista *m/f*; **to ~ from doing sth** rifuggire dal fare qc

shrivel [ˈʃrɪvl], **shrivel up** *vt* raggrinzare, avvizzire ▷ *vi* raggrinzirsi, avvizzire

shroud [ʃraud] *n* lenzuolo funebre ▷ *vt*: **~ed in mystery** avvolto/a nel mistero

Shrove Tuesday [ˈʃrəuv-] *n* martedì *m* grasso

shrub [ʃrʌb] *n* arbusto

shrug [ʃrʌg] *n* scrollata di spalle ▷ *vt, vi*: **to ~ (one's shoulders)** alzare le spalle, fare spallucce; **shrug off** *vt* passare sopra a

shrunk [ʃrʌŋk] *pp of* **shrink**

shudder [ˈʃʌdə^r] *n* brivido ▷ *vi* rabbrividire

shuffle [ˈʃʌfl] *vt* (*cards*) mescolare; **to ~ (one's feet)** strascicare i piedi

shun [ʃʌn] *vt* sfuggire, evitare

shut (*pt, pp* **shut**) [ʃʌt] *vt* chiudere ▷ *vi* chiudersi, chiudere; **shut down** *vt, vi* chiudere definitivamente; **shut up** *vi* (*col: keep quiet*) stare zitto/a, fare silenzio ▷ *vt* (*close*) chiudere; (*silence*) far tacere; **shutter** *n* imposta; (*Phot*) otturatore *m*

shuttle ['ʃʌtl] *n* spola, navetta; (*space shuttle*) navetta (spaziale); (*also:* **~ service**) servizio *m* navetta *inv*; **shuttlecock** *n* volano

shy [ʃaɪ] *adj* timido/a

sibling ['sɪblɪŋ] *n* (*formal*) fratello/ sorella

Sicily ['sɪsɪlɪ] *n* Sicilia

sick [sɪk] *adj* (*ill*) malato/a; (*humour*) macabro/a; **to be ~** (*vomiting*) vomitare; **to feel ~** avere la nausea; **to be ~ of** (*fig*) averne abbastanza di; **sickening** *adj* (*fig*) disgustoso/a, rivoltante; **sick leave** *n* congedo per malattia; **sickly** *adj* malaticcio/a; (*causing nausea*) nauseante; **sickness** *n* malattia; (*vomiting*) vomito

side [saɪd] *n* lato; (*of lake*) riva; (*team*) squadra ▷ *cpd* (*door, entrance*) laterale ▷ *vi*: **to ~ with sb** parteggiare per qn, prendere le parti di qn; **by the ~ of** a fianco di; (*road*) sul ciglio di; **~ by ~** fianco a fianco; **to take ~s (with)** schierarsi (con); **from ~ to ~** da una parte all'altra; **sideboard** *n* credenza; **sideboards** ['saɪdbɔːdz], (*US*) **sideburns** ['saɪdbəːnz] *npl* (*whiskers*) basette *fpl*; **sidelight** *n* (*Aut*) luce *f* di posizione; **sideline** *n* (*Sport*) linea laterale; (*fig*) attività secondaria; **side order** *n* contorno (*pietanza*); **side road** *n* strada secondaria; **side street** *n* traversa; **sidetrack** *vt* (*fig*) distrarre; **sidewalk** *n* (*US*) marciapiede *m*; **sideways** *adv* (*move*) di lato, di fianco

siege [siːdʒ] *n* assedio

sieve [sɪv] *n* setaccio ▷ *vt* setacciare

sift [sɪft] *vt* passare al crivello; (*fig*) vagliare

sigh [saɪ] *n* sospiro ▷ *vi* sospirare

sight [saɪt] *n* (*faculty*) vista; (*spectacle*) spettacolo; (*on gun*) mira ▷ *vt* avvistare; **in ~** in vista; **on ~** a vista; **out of ~** non visibile; **sightseeing** *n* giro turistico; **to go sightseeing** visitare una località

sign [saɪn] *n* segno; (*with hand etc*) segno, gesto; (*notice*) insegna, cartello ▷ *vt* firmare; (*player*) ingaggiare; **as a ~ of** in segno di; **it's a good/bad ~** è buon/brutto segno; **to show ~s/ no ~ of doing sth** accennare/non accennare a fare qc; **plus/minus ~** segno del più/meno; **to ~ one's name** firmare, apporre la propria firma; **sign for** *vt fus* (*item*) firmare per l'accettazione di; **sign in** *vi* firmare il registro (all'arrivo); **sign on** *vi* (*Mil etc*) arruolarsi; (*as unemployed*) iscriversi sulla lista (dell'ufficio di collocamento) ▷ *vt* (*Mil*) arruolare; (*employee*) assumere; **sign up** (*Mil*) *vt* (*player*) ingaggiare; (*recruits*) reclutare ▷ *vi* arruolarsi; (*for course*) iscriversi

signal ['sɪgnl] *n* segnale *m* ▷ *vt* (*person*) fare segno a; (*message*) comunicare per mezzo di segnali ▷ *vi* (*Aut*) segnalare, mettere la freccia; **to ~ to sb (to do sth)** far segno a qn (di fare qc); **to ~ a left/right turn**

signature ['sɪgnətʃəʳ] *n* firma

significance [sɪg'nɪfɪkəns] *n* significato; (*of event*) importanza

significant [sɪg'nɪfɪkənt] *adj* significativo/a

signify ['sɪgnɪfaɪ] *vt* significare

sign language *n* linguaggio dei muti

signpost ['saɪnpəust] *n* cartello indicatore

Sikh [siːk] *adj, n* sikh *mf inv*

silence ['saɪləns] *n* silenzio ▷ *vt* far tacere, ridurre al silenzio

silent ['saɪlnt] *adj* silenzioso/a; (*film*) muto/a; **to keep** *or* **remain ~** tacere, stare zitto/a

silhouette [sɪluːˈɛt] *n* silhouette *f inv*

silicon chip ['sɪlɪkən-] *n* chip *m inv* (al silicio)

silk [sɪlk] n seta ▷ cpd di seta

silly ['sɪlɪ] adj stupido/a, sciocco/a

silver ['sɪlvə^r] n argento; (money) monete da 5, 10, 20 o 50 pence; (also: **~ware**) argenteria ▷ cpd d'argento; **silver-plated** adj argentato/a

SIM card ['sɪm-] n (Tel) SIM card f inv

similar ['sɪmɪlə^r] adj: **~ (to)** simile (a); **similarity** [sɪmɪ'lærɪtɪ] n somiglianza, rassomiglianza; **similarly** adv allo stesso modo; (as is similar) così pure

simmer ['sɪmə^r] vi cuocere a fuoco lento

simple ['sɪmpl] adj semplice; **simplicity** [sɪm'plɪsɪtɪ] n semplicità; **simplify** vt semplificare; **simply** adv semplicemente

simulate ['sɪmjuleɪt] vt fingere, simulare

simultaneous [sɪməl'teɪnɪəs] adj simultaneo/a; **simultaneously** adv simultaneamente, contemporaneamente

sin [sɪn] n peccato ▷ vi peccare

since [sɪns] adv da allora ▷ prep da ▷ conj (time) da quando; (because) poiché, dato che; **~ then, ever ~** da allora

sincere [sɪn'sɪə^r] adj sincero/a; **sincerely** adv: **Yours sincerely** distinti saluti

sing [sɪŋ] (pt **sang**, pp **sung**) vt, vi cantare

Singapore [sɪŋgə'pɔː^r] n Singapore f

singer ['sɪŋə^r] n cantante m/f

singing ['sɪŋɪŋ] n canto

single ['sɪŋgl] adj solo/a, unico/a; (unmarried: man) celibe; (: woman) nubile; (not double) semplice ▷ n (BRIT: also: **~ ticket**) biglietto m (di sola) andata; (record) 45 giri m inv; **single out** vt scegliere; (distinguish) distinguere; **single bed** n letto a una piazza; **single file** n: **in single file** in fila indiana; **single-handed** adv senza aiuto, da solo/a; **single-minded** adj tenace, risoluto/a;

single parent n ragazzo padre/ ragazza madre; genitore m separato; **single parent family** famiglia monoparentale; **single room** n camera singola; **singles** npl (Tennis) singolo

singular ['sɪŋgjulə^r] adj singolare ▷ n (Ling) singolare m

sinister ['sɪnɪstə^r] adj sinistro/a

sink [sɪŋk] (pt **sank**, pp **sunk**) n lavandino, acquaio ▷ vt (ship) (fare) affondare, colare a picco; (foundations) scavare; (piles etc): **to ~ sth into** conficcare qc in ▷ vi affondare, andare a fondo; (ground etc) cedere, avvallarsi; **my heart sank** mi sentii venir meno; **sink in** vi penetrare

sinus ['saɪnəs] n (Anat) seno

sip [sɪp] n sorso ▷ vt sorseggiare

sir [sə^r] n signore m; **S~ John Smith** Sir John Smith; **yes ~** sì, signore

siren ['saɪərn] n sirena

sirloin ['sə:lɔɪn] n controfiletto

sister ['sɪstə^r] n sorella; (nun) suora; (BRIT: nurse) infermiera f caposala inv; **sister-in-law** n cognata

sit [sɪt] (pt, pp **sat**) vi sedere, sedersi; (assembly) essere in seduta; (for painter) posare ▷ vt (exam) sostenere, dare; **sit back** vi (in seat) appoggiarsi allo schienale; **sit down** vi sedersi; **sit on** vt fus (jury, committee) far parte di; **sit up** vi tirarsi su a sedere; (not go to bed) stare alzato/a fino a tardi

sitcom ['sɪtkɔm] n abbr (TV: = situation comedy) sceneggiato a episodi (comico)

site [saɪt] n posto; (also: **building ~**) cantiere m ▷ vt situare

sitting ['sɪtɪŋ] n (of assembly etc) seduta; (in canteen) turno; **sitting room** n soggiorno

situated ['sɪtjueɪtɪd] adj situato/a

situation [sɪtju'eɪʃən] n situazione f; (job) lavoro; (location) posizione f; **"~s vacant/wanted"** (BRIT) "offerte/ domande di impiego"

S

six [sɪks] *num* sei; **sixteen** *num* sedici; **sixteenth** [sɪks'tiːnθ] *num* sedicesimo/a; **sixth** *num* sesto/a; **sixth form** *n* (BRIT) ultimo biennio delle scuole superiori; **sixth-form college** *n* istituto che offre corsi di preparazione all'esame di maturità per ragazzi dai 16 ai 18 anni; **sixtieth** ['sɪkstiːθ] *num* sessantesimo/a ⊳ *pron* (in series) sessantesimo/a; (fraction) sessantesimo; **sixty** *num* sessanta

size [saɪz] *n* dimensioni *fpl*; (of clothing) taglia, misura; (of shoes) numero; (glue) colla; **sizeable** *adj* considerevole

sizzle ['sɪzl] *vi* sfrigolare

skate [skeɪt] *n* pattino; (fish: pl inv) razza ⊳ *vi* pattinare; **skateboard** ['skeɪtbɔːd] *n* skateboard *m inv*; **skateboarding** *n* skateboard *m inv*; **skater** *n* pattinatore/trice; **skating** *n* pattinaggio; **skating rink** *n* pista di pattinaggio

skeleton ['skɛlɪtn] *n* scheletro

skeptical ['skɛptɪkl] (US) *adj* = **sceptical**

sketch [skɛtʃ] *n* (drawing) schizzo, abbozzo; (Theat etc) scenetta comica, sketch *m inv* ⊳ *vt* abbozzare, schizzare

skewer ['skjuːə^r] *n* spiedo

ski [skiː] *n* sci *m inv* ⊳ *vi* sciare; **ski boot** *n* scarpone *m* da sci

skid [skɪd] *n* slittamento ⊳ *vi* slittare

ski: skier ['skiːə^r] *n* sciatore/trice; **skiing** ['skiːɪŋ] *n* sci *m*

skilful, (US) **skillful** ['skɪlful] *adj* abile

ski lift *n* sciovia

skill [skɪl] *n* abilità *f inv*, capacità *f inv*; **skilled** *adj* esperto/a; (worker) qualificato/a, specializzato/a

skim [skɪm] *vt* (milk) scremare; (glide over) sfiorare ⊳ *vi*: **to ~ through** (fig) scorrere, dare una scorsa a; **skimmed milk**, (US) **skim milk** *n* latte *m* scremato

skin [skɪn] *n* pelle *f* ⊳ *vt* (fruit etc) sbucciare; (animal) scuoiare, spellare;

skinhead *n* skinhead *mf inv*; **skinny** *adj* molto magro/a, pelle e ossa *inv*

skip [skɪp] *n* saltello; (BRIT) balzo; (container) benna ⊳ *vi* saltare; (with rope) saltare la corda ⊳ *vt* saltare

ski: ski pass *n* ski pass *m inv*; **ski pole** *n* racchetta (da sci)

skipper ['skɪpə^r] *n* (Naut, Sport) capitano

skipping rope ['skɪpɪŋ-], (US) **skip rope** *n* corda per saltare

skirt [skəːt] *n* gonna, sottana ⊳ *vt* fiancheggiare, costeggiare

skirting board *n* (BRIT) zoccolo

ski slope *n* pista da sci

ski suit *n* tuta da sci

skull [skʌl] *n* cranio, teschio

skunk [skʌŋk] *n* moffetta

sky [skaɪ] *n* cielo

Skype® [skaɪp] (Internet, Tel) *n* Skype® *m* ⊳ *vt*: **to s~ sb** chiamare qn con Skype

skyscraper *n* grattacielo

slab [slæb] *n* lastra; (of meat, cheese) fetta

slack [slæk] *adj* (loose) allentato/a; (slow) lento/a; (careless) negligente; **slacks** *npl* (trousers) pantaloni *mpl*

slain [sleɪn] *pp of* **slay**

slam [slæm] *vt* (door) sbattere; (throw) scaraventare; (criticize) stroncare ⊳ *vi* sbattere

slander ['slɑːndə^r] *n* calunnia; (Law) diffamazione *f*

slang [slæŋ] *n* gergo, slang *m*

slant [slɑːnt] *n* pendenza, inclinazione *f*; (fig) angolazione *f*, punto di vista

slap [slæp] *n* schiaffo; (on face) schiaffo ⊳ *vt* dare una manata a; schiaffeggiare ⊳ *adv* (directly) in pieno; **~ a coat of paint on it** dagli una mano di vernice

slash [slæʃ] *vt* tagliare; (face) sfregiare; (fig: prices) ridurre drasticamente, tagliare

slate [sleɪt] *n* ardesia; (piece) lastra di ardesia ⊳ *vt* (fig: criticize) stroncare, distruggere

slaughter ['slɔːtər] n strage f, massacro ▷ vt (animal) macellare; (people) trucidare, massacrare; **slaughterhouse** n macello, mattatoio

Slav [slɑːv] adj, n slavo/a

slave [sleɪv] n schiavo/a ▷ vi (also: **~ away**) lavorare come uno schiavo; **slavery** n schiavitù f

slay (pt **slew**, pp **slain**) [sleɪ, sluː, sleɪn] vt (formal) uccidere

sleazy ['sliːzɪ] adj trasandato/a

sled [slɛd] (US) = **sledge**

sledge [slɛdʒ] n slitta

sleek [sliːk] adj (hair, fur) lucido/a, lucente; (car, boat) slanciato/a, affusolato/a

sleep [sliːp] n sonno ▷ vi (pt, pp **slept**) dormire; **to go to ~** addormentarsi; **sleep in** vi (oversleep) dormire fino a tardi; **sleep together** vi (have sex) andare a letto insieme; **sleeper** n (BRIT Rail: on track) traversina; (: train) treno di vagoni letto; **sleeping bag** n sacco a pelo; **sleeping car** n vagone m letto inv, carrozza f letto inv; **sleeping pill** n sonnifero; **sleepover** n il dormire a casa di amici, usato in riferimento a bambini; **sleepwalk** vi camminare nel sonno; (as a habit) essere sonnambulo/a; **sleepy** adj assonnato/a, sonnolento/a; (fig) addormentato/a

sleet [sliːt] n nevischio

sleeve [sliːv] n manica; (of record) copertina; **sleeveless** adj (garment) senza maniche

sleigh [sleɪ] n slitta

slender ['slɛndər] adj snello/a, sottile; (not enough) scarso/a, esiguo/a

slept [slɛpt] pt, pp of **sleep**

slew [sluː] vi (BRIT: also: **~ round**) girare ▷ pt of **slay**

slice [slaɪs] n fetta ▷ vt affettare, tagliare a fette

slick [slɪk] adj (skilful) brillante ▷ n (also: **oil ~**) chiazza di petrolio

slide [slaɪd] n scivolone m; (in playground) scivolo; (Phot) diapositiva; (also: **hair ~**) fermaglio (per capelli) ▷ vt (pt, pp **slid** [slɪd]) far scivolare ▷ vi (pt, pp **slid** [slɪd]) scivolare; **sliding** adj (door) scorrevole

slight [slaɪt] adj (slim) snello/a, sottile; (frail) delicato/a, fragile; (trivial) insignificante; (small) piccolo/a ▷ n offesa, affronto; **not in the ~est** affatto, neppure per sogno; **slightly** adv lievemente, un po'

slim [slɪm] adj magro/a, snello/a ▷ vi dimagrire; fare or seguire) una dieta dimagrante; **slimming** ['slɪmɪn] adj (diet, pills) dimagrante; (food) ipocalorico/a

slimy ['slaɪmɪ] adj (also fig: person) viscido/a; (covered with mud) melmoso/a

sling [slɪn] n (Med) fascia al collo; (for baby) marsupio ▷ vt (pt, pp **slung** [slʌn]) lanciare, tirare

slip [slɪp] n scivolata, scivolone m; (mistake) errore m, sbaglio; (underskirt) sottoveste f; (paper) foglietto; tagliando, scontrino ▷ vt (slide) far scivolare ▷ vi (slide) scivolare; (decline) declinare; **to ~ into/out of** (move smoothly) scivolare in/fuori da; **to give sb the ~** sfuggire qn; **a ~ of paper** un foglietto; **a ~ of the tongue** un lapsus linguae; **slip up** vi sbagliarsi

slipper ['slɪpər] n pantofola

slippery ['slɪpərɪ] adj scivoloso/a

slip road n (BRIT: to motorway) rampa di accesso

slit [slɪt] n fessura, fenditura; (cut) taglio ▷ vt (pt, pp **slit**) fendere; tagliare

slog [slɔg] (BRIT) n faticata ▷ vi lavorare con accanimento, sgobbare

slogan ['sləʊgən] n motto, slogan m inv

slope [sləʊp] n pendio; (side of mountain) versante m; (ski slope)

s

pista; (of roof) pendenza; (of floor)
inclinazione f ▷ vi: **to ~ down**
declinare; **to ~ up** essere in salita;
sloping adj inclinato/a

sloppy ['slɔpɪ] adj (work) tirato/a via;
(appearance) sciatto/a

slot [slɔt] n fessura ▷ vt: **to ~ into**
infilare in; **slot machine** n (BRIT:
vending machine) distributore m
automatico; (for amusement) slot-
machine f inv

Slovakia [sləʊˈvækɪə] n Slovacchia

Slovene ['sləʊviːn] adj sloveno/a ▷ n
sloveno/a; (Ling) sloveno

Slovenia [sləʊˈviːnɪə] n Slovenia;
Slovenian adj, n = **Slovene**

slow [sləʊ] adj lento/a; (watch): **to be
~** essere indietro ▷ adv lentamente
▷ vt, vi (also: **~ down, ~ up**) rallentare;
"~" (road sign) "rallentare"; **slowly**
adv lentamente; **slow motion** n: **in
slow motion** al rallentatore

slug [slʌg] n lumaca; (bullet)
pallottola; **sluggish** adj lento/a;
(business, market, sales) stagnante

slum [slʌm] n catapecchia

slump [slʌmp] n crollo, caduta;
(economic) depressione f, crisi f inv
▷ vi crollare

slung [slʌŋ] pt, pp of **sling**

slur [sləːʳ] n (smear): **~ (on)** macchia
(su) ▷ vt pronunciare in modo
indistinto

sly [slaɪ] adj (smile, remark)
sornione/a; (person) furbo/a

smack [smæk] n (slap) pacca; (on
face) schiaffo ▷ vt schiaffeggiare;
(child) picchiare ▷ vi: **to ~ of**
puzzare di

small [smɔːl] adj piccolo/a; **small
ads** npl (BRIT) piccoli annunci mpl;
small change n moneta, spiccioli
mpl

smart [smɑːt] adj elegante;
(fashionable) alla moda; (clever)
intelligente; (quick) sveglio/a ▷ vi
bruciare; **smartcard** ['smɑːtkɑːd] n
smartcard f inv, carta intelligente

smash [smæʃ] n (also: **~-up**) scontro,
collisione f; (smash hit) successone m
▷ vt frantumare, fracassare; (Sport:
record) battere ▷ vi frantumarsi,
andare in pezzi; **smashing** adj (col)
favoloso/a, formidabile

smear [smɪəʳ] n macchia; (Med)
striscio ▷ vt ungere; (make dirty)
sporcare; (fig) denigrare, diffamare;
**his hands were ~ed with oil/
ink** aveva le mani sporche di olio/
inchiostro; **smear test** n (BRIT Med)
Pap-test m inv

smell (pt, pp **smelt** or **smelled**) [smɛl,
smɛlt, smɛld] n odore m; (sense)
olfatto, odorato ▷ vt sentire (l')odore
di ▷ vi (food etc): **to ~ (of)** avere odore
(di); (pej) puzzare, avere un cattivo
odore; **smelly** adj puzzolente

smelt [smɛlt] pt, pp of **smell** ▷ vt
(ore) fondere

smile [smaɪl] n sorriso ▷ vi sorridere

smirk [sməːk] n sorriso furbo; sorriso
compiaciuto

smog [smɔg] n smog m

smoke [sməʊk] n fumo ▷ vt, vi
fumare; **smoke alarm** n rivelatore
f di fumo; **smoked** adj (bacon, glass)
affumicato/a; **smoker** n (person)
fumatore/trice; (Rail) carrozza per
fumatori; **smoking** n fumo; **"no
smoking"** (sign) "vietato fumare";
smoky adj fumoso/a; (taste, surface)
affumicato/a

smooth [smuːð] adj liscio/a; (sauce)
omogeneo/a; (flavour, whisky)
amabile; (movement) regolare;
(person) mellifluo/a ▷ vt lisciare,
spianare; (also: **~ out**) (difficulties)
appianare

smother ['smʌðəʳ] vt soffocare

SMS n abbr (= short message service)
SMS m; **SMS message** n SMS m inv,
messaggino

smudge [smʌdʒ] n macchia,
sbavatura ▷ vt imbrattare, sporcare

smug [smʌg] adj soddisfatto/a,
compiaciuto/a

smuggle ['smʌgl] vt
contrabbandare; **smuggling** n
contrabbando

snack [snæk] n spuntino; **snack bar**
n tavola calda, snack bar m inv

snag [snæg] n intoppo, ostacolo
imprevisto

snail [sneɪl] n chiocciola

snake [sneɪk] n serpente m

snap [snæp] n (sound) schianto, colpo
secco; (photograph) istantanea ▷ adj
improvviso/a ▷ vt (far) schioccare;
(break) spezzare di netto ▷ vi spezzarsi
con un rumore secco; (fig: person)
crollare; **to ~ at sb** (dog) cercare di
mordere qn; **to ~ open/shut** aprirsi/
chiudersi di scatto; **snap up** vt
afferrare; **snapshot** n istantanea

snarl [snɑːl] vi ringhiare

snatch [snætʃ] n (small amount): **~es
of** frammenti mpl di ▷ vt strappare
(con violenza); (steal) rubare

sneak [sniːk] ((us) pt **snuck**) vi:
to ~ in/out entrare/uscire di
nascosto ▷ n spione/a; **to ~ up on
sb** avvicinarsi quatto quatto a qn;
sneakers npl scarpe fpl da ginnastica

sneer [snɪə'] vi sogghignare; **to ~ at
sb/sth** farsi beffe di qn/qc

sneeze [sniːz] n starnuto ▷ vi
starnutire

sniff [snɪf] n fiutata, annusata
▷ vi tirare su col naso ▷ vt fiutare,
annusare

snigger ['snɪgə'] vi ridacchiare, ridere
sotto i baffi

snip [snɪp] n pezzetto; (bargain)
(buon) affare m, occasione f ▷ vt
tagliare

sniper ['snaɪpə'] n (marksman) franco
tiratore m, cecchino

snob [snɒb] n snob mf inv

snooker ['snuːkə'] n tipo di gioco
del biliardo

snoop [snuːp] vi: **to ~ about**
curiosare

snooze [snuːz] n sonnellino, pisolino
▷ vi fare un sonnellino

snore [snɔː'] vi russare

snorkel ['snɔːkl] n (of swimmer)
respiratore m a tubo

snort [snɔːt] n sbuffo ▷ vi sbuffare

snow [snəu] n neve f ▷ vi nevicare;
snowball n palla di neve ▷ vi (fig)
crescere a vista d'occhio; **snowstorm**
n tormenta

snub [snʌb] vt snobbare ▷ n offesa,
affronto

snug [snʌg] adj comodo/a; (room,
house) accogliente, comodo/a

○ **KEYWORD**

so [səu] adv 1 (thus, likewise) così; **if
so** se è così, quand'è così; **I didn't
do it — you did so!** non l'ho fatto io
— sì che l'hai fatto!; **so do I, so am I**
anch'io; **it's 5 o'clock — so it is!** sono
le 5 — davvero!; **I hope so** lo spero; **I
think so** penso di sì; **so far** finora, fin
qui; (in past) fino ad allora

2 (in comparisons etc: to such a degree)
così; **so big (that)** così grande (che);
she's not so clever as her brother
lei non è (così) intelligente come
suo fratello

3: **so much** adj tanto/a; adv tanto;
I've got so much work/money ho
tanto lavoro/tanti soldi; **I love you so
much** ti amo tanto; **so many** tanti/e

4 (phrases): **10 or so** circa 10; **so long!**
(col) (goodbye) ciao!, ci vediamo!

▷ conj 1 (expressing purpose): **so as
to do** in modo or così da fare; **we
hurried so as not to be late** ci
affrettammo per non fare tardi; **so
(that)** affinché + sub, perché + sub

2 (expressing result): **he didn't arrive
so I left** non è venuto così me ne sono
andata; **so you see, I could have
gone** vedi, sarei potuto andare

soak [səuk] vt inzuppare; (clothes)
mettere a mollo ▷ vi (clothes) essere a
mollo; **soak up** vt assorbire; **soaking**
adj (also: **soaking wet**) fradicio/a

S

so-and-so ['səuənsəu] n (somebody) un tale; **Mr/Mrs ~** signor/signora tal dei tali

soap [səup] n sapone m; **soap opera** n soap opera f inv; **soap powder** n detersivo

soar [sɔːʳ] vi volare in alto; (price, morale, spirits) salire alle stelle; (building) ergersi

sob [sɔb] n singhiozzo ▷ vi singhiozzare

sober ['səubəʳ] adj non ubriaco/a; (moderate) moderato/a; (colour, style) sobrio/a; **sober up** vt far passare la sbornia a ▷ vi farsi passare la sbornia

so-called ['səu'kɔːld] adj cosiddetto/a

soccer ['sɔkəʳ] n calcio

sociable ['səuʃəbl] adj socievole

social ['səuʃl] adj sociale ▷ n festa, serata; **socialism** n socialismo; **socialist** adj, n socialista m/f; **socialize** vi: **to socialize with** socializzare con; **social life** n vita sociale; **socially** adv socialmente, in società; **social media** npl social media mpl; **social network** n social network m inv; **social networking** n il comunicare tramite social network; **social networking site** n social network m; **social security** n previdenza sociale; **social services** npl servizi mpl sociali; **social work** n servizio sociale; **social worker** n assistente m/f sociale

society [sə'saɪətɪ] n società f inv; (club) società, associazione f; (also: **high ~**) alta società

sociology [səusɪ'ɔlədʒɪ] n sociologia

sock [sɔk] n calzino

socket ['sɔkɪt] n cavità f inv; (of eye) orbita; (BRIT Elec: also: **wall ~**) presa di corrente

soda ['səudə] n (Chem) soda; (also: **~ water**) acqua di seltz; (US: also: **~ pop**) gassosa

sodium ['səudɪəm] n sodio

sofa ['səufə] n sofà m inv; **sofa bed** n divano m letto inv

soft [sɔft] adj (not rough) morbido/a; (not hard) soffice; (not loud) sommesso/a; (not bright) tenue; (kind) gentile; **soft drink** n analcolico; **soft drugs** npl droghe fpl leggere; **soften** ['sɔfn] vt ammorbidire; addolcire; attenuare ▷ vi ammorbidirsi; addolcirsi; attenuarsi; **softly** adv dolcemente; morbidamente; **software** ['sɔftwɛəʳ] n (Comput) software m

soggy ['sɔgɪ] adj inzuppato/a

soil [sɔɪl] n terreno ▷ vt sporcare

solar ['səuləʳ] adj solare; **solar power** n energia solare; **solar system** n sistema m solare

sold [səuld] pt, pp of **sell**

soldier ['səuldʒəʳ] n soldato, militare m

sold out adj (Comm) esaurito/a

sole [səul] n (of foot) pianta (del piede); (of shoe) suola; (fish: pl inv) sogliola ▷ adj solo/a, unico/a; **solely** adv solamente, unicamente; **I will hold you solely responsible** la considererò io sola responsabile

solemn ['sɔləm] adj solenne

solicitor [sə'lɪsɪtəʳ] n (BRIT: for wills etc) ≈ notaio; (in court) ≈ avvocato

solid ['sɔlɪd] adj (not hollow) pieno/a; (strong, sound, reliable, not liquid) solido/a; (meal) sostanzioso/a ▷ n solido

solitary ['sɔlɪtərɪ] adj solitario/a

solitude ['sɔlɪtjuːd] n solitudine f

solo ['səuləu] n assolo; **soloist** n solista m/f

soluble ['sɔljubl] adj solubile

solution [sə'luːʃən] n soluzione f

solve [sɔlv] vt risolvere

solvent ['sɔlvənt] adj (Comm) solvibile ▷ n (Chem) solvente m

sombre, (US) **somber** ['sɔmbəʳ] adj scuro/a; (mood, person) triste

 KEYWORD

some [sʌm] adj **1** (a certain amount or number of): **some tea/water/cream**

del tè/dell'acqua/della panna; **some children/apples** dei bambini/delle mele

2 (*certain: in contrasts*) certo/a; **some people say that …** alcuni dicono che …, certa gente dice che …

3 (*unspecified*) un/a certo/a, qualche; **some woman was asking for you** una tale chiedeva di lei; **some day** un giorno; **some day next week** un giorno della prossima settimana

▸ *pron* **1** (*a certain number*) alcuni/e, certi/e; **I've got some** (*books etc*) ne ho alcuni; **some (of them) have been sold** alcuni sono stati venduti

2 (*a certain amount*) un po'; **I've got some** (*money, milk*) ne ho un po'; **I've read some of the book** ho letto parte del libro

▸ *adv*: **some 10 people** circa 10 persone

somebody ['sʌmbədɪ] *pron* qualcuno

somehow ['sʌmhaʊ] *adv* in un modo o nell'altro, in qualche modo; (*for some reason*) per qualche ragione

someone ['sʌmwʌn] *pron* = **somebody**

someplace ['sʌmpleɪs] *adv* (*US*) = **somewhere**

something ['sʌmθɪŋ] *pron* qualcosa, qualche cosa; **~ nice** qualcosa di bello; **~ to do** qualcosa da fare

sometime ['sʌmtaɪm] *adv* (*in future*) una volta o l'altra; (*in past*): **~ last month** durante il mese scorso; **sometimes** *adv* qualche volta

somewhat ['sʌmwɔt] *adv* piuttosto

somewhere ['sʌmwɛəʳ] *adv* in *or* da qualche parte

son [sʌn] *n* figlio

song [sɒŋ] *n* canzone *f*

son-in-law ['sʌnɪnlɔː] *n* genero

soon [suːn] *adv* presto, fra poco; (*early*) presto; **~ afterwards** poco dopo; **as ~ as possible** prima possibile; **sooner** *adv* (*time*) prima; (*preference*): **I would sooner do**

preferirei fare; **sooner or later** prima o poi

soothe [suːð] *vt* calmare

sophisticated [səˈfɪstɪkeɪtɪd] *adj* sofisticato/a; raffinato/a; complesso/a

sophomore ['sɒfəmɔːʳ] *n* (*US*) studente/essa del secondo anno

soprano [səˈprɑːnəʊ] *n* (*voice*) soprano *m*; (*singer*) soprano *m/f*

sorbet ['sɔːbeɪ] *n* sorbetto

sordid ['sɔːdɪd] *adj* sordido/a

sore [sɔːʳ] *adj* (*painful*) dolorante ▹ *n* piaga

sorrow ['sɒrəʊ] *n* dolore *m*

sorry ['sɒrɪ] *adj* spiacente; (*condition, excuse*) misero/a; **~!** scusa! (*or* scusi! *or* scusate!); **to feel ~ for sb** rincrescersi per qn

sort [sɔːt] *n* specie *f*, genere *m* ▹ *vt* (*also: ~ out*) (*papers*) classificare; ordinare; (*letters etc*) smistare; (*problems*) risolvere; (*Comput*) ordinare

SOS *n* S.O.S. *m inv*

so-so ['səʊsəʊ] *adv* così così

sought [sɔːt] *pt, pp of* **seek**

soul [səʊl] *n* anima

sound [saʊnd] *adj* (*healthy*) sano/a; (*safe, not damaged*) solido/a, in buono stato; (*reliable, not superficial*) solido/a; (*sensible*) giudizioso/a, di buon senso ▹ *adv*: **~ asleep** profondamente addormentato ▹ *n* (*noise*) suono; rumore *m*; (*Geo*) stretto ▹ *vt* (*alarm*) suonare ▹ *vi* suonare; (*fig: seem*) sembrare; **to ~ like** rassomigliare a; **soundtrack** *n* (*of film*) colonna sonora

soup [suːp] *n* minestra; (*clear*) brodo; (*thick*) zuppa

sour ['saʊəʳ] *adj* aspro/a; (*fruit*) acerbo/a; (*milk*) acido/a; (*fig*) arcigno/a, acido/a; **it's ~ grapes** è soltanto invidia

source [sɔːs] *n* fonte *f*, sorgente *f*; (*fig*) fonte

south [saʊθ] *n* sud *m*, meridione *m*, mezzogiorno ▹ *adj* del sud,

sud *inv*, meridionale ▷ *adv* verso
sud; **South Africa** *n* Sudafrica *m*;
South African *adj*, *n* sudafricano/a;
South America *n* Sudamerica *m*,
America del sud; **South American**
adj, *n* sudamericano/a; **southbound**
['sauθbaund] *adj* (*gen*) diretto/a
a sud; (*carriageway*) sud *inv*;
southeastern [sauθ'i:stən] *adj*
sudorientale; **southern** ['sʌðən] *adj*
del sud, meridionale; (*wall*) esposto/a
a sud; **South Korea** *n* Corea *f*
del sud; **South Pole** *n* Polo Sud;
southward(s) *adv* verso sud; **south-
west** *n* sud-ovest *m*; **southwestern**
[sauθ'westən] *adj* sudoccidentale
souvenir [su:və'nɪəʳ] *n* ricordo,
souvenir *m inv*
sovereign ['sɔvrɪn] *adj*, *n* sovrano/a
sow¹ [səu] (*pt* **sowed**, *pp* **sown**) *vt*
seminare
sow² [sau] *n* scrofa
soya ['sɔɪə], (*us*) **soy** *n*: **~ bean** seme
m di soia; **~ sauce** salsa di soia
spa [spɑ:] *n* (*resort*) stazione *f* termale;
(*us: also*: **health ~**) centro di cure
estetiche
space [speɪs] *n* spazio; (*room*) posto;
spazio; (*length of time*) intervallo ▷ *cpd*
spaziale ▷ *vt* (*also*: **~ out**) distanziare;
spacecraft *n* (*pl inv*) veicolo spaziale;
spaceship *n* astronave *f*, navicella
spaziale
spacious ['speɪʃəs] *adj* spazioso/a,
ampio/a
spade [speɪd] *n* (*tool*) vanga; pala;
(*child's*) paletta; **spades** *npl* (*Cards*)
picche *fpl*
spaghetti [spə'gɛtɪ] *n* spaghetti *mpl*
Spain [speɪn] *n* Spagna
spam [spæm] (*Comput*) *n* spamming
m ▷ *vt*: **to ~ sb** inviare a qn messaggi
pubblicitari non richiesti via email
span [spæn] *n* (*of bird, plane*) apertura
alare; (*of arch*) campata; (*in time*)
periodo; durata ▷ *vt* attraversare;
(*fig*) abbracciare
Spaniard ['spænjəd] *n* spagnolo/a

Spanish ['spænɪʃ] *adj* spagnolo/a
▷ *n* (*Ling*) spagnolo; **the ~** *npl* gli
Spagnoli
spank [spæŋk] *vt* sculacciare
spanner ['spænəʳ] *n* (*BRIT*) chiave
f inglese
spare [speəʳ] *adj* di riserva, di scorta;
(*surplus*) in più, d'avanzo ▷ *n* (*part*)
pezzo di ricambio ▷ *vt* (*do without*)
fare a meno di; (*afford to give*)
concedere; (*refrain from hurting, using*)
risparmiare; **to ~** (*surplus*) d'avanzo;
spare part *n* pezzo di ricambio;
spare room *n* stanza degli ospiti;
spare time *n* tempo libero; **spare
tyre**, (*us*) **spare tire** *n* (*Aut*) gomma
di scorta; **spare wheel** *n* (*Aut*) ruota
di scorta
spark [spɑ:k] *n* scintilla
sparkle ['spɑ:kl] *n* scintillio, sfavillio
▷ *vi* scintillare, sfavillare
spark plug *n* candela
sparrow ['spærəu] *n* passero
sparse [spɑ:s] *adj* sparso/a, rado/a
spasm ['spæzəm] *n* (*Med*) spasmo;
(*fig*) accesso, attacco
spat [spæt] *pt*, *pp* of **spit**
spate [speɪt] *n* (*fig*): **~ of** diluvio *or*
fiume *m* di
spatula ['spætjulə] *n* spatola
speak (*pt* **spoke**, *pp* **spoken**) [spi:k,
spəuk, 'spəukn] *vt* (*language*)
parlare; (*truth*) dire ▷ *vi* parlare; **to ~
to sb/of** *or* **about sth** parlare a qn/
di qc; **~ up!** parli più forte!; **speaker**
n (*in public*) oratore/trice; (*also*:
loudspeaker) altoparlante *m*; (*Pol*):
the Speaker il presidente della Camera
dei Comuni *or* (US) dei Rappresentanti
spear [spɪəʳ] *n* lancia ▷ *vt* infilzare
special ['spɛʃl] *adj* speciale; **special
delivery** *n* (*Post*): **by special
delivery** per espresso; **special
effects** *npl* (*Cine*) effetti *mpl* speciali;
specialist *n* specialista *m/f*;
speciality [spɛʃɪ'ælɪtɪ] *n* specialità
f inv; **specialize** *vi*: **to specialize
(in)** specializzarsi (in); **specially** *adv*

specialmente, particolarmente; **special needs** adj: **special needs children** bambini mpl con difficoltà di apprendimento; **special offer** n (Comm) offerta speciale; **special school** n (BRIT) scuola speciale (per portatori di handicap); **specialty** n (esp US) = **speciality**

species ['spi:ʃi:z] n (pl inv) specie f inv

specific [spə'sɪfɪk] adj specifico/a; preciso/a; **specifically** adv esplicitamente; (especially) appositamente

specify ['spesɪfaɪ] vt specificare, precisare; **unless otherwise specified** salvo indicazioni contrarie

specimen ['spesɪmən] n esemplare m, modello, (Med) campione m

speck [spek] n puntino, macchiolina; (particle) granello

spectacle ['spektəkl] n spettacolo; **spectacles** npl occhiali mpl; **spectacular** [spek'tækjulə^r] adj spettacolare

spectator [spek'teɪtə^r] n spettatore/trice

spectrum (pl **spectra**) ['spektrəm, -rə] n spettro

speculate ['spekjuleɪt] vi speculare; (try to guess): **to ~ about** fare ipotesi su

sped [sped] pt, pp of **speed**

speech [spi:tʃ] n (faculty) parola; (talk, Theat) discorso; (manner of speaking) parlata; **speechless** adj ammutolito/a, muto/a

speed [spi:d] n velocità f inv; (promptness) prontezza; **at full** or **top ~** a tutta velocità; **speed up** vi, vt accelerare; **speedboat** n motoscafo; **speeding** n (Aut) eccesso di velocità; **speed limit** n limite m di velocità; **speedometer** [spɪ'dɔmɪtə^r] n tachimetro; **speedy** adj veloce, rapido/a; (reply) pronto/a

spell [spel] n (also: **magic ~**) incantesimo; (period of time) (breve) periodo ▷ vt (pt, pp **spelt** or **spelled**) (in writing) scrivere (lettera per lettera); (aloud) dire lettera per lettera; (fig) significare; **to cast a ~ on sb** fare un incantesimo a qn; **he can't ~** fa errori di ortografia; **spell out** vt (letter by letter) dettare lettera per lettera, (explain): **to ~ sth out for sb** spiegare qc a qn per filo e per segno; **spellchecker** ['speltʃekə^r] n correttore m ortografico; **spelling** n ortografia

spelt [spelt] pt, pp of **spell**

spend (pt, pp **spent**) [spend, spent] vt (money) spendere; (time, life) passare; **spending** ['spendɪŋ] n: **government spending** spesa pubblica

spent [spent] pt, pp of **spend**

sperm [spə:m] n sperma m

sphere [sfɪə^r] n sfera

spice [spaɪs] n spezia ▷ vt aromatizzare

spicy ['spaɪsɪ] adj piccante

spider ['spaɪdə^r] n ragno

spike [spaɪk] n punta

spill (pt, pp **spilt** or **spilled**) [spɪl, -t, -d] vt versare, rovesciare ▷ vi versarsi, rovesciarsi

spin [spɪn] (pt, pp **spun**) n (revolution of wheel) rotazione f; (Aviat) avvitamento; (trip in car) giretto ▷ vt (wool etc) filare; (wheel) far girare ▷ vi girare

spinach ['spɪnɪtʃ] n spinacio; (as food) spinaci mpl

spinal ['spaɪnl] adj spinale

spin doctor n (col) esperto di comunicazioni responsabile dell'immagine di un partito politico

spin-dryer [spɪn'draɪə^r] n (BRIT) centrifuga

spine [spaɪn] n spina dorsale; (thorn) spina

spiral ['spaɪərl] n spirale f ▷ vi (prices) salire vertiginosamente

spire ['spaɪə^r] n guglia

spirit ['spɪrɪt] n spirito; (ghost) spirito, fantasma m; (mood) stato d'animo,

S

umore *m*; (*courage*) coraggio; **spirits**
npl (*drink*) alcolici *mpl*; **in good ~s** di
buon umore

spiritual ['spɪrɪtjuəl] *adj* spirituale

spit [spɪt] *n* (*for roasting*) spiedo;
(*spittle*) sputo; (*saliva*) saliva ▷ *vi* (*pt,
pp* **spat** [spæt]) sputare; (*fire, fat*)
scoppiettare

spite [spaɪt] *n* dispetto ▷ *vt*
contrariare, far dispetto a; **in ~ of**
nonostante, malgrado; **spiteful** *adj*
dispettoso/a

splash [splæʃ] *n* spruzzo; (*sound*)
tonfo; (*of colour*) schizzo ▷ *vt*
spruzzare ▷ *vi* (*also*: **~ about**)
sguazzare; **splash out** (*col*) *vi* (*BRIT*)
fare spese folli

splendid ['splɛndɪd] *adj* splendido/a,
magnifico/a

splinter ['splɪntə*r*] *n* scheggia ▷ *vi*
scheggiarsi

split [splɪt] (*pt, pp* **split**) *n* spaccatura;
(*fig: division, quarrel*) scissione *f* ▷ *vt*
spaccare; (*party*) dividere; (*work,
profits*) spartire, ripartire ▷ *vi*
(*divide*) dividersi; **split up** *vi* (*couple*)
separarsi, rompere; (*meeting*)
sciogliersi

spoil (*pt, pp* **spoilt** *or* **spoiled**) [spɔɪl,
-t, -d] *vt* (*damage*) rovinare, guastare;
(*mar*) sciupare; (*child*) viziare

spoilt [spɔɪlt] *pt, pp of* **spoil**

spoke [spəʊk] *pt of* **speak** ▷ *n* raggio

spoken ['spəʊkn] *pp of* **speak**

spokesman ['spəʊksmən] *n* (*irreg*)
portavoce *m inv*

spokesperson ['spəʊkspɜːsn] *n*
portavoce *m/f*

spokeswoman ['spəʊkswumən] *n*
(*irreg*) portavoce *f inv*

sponge [spʌndʒ] *n* spugna; (*also*:
~ cake) pan *m* di Spagna ▷ *vt*
spugnare, pulire con una spugna ▷ *vi*:
to ~ on *or* **off** scroccare a; **sponge
bag** (*BRIT*) *n* nécessaire *m inv*

sponsor ['spɒnsə*r*] *n* (*Radio, TV, Sport
etc*) sponsor *m inv*; (*of enterprise, bill*)
promotore/trice ▷ *vt* sponsorizzare;

(*bill*) presentare; **sponsorship** *n*
sponsorizzazione *f*

spontaneous [spɒn'teɪnɪəs] *adj*
spontaneo/a

spooky ['spuːkɪ] *adj* (*col*) che fa
accapponare la pelle

spoon [spuːn] *n* cucchiaio; **spoonful**
n cucchiaiata

sport [spɔːt] *n* sport *m inv*; (*person*)
persona di spirito ▷ *vt* sfoggiare;
sport jacket *n* (*US*) = **sports jacket**;
sports car *n* automobile *f* sportiva;
sports centre *n* (*BRIT*) centro
sportivo; **sports jacket** *n* (*BRIT*)
giacca sportiva; **sportsman** *n* (*irreg*)
sportivo; **sportswear** *n* abiti *mpl*
sportivi; **sportswoman** *n* (*irreg*)
sportiva; **sporty** *adj* sportivo/a

spot [spɒt] *n* punto; (*mark*) macchia;
(*dot: on pattern*) pallino; (*pimple*)
foruncolo; (*place*) posto; (*Radio,
TV*) spot *m inv*; (*small amount*):
a ~ of un po' di ▷ *vt* (*notice*)
individuare, distinguere; **on the
~** sul posto; **to do sth on the ~**
fare qc immediatamente *or* su
due piedi; **to put sb on the ~**
mettere qn in difficoltà; **spotless**
adj immacolato/a; **spotlight** *n*
proiettore *m*; (*Aut*) faro ausiliario

spouse [spauz] *n* sposo/a

sprain [spreɪn] *n* storta, distorsione
f ▷ *vt*: **to ~ one's ankle** storcersi
una caviglia

sprang [spræŋ] *pt of* **spring**

sprawl [sprɔːl] *vi* sdraiarsi (in modo
scomposto); (*place*) estendersi
(disordinatamente)

spray [spreɪ] *n* spruzzo; (*container*)
nebulizzatore *m*, spray *m inv*; (*of
flowers*) mazzetto ▷ *vt* spruzzare;
(*crops*) irrorare

spread [sprɛd] (*pt, pp* **spread**) *n*
diffusione *f*; (*distribution*) distribuzione
f; (*Culin*) pasta (da spalmare); (*col:
food*) banchetto ▷ *vt* (*cloth*) stendere,
distendere; (*butter etc*) spalmare;
(*disease, knowledge*) propagare,

diffondere ▷ vi stendersi, distendersi; spalmarsi; propagarsi, diffondersi; **spread out** vi (move apart) separarsi; **spreadsheet** n foglio elettronico

spree [spri:] n: **to go on a ~** fare baldoria

spring [sprɪŋ] n (leap) salto, balzo; (coiled metal) molla; (season) primavera; (of water) sorgente f ▷ vi (pt **sprang**, pp **sprung**) saltare, balzare; **spring up** vi (problem) presentarsi; **spring onion** n (BRIT) cipollina

sprinkle ['sprɪŋkl] vt spruzzare; spargere; **to ~ water** etc **on, ~ with water** etc spruzzare dell'acqua etc su

sprint [sprɪnt] n scatto ▷ vi scattare

sprung [sprʌŋ] pp of **spring**

spun [spʌn] pt, pp of **spin**

spur [spəːʳ] n sperone m; (fig) sprone m, incentivo ▷ vt (also: **~ on**) spronare; **on the ~ of the moment** lì per lì

spurt [spəːt] n (of water) getto; (of energy) esplosione f ▷ vi sgorgare

spy [spaɪ] n spia ▷ vi: **to ~ on** spiare ▷ vt (see) scorgere

sq. abbr = **square**

squabble ['skwɔbl] vi bisticciarsi

squad [skwɔd] n (Mil) plotone m; (Police) squadra

squadron ['skwɔdrn] n (Mil) squadrone m; (Aviat, Naut) squadriglia

squander ['skwɔndəʳ] vt dissipare

square [skwɛəʳ] n quadrato; (in town) piazza ▷ adj quadrato/a; (col: ideas, person) di vecchio stampo ▷ vt (arrange) regolare; (Math) elevare al quadrato; (reconcile) conciliare; **a ~ meal** un pasto abbondante; **2 metres ~** di 2 metri per 2; **1 ~ metre** 1 metro quadrato; **all ~** pari; **square root** n radice f quadrata

squash [skwɔʃ] n (vegetable) zucca; (Sport) squash m; **lemon/orange ~** (BRIT) sciroppo di limone/arancia ▷ vt schiacciare

squat [skwɔt] adj tarchiato/a, tozzo/a ▷ vi accovacciarsi; **squatter** n occupante m/f abusivo/a

squeak [skwi:k] vi squittire

squeal [skwi:l] vi strillare

squeeze [skwi:z] n pressione f; (also Econ) stretta ▷ vt premere; (hand, arm) stringere

squid [skwɪd] n calamaro

squint [skwɪnt] vi essere strabico/a ▷ n: **he has a ~** è strabico

squirm [skwəːm] vi contorcersi

squirrel ['skwɪrəl] n scoiattolo

squirt [skwəːt] vi schizzare, zampillare ▷ vt spruzzare

Sr abbr = **senior; sister**

Sri Lanka [srɪ'læŋkə] n Sri Lanka m

St abbr = **saint; street**

stab [stæb] n (with knife etc) pugnalata; (of pain) fitta; (col: try): **to have a ~ at (doing) sth** provare a fare qc ▷ vt pugnalare

stability [stə'bɪlɪtɪ] n stabilità

stable ['steɪbl] n (for horses) scuderia; (for cattle) stalla ▷ adj stabile

stack [stæk] n catasta, pila ▷ vt accatastare, ammucchiare

stadium ['steɪdɪəm] n stadio

staff [stɑːf] n (work force: gen) personale m; (: BRIT Scol) personale insegnante ▷ vt fornire di personale

stag [stæg] n cervo

stage [steɪdʒ] n (platform) palco; palcoscenico; **the ~** il teatro, la scena; (point) fase f, stadio ▷ vt (play) allestire, mettere in scena; (demonstration) organizzare; **in ~s** per gradi; a tappe

stagger ['stægəʳ] vi barcollare ▷ vt (person) sbalordire; (hours, holidays) scaglionare; **staggering** adj (amazing) sbalorditivo/a

stagnant ['stægnənt] adj stagnante

stag night, stag party n festa di addio al celibato

stain [steɪn] n macchia; (colouring) colorante m ▷ vt macchiare; (wood) tingere; **stained glass**

[ˌsteɪnd'glɑːs] n vetro colorato; **stainless** adj (steel) inossidabile

stair [stɛəʳ] n (step) gradino; **stairs** npl (flight of stairs) scale fpl, scala

staircase ['stɛəkeɪs], **stairway** ['stɛəweɪ] n scale fpl, scala

stake [steɪk] n palo, piolo; (Comm) interesse m; (Betting) puntata, scommessa ▷ vt (bet) scommettere; (risk) rischiare; **to be at ~** essere in gioco

stale [steɪl] adj (bread) raffermo/a; (food) stantio/a; (air) viziato/a; (beer) svaporato/a; (smell) di chiuso

stalk [stɔːk] n gambo, stelo ▷ vt inseguire

stall [stɔːl] n bancarella; (in stable) box m inv di stalla ▷ vt (Aut) far spegnere; (fig) bloccare ▷ vi (Aut) spegnersi, fermarsi; (fig) temporeggiare

stamina ['stæmɪnə] n vigore m, resistenza

stammer ['stæməʳ] n balbuzie f ▷ vi balbettare

stamp [stæmp] n (postage stamp) francobollo; (implement) timbro; (mark, also fig) marchio, impronta; (on document) bollo; timbro ▷ vi (also: **~ one's foot**) battere il piede ▷ vt battere; (letter) affrancare; (mark with a stamp) timbrare; **~ed addressed envelope** busta affrancata per la risposta; **stamp out** vt (fire) estinguere; (crime) eliminare; (opposition) soffocare

▮ Be careful not to translate stamp by the Italian word stampa.

stampede [stæm'piːd] n fuggi fuggi m inv

stance [stæns] n posizione f

stand [stænd] (pt, pp **stood**) n (position) posizione f; (for taxis) posteggio; (structure) supporto, sostegno; (at exhibition) stand m inv; (in shop) banco; (at market) bancarella; (booth) chiosco; (Sport) tribuna ▷ vi stare in piedi; (rise) alzarsi in piedi; (be placed) trovarsi ▷ vt (place) mettere, porre; (tolerate, withstand) resistere, sopportare; **to make a ~** prendere posizione; **to ~ for parliament** (BRIT) presentarsi come candidato (per il parlamento); **to ~ sb a drink/meal** offrire da bere/un pranzo a qn; **stand back** vi prendere le distanze; **stand by** vi (be ready) tenersi pronto/a ▷ vt fus (opinion) sostenere; **stand down** vi (withdraw) ritirarsi; **stand for** vt fus (signify) rappresentare, significare; (tolerate) sopportare, tollerare; **stand in for** vt fus sostituire; **stand out** vi (be prominent) spiccare; **stand up** vi (rise) alzarsi in piedi; **stand up for** vt fus difendere; **stand up to** vt fus tener testa a, resistere a

standard ['stændəd] n modello, standard m inv; (level) livello; (flag) stendardo ▷ adj (size etc) normale, standard inv; **standards** npl (morals) principi mpl, valori mpl; **~ of living** livello di vita

stand-by ['stændbaɪ] n riserva, sostituto; **to be on ~** (gen) tenersi pronto/a; (doctor) essere di guardia; **stand-by ticket** n (Aviat) biglietto senza garanzia

standing ['stændɪŋ] adj diritto/a, in piedi; (permanent) permanente ▷ n rango, condizione f, posizione f: **of many years' ~** che esiste da molti anni; **standing order** n (BRIT: at bank) ordine m di pagamento (permanente)

stand: standpoint ['stændpɔɪnt] n punto di vista; **standstill** ['stændstɪl] n: **at a standstill** fermo/a; (fig) a un punto morto; **to come to a standstill** fermarsi; giungere a un punto morto

stank [stæŋk] pt of **stink**

staple ['steɪpl] n (for papers) graffetta ▷ adj (food etc) di base ▷ vt cucire

star [stɑːʳ] n stella; (celebrity) divo/a ▷ vi: **to ~ (in)** essere il (or la) protagonista (di) ▷ vt (Cine) essere interpretato/a da; **the stars** npl (Astrology) le stelle

starboard ['stɑːbəd] n dritta

starch [stɑːtʃ] n amido

stardom ['stɑːdəm] n celebrità

stare [steəʳ] n sguardo fisso ▷ vi: **to ~ at** fissare

stark [stɑːk] adj (bleak) desolato/a ▷ adv: **~ naked** completamente nudo/a

start [stɑːt] n inizio; (of race) partenza; (sudden movement) sobbalzo; (advantage) vantaggio ▷ vt cominciare, iniziare; (car) mettere in moto ▷ vi cominciare; (on journey) partire, mettersi in viaggio; (jump) sobbalzare; **to ~ doing sth** (in) cominciare a fare qc; **start off** vi cominciare; (leave) partire; **start out** vi (begin) cominciare; (set out) partire; **start up** vi cominciare; (car) avviarsi ▷ vt iniziare; (car) avviare; **starter** n (Aut) motorino d'avviamento; (Sport: official) starter m inv; (BRIT Culin) primo piatto; **starting point** n punto di partenza

startle ['stɑːtl] vt far trasalire; **startling** adj sorprendente

starvation [stɑːˈveɪʃən] n fame f, inedia

starve [stɑːv] vi morire di fame; soffrire la fame ▷ vt far morire di fame, affamare

state [steɪt] n stato ▷ vt dichiarare, affermare; annunciare; **to be in a ~** essere agitato/a; **statement** n dichiarazione f; **States** npl: **the States** (USA) gli Stati Uniti; **state school** n scuola statale; **statesman** n (irreg) statista m

static ['stætɪk] n (Radio) scariche fpl ▷ adj statico/a

station ['steɪʃən] n stazione f ▷ vt collocare, disporre

stationary ['steɪʃənərɪ] adj fermo/a, immobile

stationer ['steɪʃənəʳ] n cartolaio/a; **~'s shop** cartoleria

stationery ['steɪʃənərɪ] n articoli mpl di cancelleria

station wagon n (US) giardinetta

statistic [stəˈtɪstɪk] n statistica; **statistics** n (science) statistica

statue ['stætjuː] n statua

stature ['stætʃəʳ] n statura

status ['steɪtəs] n posizione f, condizione f sociale; (prestige) prestigio; (legal, marital) stato; **status quo** [-ˈkwəʊ] n: **the status quo** lo statu quo

statutory ['stætjutərɪ] adj stabilito/a dalla legge, statutario/a

staunch [stɔːntʃ] adj fidato/a, leale

stay [steɪ] n (period of time) soggiorno, permanenza ▷ vi rimanere; (reside) alloggiare, stare; (spend some time) trattenersi, soggiornare; **to ~ put** non muoversi; **to ~ the night** passare la notte; **stay away** vi (from person, building) stare lontano (from da) (from event) non andare (**from** a); **stay behind** vi restare indietro; **stay in** vi (at home) stare in casa; **stay on** vi restare, rimanere; **stay out** vi (of house) rimanere fuori (di casa); **stay up** vi (at night) rimanere alzato/a

steadily ['stedɪlɪ] adv (firmly) saldamente; (constantly) continuamente; (fixedly) fisso; (walk) con passo sicuro

steady ['stedɪ] adj (not wobbling) fermo/a; (regular) costante; (person, character) serio/a; (: calm) calmo/a, tranquillo/a ▷ vt stabilizzare; calmare

steak [steɪk] n (meat) bistecca; (fish) trancia

steal (pt **stole**, pp **stolen**) [stiːl, stəul, ˈstəuln] vt rubare ▷ vi rubare; (move) muoversi furtivamente

steam [stiːm] n vapore m ▷ vt (Culin) cuocere a vapore ▷ vi fumare; **steam up** vi (window) appannarsi; **to get ~ed up about sth** (fig) andare in bestia per qc; **steamy** adj (room) pieno/a di vapore; (window) appannato/a

S

steel [sti:l] n acciaio ▷ cpd di acciaio

steep [sti:p] adj ripido/a, scosceso/a; (price) eccessivo/a ▷ vt inzuppare; (washing) mettere a mollo

steeple ['sti:pl] n campanile m

steer [stɪəʳ] vt guidare ▷ vi (Naut: person) governare; (car) guidarsi; **steering** n (Aut) sterzo; **steering wheel** n volante m

stem [stɛm] n (of flower, plant) stelo; (of tree) fusto; (of glass) gambo; (of fruit, leaf) picciolo ▷ vt contenere, arginare; **stem cell** n cellula staminale

step [stɛp] n passo; (stair) gradino, scalino; (action) mossa, azione f ▷ vi: **to ~ forward/back** fare un passo avanti/indietro; **steps** npl (BRIT) = **stepladder**; **to be in/ out of ~ with** stare/non stare al passo con; **step down** vi (fig) ritirarsi; **step in** vi fare il proprio ingresso; **step up** vt aumentare; intensificare; **stepbrother** n fratellastro; **stepchild** n figliastro/a; **stepdaughter** n figliastra; **stepfather** n patrigno; **stepladder** n scala a libretto; **stepmother** n matrigna; **stepsister** n sorellastra; **stepson** n figliastro

stereo ['stɛrɪəʊ] n (system) sistema m stereofonico; (record player) stereo m inv ▷ adj (also: **~phonic**) stereofonico/a

stereotype ['stɪərɪətaɪp] n stereotipo

sterile ['stɛraɪl] adj sterile; **sterilize** ['stɛrɪlaɪz] vt sterilizzare

sterling ['stə:lɪŋ] adj (gold, silver) di buona lega ▷ n (Econ) (lira) sterlina; **a pound ~** una lira sterlina

stern [stə:n] adj severo/a ▷ n (Naut) poppa

steroid ['stɛrɔɪd] n steroide m

stew [stju:] n stufato ▷ vt cuocere in umido

steward ['stju:əd] n (Aviat, Naut, Rail) steward m inv; (in club etc) dispensiere

m; **stewardess** n assistente f di volo, hostess f inv

stick [stɪk] (pt, pp **stuck**) n bastone m; (of rhubarb, celery) gambo; (of dynamite) candelotto ▷ vt (glue) attaccare; (thrust): **to ~ sth into** conficcare or piantare or infiggere qc in; (col: put) ficcare; (: tolerate) sopportare ▷ vi attaccarsi; (remain) restare, rimanere; **stick out** vi sporgere, spuntare; **stick up** vi sporgere, spuntare; **stick up for** vt fus difendere; **sticker** n cartellino adesivo; **sticking plaster** n cerotto adesivo; **stick insect** n insetto m stecco inv; **stick shift** n (us Aut) cambio manuale

sticky ['stɪkɪ] adj attaccaticcio/a, vischioso/a; (label) adesivo/a; (fig: situation) difficile

stiff [stɪf] adj rigido/a, duro/a; (muscle) legato/a, indolenzito/a; (difficult) difficile, arduo/a; (cold) freddo/a, formale; (strong) forte; (high: price) molto alto/a ▷ adv: **bored ~** annoiato/a a morte

stifling ['staɪflɪŋ] adj (heat) soffocante

stigma ['stɪgmə] n stigma m

stiletto [stɪ'lɛtəʊ] n (BRIT: also: **~ heel**) tacco a spillo

still [stɪl] adj fermo/a; (quiet) silenzioso/a ▷ adv (up to this time, even) ancora; (nonetheless) tuttavia, ciò nonostante

stimulate ['stɪmjʊleɪt] vt stimolare

stimulus (pl **stimuli**) ['stɪmjʊləs, 'stɪmjʊlaɪ] n stimolo

sting [stɪŋ] (pt, pp **stung**) n puntura; (organ) pungiglione m ▷ vt pungere

stink [stɪŋk] n fetore m, puzzo ▷ vi (pt **stank**, pp **stunk**) puzzare

stir [stə:ʳ] n agitazione f, clamore m ▷ vt mescolare; (fig) risvegliare ▷ vi muoversi; **stir up** vt provocare, suscitare; **stir-fry** vt saltare in padella ▷ n pietanza al salto

stitch [stɪtʃ] n (Sewing) punto; (Knitting) maglia; (Med) punto (di sutura); (*pain*) fitta ▷ *vt* cucire, attaccare; suturare

stock [stɔk] *n* riserva, provvista; (*Comm*) giacenza, stock *m inv*; (*Agr*) bestiame *m*; (*Culin*) brodo; (*Finance*) titoli *mpl*, azioni *fpl*; (*descent, origin*) stirpe *f* ▷ *adj* (*fig: reply etc*) consueto/a, classico/a ▷ *vt* (*have in stock*) avere, vendere; **to have sth in ~** avere qc in magazzino; **out of ~** esaurito/a; **~s and shares** valori *mpl* di borsa; **stockbroker** ['stɔkbrəukəʳ] *n* agente *m* di cambio; **stock cube** *n* (*BRIT*) dado; **stock exchange** *n* Borsa (valori); **stockholder** ['stɔkhəuldəʳ] *n* (*Finance*) azionista *m/f*

stocking ['stɔkɪŋ] *n* calza

stock market *n* Borsa, mercato finanziario

stole [stəul] *pt of* **steal** ▷ *n* stola

stolen ['stəuln] *pp of* **steal**

stomach ['stʌmək] *n* stomaco; (*belly*) pancia ▷ *vt* sopportare, digerire; **stomach ache** *n* mal *m* di stomaco

stone [stəun] *n* pietra; (*pebble*) sasso, ciottolo; (*in fruit*) nocciolo; (*Med*) calcolo; (*BRIT: weight*) 6.348 kg; 14 libbre ▷ *cpd* di pietra ▷ *vt* lapidare; (*fruit*) togliere il nocciolo a

stood [stud] *pt, pp of* **stand**

stool [stuːl] *n* sgabello

stoop [stuːp] *vi* (*also*: **have a ~**) avere una curvatura; (*also*: **~ down**) chinarsi, curvarsi

stop [stɔp] *n* arresto; (*stopping place*) fermata; (*in punctuation*) punto ▷ *vt* arrestare, fermare; (*break off*) interrompere; (*also*: **put a ~ to**) porre fine a ▷ *vi* fermarsi; (*rain, noise etc*) cessare, finire; **to ~ doing sth** cessare or finire di fare qc; **to ~ dead** fermarsi di colpo; **stop by** *vi* passare, fare un salto; **stop off** *vi* sostare brevemente; **stopover** *n* breve sosta; (*Aviat*) scalo; **stoppage** ['stɔpɪdʒ] *n* arresto, fermata; (*of pay*) trattenuta; (*strike*) interruzione *f* del lavoro

storage ['stɔːrɪdʒ] *n* immagazzinamento

store [stɔːʳ] *n* provvista, riserva; (*depot*) deposito; (*BRIT: department store*) grande magazzino; (*US: shop*) negozio ▷ *vt* immagazzinare; **in ~** di riserva; in serbo; **storekeeper** *n* (*US*) negoziante *m/f*

storey, (*US*) **story** ['stɔːrɪ] *n* piano

storm [stɔːm] *n* tempesta; temporale *m*, burrasca; uragano; (*fig*) infuriarsi ▷ *vt* prendere d'assalto; **stormy** *adj* tempestoso/a, burrascoso/a

story ['stɔːrɪ] *n* storia; favola; racconto; (*US*) = **storey**

stout [staut] *adj* solido/a, robusto/a; (*supporter*) tenace; (*fat*) corpulento/a, grasso/a ▷ *n* birra scura

stove [stəuv] *n* (*for cooking*) fornello; (: *small*) fornelletto; (*for heating*) stufa

straight [streɪt] *adj* dritto/a; (*frank*) onesto/a, franco/a; (*plain, uncomplicated*) semplice ▷ *adv* diritto; (*drink*) liscio; **to put** or **get ~** mettere in ordine, mettere ordine in; **~ away**, **~ off** (*at once*) immediatamente; **straighten** *vt* (*also*: **straighten out**) raddrizzare; **straighteners** ['streɪtnəz] *npl* (*for hair*) piastra *f* per capelli; **straightforward** *adj* semplice; (*frank*) onesto/a, franco/a

strain [streɪn] *n* (*Tech*) sollecitazione *f*; (*physical*) sforzo; (*mental*) tensione *f*; (*Med*) strappo; distorsione *f*; (*streak, trace*) tendenza; elemento ▷ *vt* tendere; (*muscle*) stirare; (*ankle*) slogar; (*resources*) pesare su; (*food*) colare; passare; **strained** *adj* (*muscle*) stirato/a; (*laugh etc*) forzato/a; (*relations*) teso/a; **strainer** *n* passino, colino

strait [streɪt] *n* (*Geo*) stretto; **straits** *npl*: **to be in dire ~s** (*fig*) essere nei guai

strand [strænd] *n* (*of thread*) filo; **stranded** *adj* nei guai; senza mezzi di trasporto

S

strange [streɪndʒ] adj (not known) sconosciuto/a; (odd) strano/a, bizzarro/a; **strangely** adv stranamente; **stranger** n sconosciuto/a; (from another place) estraneo/a

strangle ['stræŋgl] vt strangolare

strap [stræp] n cinghia; (of slip, dress) spallina, bretella

strategic [strə'tiːdʒɪk] adj strategico/a

strategy ['strætɪdʒɪ] n strategia

straw [strɔː] n paglia; (drinking straw) cannuccia; **that's the last ~!** è la goccia che fa traboccare il vaso!

strawberry ['strɔːbərɪ] n fragola

stray [streɪ] adj (animal) randagio/a; (bullet) vagante; (scattered) sparso/a ▷ vi perdersi

streak [striːk] n striscia; (of hair) mèche f inv ▷ vt striare, screziare ▷ vi: **to ~ past** passare come un fulmine

stream [striːm] n ruscello; corrente f; (of people, smoke etc) fiume m ▷ vt (Scol) dividere in livelli di rendimento ▷ vi scorrere; **to ~ in/out** entrare/uscire a fiotti

street [striːt] n strada, via; **streetcar** n (us) tram m inv; **street light** n lampione m; **street map** n pianta (di una città); **street plan** n pianta (di una città)

strength [streŋθ] n forza; **strengthen** vt rinforzare; fortificare; (economy, currency) consolidare

strenuous ['strɛnjuəs] adj vigoroso/a, energico/a; (tiring) duro/a, pesante

stress [strɛs] n (force, pressure) pressione f; (mental strain) tensione f; (accent) accento ▷ vt insistere su, sottolineare; accentare; **stressed** adj (tense: person) stressato/a; (Ling, Poetry: syllable) accentato/a; **stressful** adj (job) difficile, stressante

stretch [strɛtʃ] n (of sand etc) distesa ▷ vi stirarsi; (extend): **to ~ to** or **as far as** estendersi fino a ▷ vt tendere, allungare; (spread) distendere; (fig) spingere (al massimo); **stretch out** vi allungarsi, estendersi ▷ vt (arm etc) allungare, tendere; (spread) distendere

stretcher ['strɛtʃər] n barella, lettiga

strict [strɪkt] adj (severe) rigido/a, severo/a; (precise) preciso/a, stretto/a; **strictly** adv severamente; rigorosamente; strettamente

stride [straɪd] n passo lungo ▷ vi (pt **strode**, pp **stridden**) camminare a grandi passi

strike [straɪk] (pt, pp **struck**) n sciopero; (of oil etc) scoperta; (attack) attacco ▷ vt colpire; (oil etc) scoprire, trovare; (bargain) fare; (fig): **the thought** or **it ~s me that …** mi viene in mente che … ▷ vi scioperare; (attack) attaccare; (clock) suonare; **on ~** (workers) in sciopero; **to go on** or **come out on ~** mettersi in sciopero; **to ~ a match** accendere un fiammifero; **striker** n scioperante m/f; (Sport) attaccante m; **striking** adj impressionante

string [strɪŋ] n spago; (row) fila; sequenza; catena; (Mus) corda ▷ vt (pt, pp **strung**): **to ~ out** disporre di fianco; **to ~ together** (words, ideas) mettere insieme; **the strings** npl (Mus) gli archi; **to pull ~s for sb** (fig) raccomandare qn

strip [strɪp] n striscia ▷ vt spogliare; (paint) togliere; (also: **~ down**) (machine) smontare ▷ vi spogliarsi; **strip off** vt (paint etc) staccare ▷ vi (person) spogliarsi

stripe [straɪp] n striscia, riga; (Mil, Police) gallone m; **striped** adj a strisce or righe

stripper ['strɪpər] n spogliarellista m/f

strip-search ['strɪpsəːtʃ] vt: **to ~ sb** perquisire qn facendolo/a spogliare ▷ n perquisizione f (facendo spogliare il perquisito)

strive (pt **strove**, pp **striven**) [straɪv, strəuv, 'strɪvn] vi: **to ~ to do** sforzarsi di fare

strode [strəud] *pt of* **stride**

stroke [strəuk] *n* colpo; (*Med*) colpo apoplettico; (*Swimming*) bracciata; (: *style*) stile *m* ▷ *vt* accarezzare; **at a ~** in un attimo

stroll [strəul] *n* giretto, passeggiata ▷ *vi* andare a spasso; **stroller** *n* (*US*) passeggino

strong [strɒŋ] *adj* (*gen*) forte; (*sturdy: table, fabric etc*) robusto/a; **they are 50 ~** sono in 50; **stronghold** *n* (*also fig*) roccaforte *f*; **strongly** *adv* fortemente, con forza; energicamente

strove [strəuv] *pt of* **strive**

struck [strʌk] *pt, pp of* **strike**

structure ['strʌktʃər] *n* struttura; (*building*) costruzione *f*, fabbricato

struggle ['strʌgl] *n* lotta ▷ *vi* lottare

strung [strʌŋ] *pt, pp of* **string**

stub [stʌb] *n* mozzicone *m*; (*of ticket etc*) matrice *f*, talloncino ▷ *vt*: **to ~ one's toe (on sth)** urtare *or* sbattere il dito del piede (contro qc); **stub out** *vt* schiacciare

stubble ['stʌbl] *n* stoppia; (*on chin*) barba ispida

stubborn ['stʌbən] *adj* testardo/a, ostinato/a

stuck [stʌk] *pt, pp of* **stick** ▷ *adj* (*jammed*) bloccato/a

stud [stʌd] *n* bottoncino; borchia; (*also: ~ earring*) orecchino a pressione (*of horses*) scuderia, allevamento di cavalli; (*also: ~ horse*) stallone *m* ▷ *vt* (*fig*): **~ded with** tempestato/a di

student ['stju:dənt] *n* studente/essa ▷ *cpd* studentesco/a; universitario/a; degli studenti; **student driver** *n* (*US*) conducente *m/f* principiante; **students' union** *n* (*BRIT: association*) circolo universitario; (: *building*) sede *f* del circolo universitario

studio ['stju:dɪəu] *n* studio; **studio flat**, (*US*) **studio apartment** *n* monolocale *m*

study ['stʌdɪ] *n* studio ▷ *vt* studiare; esaminare ▷ *vi* studiare

stuff [stʌf] *n* (*substance*) materiale *m*; (*belongings*) roba ▷ *vt* imbottire; (*animal: for exhibition*) impagliare; (*Culin*) farcire; (*col: push*) ficcare; **stuffing** *n* imbottitura; (*Culin*) ripieno; **stuffy** *adj* (*room*) mal ventilato/a, senz'aria; (*ideas*) antiquato/a

stumble ['stʌmbl] *vi* inciampare; **to ~ across** (*fig*) imbattersi in

stump [stʌmp] *n* ceppo; (*of limb*) moncone *m* ▷ *vt*: **to be ~ed** essere sconcertato/a

stun [stʌn] *vt* stordire; (*amaze*) sbalordire

stung [stʌŋ] *pt, pp of* **sting**

stunk [stʌŋk] *pp of* **stink**

stunned [stʌnd] *adj* (*from blow*) stordito/a; (*amazed, shocked*) sbalordito/a

stunning ['stʌnɪŋ] *adj* sbalorditivo/a; (*girl, dress*) stupendo/a

stunt [stʌnt] *n* bravata; trucco pubblicitario

stupid ['stju:pɪd] *adj* stupido/a; **stupidity** [stju:'pɪdɪtɪ] *n* stupidità *f inv*, stupidaggine *f*

sturdy ['stə:dɪ] *adj* robusto/a, vigoroso/a; solido/a

stutter ['stʌtər] *n* balbuzie *f* ▷ *vi* balbettare

style [staɪl] *n* stile *m*; (*distinction*) eleganza, classe *f*; **stylish** *adj* elegante; **stylist** *n*: **hair stylist** parrucchiere/a

sub... [sʌb] *prefix* sub..., sotto...; **subconscious** *adj*, *n* subcosciente *m*

subdued [səb'dju:d] *adj* pacato/a; (*light*) attenuato/a

subject *n* ['sʌbdʒɪkt] soggetto; (*citizen etc*) cittadino/a; (*Scol*) materia ▷ *vt* [səb'dʒɛkt]: **to ~ to** sottomettere a; esporre a; **to be ~ to** (*law*) essere sottomesso/a a; (*disease*) essere soggetto/a a; **subjective** [səb'dʒɛktɪv] *adj* soggettivo/a; **subject matter** *n* argomento; contenuto

s

subjunctive [səb'dʒʌŋktɪv] *adj* congiuntivo/a ▷ *n* congiuntivo

submarine [sʌbmə'riːn] *n* sommergibile *m*

submission [səb'mɪʃən] *n* sottomissione *f*; (*to committee etc*) richiesta

submit [səb'mɪt] *vt* sottomettere ▷ *vi* sottomettersi

subordinate [sə'bɔːdɪnət] *adj*, *n* subordinato/a

subscribe [səb'skraɪb] *vi* contribuire; **to ~ to** (*opinion*) approvare, condividere; (*fund*) sottoscrivere a; (*newspaper*) abbonarsi a; essere abbonato/a a

subscription [səb'skrɪpʃən] *n* sottoscrizione *f*; abbonamento

subsequent ['sʌbsɪkwənt] *adj* successivo/a, seguente; conseguente; **subsequently** *adv* in seguito, successivamente

subside [səb'saɪd] *vi* cedere, abbassarsi; (*flood*) decrescere; (*wind*) calmarsi

subsidiary [səb'sɪdɪərɪ] *adj* sussidiario/a; accessorio/a ▷ *n* filiale *f*

subsidize ['sʌbsɪdaɪz] *vt* sovvenzionare

subsidy ['sʌbsɪdɪ] *n* sovvenzione *f*

substance ['sʌbstəns] *n* sostanza

substantial [səb'stænʃl] *adj* solido/a; (*amount, progress etc*) notevole; (*meal*) sostanzioso/a

substitute ['sʌbstɪtjuːt] *n* (*person*) sostituto/a; (*thing*) succedaneo, surrogato ▷ *vt*: **to ~ sth/sb for** sostituire qc/qn a; **substitution** [sʌbstɪ'tjuːʃən] *n* sostituzione *f*

subtle ['sʌtl] *adj* sottile

subtract [səb'trækt] *vt* sottrarre

suburb ['sʌbəːb] *n* sobborgo; **the ~s** la periferia; **suburban** [sə'bəːbən] *adj* suburbano/a

subway ['sʌbweɪ] *n* (*US: underground*) metropolitana; (*BRIT: underpass*) sottopassaggio

succeed [sək'siːd] *vi* riuscire; avere successo ▷ *vt* succedere a; **to ~ in doing** riuscire a fare

success [sək'sɛs] *n* successo; **successful** *adj* (*venture*) coronato/a da successo, riuscito/a; **to be successful (in doing)** riuscire (a fare); **successfully** *adv* con successo

succession [sək'sɛʃən] *n* successione *f*

successive [sək'sɛsɪv] *adj* successivo/a; consecutivo/a

successor [sək'sɛsəʳ] *n* successore *m*

succumb [sə'kʌm] *vi* soccombere

such [sʌtʃ] *adj* tale; **~ books** tali libri, libri del genere; (*so much*): **~ courage** tanto coraggio; (*of that kind*): **~ a book** un tale libro, un libro del genere ▷ *adv* talmente, così; **~ a long trip** un viaggio così lungo; **~ a lot of** talmente *or* così tanto/a; **~ as** (*like*) come; **as ~** come *or* in quanto tale; **such-and-such** *adj* tale (*after noun*)

suck [sʌk] *vt* succhiare; (*baby*) poppare

Sudan [suː'dɑːn] *n* Sudan *m*

sudden ['sʌdn] *adj* improvviso/a; **all of a ~** improvvisamente, all'improvviso; **suddenly** *adv* bruscamente, improvvisamente, di colpo

sudoku [su'dəuku:] *n* sudoku *m inv*

sue [suː] *vt* citare in giudizio

suede [sweɪd] *n* pelle scamosciata

suffer ['sʌfəʳ] *vt* soffrire, patire; (*bear*) sopportare, tollerare ▷ *vi* soffrire; **to ~ from** soffrire di; **suffering** *n* sofferenza

suffice [sə'faɪs] *vi* essere sufficiente, bastare

sufficient [sə'fɪʃənt] *adj* sufficiente; **~ money** abbastanza soldi

suffocate ['sʌfəkeɪt] *vi* (*have difficulty breathing*) soffocare; (*die through lack of air*) asfissiare

sugar ['ʃugəʳ] *n* zucchero ▷ *vt* zuccherare

suggest [sə'dʒɛst] *vt* proporre, suggerire; (*indicate*) indicare; **suggestion** [sə'dʒɛstʃən] *n* suggerimento, proposta; indicazione *f*

suicide ['suɪsaɪd] *n* (*person*) suicida *m/f*; (*act*) suicidio; **to commit ~** suicidarsi; **suicide bomber** *n* kamikaze *mf inv*, attentatore/trice suicida; **suicide bombing** *n* attentato suicida

suit [su:t] *n* (*man's*) vestito; (*woman's*) completo, tailleur *m inv*; (*lawsuit*) causa; (*Cards*) seme *m*, colore *m* ▷ *vt* andar bene a *or* per; essere adatto/a a *or* per; (*adapt*): **to ~ sth to** adattare qc a; **well ~ed** (*couple*) ben assortito/a; **suitable** *adj* adatto/a; appropriato/a; **suitcase** ['su:tkeɪs] *n* valigia

suite [swi:t] *n* (*of rooms*) appartamento; (*Mus*) suite *f inv*; (*furniture*): **bedroom/dining room ~** arredo *or* mobilia per la camera da letto/sala da pranzo

sulfur *etc* ['sʌlfər] (*US*) = **sulphur** *etc*

sulk [sʌlk] *vi* fare il broncio

sulphur, (*US*)**sulfur** ['sʌlfər] *n* zolfo

sultana [sʌl'tɑ:nə] *n* (*fruit*) uva (secca) sultanina

sum [sʌm] *n* somma; (*Scol etc*) addizione *f*; **sum up** *vt* ▷ *vi* riassumere

summarize ['sʌməraɪz] *vt* riassumere, riepilogare

summary ['sʌmərɪ] *n* riassunto

summer ['sʌmər] *n* estate *f* ▷ *cpd* d'estate, estivo/a; **summer holidays** *npl* vacanze *fpl* estive; **summertime** *n* (*season*) estate *f*

summit ['sʌmɪt] *n* cima, sommità; (*Pol*) vertice *m*

summon ['sʌmən] *vt* chiamare, convocare

sun [sʌn] *n* sole *m*

Sun. *abbr* (= *Sunday*) dom.

sun: sunbathe *vi* prendere un bagno di sole; **sunbed** *n* lettino solare; **sunblock** *n* crema solare a protezione totale; **sunburn** *n*

(*painful*) scottatura; **sunburnt** ['sʌnbə:nt], **sunburned** ['sʌnbə:nd] *adj* abbronzato/a; (*painfully*) scottato/a dal sole

Sunday ['sʌndɪ] *n* domenica

Sunday paper *n* giornale *m* della domenica

sunflower ['sʌnflauər] *n* girasole *m*

sung [sʌŋ] *pp of* **sing**

sunglasses ['sʌnglɑ:sɪz] *npl* occhiali *mpl* da sole

sunk [sʌŋk] *pp of* **sink**

sun: sunlight *n* (luce *f* del) sole *m*; **sun lounger** *n* sedia a sdraio; **sunny** *adj* assolato/a, soleggiato/a; (*fig*) allegro/a, felice; **sunrise** *n* levata del sole, alba; **sunroof** *n* (*Aut*) tetto apribile; **sunscreen** *n* (*protective ingredient*) filtro solare; (*cream*) crema solare protettiva; **sunset** *n* tramonto; **sunshade** *n* parasole *m*; **sunshine** *n* (luce *f* del) sole *m*; **sunstroke** *n* insolazione *f*, colpo di sole; **suntan** *n* abbronzatura; **suntan lotion** *n* lozione *f* solare; **suntan oil** *n* olio solare

super ['su:pər] *adj* (*col*) fantastico/a

superb [su:'pə:b] *adj* magnifico/a

superficial [su:pə'fɪʃəl] *adj* superficiale

superintendent [su:pərɪn'tɛndənt] *n* direttore/trice; (*Police*) ≈ commissario (capo)

superior [su'pɪərɪər] *adj*, *n* superiore *m/f*

superlative [su'pə:lətɪv] *adj* superlativo/a, supremo/a ▷ *n* (*Ling*) superlativo

S

supermarket ['su:pəmɑ:kɪt] n
supermercato

supernatural [su:pə'nætʃərəl] adj,
n soprannaturale m

superpower ['su:pəpauəʳ] n (Pol)
superpotenza

superstition [su:pə'stɪʃən] n
superstizione f

superstitious [su:pə'stɪʃəs] adj
superstizioso/a

superstore ['su:pəstɔ:ʳ] n (BRIT)
grande supermercato

supervise ['su:pəvaɪz] vt (person
etc) sorvegliare; (organization)
soprintendere a; **supervision**
[su:pə'vɪʒən] n sorveglianza;
supervisione f; **supervisor** n
sorvegliante m/f; soprintendente
m/f; (in shop) capocommesso/a

supper ['sʌpəʳ] n cena

supple ['sʌpl] adj flessibile; agile

supplement n ['sʌplɪmənt]
supplemento ▷ vt [sʌplɪ'mɛnt]
completare, integrare

supplier [sə'plaɪəʳ] n fornitore m

supply [sə'plaɪ] vt: **to ~ sth
(to sb)** (goods) fornire qc (a qn);
to ~ sth (with sth) (system,
machine) alimentare qc (con qc)
▷ n riserva, provvista; (supplying)
approvvigionamento; (Tech)
alimentazione f; **supplies** npl (food)
viveri mpl; (Mil) sussistenza

support [sə'pɔ:t] n (moral, financial etc)
sostegno, appoggio; (Tech) supporto
▷ vt sostenere; (financially) mantenere;
(uphold) sostenere, difendere;
supporter n (Pol etc) sostenitore/
trice, fautore/trice; (Sport) tifoso/a

> Be careful not to translate
> support by the Italian word
> sopportare.

suppose [sə'pəuz] vt supporre;
immaginare; **to be ~d to do** essere
tenuto/a a fare; **supposedly**
[sə'pəuzɪdlɪ] adv presumibilmente;
supposing conj se, ammesso che
+ sub

suppress [sə'prɛs] vt reprimere;
sopprimere; occultare

supreme [su'pri:m] adj supremo/a

surcharge ['sə:tʃɑ:dʒ] n
supplemento

sure [ʃuəʳ] adj sicuro/a; (definite,
convinced) sicuro/a, certo/a; **~!** (of
course) senz'altro!, certo!; **~ enough**
infatti; **to make ~ of** assicurarsi
di; **surely** adv sicuramente;
certamente

surf [sə:f] n (waves) cavalloni mpl;
(foam) spuma

surface ['sə:fɪs] n superficie f ▷ vt
(road) asfaltare ▷ vi risalire alla
superficie; (fig: person, news, feeling)
venire a galla

surfboard ['sə:fbɔ:d] n tavola per
surfing

surfer ['sə:fəʳ] n (in sea) surfista m/f;
(on the Internet) navigatore/trice

surfing ['sə:fɪŋ] n surfing m

surge [sə:dʒ] n (strong movement)
ondata; (of feeling) impeto ▷ vi
gonfiarsi; (people) riversarsi

surgeon ['sə:dʒən] n chirurgo

surgery ['sə:dʒərɪ] n chirurgia; (BRIT:
room) studio or gabinetto medico,
ambulatorio; (also: **~ hours**) orario
delle visite or di consultazione; **to
undergo ~** subire un intervento
chirurgico

surname ['sə:neɪm] n cognome m

surpass [sə:'pɑ:s] vt superare

surplus ['sə:pləs] n eccedenza;
(Econ) surplus m inv ▷ adj eccedente,
d'avanzo

surprise [sə'praɪz] n sorpresa;
(astonishment) stupore m ▷ vt
sorprendere; stupire; **surprised**
[sə'praɪzd] adj (look, smile)
sorpreso/a; **to be surprised** essere
sorpreso, sorprendersi; **surprising**
adj sorprendente, stupefacente;
surprisingly adv (easy, helpful)
sorprendentemente

surrender [sə'rɛndəʳ] n resa,
capitolazione f ▷ vi arrendersi

surround [sə'raʊnd] vt circondare; (Mil etc) accerchiare; **surrounding** adj circostante; **surroundings** npl dintorni mpl; (fig) ambiente m

surveillance [səː'veɪləns] n sorveglianza, controllo

survey n ['səːveɪ] quadro generale; (study) indagine f; (in housebuying etc) perizia; (of land) rilevamento, rilievo topografico ▷ vt [səː'veɪ] osservare; esaminare; (building) fare una perizia di; (land) fare il rilevamento di; **surveyor** n perito; geometra m; (of land) agrimensore m

survival [sə'vaɪvl] n sopravvivenza; (relic) reliquia, vestigio

survive [sə'vaɪv] vi sopravvivere ▷ vt sopravvivere a; **survivor** n superstite m/f, sopravvissuto/a

suspect adj ['sʌspɛkt] sospetto/a ▷ n ['sʌspɛkt] persona sospetta ▷ vt [səs'pɛkt] sospettare; (think likely) supporre; (doubt) dubitare di

suspend [səs'pɛnd] vt sospendere; **suspended sentence** n condanna con la condizionale; **suspenders** npl (BRIT) giarrettiere fpl; (US) bretelle fpl

suspense [səs'pɛns] n apprensione f; (in film etc) suspense m; **to keep sb in ~** tenere qn in sospeso

suspension [səs'pɛnʃən] n (gen, Aut) sospensione f; (of driving licence) ritiro temporaneo; **suspension bridge** n ponte m sospeso

suspicion [səs'pɪʃən] n sospetto; **suspicious** [səs'pɪʃəs] adj (suspecting) sospettoso/a; (causing suspicion) sospetto/a

sustain [səs'teɪn] vt sostenere; sopportare; (Law: charge) confermare; (suffer) subire

SUV n abbr (= sports utility vehicle) SUV m inv

swallow ['swɔləʊ] n (bird) rondine f ▷ vt inghiottire; (fig: story) bere

swam [swæm] pt of **swim**

swamp [swɔmp] n palude f ▷ vt sommergere

swan [swɔn] n cigno

swap [swɔp] vt: **to ~ (for)** scambiare (con)

swarm [swɔːm] n sciame m ▷ vi (bees) sciamare; (people) brulicare; (place): **to be ~ing with** brulicare di

sway [sweɪ] vi (tree) ondeggiare; (person) barcollare ▷ vt (influence) influenzare, dominare

swear [swɛər] (pt **swore**, pp **sworn**) vi (curse) bestemmiare, imprecare ▷ vt: **to ~ to sth** giurare qc; **swear in** vt prestare giuramento a; **swearword** n parolaccia

sweat [swɛt] n sudore m, traspirazione f ▷ vi sudare

sweater ['swɛtər] n maglione m

sweatshirt ['swɛtʃəːt] n felpa f

sweaty ['swɛtɪ] adj sudato/a; bagnato/a di sudore

Swede [swiːd] n svedese m/f

swede [swiːd] n (BRIT) rapa svedese

Sweden ['swiːdn] n Svezia; **Swedish** ['swiːdɪʃ] adj svedese ▷ n (Ling) svedese m

sweep [swiːp] (pt, pp **swept**) n spazzata; (also: **chimney ~**) spazzacamino ▷ vt spazzare, scopare; (current) spazzare ▷ vi (hand) muoversi con gesto ampio; (wind) infuriare

sweet [swiːt] n (BRIT: pudding) dolce m; (candy) caramella ▷ adj dolce; (fresh) fresco/a; (fig) piacevole; delicato/a, grazioso/a; (kind) gentile; **sweetcorn** n granturco dolce; **sweetener** ['swiːtnər] n (Culin) dolcificante m; **sweetheart** n innamorato/a; **sweetshop** n (BRIT) ≈ pasticceria

swell [swɛl] (pt **swelled**, pp **swollen** or **swelled**) n (of sea) mare m lungo ▷ adj (US col: excellent) favoloso/a ▷ vt gonfiare, ingrossare; (numbers, sales etc) aumentare ▷ vi gonfiarsi, ingrossarsi; (sound) crescere; (Med: also: **~ up**) gonfiarsi; **swelling** n (Med) tumefazione f, gonfiore m

s

swept [swɛpt] *pt, pp of* **sweep**

swerve [swəːv] *vi* deviare; (*driver*) sterzare; (*boxer*) scartare

swift [swɪft] *n* (*bird*) rondone *m* ▷ *adj* rapido/a, veloce

swim [swɪm] (*pt* **swam**, *pp* **swum**) *n*: **to go for a ~** andare a fare una nuotata ▷ *vi* nuotare; (*Sport*) fare del nuoto; (*head, room*) girare ▷ *vt* (*river, channel*) attraversare *or* percorrere a nuoto; (*length*) nuotare; **swimmer** *n* nuotatore/trice; **swimming** *n* nuoto; **swimming costume** *n* (BRIT) costume *m* da bagno; **swimming pool** *n* piscina; **swimming trunks** *npl* costume *m* da bagno (da uomo); **swimsuit** *n* costume *m* da bagno

swine flu *n* influenza suina

swing [swɪŋ] (*pt, pp* **swung**) *n* altalena; (*movement*) oscillazione *f*; (*Mus*) ritmo; (*also:* **~ music**) swing *m* ▷ *vt* dondolare, far oscillare; (*also:* **~ round**) far girare ▷ *vi* oscillare, dondolare; (*also:* **~ round**) (*object*) roteare; (*person*) girarsi, voltarsi; **to be in full ~** (*activity*) essere in piena attività; (*party etc*) essere nel pieno

swipe card *n* tessera magnetica

swirl [swəːl] *vi* turbinare, far mulinello

Swiss [swɪs] *adj, n* (*pl inv*) svizzero/a

switch [swɪtʃ] *n* (*for light, radio etc*) interruttore *m*; (*change*) cambiamento ▷ *vt* (*also:* **~ round, ~ over**) cambiare; scambiare; **switch off** *vt* spegnere; **switch on** *vt* accendere; (*engine, machine*) mettere in moto, avviare; **switchboard** *n* (*Tel*) centralino

Switzerland ['swɪtsələnd] *n* Svizzera

swivel ['swɪvl] *vi* (*also:* **~ round**) girare

swollen ['swəulən] *pp of* **swell**

swoop [swuːp] *n* incursione *f* ▷ *vi* (*also:* **~ down**) scendere in picchiata, piombare

swop [swɔp] *n, vt* = **swap**

sword [sɔːd] *n* spada; **swordfish** *n* pesce *m* spada *inv*

swore [swɔːʳ] *pt of* **swear**

sworn [swɔːn] *pp of* **swear** ▷ *adj* giurato/a

swum [swʌm] *pp of* **swim**

swung [swʌŋ] *pt, pp of* **swing**

syllable ['sɪləbl] *n* sillaba

syllabus ['sɪləbəs] *n* programma *m*

symbol ['sɪmbl] *n* simbolo

symbolic(al) [sɪm'bɔlɪk(l)] *adj* simbolico/a; **to be ~ of sth** simboleggiare qc

symmetrical [sɪ'mɛtrɪkl] *adj* simmetrico/a

symmetry ['sɪmɪtrɪ] *n* simmetria

sympathetic [sɪmpə'θɛtɪk] *adj* (*showing pity*) compassionevole; (*kind*) comprensivo/a; **~ towards** ben disposto/a verso

> Be careful not to translate *sympathetic* by the Italian word *simpatico*.

sympathize ['sɪmpəθaɪz] *vi*: **to ~ with sb** compatire qn; partecipare al dolore di qn; **to ~ with a cause** simpatizzare per una causa

sympathy ['sɪmpəθɪ] *n* compassione *f*

symphony ['sɪmfənɪ] *n* sinfonia

symptom ['sɪmptəm] *n* sintomo; indizio

synagogue ['sɪnəgɔg] *n* sinagoga

syndicate ['sɪndɪkɪt] *n* sindacato

syndrome ['sɪndrəum] *n* sindrome *f*

synonym ['sɪnənɪm] *n* sinonimo

synthetic [sɪn'θɛtɪk] *adj* sintetico/a

Syria ['sɪrɪə] *n* Siria

syringe [sɪ'rɪndʒ] *n* siringa

syrup ['sɪrəp] *n* sciroppo; (*also:* **golden ~**) melassa raffinata

system ['sɪstəm] *n* sistema *m*; (*order*) metodo; (*Anat*) apparato; **systematic** [sɪstə'mætɪk] *adj* sistematico/a; metodico/a; **systems analyst** *n* analista *m/f* di sistemi

t

ta [tɑ:] excl (BRIT col) grazie!
tab [tæb] n (loop: on coat etc) laccetto; (label) etichetta; **to keep ~s on** (fig) tenere d'occhio
table ['teɪbl] n tavolo, tavola; (Math, Chem etc) tavola ▷ vt (BRIT: motion etc) presentare; **to lay** or **set the ~** apparecchiare or preparare la tavola; **tablecloth** n tovaglia; **table d'hôte** [tɑ:bl'dəut] adj (meal) a prezzo fisso; **table lamp** n lampada da tavolo; **tablemat** n sottopiatto; **tablespoon** n cucchiaio da tavola; (also: **tablespoonful**: as measurement) cucchiaiata
tablet ['tæblɪt] n (Med) compressa; (of stone) targa
table tennis n tennis m da tavolo, ping-pong® m
tabloid ['tæblɔɪd] n (newspaper) tabloid m inv (giornale illustrato di formato ridotto); **the ~s, the ~ press** i giornali popolari

taboo [tə'bu:] adj, n tabù m inv
tack [tæk] n (nail) bulletta; (fig) approccio ▷ vt imbullettare; imbastire ▷ vi bordeggiare
tackle ['tækl] n attrezzatura, equipaggiamento; (for lifting) paranco; (Rugby) placcaggio; (Football) contrasto ▷ vt (difficulty) affrontare; (Rugby) placcare; (Football) contrastare
tacky ['tækɪ] adj appiccicaticcio/a; scadente
tact [tækt] n tatto; **tactful** adj delicato/a, discreto/a
tactics ['tæktɪks] n, npl tattica
tactless ['tæktlɪs] adj che manca di tatto
tadpole ['tædpəul] n girino
taffy ['tæfɪ] n (US) caramella f mou inv
tag [tæg] n etichetta
tail [teɪl] n coda; (of shirt) falda ▷ vt (follow) seguire, pedinare; **tails** npl (formal suit) frac m inv
tailor ['teɪləʳ] n sarto
Taiwan [taɪ'wɑ:n] n Taiwan m; **Taiwanese** [taɪwə'ni:z] adj, n taiwanese
take [teɪk] (pt **took**, pp **taken**) vt prendere; (gain: prize) ottenere, vincere; (require: effort, courage) occorrere, volerci; (tolerate) accettare, sopportare; (hold: passengers etc) contenere; (accompany) accompagnare; (bring, carry) portare; (exam) sostenere, presentarsi a; **to ~ a photo/a shower** fare una fotografia/una doccia; **I ~ it that** suppongo che; **take after** vt fus assomigliare a; **take apart** vt smontare; **take away** vt portare via; togliere; **take back** vt (return) restituire; riportare; (one's words) ritirare; **take down** vt (building) demolire; (letter etc) scrivere; **take in** vt (lodger) prendere, ospitare; (deceive) imbrogliare, abbindolare; (understand) capire; (include) comprendere, includere;

t

take off vi (Aviat) decollare; (go away) andarsene ▷ vt (remove) togliere; **take on** vt (work) accettare, intraprendere; (employee) assumere; (opponent) sfidare, affrontare; **take out** vt portare fuori; (remove) togliere; (licence) prendere, ottenere; **to ~ sth out of** (drawer, pocket etc) tirare qc fuori da; (extract) estrarre qc da; **take over** vt (business) rilevare ▷ vi: **to ~ over from sb** prendere le consegne or il controllo da qn; **take up** vt (dress) accorciare; (occupy: time, space) occupare; (engage in: hobby etc) mettersi a; **to ~ sb up on sth** accettare qc da qn; **takeaway** ['teɪkəweɪ] (BRIT) n (shop etc) ≈ rosticceria; (food) pasto per asporto; **taken** pp of **take**; **takeoff** n (Aviat) decollo; **takeout** ['teɪkaut] adj, n (US) = **takeaway**; **takeover** n (Comm) assorbimento; **takings** ['teɪkɪŋz] npl (Comm) incasso

talc [tælk] n (also: **~um powder**) talco

tale [teɪl] n racconto, storia; **to tell ~s** (fig: to teacher, parent etc) fare la spia

talent ['tælənt] n talento; **talented** adj di talento

talk [tɔːk] n discorso; (gossip) chiacchiere fpl; (conversation) conversazione f; (interview) discussione f ▷ vi parlare; **talks** npl (Pol etc) colloqui mpl; **to ~ about** parlare di; **to ~ sb out of/into doing** dissuadere qn da/convincere qn a fare; **to ~ shop** parlare di lavoro or di affari; **talk show** n talk show m inv

tall [tɔːl] adj alto/a; **to be 6 feet ~** ≈ essere alto 1 metro e 80

tambourine [tæmbə'riːn] n tamburello

tame [teɪm] adj addomesticato/a; (fig: story, style) insipido/a, scialbo/a

tamper ['tæmpər] vi: **to ~ with** manomettere

tampon ['tæmpɔn] n tampone m

tan [tæn] n (also: **sun~**) abbronzatura ▷ vi abbronzarsi ▷ adj (colour) marrone rossiccio inv

tandem ['tændəm] n tandem m inv

tangerine [tændʒə'riːn] n mandarino

tangle ['tæŋgl] n groviglio; **to get in(to) a ~** aggrovigliarsi; (fig) combinare un pasticcio

tank [tæŋk] n serbatoio; (for fish) acquario; (Mil) carro armato

tanker ['tæŋkər] n (ship) nave f cisterna inv; (truck) autobotte f, autocisterna

tankini [tæn'kiːnɪ] n tankini m inv

tanned [tænd] adj abbronzato/a

tantrum ['tæntrəm] n accesso di collera

Tanzania [tænzə'nɪə] n Tanzania

tap [tæp] n (on sink etc) rubinetto; (gentle blow) colpetto ▷ vt dare un colpetto a; (resources) sfruttare, utilizzare; (telephone) mettere sotto controllo; **on ~** (fig: resources) a disposizione; **tap-dancing** n tip tap m

tape [teɪp] n nastro; (also: **magnetic ~**) nastro (magnetico); (sticky tape) nastro adesivo ▷ vt (record) registrare (su nastro); (stick) attaccare con nastro adesivo; **tape measure** n metro a nastro; **tape recorder** n registratore m (a nastro)

tapestry ['tæpɪstrɪ] n arazzo; tappezzeria

tar [tɑːr] n catrame m

target ['tɑːgɪt] n bersaglio; (fig: objective) obiettivo

tariff ['tærɪf] n tariffa

tarmac ['tɑːmæk] n (BRIT: on road) macadam m al catrame; (Aviat) pista di decollo

tarpaulin [tɑː'pɔːlɪn] n tela incatramata

tarragon ['tærəgən] n dragoncello

tart [tɑːt] n (Culin) crostata; (BRIT col, pej: woman) sgualdrina ▷ adj (flavour) aspro/a, agro/a

tartan ['tɑːtn] n tartan m inv

tartar(e) sauce n salsa tartara

task [tɑːsk] n compito; **to take to ~** rimproverare

taste [teɪst] n gusto; (flavour) sapore m, gusto; (sample) assaggio; (fig: glimpse, idea) idea ▷ vt gustare; (sample) assaggiare ▷ vi: **to ~ of** or **like** (fish etc) sapere di, avere sapore di; **in good/bad ~** di buon/cattivo gusto; **you can ~ the garlic (in it)** (ci) si sente il sapore dell'aglio; **can I have a ~?** posso assaggiarlo?; **tasteful** adj di buon gusto; **tasteless** adj (food) insipido/a; (remark) di cattivo gusto; **tasty** adj saporito/a, gustoso/a

tatters ['tætəz] npl: **in ~**; a brandelli

tattoo [tə'tuː] n tatuaggio; (spectacle) parata militare ▷ vt tatuare

taught [tɔːt] pt, pp of **teach**

taunt [tɔːnt] n scherno ▷ vt schernire

Taurus ['tɔːrəs] n Toro

taut [tɔːt] adj teso/a

tax [tæks] n (on goods) imposta; (on services) tassa; (on income) imposte fpl, tasse fpl ▷ vt tassare; (fig: strain: patience etc) mettere alla prova; **tax-free** adj esente da imposte

taxi ['tæksɪ] n taxi m inv ▷ vi (Aviat) rullare; **taxi driver** n tassista m/f; **taxi rank**, (US) **taxi stand** n posteggio dei taxi

tax payer n contribuente m/f

TB n abbr (= tuberculosis) TBC f

tea [tiː] n tè m inv; (BRIT: snack: for children) merenda; **high ~** (BRIT) cena leggera (presa nel tardo pomeriggio); **tea bag** n bustina di tè; **tea break** n (BRIT) intervallo per il tè

teach (pt, pp **taught**) [tiːtʃ, tɔːt] vt: **to ~ sb sth, ~ sth to sb** insegnare qc a qn ▷ vi insegnare; **teacher** n insegnante m/f; (in secondary school) professore/essa; (in primary school) maestro/a; **teaching** n insegnamento

tea: tea cloth n (for dishes) strofinaccio; (BRIT: for trolley) tovaglietta da tè; **teacup** ['tiːkʌp] n tazza da tè; **tea leaves** npl foglie fpl di tè

team [tiːm] n squadra; (of animals) tiro; **team up** vi: **to ~ up (with)** mettersi insieme (a)

teapot ['tiːpɔt] n teiera

tear¹ [tɪəʳ] n lacrima; **in ~s** in lacrime

tear² [tɛəʳ] (pt **tore**, pp **torn**) n strappo ▷ vt strappare ▷ vi strapparsi; **tear apart** vt (also fig) distruggere; **tear down** vt (building, statue) demolire; (poster, flag) tirare giù; **tear off** vt (sheet of paper etc) strappare; (one's clothes) togliersi di dosso; **tear up** vt (sheet of paper etc) strappare; **tearful** ['tɪəful] adj piangente, lacrimoso/a; **tear gas** n gas m lacrimogeno

tearoom ['tiːruːm] n sala da tè

tease [tiːz] vt canzonare; (unkindly) tormentare

tea: teaspoon n cucchiaino da tè; (also: **teaspoonful**) (as measurement) cucchiaino; **teatime** n ora del tè; **tea towel** n (BRIT) strofinaccio (per i piatti)

technical ['tɛknɪkl] adj tecnico/a

technician [tɛk'nɪʃən] n tecnico/a

technique [tɛk'niːk] n tecnica

technology [tɛk'nɔlədʒɪ] n tecnologia

teddy (bear) ['tɛdɪ-] n orsacchiotto

tedious ['tiːdɪəs] adj noioso/a, tedioso/a

tee [tiː] n (Golf) tee m inv

teen [tiːn] adj = **teenage** ▷ n (US) = **teenager**

teenage ['tiːneɪdʒ] adj (fashions etc) per giovani, per adolescenti; **teenager** n adolescente m/f

teens [tiːnz] npl: **to be in one's ~** essere adolescente

teeth [tiːθ] npl of **tooth**

teetotal ['tiː'təutl] adj astemio/a

t

telecommunications
[ˈtɛlɪkəmjuːnɪˈkeɪʃənz] *n*
telecomunicazioni *fpl*
telegram [ˈtɛlɪɡræm] *n*
telegramma *m*
telegraph pole *n* palo del telegrafo
telephone [ˈtɛlɪfəun] *n* telefono
▷ *vt* (*person*) telefonare a; (*message*)
comunicare per telefono; **telephone
book** *n* elenco telefonico; **telephone
box**, (*US*) **telephone booth** *n*
cabina telefonica; **telephone call** *n*
telefonata; **telephone directory**
n elenco telefonico; **telephone
number** *n* numero di telefono
telesales [ˈtɛlɪseɪlz] *n* vendita per
telefono
telescope [ˈtɛlɪskəup] *n* telescopio
televise [ˈtɛlɪvaɪz] *vt* teletrasmettere
television [ˈtɛlɪvɪʒən] *n* televisione *f*;
on ~ alla televisione; **television
programme** *n* programma *m*
televisivo
tell [tɛl] (*pt, pp* **told**) *vt* dire; (*relate:
story*) raccontare; (*distinguish*): **to
~ sth from** distinguere qc da ▷ *vi*
(*talk*): **to ~ (of)** parlare (di); (*have
effect*) farsi sentire, avere effetto; **to
~ sb to do** dire a qn di fare; **tell off** *vt*
rimproverare, sgridare; **teller** *n* (*in
bank*) cassiere/a
telly [ˈtɛlɪ] *n abbr* (*BRIT*) (*col*)
(= *television*) tivù *f inv*
temp [tɛmp] *abbr* (*BRIT col*);
= **temporary** ▷ *n* impiegato/a
interinale
temper [ˈtɛmpəʳ] *n* (*nature*) carattere
m; (*mood*) umore *m*; (*fit of anger*)
collera ▷ *vt* (*moderate*) moderare; **to
be in a ~** essere in collera; **to lose
one's ~** andare in collera
temperament [ˈtɛmprəmənt]
n (*nature*) temperamento;
temperamental [tɛmprəˈmɛntl]
adj capriccioso/a
temperature [ˈtɛmprətʃəʳ] *n*
temperatura; **to have** *or* **run a ~**
avere la febbre

temple [ˈtɛmpl] *n* (*building*) tempio;
(*Anat*) tempia
temporary [ˈtɛmpərərɪ] *adj*
temporaneo/a; (*job, worker*)
avventizio/a, temporaneo/a
tempt [tɛmpt] *vt* tentare; **to ~
sb into doing** indurre qn a fare;
temptation [tɛmpˈteɪʃən] *n*
tentazione *f*; **tempting** *adj* allettante
ten [tɛn] *num* dieci
tenant [ˈtɛnənt] *n* inquilino/a
tend [tɛnd] *vt* badare a, occuparsi
di ▷ *vi*: **to ~ to do** tendere a fare;
tendency [ˈtɛndənsɪ] *n* tendenza
tender [ˈtɛndəʳ] *adj* tenero/a; (*sore*)
dolorante ▷ *n* (*Comm: offer*) offerta;
(*money*): **legal ~** moneta in corso
legale ▷ *vt* offrire
tendon [ˈtɛndən] *n* tendine *m*
tenner [ˈtɛnəʳ] *n* (*BRIT col*)
(banconota da) dieci sterline *fpl*
tennis [ˈtɛnɪs] *n* tennis *m*; **tennis
ball** *n* palla da tennis; **tennis court**
n campo da tennis; **tennis match**
n partita di tennis; **tennis player**
n tennista *m/f*; **tennis racket** *n*
racchetta da tennis
tenor [ˈtɛnəʳ] *n* (*Mus*) tenore *m*
tenpin bowling [ˈtɛnpɪn-] *n*
bowling *m*
tense [tɛns] *adj* teso/a ▷ *n* (*Ling*)
tempo
tension [ˈtɛnʃən] *n* tensione *f*
tent [tɛnt] *n* tenda
tentative [ˈtɛntətɪv] *adj* esitante,
incerto/a; (*conclusion*) provvisorio/a
tenth [tɛnθ] *num* decimo/a
tent: tent peg *n* picchetto da
tenda; **tent pole** *n* palo da tenda,
montante *m*
tepid [ˈtɛpɪd] *adj* tiepido/a
term [təːm] *n* termine *m*; (*Scol*)
trimestre *m*; (*Law*) sessione *f* ▷ *vt*
chiamare, definire; **terms** *npl*
(*conditions*) condizioni *fpl*; (*Comm*)
prezzi *mpl*, tariffe *fpl*; **in the short/
long ~** a breve/lunga scadenza; **to
be on good ~s with** essere in buoni

rapporti con; **to come to ~s with** (*problem*) affrontare

terminal ['tə:mɪnl] *adj* finale, terminale; (*disease*) terminale ▷ *n* (*Elec, Comput*) morsetto; (*Aviat, for oil, ore etc*) terminal *m inv*; (BRIT: *also:* **coach ~**) capolinea *m*

terminate ['tə:mɪneɪt] *vt* mettere fine a

termini ['tə:mɪnaɪ] *npl of* **terminus**

terminology [tə:mɪ'nɔlədʒɪ] *n* terminologia

terminus (*pl* **termini**) ['tə:mɪnəs, 'tə:mɪnaɪ] *n* (*for buses*) capolinea *m*; (*for trains*) stazione *f* terminale

terrace ['tɛrəs] *n* terrazza; (BRIT: *row of houses*) fila di case a schiera; **terraced** *adj* (*garden*) a terrazze

terrain [tɛ'reɪn] *n* terreno

terrestrial [tɪ'rɛstrɪəl] *adj* (*life*) terrestre; (BRIT: *channel*) terrestre

terrible ['tɛrɪbl] *adj* terribile; **terribly** *adv* terribilmente; (*very badly*) malissimo

terrier ['tɛrɪəʳ] *n* terrier *m inv*

terrific [tə'rɪfɪk] *adj* incredibile, fantastico/a; (*wonderful*) formidabile, eccezionale

terrified ['tɛrɪfaɪd] *adj* atterrito/a

terrify ['tɛrɪfaɪ] *vt* terrorizzare; **terrifying** *adj* terrificante

territorial [tɛrɪ'tɔ:rɪəl] *adj* territoriale

territory ['tɛrɪtərɪ] *n* territorio

terror ['tɛrəʳ] *n* terrore *m*; **terrorism** *n* terrorismo; **terrorist** *n* terrorista *m/f*

test [tɛst] *n* (*trial, check: of courage etc*) prova; (*Med*) esame *m*; (*Chem*) analisi *f inv*; (*exam: of intelligence etc*) test *m inv*; (: *in school*) compito in classe; (*also:* **driving ~**) esame *m* di guida ▷ *vt* provare; esaminare; analizzare; sottoporre ad esame; **to ~ sb in history** esaminare qn in storia

testicle ['tɛstɪkl] *n* testicolo

testify ['tɛstɪfaɪ] *vi* (*Law*) testimoniare, deporre; **to ~ to**

sth (*Law*) testimoniare qc; (*gen*) comprovare *or* dimostrare qc

testimony ['tɛstɪmənɪ] *n* (*Law*) testimonianza, deposizione *f*

test: test match *n* (*Cricket, Rugby*) partita internazionale; **test tube** *n* provetta

tetanus ['tɛtənəs] *n* tetano

text [tɛkst] *n* testo; (*Tel*) sms *m inv*, messaggino ▷ *vt*: **to ~ sb** (*col*) mandare un sms a ▷ *vi* messaggiarsi; **textbook** *n* libro di testo

textile ['tɛkstaɪl] *n* tessile *m*

text message *n* (*Tel*) sms *m inv*, messaggino

text messaging [-'mɛsɪdʒɪŋ] *n* il mandarsi sms

texture ['tɛkstʃəʳ] *n* tessitura; (*of skin, paper etc*) struttura

Thai [taɪ] *adj* tailandese ▷ *n* tailandese *m/f*; (*Ling*) tailandese *m*

Thailand ['taɪlænd] *n* Tailandia

Thames [tɛmz] *n*: **the ~** il Tamigi

than [ðæn, ðən] *conj* (*in comparisons*) che; (*with numerals, pronouns, proper names*) di; **more ~ 10/Maria/once** più di 10/Maria/una volta; **I have more/less ~ you** ne ho più/meno di te; **she has more apples ~ pears** ha più mele che pere; **she is older ~ you think** è più vecchia di quanto tu (non) pensi

thank [θæŋk] *vt* ringraziare; **~ you (very much)** grazie (tante); **thankfully** *adv* con riconoscenza; con sollievo; **thankfully there were few victims** grazie al cielo ci sono state poche vittime; **thanks** *npl* ringraziamenti *mpl*, grazie *fpl* ▷ *excl* grazie!; **thanks to** grazie a

Thanksgiving (Day) *n* giorno del ringraziamento

⬡ **THANKSGIVING (DAY)**
⬡
⬡ Negli Stati Uniti il quarto giovedì
⬡ di novembre ricorre il *Thanksgiving*

t

(Day), festa nazionale in ricordo della celebrazione con cui i Padri Pellegrini, i puritani inglesi che fondarono la colonia di Plymouth nel Massachusetts, ringraziarono Dio del buon raccolto del 1621.

KEYWORD

that [ðæt ʃ] (pl **those**) adj (demonstrative) quel (quell', quello) m; quella (quell') f; **that man/woman/book** quell'uomo/quella donna/quel libro; (not "this") quell'uomo/quella donna/quel libro là; **that one** quello/a là
▶ pron 1 (demonstrative) ciò; (: not "this one") quello/a; **who's that?** chi è?; **what's that?** cos'è quello?; **is that you?** sei tu?; **I prefer this to that** preferisco questo a quello; **that's what he said** questo è ciò che ha detto; **what happened after that?** che è successo dopo?; **that is (to say)** cioè
2 (relative: direct) che; (: indirect) cui; **the book (that) I read** il libro che ho letto; **the box (that) I put it in** la scatola in cui l'ho messo; **the people (that) I spoke to** le persone con cui or con le quali ho parlato
3 (relative: of time) in cui; **the day (that) he came** il giorno in cui è venuto
▶ conj che; **he thought that I was ill** pensava che io fossi malato
▶ adv (demonstrative) così; **I can't work that much** non posso lavorare (così) tanto; **that high** così alto; **the wall's about that high and that thick** il muro è alto circa così e spesso circa così

thatched [θætʃt] adj (roof) di paglia
thaw [θɔː] n disgelo ▶ vi (ice) sciogliersi; (food) scongelarsi ▶ vt (food) (fare) scongelare

KEYWORD

the [ðiː, ðə] def art 1 (gen) il (lo, l') m; la (l') f; i (gli) mpl; le fpl; **the boy/girl/ink** il ragazzo/la ragazza/l'inchiostro; **the books/pencils** i libri/le matite; **the history of the world** la storia del mondo; **give it to the postman** dallo al postino; **I haven't the time/money** non ho tempo/soldi; **the rich and the poor** i ricchi e i poveri
2 (in titles): **Elizabeth the First** Elisabetta prima; **Peter the Great** Pietro il Grande
3 (in comparisons): **the more he works, the more he earns** più lavora più guadagna

theatre, (us) **theater** ['θɪətər] n teatro; (also: **lecture ~**) aula magna; (also: **operating ~**) sala operatoria
theft [θɛft] n furto
their [ðɛər] adj il (la) loro; (pl) i (le) loro; **theirs** pron il (la) loro; (pl) i (le) loro; see also **my; mine**[1]
them [ðɛm, ðəm] pron (direct) li(le); (indirect) gli, loro (after vb); (stressed, after prep: people) loro; (: people, things) essi/e; see also **me**
theme [θiːm] n tema m; **theme park** n parco a tema
themselves [ðəm'sɛlvz] pl pron (reflexive) si; (emphatic) loro stessi/e; (after prep) se stessi/e
then [ðɛn] adv (at that time) allora; (next) poi, dopo; (and also) e poi ▶ conj (therefore) perciò, dunque, quindi ▶ adj: **the ~ president** il presidente di allora; **by ~** allora; **from ~ on** da allora in poi
theology [θɪ'ɔlədʒɪ] n teologia
theory ['θɪərɪ] n teoria
therapist ['θɛrəpɪst] n terapista m/f
therapy ['θɛrəpɪ] n terapia

KEYWORD

there [ðɛər] adv 1: **there is** c'è; **there are** ci sono; **there are 3 of them**

(*people*) sono in 3; (*things*) ce ne sono 3; **there is no-one here** non c'è nessuno qui; **there has been an accident** c'è stato un incidente **2** (*referring to place*) là, lì; **up/in/down there** lassù/là dentro/laggiù; **he went there on Friday** ci è andato venerdì; **I want that book there** voglio quel libro là *or* lì; **there he is!** eccolo! **3**: **there, there** (*esp to child*) su, su; **thereabouts** ['ðɛərəbauts] *adv* (*place*) nei pressi, da quelle parti; (*amount*) giù di lì, all'incirca; **thereafter** [ðɛərˈɑːftər] *adv* da allora in poi; **thereby** [ðɛəˈbaɪ] *adv* con ciò; **therefore** ['ðɛəfɔːr] *adv* perciò, quindi; **there's** [ðɛəz] = **there is**; **there has**

thermal ['θəːml] *adj* termico/a
thermometer [θəˈmɒmɪtər] *n* termometro
thermostat ['θəːməstæt] *n* termostato
these [ðiːz] *pl pron, adj* questi/e
thesis (*pl* **theses**) ['θiːsɪs, 'θiːsiːz] *n* tesi *f inv*
they [ðeɪ] *pl pron* essi(esse); (*people only*) loro; **~ say that ...** (*it is said that*) si dice che ...; **they'd** [ðeɪd] = **they would**; **they had**; **they'll** [ðeɪl] = **they will**; **they shall**; **they're** [ðɛər] = **they are**; **they've** [ðeɪv] = **they have**

thick [θɪk] *adj* spesso/a; (*crowd*) compatto/a; (*stupid*) ottuso/a, lento/a ▷ *n*: **in the ~ of** nel folto di; **it's 20 cm ~** ha uno spessore di 20 cm; **thicken** *vi* ispessire ▷ *vt* (*sauce etc*) ispessire, rendere più denso/a; **thickness** *n* spessore *m*
thief (*pl* **thieves**) [θiːf, θiːvz] *n* ladro/a
thigh [θaɪ] *n* coscia
thin [θɪn] *adj* sottile; (*person*) magro/a; (*soup*) poco denso/a ▷ *vt*: **to ~ (down)** (*sauce, paint*) diluire

thing [θɪŋ] *n* cosa; (*object*) oggetto; (*mania*): **to have a ~ about** essere fissato/a con; **things** *npl* (*belongings*) cose *fpl*; **the best ~ would be to** la cosa migliore sarebbe di; **poor ~** poveretto/a
think (*pt, pp* **thought**) [θɪŋk, θɔːt] *vi* pensare, riflettere ▷ *vt* pensare, credere; (*imagine*) immaginare; **to ~ of** pensare a; **what did you ~ of them?** cosa ne ha pensato?; **to ~ about sth/sb** pensare a qc/qn; **I'll ~ about it** ci penserò; **to ~ of doing** pensare di fare; **I ~ so/not** penso or credo di sì/no; **to ~ well** avere una buona opinione di; **think over** *vt* riflettere su; **think up** *vt* ideare
third [θəːd] *n* terzo/a ▷ *n* terzo/a; (*fraction*) terzo, terza parte *f*; (*Aut*) terza; (*BRIT Scol: degree*) laurea col minimo dei voti; **thirdly** *adv* in terzo luogo; **third party insurance** *n* (*BRIT*) assicurazione *f* contro terzi; **Third World** *n*: **the Third World** il Terzo Mondo
thirst [θəːst] *n* sete *f*; **thirsty** *adj* (*person*) assetato/a, che ha sete
thirteen [θəːˈtiːn] *num* tredici; **thirteenth** [-ˈtiːnθ] *num* tredicesimo/a
thirtieth ['θəːtɪɪθ] *num* trentesimo/a
thirty ['θəːtɪ] *num* trenta

KEYWORD

this [ðɪs ʃ] (*pl* **these**) *adj* (*demonstrative*) questo/a; **this man/woman/book** quest'uomo/questa donna/questo libro; (*not "that"*) quest'uomo/questa donna/questo libro qui; **this one** questo/a qui, **who/what is this?** chi è/che cos'è questo?; **I prefer this to that** preferisco questo a quello; **this is where I live** io abito qui; **this is what he said** questo è ciò che ha detto; **this is Mr Brown**

t

(*in introductions, photo*) questo è il signor Brown; (*on telephone*) sono il signor Brown
▶ *adv* (*demonstrative*): **this high/long** *etc* alto/lungo *etc* così; **I didn't know things were this bad** non sapevo andasse così male

thistle ['θɪsl] *n* cardo

thorn [θɔːn] *n* spina

thorough ['θʌrə] *adj* (*search*) minuzioso/a; (*knowledge, research*) approfondito/a, profondo/a; (*person*) coscienzioso/a; (*cleaning*) a fondo; **thoroughly** *adv* (*search*) minuziosamente; (*wash, study*) a fondo; (*very*) assolutamente

those [ðəuz] *pl pron* quelli/e ▶ *pl adj* quei (quegli) *mpl*; quelle *fpl*

though [ðəu] *conj* benché, sebbene ▶ *adv* comunque

thought [θɔːt] *pt, pp of* **think** ▶ *n* pensiero; (*opinion*) opinione *f*; **thoughtful** *adj* pensieroso/a, pensoso/a; (*considerate*) premuroso/a; **thoughtless** *adj* sconsiderato/a; (*behaviour*) scortese

thousand ['θauzənd] *num* mille; **one ~** mille; **~s of** migliaia di; **thousandth** *num* millesimo/a

thrash [θræʃ] *vt* picchiare; bastonare; (*defeat*) battere; **thrash about** *vi* dibattersi

thread [θrɛd] *n* filo; (*of screw*) filetto ▶ *vt* (*needle*) infilare

threat [θrɛt] *n* minaccia; **threaten** *vi* (*storm*) minacciare ▶ *vt*: **to threaten sb with sth/to do** minacciare qn con qc/di fare; **threatening** *adj* minaccioso/a

three [θriː] *num* tre; **three-dimensional** *adj* tridimensionale; (*film*) stereoscopico/a; **three-piece suite** *n* salotto comprendente un divano e due poltrone; **three-quarters** *npl* tre quarti *mpl*; **three-quarters full** pieno per tre quarti

threshold ['θrɛʃhəuld] *n* soglia

threw [θruː] *pt of* **throw**

thrill [θrɪl] *n* brivido ▶ *vt* (*audience*) elettrizzare; **to be ~ed** (*with gift etc*) essere elettrizzato/a; **thrilled** *adj*: **I was thrilled to get your letter** la tua lettera mi ha fatto veramente piacere; **thriller** *n* thriller *m inv*; **thrilling** *adj* (*book, play etc*) pieno/a di suspense; (*news, discovery*) elettrizzante

thriving ['θraɪvɪŋ] *adj* fiorente

throat [θrəut] *n* gola; **to have a sore ~** avere (un *or* il) mal di gola

throb [θrɔb] *vi* palpitare; (*engine*) vibrare; (*with pain*) pulsare

throne [θrəun] *n* trono

through [θruː] *prep* attraverso; (*time*) per, durante; (*by means of*) per mezzo di; (*owing to*) a causa di ▶ *adj* (*ticket, train, passage*) diretto/a ▶ *adv* attraverso; **to put sb ~ to sb** (*Tel*) passare qn a qn; **to be ~** (*Tel*) ottenere la comunicazione; (*have finished*) avere finito; **"no ~ road"** (BRIT) "strada senza sbocco"; **throughout** *prep* (*place*) dappertutto in; (*time*) per *or* durante tutto/a ▶ *adv* dappertutto; sempre

throw [θrəu] *n* tiro; (*Sport*) lancio ▶ *vt* (*pt* **threw**, *pp* **thrown**) tirare, gettare; (*Sport*) lanciare; (*rider*) disarcionare; (*fig*) confondere; **to ~ a party** dare una festa; **throw away** *vt* gettare *or* buttare via; **throw in** *vt* (*Sport: ball*) rimettere in gioco; (*include*) aggiungere; **throw off** *vt* sbarazzarsi di; **throw out** *vt* buttare fuori; (*reject*) respingere; **throw up** *vi* vomitare

thru [θruː] *prep, adj, adv* (US) = **through**

thrush [θrʌʃ] *n* tordo

thrust [θrʌst] *vt* (*pt, pp* **thrust**) spingere con forza; (*push in*) conficcare

thud [θʌd] *n* tonfo

thug [θʌg] *n* delinquente *m*

thumb [θʌm] n (Anat) pollice m; **to ~ a lift** fare l'autostop; **thumbtack** n (US) puntina da disegno

thump [θʌmp] n colpo forte; (sound) tonfo ▷ vt (person) picchiare; (object) battere su ▷ vi picchiare; battere

thunder ['θʌndəʳ] n tuono ▷ vi tuonare; (train etc) **to ~ past** passare con un rombo; **thunderstorm** n temporale m

Thur(s). abbr (= Thursday) gio.

Thursday ['θəːzdɪ] n giovedì m inv

thus [ðʌs] adv così

thwart [θwɔːt] vt contrastare

thyme [taɪm] n timo

Tiber ['taɪbəʳ] n: **the ~** il Tevere

Tibet [tɪ'bɛt] n Tibet m

tick [tɪk] n (sound, of clock) tic tac m inv; (mark) segno, spunta; (Zool) zecca; (BRIT col): **in a ~** un attimo ▷ vi fare tic tac ▷ vt spuntare; **tick off** vt spuntare; (person) sgridare

ticket ['tɪkɪt] n biglietto m; (in shop: on goods) etichetta; (for library) scheda; **to get a (parking) ~** (Aut) prendere una multa (per sosta vietata); **a single/return ~ to ...** un biglietto di sola andata/di andata e ritorno per...; **ticket barrier** n (BRIT Rail) cancelletto d'ingresso; **ticket collector** n bigliettaio; **ticket inspector** n controllore m; **ticket machine** n distributore m di biglietti; **ticket office** n biglietteria

tickle ['tɪkl] vt fare il solletico a ▷ vi: **it ~s** mi (or gli etc) fa il solletico; **ticklish** ['tɪklɪʃ] adj che soffre il solletico; (which tickles: blanket, cough) che provoca prurito; (problem) delicato/a

tide [taɪd] n marea; (fig: of events) corso; **high/low ~** alta/bassa marea

tidy ['taɪdɪ] adj (room) ordinato/a, lindo/a; (dress, work) curato/a, in ordine; (person) ordinato/a ▷ vt (also: **~ up**) riordinare, mettere in ordine

tie [taɪ] n (string etc) legaccio; (BRIT: also: **neck~**) cravatta; (fig: link) legame m; (Sport: draw) pareggio ▷ vt (parcel) legare; (ribbon) annodare ▷ vi (Sport) pareggiare; **to ~ sth in a bow** annodare qc; **to ~ a knot in sth** fare un nodo a qc; **tie down** vt legare, assicurare con una corda; **to ~ sb down to** (price etc) costringere qn ad accettare; **tie up** vt (parcel, dog) legare; (boat) ormeggiare; (arrangements) concludere; **to be ~d up** (busy) essere occupato or preso

tier [tɪəʳ] n fila; (of cake) piano, strato

tiger ['taɪgəʳ] n tigre f

tight [taɪt] adj (rope) teso/a, tirato/a; (money) poco/a; (clothes, budget, programme, bend) stretto/a; (control) severo/a, fermo/a; (col: drunk) sbronzo/a ▷ adv (squeeze) fortemente; (shut) ermeticamente; **tighten** vt (rope) tendere; (screw) stringere; (control) rinforzare ▷ vi tendersi; stringersi; **tightly** adv (grasp) bene, saldamente; **tights** npl (BRIT) collant m inv

tile [taɪl] n (on roof) tegola; (on floor, wall) mattonella, piastrella

till [tɪl] n registratore m di cassa ▷ vt (land) coltivare ▷ prep, conj = **until**

tilt [tɪlt] vt inclinare, far pendere ▷ vi inclinarsi, pendere

timber ['tɪmbəʳ] n (material) legname m

time [taɪm] n tempo; (epoch: often pl) epoca, tempo; (by clock) ora; (moment) momento; (occasion) volta; (Mus) tempo ▷ vt (race) cronometrare; (programme) calcolare la durata di; (fix moment for) programmare; **a long ~** molto tempo; **for the ~ being** per il momento; **4 at a ~** 4 per or alla volta; **from ~ to ~** ogni tanto; **in ~** (soon enough) in tempo; (after some time) col tempo; (Mus) a tempo; **at ~s** a volte; **in a week's ~** fra una settimana; **in no ~** in un attimo; **any ~** in qualsiasi momento; **on ~** puntualmente; **5 ~s 5** 5 volte 5, 5 per 5; **what ~ is it?** che ora è?, che ore sono?; **to have a good ~** divertirsi; **time limit** n limite *m* di tempo; **timely** *adj* opportuno/a; **timer** *n* (*in kitchen*) contaminuti *m inv*; (*time switch*) temporizzatore *m*; **time-share** *adj*: **time-share apartment/villa** appartamento/villa in multiproprietà; **timetable** *n* orario; **time zone** *n* fuso orario

timid ['tɪmɪd] *adj* timido/a; (*easily scared*) pauroso/a

timing ['taɪmɪŋ] *n* (*fig*) scelta del momento opportuno; (*Sport*) cronometraggio

tin [tɪn] *n* stagno; (*also:* **~ plate**) latta; (*BRIT: can*) barattolo (di latta), lattina; (*container*) scatola; **tin foil** *n* stagnola

tingle ['tɪŋgl] *vi* pizzicare

tinker ['tɪŋkəʳ]; **tinker with** *vt fus* armeggiare intorno a; cercare di riparare

tinned [tɪnd] *adj* (*BRIT: food*) in scatola

tin-opener ['tɪnəupnəʳ] *n* (*BRIT*) apriscatole *m inv*

tint [tɪnt] *n* tinta; **tinted** *adj* (*hair*) tinto/a; (*spectacles, glass*) colorato/a

tiny ['taɪnɪ] *adj* minuscolo/a

tip [tɪp] *n* (*end*) punta; (*gratuity*) mancia; (*BRIT: for rubbish*) immondezzaio; (*advice*) suggerimento ▷ *vt* (*waiter*) dare la mancia a; (*tilt*) inclinare; (*overturn: also:* **~ over**) capovolgere; (*empty: also:* **~ out**) scaricare; **tip off** *vt* fare una soffiata a

tiptoe ['tɪptəu] *n*: **on ~** in punta di piedi

tire ['taɪəʳ] *vt* stancare ▷ *vi* stancarsi ▷ *n* (*US*) = **tyre**; **tired** *adj* stanco/a; **to be tired of** essere stanco *or* stufo di; **tire pressure** *n* (*US*) = **tyre pressure**; **tiring** *adj* faticoso/a

tissue ['tɪʃuː] *n* tessuto; (*paper handkerchief*) fazzoletto di carta; **tissue paper** *n* carta velina

tit [tɪt] *n* (*bird*) cinciallegra; **to give ~ for tat** rendere pan per focaccia

title ['taɪtl] *n* titolo

T-junction ['tiː'dʒʌŋkʃən] *n* incrocio a T

TM *n abbr* = **trademark**

KEYWORD

to [tuː, tə] *prep* **1** (*direction*) a; **to go to France/London/school** andare in Francia/a Londra/a scuola; **to go to Paul's/the doctor's** andare da Paul/dal dottore; **the road to Edinburgh** la strada per Edimburgo; **to the left/right** a sinistra/destra

2 (*as far as*) (fino) a; **from here to London** da qui a Londra; **to count to 10** contare fino a 10; **from 40 to 50 people** da 40 a 50 persone

3 (*with expressions of time*): **a quarter to 5** le 5 meno un quarto; **it's twenty to 3** sono le 3 meno venti

4 (*for, of*): **the key to the front door** la chiave della porta d'ingresso; **a letter to his wife** una lettera per la moglie

5 (*expressing indirect object*) a; **to give sth to sb** dare qc a qn; **to talk to sb** parlare a qn; **to be a danger to sb/sth** rappresentare un pericolo per qn/qc

6 (*in relation to*) a; **3 goals to 2** 3 goal a 2; **30 miles to the gallon** ≈ 11 chilometri con un litro

7 (*purpose, result*): **to come to sb's aid** venire in aiuto a qn; **to sentence sb to death** condannare a morte qn; **to my surprise** con mia sorpresa

▶ *with vb* **1** (*simple infinitive*): **to go/eat** *etc* andare/mangiare *etc*

2 (*following another vb*): **to want/try/start to do** volere/cercare di/cominciare a fare

3 (*with vb omitted*): **I don't want to** non voglio (farlo); **you ought to** devi (farlo)

4 (*purpose, result*) per; **I did it to help you** l'ho fatto per aiutarti

5 (*equivalent to relative clause*): **I have things to do** ho da fare; **the**

main thing is to try la cosa più importante è provare
6 (after adjective etc): **ready to go** pronto/a a partire; **too old/young to …** troppo vecchio/a/giovane per …
▶ adv: **to push the door to** accostare la porta

toad [təud] n rospo; **toadstool** n fungo (velenoso)
toast [təust] n (Culin) pane m tostato; (drink, speech) brindisi m inv ▷ vt (Culin) tostare; (drink to) brindare a; **a piece** or **slice of ~** una fetta di pane tostato; **toaster** n tostapane m inv
tobacco [tə'bækəu] n tabacco
toboggan [tə'bɔgən] n toboga m inv
today [tə'deɪ] adv, n (also fig) oggi m inv
toddler ['tɔdlə'] n bambino/a che impara a camminare
toe [təu] n dito del piede; (of shoe) punta ▷ vt: **to ~ the line** (fig) stare in riga, conformarsi; **toenail** n unghia del piede
toffee ['tɔfɪ] n caramella
together [tə'gɛðə'] adv insieme; (at same time) allo stesso tempo; **~ with** insieme a
toilet ['tɔɪlət] n (BRIT: lavatory) gabinetto ▷ cpd (soap etc) da toletta; **toilet bag** n (BRIT) nécessaire m inv da toilette; **toilet paper** n carta igienica; **toiletries** npl articoli mpl da toletta; **toilet roll** n rotolo di carta igienica
token ['təukən] n (sign) segno ▷ cpd (substitute coin) gettone m; **book/record/gift ~** (BRIT) buono-libro/-disco/-regalo
Tokyo ['təukjəu] n Tokyo f
told [təuld] pt, pp of **tell**
tolerant ['tɔlərnt] adj: **~ (of)** tollerante (nei confronti di)
tolerate ['tɔləreɪt] vt sopportare; (Med, Tech) tollerare

toll [təul] n (tax, charge) pedaggio ▷ vi (bell) suonare; **the accident ~ on the roads** il numero delle vittime della strada; **toll call** n (US Tel) (telefonata) interurbana; **toll-free** (US) adj senza addebito, gratuito/a ▷ adv gratuitamente; **toll-free number** ≈ numero verde
tomato [tə'mɑːtəu] (pl **tomatoes**) n pomodoro; **tomato sauce** n salsa di pomodoro
tomb [tuːm] n tomba; **tombstone** ['tuːmstəun] n pietra tombale
tomorrow [tə'mɔrəu] adv, n (also fig) domani m inv; **the day after ~** dopodomani; **~ morning** domani mattina
ton [tʌn] n tonnellata (Brit = 1016 kg; 20 cwt; US = 907 kg; metric = 1000 kg); **~s of** (col) un mucchio or sacco di
tone [təun] n tono ▷ vi (also: **~ in**) intonarsi; **tone down** vt (colour, criticism, sound) attenuare
tongs [tɔŋz] npl tenaglie fpl; (for coal) molle fpl; (for hair) arricciacapelli m inv
tongue [tʌŋ] n lingua; **~ in cheek** (say, speak) ironicamente
tonic ['tɔnɪk] n (Med) ricostituente m; (also: **~ water**) acqua tonica
tonight [tə'naɪt] adv stanotte; (this evening) stasera ▷ n questa notte; questa sera
tonne [tʌn] n (BRIT: metric ton) tonnellata
tonsil ['tɔnsl] n tonsilla; **tonsillitis** [tɔnsɪ'laɪtɪs] n tonsillite f
too [tuː] adv (excessively) troppo; (also) anche; **~ much** adv troppo; adj troppo/a; **~ many** troppi/e
took [tuk] pt of **take**
tool [tuːl] n utensile m, attrezzo; **tool box** n cassetta f portautensili; **tool kit** n cassetta di attrezzi
tooth (pl **teeth**) [tuːθ, tiːθ] n (Anat, Tech) dente m; **toothache** n mal m di denti; **toothbrush** n spazzolino da denti; **toothpaste** n dentifricio; **toothpick** n stuzzicadenti m inv

t

top [tɒp] n (of mountain, page, ladder) cima; (of box, cupboard, table) sopra m inv, parte f superiore; (lid: of box, jar) coperchio; (: of bottle) tappo; (toy) trottola; (blouse etc) camicia (or maglietta etc) ▷ adj più alto/a; (in rank) primo/a; (best) migliore ▷ vt (exceed) superare; (be first in) essere in testa a; **on ~** sopra, in cima a; (in addition to) oltre a; **from ~ to bottom** da cima a fond; **top up**, (US) **top off** vt riempire; (salary) integrare; **top floor** n ultimo piano; **top hat** n cilindro

topic ['tɒpɪk] n argomento; **topical** adj d'attualità

topless ['tɒplɪs] adj (bather etc) col seno scoperto

topping ['tɒpɪŋ] n (Culin) guarnizione f

topple ['tɒpl] vt rovesciare, far cadere ▷ vi cadere; traballare

top-up ['tɒpʌp] n (for mobile phone: also: **~ card**) ricarica

torch [tɔːtʃ] n torcia; (BRIT: electric) lampadina tascabile

tore [tɔːr] pt of **tear²**

torment n ['tɔːmɛnt] tormento ▷ vt [tɔː'mɛnt] tormentare

torn [tɔːn] pp of **tear²**

tornado [tɔː'neɪdəu] (pl **tornadoes**) n tornado

torpedo [tɔː'piːdəu] (pl **torpedoes**) n siluro

torrent ['tɒrnt] n torrente m; **torrential** [tɔ'rɛnʃl] adj torrenziale

tortoise ['tɔːtəs] n tartaruga

torture ['tɔːtʃər] n tortura ▷ vt torturare

Tory ['tɔːrɪ] adj, n (BRIT Pol) tory mf inv, conservatore/trice

toss [tɒs] vt gettare, lanciare; (head) scuotere; **to ~ a coin** fare a testa o croce; **to ~ up for sth** fare a testa o croce per qc; **to ~ and turn** (in bed) girarsi e rigirarsi

total ['təutl] adj totale ▷ n totale m ▷ vt (add up) sommare; (amount to) ammontare a

totalitarian [təutælɪ'tɛərɪən] adj totalitario/a

totally ['təutəlɪ] adv completamente

touch [tʌtʃ] n tocco; (sense) tatto; (contact) contatto ▷ vt toccare; **a ~ of** (fig) un tocco di; un pizzico di; **to get in ~ with** mettersi in contatto con; **to lose ~** (friends) perdersi di vista; **touch down** vi (on land) atterrare; **touchdown** n atterraggio; (on sea) ammaraggio; (US Football) meta; **touched** adj commosso/a; **touching** adj commovente; **touchline** n (Sport) linea laterale; **touch screen** n (Tech) schermo touch screen; **touch-screen mobile** telefono touch screen; **touch-screen technology** tecnologia touch screen; **touch-sensitive** adj sensibile al tatto

tough [tʌf] adj duro/a; (resistant) resistente

tour [tuər] n viaggio; (also: **package ~**) viaggio organizzato or tutto compreso (of town, museum) visita; (by artist) tournée f inv ▷ vt visitare; **tour guide** n guida turistica

tourism ['tuərɪzəm] n turismo

tourist ['tuərɪst] n turista m/f ▷ adv (travel) in classe turistica ▷ cpd turistico/a; **tourist office** n pro loco f inv

tournament ['tuənəmənt] n torneo

tour operator n (BRIT) operatore m turistico

tow [təu] vt rimorchiare; **"on ~"**, (US) **"in ~"** (Aut) "veicolo rimorchiato"

toward(s) [tə'wɔːd(z)] prep verso; (of attitude) nei confronti di; (of purpose) per

towel ['tauəl] n asciugamano; (also: **tea ~**) strofinaccio; **towelling** n (fabric) spugna

tower ['tauər] n torre f; **tower block** n (BRIT) palazzone m

town [taun] n città f inv; **to go to ~** andare in città; (fig) mettercela tutta; **town centre** n centro (città); **town hall** n ≈ municipio

tow truck n (US) carro m attrezzi inv
toxic ['tɔksɪk] adj tossico/a; **toxic asset** n (Econ) titolo tossico; **toxic bank** n (Econ) banca cattiva (che investe in titoli tossici)
toy [tɔɪ] n giocattolo; **toy with** vt fus giocare con; (idea) accarezzare, trastullarsi con; **toyshop** n negozio di giocattoli
trace [treɪs] n traccia ▷ vt (draw) tracciare; (follow) seguire; (locate) rintracciare
track [træk] n (of person, animal) traccia; (on tape, Sport: path: gen) pista; (: of bullet etc) traiettoria; (: of suspect, animal) pista, tracce fpl; (Rail) rotaie fpl ▷ vt seguire le tracce di; **to keep ~ of** seguire; **track down** vt (prey) scovare; snidare; (sth lost) rintracciare; **tracksuit** n tuta sportiva
tractor ['træktə'] n trattore m
trade [treɪd] n commercio; (skill, job) mestiere m ▷ vi commerciare; **to ~ with/in** commerciare con/in ▷ vt: **to ~ sth (for sth)** barattare qc (con qc); **trade in** vt (old car etc) dare come pagamento parziale; **trademark** n marchio di fabbrica; **trader** n commerciante m/f; **tradesman** n (irreg) fornitore m; (shopkeeper) negoziante m; **trade union** n sindacato
trading ['treɪdɪŋ] n commercio
tradition [trə'dɪʃən] n tradizione f; **traditional** adj tradizionale
traffic ['træfɪk] n traffico ▷ vi: **to ~ in** (pej: liquor, drugs) trafficare in; **traffic circle** n (US) isola rotatoria; **traffic island** n salvagente m, isola f, spartitraffico inv; **traffic jam** n ingorgo (del traffico); **traffic lights** npl semaforo; **traffic warden** n addetto/a al controllo del traffico e del parcheggio
tragedy ['trædʒədɪ] n tragedia
tragic ['trædʒɪk] adj tragico/a

trail [treɪl] n (tracks) tracce fpl, pista; (path) sentiero; (of smoke etc) scia ▷ vt trascinare, strascicare; (follow) seguire ▷ vi essere al traino; (dress etc) strusciare; (plant) arrampicarsi, strusciare; (in game) essere in svantaggio; **trailer** n (Aut) rimorchio; (US) roulotte f inv; (Cine) prossimamente m inv
train [treɪn] n treno; (of dress) coda, strascico ▷ vt (apprentice, doctor etc) formare; (sportsman) allenare; (dog) addestrare; (memory) esercitare; (point: gun etc): **to ~ sth on** puntare qc contro ▷ vi formarsi; allenarsi; **one's ~ of thought** il filo dei propri pensieri; **trainee** [treɪ'niː] n (in trade) apprendista m/f; **trainer** n (Sport) allenatore/trice; (of dogs etc) addestratore/trice; **trainers** npl (shoes) scarpe fpl da ginnastica; **training** n formazione f; allenamento; addestramento; **in training** (Sport) in allenamento; **training course** n corso di formazione professionale; **training shoes** npl scarpe fpl da ginnastica
train wreck n (fig) persona distrutta; (: pej) rottame m; **he's a complete ~** è completamente distrutto, è un rottame
trait [treɪt] n tratto
traitor ['treɪtə'] n traditore/trice
tram [træm] n (BRIT: also: **~car**) tram m inv
tramp [træmp] n (person) vagabondo/a; (col, pej: woman) sgualdrina
trample ['træmpl] vt: **to ~ (underfoot)** calpestare
trampoline ['træmpəliːn] n trampolino
tranquil ['træŋkwɪl] adj tranquillo/a; **tranquillizer**, (US) **tranquilizer** n (Med) tranquillante m
transaction [træn'zækʃən] n transazione f
transatlantic ['trænzət'læntɪk] adj transatlantico/a

t

transcript ['trænskrıpt] n
trascrizione f
transfer n ['trænsfəʳ] (gen, also
Sport) trasferimento; (Pol: of
power) passaggio; (picture, design)
decalcomania; (: stick-on) autoadesivo
▷ vt [træns'fəːʳ] trasferire; passare;
to ~ the charges (BRIT Tel) fare una
chiamata a carico del destinatario
transform [træns'fɔːm] vt
trasformare; **transformation** n
trasformazione f
transfusion [træns'fjuːʒən] n
trasfusione f
transit ['trænzɪt] n: **in ~** in transito
transition [træn'zɪʃən] n passaggio,
transizione f
transitive ['trænzɪtɪv] adj (Ling)
transitivo/a
translate [trænz'leɪt] vt tradurre;
translation [trænz'leɪʃən] n
traduzione f; **translator** n
traduttore/trice
transmission [trænz'mɪʃən] n
trasmissione f
transmit [trænz'mɪt] vt
trasmettere; **transmitter** n
trasmettitore m
transparent [træns'pærnt] adj
trasparente
transplant vt [træns'plɑːnt]
trapiantare ▷ n ['trænsplɑːnt] (Med)
trapianto
transport n ['trænspɔːt] trasporto
▷ vt [træns'pɔːt] trasportare;
transportation ['trænspɔːˈteɪʃən] n
(mezzo di) trasporto
transvestite [trænz'vɛstaɪt] n
travestito/a
trap [træp] n (snare, trick) trappola;
(carriage) calesse m ▷ vt prendere in
trappola, intrappolare
trash [træʃ] n (col: goods) ciarpame m;
(: nonsense) sciocchezze fpl; **trash can**
n (US) secchio della spazzatura
trauma ['trɔːmə] n trauma m;
traumatic [trɔːˈmætɪk] adj
traumatico/a

travel ['trævl] n viaggio; viaggi
mpl ▷ vi viaggiare ▷ vt (distance)
percorrere; **travel agency** n agenzia
(di) viaggi; **travel agent** n agente
m di viaggio; **travel insurance** n
assicurazione f di viaggio; **traveller**,
(US) **traveler** n viaggiatore/trice;
traveller's cheque, (US) **traveler's
check** n assegno turistico; **travelling**,
(US) **traveling** n viaggi mpl; **travel-
sick** adj: **to get travel-sick** (in vehicle)
soffrire di mal d'auto; (in aeroplane)
soffrire di mal d'aria; (in boat) soffrire di
mal di mare; **travel sickness** n mal m
d'auto (or di mare or d'aria)
tray [treɪ] n (for carrying) vassoio; (on
desk) vaschetta
treacherous ['trɛtʃərəs] adj infido/a
treacle ['triːkl] n melassa
tread [trɛd] n passo; (sound) rumore
m di passi; (of stairs) pedata; (of tyre)
battistrada m inv ▷ vi (pt trod, pp
trodden) camminare; **tread on** vt
fus calpestare
treasure ['trɛʒəʳ] n tesoro ▷ vt (value)
tenere in gran conto, apprezzare
molto; (store) custodire gelosamente;
treasurer [trɛʒərəʳ] n tesoriere/a
treasury ['trɛʒərɪ] n: **the T~**
(BRIT), **the T~ Department** (US) ≈ il
Ministero del Tesoro
treat [triːt] n regalo ▷ vt trattare;
(Med) curare; **to ~ sb to sth** offrire
qc a qn; **treatment** ['triːtmənt] n
trattamento
treaty ['triːtɪ] n patto, trattato
treble ['trɛbl] adj triplo/a, triplice ▷ vt
triplicare ▷ vi triplicarsi
tree [triː] n albero
trek [trɛk] n (hike) escursione
f a piedi; (in car) escursione f in
macchina; (tiring walk) camminata
sfiancante ▷ vi (as holiday) fare
dell'escursionismo
tremble ['trɛmbl] vi tremare
tremendous [trɪˈmɛndəs] adj
(enormous) enorme; (excellent)
meraviglioso/a, formidabile

Be careful not to translate *tremendous* by the Italian word *tremendo*.

trench [trɛntʃ] n trincea

trend [trɛnd] n (*tendency*) tendenza; (*of events*) corso; (*fashion*) moda; **trendy** adj (*idea*) di moda; (*clothes*) all'ultima moda

trespass ['trɛspəs] vi: **to ~ on** entrare abusivamente in; **"no ~ing"** "proprietà privata", "vietato l'accesso"

trial ['traɪəl] n (*Law*) processo; (*test: of machine etc*) collaudo; **to be on ~** (*Law*) essere sotto processo; **trial period** n periodo di prova

triangle ['traɪæŋgl] n (*Math, Mus*) triangolo

triangular [traɪ'æŋgjuləʳ] adj triangolare

tribe [traɪb] n tribù f inv

tribunal [traɪ'bju:nl] n tribunale m

tribute ['trɪbju:t] n tributo, omaggio; **to pay ~ to** rendere omaggio a

trick [trɪk] n trucco; (*joke*) tiro; (*Cards*) presa ▷ vt imbrogliare, ingannare; **to play a ~ on sb** giocare un tiro a qn; **that should do the ~** vedrai che funziona

trickle ['trɪkl] n (*of water etc*) rivolo, gocciolio ▷ vi gocciolare

tricky ['trɪkɪ] adj difficile, delicato/a

tricycle ['traɪsɪkl] n triciclo

trifle ['traɪfl] n sciocchezza; (*BRIT Culin*) ≈ zuppa inglese ▷ adv: **a ~ long** un po' lungo

trigger ['trɪgəʳ] n (*of gun*) grilletto

trim [trɪm] adj (*house, garden*) ben tenuto/a; (*figure*) snello/a ▷ n (*haircut etc*) spuntata, regolata; (*embellishment*) finiture fpl; (*on car*) guarnizioni fpl ▷ vt spuntare; (*Naut: a sail*) orientare; (*decorate*): **to ~ (with)** decorare (con)

trio ['tri:əu] n trio

trip [trɪp] n viaggio; (*excursion*) gita, escursione f; (*stumble*) passo falso ▷ vi inciampare; (*go lightly*) camminare con passo leggero; **on a ~** in viaggio; **trip up** vi inciampare ▷ vt fare lo sgambetto a

triple ['trɪpl] adj triplo/a

triplets ['trɪplɪts] npl bambini/e trigemini/e

tripod ['traɪpɔd] n treppiede m

triumph ['traɪʌmf] n trionfo ▷ vi: **to ~ (over)** trionfare (su); **triumphant** [traɪ'ʌmfənt] adj trionfante

trivial ['trɪvɪəl] adj insignificante; (*excuse, comment*) banale

Be careful not to translate *trivial* by the Italian word *triviale*.

trod [trɔd] pt of **tread**

trodden ['trɔdn] pp of **tread**

trolley ['trɔlɪ] n carrello

trombone [trɔm'bəun] n trombone m

troop [tru:p] n gruppo; (*Mil*) squadrone m; **troops** npl (*Mil*) truppe fpl

trophy ['trəufɪ] n trofeo

tropical ['trɔpɪkəl] adj tropicale

trot [trɔt] n trotto ▷ vi trottare; **on the ~** (*BRIT fig*) di fila, uno/a dopo l'altro/a

trouble ['trʌbl] n difficoltà f inv, problema m; (*problems*) difficoltà fpl, problemi mpl; (*worry*) preoccupazione f; (*bother, effort*) sforzo; (*Pol*) conflitti mpl, disordine m; (*Med*): **stomach etc ~** disturbi mpl gastrici etc ▷ vt disturbare; (*worry*) preoccupare ▷ vi: **to ~ to do** disturbarsi a fare; **troubles** npl (*Pol etc*) disordini mpl; **to be in ~** avere dei problemi; **it's no ~!** di niente!; **what's the ~?** cosa c'è che non va?; **troubled** adj (*person*) preoccupato/a, inquieto/a; (*epoch, life*) agitato/a, difficile; **troublemaker** n elemento disturbatore, agitatore/trice; (*child*) disloco/a; **troublesome** adj fastidioso/a, seccante

trough [trɔf] n (*also*: **drinking ~**) abbeveratoio; (*also*: **feeding ~**) trogolo, mangiatoia; (*channel*) canale m

t

trousers ['trauzəz] npl pantaloni mpl, calzoni mpl; **short ~** calzoncini mpl

trout [traut] n (pl inv) trota

trowel ['trauəl] n cazzuola

truant ['truənt] n: **to play ~** (BRIT) marinare la scuola

truce [tru:s] n tregua

truck [trʌk] n autocarro, camion m inv; (Rail) carro merci aperto; (for luggage) carrello m portabagagli inv; **truck driver** n camionista m/f

true [tru:] adj vero/a; (accurate) accurato/a, esatto/a; (genuine) reale; (faithful) fedele; **to come ~** avverarsi

truly ['tru:lɪ] adv veramente; (truthfully) sinceramente; **yours ~** (in letter-writing) distinti saluti

trumpet ['trʌmpɪt] n tromba

trunk [trʌŋk] n (of tree, person) tronco; (of elephant) proboscide f; (case) baule m; (us Aut) bagagliaio; **trunks** npl (also: **swimming trunks**) calzoncini mpl da bagno

trust [trʌst] n fiducia; (Law) amministrazione f fiduciaria; (Comm) trust m inv ⊳ vt (rely on) contare su; (entrust): **to ~ sth to sb** affidare qc a qn; (hope): **to ~ (that)** sperare (che); **trusted** adj fidato/a; **trustworthy** adj fidato/a, degno/a di fiducia

truth (pl **truths**) [tru:θ, tru:ðz] n verità f inv; **truthful** adj (person) sincero/a; (description) veritiero/a, esatto/a

try [traɪ] n prova, tentativo; (Rugby) meta ⊳ vt (Law) giudicare; (test: also: **~ out**) provare; (strain) mettere alla prova ⊳ vi provare; **to have a ~** fare un tentativo; **to ~ to do** (seek) cercare di fare; **try on** vt (clothes) provare; **trying** adj (day, experience) logorante, pesante; (child) difficile, insopportabile

T-shirt ['ti:ʃə:t] n maglietta

tsunami [tsu'nɑ:mɪ] n tsunami m inv

tub [tʌb] n tinozza; mastello; (bath) bagno

tube [tju:b] n tubo; (BRIT: underground) metropolitana, metrò m inv; (for tyre) camera d'aria

tuberculosis [tjubə:kju'ləusɪs] n tubercolosi f inv

tube station n (BRIT) stazione f della metropolitana

tuck [tʌk] n piega ⊳ vt (put) mettere; **tuck away** vt riporre; (building): **to be ~ed away** essere in un luogo isolato; **tuck in** vt mettere dentro; (child) rimboccare ⊳ vi (eat) mangiare di buon appetito; abbuffarsi

tucker ['tʌkər] n (AUST, NZ col) cibo

tuck shop n negozio di pasticceria (in una scuola)

Tue(s). abbr (= Tuesday) mar.

Tuesday ['tju:zdɪ] n martedì m inv

tug [tʌg] n (ship) rimorchiatore m ⊳ vt tirare con forza

tuition [tju:'ɪʃən] n (BRIT) lezioni fpl; (: private tuition) lezioni fpl private; (us: fees) tasse fpl scolastiche (or universitarie)

tulip ['tju:lɪp] n tulipano

tumble ['tʌmbl] n (fall) capitombolo ⊳ vi capitombolare, ruzzolare; **to ~ to sth** (col) realizzare qc; **tumble dryer** n (BRIT) asciugatrice f

tumbler ['tʌmblər] n bicchiere m senza stelo

tummy ['tʌmɪ] n (col) pancia

tumour, (us) **tumor** ['tju:mər] n tumore m

tuna ['tju:nə] n (pl inv: also: **~ fish**) tonno

tune [tju:n] n (melody) melodia, aria ⊳ vt (Mus) accordare; (Radio, TV, Aut) regolare, mettere a punto; **to be in/out of ~** (instrument) essere accordato/a/scordato/a; (singer) essere intonato/a/stonato/a; **tune in** vi (Radio, TV): **to ~ in (to)** sintonizzarsi (su); **tune up** vi (musician) accordare lo strumento

tunic ['tju:nɪk] n tunica

Tunisia [tju:'nɪzɪə] n Tunisia

tunnel ['tʌnl] n galleria ▷ vi scavare una galleria

turbulence ['tə:bjuləns] n (Aviat) turbolenza

turf [tə:f] n terreno erboso; (clod) zolla ▷ vt coprire di zolle erbose

Turin [tjuə'rɪn] n Torino f

Turk [tə:k] n turco/a

Turkey ['tə:kɪ] n Turchia

turkey ['tə:kɪ] n tacchino

Turkish ['tə:kɪʃ] adj turco/a ▷ n (Ling) turco

turmoil ['tə:mɔɪl] n confusione f, tumulto

turn [tə:n] n giro; (change) cambiamento; (in road) curva; (tendency: of mind, events) tendenza; (performance) numero; (chance) turno; (Med) crisi f inv, attacco ▷ vt girare, voltare; (change): **to ~ sth into** trasformare qc in ▷ vi girare; (person: look back) girarsi, voltarsi; (reverse direction) girarsi indietro; (change) cambiare; (milk) andare a male; (become) diventare; **a good ~** un buon servizio; **it gave me quite a ~** mi ha fatto prendere un bello spavento; **"no left ~"** (Aut) "divieto di svolta a sinistra"; **it's your ~** tocca a lei; **in ~** a sua volta; a turno; **to take ~s (at sth)** fare (qc) a turno; **turn away** vi girarsi (dall'altra parte) ▷ vt mandar via; **turn back** vi ritornare, tornare indietro ▷ vt far tornare indietro; (clock) spostare indietro; **turn down** vt (refuse) rifiutare; (reduce) abbassare; (fold) ripiegare; **turn in** vi (col: go to bed) andare a letto ▷ vt (fold) voltare in dentro; **turn off** vi (from road) girare, voltare ▷ vt (light, radio, engine etc) spegnere; **turn on** vt (light, radio etc) accendere; **turn out** vt (light, gas) chiudere; spegnere ▷ vi (troops, doctor, voters etc) presentarsi; **to ~ out to be ...** rivelarsi ..., risultare ...; **turn over** vi (person) girarsi ▷ vt girare; **turn round** vi girare; (person) girarsi; **turn**

to vt fus: **to ~ to sb** girarsi verso qn; **to ~ to sb for help** rivolgersi a qn per aiuto; **turn up** vi (person) arrivare, presentarsi; (lost object) saltar fuori ▷ vt (collar, sound, gas etc) alzare; **turning** n (in road) curva; **turning point** n (fig) svolta decisiva

turnip ['tə:nɪp] n rapa

turn: turnout ['tə:naut] n presenza, affluenza; **turnover** ['tə:nəuvəʳ] n (Comm) giro di affari; (Culin): **apple** etc **turnover** sfogliatella alle mele etc; **turnstile** ['tə:nstaɪl] n tornella; **turn-up** n (BRIT: on trousers) risvolto

turquoise [tə:kwɔɪz] n turchese m ▷ adj turchese

turtle ['tə:tl] n testuggine f; **turtleneck (sweater)** ['tə:tlnɛk-] n maglione m con il collo alto

Tuscany ['tʌskənɪ] n Toscana

tusk [tʌsk] n zanna

tutor ['tju:təʳ] n (in college) docente m/f (responsabile di un gruppo di studenti); (private teacher) precettore m; **tutorial** [tju:'tɔ:rɪəl] n (Scol) lezione f con discussione (a un gruppo limitato)

tuxedo [tʌk'si:dəu] n (US) smoking m inv

TV [ti:'vi:] n abbr (= television) tivù f inv

tweed [twi:d] n tweed m inv

tweet [twi:t] n (on Twitter) post m su Twitter ▷ vt, vi (on Twitter) scrivere su Twitter

tweezers ['twi:zəz] npl pinzette fpl

twelfth [twɛlfθ] num dodicesimo/a

twelve [twɛlv] num dodici; **at ~** alle dodici, a mezzogiorno; (midnight) a mezzanotte

twentieth ['twɛntɪɪθ] num ventesimo/a

twenty ['twɛntɪ] num venti; **in ~ fourteen** nel duemilaquattordici

twice [twaɪs] adv due volte; **~ as much** due volte tanto; **~ a week** due volte alla settimana

twig [twɪg] n ramoscello ▷ vt, vi (col) capire

twilight ['twaɪlaɪt] *n* crepuscolo
twin [twɪn] *adj, n* gemello/a ▷ *vt*:
  to ~ one town with another fare il
  gemellaggio di una città con un'altra;
  twin-bedded room *n* stanza con
  letti gemelli; **twin beds** *npl* letti
  mpl gemelli
twinkle ['twɪŋkl] *vi* scintillare; (*eyes*)
  brillare
twist [twɪst] *n* torsione *f*; (*in wire, flex*)
  piega; (*in story*) colpo di scena; (*bend*)
  svolta, piega; (*in road*) curva ▷ *vt*
  attorcigliare; (*ankle*) slogare; (*weave*)
  intrecciare; (*roll around*) arrotolare;
  (*fig*) distorcere ▷ *vi* (*road*) serpeggiare
twit [twɪt] *n* (*col*) cretino/a
twitch [twɪtʃ] *n* tiratina; (*nervous*) tic
  m inv ▷ *vi* contrarsi
Twitter® [twɪtəʳ] *n* Twitter® *m*
two [tuː] *num* due; **to put ~ and ~**
  together (*fig*) fare uno più uno
type [taɪp] *n* (*category*) genere *m*;
  (*model*) modello; (*example*) tipo;
  (*Typ*) tipo, carattere *m* ▷ *vt* (*letter etc*)
  battere (a macchina), dattilografare;
  typewriter *n* macchina da scrivere
typhoid ['taɪfɔɪd] *n* tifoidea
typhoon [taɪ'fuːn] *n* tifone *m*
typical ['tɪpɪkl] *adj* tipico/a;
  typically *adv* tipicamente;
  typically, he arrived late come al
  solito è arrivato tardi
typing ['taɪpɪŋ] *n* dattilografia
typist ['taɪpɪst] *n* dattilografo/a
tyre, (*us*) **tire** ['taɪəʳ] *n* pneumatico,
  gomma; **I've got a flat ~** ho una
  gomma a terra; **tyre pressure** *n*
  pressione *f* (delle gomme)

U

UFO ['juːfəu] *n abbr* (= *unidentified*
  flying object) UFO *m inv*
Uganda [juː'gændə] *n* Uganda
ugly ['ʌglɪ] *adj* brutto/a
UHT *adj abbr* (= *ultra heat treated*) UHT
  inv, a lunga conservazione
UK *n abbr* = **United Kingdom**
ulcer ['ʌlsəʳ] *n* ulcera; **mouth ~**
  afta
ultimate ['ʌltɪmɪt] *adj* ultimo/a,
  finale; (*authority*) massimo/a,
  supremo/a; **ultimately** *adv* alla fine;
  in definitiva, in fin dei conti
ultimatum (*pl* **ultimatums** or
  ultimata) [ʌltɪ'meɪtəm, -tə] *n*
  ultimatum *m inv*
ultrasound [ʌltrə'saund] *n*
  ultrasuono; (*Med*) ecografia
ultraviolet ['ʌltrə'vaɪəlɪt] *adj*
  ultravioletto/a
umbrella [ʌm'brɛlə] *n* ombrello
umpire ['ʌmpaɪəʳ] *n* arbitro
UN *n abbr* (= *United Nations*) ONU *f*

unable [ʌnˈeɪbl] *adj*: **to be ~ to** non potere, essere nell'impossibilità di; (*not to know how to*) essere incapace di

unacceptable [ʌnəkˈsɛptəbl] *adj* (*proposal, behaviour*) inaccettabile; (*price*) impossibile

unanimous [juːˈnænɪməs] *adj* unanime

unarmed [ʌnˈɑːmd] *adj* (*person*) disarmato/a; (*combat*) senz'armi

unattended [ʌnəˈtɛndɪd] *adj* (*car, child, luggage*) incustodito/a

unattractive [ʌnəˈtræktɪv] *adj* poco attraente

unavailable [ʌnəˈveɪləbl] *adj* (*article, room, book*) non disponibile; (*person*) impegnato/a

unavoidable [ʌnəˈvɔɪdəbl] *adj* inevitabile

unaware [ʌnəˈwɛər] *adj*: **to be ~ of** non sapere, ignorare; **unawares** *adv* di sorpresa, alla sprovvista

unbearable [ʌnˈbɛərəbl] *adj* insopportabile

unbeatable [ʌnˈbiːtəbl] *adj* imbattibile

unbelievable [ʌnbɪˈliːvəbl] *adj* incredibile

unborn [ʌnˈbɔːn] *adj* non ancora nato/a

unbutton [ʌnˈbʌtn] *vt* sbottonare

uncalled-for [ʌnˈkɔːldfɔːr] *adj* (*remark*) fuori luogo *inv*; (*action*) ingiustificato/a

uncanny [ʌnˈkænɪ] *adj* misterioso/a, strano/a

uncertain [ʌnˈsəːtn] *adj* incerto/a; dubbio/a; **uncertainty** *n* incertezza

unchanged [ʌnˈtʃeɪndʒd] *adj* immutato/a

uncle [ˈʌŋkl] *n* zio

unclear [ʌnˈklɪər] *adj* non chiaro/a; **I'm still ~ about what I'm supposed to do** non ho ancora ben capito cosa dovrei fare

uncomfortable [ʌnˈkʌmfətəbl] *adj* scomodo/a; (*uneasy*) a disagio, agitato/a; (*unpleasant*) fastidioso/a

uncommon [ʌnˈkɔmən] *adj* raro/a, insolito/a, non comune

unconditional [ʌnkənˈdɪʃənl] *adj* incondizionato/a, senza condizioni

unconscious [ʌnˈkɔnʃəs] *adj* privo/a di sensi, svenuto/a; (*unaware*) inconsapevole, inconscio/a ▷ *n*: **the ~** l'inconscio

uncontrollable [ʌnkənˈtrəuləbl] *adj* incontrollabile; indisciplinato/a

unconventional [ʌnkənˈvɛnʃənl] *adj* poco convenzionale

uncover [ʌnˈkʌvər] *vt* scoprire

undecided [ʌndɪˈsaɪdɪd] *adj* indeciso/a

undeniable [ʌndɪˈnaɪəbl] *adj* innegabile, indiscutibile

under [ˈʌndər] *prep* sotto; (*less than*) meno di; al disotto di; (*according to*) secondo, in conformità a ▷ *adv* (al) disotto; **~ there** là sotto; **~ repair** in riparazione; **undercover** *adj* segreto/a, clandestino/a; **underdone** *adj* (*Culin*) al sangue; (*pej*) poco cotto/a; **underestimate** *vt* sottovalutare; **undergo** *vt* (*irreg*) subire; (*treatment*) sottoporsi a; **undergraduate** *n* studente/essa universitario/a; **underground** *n* (BRIT: *railway*) metropolitana; (*Pol*) movimento clandestino ▷ *adj* sotterraneo/a; (*fig*) clandestino/a ▷ *adv* sottoterra; **to go underground** (*fig*) darsi alla macchia; **undergrowth** *n* sottobosco; **underline** *vt* sottolineare; **undermine** *vt* minare; **underneath** [ʌndəˈniːθ] *adv* sotto, disotto ▷ *prep* sotto, al di sotto di; **underpants** *npl* mutande *fpl*, slip *m inv*; **underpass** *n* (BRIT) sottopassaggio; **underprivileged** *adj* svantaggiato/a; **underscore** *vt* sottolineare; **undershirt** *n* (US) maglietta; **underskirt** (BRIT) *n* sottoveste *f*

understand [ʌndəˈstænd] (*irreg: like* **stand**) *vt*, *vi* capire, comprendere;

I don't ~ non capisco; **I ~ that ...** sento che ...; credo di capire che ...; **understandable** adj comprensibile; **understanding** adj comprensivo/a ▷ n comprensione f; (agreement) accordo

understatement [ʌndə'steɪtmənt] n: **that's an ~!** a dire poco!

understood [ʌndə'stud] pt, pp of **understand** ▷ adj inteso/a; (implied) sottinteso/a

undertake [ʌndə'teɪk] vt (irreg: like **take**) intraprendere; **to ~ to do sth** impegnarsi a fare qc

undertaker ['ʌndəteɪkə'] n impresario di pompe funebri

undertaking [ʌndə'teɪkɪŋ] n impresa; (promise) promessa

under: underwater [ʌndə'wɔːtə'] adv sott'acqua ▷ adj subacqueo/a; **underway** [ʌndə'weɪ] adj: **to be underway** essere in corso; **underwear** ['ʌndəwɛə'] n biancheria (intima); **underwent** [ʌndə'wɛnt] vb see **undergo**; **underworld** ['ʌndəwəːld] n (of crime) malavita

undesirable [ʌndɪ'zaɪərəbl] adj indesiderato/a

undisputed [ʌndɪs'pjuːtɪd] adj indiscusso/a

undo [ʌn'duː] vt (irreg) disfare

undone [ʌn'dʌn] pp of **undo**; **to come ~** slacciarsi

undoubtedly [ʌn'daʊtɪdlɪ] adv senza alcun dubbio

undress [ʌn'drɛs] vi spogliarsi

unearth [ʌn'əːθ] vt dissotterrare; (fig) scoprire

uneasy [ʌn'iːzɪ] adj a disagio; (worried) preoccupato/a; (peace) precario/a

unemployed [ʌnɪm'plɔɪd] adj disoccupato/a ▷ npl: **the ~** i disoccupati

unemployment [ʌnɪm'plɔɪmənt] n disoccupazione f; **unemployment benefit**, (US) **unemployment compensation** n sussidio di disoccupazione

unequal [ʌn'iːkwəl] adj (length, objects) disuguale; (amounts) diverso/a; (division of labour) ineguale

uneven [ʌn'iːvən] adj ineguale; (heartbeat) irregolare

unexpected [ʌnɪk'spɛktɪd] adj inatteso/a, imprevisto/a; **unexpectedly** adv inaspettatamente

unfair [ʌn'fɛə'] adj: **~ (to)** ingiusto/a (nei confronti di)

unfaithful [ʌn'feɪθful] adj infedele

unfamiliar [ʌnfə'mɪlɪə'] adj sconosciuto/a, strano/a; **to be ~ with sth** non avere familiarità con qc

unfashionable [ʌn'fæʃnəbl] adj (clothes) fuori moda inv; (district) non alla moda

unfasten [ʌn'fɑːsn] vt slacciare; sciogliere

unfavourable, (US) **unfavorable** [ʌn'feɪvərəbl] adj sfavorevole

unfinished [ʌn'fɪnɪʃt] adj incompiuto/a

unfit [ʌn'fɪt] adj (ill) non in forma; (incompetent): **~ (for)** incompetente (in); (work, Mil) inabile (a)

unfold [ʌn'fəuld] vt spiegare ▷ vi (story) svelarsi

unforgettable [ʌnfə'gɛtəbl] adj indimenticabile

unfortunate [ʌn'fɔːtʃnɪt] adj sfortunato/a; (event, remark) infelice; **unfortunately** adv sfortunatamente, purtroppo

unfriend [ʌn'frɛnd] vt (Internet) cancellare dagli amici

unfriendly [ʌn'frɛndlɪ] adj poco amichevole, freddo/a

unfurnished [ʌn'fəːnɪʃt] adj non ammobiliato/a

unhappiness [ʌn'hæpɪnɪs] n infelicità

unhappy [ʌn'hæpɪ] adj infelice; **~ about/with** (arrangements etc) insoddisfatto/a di

unhealthy [ʌnˈhɛlθɪ] *adj* (*gen*) malsano/a; (*person*) malaticcio/a

unheard-of [ʌnˈhəːdɒv] *adj* inaudito/a, senza precedenti

unhelpful [ʌnˈhɛlpful] *adj* poco disponibile

unhurt [ʌnˈhəːt] *adj* incolume, illeso/a

unidentified [ʌnaɪˈdɛntɪfaɪd] *adj* non identificato/a

uniform [ˈjuːnɪfɔːm] *n* uniforme *f*, divisa ▷ *adj* uniforme

unify [ˈjuːnɪfaɪ] *vt* unificare

unimportant [ʌnɪmˈpɔːtənt] *adj* senza importanza, di scarsa importanza

uninhabited [ʌnɪnˈhæbɪtɪd] *adj* disabitato/a

unintentional [ʌnɪnˈtɛnʃənəl] *adj* involontario/a

union [ˈjuːnjən] *n* unione *f*; (*also*: **trade ~**) sindacato ▷ *cpd* sindacale, dei sindacati; **Union Jack** *n* bandiera nazionale britannica

unique [juːˈniːk] *adj* unico/a

unisex [ˈjuːnɪsɛks] *adj* unisex *inv*

unit [ˈjuːnɪt] *n* unità *f inv*; (*section: of furniture etc*) elemento; (*team, squad*) reparto, squadra

unite [juːˈnaɪt] *vt* unire ▷ *vi* unirsi; **united** *adj* unito/a, unificato/a; (*efforts*) congiunto/a; **United Kingdom** *n* Regno Unito; **United Nations (Organization)** *n* (Organizzazione *f* delle) Nazioni Unite; **United States (of America)** *n* Stati *mpl* Uniti (d'America)

unity [ˈjuːnɪtɪ] *n* unità *f*

universal [juːnɪˈvəːsl] *adj* universale

universe [ˈjuːnɪvəːs] *n* universo

university [juːnɪˈvəːsɪtɪ] *n* università *f inv*

unjust [ʌnˈdʒʌst] *adj* ingiusto/a

unkind [ʌnˈkaɪnd] *adj* poco gentile, scortese

unknown [ʌnˈnəun] *adj* sconosciuto/a

unlawful [ʌnˈlɔːful] *adj* illecito/a, illegale

unleaded [ˈʌnˈlɛdɪd] *adj* senza piombo; **~ petrol** benzina verde *or* senza piombo

unleash [ʌnˈliːʃ] *vt* (*fig*) scatenare

unless [ʌnˈlɛs] *conj* a meno che (non) + *sub*

unlike [ʌnˈlaɪk] *adj* diverso/a ▷ *prep* a differenza di, contrariamente a

unlikely [ʌnˈlaɪklɪ] *adj* improbabile

unlimited [ʌnˈlɪmɪtɪd] *adj* illimitato/a

unlisted [ʌnˈlɪstɪd] *adj* (*US Tel*): **to be ~** non essere sull'elenco

unload [ʌnˈləud] *vt* scaricare

unlock [ʌnˈlɔk] *vt* aprire

unlucky [ʌnˈlʌkɪ] *adj* sfortunato/a; (*object, number*) che porta sfortuna

unmarried [ʌnˈmærɪd] *adj* non sposato/a; (*man only*) scapolo, celibe; (*woman only*) nubile

unmistak(e)able [ʌnmɪsˈteɪkəbl] *adj* inconfondibile

unnatural [ʌnˈnætʃrəl] *adj* innaturale; contro natura

unnecessary [ʌnˈnɛsəsərɪ] *adj* inutile, superfluo/a

UNO [ˈjuːnəu] *n abbr* (= *United Nations Organization*) ONU *f*

unofficial [ʌnəˈfɪʃl] *adj* non ufficiale; (*strike*) non dichiarato/a dal sindacato

unpack [ʌnˈpæk] *vi* disfare la valigia (*or* le valigie) ▷ *vt* disfare

unpaid [ʌnˈpeɪd] *adj* (*holiday*) non pagato/a; (*work*) non retribuito/a; (*bill, debt*) da pagare

unpleasant [ʌnˈplɛznt] *adj* spiacevole

unplug [ʌnˈplʌg] *vt* staccare

unpopular [ʌnˈpɔpjuləʳ] *adj* impopolare

unprecedented [ʌnˈprɛsɪdəntɪd] *adj* senza precedenti

unpredictable [ʌnprɪˈdɪktəbl] *adj* imprevedibile

unprotected [ˈʌnprəˈtɛktɪd] *adj* (*sex*) non protetto/a

u

unqualified [ʌnˈkwɔlɪfaɪd] *adj (in professions)* non abilitato/a; *(success)* assoluto/a, senza riserve

unravel [ʌnˈrævl] *vt* dipanare, districare

unreal [ʌnˈrɪəl] *adj* irreale

unrealistic [ʌnrɪəˈlɪstɪk] *adj* non realistico/a

unreasonable [ʌnˈriːznəbl] *adj* irragionevole

unrelated [ʌnrɪˈleɪtɪd] *adj*: ~ **(to)** senza rapporto (con); *(by family)* non imparentato/a (con)

unreliable [ʌnrɪˈlaɪəbl] *adj (person, machine)* che non dà affidamento; *(news, source of information)* inattendibile

unrest [ʌnˈrɛst] *n* agitazione *f*

unroll [ʌnˈrəul] *vt* srotolare

unruly [ʌnˈruːlɪ] *adj* indisciplinato/a

unsafe [ʌnˈseɪf] *adj* pericoloso/a, rischioso/a

unsatisfactory [ˈʌnsætɪsˈfæktərɪ] *adj* che lascia a desiderare, insufficiente

unscrew [ʌnˈskruː] *vt* svitare

unsettled [ʌnˈsɛtld] *adj (person, future)* incerto/a; indeciso/a; turbato/a; *(weather, market)* instabile

unsettling [ʌnˈsɛtlɪŋ] *adj* inquietante

unsightly [ʌnˈsaɪtlɪ] *adj* brutto/a, sgradevole a vedersi

unskilled [ʌnˈskɪld] *adj*: ~ **worker** operaio/a specializzato/a

unspoiled [ˈʌnˈspɔɪld], **unspoilt** [ˈʌnˈspɔɪlt] *adj (place)* non deturpato/a

unstable [ʌnˈsteɪbl] *adj (gen)* instabile; *(mentally)* squilibrato/a

unsteady [ʌnˈstɛdɪ] *adj* instabile, malsicuro/a

unsuccessful [ʌnsəkˈsɛsful] *adj (writer, proposal)* che non ha successo; *(marriage, attempt)* mal riuscito/a, fallito/a; **to be ~** *(in attempting sth)* non avere successo

unsuitable [ʌnˈsuːtəbl] *adj* inadatto/a; *(moment)* inopportuno/a; *(moment)* sconveniente

unsure [ʌnˈʃuəʳ] *adj*: ~ **(of** or **about)** incerto/a (su); **to be ~ of o.s.** essere insicuro/a

untidy [ʌnˈtaɪdɪ] *adj (room)* in disordine; *(appearance, work)* trascurato/a; *(person, writing)* disordinato/a

untie [ʌnˈtaɪ] *vt (knot, parcel)* disfare; *(prisoner, dog)* slegare

until [ʌnˈtɪl] *prep* fino a; *(after negative)* prima di ▷ *conj* finché, fino a quando; *(in past, after negative)* prima che + *sub*, prima di + *infinitive*: ~ **he comes** finché or fino a quando non arriva; ~ **now** finora; ~ **then** fino ad allora

untrue [ʌnˈtruː] *adj (statement)* falso/a, non vero/a

unused [ʌnˈjuːzd] *adj* nuovo/a

unusual [ʌnˈjuːʒuəl] *adj* insolito/a, eccezionale raro/a; **unusually** *adv* insolitamente

unveil [ʌnˈveɪl] *vt* scoprire; svelare

unwanted [ʌnˈwɔntɪd] *adj (clothing)* smesso/a; *(child)* non desiderato/a

unwell [ʌnˈwɛl] *adj* indisposto/a; **to feel ~** non sentirsi bene

unwilling [ʌnˈwɪlɪŋ] *adj*: **to be ~ to do** non voler fare

unwind [ʌnˈwaɪnd] *(irreg: like* **wind²**) *like vt* svolgere, srotolare ▷ *vi (relax)* rilassarsi

unwise [ʌnˈwaɪz] *adj* poco saggio/a

unwittingly [ʌnˈwɪtɪŋlɪ] *adv* senza volerlo

unwrap [ʌnˈræp] *vt* disfare; *(present)* aprire

unzip [ʌnˈzɪp] *vt* aprire (la chiusura lampo di); *(Comput)* dezippare

 KEYWORD

up [ʌp] *prep*: **he went up the stairs/ the hill** è salito su per le scale/sulla collina; **the cat was up a tree** il gatto era su un albero; **they live**

further up the street vivono un po' più su nella stessa strada
▶ adv **1** (*upwards, higher*) su, in alto; **up in the sky/the mountains** su nel cielo/in montagna; **up there** lassù; **up above** su in alto
2: **to be up** (*out of bed*) essere alzato/a; (*prices, level*) essere salito/a
3: **up to** (*as far as*) fino a; **up to now** finora
4: **to be up to** (*depending on*): **it's up to you** sta a lei, dipende da lei; (*equal to*): **he's not up to it** (*job, task etc*) non ne è all'altezza; (*be doing: col*): **what is he up to?** cosa sta combinando?
▶ n: **ups and downs** alti e bassi mpl

up-and-coming ['ʌpənd'kʌmɪŋ] adj pieno/a di promesse, promettente
upbringing ['ʌpbrɪŋɪŋ] n educazione f
update [ʌp'deɪt] vt aggiornare
upfront [ʌp'frʌnt] adj (col) franco/a, aperto/a ▶ adv (pay) subito
upgrade [ʌp'greɪd] vt (job) rivalutare; (house) rimodernare; (employee) avanzare di grado
upheaval [ʌp'hiːvl] n sconvolgimento; tumulto
uphill [ʌp'hɪl] adj in salita; (fig: task) difficile ▶ adv: **to go ~** andare in salita, salire
upholstery [ʌp'həʊlstərɪ] n tappezzeria
upload ['ʌpləʊd] vt caricare
up-market [ʌp'mɑːkɪt] adj (product) che si rivolge ad una fascia di mercato superiore
upon [ə'pɔn] prep su
upper ['ʌpəʳ] adj superiore ▶ n (of shoe) tomaia; **upper-class** adj dell'alta borghesia
upright ['ʌpraɪt] adj diritto/a; verticale; (fig) diritto/a, onesto/a
uprising ['ʌpraɪzɪŋ] n insurrezione f, rivolta

uproar ['ʌprɔːʳ] n tumulto, clamore m
upset n ['ʌpsɛt] (to plan etc) contrattempo ▶ vt [ʌp'sɛt] (irreg: like **set**) (glass etc) rovesciare; (plan, stomach) scombussolare; (person: offend) contrariare; (: grieve) addolorare; sconvolgere ▶ adj [ʌp'sɛt] contrariato/a, addolorato/a; (stomach) scombussolato/a; **to have a stomach ~** avere lo stomaco in disordine or scombussolato
upside down ['ʌpsaɪd-] adv sottosopra
upstairs [ʌp'stɛəz] adv, adj di sopra, al piano superiore ▶ n piano di sopra
up-to-date ['ʌptə'deɪt] adj moderno/a; aggiornato/a
uptown ['ʌptaʊn] (us) adv verso i quartieri residenziali ▶ adj dei quartieri residenziali
upward ['ʌpwəd] adj ascendente; verso l'alto ▶ adv = **upwards**
uranium [juə'reɪnɪəm] n uranio
Uranus [juə'reɪnəs] n (planet) Urano
urban ['əːbən] adj urbano/a
urge [əːdʒ] n impulso; stimolo; forte desiderio ▶ vt: **to ~ sb to do** esortare qn a fare, spingere qn a fare; raccomandare a qn di fare
urgency ['əːdʒənsɪ] n urgenza; (of tone) insistenza
urgent ['əːdʒənt] adj urgente; (tone, voice) insistente
urinal ['juərɪnl] n (BRIT: building) vespasiano; (: vessel) orinale m, pappagallo
urinate ['juərɪneɪt] vi orinare
urine ['juərɪn] n orina
URL n abbr (= uniform resource locator) URL m inv
us [ʌs] pron ci; (stressed, after prep) noi; see also **me**
USA n abbr = **United States of America**
USB stick n pennetta USB
use n [juːs] uso; impiego, utilizzazione f ▶ vt [juːz] usare, utilizzare, servirsi di; **she ~d to do**

it lo faceva (una volta), era solita farlo; **in ~** in uso; **out of ~** fuori uso; **to be of ~** essere utile, servire; **it's no ~** non serve, è inutile; **to be ~d to** avere l'abitudine di; **use up** vt finire; (left-overs) consumare; **used** adj (car, object) usato/a; **useful** adj utile; **useless** adj inutile; (person) inetto/a; **user** n utente m/f; **user-friendly** adj (computer) di facile uso

usual ['juːʒuəl] adj solito/a; **as ~** come al solito, come d'abitudine; **usually** adv di solito

ute [juːt] n (AUST, NZ) pick-up m inv

utensil [juː'tɛnsl] n utensile m; **kitchen ~s** utensili da cucina

utility [juː'tɪlɪtɪ] n utilità; (also: **public ~**) servizio pubblico

utilize ['juːtɪlaɪz] vt utilizzare; sfruttare

utmost ['ʌtməust] adj estremo/a ▷ n: **to do one's ~** fare il possibile or di tutto

utter ['ʌtər] adj assoluto/a, totale ▷ vt pronunciare, proferire; emettere; **utterly** adv completamente, del tutto

U-turn ['juːtəːn] n inversione f a U

V

v abbr (= verse) v.; (= vide) v., vedi; (= volt) V.; (= versus) contro

vacancy ['veɪkənsɪ] n (job) posto libero; (room) stanza libera; **"no vacancies"** "completo"

> Be careful not to translate *vacancy* by the Italian word *vacanza*.

vacant ['veɪkənt] adj (job, seat etc) libero/a; (expression) assente

vacate [və'keɪt] vt lasciare libero/a

vacation [və'keɪʃən] n (esp US) vacanze fpl; **vacationer**, **vacationist** (US) n vacanziere/a

vaccination [væksɪ'neɪʃən] n vaccinazione f

vaccine ['væksiːn] n vaccino

vacuum ['vækjum] n vuoto; **vacuum cleaner** n aspirapolvere m inv

vagina [və'dʒaɪnə] n vagina

vague [veɪg] adj vago/a; (blurred: photo, memory) sfocato/a

vain [veɪn] adj (useless) inutile, vano/a; (conceited) vanitoso/a; **in ~** inutilmente, invano

Valentine's Day ['væləntaɪnzdeɪ] n San Valentino m

valid ['vælɪd] adj valido/a, valevole; (excuse) valido/a

valley ['vælɪ] n valle f

valuable ['væljuəbl] adj (jewel) di (grande) valore; (time, help) prezioso/a; **valuables** npl oggetti mpl di valore

value ['vælju:] n valore m ▷ vt (fix price) valutare, dare un prezzo a; (cherish) apprezzare, tenere a; **values** npl (principles) valori mpl

valve [vælv] n valvola

vampire ['væmpaɪə'] n vampiro

van [væn] n (Aut) furgone m; (BRIT Rail) vagone m

vandal ['vændl] n vandalo/a; **vandalism** n vandalismo; **vandalize** vt vandalizzare

vanilla [və'nɪlə] n vaniglia ▷ cpd (ice cream) alla vaniglia

vanish ['vænɪʃ] vi svanire, scomparire

vanity ['vænɪtɪ] n vanità

vapour, (US) **vapor** ['veɪpə'] n vapore m

variable ['vɛərɪəbl] adj variabile; (mood) mutevole

variant ['vɛərɪənt] n variante f

variation [vɛərɪ'eɪʃən] n variazione f; (in opinion) cambiamento

varied ['vɛərɪd] adj vario/a, diverso/a

variety [və'raɪətɪ] n varietà f inv; (quantity) quantità, numero

various ['vɛərɪəs] adj vario/a, diverso/a; (several) parecchi/e, molti/e

varnish ['vɑːnɪʃ] n vernice f; (nail varnish) smalto ▷ vt verniciare; mettere lo smalto su

vary ['vɛərɪ] vt, vi variare, mutare

vase [vɑːz] n vaso

Vaseline® ['væsɪliːn] n vaselina

vast [vɑːst] adj vasto/a; (amount, success) enorme

VAT [væt] n abbr (BRIT: = value added tax) I.V.A. f

Vatican ['vætɪkən] n: **the ~** il Vaticano

vault [vɔːlt] n (of roof) volta; (tomb) tomba; (in bank) camera blindata ▷ vt (also: **~ over**) saltare (d'un balzo)

VCR n abbr = **video cassette recorder**

VDU n abbr = **visual display unit**

veal [viːl] n vitello

veer [vɪə'] vi girare; virare

vegan ['viːgən] n vegetaliano/a

vegetable ['vɛdʒtəbl] n verdura, ortaggio ▷ adj vegetale

vegetarian [vɛdʒɪ'tɛərɪən] adj, n vegetariano/a

vegetation [vɛdʒɪ'teɪʃən] n vegetazione f

vehicle ['viːɪkl] n veicolo

veil [veɪl] n velo

vein [veɪn] n vena; (on leaf) nervatura

Velcro® ['vɛlkrəu] n velcro® m inv

velvet ['vɛlvɪt] n velluto ▷ adj di velluto

vending machine ['vɛndɪŋ-] n distributore m automatico

vendor ['vɛndə'] n venditore/trice

vengeance ['vɛndʒəns] n vendetta; **with a ~** (fig) davvero; furiosamente

Venice ['vɛnɪs] n Venezia

venison ['vɛnɪsn] n carne f di cervo

venom ['vɛnəm] n veleno

vent [vɛnt] n foro, apertura; (in dress, jacket) spacco ▷ vt (fig: one's feelings) sfogare, dare sfogo a

ventilation [vɛntɪ'leɪʃən] n ventilazione f

venture ['vɛntʃə'] n impresa (rischiosa) ▷ vt rischiare, azzardare ▷ vi arrischiarsi; **a business ~** un'iniziativa commerciale

venue ['vɛnjuː] n luogo (designato) per l'incontro

Venus ['viːnəs] n (planet) Venere m

verb [vəːb] n verbo; **verbal** adj verbale; (translation) orale

verdict ['vəːdɪkt] n verdetto

V

verge [vəːdʒ] n bordo, orlo; **"soft ~s"** (BRIT) "banchina cedevole"; **on the ~ of doing** sul punto di fare

verify ['vɛrɪfaɪ] vt verificare; (prove the truth of) confermare

versatile ['vəːsətaɪl] adj (person) versatile; (machine, tool etc) (che si presta) a molti usi

verse [vəːs] n (stanza) stanza, strofa; (in bible) versetto; (no pl: poetry) versi mpl

version ['vəːʃən] n versione f

versus ['vəːsəs] prep contro

vertical ['vəːtɪkl] adj, n verticale (m)

very ['vɛrɪ] adv molto ▷ adj: **the ~ book which** proprio il libro che; **~ much** moltissimo; **the ~ last** proprio l'ultimo; **at the ~ least** almeno

vessel ['vɛsl] n (Anat) vaso; (Naut) nave f; (container) recipiente m

vest [vɛst] n (BRIT) maglia; (: sleeveless) canottiera; (US: waistcoat) gilè m inv

vet [vɛt] n abbr (BRIT: = veterinary surgeon) veterinario ▷ vt esaminare minuziosamente

veteran ['vɛtərn] n veterano; (also: **war ~**) veterano, reduce m

veterinary surgeon ['vɛtrɪnərɪ-], (US) **veterinarian** [vɛtrɪ'nɛərɪən] n veterinario

veto ['viːtəu] (pl **vetoes**) n veto ▷ vt opporre il veto a

via ['vaɪə] prep (by way of) via; (by means of) tramite

viable ['vaɪəbl] adj attuabile; vitale

vibrate [vaɪ'breɪt] vi: **to ~ (with)** vibrare (di); (resound) risonare (di)

vibration [vaɪ'breɪʃən] n vibrazione f

vicar ['vɪkər] n pastore m

vice [vaɪs] n (evil) vizio; (Tech) morsa; **vice-chairman** n (irreg) vicepresidente m

vice versa ['vaɪsɪ'vəːsə] adv viceversa

vicinity [vɪ'sɪnɪtɪ] n vicinanze fpl

vicious ['vɪʃəs] adj (remark) cattivo/a; (dog) cattivo/a; (blow) violento/a

victim ['vɪktɪm] n vittima

victor ['vɪktər] n vincitore m

Victorian [vɪk'tɔːrɪən] adj vittoriano/a

victorious [vɪk'tɔːrɪəs] adj vittorioso/a

victory ['vɪktərɪ] n vittoria

video ['vɪdɪəu] cpd video... ▷ n (video film) video m inv; (also: **~ cassette**) videocassetta; (also: **~ recorder**) videoregistratore m; **video call** n videochiamata; **video camera** n videocamera; **video game** n videogioco; **videophone** n videotelefono; **video shop** n videonoleggio; **video tape** n videotape m inv; **video wall** n schermo m multivideo inv

vie [vaɪ] vi: **to ~ with** competere con, rivaleggiare con

Vienna [vɪ'ɛnə] n Vienna

Vietnam [vjɛt'næm] n Vietnam m; **Vietnamese** adj, n vietnamita m/f

view [vjuː] n vista, veduta; (opinion) opinione f ▷ vt (also fig: situation) considerare; (house) visitare; **on ~** (in museum etc) esposto/a; **to be in** or **within ~ (of sth)** essere in vista (di qc); **in my ~** a mio parere; **in ~ of the fact that** considerato che; **viewer** n telespettatore/trice; **viewpoint** n punto di vista; (place) posizione f

vigilant ['vɪdʒɪlənt] adj vigile

vigorous ['vɪgərəs] adj vigoroso/a

vile [vaɪl] adj (action) vile; (smell) disgustoso/a, nauseante; (temper) pessimo/a

villa ['vɪlə] n villa

village ['vɪlɪdʒ] n villaggio; **villager** n abitante m/f di villaggio

villain ['vɪlən] n (scoundrel) canaglia; (BRIT: criminal) criminale m; (in novel etc) cattivo

vinaigrette [vɪneɪ'grɛt] n vinaigrette f inv

vine [vaɪn] n vite f; (climbing plant) rampicante m

vinegar ['vɪnɪgər] n aceto

vineyard ['vɪnjɑːd] n vigna, vigneto
vintage ['vɪntɪdʒ] n (year) annata, produzione f ▷ cpd d'annata
vinyl ['vaɪnl] n vinile m
viola [vɪ'əulə] n viola
violate ['vaɪəleɪt] vt violare
violation [vaɪə'leɪʃən] n violazione f; **in ~ of sth** violando qc
violence ['vaɪələns] n violenza
violent ['vaɪələnt] adj violento/a
violet ['vaɪələt] adj (colour) viola inv, violetto/a ▷ n (plant) violetta; (colour) violetto
violin [vaɪə'lɪn] n violino
VIP n abbr (= very important person) V.I.P. mf inv
virgin ['vəːdʒɪn] n vergine f ▷ adj vergine inv
Virgo ['vəːgəu] n (sign) Vergine f
virtual ['vəːtjuəl] adj effettivo/a, vero/a; (Comput, Physics) virtuale; (in effect): **it's a ~ impossibility** è praticamente impossibile; **the ~ leader** il capo all'atto pratico; **virtually** ['vəːtjuəlɪ] adv (almost) praticamente; **virtual reality** n (Comput) realtà f inv virtuale
virtue ['vəːtjuː] n virtù f inv; (advantage) pregio, vantaggio; **by ~ of** grazie a
virus ['vaɪərəs] n (also Comput) virus m inv
visa ['viːzə] n visto
vise [vaɪs] n (US Tech) = **vice**
visibility [vɪzɪ'bɪlɪtɪ] n visibilità
visible ['vɪzəbl] adj visibile
vision ['vɪʒən] n (sight) vista; (foresight, in dream) visione f
visit ['vɪzɪt] n visita; (stay) soggiorno ▷ vt (person: US: also: **~ with**) andare a trovare; (place) visitare; **visiting hours** npl (in hospital etc) orario delle visite; **visitor** n visitatore/trice; (guest) ospite m/f; **visitor centre**, (US) **visitor center** n centro informazioni per visitatori di museo, zoo, parco ecc
visual ['vɪzjuəl] adj visivo/a; visuale; ottico/a; **visualize** ['vɪzjuəlaɪz]

vt immaginare, figurarsi; (foresee) prevedere
vital ['vaɪtl] adj vitale
vitality [vaɪ'tælɪtɪ] n vitalità
vitamin ['vɪtəmɪn] n vitamina
vivid ['vɪvɪd] adj vivido/a
V-neck ['viːnɛk] n maglione m con lo scollo a V
vocabulary [vəu'kæbjulərɪ] n vocabolario
vocal ['vəukl] adj (Mus) vocale; (communication) verbale
vocational [vəu'keɪʃənl] adj professionale
vodka ['vɔdkə] n vodka f inv
vogue [vəug] n moda; (popularity) popolarità, voga
voice [vɔɪs] n voce f ▷ vt (opinion) esprimere; **voice mail** n servizio di segreteria telefonica
void [vɔɪd] n vuoto ▷ adj (invalid) nullo/a; (empty): **~ of** privo/a di
volatile ['vɔlətaɪl] adj volatile; (fig) volubile
volcano [vɔl'keɪnəu] (pl **volcanoes**) n vulcano
volleyball ['vɔlɪbɔːl] n pallavolo f
volt [vəult] n volt m inv; **voltage** n tensione f, voltaggio
volume ['vɔljuːm] n volume m
voluntarily ['vɔləntrɪlɪ] adv volontariamente; gratuitamente
voluntary ['vɔləntərɪ] adj volontario/a; (unpaid) gratuito/a, non retribuito/a
volunteer [vɔlən'tɪəʳ] n volontario/a ▷ vt offrire volontariamente ▷ vi (Mil) arruolarsi volontario; **to ~ to do** offrire (volontariamente) di fare
vomit ['vɔmɪt] n vomito ▷ vt, vi vomitare
vote [vəut] n voto, suffragio; (cast) voto; (franchise) diritto di voto ▷ vi votare ▷ vt (propose): **to ~ that** approvare la proposta che; **he was ~d secretary** è stato eletto segretario; **~ of thanks** discorso di

ringraziamento; **voter** *n* elettore/ trice; **voting** *n* scrutinio

voucher ['vautʃə^r] *n* (*for meal, petrol*) buono

vow [vau] *n* voto, promessa solenne ▷ *vt*: **to ~ to do/that** giurare di fare/che

vowel ['vauəl] *n* vocale *f*

voyage ['vɔɪɪdʒ] *n* viaggio per mare, traversata

vulgar ['vʌlgə^r] *adj* volgare

vulnerable ['vʌlnərəbl] *adj* vulnerabile

vulture ['vʌltʃə^r] *n* avvoltoio

waddle ['wɔdl] *vi* camminare come una papera

wade [weɪd] *vi*: **to ~ through** camminare a stento in; (*fig: book*) leggere con fatica

wafer ['weɪfə^r] *n* (*Culin*) cialda

waffle ['wɔfl] *n* (*Culin*) cialda; (*col*) ciance *fpl* ▷ *vi* cianciare

wag [wæg] *vt* agitare, muovere ▷ *vi* agitarsi

wage [weɪdʒ] *n* (*also:* **~s**) salario, paga ▷ *vt*: **to ~ war** fare la guerra

wag(g)on ['wægən] *n* (*horse-drawn*) carro; (BRIT Rail) vagone *m* (merci)

wail [weɪl] *n* gemito; (*of siren*) urlo ▷ *vi* gemere; urlare

waist [weɪst] *n* vita, cintola; **waistcoat** *n* (BRIT) panciotto, gilè *m inv*

wait [weɪt] *n* attesa ▷ *vi* aspettare, attendere; **to ~ for** aspettare; **~ for me, please** aspettami, per favore; **I can't ~ to ...** (*fig*) non vedo l'ora di

...; **to lie in ~ for** stare in agguato a; **wait behind** vi rimanere (ad aspettare); **wait on** vt fus servire; **waiter** n cameriere m; **waiting list** n lista d'attesa; **waiting room** n sala d'aspetto or d'attesa; **waitress** n cameriera

waive [weɪv] vt rinunciare a, abbandonare

wake [weɪk] (pt **woke, waked**, pp **woken, waked**) vt (also: **~ up**) svegliare ▷ vi (also: **~ up**) svegliarsi ▷ n (for dead person) veglia funebre; (Naut) scia

Wales [weɪlz] n Galles m

walk [wɔːk] n passeggiata; (short) giretto; (gait) passo, andatura; (path) sentiero; (in park etc) sentiero, vialetto ▷ vi camminare; (for pleasure, exercise) passeggiare ▷ vt (distance) fare or percorrere a piedi; (dog) accompagnare, portare a passeggio; **10 minutes' ~ from** 10 minuti di cammino or a piedi da; **from all ~s of life** di tutte le condizioni sociali; **walk out** vi (audience) andarsene; (strike) scendere in sciopero; **walker** n (person) camminatore/trice; **walkie-talkie** ['wɔːkɪ'tɔːkɪ] n walkie-talkie m inv; **walking** n camminare m; **walking shoes** npl scarpe fpl da passeggio; **walking stick** n bastone m da passeggio; **Walkman®** ['wɔːkmən] n walkman® m inv; **walkway** n passaggio pedonale

wall [wɔːl] n muro; (internal, of tunnel, cave) parete f

wallet ['wɒlɪt] n portafoglio

wallpaper ['wɔːlpeɪpəʳ] n carta da parati ▷ vt (room) mettere la carta da parati in

walnut ['wɔːlnʌt] n noce f; (tree) noce m

walrus ['wɔːlrəs] (pl **walrus** or **walruses**) n tricheco

waltz [wɔːlts] n valzer m inv ▷ vi ballare il valzer

wand [wɒnd] n (also: **magic ~**) bacchetta (magica)

wander ['wɒndəʳ] vi (person) girare senza meta, girovagare; (thoughts) vagare ▷ vt girovagare per

want [wɒnt] vt volere; (need) aver bisogno di ▷ n: **for ~ of** per mancanza di; **wanted** adj (criminal) ricercato/a; **"wanted"** (in adverts) "cercasi"

war [wɔːʳ] n guerra; **to make ~ (on)** far guerra (a)

ward [wɔːd] n (in hospital: room) corsia; (: section) reparto; (Pol) circoscrizione f; (Law: child: also: **~ of court**) pupillo/a

warden ['wɔːdn] n (of institution) direttore/trice; (of park, game reserve) guardiano/a; (BRIT: also: **traffic ~**) addetto/a al controllo del traffico e del parcheggio

wardrobe ['wɔːdrəub] n (cupboard) guardaroba m inv, armadio; (clothes) guardaroba; (Theat) costumi mpl

warehouse ['wɛəhaus] n magazzino

warfare ['wɔːfɛəʳ] n guerra

warhead ['wɔːhɛd] n (Mil) testata

warm [wɔːm] adj caldo/a; (welcome, applause) caloroso/a; (person, greeting) cordiale; **it's ~** fa caldo; **I'm ~** ho caldo; **warm up** vi scaldarsi, riscaldarsi ▷ vt scaldare, riscaldare; (engine) far scaldare; **warmly** adv (applaud, welcome) calorosamente; (dress) con abiti pesanti; **warmth** n calore m

warn [wɔːn] vt: **to ~ sb not to do sth** or **against doing sth** avvertire or avvisare qn di non fare qc; **to ~ sb that** avvertire or avvisare qn che; **warning** n avvertimento; (notice) avviso; (signal) segnalazione f; **warning light** n spia luminosa

warrant ['wɒrnt] n (voucher) buono; (Law: to arrest) mandato di cattura; (: to search) mandato di perquisizione

warranty ['wɒrəntɪ] n garanzia

warrior ['wɔrɪər] n guerriero/a
Warsaw ['wɔːsɔː] n Varsavia
warship ['wɔːʃɪp] n nave f da guerra
wart [wɔːt] n verruca
wartime ['wɔːtaɪm] n: **in ~** in tempo di guerra
wary ['wɛərɪ] adj prudente
was [wɒz] pt of **be**
wash [wɒʃ] vt lavare ▷ vi lavarsi; (sea): **to ~ over/against sth** infrangersi su/contro qc ▷ n lavaggio; (of ship) scia; **to give sth a ~** lavare qc, dare una lavata a qc; **to have a ~** lavarsi; **wash up** vi (BRIT) lavare i piatti; (US: have a wash) lavarsi; **washbasin**, **washbowl** n lavabo; **washcloth** n (US) pezzuola (per lavarsi); **washer** n (Tech) rondella; **washing** n (linen etc) bucato; **washing line** n (BRIT) corda del bucato; **washing machine** n lavatrice f; **washing powder** n (BRIT) detersivo (in polvere)
Washington ['wɒʃɪŋtən] n Washington f
wash: washing-up n (dishes) piatti mpl sporchi; **washing-up liquid** n detersivo liquido (per stoviglie); **washroom** n gabinetto
wasn't ['wɒznt] = **was not**
wasp [wɒsp] n vespa
waste [weɪst] n spreco; (of time) perdita; (rubbish) rifiuti mpl; (also: **household ~**) immondizie fpl ▷ adj (material) di scarto; (food) avanzato/a; (land, ground) incolto/a ▷ vt sprecare; **waste ground** n (BRIT) terreno incolto or abbandonato; **wastepaper basket** ['weɪstpeɪpə-] n cestino per la carta straccia
watch [wɒtʃ] n (wristwatch) orologio (da polso); (act of watching, vigilance) sorveglianza; (guard: Mil, Naut) guardia; (Naut: spell of duty) quarto ▷ vt (look at) osservare; (: match, programme) guardare; (spy on, guard) sorvegliare, tenere d'occhio; (be careful of) fare attenzione a ▷ vi

osservare, guardare; (keep guard) fare or montare la guardia; **watch out** vi fare attenzione; **watchdog** n cane m da guardia; **watch strap** n cinturino da orologio
water [wɔːtər] n acqua ▷ vt (plant) annaffiare ▷ vi (eyes) lacrimare; **in British ~s** nelle acque territoriali britanniche; **to make sb's mouth ~** far venire l'acquolina in bocca a qn; **water down** vt (milk) diluire; (fig: story) edulcorare; **watercolour**, (US) **watercolor** n acquerello; **watercress** n crescione m; **waterfall** n cascata; **watering can** n annaffiatoio; **watermelon** n anguria, cocomero; **waterproof** adj impermeabile; **water-skiing** n sci m acquatico
watt [wɒt] n watt m inv
wave [weɪv] n onda; (of hand) gesto, segno; (in hair) ondulazione f; (fig: of enthusiasm, strikes etc) ondata ▷ vi fare un cenno con la mano; (branches, grass) ondeggiare; (flag) sventolare ▷ vt (hand) fare un gesto con; (handkerchief) sventolare; (stick) brandire; **wavelength** n lunghezza d'onda
waver ['weɪvər] vi esitare; (voice) tremolare
wavy ['weɪvɪ] adj ondulato/a; ondeggiante
wax [wæks] n cera ▷ vt dare la cera a; (car) lucidare ▷ vi (moon) crescere
way [weɪ] n via, strada; (path, access) passaggio; (distance) distanza; (direction) parte f, direzione f; (manner) modo, stile m; (habit) abitudine f; **which ~? — this ~** da che parte or in quale direzione? — da questa parte or per di qua; **on the ~** (en route) per strada; **to be on one's ~** essere in cammino or sulla strada; **to be in the ~** bloccare il passaggio; (fig) essere tra i piedi or d'impiccio; **to go out of one's ~ to do** (fig) mettercela tutta or fare di tutto per fare; **to**

be under ~ (*work, project*) essere in corso; **to lose one's ~** perdere la strada; **in a ~** in un certo senso; **in some ~s** sotto certi aspetti; **"~ in"** (BRIT) "entrata", "ingresso"; **"~ out"** (BRIT) "uscita"; **the ~ back** la via del ritorno; **"give ~"** (BRIT Aut) "dare la precedenza"; **no ~!** (*col*) neanche per idea!; **by the ~ ...** a proposito ...

WC ['dʌblju:'si:] *n abbr* (BRIT: = *water closet*) W.C. *m inv*, gabinetto

we [wi:] *pl pron* noi

weak [wi:k] *adj* debole; (*health*) precario/a; (*beam etc*) fragile; (*tea, coffee*) leggero/a; **weaken** *vi* indebolirsi ▷ *vt* indebolire; **weakness** *n* debolezza; (*fault*) punto debole, difetto; **to have a weakness for** avere un debole per

wealth [wɛlθ] *n* (*money, resources*) ricchezza, ricchezze *fpl*; (*of details*) abbondanza, profusione *f*; **wealthy** *adj* ricco/a

weapon ['wɛpən] *n* arma; **~s of mass destruction** armi di distruzione di massa

wear [wɛəʳ] (*pt* **wore**, *pp* **worn**) *n* (*use*) uso; (*deterioration through use*) logorio, usura; (*clothing*): **sports/ baby ~** abbigliamento sportivo/ per neonati ▷ *vt* (*clothes*) portare; (*put on*) mettersi; (*damage: through use*) consumare ▷ *vi* (*last*) durare; (*rub etc through*) consumarsi; **town/evening ~** abiti *mpl or* tenuta da città/sera; **wear off** *vi* sparire lentamente; **wear out** *vt* consumare; (*person, strength*) esaurire

weary ['wɪərɪ] *adj* stanco/a ▷ *vi*: **to ~ of** stancarsi di

weasel ['wi:zl] *n* (*Zool*) donnola

weather ['wɛðəʳ] *n* tempo ▷ *vt* (*storm, crisis*) superare; **what's the ~ like?** che tempo fa?; **under the ~** (*fig: ill*) poco bene; **weather forecast** *n* previsioni *fpl* del tempo, bollettino meteorologico

weave (*pt* **wove**, *pp* **woven**) [wi:v, wəʊv, 'wəʊvn] *vt* (*cloth*) tessere; (*basket*) intrecciare

web [wɛb] *n* (*of spider*) ragnatela; (*on foot*) palma; (*fabric, also fig*) tessuto; **the (World Wide) W~** la Rete; **web address** *n* indirizzo Internet; **webcam** *n* webcam *f inv*; **web page** *n* (*Comput*) pagina *f* web *inv*; **website** *n* (*Comput*) sito (Internet)

wed [wɛd] *vt* (*pt, pp* **wedded**) sposare ▷ *vi* sposarsi

Wed. *abbr* (= *Wednesday*) mer.

we'd [wi:d] = **we had;** = **we would**

wedding ['wɛdɪŋ] *n* matrimonio; **wedding anniversary** *n* anniversario di matrimonio; **wedding day** *n* giorno delle nozze *or* del matrimonio; **wedding dress** *n* abito nuziale; **wedding ring** *n* fede *f*

wedge [wɛdʒ] *n* (*under door etc*) zeppa; (*of cake*) fetta ▷ *vt* (*fix*) fissare con zeppe; (*pack tightly*) incastrare

Wednesday ['wɛdnzdɪ] *n* mercoledì *m inv*

wee [wi:] *adj* (SCOTTISH) piccolo/a

weed [wi:d] *n* erbaccia ▷ *vt* diserbare; **weed-killer** *n* diserbante *m*

week [wi:k] *n* settimana; **a ~ on Tuesday** martedì a otto; **a ~ today** oggi a otto; **weekday** *n* giorno feriale; (*Comm*) giornata lavorativa; **weekend** *n* fine settimana *m inv or f inv*, weekend *m inv*; **weekly** *adv* ogni settimana, settimanalmente ▷ *adj, n* settimanale (*m*)

weep (*pt, pp* **wept**) [wi:p, wɛpt] *vi* (*person*) piangere

weigh [weɪ] *vt, vi* pesare; **to ~ anchor** salpare *or* levare l'ancora; **weigh up** *vt* valutare

weight [weɪt] *n* peso; **to put on/ lose ~** ingrassare/dimagrire; **weightlifting** *n* sollevamento pesi

weir [wɪəʳ] *n* diga

weird [wɪəd] *adj* strano/a, bizzarro/a; (*eerie*) soprannaturale

w

welcome ['wɛlkəm] *adj*
benvenuto/a ▷ *n* accoglienza,
benvenuto ▷ *vt* dare il benvenuto
a; (*be glad of*) rallegrarsi di; **you're ~**
(*after thanks*) prego

weld [wɛld] *n* saldatura ▷ *vt* saldare

welfare ['wɛlfɛə'] *n* benessere *m*;
welfare state *n* stato sociale

well [wɛl] *n* pozzo ▷ *adv* bene ▷ *adj*:
to be ~ (*person*) stare bene ▷ *excl*
allora!; ma!; ebbene!; **~ done!**
bravo/a!; **get ~ soon!** guarisci
presto!; **to do ~** andare bene; **as
~** anche

we'll [wi:l] = **we will; we shall**

well: well-behaved *adj* ubbidiente;
well-built *adj* (*person*) ben fatto/a;
well-dressed *adj* ben vestito/a,
vestito/a bene

wellies (*col*) ['wɛlɪz] *npl* (*BRIT*) stivali
mpl di gomma

well: well-known *adj* noto/a,
famoso/a; **well-off** *adj* benestante,
danaroso/a; **well-paid** [wɛl'peɪd]
adj ben pagato/a

Welsh [wɛlʃ] *adj* gallese ▷ *n* (*Ling*)
gallese *m*; **Welshman** *n* (*irreg*) gallese
m; **Welshwoman** *n* (*irreg*) gallese *f*

went [wɛnt] *pt of* **go**

wept [wɛpt] *pt, pp of* **weep**

were [wə:'] *pt of* **be**

we're [wɪə'] = **we are**

weren't [wə:nt] = **were not**

west [wɛst] *n* ovest *m*, occidente
m, ponente *m* ▷ *adj* (a) ovest *inv*,
occidentale ▷ *adv* verso ovest;
the W~ l'Occidente; **westbound**
['wɛstbaund] *adj* (*traffic*) diretto/a
a ovest; (*carriageway*) ovest *inv*;
western *adj* occidentale, dell'ovest
▷ *n* (*Cine*) western *m inv*; **West
Indian** *adj* delle Indie Occidentali
▷ *n* abitante *m/f* (*or* originario/a)
delle Indie Occidentali; **West Indies**
[-'ɪndɪz] *npl*: **the West Indies** le Indie
Occidentali

wet [wɛt] *adj* umido/a, bagnato/a;
(*soaked*) fradicio/a; (*rainy*) piovoso/a

▷ *n* (*BRIT Pol*) politico moderato; **to
get ~** bagnarsi; **"~ paint"** "vernice
fresca"; **wet suit** *n* tuta da sub

we've [wi:v] = **we have**

whack [wæk] *vt* picchiare, battere

whale [weɪl] *n* (*Zool*) balena

wharf (*pl* **wharves**) [wɔ:f, wɔ:vz] *n*
banchina

KEYWORD

what [wɔt] *adj* **1** (*in direct/indirect
questions*) che; quale; **what size is
it?** che taglia è?; **what colour is it?**
di che colore è?; **what books do you
want?** quali *or* che libri vuole?
2 (*in exclamations*) che; **what a mess!**
che disordine!
▷ *pron* **1** (*interrogative*) che cosa,
cosa, che; **what are you doing?**
che *or* (che) cosa fai?; **what are you
talking about?** di che cosa parli?;
what is it called? come si chiama?;
what about me? e io?; **what about
doing …?** e se facessimo …?
2 (*relative*) ciò che, quello che; **I saw
what you did** ho visto quello che hai
fatto; **I saw what was on the table**
ho visto cosa c'era sul tavolo
3 (*indirect use*) (che) cosa; **he asked
me what she had said** mi ha chiesto
che cosa avesse detto; **tell me what
you're thinking about** dimmi a cosa
stai pensando
▷ *excl* (*disbelieving*) cosa!, come!

whatever [wɔt'ɛvə'] *adj*: **~ book**
qualunque *or* qualsiasi libro + *sub*
▷ *pron*: **do ~ is necessary/you want**
faccia qualunque *or* qualsiasi cosa
sia necessaria/lei voglia; **~ happens**
qualunque cosa accada; **no reason
~** *or* **whatsoever** nessuna ragione
affatto *or* al mondo; **nothing ~**
proprio niente

whatsoever [wɔtsəu'ɛvə'] *adj*
= **whatever**

wheat [wi:t] *n* grano, frumento

wheel [wiːl] n ruota; (Aut: also: **steering ~**) volante m; (Naut) (ruota del) timone m ▷ vt spingere ▷ vi (birds) roteare; (also: **~ round**) girare; **wheelbarrow** n carriola; **wheelchair** n sedia a rotelle; **wheel clamp** n (Aut): **wheel clamps** ganasce fpl (per vetture in sosta vietata)

wheeze [wiːz] vi ansimare

○ KEYWORD

when [wɛn] adv quando; **when did it happen?** quando è successo? ▷ conj 1 (at, during, after the time that) quando; **she was reading when I came in** quando sono entrato lei leggeva; **that was when I needed you** era allora che avevo bisogno di te 2 (on, at which): **on the day when I met him** il giorno in cui l'ho incontrato; **one day when it was raining** un giorno che pioveva 3 (whereas) quando, mentre; **you said I was wrong when in fact I was right** mi hai detto che avevo torto, quando in realtà avevo ragione

whenever [wɛnˈɛvər] adv quando mai ▷ conj quando; (every time that) ogni volta che

where [wɛər] adv, conj dove; **this is ~** è qui che; **whereabouts** adv dove ▷ n: **sb's whereabouts** luogo dove qn si trova; **whereas** conj mentre; **whereby** adv per cui; **wherever** [wɛərˈɛvər] conj dovunque + sub; (interrogative) dove mai

whether ['wɛðər] conj se; **I don't know ~ to accept or not** non so se accettare o no; **it's doubtful ~** è poco probabile che; **~ you go or not** che lei vada o no

○ KEYWORD

which [wɪtʃ] adj 1 (interrogative, direct, indirect) quale; **which picture do**

you want? quale quadro vuole?; **which one?** quale?; **which one of you did it?** chi di voi lo ha fatto? 2: **in which case** nel qual caso ▷ pron 1 (interrogative) quale; **which (of these) are yours?** quali di questi sono suoi?; **which of you are coming?** chi di voi viene? 2 (relative) che; (: indirect) cui, il (la) quale; **the apple which you ate/ which is on the table** la mela che hai mangiato/che è sul tavolo; **the chair on which you are sitting** la sedia sulla quale or su cui sei seduto; **he said he knew, which is true** ha detto che lo sapeva, il che è vero; **after which** dopo di che

whichever [wɪtʃˈɛvər] adj: **take ~ book you prefer** prenda qualsiasi libro che preferisce; **~ book you take** qualsiasi libro prenda

while [waɪl] n momento ▷ conj mentre; (as long as) finché; (although) sebbene + sub; per quanto + sub; **for a ~** per un po'

whilst [waɪlst] conj = **while**

whim [wɪm] n capriccio

whine [waɪn] n gemito ▷ vi gemere; uggiolare; piagnucolare

whip [wɪp] n frusta; (for riding) frustino; (Pol: person) capogruppo (che sovrintende alla disciplina dei colleghi di partito) ▷ vt frustare; (Culin: cream, eggs etc) sbattere; **whipped cream** n panna montata

whirl [wəːl] vt (far) girare rapidamente; (far) turbinare ▷ vi (dancers) volteggiare; (leaves, water, dust) sollevarsi in un vortice

whisk [wɪsk] n (Culin) frusta; frullino ▷ vt sbattere, frullare; **to ~ sb away** or **off** portar via qn a tutta velocità

whiskers ['wɪskəz] npl (of animal) baffi mpl; (of man) favoriti mpl

whisky, (IRISH, US) **whiskey** ['wɪskɪ] n whisky m inv

W

whisper ['wɪspə'] n sussurro ▷ vt, vi
sussurrare
whistle ['wɪsl] n (sound) fischio;
(object) fischietto ▷ vi fischiare
white [waɪt] adj bianco/a; (with
fear) pallido/a ▷ n bianco; (person)
bianco/a; **whiteboard** ['waɪtbɔ:d]
n lavagna bianca; **interactive
whiteboard** lavagna interattiva;
White House n: **the White House**
la Casa Bianca; **whitewash** n (paint)
bianco di calce ▷ vt imbiancare;
(fig) coprire
whiting ['waɪtɪŋ] n (pl inv: fish)
merlango
Whitsun ['wɪtsn] n Pentecoste f
whittle ['wɪtl] vt: **to ~ away** or
down ridurre, tagliare
whizz [wɪz] vi: **to ~ past** or **by**
passare sfrecciando

KEYWORD

who [hu:] pron **1** (interrogative) chi;
who is it?, who's there? chi è?
2 (relative) che; **the man who spoke
to me** l'uomo che ha parlato con
me; **those who can swim** quelli che
sanno nuotare

whoever [hu:'ɛvə'] pron: **~ finds
it** chiunque lo trovi; **ask ~ you like**
lo chieda a chiunque vuole; **~ she
marries** chiunque sposerà, non
importa chi sposerà; **~ told you
that?** chi mai gliel'ha detto?
whole [həul] adj (complete) tutto/a,
completo/a; (not broken) intero/a,
intatto/a ▷ n (all): **the ~ of** tutto/a
il; (not broken) tutto; **the ~ lot (of
it)** tutto; **the ~ of the town** tutta
la città, la città intera; **on the ~,
as a ~** nel complesso, nell'insieme;
wholefood(s) n(pl) cibo integrale;
wholeheartedly [həul'hɑ:tɪdlɪ]
adv sentitamente, di tutto cuore;
wholemeal ['həulmi:l] adj (BRIT:
flour, bread) integrale; **wholesale** n

commercio or vendita all'ingrosso
▷ adj all'ingrosso; (destruction) totale;
wholewheat adj = **wholemeal**;
wholly adv completamente, del tutto

KEYWORD

whom [hu:m] pron **1** (interrogative)
chi; **whom did you see?** chi hai
visto?; **to whom did you give it?** a
chi lo hai dato?
2 (relative) che, prep + il (la) quale; **the
man whom I saw** l'uomo che ho
visto; **the man to whom I spoke**
l'uomo al or con il quale ho parlato

whore [hɔ:'] n (col, pej) puttana

KEYWORD

whose [hu:z] adj **1** (possessive,
interrogative) di chi; **whose book is
this?, whose is this book?** di chi è
questo libro?; **whose daughter are
you?** di chi sei figlia?
2 (possessive, relative): **the man
whose son you rescued** l'uomo il cui
figlio hai salvato or a cui hai salvato
il figlio; **the girl whose sister you
were speaking to** la ragazza alla cui
sorella stavi parlando
▷ pron di chi; **whose is this?** di chi
è questo?; **I know whose it is** so
di chi è

KEYWORD

why [waɪ] adv perché; **why not?**
perché no?; **why not do it now?**
perché non farlo adesso?
▷ conj perché; **I wonder why he said
that** mi chiedo perché l'abbia detto;
that's not why I'm here non è
questo il motivo per cui sono qui; **the
reason why** il motivo per cui
▷ excl (surprise) ma guarda un po'!;
(remonstrating) ma (via)!; (explaining)
ebbene!

wicked ['wɪkɪd] *adj* cattivo/a, malvagio/a; (*mischievous*) malizioso/a; (*terrible: prices, weather*) terribile

wicket ['wɪkɪt] *n* (Cricket) porta; area tra le due porte

wide [waɪd] *adj* largo/a; (*region, knowledge*) vasto/a; (*choice*) ampio/a ▷ *adv*: **to open ~** spalancare; **to shoot ~** tirare a vuoto *or* fuori bersaglio; **widely** *adv* (*different*) molto, completamente; (*believed*) generalmente; **widely spaced** molto distanziati/e; **widen** *vt* allargare, ampliare; **wide open** *adj* spalancato/a; **widescreen** *adj* (*television, TV*) a schermo panoramico; **widespread** *adj* (*belief etc*) molto *or* assai diffuso/a

widget ['wɪdʒɪt] *n* (Comput) widget *m inv*

widow ['wɪdəu] *n* vedova; **widower** *n* vedovo

width [wɪdθ] *n* larghezza

wield [wiːld] *vt* (*sword*) maneggiare; (*power*) esercitare

wife (*pl* **wives**) [waɪf, waɪvz] *n* moglie *f*

Wi-Fi ['waɪfaɪ] *n* WiFi *m*

wig [wɪg] *n* parrucca

wild [waɪld] *adj* selvatico/a; (*countryside, appearance*) selvaggio/a; (*sea, weather*) tempestoso/a; (*idea, life*) folle; stravagante; (*applause*) frenetico/a; **wilderness** ['wɪldənɪs] *n* deserto; **wildlife** *n* natura; **wildly** *adv* selvaggiamente; (*applaud*) freneticamente; (*hit, guess*) a casaccio; (*happy*) follemente

KEYWORD

will [wɪl] *aux vb* **1** (*forming future tense*): **I will finish it tomorrow** lo finirò domani; **I will have finished it by tomorrow** lo finirò entro domani; **will you do it? — yes I will/no I**

won't lo farai? — sì (lo farò)/no (non lo farò)

2 (*in conjectures, predictions*): **he will** *or* **he'll be there by now** a quest'ora dovrebbe essere arrivato; **that will be the postman** sarà il postino

3 (*in commands, requests, offers*): **will you be quiet!** vuoi stare zitto?; **will you come?** vieni anche tu?; **will you help me?** mi aiuti?, mi puoi aiutare?; **will you have a cup of tea?** vorrebbe una tazza di tè?; **I won't put up with it!** non lo accetterò!

▷ *vt* (*pt, pp* **willed**): **to will sb to do** volere che qn faccia; **he willed himself to go on** continuò grazie a un grande sforzo di volontà

▷ *n* **1** volontà

2 (*Law*) testamento

willing ['wɪlɪŋ] *adj* volonteroso/a; **~ to do** disposto/a a fare; **willingly** *adv* volentieri

willow ['wɪləu] *n* salice *m*

willpower ['wɪlpauəʳ] *n* forza di volontà

wilt [wɪlt] *vi* appassire

win [wɪn] (*pt, pp* **won**) *n* (*in sports etc*) vittoria ▷ *vt* (*battle, prize, money*) vincere; (*popularity*) guadagnare ▷ *vi* vincere; **win over** *vt* convincere

wince [wɪns] *vi* trasalire

wind[1] [wɪnd] *n* vento; (Med) flatulenza; (*breath*) respiro, fiato ▷ *vt* (*take breath away*) far restare senza fiato

wind[2] (*pt, pp* **wound**) *vt* attorcigliare; (*wrap*) avvolgere; (*clock, toy*) caricare ▷ *vi* (*road, river*) serpeggiare; **wind down** *vt* (*car window*) abbassare; (*fig: production, business*) diminuire; **wind up** *vt* (*clock*) caricare; (*debate*) concludere

windfall ['wɪndfɔːl] *n* (*money*) guadagno insperato

wind farm *n* centrale *f* eolica

winding ['waɪndɪŋ] *adj* (*road*) serpeggiante; (*staircase*) a chiocciola

w

windmill ['wɪndmɪl] n mulino a vento

window ['wɪndəu] n finestra; (in car, train, plane) finestrino; (in shop etc) vetrina; (also: **~ pane**) vetro; **window box** n cassetta di fiori; **window cleaner** n (person) pulitore m di finestre; **window pane** n vetro; **window seat** n posto finestrino; **windowsill** n davanzale m

wind: wind power n energia eolica; **windscreen** ['wɪndskriːn], (US) **windshield** n parabrezza m inv; **windscreen wiper**, (US) **windshield wiper** n tergicristallo; **windsurfing** ['wɪndsəːfɪŋ] n windsurf m inv; **wind turbine** ['wɪndtəːbaɪn] n pala eolica; **windy** ['wɪndɪ] adj ventoso/a; **it's windy** c'è vento

wine [waɪn] n vino; **wine bar** n enoteca (per degustazione); **wine glass** n bicchiere m da vino; **wine list** n lista dei vini; **wine tasting** n degustazione f dei vini

wing [wɪŋ] n ala; (Aut) fiancata; **wing mirror** n (BRIT) specchietto retrovisore esterno

wink [wɪŋk] n occhiolino ▷ vi ammiccare, fare l'occhiolino; (light) baluginare

winner ['wɪnəʳ] n vincitore/trice

winning ['wɪnɪŋ] adj (team) vincente; (goal) decisivo/a; (charming) affascinante

winter ['wɪntəʳ] n inverno; **winter sports** npl sport mpl invernali; **wintertime** n inverno, stagione f invernale

wipe [waɪp] n pulita, passata ▷ vt pulire (strofinando); (erase: tape) cancellare; **wipe out** vt (debt) pagare, liquidare; (memory) cancellare; (destroy) annientare; **wipe up** vt asciugare

wire ['waɪəʳ] n filo; (Elec) filo elettrico; (Tel) telegramma m ▷ vt (house) fare l'impianto elettrico di; (also: **~ up**) collegare, allacciare; (person) telegrafare a

wireless ['waɪəlɪs] adj wireless inv, senza fili; **wireless technology** n tecnologia wireless

wiring ['waɪərɪŋ] n impianto elettrico

wisdom ['wɪzdəm] n saggezza; (of action) prudenza; **wisdom tooth** n dente m del giudizio

wise [waɪz] adj saggio/a; (advice, remark) prudente; giudizioso/a

wish [wɪʃ] n (desire) desiderio; (specific desire) richiesta ▷ vt desiderare, volere; **best ~es** (on birthday etc) migliori auguri; **with best ~es** (in letter) cordiali saluti, con i migliori saluti; **to ~ sb goodbye** dire arrivederci a qn; **he ~ed me well** mi augurò di riuscire; **to ~ to do/sb to do** desiderare or volere fare/che qn faccia; **to ~ for** desiderare

wistful ['wɪstful] adj malinconico/a

wit [wɪt] n (gen pl) intelligenza; presenza di spirito; (wittiness) spirito, arguzia; (person) bello spirito

witch [wɪtʃ] n strega

🔘 **KEYWORD**

with [wɪð, wɪθ] prep 1 (in the company of) con; **I was with him** ero con lui; **we stayed with friends** siamo stati da amici; **I'll be with you in a minute** vengo subito

2 (descriptive) con; **a room with a view** una camera con vista (sul mare or sulle montagne etc); **the man with the grey hat/blue eyes** l'uomo con il cappello grigio/gli occhi blu

3 (indicating manner, means, cause): **with tears in her eyes** con le lacrime agli occhi; **red with anger** rosso/a dalla rabbia; **to shake with fear** tremare di paura

4: **I'm with you** (I understand) la seguo; **to be with it** (col: up-to-date)

essere alla moda; (: *alert*) essere sveglio/a; **I'm not really with it today** (*col*) oggi sono un po' fuori

withdraw (*irreg: like* **draw**) [wɪθ'drɔː] vt ritirare; (*money from bank*) ritirare; prelevare ▷ vi ritirarsi; **withdrawal** n ritiro; prelievo; (*of army*) ritirata; **withdrawal symptoms** npl (*Med*) crisi f di astinenza; **withdrawn** adj (*person*) distaccato/a

withdrew [wɪθ'druː] pt of **withdraw**

wither ['wɪðəʳ] vi appassire

withhold [wɪθ'həuld] vt (*irreg: like* **hold**) (*money*) trattenere; (*permission*): **to ~ (from)** rifiutare (a); (*information*) nascondere (a)

within [wɪð'ɪn] prep all'interno di; (*in time, distances*) entro ▷ adv all'interno, dentro; **~ reach (of)** alla portata (di); **~ sight (of)** in vista (di); **~ a mile of** entro un miglio da; **~ the week** prima della fine della settimana

without [wɪð'aut] prep senza; **to go** or **do ~ sth** fare a meno di qc

withstand [wɪθ'stænd] vt (*irreg: like* **stand**) resistere a

witness ['wɪtnɪs] n (*person, also Law*) testimone m/f ▷ vt (*event*) essere testimone di; (*document*) attestare l'autenticità di

witty ['wɪtɪ] adj spiritoso/a

wives [waɪvz] npl of **wife**

wizard ['wɪzəd] n mago

wk abbr = **week**

wobble ['wɔbl] vi tremare; (*chair*) traballare

woe [wəu] n dolore m; disgrazia

woke [wəuk] pt of **wake**

woken ['wəukn] pp of **wake**

wolf (pl **wolves**) [wulf, wulvz] n lupo

woman (pl **women**) ['wumən, 'wɪmɪn] n donna

womb [wuːm] n (*Anat*) utero

women ['wɪmɪn] npl of **woman**

won [wʌn] pt, pp of **win**

wonder ['wʌndəʳ] n meraviglia ▷ vi: **to ~ whether/why** domandarsi se/

perché; **to ~ at** essere sorpreso/a di; meravigliarsi di; **to ~ about** domandarsi di; pensare a; **it's no ~ that** c'è poco or non c'è da meravigliarsi che + *sub*; **wonderful** adj meraviglioso/a

won't [wəunt] = **will not**

wood [wud] n legno; (*timber*) legname m; (*forest*) bosco; **wooden** adj di legno; (*fig*) rigido/a; inespressivo/a; **woodwind** npl (*Mus*): **the woodwind** i legni; **woodwork** n (*craft, subject*) falegnameria

wool [wul] n lana; **to pull the ~ over sb's eyes** (*fig*) gettare fumo negli occhi a qn; **woollen**, (*US*) **woolen** adj di lana; (*industry*) laniero/a; **woolly**, (*US*) **wooly** adj di lana; (*fig: ideas*) confuso/a

word [wəːd] n parola; (*news*) notizie fpl ▷ vt esprimere, formulare; **in other ~s** in altre parole; **to have ~s with sb** avere un diverbio con qn; **to break/keep one's ~** non mantenere/mantenere la propria parola; **wording** n formulazione f; **word processing** n word processing m, elaborazione f testi; **word processor** n word processor m inv

wore [wɔːʳ] pt of **wear**

work [wəːk] n lavoro; (*Art, Literature*) opera ▷ vi lavorare; (*mechanism, plan etc*) funzionare; (*medicine*) essere efficace ▷ vt (*clay, wood etc*) lavorare; (*mine etc*) sfruttare; (*machine*) far funzionare; (*cause: effect, miracle*) fare; **to be out of ~** essere disoccupato/a; **how does this ~?** come funziona?; **the TV isn't ~ing** la TV non funziona; **to ~ loose** allentarsi; **work out** vi (*plans etc*) riuscire, andare bene ▷ vt (*problem*) risolvere; (*plan*) elaborare; **it ~s out at £100** fa 100 sterline; **worker** n lavoratore/trice; operaio/a; **work experience** n (*previous jobs*) esperienze fpl lavorative; (*student* *training placement*) tirocinio; **work force** *n* forza lavoro; **working class** *n* classe *f* operaia *or* lavoratrice; **working week** *n* settimana lavorativa; **workman** *n* (*irreg*) operaio; **work of art** *n* opera d'arte; **workout** *n* (*Sport*) allenamento; **work permit** *n* permesso di lavoro; **workplace** *n* posto di lavoro; **works** *n* (*BRIT: factory*) fabbrica ▷ *npl* (*of clock, machine*) meccanismo; **workshop** *n* officina; (*practical session*) gruppo di lavoro; **work station** *n* stazione *f* di lavoro; **work surface** *n* piano di lavoro; **worktop** *n* piano di lavoro

world [wə:ld] *n* mondo ▷ *cpd* (*tour, champion*) del mondo; (*record, power, war*) mondiale; **to think the ~ of sb** (*fig*) pensare un gran bene di qn; **World Cup** *n* (*Football*) Coppa del Mondo; **world-wide** *adj* universale; **World-Wide Web** *n* World Wide Web *m*

worm [wə:m] *n* (*also:* **earth~**) verme *m*

worn [wɔ:n] *pp of* **wear** ▷ *adj* usato/a; **worn-out** *adj* (*object*) consumato/a, logoro/a; (*person*) sfinito/a

worried ['wʌrɪd] *adj* preoccupato/a

worry ['wʌrɪ] *n* preoccupazione *f* ▷ *vt* preoccupare ▷ *vi* preoccuparsi; **worrying** *adj* preoccupante

worse [wə:s] *adj* peggiore ▷ *adv*, *n* peggio; **a change for the ~** un peggioramento; **worsen** *vt*, *vi* peggiorare; **worse off** *adj* in condizioni (economiche) peggiori

worship ['wə:ʃɪp] *n* culto ▷ *vt* (*God*) adorare, venerare; (*person*) adorare; **Your W~** (*BRIT*) (*to mayor*) signor sindaco; (*to judge*) signor giudice

worst [wə:st] *adj* il (la) peggiore ▷ *adv*, *n* peggio; **at ~** al peggio, per male che vada

worth [wə:θ] *n* valore *m* ▷ *adj*: **to be ~** valere; **it's ~ it** ne vale la pena; **it's not ~ the trouble** non ne vale

la pena; **worthless** *adj* di nessun valore; **worthwhile** *adj* (*activity*) utile; (*cause*) lodevole

worthy ['wə:ðɪ] *adj* (*person*) degno/a; (*motive*) lodevole; **~ of** degno di

KEYWORD

would [wud] *aux vb* **1** (*conditional tense*): **if you asked him he would do it** se glielo chiedesse lo farebbe; **if you had asked him he would have done it** se glielo avesse chiesto lo avrebbe fatto

2 (*in offers, invitations, requests*): **would you like a biscuit?** vorrebbe *or* vuole un biscotto?; **would you ask him to come in?** lo faccia entrare, per cortesia; **would you open the window please?** apra la finestra, per favore

3 (*in indirect speech*): **I said I would do it** ho detto che l'avrei fatto

4 (*emphatic*): **it WOULD have to snow today!** doveva proprio nevicare oggi!

5 (*insistence*): **she wouldn't do it** non ha voluto farlo

6 (*conjecture*): **it would have been midnight** sarà stata mezzanotte; **it would seem so** sembrerebbe proprio di sì

7 (*indicating habit*): **he would go there on Mondays** andava lì ogni lunedì

wouldn't ['wudnt] = **would not**

wound¹ [wu:nd] *n* ferita ▷ *vt* ferire

wound² [waund] *pt*, *pp of* **wind²**

wove [wəuv] *pt of* **weave**

woven ['wəuvn] *pp of* **weave**

wrap [ræp] *vt* (*also:* **~ up**) avvolgere; (*parcel*) incartare; **wrapper** *n* (*on chocolate*) carta; (*BRIT: of book*) copertina; **wrapping** ['ræpɪŋ] *n* carta; **wrapping paper** *n* carta da pacchi; (*for gift*) carta da regali

wreath (*pl* **wreaths**) [ri:θ, ri:ðz] *n* corona

wreck [rɛk] n (sea disaster) naufragio; (ship) relitto; (pej: person) rottame m ▷ vt demolire; (ship) far naufragare; (fig) rovinare; **wreckage** n rottami mpl; (of building) macerie fpl; (of ship) relitti mpl

wren [rɛn] n (Zool) scricciolo

wrench [rɛntʃ] n (Tech) chiave f; (tug) torsione f brusca; (fig) strazio ▷ vt strappare; storcere; **to ~ sth from** strappare qc a or da

wrestle ['rɛsl] vi: **to ~ (with sb)** lottare (con qn); **wrestler** n lottatore/trice; **wrestling** n lotta

wretched ['rɛtʃɪd] adj disgraziato/a; (col: weather, holiday) orrendo/a, orribile; (: child, dog) pestifero/a

wriggle ['rɪgl] vi (also: **~ about**) dimenarsi; (snake, worm) serpeggiare, muoversi serpeggiando

wring (pt, pp **wrung**) [rɪŋ, rʌŋ] vt torcere; (wet clothes) strizzare; (fig): **to ~ sth out of** strappare qc a

wrinkle ['rɪŋkl] n (on skin) ruga; (on paper etc) grinza ▷ vt (nose) torcere; (forehead) corrugare ▷ vi (skin, paint) raggrinzirsi

wrist [rɪst] n polso

write (pt **wrote**, pp **written**) [raɪt, rəʊt, 'rɪtn] vt, vi scrivere; **write down** vt annotare; (put in writing) mettere per iscritto; **write off** vt (debt, plan) cancellare; **write out** vt mettere per iscritto; (cheque, receipt) scrivere; **write-off** n perdita completa; **writer** n autore/trice, scrittore/trice

writing ['raɪtɪŋ] n scrittura; (of author) scritto, opera; **in ~** per iscritto; **writing paper** n carta da lettere

written ['rɪtn] pp of **write**

wrong [rɔŋ] adj sbagliato/a; (not suitable) inadatto/a; (wicked) cattivo/a; (unfair) ingiusto/a ▷ adv in modo sbagliato, erroneamente ▷ n (injustice) torto ▷ vt fare torto a; **you are ~ to do it** ha torto a farlo; **you are ~ about that, you've got it ~** si sbaglia; **to be in the ~** avere torto; **what's ~?** cosa c'è che non va?; **to go ~** (person) sbagliarsi; (plan) fallire, non riuscire; (machine) guastarsi; **wrongly** adv (incorrectly, by mistake) in modo sbagliato; **wrong number** n: **you have the wrong number** (Tel) ha sbagliato numero

wrote [rəʊt] pt of **write**

wrung [rʌŋ] pt, pp of **wring**

WWW n abbr = **World Wide Web**; **the ~** la Rete

w

XL *abbr* = **extra large**
Xmas ['ɛksməs] *n abbr* = **Christmas**
X-ray ['ɛks'reɪ] *n* raggio X;
  (*photograph*) radiografia ▷ *vt*
  radiografare
xylophone ['zaɪləfəun] *n* xilofono

yacht [jɔt] *n* panfilo, yacht *m inv*;
  yachting *n* yachting *m*, sport *m*
  della vela
yard [jɑːd] *n* (*of house etc*) cortile *m*;
  (*measure*) iarda (= 914 mm; 3 feet); **yard**
  sale (*us*) *n* vendita di oggetti usati nel
  cortile di una casa privata
yarn [jɑːn] *n* filato; (*tale*) lunga storia
yawn [jɔːn] *n* sbadiglio ▷ *vi*
  sbadigliare
yd. *abbr* = **yard**
yeah [jɛə] *adv* (*col*) sì
year [jɪəʳ] *n* anno; (*referring to harvest,*
  wine etc) annata; **she's three ~s old**
  ha tre anni; **an eight-~-old child**
  un(a) bambino/a di otto anni; **yearly**
  adj annuale ▷ *adv* annualmente
yearn [jəːn] *vi*: **to ~ for sth/to do**
  desiderare ardentemente qc/di fare
yeast [jiːst] *n* lievito
yell [jɛl] *n* urlo ▷ *vi* urlare
yellow ['jɛləu] *adj* giallo/a; **Yellow**
  Pages® *npl* pagine *fpl* gialle

yes [jɛs] *adv, n* sì (*m inv*); **to say ~ (to)** dire di sì (a)

yesterday ['jɛstədɪ] *adv, n* ieri (*m inv*); **~ morning/evening** ieri mattina/sera; **all day ~** ieri per tutta la giornata

yet [jɛt] *adv* ancora; già ▷ *conj* ma, tuttavia; **it is not finished ~** non è ancora finito; **the best ~** finora il migliore finora; **as ~** finora

yew [juː] *n* tasso (*albero*)

Yiddish ['jɪdɪʃ] *n* yiddish *m*

yield [jiːld] *n* produzione *f*, resa; reddito ▷ *vt* produrre, rendere; (*surrender*) cedere ▷ *vi* cedere; (*us Aut*) dare la precedenza

yob(bo) ['jɔb(əʊ)] *n* (*BRIT col*) bullo

yoga ['jəʊɡə] *n* yoga *m*

yog(h)urt ['jəʊɡət] *n* iogurt *m inv*

yolk [jəʊk] *n* tuorlo, rosso d'uovo

 KEYWORD

you [juː] *pron* **1** (*subject*) tu; (*: polite form*) lei; (*: pl*) voi; (*: formal*) loro; **you Italians enjoy your food** a voi italiani piace mangiare bene; **you and I will go** andiamo io e te (*or* lei ed io)

2 (*object: direct*) ti; la; vi; loro (*after vb*); (*: indirect*) ti; le; vi; loro (*after vb*); **I know you** ti (*or* la *or* vi) conosco; **I gave it to you** te l'ho dato; gliel'ho dato; ve l'ho dato; l'ho dato loro

3 (*stressed, after prep, in comparisons*) te; lei; voi; loro; **I told YOU to do it** ho detto a TE (*or* a LEI *etc*) di farlo; **she's younger than you** è più giovane di te (*or* lei *etc*)

4 (*impers: one*) si; **fresh air does you good** l'aria fresca fa bene; **you never know** non si sa mai

you'd [juːd] = **you had; you would**

you'll [juːl] = **you will; you shall**

young [jʌŋ] *adj* giovane ▷ *npl* (*of animal*) piccoli *mpl*; **the ~** i giovani, la gioventù; **youngster** *n*

giovanotto/a, ragazzo/a; (*child*) bambino/a

your [jɔːʳ] *adj* il (la) tuo/a; (*pl*) i (le) tuoi (tue); (*polite form*) il (la) suo/a; (*pl*) i (le) suoi (sue); (*pl*) il (la) vostro/a; (*pl*) i (le) vostri/e; (*: formal*) il (la) loro; (*pl*) i (le) loro

you're [jʊəʳ] = **you are**

yours [jɔːz] *pron* il (la) tuo/a; (*pl*) i (le) tuoi (tue); (*polite form*) il (la) suo/a; (*pl*) i (le) suoi (sue); (*pl*) il (la) vostro/a; (*pl*) i (le) vostri/e; (*: formal*) il (la) loro; (*pl*) i (le) loro; **~ sincerely/faithfully** (*in letter*) cordiali/distinti saluti; *see also* **mine**[1]

yourself [jɔːˈsɛlf] *pron* (*reflexive*) ti; (*: polite form*) si; (*after prep*) te; sé; (*emphatic*) tu stesso/a; lei stesso/a; **yourselves** *pl pron* (*reflexive*) vi; (*: polite form*) si; (*after prep*) voi; loro; (*emphatic*) voi stessi/e; loro stessi/e; *see also* **oneself**

youth [juːθ] *n* gioventù *f*; (*young man*) giovane *m*, ragazzo; **youth club** *n* centro giovanile; **youthful** *adj* giovane; da giovane; giovanile; **youth hostel** *n* ostello della gioventù

you've [juːv] = **you have**

Yugoslavia [juːɡəʊˈslɑːvɪə] *n* (*formerly*) Jugoslavia

zoom [zu:m] *vi*: **to ~ past** sfrecciare; **zoom lens** *n* zoom *m inv*, obiettivo a focale variabile
zucchini [zu:'ki:nɪ] *n* (*pl inv*: *US*) zucchina

Z

zeal [zi:l] *n* zelo; entusiasmo
zebra ['zi:brə] *n* zebra; **zebra crossing** *n* (*BRIT*) (passaggio pedonale a) strisce *fpl*, zebre *fpl*
zero ['zɪərəu] *n* zero
zest [zɛst] *n* gusto; (*Culin*) buccia
zigzag ['zɪgzæg] *n* zigzag *m inv* ▷ *vi* zigzagare
Zimbabwe [zɪm'bɑ:bwɪ] *n* Zimbabwe *m*
zinc [zɪŋk] *n* zinco
zip [zɪp] *n* (*also*: **~ fastener**) chiusura *f* or cerniera *f* lampo *inv* ▷ *vt* (*Comput*) zippare; (*also*: **~ up**) chiudere con una cerniera lampo; **zip code** *n* (*US*) codice *m* di avviamento postale; **zipper** (*US*) *n* cerniera *f* lampo *inv*
zit [zɪt] *n* brufolo
zodiac ['zəudɪæk] *n* zodiaco
zone [zəun] *n* (*also Mil*) zona
zoo [zu:] *n* zoo *m inv*
zoology [zu:'ɔlədʒɪ] *n* zoologia

VERB TABLES

Introduction

The **Verb Tables** in the following section contain 32 tables of the most
common Italian verbs (some regular and some irregular) in alphabetical order.
Each table shows you the following forms: **Present**, **Perfect**, **Imperfect**,
Future, **Conditional**, **Present Subjunctive**, **Imperative** and the **Past Participle**
and **Gerund**.

In order to help you use the verbs shown in Verb Tables correctly, there are also a
number of example phrases at the bottom of each page to show the verb as it is
used in context.

In Italian there are **regular** verbs (their forms follow the regular patterns of -are,
-ere or -ire verbs), and **irregular** verbs (their forms do not follow the normal
rules). Examples of regular verbs in these tables are:

> **parlare** (regular -**are** verb, Verb Table 16)
> **credere** (regular -**ere** verb, Verb Table 7)
> **capire** (regular -**ire** verb, Verb Table 6)

Some irregular verbs are irregular in most of their forms, while others may only
have a couple of irregular forms.

▶ addormentarsi (to go to sleep)

PRESENT

(io)	mi addormento
(tu)	ti addormenti
(lui/lei) (lei/Lei)	si addormenta
(noi)	ci addormentiamo
(voi)	vi addormentate
(loro)	si addormentano

FUTURE

(io)	mi addormenterò
(tu)	ti addormenterai
(lui/lei) (lei/Lei)	si addormenterà
(noi)	ci addormenteremo
(voi)	vi addormenterete
(loro)	si addormenteranno

PERFECT

(io)	mi sono addormentato/a
(tu)	ti sei addormentato/a
(lui/lei) (lei/Lei)	si è addormentato/a
(noi)	ci siamo addormentati/e
(voi)	vi siete addormentati/e
(loro)	si sono addormentati/e

CONDITIONAL

(io)	mi addormenterei
(tu)	ti addormenteresti
(lui/lei) (lei/Lei)	si addormenterebbe
(noi)	ci addormenteremmo
(voi)	vi addormentereste
(loro)	si addormenterebbero

IMPERFECT

(io)	mi addormentavo
(tu)	ti addormentavi
(lui/lei) (lei/Lei)	si addormentava
(noi)	ci addormentavamo
(voi)	vi addormentavate
(loro)	si addormentavano

PRESENT SUBJUNCTIVE

(io)	mi addormenti
(tu)	ti addormenti
(lui/lei) (lei/Lei)	si addormenti
(noi)	ci addormentiamo
(voi)	vi addormentiate
(loro)	si addormentino

IMPERATIVE

addormentati
addormentiamoci
addormentatevi

PAST PARTICIPLE

addormentato

GERUND

addormentando

EXAMPLE PHRASES

Non voleva **addormentarsi**. *He didn't want to go to sleep.*
Mi si **è addormentato** un piede. *My foot has gone to sleep.*
Sono stanco: stasera **mi addormenterò** subito. *I'm tired: I'll go to sleep immediately tonight.*

Remember that subject pronouns are not used very often in Italian.

▶ andare (to go)

PRESENT

(io)	vado
(tu)	vai
(lui/lei) (lei/Lei)	va
(noi)	andiamo
(voi)	andate
(loro)	vanno

PERFECT

(io)	sono andato/a
(tu)	sei andato/a
(lui/lei) (lei/Lei)	è andato/a
(noi)	siamo andati/e
(voi)	siete andati/e
(loro)	sono andati/e

IMPERFECT

(io)	andavo
(tu)	andavi
(lui/lei) (lei/Lei)	andava
(noi)	andavamo
(voi)	andavate
(loro)	andavano

IMPERATIVE

vai
andiamo
andate

FUTURE

(io)	andrò
(tu)	andrai
(lui/lei) (lei/Lei)	andrà
(noi)	andremo
(voi)	andrete
(loro)	andranno

CONDITIONAL

(io)	andrei
(tu)	andresti
(lui/lei) (lei/Lei)	andrebbe
(noi)	andremmo
(voi)	andreste
(loro)	andrebbero

PRESENT SUBJUNCTIVE

(io)	vada
(tu)	vada
(lui/lei) (lei/Lei)	vada
(noi)	andiamo
(voi)	andiate
(loro)	vadano

PAST PARTICIPLE

andato

GERUND

andando

EXAMPLE PHRASES

Andremo in Grecia quest'estate. *We're going to Greece this summer.*
Su, **andiamo**! *Come on, let's go!*
Com'è **andata**? *How did it go?*
Come **va**? – bene, grazie! *How are you? – fine thanks!*
Stasera **andrei** volentieri al ristorante. *I'd like to go to a restaurant this evening.*

Italic letters in Italian words show where stress does not follow the usual rules.

▶ avere (to have)

PRESENT

(io)	ho
(tu)	hai
(lui/lei) (lei/Lei)	ha
(noi)	abbiamo
(voi)	avete
(loro)	hanno

FUTURE

(io)	avrò
(tu)	avrai
(lui/lei) (lei/Lei)	avrà
(noi)	avremo
(voi)	avrete
(loro)	avranno

PERFECT

(io)	ho avuto
(tu)	hai avuto
(lui/lei) (lei/Lei)	ha avuto
(noi)	abbiamo avuto
(voi)	avete avuto
(loro)	hanno avuto

CONDITIONAL

(io)	avrei
(tu)	avresti
(lui/lei) (lei/Lei)	avrebbe
(noi)	avremmo
(voi)	avreste
(loro)	avrebbero

IMPERFECT

(io)	avevo
(tu)	avevi
(lui/lei) (lei/Lei)	aveva
(noi)	avevamo
(voi)	avevate
(loro)	avevano

PRESENT SUBJUNCTIVE

(io)	abbia
(tu)	abbia
(lui/lei) (lei/Lei)	abbia
(noi)	abbiamo
(voi)	abbiate
(loro)	abbiano

IMPERATIVE

abbi
abbiamo
abbiate

PAST PARTICIPLE

avuto

GERUND

avendo

EXAMPLE PHRASES

All'inizio **ha avuto** un sacco di problemi. *He had a lot of problems at first.*
Ho già **mangiato**. *I've already eaten.*
Ha la macchina nuova. *She's got a new car.*
Aveva la mia età. *He was the same age as me.*
Quanti ne **abbiamo** oggi? *What's the date today?*

Remember that subject pronouns are not used very often in Italian.

▶ **bere** (to drink)

PRESENT

(io)	bevo
(tu)	bevi
(lui/lei) (lei/Lei)	beve
(noi)	beviamo
(voi)	bevete
(loro)	bevono

PERFECT

(io)	ho bevuto
(tu)	hai bevuto
(lui/lei) (lei/Lei)	ha bevuto
(noi)	abbiamo bevuto
(voi)	avete bevuto
(loro)	hanno bevuto

IMPERFECT

(io)	bevevo
(tu)	bevevi
(lui/lei) (lei/Lei)	beveva
(noi)	bevevamo
(voi)	bevevate
(loro)	bevevano

IMPERATIVE

bevi
beviamo
bevete

FUTURE

(io)	berrò
(tu)	berrai
(lui/lei) (lei/Lei)	berrà
(noi)	berremo
(voi)	berrete
(loro)	berranno

CONDITIONAL

(io)	berrei
(tu)	berresti
(lui/lei) (lei/Lei)	berrebbe
(noi)	berremmo
(voi)	berreste
(loro)	berrebbero

PRESENT SUBJUNCTIVE

(io)	beva
(tu)	beva
(lui/lei) (lei/Lei)	beva
(noi)	beviamo
(voi)	beviate
(loro)	bevano

PAST PARTICIPLE

bevuto

GERUND

bevendo

EXAMPLE PHRASES

Vuoi **bere** qualcosa? *Would you like something to drink?*
Berrei volentieri un bicchiere di vino bianco. *I'd love a glass of white wine.*
Beveva sei caffè al giorno, ma ora ha smesso. *He used to drink six cups of coffee a day, but he's stopped now.*

Italic letters in Italian words show where stress does not follow the usual rules.

▶ **cadere** (to fall)

PRESENT

(io)	cado
(tu)	cadi
(lui/lei) (lei/Lei)	cade
(noi)	cadiamo
(voi)	cadete
(loro)	cadono

FUTURE

(io)	cadrò
(tu)	cadrai
(lui/lei) (lei/Lei)	cadrà
(noi)	cadremo
(voi)	cadrete
(loro)	cadranno

PERFECT

(io)	sono caduto/a
(tu)	sei caduto/a
(lui/lei) (lei/Lei)	è caduto/a
(noi)	siamo caduti/e
(voi)	siete caduti/e
(loro)	sono caduti/e

CONDITIONAL

(io)	cadrei
(tu)	cadresti
(lui/lei) (lei/Lei)	cadrebbe
(noi)	cadremmo
(voi)	cadreste
(loro)	cadrebbero

IMPERFECT

(io)	cadevo
(tu)	cadevi
(lui/lei) (lei/Lei)	cadeva
(noi)	cadevamo
(voi)	cadevate
(loro)	cadevano

PRESENT SUBJUNCTIVE

(io)	cada
(tu)	cada
(lui/lei) (lei/Lei)	cada
(noi)	cadiamo
(voi)	cadiate
(loro)	cadano

IMPERATIVE

cadi
cadiamo
cadete

PAST PARTICIPLE

caduto

GERUND

cadendo

EXAMPLE PHRASES

Ho inciampato e **sono caduta**. *I tripped and fell.*
Il mio compleanno **cade** di lunedì. *My birthday is on a Monday.*
Ti **è caduta** la sciarpa. *You've dropped your scarf.*
Attento che fai **cadere** il bicchiere. *Mind you don't knock over your glass.*

Remember that subject pronouns are not used very often in Italian.

▶ capire (to understand)

PRESENT

(io)	capisco
(tu)	capisci
(lui/lei) (lei/Lei)	capisce
(noi)	capiamo
(voi)	capite
(loro)	capiscono

PERFECT

(io)	ho capito
(tu)	hai capito
(lui/lei) (lei/Lei)	ha capito
(noi)	abbiamo capito
(voi)	avete capito
(loro)	hanno capito

IMPERFECT

(io)	capivo
(tu)	capivi
(lui/lei) (lei/Lei)	capiva
(noi)	capivamo
(voi)	capivate
(loro)	capivano

IMPERATIVE

capisci
capiamo
capite

FUTURE

(io)	capirò
(tu)	capirai
(lui/lei) (lei/Lei)	capirà
(noi)	capiremo
(voi)	capirete
(loro)	capiranno

CONDITIONAL

(io)	capirei
(tu)	capiresti
(lui/lei) (lei/Lei)	capirebbe
(noi)	capiremmo
(voi)	capireste
(loro)	capirebbero

PRESENT SUBJUNCTIVE

(io)	capisca
(tu)	capisca
(lui/lei) (lei/Lei)	capisca
(noi)	capiamo
(voi)	capiate
(loro)	capiscano

PAST PARTICIPLE

capito

GERUND

capendo

EXAMPLE PHRASES

Va bene, **capisco**. *OK, I understand.*
Non **ho capito** una parola. *I didn't understand a word.*
Fammi **capire**... *Let me get this straight...*
Non ti **capirò** mai. *I'll never understand you.*

Italic letters in Italian words show where stress does not follow the usual rules.

▶ **credere** (to believe)

PRESENT

(io)	credo
(tu)	credi
(lui/lei) (lei/Lei)	crede
(noi)	crediamo
(voi)	credete
(loro)	credono

PERFECT

(io)	ho creduto
(tu)	hai creduto
(lui/lei) (lei/Lei)	ha creduto
(noi)	abbiamo creduto
(voi)	avete creduto
(loro)	hanno creduto

IMPERFECT

(io)	credevo
(tu)	credevi
(lui/lei) (lei/Lei)	credeva
(noi)	credevamo
(voi)	credevate
(loro)	credevano

IMPERATIVE

credi
crediamo
credete

FUTURE

(io)	crederò
(tu)	crederai
(lui/lei) (lei/Lei)	crederà
(noi)	crederemo
(voi)	crederete
(loro)	crederanno

CONDITIONAL

(io)	crederei
(tu)	crederesti
(lui/lei) (lei/Lei)	crederebbe
(noi)	crederemmo
(voi)	credereste
(loro)	crederebbero

PRESENT SUBJUNCTIVE

(io)	creda
(tu)	creda
(lui/lei) (lei/Lei)	creda
(noi)	crediamo
(voi)	crediate
(loro)	credano

PAST PARTICIPLE

creduto

GERUND

credendo

EXAMPLE PHRASES

Non dirmi che **credi** ai fantasmi! *Don't tell me you believe in ghosts!*
Non **credeva** ai suoi occhi. *She couldn't believe her eyes.*
Non ti **crederò** mai. *I'll never believe you.*

Remember that subject pronouns are not used very often in Italian.

▶ **dare** (to give)

PRESENT

(io)	do
(tu)	dai
(lui/lei) (lei/Lei)	dà
(noi)	diamo
(voi)	date
(loro)	danno

PERFECT

(io)	ho dato
(tu)	hai dato
(lui/lei) (lei/Lei)	ha dato
(noi)	abbiamo dato
(voi)	avete dato
(loro)	hanno dato

IMPERFECT

(io)	davo
(tu)	davi
(lui/lei) (lei/Lei)	dava
(noi)	davamo
(voi)	davate
(loro)	davano

IMPERATIVE

dai
diamo
date

FUTURE

(io)	darò
(tu)	darai
(lui/lei) (lei/Lei)	darà
(noi)	daremo
(voi)	darete
(loro)	daranno

CONDITIONAL

(io)	darei
(tu)	daresti
(lui/lei) (lei/Lei)	darebbe
(noi)	daremmo
(voi)	dareste
(loro)	darebbero

PRESENT SUBJUNCTIVE

(io)	dia
(tu)	dia
(lui/lei) (lei/Lei)	dia
(noi)	diamo
(voi)	diate
(loro)	diano

PAST PARTICIPLE

dato

GERUND

dando

EXAMPLE PHRASES

Gli **ho dato** un libro. *I gave him a book.*
Dammelo. *Give it to me.*
La mia finestra **dà** sul giardino. *My window looks onto the garden.*
Domani sera **daranno** un bel film in tv. *There's a good film on TV tomorrow evening.*
Dandoti da fare, potresti ottenere molto di più. *If you exerted yourself you could achieve a lot more.*

Italic letters in Italian words show where stress does not follow the usual rules.

▶ dire (to say)

PRESENT

(io)	dico
(tu)	dici
(lui/lei)(lei/Lei)	dice
(noi)	diciamo
(voi)	dite
(loro)	dicono

FUTURE

(io)	dirò
(tu)	dirai
(lui/lei)(lei/Lei)	dirà
(noi)	diremo
(voi)	direte
(loro)	diranno

PERFECT

(io)	ho detto
(tu)	hai detto
(lui/lei)(lei/Lei)	ha detto
(noi)	abbiamo detto
(voi)	avete detto
(loro)	hanno detto

CONDITIONAL

(io)	direi
(tu)	diresti
(lui/lei)(lei/Lei)	direbbe
(noi)	diremmo
(voi)	direste
(loro)	direbbero

IMPERFECT

(io)	dicevo
(tu)	dicevi
(lui/lei)(lei/Lei)	diceva
(noi)	dicevamo
(voi)	dicevate
(loro)	dicevano

PRESENT SUBJUNCTIVE

(io)	dica
(tu)	dica
(lui/lei)(lei/Lei)	dica
(noi)	diciamo
(voi)	diciate
(loro)	dicano

IMPERATIVE

di'
diciamo
dite

PAST PARTICIPLE

detto

GERUND

dicendo

EXAMPLE PHRASES

Ha detto che verrà. *He said he'll come.*
Come si **dice** "quadro" in inglese? *How do you say "quadro" in English?*
Che ne **diresti** di andarcene? *Shall we leave?*
Ti **dirò** un segreto. *I'll tell you a secret.*
Dimmi dov'è. *Tell me where it is.*

Remember that subject pronouns are not used very often in Italian.

▶ dormire (to sleep)

PRESENT

(io)	dormo
(tu)	dormi
(lui/lei) (lei/Lei)	dorme
(noi)	dormiamo
(voi)	dormite
(loro)	dormono

PERFECT

(io)	ho dormito
(tu)	hai dormito
(lui/lei) (lei/Lei)	ha dormito
(noi)	abbiamo dormito
(voi)	avete dormito
(loro)	hanno dormito

IMPERFECT

(io)	dormivo
(tu)	dormivi
(lui/lei) (lei/Lei)	dormiva
(noi)	dormivamo
(voi)	dormivate
(loro)	dormivano

IMPERATIVE

dormi
dormiamo
dormite

FUTURE

(io)	dormirò
(tu)	dormirai
(lui/lei) (lei/Lei)	dormirà
(noi)	dormiremo
(voi)	dormirete
(loro)	dormiranno

CONDITIONAL

(io)	dormirei
(tu)	dormiresti
(lui/lei) (lei/Lei)	dormirebbe
(noi)	dormiremmo
(voi)	dormireste
(loro)	dormirebbero

PRESENT SUBJUNCTIVE

(io)	dorma
(tu)	dorma
(lui/lei) (lei/Lei)	dorma
(noi)	dormiamo
(voi)	dormiate
(loro)	dormano

PAST PARTICIPLE

dormito

GERUND

dormendo

EXAMPLE PHRASES

Sta dormendo. *She's sleeping.*
Vado a **dormire**. *I'm going to bed.*
Stanotte **dormirò** come un ghiro. *I'll sleep like a log tonight.*

Italic letters in Italian words show where stress does not follow the usual rules.

▶ **dovere** (to have to)

PRESENT

(io)	devo
(tu)	devi
(lui/lei) (lei/Lei)	deve
(noi)	dobbiamo
(voi)	dovete
(loro)	devono

FUTURE

(io)	dovrò
(tu)	dovrai
(lui/lei) (lei/Lei)	dovrà
(noi)	dovremo
(voi)	dovrete
(loro)	dovranno

PERFECT

(io)	ho dovuto
(tu)	hai dovuto
(lui/lei) (lei/Lei)	ha dovuto
(noi)	abbiamo dovuto
(voi)	avete dovuto
(loro)	hanno dovuto

CONDITIONAL

(io)	dovrei
(tu)	dovresti
(lui/lei) (lei/Lei)	dovrebbe
(noi)	dovremmo
(voi)	dovreste
(loro)	dovrebbero

IMPERFECT

(io)	dovevo
(tu)	dovevi
(lui/lei) (lei/Lei)	doveva
(noi)	dovevamo
(voi)	dovevate
(loro)	dovevano

PRESENT SUBJUNCTIVE

(io)	debba
(tu)	debba
(lui/lei) (lei/Lei)	debba
(noi)	dobbiamo
(voi)	dobbiate
(loro)	debbano

IMPERATIVE

–

PAST PARTICIPLE

dovuto

GERUND

dovendo

EXAMPLE PHRASES

È **dovuto** partire. *He had to leave.*
Devi finire i compiti prima di uscire. *You must finish your homework before you go out.*
Dev'essere tardi. *It must be late.*
Dovrebbe arrivare alle dieci. *He should arrive at ten.*
Gli **dovevo** 30 euro e così l'ho invitato a cena. *I owed him 30 euros so I took him out to dinner.*

Remember that subject pronouns are not used very often in Italian.

▶ *essere* (to be)

PRESENT

(io)	sono
(tu)	sei
(lui/lei) (lei/Lei)	è
(noi)	siamo
(voi)	siete
(loro)	sono

PERFECT

(io)	sono stato/a
(tu)	sei stato/a
(lui/lei) (lei/Lei)	è stato/a
(noi)	siamo stati/e
(voi)	siete stati/e
(loro)	sono stati/e

IMPERFECT

(io)	ero
(tu)	eri
(lui/lei) (lei/Lei)	era
(noi)	eravamo
(voi)	eravate
(loro)	erano

IMPERATIVE

sii
siamo
siate

FUTURE

(io)	sarò
(tu)	sarai
(lui/lei) (lei/Lei)	sarà
(noi)	saremo
(voi)	sarete
(loro)	saranno

CONDITIONAL

(io)	sarei
(tu)	saresti
(lui/lei) (lei/Lei)	sarebbe
(noi)	saremmo
(voi)	sareste
(loro)	sarebbero

PRESENT SUBJUNCTIVE

(io)	sia
(tu)	sia
(lui/lei) (lei/Lei)	sia
(noi)	siamo
(voi)	siate
(loro)	siano

PAST PARTICIPLE

stato

GERUND

essendo

EXAMPLE PHRASES

Sono italiana. *I'm Italian.*
Mario **è** appena partito. *Mario has just left.*
Siete mai **stati** in Africa? *Have you ever been to Africa?*
Quando **è** arrivato erano le quattro in punto. *It was exactly four o'clock when he arrived.*
Alla festa ci **saranno** tutti i miei amici. *All my friends will be at the party.*

Italic letters in Italian words show where stress does not follow the usual rules.

▶ **fare** (to do; make)

PRESENT

(io)	faccio
(tu)	fai
(lui/lei) (lei/Lei)	fa
(noi)	facciamo
(voi)	fate
(loro)	fanno

FUTURE

(io)	farò
(tu)	farai
(lui/lei) (lei/Lei)	farà
(noi)	faremo
(voi)	farete
(loro)	faranno

PERFECT

(io)	ho fatto
(tu)	hai fatto
(lui/lei) (lei/Lei)	ha fatto
(noi)	abbiamo fatto
(voi)	avete fatto
(loro)	hanno fatto

CONDITIONAL

(io)	farei
(tu)	faresti
(lui/lei) (lei/Lei)	farebbe
(noi)	faremmo
(voi)	fareste
(loro)	farebbero

IMPERFECT

(io)	facevo
(tu)	facevi
(lui/lei) (lei/Lei)	faceva
(noi)	facevamo
(voi)	facevate
(loro)	facevano

PRESENT SUBJUNCTIVE

(io)	faccia
(tu)	faccia
(lui/lei) (lei/Lei)	faccia
(noi)	facciamo
(voi)	facciate
(loro)	facciano

IMPERATIVE

fai
facciamo
fate

PAST PARTICIPLE

fatto

GERUND

facendo

EXAMPLE PHRASES

Ho fatto un errore. *I made a mistake.*
Due più due **fa** quattro. *Two and two makes four.*
Cosa **stai facendo**? *What are you doing?*
Fa il medico. *He is a doctor.*
Fa caldo. *It's hot.*

Remember that subject pronouns are not used very often in Italian.

▶ **mettere** (to put)

PRESENT

(io)	metto
(tu)	metti
(lui/lei) (lei/Lei)	mette
(noi)	mettiamo
(voi)	mettete
(loro)	mettono

FUTURE

(io)	metterò
(tu)	metterai
(lui/lei) (lei/Lei)	metterà
(noi)	metteremo
(voi)	metterete
(loro)	metteranno

PERFECT

(io)	ho messo
(tu)	hai messo
(lui/lei) (lei/Lei)	ha messo
(noi)	abbiamo messo
(voi)	avete messo
(loro)	hanno messo

CONDITIONAL

(io)	metterei
(tu)	metteresti
(lui/lei) (lei/Lei)	metterebbe
(noi)	metteremmo
(voi)	mettereste
(loro)	metterebbero

IMPERFECT

(io)	mettevo
(tu)	mettevi
(lui/lei) (lei/Lei)	metteva
(noi)	mettevamo
(voi)	mettevate
(loro)	mettevano

PRESENT SUBJUNCTIVE

(io)	metta
(tu)	metta
(lui/lei) (lei/Lei)	metta
(noi)	mettiamo
(voi)	mettiate
(loro)	mettano

IMPERATIVE

metti
mettiamo
mettete

PAST PARTICIPLE

messo

GERUND

mettendo

EXAMPLE PHRASES

Hai messo i bambini a letto? *Have you put the children to bed?*
Metterò un annuncio sul giornale. *I'll put an advert in the paper.*
Mettiti là e aspetta. *Wait there.*
Quanto tempo ci **hai messo**? *How long did it take you?*
Non **metto** più quelle scarpe. *I don't wear those shoes any more.*

Italic letters in Italian words show where stress does not follow the usual rules.

▶ **parere** (to appear)

PRESENT

(io)	paio
(tu)	pari
(lui/lei) (lei/Lei)	pare
(noi)	pariamo
(voi)	parete
(loro)	paiono

FUTURE

(io)	parrò
(tu)	parrai
(lui/lei) (lei/Lei)	parrà
(noi)	parremo
(voi)	parrete
(loro)	parranno

PERFECT

(io)	sono parso/a
(tu)	sei parso/a
(lui/lei) (lei/Lei)	è parso/a
(noi)	siamo parsi/e
(voi)	siete parsi/e
(loro)	sono parsi/e

CONDITIONAL

(io)	parrei
(tu)	parresti
(lui/lei) (lei/Lei)	parrebbe
(noi)	parremmo
(voi)	parreste
(loro)	parrebbero

IMPERFECT

(io)	parevo
(tu)	parevi
(lui/lei) (lei/Lei)	pareva
(noi)	parevamo
(voi)	parevate
(loro)	parevano

PRESENT SUBJUNCTIVE

(io)	paia
(tu)	paia
(lui/lei) (lei/Lei)	paia
(noi)	paiamo
(voi)	paiate
(loro)	paiano

IMPERATIVE
pari
pariamo
parete

PAST PARTICIPLE
parso

GERUND
parendo

EXAMPLE PHRASES

Mi **pare** che sia già arrivato. *I think he's already here.*
Ci **è parso** che foste stanchi. *We thought you were tired.*
Faceva solo ciò che gli **pareva**. *He did just what he wanted.*

Remember that subject pronouns are not used very often in Italian.

▶ **parlare** (to speak)

PRESENT	
(io)	parlo
(tu)	parli
(lui/lei)(lei/Lei)	parla
(noi)	parliamo
(voi)	parlate
(loro)	parlano

FUTURE	
(io)	parlerò
(tu)	parlerai
(lui/lei)(lei/Lei)	parlerà
(noi)	parleremo
(voi)	parlerete
(loro)	parleranno

PERFECT	
(io)	ho parlato
(tu)	hai parlato
(lui/lei)(lei/Lei)	ha parlato
(noi)	abbiamo parlato
(voi)	avete parlato
(loro)	hanno parlato

CONDITIONAL	
(io)	parlerei
(tu)	parleresti
(lui/lei)(lei/Lei)	parlerebbe
(noi)	parleremmo
(voi)	parlereste
(loro)	parlerebbero

IMPERFECT	
(io)	parlavo
(tu)	parlavi
(lui/lei)(lei/Lei)	parlava
(noi)	parlavamo
(voi)	parlavate
(loro)	parlavano

PRESENT SUBJUNCTIVE	
(io)	parli
(tu)	parli
(lui/lei)(lei/Lei)	parli
(noi)	parliamo
(voi)	parliate
(loro)	parlino

IMPERATIVE
parla
parliamo
parlate

PAST PARTICIPLE
parlato

GERUND
parlando

EXAMPLE PHRASES

Pronto, chi **parla**? *Hello, who's speaking?*
Non **parliamone** più. *Let's just forget about it.*
Abbiamo parlato per ore. *We talked for hours.*
Gli **parlerò** di te. *I'll talk to him about you.*
Di cosa **parla** quel libro? *What is that book about?*

Italic letters in Italian words show where stress does not follow the usual rules.

▶ piacere (to be pleasing)

PRESENT

(io)	piaccio
(tu)	piaci
(lui/lei) (lei/Lei)	piace
(noi)	piacciamo
(voi)	piacete
(loro)	piacciono

FUTURE

(io)	piacerò
(tu)	piacerai
(lui/lei) (lei/Lei)	piacerà
(noi)	piaceremo
(voi)	piacerete
(loro)	piaceranno

PERFECT

(io)	sono piaciuto/a
(tu)	sei piaciuto/a
(lui/lei) (lei/Lei)	è piaciuto/a
(noi)	siamo piaciuti/e
(voi)	siete piaciuti/e
(loro)	sono piaciuti/e

CONDITIONAL

(io)	piacerei
(tu)	piaceresti
(lui/lei) (lei/Lei)	piacerebbe
(noi)	piaceremmo
(voi)	piacereste
(loro)	piacerebbero

IMPERFECT

(io)	piacevo
(tu)	piacevi
(lui/lei) (lei/Lei)	piaceva
(noi)	piacevamo
(voi)	piacevate
(loro)	piacevano

PRESENT SUBJUNCTIVE

(io)	piaccia
(tu)	piaccia
(lui/lei) (lei/Lei)	piaccia
(noi)	piacciamo
(voi)	piacciate
(loro)	piacciano

IMPERATIVE

piaci
piacciamo
piacciate

PAST PARTICIPLE

piaciuto

GERUND

piacendo

EXAMPLE PHRASES

Questa musica non **mi piace**. *I don't like this music.*
Cosa **ti piacerebbe** fare? *What would you like to do?*
Da piccola non **mi piacevano** i ragni. *When I was little I didn't like spiders.*

Remember that subject pronouns are not used very often in Italian.

▶ potere (to be able)

PRESENT

(io)	posso
(tu)	puoi
(lui/lei) (lei/Lei)	può
(noi)	possiamo
(voi)	potete
(loro)	possono

FUTURE

(io)	potrò
(tu)	potrai
(lui/lei) (lei/Lei)	potrà
(noi)	potremo
(voi)	potrete
(loro)	potranno

PERFECT

(io)	ho potuto
(tu)	hai potuto
(lui/lei) (lei/Lei)	ha potuto
(noi)	abbiamo potuto
(voi)	avete potuto
(loro)	hanno potuto

CONDITIONAL

(io)	potrei
(tu)	potresti
(lui/lei) (lei/Lei)	potrebbe
(noi)	potremmo
(voi)	potreste
(loro)	potrebbero

IMPERFECT

(io)	potevo
(tu)	potevi
(lui/lei) (lei/Lei)	poteva
(noi)	potevamo
(voi)	potevate
(loro)	potevano

PRESENT SUBJUNCTIVE

(io)	possa
(tu)	possa
(lui/lei) (lei/Lei)	possa
(noi)	possiamo
(voi)	possiate
(loro)	possano

IMPERATIVE

–

PAST PARTICIPLE

potuto

GERUND

potendo

EXAMPLE PHRASES

Si **può** visitare il castello tutti i giorni dell'anno. *You can visit the castle any day of the year.*
Non **è potuto** venire. *He couldn't come.*
Non **potrò** venire domani. *I won't be able to come tomorrow.*
Può aver avuto un incidente. *He may have had an accident.*
Potrebbe essere vero. *It could be true.*

Italic letters in Italian words show where stress does not follow the usual rules.

▶ **prendere** (to take)

PRESENT

(io)	prendo
(tu)	prendi
(lui/lei) (lei/Lei)	prende
(noi)	prendiamo
(voi)	prendete
(loro)	prendono

PERFECT

(io)	ho preso
(tu)	hai preso
(lui/lei) (lei/Lei)	ha preso
(noi)	abbiamo preso
(voi)	avete preso
(loro)	hanno preso

IMPERFECT

(io)	prendevo
(tu)	prendevi
(lui/lei) (lei/Lei)	prendeva
(noi)	prendevamo
(voi)	prendevate
(loro)	prendevano

IMPERATIVE

prendi
prendiamo
prendete

FUTURE

(io)	prenderò
(tu)	prenderai
(lui/lei) (lei/Lei)	prenderà
(noi)	prenderemo
(voi)	prenderete
(loro)	prenderanno

CONDITIONAL

(io)	prenderei
(tu)	prenderesti
(lui/lei) (lei/Lei)	prenderebbe
(noi)	prenderemmo
(voi)	prendereste
(loro)	prenderebbero

PRESENT SUBJUNCTIVE

(io)	prenda
(tu)	prenda
(lui/lei) (lei/Lei)	prenda
(noi)	prendiamo
(voi)	prendiate
(loro)	prendano

PAST PARTICIPLE

preso

GERUND

prendendo

EXAMPLE PHRASES

Prendi quella borsa. *Take that bag.*
Ho preso un bel voto. *I got a good mark.*
Prende qualcosa da bere? *Would you like something to drink?*
Per chi mi **prendi**? *Who do you think I am?*

Remember that subject pronouns are not used very often in Italian.

▶ rimanere (to stay)

PRESENT

(io)	rimango
(tu)	rimani
(lui/lei) (lei/Lei)	rimane
(noi)	rimaniamo
(voi)	rimanete
(loro)	rimangono

PERFECT

(io)	sono rimasto/a
(tu)	sei rimasto/a
(lui/lei) (lei/Lei)	è rimasto/a
(noi)	siamo rimasti/e
(voi)	siete rimasti/e
(loro)	sono rimasti/e

IMPERFECT

(io)	rimanevo
(tu)	rimanevi
(lui/lei) (lei/Lei)	rimaneva
(noi)	rimanevamo
(voi)	rimanevate
(loro)	rimanevano

IMPERATIVE

rimani
rimaniamo
rimanete

FUTURE

(io)	rimarrò
(tu)	rimarrai
(lui/lei) (lei/Lei)	rimarrà
(noi)	rimarremo
(voi)	rimarrete
(loro)	rimarranno

CONDITIONAL

(io)	rimarrei
(tu)	rimarresti
(lui/lei) (lei/Lei)	rimarrebbe
(noi)	rimarremmo
(voi)	rimarreste
(loro)	rimarrebbero

PRESENT SUBJUNCTIVE

(io)	rimanga
(tu)	rimanga
(lui/lei) (lei/Lei)	rimanga
(noi)	rimaniamo
(voi)	rimaniate
(loro)	rimangano

PAST PARTICIPLE

rimasto

GERUND

rimanendo

EXAMPLE PHRASES

Sono rimasto a casa tutto il giorno. *I stayed at home all day.*
Mi piacerebbe **rimanere** qualche altro giorno. *I'd like to stay a few more days.*
Ci **rimarrebbero** molto male. *They'd be very upset.*

Italic letters in Italian words show where stress does not follow the usual rules.

▶ sapere (to know)

PRESENT

(io)	so
(tu)	sai
(lui/lei) (lei/Lei)	sa
(noi)	sappiamo
(voi)	sapete
(loro)	sanno

FUTURE

(io)	saprò
(tu)	saprai
(lui/lei) (lei/Lei)	saprà
(noi)	sapremo
(voi)	saprete
(loro)	sapranno

PERFECT

(io)	hai saputo
(tu)	ha saputo
(lui/lei) (lei/Lei)	abbiamo saputo
(noi)	avete saputo
(voi)	hanno saputo
(loro)	ho saputo

CONDITIONAL

(io)	saprei
(tu)	sapresti
(lui/lei) (lei/Lei)	saprebbe
(noi)	sapremmo
(voi)	sapreste
(loro)	saprebbero

IMPERFECT

(io)	sapevo
(tu)	sapevi
(lui/lei) (lei/Lei)	sapeva
(noi)	sapevamo
(voi)	sapevate
(loro)	sapevano

PRESENT SUBJUNCTIVE

(io)	sappia
(tu)	sappia
(lui/lei) (lei/Lei)	sappia
(noi)	sappiamo
(voi)	sappiate
(loro)	sappiano

IMPERATIVE
sappi
sappiamo
sappiate

PAST PARTICIPLE
saputo

GERUND
sapendo

EXAMPLE PHRASES

Sai dove abita? *Do you know where he lives?*
Non **sapeva** andare in bicicletta. *He couldn't ride a bike.*
Sa di fragola. *It tastes of strawberries.*

Remember that subject pronouns are not used very often in Italian.

▶ **scegliere** (to choose)

PRESENT

(io)	scelgo
(tu)	scegli
(lui/lei) (lei/Lei)	sceglie
(noi)	scegliamo
(voi)	scegliete
(loro)	scelgono

FUTURE

(io)	sceglierò
(tu)	sceglierai
(lui/lei) (lei/Lei)	sceglierà
(noi)	sceglieremo
(voi)	sceglierete
(loro)	sceglieranno

PERFECT

(io)	ho scelto
(tu)	hai scelto
(lui/lei) (lei/Lei)	ha scelto
(noi)	abbiamo scelto
(voi)	avete scelto
(loro)	hanno scelto

CONDITIONAL

(io)	sceglierei
(tu)	sceglieresti
(lui/lei) (lei/Lei)	sceglierebbe
(noi)	sceglieremmo
(voi)	scegliereste
(loro)	sceglierebbero

IMPERFECT

(io)	sceglievo
(tu)	sceglievi
(lui/lei) (lei/Lei)	sceglieva
(noi)	sceglievamo
(voi)	sceglievate
(loro)	sceglievano

PRESENT SUBJUNCTIVE

(io)	scelga
(tu)	scelga
(lui/lei) (lei/Lei)	scelga
(noi)	scegliamo
(voi)	scegliate
(loro)	scelgano

IMPERATIVE
scegli
scegliamo
scegliete

PAST PARTICIPLE
scelto

GERUND
scegliendo

EXAMPLE PHRASES

Chi **sceglie** il vino? *Who's going to choose the wine?*
Hai scelto il regalo per lei? *Have you chosen her present?*
Sceglievano sempre il vino più costoso. *They always chose the most expensive wine.*
Scegli la pizza che vuoi. *Choose which pizza you want.*
Non sa ancora quale abito **sceglierà**. *She hasn't decided yet which dress she'll choose.*
Stavo **scegliendo** le pesche più mature. *I was choosing the ripest peaches.*

Italic letters in Italian words show where stress does not follow the usual rules.

▶ sedere (to sit)

PRESENT

(io)	siedo
(tu)	siedi
(lui/lei) (lei/Lei)	siede
(noi)	sediamo
(voi)	sedete
(loro)	siedono

FUTURE

(io)	sederò
(tu)	sederai
(lui/lei) (lei/Lei)	sederà
(noi)	sederemo
(voi)	sederete
(loro)	sederanno

PERFECT

(io)	sono seduto/a
(tu)	sei seduto/a
(lui/lei) (lei/Lei)	è seduto/a
(noi)	siamo seduti/e
(voi)	siete seduti/e
(loro)	sono seduti/e

CONDITIONAL

(io)	sederei
(tu)	sederesti
(lui/lei) (lei/Lei)	sederebbe
(noi)	sederemmo
(voi)	sedereste
(loro)	sederebbero

IMPERFECT

(io)	sedevo
(tu)	sedevi
(lui/lei) (lei/Lei)	sedeva
(noi)	sedevamo
(voi)	sedevate
(loro)	sedevano

PRESENT SUBJUNCTIVE

(io)	sieda
(tu)	sieda
(lui/lei) (lei/Lei)	sieda
(noi)	sediamo
(voi)	sediate
(loro)	siedano

IMPERATIVE

siedi
sediamo
sedete

PAST PARTICIPLE

seduto

GERUND

sedendo

EXAMPLE PHRASES

Era seduta accanto a me. *She was sitting beside me.*
Si **è seduto** per terra. *He sat on the floor.*
Siediti qui! *Sit here!*

Remember that subject pronouns are not used very often in Italian.

▶ spegnere (to put out)

PRESENT

(io)	spengo
(tu)	spegni
(lui/lei)(lei/Lei)	spegne
(noi)	spegniamo
(voi)	spegnete
(loro)	spengono

FUTURE

(io)	spegnerò
(tu)	spegnerai
(lui/lei)(lei/Lei)	spegnerà
(noi)	spegneremo
(voi)	spegnerete
(loro)	spegneranno

PERFECT

(io)	ho spento
(tu)	hai spento
(lui/lei)(lei/Lei)	ha spento
(noi)	abbiamo spento
(voi)	avete spento
(loro)	hanno spento

CONDITIONAL

(io)	spegnerei
(tu)	spegneresti
(lui/lei)(lei/Lei)	spegnerebbe
(noi)	spegneremmo
(voi)	spegnereste
(loro)	spegnerebbero

IMPERFECT

(io)	spegnevo
(tu)	spegnevi
(lui/lei)(lei/Lei)	spegneva
(noi)	spegnevamo
(voi)	spegnevate
(loro)	spegnevano

PRESENT SUBJUNCTIVE

(io)	spenga
(tu)	spenga
(lui/lei)(lei/Lei)	spenga
(noi)	spegniamo
(voi)	spegniate
(loro)	spengano

IMPERATIVE

spegni
spegniamo
spegnete

PAST PARTICIPLE

spento

GERUND

spegnendo

EXAMPLE PHRASES

Hai spento la sigaretta? *Have you put your cigarette out?*
Spegnete le luci che guardiamo il film. *Turn off the lights and we'll watch the film.*
La luce si **è spenta** all'improvviso. *The light went off suddenly.*

Italic letters in Italian words show where stress does not follow the usual rules.

▶ stare (to be)

PRESENT		
(io)	sto	
(tu)	stai	
(lui/lei) (lei/Lei)	sta	
(noi)	stiamo	
(voi)	state	
(loro)	stanno	

FUTURE		
(io)	starò	
(tu)	starai	
(lui/lei) (lei/Lei)	starà	
(noi)	staremo	
(voi)	starete	
(loro)	staranno	

PERFECT		
(io)	sono stato/a	
(tu)	sei stato/a	
(lui/lei) (lei/Lei)	è stato/a	
(noi)	siamo stati/e	
(voi)	siete stati/e	
(loro)	sono stati/e	

CONDITIONAL		
(io)	starei	
(tu)	staresti	
(lui/lei) (lei/Lei)	starebbe	
(noi)	staremmo	
(voi)	stareste	
(loro)	starebbero	

IMPERFECT		
(io)	stavo	
(tu)	stavi	
(lui/lei) (lei/Lei)	stava	
(noi)	stavamo	
(voi)	stavate	
(loro)	stavano	

PRESENT SUBJUNCTIVE		
(io)	stia	
(tu)	stia	
(lui/lei) (lei/Lei)	stia	
(noi)	stiamo	
(voi)	stiate	
(loro)	stiano	

IMPERATIVE
stai
stiamo
state

PAST PARTICIPLE
stato

GERUND
stando

EXAMPLE PHRASES

Sei mai **stato** in Francia? *Have you ever been to France?*
Come **stai**? *How are you?*
Stavo andando a casa. *I was going home.*
A Londra **starò** da amici. *I'll be staying with friends in London.*
Stavo per uscire quando ha squillato il telefono. *I was about to go out when the phone rang.*

Remember that subject pronouns are not used very often in Italian.

▶ **tenere** (to hold)

PRESENT

(io)	tengo
(tu)	tieni
(lui/lei) (lei/Lei)	tiene
(noi)	teniamo
(voi)	tenete
(loro)	tengono

FUTURE

(io)	terrò
(tu)	terrai
(lui/lei) (lei/Lei)	terrà
(noi)	terremo
(voi)	terrete
(loro)	terranno

PERFECT

(io)	ho tenuto
(tu)	hai tenuto
(lui/lei) (lei/Lei)	ha tenuto
(noi)	abbiamo tenuto
(voi)	avete tenuto
(loro)	hanno tenuto

CONDITIONAL

(io)	terrei
(tu)	terresti
(lui/lei) (lei/Lei)	terrebbe
(noi)	terremmo
(voi)	terreste
(loro)	terrebbero

IMPERFECT

(io)	tenevo
(tu)	tenevi
(lui/lei) (lei/Lei)	teneva
(noi)	tenevamo
(voi)	tenevate
(loro)	tenevano

PRESENT SUBJUNCTIVE

(io)	tenga
(tu)	tenga
(lui/lei) (lei/Lei)	tenga
(noi)	teniamo
(voi)	teniate
(loro)	tengano

IMPERATIVE

tieni
teniamo
tenete

PAST PARTICIPLE

tenuto

GERUND

tenendo

EXAMPLE PHRASES

Tiene la racchetta con la sinistra. *He holds the racket with his left hand.*
Tieniti forte! *Hold on tight!*
Si **tenevano** per mano. *They were holding hands.*
Tieniti pronta per le cinque. *Be ready by five.*
Tieni, questo è per te. *Here, this is for you*

Italic letters in Italian words show where stress does not follow the usual rules.

▶ uscire (to go out)

PRESENT

(io)	esco
(tu)	esci
(lui/lei) (lei/Lei)	esce
(noi)	usciamo
(voi)	uscite
(loro)	escono

PERFECT

(io)	sono uscito/a
(tu)	sei uscito/a
(lui/lei) (lei/Lei)	è uscito/a
(noi)	siamo usciti/e
(voi)	siete usciti/e
(loro)	sono usciti/e

IMPERFECT

(io)	uscivo
(tu)	uscivi
(lui/lei) (lei/Lei)	usciva
(noi)	uscivamo
(voi)	uscivate
(loro)	uscivano

IMPERATIVE

esci
usciamo
uscite

FUTURE

(io)	uscirò
(tu)	uscirai
(lui/lei) (lei/Lei)	uscirà
(noi)	usciremo
(voi)	uscirete
(loro)	usciranno

CONDITIONAL

(io)	uscirei
(tu)	usciresti
(lui/lei) (lei/Lei)	uscirebbe
(noi)	usciremmo
(voi)	uscireste
(loro)	uscirebbero

PRESENT SUBJUNCTIVE

(io)	esca
(tu)	esca
(lui/lei) (lei/Lei)	esca
(noi)	usciamo
(voi)	usciate
(loro)	escano

PAST PARTICIPLE

uscito

GERUND

uscendo

EXAMPLE PHRASES

È uscita a comprare il giornale. *She's gone out to buy a newspaper.*
Uscirà dall'ospedale domani. *He's coming out of hospital tomorrow.*
L'ho incontrata che **usciva** dalla farmacia. *I met her coming out of the chemist's.*
La rivista **esce** di lunedì. *The magazine comes out on Mondays.*

Remember that subject pronouns are not used very often in Italian.

▶ valere (to be worth)

PRESENT		FUTURE	
(io)	valgo	(io)	varrò
(tu)	vali	(tu)	varrai
(lui/lei) (lei/Lei)	vale	(lui/lei) (lei/Lei)	varrà
(noi)	valiamo	(noi)	varremo
(voi)	valete	(voi)	varrete
(loro)	valgono	(loro)	varranno

PERFECT		CONDITIONAL	
(io)	sono valso/a	(io)	varrei
(tu)	sei valso/a	(tu)	varresti
(lui/lei) (lei/Lei)	è valso/a	(lui/lei) (lei/Lei)	varrebbe
(noi)	siamo valsi/e	(noi)	varremmo
(voi)	siete valsi/e	(voi)	varreste
(loro)	sono valsi/e	(loro)	varrebbero

IMPERFECT		PRESENT SUBJUNCTIVE	
(io)	valevo	(io)	valga
(tu)	valevi	(tu)	valga
(lui/lei) (lei/Lei)	valeva	(lui/lei) (lei/Lei)	valga
(noi)	valevamo	(noi)	valiamo
(voi)	valevate	(voi)	valiate
(loro)	valevano	(loro)	valgano

IMPERATIVE
vali
valiamo
valete

PAST PARTICIPLE
valso

GERUND
valendo

EXAMPLE PHRASES

L'auto **vale** tremila euro. *The car is worth three thousand euros.*
Non ne **vale** la pena. *It's not worth it.*
Senza il giardino, la casa non **varrebbe** niente. *Without the garden the house wouldn't be worth anything.*

Italic letters in Italian words show where stress does not follow the usual rules.

▶ vedere (to see)

PRESENT			FUTURE	
(io)	vedo		(io)	vedrò
(tu)	vedi		(tu)	vedrai
(lui/lei) (lei/Lei)	vede		(lui/lei) (lei/Lei)	vedrà
(noi)	vediamo		(noi)	vedremo
(voi)	vedete		(voi)	vedrete
(loro)	vedono		(loro)	vedranno

PERFECT			CONDITIONAL	
(io)	ho visto		(io)	vedrei
(tu)	hai visto		(tu)	vedresti
(lui/lei) (lei/Lei)	ha visto		(lui/lei) (lei/Lei)	vedrebbe
(noi)	abbiamo visto		(noi)	vedremmo
(voi)	avete visto		(voi)	vedreste
(loro)	hanno visto		(loro)	vedrebbero

IMPERFECT			PRESENT SUBJUNCTIVE	
(io)	vedevo		(io)	veda
(tu)	vedevi		(tu)	veda
(lui/lei) (lei/Lei)	vedeva		(lui/lei) (lei/Lei)	veda
(noi)	vedevamo		(noi)	vediamo
(voi)	vedevate		(voi)	vediate
(loro)	vedevano		(loro)	vedano

IMPERATIVE
vedi
vediamo
vedete

PAST PARTICIPLE
visto

GERUND
vedendo

EXAMPLE PHRASES

Non ci **vedo** senza occhiali. *I can't see without my glasses.*
Ci **vediamo** domani! *See you tomorrow!*
Non **vedevo** l'ora di conoscerlo. *I couldn't wait to meet him.*

Remember that subject pronouns are not used very often in Italian.

▶ venire (to come)

PRESENT

(io)	vengo
(tu)	vieni
(lui/lei) (lei/Lei)	viene
(noi)	veniamo
(voi)	venite
(loro)	vengono

PERFECT

(io)	sono venuto/a
(tu)	sei venuto/a
(lui/lei) (lei/Lei)	è venuto/a
(noi)	siamo venuti/e
(voi)	siete venuti/e
(loro)	sono venuti/e

IMPERFECT

(io)	venivo
(tu)	venivi
(lui/lei) (lei/Lei)	veniva
(noi)	venivamo
(voi)	venivate
(loro)	venivano

IMPERATIVE

vieni
veniamo
venite

FUTURE

(io)	verrò
(tu)	verrai
(lui/lei) (lei/Lei)	verrà
(noi)	verremo
(voi)	verrete
(loro)	verranno

CONDITIONAL

(io)	verrei
(tu)	verresti
(lui/lei) (lei/Lei)	verrebbe
(noi)	verremmo
(voi)	verreste
(loro)	verrebbero

PRESENT SUBJUNCTIVE

(io)	venga
(tu)	venga
(lui/lei) (lei/Lei)	venga
(noi)	veniamo
(voi)	veniate
(loro)	vengano

PAST PARTICIPLE

venuto

GERUND

venendo

EXAMPLE PHRASES

È venuto in macchina. *He came by car.*
Da dove **vieni**? *Where do you come from?*
Vieni a trovarci. *Come and see us!*
Quanto **viene**? *How much is it?*

Italic letters in Italian words show where stress does not follow the usual rules.

▶ **volere** (to want)

PRESENT

(io)	voglio
(tu)	vuoi
(lui/lei) (lei/Lei)	vuole
(noi)	vogliamo
(voi)	volete
(loro)	vogliono

FUTURE

(io)	vorrò
(tu)	vorrai
(lui/lei) (lei/Lei)	vorrà
(noi)	vorremo
(voi)	vorrete
(loro)	vorranno

PERFECT

(io)	ho voluto
(tu)	hai voluto
(lui/lei) (lei/Lei)	ha voluto
(noi)	abbiamo voluto
(voi)	avete voluto
(loro)	hanno voluto

CONDITIONAL

(io)	vorrei
(tu)	vorresti
(lui/lei) (lei/Lei)	vorrebbe
(noi)	vorremmo
(voi)	vorreste
(loro)	vorrebbero

IMPERFECT

(io)	volevo
(tu)	volevi
(lui/lei) (lei/Lei)	voleva
(noi)	volevamo
(voi)	volevate
(loro)	volevano

PRESENT SUBJUNCTIVE

(io)	voglia
(tu)	voglia
(lui/lei) (lei/Lei)	voglia
(noi)	vogliamo
(voi)	vogliate
(loro)	vogliano

IMPERATIVE

–

PAST PARTICIPLE

voluto

GERUND

volendo

EXAMPLE PHRASES

Voglio comprare una macchina nuova. *I want to buy a new car.*
Devo pagare subito o posso pagare domani? – Come **vuole**. *Do I have to pay now or can I pay tomorrow? – As you prefer.*
Quanto ci **vorrà** prima che finiate? *How long will it take you to finish?*
La campanella **voleva** dire che la lezione era finita. *The bell meant that the lesson was over.*
Anche **volendo** non posso invitarti: la festa è sua. *I'd like to, but I can't invite you: it's his party.*

Remember that subject pronouns are not used very often in Italian.